WORD & WORSHIP WORKBOOK
FOR YEAR B

*For Ministry in Initiation, Preaching,
Religious Education and Formation*

Mary Birmingham

Paulist Press
New York, N.Y. • Mahwah, N.J.

Acknowledgments

Permission to reprint *Reading the Old Testament* by Lawrence Boadt, copyright © 1984 by Paulist Press, Inc., from *Reading the New Testament,* copyright © 1978, 1988 by Pheme Perkins, and from *The Wellspring of Worship* by Jean Corbon, translated by Matthew J. O'Connell, copyright © 1980 by Les Editions du Cerf, © 1984 by Paulist Press, Inc., is controlled by Paulist Press. All rights reserved. Excerpts from *Sharing the Light of Faith, National Catechetical Directory for Catholics of the United States* and *Sharing the Light of Faith, an Official Commentary* are reprinted by permission of the United States Catholic Conference. Material from *Reading John* by Charles H. Talbert, copyright © 1994 by Charles H. Talbert, is reprinted by permission of Crossroad Publishing Co. and SPCK, London. Permission to reprint material from *The Liturgical Year* by Adolf Adam, translated by Matthew J. O'Connell, copyright © 1981 by Pueblo Publishing Co., Inc., © 1990 by The Order of St. Benedict, Inc., from *Days of the Lord,* volumes 1–7, copyright © 1999 by The Order of St. Benedict, Inc., from *Preaching the Lectionary* by Reginald H. Fuller, © 1974 by The Order of St. Benedict, Inc., from *The Crucified Christ in Holy Week* by Raymond E. Brown, copyright © 1986 by The Order of St. Benedict, Inc., from *Mark* by Wilfrid Harrington, O.P., copyright © 1979 by Michael Glazier, Inc., from *The Cultural World of Jesus, Year B,* by John Pilch, copyright © 1996 by The Order of St. Benedict, Inc., and from *Richer Fare for the Christian People* by Gail Ramshaw, copyright © 1990 by Pueblo Publishing Co. Inc., are reprinted by permission of Liturgical Press, Collegeville, Minn. Excerpts from *The Birth of the Messiah* by Raymond E. Brown, copyright © 1977 by Raymond E. Brown, are used by permission of Doubleday, a division of Random House, Inc. Excerpts from *The Word We Celebrate* by Patricia Datchuck Sanchez is reprinted by permission if Sheed & Ward, an Apostolate of the Priests of the Sacred Heart, 7373 South Lover's Lane Road, Franklin, Wisconsin 53132. The English translation of the opening prayers, antiphons, solemn blessings, prefaces and other texts from *The Roman Missal* © 1973, International Committee on English in the Liturgy, Inc. (ICEL); excerpts from the English translation of *Documents on the Liturgy* © 1963–1979: *Conciliar, Papal and Curial Text* © 1982, ICEL; excerpts from the English translation of the *Rite of Christian Initiation of Adults* © 1985, ICEL, are reprinted by permission. All rights reserved. Material from *Binding the Strong Man: A Political Reading of Mark's Story of Jesus* by Ched Myers, © 1988 by Orbis Books, and *Sharing the Word through the Liturgical Year* by Gustavo Guiiérrez, © 1997 by Orbis Books, is reprinted by permission of Orbis Books. Excerpts from the *New Jerome Biblical Commentary,* edited by Raymond E. Brown and Joseph A. Fitzmyer, copyright © 1989, are reprinted by permission of Prentice-Hall Inc. Upper Saddle River, N.J. Permission to reprint material from *The Study of Liturgy,* edited by Cheslyn Jones et al., © 1978 by Cheslyn Jones, Geoffrey Wainwright and Edward Yarnold, S.J., © 1992 by Geoffrey Wainwright, Edward Yarnold, S.J., and Paul Bradshaw, has been granted by Oxford University Press, Inc.

--- A NOTE TO READERS ---

In addition to its commentaries on the Year B texts, the present volume contains exegeses on Year C readings for the Feasts of the Holy Family, Baptism of the Lord, Ascension and Pentecost, since a new version of the lectionary, containing additional readings, was issued after the publication of the *Word & Worship Workbook for Year C.* The lectionary also mandates new Year B and Year C readings for the Feast of the Transfiguration, August 6. Commentaries on those texts can be found in the Second Sunday of Lent of the respective volumes.

Book design by Céline Allen. Cover design by Tim McKeen. Cover illustration by Julie Lonneman.

Library of Congress Cataloging-in-Publication Data

Birmingham, Mary.
    Word & worship workbook : for ministry in initiation, preaching,
religious education, and formation / Mary Birmingham.
       p. ; cm.
    Includes bibliographical references and index.
    Contents: [1] For year A   — [3] For year C.
    ISBN 0–8091–3898–0 (alk. paper)
    1. Catechetics—Catholic Church. 2. Church year—Study and
teaching. 3. Catholic Church. Lectionary for Mass (U.S.) Year B.
I. Title. II. Title: Word and worship workbook.
BX1968.B54 1999
268´.82—DC21
                                      97–22382
                                         r98

Published by Paulist Press
997 Macarthur Blvd.
Mahwah, N.J. 07430

www.paulistpress.com

Printed and bound in the United States of America

CONTENTS

1. INTRODUCTION

If you hope to become part of God's reign, you must let yourself be overtaken, knocked breathless, by a Presence, a Reality you can neither invent nor control. In a word, you have to open your life to the holy violence of conversion—a tumultuous experience that is liable to leave you feeling drenched and exhausted, as though the seas had seized, swallowed and spat you back alive on the shore. Newborn and salted, you sense that nothing looks the same, nothing can ever be the same.[1]

Nathan Mitchell's metaphor captures the heart of this book's purpose or, more humbly, its hope! While you may not find yourself spat back salted and drenched on the local beach, it is hoped that through the use of the methods and proposed sessions, you, as a catechist or small group facilitator, will share in the experience of empowering and being awed by the conversion of the adults and children with and to whom you minister and perhaps even by your own heightened faith life. Hope springs eternal in the human heart. One might therefore hope to light a spark, fan a flame, or at the very least prompt bold new questions to be raised regarding our Christian/Catholic story.

What was the experience and understanding of bread and gospel to the generations who went before us? Where work needs to begin and proceed is in helping people ask the right questions in finding meaning for their lives.

The genesis of this resource flows from the conviction that "...as many ministers of the divine word as possible will be able to effectively provide the nourishment of the Scriptures for the People of God, thereby enlightening their minds, strengthening their wills, and setting their hearts on fire with the love of God."[2] Catechists are ministers of that divine word. "The study of the sacred page is the soul of sacred theology. Sacred theology rests on the written word of God, together with sacred tradition, as its primary and perpetual foundation."[3] Catechesis that enlightens, strengthens, and inflames the love of God leads to deep conversion, which in turn leads to transformation of people's lives. This catechesis begins with the lived experience of people. It helps them celebrate and reflect on the presence of Christ in word and sacrament, in one another, and in the life and mission of the church. Hopefully this resource will assist in that noble endeavor.

This book is intended to help catechists plan engaging sessions for adults and children around the Sunday experience of word and worship. You, the catechist or group leader, may use this as a resource for planning your sessions or working with your specific group.

The structure of *Word & Worship Workbook* is based on the liturgical calendar. There are weekly planning sessions that include prayers and blessings from the liturgy, scholarly exegesis of the Lectionary scriptures, reflection questions, and suggestions for doctrinal themes. A doctrinal appendix is included for the catechist's reference.

One might ask, "How is this different from other resources that provide exegetical or catechetical material?" The answer is three-fold:

1. This book provides, under one jacket cover, condensed, scholarly exegetical material relating to both scripture and tradition and drawn from multiple and varied sources.
2. It includes ritual prayers and blessings, as well as questions, options, and possibilities for "unpacking" the experience of worship in the liturgical year.
3. It suggests themes from among the repertoire of hierarchical truths that naturally flow from interpreted texts of the Lectionary.

---

[1]Nathan Mitchell, "The Kingdom of Justice," in *Modern Liturgy*, 18: 8.

[2]*Dogmatic Constitution on Divine Revelation (Dei Verbum)*, #23, in *DVII*.

[3]Ibid., #24.

Jim Dunning, in his book, *Echoing God's Word*, challenged us to view liturgical catechesis from a new perspective. Jim asserted that we as ministers must allow ourselves to be transformed by such catechesis if we are to pass it on to others. For this reason, *Word & Worship Workbook* is not a book of lesson plans. It is a resource that committed Christians can use to prayerfully, ritually, and in an informed manner prepare for ministry in the church.

> We need formation and transformation, not just information. We need to take the journey ourselves. As ministers we need both the what (such as the vision of the church, faith, conversion, liturgical catechesis in these rites) and also some how's (some practical ways for pastoral ministers and catechumens to do that liturgical catechesis). We need methods, especially for catechists and homilists, that bring the word of God to echo in and through our lives in the community and that situate doctrine and law within the good news.[4]

This book is an attempt to provide such a method. It also seeks to tap into the current phenomenon of people's need for conversion and for renewed interest in scripture and in Jesus.

How might *Word & Worship Workbook* be used in a parish setting? The possibilities require only imagination. Obvious applications include:

1. Initiation Ministry
Catechists who work with catechumens and candidates could use this workbook to prepare sessions in which the central task is formation of the catechumen or candidate into the mystery of absorption in the paschal mystery of Christ as it unfolds in one liturgical cycle. "By means of the yearly cycle the Church celebrates the whole mystery of Christ, from his incarnation until the day of Pentecost and the expectation of his coming again."[5]

2. Small Christian Communities
Facilitators could use this workbook to plan group sessions. Liturgy is about life. Reflection on the experience of liturgy is a wonderful way to share life in the context of our Catholic Christian experience. In order to be *community*, one must reflect on

what it is the community celebrates as well as on what it believes, professes, and holds to be true.

3. Formation in Ministry
This workbook could be used by facilitators working with parish catechists who minister to adults and children through catechumenal ministry, scripture study, and adult enrichment.

4. Liturgy Teams
Liturgy teams could use *Word & Worship Workbook* as a source of reflection as they engage in planning liturgies, celebrations, and rituals for the parish.

5. Religious Education for Young People
There is much talk today regarding Lectionary-based catechesis in our schools and religious education programs. *Word & Worship Workbook* could assist religious educators in preparing Lectionary-based catechesis for their young people. At the very least it would help all who catechize be more informed about the "work" (read "liturgy") that we, as the people of God, do every Sunday throughout the liturgical cycle.

There are two final points. First, you will notice that there is an "agenda" in each of the weekly sessions. While attempting to avoid scriptural and doctrinal fundamentalism, there is nevertheless one constant lens through which the information contained in these pages has been redacted. This agenda is a radical option for the poor, the marginalized, and the less fortunate. In their document, *Communities of Salt and Light: Reflection on the Social Mission of the Parish*, the U.S. bishops state that

> The parish is where the church lives. Parishes are communities of faith, of action, and of hope. They are where the gospel is proclaimed and celebrated, where believers are formed and sent to renew the earth. Communities are measured by how they serve the "least of these" in our parish and beyond its boundaries—the hungry, the homeless, the sick, those in prison, the stranger. The Church teaches that social justice is an integral part of evangelization, a constitutive dimension of preaching the gospel, and an essential part of the Church's mission.[6]

---

[4] *EGW*, 20.
[5] *GNLY*, #17.

---

[6] *Communities of Salt and Light: Reflection on the Social Mission of the Parish* (Washington: NCCB, 1993), 1–3.

If this is true, it follows that justice is at the very heart of the gospel. The Hebrew understanding of justice (*hesed*) is right relationship. To be in right relationship with God means that one must show care and concern for God's *anawim*—the poor, the powerless, widows, orphans, and the marginalized. Thus, every weekly session is crafted in such a way as to raise questions of social responsibility. Justice is truly the agenda of the gospels. It is truly the agenda of this workbook.

Second, to be Catholic, says James Joyce, means, "Here comes everybody." We are diverse and we are to be inclusive. There is to be no "Jesus and me" mentality in the Catholic experience. Catholicism assumes community. We inherited the understanding that we are in relationship to God "as a people" from our Jewish ancestors. A personal relationship with God is essential. But we are corporate by nature and by intention. Thus, the first perspective in each session will be communal. The first question will always be, "What are the implications and challenges for our community, for the wider community?" Only after this question has been addressed is there movement toward the personal context, "What do the gospel and the liturgy call me to as a member of that corporate body?"

There is no doubt that Jesus maintained a radical stance toward the inclusion of all people. Language expresses our deepest held beliefs, convictions, and biases. To use exclusive language is against the spirit of the basic message of Jesus' gospel. Thus, I have tried to be as inclusive as possible throughout this text.

Since God is neither male nor female, our descriptive language is extremely limited. There are no adequate pronouns. The ancients struggled with naming God too, thus their designation, *YHWH*. However, I am a product of my own cultural and religious conditioning. While I desperately tried to avoid specific male pronouns in reference to the Transcendent Other, I found my efforts futile. Suffice it to say that the use of "him" when it comes to God is solely a literary concession. There were no other choices that allowed the text to make sense and to flow smoothly. Also, quoted material was included as originally written; there were no changes made to texts from other sources.

Finally, the springboard for jumping into these often uncharted waters with both feet is to pro-

ceed with courage. As we embark on this sometimes perilous voyage, may we be seized, salted, drenched, swallowed, and spat back alive on that not so distant shore we call "the Kingdom of God."

I would like to acknowledge those special people in my life who made the writing of this book possible. My first thanks and heartfelt appreciation go to my loving family and friends, especially my husband, who held down the family fort during the last year. Their support, love, and encouragement kept me going, especially in those rare moments when being spat out on the local beach looked far more inviting than spending one more hour at the computer. Without them this book would have been nothing more than a dream. I also extend my appreciation to all who have been a part of my life, and to the wonderful community of Our Saviour's Parish who have taught me what it means to be a disciple.

Mary Birmingham, 1998

2. THE SUBSTANCE OF CATECHESIS

Before proceeding further, it is important to understand *catechesis* as it is referred to in *Word & Worship Workbook*. The *catechesis* of subsequent pages embodies a broader interpretation than just the "Catholic stuff" that many have traditionally assumed is its definition. Catechesis refers to a radical relationship with Jesus Christ. Catechesis explores and recognizes God's action and presence in our natural lives, in scripture, and in the life, faith, and worship of the church. This chapter will dissect what that means in practical terms. Whether you are a small group facilitator with little or no formal catechetical training or a learned catechist, *Word & Worship Workbook* could be a useful tool as you "do" the work of catechesis.

CATECHESIS

Many people operate out of an erroneous assumption that catechesis refers to subject matter such as specific doctrines or theologies. In other words, catechesis implies content or head knowledge. However, catechesis supersedes that narrow interpretation. What, then, is it? One need look no further than church documents and the teaching authority of the church to gain insight.

The literal translation of the Greek word *catechesis* is "a sounding down, a resounding, and re-echoing." What and who is the object of this resounding? The "Who" is Jesus Christ. The "What" is the Good News of salvation offered by his life, death, and resurrection. Pope John Paul II, in his apostolic exhortation, *Catechesi tradendae*, states that "the heart of catechesis is in essence a Person, the Person of Jesus of Nazareth, the only Son from the Father...who suffered and died for us, and who now, after rising, is living with us forever."[1] When people catechize, they reveal God's plan of salvation realized in the person of Jesus. Catechesis explores the meaning of Jesus' life, his words, and the marvelous works (signs) he accomplished. Catechesis is about relationship. It concerns a radical, personal, communal relationship with the living God encountered in Jesus Christ through the Holy Spirit. Catechesis helps us interpret the story of our lives in dialogue with the story of the scriptures and the story of the church throughout the ages.

The *National Catechetical Directory* (NCD) asserts that catechesis is God's word revealed through Jesus and operative in the lives of people exercising their faith. Catechesis supports the mission of the church to proclaim and teach God's message, to celebrate the sacred mysteries and to serve God's people.[2] In this way the church establishes the reign of God on earth. The aim of catechesis is to nurture a mature faith in adults, who will in turn help nurture a growing faith in children. "The content of catechesis, then, is no more (but no less) than God's self revelation."[3]

THE FOUR SIGNS OF CATECHESIS

The catechesis referred to above is experienced through four signs of God's presence. God manifests the divine presence to humanity through signs. There are four signs of God's communication with humanity. God is present through natural, biblical, ecclesial, and liturgical signs.

I: Natural Signs

God, through Jesus Christ, is revealed in everyday life through natural signs. God resides and is revealed in the very substances of nature: creation, symbols, and our sensory world. God presides at the banquet of everyday life! God communicates to us through our own experience of life: through science, technology, and the arts, through all that is human and all that supports or enhances human life. Our first awareness of God comes to us through *natural signs*.

---

[1] John Paul II, *Catechesi tradendae*, #43.

[2] *Sharing the Light of Faith, National Catechetical Directory for Catholics of the United States* (NCD), USCC, 1979, #30.

[3] *Sharing the Light of Faith, An Official Commentary* (Washington: USCC/NCCB, 1981), 19.

The elements of life such as water, light, fire, bread, and oil reveal and point to God. For example, we know that water is necessary for life. We cannot survive without it. God created this life-sustaining element. Through the natural properties of water we are reminded that God is necessary for life. Humanity depends on the benevolence of God.

God is revealed through the gift of science. God is encountered through the intervention of medical science and the healing arts. Believers recognize God's presence in the fields of science and technology. We are called to use the insights of secular sciences and appropriate them into catechetics. For example, catechetics is in great debt to the human secular sciences for a contemporary understanding of adult faith development, stages of faith, and childhood spirituality and faith development.[4]

This resource celebrates the God of everyday life. *Word & Worship Workbook* hopes to assist people to recognize God's presence in the natural order by providing questions that probe the awareness of God in the normal routine of life and its environment. At the heart of the natural sign is the realization that Christ is present in all things and throughout all creation. The task of catechesis is to help people become aware of his presence.

II: Biblical Signs

God, in Jesus Christ, through the Spirit, is revealed through *biblical signs.* Through the proclamation of God's word in worship and through the study of sacred scripture we are able to more fully live the Christian message. The gospel is the "principal witness of the life and teachings of Jesus."[5] Thus, in the course of one complete liturgical cycle, Christ of the gospels is encountered in the liturgical proclamation of the word. "By means of the yearly cycle the Church celebrates the whole mystery of Christ, from his incarnation until the day of Pentecost and the expectation of his coming again."[6] Christ is present to us through *biblical*

signs when we proclaim, listen, study, and live the sacred word.

First and foremost, scripture is experienced as the sacramental presence of God alive in the proclamation of the word. Every time the word is proclaimed in liturgy, Christ is truly present.[7] Scripture is the story of people in covenant relationship with their God. The task of Christians is to connect the story of their everyday lives with the story of Christ in the scriptures. There are a few basic, high priority themes that are woven through the Hebrew scriptures (Old Testament) and the New Testament. These biblical themes show us how God has been present and attentive to the work of salvation throughout all of human history. They give us a glimpse of how God views his relationship with us and how we, in turn, are to view our relationship with God. These basic themes are Creation, Covenant, Exodus, and People of God (community). These recurring themes emphasize the manner in which God has been present to us. They are standard themes that occur in both testaments.

Biblical Themes

a. Creation

God's power and divinity are witnessed through the things God has made, through *creation.* "Ever since the creation of the world, his invisible attributes of eternal power and divinity have been able to be understood and perceived in what he has made" (Rom 1:20). One need only gaze through the window of a 747 jetliner to be awesomely jolted by the explosive, generative, and creative power of the Almighty. Conversely, a quiet repose while watching bugs making trails on the shimmering waves of a gurgling brook serves as a peaceful reminder of God's order, symmetry, and artistry in the creation of nature's intricate designs.

During the Easter Vigil the story of creation is told to remind us that the Easter event, the paschal mystery, was part of God's plan from the beginning. What God accomplished through Jesus began with the creation of the world. Creation was not a one-time event; it is not static, but

[4]Linda Gaupin, "Special Certification in Sacramental Catechesis," class session I, Diocese of Orlando, Florida, October 23, 1996.

[5]NCD, #60a; I.

[6]*GNLY,* #17.

[7]Gaupin, "Special Certification in Sacramental Catechesis."

exists on a continuum. It continues through history. God's creative power continues in the process of transformation. God's evolving work of creation continues in the presence of the risen Christ in the church today in the lives of men and women. All creation groans in grateful praise of the Creator.

b. Covenant

The theme of *covenant* began with the promise made to Abraham, continued on with Moses, and was fully revealed in the life and person of Jesus Christ. God is in covenant relationship with us today. It is the same covenant that began with Abraham, was fulfilled in Jesus, and continues to be lived by people of faith throughout the ages. *God promises to be with us.* That covenant relationship is experienced each day as people of faith live in the risen presence of Jesus. One need look no further than the sick bed of a dying child to find a mother sustained by the presence of her living God.

The covenant made with Abraham and Moses and fulfilled through Jesus continues today as people live in radical, reciprocal relationship with the living God. This relationship is ratified and renewed as people live in biblical justice. Biblical justice demands that one love the Lord God with one's whole heart, soul, and entire being and extend that same love to others and to self. Thus, people are to be treated as God would treat them: as children of God who deserve the highest dignity. To be in covenant with God means that the disciple has a duty to respect the dignity of all human persons. The poor, marginalized, oppressed, and powerless become the object of the disciple's care, concern, and love. Catechesis seeks to help people encounter the abiding presence of their covenant God and to instill in them zeal for a life of loving, apostolic service.

c. Exodus

The *exodus*, the premier symbol of God's saving love for the Hebrew people, ultimately reaches perfect fulfillment and profundity in the "passage from death to life accomplished by Christ's paschal mystery."[8] This sign so clearly defines the Christian life that nearly every catechetical en-

counter addresses the mystery it contains. The ultimate goal of catechesis is transformation. Exodus asks the question, "How have I/you/we been transformed, changed, brought from death to life, in the story we just shared?" Every Christian has an exodus, a passover story; it is the heart of conversion. Each Christian's exodus story constitutes participation in the cherished life, death, and resurrection of Jesus Christ, the paschal mystery.

d. People of God

Another important sign throughout the scriptures is the image of God in relationship to a "people." In the Hebrew scriptures the community was a tangible sign of God's presence. In the New Testament that same sign was transferred to the church, the people of God. By remembering this sign we are better able to move beyond an individualistic "Jesus and me" mentality and embrace the God of Inclusion who is in relationship to us as a "people." The first perspective in scripture's challenge is communal: How does this word challenge "us" as a community? What is the parish, diocesan, universal church's response in the civic, local, and national world? Are parishes responding to the culture as Christ would respond?

The people of God, the church, is in covenant relationship with God. The people of God, the church, is *one body* and is often called the sacrament of Christ. "As a divine reality inserted into human history, the Church is a kind of sacrament. Its unique relationship with Christ makes it both sign and instrument of God's unfathomable union with humanity and of the unity of human beings among themselves."[9] God is in intimate union with the church. Do our communities reveal the story of a people responding in faith to a God who is in relationship with and living within *them*? God's word is spoken first to a people. Every page of the Hebrew scriptures unveils God's self communication to *Israel.* Formation in the word of God assumes a communal relationship. The church is to respond to the world and the culture as a corporate body.

The biblical themes of creation, covenant, exodus, and community are like yeast is to bread.

---

[8] NCD, #43.

[9] Ibid., #63.

They are the leaven that allows the meaning of God's relationship with humanity to rise to fullness. Effective ministry of the word remembers and makes present the God of all creation and new life, the God of exodus who leads us out of slavery into that new life, and the God who invites the people of God into radical, reciprocal, covenant relationship.

III: Ecclesial Signs

Ecclesial signs usually are assumed to be the "content" of catechesis. Biblical signs help us encounter the presence of God in the proclamation of the word and remember and make present the saving works of God throughout salvation history. Ecclesial signs uncover the presence of God throughout the history of the church through its creed and through the way it lives its faith. Ecclesial signs get us in touch with the manner in which people lived the gospel message and celebrated their experience of God's revelation to the church. Over time, these people formulated their creed and the principles that would define behavior (tradition).

The Second Vatican Council's document on divine revelation, *Dei Verbum,* states:

> In His gracious goodness, God has seen to it that what He had revealed for the salvation of all nations would abide perpetually in its full integrity and be handed on to all generations.... This sacred tradition, therefore, and Sacred Scripture of both the Old and New Testament are like a mirror in which the pilgrim Church on earth looks at God, from whom she has received everything, until she is brought to see Him as He is, face to face (cf. 1 Jn. 3:2).
> ... Now what was handed on by the apostles includes everything which contributes to the holiness of life, and the increase of faith of the People of God; and so the Church, in her teaching, life, and worship, perpetuates and hands on to all generations all that she herself is, all that she believes.[10]

Catechesis continues what began with the apostles: handing down the tradition to present and future generations. That tradition encompasses the revelation of Jesus Christ as handed down through history, through faith, creed, worship, and way of life. Catechesis encompasses not only natural and biblical signs of God's presence, but also the witness of God in the life of the church in its creed, code, and cult.[11]

Ecclesial signs (tradition) are but one of four ways God is revealed to us. There is often a tendency to believe that to be a good practicing Catholic is to know all the "Catholic stuff" from treatises on the Trinity to the historical development and understanding of indulgences. Many well-intentioned parish catechumenates, for example, are more concerned with the *information* about Catholic beliefs and practices (ecclesial signs) than they are with *formation* in the Christian/Catholic experience (all four signs). There is an assumption that *knowing* the Catholic information will automatically make good disciples. While not wishing to minimize the necessity of passing on Catholic teaching in its entirety, catechesis is the work of an entire lifetime. How many average Catholics know "all Catholic teaching in its entirety?"

The *Rite of Christian Initiation of Adults* states that there must be a "suitable catechesis, accommodated to the liturgical year...."[12] Too often that has been translated, "every jot and tittle of Catholicity." The question should not be, "Do they know everything?" Rather, the questions should be, "Have they encountered Christ in word, worship, and sacrament? Have they encountered Christ in the life and mission of the church? How does post-biblical teaching (doctrine) impact the Christian life? Where is the challenge for the community, the individual?"

Foundational issues deserve the highest priority as they help move adults toward a mature, faith-filled Christian life. St. Augustine was once asked for a handbook of Christian doctrine. He complied by making his own handbook of basic beliefs. It includes an explanation of the creed, the Lord's Prayer, and the two great commandments—love of

---

[10]*Dei Verbum* #7, #8, in *DVII.*

[11]NCD, #45.
[12]*RCIA,* #75.

God and love of neighbor. Augustine asserted that "what we are to believe, what we are to hope for, and what we are to love, is the sum total of Christian doctrine."

The church recognizes that there is a hierarchy of truths around which other truths are rooted. There are many teachings that comprise the Catholic story. The focus of *Word & Worship Workbook* will be those foundational truths that form and flow from the core content of the Catholic/Christian experience. Both the *General Catechetical Directory* and the *National Catechetical Directory* name four basic truths that hold priority of place within the tradition and are the norm for catechesis. They are: "[1] the mystery of the Father, the Son and the Holy Spirit, Creator of all things; [2] the mystery of Jesus Christ, the incarnate Word, who was born of the Virgin Mary, and who suffered, died, and rose for our salvation; [3] the mystery of the Holy Spirit, who is present in the Church, sanctifying it and guiding it until the glorious coming of Christ, our Savior and Judge; and [4] the mystery of the Church, which is Christ's Mystical Body, in which the Virgin Mary holds the preeminent place."[13]

However, lest I give the impression that mature Catholics need not grow in the fullness of Catholic faith and life, I would suggest that we allow Richard McBrien's distinction between catechesis and theology to give us serious food for thought as we approach our various ministries of the word.

> A doctrine is an official teaching that derives from theology, not from direct inspiration of the Holy Spirit. Before the official Church can propose a statement of faith for the acceptance of its members, it must first think about and struggle with its possible meanings and with various possible expressions of meaning. That process of struggle to understand faith, leading to some official expression of faith, is called theology.... Theology, however, does not consist simply of a listing, explanation, and defense of doctrines. The theologian's task is not only explicative, but critical—critical even of doctrines, or at least of a doctrine's language

and conceptual framework so that the doctrine's truth can become accessible anew in a fresh formulation....

> Theology is not catechesis. Catechesis is, literally, an "echoing" of the faith. Unlike theology, catechesis is for the potential member (known as the catechumen) or for a newly initiated member of the Church (whether a young child or an adult convert). Catechesis teaches the faith by highlighting and explaining the main elements of the faith-tradition and their relationships, as well as their personal and pastoral implications.

> The catechist's task is not to invite potential or new members of the Church to think critically about their faith, but rather to understand and appropriate it in as clear and spiritually fruitful a way as possible. The theologian's task, by contrast, is critical. The mature member of the Church is invited to think critically, to question, even to challenge certain elements of the faith-tradition.[14]

Many good people in the church have not had the opportunities to know and grapple with the basic, core elements of our faith and the implication for living the Christian life. Catechesis must, then, be the starting point.

Located in the Doctrinal Appendix of this workbook is a list of the priority tenets of faith that *flow from* the hierarchy of truths and that are experienced in the liturgical cycle. Included with each post-biblical teaching are reflection questions that help connect ecclesial signs (tradition) and everyday life. Like biblical, natural, and liturgical signs, ecclesial signs intrinsically require a response. Such signs pave the way and point out the path toward bringing about God's reign on earth. This reign proclaims the Good News and demands liberty for those still held captive to oppression's grip.

---

[13]NCD, #47.

[14]Richard P. McBrien, "On What Theology Is and Is Not," excerpted in *America,* June 8, 1996, pp. 14–15. [Excerpts reprinted with permission from *The Tidings* (Southern California's Catholic weekly) of April 12 and 26, 1996.]

IV: Liturgical Signs

God, through Jesus Christ, is revealed and encountered in the celebration of liturgy, the liturgical year, and the sacramental rites of the church. God, through Jesus Christ, is manifest through the church (ecclesial signs) by the way she appropriates her theology, formulates her creed, and lives her mission in the world.[15] Liturgical signs have their home in ecclesial signs, just as ecclesial signs reside within liturgical signs. All four signs are not independent of each other, though they are distinct. Liturgy, through ritual, symbols, and gestures, celebrates, remembers, and manifests God in the natural elements of life: fire, light, water, oil, bread, and wine. Liturgy celebrates, remembers, and makes present the signs of God in scripture. It is a living, ongoing testimony to the scriptural themes of creation, covenant, exodus, and community. Every time the church gathers for eucharist, those themes embody the language of God's continued relationship to the church. Liturgy proclaims the core creed of Christian faith. The church prays and from her prayer flows her belief: *lex orandi, lex credendi.* The creed is a living testimony to the faith and life of men and women of all generations, past, present, and future, the *communion of saints.* Liturgy, then, sends forth the church with a mission to live that faith, life, and creed for the transformation of the world.

One precious contribution of the Second Vatican Council was to describe liturgy as "the source and summit toward which the activity of the Church is directed and the font from which her power flows."[16] If the aim of catechesis is to reveal Jesus Christ, the gospel that is proclaimed in the liturgy is the "principal witness of the life and teachings of Jesus."[17] Jesus is truly present in proclamation of sacred scripture and in the eucharist, in the elements of bread and wine, transformed to body and blood, as well as in the celebrating assembly. Catechesis prepares the community to celebrate and ritualize partnership with Jesus in the paschal mystery (his life, death, and resurrection) and to be sent as a sign into the world.

Catechesis is intrinsically connected to liturgical and sacramental activity. In the Apostolic Exhortation, *Catechesi tradendae* (#23), Pope John Paul II asserts that Christ works for the transformation of humanity in the sacraments, especially the eucharist. Catechesis has the power to change and originates in the liturgy. Liturgical catechesis has as its aim initiating people into the mystery of Christ. Catechesis helps the community reflect on the meaning and implication of the liturgy and sacraments. The purpose of catechesis is to assist believers so that their faith can "become living, conscious and active, through the light of instruction."[18]

God is present in the church as it gathers for prayer. The task of the church, then, is to reflect upon the deeper meaning of the experience of the risen Christ in the liturgy and the sacraments and to make appropriate life connections. Liturgy is the privileged environment for catechesis. It is where the people of God gather to encounter the biblical, ecclesial, and liturgical signs of God's presence during the liturgical year. From that encounter flow action and the mandate to go, do, and be what was just celebrated.

Liturgical Catechesis

The type of catechesis explored in this workbook is often referred to as liturgical catechesis. Liturgical catechesis uses as its source the liturgy, the sacramental rites of the church, and the church year.[19] Liturgical prayer is the church's official, public prayer celebrated in the midst of community. It is the way we are "church." The *Constitution on the Sacred Liturgy* states that "Liturgical services are not private functions, but are celebrations belonging to the Church" (#26). Through liturgy we celebrate the seasons of the church year and we ritualize the significant transition moments in the lives of individuals and the community (baptisms, funerals, weddings, etc.).

While liturgical catechesis admittedly does not give a syllabus for doctrinal curriculum, it seeks to reveal and uncover the basic truths of our faith inherent in the celebration of the liturgy. "Although the liturgy is above all things the worship

---

[15]NCD, #41–46.

[16]*Constitution on the Sacred Liturgy (CSL),* #10, in *DVII.*

[17]NCD, #60.

[18]NCD, #5.

[19]NCD, #44.

of divine majesty, it likewise contains rich instruction for the faithful."[20] As the church prays the scriptures and ritual prayers in the context of the liturgical year, as she shares eucharist and is sent forth, she internalizes, professes, and celebrates her creed about God, Jesus, and Spirit, the profound mystery of the church, and Mary's preeminent role.

The church at prayer ritualizes, lives, and celebrates the life and mission of Jesus. Liturgical prayer teaches us what it means to be Christian, Catholic, and disciples. Liturgical catechesis helps us articulate and enflesh it for our lives.

The Second Vatican Council's vision was for all people to be instructed and prepared for full participation in the church's liturgy. Since one of the principal signs of catechesis is liturgy, the church holds that catechesis begins with liturgical prayer and flows from it. "While every liturgical celebration has educative and formative value, liturgy should not be treated as subservient to catechesis."[21] There is a complementarity between liturgy and catechesis. Catechesis serves the liturgy and prepares people for full and engaging participation in it. Liturgy, on the other hand, provides rich food for the substance and basis of catechesis.

Every catechetical endeavor of the church must have liturgy as its anchor. The weekly sessions contained in this workbook are centered in liturgy. Catechist preparation sessions and the sample catechetical session take place within a liturgy of the word format. The ritual prayers of the church and the readings from the Sunday liturgy are formally and ritually proclaimed.

Many think of liturgy only in terms of the Sunday experience, but our church enjoys a vast repertoire of liturgical prayers and blessings: eucharistic celebrations, liturgies of the word, liturgy of the hours, blessings,[22] the Rite of Christian Initiation of Adults, the Rite of Baptism for Children, the Order of Christian Funerals, sacramental rites such as penance, marriage, ordination, confirmation, anointing of the sick and viaticum. In the midst of such liturgy, the living, dying, and rising Christ is encountered. Liturgical catechesis gives us a language with which to express the encounter.

Liturgical catechesis encourages people to name their experience of liturgy and ritual, articulate an understanding of the experience, and then make appropriate, informed decisions to live the message and become agents of change in the world. Thus, liturgical prayer is transformative. Like bread and wine, liturgy seeks to change us into a new reality: vibrant life-giving disciples.

Thus, the catechesis within the pages of *Word & Worship Workbook* is situated in the liturgical cycle: the Sundays, seasons, solemnities, and feasts of the year. As liturgy is the source and summit of all we do, and since catechesis prepares people for full and active participation in and reflection on the experience of liturgy, conversation in this workbook always begins with the presence of Christ encountered in people's experience of liturgical worship. This experience is on two levels: the liturgical worship of the catechetical gathering and reflection on and preparation for the Sunday experience of liturgy—the place from which the church's power flows.

In summary, then, catechesis echoes the four ways God makes his presence known to humanity—through natural, biblical, ecclesial, and liturgical signs. Catechesis is not solely a cognitive rendering of the articles of faith. Catechesis initiates an encounter with the risen Christ of biblical history and helps express an understanding of that encounter. Catechesis shows how the Christ encounter is celebrated in ritual and how the church remains a perpetual institution of living faith expressed in precept, dogma, life, and mission.

---

[20] *CSL*, #33.

[21] NCD, #36.

[22] Between *The Book of Blessings* and the *Catholic Household Blessings and Prayers*, there is a blessing for nearly every circumstance in life.

3. SCRIPTURE

PART ONE:
THE LECTIONARY

The Lectionary is the book that contains the chosen scriptural texts from the Old and New Testaments for proclamation in the liturgy throughout the liturgical cycle. The Lectionary begins with the readings from the three cycles of the First Sunday of Advent, continues through all the liturgical seasons, the Sundays of Ordinary Time, solemnities, weekdays, feasts, ritual and votive masses, and readings for masses for various needs and occasions. The Lectionary is the way Catholics encounter the bible, the living word of God, in their worship.

The liturgy by nature is biblical. The eucharistic liturgy is no exception. Most of the ritual prayers of the mass are inspired by biblical passages or images. "The Lord's Supper is an act of obedience to a biblical injunction (Lk 22:14c). From the opening sign of the cross (Mt 28:19) to the final dismissal (Ps 29:11b; Jdt 8:35), the participants are invited to live in the world of the Bible as one people with its people."[1]

The word of God is the heart of all liturgical gatherings. The mystery of Christ is unfolded during the liturgical year in the celebration of the church's sacraments and sacramentals. As each celebration is built upon the word of God "and sustained by it," every time the church gathers for liturgical prayer it "becomes a new event and enriches the word itself with new meaning and power."[2] In other words, Christ is sacramentally present to us in the proclamation of the biblical texts and continues to teach, form us, and provide new, life-changing insight into the living word of God.

The first and second (Old and New) Testaments are both proclaimed in order to demonstrate that there is continuity in God's plan of salvation begun with Israel and brought to completion through Jesus Christ.

We are to respond with assent and commit our lives to God's word in the person of Jesus experienced in the proclamation of the word and the celebration of the eucharist. The word brings us to the awareness of the paschal mystery of Christ we celebrate and make present in every celebration of the eucharist.

The Cycles

There are three liturgical cycles: A, B and C. Each new liturgical cycle begins on the first Sunday of Advent each year and lasts for one complete year. The three cycles make it possible for the fullness of the biblical texts to be proclaimed in the assembly over a three-year period. Each cycle's primary vehicle for encountering the mystery of Christ is one of the synoptic gospels: Matthew (A), Mark (B), Luke (C).[3] The gospel of John is interspersed in each cycle. At the beginning of the liturgical cycle the readings are concerned with the inauguration of Christ's manifestation and the beginning of his ministry. The end of the year focuses on chapters leading up to the passion.

How and Why the Readings Were Chosen

The biblical texts chosen for use at liturgy are intended to proclaim God's word so that the faithful may grow in the faith they profess. The history of salvation is broken open, especially during the seasons of Easter, Lent, and Advent, but also throughout the entire liturgical year. The readings correspond to the purpose and focus of the liturgical seasons and the principles of scriptural interpretation.

The Sundays and solemnities contain the most important biblical passages so that the faithful may experience God's revealed Word and plan of salvation over a reasonable period of time. The week-

---

[1] Gerard S. Sloyan, "Overview of the Lectionary for Mass: Introduction," in *TLD,* 118.

[2] "Lectionary for Mass: Introduction," Chapter 1, #3, in *TLD,* 127–128.

[3] Refer to chapter 9 on this year's liturgical cycle.

day readings contain a second series of readings that complement but are independent of the Sunday readings. "The Order of Readings for Sunday and the solemnities of the Lord extends over three years; for weekdays, over two. Thus, each runs its course independently."[4]

In addition, there are other sets of readings that follow their own set of rules depending upon their use, such as readings for celebrations of the saints, ritual masses, masses for various needs and occasions, votive masses, or masses for the dead.

Structure of Readings for Sundays, Seasons, and Solemnities

Each Sunday mass has three readings. The first reading is generally taken from the Hebrew scriptures (Old Testament). The second reading is from one of the apostles (either a letter or the book of Revelation, depending on the season), and the third reading is from the gospel. The responsorial psalm is a chant response following the first reading. It is from the psalter and usually is directly related to the first reading. However, there is allowance for the use of psalms common to a particular season, feast, or celebration. The psalm is generally sung, as the psalms were written as songs and best fit that mode of expression. The gospel acclamation (the Alleluia or the Lenten acclamation) is "a shout of joy which arises from the whole assembly as a forceful assent to God's Word and Action."[5] It is an acclamation of praise in preparation for the proclamation of the gospel.

There is a continuity between the Old and New Testaments that is best demonstrated when the first reading is directly related to the readings and the liturgy of the day, particularly the gospel. The Old Testament texts were chosen with that perspective in mind.

The order of proclamation is: first reading (Old Testament), responsorial psalm, second reading (from apostolic letters or Revelation), gospel acclamation, gospel.

There is also a unity and harmony evident in the readings chosen for liturgical seasons. The seasonal readings reflect the meaning of the seasons of Advent, Christmas, Lent, and Easter, which have their own distinctive character.

The Readings for the Seasons of the Year

Advent Season

The gospels for the Sundays of Advent are concerned with the theme of Jesus' coming at the end of time and preparation for his birth at Christmas. The Old Testament readings are prophecies about the future messiah and messianic age. The apostolic letters are exhortations and proclamations that center around the themes of Advent. There are two series of readings for use during the weekdays of Advent. During the early weeks (first Sunday through Dec. 16) we hear from John the Baptist and extensively from the prophet Isaiah. The last weeks are concerned with events that immediately prepared for Jesus' birth (chapter 1 from Luke and Matthew).

Christmas Season

The readings of Christmas reflect important themes in the Christian tradition. On the feast of the Holy Family the readings are about the childhood of Jesus and the virtues of family life. The readings for the octave of Christmas, the solemnity of Mary, Mother of God, are about the Virgin Mother of God and the giving of the holy Name of Jesus. The readings for the Second Sunday after Christmas profess our belief in the Incarnation; the Epiphany readings are about the calling of all people to salvation. The texts for the feast of the Lord's baptism reflect the mystery of that event. The weekday readings center around themes of the Lord's manifestation.

Lenten Season

The first and second Sundays recount the Lord's temptation in the desert and the transfiguration. The third, fourth, and fifth weeks in Cycle A tell the story of the Samaritan woman, the man born blind, and the raising of Lazarus from the dead. These gospels may be used in place of the readings of Cycle B and C every year, as they are especially important to the Christian initiation process.

Passion (Palm) Sunday's gospel preceding the procession is a passage from the synoptic gospels that relates the story of Jesus' triumphant entry

---

[4]"Lectionary for Mass: Introduction," #65, in *TLD*, 140.
[5]"Music in Catholic Worship," #53, in *TLD*, 286.

into Jerusalem. An account of the Lord's passion from one of the synoptics is read during the mass.

During Lent, the first readings are about the main aspects of our salvation history from the beginning up until the new covenant in Christ. The apostolic letters were chosen to reflect the first reading and the gospel.

The weekday readings from the Old Testament and gospel readings are related to each other. Readings that highlight proper Lenten spirituality and catechesis are used throughout the season during the week. The early days of Holy Week center around the mystery of the passion; the chrism mass celebrates Jesus' messianic mission and its continuation in the church by means of the sacraments.

Easter Triduum
Holy Thursday recounts the story of the last supper and its implication in the washing of the disciples' feet as well as Paul's telling of the institution of the eucharist, the new Passover in Christ. Good Friday always proclaims the passion event from John's perspective. Jesus as the prophesied suffering servant of Isaiah is the high priest who offered himself in sacrifice for all. The Easter Vigil's Old Testament readings (there are seven) tell the wondrous deeds of our salvation history beginning with the creation of the world. The resurrection story from one of the synoptic gospels and St. Paul's letter to the Romans about Christian baptism as the sacrament of Christ's resurrection are the two New Testament readings proclaimed at the Vigil.

Easter Sunday's gospel is from John and is about the finding of the empty tomb. However, we are allowed to use the gospel from one of the synoptics. If there is an Easter Sunday evening mass, the story of the disciples on the road to Emmaus may be used. The apostolic letter is from Paul and is concerned with living the paschal mystery.

Easter Season
The gospels for the first three Sundays of the season center around post-resurrection appearances of Jesus. The fourth Sunday is about Jesus, the Good Shepherd, and the fifth, sixth, and seventh

Sunday gospels are taken from the teaching, conversation, and prayer of Jesus at the last supper. Throughout the Easter season the Old Testament reading is replaced by passages from the Acts of the Apostles in which the life, witness, and growth of the early church are unfolded. The apostolic readings that best reflect the spirit, faith, hope, and joy of the Easter season are taken from: year A–1 Peter; year B–1 John; year C–Revelation. During the first week (octave) of Easter, Acts is read semi-continuously at the weekday liturgies. The weekday gospel recounts the appearance of the risen Christ. The rest of the season proclaims John's gospel of the last supper discourse, especially themes that emphasize the paschal mystery.

Solemnity of Ascension
The first reading is a proclamation of the Ascension of Christ as described in the Acts of the Apostles. The apostolic letters are about Christ who sits at the Father's right hand in glory and the gospel proclaims the Ascension event from the view of a particular year's synoptic gospel.

Solemnity of Pentecost
The vigil readings for Pentecost give us the choice of four possible readings from the Old Testament that best reflect the many dimensions of the mystery of Pentecost. The apostolic readings depict the Holy Spirit alive and working in the church and the gospel remembers Christ's promise to send the Spirit. Pentecost day has us immersed in the account of Pentecost taken from the Acts of the Apostles (first reading). The apostolic letter from Paul highlights the workings of the Spirit in the church and the gospel remembers Jesus' gift of the Spirit to the disciples on Easter night.

Ordinary Time
Ordinary Time is not really a liturgical season, but it is the thirty-three to thirty-four Sundays of the year in which the fullness of the paschal mystery is unfolded through the life and mission of Jesus proclaimed in the Sunday gospel. Thus, even though Easter is the "mother of all feasts" and the pinnacle of the liturgical year (the very axis upon which it spins), each Sunday is a remembrance and celebration of Easter. Every liturgical celebration is an Easter, paschal event.

During Ordinary Time there is no distinctive character to the readings. The arrangement of the apostolic readings and the gospel is semi-continuous, and, as stated before, the first reading is chosen for its connection to the gospel.

The Second Sunday of Ordinary Time centers on the manifestation of the Lord (which Epiphany also celebrates) with the story of the wedding feast of Cana. The Third Sunday begins a semi-continuous reading of the synoptic gospels in which Jesus' life, mission, and work are unfolded in their fullness according to the perspective of each gospel. The readings form a continuity with the liturgical cycle. For example, the beginning of the year is concerned with the beginning of Jesus' life and work and develops from there accordingly as his story is proclaimed and celebrated throughout the year. The end of the year moves us toward endings and last things. It centers around the ending of Jesus' earthly life and work and eschatological considerations.

Solemnities of the Lord During Ordinary Time
The feasts of Holy Trinity, Corpus Christi, and the Sacred Heart (some call them idea feasts, as they do not celebrate an event in Jesus' life) all have biblical texts that express the meaning particular to each celebration.

Weekdays of Ordinary Time
During weeks one through nine, the gospel of Mark is proclaimed at the weekday masses. Matthew is read from the tenth to the twenty-first week; Luke is read from the twenty-second to the thirty-fourth week. Mark is read in its entirety with the exception of two passages that are read during a different season. Matthew and Luke contain all the passages not included in Mark. The first readings of the weekday masses are continuous readings that are taken first from the Old Testament books, then from the New Testament books. The number of weeks depends on how long it takes to get through a particular book.

The Old Testament passages were selected to recount the overall story of our salvation history and to reflect the general character of the individual books. The only Old Testament books that do not appear in some form in the Lectionary in the weekday cycle are two small prophetic books, Oba-diah and Zephaniah, Esther, Judith, and the poetic Song of Solomon. Esther and Judith are read on Sundays and weekdays at other times of the year, however.

The readings from apostolic letters were chosen in order that the basic intent, message, and teaching of each letter be presented. Keeping in the spirit of beginning and last things, the end of the year weekday readings are from Daniel and Revelation and reflect the eschatological nature of the end of the liturgical cycle.

Lectionary-based Catechesis

This phrase is used to describe a method of catechesis based on the word of God proclaimed at the Sunday liturgy. In practice it is sometimes reduced to a simplistic approach that listens to the word of God and appropriates personal meaning from the word, and then chooses a doctrine that best complements our personal understanding. Often, however, the doctrinal teaching has little to do with the spirit of the season, solemnity, feast, or Sunday of the year.

The church, however, has left us a marvelous tool for the ordering of catechesis: the Lectionary and the liturgical cycle. As one can see from the above descriptions of the readings chosen for use in liturgy through the seasons and Ordinary Time, the liturgy itself dictates what issues of doctrine emanate from our worship.

The liturgical year provides the vehicle for the ordering of doctrine through the selected biblical texts for a specific season, Sunday, solemnity, feast, sacrament, or celebration. The readings, liturgical prayers, and gestures and symbols reflect the meaning of the celebration and the doctrine that flows from it. For example, during the Christmas season, the readings express our belief in the Incarnation, the manifestation of God, Mary as Mother of God, and the salvation offered to all people. The liturgy suggests and sets forth the thematic content of our catechesis during the season of Christmas: Incarnation, soteriology (salvation), manifestation, Mary Mother of God.

It is evident from the description, structure, and ordering of readings throughout the liturgical cycle that the major tenets of the Christian faith are unfolded in the readings and liturgies of the liturgical year. The liturgy provides us with the basis of catechesis. The implication, then, is that catechists must become very familiar with what the liturgy truly expresses, rather than with what they think it appears to be saying, or what seems to be compatible with our personal (often fundamentalist) interpretation of the readings of a particular Sunday.

Thus, catechists need to be familiar with documents such as the Introduction to the Lectionary, General Norms for the Liturgical Year, and all liturgical documents that define and express what it is we celebrate. This is one reason why a resource such as this is an important tool. While it does not answer all questions, it does provide interpretation of the biblical texts and it proposes inherent meaning in the liturgical celebration itself. It is in no way a substitute for the primary documents that truly inform and provide the praxis and rationale for the practice of our worship, faith, and life.

PART TWO:
THE INTERPRETATION OF SCRIPTURE

A word about the interpretation of scripture is in order at this juncture. *Word & Worship Workbook* is centered around the interpreted texts of the Lectionary scriptures. When I first entered the world of scriptural interpretation I had many questions. How can one scholar propose one interpretation, and another propose something altogether different? If these are respected scholars, who is right and who is wrong? Which interpretation is the most authentic? Do I really have the authority to present interpretations that are boldly new and unfamiliar to our common literal understanding of the texts?

Recently a man challenged me, "How is it possible that we could have heard a scripture in a certain way all our lives, and yet the discovery of the possible mistranslation of one word might change the entire meaning of a text? How can that be?" It is a valid question, one that I asked myself many times over in the early days. Hopefully, this chapter will answer some of those questions.

I make no claims to be a scripture scholar. In my role as catechist I have worked with scriptural exegesis in a parish setting for a long time and have used multiple resources and commentaries by various respected biblical scholars. As a compiler and redactor (editor), I have chosen exegeses according to a certain point of view. As a human person, I bring my own personality, beliefs, biases, and heart's desires to every reading of scripture. My first hearing of the scriptures is influenced by my limited perspective. Awareness of this limited perspective grew as the role of facilitating exegesis in our community was shared by members of a team. Each interpretation bore the personality traits of the facilitator who prepared it. The material might have been the same, but it was always nuanced from the perspective of the facilitator.

Bernard Lee maintains that we all enter every experience biased, "that is, with presuppositions, and rarely with much self consciousness about our ideological convictions. It is not wrong to have them. It is natural. It is disastrous not to know we have them."[6] Lee suggests that our safeguard is the Christian community as this is where discernment takes place. Thus, my effort to interpret the interpreters and to choose which interpretations to use comes with no official approbation. It is the result of one pastoral minister/liturgist's attempts to struggle with the insights of such interpretation in the midst of a faith-filled, life-giving Christian community. The efficacy of the redacted exegeses in this text will only be borne out (or not) in the midst of communities that seek to find God's compelling word in the midst of praying, studying, celebrating, and sharing the scriptures.

There is comfort in Jim Dunning's citation of Bernard Lee's[7] encouragement to ministers of the word:

> If we truly converse with scripture and allow the texts in their strangeness to interpret, change, challenge and call us to conversion, we need some guides to invite us

---

[6]*TFC,* 64–65.

[7]Bernard J. Lee, "Shared Homily: Conversation that Puts Communities at Risk," in *Alternative Futures for Worship, Volume 3: The Eucharist,* ed. Bernard J. Lee (Collegeville: The Liturgical Press, 1987), 157.

into their world. Lee insists that the model for such guides is not the scholar who knows all the nuances of form criticism, redaction criticism, literary criticism and structural analysis but who cannot lead us toward any pastoral "so what's." We require, rather, a new kind of minister of the word and a new sense of community urgency to have someone prepared to help us converse with the word in our own world.[8]

This workbook's purpose is to assist people in the art of conversing with the word "in our own world." Such conversation leads to conversion that is at the heart of the liturgy and the scriptures.

Different models of biblical criticism (historical critical, literary, redaction, and others) are employed in some form or another throughout all the exegeses in this workbook. Different scholars employ different methods in their analyses. The vehicle used to travel the road of exegesis is far less important than the destination. What is important is the heart and soul of the text: "How have we/I been transformed as a result of our conversation with the scriptures?" To simply read the information within these pages without grappling with the interpretive questions in a communal setting of some sort is to miss the opportunity to allow the texts to overtake us. To reiterate this book's opening hope, "We miss the chance to be knocked breathless by the holy violence of conversion that will leave us drenched and exhausted as though swallowed by the sea and spat back newly salted upon the shore"[9] never to be the same again. Interpretation allows the texts to interpret us, to tell us who we are: God's beloved and chosen people.

The type of agenda, interpretation, and reflection process used in this workbook is pastoral and theological and employs historical and literary criticism. It is pastoral as it deals with real issues from real people's lives in the midst of their everyday existence. It is theological as it seeks to answer the question: "Who is the God of Jesus and what is the meaning of human life lived in the Spirit?" Histor-

ical criticism allows us to listen with the ears and cultural experience of a first-century Palestinian in order to better illuminate the meaning for listeners of the twenty-first century. The historical critical method allows us to move beyond a fundamental or purely historical meaning of the texts. The historical critical method studies scripture in the context of the history, culture, customs, religious beliefs, and economy of the original community for which the word was written. This methodology recovers and discovers the past of the text in order to bring it into today. "Since the Bible points to the mystery of God and of the divine-human relationship, it makes claims not simply on its original audience but on subsequent generations."[10] We not only strive to understand biblical interpretation historically, but we also engage in a hermeneutic to translate or explain it for today. Scripture is not approached as an historical, literally interpreted representation of the events that took place and the people who were involved. Rather, it uncovers the heart and soul of the message, the reason and meaning for the retold event.

Through literary criticism, the nuances and translations of language, cultural idioms, past and present meanings, and literary devices are explored. Literary criticism helps us get inside the story-world of the text to allow the drama to touch, impact, and transform us.[11]

Scriptural interpretation draws on the wisdom and lived experience of past Christian communities through the centuries of the church's existence. Such communities struggled to live the gospel as it was passed on to them. Because of the struggle, the church today is the beneficiary of a rich deposit of faith emanating from the scriptures. Biblical archaeology and study over the past forty years have contributed greatly to our understanding of the sacred text.

The doors to biblical scholarship were opened on September 30, 1943 by Pope Pius XII's encyclical, *Divino Afflante Spiritu* ("Inspired by the Holy Spirit"). The encyclical exhorted the church and biblical scholars to use the modern methods of in-

---

[8]*EGW,* 180.

[9]Refer to opening sentence of chapter 1: quote by Nathan Mitchell.

---

[10]*EGW,* 166.

[11]Ibid., 177.

terpretation that Protestant churches had already been using. The intent was to "describe the literal sense of the scriptures, i.e. 'what the writer intended to express.'"[12] Prior to this time, much of our understanding of scripture had been figurative and allegorical. The encyclical moved us beyond allegory to the story-world of the text. *Divino Afflante Spiritu* challenged exegetes to uncover what the scriptures meant to the original authors and hearers of the texts.

Raymond Brown reminds us that the Roman Catholic Church issued a pronouncement on the historical accuracy of the gospels. Citing the Pontifical Commission's Instruction on *The Historical Truth of the Gospels* issued in 1964, Brown tells us:

> Rome has insisted that one should speak of the Gospels as historical in the sense that the four accounts of the ministry of Jesus took their origin in words that Jesus spoke and deeds that he performed. Nevertheless, the pronouncement made clear that those words and deeds underwent considerable adaptation from the time of Jesus' ministry until the time when they were written down in the Gospels. For instance, there was a period of oral transmission wherein the apostles preached what Jesus had said and done; but they infused their accounts of Jesus with a post-resurrectional insight into his divinity—an insight they had not had when he was alive. Then in the commission to writing by the evangelists there was a further selection, synthesis and explication of the accounts that had come down from apostolic preaching with the result that the final Gospel narratives of the ministry are not necessarily literal accounts of what Jesus did and said.[13]

Brown cites the Roman document's position that the inherent truth of the story is not affected by the fact that the authors relate the words and actions of Christ in a different order and that they do not recount his sayings literally, but rather differently, while still preserving their sense.

Brown also reminds us that most Catholics are not aware of this position of the church and are still uneasy when someone suggests that "a particular section dealing with Jesus' ministry is not literal history."[14] Contemporary students of the scriptures must keep in mind that "in the course of transmission from Jesus to the evangelists, all Gospel material has been colored by the faith and experience of the Church of the first century."[15]

Matthew, Mark, and Luke are called synoptic gospels. Their overall vision of Jesus is fairly similar. In the synoptic gospels Jesus is very busy establishing his reign and teaching his disciples what it means to live and work toward building that reign. Thus, there is little time or concern for proclaiming a theology about himself. John's Jesus, on the other hand, provides us with a refined christology. Each gospel was written from the vantage point of the community for which it was written. There was a significant difference in the way a story was told depending on the economic and class status of the listener. The stories were told with the community in mind, according to their needs and life situation. Since each evangelist was writing for his own community and from his own perspectives, each gospel is marked by the distinctive personality and specific agenda of its author.

It was once thought that Matthew was the earliest gospel. However, research has shown that Mark was the first evangelist, since his text appears in both Matthew and Luke. Matthew and Luke also share similar material that is not included in Mark. Thus, most scholars would agree that there must have been another source that was familiar to both Matthew and Luke. This lost reference is called *Quelle* (German for source) or "Q."

As the Hellenized, Greek speaking world became Christianized, the original biblical texts were translated into Greek. Translation from one language to another automatically involves interpretation. Jesus spoke Aramaic, not Greek. Every gospel was interpreted not only in a new language, but in a different cultural system and world view as well. By the time the Greek texts were compiled, Christian culture had already embraced Greek

---

[12]*HCEC*, 423.
[13]*ACC*, 2.

[14]Ibid.
[15]Ibid., 3.

philosophical thought that colored the translations according to Greek constructs.

Very often there are no words that capture the complexity of meaning in the original language, so the translator opts for an approximation. Language is limited. Scholarship, study, and archaeological efforts have advanced the quest to unearth authentic interpretation of the ancient texts. Exegesis is not an exact science. Yet that need not shake our faith too greatly, as the synoptic gospels are not always consonant with one another either. In many instances they contradict each other. For example, Luke's Jesus dies on the cross with a sense of peaceful confidence (23:46; cf. 23:34, 43) whereas Mark's Jesus cries out in desolation (15:34ff.).

Each evangelist has his own perspective and all draw upon the corporate memory of their different communities. New Testament scholarship recognizes that "the Gospels themselves are not histories of Jesus but the record of how communities remembered Jesus and taught new generations what and how they remembered."[16]

All scriptural interpretation is biased in one way or another. There is no such thing as an uninterpreted fact. History, for example, is shaded according to the bias of the historian. I was once struck by a comment made by a school principal who said that she would not use the Encyclopaedia Britannica in her school as it colored the events of the American Revolution according to a British bias. It was an eye-opening moment for me. Of course, it made perfect sense. Historians would naturally portray the "facts" of their history from a biased viewpoint. Facts, no matter how certain they are, are interpreted through the lens of the messenger, scribe, or historian.

Most scholars agree that none of the evangelists were eyewitnesses to Jesus' life and ministry. They had to rely on an oral account (a previous tradition) of his life. Raymond Brown asserts that the gospels developed over a long period of time and were based on the memory and tradition of communities that lived and celebrated Jesus' words and deeds. "Apostolic faith and preaching has reshaped those memories, as has also the individual viewpoint of each evangelist who selected, synthesized and explicated the traditions that came down to him."[17] The implication for our understanding of the gospels is that each evangelist gives us a multi-faceted prism's view of the God/man called Jesus. Brown suggests that we should not be disconcerted when we read the contrasting views of Jesus in the gospels. Nor should we attempt to decide which view is the most correct. Each view is given to us "by the inspiring Spirit, and no one of them exhausts the meaning of Jesus. It is as if one walks around a large diamond to look at it from three different angles. A true picture of the whole emerges only because the viewpoints are different."[18]

What does all this mean for the average minister of the word in a parish? An effective minister of the word is armed not only with a personal understanding of scripture, but also with "the work of biblical scholars . . . [who] provide historical and literary insights which help uncover the meaning of the sacred texts."[19] When reflecting upon the scriptures people often focus on an affective, "warm fuzzy," personalist/literalist/fundamentalist hearing and understanding. "This is what it must mean because this is what it says," or "How did it make me *feel*?" There is nothing wrong with approaching the scriptures this way. It is the first way we are to approach the bible, as a hermeneutic of experience. It is beneficial insofar as it touches the person's lived experience (natural sign). However, sometimes this initial reaction becomes the final perspective and people unwittingly are left with a fundamentalist understanding of the text. "This is what it means because this is what it says and since it is in the bible it must be right." They are not challenged to move beyond their basic assumptions regarding the meanings of texts and the implications for Christian living. The opportunity to be challenged by the heart and soul of the text is often missed. The role of the minister of the word is to move people beyond this initial literal understanding to one that provides the foundation for a renewed praxis of Christian living.

[16] *TFC*, 38.

[17] *CCHW*, 68.

[18] Ibid., 71.

[19] *Sharing the Light of Faith, An Official Commentary*, 20.

For example, on the sixth Sunday of Ordinary time, Cycle C, we hear Luke's version of the beatitudes. "Blest are you poor; the reign of God is yours" (6:20). An exclusively personal hearing of this scripture might prompt someone who is not literally poor to identify with the poor of Luke. They might think, "Surely, this means all who are poor in any way, such as the lonely, the stressed, those who are poor in spirit. I certainly am in that category." While Matthew's gospel does indeed make this extension, Luke's does not. The person's identification with the poor and assigning of personal meaning to the text perhaps is due to a life situation such as stress, sorrow, or grief, etc. This identification is not only logical, but desirable. It helps the person encounter God's love and compassion.

However, exegesis on the text presents a challenge. After conversing with the interpretation of the passage, that same person, given the opportunity, is invited to move beyond self, to a world view that embraces the heart of Luke's gospel: radical concern for the poor and the marginalized. Raymond Brown suggests:

> Luke's poor are the real "have-nots" of this world; his hungry know the misery of an empty stomach; his unfortunate are weeping. And just so that we do not miss the realism of the beatitudes, Luke narrates a series of corresponding "woes," stark anathemas hurled against the rich and the content who do not know the meaning of need.[20]

After such reflection on Luke's beatitudes, the person's original understanding is challenged. A decision is in order. He or she must make a decision: Am I willing to have my original assumption and understanding challenged? Is it in harmony with the exegesis? If not, where is the difficulty? Transformation takes place through honest conversation with the interpretation. Concern for self moves to concern for others, in this case, the poor and marginalized. Conversion moves us beyond the personal (me only) to the corporate and/or the global (us together). Herein lies the impetus for Christian apostolic action. Catechesis of this

sort always asks the communal question: How is the community and how am I challenged by such a word?

There is one powerful bias in the gospels: the thread that weaves their intricate design. This bias, which permeates all of scripture, is a radical option for the oppressed, the poor, and those without power or use of the world's resources. One cannot ignore it or deny it. It is so blatant that one would have to fall over it, were it to be in one's path. A preferential option for the poor (in the words of the bishops) influences the way we are to hear the word of God. Love of God and love of neighbor demand that we be responsible for all members of the human family. For many, however, this bias is the biggest stumbling block in the scriptures. It is extremely counter-cultural and very politically incorrect. In an individualistic society such as ours, our creed often becomes, "Just pick yourself up by the bootstraps and take care of yourself." While such a platitude is grounded in the American work ethic, it ignores those factors that make it all but impossible for today's marginalized to even find their boots in the first place! To be Christian today means that we are to become bootmakers. Then and only then will the disenfranchised gain access to the world's possibilities. The decision ("so-what") questions, therefore, are critical to this process. When one is faced with having to commit to a transformed world view by the assent of one's actions, true metanoia is possible.

We are taught that the word of God proclaimed at liturgy is one of our primary symbols. What is the function of symbol? Symbols provide a language system between God and humanity. Symbols speak to us in ways that words cannot. Symbols convey many different layers of meaning. Water as symbol evokes images of life giving, thirst quenching, and death-dealing all at the same time. Some have called the Vietnam wall a national symbol. Imagine a war protester and a U. S. Army officer standing before that symbol. The wall no doubt speaks two different things to both men. One can only imagine. But a loud word it speaks!

A comparison between sign and symbol helps us understand the complexities of the word of God as symbol. A sign is uni-dimensional. It points to

---

[20] *BAL*, 336.

one reality. A stop sign has one literal meaning: STOP. There is no other way to read STOP. One had better heed the sign. It means what it expresses. There are no ambiguities regarding the meaning of sign. A symbol, on the other hand, is complex, ambiguous, and powerfully enriches our lives. Symbols do not mean the same thing to every person who encounters them. Symbols touch the inner recesses of our being. They provide a vehicle for divine communication. A woman whose husband had just committed suicide was particularly moved by the symbol of breaking bread at her husband's funeral. She fully understood the meaning of one of the liturgy's primary symbols as if she had encountered it for the first time. The breaking bread recalled Christ's broken body. That day, the torn bread recalled her broken body as well. The symbol of breaking bread communicated a new truth to her. God spoke thunderous words through that symbol. Christ would have died on the cross even if she, in her unbearable grief, had been the only person in the world.

The linguistic symbol world of the gospel touches us on many different levels. How it touches us depends on the events of our lives. The story of Jesus healing the widow's son is going to speak something entirely different to a woman who has just lost her teenage son than it will to someone whose life experience is altogether different. Symbols never get exhausted of possible meanings.

The word *love* is a linguistic symbol. Its meaning will never be exhausted. We celebrate eucharist over and over because we have not experienced all there is to experience in the eucharist. What speaks to us today may not speak to us tomorrow. The word of God is living word. We are living people. Living things are fluid. Through the will of the Spirit, we move, change, and await new possibilities at the horizon of each new day. Symbols evolve. So do we. Consequently, we will never exhaust the symbol world of the scriptures. It is why we can return to Matthew, three cycles later, and hear a word in a way that we never heard it before.

Sunday to Sunday and celebration to celebration, we encounter the sacramental, risen presence of Christ. How will we interpret the experience for our lives? Ancient wisdom assumed that Christians would engage in mystagogical reflection that would give meaning to their lives. Liturgy leads us to reflection. From the experience of Christ present in word and sacrament we order our Christian life. Mystagogical reflection as it is envisioned in this resource begins and begins again with the experience of Christ present in eucharistic liturgy; in the community of believers; in the church, *called and sent*; in the word, first experienced, then illuminated by informed scholarship and in the handed-down tradition of previous generations.

Catechists are charged with planting seeds. They are to plant the interpreted experience of liturgy, scripture, and tradition. God, the Creator/Harvester, then, will water, fertilize, and bring to fullness of life those who seek authentic worship and life in Spirit and in truth.

4. THE CATECHIST

Many unsuspecting persons find themselves in the role of catechist quite by accident. We have all heard the whimsical story of the person who comes to the church office to buy a mass card and is asked to be the Director of Religious Education. While this story is more myth and mirth than fact (we hope!), there are still many eager ministers who have not had the opportunity to pursue advanced instruction to prepare for catechetical ministry. In order to "re-echo" the person of Christ encountered in everyday life, in scripture, in the faith and belief of the church, and in liturgical celebrations, catechists need hearts that are on fire with the love of God and the desire to share that love with others.

However, more is needed. Catechists must be familiar with the authentic Christian/Catholic story: scripture and tradition. Formal instruction is important. Many, if not most diocesan offices provide good catechist training. Most people who will use this resource are probably familiar with the principles of catechesis articulated in previous chapters. However, review is often an enlightening and renewing endeavor.

Catechists should be confident that the heritage they are "handing down" is truly the official understanding of the church's tradition. Many folks make assumptions regarding church teaching, when in fact their assumptions are incorrect. For example, the church has no official position regarding recent Marian apparitions. While making no judgment one way or another regarding the authenticity of such apparitions, it is not necessary for a Catholic to consider them a part of the deposit of faith. To teach such apparitions as fact and precept would be grossly incorrect. It is one thing to share a personal and private experience of faith enrichment; it is quite another for a minister of the church to pass it on as divinely inspired revelation. Such apparitions come under the heading of private revelation and do not constitute "...all that the Catholic Church believes, teaches, and proclaims to be revealed by God."[1]

Also, while there is certainly disagreement and tension regarding the use of "male" centered God language, the church teaches that God transcends the human limitations of male and female. If one were to insist that the church teach that God is male, that person would be wrong.

Therefore, it is always wise to check with primary sources to either affirm or challenge one's understanding of church teaching. It is always good to seek out and refer to sources such as the Vatican II documents, the *General Catechetical Directory,* the *National Catechetical Directory, Sharing the Light of Faith,* and its companion, *Sharing the Light of Faith: An Official Commentary,*[2] the *Catechism of the Catholic Church,* and other catechetical documents, liturgical documents, encyclicals, apostolic exhortations, pastoral letters, canon law, etc. Secondary resources would include various works and commentaries of respected scholars and theologians.

Finally, catechists must be willing to enter into and immerse themselves in the conversion world of catechesis. It is a lifelong pursuit. The Christian life is not static. It is a life. To live is to grow. To grow means one has to learn. To learn means to live in a new way. "Catechesis is a lifelong process for the individual and a constant and concerted pastoral activity of the Christian community."[3]

Catechesis empowers men, women, and children and brings the light of faith to life. A noted atheist once mused that he might consider Christianity if

---

[1] *RCIA,* #491, #585.

[2] The *National Catechetical Directory* (NCD), *Sharing the Light of Faith,* was formulated in response to the urging of the Sacred Congregation for the Clergy following formulation of the *General Catechetical Directory.* The GCD was prepared by that same Congregation after the Second Vatican Council called for a document that would provide the basic fundamentals of catechesis for the universal church. The intent of the Council was to assist Catholics in an informed and living faith. The bishop's conferences were urged to prepare national directories in order to apply the principles and guidelines of the *General Catechetical Directory.*

[3] NCD, #32.

he were to observe disciples truly living the message they allege to proclaim. It is a sad critique that he has not encountered such disciples (if, indeed, his observation constitutes more than a tongue in cheek commentary!)

The church's vision of catechesis seeks to create living, conscious, and active followers of Christ evidenced by the way they live their lives. Enormous gratitude goes to all faithful servants who strive to bring that life to birth in the people they serve. May your lives be richly blessed as you encounter Christ in this catechesis of transformation.

5. A Story of Transformative Catechesis

Credos often have little life of their own. It takes the power of the human person to bring them to life. Stories put flesh and bones on the catechesis we profess. The following vignette is a real, though composite story that takes place in the context of Christian initiation. It is a story that is or should be repeated in the lives of all Catholics who walk the ongoing journey of faith.

Her name was Rita. She was preparing for the sacraments of initiation. Rita's preparation, her "suitable catechesis"[1] consisted in helping her strengthen the relationship she was developing with God by sharing common stories and experiences of Jesus' presence. She reflected upon the life of Jesus found in the Lectionary scriptures and the church's understanding of those scriptures. There were also stories of Christians and saints throughout the ages who tried to live the message of Jesus in their daily lives, some by offering their lives for others.

Folks shared with Rita how, in their struggle to live a gospel life, those earlier Christians wisely formulated and handed down the beliefs and practices that helped conform them to the life of Christ. Christians from the very beginning gathered to celebrate their common faith in Jesus and to be strengthened and nourished for mission in their world. Early Christians had inherited a tradition from their ancestors, the Hebrew people. To be in right relationship (*hesed*) with the God of Abraham and Moses assumed an action, a response. This response involved inclusive care and concern for the poor, widows and orphans, outcasts, and the marginalized.

Jesus lived *hesed* in word and practice. It was the hallmark of his ministry and was to be the hallmark of the Christian life. While often falling short of the mark, Christians relied on Jesus' two great commandments: love of God and love of neighbor. They gathered together to worship and be strengthened to go out and strengthen others. Rita was told how the same thing still happens

___

[1] *RCIA*, #75.

today when the community gathers for liturgy. Rita understood what that meant. She, too, received similar strength in her encounter with Christ and his people in the celebration of the word each Sunday.

Over time Rita shared her experience of God. She had come to know that God was always a part of her life. She felt personally called into relationship with Jesus. This relationship brought her to the doors of the Catholic Church. Her faith was personal. The communal dimension frightened her, however, as it might ask more than she was willing to give.

Over time Rita's relationship with Jesus grew and her life began to change. Her angry, bitter edge began to melt away with the passing of each Sunday. The Christ of word and worship was impacting her life. She began to see areas and attitudes that were not in conformity with Jesus of the gospels. The Christ she encountered was reconciling and inclusive. The church she sought celebrated reconciliation and challenged one to conversion and transformation. The church was a vision and a source of biblical justice.

The social teaching of this church became Rita's proverbial thorn in the flesh, however. Jesus was far more inclusive of others than she was. Rita's new church insisted that *all* persons deserve to be treated with rightful, equal human dignity and respect. She wanted to change her inner disposition, but letting go was difficult. There was a cloud of darkness hanging over her. She tried to ignore it, but the gospel was persistent. Something was wrong. Denial is illusion's safety net. The "so-what" questions of each week began to haunt her. She responded to her new Christian life by working with needy mothers and their children. Yet, something was still wrong.

In the lenten season, those preparing for baptism—along with all the faithful—enter a period of purification and renewal. During the ritual celebration of scrutiny, Rita became conscious of the barrier that still existed in her life. In the proclamation and preaching of the story about the man born blind, Rita became aware of her own "blindness from birth." It was a blindness that had its roots in her family system. Rita was raised in a climate of hate, prejudice, and racial bigotry. This hatred was normative behavior for her and her entire family. It was the "code and creed" she knew. The response of hate is to act hatefully, just as the response of love is to act lovingly. There had been responses of hate in her life. How could she reconcile such hatred? There was obviously no room for hatred in Jesus' reign. Jesus preached a gospel of reconciliation and inclusion.

Through catechesis that echoed Jesus' life to Rita, she was able to listen and respond to God's word. Scripture and tradition had been forming her. In spite of her environmentally conditioned hatred, Rita was captured by the inclusive God of scripture and a church struggling to live the gospel. She resolved to release the hatred.

After the Vigil's cleansing bath of baptism, the slathered, scented, and sealed anointing of the Spirit in confirmation, and the uniting, healing, and nourishing reception of Jesus in the eucharist, Rita was drained of emotion. She was well aware of her personal story of creation, covenant, exodus, and community experienced throughout her life's journey. Rita was not to remain in the safe haven of the Sunday table. She was sent forth to become the gift she had received.

The Vigil was not the end for Rita. Nor is any celebration of sacrament a port of arrival rather than departure. Rita realized a deeper reality. She was empowered for action in response to the Christ encountered in *word*, *eucharist*, and *community*. Her role was one of servanthood. Her mission was clear. She would do what she could to right the wrong that had been so much a part of the life she knew before. Christ had brought something to birth in her. Her exodus from death to life meant that she had to bury the seeds of hatred she had known. Rita's heart would permanently change through her decision to act. She resolved to become a voice for those she had once hated. Her most feared platform would be her family's own front porch. She was well aware of what it might cost. Yet she was willing. "Lord, help my unwillingness." A new joy crept into her life.

Rita's catechesis not only prepared her for full and vibrant celebration of the liturgy, but it also helped her realize that she was changed because of it. Rita could not wait to share her new life with the community that had nurtured her and assisted in God's creative work in her life. Rita unabashedly shared her passover story with the Sunday assembly during the Easter season. Rita had presided over the death of *hatred* at the Easter Vigil. In its place was resurrection of *love*: the new life of Christ's healing, sacramental joy. She thanked the community for nurturing her in her many months of formation. She credited God's word, the Catholic story, and her new family of friends for assisting in birthing her transformation.

The meaning Rita extracted from her experience was nothing less than a refined articulation of the church's foundational belief: the paschal mystery of Jesus Christ. Rita engaged in liturgical catechesis with the community. She recalled the threshold moments of the Easter Vigil. As she was immersed for the first time, gasping for air in the stirring waters, Rita experienced an interior cleansing. She waged her last battle with *hatred*. That old demon was being washed away while frantically holding on for one last breath of life. On the third plunge Rita thought of what it meant to die. "I came up the third time gasping for air." In those split seconds she sensed the fear of the Israelites sloshing through the watery wall toward an unknown land of promised freedom, leaving behind their despised, yet familiar life of bondage.

Water soaked and Spirit drenched, Rita exited the font aware that it was more than excess moisture dripping off her waterlogged robe. Her familiar, nasty companion was slithering back into the murky waters, never to surface again. She sensed new life. "If Jesus died for me and for everybody else, then I have to do the same. I have to let hatred die and I have to live for other people, just like Jesus did."

Rita's experience of baptism taught her more about the theology of baptism than any creedal statement could ever articulate. When the church teaches that baptism is the washing of sin, incorporation into the Body of Christ and the mission of discipleship, it is because generation after generation has experienced what Rita experienced.

Theology is not as lofty as it sometimes appears to be. It is simply a vehicle for the expression of faith.

Rita was catechized by the belief, story, and tradition of a people (both present and past) who share a common faith in Jesus Christ. She was further catechized by a rich, sensory ritual experience (liturgy) laden with meaning. With the entire church, Rita began the life-long process of experiencing celebration that leads to reflection that leads to meaning for life. The ancients called it mystagogical catechesis, uncovering the deep layers of mystery.

The *Rite of Christian Initiation of Adults* points out that catechesis for catechumens "enlightens faith, directs the heart toward God, fosters participation in the liturgy, inspires apostolic activity and nurtures a life completely in accord with the Spirit of God."[2] Rita experienced a suitable catechesis. Such catechesis should be the agenda of the entire Christian dispensation. It is not reserved only for those seeking entry into the church. Initiation is only the gateway, the beginning. Sacramental/liturgical/ritual catechesis is the conversion work of an entire lifetime.

---

[2]*RCIA*, #78.

6. FORMAT FOR CATECHIST'S PLANNING SESSION

Catechists participate in the following reflection process prior to the Sunday liturgy in order to prepare catechesis for their particular ministry group.

The weekly sessions in this book are intended to help prepare facilitators to lead a "Breaking Open the Word" session that begins with a liturgy of the word and is followed by an adult learning session that explores the word just celebrated. Refer to chapter 7, "Preparing the Catechetical Session," for assistance in crafting catechetical sessions after participating in the weekly sessions provided in this workbook.

The prayers provided in the weekly sessions are the ritual prayers from the Sacramentary for that particular Sunday or feast. The entrance antiphon, opening prayers, prayers over the gifts, preface, prayer after communion, and final blessings serve to reveal the meaning inherent in the liturgy and the scriptures. Thus, the prayers chosen for the weekly preparation session might be any one of the prayers from the liturgy of the day and are chosen for their connection to the liturgy's obvious themes. The closing prayer of the weekly session, you will discover, is not necessarily the closing prayer of the liturgy.

PREPARATION

Liturgical Prayer

The entrance antiphon, the opening prayer, the final prayer, and assorted blessings are taken from the liturgy of the coming Sunday or feast. Other ritual prayers are also included throughout the workbook as appropriate and are taken from the Roman Missal, the *Rite of Christian Initiation of Adults,* the Liturgy of the Hours, or approved books of blessing such as *The Book of Blessings* and *Catholic Household Blessings and Prayers.*

Environment

As the preparation session occurs in the context of a liturgy of the word, it is worthy of a prayerful space decorated with the symbols of the liturgical season. Suggestions and available directives regarding the liturgical space are given at the start of each new liturgical season to assist you in creating a prayerful place for your gathering.

Music

While musical selections are not suggested in this workbook, it is nevertheless important to begin each gathering with music that is familiar to all gathered. Simple refrains are easily mastered by even the most challenged singer. Music is important to the catechetical gathering as it serves a critical function in the celebration of liturgy.[1] The psalm refrain could be chanted on one tone and ended on a lower note than the central tone, much like the chanting of the presider/celebrant when he chants, "The Lord be with you," and all respond, "And also with you." The entrance antiphon could be chanted in the same manner.

LITURGY OF THE WORD

The readings are proclaimed in a brief liturgy of the word format with song, proclamation, and gesture (standing, sitting, sign of the cross, etc.).

Proclaim the Readings from the Lectionary

(Perhaps a copy of the text can be made available and given to each person *after* the proclamation.

---

[1] "Among the many signs and symbols used by the church to celebrate its faith, music is of preeminent importance. As sacred song unites to words, it forms a necessary or integral part of the solemn liturgy" (*Constitution on the Sacred Liturgy,* #112, in *TLD).* "The quality of joy and enthusiasm which music adds to community worship cannot be gained in any other way. It imparts a sense of unity to the congregation and sets the appropriate tone for a particular celebration. In addition to expressing texts, music can also unveil a dimension of meaning and feeling, a communication of ideas and intuitions which words alone cannot yield. This dimension is integral to human personality and to growth in faith. It cannot be ignored if the signs of worship are to speak to the whole person" ("Music in Catholic Worship," #23, #24, in *TLD).*

Some like to make notes on the text during the exegesis.

STEP 1
NAMING ONE'S EXPERIENCE

All share their initial impressions. All listen without agreeing or disagreeing. In this case, the hearing of scripture constitutes the experience. What are your initial impressions? What were the feelings, mood, words that captured your attention? How did the readings (particularly the gospel) affect you? Stay with your initial feelings. Do not try to explain or give a rationale at this point. This first exercise is an attempt to name your initial experience.

STEP 2
UNDERSTANDING THE EXPERIENCE

Why did the text touch you? Were there any experiences in your life that may have shaped the way you heard the story? What understanding of this gospel or readings do you already bring with you to this dialogue? What are your biases? What do you think the gospel readings are trying to convey? In your opinion, what does it mean?

STEP 3
INPUT FROM VISION/STORY/TRADITION

The readings are interpreted in the context and from the vantage point of their original setting, culture, time, and hearers.

Liturgical Context

The facilitator gives *brief* input regarding the liturgical context of the readings. In a few sentences the facilitator explains why this reading occurs where it does in the liturgy in the present cycle. Most often the ritual prayers of the liturgy support the intent of the readings. Readings point to and focus the season, cycle, sacrament, feast, or theology.[2] The readings are interconnected with the liturgy and

shed light on the celebration. Similarly, the liturgy being celebrated also helps focus the readings. The liturgy is not only the liturgy of the word. It is much more. There are four equal signs of God's presence in the liturgy: God's presence in the assembly, the word, the eucharist, and the presider/celebrant. The readings, therefore, and all the elements of liturgy are interdependent. To provide biblical interpretation without the liturgical context is to present a distorted view of the liturgy.

Gospel Exegesis

The facilitator provides the critical biblical scholarship, using the insights of various biblical scholars. The world of the text is penetrated by looking at its structure, context, and literary devices, as well as by deepening our understanding of the author's intent or the church's reasons for using the text. What was the text saying to the early Palestinian community? Why was it said? Who was the audience and what was the background?

We ask: What does critical biblical scholarship have to say about this text? How would people have heard it in Jesus' time? Sometimes the meaning of the text is crystal clear and obvious. However, very often help is needed to appreciate the story-world, biases, and agenda of the original teller and listeners of the stories.

Proclaim the gospel again.

Listening to the gospel following the presentation of biblical interpretation often allows the text to be heard with new ears. The exegesis is brought to bear on this second reading of the gospel and helps implant (or perhaps cast doubt on) the insights that were shared.

STEP 4
TESTING ORIGINAL ASSUMPTIONS

This conversation gets the meaning out in front. Testing helps make the connection between the

---

[2]In the Rite of Confirmation there is a list of scripture citations for use in the ritual celebration. All of the citations,

taken together, shed light on the meaning of the sacrament, making it beneficial to include and use all of the readings in preparation for confirmation. The suggested readings are not simply for the purpose of choosing texts for the liturgical celebration. They help express the meaning as well.

original story and the listener's initial assumptions and understanding. It either strengthens or challenges first impressions. Initial impressions are contrasted with or related to the exegesis. A person may experience excitement, challenge, discomfort, surprise, disagreement, vulnerability, or affirmation. It is at this point that we test our earliest assumptions and prior understandings in order to allow the text to transform us. Sometimes it is very difficult to let go of our previous biases, particularly when they have been informed by a prior fundamentalist hearing of the scriptures. It is at this juncture in the process that the adult is gently led toward a new outlook. As said earlier, the stories of scripture are like a prism; they can be viewed from various perspectives depending on how the light hits the prism at a given moment. People are asked: Now that you've heard the biblical scholarship concerning this text, how do you feel about it? How does your original interpretation fit with the opinions of scholars? What was the message to the community then and now? How would you articulate an understanding of the readings now?

STEP 5
DECISION

After an in-depth dialogue with the scriptural exegesis, a decision is in order. We decide if our original understanding is adequate or if it is in need of transformation. If the latter is true, opportunity is given to articulate a new or renewed course of action, practice, and/or attitude for the future. Scripture and tradition demand a response. Discipleship demands action. We are called to and empowered for service by the word of God and by the mission of the church. *This step is critical.* Transformation is observable in the life one lives, in the attitudes one professes, and in one's work of service in the world. "The proof is in the pudding."[3]

---

[3]While Christian life is not all action and no "being," one cannot ignore the gospel imperative to live the gospel we profess. As in all things, there is to be balance, however. Action is balanced with prayer. Also, action may simply mean living a life of love in our home environments or changing an attitude or perspective and having the courage to speak up for what we believe. Some people are definitely called to public, active, pavement-pounding ministry. Others are called to

If people are not given the chance to move beyond steps one and two (naming their experience and articulating an understanding of the experience), there is a tendency to unwittingly engage in their own form of scriptural or doctrinal fundamentalism.

Reflection, study, and dialogue of this sort demand a decision, even if the decision is not to decide. If one has difficulty or disagrees with a particular interpretation, then the decision is to disagree. The decision then becomes a conscious resolution to ignore or be unaffected by what was shared. This is not a value judgment. Again, there is nothing that states that every biblical interpretation must be accepted as fact. That is one reason why it is wise to consult multiple commentators.[4] One scholar may shed light on one piece of the puzzle, while another sheds light on a different piece. Scripture scholarship is a growing, evolving discipline and unfolds as advances in biblical scholarship and biblical archaeology continue.

People are asked: How does this biblical scholarship challenge our community's (church's, parish's, neighborhood's, world's) attitudes and apostolic works? In what practical way can our parish respond to this biblical challenge? How has this biblical scholarship changed or challenged my attitudes and apostolic action? In what practical way can we/I respond to this biblical challenge?

DOCTRINAL ISSUES

Following the scriptural and liturgical segment of the preparation session, participants engage in dialogue and conversation with an issue from tradition, a doctrinal issue. Participants begin by suggesting possible doctrinal themes that flow from the readings. Whether or not this exercise results in choosing the actual topic for discussion, it is a worthwhile exercise. It helps people realize that there are connections to be made between the

---

ministry in the home and the marketplace. We are all invited to take the gospel with us to inform our posture, our actions, and our attitudes wherever we practice our ministry.

[4]You will note that each week's exegesis in this workbook contains insights from a variety of respected biblical scholars.

liturgy and the basic truths of our faith. Often multiple themes surface. Some are listed at the end of each week's session.

There are two possible approaches to choosing a topic for discussion.

a) The facilitator invites participants to name and list possible doctrinal issues/themes. Participants choose an appropriate topic for their particular parish and ministry group. Once the topic is chosen, they consult primary sources (such as catechetical and liturgical documents and/or *The Catechism of the Catholic Church*, etc.) and/or read a doctrinal issue from the Doctrinal Appendix. All then respond to questions like the questions found in each topic of the Doctrinal Appendix. Or

b) A facilitator prepares and presents a specific doctrinal theme of his or her choosing.

Participants respond using the same five-step process described above.

The prepared doctrinal material should include the church's understanding of a particular doctrinal issue, including appropriate church documents, the perspective of the *Catechism of the Catholic Church*, expansion material by respected theologians, perhaps some background on historical context. The doctrinal segment is not "everything you ever wanted to know about a topic"; it is, rather, **brief input** on a particular post-biblical teaching, creed, or practice. Doctrine comes to us from the lived experience of past communities. Much of it comes to us from the scriptures; the rest comes to us from post-biblical generations[5] that

struggled to live the gospel in the presence of the risen Christ, and as a result formulated their creed out of their experience and understanding.

The hierarchy of truths is proclaimed at liturgy every time the church gathers. Either the liturgy itself or the readings from scripture address the principal tenets of our faith.[6] From the church's prayer comes her rule of faith (*lex orandi, lex credendi).*

The Doctrinal Appendix provides *some* core doctrinal material. A resource of this size could not possibly address all doctrinal issues. *Word & Worship Workbook* is not intended to be a sole resource. However, by providing a sampling of core material, we hope that catechists will become familiar with the kinds of issues that need to be addressed, and that they will be able to use church documents in addressing any subjects not included in this workbook. The doctrinal material is presented in a reflection process format to facilitate dialogue with the material. The five-step reflection process (Naming, Understanding, Input, Testing, Decision) provides a framework for sharing. Following each doctrinal session there are instructions to return to the planning guide chapter that will assist you in preparing the catechetical session.

---

[5]Doctrine (tradition) is and has been formulated by the teaching authority of the church, the magisterium including the *sensus fidelium,* the sense of the faithful. The Second Vatican Council document, *Dogmatic Constitution on Divine Revelation (Dei Verbum)* asserts: "The tradition which comes from the apostles develops in the Church with the help of the Holy Spirit. For there is a growth in understanding of the realities and the words which have been handed down. This happens through the contemplation and the study made by believers who treasure these things in their heart (cf. Lk 2:19, 51), through the intimate understanding of spiritual things they experience, and through the preaching of those who have received through episcopal succession the sure gift of truth." (*Dei Verbum* #8, in *DVII.)*

---

[6]For further expansion on the topic of doctrine, refer to the Doctrinal Appendix. Also see the list of doctrinal issues that are encountered in the liturgical year.

7. PREPARING THE CATECHETICAL SESSION

At the end of each doctrinal teaching in the Doctrinal Appendix you will be instructed to refer to this chapter. This guide assists in planning an actual catechetical session. It provides general suggestions and ideas (painted with broad strokes) for crafting your session. It is in no way exhaustive, nor is it the *only way* to work with your group. It is merely the impetus and launching pad for using your own gifts of creativity as you work with your particular ministry group. This chapter is merely a suggested outline. Use as little or as much of it as suits your needs. Be sure that your planning considers the emotional, developmental, and age appropriate abilities of various groups within a ministerial setting.[1]

If your ministry is with adults, the same five-step reflection process is used: Naming, Understanding, Input, Testing, Decision.

THE LITURGY OF THE WORD

When a catechetical session for some reason does not follow directly upon the liturgy of the word at mass (if, for example, the catechumens are *not* dismissed following the liturgy of the word to break open the word), the session that meets during the following week should begin with a liturgy of the word as outlined on the right, followed by extended catechesis (see steps 1–8). It is not necessary to do all three readings. Perhaps the Old Testament reading, a psalm, and the gospel are all you will need to proclaim for that session. Or perhaps only the gospel is necessary. Adapt the outline to your particular needs for each specific session.[2]

---

[1]It would be beneficial for people in ministry to be familiar with the study of faith development in children and adults. Basic resources might be James Fowler's *Stages of Faith,* and *Becoming Adult, Becoming Christian* (Harper SanFrancisco).

[2]Please note that if the catechetical session follows directly upon the Sunday liturgy of the word, *there is no need to repeat a complete liturgy of the word.* The liturgy continues for them. Thus a brief centering prayer (perhaps taken from that day's liturgy), or psalm refrain and the proclamation or recall of the gospel are all that is necessary (refer to steps 1–8).

A MODEL LITURGY OF THE WORD

When gathering for a liturgy of the word, the following format is used or is adapted for your particular group. It is important to prepare a liturgical environment with appropriate symbols, music, and gestures.

Introductory Rites

Entrance Antiphon (sung) or

Psalm (sung) or

Appropriate Song

Entrance Procession
- Reader carries Lectionary or the Book of the Gospels.

Greeting
- Sign of the Cross

Opening Prayer
- The Opening Prayer from the Sunday or feast may be used.

Word of God

Reading (from Old Testament, Sunday or feast, or sacramental celebration)

Responsorial Psalm (always sung)

Reading (from apostolic letters of the Sunday, feast, or sacramental celebration)

Gospel Acclamation (always sung)

Gospel (from Sunday, feast, or sacramental celebration)

Homily

General Intercessions (adapted to occasion)

Lord's Prayer

Concluding Rites

Prayer/Blessing

Sign of Peace

Dismissal

FORMAT FOR CATECHETICAL SESSIONS WITH A MINISTRY GROUP

1. *Breaking Open the Word.* When catechumens are dismissed following the liturgy of the word to further reflect on the word of God in a different space, they begin the session with a brief centering prayer or psalm refrain. (RCIA # 81–101 suggests that the minor rites can be used to open or close a catechetical gathering.) The gospel is then proclaimed or recalled. Remember that their session is a continuation of the liturgy from which they were just dismissed. Their worship resumes.

   Cetechumenal groups (and/or other ministry groups such as small Christian communities) that meet during the week rather than following the liturgy of the word at the Sunday liturgy, celebrate the liturgy of the word (using last week's readings) as outlined above before they break open the scriptures.

   Participants then crack open the liturgy of the word. They name their experience of the gospel (there is generally not enough time to address all three readings) and articulate their understanding of it. *Brief* input is then provided regarding the liturgical context and the exegesis of the gospel.

2. *Testing the Scriptures.* The participants then enter into dialogue with their own experience and the exegesis. Participants name any new or renewed insights that may have resulted from their conversation.

3. *Catechumens Reconnect with Sponsors and Community.* In a catechetical setting it is at this point that the session stops and the group joins the community and their sponsors for hospitality (coffee and doughnuts) after mass. Sponsors then join the catechumens and candidates for extended catechesis. If the ministry group is not catechumenal, step 3 is obviously omitted.

4. *Extended Catechesis.* The church's tradition is presented. The catechist helps make the connection between the scriptures, the liturgy, and the doctrinal material that is presented: How does this particular doctrinal issue flow from the celebration of the liturgy? Elements of the four signs of catechesis—the person's personal experience (natural sign), possible scriptural connections (scriptural sign), the church's perspective, teaching and/or way of life (ecclesial sign), and the way in which the tradition is celebrated or reflected in the liturgy (liturgical sign), are included in the *brief* presentation.

5. *Testing the Tradition.* The group discusses the doctrinal issue, and tests it against their previous assumptions. They articulate any new or renewed insights or experiences of transformation that resulted from their sharing.

6. *Making the Appropriate Life Connections.* Participants share an experience from their lives. How do their new or renewed insights, their experience of the liturgy of the word, the scriptures, and tradition relate to an experience in their lives?

7. *Decision.* Participants articulate the implications of their sharing and what, if any, decisions for action, transformation, or commitment they are considering.

8. *Closing Prayer.* For catechumenal groups, the session might close with one of the minor rites: a blessing or exorcism. For other ministry groups, the session closes with any prayer form of their choosing: blessings, prayers from the liturgy, intercessions, etc.

CLARIFICATIONS

Scripture

Simplify the exegesis as much as possible. Be brief. The same or similar reflection questions used in your preparation session may be used, if they are appropriate for your specific group. Sessions take place *after* the experience of Sunday liturgy. Reflection takes place in light of the liturgical experience of the word. Remember to include insights and memories gleaned from the ritual experience of the community's liturgy, including symbols, homily, music, etc. Consider the questions you will use in light of the composition of your group. For example, you might not use the same language or questions for people in the catechumenate as you would for catechists or someone in a small Christian community. Avoid "churchy" language. Make no assumptions that people know what you are talking about. Remember that this is formation, not religious education.

Tradition

Present the doctrinal material in the same dialogical, formational fashion as scripture was presented. Allow people time to reflect, observe, and react. Allow them the opportunity to articulate the meaning for themselves. Provide accurate, informed input regarding the issue (church documents). Be careful to keep the input section brief, no more than ten minutes. It is not meant to be an exhaustive study of the church's theology. It is a sharing of the church's story in light of our own story and the implications for living the Christian life. The purpose of passing on the church's tradition is to help people live the life of faith encountered through God's presence in community, word, and eucharist and apply it to the Christian life. Doctrine often points the way. Make sure that *transformation* rather than *information* is a primary focus.[3]

Allow testing and discussion with the doctrinal input piece in order to challenge original assumptions and understanding of the issue. Encourage people to grapple with the "decision for action" questions. There is a common tendency to reduce challenge questions to ethereal mind-sets rather than praxis (practice informed by theory/theology). "What difference does this issue make in my life?" "In what way am I/we called to change due to the scriptural and doctrinal material we have shared today?"

---

[3]Please make no mistake in regard to my bias concerning transformation vs. information. Information is not bad; it is desirable and laudable. Catholics should be doctrinally literate. I am not only in favor of passing on information, I love teaching Catholic doctrine. However, in the past, most of our efforts were centered around imparting information while assuming the information would provide the impetus for transformation. Experience has taught me that most people encounter the living God before doctrine impacts them on any meaningful level. Thus, balance is imperative: transformation and information.

The Planning Session:
Things to remember as you plan your session.

1. Try to make connections with the previous week's liturgy. Where were we last week and where are we going today? What are the connections?

   Is there something that can be brought over into the sharing today? In a brief statement, how was your life different as a result of our sharing last week? Is there any unfinished business? Is there an overall thematic statement we can make as we move into this session?

2. Decide what direction to take in light of the sharing that took place in your preparation session.

   How does what we just shared [in our preparation session] specifically impact and affect the people in our ministry group? Is there a specific aspect of biblical scholarship that is more pertinent to their journey? Can all the material that we shared be covered? If so, how? If not, what are priority issues?

3. Decide what areas might be problematic.

   Are there issues we have discussed that will cause unnecessary tension and difficulty for the group? If so, how do we deal with that?

4. Decide what questions need to be asked in order to effectively and concretely move group members through the reflection process.

   What questions should we ask to help them move, as we did, from naming their initial impressions and understanding to allowing the scholarship to test their assumptions and biases in order to appropriate renewed meaning and praxis (practice informed by theology) for action? What challenge questions need to be asked? What are the implications for the community and for the individual?

5. Decide on the practical format and techniques.

   How should the material be presented? What is the format for the questions: write in journal, one-to-one sharing, wider group, small group sharing, etc? What equipment (e.g., flip chart, paper, pencils, markers, overhead projector, journals, bibles, etc.) is needed?

6. Decide on supplementary materials.

   Are there any supplementary materials that we would like to use such as Catholic Updates, bulletin inserts, articles, books, etc.?

7. Discuss current issues and events that might impact the group's sharing.

   What are the current, pertinent issues in the church, neighborhood, civic community, and world that might enter the conversation? (Never ignore a local crisis issue that is weighing heavily on the community. It impacts people's lives and so should be included in their dialogue with the gospel.)

   For example, the major employer in my parish is the Kennedy Space Center. It would have been an affront not to spend considerable time lamenting the Challenger explosion so many years ago. There was not a person in the parish who was not impacted in some way either directly (having worked on the Challenger) or indirectly. Liturgy, the gospel, and worship are connected to our everyday lives. That event impacted our community in untold ways for years as we lamented, prayed, and celebrated the resumption of the suspended shuttle program in our Sunday gatherings. While that is a dramatic example, be sure to pay attention to what is happening in the local civic community that will impact those in your ministry groups.

8. Determine what doctrinal issues might surface from within the group other than the issue being prepared.

   What issues of post-biblical teaching might surface in addition to, or other than, what we have prepared? Would we be ready to address those issues?

9. Remember to connect the doctrinal material to everyday life.

   How do we connect the post-biblical teaching (doctrine) to the lived experience of those in our ministry group? What are the appropriate questions to help them see the relevance for their lives?

10. Determine what types of prayers and/or blessings will be used.

    What prayer experiences are we going to incorporate: rituals, prayers, spontaneous prayer, prayers from *The Book of Blessings* or *Catholic Household Blessings and Prayers,* catechumenal minor rites such as blessings, exorcisms, and anointing? (The Minor Rites of the RCIA, #81–101, are normative closing and opening prayers for the catechumenate and should be used over and over as they, like liturgy, are formative.)

11. Invite (when appropriate and possible) other parishioners to share their stories and lives with the ministry group.

    Should others from the community be invited to share their story or experience with the ministry group? Who are they and why should they be present?

12. Invite the people to serve in apostolic ministry.

    In what ways are we encouraging and challenging the mission activities in the lives of people in our group? When did we last address those questions? Are we asking concrete questions that require a practical response?

13. Determine the foundational issue.

    Did we ask the bottom-line question: What are the "so what's" of this session? In what way does this experience of liturgy, scripture, and tradition challenge the community and the individual? What action will be taken?

14. Remember the ongoing issues.

    Did we remember to: a) include questions that center on the four signs of catechesis:

natural, biblical, liturgical, and ecclesial, and b) include questions that touch the basic themes of the scripture: covenant, creation, exodus, and community?

15. Determine necessary praxis for working with children.

    If our work is with children, have we chosen age and developmentally appropriate as well as sensory and concrete ways of passing on the message of what has just been shared?

16. Determine music and environment questions.

    What music will we use in our session? Where and when will we use it? Are books or song sheets to be used? How will we create a prayerful environment that will enhance and highlight the symbols of the season?

8. TIME AND THE LITURGICAL CALENDAR

Sacred Time

God resides in the space of our temporal lives. Our daily lives are ordered by the sequence of time. It marks our coming and our going. Time determines when we will work, when we will play, and when we will pray. Time is sacred. Our lives as Catholic Christians are ordered by the sacred observance of time. Each day is holy. Each day, each hour, brings a renewed encounter with the Morning Star, the Dawn of Salvation, our Evening Light, the Prince of Peace. The hand of God at creation sanctified all created things, among them, the ordering of days and nights. God, the Master Artist, captured the fleeting moment and fixed it with other moments to form the hour. The hour was multiplied to fix the day, the day to form the week, the week to order the year. In order to understand the significance of our own liturgical calendar and what it expresses, it would be helpful to plumb the religious history of how our ancestors understood the division and ordering of time.

In the Hebrew scriptures time was regarded in a way that was far different from the way in which we regard it in modern times. There was no Hebrew word for *time* meaning duration. Time was seen as the "moment or period during which something happens."[1] Human life was a compilation of the events of time. "There is a time for everything under the sun; a time to be born and a time to die" (Eccl 3:13).

There were various perceptions of time: enduring time, appointed time, liturgical time, and measuring time. *Enduring time* was the measuring of time that formed a beginning and an ending, time that resembled eternity, an abstract sense of timelessness.[2] Current events were "perceived as stretching backward or forward or as continuing indefinitely, but this is not the same as eternity, as a life or event outside of time."[3] *Appointed time* was a reference term to identify a specific event, particularly the "prescribed feasts."[4] At the *appointed time* the assembly would gather for celebration of ritual feasts. *Measuring time* viewed the work of God at creation as that of ordering time into fixed hours, days, months, and years. God was the creator of time and sustained and ordained every facet of life. Time was the servant of God's purpose. Human beings were to use time for establishing God's shalom and justice as they ordered their lives and relationships in tune with God's will. The Israelites eventually moved toward an understanding of time as historical. Time was seen in relationship to the saving events of Yahweh.

The New Testament viewed time through the lens of Judaism. A day extended from sundown on one day to sundown the next. Thus, the Last Supper and the crucifixion took place on the same day. In first-century Palestine, time was measured in far less stressful terms than today. Time seemed to stand suspended in an extended *present*. There was no rush or anxiety about the future. The moment had its own concerns. Time in the New Testament was seen in terms of its eternal or everlasting quality (*aion*—the modern word "eon" comes from this Greek origin). Everlasting time had already begun for the Christian *in this life*. It began at the paschal event of Jesus. Even though the synoptic gospels looked at everlasting time as a future event, John referred to it as a present reality. For John, "eternal life begins now, as soon as one turns to Jesus in faith."[5]

Another concept of time in the New Testament is that which refers to a determined, specific, set time, "ordinary calendar time as a quantity" (Greek—*chronos*). Chronos time ruled the ancients' daily lives and kept society functioning. A spiritual rendering of time in the New Testament

---

[1] Kathleen O'Connor, "Time," in *CPD*, 998.

[2] However, the concept of eternity as life after death, everlasting life, did not evolve until much later in Israel's history. The timelessness of enduring time was *not* an allusion to life after death or eternity as we understand it. It had more to do with extended time; time that stood still, suspended in the timelessness of God.

[3] O'Connor, "Time," in *CPD*, 999.

[4] Ibid., 1001.

[5] Sean P. Kealy, C.S.S.P., "Time," in *CPD*, 1000–1002.

is referred to as *kairos*. *Kairos* refers to those moments of spiritual significance, such as Jesus' coming and the moments and events of his life. It also refers to the circumstances in an individual's or community's life that are transitional, significant moments in the faith journey. All time was seen in relationship to Jesus Christ.

Historical time moved from the past to the present fulfillment in Jesus. Early Christians saw themselves as living in the last age; that is, they lived in the future. The future began with Christ's death and resurrection while they awaited the day of his second coming (as do we in this last age). The resurrection launched eternity. *Kairos* time envisions time and all the events of history in relationship to the Christ event.

Judaism understood time as cyclic. The events of God's intervention in human history were remembered and made present for each generation. They could not be repeated, but in the remembering, God's action was made effective for each succeeding age. Christians celebrate, recall, and make present the saving acts of Jesus every time they gather. The paschal mystery—Jesus' life, death, and resurrection—was considered the hallmark event of history. Through the paschal mystery humanity shares in Jesus' special relationship to the Father through the Holy Spirit as well as in his passion, death, and resurrection. We unite our lives to Christ's in order to share in the Father's community of love with the Son and the Holy Spirit. We seek to model our lives after Christ's and thus offer our lives as Christ offered his: then, today, and in the future. We do this when we remember (*anamnesis*) Jesus' saving events. Those same events are made present for each generation.

The early Christians ordered their entire lives around Jesus' *pasch*. The *pasch* identified who they were, how they were to live, how they were to wait for his return. Time was seen as a memorial to his passion, death, and resurrection. The morning and evening temple sacrifices were "reinterpreted as symbols of Jesus' own sacrifice."[6] The sun's slumber and awakening were seen in terms of Jesus' death and resurrection. Sundown symbolized Jesus' death and our hope for his return and for everlasting life. Sunup symbolized his resurrection. Israel's feasts were transposed into a Christian re-ordering. The yearly Passover became a metaphor for Jesus' passage from death to life.[7]

The early Christian community celebrated an annual *pasch* in which they remembered Jesus' passion, death, and resurrection. Otherwise, the only set time for prayer and worship in the first two centuries occurred on Sunday. A shift took place in the third century. As it became apparent that Jesus' return was not as immanent as once thought, there was a need to establish regulated practices of worship for the expanding church. A new ordering of time emerged.

As a response to scripture's exhortation to pray always, there emerged the practice of praying at various hours of the day. In the sixth century, monastic communities gathered for prayer at eight fixed times throughout a twenty-four hour period (the liturgy of the hours). The Middle Ages experienced a diminishment of natural symbols and metaphors. Symbols of sun and dawn in relationship to death and resurrection gave way to recitation of the Divine Office at no specific, fixed time during the day.

The liturgical year developed in similar manner. In the very early days of the church, Christians celebrated a yearly commemoration of the *pasch* and gathered only on Sunday. By the third century, Epiphany and commemorations of martyrs were added to the Christian observance. By the fourth century other remembrances of Christian events were added to the repertoire of observable feasts with the inclusion of the Nativity, the Ascension, Pentecost, and martyrs' feasts. Each of these feasts celebrated the entire mystery of Jesus' life, death, and resurrection. "At their inception these feasts were unitive feasts, each embracing the whole paschal mystery through the prism of a particular faith symbol or event. Thus, Augustine (d. 430) could call them sacraments."[8]

All ritual observances had been celebrated as remembrances and symbols of the paschal mystery.

---

[6]Edward Foley, O.F.M.Cap., "Time," in *CPD*, 1003.

[7]Ibid.
[8]Ibid., 1005.

However, usage of symbols and metaphors waned during the Middle Ages. Efforts were made to determine literal historical times, dates, and places of the circumstances of Jesus' life. Time was marked by literal observances of events in his ministry, passion, death, and resurrection. (For example, the secular calendar proceeds from the date of Jesus' birth.)

Nature's rhythms (light and darkness) provide obvious metaphors for the paschal mystery. The light and darkness of day and night are cohesive with body rhythms of the human person. The slumber of night awakens in us the desire for the resurrection brightness of a new day. All parts of creation, its images and its life cycles, are metaphors of life and death. Recent reforms sought to restore the obvious, natural symbols that speak of Christ's paschal mystery: light, darkness, seasons, and feasts. In this way we immerse ourselves in the mystery of Christ's greatest act of redemption as we wait in hope for his return.

The Liturgical Calendar

Due to the reform of the liturgical calendar, Christian observances have been restored to their original context through the renewed, ritual ordering of time. All time is sanctified. The paschal mystery is the centerpiece of all liturgical celebration and ritual observances. "Christ's saving work is celebrated in sacred memory by the Church on fixed days throughout the year. Each week on the day called the Lord's Day, the Church commemorates the Lord's resurrection. Once a year at Easter the Church honors this resurrection and passion with utmost solemnity. Through the yearly cycle the Church unfolds the entire mystery of Christ and keeps the anniversaries of the saints."[9] Thus, the paschal mystery is the root and the heart of the liturgical cycle. "By means of the liturgical cycle the Church celebrates the whole mystery of Christ, from his incarnation until the day of Pentecost and the expectation of his coming again."[10] The Lord's day, Sunday, commemorates this mystery each week even though the entire Easter season is devoted to its celebration and commemoration.

The church declares that each day is holy,[11] particularly as it gathers for daily worship. Our observance of Sunday is the earliest tradition of worship handed to us from the apostles. This day of the Lord is a weekly paschal event. "Thus Sunday must be ranked as the first holy day of all."[12] Since Sunday is held in such high esteem, nothing preempts it except solemnities and feasts of the Lord. "Only nine festivals can displace the celebration of the Sunday itself."[13] The Sundays of Advent, Lent, and Easter, however, "take precedence over all solemnities and feasts of the Lord."[14] Easter is an extended meditation on the multifaceted dimensions of the paschal mystery and each Sunday is our ongoing remembrance and expression of devotion to it. We live our lives in the shadow of the cross and resurrection.

Thus, the "mother of all feasts" is Easter. Easter is to the liturgical year what Sunday is to the week. It is the premier ritual, whose life blood flows throughout the year to each and every ritual celebration. The Easter Triduum is the "culmination of the entire liturgical year."[15] The Triduum begins with the celebration of the Lord's Supper on Holy Thursday, continues with the celebration of the Lord's Passion on Good Friday, and culminates at the Easter Vigil in the darkness of night.

The Easter season continues for fifty days and culminates on the feast of Pentecost. Forty days after Easter, the feast of the Ascension is celebrated. The days from Ascension until Pentecost anticipate the coming of the Holy Spirit.

Lent is a time of preparation for the celebration of Easter.[16] It is also a time of preparation for baptism. Catechumens prepare for celebration of the sacrament itself and the faithful prepare to renew their baptismal promises at Easter. It is also a time of renewal and penitence.

---

[9] *GNLY*, #1, in *TLD*.

[10] Ibid., #17

[11] Ibid., #3.

[12] *Constitution on the Sacred Liturgy (Sacrosanctum Concilium)*, #106, in *TLD*.

[13] Laurence E. Mick, Timothy Fitzgerald DiCello, Kathleen Hughes, RSCJ, *Sourcebook for Sundays and Seasons* (Chicago: Liturgy Training Publications, 1995), 61.

[14] *GNLY*, #5.

[15] Ibid., #18.

[16] Ibid., #27.

Christmas is second only to Easter and celebrates the Incarnation and manifestation of Christ/Spirit/God to the world. "Advent has a twofold character: as a season of preparation for Christmas when Christ's first coming to us is remembered, as a season when that remembrance directs the mind and heart to await Christ's second coming at the end of time. Advent is thus a period of devout and joyful expectation."[17]

Separate from the seasons that remember a particular aspect of Christ's salvific action, there are thirty-three or thirty-four weeks that are not devoted to any one facet of the Christian mystery. For those extended Sundays of the year, the church unfolds and observes all aspects of the mystery of Christ. Those Sundays are referred to as Ordinary Time.

Ordinary Time begins on the Monday after January 6 and continues until the Tuesday before Ash Wednesday. It resumes on the Monday after Pentecost and ends with the First Sunday of Advent.

Throughout the liturgical cycle, the church also remembers and venerates Mary, the mother of God, and commemorates the feasts of various saints and martyrs. The way the importance and significance of the celebration are determined is by its classification as a solemnity, feast, or memorial. Solemnities are principal celebrations of the church. Easter and Christmas are the most important solemnities and continue for eight days (octave).[18]

Feasts are next in importance and they generally fall on the natural days unless they fall on Sunday and commemorate the Lord during Ordinary Time and the Christmas season.[19] Memorials are observances that fall on weekdays. They are either obligatory or optional. Obligatory memorials must be celebrated on the designated day.

All ritual celebrations of the church cycle recall and make present the saving event of Jesus Christ through his life, death, and resurrection. "In the last analysis the paschal mystery is celebrated in every liturgical feast and in every feast the Lord who emptied himself, sacrificed himself in obedience unto death, and is now glorified, is present to his community and acts efficaciously in it."[20]

---

[17]Ibid., #39.
[18]Ibid., #11.
[19]Ibid., #13.

---

[20]*LY*, 31.

9. LITURGICAL CYCLE B: OVERVIEW OF MARK'S GOSPEL

At one time Mark was considered to be a theologian of lesser stature than the other synoptic evangelists. Biblical scholarship has been kinder to him in recent years, however, due to more discriminating study and reflection. Mark was believed to be the one who brought us the earliest, unembellished, simple version of the Jesus story. His gospel was considered the "no-frills" gospel. Prior to the Second Vatican Council, Mark's gospel was almost never proclaimed in the Sunday assembly. Thus, Mark is usually understood through the context and lens of Matthew's and Luke's perspectives by many Catholics. Today, however, Mark takes his rightful place as a distinguished theologian. He is even considered "a pioneer, a breaker of new ground."[1] Mark was a gifted writer with an eye for detail. He fully grasped the mystery of the incarnation and the paschal event and grippingly and passionately proclaimed it.

Papias, an early-second-century bishop, attested that Mark was a follower and the "interpreter" of Peter. It was commonly believed that he was the John Mark who escorted Paul and Barnabas on the "First Missionary Journey," who helped Peter and Paul in Rome, and whose mother owned a house in Jerusalem.[2] Since Mark was a common name at the time, however, there is simply no way to be certain that Mark the evangelist is also the Mark of Pauline missionary fame.

Mark wrote for his community, which was well formed in the Christian tradition. He wrote with skill and "surprising theological sophistication."[3] All the gospels had as their primary goal to proclaim the good news of Jesus Christ. They were not written as biographical histories of the Master, but were intended to reveal "who" he was and the "way of life" he came to initiate.[4]

Mark's brilliance lies in the fact that he was the first to proclaim the good news in gospel form. He was the first to proclaim the Christian kerygma in the context of Jesus' life. Mark knew that God's plan of salvation unfolded in the context of the human experience and story. It was thus a logical extension for Mark to proclaim God's plan of salvation through Jesus Christ in the context of experience and story.

---

beliefs into question. Often Catholics have been raised with a fundamentalist or literalist understanding of the scriptures—"if it is in the book, it must have happened just as the book says." Often when catechists teach the Catholic perspective regarding the scriptures they are accused of not being faithful to Church teaching. The late Father Raymond Brown, in his final book, *Christ in the Gospels of the Ordinary Sundays*, powerfully addressed this issue. The following is an excerpt.

"Many people think of the Gospels as biographies of Jesus. In any modern sense they are not. Some of the most basic biographical information about Jesus (when and where born, name of one parent) is absent from Mark and from John. Even more people would be unaware of how much one Gospel differs from another. The sharp differences not only raise further difficulties for the biographical approach (and perhaps create fears about the historical truth of the Gospels) but also lead into the question of the origin and goal of the Gospels.

Fortunately the Church has given us a very helpful guide for dealing with these issues—a guide that wins the approval of most centrist scholars. I refer to the Instruction on the Historical Truth of the Gospels issued by the Roman Pontifical Commission in 1964 (the substance of which was incorporated into Vatican II's Dogmatic Constitution on Divine Revelation in 1965).

When some Catholics are told that the Gospels are not necessarily literal accounts of the ministry of Jesus, they become suspicious of the "orthodoxy" of the person who makes such a claim. It may be important, therefore, to stress that this instruction, which offers that evaluation, *constitutes binding teaching of the Catholic Church on all its members* [*italics mine*].

...The 'bottom line' of this discussion based on the Roman Instruction is that modern scholarship creates no embarrassment about the Church's traditional insistence that the Gospels are historical accounts of the ministry of Jesus, provided that, as the Church also insists, 'historical' not be understood in any crassly literal sense. Indeed, a 1993 Pontifical Biblical Commission statement about different methods of interpretation is harsher than the 1964 instruction in

---

[1]Wilfred Harrington, O.P., *MK*, ix.

[2]*CGOS*, 38.

[3]Ibid., x.

[4]Often when persons struggle for the first time over the gospel's historical and biographical accuracy, it causes confusion and at the very worst a crisis that brings all cherished

Mark wrote his gospel for a community of believers comprised of both gentiles and Jews. Mark took great pains to explain Jewish customs and religious traditions, which is evidence that gentiles were a part of his community and were included in the mission of Christ. Mark's desire to unite his community is evident in the way he respected his community's Jewish roots as well as offering sensitivity to its gentile members. Faith in Jesus Christ is the glue that binds the community together.

There is debate over the date of composition. One school of thought suggests that chapter 13 was written with the destruction of the Jerusalem Temple in mind. The Temple was destroyed in A.D. 70. This places the time of composition shortly after that date. Since Mark displays an inadequate acquaintance with the Palestinian geography, it is suggested that his community may have been situated in the Roman province of Syria.

There is little confusion when it comes to Mark's reason for writing the gospel. There are two main issues: "suffering messiahship and suffering discipleship."[5] Mark's community is living in the reality of the risen lordship of Christ. There is a strong eschatological thread throughout the gospel. Mark is aware of the transitory times in which his community is living. His community is in waiting. It is living in the postresurrection (messianic) age while awaiting the last day and Christ's return. The reign of God *now and not yet* occupies a great deal of Mark's thematic thrust. Victory already belongs to the Christian. The Christian is living in the reality of salvation already won. Christ was victorious over sin and death and won salvation for all the world—now and for eternity. "Mark acknowledges that christian existence is paradoxical. He finds it normal that it should be so. Jesus won his victory through suffering and death. There is no other way of Christian living nor path to Christian victory. Mark has written that his Christians should understand and accept this."[6] Joy and pain dine together at the same earthly banquet.

There are three major movements in the Cycle B gospel. Chapters 1 through 8 are concerned with the question: "Who is this Jesus?" Only the readers and the demons know the answer. The characters are in the dark. There is emphasis on Jesus' miracles and very little on his teaching. Jesus' ministry is centered in Galilee. This section moves to a climax in which Peter confesses the identity of Jesus, the Christ.

The second movement includes chapters 9 through 15 and deals with the question, "What kind of Messiah is this?" Jesus' life and mission are gradually revealed. Emphasis is on his teaching and is directed to the disciples. There is an ongoing conflict between Jesus and his disciples. They try to follow him, they believe he is the Christ—but they consistently fail. They simply do not understand the implications of Jesus' preaching and teaching. The way of the cross is hardly attractive. They cannot comprehend the paradox that the cross is the threshold to life. They ultimately fail their Master during his mortal life. Understanding will only come after his death and resurrection.

Jesus' teaching and ministry are placed within the context of the journey to Jerusalem. What awaits him in Jerusalem is ever-present. Like a shadow behind a stage scrim, the events of Golgotha loom ominously as the curtain begins its slow ascent before opening to the drama that awaits. This portion of Mark's kerygma climaxes with the proclamation of Jesus' Passion.

The evangelist's third movement begins in chapter 16 with the proclamation of the resurrection and post-Easter origin of the fledgling church. Mark's theology asserts that Jesus is God's Son. He is the long-awaited one. Jesus was sent by God to

---

criticizing undue stress on historical inerrancy and the historicizing of material that was not historical from the start.

To some Christians any thesis that does not present the Gospels as literal history implies that they are not true accounts of Jesus. Truth, however, must be evaluated in terms of the intended purpose. The Gospels might be judged untrue if the goal was strict reporting or exact biography. If the goal, however, was to bring readers/hearers to a faith in Jesus that leads them to accept God's rule or kingdom, then adaptations that made the Gospels less than literal by adding the dimensions of faith and by adjusting to new audiences facilitated that goal and thus enhanced the truth of the Gospels. The Instruction is lucidly clear: 'The doctrine and life of Jesus were not simply reported for the sole purpose of being remembered, but were "preached" so as to offer the church a basis of faith and morals'" (Raymond Brown, *CGOS*, 1, 2, 11).

[5]Ibid., xiii.

[6]Ibid.

gather his elect and take them home. Jesus is the "suffering Son of Man, who walked a lone path to his death."[7] Jesus emptied himself and accepted death on the cross in complete submission to his Father's will. This is why people were able to profess that he was truly God's Son. Jesus freely gave his life for the sins of the world. He humiliated himself in order to give life to sinners. His agenda was not chastisement. He offered the gift of himself and his forgiveness. It need only be received.

Mark insists that there is responsibility involved in accepting the reign of Christ. Discipleship is difficult. Christianity is always on the road to Jerusalem. The way to life is the cross. Disciples cannot know Jesus without accepting and entering into his life—*all of it*—his life, death, and resurrection. The pivotal center of Mark's entire gospel is Christ's Passion and resurrection.

The frailty of humanity jumps off the page in the foibles and failings of Peter and the disciples. Readers are to see themselves in these very human characters. Jesus invited them to accept a new way of life. They accepted his invitation, but they were human; and, like all of us, they fell short.[8] But Jesus picked them up by their broken bootstraps and set them once again on the road to life. He continues to do that for all of us.

---

[7]Ibid., xviii.

[8]Wilfrid Harrington, O.P., posits an interesting, perhaps to some, controversial footnote to this marvelous gospel. "Not all had failed: the silent, steadfast women had remained faithful to the end (15:40–16:8). Perhaps a lesson of Mark, yet to be learned, is that the community of Christ will come of age when the dignity of woman and her place in his church are acknowledged not only in word but in truth."

THE SEASON OF ADVENT

THE SEASON OF ADVENT: AN OVERVIEW

"Advent begins with the first evening prayer of the Sunday that falls closest to November 30 and ends before the first evening prayer of Christmas."[1] The document *General Norms for the Liturgical Year and the Calendar* states: "The season of Advent has a twofold character. It is a time of preparation for Christmas when the first coming of God's son to men is recalled. It is also a season when minds are directed by this memorial to Christ's second coming at the end of time. It is thus a time of joyful and spiritual expectation."[2]

The origin of Advent dates back to the fifth century and is influenced by the Eastern Church. The primary focus of this liturgy was expectation of the Lord's birth at Christmas. The first evidence of Roman observance of the season occurred around the sixth century. There was little emphasis placed on the parousia. The focus was on preparation for the celebration of Christ's birth.

At the same time, however, there were other shifts taking place that would eventually impact Advent's original focus. The Irish missionaries had descended upon Gaul with a compelling message concerning the final judgment of humanity. They exhorted people to repent in the face of eventual judgment. Thus, Advent became laden with penitential overtones. This influence reached the Roman church by the twelfth century as evidenced by the wearing of purple vestments and the exclusion of the Gloria during the liturgy. Yet, in spite of this, the penitential character of Advent was different in tone from that of Lent. There was an inherent joy to the penitential observance. There was clear intention that omission of the Gloria was an anticipatory gesture rather than a penitential gesture. "It is not omitted for the same reason as it is omit-

ted in Lent, but in order that on the night of Christmas the angels' song may ring out again in all its newness."[3]

The first Sunday of Advent begins a new liturgical year and liturgical cycle: CYCLE B. During this year we encounter Jesus through the eyes of Mark, the evangelist. Mark wrote his gospel for a community of believers comprised of both gentiles and Jews. For more information on the context and perspective of the gospel according to Mark, see the chapter entitled, "Overview of the Gospel of Mark."

Advent prepares us for the coming of the Savior. We must ask ourselves, "From what do we need saving?" The scriptures of Advent challenge us to wait for the day of the Lord, but they also demand that justice reign. In the biblical sense, justice (Hebrew: *hesed*) refers to right relationship with God as evidenced by one's behavior toward God and God's people. The demands of justice are not suggestions; they are commands. Advent asks the tough question: How are we living *hesed* relationship with our God? If we are God's people, if we are in covenant relationship with God, then we must be advocates of justice wherever injustice takes center stage.

Another theme that echoes through the season is penitential. God's people are to recognize, name, and lament over the evil that permeates the world and work to eradicate it. Throughout Advent we hear from the ancient prophets who cry, "Repent and change your lives!" The prophets' cry is as relevant today as it was then. They foretold the light that would shine in the midst of darkness. Christ is that light. We are to embrace the light and become the light of Christ in the world.

---

[1] *GNLY*, #40.
[2] Ibid., #39.

[3] *Commetarius In Annum Liturgicum Instauratum*, chap. I, sect. II, 2 (p. 61), published by the Consilium for the Implementation of the Constitution on the Sacred Liturgy.

Advent explores two realities: the kingdom *here and now* and the kingdom *yet to come*. We live in the midst of that tension. We struggle to maintain the proper balance between passive waiting and proactive waiting. When we are proactive we cooperate in the work of *history making*. We enter salvation history with God and seek to alter injustice when we see it. We enter the struggle of the kingdom *here and now* with a vigilant eye and hopeful anticipation of the kingdom *yet to come*.

As consumerism seems to preoccupy the culture in the waning days of Advent, our liturgy seeks to bring us back to the "reason for the season." Advent is a wake-up call to the world. Advent's message is a counter-cultural plea to engage in the deeper meaning of the season. It is a mandate to reflect upon and prepare for the second coming of Christ, while looking forward to the celebration of the Incarnation, the ultimate gift of God's personhood to the world. We can do nothing less than ask ourselves the questions of human response and responsibility in the face of such a gratuitous gift.

St. Bernard (1090–1153) gave us a wonderful summation of the meaning of Advent when he wrote:

> We know that there are three comings of the Lord. The third lies between the other two. It is invisible, while the other two are visible. In the first coming he was seen on earth, dwelling among men [and women]; he himself testifies that they saw him and hated him. In the final coming "all flesh will see the salvation of our God," and "they will look on him whom they pierced." The intermediate coming is a hidden one; in it only the elect see the Lord within their own selves, and they are saved. In his first coming our Lord came in the flesh and in our weakness; in this middle coming he comes in spirit and in power; in the final coming he will be seen in glory and majesty. Because this coming lies between the other two, it is like a road on which we travel from the first coming to the last. In the first, Christ was our redemption; in the last, he will appear as our

life; in this middle coming, he is our rest and consolation.[4]

The First and Second Sunday of Advent center around the future coming of Christ. The Third Sunday's focus is on the present coming and the Fourth Sunday is on the birth of Jesus, the past coming.

Advent and Christmas form a unity. We cannot engage in one season without reflection upon the other. Both seasons complement one another and do not stand alone. Yet Advent and Christmas are also viewed through the lens of Lent and Easter. Advent/Christmas looks toward the fulfillment of the Incarnation that is celebrated through the paschal mystery at Easter.

As in all good liturgy, we are to properly prepare ourselves for full and vibrant participation. Advent prepares the heart and the church for just such participation in the mystery of Christ's Incarnation.

---

[4] *Homelie pour l'Advent*, 5:1–3, *Edition cistercienne*, 4, 1966, pp. 188–190, in *Liturgy of the Hours* (New York: Catholic Book Publishing Co., 1975), p. 169.

FIRST SUNDAY OF ADVENT

Environment

Advent is more than a time of personal conversion and preparation. The scriptures of Advent remind us that we are preparing for a renewal of cosmic proportions. The universe groans in longing anticipation for the *One Who Came*, the *One Who Comes*, and the *One Who Will Come Again*. The worship space and meeting space for catechesis should immediately awaken us from the slumber of complacency and speak to us through the thunderous silence of symbols, color, wreath, and candle. The possibilities are limited only by the imagination. Not only should the Advent environment reflect the hopeful, anticipatory images of the season, but also the harsh, Baptist-like demand for justice and reformation. The theme of final judgment resounds throughout the season. How might an environment be crafted to help disquiet the comfortable and ignite the complacent? One way to remain true to the spirit of Advent is to avoid trite images and saccharin art; to clothe the space in Advent's liturgical color, the violet hues of purple; and to simply and starkly use symbols or art that reflect anticipation, justice, and the final eschaton. Perhaps the bold use of color (purples laced with traces of navy, black, and the silver of the midnight sky) alongside an austere, but striking Advent wreath is all that is needed to convey the cosmic nature of the season. The symbolism of the Advent wreath "lies in the tension between light and darkness. . . . It represents the long time when people lived in spiritual darkness, waiting for the coming of the Messiah, the light of the world."[1] Each week a new candle is lit: "light increases, pushing out darkness. . . until all four are burning."[2] The Advent wreath cradles our primary symbols—wood and light. "The wood refers to the 'living greens' that are used to make the wreath. . . . The wood or pine embodies the primary symbol of the cross. It is the wood of the cross which will become the sign of our salvation at Easter whereby all are saved by the 'wood of the cross.'. . . The four can-

dles represent Christ, the Light of the World!"[3] A carved-out log or a grouping of branches laced with evergreens could be used to cradle the four candles. Four purple candles, or three purple candles and one rose candle (for *Gaudete* Sunday, the Third Sunday of Advent), or four white candles may be used in the wreath.

Mary certainly plays a supporting role in Advent's unfolding drama. However, she waits in the wings (careful not to upstage the season's central themes) for her center stage arrival and the role she will play during the latter days of the season. Perhaps iconography might be the medium to bring appropriate images of Mary's role in the history of salvation into the environment during the waning days of the season. John the Baptist leaps front and center on the first Sunday and screams to us from art both ancient and contemporary: "Repent, change your lives!" An artist's rendering (i.e., an icon) of the Baptist would be a wonderful addition to your Advent meeting space. The four archangels are also Advent images: "Gabriel blowing the trumpet, Michael with the scales of justice, Raphael with healing gall, and Uriel darkening the sun and moon—all assisting in the resurrection of the dead."[4] Icons of the archangels or of John the Baptist, pictured with wings (because he is God's messenger), might be artistically incorporated.

Flowers, while not prohibited, should be used sparingly and simply. Advent does reflect a spirit of joy. However, the joy is minimized in comparison to the cosmic bliss of Christmas. Thus, the Advent environment should never overpower the Christmas environment to come. Christmas and Advent are understood as unified and complementary. Christmas should build upon Advent.

Blessing of an Advent Wreath

Before your group lights the first candle of the Advent wreath, the following blessing taken from

---

[1] Greg Dues, *CCT*, 49.
[2] Ibid.

[3] Linda Gaupin, *Catechesis and Liturgy, Course Text*, 52.
[4] Peter Mazar, *TCY*, 210.

Catholic Household Blessings and Prayers (NCCB, 1988) may be used.

All make the sign of the cross.

Leader: Our help is in the name of the Lord.

All respond: Who made heaven and earth.

Leader: In the short days and long nights of Advent, we realize how we are always waiting for deliverance, always needing salvation by our God. Around this wreath, we shall remember God's promise.

Scripture is read.

Listen to the words of the prophet Isaiah:
the people who walked in darkness have seen a
    great light;
Upon those who dwelt in the land of gloom a light
    has shown.
You have brought them abundant joy and great re-
    joicing.
The word of the Lord.

All respond: Thanks be to God.

After a time of silence, all join in prayers of intercessions and in the Lord's Prayer.

Then the leader invites:
Let us now pray for God's blessing upon us and this wreath.

After a short silence, the leader prays:

Lord our God,
we praise you for your Son, Jesus Christ:
he is Emmanuel, the hope of the peoples,
he is the wisdom that teaches and guides us,
he is the Savior of every nation.
Lord God,
let your blessing come upon us
as we light the candles of this wreath.
May the wreath and its light
be a sign of Christ's promise to bring salvation.
May he come quickly and not delay.
We ask this through Christ our Lord.

The first candle is then lighted.

Leader: Let us bless the Lord.

All respond, making the sign of the cross:
Thanks be to God.

The blessing concludes with a verse from "O Come O Come, Emmanuel."[5]

INTRODUCTORY RITES

Entrance Antiphon[6] (or Opening Song)

To you, my God, I lift my soul, I trust in you; let me never come to shame. Do not let my enemies laugh at me. No one who waits for you is ever put to shame. (Ps 24:1–3)[7]

Opening Prayer

The facilitator of the session may lead the prayer. Others in the group may be asked to proclaim the readings.

Let us pray
[that we may take Christ's coming seriously]

Pause for silent prayer.

All-powerful God,
increase our strength of will for doing good
that Christ may find an eager welcome at his coming
and call us to his side in the
kingdom of heaven,
where he lives and reigns with
you and the Holy Spirit,
one God, for ever and ever.[8]

----

[5] *CHBP*, 64.

[6] Each mass has an assigned "Entrance Antiphon." This is usually a phrase from the scriptures (most often psalmody, intended to be sung) and, in a sense, is considered an official part of the liturgy—its opening song. However, very often the general practice in this country has been to sing a hymn because the appropriate antiphon or psalm was not yet set to music. The first option is to sing the assigned psalm or antiphon of the liturgy. The choice of a hymn is the last option. It used to be that each Sunday liturgy was given a title. The title was in Latin and was the first word of the Entrance Antiphon.

[7] First Sunday of Advent: "Entrance Antiphon," *The Sacramentary.*

[8] First Sunday of Advent: "Opening Prayer," *The Sacramentary.*

LITURGY OF THE WORD

The readings are proclaimed.

First Reading[9]
Isaiah 63:16b–17, 19b; 64:2–7

Overview of Isaiah: Isaiah was a prophet of the Southern Kingdom of Judah who served in that role for over forty years (c. 740–700 B.C.). Isaiah of Jerusalem is believed to be the author of the first thirty-nine chapters (First Isaiah: chapters 1–39; Deutero-Isaiah: chapters 40–66). It is probable that Isaiah came from privileged roots, as he seems to have had free access to the royal courts and to the king. Isaiah was intensely involved in the political life of the day. Two events during those forty years consumed much of Isaiah's attention. In the year 734, the Northern Kingdom under the rule of King Hoshea joined forces with Damascus against Assyria. Both Israel and Damascus were afraid that Judah would not go along with the plan, so they attacked Judah first. Desperate to defend itself, Judah joined forces with Assyria and thus became Assyria's vassal. Isaiah found King Ahaz's decision to align with pagan Assyria repugnant.

The defeat delivered a disastrous blow to Israel and Damascus. Damascus was destroyed and Israel was divided into three provinces under the control of an Assyrian governor. Only a small area near the capital city of Samaria was left for King Hoshea to govern. Isaiah begged Judah not to get involved with Assyria, but no one would listen. Chapters 6–11 deal with this tragic situation in great detail.

The second event that concerned Isaiah was the attempt by King Ahaz's son, King Hezekiah, to free Judah from Assyrian domination. Hezekiah led the revolt and won Judah's liberation in 705. B.C. against the Assyrian king's son, Sennacherib. Four years later Sennacherib attacked Judah. Isaiah tells us that a plague destroyed the Assyrian army, forcing them to return to their homeland. However, nearly every Judean city was destroyed except Jerusalem. Hezekiah paid a huge booty to Assyria to keep them from attacking again.

Isaiah's agenda is ardently set forth in his oracles. He railed against injustice, oppression, and idolatry. He implored the people to turn from their wicked ways and return to Yahweh. Isaiah proclaimed a God who was in control of the whole world, a God who blessed and disciplined those who were in covenant with him. Isaiah exhorted Israel and Judah to subject themselves only to Yahweh and not to the domination of foreign powers. In spite of Isaiah's warnings, Israel's kings did not heed his advice. They refused to believe the promise that Yahweh would protect and defend their nation. "As a result, Isaiah turned his hopes to a future king who would obey Yahweh. From this moment, the words of Isaiah inspired hopes of a messiah, a new king in Israel's future who would better serve God and bring about a full measure of the divine blessing on the land (see Is 9:1–6 and 11:1–9)."[10]

Isaiah also proclaimed the holiness of God. Yahweh, Creator of the universe, ruled his people in splendor and majesty and was worthy of honor and praise. Yahweh resided in the midst of Israel and as a result the people were to live in holiness. This holiness was evidenced by the ethical demands of a well-lived life, committed to the justice of God. Nothing disrupts the way of this holiness like human pride. Such pride invites God's discipline. But the God who punishes also forgives and restores. Isaiah prophesied about the destruction of Israel and Judah. However, he promised that a remnant would survive that would be the source of Israel's hope.

Second Isaiah/Deutero-Isaiah. It is believed that beginning with chapter 40 of Isaiah, a new school or author emerges. The history, doctrine, and literary style are different than in the first thirty-nine chapters. The locus for Second Isaiah is near the end of the exile. Cyrus is mentioned by name.

---

[9]The exegesis for the first and second readings may or may not be the focus of your group's reflection, as there may only be time to give adequate attention to the gospel, your primary concern. However, the exegesis is included here in order to provide a thorough investigation of the entire liturgy of the word as there may be parts (or all) that would be essential to the direction you wish to take with your particular ministry group.

[10]*ROT*, 329.

Cyrus is a threat to Babylon and in the end will free Israel. This portion of Isaiah was probably written between 550 and 540 B.C. The literary style is quite distinct from the first section of the book and thus cannot be confused with Isaiah. This author is called Deutero-Isaiah. In 1908 the Pontifical Biblical Commission asserted that the arguments in favor of a second author of chapter 40 and upward were not compelling. However, advances in biblical scholarship make the belief in Second Isaiah authorship more widely accepted than ever before. The chapters are divided into two sections: chapters 40–48 are known as "hymns of Yahweh and Israel" and chapters 49–55 are known as "hymns of Jerusalem and Zion." Second Isaiah's poetic expression of doctrine unites Israel's belief in creation and in the divine will for the salvation of the world. World powers, no matter how strong or oppressive, are subject to the majesty and sovereign will of Yahweh. The deliverance of Israel is a prerequisite to the establishment of Yahweh's reign—Israel is Yahweh's servant. Salvation is understood as the coming of Yahweh, not simply his words and deeds.[11] Israel's self-identity was wrapped up in the belief that they were the *people of God.* Second Isaiah develops Israel's self-understanding even further. Israel is in relationship with a God who expresses tender love and compassion and offers "forgiveness now magnificently manifested in His restoration to life of a people who deserve to remain dead."[12] Second Isaiah expresses belief in the *One* God—monotheism—expressed in a way never before articulated.

Third Isaiah/Trito-Isaiah. Some scholars believe that, beginning with chapter 56, a new style emerges in the Isaiah corpus. Scholars refer to a new author as Trito-Isaiah—Third Isaiah. There is debate concerning the date of authorship. Some believe it was written in the sixth century B.C. Some suggest the third or fourth. The difficulty dating the text comes from the lack of allusions to historical situations in the text. The theology of Trito-Isaiah resembles the theology of Second Isaiah. In many ways it seems dependent on the former. There are differences, however. Third Isaiah refers to national guilt as an obstacle to the salvation of Israel. This guilt is characteristic of other postexilic biblical literature such as the psalms. Salvation may be delayed but it is immanent. The reign of God was understood (as in most Israelite prophetic traditions) to be the establishment of Israelite institutions—a nationalistic understanding. For Third Isaiah, salvation is understood in terms of new creation fashioned after the paradise of Eden. Judgment is severe and graphic. Next to the Pentateuch and the psalms, Isaiah is the most quoted source in the New Testament—forty-one passages are quoted. The Book of the Prophet Isaiah had a great influence on New Testament thinking.

Today's Pericope:[13] We turn to Isaiah to begin the proclamation of Christ's coming. In the last weeks of the previous cycle our attention concentrated on eschatological concerns. We begin the liturgical year with the same focus. Isaiah paves the way for us. Today's pericope is taken from an oracle that describes the morale of the exiles following their return from Babylon. It is a lament and has been called one of the Bible's priceless jewels. The people were demoralized. The delay in Jerusalem's restoration was understood as the result of the sins of the nation. Life had been drained from the people and hope was waning. Ezra and Nehemiah had not yet mobilized their efforts to rally the people and restore their hope.

The author of Trito-Isaiah, believed to be a student of Deutero-Isaiah, speaks with his teacher's sense of hope and belief in God's salvation for all the world. However, he is also aware that a depressing pall of gloom hangs in the air. Israel accepted culpability for their exile. They were sinners; they deserved punishment for their sins. But they were home and for the most part enjoyed a certain level of freedom under the rule of the Persian governor. Now was the time to begin the enormous task of rebuilding and restoration. The task seemed almost too much for them—they were beginning to think that God had deserted them. Despair had set in.

The author led the people in a community lament in hopes that God would listen and respond. The prophet stressed the powerlessness of

---

[11] *DOB*, 401.
[12] Ibid.

[13] A pericope is a particular portion or segment of scripture that is chosen for a specific proclamation.

the people. Sin had ravaged them and without God they were nothing. God was their only reason for existence and God deserted them. Trito-Isaiah begged God to return his *hesed* love and care for the people. The people longed for a return to the covenant relationship they had broken. They longed for a return to the days when Yahweh cared for them, protected them from their enemies, and sustained them in times of exile. The prophet's supplicant request was that Yahweh remember the wonderful deeds of the past and make them present. Isaiah was asking for an anamnesis. He was asking God to remember the events of old and restore the benefits in the present generation. "Remember that you are the Master of these people and restore your acts of salvation on their behalf."

God is the potter and the people are but clay in God's hands. Weathered by the storm of exilic life, they are humbly ready to be molded into the image God would fashion. The prosperity, individualism, and self-dependence of former times melted away. The people were all the more conscious of God's absence and lack of relationship in their lives.

Trito-Isaiah insisted that God is the Father of the people, their Redeemer. The Israelites referred to God as Redeemer in relation to their covenant relationship with God. God as Redeemer was a reference to the way God functions as next of kin. It referred to deliverance from dangerous and oppressive human situations but also deliverance from sin. The term *redeemer* was understood in the Hebrew (*go'el*) to refer to a person who defended the interests of a group, especially the most vulnerable members of the group, clan, or family. The term *redeemer* was rooted in family law. It was the responsibility of the nearest male relative to "buy back" a relative sold to another household in slavery. It was his role to restore the former "integrity of family membership and property."[14] Redemption also was rooted in matters having to do with sacrifice. Animals were offered as holocaust to God. People could redeem the animal (purchase or buy back) by offering money in return for the animal. Also, the redeemer continued the

posterity of a family by marrying the widow of the family and fathering a child. The redeemer also paid the debts of a family member who fell into difficult times. The Israelites considered themselves "ransomed" from exile in Babylon (but not for a price, however). Thus, redemption was understood as "God's wonderful initiative in bringing about the possibility of renewed friendship and divine reconciliation."[15]

Advent's cry is to prepare the way for the *Redeemer* who is to come. "The Church still looks for a final rending of the heavens when the Son of Man will come again. Indeed, the Church experiences a rending of the heavens in each liturgy, when Christ comes down in his sacrament to visit the people in their need."[16]

Responsorial Psalm
Psalm 80:2–3, 15–16, 18–19

The psalm appointed for today's liturgy is a community lament. As a lament it is a perfect companion to the first reading. It is a plea for divine intervention.

Second Reading
1 Corinthians 1:3–9

(Please refer to the second Sunday in Ordinary Time for an overview of Paul's Letters to the Corinthians.)

Today's Pericope: In actuality, today's letter from Paul is not his first letter to that community. He tells us in chapter 5 that he had written to them before. Today's reading includes the opening address, blessing, and thanksgiving.

Paul's thanksgiving includes thanks to God who has gifted his community with charismatic gifts that include special gifts of knowledge and speech. Even though he thanks God for these gifts and the way in which they build up the community, he later criticizes their use in the community.

Paul views the charismatic gifts through an eschatological lens. Even though they are imbued with

---

[14]Joseph F. Wimmer, O.S.A., "Redemption/Redeemer," *CPDBT*, 811.

[15]Ibid.
[16]*PL*, 202.

special gifts of knowledge, the ultimate knowledge to come will be when Jesus returns as the final revelation. They are to remain sinless as they await the Day of the Lord. Paul gives the Corinthians three reminders of the reign of God yet to come. They would later be dangerously close to forgetting the Day of the Lord as they reveled in their obsession over their charismatic gifts. Later in Paul's letter he challenges the Corinthians' abuse of the gifts.

The gospel is proclaimed.

Gospel[17]
Mark 13:33–37. Be watchful! You do not know when the Lord of the house is coming.

STEP 1
NAMING ONE'S EXPERIENCE

What were your first impressions? What was your first response to the gospel (or the other readings)?[18] What captured your attention?

Each person names his or her initial impression. Statements should be brief. No reasons should be given at this time. All simply listen without agreeing or disagreeing.

STEP 2
UNDERSTANDING

In a brief statement, explain what you think this gospel is trying to convey.

---

[17]The gospel exegesis is provided later in this session so that it may be presented in the proper sequence where it occurs in the adult five-step reflection process. The exegesis is provided for the first and second readings for your information and edification and for you to use at your discretion. Once again, the gospel is the primary source of reflection. If there is time for reflection on the other readings, all the better.

[18]The primary focus of reflection is the gospel. However, often the other readings demand attention and must be brought into the dialogue.

STEP 3
INPUT FROM VISION/STORY/TRADITION

Liturgical Context[19]

The first and second Sundays of Advent open the unfolding drama of history's premier event on an eschatological tone. The scope transcends the immanent expectation of the coming of Christ in history as well as the Christ who dwells in our midst and who will one day return in glory. The first two Sundays bespeak the cosmic liturgy that will usher in the culmination of all history and the final eschaton. "The prophetic oracles glimpse the day when the Lord will call together all nations in eternal peace of the kingdom of God (Isa 2:1–5: First Sunday, Year A), when God will judge the poor with justice (Isa 11:1–10: Second Sunday, Year A), when he will manifest his glory (Bar 5:1–9: Second Sunday, Year C). They shout out the hope of believers in God, our justice (Jer 33:14–16: First Sunday, Year C): 'O that you would rend the heavens come down!' (Is 63:16–19; 64:2–7: First Sunday, Year B). They call for the preparation of the way of the Lord (Isa 40:1–5, 9–11: Second Sunday, Year B)."[20]

The Baptist exhorts us to prepare for the coming reign of God. We are to be as watchful as a sentry at his post. The Entrance Antiphon reminds us that no one who waits on the Lord will be disappointed. While ever mindful of the earthly reality of God's reign, we are not to forget that we live in the constant tension between the reign of God *now* and *not yet*, reflected in today's communion antiphon:

> Father,
> May our communion teach us to love
>   heaven.
> May its promise guide our way on earth.[21]

---

[19]The scriptures in the Lectionary, the seasons of the year, and the ritual prayers of the mass are interrelated and form the basis for liturgical catechesis. The *liturgical context* attempts to explore and clarify the themes and this interrelatedness.

[20]*DL* (I), 25.

[21]First Sunday of Advent: "Communion Antiphon," *The Sacramentary.*

We can look to the preface of the liturgy for an understanding of what it is we believe about a feast or season. The prefaces for Advent remind us that Jesus fulfilled the plan of salvation inaugurated by God at the creation of the world. We wait now for the final fulfillment when Christ returns again (Advent Preface I, for use until December 16). We are reminded that Christ's coming was foretold by the prophets, that the virgin Mary bore him with the greatest love, and that the Baptist paved the way for and announced his coming. We are to be confident as we prepare to celebrate his birth because Christ himself fills us with joy so that we may be watchful and ready when he returns (Advent Preface II, for use the last eight days, December 17–24.).

The liturgies of Advent begin in preparation for the Lord's second coming. By the third week and fourth week the focus is on the immediate preparation for the Feast of the Incarnation of Christ at Christmas.

Advent prepares us to enter fully into the mystery of the incarnation. Jesus dwells among us as we remember and celebrate his historical coming and anticipate his second coming at the end of time. We are immersed in Christ's explosion into human history. The liturgy engages in a sacred remembering (anamnesis) of God's salvific action in history and the role of humanity in that action. The prophets of old cry to us from their ancient graves with the same plea we hear from contemporary prophetic voices: "Reform your lives, the Day of the Lord is near." Whether that final day comes in our lifetime or in the future makes no difference. Our lives are to reflect prayerful diligence and attentiveness to the task of waiting in joyful hope. The liturgies of Advent give us the opportunity to observe and reflect upon that future kingdom as well as the kingdom of God in our midst. The Advent liturgies powerfully remind us of our need to conform our lives to the will of God. According to Karl Rahner, Advent is the time of "*the secret experience of the apparently inexperienceable.*"[22] "So the period of Advent is actually not simply just the time before something that has not yet occurred. But just as well it can be understood as the period for the quiet growth of a life already given;

and it works just like the time when, like the seed long since sown in springtime, God's inward arrival comes through unobtrusively and slowly, but with terrific force, and becomes manifest in all the seeming banality of our lives."[23]

Gospel Exegesis

The facilitator provides input from critical biblical scholarship on this text. This input includes insights as to how people would have heard the gospel in Jesus' time.

The focus at the end of each liturgical cycle and the beginning of every new liturgical cycle is always eschatological. For this reason the gospels proclaimed at the beginning of every cycle are not taken from the beginning of each synoptic gospel. They are taken instead from the future-oriented eschatological material in the gospels—the apocalyptic material. All three synoptic gospels' apocalypses end with a series of eschatological parables. Today's gospel is the parable of the doorkeeper.

The first-century Mediterranean world had little appreciation of a future time or a future world. The culture was extremely present-oriented. Activities that were not of immediate concern were postponed until the proverbial "later." Even Jesus exhorted his disciples to worry only about today. Yet their understanding of the present did include seeds of tomorrow.

The patron/client relationship of first-century Palestine provided the grist for many of Jesus' parables. The master/servant relationship was common to the experience of ancient Palestine. The master and servant model is the way in which society organized itself.[24] The patron/client system was the way in which society defined power and wealth and allocated resources. This system defined a way of life for those who lived in the first century—their thought processes were centered around this organizational structure. Their entire worldview centered around the client/patron model, just as the worldview of the Western world is the capitalist model. The patron/client model looks nothing like the employer/employee model of the Western world. It is more familial than con-

---

[22] *GCY*, 9.

[23] Ibid., 10.
[24] *HTP*, 205.

tractual. It is a voluntary model and exists over a long period of time. Roles and responsibilities are carefully defined. Strong bonds of solidarity exist.

One characteristic of this model, however, is ambiguity. There are differences in equality and power. Even though there is strong solidarity and association in this voluntary relationship, there is often social coercion. Social chaos easily erupts in volatile situations, the likes of which existed during the time of Jesus. Many of Jesus' parables play upon the ambiguities that existed in the client/patron system. Client/patron systems are unstable not simply because they are unequal, but also because they are legislated by custom rather than law. There is no legal recourse for grievances. However, the client/patron system does afford a certain level of stability in society. It provides protection from unbridled, abusive power. In payment for providing protection to the client, the client promises submission to the power and control of the patron.

The organized hierarchical power structure was not only excessively controlling, it promoted isolation between the patron and client. The elites often administered from afar, which meant the patron was usually absent. Absentee landlords were common and a mixed population of peoples existed at the very bottom of society's social structure. Jesus often placed the absentee landlord in the role of antagonist in his parables. Jesus' parables took advantage of the pent-up resentments that were common between patron and client, master and servant. He invited the listener to sympathize with the servant.[25]

The client/patron relationship was often used as a metaphor for the way God was in relationship with Israel. God is the patron, Israel the client. The early church transferred that same role to Jesus. "When Jesus becomes the church's Lord (*kyrios* is both master and lord) or returning Son of man, he becomes their patron."[26] The way in which the gospel interprets the master/servant parables is to connect them with the expectation of Jesus' return at the parousia. Jesus, the patron, will enter into final solidarity with his faithful clients.

In the parable of the doorkeeper, it is obvious that the master is the Son of Man—Jesus. The warning inherent in today's parable is eschatological. This parable belongs to a genre of parables referred to as departure/return parables. The master's return is delayed. His delay initiates a test for the servant. The servant is entrusted with care of the master's property until his return. "[T]he departure is a test, with the return the denouement."[27] Jesus proclaimed the reign of God as a reality that was both present and absent. The master's delay does provide a logical metaphor for Jesus to use to advantage. However, Kenneth Bailey argues that the metaphor would have also been an extremely useful way for the early church to describe how it understood the loss of their Lord.[28] He therefore concludes that this parable is probably a parable of the early church.

Wilfrid Harrington asserts that chapter 13's narrative brings Jesus' ministry to a close and prepared the disciples for events yet to take place.[29] Its literary form is that of farewell discourse as well as apocalypse. Prior to verse 14, everything took place in the present time. From verse 14 on, everything is future-oriented. What is taking place in Mark's narrative is directly related to the historical situation of his community. Jerusalem has fallen and Mark's community is in the midst of chaos—the great tribulation. Verses 15–18 of chapter 13 deal directly with the siege threat facing the inhabitants of Jerusalem. As far as Mark is concerned Satan rules the throne in Judea (revealing Mark's anti-Jerusalem bias). Christians' future lies beyond Judaism and Jerusalem.

In verses prior to the verse chosen for today's proclamation Mark warns the readers against the false fanaticism that plagued the church earlier and was resurfacing during this time of tribulation. Jesus preached a message of suffering. False teachers, now in the throes of the great tribulation, taught a contrary message. Mark warned believers not to listen to false teachers who "make appeal to the Christ of their own desire and imaging."[30] There is confidence that Christians will stand firm as the chosen ones of God. Yet there is nevertheless a clear warning—"be careful, *take heed!*"

---

[25]Ibid., 207.
[26]Ibid.

[27]Ibid., 213.
[28]Ibid.
[29]*MARK*, 193.
[30]Ibid., 204.

Mark is careful to ward off any hopes for a false belief in the parousia. He believes that Jesus will return and he believes that his return is imminent. For Mark, the parousia is not part of the present tribulation facing the church; it is to follow. Mark's apocalypse draws from scriptural sources, evidenced by his incorporation of prophetic texts from the Old Testament. The cosmic disturbances Mark describes are taken from Jewish apocalyptic literature that describes the *Day of the Lord*.

Everything is ready—the Son of Man can return in his final act of revelation. Jesus will be seen for who he really is at the parousia. No longer will he be dimly seen. All will know that he is the Christ, the Son of Man who sits on the throne of glory! This is the hope that will sustain Christians as they deal with his absence. No longer will they be ashamed of their suffering prophet. At the parousia they will see him in all his glory. Mark insists that the community be ready and prepared for his return. Jesus will not come to judge them. Believers will find it to be a time of great joy and rejoicing. Jesus will return to gather the elect.

Mark insists that Jesus' return is near. There is no room for complacency. People are to be ready at all times. (Refer to the gospel exegesis for the thirty-third Sunday in Ordinary Time for further elaboration of the eschatological issues in chapter 13.) We are not to fall asleep. "Mark's Jesus urges his listeners and subsequent generations of believers to be ever watchful for the return of a beloved family member. It is, after all, a fact of our faith: the beloved Master will indeed return and expect to be welcomed by family in fitting fashion. Are we ready?"[31]

Mark used a parable already in the tradition (the Watching Servants, Lk 2:35–38) and fashioned it according to the needs of his community. Mark changes the focus of the original parable to be specifically Christological. "Christ is the departing Lord and the parousia will mark his return."[32] The doorkeeper represents the waiting disciples, the elect of God, the Christian community. The designations of time ("whether in the evening, or at midnight") symbolize the span of time before Jesus' return. Mark adds to the original parable by inserting the phrase "and he puts his servants in charge." This translates "he gave them authority (*exousia*)." Mark consistently used the word *exousia* in the gospel. He associated it with the teaching authority of Jesus himself. The disciples were bestowed with Jesus' own authority. Mark called the apostles slaves (*doulos*), yet even as slaves in the Lord's service they are endowed with authority that comes directly from him. Mark is not talking about some past reality; he is talking about a present one. Jesus' authority given to the apostles is operative in Mark's community.

Mark understands that his community questions why the Lord's return has taken so long, especially when the Lord himself assured them that it would be soon. Mark answers that even though it is indeed close at hand, only God knows the day or the hour. Verse 35 acknowledges that the Lord's coming has been delayed—readiness and watchfulness are exhorted.

In the final analysis, Mark's exhortation is for all Christians for all time. He wanted the parable and the entire discourse understood "not as a guide in calculating a deadline, but as an inspiration and a warning, to live one's life at each moment in preparedness for the meeting with Christ."[33] Mark's intention in chapter 13 is to invite his readers to accept the tribulation of their present situation with the hope that the parousia would soon follow. Armed with that hope, they will be fortified to endure the trials they face as Jesus endured his own Passion and death.

Ched Myers suggests that this is one parable in which Jesus does not address his political opponents.[34] This parable is addressed instead to his community of disciples. Those who are left in charge are not tenants, they are slaves. They are slaves who have been given authority. All the servants/slaves have been given their own specific tasks. The task of the doorkeeper is to be vigilant about what is at the door. The one who is coming is the expected Messiah, but the unexpected one as well. Israel expected a militaristic Messiah who would reinstate the golden age, restoring Israel to its former glory as a political entity. Jesus was not that Messiah. Jesus was a Suffering Servant Mes-

---

[31]*CWJB*, 3.
[32]*MARK*, 208.

[33]Ibid., 209.
[34]*BSM*, 347.

siah. No wonder so many missed it—their hopes were false and fashioned according to their own human desires.

In today's parable the disciples are told to vigil through the night. The night watches correspond to the moments of our Lord's Passion. 1. Evening (*opse*) = time (*opsia*) of the Lord's Supper (14:17) and the time (*opsia*) after the crucifixion (15:42); 2. midnight (*mesonuktion*): night (*nux*) general time of Peter's denial; 3. the "cock crow" (*alektorophōnias*): actual time (*alektōr*) of Peter's denial; 4. dawn (*prōi*): the time Jesus was handed over to the officials.[35] The parable's connection to the Passion is not to be missed. The exhortation not to be found *asleep* is elaborated even further in the Gethsemane exchange. "Not to be found asleep" is directly related to the events of Jesus' final hour— the hour in which his own disciples betrayed him, fell asleep, and abandoned him in his final watch. They did not understand his call to the cross.[36]

The call to watchfulness was a common exhortation in the early church. "It was the cornerstone of the primitive church's understanding of eschatological existence on the edge of history, and perhaps the most strongly attested of all New Testament catechetical/parenetic traditions. . . . For Mark, it is the culmination of Jesus' sermon on revolutionary patience. The discipleship community is exhorted to embrace the world as Gethsemane: to stay awake in the darkness of history, to refuse to compromise the politics of the cross."[37] The call to watchfulness is a call to join the nonviolent struggle against those who oppress—against the domination of those in power. The nonviolent revolution against powers that oppress will prevail because the Lord, and the Lord alone, is in charge of his house. It may seem that the "powers" (religious and political) are in charge, but in truth, God is sovereign. Mark exhorts his community to stand firm in the midst of growing persecution.

The entire gospel of Mark is cyclical—its axis spins on the Passion-event. One prism with which to view every story in Mark's gospel is through the lens of Jesus' Passion and death. Mark's gospel is a catechism of the cross. "Be watchful!" we are exhorted.

Embrace the cross, walk with Christ to it and through it. When we stand with those on the bottom of society's social order, we will ultimately walk with Christ to the cross. Jesus' faithfulness to God's will led him to the cross. His faithfulness to God's will led him to be a voice for the voiceless and to nonviolently, but aggressively, resist domination. He upset the apple carts of those wielding domination and control. That never works in a hierarchical society. Those on top are fond of their lofty perches. They have a vested interest in staying there. When someone suggests that their perch be shared, it makes them nervous. No wonder Jesus exhorted his disciples to be last in the kingdom instead of first. Throughout history those who seek to nonviolently overthrow the perches of power and control are always resisted, stopped, annihilated, and put to death. Today's parable was a reminder to the disciples to be ready to follow the catechism of the cross. Discipleship always leads there. Never fear, stand firm, watch, be ready—for the Lord is coming and he is coming soon!

Proclaim the gospel again.

Sometimes we gain new insights when we hear the text after the interpretation is given. Someone from the group proclaims the gospel a second time.

STEP 4
TESTING

Conversation with the Liturgy and the Scriptures

Test your original understanding in dialogue with the text.

(You might consider breaking into smaller groups.)

Now that you've heard the exegesis, were there any new insights? How do you feel about it? How does your original understanding of this gospel compare with what we just shared? How does this story speak to your life?

Sharing Life Experience

Participants share an experience from their lives that connects with the biblical interpretation just presented.

---

[35]Ibid.

[36]Ibid.

[37]Ibid., 348.

Today's gospel invites watchfulness. It invites me to be prepared for the Lord's return. Even though this Advent poises us for eruption into the new millennium, I must admit that I doubt the Lord's immanent return. Y2K notwithstanding, I believe that we will all still be wildly kicking our heels and running off our mouths in the year 2001. Changes in centuries and certainly changes in millenniums bring out the apocalypticist in all of us. In the year 999 everyone (including the church) thought that Jesus would return in the year 1000 (remember the thousand-year reign of Christ mentioned in Revelation?). They had to rethink things when life continued. Do I believe the Lord will return? Yes. Do I believe that it will be soon? No. Do I believe that it could be soon for me? It is possible. However, the Lord does come and he comes today. Day in and day out the Lord comes. He comes in the everyday events of my life, the life of my community, and the life of the world. Epiphanies occur all around us. Sometimes we are blind to them, and sometimes we are able to shake off the sleep and awaken to the reality of Emmanuel in our midst. Today's gospel is a clarion call to be attentive to those moments—to listen, watch, and be ready.

A few years ago a very beautiful woman announced that she believed that the Lord was going to return soon. She was prepared for his second coming. Like Mark, she believed it to be immanent. We recently buried this precious lady. Her prediction was indeed accurate. The Lord did return—for her. She now sees him face to face. Was she ready? If she was not ready, then no one is ready! This woman lived each day as if the Lord was coming for her on that day. Her thoughts were always "other"-centered. I never heard a harsh word come from this lovely lady's mouth. Her gift was the ability to see the good—no, the precious—in every person. She not only saw the good, she affirmed it.

In her own way she lived the cross. All her pain, her struggles, and her suffering of the last days of her life were offered for others. She resisted pain medication so she could be present to her life and to the concerns she took to the Lord each day. Weeks before her death, she was still calling the parish office to see how she could help or to pass along something that might be helpful to another person, another parish.

Her suffering was not the type that led her to the picket line—but her suffering was the quiet suffering of a servant in love with her God. She was a servant who prayed in earnest every day for those she felt were in need of her prayers. Her sacrifice of praise and prayer changed lives.

When it would have been easy to give up and rest in her dying days, she continued her prayer vigil. She remembered those who most needed her prayers, she asked about them, and she continued her vigil to the end. She will never know how her deathbed prayers impacted someone very close to me.

Our crosses do not always call us to lay down our lives in a bloody show of solidarity with the world's suffering. They do call us to sacrifice, however. Our daily struggles, our pain, suffering, and sorrow, can be offered for suffering and oppressed people in the world. I am awed by all the people who benefited from this great lady's prayers and action. Her life was lived in a state of constant readiness. I have known her for twelve years. There was not a day in those twelve years that this precious woman of God was not ready to meet her God. She has now had her day of the Lord. All of us are beneficiaries of her encounter. She is our advocate, only now she advocates from a far more special place than before. I am humbled and graced to have had the experience of her love and friendship. She loved the Christ of history, she celebrated the Christ of her present, and now she dances with the Christ of her future.

What was Mark trying to tell his community? How might we relate to the eschatological issues in today's gospel? What relevance is there for us today? In what way does this gospel challenge your community today? In what way has this conversation with the scriptures for today's liturgy invited change in your life? In what way are the biblical themes of covenant, exodus, creation, and community evident in today's readings? Do you still feel the same way about this text as when you began? Has your original understanding been stretched, challenged, or affirmed?

STEP 5
DECISION

The gospel demands a response.

In what concrete way might your parish be invited to respond? Are there any attitudes or behaviors you would like to change as a result of today's conversation? What one concrete action will you take this week in response to the liturgy today?

Pastoral Considerations: Advent is a time of spiritual preparation and conversion. How might we assist families in keeping the spirituality of Advent in the fore in light of the season's rampant consumerism? Every household might be encouraged to have a copy of *Catholic Household Blessings and Prayers* (NCCB) that includes pertinent prayers and blessings for use in the Advent season: "At Table During Advent," 64–69; "Blessing of an Advent Wreath," 110–112; "Blessing of a Christmas Tree," 113; "Blessing of a Christmas Creche or Manger Scene," 117. A beautiful, scripturally based Advent calendar is available from Liturgy Training Publications for use in homes and classrooms.

Advent is a time for increased efforts to uphold the values of justice that we should be emphasizing throughout the year. What are some creative ways to call attention to the ongoing ministries of justice in your parish? Who are the poor in our midst? In what way are the needs of the poor addressed in our parishes? If there are no organized efforts, perhaps groups might join forces with civic groups dedicated to providing necessities, meals, and gifts for the poor. What local agencies might benefit from our increased participation?

Christian Initiation: What rites might be celebrated during Advent? The RCIA insists that the catechumenate proper should last at least one year from the rite of acceptance until initiation at the Easter Vigil (National Statues #6). Catechumens are thus formed in the life, death, and resurrection of Christ as it unfolds in the gospel proclaimed in the liturgy in one complete liturgical cycle. Parishes that celebrate the rite of acceptance on the first Sunday of Advent and initiation at the vigil, have a catechumenate that lasts only four months at best. Catechumens are thus formed in only a third of the paschal mystery of Jesus Christ! This deserves serious reflection, discernment, and attention and invites us to ask ourselves what informs our pastoral practices. In a year-round catechumenate, the rite of acceptance is celebrated about four times a year, thus giving people the opportunity to move in and

out of the process according to *their* timetable, not ours.

One rite that might be celebrated is the *anointing of catechumens.* This rite "symbolizes their need for God's help and strength so that, undeterred by the bonds of the past and overcoming the opposition of the devil, they will forthrightly take the step of professing their faith and will hold fast to it unfalteringly throughout their lives (RCIA #99)." Advent, with its emphasis on repentance and conversion, might be an excellent time to celebrate it.

The blessings (RCIA ##95–96) and minor exorcisms (RCIA ##90–93) should be used regularly (perhaps each time the catechumens gather). If blessings are used with baptized candidates, remember to adapt the blessings to reflect that they are one with us by virtue of the baptism we share.

DOCTRINAL ISSUES

What Church truth/teaching/doctrinal issue could be drawn from the gospel for the first Sunday of Advent?

Participants suggest possible doctrinal themes that flow from the readings.

Possible Doctrinal Themes

Advent; Christ's coming—past, present, and future; eschatology; parousia; soteriology; manifestation; paschal mystery; conversion; heaven, hell, and purgatory

Present the doctrinal material at this time.

1. The facilitator gives input on a particular doctrinal issue of his or her prior choosing. OR
2. The group chooses a doctrinal issue from the list they created. They read together from the Doctrinal Appendix or other appropriate, official Church documents and the works of respected theologians.

(Many doctrinal issues are found in the Doctrinal Appendix at the back of this workbook. If you are choosing an issue from this resource, please refer to it now.)

Reflection questions centered around the chosen doctrinal theme can be found at the end of each topic in the Doctrinal Appendix. The questions are based on the five-step reflection process. If you choose a topic not included in the Doctrinal Appendix, craft your own questions according to the same five-step process.

Following the reflection questions you will be reminded to return to chapter 7, "Preparing the Catechetical Session," to assist you in crafting your own session.

Closing Prayer

Faithful Covenant God,
During this Advent time of prayer and recollection,
we turn our gaze toward you.
We acknowledge our total dependence on your mercy.
Look with kindness on your people.
Nourish us with the food of expectant faith.
Allow our hidden hopes to discover the possibilities that lie within.
Help us to risk, to reach beyond our normal, safe solutions to life's queries.
O Father and Mother of the Universe, your Son is coming and will not delay.
You will bring every hidden hope to light and reveal yourself in our secret desires.
Lead us deeper into the dim lit shadows of winter's dusk and have pity on us.
We ask this through your Son, Jesus Christ, our Savior and Lord. Amen.[38]

---

[38]Inspired by: Carroll Stuhlmueller, C.P., *Biblical Meditations for Advent and the Christmas Season* (New York/Ramsey: Paulist Press, 1980).

SECOND SUNDAY OF ADVENT

Environment (see first Sunday of Advent)

John the Baptist is a primary character in today's gospel. Perhaps an icon bearing his image might be included in the gathering space.

Lighting the Advent Candles

Prayer to accompany the lighting of the remaining candles throughout Advent:

The following prayer may be used each time your group gathers and a new candle is lit each week.

Two Advent candles are lighted as the leader says:
Blessed are you, Lord God of all creation:
in the darkness and in the light.
Blessed are you as we wait in joyful hope
for the coming of our Savior, Jesus Christ.

All respond:
For the kingdom, the power, and the glory are
　　yours, now and for ever.

The leader says:
Come, Lord Jesus!

All respond:
Come quickly!

The leader says:
Let us live soberly, justly, and devoutly in this
　　world
as we wait in joyful hope
for the coming of our Savior, Jesus Christ.

All respond:
For the kingdom, the power, and the glory are
　　yours, now and for ever.

(Adapted from *Catholic Household Blessings and Prayers*, NCCB, 1988, 64–67.)

INTRODUCTORY RITES

Entrance Antiphon (or Opening Song)

People of Zion, the Lord will come to save all the nations, and your hearts will exult to hear his majestic voice. (Is 20:19, 20)[1]

Opening Prayer

The facilitator of the session may lead the prayer. Others in the group may be asked to proclaim the readings.

Let us pray
[in Advent for the coming Savior to teach us wisdom]

　　Pause for silent prayer.

Father in heaven,
the day draws near when the glory of your Son
will make radiant the night of the waiting world.
May the lure of greed not impede us from the joy
which moves the hearts of those who seek him.
May the darkness not blind us
to the vision of wisdom
which fills the minds of those who find him.
We ask this in the name of Jesus the Lord.[2]

LITURGY OF THE WORD

The readings are proclaimed.

First Reading
Isaiah 40:1–5, 9–11

(Please refer to the first Sunday of Advent for an overview of the Book of the Prophet Isaiah.)

Today's Pericope: Today's reading from Isaiah is one of the most commonly known texts in the He-

---

[1]Second Sunday of Advent, "Entrance Antiphon," *The Sacramentary.*

[2]Second Sunday of Advent: "Alternative Opening Prayer," *The Sacramentary.*

brew scriptures. The prophet did not have the Christ-event in mind when writing, however. His reference was the restoration of Israel after the Babylonian exile. Persia's Cyrus had already won initial victory and Babylon's power and influence were growing weaker. The prophet of the text is the one who cried from the wilderness.

The word *gospel* is derived from the original Hebrew word for good tidings. Good tidings in this text refers to the wonderful news that God will soon intervene in human history and bring the people back from exile. It is an event likened to the first exodus (it is often referred to as the second exodus).

This text is typological. Reginald Fuller suggests that Second Isaiah might be referred to as the father of typology (see the glossary).[3] It was understood, then, as a type of an expected future eschatological event and Christianity embraced it as a type of the Christ-event. We read it today in that context. "Typology is based upon the conviction, not that history repeats itself, but that God's mighty acts in history follow a consistent pattern because God is true to himself and his purpose."[4] The great *Day of the Lord*, the eschatological event, is a day in which the glory of God will be revealed in all its fullness. In the New Testament, *glory* is a word that is synonymous with salvation history. It is understood as an event. The glory of the Lord is the saving event of God's intervention in human history.

The event foreshadowed in the Isaiah reading is the Christ-event. Thus, the prophet of the text foreshadows John the Baptist. He is the voice who will cry from next week's gospel pericope, "prepare the way of the Lord." John's work of preparation will be to preach a word of repentance.[5]

Today's prophet seeks to help Israel interpret the events of the exile. All seemed lost before, but now hope loomed large over the horizon. After a generation in exile, the end was fast approaching. Isaiah reminded the people that the political situation in which Cyrus was gaining power was directed by none other than Yahweh—God was acting on behalf of Israel. Thus, Deutero-Isaiah helped Israel interpret the political realities of the day through a religious perspective. Cyrus's rise to power was another example of God's continued intervention in human affairs. Only God can restore God's people.

Today's reading refers to Israel's immanent return home as well as the prophet's commissioning. The heavenly court witnesses and approves God's command, call, and commissioning of the prophet. So commissioned, the prophet's word announces a new age of restoration for the people. Through the *power of God's Word* the world will be reconciled. The people stood on the threshold of a new age. The creative Word of God had spoken as it was spoken at the dawn of an earlier age, the creation of the world, and into the hearts of all believers was infused the seeds of new life. God's glory would be revealed when the people were safely restored and in their own land. For Christians the glory of the Lord is revealed in the advent of the *One Who Is to Come*.

Responsorial Psalm
Psalm 85:9–10, 11–12, 13–14

Today's psalm is a lament. It is unknown what situation the psalm laments. It is possible that the psalm was composed around the same time as the reading from Isaiah. The psalm looks to the future day of divine intervention in salvation history. There are threads of similar images in the reading from Isaiah, the psalm, and the description of the Baptist's mission.

Second Reading
2 Peter 3:8–14

Overview of 1 and 2 Peter: The letters of Peter are part of a group of letters known as "general" or "catholic" because "they are not addressed to a specific church."[6] Included in the classification of "catholic" epistles are 1 and 2 Peter, James, Jude, and 1, 2, and 3 John.

First Peter. Even though 1 Peter was written as a letter, including an opening thanksgiving, the

---

[3]*PL*, 205.
[4]Ibid.
[5]Ibid.

[6]*RNT*, 293.

body of the letter does not have the personal elements that are usually found in a letter. The letter was written to the church in Asia Minor; some scholars believe that it was written in the Roman church by an associate of Paul's named Silvanus (5:12). Some scholars doubt Peter's authorship of the letter for a variety of reasons, one of which was the fact that the church during Peter's time did not experience the persecution referred to throughout the letter. Those that opt for Petrine authorship, however, cite the primitive theology based on eschatology, servant Christology, and church order inherent in the letter. If Peter did not write the letter and it was written at a later time, William Dalton maintains that in light of the persecutions mentioned in the letter, it would have been unlikely that there was no mention of the persecutions by Nero shortly after Peter's death (ca. A.D. 64).[7]

Scholars suggest a parallel between 1 Peter and Paul's Letter to the Romans, not only thematically but regionally as well. The region addressed in the letter parallels Paul's missionary tour. Thematically both letters address relationship to civil governments and brotherly love, and both express liturgical language common in the early Christian community.

One of the primary concerns of 1 Peter is the life of the community in the face of growing persecution. It tries to answer the question, "What does it mean to be a Christian in a persecuted church?" First Peter's concern was to exhort Christians to faithfulness in Christ amid persecution and pagan animosities. "By recalling the greatness of their vocation and by showing that persecution is a sign of their calling, the writer encourages and exhorts his readers to stand firm (5:12)."[8] The letter also addresses the duties of Christians in the midst of such persecution. Slaves and women might find themselves abused by antagonistic non-Christian masters and husbands. "In each instance exemplary behavior may also be a strategy for alleviating the tension in the situation."[9]

The letter refers to the Christian as a resident in an alien land. This was understood not only eschatologically and metaphorically, as referring to the Christian's eventual heavenly destination, but also in a geopolitical way. Christians did not see themselves as citizens of the cities in which they lived. "The 'resident alien' at least had some status as a 'registered' member of the city."[10] Christians were particularly susceptible to suspicion not only because of their Christianity, but their legal status was also questionable. The letter asserted that the Christians' new life is evident to outsiders and thus their persecution was a reaction to this new way of life, changed patterns of living, and newly formed relationships. Conversion has meant breaking off past ties and associations (1:3–5, 10–12, 18, 21; 2:4–10) to enter the new familial community of mutual love which is God's holy people (1:17; 2:5, 10; 5:9).[11] Abuse was not isolated to one specific cause. Christians were harassed due to ignorance, the suspicion of wrongdoing, and curiosity that prompted a test of their newfound faith. Christians were to turn to the crucified Christ as an example in the midst of suffering. They were to turn their faces with hope to the resurrected Christ and the promise of eternal glory.

First Peter is known as a pastoral letter. "By emphasizing the dignity of the Christian vocation, which provides a God-given 'home' (*oikos*, 2:5, 4:17) for the "homeless" (paroikoi, 2:11; cf. 1:17), and the positive value of sharing the passion of Christ through persecution, the writer reminds his readers to remain faithful."[12]

Second Peter. The time between Jesus' lifetime sojourn and his expected return was growing longer each day. Some of the first followers of Christ were discouraged and wondered if Christ would ever return. To make matters worse, false teachers who insisted that belief in the parousia was folly dotted the early church landscape. Their proof was obvious—Jesus had yet to return. Second Peter is a pseudonymous work attributed to the apostle Peter. It reflects a more sophisticated community of believers. Most scholars date it

---

[7]William J. Dalton, S.J., "The First Epistle of Peter," *NJBC*, 903.

[8]Ibid., 904.

[9]*RNT*, 295.

---

[10]Ibid.

[11]Ibid.

[12]*NJBC*, 904.

around the mid-second century. It is probably the last letter written of all the canonical New Testament documents.

The letter bears a resemblance to the Letter of Jude, another late document. It obviously antedates the apostles, evidenced by references to the apostles in the past tense. Another indication of the postapostolic time frame of the letter is the reference to the Pauline letters as "scripture" and the allusion to the second-century problem of gnosticism. The letter was written to the churches in Asia Minor to support the Christian believers and to gird them against the heretical teaching of the false teachers.

False teachers denied that Jesus would return (3:3–4). Philosophers of the day insisted that the world itself was eternal and Christian antagonists may have used that philosophical argument in their teaching. The author of 2 Peter accuses the false teachers of misreading and misinterpreting Paul's letters. Second Peter is an apologetic in favor of traditional Christian eschatology. It is constructed as a farewell address given to the community by the dying Peter himself.[13] The author of 2 Peter expanded the arguments of the Letter of Jude. He also excerpted portions of the Hebrew scriptures. He insists that the Christian belief in divine judgment is not a human-made construct, but rather comes directly from the tradition of the prophets, inspired by the Holy Spirit. Thus, if anyone wants to argue about the validity of divine judgment, they will, in effect, have to argue with scripture itself.

Second Peter stands on the authority of the apostle Peter as testimony to the truth of the Christian position. The letter insists that the testimony of Peter should provide the necessary credence; thus its foundation is based on the recollection of the testimony and teaching of Peter. The author affirms that Peter's witness of the transfiguration is proof enough of the parousia.

Second Peter's reference to the transfiguration is an indication that at least one of the synoptic gospels (which contained the account of the transfiguration story) enjoyed "authoritative status as apostolic testimony."[14] Pheme Perkins reminds us that 2 Peter confronts the matter of apostolic authority and the continuity of the apostolic tradition.[15] It also makes reference to a collection of Paul's letters, which were considered authoritative. Thus there emerges in this letter the issue of authentic, authoritative Christian scripture. The author of 2 Peter does not maintain that everything in scripture is directly inspired. He does, however, insist that belief that the world will be judged is affirmed by the consistent witness in the prophetic and apostolic tradition and in the sayings of Jesus. The false teachers' interpretation of Paul's letters are simply antithetical to the gospel. Second Peter aggressively attacks the adversarial position that traditional Christian teaching regarding the second coming is irrational.

Today's Pericope: The author takes the offensive. To those who insist that the parousia will never take place (or Jesus would have returned by now if he were going to) the author counterattacks by insisting that divine timetables cannot be measured by human standards. We simply have no way of knowing *when* Christ will return, but we can be assured that he will indeed return—"a thousand years are as a day in the Lord's eyes." Perhaps the Lord's delay is another example of God's incredible compassion and mercy for the human race. We simply have no way of knowing. However, the author exhorts believers to take advantage of the time at hand. The interval time of waiting is to be a time of *metanoia*—conversion, repentance, and reconciliation. If the time is spent wisely, then all will be ready to meet the Lord when he does indeed return. The author insists that the day can be shortened by growing in holiness and performing good works. Proponents of gnosticism insisted that future judgment was not in the forecast so ill behavior and immorality were of no consequence.

The letter contains apocalyptic imagery. Today's pericope is unique in all of scripture in its account of a final conflagration (v. 10), but this idea is not unique to Christianity. Belief in the total destruction by fire at the end of time had spread from Persia to the Greco-Roman world, where it was a favorite topic of philosophers. Similar ideas are

---

[13]*RNT*, 300.

[14]Ibid.
[15]Ibid.

also found in Jewish apocalyptic. "Such opinions are not scientific assertions but mythopoeic images. Some scholars suggest that *heurethesetai* (v. 10) should be rendered 'will be laid bare' rather than 'will be burned up.' In any event, the author's point is clear, regardless of its mythic presentation, i.e. there will be a transformation of all creation at the Lord's second advent."[16] Thus, it is important that Christians be ever watchful, constantly awake, and enter fully into the process of ongoing conversion as we await that great and awesome *Day of the Lord*.

The gospel is proclaimed.

Gospel
Mark 1:1–8.

STEP 1
NAMING ONE'S EXPERIENCE

What were your first impressions? What was your first response to the gospel (or the other readings)? What captured your attention?

Each person names his or her initial impression. Statements should be brief. No reasons should be given at this time. All simply listen without agreeing or disagreeing.

STEP 2
UNDERSTANDING

In a brief statement, explain what you think this gospel is trying to convey.

STEP 3
INPUT FROM VISION/STORY/TRADITION

Liturgical Context

The Entrance Antiphon for the second Sunday of Advent reveals the mood surrounding today's liturgy: "and your hearts will exult to hear his

---

[16]*WWC*, 136.

majestic joy."[17] Today is the day we hear from the one who will prepare the way of the Lord. John the Baptist takes his place on salvation history's center stage to herald the *One More Powerful* who will follow him. One can almost feel the acceleration of time in forward motion. There is a "sense of nearness to the time of the Lord's coming, but there is also a sense of the universality of salvation."[18]

Today's liturgy is an invitation to enter deeply into the work of transformation—to become attentive to one's relationship with God. Today's second reading puts it in perspective for us. The Lord will not delay; he wants everyone to repent so no one will perish. Yet we are aware that without God we are powerless. We are particularly reminded of this truth in today's Prayer over the Gifts:

> "Lord,
> we are nothing without you.
> As you sustain us in your mercy,
> receive our prayers and offerings...."

Our hope, however, is revealed in the opening prayer. We ask God to open our hearts and to keep us from any obstacle that would prevent us from accepting Christ in our lives. We pray this so we might be filled with the wisdom of Christ, thereby becoming one with him when he returns in glory.

Today's liturgy in the person of John the Baptist reminds us that the world continues to need such prophet-precursors who will sound the clarion call from the belfries of the world's towers to wake up and repent. "Wherever they appear, *there* is the 'beginning of the gospel' for those who do not yet know Christ. In the Church, in the Christian communities at the heart of all renewal, of all new beginnings, we find prophets, sometimes invested with a ministry, often without any official title, but in every case animated by the Spirit of the Father, who reveals his secrets to the meek and the humble".[19]

---

[17]Second Sunday of Advent, "Entrance Antiphon," *The Sacramentary*.
[18]*DL* (I), 67.
[19]Ibid., 79.

Gospel Exegesis

The facilitator provides input from critical biblical scholarship on this text. This input includes insights as to how people would have heard the gospel in Jesus' time.

"The beginning of the gospel of Jesus Christ the Son of God." Thus Mark dramatically begins his narrative. One can almost hear the trumpet fanfare in the imagination of the evangelist as the proclamation is sounded. He sets the stage immediately for the thematic house he intends to build. It is almost as if the anonymous narrator steps in front of the curtain before it is raised upon the human drama unfolding behind its cascading folds to make sure his audience will understand the events about to be related. He provides the context and lens. This is the story of Christ, the Son of God. Mark's prologue also tells the listener how he or she ought to hear what is about to be spoken. The opening verse of Mark's gospel also serves as the motto and title of his entire work. The reader is to be critically aware that every character who enters the scene after the opening scene of Mark's narrative has not been privy to what the reader and listener just heard proclaimed. They are "consequently deprived of essential information relating to the identity of both the Baptist and Jesus himself."[20]

Mark asserts that the story of Christ really begins with the arrival of the Baptist. The story begins in the desert by the Jordan's banks—a place that evokes images from the Hebrew scriptures. The desert was always known as a place of numinous encounters between God and human beings. The desert was also known as a place of retreat, where one could disassociate from the world and enter into Yahweh's divine presence. The Essene community is one such example. The Essenes made their home in the desert at Qumran by the Dead Sea in protest of what they believed to be the unlawful way in which those who were in power at the Temple in Jerusalem came into that power. The Essenes wished to establish a new community of Israel that was pleasing in the eyes of God. False messiahs also fled to the desert to strengthen their own messianic liberation movements. "The desert is, in short, a place where people of kindred spirit assemble for the sake of pursuing a new way of life together."[21]

Jesus' gospel is thus inaugurated with the preaching of John. Jesus has the distinction of being both the *messenger* and the *message* of the gospel. Mark uses the term *the gospel* seven times in his narrative. The term was part of the evangelical language of the early church. However, Mark's Jesus is the only person that uses it. Matthew's gospel heralded the reign of God. Mark's gospel heralds the person of Jesus Christ. His is the only gospel that puts the name *Jesus* with *Christ* and uses it together—"Jesus Christ."[22]

Mark's gospel exalts the crucified and risen Lord. The term *gospel* is almost synonymous with the person of Jesus himself. Jesus and his gospel are one, which is why believers are invited to die for the gospel. Embodied in the gospel is Jesus' presence and saving power.[23] Mark designates Jesus as Messiah and Son of God from the outset. The story of Christ is the story of a people with Easter faith who experienced him as God's own Son.

Mark wastes no time. He succinctly and abruptly takes us right into the story. Immediately John the Baptizer enters the scene. He announces that *One* greater than he is about to take center stage. This *One Who Is to Come* will usher in the Spirit of God. Even the advent of John was foretold in scriptures. John is the messenger of Malachi and the wilderness prophet of Isaiah (Mal 3:1 and Is 40:3). It was believed that Elijah would return to purify Israel before the Day of Yahweh (*Kyrios*). Mark nearly quotes directly from 2 Kings 1:8 in his description of how one might expect the appearance of Elijah to be upon his arrival. When early Christian faith understood the Christ-event as fulfillment of what the Hebrew scriptures referred to as the *Day of the Lord*, it was a logical step to refer to John as the new Elijah. "Jesus' power is as much greater than his as wind is stronger than water, and the molding spirit more vigorous than the primordial chaos. Being greater than the Baptist, Jesus is allowed to see and hear what is not seen and heard by anyone else: the breaking open of the heavens,

[20] *RM*, 34.

[21] Ibid., 37.
[22] *MARK*, 2.
[23] Ibid.

the spirit descending, and the voice speaking from heaven."[24]

Thus, John comes dressed like the prophet of old; he feasted on wilderness fodder just as his ancient predecessor had similarly feasted. John is a sign that God is about to renew his covenant with Israel. John's call to repentance is rooted in this renewal of covenant. John demands a complete *metanoia*—a change of heart and conduct, a radical change in outlook that will be outwardly attested to by submitting to the baptism he preached. The recipients of John's preaching were the "people of the whole Judean countryside and all the inhabitants of Jerusalem"—in other words, God's invitation to repent is addressed to *all of Israel.* John's ministry is reminiscent of the prophets who went before him and who understood the wilderness to be the place where God's manifestation and final salvation would be revealed.

John baptized with water. Christ would follow and baptize with the Holy Spirit. Mark draws from Isaiah and appropriates the prophetic text to refer to Christ. Mark changed Isaiah's "paths of our God" to "his paths." This is the *One* whose path is made straight and for whom John prepares the way.

Mark is not concerned with the ethical nature of John's preaching as was Matthew. He is more concerned that John is the precursor who pointed the way to Christ. The prophets Joel and Ezekiel promised that in the day of salvation God would pour out his Spirit. When John insists that the *One to Come* will baptize with the Holy Spirit, this is a direct reference to the prophetic tradition of the First Testament. Jesus' baptism in the Holy Spirit is the same *Spirit* Joel and Ezekiel promised would be lavishly poured out upon the earth. Mark constructs the foundation he will use to house the catechism he intends to craft throughout the gospel narrative—Jesus is the fulfillment of all that was prophesied.

Luke and Matthew insisted that the baptism would be with fire—a baptism of judgment. It is probable that John used the language of baptism with fire also. Time perhaps mellowed the memory of the

Baptist's probable words and rather than a forecast of immanent judgment, the Baptist prophesies about the effects of Christ's act of redemption—the outpouring of the Spirit upon the earth. Mark's Jesus is not a fire and brimstone preacher; nor is Mark's characterization of John.

John Pilch reminds us that the honor/shame culture in which Jesus lived had an integral influence on Mark's gospel.[25] As said earlier, Mark announces the gospel of Jesus. *Gospel* is better translated *proclamation.* Proclamations were common, but they were usually made on behalf of some great dignitary or ruler. Listeners to Mark's gospel would wonder by what authority Jesus had the right to the honor rendered him by such a proclamation. He was, after all, from "Nowheresville"—Nazareth, a place unrecorded in antiquity. A village craftsman had no right to step out of his social sphere and make such a proclamation. Mark insists that Jesus had every right. The source of his honor or his claim to fame is that he is the Son of God. In antiquity "son of..." meant that the person who was the "son of" someone possessed the attributes of the one he claimed to be the "son of." Thus, Jesus possessed the attributes of God—he was *One* who is divine or God-like. Jesus had all the authority he needed to lay claim to his title, Son of God.

One biblical exegete we will hear from throughout this resource is Ched Myers.[26] Myers's approach is not what one would call typical or even mainstream. However, he brings an understanding to Mark's gospel that is fresh, challenging, upsetting, and convicting. Myers insists that all approaches to interpreting Mark's gospel are biased. He admits even to his own bias. Biblical exegetes are not objective reporters. Most of them bring their own cultural, religious, gender, racial, and cultural perspective into their interpretive work. The emergence of women exegetes and liberation theologians has helped us to understand that much of the interpretive work of the scriptures has been colored, quite naturally so, by the bias of the interpreter's assumptions about the text as well as his or her social class and political commitments in the real world. Biblical scholarship, cor-

---

[24]*RM,* 38–39.

[25]*CWJB,* 5.
[26]*BSM,* 8.

rectly understood, speaks to the politics of living—the injustices, the divisions, the stupidities, and the sin. Myers's commentary allows another voice to speak from the pages of Mark—a necessary voice, one we do not always hear. Much of what Myers suggests stands in direct contrast to commonly held interpretations of the scriptures. Some of his ideas are presented here in order to bring another voice into the conversation with Mark that we will be having throughout the liturgical year.

Myers's commentary is an analysis of the politics of Jesus. He insists that the *Way* Jesus suggested was a *Way* of nonviolence—a *Way* of defiant, yet loving and courageous, behavior toward the religious (the Temple authorities) and civil (imperial Rome) powers of his day. Those powers oppress and denigrate the human dignity of the powerless. They continue to do the same thing centuries later.

Myers uses the language of Gandhi to help modern readers understand the politics of Mark's narrative world—the language of nonviolence, liberation, and truth force. His work is a socioliterary criticism of Mark's gospel. Myers describes two prominent themes in his work:

> The first is *repentance*, which for us implies not only a conversion of heart, but a concrete process of turning away from empire, its distractions and seductions, its hubris and iniquity. The second is *resistance*, which involves shaking off the powerful sedation of a society that rewards ignorance and trivializes everything political, in order to discern and take concrete stands in our historical moment, and to find meaningful ways to "impede imperial progress." Both themes demand a commitment to nonviolence, as a personal and interpersonal way of life and as a militant and revolutionary political practice....

> Because we understand the present crisis of empire to have everything to do with the ordering of power, the distribution of wealth, and the global plague of militarism, radical discipleship necessarily approaches the Bible with social, political,

and economic questions in mind. What does Mark have to say concerning our struggles to overcome racism? Or to find more proximate forms of solidarity with the poor while we work for justice? Or to deepen our use of nonviolent direct action? These questions explain why I have chosen to entitle this commentary a "political reading," despite the fact that such an idiom will inevitably arouse the suspicion of most North Americans. There is another reason, however: I use it in order to distance myself at the outset from the prevailing approaches to biblical interpretation in North Atlantic circles.[27]

Mark's gospel is a gospel about and for the common people. It reflects the conditions of first-century Palestine—disease, marginalization, and poverty. John promises a new order and the people flock to him. Then the people flocked to Jesus. Compassion for them and their overwhelming need flowed from every corpuscle of his being. He reached out to them in their hunger, in their hopes for a better life and for liberation. At the end of the story the crowds are manipulated by the Jerusalem politicians, who fear insurrection. The crowds insist on Jesus' execution. As far as they were concerned, he failed to deliver on his promise to liberate them—as they understood liberation.

The first scene opens with a messenger whose coming inaugurates the mission of the *One* who is strong enough to wrestle the world away from the powers that dominate. Mark's gospel upholds an understanding of liberation that insists that people be delivered from the structures of oppression found within the dominant social structure of first-century Palestine. He also addresses the "spirit and practice of domination ultimately imbedded in the human personality and corporately in human history as a whole."[28] Wherever domination rears its ugly head, whether by those in power or in the human will, Mark addresses it. Jesus came to deliver people from domination and to show them the way to resist it in all its ugly forms.

---

[27]Ibid., 8.
[28]Ibid., 103.

Mark refers to the beginning (*arche*) of the gospel. He uses the same word later in his narrative in reference to creation. Thus, we are taken to the dawn of creation by Mark's opening proclamation. Mark wants his reader to understand that what is taking place here is a renewal of salvation history begun at the creation of the world. It is the story about a new heaven and a new earth—a new political entity.

Jesus never appropriates the title *Messiah* for himself. He prefers to use the apocalyptic image from Daniel—Son of Man, translated—the *Human One*. Mark was careful not to use the term *Messiah,* as it was laden with political overtones—it referred to popular kingship. It might have easily been misunderstood by the zealot-type messianic movements. Even though Mark opens his narrative with the proclamation that Jesus is the Messiah, he immediately places the title in its appropriate context. He wants his reader to understand what the true mission of *messiahship* is all about. He similarly wants to demonstrate what it is not.

Caesar referred to himself as the divine man. Even the coinage of the day reflected belief in imperial divinity. Mark insists from the outset that Jesus is the divine, anointed leader, appointed by God, who proclaims a new kingdom.

Mark's reference to the prophetic text of Isaiah envisions a people in search of a new way of liberation and freedom. The *path* being forged by Jesus is a new way of life built out of the old. Many of Mark's Jewish contemporaries believed that the voice of prophecy had fallen silent forever. Mark insists that the Word of Yahweh is once again alive and being spoken in their midst. Malachi's prophecy inserted in the text is an announcement that something wonderful is about to happen. The eschatological *Day of the Lord* is about to enter the stage of human history. Where? It was believed that this epiphany would take place at the Temple in Jerusalem. Mark jumps the page to Isaiah and insists that the *Day of the Lord* would take place, not in the Temple, but in the wilderness.

According to Myers, the *wilderness* conjures other images than the ones mentioned above.[29] It con-

jures images of desolation—an uninhabited, desolate place. One can only marginally exist in the desert—people hunger in the desert. Israel understood the desert on a symbolic level to mean a place where a community takes flight (exodus-event). It was also understood as a place of refuge for the faithful who wait to be delivered. Jesus (and Israel) were tested in the desert. Jesus went to the desert to be alone and to take flight. Elijah fled to the desert to escape the political authorities who were in hot pursuit. The wilderness was known as the place where revolutionary movements were spawned and nurtured. Mark's point is clear. Rather than return to Zion (Jerusalem) for the advent of salvation, the people instead flee to the desert, to the margins, in order to repent. The Jerusalem Temple establishment would not be thrilled over this desert tent revival. They believed themselves to be in control of the spirituality of the masses.

Mark paints an austere portrait of the locust-eating, bearded, and bedraggled prophet of the Lord. Immediately the reader would be drawn to images of Elijah. Myers points out an often missed understanding of the Elijah tradition, however.[30] He insists that role of the prophetic tradition was to bring judgment down upon the king and his court for failing to keep the covenant with Yahweh. John is certainly akin to that tradition. He is remembered in part for "taking on" Herod and his court, which earned him the prophet's reward of martyrdom. Since the prophet Malachi's oracle insisted that the reappearance of Elijah was the sign of arrival of the *Day of the Lord,* it would not take much for contemporaries of Jesus to wonder if John the Baptist was indeed Elijah. And was he inaugurating the beginning or the end?

John insists that the one who will follow him is so much greater that he is not fit to loosen his sandals. This was a Semitic phrase for subordination. (The allusion to sandals might also be a reference to the *Way.* Later in the gospel sandals appear again as the mode of travel as Jesus sent the disciples out on their missionary tour.) John was subordinate to Jesus. John insisted that his baptism was a prelude to the baptism Jesus would inaugurate—

---

[29]Ibid., 125.

[30]Ibid., 126.

a baptism by the Holy Spirit. The mission of Jesus (represented by the sandals) will involve the overthrow of the stronger one (an allusion to the controlling powers). This would all take place by the power of the Holy Spirit. This overthrow of dominant, controlling, abusive power would not be accomplished by military means. The zealot types who were counting on a military solution were sorely mistaken. Jesus challenged the power structures through his gospel of nonviolent resistance. We know what happens to those who resist similarly. We will continue to reflect upon the exegetical point of view of this scholar throughout the church year. Perhaps our conversation with his perspective will help us become more aware of the justice thread that runs throughout all of the scriptures.

Nonviolence, repentance, and reconciliation are Advent's watchwords. Ultimately Advent invites us all into a radical discipleship that is driven and empowered by those words. John calls for nothing less than complete *metanoia*. He calls us to "seek justice and to prepare earnestly for the encounter with the Lord who comes daily in the midst of what is insignificant in this world."[31] Gustavo Gutierrez reminds us that God comes to us in love.[32] We eagerly expect and await this joyful encounter with the Lord. Advent's challenge is for us to let go of our idols ("objects of a trust which is due to God alone")[33] and learn to turn to the living God with our entire beings. The people did not run to the Temple to find the living God. They ran to the desert, to a man society would cast off as crazy, who in turn announced the arrival of *One* whose manifestation and presence had been planned before the world began. Yet so many missed it. They were expecting something else— they failed to see the Shekinah Glory who stood in their very midst. Will we miss it too?

Proclaim the gospel again.

Sometimes we gain new insights when we hear the text after the interpretation is given. Someone from the group proclaims the gospel a second time.

---

[31] *SWTLY*, 9.
[32] Ibid.
[33] Ibid.

Conversation with the Liturgy and the Scriptures

Test your original understanding in dialogue with the text.

(You might consider breaking into smaller groups.)

Now that you've heard the exegesis, were there any new insights? How do you feel about it? How does your original understanding of this gospel compare with what we just shared? How does this story speak to your life?

Sharing Life Experience

Participants share an experience from their lives that connects with the biblical interpretation just presented.

> *Today's gospel reminds me of all the John the Baptist/Elijah figures who have been a part of my life. I look at the people who have paved the way for Christ to enter my life. The first place I have to look is in my family of origin. I grew up in a family that was committed to living the gospel, albeit imperfectly. Our family life revolved around our parents' relationship with God. My parents prayed with us and taught us what it meant to have a deep, abiding relationship with God. Dad used to tell us every day that God was his co-pilot and that God would see him through anything that life had to throw his way. He did not know how true that statement would hold to be. My parents both spent an hour a week on their knees participating in the parish perpetual adoration. My father kept the same hour at 1:00 in the morning for twenty years. He seldom missed in those twenty years. We spent most of our leisure time at our local parish church. It was the center of our lives. Both of my parents started and ended each day with prayer. There was no problem so small in our family that we did call on God to be with us, to guide us, and to show us the way. My mother was a champion of the poor and the downtrodden. She taught us racial equality when it was not fashionable. There was not a day in my life in which my father did not take us by the hand and tell us how much he loved us—no matter what we did. He was a mirror image of the love of God.*

My mother was one of the holiest women I have ever known. She would not speak ill of anyone. She refused to engage in malicious talk and gossip. The repentance and conversion John calls for in today's gospel is a conversion that sometimes costs us the world. My mother paid dearly. Once many years ago (I was in eighth grade), back when scandals in the church were a rarity (late 1950s, early 1960s), our associate pastor was having an affair with a married woman from the parish. Talk was rampant. My mother refused to get involved. People would call her and goad her to join them in their gossip, innuendos, and nasty reveling over the sins of this couple, which sent our little parish community into a tailspin. Still she refused to say anything bad about the young priest or the woman. People sometimes simply cannot deal with that kind of goodness. Word of the scandal made it back to the husband of the woman. The way the offending couple dealt with the charge was, of course, to deny it. "Someone must be spreading malicious rumors." They set out to find out just who that culprit might be.

The guilty gossip spreaders were quick to direct the charges in any direction other than where it belonged, so they pointed a finger at my mother. They accused her of spreading false and malicious rumors. It was a bold-face lie and they knew it. They were furious that she would not join in their futile machinations of small-minded, gossip-ridden busybodies.

I will never forget the night when the pastor of the parish, the husband of the woman, and the associate pastor showed up at my parents' door to accuse my mother of destroying their family. My mother was devastated. She insisted that not only was she not a part of the gossip, she refused to participate in it. The husband threatened lawsuit, the pastor castigated my mother, and when they left, this good, God-loving woman was a shambles in our living room.

The following Sunday, in this small-town, Catholic community, the parish pastor preached about the evil woman from our parish who spread scandalous rumors about the young associate. Every face in the church turned in the direction of my mother.

Did my mother leave that parish? No. Did she blame God for this terrible injustice? No. She reminded us that this is what happens sometimes when people try

to live the gospel. The stress, however, nearly destroyed her. It was a key factor in a medical breakdown she would have. She was eventually able to bounce back from that horrific time in our lives. Both my mother and father prayed together through those horrible events. God walked with them. Their pain taught me a very important lesson.

Good guys do not always come out on top. The world sometimes perceives the "real" good guys as the bad guys. My mother and father lived a life that was constantly in a state of readiness. They were prepared. Were they perfect? Hardly. Were they faithful? Absolutely. The foundation in faith that they built for themselves was one of prayer, commitment to God, and the assurance that God would see them through the bitter travails of life. I watched my father cry as he suffered with my mother through those very dark days. He never gave up on the God who gifted him with abiding presence. Hope was the guiding wind that steered both of them on the course they would take through every mishap of their short lives together (both died young—my mother died on Easter Sunday at the age of 58 and my father died two years later at the age of 60 on Easter Monday).

God gifted my mother with the courage of her convictions. She refused to be controlled by people who demanded that she follow the crowd and go down that path of status-quo living. Together my parents functioned as John the Baptist for me and my two sisters. They prepared the way for me to embrace the gospel of Christ and to take it with me as I forged my own life.

Our family paid a dear price for the choice my mother made to refuse to participate in the evil that had taken over our community. I think if she were alive today I am confident she would say that she would do the same thing again if faced with a similar choice.[34]

John the Baptist serves as a stark reminder that the path he paved for Christ was littered with rough edges and dangerous precipices. Jesus is the one who leads us down that path. He will not let us fall off

---

[34]A postscript to this story—six months after the fateful night in our living room, the young priest and the woman left town together and ended up getting married and subsequently divorced. They broke up a family with six children.

the edge. He simply invites us to be ready when the invitation comes to walk the Way he carves for each of us. He invites us to be ready to welcome the "One Who Comes" each and every day.

What was Mark trying to tell his community? How does the character of John the Baptist speak to you? How can you relate to him? Imagine what it must have been like to have stood on the Jordan's banks and witnessed the marvels recounted in today's gospel. Judging from the way you view the world today, where would you have found yourself? With the peasants and common people? With the religious authorities? A follower of John the Baptist? A follower of Jesus? How do you feel about the message of nonviolence suggested in the exegesis? In what way does this gospel challenge your community today? In what way has this conversation with the scriptures for today's liturgy invited change in your life? In what way are the biblical themes of covenant, exodus, creation, and community evident in today's readings? Do you still feel the same way about this text as when you began? Has your original understanding been stretched, challenged, or affirmed?

STEP 5
DECISION

The gospel demands a response.

In what concrete way might your parish be invited to respond? Are there any attitudes or behaviors you would like to change as a result of today's conversation? What one concrete action will you take this week in response to the liturgy today?

Pastoral Considerations: Today's gospel invites a conversation about the ways in which parish structures are oppressive to the marginalized members of the community. Who are the marginalized in your community (those without a voice or those who seem to have little credibility)? What might you do to reach out to them? Do the programs and services offered by your community take into consideration the needs of all the members—even those considered insignificant by the standards of the world? Are there multicultural tensions that need to be addressed in your community? How is

your parish exercising a preferential option for the poor? In what way does your parish reach out to the poor in your community? In Third World countries? If your parish is not celebrating the sacrament of reconciliation during Advent, you might consider celebrating a nonsacramental service (chapter V, Rite of Penance).

Christian Initiation: The minor rites, blessings, and exorcisms are intended for use throughout the catechumenate, whenever catechumens gather. Remember to adapt your language to respect the status of the baptized when using a blessing. What might your strategies be for including those in your initiation process in the ministries of justice and the apostolate in your parish? Perhaps those who minister to the sick and the poor in your parish would be willing to invite a catechumen to join them. How are you welcoming inquirers who come to you at this time? If you do not have a continuous process, are you ministering to them or asking them to wait until next year? This issue needs your serious consideration.

DOCTRINAL ISSUES

What Church truth/teaching/doctrinal issue could be drawn from the gospel for the second Sunday of Advent?

Participants suggest possible doctrinal themes that flow from the readings.

Possible Doctrinal Themes

Advent; Jesus' coming—past, present, future; parousia; eschatology; conversion; nonviolence; cost of discipleship; authenticity of scriptures; Word of God; prophetic tradition; typology; Christ, the fulfillment of the scriptures

Present the doctrinal material at this time.

1. The facilitator gives input on a particular doctrinal issue of his or her prior choosing. OR
2. The group chooses a doctrinal issue from the list they created. They read together from the Doctrinal Appendix or other appropriate, official Church documents and the works of respected theologians.

(Many doctrinal issues are found in the Doctrinal Appendix at the back of this workbook. If you are choosing an issue from this resource, please refer to it now.)

Reflection questions centered around the chosen doctrinal theme can be found at the end of each topic in the Doctrinal Appendix. The questions are based on the five-step reflection process. If you choose a topic not included in the Doctrinal Appendix, craft your own questions according to the same five-step process.

Following the reflection questions you will be reminded to return to chapter 7, "Preparing the Catechetical Session," to assist you in crafting your own session.

Closing Prayer

Preface—Advent I
Father, all-powerful and ever-living God,
we do well always and everywhere to give you
    thanks
through Jesus Christ our Lord.
When he humbled himself to come among us as a
    man,
he fulfilled the plan you formed long ago
and opened for us the way to salvation.
Now we watch for the day,
hoping that the salvation promised us will be ours
when Christ our Lord will come again in his
    glory.[35]

---

[35]"Preface—Advent I," *The Sacramentary.*

THIRD SUNDAY OF ADVENT

Environment

John the Baptist is still a figure in today's gospel. Today is Gaudete Sunday. The name comes from the Entrance Antiphon from today's liturgy. Every mass has an Entrance Antiphon [usually a phrase from scripture] assigned to it, and it used to be a custom to assign a title to every Sunday mass. The title was a Latin word taken from the first word of the Entrance Antiphon. The first word today is re-joice—Gaudete! The color of vestments for today's liturgy is rose, which might be creatively incorporated into the gathering space.

Lighting the Advent Candles

Prayer to accompany the lighting of the remaining candles throughout Advent:

The following prayer may be used each time your group gathers and a new candle is lit each week.

Three Advent candles are lighted as the leader says:
Blessed are you, Lord God of all creation:
in the darkness and in the light.
Blessed are you as we wait in joyful hope
for the coming of our Savior, Jesus Christ.

All respond:
For the kingdom, the power, and the glory are
    yours, now and for ever.

The leader says:
Come, Lord Jesus!

All respond:
Come quickly!

The leader says:
Let us live soberly, justly, and devoutly in this
    world
as we wait in joyful hope
for the coming of our Savior, Jesus Christ.

All respond:
For the kingdom, the power, and the glory are
    yours, now and for ever.

(Adapted from *Catholic Household Blessings and Prayers*, NCCB, 1988, 64–67.)

INTRODUCTORY RITES

Entrance Antiphon (or Opening Song)

Rejoice in the Lord always; again I say, rejoice! The Lord is near. (Phil 4:4, 5)[1]

Opening Prayer

The facilitator of the session may lead the prayer. Others in the group may be asked to proclaim the readings.

Let us pray
[that God will fill us with joy at the coming of Christ]

Pause for silent prayer.

Lord God, may we, your people,
who look forward to the birthday of Christ
experience the joy of salvation
and celebrate that feast with love and thanksgiv-
    ing.
We ask this through our Lord Jesus Christ, your
    Son,
who lives and reigns with you and the Holy Spirit,
one God forever and ever. Amen.[2]

LITURGY OF THE WORD

The readings are proclaimed.

First Reading
Isaiah 61:1–2a, 10–11

(Please refer to the first Sunday of Advent for an overview of the Book of the Prophet Isaiah.)

---

[1]Third Sunday of Advent, "Entrance Antiphon," *The Sacramentary.*

[2]Third Sunday of Advent, "Opening Prayer," *The Sacramentary.*

Today's Pericope: Today's reading from Trito-Isaiah is one of its most familiar passages. It is reminiscent of the Servant Songs of Second Isaiah. The prophet describes his call in terms of servanthood. Jesus' own mission was influenced by this text, as evidenced by his reference to it in his answer to John in the Lukan narrative. One cannot listen to today's reading without thinking of Jesus rising to proclaim this text in the synagogue.

Joy is also a theme in the reading. There is to be great rejoicing over the salvation that is about to be showered upon the face of the earth. Jesus used the words from this reading to announce that the messianic age had indeed arrived. The "Spirit of the Lord is upon me...." "Spirit" always signaled an incredible work of God in progress. The messianic king was promised that the Spirit would be bestowed on him. The people were given a similar promise. In the creation narrative the Spirit hovered over the waters, and God creates a new paradise. The anointing by the Lord empowers preaching and listening with faith. Anointing strengthens the anointed ones to know the Word of God, to listen to it, and to heed it. The metaphors employed by the prophet announce the advent of God's salvation for all people. Prisoners will be led out into the light of day—out of dark prison cells they will be led, unfettered, they will be free and unencumbered. The prophet envisions a salvation that is total—spiritual, individual, and social. The year of favor refers to the messianic jubilee in which debts are forgiven and all things begin anew.

The second paragraph of today's reading refers to the relationship between Yahweh and Jerusalem. It is a love relationship. The joy of salvation springs from the earth—through human beings, but through the power of God, the source of all life. Thus, there is reason to rejoice.

The Book of Isaiah is to be viewed in the context of the coming of Christ in history and the coming of the Lord at the end of time. Christians understand the "year of favor" to have arrived with the advent of Jesus. The passage may have been fulfilled in their hearing, but it will be consummated at the end of all time.

The poor are the recipients of this good news—the *anawim* of God. The Hebrew origin of the word *poor* means "bowed down"—humble submission. The poor of God will stand in humble submission to their God. They will realize their total dependence upon him. They will wait with complete faith and trust that God will do what God promises. The poor, afflicted, persecuted, and alienated—all will know the salvation of God. These are the ones who call on God and God will call them blessed.

Responsorial Psalm
Luke 1:46–48, 49–50, 53–54

Today's psalm is taken from Luke's gospel and is also known as the Magnificat, the canticle of praise sung by Mary and all the assembled poor and most often associated with Advent.

Second Reading
1 Thessalonians 5:16–24

Overview of the Letter to the Thessalonians: The letters to the Thessalonians are probably the beginning of Christian literature. Thessalonica was a city in northern Greece. Paul had attempted to evangelize the Jews of the city, but when his attempts failed, he turned his efforts to the Greeks. This enraged the Jews and they expelled Paul and his disciples from the city. The Pauline letters are evidence of Paul's mission. Paul was concerned about the identity of the Christian community. He sent messengers to Thessalonica to relay his concern that the Thessalonian church might be tempted to turn away from God in the face of persecution. There was no immediate crisis. Paul simply wanted to affirm the work already accomplished by Timothy and challenge the community to continued diligence. His letter[3] is an admonition against future temptations while affirming community members in their present adherence to gospel living. Paul sought to offer strength and consolation to the communities as they awaited the fulfillment of Christ's promise to return. While encouraging them in their progress, Paul nevertheless exhorted them to an even greater commitment to the Christian life.

---

[3]Paul wrote both letters and epistles. A letter was personal communication between two parties who were separated. The letter was usually occasioned by a particular situation. An epistle was a form of literature that resembled a letter only in style and form. There was little else about it that resembled a letter. The epistle was a written essay for the purpose of public instruction or discussion of a disputed subject.

Much of the first letter is comprised as a thanksgiving for the Thessalonians. Paul thanked them for the way in which they welcomed him and for the way in which their faithfulness served as an example to others. The second letter hints that perhaps the Thessalonians had fallen prey to false teaching. Letters purported to be from Paul spoke of the day of judgment that had already arrived. Second Thessalonians insists that there are a number of figures and mysterious events that must still come before the day of judgment.[4] The letter reminds the community that Christians are to keep working at their trade and mind their own business. They are not to be engaging in slothful activities, nor meddling in the affairs of others.

Some scholars suggest that the second letter differs in style from the first. They suggest that perhaps Paul is not its author. The second letter is less personal than the first. There is no mention of Paul's travels or activities. Some think that perhaps Timothy or Silvanus penned the second letter while Paul was imprisoned in Rome. It is possible that upon hearing about all the confusion in Thessalonica, they would have sent the letter in Paul's name.

The letters exhort Christians to conform their lives to Christ—to turn from the worship of idols and follow the gospel. Salvation is understood as a future reality which will ultimately mean that those who are recipients will be spared the judgment against unrighteous, evil people. It is understood that this judgment will take place at the "'parousia,' a Greek word that was used for the visit of an important figure like the emperor (or like a papal visit today). Christians took over the word 'parousia' to mean the second coming of Christ when Christ would have the power of God and would judge the world."[5] Paul reminds Christians how they are to live and what is meant and understood by the second coming.

Paul refers to a basic theme: love. Christians are to love one another. Paul also preached a catechism of morality. Sexual promiscuity was rampant in the ancient pagan world. The Christian perspective insists that sexual activity is the purview of the married state.

Paul demands that Christians find a trade and keep busy. Those who were well off could live off the proceeds of their land holdings. They were able to spend time reading and engaging in public affairs. Some people were able to secure benefactors, which would allow them the same luxury. It is even possible that some Christians were living off the kindness of other Christians. Paul demands that Christians are not be dependent on anyone. They are to be self-sufficient and hardworking, and they are to keep busy.

As far as the expectations of the great eschaton are concerned, Paul insists that the end of the world was being held back by God. We have no way of knowing when the end will arrive. Christians are to be ready at all times. They are to live holy lives, each day, every day. Thus, worry about the end is a futile waste of time. The end will actually be a time of great rejoicing.

There was concern over the plight of Christians who were already dead. Paul reminded the Thessalonians that when Christ returns, the risen Christians will accompany him and the entire community will be transformed. Death is not something to fear. The pagans fear death. Christians share the hope that one day all will be united with Jesus and share the glory of eternity.

Today's Pericope: The opening of today's letter continues the theme of rejoicing. The reading calls for a profound joy that is a fruit of the Holy Spirit. We rejoice because we know the Day of the Lord will bring us into the fullness of Christ's glory. Christian joy is rooted in hope that will never fail us.

Paul reminds the Christian community that holiness resides in works of charity and in joy born of the Spirit and a life of prayer and thanks. Even though it is God's work, we are to cooperate with this gift of sanctification.

The gospel is proclaimed.

Gospel
John 1:6–8, 19–28. There is one among you whom you do not recognize.

---

[4] *RNT*, 151.
[5] Ibid., 153.

What were your first impressions? What was your first response to the gospel (or the other readings)? What captured your attention?

Each person names his or her initial impression. Statements should be brief. No reasons should be given at this time. All simply listen without agreeing or disagreeing.

STEP 2
UNDERSTANDING

In a brief statement, explain what you think this gospel is trying to convey.

STEP 3
INPUT FROM VISION/STORY/TRADITION

Liturgical Context

Today is Gaudete Sunday and *Gaudete* means *rejoice*. The Entrance Antiphon for today's liturgy echoes Isaiah, "The desert and the parched land will exult; the steppe will rejoice and bloom." In this midpoint through Advent, the sense of anticipated joy heightens. The purple hues reminiscent of Lenten repentance are not so subtle as to be missed altogether. However, always at the center of Advent's repentance is the undercurrent of joyful expectation. "It is a joy that guards against anxiety...that frequently goes hand in hand with the unshakable feeling of being abandoned by God. Above all, it is an interior peace 'In the Lord,' a surrendering to his providence and love, which Jesus, in the Sermon on the Mount, makes a fundamental requirement for the kingdom (Matt. 6:24–34)."[6] The reserved joy of this transition point in Advent is evidenced by the plea that all be prepared and sadness removed, for it "hinders us from feeling the joy and hope which his presence will bestow."[7]

---

[6]*DL*, (I), 117.
[7]Third Sunday of Advent, "Alternative Opening Prayer," *The Sacramentary*.

John is the prophet who explodes onto the scene during Advent and Lent in the readings as the one who exhorts us to repent and tells us of our need for God's forgiveness and redemption. John is a symbol of the preaching ministry and reminds us that we are all called to preach the living Word of God. John is the prophet who heralds the Savior and reminds us of our appointed task in this day and age. We, too, are to herald the Christ in our everyday lives.

In addition to repentance we are reminded that through the eucharist we are given God's help and freedom from sin. The eucharist, too, prepares us for the incarnation, the coming of Christ in our lives: "may this Eucharist bring us your divine help, free us from our sins, and prepare us for the birthday of Our Savior."[8] We must not forget that Advent celebrates the *kingdom here and now* and the *kingdom not yet*. We look forward to the day when Jesus will return as we recall his first coming and prepare for his present coming that will explode anew at Christmas but is ongoing throughout our Christian lives. Our Advent cries continue to long for that final day of eternal unity. Until that day we live with imperfect messengers in the midst of an imperfect church. But in the midst of our imperfection we strive for the perfect unity of encounter and presence. Advent gives us the necessary time out to reflect upon that encounter.

Karl Rahner gives us an Advent reflection:

> We have to hear the voice of one crying in the wilderness, even if it confesses: it is not I. We must have the patience of men and women of Advent. The church is only the voice of one crying in the wilderness, announcing that the final radiant kingdom of God is still coming and that when God wills, not when it suits us. We cannot try to ignore that voice simply because it comes from the mouths of human beings; we cannot disregard the messengers of the church because they too are not worthy to loosen the sandals of the Lord whose forerunners they are, or because they cannot call down fire from heaven like Elijah.

---

[8]Third Sunday of Advent, "Prayer After Communion," *The Sacramentary*.

For it is still Advent. The church itself is still an advent church; for we are still waiting for him who is to come in the unveiled radiance of unconditional Godhead with the eternal kingdom. And that church rightly tells the impatient who want to see God directly here and now: Prepare for this God the true way, the way of faith, of love, of humility, and the way of patience with its unimpressive provisional messengers and their poor words and small signs. For then God will certainly come. He only comes to those who in patience love his forerunners and the provisional. The Pharisees of the Gospel, however, who rejected the forerunner of the messiah because he was not the definitive reality, did not recognize him who was the definitive reality either.[9]

Gospel Exegesis

The facilitator provides input from critical biblical scholarship on this text. This input includes insights as to how people would have heard the gospel in Jesus' time.

John's gospel (his prologue) begins from the perspective of eternity. "In the beginning was the Word...." The Word is responsible for breathing life into the created order. The Word brought the light, yet the light is either misunderstood or not overcome by darkness.[10] Then, in verse 6, we are introduced to John the Baptist. John was not the light sent by the Word, but rather was a witness to it. This is the John who takes center stage again in today's proclamation of the Advent gospel.

Christians worship the Christ as the incarnate Word proclaimed in John's gospel. John is the only evangelist who records this episode in the Jesus story. Jesus arrived on the human stage during a time when the world was pregnant with messianic expectations. Questions about the Christ were rampant. Who would he be? What would he look like? Added to this speculation was the expectation of other long awaited end-time personages. The Messiah had been foretold long before Christ. Nathan promised David (2 Sm 7:14) that Israel's future king would come from David's

house; thus there were expectations of a David-like king. "As David had achieved hegemony over the land of Israel and had unified the separate tribes, the awaited king was expected to restore Jewish control over the land of Palestine and reunite Jews then in dispersion. His appearance was to be an effective sign of the reign of God, for then the theocracy of Israel would be fully and finally established."[11] In the Book of Enoch, an intertestamental apocryphal book written about two centuries before Christ, it was claimed that there would be a future person who would come into the world with a saving mission. This person would be referred to as the Son of Man, savior of the people. "Many of the prophetic passages tell of an extraordinary figure who will not only proclaim the advent of this time of salvation but will usher it in as well.... They instructed Israel to look forward to the time when an 'anointed one,' a messiah, would be the vehicle of God's salvation to save the people."[12] There is also evidence of another, a second mysterious figure, referred to as the Servant of the Lord. This person was closely associated with the Messiah, but distinct from him. This Servant was to be presented to the people as a light to all nations, demonstrating the universality of God's saving action. Samaritans believed that Moses would one day return to deliver Israel. The cast of characters who were to appear at the end of time was growing. It is clear that messianic expectations were at a fever pitch around the time of Christ, and lasted until the second century.

The opening verses of today's pericope served to clarify the role of John in contrast with the role of Christ. The evangelist John set out to dispel any misconstructions from the outset.[13] John was the baptizer and Jesus the Savior. The evangelist is so adamant on this point that he repeats it later in verses 19–28. John is the witness, the one the prophet Malachi referred to as the messenger.

John the Baptist is used by the fourth evangelist as a player in a cast of characters who would stand as witnesses to Christ, the Light. John was a witness

---

[9] *GCY*, 33.

[10] *RJ*, 67.

[11] *JHW*, 11.

[12] Dianne Bergant, C.S.A., "Salvation," *CPDBT*, 868.

[13] Some followers of John the Baptist believed that he, not Jesus, was the Messiah. John makes it clear from the outset. There is to be no mistake: *Jesus* is the Messiah and Savior of the world.

par excellence, one among others, who would testify on behalf of Jesus. In the gospel of John, John the Baptist is the first to witness to Jesus, then the Samaritan woman, followed by Jesus' own testimony about himself. The Hebrew scriptures then provide testimony, followed by the Father, and, ultimately, the author of the gospel himself. Witness and testimony are key in bringing people to an awareness of Christ, who is the Light who has come into the world. Jesus later refers to the Baptist as the *bearer of light*, the light who is Jesus.[14]

The curtain rises on a courtroom drama. The grand inquisitors are the priests and Levites and those associated with the Temple and John is a witness. In verse 19 we are told that the Jews have come to check on John. He would rouse great interest in Jerusalem. Just who is this man that draws such crowds? Who does he think he is? Whenever the "Jews" are mentioned, it is usually a reference to antagonistic religious authorities who want to trap Jesus. The drama builds as the interrogations come to a dead end. To every question lobbed in John's direction, he responds by telling them who he is not. "The posture of the witness who is so reluctant to identify himself contributes to the drama about to unfold."[15] John answered them by telling them *who he was not*. Students of scripture immediately make the connection between the "*I am not*" statements of John and the "*I am*" (*ego eimi*) statements of Jesus, such as "I am the Good Shepherd," "I am the Bread of Life," "I am the Way, the Truth, and the Life." John is adamant. He is not Moses (*redivivus*) come back to life; he is not Elijah; nor is he any other awaited end-time Messiah. He is certainly not the long-awaited Christ.

The synoptic gospels (Matthew, Mark, and Luke) associated the role of John the Baptist with Elijah. The gospel of John disassociates itself from that understanding. By the time John wrote his gospel there was a belief circulating that Elijah would return to initiate the reign of God. Today many observant Jews still await the return of Elijah.

Even though many scholars believe that John was a member of the Essene community at Qumran,

much of his teaching does not fit with that supposition. John's ministry to the unclean, tax collectors, and sinners is not characteristic of the Qumran community. John's ascetic and austere style and his eschatological preaching were catalysts for many to join him and become his followers. They would participate in John's discipleship of prayer and fasting.

John's mission was effective only in relation to Jesus. John's ministry was temporal; Jesus' mission is eternal. John prepared the way for Jesus' saving work—he "paved the way" for Jesus. The metaphor would have been striking in first-century Palestine. When dignitaries visited various towns, roads would be repaired, smoothed out, holes filled in, and flowers strewn about. John did not pave the road where Jesus' feet would plod, but he did pave the way of the heart. John prepared the way of spiritual and moral conversion.

Gustavo Gutierrez reminds us that "even though we come after Jesus, as Christians we are precursors like John. Therefore, the Christian community, the church does not replace Christ. In a certain sense, it has to retreat before Christ because it is not worthy to 'untie the thong of his sandals,' Jn 1:2. The whole church must have the same spirituality as the precursor, especially in the case of those who, in one way or another, are its representatives. What matters is that the Lord is coming. This is the source of our joy."[16]

Proclaim the gospel again.

Sometimes we gain new insights when we hear the text after the interpretation is given. Someone from the group proclaims the gospel a second time.

STEP 4
TESTING

Conversation with the Liturgy and the Scriptures

Test your original understanding in dialogue with the text.

---

[14]*WWC*, 139.
[15]*JHW*, 9.

[16]*SWTLY*, 14.

Now that you've heard the exegesis, were there any new insights? How do you feel about it? How does your original understanding of this gospel compare with what we just shared? How does this story speak to your life?

Sharing Life Experience

Participants share an experience from their lives that connects with the biblical interpretation just presented.

The days are getting shorter. The day we celebrate the incarnation draws nearer and we are told to rejoice. John tells us why. He also tells us that we must prepare our hearts to cradle the Christ who will come. John tells us who he is not. He tells us that he is merely a witness, that his job is to point the way. I am reminded of the many times I have lost my way throughout my life. Sometimes I was not even aware that I was lost or at least gone astray. I look at the voices who prepared the Lord's way for me and who continued to hold the glimmer of light before my eyes, lest I completely allow the darkness to overcome.

I remember one of the darkest moments of my life. There were days I felt as if I lived on the precipice of an abyss. It was a time when a savior would have been a most welcome guest. It was also a time in which I was powerless to call on God. It was simply an effort to pray for the willingness to believe—I look upon it as my dark night of the soul.

When I look back to those days the memories are painful. There were influences trying to tell me to turn from everything I believed and held dear. In my frustration it was tempting to succumb to those influences. Yet, I refused. I clung to those who supported me in love, my family, and those who supported me in prayer, my community. They were the voices of truth. They were the presence of Christ, his light in my darkness. They were the ones who paved the way and held out the light.

The world hungers for meaning. Advent and Christmas are difficult times for people. We have more funerals in our parish in the month of December than any other time. People sometimes give up on life during the holidays. Instead of rejoicing, some people become absorbed with the disappointments of life, or

worse, the loneliness they endure. John is a voice crying out to us from centuries of lived tradition. He reminds us that the only meaning in life is to be found in Christ. This is truly a time to rejoice. The Baptist tells us that all is well. That long-awaited day has finally arrived. Jesus is in our midst. When life seems to be overcome by the darkness of the world, we know that we have the only source of light and he resides right in our midst. John tells us to prepare our hearts. For the heart becomes the cradle that will house the light to come.

What was John's purpose in introducing the Baptist to the reader? What does it mean to you that John was a witness to the light? What does that have to do with your life? What relevance is there for our contemporary communities? In what way does this gospel challenge your community? How does today's invite preparedness? In what way has this conversation with the scriptures for today's liturgy invited change in your life? In what way are the biblical themes of covenant, exodus, creation, and community evident in today's readings? Do you still feel the same way about this text as when you began? Has your original understanding been stretched, challenged, or affirmed?

STEP 5
DECISION

The gospel demands a response.

In what concrete way might your parish be invited to respond? Are there any attitudes or behaviors you would like to change as a result of today's conversation? What one concrete action will you take this week in response to the liturgy today?

Christian Initiation: Perhaps in preparation for the celebration of the mystery of incarnation, catechumens, candidates, sponsors, and the faithful might gather for a nonsacramental penitential celebration (chapter V—Rite of Penance). "Penitential celebrations are gatherings of the people of God to hear the proclamation of God's word. This invites them to conversion and renewal of life and announces our freedom from sin through the death and resurrection of Christ. The structure of these services is the same as that usually followed in celebrations of the word of God and given in the *Rite for Reconciliation of Several Penitents*."[17] Refer to RP #36 for the nature and structure of the rite. It is important to consider the exhortation in #37. "Care should be taken that the faithful do not confuse these celebrations with the celebration of the sacrament of penance. Penitential celebrations are very helpful in promoting conversion of life and purification of heart. It is desirable to arrange such services especially for these purposes:

- to foster the spirit of penance within the Christian community;
- to help the faithful to prepare for confession which can be made individually later at a convenient time
- to help children gradually form their conscience about sin in human life and about freedom from sin through Christ;
- to help catechumens during their conversion.

Penitential celebrations, moreover, are very useful in places where no priest is available to give sacramental absolution."[18] Perhaps the opening prayers and the readings from "Penitential Celebrations During Advent" [Appendix II] might be chosen.

DOCTRINAL ISSUES

What Church truth/teaching/doctrinal issue could be drawn from the gospel for the third Sunday of Advent?

Participants suggest possible doctrinal themes that flow from the readings.

Possible Doctrinal Themes

Advent; reign of God; eschatology; Jesus Christ; the Messiah; discipleship; repentance and reconciliation; Christ's coming: future, present, past; Son of Man; parousia

Present the doctrinal material at this time.

1. The facilitator gives input on a particular doctrinal issue of his or her prior choosing. OR
2. The group chooses a doctrinal issue from the list they created. They read together from the Doctrinal Appendix or other appropriate, official Church documents and the works of respected theologians.

(Many doctrinal issues are found in the Doctrinal Appendix at the back of this workbook. If you are choosing an issue from this resource, please refer to it now.)

Reflection questions centered around the chosen doctrinal theme can be found at the end of each topic in the Doctrinal Appendix. The questions are based on the five-step reflection process. If you choose a topic not included in the Doctrinal Appendix, craft your own questions according to the same five-step process.

Following the reflection questions you will be reminded to return to chapter 7, "Preparing the Catechetical Session," to assist you in crafting your own session.

Closing Prayer

Father, all powerful and ever-living God,
we do well always and everywhere to give you
    thanks
through Jesus Christ our Lord.
His future coming was proclaimed by all the
    prophets.
The virgin mother bore him in her womb with
    love beyond all telling.
John the Baptist was his herald
and made him known when at last he came.
In his love Christ has filled us with joy
as we prepare to celebrate his birth,
so that when he comes he may find us watching in
    prayer,
our hearts filled with wonder and praise.[19]

---

[17]RP, #36, p. 358.
[18]Ibid., #37, p. 358.

[19]"Preface—Advent II," *The Sacramentary*.

Fourth Sunday of Advent

Environment

All four candles are lit today as Advent reaches fulfillment in the Christ-event. Perhaps an anticipatory manger of empty straw might be added as the final preparatory gesture. Our hope, longing, and conversion have created this straw berth for the Lord who comes continuously and who will come again on the last day.

Lighting the Advent Candles

Prayer to accompany the lighting of the remaining candles throughout Advent:

The following prayer may be used each time your group gathers and a new candle is lit each week.

Four Advent candles are lighted as the leader says:
Blessed are you, Lord God of all creation:
in the darkness and in the light.
Blessed are you as we wait in joyful hope
for the coming of our Savior, Jesus Christ.

All respond:
For the kingdom, the power, and the glory are
    yours, now and for ever.

The leader says:
Come, Lord Jesus!

All respond:
Come quickly!

The leader says:
Let us live soberly, justly, and devoutly in this
    world
as we wait in joyful hope
for the coming of our Savior, Jesus Christ.

All respond:
For the kingdom, the power, and the glory are
    yours, now and for ever.

(Adapted from *Catholic Household Blessings and Prayers*, NCCB, 1988, 64–67.)

INTRODUCTORY RITES

Entrance Antiphon (or Opening Song)

Let the clouds rain down the Just One, and the earth bring forth a Savior. (Is 45:8)[1]

Opening Prayer

The facilitator of the session may lead the prayer. Others in the group may be asked to proclaim the readings.

Let us pray
[as Advent draws to a close
for the faith that opens our lives
to the Spirit of God]

    Pause for silent prayer.

Father, all-powerful God,
your eternal Word took flesh on our earth
when the Virgin Mary placed her life
at the service of your plan.
Lift our minds in watchful hope
to hear the voice which announces Christ's glory
and open our minds to receive the Spirit
who prepares us for his coming.
We ask this through Christ, our Lord.[2]

LITURGY OF THE WORD

The readings are proclaimed.

First Reading
2 Samuel 7:1–5, 8–12, 14, 16

(Please refer to the second Sunday in Ordinary Time for an overview of the Books of Samuel.)

Today's Pericope: Today's reading reveals the genesis of the Davidic messianic hope. In its original

---

[1] Fourth Sunday of Advent, "Entrance Antiphon," *The Sacramentary.*

[2] Fourth Sunday of Advent, "Opening Prayer," *The Sacramentary.*

form today's scripture was not a prophecy about a future Messiah. Only later did this text take on that meaning. In its original form, it had more to do with royal ideology—belief in Israel's monarchy. Nathan promised David that his dynasty would last forever.

David was a charismatic king who ushered in the golden years of Israel. He established Jerusalem as the capital by bringing the ark of the covenant from Shiloh to be enthroned in Jerusalem. The ark was a small wooden box made of acacia wood. Tradition held that the ark was carried in front of the people as Moses and the people trekked through the desert during the exodus. It functioned much like a standard or a flag before the troops to offer them courage and support as they forged from battle to battle.[3]

David tells Nathan that he wants to build a Temple for Yahweh. He is disgusted by the difference between his dwelling and the modest dwelling for the ark. He insists that he must provide more worthy surroundings for the ark of the covenant. Nathan at first approves of David's decision, and tells him that the Lord is with him. We are not to miss the allusion to the Isaiah Emmanuel prophecy, *The Lord is with him.* It is obviously a later insertion in the text. Nathan later rescinds his approval of David's plan after the Lord spoke to him in the night. Rather than having David build a Temple for the Lord, the Lord promises to build a house for David that will last forever. The Lord's answer to David is rooted in the theological conflict regarding the desert versus the Temple. Later biases about the emptiness of sacrificial worship in the Temple were written into the text. The Temple/desert conflict reflected a hunger to return to the simplicity of desert worship in deference to the barrenness that had crept into the Temple cult.

The Lord's promise to David carries within it hints of the promises made to the patriarchs. Yahweh promised a place where Israel could rest from their enemies. These were the promises that propelled Israel to keep plodding through Canaan in its conquest of the land. Future generations would find hope and consolation in the promises of an eternal dynasty made to David. Israel would look back to Yahweh's promise when their hopes for the Davidic-like monarchy were dashed. Israel was defeated and even though all seemed lost, hope emerged as a seed out of the barren ground. A groundswell of anticipation and expectation emerged over time—Yahweh would raise up someone strong and vibrant to continue the Davidic dynasty into eternity.

This is not the prophecy that ultimately foretold the arrival of a future David-like king, however. After the fall of the monarchy the people would look back on this David/Nathan exchange and see within it a prophecy of a future Davidic Messiah. Christians appropriated this prophecy to Christ, the fulfillment of all prophetic hope.

In today's annunciation story, Jesus is proclaimed as the fulfillment of Old Testament prophecy. Jesus is the Son of David. "Gabriel's words in 1:32–33 [in today's gospel] constitute a free interpretation of II Samuel 7:8–16, the promise of the prophet Nathan to David which came to serve as the foundation of messianic expectations."[4]

Responsorial Psalm
Psalm 89:2–3, 4–5, 27, 29

The first stanza from today's psalm is a hymn in praise of Yahweh. In that hymn is reflected the faithfulness of God, who remains faithful to the promises he made with David. The second and third stanzas reflect the Davidic messianic prophecy event specifically.

Second Reading
Romans 1:1–7

Overview of Paul's Letter to the Romans: Paul wrote his Letter to the Romans before he made his last trip to Jerusalem as indicated in 15:25. It was written around A.D. 57–58, probably in Corinth. Paul sought to expand his missionary base west toward Spain. His plan was to visit the Roman church on the way, his lifelong ambition. Before his trek could begin he needed to make one last trip to Jerusalem to hand deliver the offering collected by his newly founded gentile churches. His intent was to express solidarity between the poor of the new gentile churches and the Jewish Christian

---

[3] *WWC*, 140.

[4] *BOM*, 311.

church in Jerusalem. Thus, before he left for Jerusalem he wrote to the Romans to inform them of his impending arrival, asking them to pray that the collection would be well received by the Jerusalem church.

One school of thought suggests that Romans is Paul's catechism of Christian doctrine. Another school supports the supposition that it is his last will and testament; and still another that it is the formulation of Paul's own doctrine. Since much of Christian doctrine is missing from Romans, Joseph Fitzmyer maintains that it is none of the above, but rather an essay letter stating "his missionary reflections on the historical possibility of salvation, rooted in God's uprightness and love, now offered to all human beings through faith in Christ Jesus."[5]

Paul's conflict with the Judaizers made him come to see that justification and salvation are not offered through adherence to the Law, but rather by faith in Jesus Christ crucified. Through faith and baptism we are all heirs to what Jesus accomplished through his death and resurrection. The Jerusalem church distrusted Paul because of his anti-Law sentiments. The money offering was a sign of goodwill between the gentile and Jewish Christian church.

The Letter to the Galatians began Paul's reflection on the meaning of the Christian kerygma. He was forced to seriously formulate his theology. The more he grappled with the truths of the Christian faith, the more he was certain that human beings are justified by faith, not their own merits. It was a difficult message to accept. Justification through the Law was ingrained in the people's consciousness and history.

Paul was afraid that people would simply not believe they were forgiven. He had an urgency to proclaim the good news to the entire world! While the message of Paul's Letter to the Galatians is similar in content, the tone of his Romans' letter is less crazed and defensive. Romans was well articulated, perhaps dictated to a scribe, and written in the style of Greek literature. Galatians was written from the perspective of the jail cell and reflected

his frantic situation. For Paul, all people needed to do was to accept the message of Christ and they would become transformed.

Paul's problems with the Judaizers was past history by the time he wrote to the Romans. He was probably aware of the problem that existed between the Jewish Christians [exiled by Claudius and later returned under Nero] and the gentile church. The gentile church was not concerned with dietary laws, and thus, during the Jewish exile, was quite comfortable in practicing the Christian discipline without paying heed to such long-held cherished regulations. This obviously did not set well with the returning Jews. The gentiles were the "strong" ones because they were not bound by such regulations and the Jews were the "weak" ones because they were so compelled. Paul addressed this situation in his letter.

Paul's Letter to the Romans has had a greater impact on Christian theology than any other New Testament letter.

Today's Pericope: Today's verse and the concluding doxology bring the Letter to the Romans to a close. Many scholars believe that the letter really ends at 15:33. Chapter 16 is probably a separate letter written to Phoebe, a deaconess of the church of Ephesus. Verses 25–27 deviate from Pauline style and were probably inserted into the text by later redactors. The doxology found in today's verses occurs three times in the Letter to the Romans.

The lines of praise contain with them essential Christian theology. They reveal a new understanding of the Hebrew scriptures. Paul believed that God's hidden plan of salvation gradually unfolded in human history since the beginning of time can only be fully understood in light of the Jesus-event. Christian faith understands Jesus to be the fulfillment of all that went before him—all that was foretold in the prophetic tradition. Paul insists that in keeping with sixth-century B.C. prophetic thought, God's saving work is universal—it is for all people, Jews and gentiles. Jesus ushered in a new inclusivity. The advent of his salvation extended beyond the borders of Israel. No longer was it just the purview of a nation that grew out of a tribal confederacy. The gates of exclusion were thrown open to all the world and Jesus made it

[5]Joseph A. Fitzmyer, S.J., "*The Letter to the Romans,*" *NJBC,* 830.

possible for human beings to have a deeper, intimate, more personal relationship with God. In this new, incarnate union with God in Christ no barriers exist. The distinctions of class, race, wealth, language, and culture have nothing to do with inclusion. God's salvation, God's coming, is for all people.

The gospel is proclaimed.

Gospel
Luke 1:26–38. You will conceive and bear a son.

STEP 1
NAMING ONE'S EXPERIENCE

What were your first impressions? What was your first response to the gospel (or the other readings)? What captured your attention?

Each person names his or her initial impression. Statements should be brief. No reasons should be given at this time. All simply listen without agreeing or disagreeing.

STEP 2
UNDERSTANDING

In a brief statement, explain what you think this gospel is trying to convey.

STEP 3
INPUT FROM VISION/STORY/TRADITION

Liturgical Context

Today we walk through the last door before we come face to face with the greatest story of all time, the incarnation of Jesus Christ. We move from John the Baptist and his ministry to Mary and the annunciation. Historically and chronologically, it would appear that we are moving backward in time, not forward. It seems as if we start with John the Baptist and his work of heralding

Christ, and then segue back to Mary and her role. However, scripturally and theologically it makes perfect sense. Reginald Fuller tells us that John sums up the prophecies of the Hebrew scriptures and announces the Christ-event.[6] Mary is the instrument of God's saving action through Christ. Through Mary Jesus enters the world.

In today's liturgy Mary takes her humble center stage role in order to point us to the reason for the Christmas event, the incarnation of God's Son, Jesus Christ. Mary always points us to Christ and indeed that is her role on this fourth Sunday of Advent. The liturgy increases its energy in proclaiming the coming of Christ in anticipation of the Christmas feast.

The opening prayer for today's liturgy reminds us of the paschal nature of the incarnation of Christ: "so lead us through his suffering and death to the glory of the resurrection." In this season of sentimental songs about manger babies and straw pillows, we must not forget that the reason Christmas has captured the hearts of humankind often gets obscured in its secularization. Jesus came to die and rise for us. We are to follow him and do what he did. It is driven by joy, but it is not sentimental piety. Suffering, dying, and rising are sobering realities—the real stuff of life. The liturgy offers us a reality check in the midst of our oversecularized remembrance of this feast. The Christmas event is about our salvation. "But one cannot lose sight of the fact that this birth is but the first step to Easter, and that its ultimate importance lies in the mystery of salvation in which we share."[7] The alternative opening prayer asks that we, like Mary, be given the strength and the open hearts to place our lives in the service of God's plan. "Do we really mean it?" It is the question that resounds on the fourth Sunday of Advent.

Gospel Exegesis

The facilitator provides input from critical biblical scholarship on this text. This input includes insights as to how people would have heard the gospel in Jesus' time.

The gospel of Luke was written in Greek, which is so refined that it was probably Luke's native

---

[6] *PL*, 211.
[7] *DL* (I), 137.

tongue. The gospel is lacking in Hebrew scripture references, in local cultural idioms of first-century Palestine, and in the Hebrew language. Thus, most scholars surmise that Luke's gospel was predominantly gentile Christian, whereas Matthew's community was a mixed population.

Luke's perspective of the Jesus-event is that God's plan of salvation is not only extended to the house of Israel, but to the gentile peoples as well. Many Jews encountered Christ and believed. Others were blinded to the obvious fact that he was the fulfillment of God's plan of salvation revealed to Israel. Luke did not believe that the blindness of Israel resulted in the mission to the gentiles. He insists that the Holy Spirit initiated it and was the creative agent in its inauguration.

Today's gospel is a birth announcement. In the infancy narratives of Luke there are two birth announcements. The angel appeared to Zechariah and announced the birth of John the Baptist, and in today's gospel the angel appears to Mary and announces the birth of Christ. Both annunciations are similar. They are of equal length and they contain some of the same elements. They form a diptych—two parallel panels. One side is the annunciation of John and, next to it, the annunciation of Jesus, the Christ. As parallel as they seem, the annunciation of Jesus is far more wondrous than John's, as will be later pointed out.

In our modern culture we announce the birth of a baby by sending out notices to friends and family. We announce the day of birth, the color of hair and eyes, the weight and the name of the child. Annunciations of births in antiquity served a different purpose. They were intended to alert the reader to the mission and purpose of the one about to be born.[8] Luke's purpose is not to give a detailed historical account of Jesus' birth. We are to avoid a literal rendering of the text and need to explore the religious and spiritual implications Luke is attempting to elucidate for his audience.

Luke followed the literary patterns used by past biblical authors. He used common literary techniques to posit his theology. His annunciation stories are patterned after similar annunciation sto-

ries in the Hebrew scriptures such as Samson, Samuel, and Isaac, not to mention the secular material at his disposal. The birth stories of those biblical heroes are noteworthy because of God's intervention in situations in which the age or barrenness of the parents was a factor in the prior inability of the couple to conceive. The Jesus birth narrative supersedes those previous biblical accounts. There may be similarities between the annunciations of the Old Testament and the infancy narrative concerning Jesus. However, the Christ-event follows the pattern only to a point and then transcends them, as we will see as we explore the text further.

Both Matthew and Luke prefaced their gospel stories with the infancy narrative of Jesus' birth. They were both written with the purpose of demonstrating God's divine plan of salvation and the divine origin of Jesus in light of the prophetic messianic tradition of the Hebrew scriptures. The infancy narratives posit a theology.

Unlike Matthew, Luke does not adopt an apologetic tone since he was not as directly involved in the confrontation with the Jews. Luke regards the Temple and its worship as part of history. He does not believe Christianity to be in competition with it. Luke's perspective that God's salvation moved to the ends of the earth (thus reaching out to the gentiles) is a symbolic reference for the mission of Christ that extended out toward Rome: "the focus of Christianity passed from Jerusalem of the Jews to Rome of the Gentiles."[9]

Evidence that Luke is unconcerned with apologetics is the gentleness he displays in his narrative, especially in scenes with women. Luke purposefully exalts Mary, humble handmaid of the Lord, and gives her a dominant role in the Lukan infancy narratives. Matthew highlights Joseph's role; Luke emphasizes Mary's.

Some scholars suggest that Luke crafted the entire gospel and then inserted the birth narratives later. The first two chapters stand independently of the rest of the text. The gospel is not dependent on the narratives and could stand on its own without them. Their inclusion in the final narrative proba-

---

[8] WWC, 141.

[9] BOM, 23.

bly was a result of Luke's penchant for imitating the style of classical historians. It was a common literary technique to include the infancy or early youth history of a well-known person in a biography.

We are told that in the sixth month, that is, of Elizabeth's pregnancy, the angel Gabriel was sent to Mary. Elizabeth was in seclusion for five months; thus it was by divine revelation that Mary knew that she (Elizabeth) was pregnant. This puts the reader on notice—John the Baptist's birth was truly the work of God, and so is the annunciation to Mary.

Luke and Matthew provide us with distinct perspectives of the infancy-event. Luke's text situates the annunciation in Nazareth. Matthew's annunciation scene to Joseph takes place in Bethlehem. Only after he returns from the flight into Egypt does Joseph take his family to Nazareth. Both Luke and Matthew refer to Mary's marital status in the same way, however. "She was betrothed to Joseph." The fact that she is a virgin as well as betrothed infers that she had exchanged consent with Joseph, but she had not yet moved in with him.

Mary is assured of God's favor and support. "The Lord is with you . . ." is not to be understood as a proclamation that Jesus is within her womb. It is an expression of God's favor. The manifestation of the angel startled Mary. Why was she startled? Some have tried to posit psychological reasons for Mary's alarm—she was alarmed by the visitation of an angel or she was a maiden embarrassed by the presence of a man or she was a woman of great modesty. Closer to the truth of her startled condition is that it fits a literary pattern in scripture. "[D]isturbance is part of the literary pattern of an angelic annunciation to birth . . . and Mary's wonderment is a reaction to the great grace or favor that the angel announced."[10]

Mary is told by the angel to name the child. In Matthew Joseph is given the command. However, in the Hebrew scriptures there is precedence for divinely favored women to name the child (such as the mothers of Samson and Samuel). The angel tells Mary that Jesus will be called Son of the Most High. The calling itself names the reality of what

is. Thus, *"he will be called"* means that *"he will be"* in truth what he is called, "Son of the Most High."

Mary asks the angel how it could all be possible. She, after all, "did not know man." The word used for man is the more inclusive word, *anthropos*. It is not translated "husband"—Luke is setting the record straight. Mary did not know any man; she was a virgin.

The power of the Holy Spirit came upon Mary. The word *overshadow* in the Hebrew scripture was a reference to God's presence. Luke continues to use Old Testament terminology. All early Christology is expressed in terms of Jewish prophecy reinterpreted in light of the Christ-event. For example, in verse 35b Luke tells us: "The Holy Spirit will come upon you." This is directly connected to Old Testament messianic prophecy. Isaiah 11:1–2 proclaims that the Spirit of the Lord will come upon the Davidic branch—the Davidic Messiah. Isaiah 4:2–3 insists that the "shoot of David" will be *holy* ("Therefore the child will be called *holy*. . ."—v. 35). The gospel thus connects Jesus with the expected messianic figure: the shoot of David will be *holy*, Jesus will be *holy*. The term *Son of God* is parallel to *Son of the Most High*. Both terms are directly related to God's appointment of the Davidic messiah as his "Son."

Luke cleverly weaves Old Testament images of messianic prophecy into a new context. He situates them within the framework of an already established, early Christology. Luke's theology does take a detour from Old Testament messianic expectations, however. The Holy Spirit, in this instance, does not come down upon the Davidic messiah as prophesied in the Old Testament; it comes instead upon his mother. A Davidic ruler is not crowned as God's Son or agent. God's Son is begotten in the womb of Mary through the power of the Holy Spirit. Another detour from messianic prophecy can be observed by noting that nowhere in Old Testament prophecy is there an expectation that the Messiah would be conceived without a male parent. Thus, Brown insists that the ideas in verse 35, while laced with Old Testament terminology, are really an articulation of early Christian theology.[11] "But the way these ideas

---

[10]Ibid., 288.

[11]Ibid., 312.

are combined in 1:35 takes us out of the realm of Jewish expectation of the Messiah into the realm of early Christianity."[12]

This "overshadowing" does not allude to a quasi-sexual union. God does not take the place of the male in mating with Mary. It is an allusion to creativity. Mary is fertile. God does not intervene on the part of the husband in order to make conception possible, as in the case of Zechariah. Mary is a virgin. The creation within her womb is the result of God's creative action—it is totally the work of God. The Son was begotten by God through the creative power of the Holy Spirit.

The New Testament uses the same word, "overshadow," in reference to the transfiguration as well—a cloud of glory, of divine presence, overshadowed those present. In the transfiguration scene, paralleled with Jesus' baptism, the power of the Holy Spirit—divine presence—overshadowed Jesus and he was called "Beloved Son." Jesus' baptism revealed Christ's divine status as *Son* to the reader; the transfiguration accomplished the same goal for the chosen disciples.

The angelic manifestation to Zechariah took place in Jerusalem in the Temple as a sign of continuity with the Hebrew scriptures. The angel appeared to Mary, however, in Nazareth—a place that had no Old Testament expectations. This was certainly a sign that God was doing something brand-new! The Spirit may have entered John the Baptist from his mother's womb. But the Spirit that came upon Mary is the same Spirit who hovered over the waters at the creation of the world. Like the void and formless earth, Mary's womb was void until the Spirit hovered and generated new life—the Son of God. The parents of John longed for a child. There was no previous yearning in Mary. She was a virgin and was not yearning for a child at that moment in time. She was surprised at the gift of new life before her—"the surprise of creation."[13] John's parents prayed for a child and God answered their prayer—human request and God's fulfillment. The birth of Jesus was God's initiative, going well beyond the imagination of the mother-to-be. The annunciation of John brought with it a warning that evil would have to be faced. The annunciation of Jesus was a positive message— "reflecting the word of the creator God who made everything good."[14]

For Luke, even though Jesus was understood as the Davidic Messiah, he was also understood as the Son of God. Those two beliefs are woven together. The Son of the Most High is the same as the Son of God conceived by the power of the Spirit. In Paul's Letter to the Romans, however, Jesus was designated Son of God at his resurrection (1:3–4). Luke moves the designation back to Jesus' conception. His point is clear—"there never was a moment on earth when Jesus was not the Son of God."[15]

Some scholars refer to this text to argue against the virginal conception of Jesus. Joseph Fitzmyer refers to the work of Lyonnet when he asserts "When this account is read in and for itself—without the overtones of Matthean annunciation to Joseph, every detail of it could be understood of a child to be born to Mary in the usual human way."[16] Fitzmyer suggests, therefore, that it is possible that Jesus' birth could be considered the work of the Holy Spirit even if Mary and Joseph had had marital relations. This would be possible by virtue of the fact that his birth was foretold in scriptures, it was announced by God's messenger, and the child was to become God's son. However, other scholars use this text as proof of the virginal conception, citing Luke's insistence that Mary was a virgin. Raymond Brown takes the position that there was no question as far as Luke was concerned about the virginal conception of Jesus.[17]

Raymond Brown points to another controversy surrounding this gospel pericope.[18] He asserts that this text in Luke sometimes serves as an embarrassment to those who present the theology of the preexistence of the Son of God. It is obvious that in a theology which teaches that Jesus Christ is the preexistent Son of God, it is not possible that con-

---

[12]Ibid.
[13]Ibid., 314.

[14]Ibid., 315.
[15]Ibid., 316.
[16]Fitzmyer, "Virginal Conception," 566–567, in *BOM*, 299.
[17]*BOM*, 299–301.
[18]Ibid., 291.

ception by the Holy Spirit in Mary's womb brings about the existence of God's Son. Brown responds by drawing upon the arguments of Lyonnet in "L'Annonciation" (61): "Luke is seemingly unaware of such a christology; conception is related to divine sonship for him."[19] Brown argues that he cannot accept the premise of "those theologians who try to avoid the causal connotations in the 'Therefore' which begins this line by arguing that for Luke the conception of the child does not bring the Son of God into being, but only enables us to call him 'Son of God' who already was the Son of God."[20] The power of the Most High will overshadow Mary. Therefore, her child will be called [his reality will be] God's son. Causality between the two events cannot be ignored, according to Brown. Thus, there is a direct relationship between the action of God overshadowing Mary and the result it wrought—the existence of God's Son. We are told that Jesus will be called holy. The "will be called," as mentioned before, means "he will be." Therefore—what will he be? God's Son. Put simply, according to Luke's understanding at the time, Jesus became God's Son when the Holy Spirit overshadowed Mary. In John's gospel Jesus is seemingly aware of his preexistence. Luke does not seem to share that same understanding, however. This argument is included at this juncture in the exegesis as a reminder that biblical scholarship is certainly not an exact science. Scholars do disagree with one another. It therefore behooves the Church to continue to research, study, stay in the dialogue, and wrestle with these very important issues.

As mentioned above, Luke uses the common literary pattern typical of angelic birth annunciations in the scriptures. An angel appeared, there was fear, a message was given, and objections were raised. Finally there would be a sign. In Luke's infancy narratives there are two annunciations. Angels announce the birth of John the Baptist and the birth of Jesus. Throughout the annunciation episodes the evangelist establishes the subordination of John to Jesus. It is in this argument for John's subordination and Jesus' superiority that proof of Luke's belief in the virginal conception of Jesus lies.

In comparing the annunciations we observe that John is "great before the Lord." Jesus, however, is great—period. There are no qualifications for his greatness. John is filled with the Holy Spirit even from his mother's womb. Jesus, however, has the Holy Spirit directly connected with his conception. John will prepare the way and make the people ready for the Lord, whereas Jesus will rule the house of Jacob and Israel and will establish an eternal kingdom. Zechariah asks the angel, "How can this be?" and he is struck mute. Mary asks the same question and is not. Luke uses these parallels to posit his theology. The exchange between the angel and Zechariah is patterned after the exchange between Gabriel and Daniel.[21] Daniel was also struck mute. Mary's exchange with Gabriel, on the other hand, is patterned after Hannah, the mother of Samuel. Mary's "Magnificat" is reminiscent of Hannah's canticle of praise in 1 Samuel 2. It does not serve Luke's theological purpose to have Mary suffer consequences for her similar reaction to the announcement. Luke put the question in Mary's mouth in order to give Gabriel the opportunity to answer it. What does Gabriel tell us? He tells us that the Holy Spirit came upon Mary and that she was overshadowed by the Most High. We are also informed that the child to be born will be called holy—Son of God. Mary's question was a literary tool used by Luke to present his theology. "Mary is a spokeswoman for Luke's christological message even as Gabriel is a spokesman; and between them they fill in the picture of the Messiah's conception as God's Son, a conception not through marital intercourse (Mary's contribution) but through the Holy Spirit (Gabriel's contribution)."[22] In short, Luke uses the dialogue between Mary and Gabriel to teach his Christology.

Raymond Brown further points out that this drama of comparison between the annunciation of John and the annunciation to Mary would fail completely if

> John the Baptist was conceived in an extraordinary manner and Jesus in a natural manner. But it would be continued per-

---

[19]Ibid.
[20]Ibid.

[21]The Gabriel and Daniel episode is an eschatological reference to the day of judgment—the end of times.
[22]*BOM*, 308.

fectly if Jesus was virginally conceived, since this would be something completely unattested in previous manifestations of God's power. It is to the virginal conception rather than to a natural conception that Elizabeth refers when she says of Mary: "Fortunate is she who believed that the Lord's words to her would find fulfillment" (1:4). No belief would really be required if Mary was to conceive as any other young girl would conceive.[23]

In the annunciation of John, Zechariah reminds the angel that he and Elizabeth were unable to conceive—a human difficulty. It is through divine intervention that their human problem is overcome and they do conceive. We are reminded that Mary is a virgin. She initially questions Gabriel's announcement on the grounds that she is a virgin—she had not had sexual relations with a man. The obstacle to her conception, therefore, is the fact that she is a virgin. God once again intervenes—this time Mary's virginity is overcome through the power of divine intervention. "If the age and barrenness of Zechariah and Elizabeth were divinely overcome in the conception of [John the Baptist], the human difficulty of the virginity of Mary must be overcome by divine power in the conception of Jesus. It was creatively overcome without loss of virginity through the intervention of the Holy Spirit, the 'power of the Most High', with the result that Jesus was only the 'supposed Son' of Joseph (3:23)—a designation that makes no sense if Jesus was the natural Son of Joseph. Indeed, the totality of the emphasis on Mary in ch. 1 of Luke is curious if Joseph was equally the parent of Jesus."[24]

The portrait of Mary that Luke paints in the gospel is a portrait shaped by what Luke already knew about her ministry. In the gospel of Mark, Mary is in a scene in which she and her family go to Jesus because of charges that he is mad. Following that scene, Jesus gives a teaching on family relationships—"His true family is established through a relationship to God, not by human origin."[25] One might possibly read into the Markan

account the sense that Jesus was replacing his natural family—he was rejecting them—especially in light of his later complaint that a prophet is not welcome in his own home. Luke does an about-face from the Markan perspective. He changes the story to suit his purpose: "Then his mother and his brothers came to him, but they could not reach him because of the crowd. He was told, 'Your mother and your brothers are standing outside, desiring to see you.' But he said to them, 'My mother and my brothers are those who hear the word of God and do it'" (Lk 8:19–21). The hearers of God's Word are not to replace Jesus' mother and family, as in Mark's version. Luke is making the assertion that Mary and his brothers are among the disciples. Not only is Jesus' family his natural family, but they also hear the Word of God, making them truly his family. Mary and the rest of Jesus' family are disciples. Luke reminds the reader of this fact later in the text when he places them together with the 120 gathered after the resurrection (Acts 1:14).

Thus, Mary is one who hears the Word of God and acts on it. This is emphasized in her fiat: "Behold the handmaid of the Lord. Let it happen to me according to your word" (1:38). Mary's virginal conception started her on a path of discovery that led her to deal with God's mysterious plan of salvation embodied in the birth and life of her son. The Lukan tradition insists that Mary was true to that word and spent her life as a true disciple obedient to the Word and will of God. Luke reminds his reader of that point from the outset of the story. From the beginning she was a good disciple. The first proclamation of divine favor attracted new disciples. Luke insists that his readers become acutely aware of Mary's enthusiastic, joyful response to God's Word. Luke highlights Mary's immediate responses by the parallel between the John the Baptist's annunciation story and this annunciation story.

Elizabeth and Zechariah are patterned after Abraham and Sarah. In the Abraham and Sarah story, Sarah laughs when God reveals his plan for her. She was too old to bear a child. God challenged her lack of faith. Yet the Lord came to Sarah in her sixth month and she became pregnant. So, too, with Elizabeth. The angel repeated the same challenge given to Sarah—"Nothing said of God

---

[23]Ibid., 301.
[24]Ibid.
[25]Ibid., 317.

can be impossible." Mary's response to the angel, however, is a far cry from Sarah's. Mary accepted God's Word with total, joyous consent. Mary, like Hannah, responded to similar news: "Let your handmaid find favor in your eyes" (1 Sm 1:18).

Some scholars suggest that one Old Testament symbolism associated with Mary is the term *daughter of Zion*. The greeting given to Mary by the angel, "Rejoice, O highly favored daughter," is a more accurate translation than "Hail, full of grace!" The salutation not only acknowledges Mary's special favor and role, but it also is a proclamation of the dawn of the messianic age. Zephaniah made the same proclamation to the "daughter of Zion" (Israel) when he exclaimed that God was in their midst (3:14–17). The words of Zephaniah became associated with messianic prophecy and the advent of the messianic age. The angel proclaims the dawn of the new age— Emmanuel—God is with us.

Zion eventually evolved to be a synonym for Jerusalem. The term *daughter* was a reference to a geographical entity—a suburb, subdivision, town, or village. Cities of various countries were referred to as daughters of that country. The daughters of a city were the suburbs or villages associated with the city. Micah 1:13 refers to "daughter of Zion." It has been suggested that "daughter of Zion" referred to a new quarter of Jerusalem, north of the Temple area (Zion). It was a place known to be inhabited by poor refugees after the fall of Samaria in 721. It was filled with poor, displaced people who were in dire need of hope, encouragement, and a word of consolation from Yahweh. Micah supplied that word. Eventually the term *daughter of Zion* became a reference for Jerusalem itself and then Israel itself. It is possible that in the allusion to Mary as "daughter of Zion" she personifies one who is a defender of the poor and who has compassion for the downtrodden. There is certainly evidence of this designation in her proclamation of the Magnificat. As disciple, Mary became a champion for the poor and oppressed, following the example of her son. "She is to be identified with those of low estate and the poor (Magnificat); but she is not oppressed or violated, and is totally faithful (1:45) and obedient to God's word (1:38)... . Moreover, by stressing Mary's acceptance of God's word in 1:38, Luke has begun to as-

sociate her with those in Israel who were 'poor ones' (*anawim*) in the sense of being totally dependent upon God for support. Luke will develop that theme beautifully in the Magnificat."[26]

Mary is an icon of faith. She opened herself to the generation of new life by the simple word of God's command. No way could she have understood the full implications of what her fiat would ask of her. She did, however, ponder it all in her heart. Disciple—hearer and bearer of God's Word—defender of the poor—and ponderer. She becomes an example for us today. A disciple is one who hears the Word of God, acts upon it, and makes it alive in one's life. A disciple is one who reaches out to the poor of the world and who above all spends time in communion with the God who empowers us for the work a disciple is called to perform in the service of God's kingdom. Front and center now, Mary waits with the church as the curtain is slowly raised on the event that changed the course of salvation history—that dawning *kairos* moment in which the Light has dawned, a new age has begun, and the *shalom* peace of Eden is once again restored on the face of the earth. It is certainly reason to rejoice.

Proclaim the gospel again.

Sometimes we gain new insights when we hear the text after the interpretation is given. Someone from the group proclaims the gospel a second time.

STEP 4
TESTING

Conversation with the Liturgy and the Scriptures

Test your original understanding in dialogue with the text.

(You might consider breaking into smaller groups.)

Now that you've heard the exegesis, were there any new insights? How do you feel about it? How does your original understanding of this gospel compare with what we just shared? How does this story speak to your life?

---

[26]Ibid., 321, 328.

Sharing Life Experience

Participants share an experience from their lives that connects with the biblical interpretation just presented.

I am struck by the portrait Luke paints of Mary in today's gospel. She is truly an icon of faith. I try to put myself in her shoes. How would I have responded? Twelve years old, betrothed, and all of a sudden I am visited by an angel (I wonder if he looked like Della Reese or Roma Downey?). The angel tells me I am going to have a child. I know I have not had relations so I am just a bit confused. The prospects are scary at best. I could be stoned for such a thing. Yet this twelve-year-old girl did not hesitate. She said, "Of course—let it happen."

I often wonder about such faith. How do I really know if something is God's will? The only angelic visitation I have ever had was the last gripping episode of "Touched by an Angel." In other words, I have not been similarly favored with angelic appearances.

I can indeed relate to Mary's predicament, however. How many times in our lives have we been faced with saying yes or no to God's direction for us? How many times have we stood on the precipice of something wonderful, yet were afraid to trust? My first response to God's will in my life has always been to do exactly what Mary did—question, question, question. Is that really you, God? How do I know? How can I be sure? Maybe I just think it's you. After all this time, I am still not sure I have the answer to all those questions. Perhaps careful caution is not so bad. How do I know if the voice I believe is from God is nothing more than my own wishful thinking? There have been times in my life when I have forged ahead with something, so certain of God's divinely inspired ordained will, only to find out that I was led more by my own nose and an ark full of unrealistic dreams. Sometimes it is only in looking back that I can see that God's hand was there all along—leading, nurturing, inviting, and challenging.

I am reminded of a situation recently in which I was certain that God was calling me in a certain direction. It was one of those rare moments of prayer in which the voice of God seemed so strong that to ignore it would be tantamount to saying, "Thanks, but no thanks, God." The word became stronger as

time went by, yet I still "pondered the word in my heart." Then came the test. Would I have the courage to stand on that word even if there was risk involved? What if my security was threatened? What if I would be asked to choose between two very good things? How would I respond when push came to shove and I was asked to decide? Would I choose what I believed to be God's will? Or would I choose the comfortable, status-quo, nonthreatening way?

The situation presented itself. Once I became confident of God's direction, the rest was simple. I was able to let go and trust that God would lead me where I was supposed to go. For once in my life I was at peace with my decision. My job was to respond to God's will in my life—even if it meant going out on a limb. I was amazed as I watched God weave his marvelous tapestry in the events that unfolded. I was able to stand back and allow God to accomplish what God wanted to accomplish. It was a powerful lesson.

Mary is truly an icon. She teaches us what it means to be a disciple. She reminds us of what it means to have a heart open to the Spirit of God—to allow the epicletic action of God to wash over us, overshadow us, and invite us into complete and total transformation. God favors us so we can go and favor others. Mary is truly "daughter of Zion" and she invites the rest of us to be disciple just as she was disciple. She invites us to take the Spirit we have been given and reach out to the broken, poor, and lonely people of the world. I am touched by the other "daughters of Zion" in our midst who similarly respond to God's Word and, in so doing, allow God's anawim to know of his compassion and care. Recently I was touched by a woman in the parish who responded with a fiat of her own and in the process one of society's cast-offs found a resting place and a chance to be re-created.

Isn't that what Christmas is really all about? Reconciliation? Peace? Restoration? Re-creation? The image of God's act of creation within the womb of Mary strikes a powerful chord. The Advent Christmas season invites us to be open to the generative, creative power of God. It is an invitation to hear the Word of God, to act on it, to make it my creed, and ultimately to allow the Christ of history, the Christ of my present, and the Christ of our future to shine his illumination on the darkness still lurking within this sometimes willing soul. With Mary as my

*model, and all the other grand women of faith, I
will hopefully say yes the next time I am visited by
that still voice within.*

What was Luke trying to tell his community? What
was Luke's purpose in writing the infancy narratives? What was his theology? How do you feel
about Mary's response to the angel? In what way
do you relate to Mary as she is portrayed by Luke
in today's gospel? How does Luke's gospel invite
us to be prepared for Christmas? In what way does
this gospel challenge your community today? In
what way has this conversation with the scriptures
for today's liturgy invited change in your life? In
what way are the biblical themes of covenant, exodus, creation, and community evident in today's
readings? Do you still feel the same way about this
text as when you began? Has your original understanding been stretched, challenged, or affirmed?

STEP 5
DECISION

The gospel demands a response.

In what concrete way might your parish be invited
to respond? Are there any attitudes or behaviors
you would like to change as a result of today's conversation? What one concrete action will you take
this week in response to the liturgy today?

Christian Initiation: In what way have the catechumens and candidates been invited to participate
in the ministries of justice in the parish? Are there
shut-ins to be visited? A soup kitchen to be
tended? Sick to be visited? What "Prayers of Exorcism" and "Prayers of Blessing" might be prayed
with catechumens that seem to best reflect the
spirit of the latter days of Advent and the early
days of the Christmas season? Perhaps you might
invite catechumens and candidates to purchase
Catholic Household Blessings and Prayers (NCCB) for
use in their homes. Included in this wonderful
collection and particularly appropriate during the
Advent/Christmas season are the following rituals
and blessings: "Blessing of an Advent Wreath,"
"Blessing of a Christmas Tree," "Blessing of a
Christmas Crèche or Manger Scene," "Blessing for
the New Year," "Blessing of the Home and Household on the Epiphany."

DOCTRINAL ISSUES

What Church truth/teaching/doctrinal issue
could be drawn from the gospel for the fourth
Sunday of Advent?

*Participants suggest possible doctrinal themes that flow
from the readings.*

Possible Doctrinal Themes

Jesus Christ, Son of God; Jesus Christ, fulfillment
of the Hebrew scriptures; Mary, model of the
church; faith; eschatology; reign of God; discipleship; repentance and reconciliation; Christ's coming: future, present, past; parousia

Present the doctrinal material at this time.

1. The facilitator gives input on a particular doc-
    trinal issue of his or her prior choosing. OR
2. The group chooses a doctrinal issue from the
    list they created. They read together from the
    Doctrinal Appendix or other appropriate, offi-
    cial Church documents and the works of re-
    spected theologians.

(Many doctrinal issues are found in the Doctrinal
Appendix at the back of this workbook. If you are
choosing an issue from this resource, please refer
to it now.)

Reflection questions centered around the chosen
doctrinal theme can be found at the end of each
topic in the Doctrinal Appendix. The questions
are based on the five-step reflection process. If you
choose a topic not included in the Doctrinal Appendix, craft your own questions according to the
same five-step process.

Following the reflection questions you will be reminded to return to chapter 7, "Preparing the
Catechetical Session," to assist you in crafting your
own session.

Closing Prayer

Father, all powerful and ever-living God,
we do well always and everywhere to give you
    thanks
through Jesus Christ our Lord.

His future coming was proclaimed by all the
    prophets.
The virgin mother bore him in her womb with
    love beyond all telling.
John the Baptist was his herald
and made him known when at last he came.
In his love Christ has filled us with joy
as we prepare to celebrate his birth,
so that when he comes he may find us watching in
    prayer,
our hearts filled with wonder and praise.[27]

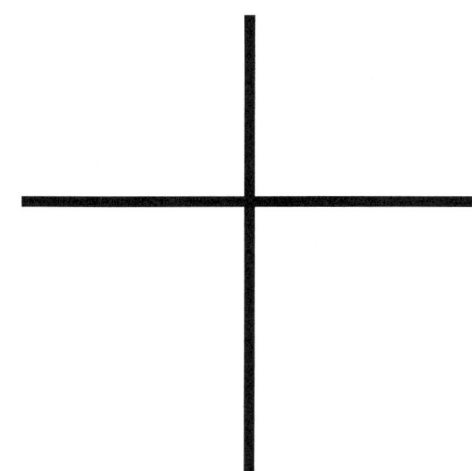

---

[27]"Preface—Advent II," *The Sacramentary.*

THE CHRISTMAS SEASON

THE CHRISTMAS SEASON:
AN OVERVIEW

There is no evidence of an official feast celebrating the nativity until the fourth century. There are two hypotheses regarding the origin of this feast. One school of thought suggests that it was adopted in response to a pagan feast inaugurated by the Roman emperor Aurelian in the hopes of strengthening and uniting his empire. The feast, *sol invictus,* was a celebration honoring the shortest day of the year when the sun reaches its lowest point. It reaches this point on December 25, the winter solstice. From that day forward the sun begins its victory over darkness by lengthening the time it will peer through the dimness of an unlit sky. Thus, the days begin to lengthen as the sun processes heavenward toward its ultimate destiny, full brightness and height during the summer solstice. Christians had no difficulty appropriating this feast to their understanding of Jesus who declared himself Light of the World. They could say very righteously to their pagan neighbors that they, in truth, were celebrating the "real" Sun of justice.

The second school of thought centers around the date of December 25 itself as the reason for establishment of the feast. Christians were very aware of the solstices and equinoxes because of the constant references to Christ as Light. Some hypothesized that John the Baptist was conceived during the autumn equinox and born during the summer solstice. As Jesus was to have been born six months later, that put his birth right at December 25th. It was once again evidence of God's incredible timing and wisdom. It seemed to be no accident that God's mighty work coincided with the temporal world's celebration of the symbols of light and darkness.

The feast spread rapidly due to the influence of the Arian heresy that "made the Son of God the highest of creatures, greater than we but less than God."[1] The Council of Nicea refuted the heresy and formulated the Nicene Creed. Through celebration of Jesus' birth, people would have an op-

portunity in their liturgy to proclaim what the council set out to accomplish.

There is an historical progression to the eventual celebration of the three masses of Christmas: night, dawn, and during the day. The first celebration of the feast of the nativity was a small papal mass. The prologue of John was proclaimed at this mass, the forerunner to our mass during the day. Jesus was honored as the Word of God made flesh. God revealed the Eternal Word to prophets throughout salvation history. The *Word* reached fulfillment in the Incarnation of the Son of God. The gospel and the celebration itself are highly christological.

Underneath the church of St. Mary Major in Rome is a small chapel designed as a replica of the cave at Bethlehem where Jesus was born. Wood was brought to the space, thus the name "mass near the crèche." The story of Jesus' birth was read at this liturgy, the forerunner of the midnight mass. The symbol of the *Christ, our Light* is highlighted in the opening prayer. In the renewed liturgical calendar, the mass at night is patterned after this early St. Mary Major observance.

On December 25, the pope went in the early morning to St. Anastasia's Church in honor of the Greek feast day honoring the church's patroness, a martyr highly venerated in the East. The story of the shepherds who arrive at the crèche seeking the heralded Child is proclaimed at this early morning liturgy, the mass at dawn. There is more reference to the "Light that will shine" in this liturgy than there is in the midnight liturgy.

In addition to the theme of Christ's manifestation to the world through the Incarnation, the liturgies of Christmas proclaim another truth that is evidenced in the opening prayer for the mass during the day and the third Christmas preface. A holy exchange takes place and humanity is elevated to the status of God's child. We share in Jesus' divine

---

[1] *CSM,* xxxiv.

nature. "Your Son shared our weakness [literally: our humanity]: may we share his glory [literally: his divinity]." "Your eternal Word has taken upon himself our human weakness, giving our mortal nature immortal value."[2]

The texts of Christmas, while not directly referring to the paschal mystery, have strong underpinnings of Christ's act of redemption. It is through the life, death, and resurrection of Jesus that we are saved. We cannot look at Christmas without remembering Easter. The Christmas season celebrates the Incarnation of Christ that ushers in God's fulfillment of salvation history. It also honors Christ's manifestation to us in human form. These two realities define and give meaning and expression to the content of our Christian theology. One liturgy cannot possibly capture all the dimensions contained within the mystery of the Incarnation. The fact that so many texts are offered to us for celebration and reflection denotes the richness and complexity of the season. Like the view through a prism, all the readings together help reflect the many facets of the profound mystery of Christ's Incarnation.[3]

The primary symbol of the Christmas liturgy is light. Christ, the light, has ushered in the messianic age. Christmas without magnificent, abundant light is like Easter without the paschal candle. Christmas without paschal themes is akin to baptism without water. Many traditional symbols from our culture remind us that Christmas draws its true meaning from Easter. Eucharistic overtones can be found in the symbol of the manger. Jesus was placed in a feed-box; he is to be our spiritual food. He was wrapped in swaddling clothes and placed in the manger. He would one day be wrapped in burial cloths and placed in a rock-carved tomb. Jesus' manifestation to the shepherds, society's lowest, reminds us that Jesus came to preach the good news to the poor. The Christmas tree was understood in its earliest conception as reminiscent of the woods of the cross. Holly is a Christmas symbol because its thorns and red berries remind us of the suffering of Christ. The wreath, an ancient symbol of victory, reminds us of Christ's victory over death.

Holy Family

The feast of the Holy Family falls on the Sunday within the octave of Christmas. This relatively new feast originated in Canada. The feast of the Holy Family lifts up the family of Nazareth as a model for struggling Christian families. Pope Leo XIII promulgated this celebration of the family of Mary, Jesus, and Joseph.

Epiphany

Epiphany means "showing forth" or manifestation. It was considered a primary feast in the area of Gaul around the third and fourth century. Epiphany, "from the Greek (*ephiphaneia*, or *theophoneia*, 'appearance or manifestation of God'), was the original feast of Christ's birth."[4] In the ancient world an epiphany referred to a visit from a god or one who was revered as a god, such as a king.

In the East, Jesus' birth and his baptism were celebrated on this day. Thus, new members were baptized on this feast. The wedding feast at Cana, where Jesus manifested his power for the first time, was also commemorated on Epiphany.

"In the second half of the fourth century East and West took over each other's birthday feast of Jesus. While the East celebrated on December 25 not only the birth of Jesus but also the coming of the Magi, and reserved January 6 for the commemoration of Jesus' baptism and his miracle at Cana and for the conferral of baptism, the West on January 6 celebrated the Epiphany of the redeemer in connection with the coming of the wise men, the baptism of Jesus, and the wedding feast at Cana."[5]

J. A. Jungman unites both feasts thematically when he states: "The mystery of the Incarnation is the proper subject of them both; but at Christmas we consider chiefly the coming down of the Son of God who became one of the poor children of men, while on the Epiphany we direct our attention to this Child's divine dignity which already is beginning to manifest itself in the world."[6]

[2]*LY*, 127.
[3]*DL* (1), 191–192.

[4]*LY*, 144.
[5]Ibid, 145.
[6]*PW*, 208.

Epiphany is also the day we remember the three magi. However, the focus is still on Christ and not the magi. In the gospel, wise men from the East come to exalt the newborn king of the Jews. The point of the story rests with Christ who comes to save the whole world, pagans and all.

Adolf Adam suggests that Epiphany is the premier celebration of Christ, the King. He proposes that the other feast designated by that title has more to do with reverence for the title, the theological concept, than it does with the inherent reality of Christ's kingship. "It is essential to the liturgical feast of Epiphany that it brings before us, in a concrete way, a royal action of Christ, an event that is an essential part of the process of salvation."[7]

Baptism of the Lord

The feast of the baptism of the Lord is celebrated on the Sunday following Epiphany. If the Sunday of Epiphany falls after January 6, then the feast of the Lord's baptism is celebrated on Monday that year. During Cycle C the gospel that is read is that of the wedding feast at Cana. During Cycle A the gospel is the account of Jesus' baptism.

This feast is important for three reasons. Jesus is named by the voice of God who calls him "Son." The Holy Spirit descends upon Jesus and thus anoints him for the destiny he is to fulfil. Since it is John who baptizes, Jesus shows his partnership with sinful humanity. This feast brings the Christmas season to an end.

Octave of Christmas

Following Christmas (and Easter) there is an entire week of liturgical feasts called an octave. The feast of St. Stephen, the first martyr (model of love for enemies and fearless witness to the faith), is on December 26. The feast of John the Apostle and Evangelist is celebrated on December 27. The feast of the Holy Innocents, the children killed by Herod, occurs on December 28. Other martyrs' feasts are celebrated on the remaining days of the week.

Christmas celebrates the manifestation of Christ, the Light of the world. The feasts of the octave

lead us into the sobering reality of what happens when one becomes a child of the Light. For the Christian there can be no complacent lapses into nostalgic reminiscence of roasted chestnuts, pine scented rooms, or cozy hearths near an open fire. The Christmas octave feasts of St. Stephen, John the Apostle, and the Holy Innocents serve as a reminder that the only open fire a true disciple can expect is that of the martyr's stake. It has been said that the three feasts are examples of the three possible forms of martyrdom: voluntary and executed (St. Stephen), voluntary, but not executed (John the Apostle), and executed but not voluntary (the Innocents). However, regardless of how martyrs offer their lives, these feasts remind the believer that the cost of discipleship is very high. The Incarnation of Christ, the Light of the world, often requires nothing less than the complete self-offering of one's life.

The first reading of the feast of St. Stephen recounts the story of his ministry and his martyrdom. Christians are reminded of the persecutions they must endure for the sake of the gospel.[8] Stephen was chosen by the apostles to help them because "he was trusted by everyone."[9] Stephen distributed food to the poor and was the first deacon because of his great charism of service. St. Stephen's commemoration is one reason for the custom of giving gifts to the poor at Christmas.

The root meaning of the word *martyr* is "witness." Stephen gave witness to Christ by the gift of his life. The etymology of Stephen's name is "wreath." War heroes and famous athletes of his day were given wreaths in honor of their achievements. Art depicting martyrs often portrays them wearing wreaths around their heads. The Christmas wreath "announces the victory of Christ who brings justice, love and peace. We remember deacon Stephen, the first witness to lay down his life for Christ."[10]

The feast of John the Apostle, celebrated first in the East, dates to the fourth century. Tradition emanating from Irenaeus holds that John ministered in Ephesus and was later banished to the island of Patmos where he wrote the book of Reve-

---

[7]*LY,* 147.

[8]Ibid., 142.
[9]*CC,* 191.
[10]Ibid.

lation. He subsequently returned to Ephesus where he composed the gospel of John and died at an old age.[11] "The symbol of John's gospel is that of the eagle that flies to the heights."[12] The liturgy of this feast stresses that God was announced to humanity through the revelation given to John. John the Apostle, the Evangelist, manifested the Word of God, the Logos, to the world. The liturgy of this feast names him a credible eyewitness to the life of Jesus.

The origin of the feast of the Holy Innocents dates to the sixth century in North Africa. This date was chosen for the feast because of its connection to the Christmas story. The liturgy of the day tells the story of the flight into Egypt and the slaughtering of the innocent children by Herod who was in search of the prophesied Child. These children are remembered and praised for their innocent martyrdom.

Very often catechetical groups do not meet during the Christmas season. While this is understandable, it is somewhat regrettable. A great part of our Christian tradition is celebrated in the days and the feasts of the Christmas season. Every attempt should be made to break open the Christmas season liturgies with groups participating in liturgical catechesis. The liturgies and feasts of Christmas are integral to complete acquaintance with the entire rich deposit of faith. The liturgies of the Christmas season celebrate and emphasize each hierarchical truth of Catholic teaching. A great deal of flexibility and creativity is needed to ensure that adequate reflection is given to this great season.

There are four liturgies of Christmas: the Christmas vigil, the mass at midnight, the mass at dawn, and the mass during the day. As a result, people will be attending different masses and will not necessarily be experiencing the same readings. It will take a great deal of imagination to effectively incorporate all the readings into a catechetical session. Perhaps it will be next to impossible, considering people's busy lives and time constraints. If there is time for reflection on the readings from only one specific mass, it would be important that the other readings be made available to partici-

pants for their personal reflection. However, all the readings of the Christmas liturgies taken as a whole reflect the broader mystery of the Incarnation. A possible solution might be to provide a Christmas season retreat in which all the readings of Christmas would be reviewed and participants would be offered an opportunity to experience the entire rich fare in the treasury of our Christmas liturgical repertoire.

... Despite all the liturgical formularies, one thing remains: it is impossible to encompass and express in only one liturgy the richness and complexity of the mystery that it celebrates. The good liturgies are those that are not limited to one perspective. This accounts for the diversity of scriptural texts that are offered for reading and meditation. They are not as distracting as one might think: they open up, rather, a greater awareness of what is being celebrated.[13]

---

[11]*LY*, 142.
[12]*CC*, 191.

---

[13]*DL* (I), 193.

CHRISTMAS

VIGIL MASS, MASS AT MIDNIGHT, MASS AT DAWN, MASS DURING THE DAY

The liturgies of Christmas are presented here: the vigil mass, mass at midnight, mass at dawn, and mass during the day. Perhaps you will have time to reflect upon only one of the liturgies. However, all of the readings shed light on the fullness of Christmas and help to unfold the meaning of the Incarnation.

The Infancy Narratives of the New Testament

Matthew and Luke are the only evangelists who tell of Jesus' birth. Raymond Brown suggests that it was not for historical purposes, but for religious reasons that the infancy narratives are told in the first place. These religious reasons are: "first, the identity of Jesus, second, his role as dramatic embodiment of the whole of history."[1] Matthew and Luke use the birth stories as a bridge between the old law, the prophets, and other scriptural books. Matthew and Luke felt that an understanding of Jesus' life and mission could be grasped only in light of the major themes and stories of the Hebrew scriptures.

One cannot help but notice that the two accounts differ considerably. Today's Christmas crèche is a combination of both stories put together. Brown warns against trying to make the stories mesh by explaining away the differences. "A greater fidelity to Scripture as we have received it would recognize that the Holy Spirit was content to give us two different accounts and that the way to interpret them faithfully is to treat them separately."[2] There is no accurate way to know where and how the two evangelists received their information. Brown suggests that when there is excessive concern for historical accuracy we are distracted from the inspired meaning of the biblical text: the identity of Jesus and his role in the fulfillment of salvation history.

Raymond Brown further reminds us that the infancy narratives had a different genesis than the stories about Jesus' life and ministry. The apostles attested to the latter. However, we have no idea where the stories of the magi and the star came from. Some suggest that such stories were orally transmitted from family sources such as Mary and Joseph. However, that is merely a supposition.

Historical accuracy becomes a problem when one considers that Matthew and Luke differ considerably in their accounts and sometimes they come close to contradiction. Another mitigating factor lies in the fact that there is no public record of the startling event of the star in the sky which should have prompted some kind of a public record—"for example, a star that moved through the heavens in a totally irregular way but left no astronomical record."[3]

Adding to the doubts about historical accuracy is the fact that nowhere else in the gospels is there a parallel between the stories of the gospels and the Old Testament like there is a parallel between the birth stories and the Old Testament. Some scholars suggest that the birth narratives were an extended meditation on stories, images, and themes from the Old Testament (a midrash).

In spite of these problems, Brown insists that scholarship has entered a positive new stage and, rather than stressing the difficulties inherent in the texts, focuses on the theology that the texts express. This new stage of biblical scholarship now asks why Matthew and Luke included the stories in the first place. How does each infancy narrative accord with the respective evangelist's theology? How do the infancy narratives convey the good news of salvation, so that they are truly and literally "gospel"?

One reason that Matthew and Luke begin their gospel with the birth story is to remind their readers that it was at Jesus' conception and birth that God revealed the identity of Jesus to the world.

Environment

While the seasonal color of Christmas is red and green in the culture, the liturgical color of Christ-

---

[1] *CCA*, 10–26.
[2] Ibid., 9.

[3] Ibid., 9–10.

mas is white. The traditional Christmas tree and crèche are appropriate adornments for the catechetical environment. Holly, a plant associated with Christmas, not only adds to the environment but carries symbolic meaning as well; the berries are reminiscent of Christ shedding his blood and the prickly leaves are an allusion to the crown of thorns. The primary symbol of the Incarnation is light. Christ, the Light of the world, came to dispel the darkness. Every environment should include ample use of candles to reflect the light that always shines.

The following blessings may be used to bless the tree and the crib. They are adapted from *Catholic Household Blessings and Prayers*.

Christmas Tree Blessing

This tree is a blessing to our space.
It reminds us of all that is filled with the gentleness and the promise of God.
It stands in our midst as a tree of light
that we might promise such beauty to one another and to our world.
It stands like the tree of paradise that God made into the tree of life, the cross of Jesus.
Lord God, let your blessing come upon us as we illumine this tree.
May the light and cheer it gives be a sign of the joy that fills our hearts.
May all who delight in this tree come to the knowledge and joy of salvation.

Blessing of a Christmas Crèche

We are at the beginning of the days of Christmas.
All through the season we will look upon these images of sheep and cattle,
of shepherds, of Mary and Joseph and of Jesus.
God of Mary and Joseph, of shepherds and animals,
bless us whenever we gaze on this manger scene.
Through all the days of Christmas
may these figures tell the story of how humans, angels, and animals
found Christ in this poor place.
Fill this place with hospitality, joy, gentleness and thanksgiving
and guide our steps in the way of peace.
We ask this through Jesus Christ the Lord.

VIGIL MASS

INTRODUCTORY RITES

Opening Song (or Entrance Antiphon)

Today you will know the glory that the Lord is coming to save us, and in the morning you will see his glory (see Ex 16:6–7).[4]

Opening Prayer

Let us pray
[that Christmas morning will find us at peace]

Pause for silent prayer.

God our Father,
every year we rejoice
as we look forward to this feast of our salvation.
May we welcome Christ as our Redeemer,
and meet him with confidence when he comes to be our judge,
who lives and reigns with you and the Holy Spirit,
one God, for ever and ever.[5]

LITURGY OF THE WORD

First Reading [6]
Isaiah 62:1–5

This was probably a song used to accompany a pilgrimage to Jerusalem. It is quite appropriate that this reading begins the Christmas celebration. It is a joyful exclamation that the day of salvation has arrived. Obviously, Christianity connected the object of Israel's joy to that which is celebrated today, the Incarnation of God's Son. The conferral of a new name designated God's almighty power over creation. When one was given a new name, that

---

[4]Christmas Vigil Mass: "Entrance Antiphon," *The Sacramentary.*
[5]Christmas Vigil Mass: "Opening Prayer," *The Sacramentary.*
[6]The exegesis for the first and second readings may or may not be the focus of your group's reflection as there may only be time to give adequate attention to the gospel, your primary concern. However, the exegesis is included here in order to provide a thorough investigation of the entire liturgy of the word as there may be parts (or all) that would be necessary to the direction you wish to take with your particular ministry group.

person was made a new creation. "To give a name is also to take possession." [7]

Responsorial Psalm
Psalm 89:4–5, 16–17, 27–29

In the first reading, Isaiah proclaims the covenant love between Yahweh and his people. The vigil of Christmas hearkens back to this covenant as it is fulfilled in the nativity of the messiah. The responsorial psalm sings of the covenant Yahweh made with Israel. This covenant is fulfilled in and through the Incarnation of Christ.

Second Reading
Acts 13:16–17, 22–25

Today's pericope consists of portions from Paul's speech in which Paul recaps Israel's salvation history and the arrival of the promised messianic era. Paul insists that Jesus and the message he came to preach belong to Israel's history. Jesus was the fulfillment of Israel's messianic hopes. Therefore, as rightful heirs of the messianic promise, Israel was entitled to be the first recipient of the good news. Paul acknowledges the election of Israel by Yahweh. He makes the case that the salvation history begun in the Old Testament is fulfilled in Christ. The Baptist played a role similar to Samuel's when he inaugurated the first of the line of ancient kings. John heralded the messiah who was foretold of old and who was the rightful heir to the messianic throne.

Gospel
Matthew 1:1–25

The genealogy of Jesus is proclaimed.

STEP 1
NAMING ONE'S EXPERIENCE

What were your first impressions? What was your first response? What captured your attention? How did the readings affect you?

Each person names his or her initial impression. Statements should be brief. No reasons should be given at this time. All simply listen without agreeing or disagreeing.

---

[7]*DL* (I), 196.

STEP 2
UNDERSTANDING

In a brief statement, what do you think this gospel is trying to convey?

STEP 3
INPUT FROM VISION/STORY/TRADITION

Liturgical Context[8]

The vigil mass is the least celebrated. It may be celebrated before or after the first vespers of Christmas. If this mass is not celebrated, the readings and prayers may be used for prayer and meditation in preparation for celebration of the feast.

A brief background will be given for the readings. Since the genealogy from Matthew's gospel is rarely heard by a gathered assembly, it is important to note that its message is worthy of serious consideration and contemplation.

In the first reading we hear that God espouses Israel. God weds humanity. One is reminded of a similar marriage metaphor sung at the Easter Vigil, the "mother of all feasts." God's betrothal to Israel culminates in the wedding event of salvation. God espouses his people. The song of the Easter Vigil is: "This is the night when heaven is wedded to earth and humanity is reconciled with God!" (Exsultet). The vigil announces the inauguration of that paschal event.

Gospel Exegesis

The facilitator gives input regarding what critical biblical scholarship has to say about this text. The input includes insights as to how people would have heard the gospel in Jesus' time.

---

[8]The scriptures in the Lectionary, the seasons of the year, and the ritual prayers of the mass are interrelated and form the basis for liturgical catechesis. The liturgical context attempts to explore and clarify the themes and this interrelatedness.

Genealogies are rarely read at liturgies. According to Raymond Brown, we miss a very important piece of salvation history if we ignore the genealogy of Jesus. Matthew's intent is to trace Jesus' origins to the house of David through Joseph. Even though Joseph was not the biological father of Jesus (the Holy Spirit is the creative power behind the conception of Christ), he was the legal[9] father because of his betrothal to Mary. Jesus, then, is rightful heir to the house of David. He possesses the necessary pedigree to claim the messianic title.

Brown asserts that the genealogy is told in order to highlight the paradox of a God who writes the story of salvation with "crooked lines." "A God who did not hesitate to use the scheming as well as the noble, the impure as well as the pure, men to whom the world hearkened and women upon whom the world frowned—this God continues to work in the same mélange."[10] The genealogy shows that God used ordinary, unknown men and women to be part of the greatest story ever told. "The message of the genealogy is an enabling invitation."[11]

God chose scoundrels and saints to be in this many-act play called salvation. There was one who pilfered his brother's birthright and one who sold his brother into slavery. God used people who would never stand up to human scrutiny. From the very beginning, God used questionable people to participate in the grand design, just like Jesus would do in his ministry to the prostitutes and tax collectors. The cast of characters in Matthew's genealogy includes scoundrel kings and the famous King David (who was not a paragon of virtue). Also included is a cast of extras, the long list of names we know nothing about. They remind us of our own minuscule place on the continuum of salvation history's time-line.

The genealogy names foreign prostitutes. It names women who give birth in questionable circumstances, and the last of these is Mary, pregnant and husband-less. God's design is certainly out of the imaginative world of human consciousness.

Yet, it stands as a clarion call, an invitation of immense significance for our lives. This God who used fallible, crafty, wily, saintly, and not-so-saintly human beings to usher in his reign continues to work with our frailty and our shortcomings.

Jesus entered our world with the intention of getting his hands dirty. He is not the image portrayed in saccharine art that shows him as a sweet, otherworldly, haloed being who exists out of our grasp or realm of understanding. Rather, the Jesus of Matthew's genealogy has a sordid family tree. He understands the "drunk uncle" hidden in everyone's closet. He understands the inherited sins of past generations. His ancestry includes the famed Davidic monarchy that, like the sinful church of any age, was used by God in spite of its corruption, sin, and vanity. Nevertheless, it was to be a vehicle for God's plan of redemption, just as the church has been and always will be. He stands as a beacon of light in the midst of relational darkness.

The genealogy portrays the unfathomable deeds of God and the gratuitous grace that has been poured out upon the world since the beginning of time, in spite of us and in communion with us. Jesus is the ultimate expression of that grace. Through his life, death, and resurrection Christ pours out a newer and fuller portion to sustain the church until his promised return.

One cannot miss the Old Testament parallels in the Matthean account of the infancy narrative. Joseph went to Egypt as a result of a dream. Joseph of the Old Testament went to Egypt for the same reason. Jesus' escape from Herod is like Moses' escape from Pharaoh. Pharaoh was warned by his scribes of the threat the child Moses posed to his throne. Pharaoh killed all the male children as a result. Moses' father was given the revelation in a dream that his pregnant wife would bear a child who would save Israel. The pre-warned parents were able to save the child from slaughter. One need not cite the obvious similarities between Herod and Pharaoh.

In the Old Testament Balaam was summoned from the East by Pharaoh to destroy Moses. David was understood as the *star* prophesied by Balaam. Instead of destroying Moses, Balaam told of the Davidic monarchy that would one day rise. "Just as

---

[9]Legal fatherhood was not a status that required physical fatherhood.

[10]*CCA*, 25.

[11]Ibid.

Balaam saw the star of David rise, the New Testament magi saw the star of the King of the Jews at its rising."[12]

Matthew uses the events of this story to follow a pattern used throughout his gospel: the good news was proclaimed, followed by a response of acceptance or rejection. Matthew begins his story in anticipation of the path that the gospel would take following Jesus' resurrection. The good news would be proclaimed. People would either accept or reject it. The bottom line—God manifested himself to the world; he became "Emmanuel—God is with us." God became one with us through his Son who lived in the midst of the human story. The faithful who accepted Jesus' revelation experienced salvation, while others saw it as offensive and contradictory. Balaam could look to a future king David. The magi could look to a future day when Jesus' kingship would only be understood as he sat victorious at heaven's throne, having vanquished the cross's apparent sign of defeat.

Proclaim the gospel again.

Sometimes we gain new insights when we hear the text after the interpretation has been given. Someone from the group proclaims the gospel a second time.

STEP 4
TESTING

Conversation with the Liturgy and the Scriptures

Test your original understanding in dialogue with the text.

(You might consider breaking into smaller groups.)

How do you feel about Matthew's genealogy in light of the interpretation just given? Were there any new insights? How does your original understanding of this story compare with what was just shared? How does this story speak to your life?

---

[12]ACC, 12

Sharing Life Experience

I am reminded of the family trees we all bring with us into adulthood. Like Jesus, we all have our share of "drunk uncles" lurking in our dark closets. Yet, when we look at the stories of our lives we are often amazed at how God works in the midst of the darkened spaces in order to bring his light into our lives. I am reminded of the story of a deceased aunt (that I never knew) who had a very sad and sordid history that was the family's deepest, darkest secret. Our mother promised to tell us the secret after the death of one of her other relatives. Unfortunately, this relative outlived my mother and today none of us know this deep, dark secret.

This secret was the source of great shame to the relatives of my mother's generation. Yet I often wonder about Eleanor. What was her story? What was the secret? How was God present to this woman with the sordid past? Did she in any way impact the people in my mother's life? Did she know my mother and in any way influence her life, thereby in some way influencing me? Was her secret really so horrible, or was it nothing more than the judgmental musings of scrutinizing relatives? Rather than a scarlet letter, perhaps Eleanor wore a saint's halo in the mind and heart of God. I will never know the answers to those questions, but I often think about Eleanor when Matthew's genealogy is read. So many unknown saints and sinners were part of Jesus' family tree. Yet even though his lineage is laced with people of shame as well as virtue, God accomplished his will in the midst of Jesus' not-so-perfect family tree. God does not expect perfection. Very often we are ashamed of the "drunk uncles" in our lives and believe that we have to be a "holy family" before God works in our lives. The reading of the genealogy reminds us that God comes to us midst the imperfections. Jesus comes to the shame-filled. Jesus comes for the Eleanors of this world in order to turn their secrets into Good News. I celebrate Eleanor and thank God that Jesus came to shed light on the secrets we all bury in our dark closets. Jesus invites us into the light of his Incarnation where there is no room for shame.

Participants share their life experience in relation to the exegesis at this time.

What was Matthew trying to tell his community? What does he have to say to our community and to me today? How is God's covenant expressed in these readings? How is the theme of liberation and deliverance (exodus) expressed in this gospel? If God is always in the process of creating things anew, how is that expressed in the readings from this liturgy? Where is the challenge in Matthew's story-telling pattern: proclamation of the good news followed by the response of acceptance or rejection? How is God speaking to a people (community)? Do you still feel the same way about this text as you did when you began? Describe your understanding of this story now. Has your original understanding been stretched, challenged, or affirmed?

STEP 5
DECISION

The gospel demands a response.

How can Matthew's rendering of the genealogy possibly speak to a contemporary church? In what concrete way are we called to respond? Have I been changed in any way as a result of this sharing? What are the implications for my life? What is one concrete action I can take this week as a response to what we have learned and shared?

Christian Initiation: As there is little opportunity for most groups to reflect on the powerful implications of the readings in the vigil mass, perhaps a Christmas season retreat could center on all the readings of the Christmas liturgies.

MASS AT MIDNIGHT

INTRODUCTORY RITES

Opening Song (or Entrance Antiphon)

The Lord said to me: You are my Son; this day I have begotten you.[13]

---

[13]Christmas Mass at Midnight: "Entrance Antiphon," *The Sacramentary.*

Opening Prayer

The facilitator of the session may lead the prayer. Others in the group could be asked to proclaim the readings.

Let us pray
[with joy and hope
as we await the dawning of the Father's Word]

Pause for silent prayer.

Lord our God,
with the birth of your Son,
your glory breaks on the world.
Through the night hours of the darkened earth
we your people watch for the coming of your
    promised Son.
As we wait, give us a foretaste of the joy that you
    will grant us
when the fullness of his glory has filled the earth,
who lives and reigns with you for ever and ever.[14]

LITURGY OF THE WORD

The readings are proclaimed.

Let us listen to God's word.

First Reading
Isaiah 9:1–6

In order to appreciate this reading in light of the Christmas event, it is important to look at the situation and the story that defines it in the book of the prophet Isaiah. King Ahaz, the youthful king of Judah (Southern Kingdom), inherited a throne in which the political problems were no match for him. The king of the Northern Kingdom (Israel) had made an alliance with Assyria. This infuriated the people, as it drastically raised their taxes. A group from the western part of the country joined forces with Damascus to overthrow Assyria, which had joined forces with Israel in the north. Thus, the Southern Kingdom, Judah, was a prime target for overthrow. King Ahaz was panic stricken and felt drawn to join forces with the North, and thus with Assyria. Isaiah met Ahaz and told him to trust Yahweh and be calm. He told Ahaz that the only

---

[14]Christmas Mass at Midnight: "Alternative Opening Prayer," *The Sacramentary.*

way to deal with the crisis was to maintain a relaxed reliance on Yahweh who was far greater than any human power. God was in covenant relationship with Judah and therefore would not abandon them. Nor would God think of abandoning the promise made to David regarding David's everlasting dynasty. Isaiah assured Ahaz that he must have faith. If his faith was secure, his throne would also be secure.

Isaiah was telling Ahaz to be strong and to resist the temptation to unite with Syria and Israel in the north. Yahweh would protect them. Ahaz did not listen to Isaiah. Isaiah promised Ahaz a sign of assurance that Yahweh would do as promised. Ahaz told Isaiah that he was not interested in asking for a sign; he would not think of putting Yahweh to the test. Isaiah became angry and told Ahaz that Yahweh would offer a sign to the house of David—to David's dynasty, not to Ahaz. The sign would confirm that the northern alliance was doomed and that God would be faithful to the promise made to David. "The purpose of a sign [in biblical history] was to make visible and to confirm dramatically the truth and power of Yahweh's word spoken by the prophet. A sign does not necessarily have to be a miracle, in our sense of the word, for its significance is not so much in its unusual character as in its power to confirm a prophetic word spoken in threat or promise."[15] The ability to see signs was an important part of Israel's faith. It enabled them to perceive God acting in human history.

Isaiah's sign was the promised birth of a child whose name was Immanuel (God is with us). Isaiah prophesied that the birth was imminent. He believed the mother to be already pregnant. One might ask how the coming of a child could be a sign for Ahaz. Isaiah attested that, unlike Ahaz, the child would be a faithful, steadfast leader of the people. Isaiah prophesied in response to a current crisis in his time. He had no idea that this prophecy would become the basis for the Jewish hope in a future messiah. Isaiah's song in chapter 7 became a part of the prophetic messianic tradition. This "child to come" was to share the suffering of his people. The child would usher in an age of judgment and an opportunity for new beginnings.

In Isaiah's prophecy the child was feasting on milk and honey, a reference to the milk and honey found in the promised land. Those listening to Isaiah realized from that reference that this child would be a sign of hope following a dismal time of misery and tribulation. "For Yahweh's purpose is not to destroy, but to refine and cleanse a remnant people. Once the Assyrian yoke is overturned the child will ascend the throne as the agent of God's rule over the people. Then the meaning of his name Immanuel will be clearly understood."[16] The early Christian community used this prophecy as the foundation for their belief in Jesus as messiah. This prophetic hymn of Isaiah sings of hope in the messiah, fulfilled in the person of Jesus Christ: Wonder Counselor, Mighty God, Everlasting Father, Prince of Peace!

Responsorial Psalm
Psalm 96:1–2a, 2b–3, 11–12, 13

The new song referred to in the psalm is the song to be sung when the messiah redeems the world. It will replace the old song sung when Moses delivered the people out of bondage.

Second Reading
Titus 2:11–14

The letter to Titus was written not to a community, but rather to an individual in regard to his pastoral duties. There are two other such letters, and they are referred to as the "pastoral epistles." There is some question as to whether Paul wrote these letters. Some believe that the letters might have been written by a disciple(s) who was trying to "publish the sort of letter he thought the master might have written had he still been alive."[17]

The reading of Titus reminds us that Advent prepared us for two comings. We do not forget the second coming of Christ even as we are steeped in celebration and remembrance of his first coming. Christ will come again; we are to live noble lives. Robert Karris asserts: "These verses are fitting for Christmas because they invite us to contemplate the new born babe as God's gracious appearance for our salvation."[18]

---

[15] *UOT*, 331–334.

[16] Ibid.
[17] *GAP*, 128.
[18] *PE*, 112.

The overall theme of the letter to Titus is that we are not to retreat from the world. We are to be a sign in the world. We are to live upright lives as we go about the task of life, remembering as we go that our final fulfillment will take place when Christ comes again.

Gospel
Luke 2:1–14

The angels appear to the shepherds and the heavenly hosts sing God's praises and announce the arrival of the messiah.

STEP 1
NAMING ONE'S EXPERIENCE

What were your first impressions? What was your first response? What understanding of this story did you bring with you to this conversation? How did the readings affect you?

Each person names his or her initial impression. Statements should be brief. No reasons should be given at this time. All simply listen without agreeing or disagreeing.

STEP 2
UNDERSTANDING

In a brief statement, what do you think this gospel is trying to convey?

STEP 3
INPUT FROM VISION/STORY/TRADITION

Liturgical Context

Read the overview of Christmas. The Christmas readings proclaim for us the reason we gather to remember the nativity event. They unfold for us a refined Christian understanding of the Incarnation. The opening prayer and the prefaces help us focus on the theological meaning of the celebration. God sent his Son as a human being to the world to redeem the world. Jesus is both fully human and fully divine. We became heirs to

Christ's divinity through his Incarnation and subsequent life, death, and resurrection. We will share eternal life with him because of the nativity and the event for which he was born: his death and resurrection. We still wait in hope for his return.

Gospel Exegesis

The facilitator gives input regarding what critical biblical scholarship has to say about this text. The input includes insights as to how people would have heard the gospel in Jesus' time.

Our culture has so romanticized and consumerized Christmas that it is difficult to remember that the scriptures of the Christmas liturgies are not intended as detailed historical narratives (while they are nonetheless historical), but as a means of communicating the awesome reality of God's explosion into human history through the person of Jesus Christ.

The story of Jesus' birth is told as good news. Why good news? Charles Talbert tells us that in the Mediterranean world every time a great ruler was born, the benefits to the people were announced. The newborn ruler was often called a savior who would bring peace. Jesus, the new ruler, the one who came to fulfill the ancient prophecies, "who has on his birthday a proclamation of the benefits of his birth,"[19] is truly good news.

Shalom (peace), according to Hebrew understanding, meant wholeness, the right ordering of relationships with one another, with God, with the earth, and with oneself. "Peace became an eschatological hope."[20] To be at peace meant that one was in complete harmony with God, neighbor, creation, and self. Obviously, the only place where the perfection of such harmony is realized is in the eternal hereafter.

Luke situates his gospel in the context of the current political situation. Persecutions were taking place when Luke was writing his account. In Luke's gospel, the origin of the child Jesus is

---

[19]*RL*, 32.
[20]Ibid.

traced back to two small inconsequential towns, Nazareth and Bethlehem. Jesus was born to poor parents. He was not what one would consider "royal material" in the earthly sense of the word. Certainly, it would be difficult to imagine one so lowly laying claim to the political power of the reigning imperial authority. Luke made it clear that the kingship of Jesus has more to do with spiritual realities than with governmental overthrow. The logical extension to this carefully devised genesis is that Jesus' followers are part of his heritage and thus are not a threat to political authority. Read: there is no reason to persecute the church.

The image of shepherds has been over-sentimentalized throughout history. Shepherds were despised individuals and considered to be in the same category as tax collectors and prostitutes. "Their testimony was not considered valid because of their reputation for dishonesty."[21] The message cannot be missed. God comes for the outcast, for those everyone hates, disregards, and leaves behind as useless. God's salvation is for everybody. The shepherds are the first to whom the message is told. Perhaps they needed it the most. This is not the last time we will hear this message from Luke.

"Angels who bring messages to accompany events are the biblical way of expressing the meaning of salvation as an act of God."[22] There are two visitations from angels in Luke's story. The first announces the birth of the messiah. The second appearance comes in the form of the heavenly host. They announce that God's favor has come to people of good will. Reginald Fuller tells us that "people of good will" is not a term of exclusion. In Hebrew, "people of good will" referred to all people who, because of this event, were the object of divine favor.[23] It also appears as if the angels came to proclaim Jesus' name and his identity. However, Eugene LaVerdiere tells us that "Luke's main point, which links God's glory in the highest with peace on earth for the humble, would have been lost had the passage merely raised the matter of Jesus' identity. The narrative called for a manifestation of Jesus' life and mission, a statement which would anticipate the actual unfolding of the implications of his name."[24] Luke's purpose is christological and ecclesial. Christ's mission is named and the church "is identified as the humble recipient and proclaimer of the gospel."[25]

Proclaim the gospel again.

Sometimes we gain new insights when we hear the text after the interpretation is given. Someone from the group proclaims the gospel a second time.

STEP 4
TESTING

Conversation with the Liturgy and the Scriptures

Test your original understanding in dialogue with the text.

(You might consider breaking into smaller groups.)

Now that you've heard what the scholars have to say about Luke's version of the nativity narrative, how do you feel about it? Were there any new insights? Was there anything you had not considered before? How does your original understanding of this story compare with what was just shared? How does this story speak to your life?

Sharing Life Experience

Participants share something from their lives that connects with the exegesis just given.

> *I am reminded of the Christmas season a few years ago when, as part of an evening of music and poetry, a group of beautiful liturgical dancers artistically pirouetted their way to the Christmas crèche accompanied by angelic voices blended in harmonious exultation of the God who comes to us in the flesh. It all sounds very beautiful and holy, doesn't it? Well it was; that is, until we spotted something happening in the back of the dancers' line. Someone (who was certainly not wrapped in the swaddling garb of angelic chiffon) decided it was appropriate to join the dancers in their gestures of praise. Bringing up the rear behind six beautiful young women*

[21]Ibid., 33.
[22]*PNL,* 467.
[23]Ibid.

[24]*LK,* 33.
[25]Ibid.

was one slovenly drunk who not-so-gracefully joined the parade—pirouettes, twists, turns, and all. I was horrified that such a beautifully choreographed work was being destroyed so haphazardly and with unconscious, alcoholic disdain. Later in the evening, there was a piece of poetry that echoed in wretched despair for those who, on Christmas night and every night, have no place to call home. Is there no place to be found where human choruses welcome the world's homeless into the sacred halls of their incense-soaked cathedrals? Suddenly, there was something very paradoxical about the scene. Christ exploded into the world for this very outcast, society's lowest. If our drunken visitor had been the only one, Christ still would have come. We cannot imagine and feel we do not deserve love like that! Who would listen, if he, like the shepherds, were to be visited by heavenly hosts with tidings of great joy? Would anybody listen?

All share at this time.

What was Luke trying to tell his community? How does the image of the shepherds resonate with our experience of the Christmas story? How does it feel to have our sentimental understanding of the Christmas story challenged? If the shepherds were unsavory characters, yet the angels appeared first to them, what is the message for our community? How would it be received? Do we still feel the same way about this text as we did when we began? What is our understanding of this story now? Has our original understanding been stretched, challenged, or affirmed?

STEP 5
DECISION

The gospel demands a response.

What would be the contemporary implications of the angels' message to the shepherds? What would be the implication for our communities today? In what concrete ways should we respond? Has this conversation with the exegesis of this Christmas gospel changed or stretched my personal attitudes? What are the implications of Jesus' Incarnation for my own life? What should be my/our response?

MASS AT DAWN

Proclaim the readings from the mass at dawn. If time is limited, focus on the gospel.

First Reading
Isaiah 62:11–12

Trito-Isaiah, the third book of Isaiah, is concerned with the sin of the people. Their sin delays salvation. Nevertheless, they still believe that salvation is not far off. Trito-Isaiah sees salvation as a new creation very much like the creation of Genesis. Judgment is harsh. In this brief pericope for use at the mass at dawn we experience the joy of the new Israel at the arrival of "messianic salvation."[26]

Responsorial Psalm
Psalm 97:1, 6, 11–12

This is an enthronement psalm. One cannot miss the light imagery and its connection with the Christmas theme of the dawning of light.

Second Reading
Titus 3:4–7

Hubert Richards cites this passage from Titus as a "fine summary of the gospel Paul made his own; it is no wonder it has been chosen as one of the readings for the Christmas liturgy. It has a lyric quality...."[27] In this third chapter of Titus, Paul points out the wonders of God. He proclaims that God is all good and wishes nothing less than the very best for his children: wholeness and salvation. Paul insists that we are to imitate God's love for us and treat others accordingly. Because we have been so gratuitously loved, we in turn must live in love and give in love. God would do no less for us. It is what God would want us to do. Paul echoes what appears to be a familiar understanding of Jewish spirituality. Covenant people are to work toward the ordering of right relationships (*hesed*). We are in *hesed* relationship when our relationships with God, one another, ourselves, and the earth are in right order. These relationships, of course, are informed by the great law of love, evidenced by our behavior to the least of God's people.

---

[26]*PNL*, 467.
[27]*GAP*, 133.

Paul provides us with a familiar schema. Robert Karris suggests that there is a movement of transformation in the *then/now* assumption apparent in this text. We were once this way, but now we are a different way. We have been made a new creation through our baptism in Jesus. We were once children in darkness, but not anymore. Now we are children in the light. Citing its use of the pronouns *we/us* rather than *you*, Karris also suggests that this pericope was once a ritual prayer used in liturgy. Titus 3:4–7 is believed to be part of an ancient baptismal hymn of thanksgiving. We give thanks that we have been made new creations in Christ through the refreshing waters of baptism. At baptism we receive the Spirit and wait in hope for the life we will share in eternity. At our baptism we share in what God accomplished through Jesus' entrance into human history at his nativity and subsequent pasch: the salvation of the world. We are to go forth transformed and make a difference in our respective worlds. "Paul insists that liturgy begets daily Christian life."[28] Paul stated that we are justified by faith and are heirs of eternal life (Ti 3:7). Through the Incarnation, we share in Jesus' divinity.

Gospel
Luke 2:15–20

The shepherds speak among themselves of the wonderful good news and decide to go and see for themselves.

STEP 1
NAMING ONE'S EXPERIENCE

What were your first impressions? What was your first response? What grabbed your attention? How did you feel?

Each person names his or her initial impression. Statements should be brief. No reasons should be given at this time. All simply listen without agreeing or disagreeing.

---

[28]*PE*, 124.

STEP 2
UNDERSTANDING

In a brief statement, what do you think this gospel is trying to convey?

STEP 3
INPUT FROM VISION/TRADITION/STORY

Liturgical Context

The light motif is even more prominent in the liturgy for the mass at dawn than it is at the midnight mass. The responsorial psalm, the entrance antiphon, and the opening prayer speak of the light that will shine this day on us and on our actions.

Gospel Exegesis

The facilitator gives input regarding what critical biblical scholarship has to say about this text. The input includes insights as to how people would have heard the gospel in Jesus' time.

This gospel is an extension of the story begun at the midnight mass. Again, we know these culturally sentimentalized stories so well that it is often easy to be blinded by their significance. Jesus came for the outcast. Shepherds were outcasts, despised and considered dishonest. Yet they were the ones who saw the Christ child. They were the ones who heard the heavenly hosts singing the hymn of praise and announcing *shalom*/peace (wholeness, *hesed*). Perhaps we could call these outcasts the first evangelists. They were the first to spread and tell the good news. Would anybody believe their testimony?

Proclaim the gospel again.

Sometimes we gain new insights when we hear the text after the interpretation is given. Someone from the group proclaims the gospel a second time.

STEP 4
TESTING

Conversation with the Liturgy and the Scriptures

Test your original understanding in dialogue with the text.

(You might consider breaking into smaller groups.)

How does it feel that some of our traditional assumptions about the Christmas story are brought into question by contemporary scholarship? How do you feel about the image of the shepherds portrayed by the scholars? How does this story speak to your life? What was Luke trying to tell his community? What does he have to say to you and to your community today? What do the Christmas readings say about God/Jesus? Do you still feel the same way about this text as you did when you began? Describe your understanding of this story now. Has your original understanding been stretched, challenged, or affirmed?

STEP 5
DECISION

The gospel demands a response.

How do these readings for Christmas challenge me and the community to action? Where is growth needed in my community, in me? What am I going to do about it?

MASS DURING THE DAY

Proclaim the readings from the mass during the day. If time is limited, focus on the gospel.

First Reading
Isaiah 52:7–10

The people of Israel had the ability to view their lives in relationship to the mighty acts of God.

They possessed a corporate conscience that allowed them to see the events of their lives in relationship to the Yahweh who saved, judged, forgave, punished, rewarded, and ordained their very life breath. Their optimism in the face of despair and oppression was of heroic proportions. Even though their exile was moving into a second generation, their hope for restoration was not to be squelched. The bondage that had ravaged their identity had the purging, yet freeing effect of giving definition to their lives.

Prophets such as Deutero-Isaiah helped them examine themselves and in the process they were formed in the heart and will of God. When it was time for their deliverance, joy overflowed and exultation filled the heart of a nation. It is this joyful song we hear from the prophet on Christmas morn. Their vindication had arrived. They were delivered from bondage. The dawn of God's saving might was upon the earth.

One need not wonder why Isaiah was chosen to sing this privileged song of joy in the liturgy of Christmas morning. It was this very event, the Christ event, that he foreshadowed in his eschatological hymn. During the time of Deutero-Isaiah, messianic prophecies began to include an eschatological element, a future hope of deliverance at the consummation of the world. Jesus ushers in the last days through his Incarnation. There was reason for joy.

Responsorial Psalm
Psalm 98:1, 2–3, 3–4, 5–6

All of the psalms of Christmas are enthronement psalms. They praise God for the acts of salvation and are most appropriate on this day of salvation.

Second Reading
Hebrews 1:1–6

St. Paul's letter to the Hebrews is not a letter at all, but rather, a *logos* of encouragement for the community. A logos was a public address, very much like a homily. This opening address is a christological hymn of praise with roots in Jewish praise of Lady Wisdom. Wisdom was personified and considered to be with God in the act of creation. Wisdom also was the agent of God's revelation of self to Israel. The early Christian community appropriated that understanding to Jesus. Jesus assumes the role of One who was with God from the beginning in the work of salvation.

Gospel
John 1:1–18 or 1:1–5, 9–14

STEP 1
NAMING ONE'S EXPERIENCE

What were your first impressions? What captured your attention?

Each person names his or her initial impression. Statements should be brief. No reasons should be given at this time. All simply listen without agreeing or disagreeing.

STEP 2
UNDERSTANDING

In a brief statement, what do you think this gospel is trying to convey?

STEP 3
INPUT FROM VISION/STORY/TRADITION

Liturgical Context

Prior to Vatican II, the prologue to John's gospel was read at the end of every mass, thus recalling for the faithful the salvation event of God through the Incarnation of the Son.

"Christmas is a feast that celebrates our redemption even though the focus of attention is on the Incarnation and the 'marvelous exchange' and not on the passion and resurrection."[29] This is clearly expressed in the second reading: "He cleansed us from our sins and took his seat at the right hand of the majesty in Heaven…"(Heb 1:3). The gospel for the mass during the day uses John's prologue to proclaim the mystery of the Incarnation. God speaks a definitive *Word* to the

---

[29]*DL* (I), 128.

world and to Israel. Salvation was at hand. The *Word* had been spoken. John's prologue and the letter to the Hebrews emphasize that the Christmas liturgy is more than a mere celebration of a baby's birth. It is God's center-stage act of communication with the world. (On this day, one might consider using the shorter form of the reading, since the longer form, including reference to John the Baptist, contains what is believed to be a later addition to the original hymn.)

This liturgy celebrates the great expression of joy inherent in all of the Christmas readings. The mystery of Jesus' Incarnation is raised to a cosmic level. John reminds us in his prologue that we must return to the beginning and remember that God began the Christmas story at the creation of the world. God had always intended that humanity be heirs of eternal life with him. We must look at the nativity alongside the cross and resurrection. Christmas is viewed through the lens of Easter.

Gospel Exegesis

The facilitator gives input regarding what critical biblical scholarship has to say about this text. The input includes insights as to how people would have heard the gospel in Jesus' time.

The prologue serves as a preface to John's gospel. It is theological and its purpose is to establish the thesis for the entire book. John's gospel tells the stories of Christ from the perspective that God, even from the beginning, from before time, from the eternal past, had been in the process of communicating. To be God means to reveal God. Creation was an act of God's self-communication. God's revelation to Israel was a continuation of his continuous activity of self-revelation. Jesus, then, was the definitive, incarnate expression of God's self-communication to Israel.

Reginald Fuller suggests that the Word became flesh throughout Jesus' entire ministry. Through Jesus' life and miracles God continued the process of revealing self to the world. Jesus manifested God to humanity. In John's prologue, *flesh* refers to all human history since the very beginning, the creation of the world. All that God had done *for* and *with* Israel is brought to this moment, to this defining moment of salvation. All of God's deeds up to this point are understood in light of God's premier saving event: the spoken Word of God, in human form, given as ultimate gift of self, to suffer for the sins of the world.

John's gospel was written in response to the situation at the end of the century in which belief in Christ's divinity was questioned. John made his case by proclaiming that Christ was a part of God's action at creation. Jesus was present at God's first act of salvation (creation) and awaited his entrance into the world (Incarnation) to inaugurate God's last, conclusive act of salvation.

Patricia Datchuck Sanchez offers an interesting observation. The Semitic understanding of the word *logos* was "a challenge a believer can accept or reject."[30] A *logos* from God could be accepted or rejected. Thus the believer was faced with a decision and a response. The Greek understanding of *logos* was "an intermediary between God and the created universe."[31] The *logos* brought order to the universe. Therefore, according to Hellenistic thought, the one who embraced the *logos* would have access to the mysteries of the heavens. John is familiar with both constructs and cleverly uses both meanings in defining the ultimate mystery of Christ. Christ is the one who invites and calls people to faith, but he is also the one who reveals the face of God to the world.

Proclaim the gospel again.

Sometimes we gain new insights when we hear the text after the interpretation has been given. Someone from the group proclaims the gospel a second time.

STEP 4
TESTING

Conversation with the Liturgy and the Scriptures

Test your original understanding in dialogue with the text.

---
[30]*WWC*, 274.
[31]Ibid.

(You might consider breaking into smaller groups.)

How does John's prologue speak to you? Did the exegesis offer any new insights? How does your original understanding of this Christmas gospel compare with the interpretation? Does John's description of Christ as the eternal spoken Word of God have anything to do with your life? If so, how? What relevance does it have today? What was John trying to say to his community? What does he have to say to your community and to you today? Do you still feel the same way about this text as you did at the beginning? Describe your understanding of this story now.

STEP 5
DECISION

The gospel demands a response.

How should our community respond to this word from John? If we accept the Semitic understanding of *logos*, how might Christ be challenging us in this reading, or in all of the readings of Christmas? What one specific, concrete thing can I do during this season to respond to the word spoken today?

DOCTRINAL ISSUES

What church truth/teaching/doctrinal issue could be drawn from the readings for Christmas ?

Participants suggest possible doctrinal themes that flow from the readings.

Possible Doctrinal Themes

Incarnation; christology; manifestation; salvation; soteriology

Present the doctrinal material at this time.

1. The facilitator gives input on a particular doctrinal issue of his/her prior choosing. OR
2. The group chooses a doctrinal issue from the list they created. They read together from the Doctrinal Appendix.

(The doctrinal issues are found in the Doctrinal Appendix in the back of this workbook. If you are choosing an issue from this resource, please refer to it now.)

Reflection questions centered around the chosen doctrinal theme can be found at the end of each topic in the Doctrinal Appendix. The questions are based on the five-step reflection process. If you choose a topic not included in the Doctrinal Appendix, craft your own questions according to the same five-step process.

Following the reflection questions you will be reminded to return to chapter 7, "Preparing the Catechetical Session," to assist you in crafting your own session.

Closing Prayer

Father, all powerful and ever living God,
we do well always and everywhere to give you thanks
through Jesus Christ our Lord.
Today in him a new light has dawned upon the
     world:
God has become one with man,
and man has become one again with God.
Your eternal Word has taken upon himself our
     human weakness,
giving our mortal nature immortal value.
So marvelous is this oneness between God and
     man
that in Christ man restores to man the gift of ever-
     lasting life.
In our joy we sing to your glory
with all the choirs of angels:
All sing or say: Holy, holy, holy, Lord, God of
     power and might,
heaven and earth are full of your glory.
Hosanna in the highest.
Blessed is he who comes in the name of the Lord.
Hosanna in the highest.[32]

---

[32]Christmas Preface III, *The Sacramentary.*

FEAST OF THE HOLY FAMILY

Environment

The environment does not change as it is still the Christmas season.

INTRODUCTORY RITES

Entrance Antiphon (or Opening Song)

The shepherds hastened to Bethlehem, where they found Mary and Joseph, and the baby lying in a manger.[1]

Opening Prayer

The facilitator of the session may lead the prayer. Others in the group may be asked to proclaim the readings.

Let us pray
[for peace in our families]

> *Pause for silent prayer.*

Father in heaven, creator of all,
you ordered the earth to bring forth life
and crowned its goodness by creating the family of
    man.
In history's moment when all was ready,
you sent your Son to dwell in time,
obedient to the laws of life in our world.
Teach us the sanctity of human love,
show us the value of family life,
and help us to live in peace with all men
that we may share in your life forever.
We ask this through Christ, our Lord.[2]

LITURGY OF THE WORD

Today it would be important to pay particular attention to all of the readings. Taken together they better express the meaning of this feast. You might want to give particular attention to the second reading.

---

[1]Feast of the Holy Family: "Entrance Antiphon," *The Sacramentary.*

[2]Feast of the Holy Family: "Alternative Opening Prayer," *The Sacramentary.*

Year ABC First Reading

Sirach 3:2–6, 12–14

Overview of Sirach: The Wisdom literature contained in the Book of Sirach was written by the person it was named after—a rare occurrence in biblical literature. It is one of the longest works in the Bible. In some translations it is referred to as "Ecclesiasticus," probably meaning the ecclesiastical book or the Church book.

Ben Sira wrote Sirach around 180 B.C. He was an educated man whose main writing concerns were reflection on the Torah and practical suggestions for upright living. He studied the Law, Prophets, and Writings and as scribe and teacher ran a school for young Jewish men.[3] Ben Sira also traveled extensively and studied the cultures of the places he visited. He gleaned much from the Wisdom traditions of those places. He included and incorporated the best of what he learned (as long as it did not compromise his Jewish beliefs, tradition, or heritage) into his teaching.

Sirach wrote his treatise on wisdom not for personal gain, but for those who sought after it. Even though the pagan philosophies of Hellenism were on the rise, his aim was not to argue against the emerging cultural trends. He simply wished to show that the Jewish life was far superior to the emerging Hellenistic culture. True wisdom had its center in Jerusalem, not Athens. Thus, good Jews should avoid the influence and lure of the new philosophies and temptations of the Greek culture.

The Book of Sirach was not accepted in the Hebrew and Protestant canons. The reason for its omission in the Jewish canon is probably due to the first-century Pharisees' dislike of the theology it contained (such as Sirach's denial of retribution in the afterlife). It was nevertheless much quoted by later rabbis. The early church fathers strongly attested to its canonicity. The Sirach text was used

---

[3]Alexander A. Di Lella, O.F.M., *JBC,* 496.

in Christian worship more than any other text with the exception of the psalms.

Today's Pericope: Sirach offers a commentary on the fifth commandment—to honor one's parents. When one follows this command, a multitude of sins are forgotten. Sirach was so serious about the Law's exhortation that to break the Law was considered tantamount to breaking the covenant relationship with God.

Israel was in covenant relationship with Yahweh (*hesed*). This *hesed* assumed a reciprocity in which love for one another flowed out of the love of God. The first persons deserving of *hesed* were one's parents. When a person uprightly and justly followed the Law, he or she could expect mercy, blessings, and God's forgiveness. Children were to respect and care for their parents. Parents who raised their children in righteousness could expect their children to be firmly planted in the faith of Israel. Children who did not heed their parents could expect to be uprooted from their firm foundation.

It was suggested in the Law that anyone who does not treat the aged with care and concern is guilty of blasphemy. The challenge of this scripture is very clear. Dysfunctional family systems were not tolerated in ancient Israel. It was assumed that all people live in the harmony God expected.

Family was a very important reality for Israel. The clan, the tribe, extended family, the people of God, all represented a form of family that was in covenant relationship with Yahweh. Covenant assumed a great respect and care for one another.

Year B First Reading

In Year B this reading may be used. Optional: Genesis 15:1–6, 21:1–3.

(Please refer to the tenth Sunday in Ordinary Time for an overview of the Book of Genesis.)

Today's Pericope: The Priestly writers introduce the story of Terah, father of Abraham (stories of individuals are introduced by the name of the father), the first ancestors of Israel.[4] We are given the rich story of our first ancestors in faith, Abraham and Sarah. Abraham, the father of a great nation, whose descendants were to be as numerous as the stars, and Sarah, who laughed over the prospects that in her old age she would bear a child, are wonderful icons for us today as we celebrate this Feast of the Holy Family. Their escapades as they forged their way and formed themselves as God's people are reminiscent of the struggles faced by families today.

The Abraham and Sarah story begins in the eleventh chapter of Genesis and continues through the twenty-fifth. There is an internal structure in the stories that takes the form of ten trials and seven blessings. "In the first trial Abraham receives a general divine promise; after each trial he receives consolation in the form of renewed assurances."[5]

Abraham was commanded by Yahweh to leave his native land and go to a land that Yahweh would designate. God promised blessings on Abraham and on his family life. Yahweh told Abraham that he would be a blessing to the people—they would use Abraham as a sign of God's blessing. Abraham followed a route to Shechem, Bethel, and then Negeb. Later Jacob, then Joshua, would follow the same route. The biblical authors posited a foretaste of what would happen to Abraham's later descendants. Abraham acknowledged Yahweh as Lord of the land.

Abraham's story is a chronicle of a family who placed their trust in Yahweh to lead and guide them throughout their life's sojourn. Today's reading marks a new episode in the Abraham saga. Yahweh promises Abraham a son and an heir. Abraham grumbled that he had still not been granted the one thing he desires—a son to carry on his name. At the rate he was going he would die without a child and would end up leaving all to his steward. God promised Abraham that his progeny would be as numerous as the stars. Not only does God promise Abraham an heir, God also promises that a great nation would descend from him. Abraham trusted Yahweh and thus found favor.

---

[4] Richard J. Clifford, S.J., "Genesis," *NJBC*, 19.

[5] Ibid.

Scrolling ahead in the Abraham and Sarah saga to chapter 21, we find that God's promise to the childless couple had been fulfilled. Isaac was born. The divine promise had been fulfilled. The birth of Isaac is a turning point in the story of Abraham and Sarah. This story was Israel's corporate myth and had been told from campfire to campfire for many generations before it was written. It was primary to their identity as a people.

Sarah did become pregnant when God stated she would the year before. Isaac was named a name that means "May God laugh in delight, smile upon." Isaac's name is a reminder that the former skepticism about this birth was unwarranted—God accomplished God's Word and provided Abraham not only with a family, but with a family that would last forever and whose name would be remembered for all generations. The couple is a reminder to us all of what can happen when we put our faith in God.

Year C First Reading

In Year C this reading may be used. Optional: 1 Samuel 1:20–22, 24–28.

(Please refer to the second Sunday in Ordinary Time for an overview of the Books of Samuel.)

Today's Pericope: Once again we come face to face with a common biblical motif—a barren, childless woman. As a typical figure in scripture, Hannah represents the oppressed and scorned woman. She is disdained by her competitor in the household. Her situation is similar to Sarah's—the connections between the two stories are clear. The point of this story is straightforward. Samuel is pure gift from God to this barren, scorned woman in Israel. As a precious gift from God, Samuel was offered to God in gratitude. Embodied in the Samuel story is the future hope for Israel as it looked to the day when Samuel would be a key player in Israel's history.

Hannah sings praise to Yahweh. She also extols the king (which is believed to be an anachronism written into the text at a later time, reflecting Israel's victory). Hannah sings praise to the Lord for his saving power. Only the Lord God is holy. Only the Lord God protects God's people. Israel will be victorious by the mighty hand of God. Israel's king

will be praised. This will be accomplished through the ministry of Samuel, the Lord's servant.

Once again today's reading elucidates a common theme of the scriptures. Trust in the Lord and the Lord will provide. When all seems impossible, trust in God and God will care for his people. On this Feast of the Holy Family, Hannah's faith resonates as a light in our midst and as a pure icon of faith in God. She reminds us to never give up hope.

Year ABC Responsorial Psalm
Psalm 128:1–2, 3, 4–5

This wisdom psalm calls on God to bless human efforts. Psalm 128 insists that the prosperity of family and society begins with a basic fear of the Lord. Prosperity and harmony as interchangeable terms are possible only when a person lives in submission to God's will, loves God with heart and soul, and extends that love to others. Herein lies the basis for fear of the Lord. This wisdom psalm beseeches the blessings of God in human efforts. "Happy" refers to the blessing of many sons. The reference to "house" ("home," NAB) is a reflection on human effort. All who do what is upright in God's eyes will be blessed with many children.

Year B Responsorial Psalm

In Year B the following responsorial psalm may be used. Optional: Psalm 105:1–6, 8–9.

Today's psalm contains the history of Israel from the exodus to the conquest put in hymnodic form. To seek the face of Yahweh, one is to seek God's presence. The psalm directly refers to the first reading and the story of Abraham and Sarah.

Year C Responsorial Psalm

In Year C the following psalm may be used. Optional: Psalm 84:2–3, 5–6, 9–10.

Today's psalm is known as a Song of Zion (see fourth Sunday of Advent, gospel exegesis), a song of Jerusalem or Israel. It is a song of pilgrimage to Jerusalem. The psalm reflects a yearning for the Temple, the joy of the one making the pilgrimage, and a prayer of blessing for the king.

Year ABC Second Reading
Colossians 3:12–21

Overview of St. Paul's Letter to the Colossians: Colossae was a city in Asia Minor, the present-day Turkey. It was a thriving center for wool and textiles. Its name comes from the dark red dye used in wool. During the time of the early church, Colossae was eclipsed by the prominence of nearby Laodicea. Colossae was ruined by earthquake (ca. A.D. 60) and was probably not rebuilt.

The Christian community in Colossae was comprised mostly of gentiles and was founded by Epaphras, one of its natives. The purpose of the letter was to strengthen the faith of the community and to correct the errors that had plagued the Christian community. The errors in question centered around prevalent false teaching. "According to the letter, the false teaching is a philosophy and an empty deceit (2:8), a human tradition (2:8); it concerns the elemental spirits of the universe (2:8), and angels (2:18); it demanded observance of food regulations and festivals, new moons, and sabbath (2:14, 16, 20, 21); and it encourages ascetic practices."[6] It appears that the Christian community incorporated pagan philosophies such as gnosticism, astrology, magic, and the mystery religions into their religious practices.

Another major error was an implied denial of Jesus as the sole redeemer and mediator of the world. Paul defends the Christian position by emphatically asserting Jesus "both as savior and as a creative and cosmic principle."[7] The letter affirms the central role of Christ in salvation and refutes the gnosticism prevalent in the church of Colossae.

Colossae experienced division in the community over the inclusion of gentiles. Aberrant religious practices threatened the Colossian church. Epaphras called on Paul in prison to chastise and challenge his community to fidelity in Christ. Paul willingly wrote to his Colossian brothers and sisters and stressed that they must remain steadfast to the Christ who is above any pagan, philosophi-

cal, or religious practice that humans might construct. Jesus is the center of the universe, our primary reality. Any other spiritual quest is idolatry.

Some contemporary biblical scholars question the Pauline authorship of this letter. There are too many differences between this letter and other confirmed Pauline letters, they insist. "Colossians contains 86 words not found in the uncontested Pauline writings, of which 34 are not found elsewhere in the New Testament."[8] It seems that the articulation of Christology is different in this letter than in other letters. "Colossians exhibits a more elaborate theology of the Church, particularly the Church as the body and Christ as the head; Colossians uses the term mystery for the plan of salvation; the idea of knowledge becomes prominent; and the cosmological-Christological synthesis, while not unparalleled in earlier writings, is here much more complex."[9] Scholars who maintain that Paul did write the letter are not disturbed by the differences. They suggest that the language difference is simply an attempt by Paul to use terms and speak in the language of the very philosophies he was attempting to combat, by incorporating that language into his Christian defense. Those who insist on Pauline authorship state that the summary of Christian belief found in the letter reflects the brilliance only Paul could expound. The letter is believed to have been written during his captivity in prison.

Some scholars believe this pericope was part of a baptismal teaching. When Paul exhorted the Colossians to "put on love," he was referring to the baptismal liturgy. At baptism a new garment was put on the neophyte as a symbol of new life in Christ. The old self dies to sin and the white color of victory triumphs over death and sin.

Today's Pericope: There is often great controversy over the latter verses of this pericope. Some people believe that the verses regarding the submission of wives should be left out of the text for the same reason that the verses regarding the submission of slaves were deleted. Those latter verses regarding slavery were deleted due to culture's view of slavery. It is a thing of the past and is intrinsi-

---

[6]Maurya P. Horgan, "The Letter to the Colossians," *NJBC*, 877.

[7]*DOB*, 146.

---

[8]Ibid.

[9]Ibid.

cally evil. Some believe the verses about "submissive wives" should be deleted for the same reason. Proponents of deleting the text suggest that it was a reality of a former time and culture. Today the value in Christian marriage is mutuality, reciprocity, and a community of covenant love. There is further, more compelling argument against reading the verses. Many times they have been cited as an apologetic for controlling, abusive husband dominance over wives.

However, Raymond E. Collins suggests a different approach. He asserts that these and similar readings were part of early Christian *Haustafel* or household codes (a compendium of household duties).[10] There were political reasons for such codes. Christians were believed to disrupt the social order. They refused submission to the gods of the state. "On the domestic scene, various women, young people and slaves had become Christians. Such phenomena led to widespread suspicion of Christians and even to the persecution of Christians, considered people who disrupted social order and disturbed domestic harmony."[11] The household codes were a way for Christians to assert their compliance with the family values of the day. Collins suggests that reading these verses serves a far greater purpose. The "submissive wives" text presents the worldview of a former time, a former culture, and a former reality. The value of this reading lies in the deeper meaning it suggests. He submits that this text affirms the concern that God has for the human family within the social culture. "One cannot make of any given society's family structures the norm of all families of all times and places. We can, however, affirm that God is not indifferent to family life, as it is actually structured within any given society."[12] Collins suggests that the household code points to God's care for the family as it is lived, not as it is idealized by some outside agency. He asserts that the basic message of the text should not be overlooked. The household codes affirm that there must be "some order for a family to function well." The use of this text in the liturgy reminds us that the Christian family has been and always will be a concern and care of the church. "The well being of families who be-

long to the church is important for the well-being of the church itself."[13]

Even though twentieth-century America has little resemblance to early Christian communities, there are corollaries to be drawn. A connection can even be drawn between the present day and the verses concerning slaves and masters. Both "submissive wives" and "obedient slaves" point to a reciprocity of relationships that is expected even today. When people work, they expect a fair wage for their labors. There is an expectation to be treated with respect and concern by their employer. In return, it is reasonable for employers to expect a fair day's work for a fair day's wage. Harmony in the human experience demands the right ordering of relationships. We are all to "do right by one another."

Collins offers a caution. He says that there is a strength and a liability to the contemporary proclamation of the household codes of early Christian communities.

> It is a strength insofar as it recalls that one must live the Christian life within the context of a socially conditioned set of human relationships. It is a liability when one attempts to make the social relationships of yesteryear a norm for the social relationships of today. When preaching household codes the homilist should not proclaim that wives should be submissive to their husbands. Such submission is no longer culturally acceptable; indeed, in our times, it may well be antithetical to the gospel itself. On the other hand, the liturgical reading of the household code may provide a pastorally sensitive homilist with an opportune occasion for reflecting on the changing nature of the family structure.[14]

Collins suggests that there be serious reflection regarding what constitutes the norm for the human family. The nuclear family of the past is no longer the present norm or a norm for all time. The extended family system was around long before the "Quaker, child centered family of the middle

---

[10]*WWC*, 276, and *PG*, 81–84.

[11]*PG*, 81.

[12]Ibid.

[13]Ibid., 83.

[14]Ibid., 84.

colonies."[15] He also cited the fact that history of the seventeenth and eighteenth centuries depicts the father as the primary caregiver following the baby's nursing period. Before we canonize the "'typical' twentieth century white American family"[16] we should rather reflect on God's presence in every family, no matter what its social circumstances. Perhaps the atypical family is pure gift in our midst. It is a reminder of our responsibility to God's *anawim*, to one another, and to those who struggle just to keep themselves afloat midst turbulent, often violent, and dysfunctional family systems. It is the responsibility of the Church, the people of God, to reflect God's care for all families, those considered typical and especially those considered atypical.

Year B Second Reading

In Year B the following reading may also be used. Optional: Hebrews 11:8, 11–12, 17–19.

(Refer to the twenty-seventh Sunday in Ordinary Time for an overview of the Letter to the Hebrews.)

Today's Pericope: The eleventh chapter of the Letter to the Hebrews is sometimes referred to as the "roll call of the heroes of faith." Today's letter looks back to Abraham's sojourn in Canaan. Abraham realized that there was no place on this earth to call home. His home would be made in the heavenly city. The Letter to the Hebrews upholds Abraham as a model for the Christian believer. Verse 11 recalls the first reading in which Abraham and Sarah are promised an offspring by Yahweh whose promises are trustworthy.

Abraham again would be called on to trust Yahweh. He offered his son Isaac as sacrifice. The author of Hebrews reminds his reader that the last example of Abraham's complete obedience to God is his response to God's command to sacrifice Isaac. Isaac was delivered from Abraham's sacrificial knife at the very last moment. Isaac is understood by the Hebrew's author as a symbol of Jesus' victory over death through the resurrection. Once again, an obvious theme in today's reading from Hebrews is its connection with the Abraham and Sarah epic, which depicts the faith of a people. As

God's family we are called to similar faith. We are to rely on God's promises—to go wherever God leads and to trust that God's will in us will be accomplished. Abraham did just that and a great nation was born. Jesus trusted that God would deliver him from the grips of death and he was raised from the dead.

Year C Second Reading

In Year C the following reading may be used. Optional: 1 John 3:1–2, 21–24.

Overview of the Johannine Epistles: There are no claims by the author of the Letters of John that he is also the author of the fourth gospel. He simply claims to represent authentic witnesses to the Johannine tradition. However, scholars suggest that there was a Johannine "school" of teachers that evolved out of John's community. The epistles were a means of communication between churches. The teachers were followers of the beloved disciple, John. The author intimates that he is part of that community. The first letter of John is a sermon on the early Johannine Christian tradition. The introduction to the letter echoes the prologue of the fourth gospel. The first letter is an exhortation to the Johannine community. The letter warns the community not to be influenced by the dissidents who refuse to accept Jesus' humanity. Some scholars suggest that the second letter does not seem to have been written by the same person as the first letter as the styles are very different. Others insist that the difference lies in the fact that the second letter was a personal letter and the first an exhortation to the community. The second and third letters of John are letters from the elders of the community. The second letter exhorts the community to expel members who threaten the community by luring others away from the tradition. The third letter is situated in the middle of a different crisis altogether. It deals with the issue of hospitality. The elder Gaius wants to extend hospitality to traveling missionaries and another elder does not. Exegetes believe that the hospitality was not offered because of misunderstanding caused over the dissident issue.

One common concern of the New Testament literature is the emergence of false teaching in the early Christian community. Much in the Johannine tradition reflects a divided church. This was

---

[15]Ibid., 85.

[16]Ibid.

not an unusual occurrence for the Johannine community as it had been divided once before when persecution by the Jews had caused some in their number to defect—to turn away from their belief in Jesus Christ, the Son of God.

It is obvious from John's gospel that love and unity of the community were strong values. Salvation relies on *agape* love and unity, rooted in Jesus. Thus the imperative to love is not to be taken lightly—it is the banner that upholds the Johannine community.

The Johannine epistles certainly speak of this love, but it is love extended to members of the community. Dissidents outside the community were regarded as the Antichrist. The language in regard to them is severe as they had been somewhat successful in enticing people away from the community. The letters exhort the readers not to be influenced by what appears to be successful attempts to win people away from the community.

John's gospel highlights the divinity of Christ. It was a popular gospel among gnostic sects, who believed that Jesus was a heavenly body who came from another world, not touched by the evil of this one. Orthodox Christianity was suspicious of John's gospel for that reason. John's insistence that Jesus came down from heaven and returned there, if not read with Jesus' humanity in mind, hinted of gnosticism. The first letter, however, reminds the reader that Christ was indeed human.

One way to combat false teaching was to establish a line of apostolic teachers whose responsibility it was to teach the true tradition. Thus, Peter plays an important role in the letters. Some scholars suggest that the emphasis on Peter was also a way in which disciples of the Johannine tradition could join with disciples of the Petrine tradition. The Johannine community's emphasis on Jesus' divinity coupled with the birth narratives is the basis of the orthodox doctrine of the incarnation of Jesus.[17]

Today's Pericope: When Christians became children of God they experienced God's goodness. Christians live in God's love now. God's love is the reason people can call themselves God's children. Now, as children of God and beneficiaries of God's love, Christians no longer belong to the world. They live holy lives in the manner of Christ, and they will become heirs to future glory—to God's marvelous salvation.

"We shall be like him because we shall see him as he is." Pheme Perkins reminds us that a common theme in Hellenistic religions was "like would know like."[18] Thus the belief that in knowing Christ we become divine—"the human being who knows God is divinized."[19] Since Jesus was equal with God, that same divinization is bestowed on his disciples, who share Christ's name, his heritage, and his life. They will share his preexistent glory.

Christians are to be confident in God, the source of forgiveness. They are to be willing to please God in all things. The letter gives a summary of the great commandments (love God, love one another) and equates believing in God with loving God. For the Johannine community believing God and loving God are synonymous. The author reminds the community that they had been anointed by the Spirit when they entered the community. They have been given the strength of God's Spirit to live the life and imperative of love. The Spirit helps the community discern false teaching from authentic teaching, thus exposing the false teachers who had become such a thorn in the flesh for the community.

We are to be comforted by the fact that God is merciful—more merciful than we are to ourselves. God will forgive us when our own conscience accuses us. God will forgive us when we ask for mercy. This will be freely offered because we (the Johannine community as opposed to the dissidents) are responding to the will of God. God's will is for people to believe in God's Son, Jesus Christ. The dissidents fail to believe because they refuse to accept his humanity. They also refuse to love. Those who obey God's commandment of love abide in God.

The gospel is proclaimed.

---

[17]*RNT,* 304–306.

[18]Pheme Perkins, "1 John," *NJBC,* 990.
[19]Ibid.

Year B Gospel

Luke 2:22–40. The child grew and became strong, filled with wisdom and God's favor.

STEP 1
NAMING ONE'S EXPERIENCE

What were your first impressions? What was your first response to the gospel (or the other readings)? What captured your attention?

Each person names his or her initial impression. Statements should be brief. No reasons should be given at this time. All simply listen without agreeing or disagreeing.

STEP 2
UNDERSTANDING

In a brief statement, explain what you think this gospel is trying to convey.

STEP 3
INPUT FROM VISION/STORY/TRADITION

Liturgical Context

Today's liturgy seeks to uphold the value of Christian family life. The gospel reminds us that the Christian family is the place where the mental, spiritual, and physical growth of children is to be nurtured and where the Christian life is developed and strengthened. The second reading suggests that a basic ingredient of family life must be the forgiveness of all its members. The Second Typical Edition of the Lectionary for Mass, Volume I, has assigned optional first and second readings for use in Years B and C. The exegesis for these readings is also included.

Like other manifestation episodes of the Christmas season, the gospel for this Sunday is another manifestation of Christ, the Son of God, to the world. Today it is Jesus' wisdom that becomes manifest. The liturgy allows us to gaze upon this Christ who, though fully human, is the personification of divine wisdom.

The Church has set aside this day to remember and uplift the Christian family. The Holy Family is offered as the model. There is much to be gleaned from the first and second readings in regard to familial relationships. After reflecting upon what it means to love in the context of family, family systems, and societal structures, the gospel reminds us that there is One who is filled with wisdom, who lavishly showers us with love, and who promises to be with us, even as we struggle to love in difficult situations. Today's liturgy is a reminder that we must turn our children and their futures over to the providential care of God. Today's liturgy is a crucial beacon of hope for contemporary family systems. It serves as a reminder to live in the mystery of God's revelation in our lives, even when difficult family experiences seem to prove the contrary. Mary and Joseph serve as models who were willing to accept the ambiguity that life often presents. They remind us that if we ponder the marvels of God in our hearts and watch God's plan unfold in our lives, we will look back on our lives and discern the mighty hand of God in even the most trying situations.

The prayers of today's liturgy ask God for the intercession of Mary and Joseph for the peace and unification of families. The Prayer over the Gifts proclaims: "Lord, accept this sacrifice and through the prayers of Mary, the virgin Mother of God, and of her husband, Joseph, unite our families in peace and love" (Sunday in the Octave of Christmas). The liturgy professes great concern for the Christian family. On this day, this Christmas season feast, we once again celebrate God's manifestation to the human race. Let us put it in the context of what can often be a most difficult place to experience such manifestation: the human family. We pray for and uplift families who struggle to submit their lives to the will of God. We thank God for the witness of their lives. We pray for those who suffer violence, hatred, and animosity within the walls of their own homes.

Gospel Exegesis

The facilitator provides input from critical biblical scholarship on this text. This input includes insights as to how people would have heard the gospel in Jesus' time.

The backdrop for today's reading from Luke is the Temple in Jerusalem. There are two different Jewish customs reflected. One custom is the presentation and consecration of a child to God. All firstborn males are consecrated to the Lord (Ex 13:1, 11). This tradition remembers the sparing of all firstborn males of Israel in the exodus-event. The original intention was that all firstborn males were consecrated into the Lord's service. However, the Levi tribe eventually took over that role, replacing the firstborn.[20] This was made possible by the legal provisions provided in the Book of Numbers. The firstborn could be purchased for five shekels and the Levites remained in the Lord's service. The money for the child was paid to the Temple, but there was no requirement that the child be brought for a presentation.

Another custom was the presentation of the mother after delivery. A woman was considered ritually unclean for seven days before the circumcision of a male child and thirty-three days after that. For forty days she was denied access to the sanctuary. When purified, she was to bring the priest an offering—a young lamb, a young pigeon, or a dove. The latter two sufficed in the event the woman was poor. The lens Luke uses for today's story is the second custom. He combines the first custom with the second, however, when he mentions the consecration of the firstborn male.

Luke presents a misunderstanding of Jewish custom. He seems to suggest that both parents are to be presented (by use of the phrase "their purification"). He does not mention the shekels needed to redeem the child, but he does mention the pigeons needed for the mother's purification. It would appear that Luke possesses a faulty understanding of Judaism. Also, his penchant for explaining the Jewish rituals leads to the assumption that Luke's audience was non-Palestinian gentiles.

Raymond Brown maintains that there may have been a theological purpose for Luke's inaccuracies.[21] Brown suggests that the emphasis on the purification rite is for the purpose of getting the family from Bethlehem to the Temple in Jerusalem.

_____

[20]BOM, 447.
[21]Ibid., 450.

The presentation is mentioned because it is the way in which Luke is able to introduce the reader to Simeon and Anna. Even though not required, the presentation of the child in the Temple allowed Luke to allude to the Old Testament story of Samuel's presentation in the sanctuary at Shiloh. Samuel was not redeemed for five shekels; he was left at Shiloh's sanctuary. Thus, since this was the model that Luke used in his story, it is clear why he did have Mary and Joseph pay the required amount to redeem their firstborn.

In the story of Hannah and Samuel (the first reading above), Hannah (or Anna) was so grateful to God for the birth of Samuel that she presented him as gift to the Lord and left him at the sanctuary. Hannah and her husband encountered the elderly priest at Shiloh. Mary and Joseph encountered the elderly priest in Jerusalem. Luke's conclusion echoes the words about Samuel, who was purported to have grown in the presence of the Lord and in stature and favor.

A primary concern of Luke is that the presentation of Jesus is in obedience to the Law of God. The Holy Spirit is mentioned three times in the text. The Spirit has been an active agent in all the Lukan birth narratives. The Spirit compelled Simeon to pray the canticle, Nunc Dimitis. The Law and the Prophets (represented by Anna and Simeon) are brought together to attest to the future mission of Christ. We are once again thrust into the comparison drama between Jesus and John. Whereas one prophet spoke of John's greatness after his circumcision, here two prophets reveal Jesus' future greatness.

The canticles in the Lukan narrative are believed to have originated with a group called the Jewish Christian _anawim_. They were people completely dependent on God, who believed that Jesus was the fulfillment of the long-awaited Day of the Lord. Simeon and Anna represent the piety of the _anawim_—faithful servants of the Lord who have patiently awaited the fulfillment of Israel and the salvation of Jerusalem. Anna, faithful servant who never left the sanctuary and who prayed and fasted day and night, is "a forerunner of the Jerusalem Christian community which devotes itself to prayer and day by day attends the Temple (Acts 2:42–46), and of its daughter community in

Antioch which worships the Lord and fasts and receives the Holy Spirit (13:2)."[22]

Zechariah received a revelation in the Temple about John the Baptist and was unable to confer the priestly blessing. Simeon, on the other hand, receives the light of revelation about Christ and blesses the parents of the child. The Law, the Spirit, and the Temple attest to Jesus whose name will be great—all attest to the greatness of the future mission of Christ. The one who is called "holy" has now been brought to the Temple. This *holy one* will himself embody all that is holy within the Temple itself. In the Lord's own house Jesus is proclaimed as a light to the nations. Jewish theology asserted that the glory of God resided in the sanctuary. Now Simeon stands within its courts and beholds the revealed glory of God in the child before him.

Simeon sings God's praises in canticle and, in so doing, proclaims that God's work of salvation is for all the world—it is universal, for Israel as well as for the gentiles. Simeon's second oracle contends that not all Israel will accept the revelation of Christ and the redemption of Israel. Simeon's second canticle is a reminder that Jesus will be the rise and fall of many in Israel. Those who reject him will face him and in facing him their inner hostility toward him will be revealed.

Lest the story end on a negative note, Luke takes us to Anna. Simeon recognized the consolation of Israel; Anna also recognized it. Anna, symbolic of the *anawim* and idealizing the virtues of the widow who prays and fasts in the Lord's courts, recognizes the Christ and speaks out. Her life of prayer and fasting prepared her heart to recognize the prophetic word revealed to her. Simeon and Anna represent for Luke an allusion to the future Pentecost in which the Spirit of God is poured out on God's sons and daughters.

Anna's widowhood is significant for Luke. Widows play an important role throughout the gospel. Anna is a widow of eighty-four years. Widows hold a high place of distinction in the Christian community. An extolled widow is widowed for at least sixty years with no expectation of remarriage so

that she might spend her days and nights praising the Lord. Anna fits the description. However, the Christian tradition of widowhood had its genesis with the Jewish *anawim*. The Book of Judith (ca. second century B.C.) exalts a heroine (Judith), a symbol of Israel. She did not remarry after her husband died; she fasted and was a devout observer of the Law. After she delivered Israel, she too sang a canticle of praise. Judith lived to the ripe old age of 105. If one were to add all the data Luke provides, this is also the age of Anna.

Luke comes closer to associating Jesus with the Wisdom tradition than any of the other synoptic evangelists. It is a wisdom that Jesus will share with his disciples. Jesus, as a child, was favored by God—thus Luke sets the stage for Jesus' adult mission. We are told in this pericope that Jesus is favored by God. We will be told again when Jesus begins his ministry and the people of Nazareth are amazed at the words of favor that come forth from him. The conclusion of today's reading prepares the reader for Jesus' future mission—"coming from Galilee and preaching a message full of wisdom and exemplifying God's gracious favor."[23]

The growth of the child Jesus is of particular importance for our reflection on today's gospel. There are three important considerations. One is doctrinal. The child, as fully human, must grow not only physically, but mentally and spiritually as well.[24] "If we are to understand the incarnation in scriptural terms, we must not think of it as entailing complete maturity from the outset. Christ is perfect man with the perfection that belongs to each stage of human growth. At each stage, too, he is the perfect manifestation of God in a manner appropriate for that stage."[25]

A second point of consideration is that Jesus' growth takes place within the human family. This scene and the scene with Jesus in the Temple as a twelve-year-old are the only scriptural references to the Holy Family. Jesus was prepared for his adult mission in a divinely inspired setting. Also, this Holy Family is a symbol for all human families. The Christian family is also divinely inspired

[22]Ibid., 453.

[23]Ibid., 469.
[24]*PL*, 221.
[25]Ibid., 221, 222.

and allows for the spiritual growth of the children within its safe enclosure.

A final point of interest in this text, insists Fuller, is that it is typological. It refers back to 1 Samuel 2:26. "Jesus stands in the prophetic succession. He is the last and the greatest of the prophets but transcends them all, for he is the eschatological prophet. But he is still a prophet."[26]

Proclaim the gospel again.

Sometimes we gain new insights when we hear the text after the interpretation is given. Someone from the group proclaims the gospel a second time.

STEP 4
TESTING

Conversation with the Liturgy and the Scriptures

Test your original understanding in dialogue with the text.

(You might consider breaking into smaller groups.)

Now that you've heard the exegesis, were there any new insights? How do you feel about it? How does your original understanding of this gospel compare with what we just shared? How does this story speak to your life?

Sharing Life Experience

Participants share an experience from their lives that connects with the biblical interpretation just presented.

> *I am reminded of when we moved to Florida. I did not want to move. I knew it was right for our lives but I did not want to leave the security of the known world for the unknown. Much prayer and discernment went into our decision. We did not receive the mandate to go in a dream—but it seemed like a dream to me. The events fell so quickly into place (we sold a house, I found a job, and we moved four kids, a dog, and a cat in a matter of three weeks). But it was difficult. Knowing that it*

> *was God's plan for our lives did not make it easy. It was the greatest challenge of our lives up to that point. I was leaving the security of my Midwestern roots for only God knew for sure! Yet, when I look back, I marvel at the ways God fulfilled the purpose of our lives through that move. Life decisions are not easy. Living in family relationships can be the most trying relationships we will ever know. Yet, it is where the paschal mystery is lived, day in and day out.*

> *I don't know what turn our lives would have taken had we not listened to that gentle nudge from God. What we learned from that story of our life would sustain us as we raised our family through the difficult years. We knew that ultimately God is with us. The incarnation is a reality in our lives.*

> *We suffered the trials that most families endure—the teenage years, near-death accidents, near-death illnesses, financial losses—all of those frustrations that prompt contemporary families to say with St. Theresa, "Lord, if this is how you treat your friends, its no wonder you have so few!" However, the truth of the incarnation is that we were not alone in any of it. We are strong because of it. And our family is better for it. Our job was to listen and trust. Sometimes we did; sometimes we fell short. But God was and is present—not only in the joys, but in the heart-wrenching sorrows. God drives our lives. God shows us what it means to love. God reminds us that the love he shows us is not only to be poured out in the midst of our family, but is to extend to others in the world—especially the poor and the marginalized.*

What was Luke trying to tell his community? In what way does Luke's theology have any relevance for our lives today? How does Luke's story of the presentation in the Temple invite us to consider the Christian family? What does Luke have to teach us about family life? In what way does this gospel challenge your community today? In what way has this conversation with the scriptures for today's liturgy invited change in your life? In what way are the biblical themes of covenant, exodus, creation, and community evident in today's readings? Do you still feel the same way about this text as when you began? Has your original understanding been stretched, challenged, or affirmed?

---

[26]Ibid.

126

Step 5
Decision

The gospel demands a response.

In what concrete way might your parish be invited to respond? Are there any attitudes or behaviors you would like to change as a result of today's conversation? What one concrete action will you take this week in response to the liturgy today?

Pastoral Considerations: Perhaps this would be a good time to bless expectant parents and families of all shapes, sizes, races, and cultures. Refer to the *Book of Blessings.* In what way does your community uphold family life? Do you schedule events that are conducive to family life, or do they interfere with it? Does your parish respect the various forms of family life within your community?

Christian Initiation: Perhaps there are candidates ready to celebrate a rite of acceptance or welcome. Also, very often the initiation process stretches relationships in some family situations. Since the "anointing of catechumens" is intended to strengthen catechumens, it might be a good time to celebrate the rite.

DOCTRINAL ISSUES

What Church truth/teaching/doctrinal issue could be drawn from the gospel for the Feast of the Holy Family?

Participants suggest possible doctrinal themes that flow from the readings.

Possible Doctrinal Themes

Christian family; incarnation; manifestation; faith; salvation—soteriology; Law and the Prophets

Present the doctrinal material at this time.

1. The facilitator gives input on a particular doctrinal issue of his or her prior choosing. OR
2. The group chooses a doctrinal issue from the list they created. They read together from the Doctrinal Appendix or other appropriate, official Church documents and the works of respected theologians.

(Many doctrinal issues are found in the Doctrinal Appendix at the back of this workbook. If you are choosing an issue from this resource, please refer to it now.)

Reflection questions centered around the chosen doctrinal theme can be found at the end of each topic in the Doctrinal Appendix. The questions are based on the five-step reflection process. If you choose a topic not included in the Doctrinal Appendix, craft your own questions according to the same five-step process.

Following the reflection questions you will be reminded to return to chapter 7, "Preparing the Catechetical Session," to assist you in crafting your own session.

Closing Prayer

Eternal Father,
we want to live as Jesus, Mary, and Joseph,
in peace with you and one another.
May this communion strengthen us to face the
    troubles of life.
Grant this through Christ, our Lord.[27]

---

[27]Feast of the Holy Family, "Prayer After Communion," *The Sacramentary.*

MARY, MOTHER OF GOD

Environment

The Christmas season environment continues.

INTRODUCTORY RITES

Opening Song (or Entrance Antiphon)

A light will shine on us this day, the Lord is born for us: he shall be called Wonderful God, Prince of peace, Father of the world to come; and his kingship will never end (see Is 9:2, 6; Lk 1:33).[1]

Opening Prayer

The facilitator of the session may lead the prayer. Others in the group may be asked to proclaim the readings.

Let us pray...

> *Pause for silent prayer.*

Father, source of light in every age,
the virgin conceived and bore your Son
who is called Wonderful God, Prince of Peace.
May her prayer, the gift of a mother's love,
be your people's joy through all ages.
May her response, born of a humble heart,
draw your Spirit to rest on your people.
Grant this through Christ, our Lord.[2]

LITURGY OF THE WORD

First Reading[3]
Numbers 6:22–27

Overview of the Book of Numbers: The name "Numbers" comes from the description of the census in chapter one. The laws contained in the Book of Numbers are directed to a people on a journey through the promised land. The material in the Book of Numbers extends over multiple centuries and from various ancient biblical sources. The narrative portion of Numbers belongs to an earlier period, while the laws were written during a later time in Israel's history. A portion of Numbers parallels the story of Exodus, especially stories of the grumbling, rebellious Israelites in the desert. "The incidents in Exodus stress the patience of Yahweh, who always listens to Israel's needs and intervenes to help. Numbers 11–21, on the other hand, stresses that the people's constant rebellion led Yahweh to **punish** them time and again. But each time Moses intervenes and begs for the sake of the people, and God softens his anger and turns back his punishments or heals the victims."[4]

Later biblical authors of Numbers looked back on the rebellion and failures of their ancestors. They believed that the trials and hardships they endured were God's punishment for rebellious behavior. "They could look back on the centuries of injustice, disobedience, and false worship, the condemnations of the prophets, the failures of the kings, and know that the loss of their freedom and land in exile had been richly deserved. God cannot be pushed too far without asserting his own justice and honor. Yet even at a late hour, he could turn from his anger and spare them, if they would only turn to him."[5] It was a constant theme for Israel: Israel sinned; God punished. Israel repented; God forgave and restored.

---

[1]Solemnity of Mary, Mother of God: "Entrance Antiphon," *The Sacramentary.*

[2]Solemnity of Mary, Mother of God: "Alternate Opening Prayer," *The Sacramentary.*

[3]The exegesis for the first and second readings may or may not be the focus of your group's reflection as there may

only be time to give adequate attention to the gospel, your primary concern. However, the exegesis is included here in order to provide a thorough investigation of the entire liturgy of the word as there may be parts (or all) that would be necessary to the direction you wish to take with your particular ministry group.

[4]*ROT,* 192.

[5]Ibid, 193.

It is at the end of Numbers that leadership of Israel is passed on to Joshua at the death of Moses, and Israel begins its conquest of the promised land.

Today's Pericope: Today's reading contains Aaron's blessing, which is an amazing anticipation of Christian belief in the Trinity. The last verse is the key verse for our purposes in this liturgy. God's name is invoked. In biblical tradition the "name" implies the totality of the person. All God is and has done throughout salvation history is brought to bear in this blessing. "To 'bless' means to invoke upon the faithful all that God is and all that he has done for his people."[6] Christians have extended this understanding to include all that has been accomplished through Jesus. "The name of Jesus is the name of the triune God made manifest and present in saving power."[7]

Responsorial Psalm
Psalm 67:2–3, 5, 6, 8

The theme of the first reading is resounded in the psalm. The psalmist asks for God's mercy. The Christian sees God's blessing fulfilled in the person of Jesus.

Second Reading
Galatians 4:4–7

Overview of Galatians: The word *Galatians* is another word for *Celtic* or *Gallic*. Galatians were from a Celtic tribe near France. The Greeks referred to it as Galatia. The Galatians eventually migrated east and settled near northern Turkey. The Romans combined other tribes in Turkey and thus formed the Province of Galatia.

Paul's letter to the Galatians is similar in tone and content to the letter written to the Romans. However, the difference between Galatians and Romans is that one was written in the heat of the moment and the other was carefully planned and crafted with deliberate intention.

Paul's agenda was to answer the religious dilemmas facing the emerging Christian church. Schol-

ars believe it was written in response to the problems going on in Corinth. Jewish Christians were insistent that Gentile converts follow Jewish ritual requirements. The problem raised questions and difficulties in the community. Should they remain strictly Jewish and observe all the practices and rituals of Judaism, or "was their Christian experience so distinctive, and [were] their claims for Jesus so absolute, that they could no longer be contained within Judaism?"[8] Unlike the first believers who saw Christianity in strictly Jewish terms (and as a sect within Judaism), the new pagan converts radically challenged the status quo. The implications were serious. How could they claim to be the heirs of the Old Testament covenant if they were no longer a part of Israel?

In the beginning Paul was sure that Jesus was doing something radically new and distinct. Thus, he felt that new converts should not be saddled with former binding, covenant rituals. This was scandalous to observant Jewish Christians. Their practice of the Christian faith was rooted in their Jewish heritage. Judaism was the foundation upon which Jesus established his reign. Jesus asserted that he had not come to abolish the law but to fulfill it. Then why were these Corinthian converts excused from Jewish formation? It did not make sense. It only proved to them that the heresies and godless practices would never have happened in the first place if these converts had been well grounded in the ethics of Judaism.

Paul was furious, but it forced him into further discernment. The issue of circumcision further exacerbated the controversy. It was only through circumcision that people were in covenant relationship with Yahweh. It was a sign of membership in the People of God (one of Israel's primary motifs). Paul was hurt and angry over the attacks by other Christians. He was not as informed as the "real" apostles. He had not known the historical Jesus. How could he be right and the others wrong? So the arguments continued. Paul dug in his heels, typically overreacting, and boldly maintained that his position was the only correct one.

Paul's rhetoric was so divisive that he polarized the community. He cut to the heart of religious obser-

---

[6]*PL*, 27.
[7]Ibid.

---

[8]*GAP*, 81.

vance. He professed Christianity to be on one side of the religious pole and Judaism to be on the other. Only one was absolutely correct, so the other was absolutely incorrect. We need not guess where Judaism fell. (Finesse was certainly not one of Paul's strong suits!)

He wisely named the potential dispositions inherent in all religious traditions and religious people. They will either be obedient or not; sincere or not; aware or blind; mature or childish. So far so good; we can all agree. However, Paul's conclusion sent chills through even the most lackadaisical Jew. Paul asserted that Christianity completely adhered to the virtuous side of those determinants while Judaism was absolutely the opposite. (Not a way to win friends and influence people!)

Paul suggested that circumcision was no more than an act of savage brutality and almost implied that he was ashamed of his own permanent Jewish branding. While his methods left a lot to be desired, Paul's intentions were to hold fast to the central gospel message.

Salvation was freely won by Christ's death and resurrection and could not be earned by one's own merit. Paul maintained that the Jewish perspective of right relationship with God (during Paul's time) evolved into total adherence to the law. This implied that salvation could be merited by one's own efforts. Paul vehemently protested. Salvation was a free, utterly gratuitous gift from God. "People do not need to prove themselves. God accepts them as they are, with all their sins. When they acknowledge this is so, of course, they will make every effort to live a life of union with God. Still it is God's unearned love, not their own effort, that puts them right with God. They become good because God is good."[9]

The way of the law, on the other hand, stressed human responsibility. Serving God was synonymous with rule-keeping. Such a perspective breeds the notion that if I am good enough, and follow the rules to the end, then God is obliged to save me.

Paul's way is not without its own set of dangers. Blindness, carelessness, and benign neglect could easily creep into the equation and prompt a person to sit on his or her laurels and passively respond to the demands of discipleship. However, Paul's vision put God in charge and offered disciples the necessary freedom to respond to God, not to restrictive religious systems. Paul's letter to the Galatians reasserts belief in the paschal mystery. Jesus suffered, died, and rose again for the sins of the world. This reality has the power to change lives.

Paul so impulsively cranked out his letter that he did not even take the time to offer the customary introductory prayers of praise. The Galatians had questioned Paul's teaching. He had to set them straight. Paul's letter defended his ministry and his position. He had not been wrong. Faith was all that was required for salvation. Jesus had paid the price; humanity reaped the benefits. The law and all the ritual requirements of the law were no longer necessary. Furthermore, his right to apostolic succession was given credence by Jesus' post-resurrection appearance to Paul.

This was a significant shift for the early church. One position embraced works as a means of salvation; the other maintained that salvation through faith automatically leads to good works. Early Christians were put in a position of having to make a choice.

Paul's letter to the Romans took up the same passionate conviction. However, it was more thoughtfully crafted and was not as influenced by his "knee jerk" reaction to the accusations leveled against him.[10]

Implications for This Feast: St. Paul is particularly relevant on this New Year's Day as a reminder that we are children of God and heirs to the salvation won through the paschal mystery of Christ. We inaugurate the new year with the resolve to live in the fullness of Christ's light. His letter to the Galatians reminds us that since we have been elevated to God's divine life through the coming of Jesus, we must own that divine heritage and live accordingly.

---

[9]Ibid, 84.

[10]The primary source for the exegesis concerning Paul's letter is taken from *The Gospel According to St. Paul* (*GAP*) by Hubert Richards.

Gospel[11]
Luke 2:16–21

The shepherds go to Bethlehem in haste to see the babe they had been told about. Mary treasures it all in her heart and on the eighth day they took Jesus to be circumcised and to be given his name.

STEP 1
NAMING ONE'S EXPERIENCE

What were your first impressions? What was your first response?

Each person names his or her initial impression. Statements should be brief. No reasons should be given at this time. All simply listen without agreeing or disagreeing.

STEP 2
UNDERSTANDING

In a brief statement, what do you think this gospel is trying to convey?

STEP 3
INPUT FROM VISION/STORY/TRADITION

Liturgical Context

The Solemnity of Mary is the oldest of Marian feasts. This feast is christological and defines Mary's role in the church. It also defines Marian devotion. The Vatican II document *Lumen Gentium* states:

> Devotion to Mary as it has always existed in the Church, even though it is altogether special, is essentially distinct from the worship of adoration paid equally to the Word incarnate, the Father, and the Holy Spirit. For the various forms of Marian devotions sanctioned by the Church, within the limits of sound orthodoxy and suited circumstances of time and place as well as to the character and cultures of peoples, have the effect that as we honor the Mother we also truly know the Son and give love, glory and obedience through him, through whom all things have their being (see Col 1:15–16) and in whom it has pleased the eternal Father that all fullness should dwell.[12]

To reiterate: this feast is christological. It is primarily about the birth of Christ, the fulfillment of God's plan of salvation. However, it also points to Mary as an example of faith. She is a model for all believers and exemplifies the true Israel. Mary was a willing vessel, ready to receive God's grace. We too are to be such vessels.

The prayers of the liturgy today ask for her intercession. The liturgy itself shows us Mary's role in the church.

> God our Father,
> may we always profit by the prayers
> of the Virgin Mary,
> for you bring us life and salvation
> through Jesus Christ, her Son.
> (Opening Prayer)

> God our Father,
> we celebrate this season
> the beginning of our salvation.
> On this feast of Mary, the Mother of God,
> we ask that our salvation
> will be brought to its fulfillment.
> (Prayer over the Gifts)

> Father,
> as we proclaim the Virgin Mary
> to be the mother of Christ and the mother of the Church,
> may our communion with her Son
> bring us salvation.
> (Prayer after Communion)

---

[11]The gospel exegesis is provided later in this session so that it may be presented in the proper sequence where it occurs in the adult five-step reflection process. The exegesis is provided for the first and second readings for your information and edification, and for you to use at your discretion. Once again, the gospel is the primary source of reflection. If there is time for reflection on the other readings, all the better.

---

[12]*Lumen gentium* #31, in *DVII*.

Mary is our intercessor. She stands with the pilgrim church as we wait in hope for Jesus' return.

We cannot ignore the fact that this feast also initiates the new year. As each new year brings solemn promises of transformation, the feast of Mary, Mother of God, reminds us that Christian discipline involves striving to live in harmony with God's will. Mary opened herself to receive God's grace and blessing. In this new year, we, too, ask for God's grace and blessing. Our prayer is for the openness to embrace salvation when it comes our way.

If catechetical groups are unable to center a session around this solemnity, it would be very important to address the themes and truths inherent in this celebration during another session.

Gospel Exegesis

The facilitator provides input regarding critical biblical scholarship on this text. The input includes insights as to how people would have heard the gospel in Jesus' time.

This gospel is almost identical to the gospel for the mass at dawn of Christmas day. It adds the event of Jesus' circumcision and the conferral of his name. Mary follows the prescriptions of the law by having Jesus baptized according to the law. In biblical tradition, the "name" often designated the person's mission. The name "Jesus" means "the one who saves." Thus, his very name identifies his role and his destiny. Throughout the Christian scriptures we are shown the power of Jesus' name to heal, expel demons, and liberate people. Jesus' name is to be used in faith.

However, in and of themselves, the events of today's gospel were not extraordinary. Many biblical figures have been given a new name; Jesus' name was not exceedingly significant in biblical times, as there were others with the same name; presenting Jesus at the temple for the circumcision was prescribed by the law. Thus, the intent is to show that Mary did all that the angel told her to do. She was a willing, obedient servant.

Yet Christians know the story and they know well that the name indeed tells us who Jesus is: "the

one who saves." We know from this story and beyond this story that Jesus' mission is extraordinary and is the fulfillment of all that was promised by the prophets of old. Jesus' name was power. His healing ministry was evidence of that power. When we call on Jesus in faith, we invoke the power of his name and place our lives under his care. It requires a great leap of faith. Mary did not ask how her son would become great as the angel had proclaimed. Hers was not to question or to know, but simply to accept in trust.

God's grace was shown to sinners in the revelation given to the shepherds. The peace offered is offered freely for all people, equally, not just for the pious righteous. We recall from a previous Sunday that peace implies wholeness, all things in right relationship, harmony. The peace brought by God's Son is a peace whereby people live in *hesed* love. Relationships are brought under the dominion of God. "The recovery of wholeness in human relationships, which is due to God's acts in Jesus, reflects honor to God."[13] This is understood in terms of our relationship to the human race, to one another, to the stranger, the lost, the alien, the misfit, and the outcast. Gustavo Gutierrez expresses it beautifully: "By becoming human, the Son of God transforms every human face into the expression of God's presence and exigency."[14] He further added comments by the Latin American bishops in Puebla, Mexico in which they exhorted the faithful to discover the presence of Jesus in the faces of the world's poor. Gutierrez tells us that such faces serve as a reminder and an invitation to us all to become more faithful to living the gospel of Christ. If we, like Mary, ponder such things in our heart, perhaps then will the "insignificant and the excluded of this world become an epiphany (a revelation) of God for us."[15]

Mary accepted in faith what she had been told. She did not question. She allowed the events to unfold and was a willing, obedient servant in God's grand design. We are called to the same mission.

Proclaim the gospel again.

---

[13]*RL*, 34.
[14]*SWTLY*, 34.
[15]Ibid.

Sometimes we gain new insights when we hear the text after the interpretation has been given. Someone from the group proclaims the gospel a second time.

STEP 4
TESTING

Conversation with the Liturgy and the Scriptures

Test your original understanding in dialogue with the text.

(You might consider breaking into smaller groups.)

How does the feast of Mary the Mother of God touch your life? Does this feast have any relevance for the church today? Were there any new insights? How does your original understanding of this story compare with what we just shared?

How does this story speak to your life?

Sharing Life Experience

Parish life is the incredible, living sign of God's presence in the world. It is filled with faith-filled people who, like Mary, trust God in the midst of life's difficulties and ambiguities. The week before and after Christmas this year, a forty-six-year-old woman (and friend) died suddenly in the shower, another woman died unexpectedly on a family outing, another woman's son was stabbed to death, and another parishioner's sister committed suicide. It is so difficult to lose loved ones, especially in untimely, unexpected ways, and especially during the holidays. In the midst of such tragedy it would be easy to wonder where God is. Yet over and over I experience the living faith of people who face such pain with courage—people who have the assurance that God is in control of their lives and will give them the strength that will see them through their grief. I am awestruck by the presence and compassion of the community as it embraces families through the tragedies of their lives.

On this day, New Year's Day, I am reminded that life is a precious gift. The death of my friend, and of the other parishioners who died so unexpectedly over the holidays, is a stark reminder of how tenuous life is. Mary did not question the future. She simply put her

trust in God and walked into it with the assurance that God would lead her. We may only have today to live the love that God invites us to live. Mary walked into her future with a willing, obedient heart.

Mary is a model for all mothers who worry about their children, and for families who worry about their loved ones. Ancient Palestinian existence was fraught with danger, yet Mary trusted. She trusted even when she knew that her pregnancy might, at the very least, cause public scandal. Mary is our anchor whenever concerns over family, friends, and loved ones lead us to the brink of despair.

Today's liturgy is a wake-up call for me to live each day to the fullest, to trust God to lead and guide me through life's difficulties, and to respond in love to the world's suffering, poor, and downcast. Today might be the day God wants to use me as a vessel of his love. Perhaps there is someone in dire need of God's love (maybe even someone the world judges as unworthy of that love). Will I respond?

Participants share an experience from their lives that connects with the biblical interpretation just shared.

What was Luke trying to tell his community? What does he have to say to your community and to you today? The biblical themes of covenant, exodus, creation, and community are in full expression in the readings for today's liturgy. What difference does it make? Do you still feel the same way about this text as you did when you began? Has your original understanding been stretched, challenged, or affirmed?

STEP 5
DECISION

The gospel demands a response.

How does our understanding of these scriptures and today's liturgy call us to transformation? In what way are we, like Mary, to grow in faith? In what way does our community need to grow in the fullness of today's scriptures? In what concrete ways is our parish called to respond? Has this conversation with the exegesis changed or stretched my personal attitudes? What are the implications of this gospel in my life? What is one concrete action I will take this week as a response to the liturgy today?

DOCTRINAL ISSUES

What church truth/teaching/doctrinal issue could be drawn from the gospel for the Solemnity of Mary, Mother of God?

Participants suggest possible doctrinal themes that flow from the readings.

Possible Doctrinal Themes

Christology; salvation; Mary's role as disciple; Mary as model of church; Incarnation

Present the doctrinal material at this time.

1. The facilitator gives input on a particular doctrinal issue of his/her prior choosing. OR
2. The group chooses a doctrinal issue from the list they created. They read together from the Doctrinal Appendix.

(The doctrinal issues are found in the Doctrinal Appendix in the back of this workbook. If you are choosing an issue from this resource, please refer to it now.)

Reflection questions centered around the chosen doctrinal theme can be found at the end of each topic in the Doctrinal Appendix. The questions are based on the five-step reflection process. If you choose a topic not included in the Doctrinal Appendix, craft your own questions according to the same five-step process.

Following the reflection questions you will be reminded to return to chapter 7, "Preparing the Catechetical Session," to assist you in crafting your own session.

Closing Prayer

Father, as we proclaim the Virgin Mary
to be the mother of Christ and the mother of the
    Church,

may our communion with her Son bring us to
    salvation.
We ask this through Christ, our Lord.[16]

---

[16]Solemnity of Mary, Mother of God, "Prayer After Communion," *The Sacramentary.*

SECOND SUNDAY AFTER CHRISTMAS

INTRODUCTORY RITES

Entrance Antiphon (or Opening Song)

When peaceful silence lay over all, and night had run half of her swift course, your all powerful word, O Lord, leaped down from heaven, from the royal throne. (Wis 1:14, 15)[1]

Opening Prayer

The facilitator of the session may lead the prayer. Others in the group may be asked to proclaim the readings.

Let us pray
[that all mankind may be enlightened by the gospel]

> *Pause for silent prayer.*

God of power and life,
glory of all who believe in you,
fill the world with your splendor
and sow the nations the light of your truth.
We ask this through our Lord Jesus Christ your Son,
who lives and reigns with you and the Holy Spirit,
one God, for ever and ever.[2]

LITURGY OF THE WORD

The readings are proclaimed.

First Reading
Sirach 24:1–2, 8–12

(Please refer to the Feast of the Holy Family for an overview of the Book of Sirach.)

Today's Pericope: Today's reading has Ben Sira presenting a treatise on wisdom and the Law. He elo-

quently and creatively paints a portrait of wisdom and its qualities. He models his treatise after chapter 8 of the Book of Proverbs. It is a poem in praise of wisdom. Verses 1 and 2 serve as the introduction to the poem. The author personifies Wisdom and situates her in the heavenly council. She speaks to the people of Israel, portrayed assembled in Jerusalem. In this poem Wisdom is the same as the Law. Wisdom is understood to be a word or utterance from God. In verses 3–7 Wisdom has just explained her origins—that her genesis is divine and is born of Israel. After Wisdom was created, she explored the heavens and the abyss for a place to dwell. Wisdom is personified in the feminine. "That wisdom is feminine is a natural development from the feminine gender 'hokmah'; but this may also fulfill some need to see a feminine side to the Deity."[3]

Wisdom was created by the Word of God. She is a Spirit who covers the earth—an allusion to the Spirit who hovered over the waters of chaos at the creation of the world. Wisdom has always been present and an active agent in God's plan of salvation.

God insists that Wisdom abide in Israel, elucidating Wisdom's subservience to God. God has gifted Israel and God's gift is Wisdom. Since Wisdom and the Law are one and the same, Wisdom provides the rules whereby the people are to worship and honor God.

Responsorial Psalm
Psalm 147:12–15, 19–20

The psalm appointed to today's liturgy is a communal hymn, dated after the exile. The rebuilding of Jerusalem by Yahweh and the gathering of the exiles are major themes in the psalm. The psalm exhorts and invites the people of God to give praise to God, who provides for the afflicted. The psalm gives praise to Yahweh for his care and protection of Jerusalem. The psalm refrain appointed

---

[1] Second Sunday after Christmas: "Entrance Antiphon," *The Sacramentary.*

[2] Second Sunday after Christmas: "Opening Prayer," *The Sacramentary.*

[3] John E. Rybolt, C.M., "Sirach," *CBC,* 3.

for Psalm 147 extols the Word of God, who became human and lived among us. We can do no less than sing praise to God for the salvation he destined for the world from the very beginning.

Second Reading
Ephesians 1:3–6, 15–18

(Please refer to the fifteenth Sunday in Ordinary Time for an overview of the Letter to the Ephesians.)

Today's Pericope: Today's reading from Ephesians is a Jewish/Christian benediction. The author of Ephesians inserts this poetic hymn of praise to emphasize what God accomplished through Jesus by the power of the Spirit. We are to "bless" God because God has "blessed" us with every spiritual blessing. These poetic words of praise were typical of the Jewish/Christian benediction. In this benediction God is named and addressed. Even though God's plan was destined from all time and is cosmic in nature, it is all accomplished through Christ.

God's plan for the world began even before creation. We were chosen by God in Christ to be holy. We were destined to be God's children before the world began. God willed that we become God's children through Jesus Christ. We are adopted children. The author of Colossians understands that this adoption takes place through our dying with Christ in baptism. The author of Ephesians insists that our adoption took place before the world began. This is our redemption. We have been redeemed through the blood of Jesus and through the forgiveness of our sins.

The author writes as though he were Paul. He believes that the letter to the Colossians is a genuine letter from the Apostle Paul and he uses many of the ideas from that letter in his letter to the Ephesians. Thus, verses 15 and 16 are variations of Colossians 1:3–4. God is named as both as "the God of our Lord Jesus Christ" and "the Father of glory." The author prays that the reader be bestowed with God's wisdom which is experienced in God's knowledge. By the power of the Spirit the author prays that his readers will be enlightened to know the hope that resides in the Christian vocation, the glory that belongs to those who are God's own, and the immeasurable greatness of God's power for those who believe.

The gospel is proclaimed.

Gospel
John 1:18. The Word became flesh and made his dwelling among us.

STEP 1
NAMING ONE'S EXPERIENCE

What were your first impressions? What was your first response to the gospel (or the other readings)?[4] What captured your attention?

Each person names his or her initial impression. Statements should be brief. No reasons should be given at this time. All simply listen without agreeing or disagreeing.

STEP 2
UNDERSTANDING

In a brief statement, explain what you think this gospel is trying to convey.

STEP 3
INPUT FROM VISION/STORY/TRADITION

Liturgical Context

The second Sunday after Christmas is celebrated only when a Sunday falls between January 2 and January 6. "In most countries, the solemnity of the Epiphany is celebrated on the second Sunday after Christmas. But when the feast is set for January, there is a formulary that is an extension of Christmas Mass during the day. It is the same for years A, B, and C."[5] Today's liturgy centers on the incarnation of Christ, the primary theme of the

---

[4] The primary focus of reflection is the gospel. However, often the other readings demand attention and must be brought into the dialogue.

[5] *DL* (I), 248.

entire Christmas season, and an extension of the Christmas liturgy. The antiphon appointed for the psalm serves as a thematic statement for the liturgy: "The Word of God became man and lived among us." The prologue to John's gospel prior to Vatican II was read at the end of every eucharist, thus recalling for the faithful the salvation event of God through the incarnation of the Son. On this second Sunday, we read the same gospel appointed for Christmas Day.

"Christmas is a feast that celebrates our redemption even though the focus of attention is on the Incarnation and the 'marvelous exchange' and not on the passion and resurrection."[6] Hints of this holy exchange are particularly evident in the reading from Ephesians, in which the author insists that our adoption in Christ took place at the creation of the world. The gospel for the mass during the day (at Christmas) uses John's prologue to proclaim the mystery of the incarnation. We use it again on this second Sunday for the same reason. It is a message we never tire of hearing. John's prologue reminds us that oversentimentalization over the birth of the baby is misplaced when we put this event where it belongs—at the cosmic, timeless center of the universe. The Grand Conductor stood on the precipice of creation's formless wasteland, and with one breath of the spoken Word created a cosmic song. The music still plays today as we celebrate the holy exchange made possible by the incarnation of God's Son.

Every liturgy of the Christmas season celebrates the great mystery of the incarnation. Jesus' incarnation is raised to a cosmic level. John reminds us in his prologue that we must return to our cosmic genesis and remember that the incarnation began at the creation of the world. God always intended that human beings be heirs of eternal life. The incarnation is viewed in tandem with the cross and resurrection.

Gospel Exegesis

The facilitator provides input from critical biblical scholarship on this text. This input includes insights as to how people would have heard the gospel in Jesus' time.

---

[6]Ibid., 128.

The prologue for John is also proclaimed on Christmas Day—Mass During the Day. Please refer to that liturgy for the gospel exegesis.

Proclaim the gospel again.

Sometimes we gain new insights when we hear the text after the interpretation is given. Someone from the group proclaims the gospel a second time.

STEP 4
TESTING

Conversation with the Liturgy and the Scriptures

Test your original understanding in dialogue with the text.

(You might consider breaking into smaller groups.)

Now that you've heard the exegesis, were there any new insights? How do you feel about it? How does your original understanding of this gospel compare with what we just shared? How does this story speak to your life?

Sharing Life Experience

Participants share an experience from their lives that connects with the biblical interpretation just presented.

See Christmas Day—Mass During the Day.

How does John's prologue speak to you? Did the exegesis offer any new insights? Does John's description of Christ as the eternal spoken word of God have anything to do with your life? What relevance does it have today? What was John trying to say to his community? In what way does this gospel challenge your community today? In what way has this conversation with the scriptures for today's liturgy invited change in your life? In what way are the biblical themes of covenant, exodus, creation, and community evident in today's readings? Do you still feel the same way about this text as when you began? Has your original understanding been stretched, challenged, or affirmed?

STEP 5
DECISION

The gospel demands a response.

In what concrete way might your parish be invited to respond? Are there any attitudes or behaviors you would like to change as a result of today's conversation? What one concrete action will you take this week in response to the liturgy today?

DOCTRINAL ISSUES

What Church truth/teaching/doctrinal issue could be drawn from the gospel for the second Sunday after Christmas?

Participants suggest possible doctrinal themes that flow from the readings.

Possible Doctrinal Themes

Incarnation; soteriology; salvation; paschal mystery; holy exchange; Jesus Christ; Son of God

Present the doctrinal material at this time.

1. The facilitator gives input on a particular doctrinal issue of his or her prior choosing. OR
2. The group chooses a doctrinal issue from the list they created. They read together from the Doctrinal Appendix or other appropriate, official Church documents and the works of respected theologians.

(Many doctrinal issues are found in the Doctrinal Appendix at the back of this workbook. If you are choosing an issue from this resource, please refer to it now.)

Reflection questions centered around the chosen doctrinal theme can be found at the end of each topic in the Doctrinal Appendix. The questions are based on the five-step reflection process. If you choose a topic not included in the Doctrinal Appendix, craft your own questions according to the same five-step process.

Following the reflection questions you will be reminded to return to chapter 7, "Preparing the Catechetical Session," to assist you in crafting your own session.

Closing Prayer

Let us pray
[aware of the dignity to which we are called by the love of Christ]

Father of our Lord Jesus Christ,
our glory is to stand before the world
as your own sons and daughters.
May the simple beauty of Jesus' birth
summon us always to love what is most deeply
    human
and to see your Word made flesh
reflected in those whose lives we touch.
We ask this through Christ our Lord.[7]

[7]Second Sunday after Christmas, "Alternative Opening Prayer," *The Sacramentary*.

Epiphany

Environment

The liturgical color of the Christmas season is white. This celebration is centered around the manifestation of Christ, the Light. Epiphany is also the day on which we hear about the wise men from the East. Perhaps a Christ candle could be lit as you pray the opening prayer.

INTRODUCTORY RITES

Opening Song (or Entrance Antiphon)

The Lord and ruler is coming: kingship is his, and government and power (see Mal 3:1; 1 Chron 19:12).[1]

Opening Prayer

The facilitator of the session may lead the prayer. Others in the group may be asked to proclaim the readings.

Let us pray
[Grateful for the glory revealed today through God made man]

Pause for silent prayer.

Father of light, unchanging God,
today you reveal to men of faith
the resplendent fact of the Word made flesh.
Your light is strong,
your love is near;
draw us beyond the limits which this world imposes
to the life where your Spirit makes all life
    complete.
We ask this through Christ, our Lord.[2]

LITURGY OF THE WORD

The readings are proclaimed.

Let us listen to God's word.

---

[1]Epiphany: "Entrance Antiphon," *The Sacramentary.*
[2]Epiphany: "Alternative Opening Prayer," *The Sacramentary.*

First Reading
Isaiah 60:1–6

The return from exile in Trito-Isaiah foreshadows the liberation won by Christ through his manifestation to the world. The Gentiles converging upon Jerusalem provide a glimpse of the manifestation of Christ—not just to the chosen people, but to the Gentiles and to the entire world.

In the poems of Trito-Isaiah there is great excitement and expectancy regarding what is about to take place. "It is as if the hell and horror had been left behind, and one is moving up a high, sun drenched summit to the very doors of the Kingdom of God."[3]

Prophets were often gifted by the Spirit to utter oracles that transcended the immediate reality. They were able to understand the meaning of God's plan in the present as well as in the future. When we hear these prophetic utterances over and over in scripture, we begin to see God's plan for the human race. It all makes perfect sense in light of what has been proclaimed throughout the generations. The prophet saw the fulfillment of God's action. He saw the magnificent light that would illumine the darkness created by humanity's sin. He saw the future city in which God's power would be seen by all. The prophet of Isaiah's time knew well about God's manifestation. It was called *shekina* glory, the unveiled, glorious presence of Yahweh. The prophet saw a future where all would live in *shekina* glory. The new city would be illumined for all to see. St. John would also see this prototype city aglow with the magnificence of Yahweh's *shekina* in the prophecies of Revelation. Even though there is an eschatological promise inherent in such prophecies, we know that Christ is the manifestation of God's glory.

We are reminded of the typological aspects of this text when we read of Gentiles riding on camels and bearing gifts of gold, frankincense, and myrrh. When we read of them converging upon the city of

---

[3]*TKG,* 137.

Jerusalem singing praises, our attention is immediately drawn to the heart of the Christian story.

Responsorial Psalm
Psalm 72:1–2, 7–8, 10–11, 12–13

This psalm, originally a hymn composed for the Davidic monarchy, speaks of the future messiah and describes those bearing gifts and bowing in worship before the messiah who was to come. This psalm was appropriated by the Christian community as a foreshadowing of Jesus. The messiah/king would come to bring God's justice-liberation and help for the oppressed and the needy.

Second Reading
Ephesians 3:2–3, 5–6

Overview to St. Paul's Letter to the Ephesians: The letter to the Ephesians is directly related to the letter to the Colossians. Duling and Perrin attest that Ephesians quotes and develops the themes found in the letter to the Colossians. Nearly a third of the words from Colossians appear in Ephesians.

There is a question as to the Pauline authorship of both letters. Those who insist on Paul as the author say that it is highly probable that one man could have written the letters in a short amount of time, thus their similarity. Those who argue that Paul did not write the letters suggest that both letters (Colossians and Ephesians) were reiterations of Paul's previous writings. Those former letters were probably used as a reference for the writing of Colossians and Ephesians. Those who do not believe that Paul wrote Ephesians also point to the many words (forty) that are not found in Paul's other letters, but are instead found in later Christian literature.

Another reason scholars deny Pauline authorship lies in the differences between Paul's usual theology and the theology inherent in this letter. In the letter to the Ephesians, the author refers to the "holy apostles" as having special insight. Duling and Perrin suggest that "Paul never distinguishes apostles in this way and never regards them as 'holy' in a way other Christians are not."[4] Ephesians uses the word church exclusively as a term for the universal church (resonant with the theme

of the "Great Church" of later centuries). Paul used the word to mean local community as well.

The letter to the Ephesians is also not a letter in the usual Pauline form. Paul usually wrote in response to problems or an occasion in his life. The letter is certainly different from Paul's other letters. Whether it be the work of a calmer, more reflective imprisoned Paul, or the brilliant work of a later disciple of Paul's who was eager to make his master's ideas known, what is certain is the plentiful adherents to both sides of the controversy.

The context for the letters: Paul established a mission in Ephesus and Colossae ten years earlier on his third missionary tour. Ephesus was his headquarters. The letters to the Colossians and Ephesians are known as the "Captivity Epistles" because they were written from his jail cell. Paul had left Corinth for Jerusalem. He was constantly in trouble with his pursuers, the Jewish authorities. They accused him of defacing the temple and he was subsequently thrown into prison. He spent three years in prison in Jerusalem and Caesarea.

A great concern for Paul in Ephesus and Colossae was dilution of the gospel due to the influence of gnosticism. Paul was concerned with promoting an authentic gospel, not one made of people's own agendas and exclusive concerns. Even though Paul passionately preached the universality of the Christ event, he was appalled at the way in which the gnostics distorted his teaching and in the process diluted the Christ-event. They relegated the person of Christ to angelic being or heavenly body. Paul would have none of it. "Christ is no mere angel or semi-god. He is the very image of the invisible God, a window through which men can finally see without distortion God as he really is."[5] To reduce Christ to a mere heavenly body was to deny his role as Savior of the world. The letter to the Ephesians addresses and refutes this gnosticism.

Today's Pericope: Today's reading from Ephesians is read every year in all three cycles on the feast of Epiphany. Today's text resonates with the reading from Isaiah when it asserts that the Gentiles along with the Jews are also heirs to the promise of salvation. All men and women from every nation on

---

[4]*NTI*, 220.

[5]*GAP*, 113.

140

earth will converge on the holy city singing God's praise. Matthew picks up the same theme with the arrival of the magi bearing gifts. The message of all three readings is not to be missed. Salvation is for all people. No one is excluded. Jew and Gentile alike share the covenant. Two themes are represented in this pericope: Jesus, the revelation of God and the universal message of salvation.[6]

Gospel
Matthew 2:1–12

Today's gospel tells the story of the magi who come bearing gifts to the messiah who was to be born. Herod tries to trick them into divulging the location of this great event.

STEP 1
NAMING ONE'S EXPERIENCE

What was your first impression? What captured your attention?

Each person names his or her initial impression. Statements should be brief. No reasons should be given at this time. All simply listen without agreeing or disagreeing.

STEP 2
UNDERSTANDING

What understanding did you bring with you to these readings? In a brief statement, what do you think this gospel is trying to convey?

STEP 3
INPUT FROM VISION/STORY/TRADITION

Liturgical Context

Please read the Christmas Overview for background on this feast. The Epiphany texts need to be understood in the context of the entire Christmas season. Epiphany is another celebration of Christ's manifestation to the world. Even though

there is great emphasis placed on the story of the magi, the theme of this feast transcends the manifestation of God to the gentiles; it centers on God's self-revelation to humanity in the person of Christ. This is another manifestation in a line of manifestations during the season: to the shepherds, to Mary, the Mother of God, through baptism, and now to all the world.

In the overview of the Christmas season it was stated that the feast of the Epiphany has undergone a few shifts in the Eastern and Western Church. When East and West transposed their feasts, the West preserved Christmas overtones in its observance of Epiphany. "The connection is especially clear in the insertions in the first eucharistic prayer, since they speak of the celebration of this most holy day 'when your only Son, sharing your eternal glory, showed himself in a human body.'"[7] However, Epiphany was also the day to remember the magi. As the magi were considered Gentiles, the feast proclaimed the manifestation of God's mission to the Gentiles and to all nations.

Today's liturgy remembers and makes present the very mystery it celebrates—that is, the manifestation of God's power, God's salvation to the entire human race. The opening prayers of this liturgy exhort us to listen to the readings "as an announcement of a mystery, of the good news, of what is and will be."[8] The celebration calls us to live in the glory that is ours. In the Epiphany liturgy when we pray the "Prayer over the Gifts" we ask God to accept our offerings, not of gold, frankincense, and myrrh, but our very selves—our hearts and our humanity. The preface for Epiphany proclaims the feast's central theme, Christ, the Light of the Nations: "Today you revealed in Christ your eternal plan of salvation and showed him as the light of all peoples. Now that his glory has shown among us you have renewed humanity in his immortal image."

Gospel Exegesis

The facilitator provides input regarding critical biblical scholarship on this text. The input includes insights as to how people would have heard the gospel in Jesus' time.

---

[6]*PNL*, 478.

[7]*LY*, 147.
[8]*DL* (I), 254.

Detailed historicity is not the object of this story. A far greater concern is the meaning of God's manifestation to the world expressed through the symbolic language of the story. That does not mean that the story is not based on a factual occurrence. Certainly, something happened to elicit such a narrative. However, the author cares little about the details. It is the point of the story that has captured his imagination, and in the process of telling that story he hopes to capture ours.

The way Matthew tells the story is "colored by the faith which enlightened the evangelist when he wrote his work; it expresses and clarifies the faith of the Church at the time; he intended it to be an aid to the faith of those Christians for whom he wrote. But faith is not simply a matter of acknowledging that Jesus is Messiah, Lord and Son of God. It involves obedience to him now. The Gospel is not only 'kerygma,' that is to say, proclamation of faith; it is also 'catechesis,' instruction on how to unify one's faith and life. This part of the message is especially stressed in Matthew."[9]

"After Jesus' birth . . ." begins the narrative regarding the approaching magi. Matthew puts this story in the context of the wider political arena. Herod was reputed to be compulsive and neurotic with regard to the possible political overthrow of his power. One cannot miss the subtlety of Herod's part in this drama. The scribes and Pharisees in Matthew's gospel quote Micah regarding the messiah's projected birthplace and are unaffected and unimpressed. Herod, on the other hand, takes the story of the "King of the Jews" quite literally and seriously. Those who knew better and *should have gotten it*, ignored it; and those who should have had no understanding or interest *did get it*, and as a result set out to do violence.

The mysterious magi enter the scene. The story tells us little of their origin. However, because of Psalm 72, where kings from Tarshish and the Isles come bearing gifts, it is assumed that the magi are those referred to in the psalm. This puts their place of origin in Persia. The only reason we have assumed there were three is due to the three gifts of frankincense, gold, and myrrh. In later Western tradition they were given the names Balthasar, Melchior, and Caspar. They became symbols of the diversity of the church, of God's manifestation to the Gentile world, to all peoples.

Jesus is called the "King of the Jews" in order to name him the messiah. The *star* is a reference to a messianic prophecy in the Old Testament book of Numbers in which a star was identified with the messiah (Num 24:17). For Matthew, the magi signify that Christ has always manifested his glory to people from distant lands. There is noticeable irony in the fact that it is the very scribes and Pharisees who supply the magi with the scriptures that direct them to the place where their search will end.

The magi find the child and their search ends. They learn of Herod's evil plotting and thus return home by a different route. Having found the child Jesus, their lives were forever touched. They were transformed. Their change in direction alerts us to this transformation. A change in direction in the Bible assumes a change of heart, conversion, a *metanoia*.

In ancient times, people were often attracted to astral religions because of the cold predictability of the stars.[10] These religions were very burdensome as people believed themselves under submission to powers beyond their control. Some early Christians were offended by this story as it appeared to tolerate astrology. However, their problem was not Matthew's problem. The star merely served a purpose. The star was the instrument that would lead people to the One who would break the power of any force that would bind people to a predetermined fate. When people are in God's hands, their fate is secure in and through Jesus.

Later the gifts of gold, frankincense, and myrrh became symbols of Christ's kingship, his divinity, and his suffering. Like Christmas, Epiphany is a feast of redemption. Christ became incarnated in our world and manifested the presence of God in order to save the world from itself. Sin could be conquered only through the life, death, and resurrection of the One who was born and the One who revealed his glory to all the nations. The call

---

[9]J. Dupont, "L'evangile de saint Matthieu: quelques cles de lecture," in *Communautes et liturgies* 57 (1975): 21.

[10]Benedict T. Viviano, O.P., "The Gospel of Matthew," *NJBC*, 636.

of this gospel is to proclaim the *shekina* glory of God through Christ.

This is a feast of manifestation. God manifests himself to the world. He elevates the human heart and offers humanity his divine dignity. God sits on the throne of heaven and earth and is Lord over all the world. God is a God not just for a select few, but for the whole world. This is a missionary feast par excellence. "All nations will come to this light (v. 3); all are called to become disciples of Jesus Christ (Mt 28:19). This is why Epiphany is the great missionary feast. A church which is not missionary is a contradiction as the community of Christ's followers. This is true for all Christians, for faith is not a private and interior matter; rather it impels communication and life in community."[11]

Proclaim the gospel again.

Sometimes we gain new insights when we hear the text after the interpretation has been given. Someone from the group proclaims the gospel a second time.

STEP 4
TESTING

Conversation with the Liturgy and the Scriptures

Test your original understanding in dialogue with the text.

(You might consider breaking into smaller groups.)

Were there any new insights? Was there anything you had not considered before? There are many levels of meaning in this text, such as inclusivity, the manifestation of God's power, and the fact that the Gentiles appropriated the faith while the chosen ones missed it. How are these themes relevant for our community today? Has your original understanding of these stories been transformed in any way? How? How does this story speak to your life?

Sharing Life Experience

This feast reminds me of a special young man who is on an odyssey of discovery. God is compelling him

[11]*SWTLY*, 38.

toward God's incredible light. I am honored to be a part of this young man's life. In willing obedience, he is following a star, not knowing where it will lead. I am awed by his journey (even though I often find myself frustrated by it, as it does not always conform to the norms that society sets out for those preparing for the adult world).

As a young adult he does not come across many peers who understand his faith journey. In some ways it is a lonely road for him. Yet he has heard the voice of God within. It beckons him. The miracle lies in his ability to hear the voice midst the pressures and lures of his everyday experiences. He sees God in all the experiences of his life. He is open to discovery and to the mysteries God reveals to him. This manifestation of God in his life is not the pious imaginings of a dreamer. His epiphany has radically transformed his life. He has been on several wrong roads, and like the magi (and because of the promptings of God) has moved toward his destiny by taking the difficult road of conversion. He listens to God's voice and at age twenty-two works very hard to act on the word he hears. He has allowed God to change his life and is grateful for the gift of divine energy. When dealing with someone who is difficult, he feels that it is his responsibility to offer the gift of God's divine energy to that person, because it is the only thing that has the power to transform. I have seen a huge change in his life and his change invites change within me. I watch his response to the God within and I marvel at his ability to listen, respond, and then to allow his shortcomings to be tested and changed. Evidence of this young sojourner's relationship with God is readily observable. He offers love to everyone—the poor, the outcast, and even those he finds most difficult to love. He believes his life's mission is to offer the gift of himself to the less fortunate. He is not an idyllic, superhuman young adult. He struggles with the same issues of all young people today. Yet he is incredibly and refreshingly unique in his ability to listen to, and be conscious of, the God who is manifested to him in his everyday life. Watching this young man respond to the word and will of God invites change within me. I thank God for his witness in my life.

Epiphany is a reminder that God continues to make his presence known to us and invites us to respond to that presence. This feast also prompts us to share with others the divine energy that has been given to us. There is responsibility attached to our relationship with God.

All share their life experience.

What was Matthew's message to his community? Is it relevant today? How do these scriptures speak to you as church and to you personally? Are the biblical images of covenant, creation, exodus, and community in full view in today's liturgy? How? Do you still feel the same way about this text as you did when you began? How would you explain these readings to a stranger?

STEP 5
DECISION

The gospel demands a response.

In what way are we called to respond to this gospel? How are our attitudes challenged in this liturgy? Would there be any contemporary corollary for the issue of Gentile inclusion today? Has this conversation with the exegesis of the Epiphany called for transformation of my actions or attitudes? Name one concrete action we/I will take this week as a response to today's liturgy.

Christian Initiation: The baptism of Jesus was originally associated with the feast of Epiphany. In the East baptisms were celebrated on this day. Since initiation has an historical connection with this feast, perhaps today would be an appropriate time to celebrate the baptism of people with special circumstances (such as catechized, unbaptized persons) or with infants. It might also be a good time to celebrate a rite of full communion in the Catholic Church, or a rite of acceptance, or a rite of welcome.

DOCTRINAL ISSUES

What church truth/teaching/doctrinal issue could be drawn from the gospel for the feast of the Epiphany?

Participants suggest possible doctrinal themes that flow from the readings.

Possible Doctrinal Themes

Epiphany; manifestation; christology; missiology; evangelization; ecumenism

Present the doctrinal material at this time.

1. The facilitator gives input on a particular doctrinal issue of his/her prior choosing. OR
2. The group chooses a doctrinal issue from the list they created. They read together from the Doctrinal Appendix.

(The doctrinal issues are found in the Doctrinal Appendix in the back of this workbook. If you are choosing an issue from this resource, please refer to it now.)

Reflection questions centered around the chosen doctrinal theme can be found at the end of each topic in the Doctrinal Appendix. The questions are based on the five-step reflection process. If you choose a topic not included in the Doctrinal Appendix, craft your own questions according to the same five-step process.

Following the reflection questions you will be reminded to return to chapter 7, "Preparing the Catechetical Session," to assist you in crafting your own session.

Closing Prayer

God has called you out of darkness
into his wonderful light.
May you experience his kindness and blessings,
and be strong in faith, in hope and in love. Amen.
Because you are followers of Christ,
who appeared in this day as a light shining in
    darkness,
may he make you a light to all your sisters and
    brothers.

Response: Amen.

The wise men followed the star,
and found Christ who is light from light.
May you find the Lord
when your pilgrimage is ended.

Response: Amen.[12]

---

[12]Epiphany: "Solemn Blessing," *The Sacramentary.*

BAPTISM OF THE LORD

Environment

This feast brings the Christmas season to an end.

INTRODUCTORY RITES

Entrance Antiphon (or Opening Song)

When the Lord had been baptized, the heavens opened, and the Spirit came down like a dove to rest on him. Then the voice of the Spirit came down like a dove to rest on him. Then the voice of the Father thundered: This is my beloved Son, with him I am well pleased. (Mt 3:16–17)[1]

Opening Prayer

The facilitator of the session may lead the prayer. Others in the group may be asked to proclaim the readings.

Let us pray
[that we will be faithful to our baptism]

   Pause for silent prayer.

Almighty, eternal God,
when the Spirit descended upon Jesus
at his baptism in the Jordan,
you revealed him as your own beloved Son.
Keep us, your children, born of water and the Spirit,
faithful to our calling.
We ask this through our Lord Jesus, Christ, your
   Son,
who lives and reigns with you and the Holy Spirit,
one God, forever, and ever.[2]

LITURGY OF THE WORD

The readings are proclaimed.

---

[1]Baptism of the Lord: "Entrance Antiphon," *The Sacramentary.*

[2]Baptism of the Lord: "Opening Prayer," *The Sacramentary.*

Year ABC First Reading
Isaiah 42:1–4, 6–7

(Please refer to the first Sunday of Advent for an overview of the Book of the Prophet Isaiah.)

Today's Pericope: Scholars believe that the Suffering Servant in Deutero-Isaiah represents Israel and her role as covenant people in relationship to Yahweh. There is strong evidence that the writer is referring specifically to Israel. Israel was servant from the very beginning, from her very origins in the womb of Sarah. Servant Israel is Yahweh's agent who quietly brings the idolatrous nations to justice. "Israel's election is for responsibility."[3] The image of Suffering Servant belongs to Israel who, through exile, was tried by God for her transgressions and was re-created in order to participate in God's plan of salvation.

Bernard Anderson suggests that there are flaws in this interpretation. The second poem clearly refers to an *individual* whose mission is *to* Israel. The "Servant" of Deutero-Isaiah acclaims that Yahweh called him from the womb to be a light to the nations. Thus, the Servant is an individual, not the collective Israel.

Some believe the servant was Moses; others believe it to be Deutero-Isaiah himself. Some believe the Suffering Servant was a remnant few who would remain faithful to Yahweh. Others believe the Servant was some future messianic person. (Jesus referred to himself as the Suffering Servant.) The early Christian community believed Deutero-Isaiah to be prophesying about their Messiah and Lord, Jesus Christ.

In today's liturgy it makes no difference which hypothesis is correct. Deutero-Isaiah is chosen on this feast to shed light on the mission of Christ. Jesus is the fulfillment of Second Isaiah's word to Israel. It is Jesus who establishes God's justice. It is Jesus who reaches out to the poor and the power-

---

[3]*UOT,* 490.

less. It is Christ who, assuming the role of Suffering Servant, dies for the transgressions of many. Today this reading does not stand on its own. It prefigures Jesus' baptism in the River Jordan.

Year B First Reading

In Year B, this reading may be used. Optional: Isaiah 55:1–11.

(Refer to the first Sunday in Advent for an overview of the Book of the Prophet Isaiah.)

Today's Pericope: Today's reading from Isaiah invites us to look back on salvation history to a more present, sacramental stance. We are brought into the presence and action of Christ. Isaiah's conclusion to the "Book of Consolations" speaks of that day in which God's people will be lavished with rich fare and flowing water. "Deutero-Isaiah invites poor people to a joyful banquet."[4] Throughout the Bible, the banquet image is used to demonstrate God's care for Israel. The messianic age and everlasting life in heaven are often described as a banquet.

Yahweh insists that the only requirement for this banquet is thirst for God. People are to seek God, who is transcendent and elusive. God is near enough to be troubled by the sin of humanity, however. What Christian does not turn her or his eyes toward baptism and eucharist when hearing of quenched thirst and rich food, spread for all, rich and poor alike? How could a Christian not think of the eucharistic banquet when hearing of Isaiah's admission-free banquet for the salvation of all people?

The Word of God again plays a very important, sacramental role in this reading. "God's word is the initiator: from it comes salvation."[5] Stuhlmueller suggests that, in Isaiah, God's Word is not so much a message as it is an event in the mystery of salvation history. God's Word is not static, but living; it causes action. God's Word will accomplish what God intends. God's Word will restore Israel. The world rejoices as God brings Israel home. Sin will be no more in the new

Jerusalem. Sin and death will not be invited guests at the eternal banquet; they will be gone forever. The *shalom* peace of God will reside eternally in God's restored Paradise. Jesus, Word of God, brings salvation to the world. We draw deeply and joyfully from the springs of our sacramental salvation.

Year C First Reading

In Year C this reading may be used. Optional: Isaiah 40:1–5, 9–11.

Today's Pericope: Today's reading comes from a section of Isaiah referred to as the "Book of Consolation." The context is the return from Babylonian exile. Great news is proclaimed—the exile is over. It is an opportunity to compare the empty gods of Babylon with the omniscient and omnipowerful God of Israel. The scene of today's reading is God's heavenly council and the commissioning of the prophet. It was a common ancient belief that the gods assembled together in a heavenly court. The Israelites appropriated that understanding to Yahweh. As King, the people assumed Yahweh was surrounded by a royal court.

The exile was understood as a punishment for Israel's sin. The author does admit that Israel received a double portion of punishment, however, indicating that not all of Israel's suffering was chastisement for sin. Later in Deutero-Isaiah renewed significance will be given to the suffering endured by those in exile.

The angel announces God's decree, alluding to the triumphant procession of Yahweh from Sinai during the exodus. Freedom from bondage in Babylon is regarded by Second Isaiah as a second exodus. It is the revelation of God. In the first exodus the people followed the pillar of fire—the presence of God. Second Isaiah insists that now all people will experience God's revelation. God's Word is unshakable, whereas human life is transitory. The Babylonians who before appeared invincible are now nothing but grass in the face of God's power.

In verses 9–11 Zion/Jerusalem is told to shout the news throughout Israel. Jerusalem is a symbolic figure denoting the returning exiles who join the prophet in the work of restoration. Many Jews

---

[4]Carroll Stuhlmueller, "Deutero-Isaiah and Trito-Isaiah," *NJBC*, 343.

[5]*DL* (III), 52.

stayed in Babylon, believing that they would fare better there rather than in Israel. Thus, the prophet's message is not just an announcement that deliverance was at hand; it was also an exhortation to accept it. He reminds the people that God is with them and will care for them. God will shepherd them in their work of restoration.

This text is often referred to when speaking of the John the Baptist tradition. Even though the allusion in John 1:23 ("the voice of one crying out in the wilderness") is not an accurate interpretation of the original, it does remind us that John (like the prophet in today's reading) was also announcing a new salvation, just like the salvation/liberation announced to the people of Israel. So, too, does Jesus' baptism announce to us the good news of God's revelation on the face of the earth—a new liberation and salvation won for us by his life, death, and resurrection.

Year ABC Responsorial Psalm
Psalm 29:1–4, 9b–10

The "voice above the waters" in the psalm chosen for this liturgy is harmonious with the voice of God from heaven in today's gospel. The psalm proclaims the manifestation of God through Jesus' baptism in the River Jordan.[6]

Year B Responsorial Psalm

In Year B, this text may be used. Optional: Isaiah 12:2–3, 4b–6.

Even though this passage is found in First Isaiah, it is more reminiscent of Deutero-Isaiah. It remembers the return from Babylonian exile as a second exodus. The psalm is a song reminiscent of the Song of Moses. There is an inherent fourfold structure—"exodus/return from exile/ Christ's death and resurrection/the foundation of the Church and our initiation into it through baptism and the Eucharist."[7]

Year C Responsorial Psalm

In Year C this psalm may be used. Optional: Psalm 104:1b–4, 24–25, 27–28, 29–30.

Psalm 104 is a hymn of praise to Yahweh, Master and Creator of the world. God cares for all creation. When God cares for the world, there is abundance. Without God's providence, human beings would die. God sustains all life.

Year ABC Second Reading
Acts 10:34–38

(Refer to Easter Sunday for an overview of the Acts of the Apostles.)

Today's Pericope: This pericope from the Acts of the Apostles attests to the manifestation of God through Jesus Christ. Jesus' baptism is testimony to God's presence through Jesus' words and works. There are a few significant segments in this reading, obviously chosen for its connection to the gospel. First, the story of Cornelius was important for the early church. Cornelius was a gentile. His conversion opened the door to the gentile mission and to the inclusion, integration, and incorporation of gentile Christians with Jewish Christians. Peter proclaimed that God has no favorites, since all are called equally. "Therefore, the door is open to anyone who fears God and works righteousness as Cornelius does (cf. 10:33). Such a person is 'acceptable' to God."[8]

Second, verse 36 reflects evidence of a key theme of both Luke and Acts. Luke's primary message is the proclamation that Jesus is Lord and Messiah. "He brings peace to the Jewish people in fulfillment of scriptural promises, it applies to all peoples, for they are invited to share with Israel in this messianic peace."[9] Verse 36 is an echoing of the birth narrative in which God proclaimed to the shepherds that peace had come to all the earth. Robert Tannehill suggests that verses 36–43 are a chronological summary of Luke's gospel from the birth stories through the sending of the apostles to the world. Empowered by the Holy Spirit, Jesus' ministry manifested God's healing and forgiveness and liberated those in bondage. He established a peace that only Yahweh could give. The response to Jesus' life and work was and is apostolic witness to his life, work, and resurrection.

---

[6] *PNL,* 132.
[7] Ibid., 68.

[8] *NULA,* 137.
[9] Ibid., 140.

We encounter the story of Christ through events that reflect God's action and presence in and through Jesus' life, his work, and the ultimate fulfillment of God's plan of salvation for the human race. Jesus proclaims God's reign. God tells Mary of her role in salvation history; God tells the shepherds the good news of Jesus' birth; God manifests himself to the magi, to the gentile world, to all nations; and God manifests the fulfillment of his master plan through Jesus in the baptism at the River Jordan.[10] Reginald Fuller asserts that it is often said that a significant contrast exists between the message of Jesus and the message of the church. "Jesus preached the kingdom, but the church preached Jesus."[11] Fuller maintains that, in essence, there is really little difference. Jesus was proclaiming God's action and presence in the lives of human beings through the healing, exorcisms, and his words and works. The church, on the other hand, proclaimed and proclaims that God was and is present through the signs, words, and deeds Jesus performed. God has, is, and will continue to be present in human history.

Year B Second Reading

In Year B this second reading may be used. Optional: 1 John 5:1–9.

Please refer to the Feast of the Holy Family for an overview of the Johannine letters.

Today's Pericope: All who put their faith in Jesus Christ, the Son of God, are to love God as their Father. God commands that God's children love God just as God loves them. Such love is never burdensome. Christians are to grow in the faith they have been given. This faith is in Jesus Christ, who became one with humanity, who ministered in the world from the time of his baptism until his death and resurrection, and who gave his life for the world, thereby conquering sin and death.

The Spirit of God testifies to the truth of Christ. Ongoing living testimony to this faith is through baptism and eucharist ("So there are three that testify, the Spirit, the water, and the blood")—the living memorial of his life, death, and resurrec-

tion. Baptism and eucharist are the embodiment of Christ's presence and eternal life. Spirit, water, and blood are signs of God's presence. To deny the signs we have been given is to reject Jesus himself. The purpose of the entire letter is to remind the Christians that they are heirs of eternal life as long as they remain faithful to Jesus Christ, Son of God. On this feast of revelation of Christ, we are invited with the Johannine community to grow in faith in Christ, the Son of God.

Year C Second Reading

In Year C this reading may be used: Optional: Titus 2:11–14, 3:4–7.

Overview of the Letter to Titus: Titus was not a letter written to a community, but to an individual in regard to his pastoral duties. There are two other such letters (1–2 Timothy) and the three are referred to as the "pastoral epistles." Many biblical critics question Pauline authorship of the letters. They assert that there are too many differences of style, language, theology, and the situation surrounding the letters. Paul's letters were far less formal than the pastoral epistles. Also, pseudonymous epistles were common. In an attempt to pass on a master's legacy to later generations, authors would use his name as an official stamp of approbation. The authors would pen the master's name in hopes that his teaching would have an influence on the problems facing that later community.

There already appears to be a hierarchical church structure in place at the time the letters were written—bishops, presbyters, and deacons. It is the responsibility and mission of the bishop to teach. The teaching is based on the apostolic tradition. The letters urged church leaders to maintain structure and order. Together with the scriptures, this forms the total deposit of faith. The bishop is to safeguard the authentic teaching of the church. There is also evidence that apostolic succession was already a reality by the time the letters were written. Eschatological concerns are no longer an issue. The church now sees itself as an earthly reality. The epistles are concerned with orthodox teaching and the moral life. They are obviously influenced by Hellenistic Jewish Wisdom teaching and modern philosophy. One theme inherent in

---

[10]*PNL*, 132.
[11]Ibid.

the Letter to Titus is that Christians are not to retreat from the world—they are to be signs in the world. Christians are to live upright lives, remembering that their final fulfillment will take place when Christ comes again.

Today's Pericope: The author of Titus insists that God alone empowers us to live upright and moral lives and to have hope in the future. God's grace is personified and Jesus is the reality and incarnation of that saving grace in human history. God's favor is for all human beings. God is the source of all knowledge and bestows it freely upon human beings. God educates his people—a true education. High value was placed on the intellect in Graeco-Roman society. The education God provides helps the Christian live a virtuous life—the cardinal virtues of moderation, justice, and piety.

The pastoral epistles seem to use language which implies that Christ is subordinate to God. However, they refer to him as the "past and also yet to come manifestation of God, the same titles as God. Here he receives the very name of God."[12] The letter affirms that the promises God made in the scriptures are fulfilled and accomplished through Jesus Christ.

The gospel is proclaimed.

Gospel
Mark 1:7–11. You are my beloved Son; with you I am well pleased.

STEP 1
NAMING ONE'S EXPERIENCE

What were your first impressions? What was your first response to the gospel (or the other readings)? What captured your attention?

Each person names his or her initial impression. Statements should be brief. No reasons should be given at this time. All simply listen without agreeing or disagreeing.

---

[12]Robert A. Wild, S.J., "The Pastoral Letters," *NJBC*, 895.

STEP 2
UNDERSTANDING

In a brief statement, explain what you think this gospel is trying to convey.

STEP 3
INPUT FROM VISION/STORY/TRADITION

Liturgical Context

The focus of the Christmas season is theological rather than historical. Throughout the season we experience the multifaceted manifestations of God through Jesus Christ, his Son. Particularly in the East, the entire life of Christ is regarded as repeated manifestations of God, with the baptism of Jesus representing the most important. The East celebrated the Lord's baptism (and the manifestation at Cana) on the Feast of Epiphany. Prior to the renewed Roman calendar, this feast was not given the prominence it deserved in the Western church. Thus, without preempting Epiphany, the new calendar restored it to a prominent place. It now follows Epiphany and closes the Christmas season.

God anointed Jesus for public ministry through the power of the Holy Spirit. The baptism at the River Jordan is Jesus' ritual celebration of empowerment. He is empowered through the authority of the voice of God, Lord of the universe. Since John is intimately involved in this ritual event, the church avows that Jesus "shows his solidarity with the guilty human race and gives water the power to forgive sins."[13]

The preface of this liturgy expresses our theology succinctly and is very clear regarding God's role on the stage of salvation history. "You celebrated your new gift of baptism by signs and wonders at the Jordan. Your voice was heard from heaven to awaken faith in the presence among us of the Word made man. Your spirit was seen as a dove,

---

[13]*LY*, 148.

revealing Jesus as your servant, and anointing him with joy as the Christ, sent to bring to the poor the good news of salvation."[14]

The Second Typical Edition of the Lectionary for Mass, Volume I, has assigned optional first and second readings for use in Years B and C. The exegesis for these readings is also included.

Gospel Exegesis

The facilitator provides input from critical biblical scholarship on this text. This input includes insights as to how people would have heard the gospel in Jesus' time.

Like every gripping literary work, today's prologue opens Mark's gospel in dramatic style. We are introduced to John the Baptist. We can almost hear his gruff voice, see his straggly beard and prophet's garb, and smell the leftover whiff of one who has slept with wild animals and locusts—a bizarre character by today's standards. John proclaims that one greater than he is about to appear on the world's stage. This Great One will pour out his Spirit on the face of the earth. The reader should not be too alarmed at John's presence. He was, after all, the messenger foretold of old (Mal 3:11 and Is 4:3) who would prepare the way in the wilderness.

Malachi announced that the future messenger would be Elijah, coming on the Day of the Lord [*Kyrios*] as the eschatological promise. John was that new Elijah; he professed faith in Jesus as Lord [*Kyrios*]. The news of salvation through Jesus Christ is announced by the man named John, who not only looked like Elijah but also ate wilderness food like Elijah. God entered into the first covenant with the people of Israel *in the wilderness.* Now, John heralds a renewal of that covenant in that same wilderness. Jesus will inaugurate it. The entire scene with John is set in the context of the Old Testament prophetic tradition. The prophets foretold that God's final act of salvation would be enacted on the wilderness stage. John, the new Elijah, announces God's dawning salvation at the edge of the desert. Mark's message? The Day of the Lord was waiting in the wings to be ushered onto stage as creation's grand finale and Jesus would be its star.

---

[14]Baptism of the Lord: "Preface," *The Sacramentary.*

John's clarion call is for total repentance—a *metanoia* that requires nothing less than a coming to one's senses, turning one's life over completely, a total change of heart. John insisted on radical conversion accompanied by the sign of baptism. In light of the awesome event about to explode onto the world theater, is it any wonder? Yahweh's divine invitation was intended for all of Israel.

John's corporate call to conversion and repentance was intended to pave the way for Jesus who would baptize, not with John's water of repentance, but with the Holy Spirit. John's role in this prophetic drama was to point to Jesus. "See, there he is—I am not worthy to be his slave!" Mark is the only synoptic evangelist who puts John in the role of pointing to the coming Christ. The other evangelists stress the ethical preaching ministry of John. The prophets of old (Joel for one) promised that in the last days the Spirit would be poured out upon the world. *Baptism in the Holy Spirit* is that overflowing, cup-runneth-over outpouring of God's Spirit. (Refer also to the gospel exegesis for the second Sunday of Advent for further important background on the role of John the Baptist and further elaboration on this section of Mark's gospel.)

The locus of Mark's gospel is not only the wilderness, not only the inhabited world, but a much more cosmic space. Mark's stage is the Hebrew theology of cosmos. He refers back to a long ago, dramatic platform of revelation. The dais in which the formless wasteland, the firmaments, and the stars took their rightful bows as players is none other than the drama of genesis—creation. Now Mark remembers that thespian moment and expands our present understanding of world—a new symbolic universe. There is a place where Divinity resides and it is called heaven. For Mark there is no limitless universe. Following common belief, he understands there to be another place, just above the earth—a canopy draped over the earth's surface. Above the canopy is heaven—this is where the Voice originates, where God's voice is heard. "But it is also the heavens which may suddenly tear open to let the spirit of God pass through (1:10) and from where the voice of God is heard (1:11, 9, 7). The one who speaks from there is named by Jesus 'your father in heaven' (11:25–26), while he himself sometimes looks up to that heaven, for instance when saying a blessing (6:41)."[15]

Jesus left home to go to the desert and subsequently to John for baptism. This action in and of itself carries symbolic significance even though it is not mentioned directly. It is understood by the culture of the time, however. In the ancient Mediterranean world the family is the matrix of society. A person has no identity outside the family (see Easter vigil, symbol of church—fictive family). Jesus left his family and his village. What did this highly symbolic action mean, and what would he do? Those outside the family system might as well be dead. His action would also have been regarded as shameful. What was Jesus doing and what does it mean? John Pilch insists that Jesus' baptism holds the key to these queries.[16]

The voice from heaven opens and Jesus is proclaimed *Son* by the Father in heaven. Paternity could not be proven—for a person to be someone's son or daughter the father had to claim the child as his own. This is why it was so important for Joseph to acknowledge Jesus as his son and incorporate him into his family life. Joseph ensured that Jesus would have an honorable upbringing.

Jesus, having left home and family, now is acknowledged by none other than God the Father, who claims Jesus as his beloved Son. The heavens are torn—thus, it not a private event. If it had been meant for Jesus alone it would have been meaningless. Who are those witnesses since Mark does not mention any? Who will attest to Jesus' honor? Mark's readers. The gospel is his witness. The readers are privy to the spectacular event in the heavens. The reader (ancient and contemporary) can proclaim the source of Jesus' honor to the world.

We might think this scene an exercise in futility— our modern sensibilities would have little tolerance for stories of heavens ripping apart and voices thundering from above. Ancient readers are another matter altogether. There was a very strong belief in the spirit world. Voices from the heavens would not have been an unrealistic expectation. "In Mark's Gospel, it is chiefly this spirit world that knows and acknowledges Jesus' identity

as son of God. Here at the baptism, the divine voice is directed toward Jesus' identity as son of God."[17] Later, the evil spirits will also recognize Jesus' honorable status and acknowledge him as God's Son and God will reveal Jesus' identity to Peter, James, and John. At Jesus' trial one of the charges leveled against him was his claim to be God's Son.

Jesus' humble, lower-class standing in the social world would have been reason enough for people to question his legitimacy. Who did he think he was, anyway? By what right has he warranted a public persona? He offended them in their extreme status-conscious honor- and shame-based culture. At Jesus' baptism God legitimated his Son once and for all.

Ched Myers posits another understanding of today's pericope.[18] He suggests that this event signals the advent of a new creation. Certainly a savior would come from refined origins, with impressive credentials or genealogy! At least, that would be a first-century expectation. Mark's Jesus possesses no such credentials or genealogy. Nazareth is not even mentioned in any ancient historical source. Mark constantly drives home the point that Jesus came from humble origins. Even though Nazareth was a "nothing" place, Galilee was notorious. It was on the northern edge of Israel. People from Jerusalem and parts south regarded it with contempt. It was surrounded by Hellenistic cities, heavily populated with gentiles and comprised of mostly poor peasants. Jerusalem believed God's eschatological promises would be fulfilled in Jerusalem. Mark insists that the advent of the new creation is also a return to the spirituality of the wilderness (not the Temple). The wilderness is the locus of God's salvation, renewal, and re-creation.

Mark's drama makes a bold assertion: "Yet it is precisely upon this figure, of these doubtful social origins, in this remote location, that the divine favor falls."[19] The heavens are thus rent and the Voice speaks of Jesus' election—he is God's "Beloved Son." The allusion to an Isaiah text is not to be missed:

---

[15]*RM*, 27.
[16]*CWJB*, 20–21.

[17]Ibid., 20.
[18]*BSM*, 129.
[19]Ibid., 128.

"Oh that you would tear the heavens open
   and come down
to make known your name to your enemies,
and to make the nations tremble at your presence,
working unexpected miracles
such as no one has ever heard before"[20]
   (Is 64:1–2).

Is this obscure artisan from Nazareth the one foretold in Isaiah? In this instance the Divine Name affirms the proclamation made by John in the first verse: The beginning of the gospel of Jesus Christ, Son of God. At this point in the gospel all this is still privileged information. There were no witnesses at the Jordan. Like a Shakespearean play, Mark takes his readers off to the side and fills them in on what no one else at this point knows. We are privy to Jesus' identity. This time it is affirmed by none other than the Divine Word of God.

Jesus is thus named, we are thus privileged, and the scene ends quietly. Jesus then retreats into the desert. However, there is still more to be gleaned from the symbolic world surrounding the baptism. Is this Mark's way of proclaiming the new heavens and new earth? If so, it is rather a feeble attempt. It could be reduced to mere hallucination. There is still more going on. Jesus' baptism signals a new heaven and a new earth—"the creation of a new humanity."[21] How? Jesus' baptism is real; he is not pretending. However, it is distinct from the baptism of everyone else—those whom John baptized *in* the Jordan (v. 5). Jesus was baptized *into* the Jordan. Jesus' baptism was a complete and total act of repentance.

The Jews from Jerusalem and Judea were not submerged completely into John's baptism. They did not fully submit; they could not conform to the radical new way that John was suggesting. Jesus, on the other hand, submitted completely and in so doing repudiated and rejected the old way of *being*, the old order. It is a symbolic repudiation of the social and religious power structures. Jesus, in effect, cancels and abandons the obligations imposed by the religious system into which he was born. Jesus' death experience of repentance re-

leased him from all the obligations and the system's way of enforcing those obligations. Jesus is no longer bound by those imposed obligations. He is no longer obliged. Thus, the new creation begins by denouncing the old order. This new humanity, this new creation, will no longer be bound either. It is about liberation. Jesus' baptism is a subversive event—it sets him up as outside the Law. His mission will be to challenge the systems of order and imposed law.

Jesus' baptism sets the salvation history of God in motion again. It takes place on the edge of society—not at its center. We can appreciate that Jesus' baptism is a subversive event by what follows it. After Jesus declared himself liberated, he went to the desert to confront the ruler of the world and, in so doing, set in motion the apocalyptic combat myth (see thirty-fourth Sunday, second reading exegesis). Spirit-filled Jesus and Satan commence the struggle. The first part of Mark's gospel is a continuous struggle between Jesus and the demons. The political nature of Jesus' mission is thus sharpened by Mark's transition. Jesus begins his mission of preaching the kingdom of God (not the national kingdom that was expected, but an entirely new political and spiritual reality) after John was arrested. Jesus took up the "mantle of the fallen prophet. Jesus continues the proclamation of the kingdom and the demand for repentance—and all too soon he too will be targeted for arrest by the authorities."[22]

Mark challenges the oppressive power structures of first-century Palestine and sets the stage for what he believes is truth. Preaching a message of repentance ultimately leads to political trouble. One can expect such trouble when true to that message. Jesus reminds us of that in his last gospel. Mark keeps the reader off balance. Expectations are turned upside-down. Elijah has come and the Messiah is already on the world stage, but the expected end of the world has not come. Mark's Jesus turns the expectations of Messiah on end. The Jews believed that liberation of the Jewish nation would depend on the political and military intervention of the Messiah. One place (among others) that this expectation was alluded to was Malachi, the same citation used in today's reference to the messenger

---

[20]Revised Standard Version.
[21]Ibid.

---

[22]Ibid.

(John the Baptist). Mark, however, in using Malachi, omits reference to that type of messianic intervention. His omission is obvious. Mark also moved the center of believed messianic arrival from Jerusalem to the wilderness. Mark's narrative raises and answers the question, "Just what is a liberating messiah?" His point is clear. A liberating messiah is not a militaristic savior of the people. The rest of the gospel shows what it truly is and what was always intended by God. It is important to note that Jesus eventually left the desert. He did not stay there. His mission took him out into the world—to engage it, not to flee from it. Mark's prologue "narrates the dawn of the kingdom at the margins of the world. In it Mark announces an offensive upon the strongholds of oppression and the dawn of liberation, and launches the discipleship adventure. But from the very outset, the tone of the story anticipates conflict. This erupts in Jesus' very first public action in Capernaum."[23]

Proclaim the gospel again.

Sometimes we gain new insights when we hear the text after the interpretation is given. Someone from the group proclaims the gospel a second time.

STEP 4

TESTING

Conversation with the Liturgy and the Scriptures

Test your original understanding in dialogue with the text.

(You might consider breaking into smaller groups.)

Now that you've heard the exegesis, were there any new insights? How do you feel about it? How does your original understanding of this gospel compare with what we just shared? How does this story speak to your life?

Sharing Life Experience

Participants share an experience from their lives that connects with the biblical interpretation just presented.

---

[23]Ibid., 136.

The heavens were opened and the Divine Voice affirmed Jesus as "Son." When was the last time the Divine Voice affirmed me as "Daughter"? Certainly the heavens have never been rent, nor have I heard thunderous voices, but I have known the God who calls me "daughter" as well as "beloved" and "chosen." I have known that Divine Voice through the people of God who love me—unconditionally, not for what I do, but for who I am. I think of my family who cherishes me and I them. I am reminded of my friends who are always there, ready to uphold me in times of disaster, encourage me in times of doubt, and challenge me in times of despair. I am aware of that still, small Voice within, the Voice who exhorts us never to "settle." We are children of the "Most High God" and we deserve the best that life has to offer.

A dear friend listened to the Voice of God who called her "Beloved and Chosen" and in the process she found the charism of God-gifted vocation. That voice within urged, called, and invited her to remain steadfast. After staying home with her children for a few years, it was time for her to seek employment outside the home again. She knew the desires of her heart. She recognized that "heart voice" as the voice of God. She knew what she needed to do to be a fulfilled, "beloved," and "chosen" child. Yet, in the waiting process for fulfillment of the Voice's word, my friend was tempted to let go of her dream. "Act now, take what you can; you can get the job you want later." She made the choice to hold fast and wait for the Word she believed. "God has spoken, and God will do what God has promised." She believed that Word. She believed that her status as "beloved and chosen" was a gift from God. She would wait for God to act. She waited six weeks and watched other good positions sail on right past her. She remained steadfast. Then came her exodus day. She was offered her life's work, vocation, and ministry. She would breathe new life into the lives of children torn apart from abuse. She is an adoption counselor and today a supervisor of her department. She has made a huge difference in the lives of children and many families. Her fulfillment as a fully alive human being is the result of steadfast belief in the revelation of God, spoken to her as truth, affirming her as gift and as God's "beloved and chosen."

Would I, could I, be that courageous? Day in and day out God challenges me to listen to that Word, believe it, and act on it. Yet I resist. I still want to control. Jesus' baptism is a revelation of God's gift to the world. It is still a struggle to allow God to truly guide and direct my life. For every inch forward I take, I step back a mile. Then in a caterpillar crawl, onward I forge again. "I'll hand my life over to you, God, but this is what I want you to do with it once you get it." I do not know if I would have the tenacity to remain as steadfast as my friend. I do not know if I would have enough trust in the Voice in the first place. Yet, the Voice continues to shout to me above the din of doubt and exhorts me, "Believe it!" Still I find it difficult. Jesus was open to God's Voice, and where did it lead? To the cross. He was affirmed by the Divine Voice and was empowered to rattle cages and be a voice of truth.

Recently the voice of truth came tumbling into my life in a way that I was unprepared to hear. I was humbled in the process. Someone challenged the way I try to control the events of my life. Interior defensiveness started to prick the hairs on the back of my neck. My temperature raised and the blush in my cheeks turned to crimson as I listened to the charge. How could this person have more spiritual wisdom than I? Who is this person? Where did this person get such wisdom? This person is "out of the mainstream." What does he or she know? How could he or she be so wise? Jesus was out of the mainstream too. What struck me in today's exegesis is the notion that Jesus was no longer obligated or bound by mainstream-ism. Nor is this person of which I speak. I have never met anyone in my life who lives the gospel so innocently and so completely. I am bolstered and strengthened by this person's testimony of faith. There is part of me that refuses to legitimate God's work in his or her life. Yet this person is SO legitimate that it makes me question my own legitimacy. Perhaps I want a safe faith. Am I ready to stick my neck out like Jesus did? Or do I, in truth, really want a faith that I can control and which keeps the status quo intact? I am amazed at the way in which the gospel invites me to look at my worldview and to bring it into God's transformative love. Reflection on this gospel invites me to look at the ways in which God's revelation is present in my life, to trust it, and to let God chart the course for my life.

I am convinced that God puts these small challenges in my path in hopes that I will have opportunity to practice for the times I will be called on to be a subversive voice for the world's oppressed. I hope that I

will be up to the challenge and respond with tenacious persistence.

The message for our community is to trust that God is speaking a voice of invitation, that God has called us—we are divinely elected. With election (baptism) comes responsibility. The liturgy invites us to look beyond our complacency. Jesus was called "Beloved Son." We have Jesus as our example. It is often easy to accept the "easy, prayerful" parts of the gospel and regard the "tough things" with the attitude that this is another day—"Jesus didn't really mean THAT, for heaven's sake!" But, for "heaven's sake," he really did! When we consider that Jesus dined with the unclean, tax collectors, and prostitutes (making him ritually unclean by the religious standards of his day) and try to connect that with our everyday experience, we are forced to ask ourselves the question: "What tax collectors and prostitutes have we invited to dinner lately?" No other question has the potential to raise the angst of a parish community. Status as "beloved and chosen" invites martyrdom. I do not remember the last time many of us prayed, "Lord, please let us be martyrs for you." The gospel decisions our parish has made over the years are not without conflict and resistance. I would wonder if we are really living the gospel, if there had not been such conflicts. The challenge of today's gospel is to draw on the strength we possess because we are adopted children of God; we are divinely elected. We are beloved and chosen of God, and go forward with that positive image of self and church. If we could truly see ourselves the way God sees us, we, like Christ, have the potential to transform the world.

What was Mark trying to tell his community? Why do you suppose there are no witnesses to Jesus' baptism in today's gospel? What might that say to us today? What does it mean to you that Jesus was called "Beloved and Chosen"? How might that speak to your life? How do you feel about the possibility that Jesus' gospel was subversive for his time? In what way is that a challenge for the church today? What does the fact that the mission of Christ began at the desert's edge instead of at the center of Jerusalem say to us today? In what way does this gospel challenge your community today? In what way has this conversation with the scriptures for today's liturgy invited change in your life? In what way are the biblical themes of covenant, exodus, creation, and community evident in today's readings? Do you still feel the same way about this text as when you began? Has your original understanding been stretched, challenged, or affirmed?

STEP 5
DECISION

The gospel demands a response.

In what concrete way might your parish be invited to respond? Are there any attitudes or behaviors you would like to change as a result of today's conversation? What one concrete action will you take this week in response to the liturgy today?

Pastoral Considerations: Who are the people in your parish and neighborhood who most need the message of the Beloved and Chosen Christ? Who is not "beloved and chosen" in your parish? How do you reach out to the sick and suffering members of your community? What about the ones not in your community? No doubt this would be an excellent time for the parish to celebrate a rite of sprinkling so that all the faithful, including baptized candidates, are given an opportunity to reflect on the implications of their baptism.

Christian Initiation: This might be a good time for the anointing of catechumens. As usual the minor blessings and exorcisms can be prayed with them each week. This might also be an opportune time to once again remind candidates that we share one baptism and that we are already one with them by virtue of our baptism. Is there anyone in your parish ready to come into full communion of the Catholic Church or celebrate a rite of acceptance or welcome?

DOCTRINAL ISSUES

What Church truth/teaching/doctrinal issue could be drawn from the gospel for the Baptism of the Lord?

Participants suggest possible doctrinal themes that flow from the readings.

Possible Doctrinal Themes

Baptism; manifestation; incarnation; sacraments; sacramentality; salvation; soteriology; Jesus Christ; Son of God; discipleship; conversion

Present the doctrinal material at this time.

1. The facilitator gives input on a particular doctrinal issue of his or her prior choosing. OR
2. The group chooses a doctrinal issue from the list they created. They read together from the Doctrinal Appendix or other appropriate, official Church documents and the works of respected theologians.

(Many doctrinal issues are found in the Doctrinal Appendix at the back of this workbook. If you are choosing an issue from this resource, please refer to it now.)

Reflection questions centered around the chosen doctrinal theme can be found at the end of each topic in the Doctrinal Appendix. The questions are based on the five-step reflection process. If you choose a topic not included in the Doctrinal Appendix, craft your own questions according to the same five-step process.

Following the reflection questions you will be reminded to return to chapter 7, "Preparing the Catechetical Session," to assist you in crafting your own session.

Closing Prayer

Almighty, eternal God,
when the Spirit descended upon Jesus
at his baptism in the Jordan,
you revealed him as your own beloved Son.
Keep us, your children born of water and the Spirit,
faithful to your calling.
We ask this through our Lord Jesus Christ, your Son,
who lives and reigns with you and the Holy Spirit,
one God, for ever and ever.[24]

---

[24]Feast of the Baptism of the Lord: "Evening Prayer," *Christian Prayer: Liturgy of the Hours* (New York: Catholic Book Publishing Co., 1976).

THE SEASON OF LENT

THE SEASON OF LENT: AN OVERVIEW

The rich, liturgical color of royal purple cloaks the season in its penitential vesture. Simplicity and austerity quietly whisper images of the barren desert. Flowers are absent; music is sparse and the church quietly, but firmly, heralds its reflective "time out." Things have noticeably changed. As people and as church, we enter the poustinia of serious penitential and baptismal reflection. We take stock and assess our growth in the Christian life. We ask ourselves, "Where is there need for healing and reconciliation in our lives?"

> Lent is a preparation for the celebration of Easter. For the Lenten liturgy disposes both catechumens and the faithful to celebrate the paschal mystery: catechumens, through several stages of Christian initiation; the faithful, through reminders of their own baptism and through penitential practices.[1]

History of Lent

The history of Lent evolved over the centuries from varied and sometimes blended sources. Very early in the church's history, the Jewish Christians superimposed their worship of Jesus, the new Passover, on the annual celebration and understanding of Jewish Passover. Once this was established as an annual Christian feast, it was preceded by a day of fasting. At the same time, gentile Christians fasted on Wednesdays and Fridays, and celebrated the breaking of the bread after Sabbath, on the first day of the week. Eventually both traditions merged, and the annual Easter feast was celebrated on the Sunday closest to the Jewish Passover. The Saturday before Easter Sunday was designated a fast day and, since the Friday fast was already in observance, there emerged a two-day, pre-Easter fast. Eventually the fasting period was extended to begin the Sunday before Easter (a week-long fast).

Early in the church's history, the Christian initiation of adults was a focus of the pre-Easter fast. By the third century, more was required for an adult to become a Christian than simply converting to belief in Jesus Christ. A process of initiation emerged that extended over a period of time and included several stages marked by ritual celebrations. There was no time limit imposed and eventually the process extended over a period of three years. Initially, baptisms were not specifically assigned to the Easter celebration, but rather, were most often celebrated during the fifty days between Passover and Pentecost.

Scrolling through time to the fifth century, we find the observance of a three-week preparatory fast for baptism. By the eighth century, three scrutinies were celebrated with those preparing for baptism. The scrutinies, which took place on three consecutive Sundays, are believed to have evolved from the three-week preparatory fast of previous centuries.

The history of a defined lenten season may be loosely divided into three periods: 1. the Council of Nicea (325) until the Middle Ages; 2. Middle Ages until the Second Vatican Council; 3. the promulgation of the Missal, Lectionary, and Roman Calendar by Paul VI in 1969 until the present.[2] The Council of Nicea set forth a forty-day preparatory fast and determined a fixed date for the celebration of Easter.

At one time, the Alexandrian church (in the East) celebrated the Lord's birth and began its liturgical year on January 6. Alexandria's new year began with the proclamation of the Lord's baptism, the beginning passage from the gospel of Mark. St. Mark was considered the founding father of the

---

[1] *GNLY*, #27.

[2] *DL* (II), 1.

Eastern church. Since the next passage in Mark's gospel was the story of Jesus' forty-day trial in the desert, the Alexandrian church established a similar forty-day fast (the "Fast of Jesus") beginning on January 7th. This fast had no connection to the week-long pre-Easter fast. Once the forty-day preparatory fast before Easter was established by the Council of Nicea, it collided with Alexandria's "Jesus fast" following the feast of the Lord's baptism. Adjustments, therefore, had to be made. Some monasteries observed a hundred-day fast in order to unify the two traditions of the East and the West.

Modern scholarship suggests that the penitential nature of the Lenten season emerged and grew stronger because of the influence of Alexandria's forty-day fast which was inspired by Jesus' temptations in the desert. The baptismal nature of Lent weakened with the decline of adult initiation in the fifth and sixth centuries. The heightened sense of penitence gave rise to the observance of three penitential Sundays prior to the first Sunday of Lent. These Sundays were called Septuagesima, Sexagesima, and Quinquagesima Sundays (seventy, sixty, and fifty days before Easter) and were observed until the Second Vatican Council.

Early in the fourth century, Lent lasted six weeks, beginning on the First Sunday of Lent. However, since Sundays were not fast days, the six weeks allowed for only thirty-six, rather than forty days of fasting. Thus, in the sixth century, Wednesday, Thursday, Friday, and Saturday before the First Sunday of Lent were added to the season in order to complete the forty days of fasting.

The Second Vatican Council restored a simpler, earlier version of Lenten observance. The Council halted the observance of three penitential Sundays prior to Lent. Lent begins on Ash Wednesday and continues until the Mass of Holy Thursday (which begins the Easter Triduum). Thus, there are five Sundays of Lent, followed by Palm Sunday (also called Passion Sunday). Lent begins on a day between February 10 and March 10, depending on the year and the occurrence of the spring equinox. It ends between March 19 and April 22. Lent is the only season that begins on a weekday (Ash Wednesday).

From the very earliest days, the season of Lent prepared the church for Easter. Lent fortifies God's people for immersion into the Lord's passion, death, and glorious resurrection. The ancient stories of God's salvation history with Israel were only a prelude to the ultimate event of all time—Jesus' paschal mystery. Each Sunday during Lent, the first reading takes us on a journey back to ancient Israel and brings forward the saving benefits of God's redemptive actions into our present day experience.

Themes of Lent

The season of Lent is highly charged with images of the exodus, Israel's premier, identifying moment. Passover is for Jews what the eucharist is for Catholics. Yahweh's action of delivering Israel out of Egyptian bondage was so essential to its consciousness and identity that it was instructed to commemorate it each year as a living memorial of God's great covenant with his people. The angel of death passed over the houses of the Israelites; they were delivered out of bondage and given possession of the promised land. The covenant was forged, and a *people*, a *holy nation* was brought to birth. Lent serves as the womb for the elect who await new birth into Christ's new covenant.

Lent is penitential, baptismal, and eucharistic by its very nature. The Second Vatican Council restored the early baptismal focus of Lent. The *Constitution on the Sacred Liturgy* restored the two-fold baptismal and penitential nature of Lent. "By recalling or preparing for baptism and by repentance, this season disposes the faithful, as they more diligently listen to the word of God and devote themselves to prayer, to celebrate the paschal mystery" (#109). Both baptism and repentance were to "be given greater prominence in both the liturgy and liturgical catechesis" (#109). This is to take place in the liturgy through homilies and catechesis that emphasize the two-fold nature of the season.

Penitential Nature of Lent

Lent is an extended time of self examination. "During Lent penance should be not only inward and individual, but also outward and social."[3] In the Rite of Christian Initiation of Adults, Lent coincides with the period of purification and enlightenment for catechumens. The elect[4] enter a process of purification in which they examine their heart, mind, and intentions. They ask God to enlighten the areas of sin and darkness with the light of Christ's healing presence. The elect preparing for baptism (along with the rest of the faithful) scrutinize and uncover *(enlighten)* what is weak and sinful and ask God to heal, strengthen, and liberate us from the power of evil *(purify)*. The elect are a symbol of the penitential posture we are all to assume during the season. The elect stand before the community in the celebration of the scrutinies on the Third, Fourth, and Fifth Sundays of Lent as the premier sign of Christ's *deliverance from* and *victory over* the power of evil.

During Lent's extended penitential period, the church examines the dimension, power, and impact of personal, social, and systemic sin. It asks to be delivered from sin's illusionary power and control. Since the scrutinies are an important part of the church's lenten observance, it is important to explore the meaning of the ritual and our participation in it. The following is an extract from my article in *Christian Initiation Magazine* regarding the scrutinies.

In the scrutinies we name and uncover the sinister reality of sin; the personal sin that we commit when we reject God and fail to love; the social sin that we participate in when we do nothing to change the systems and structures that keep members of God's family oppressed, marginalized, hungry, and poor; and finally the systemic sin that encompasses total hopelessness and despair. Systemic sin is sin in which the only solution is God alone. Death already reigns in the situation and nothing short of a miracle is required to heal it. "Sin and its effects are visible everywhere: in exploitive relationships, loveless families, unjust social structures and policies,

crimes by and against individuals and against creation, the oppression of the weak and the manipulation of the vulnerable, explosive tensions among nations and among ideological, racial and religious groups and social classes, the scandalous gulf between those who waste goods and resources and those who live and die amid deprivation and underdevelopment, wars and preparation for war. Sin is a reality in the world."[5]

Lest we be brought low by its devastating effects we must not lose sight of the most important element of the scrutinies: enlightenment or grace. Grace is union with God and a share in his life. The *National Catechetical Directory* reminds us that we are unconditionally loved, adopted children and that we live in the reality of being forgiven our sins.[6] Thus, the elect are filled with the presence of Christ the Liberator, who won the victory over evil and its consequences. In the Trinitarian prayer of exorcism, God the Father is invoked and asked for strength and protection. Through the power of the Holy Spirit (the epicletic action of laying on of hands), Jesus exercises his healing and liberating power over the effects of evil. Thus, the power and presence of Christ in Word and Exorcism are the primary symbols of the scrutinies.

Lent is a time of conversion, of *metanoia*, a compete turning away from sin into the loving arms of our loving God. "What we are about when we observe this liturgical time is the correction of our habits in order to relearn normative Christian behavior,"[7] first as a church, then as individuals. While it is a somber time, it is nevertheless marked by a spirit of joy. As Christians we know the rest of the story. Christ was victorious over the power of sin and death. While it is no doubt a time of serious reflection and interior conversion, we are joyful because we know that Easter joy awaits us. Christ the Liberator continues to heal, strengthen,

---

[3]*Constitution on the Sacred Liturgy*, #110, in *TLD*.
[4]Catechumens are called *the elect* after celebration of the rite of election on the First Sunday of Lent.

[5]*NCD*, #98, in *TCD*.
[6]Ibid.
[7]*DL* (II), 6.

and free us from the bondage imposed by ourselves and by the world.

Baptismal Nature of Lent

Lent is baptismal in nature. It is the time when the *elect* prepare to be fully initiated at the Easter Vigil through the sacraments of baptism, confirmation, and eucharist. During Lent, the faithful prepare to ritually remember their baptism and their baptismal commitment. Whether the newly baptized are present or not, the faithful will recall their baptism and renew their profession of faith at the Easter liturgies.

In the earliest days of the church, the Christian community walked hand in hand with the elect in their preparation for baptism—they were in it together. In his book, *The Liturgical Year,* Adolf Adam suggests that pre-Easter fasting was a way to prepare for the reception of the Spirit and the Easter sacraments of baptism and eucharist. It was a weapon against evil spirits, and a means to help the poor with money that would otherwise have been spent on food. What the church required of candidates for baptism by way of liturgical and spiritual effort was also done by the faithful in solidarity of spirit. "An atmosphere of cooperation and reciprocity was thus established that benefited the entire community."[8]

Eucharistic Nature of Lent

The season of Lent also prepares the elect and faithful for eucharist. While focusing on the baptismal nature of the season, we must not forget that baptism is the gateway, the door that leads to the table. The goal of initiation is not baptism; it is eucharist. The eucharist is the fullest sign of incorporation into the Body of Christ; it is the ultimate sacrament of unity. Through our participation in Christ's Body we become one people. The entire Christian life is somewhat catechumenal in nature. Christians are never finished; they never arrive; they are always on the journey. St. Augustine called the eucharist the repeatable sacrament of initiation. Eucharist is always a new encounter with the risen Christ. Jesus gave us his Body and Blood for the forgiveness of sins. Thus, whenever we eat Jesus' Body and drink his Blood

at the communal feast we are made a new creation.

Each time we partake of Christ's Body and Blood, we recommit our lives to the ongoing incorporation into his life, death, and resurrection, the paschal mystery. We receive the necessary nourishment to take up our cross, to go out to the world, *to be fed off of,* and to become food for others. We come back to the table depleted; we are nourished again so that we can go out again.

The Disciplines of Lent: Prayer, Fasting, and Almsgiving

During the fifth century the church gathered for liturgical prayer on Mondays, Wednesdays, and Fridays. It was not until the sixth century that the other days of the week were added as eucharistic observances. Thus, from the earliest stages of the season, Lent was marked by prayer and communal worship. The people gathered to celebrate special "Liturgies of the Word, homilies and prayer.... Lent is a time characterized by more assiduous observance of prayer and liturgy."[9]

Fasting is regarded as the hallmark discipline of Lent. No doubt most Christians would immediately identify fasting with Lent. However, fasting is not just a lenten discipline. It should be a habit common to the Christian's entire life. Fasting does not have its origin in Christianity. The Jews fasted throughout their history. Fasting was a discipline of other pagan religions as well.

Fasting is *always* observed in tandem with prayer and almsgiving. The early Fathers of the Church considered fasting an exercise of compassion. It is expressed best in the following ancient sermon.

> There are three things, my brethren, by which faith stands firm, devotion remains constant, and virtue endures. They are prayer, fasting and mercy (almsgiving). Prayer knocks at the door, fasting obtains, mercy receives. Prayer, mercy and fasting: these three are one, and they give life to each other.

---

[8]*LY,* 91–113.

[9]*DL* (II), 4.

Fasting is the soul of prayer, mercy is the lifeblood of fasting. Let no one try to separate them; they cannot be separated. If you have only one of them or not all together, you have nothing. So if you pray, fast; if you fast, show mercy; if you want your petition to be heard, hear the petition of others. If you do not close your ear to others, you open God's ear to yourself.

When you fast, see the fasting of others. If you want God to know that you are hungry, know that another is hungry. If you hope for mercy, show mercy. If you look for kindness, show kindness. If you want to receive, give. If you ask for yourself what you deny to others, your asking is a mockery...

...Fasting bears no fruit unless it is watered by mercy. Fasting dries up when mercy dries up. Mercy is to fasting as rain to the earth. However much you cultivate your heart, clear the soil of your nature, root out vices, show virtues, if you do not release the springs of mercy, your fasting will bear no fruit.

When you fast, if your mercy is thin your harvest will be thin; when you fast, what you pour out in mercy overflows into your barn. Therefore, do not lose by saving, but gather in by scattering. Give to the poor, and you give to yourself. You will not be allowed to keep what you have refused to give to others.[10]

Prayer, fasting, and almsgiving are communal disciplines of Lent. The lenten disciplines are not for private edification but are to build up the entire church. One fasts in order to share. In antiquity, those who did not have enough to share were instructed to fast and use the money they saved on food to give to the poor. Prayer, fasting, and sharing are the agenda of the entire community. Many parishes gather during Lent for light soup suppers in which the money normally spent on a hearty meal is given instead to the poor.[11]

Prayer, fasting, and sharing must include reflection on the social dimensions of sin in our world where many people do not have an adequate share of the world's resources. Our commitment to prayer and fasting must include a commitment to issues of justice and equality for all people. It is hypocrisy to pray and fast and then assert that the poor of the world are not our problem, but are, instead, the problem of politicians and other nations.

The only obligatory fast days are Ash Wednesday and Good Friday. Some dioceses have included the Fridays during Lent as days of fast and abstinence.

The Lenten Lectionary

The Old Testament readings of Lent proclaim the salvation events wrought by Yahweh, especially the exodus. Christianity understands the readings from the Hebrew scriptures to be the foreshadowing of the salvation accomplished through Jesus Christ. Reginald Fuller maintains that during Lent, the New Testament letters profess the Christian kerygma and participation in the passion, death, and resurrection of Christ through baptism. The lenten gospels are stories from Jesus' life that foreshadow his impending death and resurrection. The scriptures of Lent are intended to prepare us to celebrate our redemption in Christ. "The emphasis of the Lenten readings is the new life to which the baptized are called and its ethical demands."[12]

Fuller also suggests that the lenten readings are penitential, but are placed in the context of the missionary implications of the gospel. On the First Sunday of Lent, the focus is the fasting of Jesus and his temptation in the desert. The Second Sunday of Lent takes us to the mountain of Jesus'

---

[10]St. Peter Chrysologus (ca. 380–450), "Sermon 43," Patrologia Latina 52, ed. J.P. Migne, in *The Liturgy of the Hours*, Vol. 2 (New York: Catholic Book Publishing Co., 1976), Office of Readings, Tuesday in the Third Week of Lent, 231–232.

[11]However, to reserve these activities only to the season of Lent diminishes Jesus' ongoing call to prayer, fasting, and sharing, the hallmarks of biblical justice. Lent serves as a reminder of what we should be doing as a matter of course throughout the entire Christian life.

[12]*PNL*, xxix.

transfiguration where we will hear the story from Matthew, Mark, or Luke's perspective. Thus, the First and Second Sundays of Lent in each cycle proclaim the same gospel event: temptation in the desert and the transfiguration. The gospels for the remaining Sundays of Lent are not the same for each cycle.

During Cycle A, we hear the powerful stories of the Samaritan woman at the well (Third Sunday of Lent, first scrutiny), the man born blind (Fourth Sunday of Lent, second scrutiny) and the raising of Lazarus (Fifth Sunday of Lent, third scrutiny). These Johannine gospels are catechumenal in nature as they best reflect the baptismal and penitential nature of the season. Through these stories we encounter sin (personal, social, and systemic) head on and are filled with "Christ the Redeemer, who is living water, the light of the world, and the resurrection and the life."[13]

The Cycle A readings are known as "the Johannine signs" and were "long viewed as symbols of the Christian experience of baptism."[14] When baptismal preparation was only three weeks long, the three Johannine gospels were used as primary catechesis because of their strong baptismal images: "water and spirit, the light of faith, and death and life."[15] Whenever there are catechumens, the Cycle A readings are to be used, regardless of the liturgical cycle. Since they were for use in catechumenal ministry and were intended to "arouse the baptismal faith" of the faithful, there is an option to use the Cycle A readings each year.

During Cycle B, the Third Sunday's gospel is John's account of the destruction of the temple and its subsequent rebuilding in three days. The Fourth Sunday's gospel (also from John) professes the Son of Man who will be raised for the salvation of all. The Fifth Sunday is about the grain that dies and bears much fruit.

The Cycle C gospel for the Third Sunday of Lent is about the need for repentance and conversion. The Fourth Sunday is the story of the prodigal son and the Fifth Sunday is the story of the woman accused of adultery.

---

[13] *RCIA*, #143.

[14] *PNL*, xxix.

[15] *DL* (II), 35.

The second reading during Lent is chosen to support the gospel. The first reading, however, is concerned with recounting significant events in salvation history. On Palm Sunday, the first and second readings are the same every year. The gospel is the passion narrative from one of the synoptic gospels. (For more on the lenten lectionary, see chapter 3 on scripture.)

As a springboard for lenten reflection, the following poem captures the heart of Lent's purpose. The protagonist of the poem is a catechumen who has journeyed with a community of faith for over a year. The catechumen has just celebrated the rite of election and has moved into the final preparatory period of purification and enlightenment. The person in this poem has encountered Jesus through the prayer and worship of his or her celebrating community in one complete liturgical cycle. This person speaks for us all.

*so what **could** be left, sister lent?*

I thought I had uncovered it all... layer by layer I
shed it all away...
*so what **could** be left, sister lent?*
like a snake squirming from the casing of his
former self
and the butterfly wrestling from the safe bondage
of her quiet hibernation...
I stand empty...
a wonderful, curious, new creation,
chosen of god...
nakedly I gaze before discernment's interior
mirror...
*so what **could** be left, sister lent?*
Sunday after Sunday, story after story, decision
after decision,
gave way to an empty, vulnerable vessel, ready for
easter filling...
*so what **could** be left, sister lent?*
like an air-dried sponge I stand waiting...
for what do I wait?
for fire light's illumination...
for baptismal water's soaking immersion...
for confirmation oil's sealing configuration...
for eucharist bread and wine's sumptuous
celebration
for dying, rising, famine, for feasting,
for those who are *out* to be one with the *in*...
to eat, to be broken, to be poured, to be filled,
to live by example, to die, to be food...

for the hungry, the lost, the blind and the
obstinate...
I wait to give more of the gift already given,
the sacrament of life for the sake of the
kingdom...
so, forty more days of repentance and ashes
to renew, to strengthen and prepare for the
banquet...
is there more? could there be?
one forgotten remnant
of a life not yet surrendered, of blindness,
repression?
be it sojourn, or Passover or exodus event
I stand with eyes opened, my heart in my hand...
what could be left? only *YOU* know for sure...
so do what *YOU* will, root out from the core
all that might keep me from the life *YOU* intend
of thanksgiving, of service and praise till the
end...

Mary Birmingham

Ash Wednesday

Environment

The catechetical space may be adorned simply with a cross, the Lectionary, and a candle; you might want to use hints of the color purple. A clay pot filled with ashes may be included as a sign of our need for repentance. Barren branches simply arranged speak of that buried seed, hibernating in its preparatory earthen cocoon awaiting the new life of Easter. Since Lent is a time of preparation for baptism, holy water fonts should be emptied.

The names and pictures of catechumens who will be initiated at the Easter Vigil might be placed in a basket nearby so all can be united with them in prayer and solidarity throughout the season.

The cross might be surrounded by purple cloth and then in the later weeks shrouded with that same purple cloth. This ancient practice is reminiscent of Isaiah's prophecy concerning the future day of the Lord: the new heaven and new earth. The veil that covers our eyes will be torn down and all will see the glory of God. Sin shrouds us from the *shekina* glory of God. The custom of veiling statues was stopped after the Second Vatican Council. However, it was reinstated in 1985 for use in the last weeks of Lent.[1]

The following ritual prayer from *Catholic Household Blessings and Prayers* may be used to bless the lenten environment:

INTRODUCTORY RITES

Opening Song (or Entrance Antiphon)

Lord, you are merciful to all, and hate nothing you have created. You overlook the sins of men to bring them to repentance. You are the Lord our God. (See Wisdom 11:24–25, 27.)[2]

---

[1] *TCY*, 42–69.
[2] Ash Wednesday: "Entrance Antiphon," *The Sacramentary*.

Ash Wednesday Blessing of the Season and of a Place of Prayer

All make the sign of the cross as the leader begins:
The Lord calls us to days of penance and mercy.
Blessed be the name of the Lord.

All respond:
Now and for ever.

Leader: Remember that we are but dust and ashes, yet by God's grace we have died in baptism and have put on the Lord Jesus Christ. Each year we keep these forty days with prayer and penance and the practice of charity so that we may come to the Easter festival ready to renew once more the life-giving commitment of our baptism. Throughout this Lent we shall gather here to read the Scriptures and ponder them and to intercede with God for the needs of the world.

Scripture
Isaiah 58:5–10

(Someone proclaims the reading from the prophet Isaiah.)

After a time of silence, members of the household offer prayers of intercession for the world, the church and its catechumens, and themselves. The leader then invites:

Let us kneel and ask for God's blessing on us and
    this holy season.
Merciful God,
you called us forth from the dust of the earth;
you claimed us for Christ in the waters of baptism.
Look upon us as we enter these Forty Days
bearing the mark of ashes,
and bless our journey through the desert of Lent
to the font of rebirth.
May our fasting be hunger for justice;
our alms, a making of peace;
our prayer, the chant of humble and grateful
    hearts.
All that we do and pray is in the name of Jesus.

Each person then kisses the cross.

All then stand, and the leader concludes.

All through these days let us be quiet and
    prayerful,
pondering the mysteries told in the Scriptures.
In the cross, we have been claimed for Christ.
In Christ, we make the prayer that fills these days
    of mercy:

Our Father...

The leader says:
Let us bless the Lord.

All respond, making the sign of the cross:
Thanks be to God.[3]

Opening Prayer

*The facilitator of the session may lead the prayer. Others
in the group may be asked to proclaim the readings.*

Let us pray
[in quiet remembrance of our need for redemption]

    Pause for silent prayer.

Father in heaven,
the light of your truth bestows sight
to the darkness of sinful eyes.
May this season of repentance bring us the bless-
    ing of your forgiveness
and the gift of your light.
Grant this through Christ our Lord.[4]

LITURGY OF THE WORD

Let us listen to God's word.

The readings are proclaimed.

First Reading
Joel 2:12–18

[3]"Ash Wednesday Blessing of the Season and of a Place
of Prayer," *CHBP,* 132–135.
[4]Ash Wednesday: "Alternative Opening Prayer," *The
Sacramentary.*

Joel's book is heavily centered in the language of
temple worship. He speaks of vegetable offerings,
libations, the fast, and a solemn assembly—the
things of ritual worship. Temple priests, ministers
of Yahweh, and ministers of the altar were part of
Joel's cast of characters. Joel was one of the twelve
minor prophets. Most scholars believe that the
book of Joel was written after the exile and after
the temple had been rebuilt (ca. 515 B.C.E.).

In chapters 1 and 2, Joel tells of a devastating
drought and locust plague and thus sets the tone
for his manuscript. His primary agenda concerns
the reversal of fortunes. The first chapters depict
the effects of the drought and plague on the people and on their worship. First, those directly involved by the effects of the plague (such as farmers) were called to lament. The effects of the
invading army of locusts were so horrific, however,
that the entire community was summoned to publicly lament.

Scholars believe that the book's main theme flows
from verse 18. There was a corporate summons to
grieve and lament. Israel was in devastation; there
was pending doom. One can almost imagine the
scene in true epic style. The ground rumbled, the
earth shook, and the invading creatures black-
ened the sky. The people pleaded and Yahweh responded—a miracle happened! Yahweh intervened; the drought and plague were lifted. Their
fortunes were reversed; Yahweh saved the day.
This day was to be remembered.

Later in the book, Joel assigned this story to the
community's corporate memory so that when all
seemed lost, Israel would remember Yahweh's
mercy. They would count on Yahweh to usher Israel into that final victorious battle. Herein lies an
important lesson regarding the power of story-
telling. Our stories of faith sustain us through the
difficult times. We remember God's action, and
are encouraged to be steadfast.

Yahweh does not act because of the ritual offerings. Yahweh acts because of his kindness and
mercy and because of "who God is." For God,
doing and being are the same thing. People repent because they are confident of his mercy.
Everyone is called to fast—no one is excluded!

Responsorial Psalm
Psalm 51

Psalm 51 is the psalm of repentance. Humans acknowledge their utter guilt before God. God not only forgives the sin and guilt, but he restores the relationship.

Second Reading
2 Corinthians 5:20–6:2

Paul expounds a beautiful theology regarding the effects of Christ's death and resurrection upon the sin of the world. When Christ died, the veil on the temple was ripped in two. Humanity was given access to the holy of holies; God was now approachable. Christ *became* the very sin he came to destroy. He lifted the weight of sin from humanity's shoulder. Jesus' act was the ultimate gift of grace. Now is the time to rejoice in the grace that was won for all the world! Like Joel, we must shout it from the rooftops—the day of salvation is upon us! It is Good News; we can do no less than share it.

Gospel
Matthew 6:1–6, 16–18

Jesus warns about ostentatious displays of prayer and fasting.

STEP 1
NAMING ONE'S EXPERIENCE

What were your first impressions? What was your first response? What grabbed your attention? How did you feel?

Each person names his or her initial impression. Statements should be brief. No reasons should be given at this time. All simply listen without agreeing or disagreeing.

STEP 2
UNDERSTANDING

In a brief statement, what do you think this gospel is trying to convey?

STEP 3
INPUT FROM VISION/STORY/TRADITION

Liturgical Context

On Ash Wednesday we receive ashes as a sign of our willingness to repent. We are sorry for our sins. At one time ashes were a public sign of repentance. They were not used in official liturgy until the thirteenth century. Until the reform of the liturgy, the ritual took place before mass. Since the reform, the blessing and distribution of ashes take place following the liturgy of the word. If mass is not celebrated, it takes place in the context of the liturgy of the word.

The ashes are given with the words, "Remember, man, that you are dust and to dust you shall return," or "Turn away from sin and be faithful to the gospel."[5] (See also "Dust," Appendix II.) The ritual prayers that accompany the blessing of ashes place the season in its appropriate pre-Easter perspective:

> Lord,
> bless the sinner who asks for your
> forgiveness
> and bless + all those who receive these
> ashes.
> May they keep this Lenten season
> in preparation for the joy of Easter.
> We ask this through Christ, our Lord.
> Bless these ashes+
> by which we show we are dust.
> Pardon our sins
> and keep us faithful to the discipline of
> Lent,
> for you do not want sinners to die
> but to live with the risen Christ,
> who reigns with you forever.[6]

On Ash Wednesday we humbly come before God seeking *metanoia*, conversion, and complete repentance. Our repentance is an act of faith because we repent trusting in God's kindness and mercy. Today's liturgy is a call to repentance for the

---

[5]Ash Wednesday: "Blessing and Distribution of Ashes," *The Sacramentary.*
[6]Ibid.

whole church. Joel sets the stage. "Proclaim a fast, call an assembly!" This is not a "Jesus and me" event. The entire community is called. Together we recognize our need for God's mercy.

We engage in a process of reflection and renewal as a community. Joel summoned the nation, the church summons its people. Fasting increases our hunger. For whom do we hunger? The resurrected Christ. What is the living memorial of his resurrected presence? The eucharist.

Gospel Exegesis

The facilitator gives input regarding what critical biblical scholarship has to say about this text. The input includes insights as to how people would have heard the gospel in Jesus' time.

Jesus' words are part of the discourse on the Mount. They are part of the evangelical section of the sermon. We must read this gospel in its evangelical context, as well as in the obvious context of prayer, fasting, and almsgiving. To live as Jesus commanded is to live according to the demands of the law, according to God's justice. God's justice (*hesed*) embodies right relationship with God as evidenced by care and concern for the poor and oppressed. Our prayer, fasting, and almsgiving must be in the spirit of the gospel and its mission orientation. Our light must shine before all, but it must shine with integrity. There can be no false airs, no hypocrisy. We are not to perform the lenten disciplines to gain the admiration of others.

The good deeds of a righteous person will cause people to see the light of Christ. Jesus invites us to look within and judge our motives. As community and as individuals we are to examine our hearts and judge our motivation for worship, prayer, fasting, and devotional practices.

Christians are to be joyful in the midst of their trials. In spite of life's difficulties they know what awaits them. Believers are to act in love toward their neighbors and invite others to Christ by the way they live their lives.

Proclaim the gospel again.

Sometimes we gain new insights when we hear the text after the interpretation has been given. Someone from the group proclaims the gospel a second time.

STEP 4
TESTING

Conversation with the Liturgy and the Scriptures

Test your original understanding in dialogue with the text.

(You might consider breaking into smaller groups.)

Were there any new insights? Was there anything you had not considered before? How do the readings for Ash Wednesday speak to your life?

Sharing Life Experience

Participants share an experience from their lives that connects with the biblical interpretation just shared.

> *I see people in my parish who live their lives in the spirit of Jesus' gospel. They live it not only during Lent, but also throughout the year. They are the real saints. They live their lives in humble submission to the word of God. They pray, fast, and reach out to the sick, the sorrowing, the infirm, the lonely, and the aged. One woman exemplifies the life Jesus calls us to live in today's gospel. She ministers to the sick and the elderly. She ministers the word of God everywhere she goes. She seeks God with every breath she takes. She speaks for truth and will not listen to gossip or destructive conversation. She exudes joy and typifies the humility demanded in today's gospel. Few people know how much she does for the reign of God. I look to her this Lent to remind me of the spirit and challenge of the season. My lenten repentance and conversion must lead me to grow more like the woman I admire so.*

All share their life experience.

What was Matthew trying to tell his community? What does he have to say to our community and to me today? What might God be creating in us through this experience of Jesus in the gospel and the lenten liturgy? In what way does this gospel point to God's promise to be with us? In what way have I/we known death/resurrection in my/our experience and understanding of this gospel? How is God speaking to us as a community? Has our original understanding been stretched, challenged, or affirmed?

STEP 5
DECISION

The gospel demands a response.

How does your sharing and this biblical interpretation challenge your community's attitudes? What will you/your community/your parish be called to do in response? Name one concrete action you will take this week as a response to what was learned and shared today.

DOCTRINAL ISSUES

What church truth/teaching/doctrinal issue could be drawn from the gospel for Ash Wednesday?

Participants suggest possible doctrinal themes that flow from the readings.

Possible Doctrinal Themes

Lent, conversion, repentance, fasting

Present the doctrinal material at this time.

1. The facilitator gives input on a particular doctrinal issue of his/her prior choosing. OR
2. The group chooses a doctrinal issue from the list they created. They read together from the Doctrinal Appendix.

(The doctrinal issues are found in the Doctrinal Appendix in the back of this workbook. If you are choosing an issue from this resource, please refer to it now.)

Reflection questions centered around the chosen doctrinal theme can be found at the end of each topic in the Doctrinal Appendix. The questions are based on the five-step reflection process. If you choose a topic not included in the Doctrinal Appendix, craft your own questions according to the same five-step process.

Following the reflection questions you will be reminded to return to chapter 7, "Preparing the Catechetical Session," to assist you in crafting your own session.

Closing Prayer

Come back to the Lord with all your heart;
leave the past in ashes,
and turn to God with tears and fasting,
for he is slow to anger and ready to forgive.
    (Joel 2:13)

Let the priests and ministers of the Lord
lament before his altar, and say:
Spare us, Lord, spare your people!
Do not let us die for we are crying out to you.
    (Joel 2:17; Est 13:17)[7]

---

[7]Ash Wednesday: "Antiphon 1 and 2," *The Sacramentary.*

170

FIRST SUNDAY OF LENT

Environment

Refer to Ash Wednesday. If not meeting on Ash Wednesday, the first Sunday of Lent would be an appropriate time to bless your catechetical space with the "Ash Wednesday Blessing of the Season and of a Place of Prayer" found in the previous session.

INTRODUCTORY RITES

Entrance Antiphon (or Opening Song)

When he calls me, I will answer; I will rescue him and give him honor. Long life and contentment will be his. (Ps 90:15–16) [1]

Opening Prayer

The facilitator of the session may lead the prayer. Others in the group may be asked to proclaim the readings.

Let us pray
(at the beginning of Lent for the spirit of repentance)

Pause for silent prayer.

Lord our God,
you formed man from the clay of the earth
and breathed into him the spirit of life,
but he turned from your face and sinned.
In this time of repentance
we call out for your mercy.
Bring us back to you
and to the life your Son won for us
by his death on the cross,
for he lives and reigns for ever and ever. [2]

LITURGY OF THE WORD

The readings are proclaimed.

---

[1] First Sunday of Lent: "Entrance Antiphon," *The Sacramentary.*

[2] First Sunday of Lent: "Alternative Opening Prayer," *The Sacramentary.*

First Reading [3]
Genesis 9:8–15

(Refer to the tenth Sunday in Ordinary Time for an overview of the Book of Genesis.)

Today's Pericope: Today's proclamation of the Noah story concludes the great Genesis epic. One purpose of the Book of Genesis was to answer a fundamental question of life: "What is the origin of evil in the world?" The story of the ravenous flood that devoured all life in its path was used to express belief in God's covenant, protection, and perpetuation of the human race. It also served as an explanation for the existence of the rainbow. Thus, the narrative is both etiological (reflection on, or study of, the origins of something) and theological (reflection on, or the study of, God).

The flood serves as a healthy reminder to all people for all time that punishment for serious sin can be severe. Noah, an upright and just person, and all his family were saved. The flood also alludes to a divine birthing. In ancient literature, flood narratives were really birth narratives. The person who survived the flood was considered the first created human being. [4] The flood, therefore, was not understood as a historical occurrence, but as a primeval happening. The story of Noah and the flood is regarded in similar fashion—it is understood as a creation story, intimately connected to the first chapter of Genesis. First there was an abyss, then God separated the waters. Then those same waters ruptured through that same abyss and there was a flood. Both creation stories speak of a mighty wind; both command the fertility and multiplication of the animals and both bless and com-

---

[3] The exegesis for the first and second readings may or may not be the focus of your group's reflection, as there may only be time to give adequate attention to the gospel, your primary concern. However, the exegesis is included here in order to provide a thorough investigation of the entire liturgy of the word as there may be parts (or all) that would be essential to the direction you wish to take with your particular ministry group.

[4] Diane Bergant, C.S.A., "Flood," *CPDBT*, 344.

mission human beings to rule over those same animals. The two epics are intimately connected.

The flood was understood as the result of wickedness. Yahweh regretted that he created human beings—they were that wicked! He also regretted the creation of other living things as well. Why did the rest of the natural world have to suffer for the sins of humanity? The earth itself was polluted and defiled by the gravity of human sin. Creation signaled victory over primordial chaos. It was also the means of ordering the universe.[5] The flood reversed the ordering of the universe—thus the ordering of nature—thus the return to chaos—thus the need for a second creation-event.

The ark was a place of sanctuary and a haven of purity. The animals were separated on the ark, clean from unclean. The ark was the embodiment of purity and order "in the midst of a world of defilement and chaos."[6]

Later in history, the ark would be understood as a means of salvation. The Hebrew word for ark (*tebah*) was also used for the basket that carried baby Moses to safety. An ark would also house and transport the tablets of the Law, a visible expression of the covenant between God and Israel. The ark became a symbol of God's protection and salvation. It also became a type for baptism in Christ and for the church. "Later, the church fathers developed the ark typology so that it became symbolic of the church itself, 'the bark of Peter,' and a popular symbol in Christian art, as the catacombs will reveal."[7] The flood is used in Christianity as a reminder that Christians must be prepared. Just as the people of Noah's day were caught unaware, the coming of the Lord will also find people unprepared. The flood also prefigured the waters of baptism (1 Pt 3:21—today's second reading). "Here the waters are neither punishment nor cleansing. They are a passage into a new life."[8]

The flood and the ark, while ambiguous, are symbols of salvation as well as destruction, demonstrating the multivalent nature of symbols (refer

---

[5]Ibid.
[6]Ibid.
[7]*WWC*, 152.
[8]"Flood," *CPDBT*, 346.

to Easter Vigil: symbols). The flood and ark were signs of death and destruction for the wicked and signs of hope and salvation for the righteous. The flood precipitated God's second salvific action. The Spirit of God hovered over the chaotic waters and creation came into being. God's act of re-creation after the flood gave birth to a *new* creation. The same word for "creation" (*tehom*) was used by the priestly biblical authors in both accounts. The destruction by the flood signaled something brand-new and marvelous—God's new creation, a new beginning for all living things. God entered into covenant with Abraham, Moses, and the people of God, so *covenant* is certainly not a new concept. However, this story is not about God's covenant with humanity. God's covenant is with *all creation*. Such a covenant demanded a worthy sign and an added epilogue to the story. The Divine Painter, palette in hand, ratified the covenant in hue and color. A translucent canopy, afloat in time and space, would be forever suspended in the post-rain heavens as a sign and reminder to God—not humanity.

The rainbow was probably an allusion to a common ancient motif—the cosmic battle between chaos and a warrior god. The bow is likely a weapon of war (evidenced by Mesopotamian artifacts depicting the gods with quiver in hand). The rainbow was a sign that the cosmic battle was over and that creation was restored to its ordered state.

Other exegetes suggest another thought for reflection. The rainbow is arched in the sky as a reminder to earth's inhabitants that they are here as stewards. What caretaker would purposefully pollute his garden or waste his produce? Would he not cherish each seed, prune each twig, and handle each seedling with tenderness, care, and concern? This is how God cares for human beings. This is how human beings are to care for the earth.

Responsorial Psalm
Psalm 25:4–9

The refrain is an appropriate companion text to the story of the flood. The psalm extols Yahweh's love and truth and the covenant.

Second Reading
1 Peter 3:18–22

(Refer to the second Sunday of Advent for an overview of 1 and 2 Peter.)

Today's Pericope: Today's passage from 1 Peter reflects an early Christological baptismal hymn. Some exegetes suggest that the letter may have been part of an ancient baptismal liturgy. The first stanzas hint of the Pauline theology of the atoning nature of Jesus' death and resurrection. Jesus died for our sins and in so doing made it possible for human beings to gain access to God. The author of the letter uses the Greek construct of two separate realms to argue his theology. "Flesh" represents the earthly realm and "spirit" the heavenly abode.

Christ's preaching to the spirits in prison takes place after the resurrection. It is not the earthly Christ, but the resurrected and ascended Christ who preached to the imprisoned spirits. Protestant scholarship based on the teaching of Clement of Alexandria and Origen believes that this passage refers to Christ's descent into hell. Reginald Fuller insists that the text simply has nothing to do with that belief. It is a proclamation of the early belief in the resurrected and exalted Christ's victory over the power of evil.[9] The spirits referred to by the author represent the cosmic powers— unadulterated evil. Jesus is not proclaiming God's love to the spirits in hopes of an eleventh-hour conversion; he preaches to them in order to announce their ultimate defeat.

The first four verses of 1 Peter comprise an early baptismal homily inserted into the original body of the letter, however.[10] The author of the letter adapted the hymn to fit his baptismal theology. The original hymn refers to the *spirits* as the cosmic powers (mentioned in the previous paragraph). This author appropriates the term *spirits* to refer to the contrary spirits during the time of Noah—embodied either in the corrupt generation of people who were destroyed by the floodwaters or in the evil angels of Genesis 6. In the adapted version of the baptismal homily, Jesus' preaching is a message of salvation. There is hope for the dead—they, too, are given an opportunity to repent. The reference to Noah provides the vehicle for establishing the author's theology—Noah and the flood become a typological sign for baptism into Christ.

Reginald Fuller contends that the insertion is difficult to interpret.[11] He suggests two possible meanings for the phrase "saved through water." Perhaps it refers to the safe passage of Noah and sons through the dangerous, death-dealing power of the waters, or it could mean that water was the means by which Noah and his family were led to safe harbor. When one considers the connections made between the flood and baptism, the latter possibility is more probable. There are two separate typological references in today's reading. The floodwater refers to future baptism in Christ and the ark and its crew refers to the future Christian community. The ark is a *type* of the church. "It is obvious that the author of 1 Peter regarded the salvation of all humanity by Jesus, and Noah's victorious emergence from the flood as a type of the victory afforded to all believers by immersion in the *baptismal* waters."[12]

The author presents his baptismal catechism. The reader is not to understand baptism as a washing—it is an invitation to conversion and new life. Baptism involves *metanoia*, a conscience turned completely and wholly toward God. The "appeal to God for a clear conscience" (v. 21) possibly reflects a response given to God by the Christian that flows from a well-formed conscience. The ancient scrutinies assumed that the candidates approached the baptismal waters with a repentant conscience and total faith in Christ. The author stresses that baptism is not only participation in God's saving initiative, but it also requires a response on the part of the one to be baptized.

The gospel is proclaimed.

Gospel[13]
Mark 1:12–15. Jesus was tempted by Satan and the angels ministered to him.

---

[9]*PL*, 231.

[10]Ibid., 232.

[11]Ibid.

[12]*WWC*, 153.

[13]The gospel exegesis is provided later in this session so that it may be presented in the proper sequence where it occurs in the adult five-step reflection process. The exegesis is

STEP 1
NAMING ONE'S EXPERIENCE

What were your first impressions? What was your first response to the gospel (or the other readings)?[14] What captured your attention?

Each person names his or her initial impression. Statements should be brief. No reasons should be given at this time. All simply listen without agreeing or disagreeing.

STEP 2
UNDERSTANDING

In a brief statement, explain what you think this gospel is trying to convey.

STEP 3
INPUT FROM VISION/STORY/TRADITION

Liturgical Context[15]

The origin of the first two Sundays of Lent (temptation and transfiguration) date back to the fourth century. The first Sunday of Lent recalls Jesus in the desert, the place of his temptation and Israel's unfaithfulness (as well as its faithfulness). The symbol of the desert has ancient roots in the Church. It was seen as a quiet, distraction-free place, where people could commune with God. Monasticism emerged out of the desert motif.

The purpose of the Lenten readings is to prepare the faithful for participation in the pasche. The

first reading on the first Sunday of Lent in all three cycles remembers God's self-revelation to humanity through the prism of salvation history. This history allows us to view the paschal mystery from the vantage point of God's saving action from the very beginning of God's relationship with the human race. What God began at the creation of the world was the first step in the forward movement toward what he would ultimately accomplish through the life, death, and resurrection of his Son.

> God, who wishes all men to be saved and come to the knowledge of truth (1 Tm. 2:4), in many and various ways...spoke of old to our fathers by the prophets (Heb. 1:1). When the fullness of time had come He sent His Son, the Word made flesh, anointed by the Holy Spirit, to preach the gospel to the poor, to heal the contrite of heart (cf. Is. 61:1; Lk. 4:18), to be a "bodily and spiritual medicine"[16] the Mediator between God and man (cf. 1 Tm. 2:5). For His humanity, united with the person of the Word, was the instrument of our salvation. ...The wonders wrought by God among the people of the Old Testament were but a prelude to the work of Christ the Lord in redeeming mankind and giving perfect glory to God. He achieved his task principally by the paschal mystery of his blessed passion, resurrection from the dead, and glorious ascension, whereby dying, he destroyed our death and, rising, he restored our life. For it was from the side of Christ as He slept the sleep of death upon the cross that there came forth the wondrous sacrament which is the whole Church.[17]

Jesus' temptation in the desert, proclaimed on every first Sunday of Lent in all three cycles, heralds Jesus' triumph over Satan as well as the mandate that we all enter with Christ into the fight against evil.[18]

"At Sunday Masses in Lent, the first reading is independent from the other two. Each of the three

---

provided for the first and second readings for your information and edification, and for you to use at your discretion. Once again, the gospel is the primary source of reflection. If there is time for reflection on the other readings, all the better.

[14] The primary focus of reflection is the gospel. However, often the other readings demand attention and must be brought into the dialogue.

[15] The scriptures in the Lectionary, the seasons of the year, and the ritual prayers of the mass are interrelated and form the basis for liturgical catechesis. The *liturgical context* attempts to explore and clarify the themes and this interrelatedness.

[16] St. Ignatius of Antioch, "To the Ephesians," 7, 2; ed. F. X. Funk, *Patres Apostolici* I, Tübingen, 1901, 218.

[17] *CL*, #105.

[18] *DL* (II), 37.

series constitutes a catechetical unity, as do the seven Old Testament readings at the Easter vigil. Hence their importance during the first five Sundays of Lent."[19] The readings serve as a stark reminder of who we are, where we came from, and where we ought to be going. The second readings during Lent are usually intended to shed light on Jesus' Passion and death or on baptism, the means by which faithful Christians are incorporated into that mystery. All the readings prepare us for the renewal of our baptismal promises at Easter and they help us to reflect on the dimensions of sin and grace in our lives.

The Lenten theme of *conversion* is highlighted in the liturgical prayers of each Sunday. Note the alternative opening prayer for today's liturgy: "In this time of repentance we call out for your mercy. Bring us *back to you* [*italics mine*] and to the life your Son won for us by his death on the cross...." The prayer over the gifts asks that the sacrifice we offer help *to change our lives;* and the prayer after communion invites us to *live by the Word* and to seek the Bread of Life. The call to conversion cannot be clearer either in scripture or in the liturgy.

Lent highlights and illumines that which should be the agenda of every day of our lives: a complete turning of our lives and our hearts to God, a true sense of sorrow for sin, and participation in our baptismal life which is, ultimately, participation in the paschal mystery of Jesus Christ. "Lent is the explicitness of that period of 'fast' and 'passion' which extends over our whole lives. Today's welfare and consumer state has accommodated itself to a permanent lie: the impression is universally given that serene happiness is everywhere the rule, or if that is not strictly true in every case, it soon will be with goodwill and the irresistible progress of humankind."[20] Yet, how can we ignore the reality of suffering in this world? Pain, death, old age, and sickness are with us forever. We cannot deny or ignore the somber reality. One thing we can do, however, is to ask how to cope with it. "Cynicism and stoicism do not go very far. In faith, hope and love a Christian understands this aspect of her life as a sharing in the Lord's passion. The acceptance in belief and hope of one's

own passion is exercised by what in Christian asceticism is called 'voluntary renunciation.' In Lent, however, that which one must necessarily suffer in life in sober realism and can live in hope as a *Christian* passion becomes publicly known, in ecclesial, liturgical and sacramental explicitness, as a freely loving participation in the passion of Christ."[21]

Jesus' temptation in the desert is his first encounter with the Evil One. It would not be his last. His final and victorious battle would be from the cross itself. Jesus' temptation is an invitation and a challenge. The elect and the entire church are invited to the desert as a prelude to the journey to Jerusalem and the challenge of the cross. Lent marks the way for us all.

Rite of Election and Rite of Sending

By the fourth century, Easter was the customary time for the celebration of baptisms. However, there is evidence that Pentecost was another suitable time.[22] At the beginning of Lent, the catechumens who desired baptism handed over their names as a request for baptism. To "give in their names" became the technical language for people's request to be baptized. "Candidates whose application was accepted were called 'applicants' (*competentes*), 'chosen' (*electi*) or 'destined for illumination' (*photizomenoi*)."[23] A description of the rite was handed down to us by the Gallican or Spanish nun, Egeria (fourth century), who, on a pilgrimage to Jerusalem, wrote down her experiences.

> I think I ought to tell you how instruction is given to those who are baptized at Easter. Those who give in their names do so the day before Lent begins; the presbyter writes down the names of all of them. This takes place before the eight weeks during which, as I told you, Lent is observed here. When the presbyter has made a note of all the names, later on another day in Lent, the day on which the eight weeks begin, the bishop's chair is set up in the middle of the great church, the

---

[19]Ibid., 36.
[20]*GCY*, 120–121.

[21]Ibid.
[22]St. Siricius (pope, 384–399) was known to have baptized people at Pentecost.
[23]Edward Yarnold, S.J., *AIRI*, 8.

church of the Martyrium. The [presbyters sit] on either side on chairs and all the clerics stand. Then the candidates are brought in one by one, the men with their "fathers," the women with their "mothers." Then the bishop one by one asks their neighbors: "Is he a good-living man? Does he respect his parents? Is he a drunkard or trustworthy?" He asks them like this about every vice, at least the more serious ones. If the bishop finds that the candidate is free from all these faults about which he has questioned the witnesses, he writes down the candidate's name with his own hand.[24]

The rite of election that is presently celebrated is an adaptation of the ancient rite.

Today begins the period of purification and enlightenment for catechumens. This marks the beginning of the final, more intense preparation for the Easter sacraments of initiation. The celebration of the rite of election and the enrollment of names is the liturgical rite that marks entry into this final period that coincides with the season of Lent. The principal celebrant for the rite of election is the bishop and it generally takes place at the diocesan cathedral. However, the great enthusiasm and ownership of the rite at the parish level has prompted an adaptation known as the rite of sending.

The rite of sending allows the parish to send their catechumens to the bishop for election and enrollment of names. The preliminary judgment of the catechumen's readiness takes place within the parish. The parish is the spiritual mother who now wishes to send her fledglings to election with assurances of love, support, and prayers. Baptized candidates are also sent to the bishop for recognition of their call to continuing conversion during this time of preparation for completion of their initiation.

At the rite of election, the catechumens make a transition into their final preparation for initiation and are conferred with a new name: the *elect*. In scripture, the conferral of a new name signified

a changed status or a new mission or vocation. The church accepts the catechumens as chosen of God; they are elected by God. On the basis of the testimony of the godparents and the catechists, as well as the catechumens' own reaffirmation, the Church judges their state of readiness to go forward for initiation at the Easter Vigil. The Church testifies to God's grace at work in the lives of the catechumens. The catechumens, then, hand their names over, and enroll for baptism.

Election is about being chosen. To be chosen assumes that one is in reciprocal covenant relationship with God. It is a relationship rooted in biblical justice. "Election as people of God requires a style of life that reflects this office. It is as much a responsibility as it is a privilege."[25] Election is a radical call to intimate relationship with God and unconditional love toward all of God's creation. In the Old Testament, election assumed that those chosen believed in their hearts and professed with their voices the ancient Shema: "The Lord God is One. We are to love the Lord God with all our heart, mind, and soul, and love our neighbor as ourselves."

Election is God's free act of gratuitous, unmerited love. However, there is always an inherent obligation on the part of the person or group chosen. "To belong to God in the special relationship of election demands that one imitate the very character and qualities of God."[26] Election reminds us that God is in charge; we are not. Election is freely given, but it is also freely received. Barbara Bowe suggests that a person's membership among the elect depends on the extent to which a person is faithful to God throughout life, especially during times of distress and tribulation. Thus, there is an eschatological dimension inherent within election. Election is participation in the messianic reign in this world and anticipation of God's reign to come.

Election is understood as vocation and responsibility rather than privilege and superiority. Election assumes a special intimacy and full commu-

[24]Egeria, *Peregrinatio*, 45, in Edward Yarnold, S.J., *AIRI*, 8.

[25]Marilyn M. Schaub, "Election," *CPDBT*, 250.
[26]Barbara E. Bowe, R.S.C.J., "Election: New Testament," *CPDBT*, 251.

nion with God as well as the vocation to witness to the marvels of God in the world.[27]

The prologue of Mark's gospel is a wonderful testament to election. The first Christians compared Jesus to the Suffering Servant of Isaiah, the "chosen one of God" (Is 42–53). Jesus, as God's beloved, stands chosen above all others as God's elect. Prior to Jesus' temptation, he was baptized by the Holy Spirit in the Jordan River. The Spirit called and empowered Jesus for mission. The Spirit then led Jesus to the desert, where he was tempted. The temptation was a prelude and preparation for Jesus' ministry.

Jesus, as God's chosen and God's elect, was faithful to his call and mission. His call ultimately led him to the desert, where his ancestors had failed miserably. They failed in their call to covenant relationship. Jesus not only succeeded in this, but he also offered us a new covenant. Jesus invites us all into the desert of Lent. On this first Sunday of Lent, Jesus shows the elect what the call of discipleship means. It is fraught with dangers; it is the emptying of self; it is a mission of service and it leads ultimately to the cross. Jesus does not leave us alone and abandoned in our testing, but rather gives us the sword of God's Word as our saber of protection. He shows us and the elect the way through purification to enlightenment.

At the rite of election, the godparents testify to the catechumens' readiness to accept God's call and subsequent challenge of election. The Church, then, declares the catechumens chosen and ready to go forward for baptism and we all prepare to renew our baptismal promises with the re-created floodwaters of Easter. Maximus, bishop of Turin (ca. 380–470), in *Sunday Sermons* (II, 349) speaks to the Church about the flood and its connection with baptism:

> The flood of those days was, as I say, a figure of baptism. For that was then prefigured which is now fulfilled; that is, just as when the fountains of water overflowed, iniquity was imperilled, and justice alone

reigned. Sin was swept into the abyss, and holiness upraised to heaven. For as Noah was saved in the ark, while human iniquity was drowned in the flood, so by the waters of baptism the church is borne close to heaven, all the superstitions of idols overthrown, and the faith reigns on earth which came forth from the ark of the Savior.[28]

Gospel Exegesis

The facilitator provides input from critical biblical scholarship on this text. This input includes insights as to how people would have heard the gospel in Jesus' time.

Jesus' baptism inaugurates his public ministry. The Voice from Heaven affirms him "Son" and so doing affirms his status and his commission. The term *Son of God* has scriptural roots. It alludes to Genesis 22, in which Abraham's beloved son is his only son, the royal Davidic Psalm 2, in which Yahweh names the Davidic king his son, and the Suffering Servant of Isaiah (42), who is *chosen* for public ministry. God affirms that Jesus is his anointed Son, from David's royal house, whom he has elected for eschatological ministry.

Thus, Jesus' baptism announces the advent of the eschatological age and with the advent of the Son, new hope is born. The hallmark of eschatological hope is the defeat of Satan. Thus, Mark connects the temptation in the desert with the baptism of Jesus. He also clarifies the role of the messenger with the one the messenger was appointed to announce. John was sent to preach and baptize. Jesus' election inaugurates a new world. This new world is proclaimed by the Voice of affirmation, empowered by the invocation and sending of the Spirit and the Spirit's power, and challenged by the encounter with Satan.

The ruler of this present age (Satan) has his first encounter with the Spirit-filled Son in the desert. Jesus, anointed by the Spirit and named *Beloved Son* by God, was driven into the desert by that same Spirit. The Spirit *drove* Jesus to face his test of strength in the desert for forty days and forty nights. Jesus was tempted, faced tribulation, en-

---

[27]Robert J. Schreiter, C.P.P.S., "Election: Pastoral Liturgical Tradition," *CPDBT*, 254.

[28]*RF*, 95.

dured the trial, and was tested. Jesus encountered Satan in the desert, but his ultimate battle with the Evil One was yet to come. Jesus would win the contest with Satan on the cross.

Mark's story is rich with Old Testament metaphors and symbolism. The allusion to the forty days and forty nights is obviously connected to the forty-year exodus sojourn in which Israel was tested in the desert. Jesus was ministered to by angels; so was Elijah. When Elijah was running from Jezebel and company, he fled to the desert. He wearily sat down under a broom tree and complained to God. God sent angels to minister to him—not once, but twice. The angels gave him bread "so the journey would not be too long for him." Bread of nourishment, bread of strength—Elijah was given bread to endure the trial at hand as he journeyed through the desert to the place of covenant and relationship with God—Horeb, Mount Sinai. The angels supplied Jesus with similar food. "At this first struggle Jesus is not God-forsaken as he will be at his last."[29]

The intention of today's gospel is not to provide an accurate historical accounting of the events of Jesus' temptation by Satan. It is also not primarily about Jesus' confrontation and subsequent vanquishing of Satan. It was written as a story about the testing of God's Son. "God, through the Spirit, intends to *test* Jesus; Satan, God's indirect agent, seeks to tempt the Messiah designate."[30]

The ancient Mediterranean culture lived in the world of spirits as much as in the ordinary plane of existence. The culture believed that spirits abounded and that they interfered in human affairs. When the Voice from Heaven named Jesus his beloved "Son," the highly charged, spirit-sensitive culture of the then-known world would have fully understood the implications of that event. The compliment paid to Jesus would have captured the attention of the underworld. The spirits would be compelled to test Jesus to see if the Voice from Heaven proclaimed the truth. They would try to trip him up in the event the Voice was speaking truth. Jesus was led into the place where the spirits lived, the place of testing—the desert.

Jesus, full of the Holy Spirit, would then do battle with the Evil One.[31]

Serious reflection on the symbolic world associated with the desert helps us appreciate Jesus' trial all the more. The desert was a place of death—to lose one's way there was a death sentence. Illustrated in the stories of Elijah and David, the desert was a place where fugitives flee. Wild animals (beasts) live in the desert. It is also the dwelling place of demons. Jeremiah (26) insisted that God's wrath changed the garden into a desert.

The desert is also the place where God's providence is manifested. Israel was led safely through the desert. God fed the people with quail and manna in the desert. The scriptural account of the exodus-event alludes to the feminine attributes of God. The responsibility of providing food rested with the mother. Thus, God became the Mother-provider to the people in the desert. God also provided military victory for the people.

God entered into covenant with the people in the desert and presented Israel with the Law. It is the place of relationship with God and the place where the terms of that relationship were made perfectly clear. The desert is the place of revelation. The prophet Hosea understood the desert as a place of encounter, a place to seek God, and a place of reconciliation between lovers—a place where Israel reconciled with Yahweh.

Jeremiah did not believe that Israel should return to the desert, but he did insist that Israel return to a desert spirituality. "I remember the devotion of your youth, how you loved me as a bride, following me in the desert, in a land unknown" (Jer 2:2). Jeremiah called for a return to the spirituality in which a people followed their God in the desert. Thus, the desert was also a place where Israel was faithful to Yahweh. It is also a place where Israel sinned, where they were forgiven, and ultimately from which they were led to the Promised Land.

The desert is clearly a place where God dealt with Israel on many levels. Every evangelist

---

[29] *MARK*, 9.
[30] *MI*, 23.

[31] John J. Pilch, *CWJA*, 49–51.

evoked the prophetic message of Isaiah to establish a connection between the mission of John and his role as herald. God's work of salvation would go forward from the desert stage. "Clearly the desert and God's plan for Israel were intimately bound together."[32] The testing of Jesus paralleled the testing of Israel. Israel failed; Jesus did not.

Jesus' desert temptation scene certainly draws on Hosea's perception of the desert. It is a place of manifestation and communication with God. Jesus retreated to the desert to determine the manner in which he would fulfill his mission. The gospel texts did not necessarily reveal the shape his mission would take, but they did reveal the shape it would *not* take. It was not a militaristic, nationalistic messiahship. His was not a mission of unbridled power. "Ultimately Jesus is experiencing the temptations of Israel in the desert. However, where Israel failed, Jesus has succeeded."[33]

The testing of Jesus paralleled the testing of Abraham. The temptation story has a parallel with the testing of Abraham in the Hebrew scriptures. Jesus became both Abraham and Isaac because he eventually placed himself on the altar of sacrifice.

John Pilch suggests that Jesus' encounter with Satan was a matter of honor.[34] In a culture that placed such a high value on honor, it was inevitable that Jesus' honor be challenged. Every claim of honor was certain to be tested. He could not have had a greater honor bestowed on him than God calling him "Son." There was always someone waiting in the wings to prove a compliment of that magnitude wrong. Satan was that someone. Jesus defended his honor and claimed his place as "Son."

Matthew and Luke provide Christians with the opportunity to reflect on the specific trials Jesus endured. Mark invites a different reflection. He does not describe Jesus' temptations. He simply uses the occasion to invite readers to question their loyalty (faith). Whom will they follow? Loyalty and solidarity were the binding forces in ancient community-centered cultures. Jesus invites total commitment—total loyalty. Jesus himself demonstrated complete and total loyalty to God.

Ched Myers posits another understanding of today's pericope.[35] In order to understand the desert scene we must put it in context with Jesus' baptism that preceded it. Myers insists that the baptism signals the advent of a new creation. Just as the flood signaled a new creation, a new beginning, so, too, does this event in the Jesus story signal a similar new creation. People would have expected a Messiah to possess more polished roots—impressive credentials or genealogy! Mark's Jesus possesses neither. He is from humble origins.

Nazareth was insignificant, but Galilee was notorious. It was regarded with contempt by the Jerusalem aristocracy. Hellenistic influence, gentiles, and poor peasants rendered it unclean. God's eschatological promises were to be fulfilled in Jerusalem (i.e., the Temple). Jesus' new creation and eschatological promise would be fulfilled where they were least expected—in the desert, not the Temple. Jesus signaled a return to wilderness spirituality, not Temple spirituality. The wilderness is the scene of God's salvation, renewal, and re-creation.

Mark's point is clear: divine favor falls on this figure of humble origins. Jesus' election names him God's "Beloved Son." This language recalls two scriptural traditions. The first tradition comes from royal messianic psalm (2:7) in which the new king is enthroned in opposition to the rulers of the earth. The second tradition, and the one that tempers the first, is the Isaiah tradition of the Suffering Servant. The triumphant militaristic tone of the Davidic tradition is tempered by Isaiah's Suffering Servant, who would be imbued with God's Spirit, who would bring justice to the world, and who would not cry or lift his voice in the street (Is 42:1). A king in opposition to the rulers of the earth and a Suffering Servant—both images shed light on Jesus' mission. At this point in the narrative only the reader knows Jesus' identity—it is privileged information.

---

[32] John F. Craghan, "Desert," *CPDBT*, 216.
[33] Ibid.
[34] *CWJB*, 69.

[35] *BSM*, 129.

The "Beloved Son" then retreats into the desert. The Voice from Heaven is Mark's way of proclaiming a new heaven and a new earth. There were no witnesses. Yet Jesus' baptism signals a new heaven and a new earth—"the creation of a new humanity."[36] How do we know? Jesus' baptism was real; he was not pretending. Jesus was baptized *into* the Jordan and the people were baptized *in* the Jordan (v. 5). Jesus' baptism was a repudiation and rejection of the old way—the Jewish/Roman structures of organized power, the social and religious power structures. Jesus symbolically declared that he was no longer bound by the obligations imposed by those old structures. Jesus' experience of repentance in the Jordan released him from all the obligations imposed by the systems that kept people bound and obligated. "Thus, the new creation begins with a renunciation of the old order."[37] The new people of God will no longer be bound either. It is about liberation. Jesus' baptism is a subversive event—it puts him outside the Law. Part of his mission will be to challenge that Law. His baptism serves as a declaration of resistance. He will die because of it.

Jesus' baptism charges the battery of salvation history—it is once again in forward motion. It takes place on the edge of society (desert wilderness), not at its center. After Jesus' liberating baptism, he went to the desert to confront the ruler of the world. Today's gospel only makes sense in tandem with Jesus' baptism that preceded it. The desert scene elucidates a common biblical motif—the apocalyptic combat myth (see thirty-fourth Sunday, second reading exegesis). Jesus, filled with God's Spirit, "Beloved Son," begins his battle with Satan. From the outset of the gospel, Jesus struggles with the demons. They know his identity when the crowds do not. Jesus inaugurates his preaching mission. The kingdom of God is at hand—not the anticipated nationalistic kingdom, but an entirely new kingdom, a new political and spiritual reality.

After John's arrest Jesus took up the "mantle of the fallen prophet. Jesus continues the proclamation of the kingdom and the demand for repen-

tance—and all too soon he too will be targeted for arrest by the authorities."[38]

Mark's Jesus confronts the oppressive power structures of first-century Palestine. He reminds his readers that preaching a message of repentance ultimately leads to political trouble—fidelity to the message leads to the cross. Mark keeps readers off balance. Expectations are turned upside-down. Elijah (John) has returned and the Messiah has already arrived. The expected end of the world did not arrive, however. Jews believed that liberation of the Jewish nation would depend on the political and military intervention of the Messiah. The place of messianic advent was the desert, not the expected Jerusalem. Mark wants his readers to understand what the role of the liberating Messiah was really meant to be. He does that by telling what the Messiah is not. The long-awaited, liberating Messiah will not be a militaristic savior of the people.

Jesus' movement to the desert evokes images of liberation from Pharaoh in Egypt. Jesus was "tempted" by his political antagonists throughout the gospel. They goad him into compromising himself. He will warn the disciples not to be swayed by similar temptations. Both sides of the contest have their own supporters. We are told that Jesus was supported by angels as he survived in the midst of wild beasts. The term *wild beasts* should take the biblically aware reader immediately to the apocalyptic Book of Daniel and the Book of Revelation. (Refer to the thirty-fourth Sunday in Ordinary Time for more information on the apocalypses of the Book of Daniel and the Book of Revelation.) Wild beasts are a euphemism in both Daniel and Revelation. The wild beasts represent ruling powers—not just one king, but a combination of earthly rulers who are directed and inspired by one invisible guardian—in this case, Satan. The apocalyptic myth now enacted in the desert, Mark announces the arrival of the new kingdom. The new creation and the cosmic battle between Jesus and Satan and the oppressive powers have now begun.

Jesus eventually leaves the desert. He did not stay there. His mission took him out to engage the world, not to flee from it. Mark's prologue "nar-

---

[36]Ibid.
[37]Ibid.

---

[38]Ibid.

rates the dawn of the kingdom at the margins of the world. In it Mark announces an offensive upon the strongholds of oppression and the dawn of liberation, and launches the discipleship adventure. But from the very outset, the tone of the story anticipates conflict. This erupts in Jesus' very first public action in Capernaum."[39]

One last perspective to bring into this dialogue is the Christology posed by Mark, reflected in the baptism and desert scene. Mark takes great pains to establish the superiority of Jesus to John. Jesus witnesses what no other human being ever witnessed. The heavens were opened, the Spirit descended, and the Voice of God thundered. As noted above, the Voice alludes to the enthronement psalm in which Yahweh installed the king as his own son. The Voice also referred to the Servant of Isaiah in whom God delighted and to whom God sent his Spirit. Bas van Iersel reminds us that the narrator of this text was not positing belief in the Trinitarian concept of God.[40] (Passages like this, however, are the basis for eventual belief in the Trinity.) The narrator had another purpose in mind: "In this story the voice from heaven designates Jesus as messianic king and as the servant of God *par excellence*."[41]

Allusion to the above-mentioned scriptures designates Jesus as both prophet and messianic king. However, Jesus' baptism and installation as prophet are both similar and dissimilar from the prophetic commissioning in the Hebrew scriptures. Jesus' election is similar to Ezekiel's. Ezekiel was installed on the banks of a river, winged creatures hovered overhead, a voice spoke from heaven, and a spirit carried him to another place.[42] The differences between Jesus' call and Ezekiel's call are nonetheless striking. In the Ezekiel tradition a human figure known as the "son of man" was sitting on a throne above the sky. Ezekiel was sent to the house of Israel with a message on a scroll, with orders to eat the scroll as a way of making the message his own. None of those elements is in Jesus' episode. Jesus is sent by no one. The Voice did not send him,

nor did the Voice tell him the nature of his mission. "It appears that Jesus' authority as messianic son of God does not derive from a higher authority, but is due him as a matter of course."[43] This, therefore, is the Jesus who engages Satan in the desert, the place of encounter, testing, and revelation. This is the Jesus who announces the day of salvation and the reign of God. This is the Jesus who is imbued with his own divine authority.

Ultimately, Jesus retreated to the place of communion with God, and as is readily observable in the various exegetical perspectives, he entered a symbolic world of meaning. The liturgy of the first Sunday of Lent invites us into the symbols and metaphors that most speak to our lives. Perhaps we need the Christ who engaged the sinister power of evil and was successful. Perhaps we need the Christ who nonviolently challenged the power structures bent on keeping people dominated, oppressed, or in bondage. Or perhaps we need the Christ who was acknowledged as "beloved" by his Father and retreated to the desert to enter into that deep, abiding intimacy, only to survive the first test of his life in preparation for the ultimate test of his life. Gustavo Gutierrez puts today's gospel in perspective:[44]

> Every mission of proclaiming and witnessing the kingdom must be prepared in the desert, where the proximity of death stirs up our will to live and makes us experience the isolation which leads us to hunger for communion. Today, on our continent, the spirit of many witnesses of the kingdom is being shaped by following the Lord in troubles, difficulties, and hostility. These witnesses know that Christ's death gave them new life.[45]

Proclaim the gospel again.

Sometimes we gain new insights when we hear the text after the interpretation is given. Someone from the group proclaims the gospel a second time.

---

[39]Ibid., 136.
[40]*RM*, 39.
[41]Ibid.
[42]Ibid.

---

[43]Ibid., 40.
[44]*SWTLY*, 49.
[45]Ibid., 47.

Conversation with the Liturgy and the Scriptures

Test your original understanding in dialogue with the text.

(You might consider breaking into smaller groups.)

Now that you've heard the exegesis, were there any new insights? How do you feel about it? How does your original understanding of this gospel compare with what we just shared? How does this story speak to your life?

Sharing Life Experience

Participants share an experience from their lives that connects with the biblical interpretation just presented.

Like Noah and clan, today signals our embarkation on a journey of serious reflection. There are two cabins in this ark, one marked baptismal, the other penitential. The church enters this Lenten time of retreat and preparation as we sail toward the waters of rebirth, restoration, and renewal at the Easter Vigil.

The invitation for me and for the Church is to be present during the voyage, not to sleep through it. Today's liturgy is a wake-up call. It is amazing how a four-verse pericope has within it the power to invite conversion and complete metanoia. Baptism is participation in the life, death, and resurrection of Jesus, death to sin, and incorporation in the community of God. With baptism comes call and responsibility. There is an election involved. Through baptism we are called by God. As the elect go forward for the rite of election, we are invited to remember our own election—that we, too, are "beloved and chosen." Jesus' own election made ours possible. Our election demands response—conversion. Lent is a time-out for the Church to reflect on the ways in which we fall short of our baptismal responsibilities. How have we failed to love God? One another? God's anawim? The least among us? The greatest among us? In what way have we engaged the "powers"? In what way do we still struggle with the power of evil? The season of Lent presents us with an invitation. We are invited to step into that penitential door in order to discover the obscure and often hidden ways we fail to love, give in to temptation, and serve our own idolatrous concerns.

Whenever we become an obstacle to promoting the reign of God, we succumb to the power of evil and are defeated in our desert contest. About ten years ago our parish was engaged in a struggle that seemed at the time to be of cosmic proportions. Both sides understood themselves to be on the side of righteousness. The more we tried to engage the demon, the more we succumbed to its power. Hatred and obsession became an aphrodisiac for both sides. There was little evidence of God's kingdom in the midst of that mess. Both sides believed themselves to be on the side of Christ, champions of the cause of justice.

"Repent and believe the good news" was far from the lips of many key players. There was an idolatrous need for each side to be right, which made reconciliation next to impossible. How does one reconcile when one does not think there is anything to be reconciled about? How does one reconcile when one thinks that one's actions are ordained by God himself? It was the most painful community experience I have ever known. We marched militantly to the table each week, believing that we needed to be strengthened for the battle ahead. There was indeed a battle. But the locus was far more internal than it was external. While the numbers of those involved in the controversy were small and somewhat contained, it nevertheless impacted our entire community. How could it not? When one member hurts we all hurt.

We are all elected by God, chosen in God's service and called "beloved." Yet through the chaos we failed to see the "beloved" in one another. We listened to the insults and allowed that "naming" to become our reality, rather than believing our status as "beloved child of God."

As we lived out our own version of the biblical combat myth, we thought it would never end. Even though our contest was only a few months in duration, the animosities continued for a year or two. Some ruptured relationships have never been fully restored. Healing in the community eventually occurred; Christ was victorious over the evil that seemed untouchable, and reconciliation finally was given a chance.

Everyone involved in the situation suffered terribly. Unfortunately, little of it was redemptive as so much of our pain was caused by the hateful vollies leveled by both sides. Today our parish is strong and vibrant. We are not without problems—every parish has them. Little skirmishes pop up here and there. But what we learned from this great test is that we will never again allow evil to gain a strong foothold in our relationships with one another. There is too much at stake. If it were not for honest pastoral leadership we might still be in the conflict many years later. Jesus entered the contest for us at the beginning of his ministry and at the end. His desert encounter is a source of hope. We are reconciled, healed, and united as a community today because Christ went before us.

Evil had its day in our community, and it will probably have others. There were no simple solutions. Everything we tried was futile until we abandoned ourselves as best we could to the imperatives of the Serenity Prayer. We did what we could do to fix the situation and then we turned it over to God to do the rest. We were truly powerless. In God's time hearts softened and we were able to worship in truth. As a community we failed. We refused to do the work of restoration and re-creation invited in today's gospel. We allowed the flood of hatred to cut a path of destruction and division in the midst of our community life. As individuals we refused to love. Those of us involved in the conflict could not imagine reconciliation with some of the people who had been the cause of so much pain. The Spirit of God is the Great Reconciler, however. Many of the people involved in the fracas are intimate friends today. Reconciliation does not just restore the status quo—it invites a new way of being. One of our primary missions as Church is reconciliation, yet sometimes it is the most difficult. Jesus engaged Satan, the initiator of all hatred and division, and gave us the promise of a better way to live.

I hope I never have to experience a contest of that nature again. However, should the situation present itself again, I pray that I will walk through it with more love and with the self-effacing attitude of Christ.

This Lent invites me to a deep personal encounter with the God Who Calls Me Beloved. It is also a time to believe those words spoken to me in love.

They may not be shouted from a ruptured heavenly ceiling, but they are certainly whispered in the quiet recesses of my soul. Perhaps if I were to own those words, I would be more prepared to withstand the struggle in my next confrontation with the sinister tempter.

What was Mark trying to tell his community? How do you feel about Jesus' battle with Satan? How does it relate to your life? The life of the community? Have you ever felt powerless over the presence and power of evil around you? Have you ever experienced the healing, reconciling power of Christ? What does it mean to you that Jesus initiated the new kingdom at his baptism? What does that have to do with you or your community? In what concrete way does this gospel challenge your community? In what way has this conversation with the scriptures for today's liturgy invited change in your life? In what way are the biblical themes of covenant, exodus, creation, and community evident in today's readings? Do you still feel the same way about this text as when you began? Has your original understanding been stretched, challenged, or affirmed?

STEP 5
DECISION

The gospel demands a response.

In what concrete way might your parish be invited to respond? Are there any attitudes or behaviors you would like to change as a result of today's conversation? What one concrete action will you take this week in response to the liturgy today?

Pastoral Considerations: The season of Lent is an opportunity to give serious attention to issues of justice. What is happening in your civic community that needs the attention of the Christian community? Are there areas where advocates are needed to speak for the rights of the poor? In what ways might your parish participate in the Lenten discipline of almsgiving—a soup kitchen, soup suppers where the profits are given to the poor, food drives, clothing drives, a project to assist the poor in Third World countries to help themselves? How is your parish addressing multicultural issues? Are there factions and divisions within the parish community that are crying out for healing? Perhaps Lent is the appropriate time to face those issues head-on!

Christian Initiation: The rite of election is usually celebrated at the diocesan cathedral. The parish will probably celebrate the rite of sending catechumens for election and candidates for recognition by the bishop. Those in the catechumenate *who will not be initiated at the Easter Vigil* continue in the period of the catechumenate. The elect begin the period of purification and enlightenment—retreat time. It is a time of discernment in which they are prepared for baptism, reflect on sin and grace, and prepare to celebrate the scrutinies. In what ways can the disciplines of prayer, fasting, and almsgiving be highlighted in the catechumenate community? Are there opportunities for catechumens, candidates, and the elect to participate in issues of justice?

Reconciliation. Perhaps baptized candidates who will enter into full communion with the Catholic Church during the Easter season might be prepared to celebrate the sacrament of reconciliation at the parish's Lenten celebration of the sacrament of penance. Perhaps the elect might join in the preparation so they can celebrate the sacrament following their initiation. Perhaps a nonsacramental penitential celebration might be celebrated with catechumens still in process.

DOCTRINAL ISSUES

What Church truth/teaching/doctrinal issue could be drawn from the gospel for the first Sunday of Lent?

Participants suggest possible doctrinal themes that flow from the readings.

Possible Doctrinal Themes

Baptismal and penitential themes of Lent; reconciliation; season of Lent; conversion; sin; grace; nonviolence; social justice; faith; covenant; prayer, fasting, almsgiving

Present the doctrinal material at this time.

1. The facilitator gives input on a particular doctrinal issue of his or her prior choosing. OR
2. The group chooses a doctrinal issue from the list they created. They read together from the Doctrinal Appendix or other appropriate, official Church documents and the works of respected theologians.

(Many doctrinal issues are found in the Doctrinal Appendix at the back of this workbook. If you are choosing an issue from this resource, please refer to it now.)

Reflection questions centered around the chosen doctrinal theme can be found at the end of each topic in the Doctrinal Appendix. The questions are based on the five-step reflection process. If you choose a topic not included in the Doctrinal Appendix, craft your own questions according to the same five-step process.

Following the reflection questions you will be reminded to return to chapter 7, "Preparing the Catechetical Session," to assist you in crafting your own session.

Closing Prayer

Father,
through the observances of Lent,
help us to understand the meaning
of your Son's death and resurrection,
and teach us to reflect it in our lives.
Grant this through our Lord
Jesus Christ, your Son,
who lives and reigns with you and the Holy Spirit,
one God, for ever and ever.[46]

---

[46]First Sunday of Lent: "Opening Prayer," *The Sacramentary.*

SECOND SUNDAY OF LENT

Environment

See Ash Wednesday.

INTRODUCTORY RITES

Entrance Antiphon (or Opening Song)

My heart has prompted me to seek your face; I seek it, Lord; so do not hide from me.[1]

Opening Prayer

The facilitator of the session may lead the prayer. Others in the group may be asked to proclaim the readings.

Let us pray
(for the grace to respond to the Word of God)

Pause for silent prayer.

God our Father,
help us to hear your Son.
Enlighten us with your word,
that we may find the way to your glory.
We ask this through our Lord
Jesus Christ, your Son,
who lives and reigns with you
and the Holy Spirit,
one God, for ever and ever.[2]

LITURGY OF THE WORD

The readings are proclaimed.

First Reading
Genesis 22:1–2a, 10–13, 15–18

Refer to the tenth Sunday in Ordinary Time for an overview of the Book of Genesis.

---

[1]Second Sunday of Lent: "Entrance Antiphon," *The Sacramentary.*

[2]Second Sunday of Lent: "Opening Prayer," *The Sacramentary.*

Today's Pericope: (For further elaboration on the Abraham saga, refer to the Feast of the Holy Family, Optional Year B, first reading.) The Lord God promises Abraham many and great things in this reading. We, however, are shocked by the demand to murder his son. We have a difficult time getting past Abraham's willingness to perform such a heinous act. Someone once raised the question, "If that is an example of the kind of God you wish me to worship, thanks, but no thanks. I want no part of him. What God would ask a father to murder his own son?" It is an honest question. Yet this story is upheld throughout all of biblical literature as a premier story of faith. There has to be and there is more to the story.

In order to understand this story we must stretch ourselves and put our Western mind-sets on hold for a brief period. This story is not about killing one's son; it is about placing one's entire life in the hands of the all-knowing, omniscient God. "The father's life is bound up with that of his child and heir; Abraham entrusts his life and his future unconditionally to the God who calls him."[3]

This is the only time in scripture that God tests one individual rather than the entire nation. Abraham, as the future leader of Israel, must "entrust his entire life and future to God."[4] The reader of this story is aware from the beginning that God is testing Abraham, but Abraham is not aware. Isaac was not Abraham's only son as the text would intimate. Rather, a better translation is *favored.* God makes sure that in this dialogue the weight of Isaac's value to Abraham is emphasized.

Abraham and Isaac ascend Mount Moriah, the place believed to be the site of Solomon's Temple. Abraham, then, is the first worshiper on the Temple site. Abraham obeys God in silence. Isaac follows and asks the whereabouts of the sacrificial animal. Abraham's reply that God would provide is

---

[3]Richard J. Clifford, S.J., and Roland E. Murphy, "Genesis," *NJBC*, 25.

[4]Ibid.

another example of trusting God to supply all needs. His life is completely in Yahweh's hands.

The angel arrives to save the day. Isaac is spared and Abraham has proved that his entire life is completely under God's providential care. "He has finally learned to give up control over his own life that he might receive it as grace."[5] God spoke the word to the angel and caused Isaac to be spared. God caused the firstborn of Israel to be spared. In Israel it was understood that each newborn child belonged to God and was symbolically sacrificed to God. As a symbolic sign of this sacrifice, a ram (or other animal) was offered in order to redeem the firstborn.

Abraham was always understood to prefigure what would be accomplished through Christ. The sacrifice of Isaac was understood as a type for the sacrifice of Christ on the cross. Today's reading from Romans bespeaks that belief. Paul was probably referring to the Isaac-event in his proclamation: "God did not spare his only Son but gave him up for us all." Jesus, God's firstborn, "beloved Son," would be sacrificed, would stand in as the sacrificial lamb and redeem Israel. Isaac, Abraham's favored son, was saved from death. In the story of the transfiguration Jesus is affirmed as God's beloved, favored Son. Through his sacrifice on the cross, he would conquer death once and for all.

In early Judaism the Abraham/Isaac story was a story about Abraham's faith. Later interpretive development combined Abraham's faith with Isaac's voluntary surrender of his life.[6] "To this voluntary surrender was attributed atoning significance, and the sacrifice of Isaac was further connected with the Passover Lamb."[7]

Responsorial Psalm
Psalm 116:10, 15–19

Verses from this psalm are proclaimed on Holy Thursday with a eucharistic context. The emphasis in this psalm is the deliverance of a just person from trials, thus connecting it with the sacrifice of Isaac.

---

[5] Ibid.
[6] *PL*, 234.
[7] Ibid.

Second Reading
Romans 8:31b–34

(Refer to the fourth Sunday of Advent for an overview of St. Paul's Letter to the Romans.)

Today's Pericope: Paul takes up the theme of the first reading even though he does not directly mention it. He insists that God does not want the death of any of his children. The story of Cain and Abel is a reminder to us that God abhors homicide. God, however, did not spare his only Son (as Isaac was spared) but gave him over for us all. Ours is not to question the wisdom of God. But this we know—God sent his Son to take on human form, the likeness of sinful humanity. God's Son was handed over to be killed, like a convicted criminal. Jesus was not a sinner, however. Jesus' death was a supreme self-sacrificing act of love for God and for human beings. Jesus' death and resurrection conquered sin and death once and for all. Once and for all time Jesus shattered the connection between sin and death. Death would not have the last word. Jesus was victorious over death and was restored to life. He rose from the dead and returned to the throne of glory, at God's right hand. God demonstrated his advocacy for the human race. Jesus' sacrifice made eternal life possible for all. In light of God's incredible, gratuitous gift, who could be against us? God gave us everything. Jesus, who gave his life for us and who interceded for us, is certainly not going to condemn us. Who then? Our salvation is assured through the death and resurrection of Jesus. We can do no less than be attentive to our responsibility as children of God. God's work and action in us will be operative in us as long as we live in faith, hope, and God's incredible love.

The gospel is proclaimed.

Gospel
Mark 9:2–10. This is my beloved Son.

STEP 1
NAMING ONE'S EXPERIENCE

What were your first impressions? What was your first response to the gospel (or the other readings)? What captured your attention?

Each person names his or her initial impression. Statements should be brief. No reasons should be given at this time. All simply listen without agreeing or disagreeing.

STEP 2
UNDERSTANDING

In a brief statement, explain what you think this gospel is trying to convey.

STEP 3
INPUT FROM VISION/STORY/TRADITION

Liturgical Context

The celebration of liturgy continues to remember and connect us with the Abraham/Isaac story. Eucharistic Prayer I calls to mind the sacrifice of Abraham and connects it with the offering of eucharist. "Look with favor on these offerings and accept them as once you accepted the sacrifice of Abraham, our father in faith." The sequence from the Mass of the Feast of the Body and Blood of Christ, the Lauda Sion (St. Thomas Aquinas), asserts that the sacrifice of Isaac prefigured the sacrifice of Christ.[8]

"Lent sends each Christian and the entire Church on a long journey of faith. It does not make use of an intense catechesis—the liturgy is not the place for this, despite its catechetical dimension—but of efficacious signs, sacraments, of a grace-bearing symbolic approach; and it leads us on the way of an exodus toward life."[9]

"Today, let us go up the mountain
On which Jesus will shine forth.
Who can withstand, O Lord, your light?
Who will face the cross?
Today, let us go up the mountain
On which Jesus will shine forth.

Today let us remain in the light.
Jesus Christ will keep us.
Heal us, Lord, by your wounds,

Create in us a new heart.
Today, let us remain in the light.
Jesus Christ will keep us.

Today, let us walk in the light.
Jesus will rise.
Open to us the doors of life,
Open to us the new times.
Today, let us walk in the light.
Jesus will rise."[10]

The liturgies of the first two Sundays of Lent date back to the fourth century, making them the oldest Lenten observance. From the fourth until the mid-sixth centuries, Lent was the beginning of the liturgical year and the continuous reading of the Bible.[11] Abraham, the father of Jewish, Muslim, and Christian believers, is remembered every second Sunday of Lent. Abraham was so important to the ancient writers that thirteen chapters of the Bible were devoted to his life, deeds, and story. Today's scriptures relate the sacrifice of Abraham and Isaac. Abraham, our ancestor in faith, reminds us of what it means to be a disciple. We are to yield to God's sovereign will for our lives and completely and totally put our trust in him. Abraham is a reminder for believers of all generations that each person is called by God and has a role in history's continuous drama.

With Abraham was born the People of God. God formed a people to be his own, a chosen race, a holy people, a people set apart to participate in God's own purposes. God was present to Israel. We continue to celebrate that presence in the community of believers today.

The story of the Lord's transfiguration is the gospel for the second Sunday of Lent. All three gospels place this event immediately after Peter's confession of Jesus, the prediction of his death and Passion, the cost of discipleship, and the promise of the parousia. However, the liturgy for this Sunday does not address those themes. The transfiguration-event stands on its own, for its own sake and meaning, as a Sunday in Lent. The carry-over of these passages into a liturgical context is not contrary to the spirit of the gospel, however.

---

[8] *DL* (II), 83.
[9] Ibid.

[10] J. Servel (text) and M.-A. Rétif (music), *Chantes notés*, vol. 4, coédition (Paris, 14), 289–290.
[11] *DL* (II), 40.

With an unerring instinct, the Lenten liturgy proposes the mystery of Jesus' transfiguration to the contemplation of the faithful, who are slowly moving toward the feast of Easter, that is, toward the mysteries—apparently separated but forming a deep unity—of the passion and the resurrection. The liturgy thus transposes the teaching that the three Synoptic Gospels sought to impart.[12]

The second Sunday of Lent and the transfiguration gospel are intended to accompany the Church on our own ascent to Jerusalem and the resurrection of Easter. The transfiguration serves as a shining beacon of hope to strengthen the Church and increase its zeal as it follows Christ to the cross and subsequent glory.[13] "The mystery of the transfiguration concerns the entire Church—all Christians! The voice is addressed to us with a particular force during Lent when the insistent call to conversion resounds."[14]

The preface for today's liturgy reminds us of the importance of this event. "He had wanted to teach them through the Law and the Prophets that the promised Christ had first to suffer and so come to the glory of his resurrection" (Preface: Second Sunday of Lent). The transfiguration was intended to strengthen the disciples for the ominous cross that was just beyond the horizon. It was also a message of hope to believers that they would one day share in the glory Christ revealed on that high mountain. This hope is reflected in the opening prayer: "Enlighten us with your word, that we may find the way to your glory"; and in the prayer after communion: "Lord, we give you thanks for these holy mysteries which bring to us here on earth, a share in the life to come."

Gospel Exegesis

The facilitator provides input from critical biblical scholarship on this text. This input includes insights as to how people would have heard the gospel in Jesus' time.

The awesome transfiguration. What was going on? On the surface it appears so surrealistic that it is natural fodder for the prone skeptic. Yet the event is found in all three synoptic gospels—a surefire sign that the early Christian communities accepted it as authentic.

In Mark's gospel Jesus' identity was constantly in question. The transfiguration was to expand the disciples' understanding of Jesus. It called for a response of obedience even in the midst of their lack of understanding. Mark uses the transfiguration-event to provide divine ratification for Peter's profession of faith and to foretell the resurrection.

Luke posited the event as an experience for both Jesus and his disciples.[15] Luke does not use the same language of transfiguration utilized by Mark and Matthew. Only Luke relates the conversation between Jesus and guests. Moses and Elijah pointed to Jesus' coming exodus. Jesus would lead the people to freedom just as a previous generation had once been so led. Luke's event proclaimed Jesus as a prophet "great in word and deed"[16] who would suffer and later be vindicated by God. Jesus stood on the threshold of the new, final age. Luke affirms Jesus as Messiah and reminds the disciples of the sobering implications of that reality: suffering, death, glory. Disciples would ultimately follow the same path.

Matthew's version is an "in-house" experience for the benefit of the three disciples. Matthew exalts Jesus as Lord and throughout the gospel is concerned with showing Jesus' superiority to Moses. Moses' and Elijah's part in this one-act encounter demonstrates that Jesus superseded and was the fulfillment of the Law and the Prophets.[17] Matthew insists that disciples hear, respond, and act on the word of Jesus. Matthew's disciples do not misunderstand. They listen to him.

Jesus and company experienced a vision. Altered states of consciousness like visions and dreams were and are not uncommon human experiences in Mediterranean cultures.[18] Our pragmatic, "show me" society looks askance at such phenom-

---

[12]X. Leon-Daffier, "La Transfiguration de Jesus (Mt. 17, 1–9)," *Assemble du Seigneur*, St. series, no. 28 (Brutes: Publications de Saint-Andre', 1962), 27, in *DL* (II), 76.

[13]Ibid.

[14]Ibid., 79.

[15]Barbara E. Reid, O.P., "Transfiguration," *CPDBT*, 1013.

[16]Ibid.

[17]Ibid.

[18]*CWJ*, 53.

ena. However, Jesus and his disciples experience just such a vision. There is much to learn from it. Jesus was considered a disgrace in many circles of his community. The transfigured Jesus experienced a reversal and an advent. While not a parable, the story's meaning makes it function like a parable. The disgraced Jesus finds favor with the Father and communes with him. It is the ultimate reversal of fortunes and advent (manifestation) of God's presence and favor. The one who was shamed was vindicated by the Father. Through this intercommunication with his Father, Jesus was immersed in a love that would assure him of exoneration.

The cross was a stumbling block for many earlier believers. If Jesus was the Messiah, and the one his disciples believed him to be, how could the Lord God have forsaken him? According to John Pilch, the transfiguration shows unequivocally that God no more abandoned Jesus than he did his predecessor, Moses. Jesus trusted his Father against all odds. When the world thought him to reside in shame and disgrace, Jesus trusted his Father. Believers are to do no less. We are to trust God; we are to be subject to the Lordship of Christ, the new Moses and Lawgiver.

It is generally believed that the mountain in the story is Mount Tabor in southern Galilee. "The high mountain symbolizes the border zone between earth and heaven, between the material and the spiritual."[19] As one who stood atop that mountain on the Feast of the Transfiguration, I can readily understand the allegory. The visitor stands transfixed as the panoramic lushness of the valley glistens like the jewels that adorn the new and eternal city, the heavenly Jerusalem. I felt I could "reach out and touch" the heavenly realm at a mere arm's length!

In the doctrine of later generations, the transfiguration was understandably interpreted as the revelation of Christ's divinity. However, the first communities were not so developed in their theology. The transfiguration is a preview of Christ's resurrected glory and rule from the heavenly throne. On the holy mountain of authority he will rule heaven and earth. It foreshadows the resurrection.

Moses and Elijah are integral to the scene. Moses foretold a prophet that would one day reveal God's will to the world. Elijah was understood as a precursor to the day of the final eschaton. Both characters signal the world that the last age has finally arrived.

True to form, the impetuous Peter responds according to his limited human perspective. He is cut short by the Divine Voice. The disciples were afraid of the Voice—a sign of "Jesus' supreme teaching authority."[20]

One is not to miss the paradox of the moment. Jesus, on this mountain, is surrounded by hero-saints of old. On the hill of Golgotha he will be surrounded by criminals. On this holy mountain Jesus' clothes dazzle brilliantly. On the hill of Golgotha they are torn from his body in disgrace. The Divine Voice heralds Jesus as Son. His executioners do the same at his murder.

The vision of transcendent glory was to be balanced with the specter of future suffering. There can be no resurrection, no power from on high, to rule supreme over the earth in resurrected glory without the cross. "His suffering was part and parcel of his glory."[21]

In order to understand Mark's intention in the story we must first consider the verse prior to today's pericope. Jesus referred to the immanent parousia. Talk of parousia and the appearance of Elijah and Moses point the reader in the direction of Mark's community and what was happening at the time of the gospel's composition. People believed that the destruction of the Temple signaled the final eschaton. Their hopes were dashed, however, and disillusionment set in when that did not take place. Doubts threatened the community. Perhaps Jesus was no greater than Moses or Elijah, who had also been swooped up into heaven. Perhaps he was not really the Messiah after all. Mark sets the record straight.

Jesus took Peter, James, and John with him, underscoring the importance of the revelation about to be given. He took them off by himself and then

---

[19]Ibid.

[20]David E. Garland, *RM*, 183.
[21]Ibid., 184.

enjoined the disciples to say nothing, again emphasizing the revelatory character of the event.[22] The word *transfigured* is used in the Letters to the Romans and Corinthians as a reference for the transformation of the believer into the spiritual image and likeness of Christ. A common apocalyptic motif is the transfiguration of the just of the world. The narrator of Mark connects the transfiguration of Jesus with his future resurrected glory. Further proof of the eschatological implications of the event can be seen in the description of Jesus' dazzling white clothes. Mark insists that the phenomenon is of divine origin.

In Luke's version of the story Jesus is given a revelation about his immanent fate—he will suffer and die. The disciples, as witnesses of Jesus' future glory, are strengthened to face the ordeal of the cross. Mark, on the other hand, uses the transfiguration primarily as the means of revelation to the disciples. Jesus led *them* up the mountain and he was transfigured before *them*. Moses and Elijah appeared to *them* and God's Voice was spoken for *their* benefit, evidenced by the Voice's use of the third person in the dialogue.

The disciples want to extend this very joyous experience. They suggest the erection of "booths," an image reminiscent of the Feast of Tabernacles, an eschatological feast evoking the heavenly dwelling of the righteous. Peter wanted to build a booth for Jesus, Moses, and Elijah, which would have put all three on an equal footing. Again, Peter misunderstands the implications of what he has just witnessed, but the Voice teaches him the truth. The cloud, the presence of God, the Shekinah glory of God passes over and was manifest to them. God names Jesus his beloved Son. However, there is something unique about this designation. In the first chapter of Mark, God addressed Jesus personally as his beloved Son. Now, in this instance, God addresses the disciples and tells them what he told the Son earlier. "This is my beloved Son." Now the disciples are privy to the word spoken only to Jesus in the gospel's prologue. The Voice exhorts the disciples to listen to the beloved Son who is also the "prophet like Moses whose teaching must be heeded."[23]

Mark wants his reader to understand that the transfiguration of Jesus was a future glimpse of his resurrected glory. Jesus is greater than Elijah and Moses; he is God's Son who was victorious over death. Mark uses Peter's misunderstanding (as he often does) to teach the truth to those who doubt that Jesus is who they thought he was—Messiah, resurrected Son of God who would one day return in glory.

The disciples are enjoined to keep the events they have witnessed to themselves. They are to tell no one. No one would understand anyway. The transfiguration could only be understood in retrospect, after the Passion, death, and subsequent resurrection. Easter faith would be required to proclaim the truth of Jesus' death and resurrection. "It is a signal to the Christian: he or she must strive to understand the mighty, transforming import of the resurrection."[24]

Ched Myers offers a different lens with which to view this scene.[25] The transfiguration follows on the previous verses in chapter 8 in which Jesus openly begins to teach to the crowds. His message is a call to radical discipleship: "deny yourself, take up your cross and follow me." The political ramifications of Mark's gospel now take center stage. "Take up your cross" had only one connotation in ancient Palestine—dissidents were executed on it. Crucifixion was the means of political and military punishment. It was reserved by the Romans for the lower classes—the slaves, criminals, and rebellious elements, anyone who threatened law and order. Jesus' call to take up the cross is a call to share the same fate (crucifixion) as those who dare to challenge the oppression of the organized structures of power.

Condemned persons were forced to carry their own cross to the place of execution. There was no greater humiliation. The one crucified was exposed naked in the public area and then executed for all to see. Mark's readers would have shuddered in horror at the implications of "taking up one's cross." There was absolutely no privatized, spiritualized connotation associated with the term. It was simply a reference to the horror of crucifixion.

[22]*MARK*, 132.
[23]Ibid., 135.

[24]Ibid., 136.
[25]*BSM*, 248–256.

Prior to carrying the cross, the call to discipleship involved denying oneself. This was not an invitation to engage in private asceticism. The term meant to risk one's life. In other words, if you really want to follow Jesus, this is what it means: when dragged before courts because of your association with Jesus, you risk the death sentence if you profess loyalty to him.

The threat of death by the state was the means by which the state controlled the populace. Fear of this punishment is what maintained order. "By resisting this fear and pursuing kingdom practice even at the cost of death, the disciple contributes to shattering the powers' reign of death in history."[26] Jesus' Messiahship was one of nonviolent confrontation with power—Rome and the Sanhedrin. Those who wish to follow Jesus must be willing to be identified with his nonviolent subversive movement. They will face a test of loyalty when interrogated before the courts. If they deny "self" they will risk the death of an insurgent. This is the way of the cross.

In Mark's gospel, John the Baptist had already faced his moment of trial and execution. Jesus was moving closer to his moment and it would be just a matter of time before the disciples would face theirs. Mark's purpose in presenting the Daniel myth in connection with Jesus' instruction on discipleship is to teach the disciples/readers the meaning of the cross and to empower them to stand with Jesus, knowing that their decision may result in their execution. It will also result in the judgment of those who seek their lives.

Daniel employs a common apocalyptic myth—the combat myth. In Daniel's vision the tyrannical rulers (beasts) cause devastation and upheaval in the world, especially for God's people. They are finally brought before the divine court and judged by the true judge (Ancient One—Dn 7:9). The judge then places earthly power in the hands of the saints (people of God). The Son of Man/Human One is the judge who adjudicates the trial and passes sovereignty to the people of God.

Mark adapts the myth to suit his purpose. The Son of Man/Human One, because of his inevitable conflict with the tyrants, becomes a defendant in their court. He is tried, convicted, and sentenced to death.[27] Mark's Son of Man/Human One is aligned with the persecuted saints in Daniel's myth—but only briefly. A few verses later (v. 38) the Son of Man comes with the angels (Daniel's saints) to be the true judge and to receive the kingdom. Thus, in Mark's adaptation of Daniel, the Son of Man is both defendant in the earthly court and prosecutor in the heavenly one.

It seems to the Danielic prophet that the tyrannical powers are invincible, untouchable, and all-powerful. They appear to have the upper hand at that historical moment. However, he looks again, reflects further, and discovers a different reality. The Son of Man is really establishing justice. Mark uses the prophet's revelation to explain the cross. What appears to be Jesus' apparent defeat is in truth his vindication. What seems to be the upper hand and triumph of Rome and the Sanhedrin is in truth their judgment and defeat. The myth functions to help the disciple understand the true meaning of the cross as Jesus' glory and vindication. It also helps disciples understand the choices before them. If they stand with Jesus in this courtroom drama, they will be executed, but they will gain their lives. If they stand "ashamed" against him they will live, but they will ultimately lose their lives. This truth is timeless—it "illuminates Christian existence at all times and in all places."[28]

The transfiguration continues the courtroom scene of chapter 8. Daniel's courtroom vision was confirmed by the appearance of a man dressed in glorified clothing. For Mark, the transfiguration performs the same function. The transfiguration confirms the teaching on the cross. The fearful Danielic prophet stood before the man in dazzling clothes and received the true interpretation of his vision that the angels would be triumphant over the beasts. The fearful disciples stand before Jesus in his dazzling garments and he confirms that his teaching on the cross is truth and will stand. Whereas most scholars consider the "coming of the Son of Man in glory" to refer to the parousia, Myers insists it has nothing to do with

---

[26] Ibid., 247.

[27] Ibid., 248.
[28] Ibid.

that. He insists that it is a reference to the Daniel myth. Compare the passages in Mark and in Daniel.

> Once again the high priest interrogated him: "are you the Messiah, the Son of the Blessed One?" Then Jesus answered: "I am; and you will see the Son of Man seated at the right hand of the Power and coming with the clouds of heaven." (NAB: Mk 14:61–62)

> I saw One like a son of man coming on the clouds of heaven; When he reached the Ancient One and was presented before him, he received dominion, glory and kingship, nations and peoples of every language serve him. His dominion is an everlasting dominion . . . his kingship shall not be destroyed. (NAB: Dn 7:13–14)

Jesus insisted that "this generation" would see the kingdom come in power. He also insisted that there would be no sign from heaven. "This rules out the possibility of the advent of the Human One as a heavenly spectacle."[29] "Do not stand around waiting around for the son of man to return. This is a moment of decision on your part." Thus, this section of Mark's gospel is not a reference to belief in the parousia as most scholars suggest; it is a reference to the cross. Thus, Myers argues that the phrase, "some of those standing here" (9:1) is a reference to those who will see and experience the event of the cross—not the parousia.

In the transfiguration scene Moses and Elijah appear as reminders that they, too, received similar mountaintop epiphanies at crucial moments of discouragement in their respective ministries. Elijah was a man hunted by the authorities. He tried to flee but Yahweh strengthened him to return to the struggle. Moses was a messenger who was rejected by the people and was forced to return to the mountain a second time. Mark uses the two characters at this point as a means to instruct the disciples. The presence of the two Old Testament figures legitimates Jesus' teaching. The theology of the cross is attested to by the Law and the Prophets. This is Mark's way of insisting that the

[29]Ibid.

Jesus story is in continuity with the old story from the Hebrew scriptures.

Jesus' radiant white robe takes us again to the Danielic courtroom. In apocalyptic literature white garments were associated with the clothing of martyrs (as attested in the Book of Revelation 3:5, 18; 4:4; 6:11; 7:9, 1–3). Following his teaching on the cross, Jesus now dons the martyr's robe.

Peter misconstrues Jesus' teaching. He addresses Jesus as Rabbi, not Messiah. The only other time the word is used in Mark's story is when the disciples support Jewish ideology rather than Jesus' teaching—when they lament over Jesus' repudiation of the Temple and when Judas addresses him as "Rabbi" and then subsequently betrays him. Peter obviously has missed Jesus' teaching on the cross. He would rather stay on the mountain and build a memorial to the event he was witnessing than face the cross.

Peter was rebuked for a second time—this time by the Voice, not Jesus. The Voice simply repeated the affirmation of Jesus as "Beloved Son" given at his baptism. No new revelation was needed. Jesus' teaching on the cross was definitive—the word had already been delivered.

The Voice (a higher authority than even Moses or Elijah) presents itself a second time in Mark's narrative in order to give credence to Jesus' teaching authority. The parallel between the baptism of Jesus and the transfiguration is obvious. Jesus' first mission was confirmed by the Voice at his baptism; now the Voice confirms his new mission. Jesus is the Beloved Son and the just judge who will, in the end, sit in judgment over those who put him to death. His new mission is his execution. His teaching on the cross has been definitively affirmed. The Voice insisted that the disciples listen to him and remember it. They will one day call on it to strengthen and empower themselves when they, too, stand with Jesus in a similar court.

The command to keep silent about the vision is given to the disciples because Mark's Jesus does not want them to get carried away with the "miracle" aspect of the transfiguration. He wants them to remember the teaching on the cross. Myers suggest that Mark's point in the narrative is that the reason the scribes were unconcerned about the end times is that they believed that Elijah had to return before judgment would take place. Elijah would soften the hearts of people, thereby forestalling Yahweh's wrath. Mark's Jesus asks the question: "What if Elijah has come and the elite ruling classes completely ignored him, and worse, murdered him?" This is the purpose of Mark's allusion to the Malachi prophecy in the first chapter. John the Baptist is the returned Elijah who preached a message of repentance and like all prophets was put to death. Jesus took over the Baptist's ministry of witnessing to the rulers. Thus, he similarly was Elijah's successor. The advent of Elijah was not some heavenly spectacle as was expected, but was realized in the ministry, trial, and execution of John. Similarly, the coming of the Son of Man is not realized by some extraterrestrial flight on the clouds, but like Elijah's and John's, is observed in his trial and execution.

The catechism of Mark can be reduced to one point: all true prophets face the same destiny. The Voice summoned all believers to this destiny—to listen. Do we have the courage to listen?

> Thomas à Kempis speaks to us of the cross:
>
> Take up your cross then, and follow Jesus, and you will enter eternal life. He went before you, carrying his cross, and on the cross he died for you, so that you too should carry your cross, and long for a death on the cross. For as you share his death, you will also share his life. If you are with him in his suffering, you will be with him in his glory.
>
> All that matters is the cross and dying on that cross.... The cross is always close by and waits for you everywhere.[30]

Proclaim the gospel again.

Sometimes we gain new insights when we hear the text after the interpretation is given. Someone from the group proclaims the gospel a second time.

---

[30]Thomas à Kempis, *Imitation of Christ*, ed. Betty I. Knott (London: Collins, 1963), 103, 104, in *RF*, 96.

Conversation with the Liturgy and the Scriptures

Test your original understanding in dialogue with the text.

(You might consider breaking into smaller groups.)

Now that you've heard the exegesis, were there any new insights? How do you feel about it? How does your original understanding of this gospel compare with what we just shared? How does this story speak to your life?

Sharing Life Experience

Participants share an experience from their lives that connects with the biblical interpretation just presented.

> Today's gospel reminds me of a wonderful man in our parish who knows well the implications of today's liturgy. He knows well the implications of the cross. His family owned a large farm in Cuba. Castro took over the farm, arrested some of his brothers, and conscripted the rest of them into his army. He was sent to deplorable, unimaginable, military action in Angola. Every time he mentions it, it conjures horrible memories and reminds him of what salvation really means. He loathed being in the Communist army. He was a good Catholic. He loved God and he loved his family. He was in love with a wonderful woman. They were going to be married. It was against the law to be married in the Church, but he and his new bride defied the law and married in the Church anyway. He was arrested the following day and spent two years in a Cuban prison for his decision.
>
> When he was finished serving his sentence, they reassigned him in the army. A few years later the oppression and inability to practice his faith took a toll on him and his wife. They knew they had to leave the country. No matter what the price, they would have religious freedom. He also was needed to join forces with the brothers who had made it out safely in order to help get the rest of the family out of the country. After many, many thousands of dollars, much hard work, and sacrifice, all of his brothers are now in this country.

When it looked as if they would send him to Angola again, he decided that no matter what the cost he would flee the country. It was a dangerous move. As a soldier in Castro's army he would be executed if caught trying to escape. He disguised himself. He and his wife and two children went without food for one full week and water for a few days in their attempt to leave the country. He was nearly caught on several occasions, but ultimately avoided detection. God sustained them in their ordeal.

This wonderful man of God moved his family to this country. When he talks about the freedom to worship God he weeps with joy. We celebrated the day he became an American citizen. Again he told his story and we all wept with him. Every couple of months we ask him to come and share his story with our catechumens and candidates as a reminder of the cost of discipleship. He knows what it means to live the gospel and carry the cross in a way most of us will never experience. His family experienced the joy of the transfiguration through the freedom they won. They knew the joy that awaited them and it sustained them as they forged ahead in their decision to stand with Christ no matter where it led them. They do not take freedom for granted. They know what it means to stand side by side with Jesus and profess his name. This disciple of God spent two years in prison for it. He could have died in Angola and he could have died when fleeing the country. When faced with the choice, he made the decision to die with Christ if that is where he was led. He was strengthened by the Shekinah glory of God—he knew that God was with him. *The man in this story is the first to help anyone in need. He knows what it means to need help. He is the first to reach out to the poor who come our way. He knows what it means to be poor and to have your land ripped out from under you. He knows what it means to have faced the cross and experienced the transfigured light of Christ who invited him to make a decision and then strengthened him to carry it out. I feel honored to call him my friend.*

What was Mark trying to tell his community? In what way have you ever experienced the transforming power of God? Have you ever experienced the light of revelation in your life? How did the experience impact your life? Put yourself in the position of Peter. How does it feel? Put yourself in the place of Jesus. What might have been

your feelings? In what way has this conversation with the scriptures for today's liturgy invited change in your life? In what way are the biblical themes of covenant, exodus, creation, and community evident in today's readings? Do you still feel the same way about this text as when you began? Has your original understanding been stretched, challenged, or affirmed?

STEP 5
DECISION

The gospel demands a response.

In what concrete way might your parish be invited to respond? Are there any attitudes or behaviors you would like to change as a result of today's conversation? What one concrete action will you take this week in response to the liturgy today?

Pastoral Considerations: In what way are you and your parish responding to the Lenten disciplines of prayer, fasting, and almsgiving? (See Lenten Overview.) What issues of social justice need the attention of your community? Are there any situations in your parish, civic community, or state or national political scene that call for a gospel voice? How are the needs of the poor in your area being addressed? In what way is your community responding to the needs of the sick, the lonely, the grieving, and the marginalized? Will your community be gathering for the celebration of the sacrament of reconciliation? If not, perhaps you might celebrate a *nonsacramental* celebration of reconciliation found in the rite of penance. This may be presided over by a nonordained person.

Christian Initiation: The RCIA designates the second Sunday of Lent for the optional penitential rite for baptized candidates. The elect continue to be dismissed to break open the Sunday scriptures, but their period of catechesis is officially over. The first Sunday of Lent began their process of purification and enlightenment. This week the elect gather to prepare to celebrate the first scrutiny next week. Catechumens who will not be baptized at the Easter Vigil continue to be dismissed from the Sunday liturgy and participate in extended catechesis.

DOCTRINAL ISSUES

What Church truth/teaching/doctrinal issue could be drawn from the gospel for the second Sunday of Lent?

Participants suggest possible doctrinal themes that flow from the readings.

Possible Doctrinal Themes

Transfiguration; doctrine on the cross; conversion; prayer; fasting and almsgiving; call of baptism; sin; paschal mystery; repentance and reconciliation; nonviolence; martyrdom; prophets

Present the doctrinal material at this time.

1. The facilitator gives input on a particular doctrinal issue of his or her prior choosing. OR
2. The group chooses a doctrinal issue from the list they created. They read together from the Doctrinal Appendix or other appropriate, official Church documents and the works of respected theologians.

(Many doctrinal issues are found in the Doctrinal Appendix at the back of this workbook. If you are choosing an issue from this resource, please refer to it now.)

Reflection questions centered around the chosen doctrinal theme can be found at the end of each topic in the Doctrinal Appendix. The questions are based on the five-step reflection process. If you choose a topic not included in the Doctrinal Appendix, craft your own questions according to the same five-step process.

Following the reflection questions you will be reminded to return to chapter 7, "Preparing the Catechetical Session," to assist you in crafting your own session.

Closing Prayer

Father, all powerful and ever-living God,
we do well always and everywhere to give you
    thanks
through Jesus Christ our Lord.

On your holy mountain he revealed himself in
    glory
in the presence of his disciples.
He had already prepared them for his approaching death.
He wanted to teach them through the Law and
    the Prophets
that the promised Christ had to first suffer
and so come to the glory of his resurrection.
In our unending joy we echo on earth
the song of the angels in heaven
as they praise your glory forever.[31]

---

[31]Second Sunday of Lent, "Transfiguration" (Preface 13), *The Sacramentary.*

195

THIRD SUNDAY OF LENT

INTRODUCTORY RITES

Entrance Antiphon (or Opening Song)

I will prove my holiness through you. I will gather you from the ends of the earth; I will pour clean water on you and wash away all your sins. I will give you a new spirit within you, says the Lord. (Ez 36:23–26)[1]

Opening Prayer

The facilitator of the session may lead the prayer. Others in the group may be asked to proclaim the readings.

Let us pray
(for confidence in the love of God
and the strength to overcome all our weakness)

Pause for silent prayer.

Father,
you have taught us to overcome our sins
by prayer, fasting and works of mercy.
When we are discouraged by our weakness,
give us confidence in your love.
We ask this through our Lord
Jesus Christ, your Son,
who lives and reigns with you and the Holy
    Spirit,
one God, for ever and ever.[2]

LITURGY OF THE WORD

The readings are proclaimed.

First Reading
Exodus 20:1–17

(Please refer to the eighteenth Sunday in Ordinary Time for an overview of the Book of Exodus.)

---

[1]Third Sunday of Lent: "Entrance Antiphon," *The Sacramentary.*

[2]Third Sunday of Lent: "Opening Prayer," *The Sacramentary.*

Today's Pericope: An image of the white-bearded Moses carrying the tablets down the mountainside with piercing eyes, flowing robes, and spirit-dazed consciousness is the imaginative picture most of us have when the Ten Commandments are mentioned. Cecil B. DeMille can certainly be lauded for permanently implanting the visual image of Israel's premier event into our corporate memory. The question for us to ask is, How do we understand the event? Israel understood the desert, mountaintop event to be God's premier saving act in their history. It embodied the most cherished thing in their lives—their covenant relationship with Yahweh. Proscribed legislation was a common phenomenon in the ancient Near East. Laws intended to structure societal life such as the Code of Hammurabi and the Hittite codes had already been around for centuries by the time the Ten Commandments were composed. The Ten Commandments, otherwise known as the Decalogue (ten words), were considered the cornerstone of all Israelite law. Israel was the only entity to associate the adherence to law with spiritual and ethical concerns.

Whether Moses is the author of the Ten Commandments has been a hotly debated topic. Contemporary scholarship assigns authorship to Moses with the understanding that he probably reworked codes already in existence according to a monotheistic religious perspective.

Israel adapted the form of the Hittite suzerainty treaty to communicate its covenant relationship with Yahweh. The Decalogue appears in two places in the Bible, Exodus and Deuteronomy. The structure of the Ten Commandments is significant. Like other laws in Israel, the Decalogue is apodictic. Apodictic laws are laws directed to a person, binding that person to practice or to refrain from practicing a specific behavior determined admirable or undesirable by the lawmaker. Two formulas are used: third-person commands and second-person commands. An example of a third-person command can be found in the seventeenth chapter of Deuteronomy: "No one shall be put to death on the testimony of one person." A second-person apodictic can be observed in a Leviticus law: "You shall not have intercourse with your father's wife." Second-person apodictic laws are characteristic of Israelite law. They reflect an intimacy between Yahweh and the people as they are addressed to an individual Israelite. This type of law is rooted in the human person, not in an impersonal system of laws.

The Fourth through Tenth Commandments flow out of tribal wisdom and the natural law. Before transcribed as official law, they were commands that were passed down in the tribes from elder to child. The elder's word carried weight and authority and thus his commands were taken seriously.

Yahweh, in this case, is the Lawmaker who acts on behalf of the community. The way the Decalogue is composed expresses the belief that Yahweh is the primary agent in the exodus. Yahweh's salvific action is the basis of all the commands that follow. Israel is obliged to live by the Ten Commandments, to own them, because God intervened decisively in its history. Such gratuitous love calls for no less than a response of total adherence to God's Law. "This opening sentence (I am the Lord your God . . .) also makes clear that the commandments are intended to be Israel's response to God's saving deed and not a condition for it."[3]

The first three commandments have to do with one's relationship with and proper conduct toward God. The First Commandment is monotheistic, even though monotheism was not observed until after the period of the classical prophets. The gods were recognized as existing and having power. Archaeology has yet to uncover any evidence of artwork depicting a representation of God, demonstrating that the First Commandment was taken seriously. No graven images have been found to date. Taking the Lord's name in vain referred to the use of perjury or magical incantations. In an extreme interpretation of the Law, Israel later substituted *Adonai* (Lord) or *Ha Shem* (the Name) when referring to God. The Third Commandment reflects practice that was already taking place in the culture. By enjoining it on the people within the structure of the Decalogue, religious significance was attached to the observance

of a day of rest. The priestly contribution to the Third Commandment is to connect it with the day of rest observed by God after the creation of the world.

Commandments four through ten have to do with people's relationship toward one another and toward society. They uphold the virtues and values that are cherished by society. In and of themselves they are not unique to Israel. What is unique is that Israel understood ethical behavior to be intimately connected to the worship of God. All of life is understood to be under the dominion of God's Law. The Law is considered absolute; thus there are no punishments assigned for transgressions. The observant Israelite is to avoid any behavior that is not in conformity with the covenant. The last seven commandments were considered equal to the first three as all were considered ordained by God. Later prophets would call upon that divine will and connect God's care for issues of social justice to the covenant. Jesus challenged those who manipulated the Law in order to ignore God's command to care for the least among them.

Responsorial Psalm
Psalm 19:8, 9, 10, 11

There are two parts to Psalm 19. The first part is a hymn in praise of the revelation of God found in creation. The second part praises God's Law. Today's appointment is taken from the second part of the psalm for obvious reasons.

Second Reading
1 Corinthians 1:22–25

(Refer to the second Sunday in Ordinary Time for an overview of Corinthians.)

Today's Pericope: Paul was a seasoned preacher. He had had a great deal of experience ministering to the Jews and gentiles. Over and over again it became apparent that the Jews would not be satisfied without a legitimating miracle, a sign to prove that his preaching carried weight. The Greeks used wisdom as a guide. If the Christian message proposed an understanding of the world and humanity's place in that world, so human beings might be reconnected with their heavenly genesis and thereby be delivered from the

---

[3]Marilyn M. Schaub, "Law." *CPDBT*, 538.

197

drudgery of earthly existence, then it was acceptable to the Greeks.

Wisdom, not signs, is the issue for the gentile Corinthian community. Later they would be impressed with the wandering Jewish Christian preachers who demonstrated signs in their ministry (evidenced in the second letter to the Corinthians). Paul does not repudiate the quest of either group; he simply puts it in perspective. The main issue for Paul is the cross. If they want signs, there is only one—it is powerful and dynamic and possesses the wisdom they seek. Is it, however, a paradox? For some it was a sign of weakness and failure, when in truth it is a sign of life. To others it is a sign of foolishness, not power and wisdom. For Jews the cross is scandalous and cause for shame; for Greeks it is foolishness. Only through eyes of faith will the believer be able to understand the foolishness as wisdom and power amid weakness wielded by the cross. (See gospel exegesis for the previous Sunday.)

The gospel is proclaimed.

Gospel
John 2:13–25. Destroy this temple, and in three days I will raise it up.

STEP 1
NAMING ONE'S EXPERIENCE

What were your first impressions? What was your first response to the gospel (or the other readings)? What captured your attention?

Each person names his or her initial impression. Statements should be brief. No reasons should be given at this time. All simply listen without agreeing or disagreeing.

STEP 2
UNDERSTANDING

In a brief statement, explain what you think this gospel is trying to convey.

STEP 3
INPUT FROM VISION/STORY/TRADITION

Liturgical Context

In today's gospel Jesus proclaims that his body replaced the Temple and all the spiritual meanings associated with the Temple. He proposed a new understanding of Temple—a living entity built on the foundation of his life, death, and resurrection. The image of "temple" became a powerful metaphor for the body of believers, a holy dwelling place of God. St. Paul's letter to the Ephesians expressed it thus: "The Church is favored, the dwelling place of God on earth, a temple built with living stones, founded on the apostles with Jesus Christ its cornerstone" (2:21–22). Thus, the Temple is the Church, founded on the tradition of the apostles, whose foundation is Christ. It is the holy abode of God. The Preface for the Rite of Dedication (of a church) beautifully expresses the fullness of the image as it has evolved from Jesus' reinterpretation of Temple in today's gospel. Temple is an image for all of creation, for God's heavenly city, and for the incarnate Christ. The Preface prays that temple is also an image for Church and the entire communion of saints, living and dead. The glue that binds it all is love born of Christ. Christ then becomes the light that illumines the holy city for all time.

The early Christian community displayed ambivalent feelings about the Temple, probably emanating from Jesus' own feelings evident in today's reading. On the one hand, he challenged Temple practice, but on the other hand he considered it a house of prayer. He insisted that his new worship would surpass the Temple. Participation in Temple worship continued for some time, which is one reason why the Christian community associated so closely with Judaism for such a long time. That fact must be balanced with Jesus' teaching that his body was the new Temple and with Paul's insistence that by extension the church, too, became a living Temple. "All salvation history finds its fulfillment in Christ and in his paschal mystery. A distinctive feature of Christian worship is that it 'memorializes' the salvation already accomplished in Christ. Christian worship is distinguished from Jewish worship not simply by the appearance of its cult, its liturgy, but its content. The victory of

Christ animates Christian liturgy with its eternally present reality of salvation already accomplished. In our celebration of the sacred mysteries Christ acts in us, head with body, in offering worship pleasing to the Father. In turn, that which the Temple symbolizes, God's dwelling with us, is fulfilled and perpetuated."[4]

In the Bible the Temple is an image of the presence of God in the midst of the people. It was also a sign that God was still bringing about salvation in time and history. The Lord's own glory springs forth from the Temple. Images of Temple destruction and rebuilding are associated with images of dispersion and gathering. Yet as significant and awesome as the Temple was in biblical history, the people still waited for a new Temple to come down from heaven that would signal God's abiding presence in their midst. It was believed that this new Temple would emerge with the coming of the Messiah. At that time the Temple would also be cleansed. This is why the Temple was such an important place of spiritual significance for the Jewish people. The exile only served to heighten this Temple spirituality. Jesus' actions in today's gospel are a parable in action, a prophetic action. He gave a new meaning to Temple spirituality. His body would become the new locus of worship.

> God prepared for himself
> a dwelling among humans,
> he has set the stone
> and lighted the fire.
> Today,
> he multiplies the bread
> and joins our hands together:
> now our hearts are but one.
> *God with us, God in us,*
> *we are the body of Christ.*
> Here is the promised land
> where the human assembly knows the love of
>   God.
> Here is the festive space
> where the human family
> gives a face to God.
> Here is the house of peace
> where those who share receive the gift of God.
> Here is the open temple
> where those who adore
> become witnesses of God.[5]

Another theme that flows from today's gospel revolves around the issue of the selling of doves for sacrifice. Doves were the only creatures the poor could afford. They are particularly mentioned in the gospel as a reminder that the practice of selling in the temple precincts was an act of injustice against the poor. They were forced to take what little money they had for subsistence, and in the name of religion purchase a sacrifice with money that was sorely needed for food and shelter. Jesus was righteously annoyed. Believers cannot afford to have such an attitude toward the poor. "In his encyclical *Centesimus Annus* (no. 58), John Paul II underscores this by asking us to sell what is luxurious, which we attempt to justify as necessary for ourselves or God's worship, in order to change it into food, drink, clothing, and housing for the poor."[6] This is a reminder in the season of Lent that our prayer, fasting, and almsgiving must not only be a Lenten discipline, but a way of life for all Christians. Today's opening prayer echoes that theme and serves as a reminder that we are strengthened through God's love to resist sin through the Lenten disciplines. Every liturgy throughout the year invites us to reach out to the poor. Eucharist commits us to the poor.

Today's gospel reveals that God was establishing a new worship for Christian believers. Above all, it was a worship rooted in relationship with God, not dependent on legalistic practice. This relationship requires an openness to God's Spirit. We pray for that Spirit in today's Entrance Antiphon. In this Lenten time of conversion we pray that God puts a new spirit within each and every one of us.

Gospel Exegesis

The facilitator provides input from critical biblical scholarship on this text. This input includes insights as to how people would have heard the gospel in Jesus' time.

All four gospels relate the events in today's gospel in which Jesus chased the merchants out of the

---

[4]Brian J. Fischer, "Temple," *CPDBT*, 983.

[5]Commission Francophone Cistercienne, *Sur la trace de Dieu* (Paris: Descl'ee, 1979), 141. (Dische de chant K 145–1), in *DL* (II), 144.

[6]*SWTLY*, 55.

Temple. Seen through the eyes of the fourth evangelist, we are to interpret the action as a sign understood only by faith. It is an example of the Church looking back on the event and interpreting it in light of its lived experience.

As usual John employs various techniques and themes in the creation of his drama. The meaning and future of the Temple are brought into his conversation. Other issues also come to the fore: the Messiah, redemption of Israel and the world, and the end times. The star of this one-act drama, however, is Jesus himself—the mystery of his life, his persona, and his mission.

John combines two key themes that are addressed in a single fashion by the other evangelists: the cleansing of the Temple and its destruction. Today's gospel is an example of a scriptural passage that represents more than one layer of tradition. That is, the pericope reflects not only an actual event in Jesus' life, but also written into the text are the perspective, meaning, discernment, or theology of an evangelist and his community. Sixty plus years of Christian living, experience, and theology are also reflected in the text. Historical-critical methods of interpretation have helped the biblical student to understand that John's use of the words *remembered* and *recalled* in today's gospel describes the means by which the community came to understand that Jesus Christ, crucified and risen, was the fulfillment of all scriptural prophecy.[7] Verses 17 and 22, therefore, do not represent the responses of Jesus' immediate followers, but the evangelist's critical reflection upon and interpretation of the event sixty years later.

The theme of John's gospel up to this point is the choosing of a new community. That first section ends with the fulfillment of Jesus' prophecy. Jesus prophesied that only through him would the bridge between heaven and earth be realized. The fulfillment of his prophecy takes place in a miracle story (at Cana) which teaches that access to the new wine, the spiritual reality, will be made readily available upon Jesus' glorification.[8] That spiritual reality is placed in direct contrast to the purification rites of the Temple. "Jesus' wine is given at

the end of the fulfillment of such rituals and supersedes them."[9] Thus, the section in the first part of John's gospel that deals with the formation of a community ends by insisting that Jesus was inaugurating a religious reality that superseded Jewish worship. It was an invitation to Jesus' disciples, the new community, to evaluate their Jewish worship in light of the worship Jesus was offering. Thus, the thesis of 2:13–12:50 is that the worship Jesus offered supersedes Jewish religious worship and practice.

What, then, were the views of worship in John's universe, the first-century Mediterranean world? How was access to God administered? What was the shape of appropriate honor and worship? One gained access to the deity (God or pagan) by erecting a sacred space (temple) and offering sacrifice in the sacred space (the temple cultus). Pagan sacrifice was practiced as was Jewish sacrifice. Historian Josephus related that those who controlled the places of sacrifice in the Temple had the Jewish nation in their power. The Jewish sacrifice and Temple worship were the heart and core of Jewish identity. Thus, by the time of the Christ-event the temple cultus and the sacrifice offered at the temple were the proper ways to worship and honor the deity in both pagan and Jewish cultures.

According to Charles Talbert this form of temple cultus was not without philosophical and prophetic critique.[10] The philosophical critique emanated from Socrates. Socrates offered sacrifice, but insisted that it be offered in humility and piety. It was not the size of the sacrifice that mattered, but the heart and piety that motivated the sacrifice in the first place. The prophetic critique stemmed from the preexilic prophets. They insisted that Temple worship must flow from right disposition, from a clean, upright, and moral heart.

> I hate, I despise your feasts, and I take no delight in your solemn assemblies. Even though you offer me your burnt offerings and cereal offerings, I will not accept them, and the peace offerings of your fatted beasts I will not look upon. Take away

---

[7] *CWJB*, 55.
[8] *RJ*, 87.

[9] Ibid.
[10] Ibid., 88.

from me the noise of your songs; to the melody of your harps I will not listen. But let justice roll down like waters, and righteousness like an ever flowing stream (Am 5:21–24; cf. Is 1:12–17; Hos 6:6; 8:11–13; for a later time, cf. Aristeas 234).[11]

The prophets were chastising Israel for a worship void of righteousness and ethical living and the refusal to be faithful to the covenant.

In addition to temple cultus and the sacrificial system there was a second prevalent understanding of worship. Sacred space was expanded to reflect a broader concept. "The universe is the temple and the holy of holies is the inner self."[12] Thus, worship was understood as knowledge of God and upright living. Those who followed this belief were critical of external forms of worship and ritual. They were advocates of rational mysticism, "the piety of which consists in the consciousness of the deity present in each individual, which issues in lofty morality."[13] There were pagans and Jews who believed that worship of God was an internal spirituality, but they did participate in some form of ritual worship. Ultimately, as long as the spiritual realization of God was not convoluted, it was appropriate to participate in some form of cultic activity. According to this perspective both literal observance of the Law and spiritual worship were advocated.

There was still another, third view of worship at the time of the gospel's writing—the emergence of the "holy man" who inspired devotees outside the Temple worship. The culture was becoming unenamored with sacred space.

> People, in their search for salvation, began to turn from temples and cultus of the temple and look to savior figures and communities revolving around such figures as havens of salvation. Rather than a sacred place, the new center and chief means of access to the deity came to be a divine man who functioned without a fixed locale. Rather than celebration, purification, and pilgrimage, the new rituals came to be conversation, identification with the divine man, and initiation into the holy man's group.[14]

The shift to this third form of worship involves a reinterpretation of the language and belief of previous forms of worship. In this third form, worship is understood not as localized in the temple cult, not as existing in the holy of holies in the human soul, and not in spiritual mysticism and ethical living, but existing in the holy man himself and his disciples. Divine presence is thus embodied in the holy man. Honor of the holy man is the same as honor to the deity. The man, his words, his actions become the revelation of deity. Participation in the holy man's group ensures access to the god and is in itself a form of worship.

Therefore, according to Talbert, appropriate traditional worship in the ancient world that existed at the time of the Christian era (1) took place in sacred space (temple), by using sacred ritual (sacrifice) and at sacred times (feasts and such) and was presided over by sacred people (priests); (2) was spiritual, not directed to the temple; the deity was encountered primarily in the soul; sacrifice was contemplation on the deity and moral living; daily living was understood as a festival of worship; or (3) access to the deity was mediated through a holy man and honor to the deity was achieved by honoring the holy man. These three perspectives are lenses through which to explore and interpret the Gospel of John.

Two different time periods are reflected in John's gospel—the time before Jesus' glorification and the time following it. Jesus' earthly life is presented in terms of the holy man in whom God's presence was revealed. Temple worship was replaced by honor given to him, thereby fulfilling one's obligation to worship and honor God. This is the reason John's Jesus is the One sent to reveal God. This Johannine perspective of Jesus follows the third form of worship described above. It is clear that the human Jesus advocated the supersession of the entire Jewish system of worship and practice. John then situates everything that happens in the gospel after Jesus' glorification within

---

[11]Ibid., 89.
[12]Ibid.
[13]Ibid.

---

[14]Ibid.

the context of Jesus' words and actions while he was on earth. During this postresurrection period in the gospel the evangelist not only honors Jesus but he also spiritualizes worship due him. Worship after Jesus' ascension is understood as through the Holy Spirit who was sent by Jesus to reveal him. Thus the old feasts and festivals celebrated in traditional Jewish worship were superseded in the Christian community.

All of the evangelists adopt the third form of prevalent worship in which the holy man is the revelation of God. However, John's emphasis is stronger. John differs from the other three in regard to cultic ritual observance. From the outset, the fourth evangelist makes his case abundantly clear. Jesus begins his public ministry by actions that halt Temple sacrifices. After Jesus' action in today's gospel of driving out the money changers and cleansing the Temple, any further participation in Temple ritual is to demonstrate that he not only fulfills it, he supersedes it. The other evangelists only minimally address the issue, and place the cleansing of the Temple at the conclusion of Jesus' ministry. They do not reject the Temple altogether, however. It remains a place of teaching, prayer, and sacrifice. John's Jesus, the holy man, demonstrates more animosity toward the Temple and traditional worship than does the Jesus portrayed by the synoptists.

Early Christianity spiritualized the Jesus-event. The church is referred to as the Temple, the sacrifices of Christians are spiritual sacrifices and include praise and ethical action and martyrdom. For the most part, the understanding of all the evangelists is that traditional Jewish worship ceased (exception can be noted in the Acts of the Apostles, in which the Christian Jews were allowed to retain their Jewish forms of worship).

John's gospel highlights another important fact about his community. It was a worshiping community and thus the reason worship is such a critical issue throughout the gospel. Jesus' earthly actions and deeds continually demonstrate that he superseded Jewish forms, but they also provide the basis of the community's new worship. There are seven episodes that demonstrate John's thesis. The first episode is obviously the gospel for today's liturgy.

Underlying today's gospel is the question: From where does Jesus' authority come? In verse 18 a sign is requested in order to answer that question. Who does Jesus think he is anyway? By what authority does he perform such an action? Verse 23 admits that Jesus' miracles are a sign for some, but he insists on looking to his resurrection as a sign. The principle of "like can only know like" demands that only those who are born of Spirit, who are of God, can understand such things.

Jesus' action was not only symbolic, but it rendered the sacrifices of the Temple impossible. The money changers exacted pledges from those who needed to purchase animal sacrifices for the daily offering to atone for the sins of Israel. They were therefore necessary for the ritual of atonement for sin to continue. Jesus' action of overturning the tables is a repudiation of Israel's most important cult, the daily offering for sin—the center and heart of all Temple worship.

The second part of today's pericope is concerned with Jesus' authority. He rendered the sacrifices of Israel impossible—why does he think he has the authority to perform such a radical action? Jesus answers by alluding to his resurrection. Jesus still has no intention in buying into their need for a miracle. The Jews, the "many," and Nicodemus wanted a miracle to legitimate Jesus' authority. Jesus points the Jews in the direction of his resurrection, he retreats from the "many," and to Nicodemus he offers a new birth in the Spirit. This new life in the Spirit is needed to recognize God's reign, since only like can know like; one must be born of God in order to understand God.

Another reason why John placed the cleansing of the Temple at the beginning of Jesus' ministry is theological. The actions of Jesus serve to demonstrate that he is the fulfillment of messianic prophecy and expectations. The prophets Malachi (3:14) and Zechariah (14:1–21) both prophesied that the Lord would come suddenly to purify and cleanse the Temple. The Day of the Lord would also mean that traders in God's house would not be seen. John's scene in the Temple is intended to announce that that day had indeed arrived. Jesus' ministry, his life and work, is not only the fulfillment of that prophecy, but also the repudiation of Jewish Law and the chastisement of hypocrisy and legalism. His body now is the new Temple. Instead of legalistic ritual, Jesus would offer a taste of intimate relationship with his heavenly Father.

Animals for sacrifice could be purchased in the Temple precincts. Pilgrims converging on the city from long distances would not have to bring their animals with them but could instead purchase them at the Temple. Doves were sold to the poor as they were the only creatures the poor could afford to purchase for the sacrifice. The money changers were needed to change Roman coins that were imprinted with the image of pagan gods to the more acceptable coins of Tyre. The Roman coins were not allowed to be used as Temple tax. However, the changers were notorious for cheating, gouging, and swindling their customers. No doubt this may have been in the back of Jesus' mind as he stormed through the precincts.

Other scriptural allusions were perhaps brought to bear by the evangelist in order to further demonstrate the fulfillment of messianic prophecy. Jeremiah prophesied that the evil deeds of people destroyed the Temple. Tobit and Zechariah prophesied that business would not be conducted in the Temple. Jesus referred to the Temple as his Father's house; he also used that term as a reference to the eternal reign of God freely available to all who believe.

If Jesus' action repudiated Temple worship and rendered it impossible, then with what did he replace it? He replaced the old forms of worship with himself. John connects the cleansing of the Temple with its destruction. Jesus insists that they can destroy this temple (himself), but it will be raised up again, an obvious reference to his resurrection.

Gustavo Gutierrez takes us to the heart of today's gospel for our contemporary world.[15] We are told that Jesus is in Jerusalem for the Feast of Passover, the feast of deliverance from oppression. Yet when he arrives at the Temple, instead of finding a place where people can come and find free access to the living God, obstacles are put in their way. "What the Lord finds is a new form of oppression of the people, which perverts the worship due the

'jealous God' (Ex. 20:5)."[16] God's house thus becomes a supermarket, rather than a place where people can come to find refuge in their providential God. Greed is the motivator of those who have placed obstacles in the path of access—greed of the high priests who profited from the sale of the animals in the temple. What is worse, this greed is supported and proselytized in the name of religious rhetoric. Temple personnel became richer, while the poor became poorer. The doves are specifically mentioned as a reminder that the practice is not only an obstacle for God's people, but especially for the poor. The poor were not only exploited, but they were exploited in the name of worship.

Proclaim the gospel again.

Sometimes we gain new insights when we hear the text after the interpretation is given. Someone from the group proclaims the gospel a second time.

STEP 4
TESTING

Conversation with the Liturgy and the Scriptures

Test your original understanding in dialogue with the text.

(You might consider breaking into smaller groups.)

Now that you've heard the exegesis, were there any new insights? How do you feel about it? How does your original understanding of this gospel compare with what we just shared? How does this story speak to your life?

Sharing Life Experience

Participants share an experience from their lives that connects with the biblical interpretation just presented.

> Very often it is easy to get caught up with the mechanics of liturgy and forget what we are all about. When I fall into that trap, echoes of the prophets ring in my ears: "Your liturgies are an abomina-

[15] *SWTLY*, 55.

[16] Ibid.

tion . . . I want your hearts." Today's liturgy boils down to relationship. God wants our hearts. If our liturgies are an obstacle to that relationship for us and for others, then we must take a serious look. Today there is so much concern and controversy centered around our common prayer. There are liturgy cops waiting in one wing to report infractions of rubrical law. There are those in the other wing insisting that there is only one way to celebrate liturgy. There are those in yet another wing who insist that anything goes if it is for a good reason. I am sometimes saddened when I consider that the liturgy, the place we come together in unity, is often the source of our great divide.

Our parish has experienced similar controversy over the years. Today, however, it is minimal. I hear of so many places embroiled in serious controversy and I wonder how we crossed the hump and are now in a good place. I believe good pastoral leadership is one reason. Our pastor has traditionally and respectfully given every person and every issue a voice. We have made a concerted effort to listen to the community, while at the same time being diligent to the instructions we are given by the church for the celebration of liturgy. We continue to try to make the symbols of the liturgy robust, so they speak the truth they are intended to reveal, knowing that we need to be continually attentive to such issues. We still get complaints about this or that point of concern, but for the most part, there is wonderful celebration, a good spirit, and a sense of people praying in unity. Above all, there is ample evidence of charity and mission.

I am thankful for a community that sings, prays, and lives the paschal mystery together in spirit and in truth. When we get sidetracked by "church" issues that keep us from relationship with God and one another it is reflected in our liturgy. During those times in our history when there have been divisions and tensions, it was difficult to celebrate liturgy together. I remember times when the sign of peace was a challenge. Thank God we have reconciled and moved beyond those days.

Today's liturgy, in this Lenten season, is a reminder for us as Church to be attentive to our relationship with God as Church and with one another. It is an invitation to look at the areas within our communities that foster division and to work toward mutual reconciliation. It is an invitation

to ask ourselves if we are living by the letter of the Law rather than by the Spirit. Does our worship reflect mutual care of one another and of those who cannot care for themselves?

What was John trying to tell his community? In what way does John's insistence on repudiating the old forms of worship speak to us as Church today? In what way do we still put obstacles in front of people and in so doing keep them from free access to God? In what way has this conversation with the scriptures for today's liturgy invited change in your life? In what way are the biblical themes of covenant, exodus, creation, and community evident in today's readings? Do you still feel the same way about this text as when you began? Has your original understanding been stretched, challenged, or affirmed?

STEP 5
DECISION

The gospel demands a response.

In what concrete way might your parish be invited to respond? Are there any attitudes or behaviors you would like to change as a result of today's conversation? What one concrete action will you take this week in response to the liturgy today?

Pastoral Considerations: In what way does your parish foster free and unlimited access to God in liturgy, sacraments, and the communal life? Does your scheduling reflect the concerns of the neediest people in your parish? In what way does your parish participate in the Lenten disciplines of prayer, fasting, and almsgiving?

Christian Initiation: This is the day scrutinies are celebrated in the Church. Please refer to the third Sunday of Lent, Cycle A for further information. For those catechumens still in the period of the catechumenate who will not be initiated at the Easter Vigil this year, perhaps it would be a good time to celebrate a rite of anointing. The rite imparts a special strength to continue the journey, and Lent is a time of deepening conversion; thus it might be an appropriate time to celebrate the anointing. This would be a particularly apt time to celebrate the minor exorcisms when gathering with catechumens. Baptized candidates may be prepared for the celebration of the sacrament of reconciliation and celebrate it with the community. Catechumens who will not be baptized at the Easter Vigil continue to be dismissed from the Sunday liturgy and participate in extended catechesis.

DOCTRINAL ISSUES

What Church truth/teaching/doctrinal issue could be drawn from the gospel for the third Sunday of Lent?

Participants suggest possible doctrinal themes that flow from the readings.

Possible Doctrinal Themes

Ten Commandments; moral life; conversion; worship/liturgy; Church; prayer; paschal mystery; Christology; disciplines of Lent; reconciliation

Present the doctrinal material at this time.

1. The facilitator gives input on a particular doctrinal issue of his or her prior choosing. OR
2. The group chooses a doctrinal issue from the list they created. They read together from the Doctrinal Appendix or other appropriate, official Church documents and the works of respected theologians.

(Many doctrinal issues are found in the Doctrinal Appendix at the back of this workbook. If you are choosing an issue from this resource, please refer to it now.)

Reflection questions centered around the chosen doctrinal theme can be found at the end of each topic in the Doctrinal Appendix. The questions are based on the five-step reflection process. If you choose a topic not included in the Doctrinal Appendix, craft your own questions according to the same five-step process.

Following the reflection questions you will be reminded to return to chapter 7, "Preparing the Catechetical Session," to assist you in crafting your own session.

Closing Prayer

The Father of mercies has given us an example of
    unselfish love
in the sufferings of his only Son.
Through your service of God and neighbor
may you receive his countless blessings.
    Amen.

You believe that by his dying
Christ destroyed death for ever.
May he give you everlasting life.
    Amen.

He humbled himself for our sakes.
May you follow his example
and share in his resurrection.
    Amen.[17]

---

[17]Third Sunday of Lent: "Solemn Blessing or Prayer Over the People," *The Sacramentary.*

THIRD SUNDAY OF LENT (CYCLE A)

Environment

Today's liturgy contains strong images of water:

The Entrance Antiphon: "I will pour clean water on you and wash away all your sins..."

The First Reading: "Yahweh instructed Moses to strike the rock and water flowed..."

The Gospel: "But whoever drinks the water I give will never be thirsty..."

The Communion Rite: "Whoever drinks the water I give...will have a spring inside..."

Imaginative display of this powerful symbol in the catechetical environment might be appropriate for today's session.

INTRODUCTORY RITES

Opening Song (or Entrance Antiphon)

I will prove my holiness through you. I will gather you from the ends of the earth; I will pour clean water on you and wash away all your sins. I will give you a new spirit within you, says the Lord. (Ez 36:23–26)[1]

Opening Prayer

The facilitator of the session may lead the prayer. Others in the group may be asked to proclaim the readings.

Let us pray
[to the Father and ask him
to form a new heart within us]

Pause for silent prayer.

God of all compassion, Father of all goodness,
to heal the wounds our sins and selfishness bring
    upon us
you bid us turn to fasting, prayer, and sharing with
    our brothers.
We acknowledge our sinfulness, our guilt is ever
    before us:
when our weakness causes discouragement,

let your compassion fill us with hope
and lead us through a Lent of repentance
to the beauty of Easter joy.
Grant this through Christ, our Lord.[2]

LITURGY OF THE WORD

Let us listen to God's word.

The readings are proclaimed

First Reading
Exodus 17:3–7

Today's reading refers to Israel's defining event: the exodus and the wanderings in the desert. Moses was instructed to strike the rock and water sprang forth. Water was a powerful symbol of God's activity. Water was a sign of life. At creation God hovered over the waters and breathed life into them. Water was a sign of destruction, purification, and God's awesome power. God sent down the rain for forty days and forty nights and submerged the earth because of the sin of human beings. Water was a sign of salvation. When the Israelites thirsted in the desert, water flowed through the power of God. In an arid land, water is an absolute need. Water is a symbol of liberation and passage from death to life. God held back the water for the Israelites to pass through.

Through the water sign there is allusion to the sacraments: water as salvation; water as sign of baptism. Lent is both penitential and baptismal in nature. The first reading touches on both themes.

The psalm for this liturgy exhorts us "not to harden our hearts." Meribah and Massah were the places where the people had sinned. This first reading reminds us of our total dependence on the God who saves, Christ who liberates, and the Spirit who leads us to the life-giving water.

---

[1] Third Sunday of Lent: "Entrance Antiphon," *The Sacramentary.*

[2] Third Sunday of Lent: "Alternative Opening Prayer," *The Sacramentary.*

Responsorial Psalm
Psalm 95

This psalm was chosen for its connection to the first reading. It especially helps focus the meaning for the first reading: "Harden not your hearts."

Second Reading
Romans 5:1–2, 5–8

Up to this point in his letter to the Romans, Paul has expressed his assurance that human beings were justified through the redeeming death of Christ. Today's pericope is concerned with the implications of our justification. Since we are justified, we share the peace of Christ. Our faith in the paschal mystery gives us free access to God's grace as we wait in hope for our future glory. Paul reminds us that the Spirit continues to shower us with the living, ever-present love of God. Reginald Fuller maintains that Paul related justification to the indwelling of the Spirit. The Spirit of God initiates and continues the work of healing transformation within those the Spirit justifies. Each person is thus raised to a state of created grace. God pours out gratuitous love through the gift of the Spirit and through the sacrifice on the cross by God's Son, Jesus Christ. The veil of the curtain was torn at the death of Jesus and sinners were given access to God. That access is the Spirit of God. The gift of the cross is God's Holy Spirit dwelling within human beings to transform them into the elevated state they were destined to attain. We also hear in Paul's letter the roots of our belief in the Holy Trinity.

Gospel
John 4:5–42

Jesus encounters the woman of Samaria.

STEP 1
NAMING ONE'S EXPERIENCE

What were your first impressions? What was your first response? What grabbed your attention? How did you feel?

Each person names his or her initial impression. Statements should be brief. No reasons should be given at this time. All simply listen without agreeing or disagreeing.

STEP 2
UNDERSTANDING

In a brief statement, what do you think this gospel is trying to convey?

STEP 3
INPUT FROM VISION/STORY/TRADITION

Liturgical Context

As stated in the lenten overview, the Johannine gospels for the three Sundays of Cycle A were used as immediate preparation for those preparing for baptism. Thematically they address the baptismal issues and symbols of water, light, and the passage from death into life. Today's readings are viewed through the lens of baptismal preparation.

The Communion Antiphon (from today's gospel) serves as a summary text for today's liturgy: "Whoever drinks the water that I shall give . . . will have a spring inside . . . welling up for eternal life" (Jn 4:13–14). Today's readings ask us where the areas of sin reside in our society, in the world, in the church, and in our personal lives. Where and how do we thirst? Where in our society, in the church, and in our personal lives, is there a need for Christ's healing liberation? When we scrutinize sin through the eyes of faith, Christ refreshes us and gives us the water of new life that springs up as a fountain within us.

Scrutinies

The Cycle A readings are designated for use when there are catechumens preparing for initiation at the Easter Vigil. In the Rite of Christian Initiation of Adults, Lent coincides with the period of *purification and enlightenment.* It is a period of final preparation for the elect. They (along with the entire church) are to seriously discern the areas of sin and weakness [purification] and allow those areas to be healed and illumined by Christ, the Liberator [enlightenment]. The church celebrates three scrutinies with the elect beginning on the Third Sunday of Lent. Scrutinies are intended to heal what is weak, defective, and sinful, to protect the elect from temptation, and to strengthen them in Christ (RCIA, #141–146). The magnitude of sin in all its forms—personal, social, and systemic—is laid bare. The elect are filled with the presence of Christ the Liberator who won the victory over evil and its consequences. God the Father is invoked and asked for strength and protection in the trinitarian prayer of exorcism. "Through the power of the Holy Spirit (the epicletic action of the laying on of hands), Jesus exercises his healing and liberating power over the effects of evil. Thus, the power and presence of Christ in word and exorcism are the primary symbols of the scrutinies." Preparation for the elect's celebration of the scrutinies includes reflection upon the scriptures from today's readings. The elect seek to uncover the many layers of sin as well as to reflect upon the ultimate source of power and grace. They explore the question, "Where does sin exist and where is liberation needed in the world, in the community, and in my life?" They search the scrutiny gospel for ways that Christ, the great Liberator, is proclaimed and imaged. They come to the scrutiny as expectant, vulnerable, and willing vessels eager to approach the freedom that awaits them.

While scrutinies are celebrated with the elect, they are also for the entire church. We and the elect are on this journey toward liberation and wholeness together. The scrutinies prepare the elect for the sacraments of initiation and they serve as preparation for our own recommitment to the baptismal promises we will profess anew at Easter.

Presentation of the Creed

The presentation of the creed generally takes place during the week following the first scrutiny, "preferably in the presence of a community of the faithful, within Mass after the homily" (RCIA, #157). The elect are to commit the creed to memory and profess it publicly prior to their official profession of faith at their baptism (RCIA, #148). The creed and the Lord's Prayer have always been considered central to Christian faith and prayer. The creed is intended to enlighten the elect with the light of faith. God's wondrous salvation deeds (of which the human race is beneficiary) are pro-

fessed. The RCIA does allow the presentations to take place during the catechumenate period as the season of Lent is rather brief and packed with multiple spiritual riches. Thus, some parishes celebrate and anticipate the presentations with their catechumens before Lent.

Gospel Exegesis

The facilitator gives input regarding what critical biblical scholarship has to say about this text. The input includes insights as to how people would have heard the gospel in Jesus' time.

The exegesis for the gospel of the Samaritan woman at the well will utilize the insights of Sandra Schneider, a biblical scholar. In my opinion, her interpretation most thoroughly uncovers the heart and soul, not only of the text, but of its place in baptismal and lenten catechesis. At a recent workshop, Donald Senior, one of this country's most respected biblical scholars, asserted that the scholarly work of Schneider in relation to this gospel is masterful and right on the mark. He was surprised that no one had stumbled across it before. He surmised that it was because most biblical scholars have been male. As male members of the community, they approach the texts primarily with a masculine hermeneutic. Biblical texts are to be interpreted not only through the science of biblical criticism, but also through the discerning wisdom of the community. For most of its history, the church has not had the privilege of the discernment of half of her members—the female half.[3] The scholar further noted that the feminine consciousness has not had the opportunity to interpret the texts. That is presently chang-

---

[3]Barbara Reid, in her book, *Choosing the Better Part* (Collegeville: The Liturgical Press, 1996), describes the vision that best informs the exegesis for this liturgy. "Patriarchy is 'any system, organization, or institution in which the men own, administer, shape, or control a major portion of all the facets of society.' [Joan Chittister, "Yesterday's Dangerous Vision: Christian Feminism in the Catholic Church," *Sojourners* (July 1987): 18.] The world of Jesus was a patriarchal world, as is our own, although that is beginning to change. Feminism, as a response to patriarchy, 'is a commitment to the humanity, dignity, and equality of all persons to such a degree that one is willing to work for changes in structures and in relationship patterns so that these occur to the

ing with the emergence of many female biblical scholars.

Schneider approaches the text with a hermeneutic of suspicion.[4] She confronts the story, suspicious of its obvious moral dilemma: a woman chastised for her sexual indiscretions. It appears as though Schneider side-steps the patriarchal literal meaning, turning instead to the images, symbols, and typology common to the time and to the Johannine community, in order to appropriate a more inclusive interpretation.

Some scholars suggest that the story of the Samaritan woman probably was not an historical story. The story served as legitimization "of the Samaritan mission in John's community; to establish full equality between Samaritan and Jewish Christians, and to affirm Jewish legitimacy as bearer of covenant faith but with a surprising recognition of the essential validity of Samaritan faith and inclusion in the covenant."[5]

Samaria was a territory north of Jerusalem. It was part of the Assyrian and Persian empire in 721–612 B.C.E. The Assyrians imported foreign colonists and deported many of Samaria's native citizens; others sought refuge in Judea. A Yahwism influenced by other religions developed that led to animosity from traditional Jews. The bad feeling between the two groups was further exacerbated when the Samaritans offered to help rebuild the temple after the exile and were turned down by their Jewish brothers and sisters. This

added fuel to the already smoldering fires of resentment. Another revolt forced the Samaritans to move to Shechem where they built a temple on Mount Gerizim.[6] Samaritans anticipated a prophet like Moses who would restore worship on Mount Gerizim in northern Israel. The Jews, on the other hand, believed the messiah would be a descendant of David who would restore worship in the Jerusalem temple. It is obvious that resentments ran deep and permeated the consciousness of the two peoples. They were bitter enemies.

In the story of the Samaritan woman, it is the unspoken text between the lines that captures our attention and imagination. The woman is nameless. Nameless people in scripture often represent more than the literal eye can see, especially in John's gospel (the beloved disciple, the royal official, the paralytic at the pool, and the man born blind). This woman is a symbolic figure who represents the Samaritan people and the New Israel (the new kingdom).

The woman was at a well—not just any well, but a famous well. Wells were important symbolic places in biblical literature. Important events in salvation history began with unions initiated at famous wells. Rebecca was found for Isaac at a well; Rachel met Jacob at the very well in this story. Before this scene in John's gospel, at the wedding in Cana, Jesus was called the new Bridegroom. Our attention in this reading, then, turns to Jesus, the new Bridegroom, present at the well of famous weddings to "claim Samaria as beloved in the New Israel."[7]

There is more to consider about the heroine of the story. She was a woman and a Samaritan, the lowest on society's totem pole. Even the pagans hated Samaritans. She was an outcast's outcast! Yet this outcast, woman and Samaritan, encountered Christ. Jesus, a Jew, not only spoke to her and noticed her, but he drank from her bucket (making him ritually unclean). The woman was trained by her culture to believe she was worthless. Yet this Jew offered her acceptance, dignity, compassion, a way out, and a way in! Donald Senior suggests that

equal good of all' (Chittister, 18).... Feminism advocates a community of equals that provides for all the members, women and men alike, to use their God-given gifts to the benefit of all. Christian feminists are women and men committed to eliminating sexism in their relations with one another, in the structures of their faith communities and in society. They see this as a work of justice that is truly faithful to the teaching and life of Jesus...." (Reid, 7)

[4] "...A hermeneutic of suspicion recognizes that the biblical texts have been written, for the most part, by men, for men, and about men, and that they serve the interests of patriarchy. One who reads with a hermeneutic of suspicion is wary that the text can be oppressive for women. This does not deny the inspiration of Scripture, but recognizes the limitations of the human authors that set forth God's word." (Reid, 9)

[5] EGW, 306.

[6] For further information, refer to: Robert F. O'Toole, S.J., "Samaria/Samaritan," in CPDBT, 872–873.

[7] EGW, 306.

this woman has much more to teach us than a lesson on morality. It is the story between the lines we dare to hear.

During the exile the Samaritans remained faithful to Yahweh, but became inculturated by their conquerors. While they still loved Yahweh, they nevertheless dabbled in the local worship of the Samaritan gods. The result was that Jews hated the Samaritans whom they judged unfaithful. Samaritans were outcasts and ritually unclean. No good Jew would drink from this woman's bucket. Yet Jesus drank from her bucket. In his encounter with her, Jesus welcomed the lost and included the sinner, the outsider.

She entered into a theological discussion with him. She interrogated him about his action toward her. He had broken Jewish tradition by speaking to her (a woman) and by using the same utensils she had used. She was dumbfounded. Samaritans would have been shocked to hear anyone claiming to be on the same plane as their patriarch Jacob who had given the well to Israel in the first place. Jesus acknowledged Samaria's rightful place in salvation history while still affirming Yahweh's covenant with the Jews. Yet he made it very clear that they had each missed the boat—both the Jews and the Samaritans. Neither had a monopoly on the truth. God was doing something new. While defending the Jewish claim to the covenant tradition, Jesus made no distinctions regarding the *territory* people worshiped in. What was important was the worship Jesus would inaugurate as messiah—worship in spirit and truth, authentic worship. The gospel would guide the worship. In the new kingdom people would live in biblical justice, in right relationship with God. They would live the law of love.

Centered in the middle of Jesus' theological discussion with the woman is his scrutiny of her adulterous liaisons—her five husbands. That she had had five husbands was unusual in the religious society of her day. "Either this is totally out of place, a trivial bit of moralism or even a shallow display of preternatural knowledge on the part of Jesus, or it is an integral part of this highly theological exchange."[8] This story is about the *inclusion* of

Samaria into the New Israel. Jesus scrutinized the woman's (Samaria's) adulterous (idolatrous) union with the gods of the five tribes. "Jesus' declaration that Samaria 'has no husband' is a classic prophetic denunciation of false worship, like Hosea's oracle in which the prophet expresses God's sentiment toward unfaithful Israel" (Hosea 2:2).[9] Thus, Jesus suggests that Samaria's relationship to Yahweh in the past was colored by her adulterous flirtations with other gods. Jesus scrutinized the false worship, named the sin, and invited repentance as he included Samaria in his New Israel.

At this wedding well, in broad daylight and at high noon so that all could see, Jesus, the new *Bridegroom*, wed Samaria and included her in the kingdom.[10] "Now the new Bridegroom who assumes the role of Yahweh, bridegroom of ancient Israel, comes to claim Samaria as an integral part of the New Israel, namely, the Christian community and specifically the Johannine community."[11]

What, then, was the woman's response? She recognized Jesus for who he was, messiah and lord. She could do no less than "go and tell everyone . . . and they all came to believe on her testimony." She was the first evangelist and the only person to bring an entire group of people to faith in Jesus. No wonder women had an important ministerial role in John's community.[12]

The implications? Jesus extended reconciliation, inclusion, and healing to alienated Samaria; everyone is included in the reign of God. Jesus shared this revelation with a woman—society's outcast (then and in many places today).[13] He treated her as he would have treated any member of his soci-

---

[8]*RT,* 190.

[9]Ibid.

[10]Contrast the woman coming to the well at high noon, in the light of day for all to see, with Nicodemus, who came in the dead of night. John's gospel is filled with the metaphor of night and day, light and darkness.

[11]*RT,* 187.

[12]See Sixteenth Sunday in Ordinary Time: the story of Martha and Mary.

[13]At the time of Christ, in order for something to be attested and affirmed, it had to be verified in a court of law. I find it very interesting that first-hand testimony and events often occurred to people who could not legally witness to them in the courts. Women could not serve as verifiable

ety—with respect and dignity. We are, by extension, invited to cast aside any idols of our making that get in the way of our authentic worship of God, and we are to welcome all who are on the bottom rung of society.

This is a story about the kingdom in which there are no outcasts and no strangers, only repentant, welcomed sinners. "In summary, the entire dialogue between Jesus and the woman is the 'wooing' of Samaria to full covenant fidelity in the New Israel by Jesus, the New Bridegroom. It has nothing to do with the woman's private moral life, but with the covenant life of the community. Nowhere in the fourth gospel is there a dialogue of such theological depth and intensity."[14]

In light of the celebration of the scrutinies, this gospel helps us name the social and personal sin that keeps us from an intimate relationship with God. We are reminded that it is God who names our sin, who scrutinizes the evil in our lives, and who invites us to turn away from anything (our personal and corporate idols) that keeps us from a full liberated life in Christ. Today's liturgy highlights the evil of exclusion on any level: in our personal lives, in our society, and in our religious structures. It demands that we ask the questions: *Who is out?* and *Who is in?* Like the woman, we are to go out and invite others in. Today's gospel invites *metanoia*—a complete turning away *from* sin *toward* the Healer, Liberator, Victor, and One who offers living water through the refreshing waters of baptism. This is the victory Christ holds out to us in today's liturgy.

---

witnesses unless the issue pertained to a household matter. Shepherds were also not allowed to testify as valid witnesses, since they were considered too untrustworthy to give truthful testimony. Yet, is it not God's irony (or perhaps humor) that the two premier events of redemptive salvation were witnessed by people who, by human standards, were not able to verify or testify to what they had witnessed? Shepherds were the first to witness the Incarnation and a woman was first on the scene following the resurrection. Once again, God writes salvation history with crooked lines and refuses to be boxed in by humanity's standards of convention. In today's story, a woman experienced the messiah. Her experience and her story alone had the power to invite people to faith.

[14]*RT,* 191.

Proclaim the gospel again.

Sometimes we gain new insights when we hear the text after the interpretation has been given. Someone from the group proclaims the gospel a second time.

STEP 4
TESTING

Conversation with the Liturgy and the Scriptures

Test your original understanding in dialogue with the text.

(You might consider breaking into smaller groups.)

Were there any new insights? How do you feel? Comfortable or uncomfortable? Why? How does your original understanding of this story compare with what was just shared? How does this story speak to your life?

Sharing Life Experience

Participants share an experience from their lives that connects with the biblical interpretation just shared.

> *A few years ago I had an encounter with this scripture. It caught my attention, challenged my attitudes, and invited me to change. This story summoned me to let go of the idol I had made of "being right." I had mentally and spiritually excluded some folks who held different points of view than I. They were my outcasts. They were wrong and I was right. Of this I was certain! I had been hurt by them and was not willing to consider how I had excluded them as a group. After wrestling with the angel of this text, I was forced to look at my idol and at the people that I had cut off and excluded. Through an interesting process of not-so-gentle persuasions, the Lord God insisted that I offer a hand in reconciliation to a person that best represented those I had discarded. Our reconciliation began a lasting bond of friendship.*

> *This word is a powerful word for communities today. Yet it is a word that often invites the greatest challenge. Try though we may, there are still many excluded people in our communities. Our hierarchical structure excludes, our parish structures exclude,*

and our personal relationships are often exclusive. The gospel continues to invite us to scrutinize the areas of elusion, sin, and idolatry, and ask Christ, the liberator, to deliver us from evil.

All share their life experience.

What was John's message to his community? What are the implications for our communities today? Is there any situation in our community that needs to be enlightened by this gospel? In what way (if at all) did the experience of God's word:

1. affirm God's promise to be with us *(covenant)*
2. lead us through a death/resurrection experience in our attitudes *(exodus)*
3. speak to us as a community *(people of God)*
4. call us to new life *(creation)*?

Do we still feel the same way about this text as we did when we began? Has our original understanding been stretched, challenged, or affirmed?

STEP 5
DECISION

The gospel demands a response.

In what concrete way does this gospel call our parish to action in the church, parish, neighborhood, or world? Has this conversation with the exegesis changed or stretched my personal attitudes? What am I /we/community/parish called to do in response? What is one concrete action I will take this week as a response to what was learned and shared today?

DOCTRINAL ISSUES

What church truth/teaching/doctrinal issue could be drawn from the gospel for the Third Sunday in Lent?

Participants suggest possible doctrinal themes that flow from the readings.

Possible Doctrinal Themes

Grace and sin, baptism, social dimension of sin, Jesus the messiah, reconciliation

Present the doctrinal material at this time.

1. The facilitator gives input on a particular doctrinal issue of his/her prior choosing. OR
2. The group chooses a doctrinal issue from the list they created. They read together from the Doctrinal Appendix.

(The doctrinal issues are found in the Doctrinal Appendix in the back of this workbook. If you are choosing an issue from this resource, please refer to it now.)

Reflection questions centered around the chosen doctrinal theme can be found at the end of each topic in the Doctrinal Appendix. The questions are based on the five-step reflection process. If you choose a topic not included in the Doctrinal Appendix, craft your own questions according to the same five-step process.

Following the reflection questions you will be reminded to return to chapter 7, "Preparing the Catechetical Session," to assist you in crafting your own session.

Closing Prayer

First Scrutiny: Exorcism

All merciful Father,
through your Son you revealed your mercy
to the woman of Samaria;
and moved by that same care
you have offered salvation to all sinners.
Look favorably on these elect,
who desire to become your adopted children
through the power of your sacraments.
Free them from the slavery of sin,
and for Satan's crushing yoke
exchange the gentle yoke of Jesus.
Protect them in every danger,
That they may serve you faithfully in peace and joy
And render you thanks forever. Amen.

Laying on of hands

Hands outstretched over the elect:

Lord Jesus,
in your merciful wisdom

you touched the heart of the sinful woman
and taught her to worship the Father
in spirit and in truth.
Now, by your power,
free these elect from the cunning of Satan,
as they draw near to the fountain of living water.
Touch their hearts with the power of the Holy
    Spirit,
that they may come to know the Father
in true faith, which expresses itself in love,
for you live and reign for ever and ever.
Amen.[15]

---

[15]Prayer of Exorcism, "First Scrutiny," *RCIA*.

FOURTH SUNDAY OF LENT

INTRODUCTORY RITES

Entrance Antiphon (or Opening Song)

Rejoice, Jerusalem! Be glad for her, you who love her; rejoice with her, you who mourned for her, and you will find contentment at her consoling breast. (Is 66:10–11)

Opening Prayer

The facilitator of the session may lead the prayer. Others in the group may be asked to proclaim the readings.

Let us pray
(that by growing in love this Lenten season
we may bring the peace of Christ to our world)

Pause for silent prayer.

God our Father,
your Word, Jesus Christ, spoke peace to a sinful
    world
and brought mankind the gift of reconciliation
by the suffering and death he endured.
Teach us, the people who bear his name,
to follow the example he gave us:
may our faith, hope and charity
turn hatred to love, conflict to peace,
death to eternal life.
We ask this through Christ our Lord.[1]

LITURGY OF THE WORD

The readings are proclaimed.

First Reading
2 Chronicles 36:14–17, 19–23

Overview of Chronicles: The Books of 1 and 2 Chronicles (as well as the Books of Ezra and Nehemiah) depict life in Israel after the exile. The Books of Chronicles describe the prayer, worship, and ritual purity of the people in postexilic Is-

rael. The world had changed. The priestly leaders believed that an updated chronicle of Israel's history was needed. Chronicles follows the Books of Kings and Samuel almost verbatim. However, there are differences. David's shadow side is minimalized and many of his most grievous sins are downplayed. The author exalts David even more than he is exalted in the Books of 1 and 2 Kings. David is depicted as a faithful servant who was devoted to the right worship of Yahweh. He is portrayed as a lawgiver nearly as important as Moses.[2]

David was the standard by which the Chronicler judged all of Israel. The exile was a result of the people's failure to worship Yahweh. David's example of faith and the failures of the people were a reminder to the Israelites of the importance of Temple worship and the quest for a king like David who would restore true worship that would glorify God.

The books' intention is to offer hope to Jerusalem and Judah in their time of great need. The books praise the great deeds of God and connect worship and observant practice to the great heroes of Israel's history.

Today's Pericope: God hates the sin but loves the sinner. God becomes offended when people of the covenant become embroiled in sin. God is always ready to forgive at the first sign of a repentant heart. God even sends messengers to exhort the people to repent. This has been the way God has been in relationship with people since the very beginning—since humanity's very first sin. God's incredible mercy is at the heart of salvation history. The books known as Chronicles together with the Books of Ezra and Nehemiah are regarded by scholars as the history of the people of Israel from their beginning through the rebuilding process that took place after the exile. All four books are similar in style and content. They were written during the period of 400 to 200 B.C.

---

[1]Fourth Sunday of Lent, "Alternative Opening Prayer," *The Sacramentary.*

[2]*ROT*, 451–453.

The books use similar language and employ the use of genealogies. The role of the Levites is regarded similarly and all four recognize Jerusalem as Israel's religious center of worship. The books place high value on the Torah. They understand the covenant made with David to be more important than the covenant made with the people at Sinai. The books provide insight into the way in which Israel understood its own history.

All recorded history is biased in one way or another. One need only compare the recorded history of the American Revolution in the *Encyclopaedia Britannica* with any American encyclopedia. It is human nature to understand events from one's own cultural, religious, and historical perspective. Israel's history is recorded not only from its own understanding of history, but also from its understanding of the religious and theological significance of the events. Israel believed that its entire history was revelatory. All the events in their history were the result of God's revelation to humanity. God was experienced in the events of history. Salvation history is evidence of relationship between God and the people of Israel.

When religious themes are the primary focus of the historian's agenda, attention to historical data is not a primary concern. There was no concept of recording historical data for the sake of providing a chronicle of history. There was no word for history in the Hebrew scriptures. Modern Hebrew's word *toledot*, which means *acts of generating*, is the closest word for describing the ancient Israelite concept of history.[3]

The Chronicler interpreted Israel's victories from the perspective of God's divine initiative, grace, and favor as a result of Israel's faithfulness to the covenant. Tragedy, natural disasters, defeats were similarly understood as God's retribution for failure to observe the covenant. Today's reading uses this argument as a reason for the travesty of the Babylonian exile. Israel refused to listen to God's Word revealed through the prophets and as a result they lost their home, their lives, their possessions, and their freedom.

During the exile, large numbers of people were deported to Mesopotamia. They formed a large community that retained its Jewish identity and greatly influenced later Israelite history. Since Temple worship was no longer possible, they centered their spirituality on study of the Torah and on developing centers of prayer and worship that served as forerunners of the synagogue. Great attention was given to the collection and preservation of the sacred books and the Babylonian Talmud was written. Some of the Jews of the diaspora returned to Palestine and were influential in the rebuilding of the Temple and the encouragement of a return to Jewish religious observance. "[T]he dispersion of the Jews, which began as cruel deportation, ended as a highly successful sowing of Jewish ideas and ideals in most parts of the then known world."[4]

The author names the time between the burning of the Temple and its reconstruction (approximately seventy years) under the Persian king Darius (586 B.C.–520/515 B.C.) as the time of Yahweh's righteous anger. Israel's failure to observe the Sabbath and to celebrate a sincere liturgy grounded in truth and justice is cited as the reason for God's displeasure. As a result the land would lie fallow for seventy years.

No one was immune from indictment. Both the priests and the people were held responsible. It has been suggested that the author was himself of the Levite class, perhaps a cantor or someone who worked in the Temple. The author has the best interest of the Jerusalem Temple as a primary concern and displays a strong bias against the Northern Kingdom and its insistence that the Samaritan temple was the true center of worship. The Chronicler believed that Jerusalem would be the locus of God's act of restoration—faithfulness to the Davidic covenant and worship at the Temple in Jerusalem would be the only true and authentic worship. The exile, therefore, was interpreted as punishment for sin and the end of the exile as forgiveness of sin and subsequent restoration.[5]

Even though the Israelite interpretation of history is foreign to our modern sensibilities, it does invite us to enter more deeply into a Lenten reflection. It strengthens our faith in Christ, the

---

[3]*WWC*, 159.

[4]Demetrius R. Dumm, O.S.B., "Diaspora/Dispersion," *CPDBT*, 218.
[5]*WWC*, 157–158.

Savior, and it invites us to trust more completely and enter more fully into a life of prayer and conversion. "This prayer joins, in particular, the entreaties of those who are bent under the weight of injustice and oppression, the consequence of sin, but we shall keep ourselves from saying—or thinking—that this sin deserved this punishment."[6]

Responsorial Psalm
Psalm 137:1–6

Reginald Fuller asserts that today's psalm is a lament of the exiles in Babylon.[7] The exiles are to remember Jerusalem and the future day when all will be restored to their homeland.

Second Reading
Ephesians 2:4–10

(Refer to the fifteenth Sunday in Ordinary Time for an overview of the Letter to the Ephesians.)

Today's Pericope: A hallmark of salvation history is God's incredible, awesome, completely gratuitous mercy. Punishment for sin is even regarded as part of God's mercy. God sent prophets to warn the people to repent and turn away from sin and when they refused to listen, God punished them. It was the only means left to prompt conversion. God's punitive action was always offered with the idea that pardon would be granted and people would return to their covenant relationship. God hides from view so that people will seek after him. The ultimate locus of God's mercy and love is the person of Jesus Christ.

God loves us so much in spite of our infidelity that we were given his Son. Jesus Christ is the perfect revelation of God's mercy. Through Christ we are saved—an unmerited salvation. Through Christ we were brought from death to life. We have been born anew in order to respond to God's unmerited mercy and grace. We can do no less than live the imperative to love. "Good works" involves the daily covenant living, but it also involves immersion into the paschal mystery. It is the offering of daily deaths and resurrections in the service of

God's people. When Christians die to sin each day they grow in their relationship with God and advance in Christian maturity. They already taste the heavenly banquet here on earth.

Ephesus was an active seaport on the coast of Asia Minor, today known as Turkey. It was the capital of Rome's Asian provinces and was also known as a "free city." It was a base of operations for Paul's second and third missionary tours. It is possible that the letter was written to all the churches in Asia Minor, rather than just the Ephesian church.

The perspective of the Letter to the Ephesians is that Christians are already participating in the resurrection of Christ. This participation is initiated through baptism. The author believes that Christians are living a realized eschatology. The letter is more concerned with the issues of church in this temporal reality. There is no strong focus on Jesus' second coming. Ephesians centers on the resurrection and exaltation of Christ, rather than on his Passion and death. The letter is an invitation to Christians to come together in unity with one common faith.

The Hebrew understanding of salvation examines history as a series of events used by God to teach the people—good behavior is rewarded, bad behavior is punished. What is learned in such a schema? It is in everyone's best interest to be good. The author of Ephesians insists that salvation is completely undeserved and unmerited, as eloquently attested in today's reading. The author's letter was also a polemic against the gnostic influences of his day which asserted that Christianity was nothing more than the inner knowledge of the disciple. Ephesians insists that Christian life depends on God's free, unmerited grace. Our response in love can be no less than the complete offering of self to God. This freely offered grace is the reason that Christians live ethical lives. They can do no less. God's grace has nothing to do with one's worthiness. Nothing can be done to earn God's grace—it is freely given. It is not given as a reward for good behavior. Christians are to understand good works as a result of God's incredible mercy and grace.

Grace is understood in terms of the client-patron relationship that existed in ancient Palestine.

---

[6] *DL* (II), 146.
[7] *PL*, 240.

When governments were ineffective in providing help for their citizens, the citizenry turned to a patron to provide the necessary care and protection. A person of higher status and wealth would make a free pledge to care for a client from a lower class of people. Particularly impoverished clients would go to great lengths to win the approval of a patron of their choice, fully aware, however, that they had no real voice in the decision. Once the patron chose the clients, they entered into a bond in which the patron promised to care for the client. Favors were granted that would not otherwise have been granted. An honorable patron took good care of his clients—it was his claim to fame and acclaim. Mistreatment of clients was a cause of serious shame. It was, therefore, in the patron's best interest to behave magnanimously toward the client.

This is how Israel understood its relationship with God. God was the patron and the people were the clients. God freely elected Israel. God chose Israel as clients; it was an unmerited choice. However, it was not without a catch. There were strings attached. The patron expected that the client would respond to the free gift with appreciation and openness to the gift. In the Letter to the Ephesians, response to God's grace is not understood as a catch. It is a response in love. As a result of the "favor" or free, undeserved gift, the people will do no less than live the precepts of love.

The gospel is proclaimed.

Gospel
John 3:14–21. God sent his Son so that the world might be saved through him.

STEP 1
NAMING ONE'S EXPERIENCE

What were your first impressions? What was your first response to the gospel (or the other readings)? What captured your attention?

Each person names his or her initial impression. Statements should be brief. No reasons should be given at this time. All simply listen without agreeing or disagreeing.

STEP 2
UNDERSTANDING

In a brief statement, explain what you think this gospel is trying to convey.

STEP 3
INPUT FROM VISION/STORY/TRADITION

Liturgical Context

This Sunday used to be called Laetare Sunday. Vestiges of that mid-Lenten joy can still be noticed in the readings today: the joy experienced in the healing, saving power of God in the wilderness (first reading), the joy of being recipients of God's mercy and grace through Christ (second reading), and the joy experienced through the love of God offered to the world through Jesus Christ, God's Son. The Entrance Antiphon proclaims this joy from the opening moments of the liturgy. We are to take note and "Rejoice!"

This love is fully manifest today in the celebration of the eucharist. The eucharist finds its fulfillment at the messianic banquet. The early church believed that Jesus would return at celebration of the pasch, the ritual memorial of his death and resurrection. When that did not occur, they celebrated the eucharist instead. The Easter eucharist has a closer connection to the heavenly banquet than any other eucharist of the year. As Easter fast approaches we are reminded of the love of God manifest through Christ that we remember, celebrate, and partake of at every eucharistic celebration. Lent is not only penitential in nature and it not only prepares for baptism, it also prepares us to receive Christ anew in the Easter eucharist. Today provides thoughtful reflection for this preparation.

John's gospel is a sermon par excellence on the mystery of God's love and midway through Lent is a wonderful time to reflect on that awesome love. We sometimes get so caught up with the darkness of our lives that it becomes difficult to experience the light which surrounds us. We encounter God's love in the person of Christ—his life, mission, death, and resurrection—and we continue to experience it in the incredible gift of eucharist, the gift of God given to us as food. The Entrance Antiphon reminds us that we are to rejoice! We rejoice because we are the children of God and heirs of God's great love and mercy. The opening prayer reminds us that as we grow in love throughout this season of Lent we become ambassadors of that love and peace in the world. We are reminded that God's Son brought peace to a sinful world and reconciled us to God through the pasch of Christ. The prayer asks that God teach us to follow Jesus' example and that our "faith, hope and charity turn hatred to love, conflict to peace, and death to eternal life."[8] St. Catherine of Sienna reminds us of the implications of the love expressed in today's liturgy.

> "O eternal Trinity!
> Eternal Trinity!
> O fire and deep well of charity!
> O you who are madly in love
> with your creature!
> O eternal truth!
> O eternal fire!
> O eternal wisdom
> given for our redemption!
> But did your wisdom come into the world
>   alone?
> No.
> For wisdom was not separate from power,
> nor was power without mercy.
> You, wisdom, did not come alone then,
> but the whole Trinity was there.
> O eternal Trinity,
> mad with love,
> of what use to you was our redemption?
> None at all,
> for you have no need of us,
> you who are our God.
> For whose good was it?
> Only humanity's.
> O boundless charity!
> Just as you gave us yourself, Wholly God and
>   wholly human,
> so you left us all of yourself as food
> so that while we are pilgrims in this life

we might not collapse in our weariness
but be strengthened by you, heavenly food! "[9]

John uses the image of light when referring to Christ and life in Christ. Without the light of Christ there is nothing but darkness. The Church has appropriated John's powerful use of light as a symbol in all liturgical celebrations. When light is burning it is a sign of the presence of Christ. (Refer to the Easter Vigil, symbol of light for further elaboration on the powerful symbol of light.) Light is the symbol that plays a prominent role in the beginning moments of the Easter Vigil. It lights the way for us to enter into the mysteries of our faith on that Mother of all Feasts. Today's liturgy is filled with anticipatory images of baptism as Easter fast approaches. The preface for this liturgy also speaks of being led out of darkness into the light. The prayer after communion seeks enlightenment from the light of the gospel. Perhaps this would be a good time to prepare the faithful to encounter the primordial symbol of light that we will soon encounter at the Easter Vigil. What does it mean in this Lenten season to prefer darkness over light? Are we really people of the Light as we claim to be?

Gospel Exegesis

The facilitator provides input from critical biblical scholarship on this text. This input includes insights as to how people would have heard the gospel in Jesus' time.

[Refer to the liturgical context and the gospel exegesis of last week for background and context for today's gospel pericope.] The author of the fourth gospel echoes the theme of the Letter to the Ephesians in today's second reading. God's free, unmerited salvation is highlighted by John's reference to the wilderness tradition. The Israelites were plagued by snake bites as a result of their interminable grumbling about their plight. They begged Moses to intercede for them. They were instructed to look upon the bronze snake attached to a pole and they would be saved. That image eventually became a symbol for the healing arts. In later Wisdom traditions it became a symbol of healing. However, John understood that action of looking and lifting up as the action of salvation. He

---

[8]Fourth Sunday of Lent, "Alternative Opening Prayer," *The Sacramentary.*

[9]*RF*, 99.

compared the saving action of looking up and lifting up to the saving action of Christ as he was lifted up on the cross. All those who embrace Jesus Christ crucified and risen will be healed just as those who trusted in God's word to Moses.

While not mentioned explicitly in this gospel passage, today's pericope comes out of a dialogue with Nicodemus, a representative of Israel's religious leadership. As a religious leader he is also of the "rich class" and thereby was one who marginalized the poor and the outcasts (which we will address in more detail later). Nicodemus saw in Jesus a certain authenticity—"he has partial faith in Jesus."[10] However, he was afraid to approach him in the light of day (unlike the Samaritan woman, who encountered Jesus at noon in the full light). Perhaps someone would see him. Nicodemus was more concerned with protecting his honor and reputation than openly coming to Christ. A ruined and lost reputation could not be regained.

It is obvious that Nicodemus joined the ranks of those who did not understand Jesus' message. However, he obviously continued to grapple with his misunderstanding, for it was Nicodemus who, in a later section of the gospel, risked shame when he insisted that Jesus had a right to a hearing. The Temple priests and Pharisees were angry with the Temple police for not arresting Jesus and Nicodemus came to Jesus' defense. Nicodemus allowed himself to be shamed and joined the ranks of those who embraced Christ in the light of day. "He stands up for Jesus, the marginalized person from Galilee."[11] Nicodemus's journey toward Christ progressed and he appears again at the end of Jesus' life. He threw caution to the wind and publicly anointed Jesus' dead body with myrrh and aloe. He anointed Jesus with an amount so lavish that it was similar to the amount used to anoint Herod. "Jesus' burial is not an ordinary one, but has some of the trappings of a royal burial."[12] The lavish oil Nicodemus used was an amount that only a very wealthy man could offer in his last tribute to Christ, the King. In this last act of homage, Nicodemus embraced Jesus as King, thereby becoming his disciple.

As an aside, it is noteworthy to mention that throughout John's gospel, John's community repudiates Jewish worship and understands Christian observance as superseding its Jewish antecedents, except in one instance. Jesus and his followers continue to observe all the ritual and religious requirements regarding almsgiving to the poor. John's community continued to uphold care for the weak, the poor, and the marginalized. Nicodemus, as one of the religious elite, participated in this corporate act of marginalizing God's people. Yet in the end he came to full faith in Christ. As a disciple of Christ he not only embraced Christ on an internal level, but also an external one. To be a disciple meant that he could no longer participate in systems of marginalization. His faith in Christ essentially placed him among the ranks of those who were considered outcast. "In his last vignette about Nicodemus, the religious leader, John portrays himself as a disciple of Jesus. Jesus died to draw all people to himself, even those who marginalize the weak. . . . The religious leader, Nicodemus the marginalizer, has become a follower of Jesus. He is representative of those marginalizers who have been drawn to Jesus and have joined the Johannine community, a community which is filled with marginalized people."[13] Nicodemus's final act of faith is a reminder that even if one begins the Christian journey halfheartedly, what matters in the end is the ultimate giving of one's life and destiny to Christ. Part of that destiny is lived out as one responds to God in love and lives in the light. Such response demands that love is not a respecter of class or social standing. There is no room for marginalization in the community of believers.

The reward for living the love required in today's gospel is eternal life. Lent is a time to assess the Christian journey and to discern the areas lost to darkness. Lent's mission is to provide the necessary signposts that will lead those lost to darkness back to the light-exposed, Christ-directed track.

Prior to today's pericope, Nicodemus had asked Jesus by what authority he had performed his signs. He told Jesus that he could see that God was obviously the power behind Jesus' actions. Drawing on the principle that only *like can see like,* Jesus

[10]*JMJG*, 97.
[11]Ibid., 99.
[12]Ibid., 98.

[13]Ibid., 100–101.

insisted that Nicodemus needed to be born again in order to see the reign of God. He needed to be *of the kingdom* in order to understand it. He also needed to be born of water and the Spirit in order to gain access to eternal life. Access to eternal life is made possible only through the death (lifting up) of Jesus. John understands the *lifting up* of Jesus on two levels. It is the lifting up of Jesus to die on the cross and the lifting of Christ to the throne of glory. John alludes to the Isaiah passage in which the Suffering Servant is lifted up to the throne of glory.

Isaiah's Suffering Servant is a source of healing for many through the vicarious nature of his suffering. Just as those who believed in the word of God to Moses were healed, all the more will those be healed and receive salvation who turn to the risen and glorified Christ. All who believe will share in his resurrection and exaltation.

The only reason for so great a gift is the gratuitous love and mercy of God. There is nothing anyone can do to earn so great a gift. The famous verse, "God so loved the world that he gave his only beloved Son," has two meanings for John. It refers to the giving of the Son through the incarnation, but it also refers to the giving of the Son to die, rise, and ascend in glory. God's love for the human race is most fully expressed in God's act of sending the Son. We can be assured of God's love for us because of Christ's presence among us. Every action, every word, every breath uttered by Jesus is a sign for the world of just how much we are loved by God.

Faith is an act of response to that love. Faith is an action that welcomes the love of God manifest through Christ. This is the love that saves us and offers us a share of eternal glory. God's saving love is available for everyone. No one is given a greater share of God's love than someone else. It is freely offered to everyone. A response is required, however. This love must be either accepted or rejected. When it is rejected, the rejection is not only of God, but also rejection of self. To reject God is the same as cutting one's self off from life itself. John tells us what rejection of God's love is tantamount to by employing an image he frequently uses throughout his gospel—darkness versus light. Rejection of God's love is the same as preferring darkness over the light. What could be more horri-

ble than to accept the darkness when one knows what it means to live in the light? For John, Christ is the Light that dispels all darkness.

John insists that people refuse the light because they prefer to engage in evil actions. Actions, for John, speak louder than words. They are essential when it comes to matters of faith. One's actions become the barometer by which the acceptance or rejection of God's love is measured. Preferring the darkness is the same as engaging in evil actions. Some continue to engage in evil so that their evil will not come into the light and thus be exposed. The implications are clear. John reminds us that only those who do what is true enter God's light. "The truth involves not only thinking, accepting, but also doing. It has to be translated into concrete gestures, commitment, and solidarity."[14]

Raymond Brown asserts that John 3:16–17 is an example of universalism (salvation of all people through Christ) even though it is modified by the dualism found in verses 18–21.[15] "The human race is divided into nonbelievers and believers, into those who prefer darkness and those who prefer light, into those who are condemned and those who already have eternal life. Since the Johannine community identifies itself with the believers, it is no surprise that most of those outside the community are looked upon as more or less shadowed by darkness."[16] The Johannine community understands itself as a communion—a family of brothers and sisters, children of God. Those who know Jesus are children of the one God and are thus joined together in solidarity, peace, harmony, and the love of Christ. The Christology of John's gospel is not just an exposition of orthodoxy unrelated to community life. "If it is crucial (in John's Gospel) to believe that Jesus is the preexistent Word of God who has come from God and is of God, it is because then we know what God is really like—He really is a God of love who so loved the world that He was willing to give of Himself, in His Son (3:1; 1 John 4:8–9), and not merely send someone else. And such an understanding of God and of Jesus demands that the Johannine Christian, who is a child of God, behave in a way worthy of His Father and of Jesus his Brother: 'By this will all identify

---

[14]*SWTLY*, 59.
[15]*TCBD*, 60.
[16]Ibid.

you as my disciples—by the love you have for one another' (John 13:35)."[17]

Brown further insists that we avoid looking at John's gospel as an "in-group manifesto meant as a triumph over outsiders; its goal is to challenge the Johannine community itself to understand Jesus more deeply. . . . Jesus is from God and therefore remains above everyone's grasp."[18] Throughout John's gospel the principal characters such as Nicodemus simply fail to understand Jesus. This motif of misunderstanding is used by John to convince nonbelievers that they should come to belief and to remind believers and readers to strip away their own self-confidence.[19]

Today's passage from John is a favorite in all religious circles. "God so loved the world that he gave his only beloved Son"—John 3:16. One sees it emblazoned on cardboard advertising posters and waved as banners during sports events. The fourth gospel promises that eternal life is the result of so great a love. John Pilch reminds us that even though this text conjures tender images and thoughts of God, there is something more lurking within the lines of this text when one considers it in light of the experience of the Johannine community.[20] This section of the gospel insists that people prefer darkness.

As far as John is concerned the "world" refers to anyone who does not come to faith in Christ—Jews and gentiles. Throughout the fourth gospel John reminds his reader that the world is against Jesus and his Spirit. Those who follow Jesus are hated. Those who hate Jesus and his followers are children who prefer darkness. "For this reason, Jesus refuses to pray for the world; instead, he defeats the world."[21] This passage from John is a stark reminder that the world is a hostile place. The world's posture in no way resembles that of the recalcitrant child who suddenly comes to the awareness of its folly and thereupon waits eagerly at the street corner to catch the first trolley waving a John 3:16 placard. On the contrary, the world is a place hostile to Christ and his message. We must not be lulled into a sentimental hearing of this scripture. There is still plenty of hostility to Christ and the message he proclaimed with his life. Raymond Brown puts it in proper perspective:

> Perhaps I may be permitted a paragraph of commentary on what the Johannine attitude toward the world means for Christians on a long-term basis. On the one hand, texts reflecting alienation from a hostile world have comforted inward-looking Christians, inclined to leave outsiders to their own devices if they are not attracted by God toward Christian truth. This has often produced a fortress mentality. On the other hand, these texts have annoyed Christians very conscious of a mission to the world, whether that mission be to infiltrate and change it, or to enable its own spiritual potentialities, or to win it for Christ. Certainly it is some facet of the latter mood that dominates in Christianity today, and especially in my own Roman Catholic community after Vatican II. Nevertheless, the Fourth Gospel remains a warning against naivete. The world is not simply unplowed ground waiting to be sown with the Gospel; it is not simply neutral terrain. There is a Prince of this world that is actively hostile to Jesus, so that the maxim *Christus contra mundum* ("Christ against the world") is not without truth. Presumably it was with an initial conviction of God's love for the world that the Johannine community had turned to Gentiles from "the Jews," and the feeling that men of all sorts preferred darkness to light must have come after bitter experience. By all means Christians must keep trying in various ways to bear a testimony about Christ to the world, but they should not be astounded if they relive in part the Johannine experience.[22]

Raymond Collins points out that John's gospel is laced with legal terminology when it comes to the profession of Christ.[23] The synoptic gospels prefer terms such as "to proclaim" or "to announce the

---

[17] Ibid., 60–61.
[18] Ibid., 62.
[19] Ibid.
[20] *CWJB*, 58.
[21] Ibid.

[22] *TCBD*, 65, 66.
[23] *JHW*, 15.

Good News." John uses legal terms such as "testify" and "verdict" probably as a result of the circumstances of the Johannine church. Most scholars agree that the fourth gospel was written in the 90s. The Temple had already been destroyed following the siege of Jerusalem (A.D. 70) and Israel was concerned with preserving its own identity. With the Temple gone, all that remained for the Jews was their tradition. It was therefore imperative that they do whatever they could to preserve that tradition. "Circumstances dictated that they do all within their power to ensure the vitality and the purity of Jewish tradition."[24]

The Pharisees, who had always been responsible for the interpretation of the Law, gathered for a meeting in Jabneh. Their purpose was to do whatever was needed to ensure the continuation of the tradition. They formulated a canon of Jewish scriptures and they dealt with the issue of prayer and assembled worship. During the tenure of Gamaliel at the academy of Jabneh (A.D. 80–115), a list of eighteen benedictions was composed. The "benediction" was a form of curse that attacked and censured heretics and slanderers. It is believed that this benediction was directed primarily toward Christians. Those who would not utter a curse against the *minim* (heretics) would be expelled from the synagogue. Christians refused to utter the curse against themselves and were thus expelled.

One school of thought suggests that Christians were considered heretics because of their belief in the divinity of Christ, which for the Jews constituted belief in ditheism and a denial of monotheism. Robert Karris, however, posits a slightly different interpretation.[25] He agrees that the Christians were threatened with expulsion from the synagogue. He maintains that rather than a reaction to Christian ditheism, the Jews were reacting to an issue of election: "I maintain that the religious leaders oppose the Christians of John's community because they perceive them as watering down the standards of election by bringing into their communion Samaritans, and Galileans, the physically incapacitated, the 'people of the land,' people who are ignorant of the law. The Jewish religious leaders cannot tolerate this view of election and do indeed 'drum' Christians out of the synagogue."[26] John, therefore, shares the view of the synoptic writers that discipleship and love of God which are evidenced by love of neighbor include all of God's people, especially the poor, the outcast, and the marginalized. One cannot live in the light without asking the question: "If I am to live as a child of the Light, then who do I not include among the chosen?"

It is obvious that a tremendous tension existed between Jews and Christians during the time of the fourth gospel. Expulsion from the synagogue was no light matter. It ultimately put Christians at risk. They became an illegal sect operating outside the protection of the formal, state-sanctioned Jewish religion. It is no wonder that John's language is juridical. "Similarly, the existence of local controversies with the proponents of Jewish orthodoxy explains why the Fourth Gospel fairly breathes the atmosphere of the courtroom."[27]

One must not forget that God's love for humanity reaches its fulfillment in the death and resurrection of Christ. Greater love has no person than to lay down her life for another. The sacrifice of Christ is a sign par excellence of God's love for the human race. It is an invitation to do the same for others. Another theme in today's gospel is the paschal mystery of the Son and our participation in that mystery. "The love of Christ even unto death becomes model and means of love for one another, so that Christ can offer a 'new' command to love one another... the newness is in loving as Christ loves, not simply following Christ's example, but drawing from the power of Christ's love which abides within each one."[28]

Salvation is yet another theme. God's intention in sending the Son is the salvation of the world. Then why is the world judged? The world condemns itself by not looking upon Christ crucified and risen, just as those in the time of Moses did not look to the serpent raised on the standard to be healed and saved. Everyone is given an opportunity to choose the Light. But choose they must. No one is exempt. John's gospel is set up as a

---

[24]Ibid., 16.
[25]*JMJG*, 100–105.

[26]Ibid., 105.
[27]Ibid., 18.
[28]Anthony J. Tombasco, "Love," *CPDBT*, 572.

polemic. Those who choose Christ choose the Light; those who engage in evil deeds and reject Christ choose the darkness.

Proclaim the gospel again.

Sometimes we gain new insights when we hear the text after the interpretation is given. Someone from the group proclaims the gospel a second time.

STEP 4
TESTING

Conversation with the Liturgy and the Scriptures

Test your original understanding in dialogue with the text.

(You might consider breaking into smaller groups.)

Now that you've heard the exegesis, were there any new insights? How do you feel about it? How does your original understanding of this gospel compare with what we just shared? How does this story speak to your life?

Sharing Life Experience

Participants share an experience from their lives that connects with the biblical interpretation just presented.

Today's gospel expresses God's love and its implications in living the Christian life. Just how does that speak to my life? As a mother I am immediately taken to my family and the way in which God has been present to us throughout our lives. I look at the times of joy and the times of sorrow. I look at the moments of great triumph and the moments of great sorrow. I think of the difficult teen years and I celebrate the young adult years in which we now watch the love of God manifested in the lives of our maturing, young adult children.

I consider the hopeful, urgent longing we all share right now as we pray with our adult children for a grandchild. When I hear the words, "God so loved the world that he sent his only Son," I plead with God to send our oldest daughter and her husband a child. Such a child would find a precious home. Yet

I know that in the midst of their longing (and ours) God is present and wants us to know how much he loves us. God so loved the world that he sent his Son, and in so doing he invites us to trust him in the midst of our longing for a child.

I consider the ways we as family have responded (or not) to God's insistence that we love as God loves us. I am reminded of the ways in which our family, especially my husband and our children, have reached out to the poor and the hungry. My heart is warmed as I think of the ways in which my children demonstrate hearts that were made for loving. I see the ways in which my youngest always offers a loving response to anyone who approaches her with a need—anyone. Night or day, she is present to them. I have experienced the love of God that has been nurtured in the bosom of family life, and I am thankful.

Today's gospel also presents a challenge. I am challenged to see the ways in which love has not been given a chance—both in my family and in my response to the world. There have been times in which unconditional love would have been a far better response than judgment and condemnation. There have been moments when I tried to determine the path of life for my adult children rather than turn them over to God's care. John describes a self-sacrificing love in today's gospel that prompts the question: "How have I failed and continue to fail to be present to those who need me, especially my family?" Today's gospel also invites me to examine the ways I refuse to set an example by loving as Christ loves. There was a time when I was embroiled in controversy that generated much disunity, gossip, and destructive behavior. It was difficult to maintain an appropriate Christian response when under fire. Sometimes I succeeded, but when I did not, it was blatant, and my children were quick to point out the error of my ways—and they were right.

In my response to the world, I look at the ways in which I marginalize or participate in the marginalization of anyone in God's family. One time in particular stands out—I stood frozen and failed to move when a poor child of God was hurting. Even though I have a strong passion for justice, and try to preach and teach a just word, living it is another matter. Living a just life is not easy. When I look at the ways I participate in social sin, yet fail to do anything about it, I am reminded that I have a long way to go to fully live the imperative of today's gospel. As long as people are not loved as God loves them, then I am called to respond. My response, however, is minimal. There is so much more I could and should do.

Nicodemus is a reminder to me that conversion is gradual and that God's love will sustain me and teach me as I strive to live the imperatives of today's gospel. Nicodemus is also a reminder to us as church that even though we often participate in structures which are oppressive and keep people from full access to God, we are called to break down those barriers and be a sign in the world of God's unconditional, sacrificial love. We must therefore seek out those who are kept on the fringes by society and even by our churches, and invite them into the midst of our communities—a sign and symbol of Christ's presence. Today's liturgy invites the question: "Does our parish really set a common table for all or are there places of honor reserved for a select few?" It is a rare experience to find a place that honestly reflects a common table, rooted in God's complete, unconditional, gratuitous love. Today's gospel offers a gentle nudge to continue to work toward setting such a table.

What were the underlying issues in John's gospel today? How might this gospel have relevance today? How might this gospel speak to the Church today? How does the figure of Nicodemus challenge you? In what way is your journey similar to Nicodemus's journey? In what way does this gospel challenge your community today? In what way has this conversation with the scriptures for today's liturgy invited change in your life? In what way are the biblical themes of covenant, exodus, creation, and community evident in today's readings? Do you still feel the same way about this text as when you began? Has your original understanding been stretched, challenged, or affirmed?

STEP 5
DECISION

The gospel demands a response.

In what concrete way might your parish be invited to respond? Are there any attitudes or behaviors you would like to change as a result of today's con-

versation? What one concrete action will you take this week in response to the liturgy today?

Christian Initiation: Today the elect celebrate the second scrutiny. Even though the Cycle A readings are to be used at all the liturgies on the Sundays in which the scrutinies are celebrated, parishes sometimes do not follow that practice. It would therefore be important to address the fact that the scrutinies are being celebrated at another liturgy and what that means to the elect as well as the faithful. Refer to the third and fourth Sundays of Lent Cycle A for further information regarding scrutinies. Catechumens who will not be baptized at the Easter Vigil continue to be dismissed from the Sunday liturgy and participate in extended catechesis.

DOCTRINAL ISSUES

What Church truth/teaching/doctrinal issue could be drawn from the gospel for the fourth Sunday of Lent?

Participants suggest possible doctrinal themes that flow from the readings.

Possible Doctrinal Themes

Cross; love of God; paschal mystery; faith; conversion; discipleship; sin; grace; social justice; salvation; Christology; symbol of light; reconciliation; baptism; soteriology

Present the doctrinal material at this time.

1. The facilitator gives input on a particular doctrinal issue of his or her prior choosing. OR
2. The group chooses a doctrinal issue from the list they created. They read together from the Doctrinal Appendix or other appropriate, official Church documents and the works of respected theologians.

(Many doctrinal issues are found in the Doctrinal Appendix at the back of this workbook. If you are choosing an issue from this resource, please refer to it now.)

Reflection questions centered around the chosen doctrinal theme can be found at the end of each topic in the Doctrinal Appendix. The questions are based on the five-step reflection process. If you choose a topic not included in the Doctrinal Appendix, craft your own questions according to the same five-step process.

Following the reflection questions you will be reminded to return to chapter 7, "Preparing the Catechetical Session," to assist you in crafting your own session.

Closing Prayer

Father, look with love upon your people,
The love which our Lord Jesus Christ showed us
when he delivered himself to evil men
and suffered the agony of the cross.
Grant this through Christ, our Lord.[29]

---

[29]Fourth Sunday of Lent, "Solemn Blessing or Prayer Over the People," *The Sacramentary.*

FOURTH SUNDAY OF LENT (CYCLE A)

Environment

Today's gospel speaks of Christ, the Light of the World. If the environment is not normally adorned with a light symbol, today would certainly be a day to incorporate a Christ candle.

INTRODUCTORY RITES

Opening Song (or Entrance Antiphon)

Rejoice, Jerusalem! Be glad for her, you who love her; rejoice with her, you who mourned for her, and you will find contentment at her consoling breast. (See Isaiah 66:10–11.)[1]

Opening Prayer

The facilitator of the session may lead the prayer. Others in the group may be asked to proclaim the readings.

Father, all powerful and ever-living God,
we do well always and everywhere to give you
    thanks
through Jesus Christ our Lord.

He came among us as a man,
to lead mankind from darkness
into the light of faith.

Through Adam's fall we were born slaves of sin,
but now through baptism in Christ
we are reborn as your adopted children.

Earth unites with heaven
to sing the new song of creation,
as we adore and praise you for ever:

Holy, holy, holy Lord, God of power and might,
heaven and earth are full of your glory.
Hosanna in the highest.
Blessed is he who comes in the name of the Lord.
Hosanna in the highest.
    (Preface, Fourth Sunday of Lent)

LITURGY OF THE WORD

Let us listen to God's word.

The readings are proclaimed.

First Reading
1 Samuel 16:6–7, 10–13

In today's reading David is chosen to be king by Yahweh from among Jesse's sons. Throughout all of scripture, it is very clear that God's election is God's own. Humans can do nothing on their own merit to achieve it. God often painted history with crooked lines by choosing people to fulfill his designs who would normally have difficulty passing human scrutiny. David was the least likely character from among Jesse's sons.

Saul anointed David king, thereby signifying the abiding, and guiding presence of God's Spirit. "Anointing means to touch some person or thing with a substance (oil, water, blood, fat, mud) to effect a change, either external or internal."[2] To be anointed by the Lord as king meant that the person was commissioned for a special mission. The new designation required protection and respect. David's anointing also signaled that he was divinely elected and was thus deserving of divine protection.

Today's reading was perhaps chosen for its baptismal images: David was elected by God and anointed for a new life in Yahweh's service.

Responsorial Psalm
Psalm 23:1–3, 3–4, 5, 6

The reasons for the choice of this psalm are ambiguous. One scholar has suggested that it could have been used because of its vague reference to the anointing of David.

Second Reading
Ephesians 5:8–14

---

[1]Fourth Sunday of Lent: "Entrance Antiphon," *The Sacramentary.*

[2]John C. Endres, S.J., "Anointing," in *CPDBT,* 28.

Some question Pauline authorship of this letter. However, if Paul was the author, it was written around 60 C.E. This would correspond with Paul's stint in the Roman jail. The letter contains allusions to gnostic influences that were plaguing the first-century church. Chapters four through six describe the difference between the pagan and Christian way of life. It is the difference between life and death, light and darkness.

Today's subject is a primary theme of our Lenten reflection: conversion. The pericope suggests a complete metanoia—a turning away from all that is darkness into the marvelous light of Christ. Some suggest that today's letter was part of an ancient baptismal liturgy because of its use of the light and darkness baptismal metaphor.

Gospel
John 9:1–41

STEP 1
NAMING ONE'S EXPERIENCE

What were your first impressions? What was your first response? What grabbed your attention? How did you feel?

Each person names his or her initial impression. Statements should be brief. No reasons should be given at this time. All simply listen without agreeing or disagreeing.

STEP 2
UNDERSTANDING

In a brief statement, what do you think this gospel is trying to convey?

STEP 3
INPUT FROM VISION/STORY/TRADITION

Liturgical Context

The Fourth Sunday of Lent is highly charged with baptismal themes. Jesus healed the man born blind and then instructed him to wash in the pool of Siloam. The man came to believe in Jesus. On this Fourth Sunday, during the period of purification and enlightenment, the elect celebrate the second scrutiny. (Refer to the overview of Lent and Third Sunday of Lent, Cycle A for further explanation of the scrutinies.) We, along with the elect, seek enlightenment. "The early church referred to baptism as 'enlightenment' and spoke of the candidates as being enlightened."[3]

The three scrutiny gospels were used to prepare people for baptism when preparation lasted only three weeks. Today these readings are still used for penitential and baptismal preparation for the Easter sacraments. Jesus, Light of the World, is important catechesis for those preparing for enlightenment (baptism).

The first reading from Samuel, the anointing of David, may also be connected to baptism. The initiation corollaries are obvious. At baptism we are given (anointed with) the gift of the Holy Spirit. We are anointed priest, prophet, and king. "Baptism is a freely given call from God; it is a gift of the Spirit and brings participation in the royal priesthood of Christ."[4] In today's first reading, Saul anoints David king, symbolizing the presence of the Spirit in his life and mission. The anointing of David signals a changed reality for him. Baptism changes our reality—we change from children of the darkness to children of the light. (The second reading from Ephesians also points to today's baptismal focus when it speaks of those who had once lived in darkness but are now children of the light.) David was anointed for a special mission. Baptism anoints us for the reconciling, evangelizing mission of Jesus Christ. David's new identity entitled him to rights and privileges: he received divine protection and was respected. Through baptism we are protected from the snares of the devil and are entitled to rights and privileges as adopted daughters and sons of God. David's anointing was a sign of God's divine election. We, too, are baptized by God's divine election. We can do nothing on our own to merit salvation.

---

[3] *LY*, 102.
[4] Ibid., 103.

Today's liturgy is filled with anticipatory images of baptism as Easter fast approaches. The preface for this liturgy also speaks of being led out of darkness into the light. The prayer after communion seeks enlightenment from the light of the gospel.

Gospel Exegesis

The facilitator gives input regarding what critical biblical scholarship has to say about this text. The input includes insights as to how people would have heard the gospel in Jesus' time.

Today's gospel is a commentary on Jesus' earlier assertion that he is the Light of the World (Jn 8:12).[5] Jesus contrasts the growing vision of the blind man with the increasing blindness of the ones who claim they already see. This story is placed in the context of the controversies between Christians and the synagogue Jews in John's community. There are seven stories in John's gospel that serve to prove that Jesus was who he said he was—the messiah. They also attest to Jesus as the fulfillment of all prior Jewish worship (in this case, the water and light rituals of the Feast of Tabernacles), thus providing the rationale and the credence for the *new worship* of the Christian community. In other words, the stories gave permission to the Christian community to break away from the rituals of the past in order to embrace the new liturgy of Christ.

Jesus met the blind man after he left the temple area during the Feast of Tabernacles. It was a huge feast that attracted many pilgrims to Jerusalem. For a solid week there was great celebrating as all joyously waved their palm fronds.

The feast was at the end of the harvest. Booths had been erected and there was jubilant dancing, song, and festivity. The feast commemorated the entrance into the promised land and the future hope of the messiah at the end of the world. Priests would go to the pool of Siloam each day, draw a golden pitcher of water, and recite their ritual prayers. "Rivers of living water

will flow from within him" (Jn 7:37–38). "I am the light of the world. Whoever follows me will not walk in darkness but will have the light of life" (8:12). They poured the water on the corner of the altar at night in the brilliantly illuminated courtyard of the women. The gospel of the man born blind is told in the contextual framework of this feast.

The collection of miracle stories in John is often referred to as the "Book of Signs." This is because, rather than referring to miracles, John speaks of signs. The stories describe the healing signs Jesus performed in his ministry and then discuss their significance (a forerunner of liturgical catechesis, to be sure!). The signs serve as windows to eternity for those who have faith: ". . . the man born blind truly sees the sign of Jesus as light of the world and the Pharisees remain in the darkness of their stubborn refusal of faith."[6]

The progression of the miracle begins with a theological discussion stating the nature of the problem. The man born blind from birth enters the scene. The disciples ask Jesus whose sin has caused the man's blindness. It was Jewish belief that sin—either of the individual or the parents—caused suffering. Jesus asserts that blindness is not due to human sin, but that God's glory will be seen through the man's blindness.

The next section of the story describes the miracle. Jesus spits into the dirt, makes a clay compress, and places it on the man's eyes, telling him to go and wash in the Siloam pool—the pool from which the water for the Feast of Tabernacles has just been drawn. The man does as he has been told and returns with his sight restored.

The story progresses to a description of reactions to the miracle. The man's neighbors are incredulous and can hardly believe this is the blind man they have always known. The blind man confesses Jesus' identity and answers their queries by reporting what Jesus instructed him to do. The Pharisees ask the man how his sight was restored. The man responds by relating the details again. Some Pharisees accuse Jesus of healing on the Sabbath. The

---

[5] For further elaboration, refer to *RJ,* 158.

[6] *WWC,* 26.

Pharisees then approach the man's parents. Fearful of expulsion from the synagogue, they send the Pharisees back to the son. Finally, the Pharisees believe the man was healed.

The Pharisees challenge the man. They state that Jesus is a sinner. The man says that he does not know whether Jesus is a sinner or not, but perhaps they should go and ask Jesus themselves; *perhaps they, too, would like to be his disciples.* This lets the reader know that the newly sighted man is now a disciple. His healing has caused conversion.

Jesus is now elevated to the status of prophet. The man pleads Jesus' case. Never has there been a known case of someone healing a person blind from birth. The man reminds the Pharisees that everyone knows that God does not hear the prayers of sinners; yet this man's prayers were heard. He recalls and names a foundational scriptural truth that God hears the prayers of those who do the will of God and who are devout. The man confesses his christology (the main agenda of John's gospel) *as a result of his experience of Jesus:* Jesus is a prophet, the Master; he comes from God; he does God's will and God hears his prayers in ways that no one has ever before experienced.

The man is then thrown out of the synagogue. His expulsion is connected to his profession of faith in Jesus and his status as disciple. Jesus hears of the man's expulsion and looks for him. Some scholars believe that the next section of this gospel is an ancient liturgical text used at baptism. The man professes belief in Jesus and then worships him. "With this, the process of conversion is complete. For him, light means salvation/sight."[7]

Jesus then challenges the Pharisees. He asserts that his ministry is to bring light to those who cannot see. The Pharisees goad Jesus: "Do you presume to consider us among the sightless?" Jesus accepts their challenge and tells them that to be given sight means they must believe that they are blind in the first place. The Pharisees very self-righteously believe themselves among the fully sighted, thus not in need of Jesus' marvelous sign. "If people can feel the need for light, the help can be forthcoming. But if they absolutize their blindness as sight, then help is impossible. For them, light means judgment/blindness."[8]

While there is progression in the story, there is also progression in the stages of awareness about Jesus's identity: first he was light, then the one sent, then prophet and Son of Man, and finally, Lord. In the first chapter of John, Jesus was named as the "Light that has come into the world." Today's story shows Jesus *in the process of doing* what God sent him to do: his mission as Light of the world. *The gospel asserts that we will know that Jesus is who he says he is by the signs he performs.*

Talbert maintains that the miracle functions as a sign—it is instruction. Miracles have three purposes. They serve as a way to legitimate and give authority to the person of Jesus. The miracle stories are also a means of evangelization—they bring people to faith. Third, they serve as a means of teaching. The story of Jesus' giving sight to the man born blind is a teaching on Jesus, the Light of the world.

Today's gospel prompts serious examination of our inner integrity and self deceptions. Where are we blind and yet think we see? Are any of our firmly held beliefs subject to the discerning challenge of Jesus' illumination?

It is no wonder this gospel was premier catechesis on baptism. The catechumen progresses, like the man born blind, from darkness to light, from unbelief to belief. This gospel reminds those preparing for baptism, as well as those preparing to renew their baptismal profession of faith at Easter, that "all will have to testify to their faith at the risk of being rejected by some or henceforth ignored by others."[9]

Proclaim the gospel again.

Sometimes we gain new insights when we hear the text after the interpretation has been given. Someone from the group proclaims the gospel a second time.

---

[7] *RJ*, 162.

[8] Ibid.

[9] *DL* (II), 126.

Conversation with the Liturgy and the Scriptures

Test your original understanding in dialogue with the text.

(You might consider breaking into smaller groups.)

Were there any new insights? Was there anything you had not considered before? How does your original understanding of this story compare with what we just shared? How does this story speak to your life?

Sharing Life Experience

Participants share an experience from their lives that connects with the biblical interpretation just shared.

> *The blindness of the Pharisees was a blindness rooted in certainty. The Pharisees were certain that they possessed the light and the only truth. It is a dangerous posture.*

> *Our society is steeped in blindness when we continue to perpetrate sins against the world's poor, oppressed, and marginalized. When we continue to foster policies that keep people under the thumb of oppression with the certainty that we are protecting the rights of our own citizenry (e.g., when we do not allow immigrant children access to medical care, etc.), we remain blind to the light of Christ.*

> *Our religious structures are steeped in blindness when we treat some of our members as marginalized people with no voice. We are blind when we dismiss members of our communities such as the uninvolved members of our parishes, the homeless, the poor, homosexuals, women, and all those who find themselves "outside the loop," whether that be at the hierarchical, diocesan, parish, or small-group level.*

> *I am blind when I hang on to personally held beliefs and positions as if they were written with hammer and chisel on the stone of my very own ego. At times I feel so strongly self-righteous about some issues that there is little room for the possibility of needed con-*

version, particularly if prayer and discernment helped formulate my position in the first place. Sometimes I call that trust; at other times I call it arrogance. Discernment takes place within the Christian community. If and when I am unwilling to listen to all the voices within the community, my discernment is incomplete. I remain in blindness when I am unwilling to allow God to transform my belligerently held convictions.

> *In my opinion, the primary sin of the Pharisees was idolatry. They presumed to know the mind, heart, and will of God better than God: all things are subject to God's interpretation and intervention. The message for me is: there is a God, and it is not me!*

All share their life experience.

What did I/we hear in this exegesis? What was John's concern for his community in today's gospel? Are there any connections that can be made to our community today? Do the baptismal implications of today's readings have anything to do with our community? What are our collective and personal responses to all of the above questions? Has our original understanding been stretched, challenged, or affirmed?

The gospel demands a response.

How might our community be challenged to change as a result of today's liturgy? In what contrete way does this gospel call our parish to action in the church, parish, neighborhood, or world? Has this conversation changed or stretched my personal attitudes? What is one concrete action I/we will take this week as a response to what we have learned and shared today?

DOCTRINAL ISSUES

What church truth/teaching/doctrinal issue could be drawn from the gospel for the Fourth Sunday in Lent?

Participants suggest possible doctrinal themes that flow from the readings.

Possible Doctrinal Themes

Baptism, conversion, election, sin—personal and corporate

Present the doctrinal material at this time.

1. The facilitator gives input on a particular doctrinal issue of his/her prior choosing. OR
2. The group chooses a doctrinal issue from the list they created. They read together from the Doctrinal Appendix.

(The doctrinal issues are found in the Doctrinal Appendix in the back of this workbook. If you are choosing an issue from this resource, please refer to it now.)

Reflection questions centered around the chosen doctrinal theme can be found at the end of each topic in the Doctrinal Appendix. The questions are based on the five-step reflection process. If you choose a topic not included in the Doctrinal Appendix, craft your own questions according to the same five-step process.

Following the reflection questions you will be reminded to return to chapter 7, "Preparing the Catechetical Session," to assist you in crafting your own session.

Closing Prayer

Second Scrutiny: Exorcism

Father of mercy,
you led the man born blind
to the kingdom of light
through the gift of your Son.
Free these elect from the false values that surround and blind them.
Set them firmly in your truth,
children of the light for ever.
We ask this through Christ our Lord.
Amen.

Laying on of hands

Presider stretches hands over the elect:

Lord Jesus,
you are the true light that enlightens the world.
Through the Spirit of truth
free those who are enslaved by the father of lies.
Stir up the desire for good in these elect,
whom you have chosen for your sacraments.
Let them rejoice in your light, that they may see,
and, like the man born blind whose sight you restored,
let them prove to be staunch and fearless witnesses to the faith,
for you are Lord for ever and ever.
Amen.[10]

_____
[10]Prayer of Exorcism, "Second Scrutiny," *RCIA*.

FIFTH SUNDAY OF LENT

INTRODUCTORY RITES

Entrance Antiphon (or Opening Song)

Give me justice, O God, and defend my cause against the wicked; rescue me from deceitful and unjust men. You, O God, are my refuge. (Ps 42:1–2)[1]

Opening Prayer

The facilitator of the session may lead the prayer. Others in the group may be asked to proclaim the readings.

Let us pray
(for the courage to follow Christ)

Pause for silent prayer.

Father,
help us to be like Christ your Son,
who loved the world and died for our salvation.
Inspire us by his love,
guide us by his example,
who lives and reigns with you and the Holy Spirit,
one God, for ever and ever.[2]

LITURGY OF THE WORD

The readings are proclaimed.

First Reading
Jeremiah 31:31–34

(Refer to the sixteenth Sunday in Ordinary Time for an overview of the Book of the Prophet Jeremiah.)

Today's Pericope: Jeremiah, prophet of God, is speaking a word of prophecy to the exiles in Babylon. He insists that the exile is the result of God's punishment for the failure to live by the old covenant forged at Sinai. In the old covenant it was understood that the successes and failures of Israel were dependent upon Israel's faithfulness to the covenant. Unfaithfulness resulted in banishment from their homeland at the hands of their Babylonian captors.

Much of the prophetic tradition was concerned with the issue of fidelity to the covenant. Jeremiah believed that the predicament of Israel was a result of people whose hearts had turned to stone. The people were unrepentant. He insisted that only God knows the human heart and that faithfulness to the covenant was a matter of interior commitment and response to God. Jeremiah promised that Yahweh would forge a new covenant with the people, a covenant etched not on stone, but on the hearts of the people. He insisted that inner dedication to Yahweh is of utmost priority. Without interior commitment, the external manifestations of obedience to the Law are without substance. When Yahweh establishes the new covenant, Jeremiah affirms that the people will embrace God's will and grow in relationship with him.

The Book of Deuteronomy exhorted that the old covenant needed to be taught to the people. Jeremiah now insists that Yahweh himself will infuse the new covenant in the hearts of people. This infusion will result in "knowing" Yahweh. "Knowing Yahweh," according to the scriptures, was a state of intimate, abiding relationship with God. The new covenant envisioned by Jeremiah assumed this type of "knowing" for the people of Israel.

Responsorial Psalm
Psalm 51:3–4, 12–15

Today's psalm is the most famous of the penitential psalms. It is the psalm appointed for Wednesday and Friday in the Liturgy of the Hours. It is also one of the appointed common psalms for the season of Lent. The psalm turns Jeremiah's prophecy that there will be a new covenant etched on the hearts of people into a prayer. It asks that hearts be changed, that sins be forgiven, and that

---

[1] Fifth Sunday of Lent: "Entrance Antiphon," *The Sacramentary.*

[2] Fifth Sunday of Lent: "Opening Prayer," *The Sacramentary.*

strength to walk according to the Lord's commands be given.

Second Reading
Hebrews 5:7–9

(Refer to the twenty-seventh Sunday in Ordinary Time for an overview of the Letter to the Hebrews.)

Today's Pericope: The author of Hebrews intended to portray Jesus as the great high priest of the everlasting covenant. Jesus won salvation and God's mercy and forgiveness for all people by his sacrifice on the cross. Today's reading elucidates Jesus' qualifications as high priest. Jesus shares the same qualifications as Melchizedek, the ideal high priest, even though he is not a Levite and thereby an automatic heir to the priesthood. Jesus has all the qualifications for his role of high priest—he is a mediator; he offered sacrifice (the sacrifice of himself on the cross), and he offered prayers of intercession to God for sins. In Jesus' role as high priest he initiated the new covenant.

Christ became perfected through his suffering. The word *perfected* is a term used in the Septuagint for the conferring of priestly power. Jesus became the eternal high priest through his sacrifice on the cross. Through his obedient sacrifice he now sits on the exalted throne of heaven where he reigns as eternal high priest. Jesus is the high priest who won salvation for all who believe in him.

The gospel is proclaimed.

Gospel
John 12:20–33. If a grain of wheat falls to the ground and dies, it produces much fruit.

STEP 1
NAMING ONE'S EXPERIENCE

What were your first impressions? What was your first response to the gospel (or the other readings)? What captured your attention?

Each person names his or her initial impression. Statements should be brief. No reasons should be given at this time. All simply listen without agreeing or disagreeing.

STEP 2
UNDERSTANDING

In a brief statement, explain what you think this gospel is trying to convey.

STEP 3
INPUT FROM VISION/STORY/TRADITION

Liturgical Context

Today brings us to the threshold of Holy Week. Stripped bare of our illusions, confronted with our blindness, and challenged by our insincere motives, the faithful and the elect prepare to enter the tomb of Christ's death and resurrection. Today's reflection by Christ on his own death prepares us to enter into this paschal week ready to embrace the cycle of death and resurrection anew. In today's prayer over the gifts we ask Almighty God that the sacrifice we offer take away the sins of those God enlightens with the Christian faith.[3] We ask that the sacrifice of Christ's Body and Blood, offered together at the Sunday liturgy, rid us of the sins of false pride and judgment. The solemn blessing asks that the Lord protect us always from every evil that we may serve God with all our hearts. *"With all our hearts"* implies that we turn toward God and not toward our own self-righteous pride and judgmental attitudes.

Today's liturgy reminds us that conversion is at the heart of it all. We ask that our stony hearts be replaced with hearts made for love. In the new covenant that Jeremiah promised God would inaugurate, people were to be more fully converted to God, and in process come to "know" him more deeply (first reading). We who "know" Christ have experienced that knowledge. Jesus is truly our high priest (second reading) who intercedes for us at the right hand of God and strengthens us to continue to live the intimate relationship of the new covenant and in so doing enter more deeply into his paschal mystery.

---

[3]Fifth Sunday of Lent, "Prayer Over the Gifts," *The Sacramentary.*

We are converted to God who is in relationship with us as God's very own people—God who is working with us in the lifelong process of transformation. We are converted to God who forgives, is infinitely merciful; who does not condemn and who demands that we, in turn, not condemn others. We are converted to God who cares for the poor, the lost, and the broken; the suffering, the poor, and rejected; and to all who are marginalized, despised, or forsaken. We are converted to God who in turn demands that we do no less. This conversion is the very heart of justice. It is the heart of our Lenten fast.

> Let us pray
> for the courage to embrace the world in the
>   name of Christ.
> Father in heaven,
> the love of your Son led him to accept
> the suffering of the cross
> that his brothers (and sisters) might glory in
>   new life.
> Change our selfishness into self-giving.
> Help us to embrace the world you have given
>   us,
> that we may transform the darkness of its pain
> into the life and joy of Easter.
> Grant this through Christ our Lord.[4]

This alterative opening prayer could very easily function as a summary of today's gospel. It is the heart of Jesus' message and worthy of our heartfelt supplication. Our time of purification and enlightenment is drawing to an end. The great feast of Easter lies just beyond the horizon. By the time of its approach we will have been emptied, poured out, examined, scrutinized, purified, and enlightened. We will stand as empty vessels, ready to be filled, overflowed, spilled, and running over with the new life of Easter joy. And in the process we have hopefully come to "know" the crucified and risen Christ more deeply.

During Lent we have entered into the process of conversion enlightened by Christ, who is the water for whom we thirst, the light of our blindness, and our very life's breath. With the elect we once again enter the womb of darkness to be born into

the dawn of Easter light. We then are sent forth renewed, refreshed, and committed to live the *pasch* we just celebrated, day in and day out; until once again depleted, we return next year to continue the paschal life cycle once again.

Gospel Exegesis

The facilitator provides input from critical biblical scholarship on this text. This input includes insights as to how people would have heard the gospel in Jesus' time.

As Palm Sunday draws nearer we hear echoes of the Passion not only throughout today's liturgy, but also in this section of John's gospel, which serves as an introduction to the remaining chapters dealing with Jesus' final hour. In John's gospel, "hour" is a reference to the time of the new covenant. The entire fourth gospel is written as one great unfolding drama in constant motion toward the ultimate destination of fulfillment— "namely, the encounter of the power of Jesus based on love with the unjust power rejecting him."[5] The "hour" of the new covenant is the time when God's incredible, awesome, completely gratuitous love, evidenced especially in his preferential treatment of the poor and outcast, encounters rejection by both religious and worldly power. This power is rooted in sin. The power's battle with love is waged on the cross. This is why the cross will have to be lifted up. The cross is where the victory will be won. Those powers responsible for sending Christ to his death will be conquered once and for all. Jesus, in loving surrender, gives up his life so that the world may live. In this paradox of paradoxes Jesus' sacrificial death reveals God, the author of life, to the world.

Jesus freely takes up the cross. It is not imposed upon him. It is a choice. Jesus could do no less than journey to the cross. His faithfulness to God, to his mission, and to his disciples led him to this moment of covenant love. "Jesus journeys to his 'hour' with the consistency of his life. His words are in accordance with his deeds and his deeds are in accordance with his words. This is what makes him dangerous to the powers of this world."[6]

---

[4]Fifth Sunday of Lent, "Alternative Opening Prayer," *The Sacramentary.*

[5]*SWTLY,* 63.
[6]Ibid., 63.

Reflection on today's gospel must necessarily begin with a reflection on the verses leading up to it as they form the context out of which today's gospel flows. The introductory section to Jesus' final hour serves to establish the time and locus of events—the remaining days and hours of Jesus' life and the approaching Passover celebration. This introductory piece also informs the reader that pilgrims were on their way to Jerusalem to observe Passover in appropriate lawful fashion and that there was a sense of expectancy in the air. Through the use of dramatic foreshadowing, the reader is informed that Jesus was a hunted man—the authorities were on the lookout for Jesus to arrest him. The first eleven verses of chapter 12 (verses directly preceding today's pericope) set the stage for Passover, the symbolism of the paschal lamb and hints of Jesus' pending death and burial. Included in those verses is the story of Mary, who unknowingly anoints the feet of Jesus in preparation for his burial. Also in these preliminary verses is the appearance of a crowd that emerges not only to encounter Jesus but also to see Lazarus who had been raised from the dead (v. 9). "This results in Lazarus being included in the death plot of the chief priests 'because on account of him many of the Jews were going away and believing in Jesus' (vv. 10–11)."

The next portion of this introductory section centers around initiatives taken by other people, initiatives that prompt a reaction from Jesus.[7] The first initiative is taken by the crowd and the second initiative is taken by the Greeks (today's pericope). Prior to the verses proclaimed today, the crowd went out to meet Jesus waving branches of palm trees. They hailed Jesus as King of Israel. The designation had little to do with spiritual realities, however. It was an acclamation of Jewish nationalism. Palms were reminiscent of a moment in Israel's history in which the Jews brought palms to the Temple when Judas Maccabees rededicated it in 165 B.C. after it had been desecrated with pagan idols by the Greek kings of Syria (1 Mc 4:52–59). Palms were also carried by the Jews when Simon conquered and took possession of the Jerusalem citadel. Palms were given to Levi (Testament of Naphtali 5:4) as a symbol of supremacy over all Israel. Waving palms, then, carried the same signifi-

cance as the waving of the American flag by people in towns that had been liberated during World War II. It was a sign of political and national liberation. Palms, therefore, were waved before Jesus as a sign and symbol of the people's expectations that he be their national liberator during their time of persecution and oppression.

"They came to meet him" reflects the practice of crowds as they went out to greet Greek rulers as they approached the city. The term *Hosanna* was used to address and salute sovereign kings. The crowd went out to meet Jesus with the expectation that he would take up the role of national political leader and liberator.

Jesus reacted to their expectations by sitting on a donkey. The underlying symbolism surrounding his parabolic action is based on imagery found in Zechariah, in which the monarch came riding on a colt if he was bearing peace, but riding on a horse if war was his agenda. Jesus' act of riding on a colt was a prophetic reaction to their nationalistic expectations. He came bearing a message of universal kingship and peace—not war. The crowd went out to him because they heard that he had raised Lazarus from the dead. Who would not follow a Messiah who could raise someone from the dead? How could they lose with someone so powerful and mighty leading them? This was the kind of Messiah they had been looking for all along. Jesus, however, turned their expectations upside down. He was not the Messiah of their own ideological and political imaginings. The kingdom Jesus came to establish was not a kingdom of political power. It was a reign of peace, a new covenant of love. John continues the theme of Jesus' universal message of salvation by having the Pharisees respond that the "world has gone after him" (v. 19). Jesus' message is for all people inclusively—all people who hear and believe.

Thus the stage having been appropriately set by the first initiative of the crowd, we are privy to the second initiative found in today's gospel—the initiative of the Greeks. It is here we see that the world indeed did go out after Jesus. Greeks converged on the city to participate in the festivities surrounding the feast of Passover (also attested to by the historian Josephus). They (the Greeks) approached Philip the Galilean from the region of

[7]*RJ*, 185.

the gentiles, and told him that they wanted to see Jesus. Philip told Andrew and together they told Jesus. Once again John establishes his symbolism: gentiles are introduced to Jesus through Hellenistic Jewish disciples.[8]

Jesus responded to the Greeks in word and action. Jesus' reaction to the Greeks' request to see him was to tell Philip and Andrew that the time for his death was near. It was time for the Son of Man to be glorified. The universal kingship he prophetically proclaimed by his action of sitting on the donkey (in the first twelve verses of the chapter) was possible only after his death and subsequent glorification. The only way his mission would bear fruit is through his death. This applies not only to Christ's mission, but also to the mission of discipleship. "Whoever hates his life in this world...." *Hate* in this instance means *a higher value than.* Thus, the text would read: "Whoever places a higher value on their life in this world will preserve it for eternal life" (vv. 25–26).

John's version of the agony in the garden is found in verses 27–30 in today's pericope. John employs a common literary technique referred to as interior monologue; it is used frequently in ancient Greek literature. In the *Iliad* the interior monologue was used when a character wrestled with fear before battle or some dangerous situation. The monologue reflected an inner psychological debate. The ego, divided in two, engaged in argument. One voice of the ego argued in favor of protecting the self, the other argued to advance toward the acceptable goal. Jesus resolved his dilemma by turning to God in prayer. Jesus proceeded toward his goal because the universal mission of salvation demanded that it happen.

His humanity wrestled with the reality. Jesus' prayer was answered by a voice from heaven. God assured Jesus that his name had indeed been glorified through the signs he accomplished. God further attested that his name would be glorified again when Jesus was lifted up—not only on the cross but also to glory and exaltation at God's right hand. Observers mistook the voice for thunder. Jesus responded by assuring onlookers

that he needed no voice from heaven—the voice was for their sake. Jesus heard the voice in the very depths of his being; he needed no external sign.

Jesus insisted that if his universal mission was to proceed he must die. He must be "lifted up." *Lifted up* refers not only to the sacrifice of the cross but also to Jesus' glorification and exaltation. Two things would be accomplished through Jesus' death and resurrection. Jesus Christ, Victor, would cast out the ruler of this world as well as draw all people into his loving embrace—"the releasing of the magnetic power of divine love that pulls people to Jesus."[9] The reader is once again privy to Jesus' divine knowledge, for we are told that "this he said to show by what death he was to die" (v. 33). Jesus informed his audience that his death would be by crucifixion, not stoning.

In summary, this introductory section of chapter 12 includes an announcement of the arrival of Jesus' hour, the anticipation of his burial, his universal, peaceful mission, and the necessity for his glorification to occur if his universal kingship is to extend out toward everyone—Jews and gentiles. "Jesus approaches his death in John 12 with an emphasis on the universal outreach of his mission."[10]

Jesus freely sacrificed his life for the world. We embrace that truth almost casually. Perhaps today's liturgy invites us to go more deeply into that reality and allow it to transform the very roots of our being. Our creed and cult profess that God sent his only begotten Son to the world to give his life in ransom for the many—that God willed the death of his Son. We call Jesus' death a sacrifice. Has anyone ever asked the question, "What kind of a God would send his son to be tortured, murdered, and sacrificed in the most heinous, shame-filled fashion known to the world?" Perhaps that question demands further reflection.

The Hebrew scriptures are filled with stories of horrible atrocities. They were not committed only by pagans either. The Israelites passed through Canaan, conquering, slaughtering, and butchering the inhabitants of the land as they forged their

---

[8]Ibid., 186.

[9]Ibid., 187.
[10]Ibid., 188.

way through the promised land. Our modern-day sensibilities are rattled to the core by their annihilating behavior. *God* ordained this savagery?

After the destruction of Jericho, its mayor sacrificed his eldest son when the new city foundations were laid and his youngest son when the gates were erected. Archaeology shows the remains of children under the gates of Shechem. In order to fulfill a vow, Jephthah of Gilead sacrificed his only daughter. Children were regularly sacrificed outside the gates of Jerusalem in the Valley of Himmon.

There is a history of child sacrifice in Israel. Outside the city walls in the Valley of Himmon, on a hillside known as Topheth, there existed a sanctuary to the god, Melek. Solomon built the sanctuary when he turned to the worship of pagan gods (ca. 950 B.C.). The tradition lasted over four hundred years. People sacrificed their children in order to gain certain favors from the god or gods. The monolithic structure of the child-eating god was foreboding and massive. Its jaws wide open to accept the child sacrifice in its fiery belly (the fire created in an opening at the back of the structure), the god was a menacing, ravenous, and vengeful presence. People would gather in revelry, dancing and singing songs at the base of the structure. The child was then ripped from its mother's arms, perhaps already dead from stab wounds, but other times offered as live sacrifice. The child would then be placed in the arms of the red-hot giant and then roll into its ravenous furnace-belly. It is beyond our comprehension.

The Deuteronomist later denounced the horror: "Do not worship the Lord your God in the way they worship their gods, for in the worship of their gods they do all the disgusting things the Lord hates. They even sacrifice their children in the fires of their altars" (Dt 12:31). Later, King Ahaz continued the practice and King Manasseh after him. Jeremiah denounced the practice: "In Himmon Valley they have built an altar called Topheth, so that they can sacrifice their sons and daughters in the fire" (7:31).... "They have built altars to Baal in Himmon Valley, to sacrifice their sons and daughters to the god Molech" (32:35). King Josiah destroyed the altars in his period of reform, but Ezekiel continued to mention them fifty years later. "The abominable practice at Topheth was like an incurable disease."[11]

We might ask if the parents back then were heartless and unable to love their children. It is doubtful—what parents could not love their children? However, the pull to acquiesce was greater than their love. God is good, yet perhaps deep within the human psyche there abides a fear that God's goodness is temporary—cannot last, is too good to be true, will one day end, and the raging fire-god Melek will come to the fore to consume us. Perhaps this is what would drive God-fearing Israelites to sacrifice one of their children. Perhaps in allowing this Melek god to have one of their children, they would, in the end, spare the rest of their family. When life is good, perhaps the human subconscious becomes incredulous, and knows that the day is coming when the shoe will fall and God will make us pay a price for such happiness. Human fear of this sort is no doubt not without precedence in the experience of most religious people. "Why did God cause this pain and suffering?" We have all heard this comment in one form or another. Fear of that sort has the potential to be contagious and collective. It was certainly a driving force in Israel. "It was a fear that naturally arose from paternalistic authority structures and from the ancient covenant's stress on curse and punishment. The god Melek, that cruel brass monster that stretched out its arms to grab children and swallow them in its fiery belly—what else is it but an archetype of the hardness projected onto God."[12]

Yet we know God is not an exacting, vengeful, child-eating God. He hated human sacrifice. Prophets constantly screamed to the people about God's disdain for such atrocities. "Do not sacrifice your children in the fires on your altars.... The Lord your God hates people who do these disgusting things" (Dt 18:10, 12). "They have built altars for Baal in order to burn their children in the fire as sacrifices. I never commanded them to do this; it never even entered my mind" (Jer 19:5). "If anyone gives one of his children to Molech and makes my sacred Tent unclean and disgraces my holy name, I will turn against him and will no

---

[11] *IMC*, 23.
[12] Ibid., 24.

longer consider him one of my people" (Lv 20:3). To misinterpret God's opinion of this horror is stupidity of the highest order. Yet they persisted. Human sacrifice was an abomination—it defiled God's holy name and holy place. God never had the intention in his mind—*never!* Thus, the genesis of child sacrifice (human sacrifice) rests within the human person, not from God, but from distorted thinking and a distorted notion of God's will.

Perhaps in the human subconscious this archetypal fear of God is so strong that only healing of divine proportions is able to overcome it. Perhaps human fear projects upon God experiences of suffering and loss, the cruelty and vindictiveness that are experienced in this world. Even theologians and theology have been guilty at times of developing an understanding of salvation that is nothing more than "a baptized version of the Melek doctrine."[13] The theology reads something like this: human beings sinned. God wanted to redeem human beings from sin, but since God's sense of justice is so strong, it had to be satisfied before redemption could occur. "In other words, God could not simply forgive sins through an act of mercy; satisfaction had to be offered to his justice."[14] God therefore decided to send his Son to die a horrible, violent death in order to pay the price for all people, thereby avenging God's justice. Having satisfied God's vengeance, only then could God forgive sinners and welcome them as his children.

Origins of this doctrine began in the Middle Ages. The word *justice* was misunderstood. St. Paul understood justice to mean "to make holy." Middle Age theology misinterpreted the word and understood it in a juridical sense. It also misinterpreted the concept of vicarious suffering as expressed in Deutero-Isaiah (the basis of interpreting the suffering of Jesus). There was a gross misunderstanding regarding the belief that God willed the death of Jesus. This misunderstanding (which asserted that God willed Jesus' death to satisfy his justice) was probably the result of a misinterpretation of Peter saying that Jesus had to "pay the price" (1 Pt 1:18–19). This misdirected doctrine reflected a Melek-type understanding of God. It sometimes

creeps into our consciousness and surfaces when we reflect on the mystery of suffering. Jesus was not sacrificed to avenge a child-sacrificing, justice-seeking God.

Theology just described defies what we know about God from scripture. Scripture is emphatic—human sacrifice does not give God satisfaction. Three times Jeremiah tells us that it never entered God's mind. "How could we expect God the Father to do to his beloved Son what he abhorred in the parents of Israel? Secondly, redemption would become a deal instead of being a free act of mercy."[15] The point of Jesus' act of redemption is that it was a completely free, gratuitous gift of God. In no way can human beings merit or win it. It cannot be "earned," nor was it based on some notion of "payback." If Jesus' death was the wage paid to God to satisfy his anger, then the resurrection would be pointless. Yet we know from St. Paul that without the resurrection our faith is delusional and we are still lost to our sinful natures (1 Cor 15:17).

John Winjgaarden invites us to take a closer look at our understanding of redemption.[16] Jesus, Word of God and God's only begotten Son, became a human person. Since Jesus had seen God, he brought grace and truth to the human race. Jesus revealed God. All who believed in Jesus were given the privilege of becoming God's children. Jesus saved us by the free gift of his life.

Thus we ask, "What about Jesus' death and resurrection?" Jesus' torture and death was a crime. It was murder. He was an innocent man. Jesus himself denounced it as a sin. How could that, in and of itself, be willed by God? How could God will such an evil action—against his Son, no less? He did not will it, not directly. What is meant, then, by all the scriptural references to the contrary? Perhaps the answer lies in understanding just what it was that God willed.

God sent his Son to be one with the human race, to save humanity and to show the world just how much he loves them. Human beings would never have believed in God's love had God not sent his Son. We could say, "You say you love us, but what

---

[13]Ibid.
[14]Ibid.

[15]Ibid., 26.
[16]Ibid.

do you know? You have not walked in our shoes. You do not know what it is like to live in this world—to endure suffering, hatred, and misery." Human beings would never have truly believed God's love or God's compassion. The only way we would ever truly enter into the mystery of that awesome, compassionate love would be if God were to send a portion of himself, God's very own child, to live among us and to endure what human beings must endure. Then and only then would we listen—actions, particularly self-sacrificing, love-centered actions speak louder than words.

Jesus was true to his mission. He lived a consistent righteous life. He stood with the poor, the outcast, and his disciples—all who listened to him—and he stood with them to the bitter end. He was a danger to those who had a vested interest in maintaining the social and religious status quo of his day. Jesus would not hide from the consequences of his faithfulness. He loved and accepted each person equally. Imagine how that set with those who believed they were somehow exalted at birth and were far more deserving of God's love and acceptance? Jesus was fearless—he minced no words; he challenged those who refused to love.

Jesus was a shepherd who cared for his sheep and who invited new sheep into his fold. He would never run or hide from the dangers involved in protecting and safeguarding them. If need be, he would die for his sheep. He could do no less than die for them, so great was his love. He was ready to do what was necessary to save his sheep, to care for them and to protect them, even if it meant giving his life. He was always ready to die for them. This is what was pleasing to God—Jesus' inner disposition of faithfulness and love and his *willingness* to die for his sheep. Today's gospel affirms Jesus' willingness to die. This is what God willed—love so deep that he was willing to sacrifice his own life for it. In this way Jesus was able to reveal the love that God has for all of us—a love that is willing to go to any length, even humiliating lengths, lengths unto death.

Jesus' death was a result of sin, hatred, prejudice, animosities, jealousies, fear, pride, and power, yet in his death he expressed the highest form of human love. The greatest expression of human love is found in the offering of one's life for another. This incredible sacrifice of love was chosen by God as the ultimate act of redemption for the human race. Jesus, the new Passover sacrifice, liberated the human race from sin. Jesus' resurrection initiated us into life in the Spirit of God.

The early Christians appropriated the "Song of the Suffering Servant" in Isaiah to explain the meaning of Jesus' death and resurrection. Jesus, like the Suffering Servant, was an innocent man who suffered immense pain and sorrow. The Suffering Servant was special because in the midst of his suffering he lived and prayed for others. Jesus' incredible gift of intercession, prayer, and life was used by God as a means to offer forgiveness to the human race.

But is it not our understanding that Jesus' suffering was preordained by God? During Jesus' agony in the garden we hear Jesus say that he accepted his suffering willingly in obedience to his Father.

> Thus, the Father wanted Jesus to die in order to make his death the sacrifice for all. Yes, it was the Father's will, and yet, it wasn't! How is this explained? It was not the Father's will in the sense that he wanted that death itself, as something determined by his absolute will. As we have seen, he could not want it like that because it involved a sin. And God cannot contradict himself by wanting an evil thing. But when the option of death faced Jesus as a consequence of being faithful to his mission, then the Father wanted it. Because he wanted Jesus to be faithful.[17]

Today's gospel insists that Jesus willingly took up his life. Jesus saved us by his life, witness, mission, death, and resurrection—by his entire life. His rising is as important as his dying. He invites us to participate in both his death and his resurrection. His death was a sacrifice of reconciliation. Just as his life was a mission of reconciliation, so was his death and resurrection. Jesus' entire mission was one of invitation. Jesus not only invited people to become part of God's family, he restored them to relationship with God and with the community. Jesus, the grain of wheat that falls to the earth and dies, did indeed produce much fruit—and that fruit is the abundance of love. By his death Jesus

---

[17]Ibid., 28.

"becomes the standing tree from which everyone can receive the fruit of life. What an extraordinary abundance!"[18] From the fruit of this tree people would be fed for generations to come.

If all this is true, then how are we to understand the story of Abraham and his mission to sacrifice his son Isaac at the behest of God? Abraham was prepared to do whatever God asked of him. Imagine Abraham's frustration. Kill Isaac? What a contradiction! God had already promised numerous offspring through Isaac. What could it mean? Could Abraham have wondered if Melek was rearing his ugly archetypal head? God is not Melek and he insisted that Abraham not lay a hand on his son. "However, God does appreciate the willingness to give what he will never demand: 'You have not kept back your only son from me' (Gn. 22:12). What seemed a contradiction, loving his son and loving God at the same time, proves not to be contradictory at all."[19]

God wept tears of thunderous anguish over the death of his Son. God allowed it to proceed because of the greatest potential in salvation history to allow love to speak a definitive, life-giving word. How else would we ever truly believe just how much we are loved by a God who did not hold back the death of his only treasured, precious, beloved Son? "This is not a cruel God demanding satisfaction. It is a loving Father who revealed to us, through the love of his Son, that he is pure love."[20]

John's version of Jesus' transfiguration takes place at the cross. It is on the eve of his Passion and death that the voice from heaven is heard. God will be glorified through Jesus' supreme act of love on the cross. God's glory will continue to be revealed through the disciples and their faithfulness to Christ's mission.

> "If hope has made you walk
> farther than fear,
> you will raise your eyes.
> Then you will be able to hold firm
> until you reach the sun of God.

---

[18]*DL* (II), 159.
[19]*IMC*, 30.
[20]Ibid.

> If anger caused you to clamor for justice for
> all,
> your heart will be wounded.
> Then you will be able to struggle
> along with the oppressed.

> If weakness made you fall along the way,
> you will know how to open your arms.
> Then you will be able to dance
> to the rhythm of forgiveness.

> If destitution made you search in the hungry
> night,
> you will have an open heart.
> Then you will be able to give
> the bread of poverty.

> If suffering made you shed tears of blood,
> you will have cleansed eyes.
> Then you will be able to pray
> with your brother on the cross.

> If sadness has made you doubt
> on one evening you felt abandoned,
> you will know how to carry your cross.
> Then you will be able to die
> in step with the God-Man."[21]

Proclaim the gospel again

Sometimes we gain new insights when we hear the text after the interpretation is given. Someone from the group proclaims the gospel a second time.

STEP 4
TESTING

Conversation with the Liturgy and the Scriptures

Test your original understanding in dialogue with the text.

(You might consider breaking into smaller groups.)

Now that you've heard the exegesis, were there any new insights? How do you feel about it? How does your original understanding of this gospel

---

[21]J. Akepsimas and M. Scouarnec, *Des mots et es notes pour c'el'ebrer*, 99 (Fiche de chant G 213), in *DL* (II), 151.

compare with what we just shared? How does this story speak to your life?

Sharing Life Experience

Participants share an experience from their lives that connects with the biblical interpretation just presented.

Today's liturgy reminds me of a woman in our initiation process who recently was received into full communion in the Catholic Church. I have come to treasure her as pure gift from God in our midst. This woman is an example of the redemptive, self-sacrificing love of Christ evidenced in today's gospel. She has been extremely touched by God's love for her, particularly a love that sustained her through some very difficult, lonely times. She is humbled by the unconditional love of a God who has loved her throughout her life, even though there were many times she fell short of what she believed God wanted of her and for her. Her search for a deeper, more intimate relationship with God brought her to our doors. She lived her faith in the context of another ecclesial communion. She had a lively faith and Christ was a living reality for her, but she felt she was missing a connection to his historical reality. So she began her search. She went to the library and her search took her to the patristic Fathers. She knew she had found a home in the Catholic Church. She was ready to live out the rest of her faith life as a Catholic. Even though she was in our process for only a few short weeks, she became a gift to us.

She discovered the Christ of history who is present to us in community, in Word, and in sacrament. She entered into the paschal mystery as never before in her life. She was awed by the fact that Christ died and rose again for us and she insisted that she could do no less than join the sorrows and joys of her life to the pasch of Christ.

This beautiful woman decided that since she had been given so much love by the risen Christ, she simply had to respond in kind. Even though she is not a young woman, one of the ways she has responded to God's love is through the foster parent program. One day she was asked to take care of two special little children. She sensed that this was somehow different than the other times. Indeed it was. The week before she completed her initiation, the adoption of these two very precious gifts of God (ages 2 and 5) became assured. The day she made her profession of faith we

also celebrated the baptism of her two newly adopted, special needs children.

These children had been abused by their parents. The youngest, a two-year-old, was completely blind due to shaking baby syndrome. She has no concept of night and day and therefore is awake most of the night. The children consume all her time and energy. She spends every waking minute meeting the needs of these very active children. She falls wearily into bed each night, thankful that the living God gave her two precious children in need of her unconditional love. She knows the road ahead for her new little family will be challenging. She does not see her action as anything but pure resurrection joy. That she could help deliver those children out of their hell and offer them love, compassion, and a new home, is simply an opportunity for her to extend the love Christ has given to her. She willingly, openly, and eagerly gives every part of herself to care for her new children. She can do no less. In the day-to-day struggles she faces, she gives her life energy for them. I am awed by her spirit and the complete trust she has that God will provide all she needs—even the energy it takes to meet their pressing concerns. This is what it means to participate in the life, death, and resurrection of Christ. This woman of God has embraced the love of Christ and allowed it to bear much fruit in her own life and in so doing touched the lives of two very wounded young people of God. She is a symbol of discipleship and a reminder of what we are all called to do—to live with paschal faith and paschal love.

What was John's message to his community? In what way can you relate to Christ's parable of the seed? In what way have you been called upon to die and subsequently to bear much fruit? In what way have you, like Christ, willingly offered your life for others? In what way are there hints and vestiges of the ancient Melek syndrome lurking in your subconscious? How might our communities today relate to the crowd in John's gospel and their need for a nationalistic liberator? Do our communities and/or the world ever entertain false expectations of God? In what way does this gospel challenge your community today? In what way has this conversation with the scriptures for today's liturgy invited change in your life? In what way are the biblical themes of covenant, exodus, creation, and community evident in today's readings? Do you still feel the same way about this text as when you began? Has your original understanding been stretched, challenged, or affirmed?

STEP 5
DECISION

The gospel demands a response.

In what concrete way might your parish be invited to respond? Are there any attitudes or behaviors you would like to change as a result of today's conversation? What one concrete action will you take this week in response to the liturgy today?

Christian Initiation: Today the elect celebrate the third scrutiny. Even though the Cycle A readings are to be used at all the liturgies on the Sundays in which the scrutinies are celebrated, parishes sometimes do not follow that practice. It would therefore be important to address the fact that the scrutinies are being celebrated at another liturgy and what that means to the elect as well as the faithful. Refer to the third, fourth, and fifth Sundays of Lent Cycle A for further information regarding scrutinies. Catechumens who will not be baptized at the Easter Vigil continue to be dismissed from the Sunday liturgy and participate in extended catechesis.

Perhaps baptized candidates who will enter into full communion with the Catholic Church during the Easter season might be prepared to celebrate the sacrament of reconciliation at the parish's Lenten celebration of the sacrament of penance. Perhaps the elect might join in the preparation so they can celebrate the sacrament following their initiation. Perhaps a nonsacramental penitential celebration might be celebrated with catechumens still in process.

DOCTRINAL ISSUES

What Church truth/teaching/doctrinal issue could be drawn from the gospel for the fifth Sunday of Lent?

Participants suggest possible doctrinal themes that flow from the readings.

Possible Doctrinal Themes

Paschal mystery; cross; mystery of suffering; Christology; redemption; soteriology; salvation; conversion; faith, hope, and love; discipleship

Present the doctrinal material at this time.

1. The facilitator gives input on a particular doctrinal issue of his or her prior choosing. OR
2. The group chooses a doctrinal issue from the list they created. They read together from the Doctrinal Appendix or other appropriate, official Church documents and the works of respected theologians.

(Many doctrinal issues are found in the Doctrinal Appendix at the back of this workbook. If you are choosing an issue from this resource, please refer to it now.)

Reflection questions centered around the chosen doctrinal theme can be found at the end of each topic in the Doctrinal Appendix. The questions are based on the five-step reflection process. If you choose a topic not included in the Doctrinal Appendix, craft your own questions according to the same five-step process.

Following the reflection questions you will be reminded to return to chapter 7, "Preparing the Catechetical Session," to assist you in crafting your own session.

Closing Prayer

Father, all powerful and ever-living God,
we do well always and everywhere to give you
    thanks.
This season of grace is your gift to your family
to renew us in spirit.
You give us strength to purify our hearts,
to control our desires,
and so to serve you in freedom.
You teach us how to live in this passing world
with our heart set on the world that will never
    end.
Now, with all the saints and angels,
we praise you for ever.[22]

---

[22] "Preface for Lent II" (P9), *The Sacramentary.*

FIFTH SUNDAY OF LENT (CYCLE A)

INTRODUCTORY RITES

Opening Song (or Entrance Antiphon)

Give me justice, O God, and defend my cause against the wicked; rescue me from deceitful and unjust men. You, O God, are my refuge. (Ps 42: 1–2)[1]

Opening Prayer

The facilitator of the session may lead the prayer. Others in the group may be asked to proclaim the readings.

Let us pray
[for the courage to embrace the
world in the name of Christ]

Pause for silent prayer.

Father in heaven,
the love of your Son led him to accept
the suffering of the cross
that his brothers might glory in new life.
Change our selfishness into self-giving.
Help us to embrace the world you have given
    us,
that we may transform the darkness of its pain
into the life and joy of Easter.
Grant this through Christ our Lord.[2]

LITURGY OF THE WORD

Let us listen to God's word.

The readings are proclaimed.

First Reading
Ezekiel 37:12–14

The book of Ezekiel is a message of judgment and a message of hope. Ezekiel is considered third in a line of the great writing prophets: Isaiah, Jeremiah, Ezekiel. Ezekiel was a priest and a prophet who was deported to Babylon along with the other inhabitants of Judah (ca. 597–538 B.C.E.). The prophetic ministry of Ezekiel was a testament to the awesome faithfulness and power of Yahweh. Only Yahweh possessed the power to bring life out of the ashes of despair and failure. Israel understood her tribulation and exile as punishment for her sinfulness. The people of Israel believed that God had punished their disobedience and unfaithfulness by inflicting political disaster. The exile was God's divine retribution and only God could breathe life into their hopeless situation. Ezekiel boldly asserted that even though the signs of God's covenant with Israel (promised land, temple, Davidic monarchy) appeared to be dead and gone, Yahweh was still sovereign and in control of their history.

The exile plays a great role in the corporate memory of this people; it is remembered as Israel's time of tribulation. Yahweh punished Israel for her sins. Yet, in spite of Israel's unfaithfulness, Yahweh was steadfast in his love for her. He never broke the covenant, but rather, in his power and love, stood with her to deliver her in her great time of distress.

Ezekiel vehemently professed God to be the sole agent in Israel's liberation. God spoke the word and caused it to be, so that all would know: "I am the Lord." Ezekiel puts these words in the mouth of the Great Author of Life at least eighty-six times throughout the book.

The great age of Israel had collapsed. The people were forced into an alien land (Babylon) without the support of their religious structures to sustain them in the midst of their ordeal. Ezekiel was a revolutionary. He demanded that Israel engage in reform that would see them through their faith-shattering trials.

Ezekiel forged a bold, new path in prophecy. His language and style were unlike those of any prophet before him. The literary text reads like an

---

[1]Fifth Sunday of Lent: "Entrance Antiphon," *The Sacramentary.*

[2]Fifth Sunday of Lent: "Alternative Opening Prayer," *The Sacramentary.*

oratory which suggests that an oral tradition preceded its writing. Ezekiel's message was clear: trust Yahweh, return to the corporate memory and celebration of God's previous saving actions. Worship and observe the law, and faith will be strengthened. Since Ezekiel stressed the Torah as central to his message, he is often called the "father of modern Judaism."

Today's pericope is concerned with the restoration of Israel. Ezekiel assured his audience that the covenant with Israel was still operative (ch. 37). Ezekiel received two visions: one vision was Israel—dead, lifeless, dry bones. In Ezekiel's vision, Yahweh literally breathed life into the dead bones and they were restored to life (37:1–14). The hopeless Israel was given hope and promise for future restoration. Ezekiel's second vision was the convergence of the twelve tribes into one people.

Ezekiel's vision was a summary of his ministry to those in exile: the dead Israel would be restored by the divine breath, wind, spirit (*ruah*) of God. Ezekiel's vision in today's pericope was not intended as a commentary on the resurrection of individuals from the dead.

Ezekiel's vision left nothing to the imagination: death presided over the bone-littered plain. Yahweh and Yahweh alone must intervene if the tables were to turn and if life was to be restored into Israel's breathless corpse.

Responsorial Psalm
Psalm 130

Today's psalm, one of the seven penitential psalms, is an individual lament. The psalmist pleads for deliverance from distress.

Second Reading
Romans 8: 8–11

Paul's letter to the Romans typifies a refined, systematic articulation of Pauline theology. It is considered his greatest theological masterpiece.

Paul insists that God freely *forgives and forgets* people's sins; they are not held against them. Each sinner is welcomed into God's loving arms as a parent would forgive a precious, wayward child. The child is treated as if she or he had never

strayed in the first place. The law can never replace the peace, freedom, and relief that only God can give. With the law, human beings work out their own salvation. With Christ, it is already won for those who accept it. Prior to Christ, the law had been a necessary guide. But now, the guide is Christ. We are set free from sin by Jesus' saving action. Jesus' death/resurrection opened the way for the Spirit to reign in the hearts of humankind.

Paul offers us the greatest gift: to see ourselves as God sees us—loved and forgiven. The law does not give us freedom; only Christ gives us freedom. This does not mean that we are no longer bound to an ethical code. Law will always serve as a reminder of our obligations and responsibilities to God, the world, other people, and ourselves. Paul insists that the law does not "capture the will of God."[3] Jesus did not come to create a new set of rigid codes that would replace the old set of rigid codes. Jesus did not denigrate the law; he simply wished to restore its heart.

Jesus came to *show us how to live*. Discipleship consists in living in the pattern of Christ—doing what he did. Thus, Christians are freed from rigid observance of the law. They are, instead, guided by a new motivator—the Spirit of God. When led by the Spirit, Christians participate in a mature, love-based faith. It is a faith based on biblical justice (*hesed*): a reciprocal, covenant relationship with God that is active, alive, and produces every good action because of the demands of love. Loving God with heart, mind, and soul is synonymous with extending that same love to all of God's creation. It is a higher law—one that is not self-determined, but rather Spirit-provoked.

Human nature is flawed because of the sinful, human condition—no one is exempt. However, we must never forget the power and affirmation of our Genesis origins: God created men and women in God's image and saw that "it was good." Thus, we have the ultimate disposition and created potential to be elevated to the divine status that has been our birthright since the beginning of the world. Yet we are nevertheless born into a sinful world and are thus subject to sin. It is sim-

---

[3] *GAP*, 97.

ply (or not so simply) the way it is. We are human beings and so we are sinners. The indwelling of the Spirit prompts, nudges, and leads us, ever so gently—and sometimes not so gently—toward the created grace that is our destiny. The Spirit gives human beings the possibility of being free from sin. Humanity is to cooperate with the work of creation taking place within each of us. It is not automatic. The Spirit provides the yeast and, out of love, we become what the flour was destined to become: one complete loaf, ready to be broken and shared.

We are new creations in Christ to the extent that we cooperate with the generating work of the Spirit within us. When we live the cycle of death and resurrection and when we lay down our lives for others, we become that which we were created to be. "Paul shows how theology and morality are intimately connected. When we speak of 'Christian being,' we are led to discern what is 'Christian acting.'"[4]

Gospel
John 11:1–45

Jesus raises Lazarus from the dead.

STEP 1
NAMING ONE'S EXPERIENCE

What were your first impressions? What was your first response? What grabbed your attention? How did you feel?

Each person names his or her initial impression. Statements should be brief. No reasons should be given at this time. All simply listen without agreeing or disagreeing.

STEP 2
UNDERSTANDING

In a brief statement, what do you think this gospel is trying to convey?

---

[4]*DL* (II), 129.

STEP 3
INPUT FROM VISION/STORY/TRADITION

Liturgical Context

The raising of Lazarus is Jesus' last sign to the world before his impending passion. These are signs because they not only reveal Yahweh, the Almighty, Powerful Creator, but they point to the One who performed the sign, Jesus, the Christ. The signs of Jesus call people to radical faith.

This story is a prelude to the cross. It leads the way; it shows us the meaning of Jesus' coming passion. Lazarus was raised from the dead for a brief respite; Jesus was raised forever. Through Jesus' death and resurrection we all share in the Lazarus sign. The raising of Lazarus prompts every believer to answer the ultimate question: "Do you believe that I am the resurrection and the life?"

Most of John's signs are accompanied by an explanation of the event, except in this instance. This gospel reads more like an unfolding liturgy with a "certain number of declarations made as the action develops. . . . 'This illness does not end in death, but is for the glory of God, that the Son of Man might be glorified through it' . . . 'Lazarus has died. And I am glad for you that I was not there, that you may believe' . . . This sort of composition has been likened to the words of a commentator explaining the unfolding of a liturgy,[5] arousing the attention, spurring the curiosity, and provoking the reflection of the assembly."[6] The declarations made in today's unfolding liturgy prompt assemblies ancient and contemporary to answer the question: "Do you believe in Jesus, the Christ, the One who raised Lazarus from the dead, and the One who can and will raise us from the death of our sinful lives?"

In this liturgy, the elect who are preparing to plunge into the baptismal waters leading to new life stand in the face of impending death and with the entire assembly proclaim with Lazarus,

---

[5]This image is attributed to M. Moret, *Assemblèes du Seigneur,* 2nd series, No 18 (Paris: Publications de Saint-André—Cerf, 1971), 22. In *DL* (II), 131.
[6]Ibid.

Martha, Mary, well wishers, and previous nay-sayers, "Yes, Lord, we do believe that you are the resurrection and the life."

Sin and death reigned in the world. Jesus shattered the choke-hold that death asserted over the neck of a powerless people. Lazarus is a sign and an explanation of the paschal event, of Jesus, the Resurrection and the Life.

The first and second readings attest to God's life-force in the world, the Holy Spirit. Through the power of the indwelling Spirit, we are left a living legacy that entails ongoing participation in the same resurrected life Lazarus was given. In the opening prayer of the Fifth Sunday of Lent, we ask to be inspired and guided by Christ's love and example. In the alternative opening prayer we are reminded of Christ's passion. We ask for the strength to embrace the cross, to work for the transformation of the world, and to be delivered from darkness that blinds us to sin and keeps us from the joy of Easter.

Today the elect celebrate the third and last scrutiny, one of the last steps before they enter into the Lord's ongoing *pasch*—the eucharistic banquet. The elect, with the entire church, celebrate Christ's victory over the systemic evil that keeps people lifeless, like dry, brittle, dead bones rotting in a worldly grave of death and despair. In the celebration of the third scrutiny we pray that the elect be "liberated from the shackles of sin that they may become like Christ by baptism, dead to sin and alive forever in God's sight" and "that they be filled with the hope of the life-giving Spirit and prepare themselves thoroughly for their birth to new life..." so the "eucharistic food, which they are soon to receive, may make them one with Christ, the source of life and of resurrection."[7] We thus pray to the Lord—for them and for ourselves.

The third scrutiny on this Fifth Sunday leads us to the premier moment in our liturgical life—the Triduum, the Easter pasch. We are poured out like a libation, ready for Easter filling.

Today brings us to the threshold of Holy Week. Stripped bare of our illusions, confronted with our blindness and insincere motives, the faithful and the elect prepare to enter the tomb of Christ's death and resurrection. We enter the darkened womb of this Holy Week enlightened by Christ who is the "water for which we thirst," the "light of our blindness" and our very "life's breath." We wait to be born anew in the dawn of Easter light. We will then go forth renewed, refreshed, and committed to live the *pasch* until, once again depleted, we will return next year to begin the paschal cycle once again.

Presentation of the Lord's Prayer

The presentation of the Lord's Prayer generally takes place during the week following the third scrutiny, "preferably in the presence of a community of the faithful, within Mass" (RCIA, #178). The Lord's Prayer has always been the prayer "proper to those who in baptism have received the spirit of adoption" (RCIA, #148). The Lord's Prayer gives the elect a better appreciation of God as their Father and thus prepares them to stand in the midst of the celebrating assembly and pray this prayer with confidence. At their baptism they will stand for the first time with the assembly and proclaim this foundational prayer. The creed and the Lord's Prayer have always been considered central to the Christian faith and prayer. The RCIA does allow the presentation of the Lord's Prayer to be deferred until the preparation rites for Holy Saturday.

Gospel Exegesis

The facilitator gives input regarding what critical biblical scholarship has to say about this text. The input includes insights as to how people would have heard the gospel in Jesus' time.

A few verses before this pericope begins, John tells us that "many came to believe in him." This is an excellent springboard for understanding the purpose of the Lazarus sign. Many came to believe in Jesus. Therefore, there was now urgency on the part of the chief priests to put Jesus to death. The stakes were higher. Jesus was having an influence on the people and they were becoming his disciples. Prior to this time, Jesus had had less impact on the Jewish community. People had been rejecting his message and fighting among themselves. Now things were changing, and many Jews were coming

---

[7] *RCIA*, #174.

to believe in him. Peter Ellis suggests that John may have been mirroring what was taking place in the Johannine community "in the divisions among the people and in the animosity of the Jewish leaders toward those who wanted to accept Jesus and abandon the synagogue" (9:22 and 16:2).[8]

Jesus' greatest "sign," the raising of Lazarus from the dead, leads to the decisive act of unbelief, the formal decision that Jesus must "die for the people" (11:1–57).[9] Thus, the plot thickens and the collaboration of the religious leaders to have Jesus put to death begins. The Lazarus event is the catalyst for their decision to put the plans for his execution into motion.

The miracle stories in chapters 5 and 9 highlight the growing tension between Jesus and the religious authorities and set up this final event. Jesus healed the paralytic in a few short verses and then engaged in a debate with the Pharisees over curing on the Sabbath. Jesus healed the blind man in a brief narrative, and in the rest of the dialogue confronted the blindness of his interrogators. Thus, the miracle signs of chapters 5 and 9 were recounted not only to attest to Jesus' miraculous power to heal (while they indeed served that function), but also as a means of illustrating the judgment Jesus was hurling at the religious establishment.

The evangelist crafted his story around the premise that Jesus' *signs*, especially the gift of life, were gifts from the Father. Ellis believes that, in this instance, the miracle is the point of the story; it demonstrates Jesus' power to raise the dead and offer eternal life.[10] Jesus waited until the fourth day before he went to the side of his grieving friends. At first glance, Jesus' delay seems callous. Perhaps first-century listeners would have thought it more than callous; they may have thought it downright cruel. They would have known without question that by the fourth day Lazarus would have been as dead as those dry, rotted, brittle bones that were littered across Ezekiel's plain. Prior to the fourth day, there might have been hope. "Rabbinical tradition taught that the life breath hovered around the body for three days.

After that, all hopes for resuscitation were pointless."[11] Why would Jesus wait so long to go to his dying friend?

By making sure that the reader and the witnesses were fully aware that Lazarus was totally, irrevocably dead, John skillfully crafted the point of the miracle. All hope was lost. There was nothing anyone could do. Like the dead bones in the first reading, only God could breathe life into the situation. It was beyond human imagination and control. ". . . For the Johannine Jesus, the impossible is merely a matter of routine."[12] Jesus' miracle, by his own confession, was to bring people to faith and to reveal and glorify God.

John always refers to life in the eternal sense. Whether human beings are offered the gift of eternal life or not, everyone is subject to the body's mortality. Just as Lazarus was raised to life for a short while only to later die a natural death, so too, are people subject to the same mortality. "As mortal human beings they face the fact of death; but as believers in the Son who possesses the gift of eternal life, here and now, they can confidently look forward to their own resurrection from the dead. Of course, you have to die before you can rise from the dead never to die again; else, the resurrection would merely be a resuscitation."[13] Yet, amidst this mysterious, awe-inspiring gift, there is a lurking dark cloud: the gift of life is also cause for people to maliciously turn against Jesus.

Jesus went to Bethany because of the news of his friend Lazarus' death. Jesus confirmed that the illness would not result in death, but would be for the glory of God. Jesus stayed where he was for two more days in spite of the anxiety and grief of his friends. In typical Johannine style, Jesus' action was a sign that the miracle was going to be at God's initiative, not because of human pressures. "The illness and Jesus' behavior were under divine control."[14]

Pharisees believed in life after death and Martha professed that belief. Jesus asserted that he was the realization of that foundational belief—"I am

[8] *GJ*, 181.
[9] Pheme Perkins, "John," in *NJBC*, 969.
[10] *GJ*, 181.

[11] *WWC*, 29.
[12] Ibid.
[13] *TGJ*, 187.
[14] *RJ*, 172.

the Resurrection and the Life." He was making eternal life possible through the gift of his life.

Jesus arrived at the tomb of Lazarus and wept. Charles Talbert suggests that John was portraying Jesus as a human figure who felt the deepest grief over the loss of a friend, the same grief he experienced over his own impending death and the same grief he experienced knowing that he would be betrayed by a disciple (12:27, 13:21). However, Jesus' weeping is contrasted to the weeping of Mary and the other mourners. Jesus wept sincere tears of sorrow, but did not wail like the other mourners. Wailing was an expression of despair. "Profound grief at such bereavement is natural enough; grief that degenerates into despair, that pours out its loss as if there were no resurrection, is an implicit denial of that resurrection."[15]

However, other scholars suggest a different interpretation of Jesus' emotion at the death of Lazarus. Jesus' weeping does not make much sense if he was aware that he was going to raise Lazarus from the dead. The Greek word *embrimasthai* suggests strong emotion. However, some scholars assert that Jesus' deep emotion is related to his justified anger "at the powers of darkness and evil with whom Jesus is about to do battle. In this emotion and the act which followed it, Jesus' victory over illness, darkness, sin, death and evil is complete and absolute."[16]

Jesus prayed a prayer of thanksgiving over the tomb of Lazarus. It was prayer rooted in ongoing intimacy with his Father. "It is not a prayer of petition, but rather for the purpose of indicating to those assembled his own close relationship with the Father."[17] Jesus' prayer demonstrated that the power he needed depended on God's gift. Jesus summoned Lazarus from the grave and gave the instruction to unbind him from his funeral wrappings. Thus, Jesus, who was called Lord throughout this gospel, completed the revival of the dead man, thereby asserting his sovereignty and authority.[18]

The reaction is two-fold: some believed through the sign he performed; others conspired to have him executed (see later verses). Jesus was a threat to the institutional and national Jewish identity. John the Baptist was killed because Herod feared a political uprising of John's followers. The Jewish leaders feared that the hard hand of government would come crashing down on their "holy place" and their "nation" as a result of Jesus' ministry. It would appear as if John was suggesting that the leaders were acting in order to protect the lives and worship of the Jewish community.

Richard Cassidy supports D. A. Carson's position that there were no such noble intentions. When Caiaphas stated that it would be better for one man to die for the many, he was in effect indicting himself and his co-conspirators. What Caiaphas really meant was that it would be better for the one man (Jesus) to die to protect Caiaphas and the Sanhedrin. They were the ones who stood to lose the most because of Jesus' alleged insurrection activities. The Romans might be angered enough to take away what little political, legal, and religious control the Sanhedrin enjoyed. Caiaphas uttered the prophetic oracle that Jesus would die for the whole nation so they would not perish. Indeed, Jesus did die to save all nations—past, present, and yet to come. There is a brilliant piece of irony in this segment. John has Caiaphas utter the prophetic meaning of Jesus' death and yet, from Caiaphas's point of view, he was merely positing the *party line* the Sanhedrin would assume when explaining their intentions to have Jesus killed. Caiaphas was rehearsing for the Sanhedrin what their response might be: "We were simply protecting the nation from Roman intervention and subsequent calamity. If we do not have him killed, the very fiber of our identity, our temple worship, may be threatened."[19]

Chapters 10 and 11 seek to show Jesus as the fulfillment of the Feast of Dedication because of the *signs* he performed. In this way, John's Jesus was authenticating the new worship emerging in the Christian community. This worship would supersede the traditional forms of Israel's worship, such as: temple sacrifices, purification rituals, temple worship on Gerazim or Jerusalem (see Samaritan woman), the water rituals that promise healing of

[15] *GAJ*, 416.
[16] *WWC*, 29.
[17] *JGNP*, 37.
[18] Ibid.

[19] Ibid., 43, 107, #8.

the body, the feasts of Passover, Tabernacles, and Dedication. The new rituals were seen as the fulfillment of the old.

According to Charles Talbert, in John's gospel, the *disbelief of the people* motif served as a fulfillment of the biblical prophecies such as: "He has blinded their eyes and hardened their heart, lest they should see with their eyes and turn to me to heal them" (Is. 6:10). While human responsibility is not negated in John's gospel, divine sovereignty is a major theme. Thus, God is the architect (planner) of salvation history. Faith is a gift from God generated by divine initiative. Governments are also under the control of God. John maintains that even though God initiates and directs history, human beings are still responsible for their decisions. Those who did not believe in Jesus were responsible for their actions, but these actions were also part of God's plan.[20]

If we make wrong decisions, the implications for our lives are disastrous. We might find ourselves standing with the Sanhedrin in opposition to the saving love of God. Perhaps we will choose our own self interests of power and control while fooling ourselves and others into believing it is for the good of others. Or worse, we may try to stand in the way of God's gift of life by discouraging people in their quest for Jesus Christ, whether by our actions, attitudes or speech, conscious or unconscious. In other words, we have the freedom to choose death over life.

However, life is far more attractive. Jesus offers us life, fulfillment, and joy. We profess and celebrate the gift of life given to us through his paschal mystery. We accept Jesus as Lord of the hopeless, Lord of sinners, and Lord of history. We are heirs to eternal life because of Jesus' saving action and we accept his radical, unconditional love and truth with eyes of faith. Thus, fear loses its control over us. Nevertheless, the ball remains in our court; we are still left with a decision.

Jesus embraced hopelessness and became hope for the world. Jesus became sin and in the process delivered the world. Jesus delivered us from the snares of death and offered us resurrection and eternal life.

_____
[20]*RJ*, 173, 174.

Proclaim the gospel again.

Sometimes we gain new insights when we hear the text after the interpretation has been given. Someone from the group proclaims the gospel a second time.

STEP 4:
TESTING

Conversation with the Liturgy and the Scriptures

Test your original understanding in dialogue with the text.

(You might consider breaking into smaller groups.)

Were there any new insights? Was there anything you had not considered before? How does your original understanding of this story compare with what we just shared? How does this story speak to your life?

Sharing Life Experience

Participants share an experience from their lives that connects with the biblical interpretation just shared.

> One night, on the first Friday of Lent, we received the call every parent of teenagers dreads: "Come to the hospital, your son has been in an accident and someone is dead." We rushed to the hospital to discover that our son had been spared, but his best friend since fifth grade had died in his arms. Thus, Adam's family, our son, and the friends of the boys were forced to reflect on the precious gift of life. Some folks would innocently and lovingly say to us: "You are so blessed that God spared your son." I found myself cringing. If God spared my son, then it meant that he had snatched Adam. I had to wrestle with the mystery: "If you ordain all life and if you are the architect of our lives [so went the argument], then you must have willed that Adam die and Joe live." For a time, I even bought into the concept. "God must really have wonderful plans for your life," I horrifically said to my son. He shuddered at the words: "Mom, don't say that. Don't you understand what a burden that puts on me?" I had to retract my untenable position. No, God is not, cannot be like that. God is the author of life; he is not a puppeteer who holds the strings and amuses himself by choosing this life over that life.

This gospel gives great consolation and meaning to Adam's death. While we grieve over his death (it is now two years later and my son is still grieving), we are assured that Adam's death will not end in despair. Adam knows perfect happiness. We are the ones who are sorrowful. As Christians, we have the eyes of faith to see us through the tragic death of a loved one, particularly a young person. There is no rhyme or reason. Life happens; we are mortal human beings. God is with us in the living of life, but God does not pull all the strings. How it works is a mystery. Death is hideous. If we were not people of faith, despair would be an understandable reaction. It would be difficult to find meaning in a tragic death such as Adam's. We grieve for those who mourn the loss of loved ones, but faith gives us the assurance to know that Adam is far happier in his glorified state than he would have been in this world's sojourn. The Order of Christian Funerals asserts that the bonds of love forged in life do not end with death, but continue into eternity.

There are some who say that faith is this world's opiate for dealing with the tragedies of life. Jesus promised us that we would share eternal life; but he also showed us the price—the cross. So many issues emerged from the experience of Adam's death. The goodness and love of the local teens flowed in the midst of the tragedy. For days they held vigil, told stories, and reflected on the meaning of his death.

Many young people came to the funeral from homes where the word "Jesus" had never been spoken. Others were in their own personal deaths of despair, meaninglessness, and disillusionment because of an adult world that had hurt them. Jesus is the life and the resurrection, but what does that mean to our young people who are hardened by cynicism? My son eulogized his friend, shared how much he cared for Adam and what Adam had meant to him. He offered a challenge. "We have to learn from Adam's death. We have to allow the experience to change us. If we do, his death will have meant something."

The liturgist in me could not help but apply symbolic meaning to the experience. It was a teachable moment for the kids and for us. The name "Adam" means red clay and the first man. Adam, the first young man among their friends to die and return to the red clay of the earth, was also the first to experience the life Jesus promised in today's gospel. He per-

haps even paved the way for others. If his death prompted one young person to consider his or her life, then Adam, the first one to return to the red clay of the earth, was like a Christ figure. He paid the price with his life.

While there is no Sanhedrin to taunt us, we face similar enemies when we try to bring life to others. We often find ourselves headed straight for the cross. There is so much death around us. One need only encounter the hopelessness of many young people to observe it first hand. But today's gospel reminds us that we have the gift of life, not only for ourselves, but as a gift to offer all those who find life meaningless and without hope. It is not only Good News, it is the best news.

All share their life experience.

What was John trying to tell his community? Are there any present-day similarities between the issues in John's community and the issues the contemporary church faces? How does this gospel call us (biblical theme of community) or me to be re-created (creation), to experience life, death, and resurrection (exodus) and commitment to my/our relationship with God (covenant)? Do I still feel the same way about this text as I did when we began? Has my original understanding been stretched, challenged, or affirmed?

STEP 5
DECISION

The gospel demands a response.

What specific thing am I/we/community/parish called to do in response to today's gospel? Has this conversation with the exegesis of the raising of Lazarus changed or stretched my personal attitudes? What are the implications for my life? What is one concrete action I will take this week as a response to what we have learned and shared today?

DOCTRINAL ISSUES

What church truth/teaching/doctrinal issue could be drawn from the gospel for the Fifth Sunday of Lent?

Participants suggest possible doctrinal themes that flow from the readings.

Possible Doctrinal Themes

Eternal life, sin, cross, baptism, soteriology, Jesus the Christ, paschal mystery, death, reconciliation

Present the doctrinal material at this time.

1. The facilitator gives input on a particular doctrinal issue of his/her prior choosing. OR
2. The group chooses a doctrinal issue from the list they created. They read together from the Doctrinal Appendix.

(The doctrinal issues are found in the Doctrinal Appendix in the back of this workbook. If you are choosing an issue from this resource, please refer to it now.)

Reflection questions centered around the chosen doctrinal theme can be found at the end of each topic in the Doctrinal Appendix. The questions are based on the five-step reflection process. If you choose a topic not included in the Doctrinal Appendix, craft your own questions according to the same five-step process.

Following the reflection questions you will be reminded to return to chapter 7, "Preparing the Catechetical Session," to assist you in crafting your own session.

Closing Prayer

Father of life and God not of the dead but of the
    living,
you sent your Son to proclaim life,
to snatch us from the realm of death,
and to lead us to the resurrection.
Free these elect
from the death-dealing power of the spirit of evil,
so that they may bear witness
to their new life in the risen Christ,
for he lives and reigns for ever and ever.

Laying on of hands

Presider stretches hands over the elect.

Lord Jesus,
by raising Lazarus from the dead
you showed that you came that we might have life
and have it more abundantly.
Free from the grasp of death
those who await your life-giving sacraments
and deliver them from the spirit of corruption.
Through your Spirit, who gives life,
fill them with faith, hope, and charity,
that they may live with you always
in the glory of your resurrection,
for you are Lord for ever and ever.[21]

---

[21] *RCIA*, #175.

PASSION SUNDAY (PALM SUNDAY)

On Passion Sunday [Palm Sunday] the Church enters into the mystery of its crucified, buried and risen Lord, who, by his entrance into Jerusalem, gave a glimpse of his own majesty. Christians carry branches as a sign of the royal triumph that Christ won by his acceptance on the cross. Since Saint Paul says: "Provided we suffer with him in order that we may also be glorified with him," the link between these two aspects of the paschal mystery should stand out clearly in the liturgical celebration and catechesis of Palm Sunday.[1]

Environment

The cross is the primary symbol of today's liturgy and should be prominently displayed in the catechetical environment.

INTRODUCTORY RITES

Opening Song (or Entrance Antiphon)

Hosanna to the Son of David,
the king of Israel.
Blessed is he who comes
in the name of the Lord.
Hosanna in the highest. (Mt 21:9)
Let us go forth in peace,
praising Jesus our Messiah,
as did the crowds who welcomed him to
    Jerusalem.[2]

Opening Prayer

The facilitator of the session may lead the prayer. Others in the group may be asked to proclaim the readings.

Let us pray
[for a closer union with Christ
during this holy season]

Pause for silent prayer.

Almighty, ever-living God
you have given the human race
Jesus Christ our Savior
as a model of humility.
He fulfilled your will
by becoming man and giving his life on the cross.
Help us to bear witness to you
by following his example of suffering
and make us worthy to share in his resurrection.
We ask this through our Lord
Jesus Christ, your Son,
who lives and reigns with you and the Holy Spirit,
one God, for ever and ever.[3]

LITURGY OF THE WORD

Let us listen to God's word.

The readings are proclaimed.

First Reading
Isaiah 50:4–7

Today's pericope is the second servant song in Deutero-Isaiah. In this song the prophet bemoans the rejection of his message. The people had grown weary of his optimism for the future while they were suffering amid the trials of the exile. However, their frustration would not stop him. He was given a word from the Lord and nothing would keep him from delivering the message. His suffering would result in vindication once Yahweh proved him right. He would not be deterred.

The Christian community thought of Jesus as the suffering servant of Isaiah. Jesus, too, would not be deterred from speaking and living the word he was given. The word he came to preach was one of love and faithfulness. His faithfulness ultimately led him to the cross. This is the fate of all prophets who faithfully proclaim and live their God-given message: a one way ticket to the cross, glory, and ultimate vindication.

---

[1] *Ceremonial of Bishops*, #263, in *TLD*, 213.

[2] Passion Sunday: "Commemoration of the Lord's Entrance into Jerusalem: The Procession," *The Sacramentary*.

---

[3] Passion Sunday: "Opening Prayer," *The Sacramentary*.

Responsorial Psalm
22:8–9, 17–18, 19–20, 23–24

This is the first Old Testament scriptural text to have been appropriated for Christian usage. To an innocent onlooker, it seems to have been specifically written with the passion events in mind. This psalm served as a proof text that Jesus indeed was the promised messiah. The psalm speaks of an innocent one's suffering. The details surrounding the suffering servant in the psalm bear an incredible resemblance to the passion and death of Jesus. It is no wonder that the early Christians related this text to the suffering of Christ.

Second Reading
Philippians 2:6–11

It is believed that Paul inserted this beautiful, previously crafted hymn into his letter to the Philippians. Some consider it a perfect expression of Pauline theology regarding the passion and death of Jesus. This hymn was probably used in ancient Christian liturgies and profoundly captures the essence and the paradox of Christian redemption. Jesus, through abject humiliation (see Fourth Sunday of Lent, Cycle C, parable of the prodigal son), offered the free gift of himself. Through such humiliation, salvation was won. Jesus left his rightful throne with Yahweh, descended into the midst of humanity, and took the form of a slave, subject to the suffering and limitations of the human person. He allowed himself to be rejected, misunderstood, and treated like a slave and a criminal. Because of this free gift of self, this abasement, Jesus ascended back to the throne victorious. Because of the resurrection, humanity was and is offered freedom from the ravages of sin and death, and the promise of eternal life. Jesus, the perfect servant, model of all perfect servants, earned the rightful title, Lord, *Kyrios* (Greek), *Adonai* (Hebrew).

Paul was addressing the factions in the Philippian community. He pleaded that all assume the posture of Jesus. If they would only assume the model of Christ's self-abasement, then harmony and peace would be restored to the community. Jesus could have claimed all the rights and privileges of royalty. But he did not. "He became sin." He entered the human condition with all its defects and in the process emptied himself. The Philippian community was exhorted to embrace *kenosis*, a vol-

untary emptying of self in the manner of Jesus. Paul challenged his community to turn away from the lure of power and control, to assume the humble stance of self-giver. Jesus, emptied and poured-out, went willingly to his passion and death. We are to follow in his footsteps.

Gospel
Mark 14:1–15:47

The Passion of our Lord Jesus Christ according to Mark.

STEP 1
NAMING ONE'S EXPERIENCE

What were your first impressions, your first response? What grabbed your attention? How did you feel?

Each person names his or her initial impression. Statements should be brief. No reasons should be given at this time. All simply listen without agreeing or disagreeing.

STEP 2
UNDERSTANDING

In a brief statement, what do you think were the primary concerns of Mark's version of the passion?

STEP 3
INPUT FROM VISION/STORY/TRADITION

Liturgical Context

The title of today's liturgy expresses its double emphasis: Passion Sunday/Palm Sunday. Today we remember Jesus' triumphant entry into Jerusalem and his passion and death on the cross. "Holy Week has as its purpose the remembrance of Christ's passion, beginning with his Messianic entrance into Jerusalem."[4] The origins of Holy Week began with a yearly celebration of the Lord's

---
[4]*GNLY*, #31, in *TLD*.

pasch in the spirit of the Jewish Passover. Jesus was celebrated as the new Passover, the one who passed from death into life. The purpose of the celebration was to remember and make present the eschatological implications of Jesus' passion, death, and resurrection. There was very little concern for recording the historical facts. "The redemptive event was a unitary feast, embracing the passion, death and resurrection and exaltation of the Messiah and the outpouring of the Spirit and the anticipation of his coming again."[5]

On the Sunday that began Holy Week, the Jerusalem Christians of the fourth century proceeded to the great church (Anastasis) called the *martyrium* (the place behind Golgotha where the Lord was crucified). Following their morning eucharist and right before the dismissal, the archdeacon announced the beginning of the "Great Week" and summoned Christians to meet each day, "beginning tomorrow" at the ninth hour in the *martyrium*. He instructed them to be ready at the seventh hour (early evening) and to meet at the church on the Mount of Olives. They met at the assigned place and together with the bishop they sang songs, antiphons, and hymns of praise and listened to lessons. At the ninth hour they moved to the place where Jesus ascended into heaven. At the eleventh hour they read the passage of the Lord's triumphant procession into Jerusalem; the bishop then led the procession from the Mount of Olives back to the *martyrium* in the city. Parents carried their small children and all waved their palm branches as they made their holy trek to the city gates. They processed through the city streets until they arrived at the Anastasis at a very late hour. They prayed the *lucernare* together, "with prayer at the cross; after which the people were sent home."[6]

From the earliest days, Passion Week began with the celebration of the eucharist, followed by a procession in honor of Christ the King to the Holy City. Antiphons and hymns were sung and the gospel of the Lord's entry into Jerusalem was proclaimed. With a few minor variations, the celebration of Palm Sunday still contains the same elements and meaning: "While the doors of his city are opened for the King, the Church already celebrates his triumph, being assured of the victory he will gain by his glorious cross."[7]

The church in the East adopted this liturgy with the exception of the procession with palms. Instead, they ritually anointed catechumens while reading John 12, the story of the anointing in Bethany. Following the anointing, they proclaimed the gospel of the entry into Jerusalem. Thus, the name Palm Sunday emerged, even though there was no procession with palm branches at the time.[8]

The *blessing of the palms* in the liturgy did not occur until around the eighth century. Ancient Latin and Greek texts referred to palms as the symbol of life, hope, and victory. However, popular devotion attached a certain magical power to the palms, in part because of the Greek and Roman secular belief that some species of trees carried magical powers. Christians carried over this secular belief by using palms in such practices as eating parts of the blessed palms to deter illness, planting or burning palms in fields to ward off storms, and placing palm branches on livestock to protect them from infestation. People took the blessed branches home in hopes they would ward off evil spirits.

The church responded to this common practice by formulating a blessing ritual for use with the palms. The blessing prayer asks that the branches be blessed and made holy. It is not an invocation of magic; rather—as with all blessings—it is a prayer that God will save us from all threat to our lives, our holiness, and our salvation. "Blessed or consecrated objects are symbols; they express and stimulate faith, hope and love, and do not possess magical power."[9]

The liturgy provides three forms for the entrance rite on Palm Sunday. The first form is reminiscent of the fourth-century liturgy. We are instructed to meet at some other suitable place. All then process to the main church waving palms, not as an historical reenactment, but rather as a sign of loving discipleship. The branches are blessed with holy

---

[5]*PNL*, 11.
[6]*DL* (II), 210–211.

---

[7]Ibid., 211.
[8]For further elaboration, refer to *LY*, 107.
[9]Ibid., 108.

water, the entrance gospel is read, a brief homily is given, and—led by cross, incense, and candles—the solemn procession to the church begins.

The second form includes the solemn entrance inside the church before the principal mass of the day. The branches are blessed outside the sanctuary where the gospel is proclaimed. Then the presider and a representative group of the faithful process to the sanctuary.

In the third form, the simple entrance, the entry into Jerusalem is commemorated by singing the prescribed antiphon as the presider processes into the church. However, the Sacramentary suggests holding a bible service the night before to commemorate the triumphant entry into Jerusalem. The church obviously sees great value in not diminishing this important aspect of the Palm Sunday liturgy. However, it is not to overshadow the passion, which is of primary focus. The triumphant entry is significant insofar as it points to the cross.

The ritual prayers of the liturgy including the opening and concluding prayer and the prayer over the gifts reflect the central saving action of Jesus Christ: his victory over death for the reparation of sin. They exalt the death and resurrection of Christ and our ongoing participation in his paschal mystery.

Thus, Palm Sunday brings us to the culmination of Lent's arduous journey. The preparation and emptying of the lenten season have readied us to enter the holy city with Jesus, to die and rise to new life with our Lord and Savior. The triumphant procession has eschatological overtones; it hints of that final day when all will process with Christ into the holy city, the new Jerusalem.

Passion/Palm Sunday is celebrated with full acknowledgment of the ultimate reality: Jesus died and rose from the dead and is now seated at the right hand of God. We do not process as if we do not know the rest of the story. Jesus is addressed as "the Son of David . . . he who comes in the name of the Lord." This antiphon from Psalm 118 is our joyful testament to the one who came, died, and rose for our sins, the one who is the fulfillment of the law and the prophets. Once again he comes to

save in every celebration of the paschal mystery. We proclaim the Lord's passion and we acclaim what we already know to be true: Christ is Victor over sin and death.

In the blessing of the branches we acknowledge Christ's triumph and we ask that he lead us to embrace the cross and to share in the resurrection. The blessing and procession of branches is not an historical reenactment of that first procession. Rather, it is a living memorial to the saints of the past with whom we join in the ongoing dying and rising of people of faith through the centuries. The cross, the book of the gospels, and the presider are signs of the living presence of Christ in our midst as we process together to the Holy City. "It is a presence in absence."[10]

It is important to reiterate that the entrance into Jerusalem is a secondary theme and serves as a preparation for the prominent focus of this liturgy—the passion of our Lord. We are joyful, yet ever mindful of the price paid by our loving Lord to heal the wounded core of humanity. This week reminds us, ever more fully, that the path Jesus chose is also the path of discipleship. It is the path that leads to the light rather than the dark, to salvation rather than death.

The Proclamation of the Passion

Today we read the passion account through the eyes of Mark. Each year on Passion Sunday we hear from a different evangelist—Matthew in Cycle A, Mark in Cycle B, and Luke in Cycle C. John's account of the passion is read every Good Friday. It is apparent to the observant listener that the passion account read on Passion Sunday and on Good Friday vary considerably. "They do not offer the same outlook of Jesus either in content or outlook."[11]

Thus, contemporary disciples are faced with the awareness that God revealed himself in the words of human beings. Various factors colored their perspectives and the telling of their stories. What family does not have stories of family events, stories that are shaped and colored by the bias or perspective of the teller? "We recall the Catholic

---

[10]*DL* (II), 213.
[11]*CCHW*, 9.

Church's official teaching that sayings uttered by Jesus have been expanded and interpreted by the apostolic preachers and the evangelists before they were put in the Gospels...."[12]

The fact that there are four different perspectives of the passion accounts serves an unconscious, blessed purpose in the lives of believers that is evident once each gospel is examined on its own ground.

> A true picture of the whole emerges only because the viewpoints are different. In presenting two diverse views of the crucified Jesus every Holy Week, one on Palm/Passion Sunday, one on Good Friday, the Church is bearing witness to that truth and making it possible for people with very different spiritual needs to find meaning in the cross.[13]

Thus, those whose lives cry out like the Jesus of Mark and Matthew, "My God, my God, why have you forsaken me?" find a Christ who resonates with their desperate, yet human pleas for deliverance. Those who need a savior who listens, is present, and can overturn hopelessness find consolation in the cross of those two evangelists. Those who find themselves in need of the tender embrace and loving forgiveness of God will find consolation in Luke's passion narrative. Others may need Christ, the reigning King of heaven and earth, who looks down from the throne of the cross to strengthen and uplift in life's burdensome travail. "To choose one portrayal of the crucified Jesus in a manner that would exclude the other portrayals or to harmonize all the Gospel portrayals into one would deprive the cross of much of its meaning."[14]

The passion narrative is the dramatic portrayal of the most significant event in human history. Its cast of characters reads like a Shakespearean tragedy complete with hero and antagonist. The church allows various readers to proclaim the text. While this serves to heighten the already powerful sense of drama, we are conscious that this is not "theater" provided for our passive enjoyment. We are all fully engaged participants in the proclamation. We are to put ourselves in the place of hero, protagonist, sympathizer, and accuser. In the process, we stand either accused or acquitted.

> The distribution of palm in church may too quickly assure me that I would have been among the crowd that hailed Jesus appreciatively. Is it not more likely that I might have been among the disciples who fled from danger, abandoning him? Or at moments in my life have I not played the role of Peter, denying Jesus, or even of Judas, betraying him? Have I not found myself like the Johannine Pilate, trying to avoid a decision between good and evil? Or, like the Matheean Pilate, have I made a bad decision and then washed my hands so that the record could show that I was blameless? Or, most likely of all, might I not have stood among the religious leaders who condemn Jesus?[15]

Brown insists that the last statement is very probable, since sincerely religious people often have binding, sometimes blinding affiliation with their tradition. However, Jesus challenged fundamentalist adherence to tradition. He always pointed out the human directives and elements that were not in keeping with the will of God. "If Jesus was treated harshly by the literal minded religious people of his time who were Jews, it is quite likely that he would be treated harshly by similar religious people of our time."[16]

Thus, our proclamation of today's passion requires that we become fully engaged, active participants. In so doing, we allow the story to impact our lives and become the leaven for transformation in the fullness of Jesus Christ's paschal mystery.

Gospel Exegesis

The facilitator provides input from critical biblical scholarship on this text. This input includes insights as to how people would have heard the gospel in Jesus' time.

---

[12]Ibid., 16.
[13]Ibid., 71.
[14]Ibid.

---

[15]Ibid., 11.
[16]Ibid., 12.

Entrance Gospel: At the Procession with Palms

Option A Mark 11:1–10

Readers of Mark definitely understand that Jesus' entry into Jerusalem is laced with messianic overtones. It was not that clear to people who were present. The event probably occurred at the Feast of Dedication, not Passover, and no doubt was a quiet, unnoticed event. Perhaps only Jesus and his disciples were present. A man riding on a donkey would not have drawn much attention, nor would the waving of palms and the singing of Psalm 118 on the Feast of Dedication. Christians looking back on the event see it as the triumphant entry of their Lord and King into Jerusalem for the final time. Mark's Jesus is not greeted by huge, cheering crowds. They spread their cloaks (a sign of royal homage) and branches (evocative of the welcome of Simon Maccabees and his followers into Jerusalem) as he passed by. They shouted "Hosanna"—translated "save now," an acclamation asserting, "Blessed be the kingdom of our father David that is coming."[17] It was not an acclamation in praise of Jesus, but the expected kingdom of David. Mark is concerned about demonstrating the type of Messiah Jesus is and the type he is not. He is not a political Messiah; he is a humble servant, willing to offer his life. Jesus entered as the "humble Messiah-King of Zechariah. But even here, there is studied reticence."[18] The reticence is connected to Mark's intention to slowly unveil the messianic secret and what Jesus' messiahship means. Throughout Mark's gospel Jesus' mission is one of servanthood and self-sacrifice. Jesus is one who lays down his life for his friends. For the first time in the gospel, Mark's Jesus acts like a Messiah, but he does so in keeping with his consistent message of humble service.

The disciples follow Jesus' instruction and prepare Jesus for his kingly entrance into Jerusalem. Jesus is praised as the one who will realize the long-awaited Davidic kingdom—the very kingdom Jesus emphatically renounces. Prior to this section of the gospel narrative Jesus healed the blind Bartimaeus, whereupon Bartimaeus followed him into Jerusalem. The faith of Bartimaeus is in sharp contrast to the lack of faith of Jesus' disciples. Jesus is now ready to enter into his final conflict with the political and religious powers. We stand on the precipice of the Passion event with two memorable figures leading us—a poor, blind disciple and a lowly king.

Mark is well aware that the portrait he paints of Jesus' entry will elicit images of a political hero's welcome and entry into a city following victory. The march is situated near the Mount of Olives, a place scripturally and apocalyptically attested to be the place of the final battle against the enemies of Israel in defense of Jerusalem.[19] The prophet Zechariah prophesied that Yahweh would go forward to battle the nations and on that day Yahweh would stand on the Mount of Olives (14:2–4).

Could Mark be suggesting that Jesus is marching forward into battle? His entry reflects that of the victorious rebel Simon Maccabees. Ched Myers suggests that even though the military symbolism is strong, there are other things going on in the text.[20] Rather than enter on a triumphant horse, Jesus rides on a colt. He seems to deliberately choreograph the symbolics. Instead of a victorious horseback ride, Jesus enters on an ass, a meek and humble entry. Even though Mark alludes to the liberation of Jerusalem tradition, Jesus has absolutely no intention to fight for Israel. The Mount of Olives will be the place of final judgment, not Jesus' military liberation of Israel. It almost seems as if Mark is creating a satire on the military messianic expectations of the Zealot movement of his day.

Not only were garments thrown on the animals, but straw was thrown on the roadway. Most commentators ignore this little detail Mark has inserted into the text. Ched Myers suggests that it is Mark's way to define the crowd.[21] He defines the crowd as rural rather than the urban elite. It is the peasants who come to meet Jesus waving the only gifts (weapons?) they can afford to give him—straw from the fields. It is the peasants who escort Jesus into Jerusalem. They shout hearty, joyful acclamations to him, which is in direct contrast to

---

[17]*MARK*, 176.

[18]Ibid., 175.

[19]*BSM*, 294.

[20]Ibid., 295.

[21]Ibid., 296.

the frozen reception he receives from the religious leaders and his own Milquetoast, half-hearted disciples.

Mark, the master of irony, once again presents a situation riddled with it. Here the crowd shouts "Hosanna"—a cry that God will preserve and save Jesus. Yet Jesus himself is determined to walk the way of the cross and death.[22] Previously Bartimaeus acclaimed him "Son of David" and now the crowd shouts in anticipation of the coming of David's kingdom. "Jesus will repudiate this ideology of restorationism."[23] Thus, later, at Jesus' trial, the cry of the crowd becomes one of condemnation and they demand the release of the political revolutionary Barabbas and the crucifixion of Jesus.

The opening scene of this narrative sets the stage and names the political expectations that are at play in this drama. Jesus—humble, nonviolent King of peace—stands in stark contrast to the political, revolutionary, Zealot, Davidic messianic movement. Jesus is not the Messiah they expected. He will show another way to liberate the world—the way of the cross.

OR

Option B John 12:1–6

Jesus' final hour has come. In John's gospel, "hour" is a reference to the time of the new covenant. The entire fourth gospel is written as one great unfolding drama in constant motion toward the ultimate destination of fulfillment.

Reflection on today's Passion must necessarily begin with a reflection on the verses leading up to it. The introductory section to Jesus' final hour serves to establish the time and locus of events—the remaining days and hours of Jesus' life and the approaching Passover celebration. This introductory piece also informs the reader that pilgrims were on their way to Jerusalem to observe Passover in appropriate, lawful fashion and that there was a sense of expectancy in the air. The first eleven verses of chapter 12 (verses directly preceding today's pericope) set the stage for Passover, the

symbolism of the Paschal lamb and hints of Jesus' pending death and burial. Included in those verses is the story of Mary, who unknowingly anoints the feet of Jesus in preparation for his burial. Also in those preliminary verses is the appearance of a crowd that emerges not only to encounter Jesus but also to see Lazarus who had been raised from the dead (v. 9). "This results in Lazarus being included in the death plot of the chief priests 'because on account of him many of the Jews were going away and believing in Jesus'" (vv. 10–11).

The next portion of this introductory section centers around initiatives taken by other people, initiatives that prompt a reaction from Jesus.[24] The first initiative is taken by the crowd and the second initiative is taken by the Greeks. The crowd went out to meet Jesus waving branches of palm trees. They hailed Jesus as King of Israel. The designation had little to do with spiritual realities, however. It was an acclamation of Jewish nationalism. Palms were reminiscent of a moment in Israel's history in which the Jews brought palms to the Temple when Judas Maccabees rededicated it in 165 B.C. after it had been desecrated with pagan idols by the Greek kings of Syria (1 Mc 4:52–59). Palms were also carried by the Jews when Simon conquered and took possession of the Jerusalem citadel. Palms were given to Levi (Testament of Naphtali 5:4) as a symbol of supremacy over all Israel. Waving palms, then, carried the same significance as the waving of the American flag by people in towns that had been liberated during World War II. It was a sign of political and national liberation. Palms, therefore, were waved before Jesus as a sign and symbol of the people's expectations that he be their national liberator during their time of persecution and oppression.

"*They came to meet him*" reflects the practice of crowds as they went out to greet Greek rulers as they approached the city. The term *Hosanna* was used to address and salute sovereign kings. The crowd went out to meet Jesus with the expectation that he would take up the role of national political leader and liberator.

Jesus reacted to their expectations by sitting on a donkey. The underlying symbolism surrounding his parabolic action is based on imagery found in

---

[22]Ibid.
[23]Ibid.

---

[24]*RJ*, 185.

Zechariah, in which the monarch came riding on a colt if he was bearing peace, but riding on a horse if war was his agenda. Jesus' act of riding on a colt was a prophetic reaction to their nationalistic expectations. He came bearing a message of universal kingship and peace—not war. The crowd went out to him because they heard that he had raised Lazarus from the dead. Who would not follow a Messiah who could raise someone from the dead? How could they lose with someone so powerful and mighty leading them? This was the kind of Messiah they had been looking for all along. Jesus, however, turned their expectations upside down. He was not the Messiah of their own ideological and political imaginings. The kingdom Jesus came to establish was not a kingdom of political power. It was a reign of peace, a new covenant of love. John continues the theme of Jesus' universal message of salvation by having the Pharisees respond that the "world has gone after him" (v. 19). Jesus' message is for all people inclusively—all people who hear and believe.

The disciples simply would not understand Jesus' mission until he returned to the throne of glory—after his death, resurrection, and exaltation. Then their eyes would be opened. Then they would remember the words of Jesus and recall the words of prophecy. Then the fullness of Christ would be completely manifest to the disciples.

Passion Exegesis

According to Reginald Fuller, the passion narratives possess a different form than the rest of the gospel. All gospel material, other than the passion narratives, was passed on as oral tradition in the short unit format. Those short pieces were preserved as individual units within the gospel. The passion narratives, on the other hand, were told in their complete form from the very beginning. The church continued its early tradition by preserving the pericopes in the Lectionary and keeping the passion narratives in their complete narrative form.[25]

Brown insists that our understanding of the passion narratives must begin with an understanding of the apologetic motives of the evangelists. One concern was to portray a balanced picture of Jesus for the Roman-controlled populace. Jesus was re-

membered by secular historians as a criminal who had been put to death. The evangelists sought to temper that portrayal, so they depicted Pilate as a fair judge who acknowledged Jesus' innocence. Pilate himself tells the Roman listeners that Jesus is not a criminal.[26]

The second bias of the evangelists centered around the controversy between the early Christians and the synagogue. Many of the gospel perspectives were shaped in relation and in response to that situation. However, Brown also points out that while there were scoundrel "ecclesiastical" politicians intent on getting rid of Jesus for their own selfish reasons, there were also no doubt some very religious men who thought they were honestly safeguarding the people from a liberal, false prophet who was leading the people astray and promoting a lackadaisical adherence to the law of God. Thus, we are prompted to remember that any one of us could stand quite unconsciously and maybe even innocently with the accusers of Jesus at any given time in the story. There were many factors involved in the portrayal handed down to us. Therefore, it behooves us to approach the text with an open mind and heart.

The intent of the evangelists was theological rather than biographical. They were primarily concerned with showing Jesus in relation to the messianic foreshadowing of the Old Testament. "The evangelists were emphasizing that through the Scriptures of Israel God had taught about his Son. Their emphasis also had an apologetic touch against Jews who rejected the crucified Jesus precisely because they did not think he fulfilled Scriptural expectations."[27]

The curtain is about to come up on the drama that will ultimately change the world! It was for this moment that Jesus came into the world. It was for this moment that humanity held its centuries-long breath. It was for this moment that the Word spoke and breathed the world scene into existence. We stand as spectators on the stage of virtual reality. We are there and it is now. The evangelists sharpen our senses, put the players in motion, and catapult us back in time while ever

---

[25]*PNL*, 15.

[26]*CCHW*, 12.
[27]Ibid., 18.

mindful that *we are there and it is now*. We are not to be lulled into the false sense that the "bad guys" are "those guys." The bad guys are those readers ancient and contemporary whose feet fit into the proverbial shoes portrayed by the antagonists and protagonists in the passion event.

Perhaps the size we wear fits Judas, the one who saw the handwriting on the wall and, concerned with his own self-interests, sold his soul and his relationship with the *Word Incarnate* for thirty pieces of silver. Perhaps many of us easily wear the shoes of those who fled the scene in terror, worrying more about their own skins than the hope of the new kingdom promised by their Master (which by all appearances seemed to have gone up in smoke). Perhaps our feet fit into the sandals of Peter, the one who professed Jesus, but also denied him. Or perhaps we fit snugly into the political shoes of the Pilates of this world who wash their hands and choose to ignore the pervasive systemic evil that looms as a giant blockade and pleads, through its stony silence, for someone to bring it crashing to the ground? "Or, most likely of all, might I [we] not have stood among the religious leaders who condemned Jesus?"[28]

The entire Gospel of Mark prepares us for this climactic moment. The cross looms large over the reading of each page as we are nudged ever closer to the heart of Christ's redemptive mission. We do not face the passion as shocked and alarmed spectators, but as participants who are fully aware that the road followed in the gospels leads directly to Calvary. "The death and triumph of Jesus are not unexpected or arbitrary endings to the Gospel drama but its inner core."[29]

Donald Senior maintains that the Passion story is a proving ground for fidelity. "Jesus himself is the model; he faces suffering and death with the same integrity and obedience that marked his life."[30] In the shame-based Mediterranean culture in which he lived, Jesus' manliness—his character—was tested. Would he go through his ordeal with head held high or would he grovel in the face of pain, persecution, and torture? Jesus was challenged and withstood the test, demonstrating great heroism.

He faced his demons head on and was victorious. The infidelity of the other characters stand in sharp contrast to the faithfulness of the *Anointed One*.

Raymond Brown reminds us that the gospel accounts were written by Christian communities, with specific concerns and life situations that impacted their telling of the passion event. "But we must remember that apologetic motives colored the Gospels. Remember our official Catholic teaching (Pontifical Biblical Commission in 1964) that, in the course of apostolic preaching and of Gospel writing, the memory of what happened in Jesus' lifetime was affected by the life-situations of local Christian communities."[31]

An immediate concern was to soft-pedal the portrayal of Jesus in a world governed by Roman law. Brown reminds us that the Roman historian Tacitus remembered Jesus as a condemned criminal who was executed by Pontius Pilate. The Christian account very cleverly uses Pilate to acknowledge Jesus' innocence.

The gospel accounts often reflect the existing tension between the synagogue and the early church. No doubt there were those religious leaders who honestly believed that Jesus was a false prophet and that they were protecting the populace from his influence. On the other hand, there were probably those who were feathering their political nests (as self-serving politicians are wont to do when a public figure appears that might be sacrificed for their self-serving ends).[32] It is with this perspective that we approach the Passion of Jesus Christ according to Mark.

Mark 14:1–15:47

The entire Gospel of Mark is in forward motion to this peak moment in the dramatic narrative—the Passion, death, and resurrection of Jesus Christ. Raymond Brown demonstrates how the groundwork is laid for the proclamation of Jesus' death throughout the entire story of his life and ministry.[33] We are given hints that this is where

---

[28]Ibid., 11.
[29]*PJGM*, 18.
[30]*IM*, 249.

[31]Ibid., 11.
[32]Brown reminds us that the "Annas high priestly family of which Caiaphas was a member gets low marks in Jewish memory," 12.
[33]*CCHW*, 21.

Jesus' journey will lead him from the very outset of the gospel and they continue throughout the narrative. John the Baptist was handed over to Herod, who succumbed to pressure and had him executed—the fate of all prophets, and the fate that would eventually befall the ultimate Prophet. When asked to respond about who this Jesus really was, Herod insisted that he was John raised from the dead. Very early in the Jesus story the reader is told that there were plots against Jesus by Pharisees and Herodians. Jesus himself predicted his own death three times. Jesus' prophetic action of purifying the Temple was the proverbial straw that broke the camel's back and increased the momentum of the priests and scribes to have Jesus killed.

A woman who honored Jesus anointed his body—a preparation for his burial. She was criticized and misunderstood for her blatant extravagance; the cost of the ointment she used was the equivalent of one year's salary for a laborer. The money would have been enough to feed many poor people for a very long time. The meaning of her action is akin to the principle that when the bridegroom is present there is no time for fasting. "There will be all the time in the world for caring for the poor; but this is a privileged moment and the pouring of this ointment is no extravagance. The woman has made a lovely gesture, more significant than she knew. Anointing for burial was not her intent; that is how Jesus chose to see it. He thereby gives notice that he expected to die a violent death and suffer a rude burial."[34]

In the Mediterranean first-century world shame and honor were priority values. During his earthly life Jesus proved that he was a worthy opponent when it came to issues of shame and honor. No one "got the best" of him; he could hold his own—"no antagonist succeeded in shaming him. Jesus successfully protected his honor against all attacks."[35] Yet it appears in the Passion narrative that Jesus was shamed not only by his enemies but even by his friends. How could the master of riposte remain silent at his final hour? He could not have died a more shameful death as crucifixion. How could the

evangelists who meticulously recorded Jesus' one-upmanship throughout his public ministry and who knew well the value placed on honor in the culture, have portrayed Jesus in such shame-ridden circumstances? Perhaps on closer inspection they allowed Jesus to remain in the honorable driver's seat after all (as only a first-century onlooker would have readily understood). Jesus turned his shameful ordeal into the highest honor. The way in which Jesus approached his death would have been held in high esteem because he acted with manliness. He was not a coward in the face of death. The woman who anointed Jesus' body was well aware of the honor due him. Jesus, the venerable Son, honored his Father at Gethsemane by agreeing to be faithful to his Father's will, no matter how fearful or ugly it would prove to be. The chief priests level their accusations against Jesus and, in an ironic twist, the charges reflected Jesus' reality, his true and honorable status. Jesus acts like a "King" in his encounter with Pilate and because of his "Kingship" he holds a higher status than Pilate. With his silence he treats Pilate like a subordinate and his honor remains intact. Everyone who mocks him is ironically acknowledging his truthful, rightful status. Jesus' ultimate honor is realized when God raises him from the dead, a distinction no human person has ever attained. "Mediterranean readers see in the passion story an ironic pronouncement of Jesus' true honor."[36]

One of Jesus' own disciples betrayed him to his enemies. Judas serves the purpose of the priests and scribes to "deliver Jesus up." He is described by Mark as one of the Twelve. This is to highlight the urgency of events. The horror and implications of Jesus' predicament are beginning to emerge. Mark wishes to connect the supper Jesus celebrated with his friends with Passover and to demonstrate Jesus' foreknowledge of events and his authority and command of the situation. Mark is the only evangelist who insists that Jesus was celebrating a Passover meal at the Last Supper, which means that Jesus died on Passover. John the evangelist, on the other hand, is just as insistent that Jesus died on the 14th of Nisan (the hour when the Passover lambs were sacrificed). For both John

---

[34]*MARK*, 213.
[35]*CWJB*, 65.

---

[36]Ibid.

and the Synoptics the point is clear—Jesus' death is intimately connected to Passover. Their agenda is more concerned with theology than with factual detail.[37] At the Last Supper with his friends Jesus affirmed that he was willing to pour out his blood as a sign of the new covenant God was forging with all people.

The Feast of Passover could only be celebrated in Jerusalem beginning at sundown. The beginning of the liturgical day of Passover commenced from sundown to sundown on the 15th of Nisan. That afternoon the lambs were slaughtered and offered in the Temple (on the 14th of Nisan). The meal was eaten between sundown and midnight (on the 15th of Nisan). The Feast of Unleavened Bread that originated as a barley harvest feast and in which the unleavened bread was eaten was celebrated between the 15th and 21st of Nisan. That feast was combined with Passover so when Mark referred to both Passover and the Feast of Unleavened Bread it was not an unusual designation.[38] Mark's reference to "two days" was his way of alerting the reader to the divine purpose in all of the events about to transpire.

After the supper Jesus went with his disciples to Gethsemane. He went with resolve. He knew that he must die for the reign of God to come to fruition. Mark's disciples still did not "get it." They believed that the Messiah would be a Davidic-like leader who would restore Israel to its past glory. Jesus' efforts to prepare them for a different reality was filtered through their own faulty biases and expectations. They simply could not hear that all would be scattered as Jesus prophesied. Peter was warned that even he would deny Jesus.

The ordeal that is about to take center stage should be no surprise to expectant readers. It was duly foreshadowed. Jesus would go to his death alone. The curtain is drawn on the Passion scene. Depression and despair hang like a mildewed blanket suspended motionless in air awaiting earth's cue to drop to the ground and suffocate everything in its path. Jesus is sorrowful unto death. More than in any other gospel, Mark's Jesus prays more earnestly that the bitter cup pass him by.

Betrayal stings his wounded heart. Even Peter? His prayer for deliverance notwithstanding, Jesus rises to begin drinking the sorrowful libation that was before him. God no doubt gave Jesus his answer—we see it in his resolve as he approached his betrayer. The hour has arrived.

Unlike the other evangelists, Mark's Jesus is resigned to his fate. He insists that the will of God go forward and that the scriptures be fulfilled. If the cup could not pass, then let it go forward. At this, his disciples desert him. Jesus' abandonment is most acutely portrayed in Mark's rendition of events. We are taken quite by surprise as a naked man appears on the scene. Raymond Brown asserts that many exegetes have linked the naked man to the man who appears after Jesus' resurrection clothed in a white robe and that he is a symbol of the Christian who descends into the baptismal waters to die with Jesus only to be clothed in new life.[39] Brown suggests that such symbolism was beyond Mark's intention and that the naked man was a symbol of the utter abandonment Jesus experienced at the hands of his intimate friends. "The first disciples to be called left nets and family... indeed everything... to follow him; but this last disciple, who at first sought to follow Jesus, ultimately leaves everything to get away from him."[40]

Mark's version of the greatest story ever told is the most difficult of all versions to swallow for both believers and nonbelievers. Well-intentioned exegetes and preachers have tried to resurrect Jesus' sorrow in the face of death. "He really did not ask to be delivered from suffering," they defend. "He was just overcome in the face of such evil." Nonbelievers simply question his divinity. "How could he be divine and yet experience fear—a very human reaction to death?" Another argument: "Since he advocated the cross for others, why would he try to avoid it himself?"

Jesus' reaction to death has a genesis and can be traced to the Hebrew understanding of death. God created men and women to be immortal. Death was a punishment for the sin of our first parents. Death was understood as alienation and total separation from God. Jesus' victory on the cross was un-

---

[37]*MARK*, 215.

[38]Ibid., 212.

[39]*CCHW*, 23.

[40]Ibid.

derstood as the last enemy to be ultimately conquered. Death is also the final enemy of the last days. Jesus engages the last enemy to be conquered. Jesus prays with the disciples that the final battle with death not come at a time when they are not prepared. Thus, "The Christian answer lies not in underplaying the apprehension of Jesus, but in stressing the importance of life in this world so that death is seen as a distortion and not as a welcome deliverance—an enemy that, because of Jesus' victory, cannot conquer but an enemy nevertheless. The obedience that Jesus showed to God's will and the trust that this demanded of him are all the more impressive when it is realized how satanic an enemy he was encountering".[41]

Mark moves us to the next scene. Jesus is led before the Sanhedrin, which enjoyed certain juridical power even under Roman occupation. Peter follows Jesus and waits out in the courtyard, roasting the apprehensive chill in his body next to a fire. Simultaneous questioning takes place. Jesus is interrogated inside while Peter is questioned outside. The dichotomy between the two interrogations is stark. The trial commences and Jesus is ultimately sentenced. Bogus witnesses falsely testify. They twist Jesus' words to make their case that Jesus blasphemed against the Temple. Brown intimates that while Mark's insertion of the charges is difficult to interpret exactly, the adjectives Mark uses (the clarifying clauses and positive and negative Greek adjectives "made with hands" and "not made with hands") "more likely represent a later Christian explanation that the Temple would be replaced by the Church."[42]

The high priest is angry with Jesus' silence (like the silence of Isaiah's Suffering Servant) and with the incompetence of the witnesses against him. The inquisitor presses Jesus further. "Are you the Messiah, Son of the Most High?" Jesus was proclaimed son at his baptism, at his transfiguration, and by Peter. Jesus answers that he is the Messiah, but not the Davidic, political Messiah expected by so many. His kingdom is not the expected restored, golden age Davidic, long-awaited kingdom. Jesus' reign will come to its completion at the end of the age. Then Jesus will judge the world and everyone will acknowledge Jesus' victory—even his enemies.

The high priest hears Jesus' pronouncement as further proof of blasphemy. No one comes to Jesus' defense. He stands alone. Adding insult to injury, the members of the Sanhedrin spit on Jesus and taunt him to prophecy, providing echoes once again of Isaiah's Suffering Servant: "I hid not my face from shame and spitting" (Is 50:6).

While Jesus was strong under scrutiny inside the court walls, Peter falters outside. He crumbles under the weight of interrogation and denies Jesus. After the third denial Peter cursed. Some exegetes believe that his curse was leveled against Jesus—he had sunk to the lowest depths of low. Peter remembered the Lord's words of prophecy about him and wept. Yet the Lord still included him in the future promise and Peter would become a symbol of hope for future martyrs who would also crumble under the weight of denying Christ. Just as Jesus was being taunted in the inside court to prophecy, his prophecy was being realized in the denials of Peter just yards away.

Jesus exits the Jewish trial and the Roman one begins. The Sanhedrin insisted that he is deserving of death, but Mark does not explain why they did not execute the sentence themselves. It is probable that the story was so well known that he didn't feel it warranted explanation. At any rate, the locus moves from a religious trial to a political one. Pilate asked Jesus if he believed he was the King of the Jews. He is inquiring whether Jesus was a threat to Rome. Jesus is silent once again. Pilate was not convinced of his guilt, so the chief priests work the crowd. They incite the crowd to ask for the customary feast-day release of a prisoner—except they ask for a criminal, an insurrectionist, not Christ. Pilate is aware of their hidden agenda and invites the crowd to choose Jesus. The priests cajole the crowd into choosing Barabbas. Pilate asked what evil Jesus had done. Those who should have enthusiastically welcomed the Son of God rejected him and insisted on his torture and death. Pilate takes the politically expedient road and hands Jesus over. Absolutely no one came to Jesus' defense. He stood alone in this travesty. Jewish and Roman powers stood together as willing accomplices in the death of Jesus. He was whipped, struck, and spit upon in both courts. Death was not enough—the shame of

---

[41]Ibid., 24.
[42]Ibid., 25.

shames had to be added as well. "His claims had to be derided."[43]

Mark moves the transfixed reader to the scene of crucifixion. He is a master of detail and many of them were carefully written into the text by a later community that was influenced by Psalms 69:22; and 22:19 (the wine mixed with myrrh and the division of garments, for example, are reminiscent of these psalms). Mark uses the symbol of *three* that he has previously used (i.e., Peter's three denials). The time of Jesus' "hour" takes place at the third, sixth, and ninth hours. Jesus is mocked by three groups between the third and sixth hours. A first group of accusers taunt him to save himself and they hurl accusations of blasphemy at him (that Jesus threatened to destroy and then rebuild the Temple, again an allusion to Psalm 22). The second group to taunt Jesus is the priests and scribes, who echo the charge that Jesus was the Messiah, King of Israel. The third group is the criminals who hung by his side—even they revile him.

Humanity shows not even one iota of compassion in the face of Jesus' horrendous hour. The earth, however, is another matter. It groans in depression emanating from the depths of its bowels. From the sixth to the ninth hours the earth releases its acrid, pungent blanket of despair and forbids any penetration of light to cut through as it grieves over what it witnessed—the life breath sucked from its innocent Master's tortured body. Mark perhaps was alluding to the warning of Amos that the "sun would go down at noon and the light would be darkened on the earth by day."[44]

At the final, ninth hour Jesus cries out with words given to him by the psalmist: "My God, why have you forsaken me?" We dare not soften Jesus' words to reflect anything other than what they express. Mark uses Jesus' desperate plea to further show the level of abandonment and antagonism by the onlookers. It is another opportunity for taunters to level their mockery. In a shame-and-honor-based culture the mockery is worse than the torture and death. The crowd asks him if he is waiting for Elijah to deliver him. Yet Jesus goes to his death knowing no such deliverance. John the

Baptist, the Elijah figure, died a martyr's death. So, too, Jesus steps in line to accept the same fate.

During Jesus' lifetime the demons screamed when they experienced the Son of God. Now the Son of God screams as he wages his war with Satan and breathes his last. Apocalyptic images dance on the pages with the scene described so carefully by Mark. The biblically astute remember the eschatological words of Joel that the sun and moon will be darkened, the Lord shall give his voice before God from Jerusalem, all the heavens and the earth will be shaken, and God will spare his people (2:10–11; 4:16).

Like the urgency of an accelerating symphony in its final moments of peak, crescendo, and finale Mark relates God's definitive response. The curtain to the Temple is torn in two from top to bottom. There is debate whether the curtain is the one that separated the Holy of Holies or the outer court from the sanctuary. It would be significant in assigning symbolism. Brown suggests that there is no way to know for certain what, if any, symbolism Mark had in mind.[45] One debate worthy of discussion, however, is whether the action was an expression of God's anger over the abandonment of the Temple or the inclusion of gentiles into the once very exclusive space. It is likely that the former is closer to Mark's intention than the latter. Images of division and schism can be heard as the curtain is ripped from top to bottom. Here the charges against Jesus come once again to the fore, and in parabolic form, they are turned on end and a new reality is breathed into them. With the veil torn, the Temple *is* destroyed and outsiders are not welcomed. Outsiders will now have to come to a Temple not crafted with human hands. And immediately one comes—the centurion—and he sees that this man truly is the Son of God. Both charges leveled against Jesus at his trial now are affirmed as truth and reality. The Temple is destroyed by the tearing of the veil. Jesus is truly the Messiah and Son of God and it is attested to by an outsider—one who has come to worship at the new Temple not made with human hands. "[F]or the first time in the Gospel a human being has recognized Jesus as the Son of God."[46] Jesus is fi-

---

[43]Ibid., 29.
[44]Ibid., 30.

[45]Ibid., 31.
[46]Ibid.

nally vindicated. "God has answered Jesus' cry by replacing the Temple as the locus of worship and by offering in its place His own Son who will be confessed by Gentile and Jew alike."[47]

After this inaugural confession Mark tells the reader that there were others who would have affirmed the same confession—the women who ministered to him and other disciples who were present at the cross. Mark introduces Joseph of Arimathea, a Jewish member of the Sanhedrin, to the epilogue's cast of characters. Joseph had been a seeker of God's kingdom. He courageously stepped forward to claim Jesus' body. Mark makes his theological point in the closing moments.

Discipleship and salvation involve accepting the cross, letting go of all human supports and relying totally on the power of God to save. Mark's portrayal of the Passion is not glossed over; it is severe and as stark as gray prison steel. More than any other portrayal of the crucifixion, Mark's is the most sobering. Perhaps that makes sense if the church was undergoing severe testing, persecution, and martyrdom. Had they perhaps witnessed the persecution of Christians under Nero? The "Good News" in Mark's gospel for persecuted Christians is that Jesus' suffering and the cross is not defeat; it is victory. Salvation exists in taking up the cross and following the example of Jesus— even unto death!

Mark is the only evangelist who tells us that Pilate checked to see whether Jesus was dead. This was perhaps a reaction to apologists who were already positing the story that Jesus was not dead and survived the tomb. Mary Magdalene and the women appear on the scene as a dramatic foreshadowing of what will take place the next morning when they return to the tomb. "For Mark, the story of Jesus' death does not close with his burial, but with his resurrection."[48]

Proclaim the gospel again.

Sometimes we gain new insights when we hear the text after the interpretation has been given. Someone from the group proclaims the gospel a second time.

---

[47]Ibid.
[48]Ibid., 33.

Conversation with the Liturgy and the Scriptures

Test your original understanding in dialogue with the text.

(You might consider breaking into smaller groups.)

Was there anything in the passion narrative you had not considered before? Were there any new insights? How does Mark's account of Jesus' passion speak to your life? How does it speak to the life of the community?

Sharing Life Experience

Participants share an experience from their lives that connects with the biblical interpretation just shared.

I cannot experience a Palm Sunday liturgy without remembering a very defining moment of healing and liberation in my life. It was a moment of passage, of crossing the Red Sea into the promised land. I have told this story before; I will tell it again. The passion, death, and resurrection of Jesus always bring me back to this very personal, yet communal experience of passage and liberation. Two years ago I participated in a retreat and study pilgrimage in Israel. One very defining moment for me occurred on the day we participated in the passion walk that closely resembled the steps of Jesus in his last days. Beginning at the place of the Last Supper, we walked down the hillside and across the Kidron Valley to the Mount of Olives. We mirrored the same walk of the fourth-century Christians described above. We stopped and prayed at the Mount of Olives, crossed the Kidron Valley, and processed up the mountainside once again to the holy city and to the Church of the Holy Sepulcher. It was about a four- to five-hour trek and I was not in the best physical shape.

As I labored up the mountainside and down into the valley, I entered the quiet space of sweat-filled, breathless interior reflection. My intention was to enter the heart of Christ as he walked those same steps for far different reasons than I. "Teach me what I need to know; show me your heart," was my earnest prayer. As each step became more strained, things began to change.

Rather than centering on my inability to breathe in the hot August Jerusalem sun, I was moved to carry others with me on the burdensome trip. My attention started to shift. How must it have been for Christ as he carried the world on his shoulders that horrible, wonderful day!

"Who am I willing to carry?" Slowly, I became aware of those who suffer and those who cause the suffering. In that land of the Jews I became aware of the millions who had been oppressed, tortured, and murdered at the hands of an evil, distorted, obsessed, and blind Nazi Germany. I was also aware of Arab families from that same ancient land who, after the war to gain Israel's independence, were taken from their homes and led on a death march across Israel. Mothers, fathers, children, grandmothers, and grandfathers had their homes and possessions ripped from them as they were marched to their new settlements. Many died on that horrendous march. How quickly the oppressed had forgotten their own tortuous past and put on the cloak of oppressor.

I invited them all to walk with me, oppressed and oppressor, and together we prayed, "Father, forgive them for they know not what they do. Father, forgive us." The day wore on and my back bent low. As we continued toward the place of freedom, a new group joined my imaginary motley entourage of the world's oppressed. It was this last group that brought me to my knees. They were the children, all the children in the world who were suffering, abused, neglected, and crying out for deliverance. "Climb on," I said, "we'll make it together." We climbed the last mount to Jerusalem huffing with each breath, singing all the way, "Father, forgive them, for they know not what they do."

As we approached the church's courtyard, the holy place where that Final Deliverance was realized, my imaginary companions and I stood still. All of us, the oppressed, the marginalized, the tortured, the poor, the children . . . all of us stood at the door, aware of who had gone before us. As if struck by lightning, I became aware of just one person—one small girl—who, as a very young child, had cried out to be saved from the horror that was happening to her. If her parents had only known, they would have saved

her, but no one knew, no one saved her. She stood frozen at the doors.

It was as if the gentle hand of Jesus, from his nail-ridden wooden throne, reached out his hand to the small girl child and beckoned her into the holy place. Inside the holy of holies, the girl child and her friends stopped motionless at the rock, the earthen rock, split in two and opening into the earth's bowels, the rock that most believe is the very place where Jesus was crucified. On that hot August afternoon, energy-spent, breathless, and emptied, that small girl child and her companions gave it all up to the crucified Christ. They handed it over: the brokenness, the devastation. They left it all on the broken rock of Golgotha. "Father, forgive them, they did not, they do not know what they do."

This girl child was obviously my own wounded inner child. While details are unnecessary, that day Christ walked with me on the steps to Calvary and gave me freedom. He extends that same freedom to every broken person in the world. We are agents of his freedom. It is our job to bring the broken and the wounded to the wooden throne of Jesus.

I left the holy city that day with a new reality. Now whenever I hear the words, "Upon this rock I will build my church," I will think less of Peter and more of the broken, split, fissured rock of Golgotha. It is upon that rock that Jesus built his church—the broken rock of people's lost and forsaken lives, including Peter's. It is Christ who reaches out and says, "I have prepared the way, I have gone before you. . . . Come, find healing and forgiveness in me . . . find your freedom."

While this was no doubt a powerful moment of liberation, it is not necessary to go to Israel to encounter the Jesus of Matthew's passion. He is encountered in every life that struggles in the pain and sorrow of life and peacefully submits to the will of God. Jesus' passion finds expression with every person who chooses love over hatred and forgiveness over resentment. As a wife and mother I am asked to live the cross of Christ in the difficult times as well as in the everyday circumstances of life. My family participates in

Jesus' passion every time we face a crisis in our lives with a willingness to love, to communicate, to listen, and to put aside our selfish interests and our selfish pride.

Every time we love one another in spite of our angers and our hurts, we live the passion of Christ. Every time we refuse to give in to despair and hopelessness in the difficult times, we live the passion of Christ. We live Christ's passion every time we refuse to submit to hatred, animosity, jealousy, gossip, and self-serving interests, and instead offer love and reconciliation to those who are different from ourselves. Jesus' passion is intimately connected to the living of our lives. As wife and mother I live it every day. As a disciple and parishioner I am given opportunities to live it every day. Jesus' passion helps me face each day with new resolve to extend his reconciling ministry in my family, in my parish, and in the world.

All share their life experience.

What was Matthew's primary agenda in his version of the passion narrative? Have there been times in my life when I have worn the shoes of Peter, Judas, Pilate? In what way? Have I ever walked the way of Jesus? What was Matthew saying to his community, to our community, and to me today? How are we called to live Jesus' passion? What does the cross mean in our lives? In what way do we live the paschal mystery as a community? How do I personally live it? Do I still feel the same way about the passion of our Lord as I did when we began? Has my original understanding been stretched, challenged, or affirmed?

STEP 5
DECISION

The gospel demands a response.

In what concrete way does the passion of Christ call us (community, parish, me) to respond? Has this conversation with the exegesis of Matthew's passion changed me in any way? What concrete action could I/we take this week as a response to what we have learned and shared today?

DOCTRINAL ISSUES

What church truth/teaching/doctrinal issue could be drawn from the gospel for Passion Sunday?

Participants suggest possible doctrinal themes that flow from the readings.

Possible Doctrinal Themes

Cross, paschal mystery, redemptive suffering, soteriology

Present the doctrinal material at this time.

1. The facilitator gives input on a particular doctrinal issue of his/her prior choosing. OR
2. The group chooses a doctrinal issue from the list they created. They read together from the Doctrinal Appendix.

(The doctrinal issues are found in the Doctrinal Appendix in the back of this workbook. If you are choosing an issue from this resource, please refer to it now.)

Reflection questions centered around the chosen doctrinal theme can be found at the end of each topic in the Doctrinal Appendix. The questions are based on the five-step reflection process. If you choose a topic not included in the Doctrinal Appendix, craft your own questions according to the same five-step process.

Following the reflection questions you will be reminded to return to chapter 7, "Preparing the Catechetical Session," to assist you in crafting your own session.

Closing Prayer

Lord,
may the suffering and death of Jesus, your only Son,
make us pleasing to you.
Alone we can do nothing,
but may this perfect sacrifice
win us your mercy and love.
We ask this in the name of Jesus the Lord.[49]

---

[49]Passion Sunday: "Prayer Over the Gifts," *The Sacramentary.*

Holy Week, Easter Triduum, The Easter Season

Holy Week, Easter Triduum, The Easter Season: An Overview

HOLY WEEK

Palm Sunday, while still part of the Lenten season, inaugurates entrance into the liturgical year's holiest, most solemn week. "Holy Week has as its purpose the remembrance of Christ's passion, beginning with his Messianic entrance into Jerusalem. The Sixth Sunday of Lent, which marks the beginning of Holy Week, is called Passion Sunday [Palm Sunday]."[1] The first days of Holy Week, like all of Lent, serve as final preparation for the celebration of Easter. As the Triduum fast approaches, our focus turns toward the suffering of Christ. In the past, Mark's passion was read on Tuesday of Holy Week and Luke's was read on Wednesday. Now the passion narratives from the synoptic gospels are read on Palm Sunday in the three-year cycle.

During the weekdays of Holy Week the scriptures point us toward the Triduum. "In the first half of Holy Week the readings are about the mystery of Christ's passion."[2] We are immersed in the "Servant Songs" of the prophet Isaiah, whose image of the suffering servant finds fulfillment in the suffering of Jesus Christ. The gospel passages relate events from Jesus' last days before his pending passion and death.

Lent does not end with much fanfare. Like a graceful dancer, she makes one last pirouette, solemnly bows, and exits to make way for the grand finale, the showcase piece, the defining moment of the entire movement. Looking back in history, we observe two things that occurred before the Triduum began. The penitents, who on Ash Wednesday entered a period of preparation for reconciliation, were reconciled to the church on Holy Thursday. The oils were blessed on that same day. Thus, before the defining celebration of Christ's premier saving action could begin, the church became whole, complete, and restored again through the reconciliation of its penitents. The oils used in the sacramental, ongoing life of the church were blessed, sent, and received by individual parishes.

Chrism Mass

Lent ends on the evening of Holy Thursday with the celebration of the Lord's Supper. On the morning of Holy Thursday the Chrism Mass is celebrated by the bishop. For pastoral reasons it may be celebrated on a day prior to Holy Thursday. "At the Chrism Mass on Holy Thursday morning the bishop, concelebrating mass with his body of priests, blesses the oils and consecrates the chrism."[3] The blessing of the oils is a very ancient tradition dating back to Hippolytus and the *Apostolic Tradition* in the third century. Three oils are blessed: oil of chrism, oil of catechumens, and oil of the sick.

The chrism is blessed for the anointing of the newly baptized, for the chrismation of candidates for confirmation, and for the anointing of the hands of priests and the heads of bishops at ordination. Chrism is also used in the dedication of churches and altars.

The oil of catechumens is used to anoint catechumens in their preparation for baptism. "The anointing with oil symbolizes their need for God's help and strength so that, undeterred by the bonds of the past and overcoming the opposition of the devil, they will forthrightly take the step of professing their faith and will hold fast to it unfalteringly throughout their lives."[4]

"The oil of the sick is used to bring comfort and support to the sick in their infirmity."[5] The holy

---

[1] *GNLY*, #30, 31, in *TLD*.

[2] "Introduction to the Lectionary for Mass," *The Lectionary for Mass*, #98.

[3] *GNLY*, #31.

[4] *RCIA*, #99.

[5] "Ceremonial of Bishops," in *TLD*, #274.

oils represent the ministry of the church. Each year we bless the new oils that are used in church life.

The premier focus of the Chrism Mass is the priesthood of Christ. The first reading and the gospel remind us that Jesus was empowered and anointed for this holy priesthood by the Holy Spirit. The second reading for the Chrism Mass from the book of Revelation reminds us that Jesus shares this priesthood with his disciples. "For the Chrism Mass the readings bring out both Christ's messianic mission and its continuation in the Church by means of the sacraments."[6] The Chrism Mass is also an expression of the unity of the priesthood and sacrifice of Jesus, which continues to be a present reality in the church today. All the priests of the diocese come together to concelebrate the Chrism Mass with their bishop and to consecrate the chrism, because they, like the bishop, share in the mission of Christ to sanctify, guide, and build up God's people.[7]

The preface of the Chrism Mass offers praise and thanks for Jesus' priesthood, for our share in it and for those who have been called "to share his sacred ministry by the laying on of hands."[8] The preface outlines the call of ministerial, ordained priesthood:

> He appoints them [presbyters] to renew in his
>   name
> the sacrifice of our redemption
> as they set before your family his paschal meal.
> He calls them to lead your holy people in love,
> nourish them by your word,
>   and strengthen them through the sacraments.
> Father, they are to give their lives in your service
> and for the salvation of your people as
> they strive to grow in the likeness of Christ
> and honor you by their courageous witness of
>   faith and love.[9]

The oils are blessed and a renewal of commitment to priestly life may also take place during the liturgy.

---

[6]"Lectionary for Mass: Introduction," #91, in *TLD*.
[7]"Ceremonial of Bishops," #274.
[8]Chrism Mass: "Preface for Priesthood" (P20), *The Sacramentary*.
[9]Ibid.

While most of the faithful will not be participating in the Chrism Mass, it is an important part of our heritage and a vital piece of our tradition. The scriptures of the Chrism Mass speak to us of Christ's priesthood and our share in his priesthood by virtue of our baptism (according to the ritual text for baptism, we are anointed *priest, prophet*, and *king*). The scriptures and the ritual texts of the Chrism Mass foreshadow and remember the rights, duties, and responsibilities of ordained priesthood. The oils used in the sacramental function of the church are blessed and distributed for use in all diocesan churches throughout the liturgical year.

The Chrism Mass is a pivotal liturgy. Catechesis based on the liturgical year must address the Chrism Mass and what it means for the ongoing life of the church. This workbook does not provide a session for the Chrism liturgy. However, the scriptures and the issues just mentioned should be shared and addressed in catechetical reflections of Holy Week. To completely ignore the Chrism Mass would be tantamount to omitting an integral piece of the church's liturgical life.

THE EASTER TRIDUUM

The Easter Triduum is the "mother of all feasts." All other feasts of the year hinge on this great feast. While each Sunday stands on its own as an observance of the paschal mystery, the entire liturgical year is in forward motion toward the fundamental commemoration of our Christian faith: the redemptive action of Jesus Christ's passion, death, and resurrection. "Theologically and historically the entire liturgical year springs from the paschal redemptive action of Christ and the celebration of this action."[10] Any treatment of the liturgical year should begin and flow from the foundation and celebration of Easter. However, the liturgical year begins on the first Sunday of Advent and liturgical books are ordered according to chronological progression rather than the preeminence of the feast. Thus, in the interest of following the liturgical year and the Lectionary and Sacramentary's layout, *Word & Worship Workbook* begins with the First Sunday of Advent rather than with the logical, primary place—Easter.

---

[10]*LY*, 57.

It is understood that the early Christians remembered Jesus' saving event in a special way during the annual Jewish celebration of Passover. Jesus, the new paschal lamb, passed from death to life. While the early Christians continued to observe the Jewish Passover, it took on new significance in light of Jesus' saving action. There was probably a gradual break from the traditional Jewish Passover.

However, according to second-century literary evidence, there was debate over the date of the annual celebration, suggesting a probable first-century observance. The earliest recorded celebration consisted of a eucharistic meal, preceded by a period of fasting. According to Adolf Adam, the focus of the feast in Rome was primarily on Christ's resurrection and exaltation. The Council of Nicea (325) definitively set the date on the first Sunday after the first full moon in the spring. This way, Easter would not fall during the annual Jewish Passover feast.

The feast takes its name from the Aramaic and Greek word, *pascha,* which is a translation from the Hebrew, *pesach.* The Hebrew word is translated as a "passing by" or "passing through." The word refers to the primary saving event of Israel. The angel of death passed over the houses of the Israelites. Hebrew slaves were led safely out of bondage through the Red Sea and were given safe passage to the Promised Land. Christians appropriated the feast of Passover to their understanding of Jesus' *pasch:* "He passed through the sea of suffering and death and led the people of God to a communion of grace with the Father."[11]

The word *Easter* has various questionable origins. It was once thought to be a reference to the worship of the spring goddess, *Eostre.* However, modern scholarship refutes that connection. Though scholars are still uncertain, it is probably derived from some connection to or translation of the word *East*, where each day meets the rising sun (an obvious metaphor for "Christ, the sun of justice who will rise again in the East after his descent into death"[12]).

The Triduum: A Celebration of the Paschal Mystery

Jesus' *pasch* includes his suffering, passion, death, and—most of all—his passage from death to new life through the resurrection. Raniero Cantalamessa expresses it as follows: "The Passover was a pre-existing institution which the Christians inherited from the Old Testament. All its symbolism was directed to immolation, blood sacrifice. Because this was so, it was easy for Christians to make transfer to the passion of Christ."[13] Thus, the term "paschal mystery" was used to express the reality we know as Jesus' suffering, death, and resurrection. According to St. Augustine, "Passover is the day on which we at the same time celebrate the Lord's passion and resurrection."[14] Therefore, Easter is the prime, exalted celebration of the paschal mystery. However, every sacramental celebration is also the ritual remembrance of the same mystery. The Great Feast, however, summons our power of remembering with greater intensity, and rouses within us greater rejoicing, awareness, and corporate memory of the Easter event itself. It brings the paschal experience to full consciousness so that we may enter the mystery of Jesus' death and resurrection with active and vigilant participation. Thus, "Christ's Passover is prolonged in the Church with three rhythms of differing frequency; an annual rhythm which is the feast of Easter; a weekly rhythm which is Sunday; and a daily rhythm which consists in the daily celebration of the Eucharist."[15]

The feast of Easter is the ritual proclamation and embodiment of the saving act of Jesus' resurrection and glorification. This saving reality is remembered and brought into the present. Through this utterly gratuitous act of self-giving love, Jesus conquered sin and death and gave the human race the promise of eternal life and perfect union with Yahweh, the Lord of all creation. Through Jesus' saving act, the church was born. Through the Holy Spirit, the church was empowered to live in perfect union with Christ and to spread his Good News. The feast of Easter cele-

---

[11]Ibid., 20.

[12]*Patrologia Latina,* ed. J.-P. Migne, Paris, 1878–90, 172:69, in *LY*, 63.

---

[13]*ME*, 37.

[14]St. Augustine, *Sermo Denis 7 (Miscellanea Agostiniana, 1,* p. 32).

[15]*ME*, 58.

brates the passage from death to life. It inaugurates the church's participation in Christ's redeeming action. The church at Easter remembers past events and makes them present. Easter also prompts the church to look forward to the new and eternal city in the next life as it works for the salvation of the world in this one.

Historical Perspective

Prior to the fourth century all the different aspects of this powerful mystery were separated into specific units that centered on particular features of the mystery. Originally the Easter Vigil was spent in fasting and mourning over the death of Jesus until midnight.[16] The joy of the resurrection thus began at the end of the evening's vigil. At the end of the fourth century there was no Easter Sunday mass, as the Easter liturgy lasted all night long.

Over time, however, the vigil prior to the mass was shortened. In response to the vigil not lasting until the appointed midnight hour, the church of the sixth century initiated an Easter Sunday liturgy. By the eighth century, an early evening vigil emerged, and by the ninth century the rituals that preceded the mass were moved back to noon, thus pushing the mass back to three o'clock. From the Middle Ages on, three o'clock in the afternoon became the starting time for all masses that took place on fast days.

Fasting laws relaxed during the fourteenth century, so masses on fast days were moved to the morning hours. This posed a serious problem, however, for the Easter Vigil. The vigil rituals had to take place in the very early hours of the morning in order for the mass to be celebrated during regular morning hours. This was made obligatory by Pius V. The result: the Easter Candle was carried into the church to the proclamation of *Lumen Christi* in the full light of day, with no one but a few clerics and a handful of the faithful gathered for participation.

Then, in 1951, Pius XII restored the early church's experience of the night vigil and moved it to the night before Easter. The rite was revised and finally made law in 1955. "The Roman Catholic liturgy had rediscovered a lost treasure."[17] Further steps were taken to restore this beautiful, awesome liturgy to its rightful place and status among the liturgies of the church. "During it [the Easter Vigil] the Church keeps watch, awaiting the resurrection of Christ and celebrating it in the sacraments. The entire celebration of this Vigil should take place at night, beginning after nightfall and ending with dawn."[18] "In accord with an ancient tradition, this night is a night of vigil for the Lord, and, as the memorial of the holy night of Christ's resurrection, the Vigil celebrated is the 'mother of all holy vigils.' The Church this night awaits the Lord's resurrection and celebrates the sacrament of initiation."[19]

By the fourth century, pieces of the Triduum gradually developed and merged into one distinct commemoration of the paschal mystery. The Triduum is the word designated for celebration of the Lord's paschal mystery that spans three days. The Triduum is one liturgy that lasts three days. There is no formal closing to the Holy Thursday or Good Friday liturgies. The liturgy continues for three days until its culmination at the Easter Vigil. For three days, the church enters and remains in the tomb with Christ. The Triduum begins with the Mass of the Lord's Supper, continues with the celebration of the Lord's passion on Good Friday, culminates with the Easter Vigil on Holy Saturday, and ends with evening prayer on Easter Sunday.

Holy Thursday

The Mass of the Lord's Supper begins the Triduum. It commemorates the Last Supper and is a living memorial of the institution of the eucharist and of the Lord's Passover in which Jesus left us sacramental signs of his new covenant. In this new covenant, Jesus promised to be with us through the signs he inaugurated (especially the eucharist). Through the *mandatum*, the washing of feet, Jesus reminds us of the self-sacrificing nature of his love. Jesus, servant of the human race, loves

---

[16]*LY*, 64.

[17]Ibid., 77.

[18]*GNLY*, #21.

[19]"Ceremonial of Bishops," #332.

us to his death. Jesus, servant of all, washes the feet of those he serves and instructs his disciples to go and do the same. We share in the servanthood of Christ. In John's gospel there is no eucharist of bread and wine. John's eucharist *is* the washing of feet. The implication? Go, do this in memory of me! The "Ceremonial of Bishops" asserts that the liturgy of Holy Thursday recalls the unconditional love of God and the height and the depth of that love—even unto death.[20]

We slowly shift into part two of our three-day liturgy as part one quietly fades into the meditative silence of darkness. The liturgy of Holy Thursday draws to its temporary intermission, and the church enters into the silence of meditation as it sets its face toward Jerusalem and the ominous events that will forever change the world.

Good Friday

Celebration of the Lord's Passion on Good Friday commemorates the redemption Jesus won for us through the free gift of his life. Jesus was the messianic fulfillment prefigured by the law and the prophets in the Old Testament scriptures. The redemptive act of the cross was the fulfillment of all the saving acts of Yahweh prior to the Incarnation.

The liturgy of Good Friday begins in silent prayer. There are three parts: the liturgy of the word, with John's account of the passion and the general intercessions; the veneration of the cross; and communion using bread consecrated at the Holy Thursday liturgy. During the liturgy of the word we encounter John's Christ, the royal victor, who is fully aware of his divine preexistence.[21] Jesus' death will return him to his former state, to the state that was his before he was sent to this life's sojourn by his Father. He is not a victim; he is the initiator of events. Jesus freely walks to his death. Jesus is aware of his victory over his enemy, Satan. The Good Friday liturgy is a cause for joyful celebration because of the infinite love of God demonstrated through his Son's passion.[22]

The intercessions of Good Friday are a sign of the priestly function of God's people. All are gathered together in the sacred assembly to offer prayers on behalf of the entire world. The veneration of the cross reminds us of the good news inherent in the cross: this instrument of torture became a sign of salvation and love for all humanity. Part two of this great three-day feast culminates with the reception of communion consecrated the night before at the Holy Thursday Mass of the Lord's Supper. The faithful then leave in silence. The church stands hopeful as it anticipates the night of the great Phoenix rising out of the ashes of sin and death. The church, then, awaits the Passover of the Lord.

The Easter Vigil

The Easter Vigil, in the words of St. Augustine, is the mother of all feasts. It takes center stage in relation to the other liturgies of the Triduum. "During it [the Easter Vigil] the Church keeps watch, awaiting the resurrection of Christ and *celebrating it in the sacraments* [italics mine]. The entire celebration of this Vigil should take place at night, beginning after nightfall and ending with the dawn."[23] There are four parts to the liturgy of this most holy night: the service of fire/light, the liturgy of the word, the service of baptism, and the liturgy of the eucharist.

The Service of Fire/Light

The service of fire/light catapults us back to the journey of the Israelites as they were led by the bright pillar of fire. The radiance of that fire, now dimmed, was replaced by the light of Christ shining in the lives of people. The primordial symbol of fire is blessed anew. The light of the Easter candle is triumphantly carried into the darkened space; the Easter proclamation of *Christ, the Light Who Dispels the Darkness* is shouted, resounded, proclaimed, and heralded in the midst of the great assembly. The *Exultet's* euphoric proclamation elevates the gathering to a communion between the saints of heaven and earth who stand exultant in an assembly of triumphant victory over the crushed head of Satan, the evil arch-villain.

---

[20]Ibid., #297.
[21]*CCHW*, 57.
[22]*DL* (III), 23.

[23]*GNLY*, #21.

The Liturgy of the Word

The liturgy of the word carries us back to the roots of our Christian genesis: creation, passover, and paschal mystery. The believer is thrust into the drama of the first passover, Israel's liberation from bondage; the second passover, Jesus' passage from death to resurrection; and the third and ongoing passover, the church's passover from sin, darkness, and death to resurrected life both now and for eternity. The Vigil scriptures move us into a world of virtual reality. We are present at the threshold of dawn's first light, water's first flow, the star's first glimmer, the animal's first ravenous howl, the seed's first agonizing rupture from earth's womb and humanity's entrance on the world stage. We are hardly passive spectators as we intimately encounter man's and woman's first cognizance of their own goodness.

We are there and it is now as we stand with Abraham and Sarah in that first perpetual covenant of faith. *We are there and it is now* as we trudge through the parted waters of death, pursued and exhausted by Pharaoh's onslaught, only to be enfolded in the protective mantle of Yahweh's liberating providence. *We are there and it is now* as we call down that great and terrible day of the Lord's visitation, when sin comes to an end and we are gathered as *one people* to process majestically to the gates of the jeweled eternal city. (The first four Old Testament readings.)

The word reminds us that this is a night of genesis, of new life. Life is reborn as we witness the baptismal passage from death to life. Water flows abundantly as it promises to quench our thirst. The God who calls us to repentance pours down the waters of forgiveness on the church. The wisdom who blesses, invites, and leads to the light also delivers us from the stain of defilement. We are sprinkled with fresh water, given new hearts, taken by the hand, and led to the font. (The last three Old Testament readings).

We are then ready to stand in the Roman assembly as Paul definitively acclaims (then and now) that baptism is the "passage from death to sin, to life for God."[24] And finally, as fully engaged, sense-sharpened celebrants, we go with Matthew to the empty tomb, where we, alongside the women witnesses,[25] are the first to hear the wondrous news: "Do not be frightened. I know you are looking for Jesus the crucified, but he is not here. He has been raised, exactly as he promised."

The Service of Baptism

Thus, our senses sated and our emotions spent, we escort the elect to the font of life to *do* what we have heard, experienced, professed, and acclaimed. We bring new life to birth and in the process initiate our own rebirth.

As this is a night of new things and new beginnings, the new water is blessed. The water carries symbols and images both ancient and new. As the new water is blessed, the presider-celebrant once again touches our corporate memory. We are reminded of how God's hand once stirred the embryonic waters of creation and deluged the earth with flood, thereby hinting at the purgation of sin through water. Scripture's water images bring us face to face with the God who parted the Red Sea of deliverance. The symbol of water takes us to the shore of the Jordan River where Jesus, the "Beloved Son" whose lanced side would inaugurate the saving flow of his water and his blood, was baptized. Finally, the holy waters of creation, the Red Sea, and the Jordan still flow through the apostolic mission to baptize in the name of the Father, Son, and Holy Spirit.[26] The service of baptism lets us once again plunge into the ancient primordial symbol of water to remind us of who God is, what God did, and what God continues to do in and through the resurrection of Jesus Christ. God immerses us in the purging waters of baptism where death sinks to the bottom and resurrected life gushes to the top, dripping and spilling over at the font's edge. With all the saints—past, present, and future—the church, in its annual ritual, celebrates resurrected life and initiates new members into its hallowed communion.

---

[24]*DL* (III), 43.

[25]In order for an event to be proclaimed as authentic, there needed to be two male witnesses. Thus, one can hardly miss the irony that the only witnesses to the empty tomb were not even officially allowed to testify to what they had seen and heard. God does not need a human court to authenticate the greatest act of redemption in salvation history.

[26]*DL* (III), 63.

Together with the elect, we commit and recommit ourselves through our baptismal promises. We pledge to enter and continue in the struggle between good and evil by renouncing evil's lure. We profess our faith in the Father, the resurrected Christ, and the Holy Spirit. Finally, the baptismal liturgy comes to a close as the newly baptized are anointed with confirmation's holy oil, permanently signed and sealed with the Spirit and delivered into God's service. Thus bathed and anointed, neophytes are ready for the joyful, exultant, and long awaited culmination of their journey: incorporation into the Body of Christ through the eucharist, the ongoing participation in Christ's paschal mystery. Purged, reconciled, and renewed through the waters of baptism, the faithful are ready for eucharist, that which St. Augustine called the repeatable sacrament of initiation.

Liturgy of the Eucharist

As the assembly breathes a sigh of intermission, the gifts of bread and wine are brought to the table and the paschal story continues in word and action. Calvary and Easter coexist boldly on our communal table. The *cross* stands triumphant in the brilliant light of the *resurrection* and we, God's people, consume both realities at the eucharistic banquet. Thus fed, we go forth, cross in hand, the resurrection in heart, and take what we have consumed to feed the starving soul of the world.

If this sounds like poetry, so it must. It is only through the language of poets that we dare come close to capturing the mystery of this sacred, awe-filled, holy night.

Symbols of the Vigil

The dominant liturgical symbols of the church—assembly, cross, fire/light, word, water, oil, white garment, laying on of hands, bread, wine—are all manifest at the Easter Vigil. The symbols speak to us of our identity as Catholic Christians. For example, the symbol of light has its genesis in Christ, the light of the world. Since we are to walk as children of the light, light identifies us and we become its reality—we become light, we become bread, etc.

Meaning is conveyed when people encounter symbols, which are repeatable and possess many layers of meaning. They are multi-faceted and have multiple forms and uses. At the Vigil alone, the symbol of light shines forth in the new fire, the Easter candle, the candles of the faithful, the incense, and the sanctuary lamp. Light's power is felt by its absence in the darkened church. The meaning of symbols is expressed in the way they are used and in the background and gestures that define them. Symbols are also understood through the words of the ritual text that are used in relation to them, and through the sacramental proclamation of God's word that accompanies their use.[27]

The Easter Vigil calls forth the symbols that illuminate our existence and that occur in all liturgies. We are people of the cross. We are chrismated into the ecclesial community. We are people of the light and the water of baptism incorporates us into the paschal mystery. We are people of the table: we are eucharistic people.

"Liturgical action depends on symbols because beings cannot be together and communicate without some kind of encounter in words (verbal symbols) and/or in gestures and actions (nonverbal symbols). All knowledge begins with our senses; this means that an encounter with God is only possible by means of sensible signs."[28] In antiquity, a symbol used to be understood as two halves, which when joined became one whole. The person who had one half would thus recognize the other half because the two put together formed the whole entity. By extension, then, a symbol can be regarded as two parts of a whole—the visible and the invisible. Just because the invisible half of the symbol is not readily observable, it is nevertheless half of the reality. When joined with the visible half of the symbol, it constitutes the whole reality. "In the language of religion and theology it is frequently the case that the concept of 'symbol' is reserved for the signs of faith, that is...in addition to their superficial, natural meaning, another and supernatural meaning that is only accessible to

---

[27]Linda Gaupin, *Sacramental Catechesis,* course text for "Special Certification in Sacramental Catechesis," Diocese of Orlando, Florida, November 1996.

[28]*MSS,* 13.

faith."[29] Through symbols we are able to touch the deep mysteries of our faith in ways that words can never express.

If symbols were to speak, they would say: "I am . . ." rather than "I am like. . . ." Symbols in the sacramental sense *are* the reality they express. Eucharist in the form of bread and wine *is* the Body and Blood of Jesus. We can say with assurance that symbols express our identity. When we consume the precious elements, we become what we have consumed: the Mystical Body of Christ. The symbols of the Easter Vigil, highlighted and set forth, give us the means to communicate with God and for God to communicate with us through our senses. They express all of our sacramental realities. The symbols of the Vigil are food for mystagogical reflection throughout the Easter season and form the basis of our sacramental catechesis.

Easter Sunday

The Easter Sunday liturgy is a later development and thus did not originally have a liturgy of its own. The Easter Vigil is considered the principal mass of the Easter feast.[30] The Easter Sunday mass, however, is a cacophony of jubilation. From the opening prayers to the dismissal alleluia, praise and thanks are rendered for the resurrection of the Lord Jesus Christ. Many people who attend Easter Sunday mass do not attend the Vigil. It is important, therefore, that the homily reflect the unity of the passion and resurrection just as it is reflected in the Easter preface and the communion antiphon. The Vigil should be upheld "as the climax of the liturgical year and thus should be explained."[31] Very often the neophytes return on Easter Sunday and take their rightful place as fully initiated, candle carrying, garmented members of the celebrating assembly. The neophytes themselves are an Easter symbol for the community: a symbol of new, resurrected life in our midst.

---

[29]Ibid.
[30]*LY,* 83.
[31]Ibid., 84.

OCTAVE OF EASTER

The first eight days after Easter are called the octave. The liturgical calendar names each day a solemnity of the Lord ("General Instruction of the Roman Missal," #24). The observance of the octave dates back to the mid-third to fourth century. Some suggest that celebration of the octave has its roots in the Jewish Passover and the seven days of Unleavened Bread. Each day of the octave was, for the neophytes, a fuller introduction to the mysteries of faith and their initiation sacraments. Observance of the octave was a universal practice of the church (*ecclesiae consensus*) in which all the faithful attended daily liturgy and refrained from work. At one time the octave was referred to as "white week," since the neophytes wore their white baptismal garments to mass. The Eastern church called it a "week of renewal."

Due to the fast-paced life we lead, it is often difficult for the neophytes to attend daily liturgy during the octave. However, the practice should be strongly encouraged. The solemnities of the octave are an integral part of the Easter mystery. Most catechetical groups do not have the opportunity to come together to experience and reflect upon each day of the octave. This workbook will not provide sessions for the days of the octave. However, the octave should not be ignored. Those in catechetical groups—actually, all Catholics—should make every effort to attend daily mass and, when possible, reflect upon the scriptures, ritual prayers, and experience of the liturgies of the octave.

FIFTY DAYS OF EASTER

"The fifty days from Easter Sunday to Pentecost are sometimes called the great 'Sunday.'"[32] Each Sunday is considered a paschal Sunday; the Sundays are called the Second, Third, Fourth, etc. Sundays *of* Easter (not after Easter) until the eighth Sunday, called Pentecost. Forty days after Easter, the Ascension of the Lord into heaven is celebrated except in places where it is not a holy day of obligation, in which case it is moved to the Seventh Sunday of Easter. Following the feast of the Ascension, the weekdays are intended as a

---

[32]*GNLY,* #22.

preparation for Pentecost. Each Sunday of the Easter season is a solemnity, a Great Feast. Each Sunday exalts an aspect of the paschal mystery.

All three scripture readings of the Sundays are taken from the New Testament. The first reading is always from the Acts of the Apostles. The second reading for Cycle A is from the first letter of Peter. The gospel readings for Cycle A are from John, with the exception of the Third Sunday of Easter, which is Luke's account of the Emmaus story.

The celebration of the fifty days is the church's extended meditation on the paschal mystery as the source, summit, and driving power of the Christian life. The paschal mystery is the heart of all celebration, liturgical and sacramental. The resurrection of Jesus is the hinge on which the doors of faith swing. Without it, the church has no purpose for existence.

The Fifty Days of Easter and the Rite of Christian Initiation

The fifty days of Easter are also called the period of mystagogia (uncovering the mysteries). In the early centuries of the church, there existed an advanced type of religious instruction called mystagogical catechesis, or an introduction to the mysteries. This was usually directed by the bishop after baptism, not before. There was a belief that neophytes were unable to comprehend the church's teaching on eucharist until they had experienced it. Once they had taken part in the ritual celebration, then and only then would they be able to grasp what the awesome mystery was about. In his first address to the neophytes, St. Ambrose began: "I shall begin now to speak of the sacraments which you have received. It was not proper for me to do so before this, because, the Christian faith must come first."[33]

The reality of the risen and crucified Christ was conveyed through the initiation rites and their powerful symbols, thus sparking faith and enthusiasm. Mystagogical catechesis infuses the truths of the faith and the sacraments through the concrete, personal, and vivid memories of water-soaked skin, oil-slathered body, and flowing white robes. St. Cyril

said it best to the neophytes: "It has long been my wish to discourse to you on these spiritual, heavenly mysteries. On the principle, however, that seeing is believing, I delayed until the present occasion, calculating that, after what you saw that night, I should find you a readier audience when I am to be your guide to the brighter and more fragrant meadows of this second Eden."[34]

Mystagogical catechesis seeks to make a connection between the events of salvation history (the prefiguring events of the Old Testament and their fulfillment through Christ) and the rites that make those saving events manifest and the benefits operative. Mystagogical catechesis explains the rite in dialogue with the experience of it. Mystagogical catechesis weds truth and experience. During their preparation for baptism, the catechumens immersed themselves in God's word and in the truths of our faith laid out in the celebration of the litugical year. As they unpacked the liturgy week after week, they discovered the truths of salvation history, and with baptism, confirmation, and eucharist they completed the rites of initiation. Now, for the first time, their prior knowledge and their experience come together.

The agenda of mystagogia is ongoing ritual catechesis. What happened? What did it mean? What are the implications and what am I going to do about them? Mystagogy is ongoing, repeated celebration leading to reflection that provides understanding which demands a response, a decision. Mystagogical catechesis is an activity of the entire church. It is what the Easter season is all about. We are *all* to spend the season asking, "What happened, what was my experience, and what does it mean?" The neophytes point to what we should all be doing.

During the season of Easter, the entire church enters a period of mystagogia in which we experience and reflect upon the meaning of the symbols of initiation that express the dying and rising of Jesus for the fifty days between Easter and Pentecost Sunday. "Mystagogy is a time for the community and the neophytes together to grow in deepening their grasp of the paschal mystery and in making it part of their lives through meditation

---

[33]St. Ambrose, *Catechesis mystagogica* 1.1. (PG 33, 1066).

[34]St. Cyril of Jerusalem 14.10 (PG 33, 836), in *ME*, 65.

on the Gospel, sharing in the Eucharist and doing the works of charity."[35] It is a time for reflection on the way we are called to die and rise and thus fully embrace the paschal mystery in our daily lives. Reflection on the Easter gospels in light of their sacramental experience is the springboard for neophytes to unpack the meaning of the sacraments. This is post-baptismal, sacramental catechesis. Mystagogia is a time to gather with the community for eucharist and to be fed at the paschal table. It is a time to become more immersed in a life of service, outreach, evangelization, and corporal and spiritual works of mercy.

The heart of mystagogy flows from ritual. We pray, we celebrate, we believe; then we seek to find meaning in our prayer, celebration, and belief. What does it mean for our lives? The ritual of mystagogia is eucharist, the "repeatable sacrament of initiation" (Augustine). The neophyte and the worshiping community become immersed in the Easter stories, symbols, and eucharists. Knowledge and understanding of the church's Easter tradition are thus based on experience. The risen Christ is experienced in word, in sacrament, and in symbol. To experience Christ is to "know" Christ.

The fifty days of Easter show us how to live the mystery of the Risen Lord as a result of plunging into the waters of rebirth, of being anointed with the Spirit, and of feasting at the Lord's table. Empty vessels become fully filled. The whole church is catechized, not just the neophytes.

Thus, while post-baptismal catechesis would appear to be only for neophytes, it is indeed the business of everyone; it is a lifelong pursuit. The scriptures and liturgies of the season invite us to engage in this ancient form of catechesis in order to become fully absorbed in the paschal mystery of Jesus Christ. The historical perspective of the fifty days will be covered in the section that deals with Pentecost.

ASCENSION

The feast of the Ascension is a solemnity that focuses on Jesus' second coming (entrance rite) and his continued risen presence in the community (communion antiphon). The liturgy's opening prayer expresses the effects of the resurrection: the elevation of human beings to the glory of Christ. The first two readings are the same every year but the gospel changes according to the cycle.

During the fourth century, the feast of the Ascension was celebrated on the fiftieth day along with the feast of Pentecost. However, there emerged a practice of celebrating the Ascension on the fortieth day after Easter. The reason for this was twofold. First, there was a strong connection to the sacred significance of the number forty. Second, there was reference in the Acts of the Apostles to "appearing during forty days . . ." and also the witness of the Ascension account in verses 9-11. The decision was made to place the celebration forty days after the resurrection.

The weekdays following Ascension serve as preparation for Pentecost, for the coming of the Holy Spirit. Thus, the old popular devotion, the Pentecost novena, was replaced by an official liturgy. During these pre-Pentecost days, the church enters the room of prayer with Mary, the women, and the disciples as they await the holy fire of the Spirit.

PENTECOST

Pentecost (*pentekoste,* the ordinal form of the number fifty) takes place fifty days after Easter and brings the Easter season to a close. It is the final, dramatic curtain call in which the church is brought on stage, commissioned, and sent out with the fire of the Holy Spirit. Pentecost inaugurates the full manifestation of the Spirit in the messianic age. Pentecost ushers us into the reality of all that was prophesied by the law and the prophets and then fulfilled through Jesus Christ. Pentecost, in its thunderous clamor from the womb of anticipation, celebrates the church's birth on Calvary. Even though Pentecost commemorates the events that took place fifty days after Easter, it continues on through time through the liturgical celebration.[36]

---

[35]*RCIA,* #244.

[36]*DL* (III), 249.

Pentecost is the day the church celebrates the conferral of the Holy Spirit. "It appears on the fiftieth day, when the Spirit was poured out on the first Christian community, giving it the strength and confidence to testify publicly to the resurrection."[37] The paschal celebration of redemption through Christ took place over the fifty days of Easter and was understood to include the "victorious passion and death, his resurrection and ascension, and the sending of the Spirit upon the Church."[38] Thus, Easter was not just a celebration of the resurrection of Christ, but also an extension of his ministry through the Spirit to the Church: ". . . Pascha was a total celebration of our redemption. . . ."[39]

The Christian feast of Pentecost has its roots and is to be understood in light of the Jewish celebration by that same name. The Jewish feast of Pentecost, or Weeks, also called *Shabuoth* ("Weeks") was the closing feast for the season of harvest that began with the feast of Unleavened Bread. Thomas Talley speaks of several hypotheses regarding the origin of Pentecost. He suggests that some scholars maintain that Pentecost represents a period of seven weeks measured from the day after Passover. The feast of Passover marked the first day. Thus, seven times a seven-day week equals forty-nine and the addition of one day for festival makes a *pentecontad*, or a period of fifty days.[40] There was dispute over how to count the days and there was an absence of dispute regarding a particular date for the feast of Weeks. Thus, it is suggested that "in the first century it was not simply the fiftieth day that was considered sacred, but the very period between that fiftieth day and the day from which it was counted, a day related in one way or another to Passover."[41] Since pilgrims from Judea and Galilee gathered in Jerusalem for the single-day feast of Pentecost, some scholars suggest that Pentecost was the celebration that brought the entire season, beginning with Passover, to a close. However, Talley maintains that there is also scriptural evidence that the feast stood on its own and was a feast celebrating the renewal of covenant and the giving

of the law (Book of Jubilees, ca. 140–100 B.C.E.).[42] During the time of Christ it was probably being observed as a feast of renewal of the covenant.

There is no solid evidence to suggest that the period between Passover and Pentecost was appropriated as one feast of rejoicing by the first-century Christian church. However, by the second century there is evidence (fasting and kneeling in prayer were forbidden during the fifty days) that Christians observed an extended festival from Easter to Pentecost.

As the feast evolved and in places where it was celebrated on Sunday, the feast of Pentecost was counted from Easter-day itself, thus making Pentecost the eighth Sunday after Easter Sunday. Easter to Pentecost was celebrated as one continuous period of rejoicing. However, by the fourth century, the unitive dimension to the fifty days of Easter waned in the Roman church as Ascension and Pentecost were regarded as distinct festivals. Adolf Adam reminds us that the East always regarded Pentecost as the close of the Easter season. The Roman liturgy, on the other hand, "made this day an independent entity and thus a more or less isolated feast of the sending of the Holy Spirit."[43] Like the great feast of Easter, Pentecost was thus afforded an octave that caused liturgical confusion as it coincided with the ember days (days of penance), which had already been established on the liturgical calendar. Thus, this feast of rejoicing over the sending of the Spirit was clouded by days of penance.

In light of historical liturgical studies, the Congregation of Rites restored Pentecost to its unity with Easter and reaffirmed the close connection between the Resurrection, Ascension, and the sending of the Spirit. The "General Norms for the Liturgical Year and the Calendar" states: "The fifty days from Easter Sunday to Pentecost are celebrated in joyful exultation as one feast day, or better as one 'great Sunday'" [#22].

There are two liturgies of Pentecost: the vigil mass and mass during the day. The vigil mass is not

[37]Ibid., 293–294.
[38]*OLY*, 57.
[39]Ibid.
[40]Ibid.
[41]Ibid., 59.

[42]Ibid., 61.
[43]*LY*, 89–90.

widely celebrated as the "mass during the day" is usually chosen for the Saturday evening liturgy prior to Pentecost Sunday. Even though we seldom participate in the vigil mass, the texts are nevertheless a wonderful preparatory meditation in anticipation of the Sunday celebration of Pentecost. The second reading and the gospel are always the same: Romans 8:22–27 and John 7:37–39. The first reading is chosen from among four possibilities: Genesis 11:1–9, Exodus 19:3–8, 16–20, Ezekiel 37:1–14, and Joel 3:1–5.

Pentecost's power is not simply in the recall of a monumental sacred event. While it is indeed just that, it is so much more. Pentecost is an ongoing event. It was inaugurated in the first Christian community, but it still continues to unfold in this messianic era. Pentecost is our eternal hope: it is the perpetual gift of the Spirit to build the Body of Christ. Pentecost celebrates within the community that which takes place in the individual through baptism and eucharist. The Spirit who breathes transforming life into the church is given at baptism and continues to be manifest through the ongoing celebration of eucharist. It is the same Spirit who challenges, teaches, seals us permanently to Christ, and leads us forward in holiness to the new Jerusalem, the holy, eternal city. Pentecost celebrates the reign of God now and not yet; it is a present and future reality. The Spirit of Pentecost continues the work of Christ on earth as we are formed and prepared for the great day of his return. Pentecost is the ongoing renewal of our participation in Christ's new covenant. The liturgy of Pentecost calls us to worship in spirit and in truth. We are strengthened for mission to the world's poor, oppressed, and spiritually hungry.

In summary then, Easter is a living memorial of the primary Christian symbol of deliverance and liberation—Christ's passion, death, and resurrection. Through his ultimate act of sacrifice, Jesus inaugurated the *new covenant*. Jesus, the New Passover, shed his blood, thereby ratifying the new covenant. Jesus' passage from death to life for the forgiveness of sins fulfilled all the promises Yahweh had made with Israel since the creation of the world. Death ultimately lost its power. Christ's death and resurrection would guarantee human beings a place at the eternal banquet. The living memorial of Christ's Passover today is our sharing in the Body and Blood of Christ in the eucharist and our incorporation into and participation in the paschal mystery.

Each year, Easter renews our participation in the paschal mystery. We recall and renew our participation in the life, passion, death, and resurrection of Jesus and the sending of the Spirit to the church. Liturgically and sacramentally we celebrate and exalt the saving effects in our lives. We recommit our lives to cross and resurrection, to dying and rising, and in the process we are renewed in the mandate to go out, teach, and baptize all nations. Such is our faith; so shall it be.

HOLY THURSDAY

INTRODUCTORY RITES

Opening Song (or Entrance Antiphon)

We should glory in the cross of our Lord Jesus Christ, for he is our salvation, our life and our resurrection; through him we are saved and made free.[1]

Opening Prayer

Let us pray.

Pause for silent prayer.

God our Father,
we are gathered here to share in the supper
which your only Son left to his Church to reveal
    his love.
He gave it to us when he was about to die
and commanded us to celebrate it as the new and
    eternal sacrifice.
We pray that in this eucharist
we may find the fullness of love and life.
Grant this through our Lord Jesus Christ, your Son,
who lives and reigns with you and the Holy Spirit,
one God, for ever and ever.[2]

LITURGY OF THE WORD

Let us listen to God's word.

The readings are proclaimed.

First Reading
Exodus 12:1–8, 11–14

The synoptic gospels place the Last Supper in the context of a Passover meal. John's gospel places it a day before Passover. While the historical facts are not certain, one thing is: the meal was cloaked in the experience and language of

Passover. It is very appropriate that the Triduum begin with this reading. The entire experience of Christ's passion, death, and resurrection was understood in light of the passover experience. Jesus naturally was seen as the fulfillment of all the promises inherent in the passover tradition.

As said multiple times throughout this workbook, the Passover was for Israel the hallmark event that celebrated Yahweh's redemptive act of salvation. Then and today every observant Jew remembers the exodus story as if he or she had actually been present for the original event.

The blood on the doorposts was considered a prefiguring of the blood that Christ would shed. This saving blood, shed for the sins of the world, is made real, active, and present at every celebration of eucharist.

This reading remembers the ritual of unleavened bread and passover lamb. Originally, the two rites were separate. Prior to the exodus, the ritual of the sacrificial lamb was used by herders to satisfy the gods as the herders moved their flocks from well-irrigated winter land to dry summer lands. The unleavened bread was used in a ritual for farmers. The rite functioned as a spring cleaning of the previous year's leaven. Tonight's text brings the sacrificial lamb ritual into the exodus story (vv. 11–13). The unleavened bread is established as a living memorial of the actual exodus narrative.[3] Thus, the ritual celebration of the passover lamb and the unleavened bread celebrated in the spring of each new year affords the descendants of the Israelites the opportunity to mark once again the liberation from the yoke of Egyptian bondage. The unleavened bread was a sign that those in bondage had to leave in haste. This urgency evolved through the generations to an expectation of the coming messiah who would return at night.

Our eucharistic bread is unleavened, just as the bread of exodus was unleavened. The nomadic

---

[1]Evening Mass of the Lord's Supper: "Entrance Antiphon," *The Sacramentary.*

[2]Evening Mass of the Lord's Supper: "Opening Prayer," *The Sacramentary.*

[3]Richard J. Clifford, S.J., "Exodus," in *NJBC,* 49.

life was a hurried life; people had to be ready to pick up and leave at a moment's notice. There was no time to wait for the leaven to rise. The Israelites, fleeing from Pharaoh, had no time to wait for the unleavened bread to rise. Eucharistic people are on the move to the new and eternal city. They also have no time to wait around for the bread to rise, but rather, are in a hurry to work for the coming reign of God. For the nomads, for the fleeing Israelites, and for Christians, the unleavened bread was food for their respective journeys.

The shedding of Jesus' blood was easily connected with the Old Testament understanding of blood. Blood was a sign of life. "Blood took on special significance for the Israelites both in the popular imagination and in the official cult. . . . Blood, as the bearer of life, was offered to God as atonement for humanity's sins."[4] The blood poured out on the altar was a substitute for the human sinner. Thus, an animal that was sacrificed served as a symbol. The animal stood in the place of the sinner who was symbolically offering his own life in order to reestablish the lost covenant relationship with God. The blood of rams was placed on the horns of the altar and on the altar as a sign of the cleansing properties of blood. "The blood removed the impurities which would defile the Israelite community and its cult."[5]

In the ancient agricultural world, blood represented the sharing of all life. Both animals and humans were in relational community. Even though animals had to die for the people to survive, there was a special life relationship with the animals. To shed the blood of an animal was a sacred event. Also, those who shed their own blood to save others were considered sacred people.[6]

The ancient rituals of blood were fulfilled through the shedding of Jesus' blood on the cross. He offered his blood for the sins of the world. In every eucharist we eat Jesus' Body and drink his Blood. Jesus is the new passover; he passed through death to life. Every time we celebrate eucharist we participate in that same passover. With Jesus, we pass from death to sin, to new life in Christ.

Responsorial Psalm
Psalm 116:12–13, 15–16, 17–18

This psalm celebrates the unity of the eucharist: a sacrifice of thanksgiving and a communion among believers.[7] This is a prayer of thanks after a difficult, terrifying ordeal.

Scholars are stumped when it comes to verse 15 in which the death of the faithful ones is precious in the eyes of the Lord. "Difficult. Just why their death should be 'precious' to Yahweh is not easy to see."[8]

Second Reading
1 Corinthians 11:23–26

This is the earliest fragment of Christian tradition preserved in the New Testament. Paul stated that he had received the tradition given in today's letter prior to his dealings with the Corinthians. He used language denoting the *passing on of tradition,* such as that which is passed on through the oral teaching of the rabbis. Paul received his revelation from the oral tradition in which human witnesses, under the inspiration of the risen Christ, shared and passed on their experience.

It is believed that today's pericope is an exegesis of a eucharistic liturgy already being celebrated. It does not completely describe the Last Supper, but rather seeks to define it in light of eucharistic theology. In the earliest celebration of the *breaking of bread,* there was a supper between the bread and the cup (as alluded to in this pericope), thus testifying to the primitive character of this text.[9]

Just as the unleavened bread was a living memorial of the events of Passover, so too is the unleavened bread of eucharist a living memorial of the events of Jesus' *passage through death to life.*

There are strong eschatological overtones in tonight's second reading. Paul reminds us of the Lord's second coming. Eucharist, for Paul and for us, was and is a ritual remembering of the cross

---

[4]Dale Launderville, O.S.B., "Blood," in *CPDBT,* 95.
[5]Ibid., 96.
[6]James A. Fischer, "Blood, New Testament," in *CPDBT,* 97.

[7]*PNL,* 17.
[8]John S. Kselman and Michael Barré, S.S., "Psalms," in *NJBC,* 546.
[9]*PNL,* 17.

with its effects made real and present. It is an anticipation of Jesus' second coming: "Christ has died, Christ is risen, Christ will come again."

Gospel
John 13:1–15

Jesus washes the feet of his disciples.

STEP 1
NAMING ONE'S EXPERIENCE

What were your first impressions? What was your first response? What grabbed your attention? How did you feel?

Each person names his or her initial impression. Statements should be brief. No reasons should be given at this time. All simply listen without agreeing or disagreeing.

STEP 2
UNDERSTANDING

In a brief statement, what do you think this gospel is trying to convey?

STEP 3
INPUT FROM VISION/STORY/TRADITION

Liturgical Context

Order of Service: Liturgy of the Word, Washing of Feet, Intercessions, Liturgy of Eucharist, Transfer of Eucharist

The observance of Holy Thursday began as a ritual celebration commemorating the Lord's Supper in Jerusalem. The story of the Christ's Last Supper is told and remembered as the event that instituted the eucharist. The Sacramentary defines the homiletic focus of tonight's liturgy: the institution of the eucharist; the institution of the priesthood; and the commandment of filial love. The first and second readings address the institution of the eucharist. The gospel hints at the institution of priesthood[10] and filial love is expressed in all three readings.

The liturgy for Holy Thursday is not unlike every liturgy of the year. However, it does have its own character and is set apart in one particular way. Holy Thursday is understood as the day Jesus was betrayed. This liturgy does *not* attempt to re-create the Last Supper. Jesus is referred to in the third person as if he were absent. "The night he *was* betrayed, he *took* bread," etc. However, the telling makes the actions and words present to us in a very concrete way. At every eucharist, the story we proclaim and the action we perform becomes a reality. The word is *anamnesis*, a remembering that brings the event forward and makes it present. This happens at every liturgy. The Holy Thursday liturgy is the same as every other liturgy in that regard. Where Holy Thursday is unique is that it highlights and exalts the connection between the free offering of Jesus' life through his passion and death and our own present celebration of eucharist.

"Eucharist is the sacrament of the Lord's presence during his absence."[11] We are not participating in an historical reenactment of an event that took place two thousand years ago. The events are historical and they do belong to the past. However, we remember them and they become presently effective. The events of Calvary build up the Body of Christ and are continued today through the sacraments, an ongoing living memorial of those events. We share in Jesus' passion,

---

[10]Reginald Fuller cautions a careful handling of the issue of priesthood. He suggests that interpreting the command to "do this" as a command for priesthood oversimplifies the meaning for two reasons. First, the Vatican II document, *Decree on the Ministry and Life of Priests*, "set the eucharistic presidency in the wider context of a total pastoral ministry of word and sacrament." Also, there is no solid evidence as to who presided at the first liturgies. It is not until the second century that the bishop presides at liturgy and only later do the priests preside. "The command, 'Do this' (plural) is addressed to the Christian church as a whole. The eucharist is an action of the whole church and the preeminent expression of its priestly character" (1 Peter 2:1–10; Ap 1:6; and perhaps Hebrews 13:15). *PNL*, 18.

[11]*DL* (III), 15.

death, and resurrection and in his saving redemption every time we tell the story and share the meal in his memory. (For further insight, see "Gospel Exegesis," Palm Sunday.)

> Lord, make us worthy to celebrate these mysteries.
> Each time we offer this memorial sacrifice,
> the work of our redemption is accomplished.
> We ask this in the name of Jesus the Lord.[12]

One can understand tonight's liturgy only through the eyes of the Passover. Ancient nomads participated in a ritual to mark the movement of their flocks to summer pastures after the first full spring moon. It was a dangerous journey and, to ward off evil, they marked their tents with the blood of lambs. "The death would propitiate the death-threatening deities."[13]

Later it was very easy to appropriate this rite into the Passover ritual: it gave new meaning to an old rite. Christianity had the same experience: new meaning was given to many of the Old Testament rituals.

The ancient ritual of Passover had two parts: unleavened bread and the sacrifice of the paschal lamb (First Reading). This passover ritual was celebrated by Jesus himself. He prayed the ritual prayers and enacted the ritual actions, perhaps many times over. Jesus was celebrating a passover supper on this night prior to his act of redemption. It was natural that the Christian psyche connect Jesus to the paschal lamb that shed its blood in order to save the Jews from the angel of death in the book of Exodus. The early Christians understood the paschal lamb of Exodus as a foreshadowing of Christ, the Paschal Lamb. John would later declare: "This is the Lamb of God who takes away the sins of the world." Christianity took an old rite and breathed new meaning into it.

So much of the Passover is integral to our understanding of eucharist. Passover was not celebrated alone; it was a family, communal event. Similarly, eucharist is a community event; it is cel-

ebrated in communion with other believers. Israel was in relationship to God as a people; so too, are Christians saved as a people. It is not a private affair.

We hear from Paul (tonight's second reading), who received the tradition of the supper from the Lord himself. Today we celebrate the same ritual of breaking bread that Paul's community celebrated. We celebrate eucharist as a living memorial of Jesus' presence in his absence as expressed in the preface for this liturgy:

> Father, all-powerful and ever-living God,
> we do well always and everywhere to give you thanks
> through Jesus Christ our Lord.
> He is the true and eternal priest
> who established this unending sacrifice.
> He offered himself as a victim for our deliverance
> and taught us to make this offering in his memory.
> As we eat his body which he gave for us,
> we grow in strength.
> As we drink his blood which he poured out for us,
> we are washed clean.
> Now, with angels and archangels,
> and the whole company of heaven,
> we sing the unending hymn of your praise.[14]

The gospel for Holy Thursday is John's account of eucharist: washing feet. Some scholars suggest that John's account of the foot-washing scene was a homily given at a eucharistic liturgy in his community. Holy Thursday is the place for us to best understand the meaning of the foot washing (*mandatum*). Holy Thursday used to be called Maundy Thursday, a derivative of the word *mandatum*. The *mandatum* makes sense only in light of Christ's approaching death and resurrection. The *mandatum* flows from Jesus' ultimate act of love: the gift of his life. We, too, are to wash feet by loving and dying for others.

During the Holy Thursday liturgy, people come forward to have their feet washed. The ritual dates back to the fifth century in Jerusalem, the latter

---

[12]Evening Mass of the Lord's Supper: "Prayer Over the Gifts," *The Sacramentary*.

[13]Launderville, "Blood," 95.

---

[14]Evening Mass of the Lord's Supper: "Preface of Holy Eucharist," *The Sacramentary*.

part of the seventh century in Gaul and Spain, and the twelfth century in Rome. The *mandatum,* at one time considered a sacrament, was commonly celebrated throughout the year by the early church as a sign of service and Christian charity.

The implication of eucharist is that we share in the paschal mystery. We are called to serve and to wash feet. We are called to love as Christ loved by offering the gift of ourselves for others. The sign of foot washing leads us into the mystery of these three days. Also, Holy Thursday used to be the day on which penitents were reconciled to the church so they could participate in the paschal celebration.

This is the only liturgy in which the church prescribes a hymn during the presentation of the gifts. Gifts for the poor are presented and the antiphon *Ubi Caritas* is sung: "Where charity and love prevail, there is God." The offering of food for the poor is the community's way of ratifying in action the directive of the *mandatum:* "This example I leave you (Antiphon 1) . . . then surely you must wash one another's feet (Antiphon 3) . . . If there is this love among you, all will know that you are my disciples (Antiphon 4) . . . love one another as I have loved you . . ."(Antiphon 5).

Sufficient bread is consecrated so that there is enough for both Holy Thursday and Good Friday. The liturgy ends with a transfer of the eucharist to a different place of reservation. We continue our vigil in prayerful meditation with solemn adoration ending at midnight. Anticipation of Christ's passion begins immediately. There is quiet solemnity as people spend a holy hour in adoration.

After the liturgy, the altar is stripped without any special notice by the assembly. In the past, special meaning was assigned to this action. It was intended to be symbolic of the stripping of Jesus. While this action no longer holds the same meaning, the practice itself was restored after the Second Vatican Council.

Gospel Exegesis

The facilitator gives input regarding what critical biblical scholarship has to say about this text. The input includes insights as to how people would have heard the gospel in Jesus' time.

One scholar calls this story "revelation in action" of the mystery of God, of Jesus and his Passover.[15] The meaning is not apparent at first glance. It unfolds as the story progresses. Jesus laid aside his garment, wrapped a towel around himself, and washed his disciples' feet. Jesus' laying aside his garment in this pericope alerts us to a prophetic symbolism. "Laying aside" is akin to "laying down" as in "laying down one's life." Jesus' action is symbolic of what will happen through his death.

The action of foot washing in Jesus' culture was a very menial task. It was considered too lowly even for Jewish male slaves; only gentile slaves, wives, and children qualified. According to ancient Mediterranean custom, people bathed either at home or in the public baths before attending a dinner party. By the time they arrived at the party, the only washing ritual left was the washing of feet. Verses 6 and 8 refer to the washing of feet. Verses 9–10 refer to the washing of the entire body. Since the body had already been washed before the party, the only remaining washing was that of feet.

Charles Talbert suggests that "the bath of the whole person is linked with becoming a disciple."[16] The foot washing was a preparation for eating with Jesus. John's disciples *were already clean through a bath* (images of baptism). Jesus *made the disciples clean* by his word. Jesus was offering something beyond the cleanliness of the bath. He was offering ongoing, continued cleansing of the dust and dirt of life's everyday journey. This was to be preparation for the meal: disciples were to wash the feet of others. Talbert maintains that the point of the story is that through Jesus' death, the daily sins of disciples (who had already been washed clean earlier from the "principle of sin") were forgiven.[17] Thus, through Jesus' action of selfless love and service, post-baptismal sins are forgiven. After Jesus washed the feet of the disciples he took back his garments and resumed his place. The symbolic meaning in taking back his garments applies to Jesus' taking back his life.

---

[15]*DL* (III), 19.

[16]*RJ*, 193.

[17]Ibid., 194.

The "do as I have done" command usually is understood to mean: to act as Jesus, the humble servant. One scholar suggests another meaning. If we are to wash one another's feet for the daily forgiveness of sin, an inherent piece of the preparation for eucharist must include forgiveness of our neighbor. There is a specific command to forgive one another's daily sins.

Images of baptism are obvious in tonight's gospel through the cleansing motif. Eucharistic overtones appear in the *mandatum* and preparation for eucharist through the daily forgiveness of sins. On this inaugural night of the Triduum, baptism, confirmation, and eucharist are foreshadowed as the elect wait on the threshold for their reception at the Easter Vigil.

We are reminded that Jesus performs the sign of foot washing right before his passion. As listeners, we expect the gospel to be an account of the institution of the eucharist. However, on this night that celebrates the institution of the eucharist, Jesus invites us into the challenge of living eucharist. John's *mandatum* provides the daily example of offering our lives for others (as Jesus would do the very next day) in service and in forgiveness, as we prepare to dine at his table.

Now we really know how much Jesus loved his disciples. Through the sign of foot washing Jesus took his place among the slaves of the world, humbled himself, and willingly gave up his life. The eucharist is an ongoing remembering of Jesus' passover from death to life. The liturgy jump-starts the Triduum with this solemn reminder: "We shall glory in the cross of our Lord Jesus Christ. Through him we are saved and made free."[18] Just as the Passover was a sign of liberation, so too is the eucharist the sign of liberation for Christians.

Proclaim the gospel again.

Sometimes we gain new insights when we hear the text after the interpretation has been given. Someone from the group proclaims the gospel a second time.

---

[18]Evening Mass of the Lord's Supper: "Introductory Rites," *The Sacramentary*.

Conversation with the Liturgy and the Scriptures

Test your original understanding in dialogue with the text.

(You might consider breaking into smaller groups.)

Were there any new insights in the readings that you had not considered before? How does your original understanding of this story compare with what was just shared? How does this story speak to your life?

Sharing Life Experience

Participants share an experience from their lives that connects with the biblical interpretation just shared.

> *I can only respond to this Holy Thursday by remembering the example of my sister and her family. Tonight's liturgy invites us to wash feet and to offer our lives in sacrifice for others. Life offers the opportunity to live that in real, often painful ways. I watched my sister and her family respond to the sudden illness of one of their children in the most incredible, sacrificial, paschal way. They put their lives on hold and researched a disease that is so new on the scene that few had ever heard of it. My sister became the epitome of Christ's unbelievable, compassionate love and mercy to her child. Due to a very severe case of this adolescent onslaught chemical disorder, their family endured the test of a lifetime. Many, if not most, would have buckled under the pressure. Each family member had a role to play in the healing that would be gradual and nearly complete. They literally "became the disease," took their beloved child by the hand and walked with her through the Red Sea of desperation to the promised land of healing and liberation. With the help of the medical community, new medical research, and an incredible amount of sacrifice and patience, and an unwillingness to be conquered by the unusual and often embarrassing dimensions of the disease, this child will live a normal life. The family became eucharist, and washed the feet of one of its hurting members in painful and often heroic ways. Wouldn't every family go to similar lengths for one of its members? Sadly this is not always true. Many*

would be tempted to believe in the apparent hopelessness of the situation rather than go to incredible lengths, die the daily deaths, and endure to the end, not knowing if it would work. They are my heroes and a living example in my life of what the power of self-sacrificing love is able to accomplish. They never knew if their efforts would help; there was little research and few who went before them who could help and support them in their trial. They simply had to trust and offer each day, sometimes each moment, to the healing compassion of God and trust that they would safely reach the other side. We celebrate that trust every time we encounter this beautiful child of God.

The Holy Thursday liturgy mandates that same self-sacrificing love to be extended to the least of the least, and the poorest of the poor. "Where charity and love prevail, there God is." What my sister's family offered for one of their children we are invited to offer for all of God's children, especially those whose feet we would rather not wash. We are to become the eucharist of this feast; we are to wash feet and love unto death. It is because of this night that we have the strength to do it.

All share their life experience.

What was John trying to tell his community? What does he have to say to our community and to me today? In what way is our community called to wash feet? Whose feet are we called to wash? How are images of creation, covenant, exodus/death/resurrection and community evident in tonight's readings? Has our original understanding of tonight's liturgy and scriptures been stretched, challenged, or affirmed?

Step 5
Decision

The gospel demands a response.

How does our sharing and this biblical interpretation challenge our community's attitudes? In what way does this gospel call our parish to action in the church, parish, neighborhood, or world? What is one concrete action we will take this week as a response to what we have learned and shared today?

DOCTRINAL ISSUES

What church truth/teaching/doctrinal issue could be drawn from the readings for Holy Thursday?

Participants suggest possible doctrinal themes that flow from the readings.

Possible Doctrinal Themes

Eucharist, bread, wine, washing feet, covenant, paschal mystery, charity, Triduum, service

Present the doctrinal material at this time.

1. The facilitator gives input on a particular doctrinal issue of his/her prior choosing. **OR**
2. The group chooses a doctrinal issue from the list they created. They read together from the Doctrinal Appendix.

(The doctrinal issues are found in the Doctrinal Appendix in the back of this workbook. If you are choosing an issue from this resource, please refer to it now.)

Reflection questions centered around the chosen doctrinal theme can be found at the end of each topic in the Doctrinal Appendix. The questions are based on the five-step reflection process. If you choose a topic not included in the Doctrinal Appendix, craft your own questions according to the same five-step process.

Following the reflection questions you will be reminded to return to chapter 7, "Preparing the Catechetical Session," to assist you in crafting your own session.

Closing Prayer

Almighty God,
we receive new life
from the supper your Son gave us in this world.
May we find full contentment
in the meal we hope to share
in your eternal kingdom.
We ask this through Christ our Lord.[19]

---

[19]Evening Mass of the Lord's Supper: "Prayer after Communion," *The Sacramentary.*

GOOD FRIDAY

Opening Prayer

Lord,
by shedding his blood for us,
your Son, Jesus Christ,
established the paschal mystery.
In your goodness, make us holy
and watch over us always.
We ask this through Christ our Lord.[1]

LITURGY OF THE WORD

Let us listen to God's word.

The readings are proclaimed.

First Reading
Isaiah 52:13–53:12

The Fourth Servant Song of Isaiah was written while Israel was still in captivity and awaiting deliverance in Babylon. Jerusalem had been destroyed and had not yet been reconstructed.[2] Deutero-Isaiah lamented the plight of the people and offered a message of consolation. Prior to the exile the people had been materialistic, greedy, and overly-prosperous. Once in captivity, that all changed. Deutero-Isaiah portrayed the people as depressed, "dazed, discouraged, and destitute, severely tempted to apostasy."[3] Deutero-Isaiah set out to console, not punish, to offer encouragement, not chastisement, and to strengthen the faith of the people as they awaited deliverance.

The early Christian community believed that Jesus Christ was the suffering servant of the first reading. They believed that Deutero-Isaiah was heralding and foretelling the passion and death of Christ and the inauguration of the messianic age. Jewish scholars are not certain who the suffering servant of Isaiah was. Christians proclaim with faithful assurance: it was Christ, the one who suffered for the many, the one who bore our infirmities. Jewish scholars maintain that the "many" referred to gentiles. It is not certain whether Jesus saw himself as the servant of this Isaian passage. But there is evidence in the scriptures that he embraced Isaiah's servant image as a metaphor for his mission.

The first reading from Isaiah sets the stage for understanding the passion. Jesus, servant of God, who by all appearances was reduced to nothing, was exalted and raised up by the living God. Vindication was his. The passage ends on a note of peace and hope and helps form our understanding and theology of the cross: "Jesus' suffering was innocent, vicarious and redemptive; it is for all people inclusively; the righteous sufferer is finally vindicated."[4]

Responsorial Psalm
Psalm 31:2, 6, 12–13, 15–16, 25

The psalm highlights the suffering of the Just One. It includes the words of Jesus spoken from the cross in Luke's gospel.

Second Reading
Hebrews 4:14–16; 5:7–9

In the letter to the Hebrews, the theme of Jesus, the high priest, is very carefully set forth. "Jesus is the high priest of his own sacrifice, the perfect sacrifice that is ever before his Father, since he dwells eternally in his presence. He is, 'in the heavens,' the eternal and definitive Passover."[5]

This letter consoles us in our humanity. Jesus identifies with our suffering and weaknesses because he was a person, just like us. He was tempted just as we are tempted. "The only difference that the author [of Hebrews] remarks between Jesus' temptations and those of his followers is that he never succumbed to them."[6] He

---

[1] Good Friday: "Opening Prayer," *The Sacramentary.*

[2] Carroll Stuhlmueller, C.P., "Deutero-Isaiah and Trito-Isaiah," in *NJBC,* 329.

[3] Ibid., 330.

[4] *PNL,* 19.

[5] *DL*(III), 3, 26.

[6] Myles M. Bourke, "The Epistle to the Hebrews," in *NJBC,* 928.

prayed for deliverance *through* his hour to come. Jesus learned obedience through the struggle of his life.[7] Jesus lived his life in complete submission to the will of God. His faithfulness prompted decisions and choices that led him ultimately to the cross.

A major theme of the letter to the Hebrews is *Jesus Christ, the exalted High Priest and Lord, reigns from heaven's throne.* Verses 5–10 are believed to reflect a hymn to "Jesus the High Priest." The author of Hebrews often referred to Jesus as the High Priest in order to accentuate his superiority over the Jewish high priest. Later in the letter to the Hebrews Jesus was contrasted with the high priest in one very important aspect. The priesthood of the Jewish high priest ended upon his death. Jesus' priesthood, on the other hand, required his death in order to be officially inaugurated. Jesus, the resurrected High Priest, reigns from his exalted heavenly throne.

Jesus' throne is a throne of grace because Christ made it possible for the human race to have access to God and to God's grace. Unlike the Jewish high priest, Jesus did not sin, even though he was fully tempted to sin. Jesus offers loud cries, tears, and prayers of supplication (v. 7) to God. In his glorified state, Jesus was no longer subject to the natural struggles of human nature, such as the fear of death.[8] The author of Hebrews maintains that God heard Jesus' cries and saved him from death. Jesus was not saved from death as we understand death. Jesus died a natural death. However, God did hear his cries and God did deliver him from death. Through the resurrection Jesus is no longer dead, but lives eternally. As reigning High Priest, Jesus empathizes with his people because he knows the trials, tribulations, and struggles of life's sojourn. Jesus cried out. He knew pain, weakness, and suffering like any other human being. However, Jesus the High Priest sacrificed the gift of his own life and now sits on heaven's throne as an advocate on our behalf.

Jesus was God's Son (v. 8) in two very distinct ways. "He became Son when exalted; he always was Son because he existed with the Father even before he appeared on earth."[9] The Jesus of John's gospel is aware of his preexistence. Jesus learned obedience through his suffering and was consecrated to the priesthood because of his obedience (v. 8). Thus, he is qualified to "to save those who are obedient to him."[10] The author of Hebrews assures his reader that the follower of Christ will receive eternal salvation because that salvation is based on Jesus' eternal priesthood. In this sense, *eternal* refers to things that exist in the permanence of the heavenly realm rather than the impermanence of the earthly domain.

Gospel

The passion of our Lord Jesus Christ according to John.

STEP 1
NAMING ONE'S EXPERIENCE

What were your first impressions? What was your first response? What grabbed your attention? How did you feel?

Each person names his or her initial impression. Statements should be brief. No reasons should be given at this time. All simply listen without agreeing or disagreeing.

STEP 2
UNDERSTANDING

In a brief statement, what do you think this gospel is trying to convey?

STEP 3
INPUT FROM VISION/STORY/TRADITION

Liturgical Context

"On this day, when 'Christ our passover was sacrificed' (1 Cor 5:7), the Church meditates on the

---

[7] *PNL*, 19.

[8] This was probably a reference to Jesus' experience in Gethsemane in Mark 14:35–36. (Bourke, "The Epistle to the Hebrews," 929.)

[9] Bourke, "The Epistle to the Hebrews," 929.
[10] Ibid.

passion of her Lord and Spouse, adores the cross, commemorates her origin from the side of Christ asleep on the cross, and intercedes for the salvation of the whole world."[11]

Scripture scholar Raymond Brown contends that John's Jesus is the all knowing, always in control Savior who conquered sin and death by carefully orchestrated design. Good Friday's message is Good News. St. John Chrysostom very eloquently summed up the reason we gather for this Good Friday feast.

> Today sees our Lord Jesus Christ on the cross; we celebrate, so that we may understand that the cross is a celebration, a solemn, spiritual feast. Before, the cross was synonymous with condemnation; now it is an object of honor. Before, a symbol of death; now, the means of salvation. It has been the source of countless blessings for us: it has delivered us from error, it has shone on us when we were in darkness. We were vanquished, yet it reconciles us with God. We were foes, yet it has regained God's friendship for us. We were estranged, yet it has brought us back to him.... We have discovered a wellspring.[12]

The liturgy is not a somber preoccupation with the wounds and suffering of Christ. It is surrounded by anticipatory joy. We do not feign ignorance of the resurrection. Liturgy is truth and authenticity, not historicization. In other words, we do not remember and make present Jesus' passion and death as if we didn't know about the resurrection. It is always a prominent piece of our consciousness, remembrance, and celebration.

There is no intention of minimizing Jesus' suffering. We grieve over his passion, so much so that we fast on this day as an expression of our grief. The Good Friday fast puts us in communion with our brothers and sisters who, from as early as the second century, observed a pre-Easter fast of no

food or water. As the centuries wore on, and a definite celebration of Good Friday evolved, the fast was observed on Good Friday and Holy Saturday.

In the very early centuries, there was no official Good Friday liturgy. The observance of Good Friday developed according to the local custom of various places. The liturgy of Good Friday today is a blending of customs, observances, and liturgies that evolved over the centuries from varied sources.

The date of Jesus' death, the 14th of Nisan, which fell on a Friday, was observed as a day of mourning and fasting inspired by compassion (a "grieving fast").[13] By the turn of the fourth century there was a non-eucharistic liturgy that is recorded in the travels of the pilgrim, Egeria (ca. 400). She records multiple liturgies on Good Friday beginning before dawn and continuing through the night. The early dawn service took place at the site where Jesus was scourged. Later in the morning they gathered to venerate the cross. (In the fourth century Empress Helena gave the church in Rome a relic of the holy cross. Any church that possessed a relic of the cross venerated it at this liturgy. The present ritual of veneration developed from these early origins.)

The Christians of Egeria's day then gathered from about noon to three for a liturgy of the word. The celebration consisted of a series of scripture readings including psalms that alluded to Jesus' suffering, the passion of Jesus, and John's account of Jesus' death. Nearly spent from the day-long liturgies, the worshipers gathered again in the evening to listen to the proclamation of Jesus' burial. Following the evening service, there was an all-night vigil for those hearty enough to endure it.

By the seventh century there was a clearly defined Roman liturgy. The pope carried the relic of the cross barefoot from the Lateran Basilica to the Church of the Holy Cross in Jerusalem. The cross was venerated by clergy and laity alike as the scriptures were proclaimed. The intercessions of the faithful ended this liturgy until communion was added in the seventh century.

---

[11] *Circular Letter Concerning the Preparation and Celebration of Easter Feasts,* Congregation for Divine Worship (Rome, USCC, 1988), #58.

[12] John Chrysostom (ca. 350–407), "Homélie pour le Vendredi saint," in *Homiliaire patristique,* Lex Orandi 8 (Paris: Cerf, 1949), 65; in *DL* (III), 27–28.

---

[13] *LY,* 69.

According to Adolf Adam, the liturgy became far more dramatic during the Middle Ages. The simple communion of the faithful became *missa praesanctificatorum* (mass with previously consecrated gifts). In other words, many parts of the mass, with the exception of the defining element, the eucharistic prayer, were added to this liturgy. The faithful were receiving communion rarely, if at all during those times; thus, only the clergy received the eucharist at the Good Friday liturgy. The Tridentine Mass of 1570 mandated this practice to last for the next four hundred years.

In 1955 the new Order reinstated the traditional three part liturgy: word, veneration of the cross, and communion. After a four-hundred year hiatus, the faithful were once again allowed to receive communion at the Good Friday liturgy. The liturgy was to begin at 3:00 P.M. unless, for pastoral reasons, it could not take place at that time. The liturgical color of the Good Friday liturgy was changed from black to red, the color of martyrs.

The liturgy of Good Friday begins with the very ancient and solemn gesture of prostration by the presiding celebrant and attending priests. The celebrant then moves to the chair and reads the opening prayer followed by the liturgy of the word. The first reading of Good Friday, the fourth Servant Song, was appropriated to the suffering of Christ very early in the Christian tradition. Psalm 31 is a lament and a prayer of trust to the faithful God. The second reading from Paul's letter to the Hebrews exalts Jesus, the great High Priest, the source of salvation. The gospel acclamation introduces the gospel with a proclamation of the exalted, obedient unto death, Jesus Christ crucified. The passion is proclaimed without candles or incense.

The intercessions of Good Friday have their roots in the early Good Friday liturgies. They are the inspiration behind the general intercessions prayed at every liturgy. The intercessions are prayers offered by God's people "for the holy Church, the pope, all states of life in the Church, catechumens, Christian unity, the Jews, all who do not believe in Christ, all who do not believe in God, rulers, those in every kind of need."[14] The intercessions allow the faithful to exercise their

"priestly function and intercede for all humanity."[15] Liturgical prayer is universal and missionary. It is not self-centered; it is communal and other-centered. The first intercession is an example of this universal dimension.

Deacon: Let us pray, dear friends,
           for the holy Church of God
           throughout the world,
           that God the almighty Father
           guide it and gather it together
           so that we may worship him
           in peace and tranquility.

Priest: Almighty and eternal God,
           you have shown your glory to all nations
           in Christ, your Son.
           Guide the work of your Church.
           Help it to persevere in faith,
           proclaim your name,
           and bring your salvation to people
               everywhere.
           We ask this through Christ our Lord.[16]

The veneration of the cross is a high point of the Good Friday liturgy: "It expresses the Church's faith in and gratitude to Christ who turned the wood of an instrument of torture into the means of redemption and the sign of God's infinite love. The cross stands as an irresistible call to love God who has loved us so well."[17] The ritual text and antiphons for the veneration proclaim our faith in the cross:

Priest: This is the wood of the cross, on which
           hung the savior of the world.
All: Come, Let us worship.

Antiphon
    We worship you, Lord,
    We venerate your cross,
    We praise your resurrection.
    Through the cross you brought joy to the world.

Psalm 66:2
    May God be gracious and bless us;
    and let his face shed its light upon us.

---

[14]Ibid., 73.

[15]General Introduction to the Roman Missal, #45.

[16]Good Friday: "Intercessions for Good Friday," *The Sacramentary.*

[17]*DL* (III), 34.

> We worship you, Lord,
> We venerate your cross,
> We praise your resurrection.
> Through the cross you brought joy to the
> world.[18]

Communion ends the Good Friday liturgy. The Lord's Prayer is recited and communion bread, consecrated the day before, is distributed. The liturgy ends in silence. We keep vigil as we await the Lord's resurrection.

The Office of Readings and Morning Prayer is to be celebrated with the faithful on both Good Friday and Holy Saturday morning.

Gospel Exegesis

The facilitator gives input regarding what critical biblical scholarship has to say about this text. The input includes insights as to how people would have heard the gospel in Jesus' time.

This exegesis of John's passion is based on Raymond E. Brown's *A Crucified Christ in Holy Week.* John's passion narrative is proclaimed every Good Friday. The context for this reading is given in the weeks preceding Holy Week in which other segments of John's gospel are proclaimed. Brown asserts that the Jesus of the Good Friday passion is a far different Jesus from the Jesus portrayed in the synoptic gospels. John's Jesus is aware of his pre-existence. Through Jesus' death he is simply returning to a state he temporarily left during his stay in this world (17:5).[19] The Jesus of Good Friday freely offers his life and freely takes it back again. Jesus is not a victim. There is no struggle. Jesus is confident of the outcome. Satan has no power over Jesus. He is a step ahead of all the characters. He knows what is going to happen. He is in complete control. Brown asserts that John's image and portrayal of Jesus is the one that was most frequently passed on to the faithful. The portrait of Jesus in the synoptic gospels is different: the Jesus of the syn-

optics was not aware of his pre-existence; he was not so all-knowing, either.

The light-darkness image in John's gospel is a strong sign that appears frequently. Jesus came as Light of the world. Judas arrived with a lantern to arrest Jesus. Judas resided in darkness and needed artificial light in order to see.

John's Jesus is the royal personage who grovels to no one. There are no blood and sweat stained moments in the garden. Jesus does not pray to be delivered from his ordeal (as he does in the reference to Mark's gospel in the second reading from Hebrews). He accepts his appointed task with awareness, purpose, and power. No worldly power has control over Jesus. Jesus Christ, Victor, is in complete control of his destiny.

Brown further points out that the Jewish trial of Jesus is different in John's gospel than it is in the other gospels. Rather than the formal court of the high priest, Caiaphas, Jesus is questioned by the police before Annas, Caiaphas's father-in-law. The interrogators try to determine if there is evidence against Jesus of insurrection, thereby prompting a Roman trial in a Roman court. Jesus is so clever with Annas that his captors abuse him.

Jesus' innocence is written all over his face while Peter's weakness stands out like a rooster's crow at first light. Peter cut off the servant's ear and denied Jesus in the garden. Contrasted with Peter is the beloved disciple of John's gospel. While no one knows for sure who this disciple is, he was nevertheless a hero in the Johannine community. It was the "Beloved Disciple" who was present at the Last Supper, the trial, the foot of the cross, the empty tomb, and the post-resurrection appearances of Jesus. This disciple is *the enlightened one, the witness,* and *the lover* par excellence. It is believed that this disciple was upheld in the Johannine community as the perfect model of discipleship and apostolic witness. The Beloved Disciple, not Peter, is the perfect disciple.

The trial of Jesus reads like a Shakespearean play. Jesus was inside with Pilate; the Jewish community was outside. Pilate was moving back and forth between both and tension was mounting. Pilate was agitated and placating. Jesus was in control, en-

---

[18]Good Friday: "Veneration of the Cross—Antiphon," *The Sacramentary.*

[19]*CCHW,* 57.

gaged and hardly silent (as in Mark's passion). Jesus assumed his own advocacy. No, he was not a king in the earthly sense, but if Pilate wanted to call him a king, so be it; his kingdom was not of this world. He simply came to testify to the truth—not to preside from a royal throne. Jesus was in control. Pilate was on trial: would he succumb to the political pressure? Pilate was aware of who Jesus was, and he was afraid. He knew who Jesus was, yet he was too afraid to bear witness to the truth.

In Mark and Matthew, Jesus was scourged as a part of his sentence. His cloak was stripped from him and then he was marched off to Calvary. In John's gospel Jesus is scourged before he is brought out from the praetorium to the crowd.

All of the gospels highlight the guilt of the crowd by their own self-recriminating cries to crucify him. However, none of the cries are more intense than those in John's gospel. Jesus, wearing a kingly cloak and crown of thorns, was ultimately abandoned. The Jews favored Caesar over Jesus and in the process abandoned all their hopes for access to the messianic reign. Thus, in the final scene of this Roman court, Pilate extracted fidelity to Caesar from the Jewish crowd and in the process they abdicated their messianic hopes.[20] Pilate then handed Jesus over to the priests to be crucified.

The curtain was about to come down as Jesus, the one who willingly offered his life, carried the cross by himself. According to all four gospels, Pilate put a *titulus* (a charge) on the cross stating that Jesus was a would-be "King of the Jews." John's theology was not without a touch of irony. Jesus, who was rejected as king by his own people, was given the legal title of king by none other than Pilate himself.

John's Jesus is wearing a seamless garment. The synoptics only make allusions to the division of the garment. Some scholars believe that the seamless garment was the one worn by the high priest. Jesus hangs not simply as king, but as priest as well. Other scholars say the garment was a symbol of unity.

In Mark and Matthew there is no one with Jesus at the cross. John places Mary and the Beloved Disciple at the cross. John uses them in a symbolic way in his narrative. Jesus named Mary the mother of the Beloved Disciple and the disciple was named her son, thus becoming Jesus' brother. "Jesus has constituted a family of preeminent disciples and the Johannine community is already in existence at the cross (which becomes the birthplace of the church)."[21]

John loaded the final verses with further symbolism. Jesus was given wine-soaked hyssop. Hyssop was a type of leaf used to sprinkle the blood of the paschal lamb on the doorposts of Israelite homes in the exodus story. Jesus was sentenced to death at noon, the time when the priests would slaughter the paschal lambs at Passover. With his last breath Jesus fulfilled the Baptist's prophetic proclamation: "Behold the Lamb of God who takes away the sins of the world." Jesus' bones were not broken, again a symbolic connection to the paschal lamb.

Jesus, still in control of his destiny, proclaimed to the world that *"It is finished"* and handed over his spirit. His resurrected spirit, then, was present at his death and at his resurrection. The Spirit was not present until this defining, crowning moment. Jesus breathed the Holy Spirit on the disciples after his resurrection.

Upon Jesus' death he was quietly removed from the cross in a reverent fashion. Contrast this with the synoptics who record all kinds of cataclysmic events upon his death. Blood and water flowed from Jesus' side (the living water that we were told would flow from his side). It is believed that the water signifies the outpouring of the Holy Spirit upon Jesus' glorification. Some scholars suggest that the water and blood are signs of baptism and eucharist. The Spirit was given to the community through baptism (water) and the eu-

---

[20]Brown alerts us to the anti-Jewish sentiment in John's gospel. He tells us that we are not to ignore it or sugarcoat it. It was real. There was tension between Christians and Jews. It was leveled not just at the leadership, but also at the synagogue. John's community suffered great persecution at the hands of their Jewish brothers and sisters. They were thrown out of the synagogue, which made them very vulnerable. The Romans allowed the Jews to coexist with them, but they were suspicious of Christians. The hostility was deep and it was bitter. However, we are not to use it as a cause and source of anti-Jewish sentiment, but rather to understand it in light of the cultural and religious problems of the first century.

---

[21]*CCHW,* 64.

charist (blood). Thus, the church was born at the foot of the cross through his water of baptism and the blood of eucharist that flowed from his side.

John makes sure that Jesus' burial befits a king; there is plenty of myrrh and oil, and there are cloth wrappings. Nicodemus, a reluctant disciple earlier, now becomes a disciple in full view. At his death, Jesus continued to reconcile sinners to himself. Jesus died as he lived in John's gospel: as a conquering, royal king, in charge of his own destiny, who overcame the sins of the world. Jesus fought the great battle with Satan and was victorious.

The cross then is a sign of victory. Disciples do not stand at this Good Friday cross in sadness or in mourning, but rather in praise and thanksgiving for the incredible mercy of God who loved so greatly that he sent his Son to die for a sinful world.

Proclaim the gospel again.

Sometimes we gain new insights when we hear the text after the interpretation has been given. Someone from the group proclaims the gospel a second time.

STEP 4
TESTING

Conversation with the Liturgy and the Scriptures

Test your original understanding in dialogue with the text.

(You might consider breaking into smaller groups.)

Were there any new insights? Was there anything you had not considered before about this liturgy and/or scriptures? How does your original understanding of Good Friday compare with what we just shared? How does this story speak to your life? Have you ever known a time in your life when the Jesus portrayed in John's gospel was necessary to your situation? How does John's Jesus compare with Matthew's Jesus? What does the Jesus of Matthew and the Jesus of John have to say to our community? To me?

Sharing Life Experience

Participants share an experience from their lives that connects with the biblical interpretation just shared.

Many years ago my husband and I were involved in a parish that gathered regularly to pray for people who were in need of healing. We often encountered people who were broken and beaten down by life's disappointments. They came seeking the healing presence of God in the gathering of our community. I remember one young woman in particular, who was extremely troubled. She had been coming to pray with us for quite some time. Our pastor approached our group with an unusual request. Would we gather to pray particularly for and with this woman? It seemed that she had been actively involved in the occult and was now under the care of a psychiatrist. The doctor had approached our pastor and said, "I am not a Catholic, but I have come up against something in this woman I have never experienced before. It could be auto-suggestion, but I am encountering what this woman believes is the presence of evil. This is new to me. Is there something you can do?" The pastor said he would talk to his bishop. We were reminded that every celebration of the eucharist is a share in the passion, death, and resurrection of Christ, and that every eucharist is an opportunity for healing and liberation. Christ was already victorious. Christ had already conquered sin and death. We know the rest of the story and we celebrate it at every mass.

The Christ of Good Friday is that same victorious, liberating Christ. The woman celebrated the sacrament of reconciliation, and together we, as a community, celebrated eucharist. It was like every other eucharist—a celebration of faith-filled people who gather to take bread, bless it, break it, and share it, and who in the process become broken and shared. The Jesus of John's gospel went to the cross on Good Friday knowing he was in charge and that he would be victorious over sin and death. That same liberating reality is present and operative in our lives today.

Over a period of time, and after continued medical care, and the self-sacrificing pastoral care of our community, the woman experienced profound healing. Today she is a vibrant member of that community. There is no power greater than the power of the

*Crucified and Risen Lord! Whether it is something as dramatic as that seemed, or something as normal as the seemingly hopeless situations we often find ourselves in throughout life, today's liturgy is a reminder that Jesus is in control. He knowingly and willingly paid the price. There is no evil in my life or in the world that can erase that reality. Ruptured relationships cannot erase it—not even death can erase it. We continue to live it in our communities when we gather to remember and celebrate the paschal mystery. Today is **Good** Friday; it is such **Good** News.*

All share their life experience.

What was the message for the Johannine community in the passion narrative? What does he have to say to our community and to me today? How does today's liturgy call us to death and resurrection? What are the implications? What are our collective and personal responses to the Good Friday liturgy? Do I still feel the same way about this text as I did at the beginning? Has our original understanding been stretched, challenged, or affirmed?

STEP 5
DECISION

The gospel demands a response.

In what concrete way does this gospel call our parish to action in the church, parish, neighborhood, or world? Has this conversation with the exegesis of the scriptures and the liturgy for Good Friday called me to change in any way? What am I/we/community/parish called to do in response? What is the challenge of the Good Friday liturgy? What will I/we do about it?

DOCTRINAL ISSUES

What church truth/teaching/doctrinal issue could be drawn from the gospel for Good Friday?

Participants suggest possible doctrinal themes that flow from the readings.

Possible Doctrinal Themes

Cross, redemptive suffering, paschal mystery, christology

Present the doctrinal material at this time.
1. Facilitator gives input on a particular doctrinal issue of his/her prior choosing. OR
2. The group chooses a doctrinal issue from the list they created. They read together from the Doctrinal Appendix.

(The doctrinal issues are found in the Doctrinal Appendix in the back of this workbook. If you are choosing an issue from this resource, please refer to it now.)

Reflection questions centered around the chosen doctrinal theme can be found at the end of each topic in the Doctrinal Appendix. The questions are based on the five-step reflection process. If you choose a topic not included in the Doctrinal Appendix, craft your own questions according to the same five-step process.

Following the reflection questions you will be reminded to return to chapter 7, "Preparing the Catechetical Session," to assist you in crafting your own session.

Closing Prayer

Lord,
send down your abundant blessing
upon your people who have recalled the death of
    your Son
in the sure hope of the resurrection.
Grant them pardon; bring them comfort.
May their faith grow stronger
and their eternal salvation be assured.
We ask this through Christ our Lord.[22]

---

[22]Good Friday: "Prayer Over the People," *The Sacramentary.*

EASTER VIGIL

The Easter Vigil sets out for the church in sign, symbol, word, and gesture the heart of our Catholic Christian faith and identity. The riches contained within the Vigil are nearly impossible to examine in one celebration or catechetical session. The Easter Vigil is the springboard not only for pre-sacramental preparation for the rites of initiation, but also for mystagogical reflection for neophytes and the entire church.[1] Rather than dealing with the segments as individual pearls scattered in other areas of this resource, this session will deal with the pearls as if on a finely crafted string. Therefore, the exegesis of the symbols, words, and ritual pieces in this liturgy will be treated as they occur in the liturgy. Obviously, the format for this session will be different from the formats for other sessions in the book. The gospel, the readings, and each ritual piece of the Vigil are vital to understanding who we are and why we gather on this night. There are enormous riches in this powerful celebration. It would be very difficult to absorb them all in one preparation session. Since the pieces of this liturgy are pivotal to understanding our Catholic heritage, it is essential that they become a benchmark for constant referral. All liturgy flows from this Mother of all Feasts.

This session is crafted in such a way that it can be used for ongoing reflection throughout the Easter season and liturgical year. The meaning, value, and function of symbols, as well as an exegesis of their biblical, ecclesial, and liturgical signs will be explored as they occur in the liturgy. Questions for mystagogical reflection are provided at the end of each section.

---

[1] The *NCD* asserts that "sacramental catechesis has traditionally been of two kinds: preparation for the initial celebration of the sacraments and continued enrichment following their first reception" (#36). The meaning of the sacraments is set forth in the scriptures assigned to the sacramental rites. Therefore, in order to prepare people for full, conscious, and active participation in the celebrations of the sacraments in the liturgy, the scriptures from those celebrations may be used for prior prayer and meditation. They may also be revisited following the celebration itself for mystagogical reflection and catechesis.

The historical development of the Easter Vigil will not be addressed in this session, as it was covered in the overview of the Easter season.

The symbols will not be repeated in the Doctrinal Appendix as they will be treated extensively in this session. However, symbols are critical to our Catholic tradition and therefore should form a major piece of our catechetical efforts. Thus, there will be questions provided for reflection on them, as well as on the scriptures and the liturgical segments.

This session is divided into seven sections: A. Holy Saturday and Rites of Preparation, B. Symbols, C. Introduction to the Easter Vigil, D. Service of Fire/Light, E. Liturgy of the Word, F. Service of Baptism, G. Liturgy of the Eucharist.

A. HOLY SATURDAY AND RITES OF PREPARATION

We are still in the midst of the Triduum; the liturgy is not over. The church gathers again for celebration of the liturgy of the hours on the morning of Holy Saturday.

Preparatory Rites

The elect are brought together for prayer and reflection in immediate preparation for the sacraments of initiation. If the presentation of the Lord's Prayer was deferred until this time [see #149, #178–180 in RCIA], it is celebrated on Holy Saturday. The "return" or recitation of the creed and the choosing of a baptismal name may also take place at this time (RCIA, #193–196, #200). Another preparatory rite is celebrated with the elect on Holy Saturday. "By the power of its symbolism, the *ephphetha rite*, or rite of opening the ears and mouth, impresses on the elect their need of grace in order that they may hear the word of God and profess it for their salvation" (RCIA, #197).

Blessing of Easter Foods

In some places there is a custom of blessing the foods that will break the lenten fast. Eggs, breads, meats, and produce are brought to the church for a special blessing. These foods used to be forbidden during Lent and blessing them is an indication that the lenten fast is over and Easter has arrived. This was easily understood when the Easter Vigil was celebrated early on Holy Saturday morning and the foods were brought to that celebration. Now, however, the blessing anticipates—rather than celebrates—the arrival of Easter. Gabe Huck suggests that rather than blessing with water (water blessing needs to wait for the Vigil) and incense, a simple extension of hands might be appropriate, if well explained. Another possibility might include inviting people to bring their foods on Easter day. "If such blessings are then given a prominent place in the liturgies of Easter day, with full use of water and incense, the blessings of food might slowly come to be seen—as they originally were—as part of the Easter liturgy."[2]

B. SYMBOLS

The symbols of the Easter Vigil are cross, fire/light, word, water, white garment, oil, laying on of hands, bread, wine, church. The nine dominant liturgical symbols of the church are all manifest at the Easter Vigil. The celebration of liturgy makes use of symbols that speak most appropriately of creation (candle, water, fire), human existence (washing, anointing, breaking bread), and the history of God's saving action in the world (the rites of Passover). The stories and actions of remembrance, the human rituals, and the above mentioned cosmic elements are subsumed into a world of faith and, through the power of the Holy Spirit, they reveal the saving action of Jesus Christ.

Symbols are encountered through the four signs of God's presence (the four signs of catechesis referred to in chapter 2). We encounter symbols through the natural, biblical, ecclesial, and liturgical signs of God's presence. Symbols speak to us of our identity as Catholic Christians. For example, the symbol of light has its genesis in Christ, Light of the World. Since we are to walk as children of the Light, light identifies us and we become its reality—we become light, we become bread, etc.

Meaning is conveyed when people encounter symbols, which are repeatable and possess many layers of meaning. They are multi-faceted and have multiple forms and uses. At the Easter Vigil, the symbol of light looms in the new fire, the Easter candle, the candles of the faithful, the incense, and the sanctuary lamp. In the darkened church, light's presence is felt in absence. The meaning of symbols is expressed in the way they are used, in the scriptures and ritual prayers that accompany their use, and in the gestures that define them.[3]

The Easter Vigil accentuates the symbols that illumine our existence and that occur in all liturgies. We are people of the cross. We enter the waters and we are chrismated into the ecclesial community. We thus become people of the light and are thereby incorporated into the paschal mystery, which we experience as we gather around the eucharistic table.

"Liturgical action depends on symbols because beings cannot be together and communicate without some kind of encounter in words (verbal symbols) and/or in gestures and actions (nonverbal symbols). All knowledge begins with our senses; this means that an encounter with God is only possible by means of sensible signs."[4] In antiquity, a symbol used to be understood as two halves which, when joined, became one whole. The person who had one half would thus recognize the other half because the two put together equaled the whole. By extension, a symbol was regarded as two parts of a whole—the visible and the invisible. Just because the invisible half of the symbol was not readily observable, it was nevertheless half of the reality. When joined with the visible half of the symbol, it constituted the whole reality. "In the language of religion and theology it is frequently the case that the concept of 'symbol' is reserved for the signs of faith, that is . . . in addition to their superficial, natural meaning, [they have] another and supernatural meaning that is only accessible to faith."[5] Through symbols we are able to touch the deep mysteries of our faith in ways that words can never express.

---

[2]Gabe Huck, *The Three Days: Parish Prayer in the Paschal Triduum* (Chicago: Liturgy Training Pub., 1981), 53.

[3]Linda Gaupin, *Sacramental Catechesis,* course text for "Specialized Certification in Sacramental Catechesis," Diocese of Orlando Florida, November 1996.

[4]*MSS,* 13.

[5]Ibid., 13.

If symbols were to speak, they would say: "I am ..." rather than, "I am like ...." Symbols in the sacramental sense *are* the reality they express. Eucharist in the form of bread and wine *is* the Body and Blood of Jesus. We can say with assurance that symbols express our identity. When we consume the precious elements, we become what we have consumed: the Mystical Body of Christ. The symbols of the Easter Vigil, highlighted and set forth, provide the means for us to communicate with God and for God to communicate with us through our senses. The symbols of the Vigil are food for mystagogical reflection throughout the Easter season and form the basis of our sacramental catechesis. Our symbol system connects us to the saints of the past with whom we share the same sacramental signs. When we experience the symbols of water, oil, and bread in their natural, biblical, ecclesial, and liturgical context, we discover new depths of meaning. God speaks to us as we crack open the meanings of the symbols and apply them to our lives. We encounter God in the natural elements of life. Those natural elements point to the hidden mystery of God in our lives. Sirach proclaimed: "Chief of all needs for human life are water and fire, iron and salt, the heart of the wheat, milk and honey, oil, the blood of the grape and cloth." If these are the chief of all human needs, no wonder they form the basis of our entire symbol system. Each one is essential for life just as God is essential for life.

The ecclesial signs provide us with the sources for understanding the nature and purpose of the symbols and rites. Ecclesial signs express what we believe about our symbols, how past communities understood them, and how we live what we believe. The first sources for understanding what the church believes about our signs and symbols are the ritual texts themselves (The Sacramentary, RCIA, rite of baptism, rite of confirmation, rite of penance, etc.).

Liturgical signs provide the vehicle for allowing our symbols to express what they were intended to convey. Liturgical signs occur in the worship of the community, in the liturgical celebration. In the liturgy, we pray the ritual prayers, perform the ritual action, and profess our ritual story. This is the night when new Christians are made in the waters of new birth; when the new oils anoint, seal, and brand the baptized to the image and likeness of Christ; and when the newly consecrated bread incorporates all the faithful in the life, death, and resurrection of Jesus Christ. The liturgy is the theater in which the symbols enact their intended roles and, in so doing, reveal the manifestation of God.

Before proceeding with the Vigil liturgy, let us explore the symbols of church and cross. The symbol of church/people of God is also addressed at this juncture because it is the context within which the Vigil is set. This is the night the church generates itself. We must approach the liturgy of this night from the perspective of church doing the work God has given it.

While the cross is a prominent symbol of this and every liturgy, it is underscored particularly in the liturgies of Good Friday, Palm Sunday, and the feast of the Triumph of the Cross. The cross is a primary symbol of the Easter Vigil as it relates to the resurrection of Christ. Without Christ's death on the cross, there could have been no resurrection. However, this liturgy does not meditate particularly on the cross, per se, but rather on its fulfillment in the resurrection.

Symbol of Church/People of God

One of the clearest symbols of God's presence in the world is the church. There are many interchangeable terms for church—community, church, people of God, assembly—but they are all the same reality. God is present to the world through the visible, tangible sign of God's love, the church. Human beings are, by nature, social beings. Belonging is a basic anthropomorphic need. From its earliest origins, Israel survived because it was *a people*. There was no life outside the community. The ancient world was a treacherous place. Food and water were scarce, and the environment was dangerous. The community was needed for basic survival and protection. The community meant life. The community provided the basic needs of shelter, food, and human companionship. When someone was exiled from the community, it was a death sentence.

One common thread running through all religious symbols is that in some way they speak to something that is essential or meaningful for human life. A symbol mirrors, images, or reflects invisible realities. Symbols provide a way of touching the intangible. God is revealed through a visible, tangible sign, something people can experience, touch, taste, smell, or feel.[6] Since community was essential for life and since there was no life, food, shelter, or protection outside the community, perhaps the community was a sign of who God is, how God acts, and what it means to be God's people. God functions like the community. God is provider, protector, and the One who sustains life.

Our experience of human community colors how we experience and understand the spiritual, biblical sense of community. Community as a symbol of God is a lived reality for people whose primary experience of the family community is nurturing. However, when the contrary is true, community as a sign of God becomes a reality only as it is experienced in the ongoing life of a faith-filled community.

The Easter Vigil celebrates the symbol of church/ people of God in the most visible way through the presence of the elect. After months of loving guidance, care, and nurturing, tender Mother Church gently brings her children to the water's edge for full immersion in the life of the community, the life of God.

Natural Sign

We exist in community. We are part of the human family. We have friends and we are social beings.

Groups can be exclusive or inclusive. They can pull together or be divisive. A unified community is capable of accomplishing many common goals. A divisive community is destructive. Community exists on many levels: family, friends, religious groups, ethnic groups, institutional groups, class groups, racial groups, civic groups, cities, states, country, world. Every family is a community. It can be nurturing and speak of the unconditional love of God, or the contrary can be true. Communities have power when they are united; they are powerless when they are not. Communities have the power to change laws and structures.

Questions: Have you ever had an experience of being part of a community other than your church community? What were the things that attracted you to this community? Did you ever have the sense that a community you were part of possessed corporate power?

Biblical Sign

The word *community* is not a term found in either the New Testament or the Old Testament. Israel was formed from tribal origins. Tribes were formed from unions between extended families, parents, brothers, sisters, cousins, in-laws, slaves, and servants. A person's identity was tied to the clan. Kinship was synonymous with tribal identity. Kinship prompted the celebration of rituals that supported the familial tribal bond, such as marriages, burials, and common festival meals. Passover was one such ritual.

In addition, there was a political understanding of community. Tribes were often forced to come together for military purposes or to support political leadership. "The basic Hebrew word for assembly, *qahal*, contains the notion of invited participation or summoning. This suggests that such large gatherings were irregular and exceptional; Israelites gathered at someone's command or request for joint military purposes or raiding."[7] Only hierarchical males in the tribe gathered for such meetings. Such was the tribal, communal structure.

Israel was a unique people, a people set apart. Beginning with Abraham, they were elected by God to become a great nation. Biblical authors be-

---

[6]This is how sacraments nourish the ongoing life of the church. Sacraments get us in touch with the living God through visible, touchable human symbols. Jesus Christ is called the sacrament of God. The reason God sent the Son to the world is that humanity does not have the capacity to comprehend the mind, heart, and inestimable love of God on its own. Human suspicion and incredulity would have always been a barrier. Unconditional love makes no sense in light of the human condition. Human beings could always say to their maker, "Sure, you love us. Those are empty words. You do not know what it means to struggle, suffer, and live the human condition. Your love is empty until you walk in our shoes. It means nothing." So the Son was sent. His name was Jesus; he walked in our shoes. Made of human flesh, Jesus, the sacrament of God, expressed for us the unfathomable love of God through death on the cross.

---

[7]Jerome H. Neyrey, S.J., "Community," in *CPDBT*, 151.

lieved Israel was "chosen by God as the means by which a special people were brought into being."[8] Israel was called and elected by God for a special purpose in his plan for the salvation of the world.

The exodus solidified the understanding of Israel's election. God called Moses to deliver *God's people* from slavery in Egypt. He formed an everlasting covenant with them and made them his precious, chosen, endeared children (Ex 19:5–6). God formed a covenant with Israel that was tied to their understanding of the tribal, family system. God would provide, sustain, and protect them. They would enjoy God's blessing, sharing, and peace, *shalom*. In return, they would live *hesed* (biblical justice) and would be obedient to God through adherence to the law and the prophets. Such obedience demanded that God's people extend the same covenant love to one another, especially the weakest members of the clan. Thus, in response to the covenant forged with Israel, they would live in obedience and biblical justice. Every time Israel sinned by going their own way, they understood their sin as disobedience to God's will. Calamity was understood as divine retribution for breaking the covenant.

The New Testament took the understanding of *people of God* one step further. The people of God were all those who were open to God's revelation in Christ, no matter what tribe or clan claimed their membership. "In referring to people of the second covenant, however, it also transcends having a common ancestry and history and is a reality of revelation, faith and historical awareness open to all human beings. This universality stems from the people's relationship to the person of Christ who died and rose in a great Passover event to be Lord of all, as well as from the creative Spirit of God manifested on Pentecost."[9] Thus, the invitation to become the people of God was open to all: Jew, Greek, gentile, who would accept the proclamation of God's reign (Acts 28).

When the Hebrew bible was translated into Greek, the term for *qahal*, an invited gathering, was *ekklesia* or *synagoge*. To the Greeks, the term meant a political gathering. There were many such gatherings that were not religious in orientation. The males would gather in a public square or gathering space for political or other reasons. They may have gathered for reading the Torah on the sabbath, but the *synagoge* was not necessarily religious in purpose.

According to Jerome Neyrey, when the Christian church adapted the term, it understood *ekklesia* (church) to mean the gathering of a new people as citizens of a new political reality—the reign of God. Christians were new citizens of the household of God (Eph 2:19).

People of Jesus' time did belong to groups outside the family structure. Neyrey calls these groups the *fictive* family. The disciples were a fictive family. When Jesus spoke of anyone who does the will of God as being his mother, brother, sister, etc., he was referring to the creation of a new fictive family, the household of God (Mk 3:34–35). Regardless of the social class structure in the tribal or political system, members of Jesus' new fictive family, or households, were to be treated with equal respect, honor, and protection, whether they were slave, servant, woman, or child. They were as deserving as blood relatives. There was no sense of individualism. "Family ideology indicates that individuals should always 'seek the good of the group' (1 Cor 10:24), and not pursue individualistic objectives."[10]

The Christian message of community centered around the eschatological hope of the new, eternal city, the new Jerusalem. It was a message of universality. God's new paradise would be open to all people inclusively without distinctions. "Later in the vision of the new creation (Rev 21:1–22:5), when salvation history is finally fulfilled, God's dwelling will be with the entire human race. 'He will dwell with them and they will be his people' (Rev 21:3)."[11]

Questions: What touched you in the biblical understanding of people of God? Was there any new insight? What does it teach you about God, Christ, Spirit, community, or yourself? What does it mean to you to be part of a com-

[8]Joseph Jensen, O.S.B., "People of God," in *CPDBT*, 720.
[9]Eugene LaVerdiere, S.S.S., "People of God: New Testament," in *CPDBT*, 721.

[10]Neyrey, *CPDBT*, 152.
[11]LaVerdiere, *CPDBT*, 723.

munity comprised of citizens of a new political reality? What are the implications? How does the notion of corporate reality versus individual identity speak to us today? Does your community live the eschatological and universal understanding of community inherent in the New Testament? In what way does your community need to grow in the awareness of its own identity and reality?

Ecclesial Sign

The Second Vatican Council, in its document, *The Dogmatic Constitution on the Church*, recaptured the biblical symbol of the church as people of God. There is a direct bearing and relationship to the scriptural understanding of covenant between God and Israel.

Justin, one of the early church fathers, eventually understood the emergence of the Christian church as coming *from* Israel, but as now being the true Israel. The church continued the work and role of Israel. Augustine described the church as on its way, since the creation of the world, to its final destination in heaven. Since church and state were one during the Middle Ages, there was little need to refer to the church's identity—it was obvious. There was no one to dispute it. During the Reformation there was, however, discussion regarding the role of the church. Rather than using the symbol, *people of God*, the language chosen during the Reformation was *communion of saints*, "the invisible communion of believers who are the true Church."[12]

The symbol did not enjoy a renaissance until the nineteenth century. "The spirit of a people binding them together as a community, works to retrieve the symbol of body of Christ to describe the organic unity of the Church, through the enlivening presence of the Holy Spirit"[13] (per the work of Johann Adam Mohler). This eventually led to the encyclical, *Mystici Corporis* in 1943. With the emergence of the field of biblical studies, the symbol *people of God* was retrieved from the church's earliest foundation, Israel and the Christian community. By 1960, the symbol was a consciously recognized aspect of ecclesiology. This led the way for reformulation of the church's theology.

---

[12]Ann Graff, "People of God in the History of Theology," in *CPDBT*, 724.

[13]Ibid.

The Second Vatican Council redefined our understanding of church. The following principles are a summary of our theology as articulated in *Sharing the Light of Faith: The National Catechetical Directory*. "The Church is a mystery. It is a reality imbued with the hidden presence of God" (from Pope Paul VI's opening allocution at the second session, September 19, 1963). "The Church is a gift coming from the love of God, Christ's redeeming action and the power of the Holy Spirit" (*National Catechetical Directory* [NCD], #63). "As a divine reality inserted into human history, the Church is a kind of sacrament. Its unique relationship with Christ makes it both a sign and instrument of God's unfathomable union with humanity and of the unity of human beings among themselves" (NCD, #63). "...As a mystery, the Church cannot be totally understood or fully defined. Its nature and mission are best captured in scriptural parables and images, taken from ordinary life, which not only express truth about its nature but challenge the Church: for example, to become more a People of God, a better servant, more faithful and holy, more united around the teaching authority of the hierarchy" (NCD, #63).

The church is a community of believers, the people of God. We are called to become a new people, a royal priesthood, a people claimed by God to proclaim the greatness of God (1 Pet 2:9). Jesus freed us from sin and because of the saving waters of baptism we are called to believe, worship, and witness to his saving works.

We are one body in Christ (Rom 12:5). Through Jesus' death, resurrection, and glorification, he remains a living presence and head of his church, of which we are all members. *We celebrate this identity most especially in the eucharist.* Through the eucharist, we become the Body and Blood of Christ.

The church is servant. The church has a mission to heal and reconcile as Jesus did. The church is to live the gospel through the works of mercy, assisting anyone who is in need of our help. The church as servant acts out of love and concern, not for personal glory. One way the church is servant is through its teaching ministry in which it witnesses to the gospel and the power of God in the world.

The church is a sign of the reign of God. The church is evidence that God is alive in our midst. In order to be that sign, the church "must be committed to justice, love and peace, to grace and holiness, truth and life, for these are the hallmarks of the kingdom of God" (NCD, #67).

The church is a pilgrim church. Aware of its sins, the church journeys to its final destination as it repents and overcomes patiently the trials and tribulations that come its way. In this way it demonstrates its steadfast faithfulness to the world.

"As mystery, people, one body in Christ, servant, sign of the kingdom, and pilgrim, the Church is conceived as God's family, whose members are united to Christ and led by the Spirit in their journey to the Father. The Church merits our prayerful reflection and wholehearted response" (NCD, #68).

Questions: Does the church's theology about church resonate with your experience of church in your own community? What are the areas of death/resurrection? What are some specific areas that are in need of growth? What does participation in your community teach you about God, Christ, Spirit, church, or yourself?

Liturgical Sign

The symbol of church as people of God is a primary symbol in the liturgy. The gathered community is a sign of God's presence in our midst. Before the book is opened or the bread shared, God is experienced in the community. "For these people are the people of God, purchased by Christ's blood, gathered together by the Lord, nourished by the word. They are a people called to offer the prayers of the entire human family, a people giving thanks in Christ, for the mystery of salvation by offering his sacrifice. Finally they are a people growing together into unity by sharing Christ's Body and Blood. These people are holy by their origin, but becoming ever more holy by conscious, active and fruitful participation in the mystery of the Eucharist" (*Constitution on the Sacred Liturgy*, #59, "General Instruction of the Roman Missal," #5).

In every liturgical celebration the community is a primary experience of God's presence. We profess the mystery of the church in our ritual prayers and, through the eucharist, we live its reality. Through all the ministries of the church, Christ is present. Thus, when the people participate and celebrate, the lector proclaims, the priest presides, the eucharistic minister serves, the cantor sings, the hospitality people welcome, etc., Christ is made manifest in our midst.

Questions: Have you ever had an experience of the presence of God in the midst of your communal worship? In what ways does your community embody the living presence of Christ in your past worship? What did your experience teach you about God, Christ, Spirit, community, yourself?

Symbol of the Cross

This object of torture and sign of disgrace and horror is a symbol of our salvation. It is the principal Christian symbol of hope. The cross is at the heart of our belief in the paschal mystery and our participation in it. Without the cross there is no resurrection. Tonight's liturgy leads us from the cross to the resurrection. We are transported through time as witnesses of God's great deeds of history and brought to this moment. God fulfilled in Christ what was begun at the creation of the world. We are called to take up our cross and follow Christ. "Apart from the cross there is no other ladder by which we may get to heaven."[14]

The cross was an absurdity to the people of Jesus' time. To imagine the cross as a symbol of salvation, victory, and honor, was as absurd to Jesus' contemporaries as imagining the electric chair as an object worthy of veneration would be in today's culture. The cross is a sign of our redemption. Christ was victorious over sin and death. St. Irenaeus reminds us of the implication of the cross: "By the wood of the Cross the work of the Word of God was made manifest to all: his hands are stretched out to gather every one together."[15]

---

[14]St. Rose of Lima, cf. P. Hansen, *Vita mirabilis* (Louvain, 1668).

[15]Quoted in Henri de Lubac, *Catholicism: A Study of Dogma in Relation to the Corporate Destiny of Mankind* (New York: New American Library, 1964), 210.

Natural Sign

Crucifixion is not a means of execution today. We have no natural concept of cross apart from what has come to us from religious sources. However, the cross is used in our culture as a sign of adornment with little or no meaning attached to it. Some in the counter-cultural strata of today's society have even made a mockery of it. The word *cross* has often been associated with a general understanding of suffering in our culture ("That poor woman has a cross to bear"). The term *cross* is somewhat universally understood to mean the trials in one's life.

Questions: How does "cross" have anything to do with your everyday life? What is your experience of the cross?

Biblical Sign

There was no mention of the cross in the Old Testament. Crucifixion was an oriental means of execution. The Greeks did not use it, but the Romans did. However, Roman citizens were never crucified. Crucifixion on the cross was reserved for slaves, insurrectionists, traitors, and anyone guilty of a grave crime. Jesus alluded to the cross in reference to his own death. The symbol of cross was fostered by Jesus who challenged his disciples to take up their cross and follow him. Cross was understood in that sense to mean the "denial of self." In order to gain one's life, one had to lose it. Disciples had to be willing to give up their personal welfare in response to the reign of God.

Paul gives us a refined theology of the cross as symbol. He preached that the cross was revolting to the Jews and folly to the Gentiles (1 Cor 1:23; 2:2). Through the power of the cross, all people who believe in it are saved. Circumcision is no longer needed; it is replaced by the cross as a sign of God's covenant with the human race (Gal 66:14). The cross is a symbol of unity; it unites Jews and gentiles. Jesus nailed the sins of the world to the cross. He became the victim of their sins (Col 2:14). Jesus freely gave up his life for all. He died once, and for the whole world. We cannot merit salvation. Jesus won it for us, once and for all.

Ecclesial Sign

The symbol of cross is understood to mean the unique sacrifice of Jesus' life for the salvation of the world. Only Christ was able to take unto himself the sins of the world by dying a horrid death on the cross.

St. Augustine exhorted those who were preparing for baptism to understand the significance of the cross: Jesus Christ suffered and died for humanity.

> "Do not hesitate, do not be ashamed. When you first believed, you received the sign of Christ on your forehead, the home of your shame. Remember your forehead and do not be afraid of another man's tongue.... Do not then be afraid of the shame of the Cross."[16]

Since the forehead is where the blush of shame appears, the catechumens were signed with the cross on their forehead as a sign that they should never be ashamed of the cross. There was another reason for signing the candidates with the cross. In antiquity slaves and soldiers were marked on their foreheads or their hands as a sign that they owed allegiance to those they served. The slave was branded with his master's sign whereas the soldier was marked with the name of the Emperor. Catechumens were thus signed as a reminder that they belonged to Christ and his cross. This was referred to as a seal as was the entire rite of initiation. The cross was signed on the forehead once again at the completion of their initiation.[17]

We are united to Jesus' cross and suffering through baptism. The cross is initiatory. We are incorporated into Christ's cross through baptism: we die to sin and are resurrected to new life in Christ. Through confirmation we are branded with the Holy Spirit. We are also sealed and joined to the cross of Christ. Through the eucharist, we share in Jesus' sacrifice of the cross. In the form of bread and wine we once again participate in the breaking, sharing, and pouring out of Jesus' life. We, too, are broken, shared, and poured out. The Christian community shares in the saving effects of Jesus' sacrifice: his paschal mystery, his death and resurrection. Like Jesus on Calvary, paschal Christians are to live, die, and empty themselves, for the sake of others, for the sins of the world.

---

[16] *Sermon* 215.5; *Patrologia Latina*, ed, J.-P. Migne, in *AIRI*, 4.
[17] Ibid.

The sacrifice of the cross continues through the broken bread and the poured cup of the eucharist.

We cannot earn salvation. Jesus won salvation on the cross and through the grace offered by the selfless sacrifice of his life we are all beneficiaries. The cross is a supreme act of love. Jesus' death on the cross fulfilled all the expectations of the old Passover. Salvation history is fulfilled with Jesus' final act of love. All sacraments participate in the cross of Christ. They invite us to live the paschal mystery in our everyday lives and supply the needed grace to do so.

St. John Chrysostom professes it best:

> Today sees our Lord Jesus Christ on the cross; we celebrate, so that we may understand that the cross is a celebration, a solemn, spiritual feast. Before, the cross was synonymous with condemnation; now it is an object of honor. Before, a symbol of death; now, the means of salvation. It has been the source of countless blessings for us: it has delivered us from error, it has shone on us when we were in darkness. We were vanquished, yet it reconciles us with God. We were foes, yet it has regained God's friendship for us. We were estranged, yet it has brought us back to him. . . . We have discovered a wellspring.[18]

Question: In light of your personal experience of the cross, the suffering in your life, can you now perhaps assign a deeper meaning to that suffering in dialogue with our tradition's belief in its saving effects?

Liturgical Sign

The cross forms us as people. Every liturgy, every sacramental celebration has as its primary focus incorporation into the paschal mystery of Jesus Christ. That is, we participate in Jesus' death and resurrection through our participation in the liturgy. Eucharist is a living memorial of that death and resurrection.

---

[18]John Chrysostom (ca. 350–407), "Homélie pour le Vendredi saint," in *Homiliaire patristique,* Lex Orandi 8 (Paris: Cerf, 1949), 65; in *DL (III),* 27–28.

Every liturgical gathering remembers the cross of Christ. We begin each liturgy with the sign of our identity, the sign of the cross. We are signed with the cross of Jesus as catechumens and at our baptism. The sign of the cross signifies the grace of salvation won for us through Jesus' passion, death on the cross, and resurrection. We make the sign of the cross before all prayer and as we enter the church.

We remember the cross of Christ especially on Good Friday, Palm Sunday, and the feast of the Triumph of the Cross. The Easter season is a meditation on its saving effects. The entire liturgical year invites us to live the cross each day. The cross is a primary symbol in every blessing, ritual, liturgy, sacrament, and sacramental of the church. (Refer to the Good Friday liturgy for the historical development of the ritual celebration of the cross.)

Questions: Do you remember a time when you were conscious of an experience of the cross in the liturgy? What did it teach you about God, Christ, the church, and yourself? What is the challenge of the cross we celebrate? How are we called to respond to the cross of Christ in our lives?

C. INTRODUCTION TO THE EASTER VIGIL

Huddled around ancient fires, our ancestors told their stories and enacted the rituals that formed them into a holy nation, a consecrated assembly, a people set apart. We, too, gather this night around similar sacred flames to remember our origins, to tell our story, and to "do" the business of making church. The ancient phallic symbol of Easter candle is plunged into the embryonic waters of font. Tonight, the church gives birth. As it labors in love, Mother Church sings its pangs of joy as neophytes are born and hearts are reborn.

This is the night when heavenly hosts gather around their Master's jeweled banquet table in triumphant exultation, awaiting the final great communion. This is the night when Christians of earth look toward their participation in that banquet while rejoicing in the one at hand. It is sacred, earthy work. We dirty our hands in groves of olives, fields of wheat, and vineyards of grapes and we wash them again and again in the murky waters of life. And somehow the fruit of our labor is sanctified and transports us into the heart of Transcendent Mystery. This is the night when heaven is truly wedded to earth.

This night (the night early Christians believed would be the time and place of Jesus' return) is the high point and premier celebration of our liturgical year. All the liturgies of the year point to this one great feast; it is foundational to our Catholic experience and identity. The Easter Vigil is divided into four parts: 1. Service of Light, 2. Liturgy of the Word, 3. Liturgy of Baptism, 4. Liturgy of the Eucharist.

D. SERVICE OF FIRE/LIGHT

Opening Prayer

Blessing of the Fire

Let us pray.
Father,
we share in the light of your glory
through your Son, the light of the world.
Make this new fire + holy, and inflame us with new
    hope.
Purify our minds by this Easter celebration
and bring us one day to the feast of eternal light.
We ask this through Christ our Lord.
Let us pray. . . .[19]

Liturgical Context

The liturgy begins with the service of light and the blessing of the new fire. Even though Christ was discovered missing from the tomb at dawn, this liturgy is celebrated in the dark of night, with the blessing of new fire and a procession. The baptized, passing from death to life, darkness to light, were once called the *illuminandi*. The church gathers to celebrate the risen Christ who, on this holy night, dispelled the darkness of death.

This is a night of new things and new beginnings. We bless the new fire that will be used to light all

the lights that were extinguished on Holy Thursday. Lit by the flame of the newly blessed fire, the Easter candle is processed into the darkened space as the acclamation of praise resounds: *"Lumen Christi*, Light of Christ, *Deo Gratias*, thanks be to God."

Like our ancestors of old who followed the pillar of light to freedom, we, too, are led to our freedom, the font and table. The procession moves through the church, the light growing brighter with the multiplication of each person's individual candle light. We stand as God's triumphant, liberated people while we listen to our hymn of praise: the Christian story in its grandeur, the mother of all prayers, the Exultet. We boldly, almost shockingly, praise God for the "necessary sin of Adam that gained for us so great a Redeemer" who is Christ our Light, the One who dispelled the darkness. In the dimness of this darkened church we listen as our salvation is unfolded before our sense-sharpened eyes and ears.

There are three ritual moments of light in the service of light: the blessing of the new fire; the procession and passing of light through the congregation with the acclamation, *Lumen Christi, Deo gratias;* and the prayer of blessing in the Exultet. "The fundamental theme of the Exultet is thanksgiving and praise for the light and the event of Easter night: redemption through the paschal mystery."[20]

Questions: How do these introductory moments of the Easter Vigil speak to your community? What do they tell you about God, the church, or you as an individual? What are the implications of blessing the new fire, processing by the light of the Easter candle, and singing our ancient hymn of praise? How does this experience call you to enter the death and resurrection of Christ?

Symbol of Light/Fire

The symbol of light in most religions is a sign of divinity. In the Christian tradition, the symbol of light is a sign of Christ's presence. Darkness symbolizes the converse: God's absence and/or the destructive force of evil. Fire is only used once in

---

[19]Easter Vigil: "Blessing of the Fire," *The Sacramentary.*

[20]*MSS*, 112.

our tradition—at the Easter Vigil. However, the symbol of fire and light overlap in many ways, so they will be treated together.

Natural Sign

Fire and light order our life. We rise to the light and go to bed in the dark. Light and darkness are known to effect mood shifts. Studies have shown that sunny, bright days impact people in a positive way, whereas repeated dark and gloomy days can cause depression. We need the light to see; we are unable to see in the dark. Too much light can burn us or hurt our eyes. Too much darkness is known to have prompted some suicides. Without light, plants do not grow. If there is too much light they are burned. When the night is illumined with light, it protects us from the unknown shadows of the dark. The light of fire protected ancient communities from intruding marauders. Food is cooked and our homes are heated with the warmth of fire. Fire and hearth are images of cozy comfort. We have no control over the light of day or the darkness of night. We are subject to their benevolence or their tyranny. Forest rangers purposely set fires to prompt new growth in the forest. The giant redwoods cannot procreate without nature's birthing, necessary fire. Fire makes it possible for acorns to gestate through the nutrients found in the charred ash. Fire also destroys.

Question: In what ways do we experience light and fire in our everyday lives? Describe your personal images and experiences of light and fire.

Biblical Sign

The Bible uses fire first in very natural ways, then in symbolic ways. The word "light" appears 257 times in the Bible and the word "fire" 457 times. These are basic, primordial elements, necessary for life. Fire is used in cooking, for heat and light, and as a weapon of war (2 Chr 35:13; Is 44:16, 19; Num 31:10). Fire, as light, is also a means of communication between cities. Fire can be a powerful sign of God's presence and protection: the burning bush (Ex 3:2) and the column of fire that escorted the Israelites (Ex 13:21–22). When fire and light appear in scripture, everyone is to take notice: it means God is present. Fire and light are signs of theophany. A fire was kept burning at the altar as a sign of God's abiding presence (Lev 6:2, 5–6). In addition to being a sign of God's presence, fire is also a sign of God's protection. God protected Elisha with fiery chariots; the three young men who were thrown into the fire by Nebuchadnezzar were not consumed by its flame. A very common Old Testament theme is that God will judge the world by fire (2 Sam 23:7) and test and purify his people by fire (Zech 13:9; Ex 32:20). Light is a reference to Torah or God's law—a lamp to light our feet (Ps 119).

The New Testament uses fire in the same way as the Hebrew scriptures used fire. God appeared to the twelve as tongues of fire. Jesus will test and purify when he baptizes with the Holy Spirit and fire (Mt 3:11). The last judgment is also seen in terms of fire. Jesus is understood as the Light, the new Word that lights our way.

Light is a prime symbol of Christ and his life. Christ is the Light; we are to walk as children of the Light (Mt 4:16; Lk 1:7–9; 2:32; Jn 12:36). For John, the evangelist, Jesus is the *Light* that dispels the darkness. Jesus, the *Light*, is the eternal Word of God. Faith calls people into the *Light*. The reign of God is characterized by light; there is no night in the heavenly sphere (Rev 21:22–27; 22:5).

Questions: What caught your attention in regard to the biblical understanding of fire and light? Why? In what way do you relate to the symbol of light/fire found in scripture? In what way does fire remind you of God's presence? In what way does the symbol of light invite you into the transcendence of God? How does the symbol of light challenge you in your Christian journey? How might light reveal the inclusivity of God? What does it teach you about God, Christ, the church, or yourself? How does it speak to the life of the community, your life?

Ecclesial Sign

The lighting of fire is not, in and of itself, characteristic of Easter. Every evening celebration in the ancient world began with a ritual of lighting. Whenever there is light, God is present: it is cause for our thanks. The blessing prayer over the fire is a prayer of longing for God, the Light that is never extinguished. The ritual of lighting probably has pagan roots. Large bonfires were lighted in the spring in hopes that pagan deities would bless the crops. Christians were forbidden to do this until the emergence of a ritual bonfire associated with Holy Saturday around the sixth century. This eventually became a part of the Easter Vigil liturgy. In the Middle Ages, people observed a custom of extinguishing all fires and lights in or around their homes. They would take a flame from the newly blessed Easter fire to light the extinguished fires in their homes as a sign of new life.

The newly-baptized are presented with a lighted candle as a sign that they have been enlightened by Christ. In antiquity there was reference to "the shining lights" of the neophytes, the "white-robed members of the heavenly kingdom."[21] The use of lighted candles probably originated as a practical necessity in a ritual that took place in the darkened shadows of early dawn. Connection between the lights and the parable of the bridesmaids was made by Gregory Nanzianus in 381: "The lamps which you will light symbolize the torchlight procession in the next world, in which our shining, virgin souls will meet the bridegroom with the shining lights of faith."[22]

Fire and light are signs of the risen Christ. They are also signs of the Holy Spirit. Fire is a symbol of the transforming power and energy of the Holy Spirit. Everything that is touched by the fire of the Spirit is transformed. Tradition understands fire as a sign of hope, consummation, sacrifice, and purification. Fire and light are symbols of sanctification. Light is initiatory in character. It is a symbol of incorporation into Christ's Body: we are to walk as children of the Light. "The presentation of the lighted candle shows that they [neophytes] are called to walk as befits the children of the light" (RCIA, #214). Light is a symbol of Christianity. Jesus is the Light that illumines the world. Light is a sign of wisdom and understanding. Light reminds us of Christ's presence. It is a sign of discipleship and righteousness. Wherever a candle is left burning, Christ is present.

Questions: How would you articulate the church's understanding of light and fire? In what way does it have anything to do with living the Christian life, our life, your life? How might light speak to you of hope, consummation, sacrifice? What does that mean? In what way do they have relevance for your life? What does tradition's understanding of light and fire teach about God, Christ, the church, or yourself?

Liturgical Sign

The church uses fire, particularly light, extensively in its liturgy. The only time fire is used as a single entity is at the Easter Vigil. Fire is blessed as a sign of the risen Christ. The Easter candle is lit from this new fire and all other candles are lit from the light of that candle. The assembly's individual candles are also signs of the resurrected Christ.

The Easter candle probably originates from the ancient ritual of the *Lucenare*, celebrated at the end of each day. Lamps were lit to ward off the darkness. Light has always been a symbol of the presence of God: Moses and the burning bush, the presence of smoke, the cloud and pillar of fire. Light is such an important symbol and sign of God's presence that it is used in every liturgical celebration. Wherever the Blessed Sacrament is reserved, a sanctuary lamp burns as a sign of Christ's presence. As the neophytes are baptized, they are given lighted candles as a sign of their new status: they now walk as children of the Light. Candles illumine the table of the word and the table of the eucharist as a sign of the living, sacramental presence of Christ. Candles are used for the blessing of throats, Candlemas, and with the sick. The Easter candle is used at baptisms and funerals. Candles are used in processions, in all liturgical celebrations, at evening prayer, weddings, religious professions, and in homes. The symbol of Christ, the *Light*, is present at every liturgy.

Questions: What is your experience of fire and light in liturgy? Has it ever touched you in a conscious way? What does it say to you about God, Christ, church, or yourself? How has the Easter fire spoken to you? What did you experience, feel, and think as you gathered around the new fire at the Easter Vigil, as you carried candles or watched the procession with the Easter candle? What do these signs say to us as a community and what is their challenge?

[21]*De Lapsu Virginis*, 5.19, *Patrologia Latina*, ed, J.-P. Migne, in *AIRI*, 34.

[22]*Oratio* 40. 46; cf. 45.2, *Patrologia Gracca*, ed, J.-P. Migne, in *AIRI*, 34.

E. THE LITURGY OF THE WORD

Liturgical Context

The biblical readings for the Easter Vigil are the same in the churches of the East and the West. The first four readings from the Old Testament (Hebrew scriptures) correspond to the Jewish tradition of the "Four Nights." The first night was when the Word of God created the world. The second night was when God appeared to Abraham and Sarah to fulfill the promise that Abraham would father Sarah's child in spite of their very old age. It was also the night when Abraham offered his son, Isaac, in sacrifice to God, thus demonstrating great faith. The third night was the night when the angel of death protected Israel's first-born from the death sentence reserved for Egypt's first-born. Pharaoh released Israel from bondage and Yahweh led the fleeing band through the desert. The fourth night is yet to come and will take place at the end of the world.

Thus, the first four readings are essential to understanding our salvation history already set in motion at the beginning of the world, fulfilled through the Incarnation, and to be culminated through Jesus' second coming.

The next three Old Testament readings are laden with baptismal images. They prepare us for this night when the church opens its fonts to the flowing waters of new birth, death, and resurrection. Paul's letter to the Romans explicitly names baptism as death to sin as the beginning of new life in Christ. The liturgy of the word culminates with the exuberant proclamation of the resurrection. We are taken to the place where death was destroyed forever: we are brought to the empty tomb of Jesus Christ.

The Word as Symbol

The Word embodies the presence of Christ in our midst. We proclaim the word of God as the living, sacramental presence of God. "In the celebration of the liturgy, the word of God is not voiced in only one way nor does it always stir the hearts of the hearers with the same power. Always, however, Christ is present in his word; as he carries out the mystery of salvation, he sanctifies us and offers the

Father perfect worship.... That word constantly proclaimed in the liturgy is always, then, a living, active word through the power of the Holy Spirit. It expresses the Father's love that never fails in its effectiveness toward us."[23] When the word is proclaimed, the church is built up and it grows. Through the symbols inherent in the liturgy, salvation events are brought into the present and we are their beneficiaries. Through the proclamation of God's word we are made a new people, heirs of God's covenant.

Natural Sign

Words can build up or tear down. They can affirm or destroy. Words express mystery and reality. Words can be spoken, written, sung, signed, or coded. Words can sell things, teach, regulate, and warn. Words can start wars. Words can create revolutions. Words can change consciousness and political perspectives. Words have power.

Questions: Can you a remember a time when words had a powerful impact on your life, positively or negatively? What did that experience teach you about the power of the word?

Biblical Sign

Word is understood as the self-revelation of God to human beings. The Hebrew word *dabar* means not only the spoken word, but also an event, a happening. The term assumes power, energy, and action. It is dynamic and alive. The word of God connotes God's acts of salvation. The power of God's word is evident in the first reading from tonight's liturgy. God's word created the heavens and the earth: "Let there be light, and there was light" (Gen 1:3). The covenant with Israel comes from the word of the Lord, "Everything the Lord has said, we will do" (Ex 19:8; 24:3, 7). The ten commandments were referred to as the spoken word of God. The word of God is synonymous with God's promises: Abraham and his descendants, the promised land, etc. God's word was spoken through the prophets. God spoke in person to Moses who, in turn, was to speak God's word to Pharaoh (Ex 33:11; Num 12:8; Deut 34:1). Samuel heard the voice of the Lord calling in the night (1 Sam 3:7–14). Prophets spoke

---

[23]*Lectionary for Mass.* Introduction, #4, in *TLD*, 128.

God's word to David. Nathan assured David that his monarchy would endure forever. Nathan also accused David of having an illicit affair with Bathsheba. Elijah and Elisha are always in dialogue with God's word. When the prophet speaks, Israel listens. What the prophet speaks is as good as accomplished.

In the Wisdom tradition, asserts Irene Nowell, the word is understood as the bearer of good things to God's people and calamity to God's enemies. *Word* is also another term for the law. The wisdom tradition begins to personify the word and give it a divine role. The word, for example, was present at creation and in salvation history (Wis 10–12).

In the New Testament, the term *logos* is used 331 times. It has many possible meanings: a statement, an assertion, a command, a report or story, a proverb, a saying, a prophecy, or a speech. It is used as a reference for the revelation of God, especially revelation as it occurred through Jesus Christ. "In many cases, the 'word of God' is simply the Christian message, the good news."[24] Apostles and preachers speak God's word. Hearers of the word are to listen and respond accordingly.

The evangelist John's use of *logos* is in direct relation to Jesus Christ. In the Jewish story of the Four Nights (the first four readings from the Vigil liturgy), God's word as a personified entity creates the world. Many believe that the identification of Jesus with *logos* comes from this concept. "The hymn in the Prologue is the clearest example in first century Christian literature of both an incarnation and a preexistence of Christology. It affirms both that the logos has become flesh in the person of Jesus of Nazareth and that Jesus of Nazareth existed before the incarnation, indeed before the creation of the world, as God's divine *logos*."[25]

Toward the end of the New Testament, the word was associated with the written word of God. "The 'good news' came to be seen in the written words of the four evangelists and in the Bible as a whole."[26]

---

[24]William G. Thompson, S.J. and Gerard S. Sloyan, "Word: New Testament," in *CPDBT*, 1097.

[25]Ibid., 1100.

[26]Anthony Tambasco, "Word of God," in *CPDBT*, 1097.

Questions: Have you ever experienced God's living presence in the scriptures? What did it teach you about God, Christ, the church, or yourself? Was there a call to respond, to action?

Ecclesial Sign

The Church Fathers sought to confirm the dynamic power of God's word through Christ in the church. "Where the Lordship (of God) is proclaimed, the Lord is present" (*Didache*, 4:1). St. Augustine linked the power of preaching to a person's absorption (or lack thereof) in the sacred scriptures. "Caesarius of Arles declared that 'the word of God is not to be treated as inferior to the body of Christ' (Sermon 78:2). For the Father, in fact, the liturgy becomes the fitting place where Jesus as the word of God is fully encountered, first in the scriptural flesh and blood of the *logos* and then in celebration of that word in the bread and wine of the eucharist."[27]

Because of the emergence of various heresies and the rise of the teaching ministry, the church of the Middle Ages was less concerned with the word as the living, dynamic, self-revelation of God and more concerned with the intellectual formulations of doctrines *about* God. Partly due to a concern over this, the Protestant reformers set forth *sola scriptura* (scripture alone) as the only source of God's word, thereby denying the teaching authority of the hierarchy. The Council of Trent insisted that the truth of God's word was in both the written sources and in the unwritten traditions. However, later developments elevated the unwritten source, tradition, to the status of a second, separate source of divine revelation.

Lines were drawn between Protestant and Catholic understandings of God's word. Protestants continued to preach God's word and to assert the importance of its power within each individual. Catholics relied on doctrinal formulations and theologies in relation to God's word. Tradition was placed in a higher position of authority than the biblical sources of God's word.

The Second Vatican Council retrieved the biblical source of God's self-revelation fulfilled through the

---

[27]Ibid.

person of Jesus Christ. The document *Dei Verbum* asserted the authenticity of scripture and tradition as one source. Thus, God is revealed through the scriptures *and* the tradition of the church. Tradition was redefined in terms of the "faith of the living church which surrounds, preserves and transmits the scriptures and makes them come alive."[28]

Questions: How does the church's experience of God's word throughout its history relate to the life of your community or yourself? What does it teach you about God, Christ, the church, or yourself?

Liturgical Signs

Dei Verbum returned us to our earliest roots in which the living word of God was best experienced in the celebration of the liturgy. Therefore, the Council prompted a renaissance in the preaching ministry of the church. "The primary duty of priests is the proclamation of the Gospel of God to all" (*Decree on Ministry and Life of Priests*). Preaching is characterized by the "proclamation of God's wonderful works in the history of salvation, that is, the mystery of Christ, which is made present and active within us, especially in the eucharistic celebration of the liturgy" (*Constitution on the Sacred Liturgy*, [CSL], #35, 2).

The church teaches that Christ is present in the proclamation of God's word in the liturgy. "He is present in his word, since it is he himself who speaks when the holy Scriptures are read in the Church" (CSL, #7). The word of God proclaimed in the liturgy is efficacious: "and it is from the continued use of Scriptures that the people of God, docile to the Holy Spirit under the light of faith, receive the power to be Christ's living witnesses before the world" (*Lectionary for Mass: Introduction*, #12).

All scripture reveals Jesus Christ. Both Testaments are about the saving work of God in Christ, the *Word* who was present at the creation of the world. God used human authors to reveal his *Word* for the salvation of all. The four gospels hold a preeminent place in the canon of the Bible as they reveal the life and work of Christ, the *Word made Flesh*. [See chapter three and chapter nine.]

---

[28]Ibid., 1098.

The word and the eucharist are in intimate relationship. "The Church is nourished spiritually at the table of God's word and at the table of the eucharist: from one it grows in wisdom and from the other in holiness. In the word of God the divine covenant is announced; in the eucharist the new and everlasting covenant is renewed. The spoken word of God brings to mind the history of salvation; the eucharist embodies it in the sacramental signs of the liturgy" (*Lectionary for Mass: Introduction*, #10).

Whenever the church gathers for prayer, God's word is primary. Whether the gathering is for sacraments, eucharist, rites, the liturgy of the hours, blessings, or sacramentals, it is the church's intention that the word be a pivotal part of all liturgical celebration.

Questions: Have you ever experienced the presence of Christ in the proclamation of God's word in the liturgy? What did it teach you about God, Christ, the church, or yourself? In what way has the word of God called your community to respond in the past? How is God's word challenging your community now?

THE WORD OF GOD

Proclaim the word of God.

First Reading
Genesis 1:1–2:2

While meditating on the reason for God's incredible action in the lives of human beings, and drawing on Babylonian images of the creation of the world, the ancient author of Genesis (ca. 5th or 6th century B.C.E.) eloquently provided all future generations with refined insight into the creative, loving, and omniscient power of the Creator. The word was spoken and God's generative power created the universe. From creation onward, the generative word of God would have a leading role in human history and experience. (Remember the centurion who told Jesus to say but the word and his servant would be healed.)

"God creates the world for humans in six days and rests on the seventh, the first week of human history; the week of six work days ending in Sabbath observance is thereby hallowed. . . . In W. Semitic enumerations, the seventh place is often climactic; God's sabbath is therefore the climax of the story, which is primarily about God, not humans."[29] No matter how chaotic the pre-creation order was, God was in control.

Thanks be to God for this inspired author of Genesis. He gave us an anchor that would inspire all generations. Genesis is a constant reference. When we are tempted to accept the hopeless depravity of the human condition, we have something that shakes our sensibilities and reminds us: "Remember? God saw that it was *good.*" "God pronounces the light good, beautiful; the phrase will be repeated six times of created elements, climaxing in the seventh climactic occurrence for the whole universe (v. 31). The declaration is not a deduction from human experience but a divine declaration that all of creation is good."[30] We are created in the image and likeness of God. "The human is a statue of the deity, not by static being, but by action, who will rule over all things previously created (v. 26). In the ancient Near East, the king was often called the image of the deity and was vested with God's authority; royal language is used here for the humans."[31] We are created to be fully alive human beings, imbued with transcendent dignity. "The human being is placed at the summit in the temple of creation: all humanity has value in God's eyes."[32] Men and women are created *equal* in the eyes of God. Men and women are given sacred rights and responsibilities.

In the creation account, men and women are to subdue the earth. They will control their harsh environment by force if necessary, but they are to treat God's creation with proper dignity. Human beings "are to respect the environment; they are not to kill for food but are to treat all life with respect... the world is made for man and woman. Plants will suffice for food for humans and animals; there will be no bloodshed. This prohibition is modified in the renewal of creation after the flood."[33] Thus, the whole created order is good. In Yahweh's world there is no evil; there is only

beauty. In an effortless stroke of the Master's brush, God's word painted the heavens and the earth.

The creation story is eschatological as it defines what God intends. "This serene, beautiful world, in which all is ordered to humans, and humans are ordered to God, is how it will be at the end. God's world will triumph."[34] The sin that will follow in subsequent chapters will not reign forever. It will not stand in the way of God's original intent. God will be victorious.

The *word* of God created the world. Christian understanding gives Jesus Christ a star role in this first theater of God's creative drama. Jesus, the spoken *Word* of God (John's prologue), was present and active in this creative, generative moment. Jesus Christ was the *Light* that dispels the darkness and chaos. We share in that light and thus can marvel and proclaim with the psalmist, "Lord, continue to send out your Spirit and renew the face of the earth, continue to create it anew and make it good."

Questions: In what way does God continue the transforming work of creation in our community? Do we really believe in the goodness of creation? What are we going to do about it?

Responsorial Psalm

Psalm 104—Lord, send out your Spirit and renew the face of the earth.
or
Psalm 33—The earth is full of the goodness of the Lord.

Second Reading
Genesis 22:1–18

The Lord God promises Abraham many and great things in this reading. We, however, are shocked by the demand to murder his son. We have a difficult time getting past Abraham's willingness to perform such a heinous act. Someone once raised the question, "If that is an example of the kind of God you wish me to worship, thanks, but no thanks, I want no part of him. What God would ask a father to murder his own son?" It is an hon-

---

[29]Richard J. Clifford, S.J. and Roland E. Murphy, O.Carm., "Genesis," in *NJBC*, 11.

[30]Ibid.

[31]Ibid.

[32]*DL* (III), 44.

[33]Clifford and Murphy, *NJBC* 11.

---

[34]Ibid.

est question. Yet this story is upheld throughout all of biblical literature as a premier story of faith. There has to be and there is more to the story.

In order to understand this story we must stretch ourselves and put our Western mind-sets on hold for a brief period. This story is not about killing one's son; it is about placing one's entire life in the hands of the all-knowing, omniscient God. "The father's life is bound up with that of his child and heir; Abraham entrusts his life and his future unconditionally to the God who calls him."[35]

This is the only time in scripture that God tests one individual rather than the entire nation. Abraham, as the future leader of Israel, must "entrust his entire life and future to God."[36] The reader of this story is aware from the beginning that God is testing Abraham, but Abraham is not aware. Isaac was not Abraham's only son as the text would intimate. Rather, a better translation is: *favored*. God makes sure that in this dialogue, the weight of Isaac's value to Abraham is emphasized.

Abraham and Isaac ascend Mount Moriah, the place believed to be the site of Solomon's first temple. Abraham, then, is the first worshiper on the temple site. Abraham obeys God in silence; Isaac follows and asks the whereabouts of the sacrificial animal. Abraham's reply that God would provide is another example of trusting God to supply all needs. Everything is completely in Yahweh's hands.

The angel arrives to save the day, Isaac is spared, and Abraham proves that his entire life is completely under God's providential care. "He has finally learned to give up control over his own life that he might receive it as grace."[37] God spoke the word to the angel and caused Isaac to be spared. God caused the first-born of Israel to be spared. In Israel it was understood that each new-born child belonged to God and was symbolically sacrificed to God. As a symbolic sign of this sacrifice, a ram (or other animal) was offered in order to redeem the first-born.

---

[35] Ibid., 25.
[36] Ibid.
[37] Ibid.

Abraham was always understood to prefigure what would be accomplished through Christ. Jesus, God's first-born, would be sacrificed, would stand in as the sacrificial lamb and redeem Israel. We can do no less than respond to such love with the unconditional trust of Abraham. Keep me safe, O God; you are my hope.

Questions: What is your first reaction to God's request to Abraham? How is Abraham a sign for your community? What difference do this reading and its implications make for the life of your community and for your own life? What is the challenge?

Responsorial Psalm
Psalm 16—Keep me safe, O God; you are my hope.

Third Reading
Exodus 14:15–15:1

The Passover is to Jews what the death and resurrection of Jesus is to Christians—the premier saving event of God. It is and has been remembered annually as a living memorial of God's saving, liberating power. It is actualized as it is remembered. Those who remember and celebrate the Passover are, in a manner of speaking, present at the first passover and are beneficiaries of its liberating action.

Thus, the exodus story is told on this night above all nights, when the passover of Jesus Christ was prefigured through the exodus event. This is why the reading from Exodus must be proclaimed at the Vigil.

Whether each detail of this epic event is based on historical fact or on the natural elaboration that goes with the telling of a great moment in the conscious collective memory of a people is not important. What is important is that the exodus event is remembered for generations as a defining moment for the people of God, the supreme initiative of God's loving and liberating action. It is a sign of God's covenant with Israel—a primary theme throughout biblical literature. (Refer to the exegesis on Holy Thursday for a more complete elaboration of the meaning and roots of Passover.)

Jesus is the new Passover, the new covenant. Jesus, the new paschal lamb, was sacrificed for the sins of all, and leads us out of bondage into the promised land of freedom and new life through baptism. The Red Sea was understood in Christian consciousness as an image of baptism. The neophyte passes through the sea of death to new life. It is no wonder that this story of Passover and passage is a baptismal scripture of great importance. We continue to live the benefits of the first Passover and Jesus' Passover from death to life. We must, then, sing triumphantly with Miriam: "Let us sing to the Lord; he has covered himself in glory."

Questions: In what way does your community resemble the Israelite community? How would you describe your communal covenant with God? What can be affirmed and where is growth needed? Are there any areas in your community life that are still in bondage and in need of liberation? How does your community live in covenant relationship with God? What is the evidence that you are in a covenant relationship with God as a community and as an individual? Where does death still reign? Where is there resurrection? What are you going to do about it?

Responsorial Psalm
Exodus 15—Let us sing to the Lord; he has covered himself in glory.

Fourth Reading
Isaiah 54:5–14

This reading is from Second Isaiah (Deutero-Isaiah) and it represents the fourth night—the fourth stage of salvation history. It is the night in which God's own people will be gathered to the heavenly city of eternal life. We are reminded on this Vigil night that lest we become mesmerized by the excitement of tonight and the joy of God's reign in the temporal sphere, there is an important reality always in our consciousness. We live in the reign of God on two planes—*the here and now* and *the not yet.*

This pericope is written from the tenuous situation of captivity. It is a word of consolation to a people in great distress. There is none of the overconfident self-assurance that was evident during the time of First Isaiah when Israel was in its shining glory. Such confidence faded into obscurity in

light of domination by a foreign power in the alien land of Babylon.

Isaiah wants his people to know that, no matter what happens, God will not forsake them. No matter how difficult things become, God's covenant with Israel will stand. We are left with the hope and the imagery of that brilliant future city, laid out for us with streets and walls lined with "cornelians, rubies, sapphires and precious stones"—a city in which God's justice will reign eternal. "The word of God emanates from the splendor of the Lord's presence."[38] We pause, then, before our great God and humbly acknowledge in heartfelt response: "I will praise you, Lord, for you have rescued me."

Questions: In what way has your community experienced the consoling love of God? Has there ever been a time in which great distress caused your complete reliance on God? What was the experience like? What does this reading teach you about God, Christ, the church, and yourself? What are you called to do in response?

Responsorial Psalm
Psalm 30—I will praise you, Lord, for you have rescued me.

Fifth Reading
Isaiah 55:1–11

This reading turns our eyes from a backward glance at salvation history to a more present, sacramental stance. We are brought into the presence and action of Christ. Isaiah's conclusion to the "Book of Consolations" speaks of that day in which God's people will be lavished with rich fare and flowing water. "Deutero-Isaiah invites poor people to a joyful banquet."[39] Throughout the Bible, the banquet image is used to demonstrate God's care for Israel. The messianic age and everlasting life in heaven are often described as a banquet.

Yahweh insists that the only requirement for this banquet is thirst for God. People are to seek God who is transcendent and elusive. God is near enough to be troubled by the sin of humanity,

---

[38]Carroll Stuhlmueller, "Deutero-Isaiah and Trito-Isaiah," in *NJBC*, 343.
[39]Ibid.

however. What Christian does not turn his or her eyes toward baptism and eucharist when hearing of quenched thirsts and rich food, spread for all, rich and poor alike? How could a Christian not think of the eucharistic banquet when hearing of Isaiah's admission-free banquet for the salvation of all people?

The word of God again plays a very important, sacramental role in this reading. "God's word is the initiator: from it comes salvation."[40] Stuhlmueller suggests that, in Isaiah, God's word is not so much a message as it is an event in the mystery of salvation history. God's word is not static, but living; it causes action. God's word will accomplish what God intends. God's word will restore Israel. The world rejoices as God brings Israel home. Sin will be no more in the new Jerusalem. Sin and death will not be invited guests at the eternal banquet; they will be gone forever. The *shalom* peace of God will reside eternally in God's restored Paradise.

Jesus, Word of God, on this night of nights, rises and returns to God. In so doing, Jesus, Word of God, brings salvation to the world. On this night, holier than all other nights, we listen to Isaiah and are invited to remember our baptismal and eucharistic life. We draw deeply and joyfully from the springs of our sacramental salvation.

Questions: Is your community—are you—inclusive? Where are there still areas of death? Where are the areas of resurrection? Do all of God's people have a place at your communal and individual banquet table? Who is not invited? In what way does your community need to grow? What does this reading say to you about God, Christ, the church, and yourself? What is the challenge? What are you going to do about it?

Responsorial Psalm
Isaiah 12—You will draw water joyfully from the springs of salvation.

Sixth Reading
Baruch 3:9–15, 32–4:4

This sixth reading extols the value of wisdom. When we stray (and we will) from God's path, wis-

dom leads us back. While on this earth, we can never completely know the extent of the mystery of God. What we do know is revealed through the power of wisdom. Wisdom reveals the mind and the heart of God through the Word of God.

Baruch upholds obedience to God's law as the highest value. Israel disobeyed the law and was punished. Prosperity and peace can occur only when the word of God is observed. Baruch understands the Mosaic law as wisdom. In later Judaism, wisdom is "personified and given divine attributes."[41] It is the greatest value, the most prized asset. Without wisdom, all is lost. Only God can offer wisdom; human beings can do nothing on their own to obtain it.

The word of God is the ongoing, sacramental presence of God's wisdom. Through the scriptures we come to know God. In our liturgy we believe that when scriptures are proclaimed we are in the living presence of Christ.

Through baptism, we live within the active, present word of God. We are strengthened and led by God's word in and through Jesus Christ and his Spirit. Thus, with assurance we together proclaim: "Lord, you have the words of everlasting life."

Questions: How is your community responding to God's wisdom? In what way, if any, do you forge ahead without seeking the will of God in your community life? How does your community listen to God? Where is there still death and where is there resurrection? What does this reading say to you about God, Christ, the church, and yourself? What is the challenge?

Responsorial Psalm
Psalm 19—Lord, you have the words of everlasting life.

Seventh Reading
Ezekiel 36:16–28

In tonight's reading from Ezekiel, we are made privy to God's conversation with Ezekiel. God reminded Ezekiel that the people had turned away from Yahweh, thinking they had no need of his providential care. They found themselves in exile

---

[40]*DL* (III), 52.

[41]Aloysius Fitzgerald, F.S.C., "Baruch," in *NJBC*, 566.

because they had sinned, blasphemed, and acted in depravity. Therefore, God punished them. Only God's power could gather the lost and scattered people.

However, the covenant continues with Israel. God blesses them. This reading is a summary of Ezekiel's theology. Paul resonates the same theology throughout his ministry: salvation is freely offered grace. Salvation and justification are from God.

Ezekiel promises the bestowal of a new heart and a new spirit. "The heart is the seat of thinking and loving, so it will be a new way of looking at life from God's point of view."[42] The new spirit bestowed upon Israel empowers it to live *as a people*. God forms them as a community, not as individuals.

This reading also foreshadows the final eschatological gathering. Before the last gathering, people must be washed clean of their idolatry. Only God is capable of such cleansing. Only God has the power to remove stony hearts and replace them with hearts of love. God's Spirit will breathe new life into these newly gathered children.

On this night of baptisms and rebirth we ask for the new heart and new spirit promised to Ezekiel. Thus, the cries of our heart resound in song: "Create in me a clean heart, O God."

Questions: This reading reminds us why we must ask the communal questions first. God deals with us as a people, yet we often have only the sense that our relationship with God is a "Jesus and me" affair. What are the "stony heart" areas in your community, in your own life? Where is God's transformative healing needed? Where is the death and where is the resurrection? How are you called to change as a community?

Responsorial Psalm
Psalm 42—As the deer longs for running streams, so my soul longs for you, my God.
or
Psalm 51—Create a clean heart in me, O God.

Epistle
Romans 6:3–11

Paul's letter to the Romans is a transition point in the liturgy of the word. We now move from the Hebrew scriptures to the Christian scriptures; from the former age to the messianic age and thus to the present. The Sacramentary instructs us to turn on the lights at this point in the liturgy. This is the moment when we turn from darkness to light. We are led to the font, the place that initiates *bearers of the light*. Baptism assures us that we no longer live in the darkness, but are children of the light.

We are no longer dead. Paul reminds us that through baptism we die to sin and become a new creation in Christ. The neophyte plunges deeply into the waters of death, suffocated by the crushing weight of water and sin, only to come up, gasping for the air of invigorating new life and freedom. (A little sprinkle of water hardly speaks of the same reality.)

"The rite of Christian initiation introduces a human being into union with Christ's suffering and dying."[43] The newly baptized are initiated into Christ's resurrected life. Baptism gives the Christian the power to live the Christian life. Paul asserts that through baptism we are dead to sin; it no longer lives in us. "The destruction of the sinful 'self' through baptism and incorporation into Christ means liberation from enslavement to sin. Hence, one's outlook can no longer be focused on sin."[44]

Reginald Fuller reminds us that the verbs used in Paul's address bring to mind the effects of baptism. When speaking of "dying to ourselves," Paul uses past tense verbs. He uses future tense verbs in relation to the resurrection. Through baptism we *died* (past tense) with Christ.[45] However, our resurrection is our future goal as we live out our baptismal commitment and moral response. We continue to renew our commitment to die to sin each day.

Paul's letter to the Romans prepares us for a key moment of the Easter Vigil liturgy: the renewal of

---

[42]Lawrence Boadt, C.S.P., "Ezekiel," in *NJBC*, 325.

[43]Joseph A. Fitzmyer, S.J., "The Letter to the Romans," in *NJBC*, 848.
[44]Ibid., 848, 849.
[45]*PNL*, 21, 22.

our baptismal vows. And so, together with the psalmist, we can joyfully sing the triple alleluia as well as our praise, awe, and trust in God's incredible, awesome mighty works!

Questions: How have you died to sin throughout this Lent as a community and as individuals? In what way have you grown? Where is growth still needed? Where is death? Resurrection? What difference has the baptism of neophytes made in your community this year? Is your community prepared to recommit to their baptismal promises? How is growth (resurrection) evident? Where is growth still needed? What is the challenge?

Responsorial Psalm

Psalm 118—Alleluia! Alleluia! Alleluia!

Gospel

Mark 16:1–7

Mark's gospel raises questions as it approaches the finale. It is difficult to decipher what is original to Mark and what were later additions. Only the first eight verses of this chapter (proclaimed at the Easter Vigil) are widely affirmed as belonging to the original gospel.[46] Verse 1 of chapter 1 begins the gospel as the Good News of Jesus Christ. Yet in verse 8 of chapter 16 we are told that the women, after being told by an angel to go and tell Peter and the others, say nothing because they are so afraid. If they are so afraid, where is the Good News? The construction of chapter 16 and Mark's resurrection account has baffled commentators since early in Christian history. Raymond Brown reminds us that verses 1 through 8 and verses 9 through 20 are usually read separately in the liturgy.[47] Verses 9 through 20 are known as the "Long Ending" and they appear in most Catholic and Protestant Bibles, sometimes with a footnote questioning their Marcan source, yet widely accepted as the ending of Mark's gospel. Brown's treatment of chapter 16 centers on the first eight verses as if Mark intended to end the gospel there.

The cast is laid before us and we have met them before—Mary Magdalene, Mary of James, and Salome. They were identified as the women who ministered to Jesus and who were his disciples. They stood as witnesses to Jesus' death on Calvary. Mark does not lump them with the disciples of the Last Supper or with the Twelve apostles. Even though the women were present at the crucifixion, they were in no position to be a support to him. Jesus was still left alone and abandoned. They also were not with Jesus at Gethsemane or privy to those private moments of intimacy to which his closest disciples were privileged to be a part of. The apostles rejected Jesus in spite of that intimacy. The women, however, did not abandon him. Brown asks whether the women are positive role models for Christians or followers who were simply, passively present to the crucifixion. Or did they not fail because, unlike the apostles, they were not tested in their faith? When Joseph of Arimathea removed Jesus' body for burial, the gospel mentioned that the women saw where Jesus was laid. That does not mean they did anything at that stage. It just means that they knew where he was buried. Period. They still seem to be in the role of passive onlooker. However, Mark later reports that after the Sabbath the women finally do get involved and take spices to minister to Jesus' dead body. Mark will use this occasion to have the women discover Jesus' resurrection.

Mark uses time intervals to tell us when events unravel in his narrative. He is particularly fond of three-hour time intervals:

> Throughout the Marcan passion narrative there has been an extraordinary sequence of precise three-hour time intervals: the story began with "evening" on the first day of unleavened bread when Jesus ate the supper with his disciples (14:12, 1); it continued through cockcrow when Peter concluded his denials (14:72) and a morning hour when Jesus was given over to Pilate (15:1); and it culminated with the third, sixth, and ninth hours as he hung on the cross (15:25, 33; i.e. 9:00 A.M., noon, 3:00 P.M.); only at "evening" was Jesus at last buried (15:42).

Not without plausibility scholars have suggested that such time precision means that already within Mark's experience there were set times of commemorative prayer as Christians recalled the death of the

---

[46] *RCE*, 9.
[47] Ibid., 10.

Lord. The references in 16:1–2 to the end of the Sabbath and to the early hour on the first day of the week may be part of the same picture.[48]

Mark relates how the sun had already risen, perhaps an allusion to the resurrection of Christ having already taken place. Perhaps Mark is also drawing on the images of light and darkness that he already used in chapter 8.

The women ask who will remove the stone. Mark wants his reader to know that it is a very large stone that covered the entrance of the tomb. Humans could not move the stone, but God's power is beyond human imagination. Mark tells the reader that the stone had already been moved—his way of alerting them that divine action had already occurred.

The women look in the tomb and they see a man sitting on the right side of the tomb (a place of dignity). He is clothed with a white robe—a divine manifestation, a "divine spokesman," an angel. As an aside, Ched Myers reminds us that there are powerful symbolic references in the scene with the angel.[49] First, he sits at the right. This is a very significant place for Mark and carries diverse meanings. It is the place of honor for which the other disciples competed. It is the place Psalm 12:36 attributed to the Messiah. It is also the place Jesus insisted was reserved for the "Human One" (Son of Man). It was also a place reserved for one of the robbers who hung next to Jesus on the cross. "It is the symbol of true power of solidarity."[50]

The young man donned a white robe. Remember the man dressed similarly at Jesus' Passion? He was wrapped in linen cloth; he let it drop and ran away naked. Jesus was wrapped in similar linen and now he is no longer in the tomb. But, alas, the angel is now wearing a white robe. Images of the transfiguration are readily observable. The language Mark uses for the robe is reminiscent of that used for Jesus' clothes at his transfiguration and the same language used in the Book of Revelation (7:9, 13) for the apparel of martyrs.

"The young man plays the role of *angelus interpres*, of interpreting angel, a feature of apocalyptic.... The evangelist intimates that, for his readers, he is this *angelus interpres*, the rightful herald of cross and resurrection."[51] The angel interprets the meaning of the empty tomb. The women react to him as all people react to divine manifestations in scripture—with amazement. Ched Myers insists that the word is "deeply troubled" (*exethambēthēsan*).[52] He insists that this verb only appears two other times in Mark's narrative. It is used in 9:15 after the crowd encountered Jesus following his transfiguration and he was teaching them about the way of the cross. It appeared again in 14:33, when Jesus struggled to come to terms with his own suffering and execution. "Each of these apocalyptic symbolics compels us to conclude that the women realize they are in the presence of a glorified martyr figure."[53]

Raymond Brown, on the other hand, equates the amazement with the same type of amazement that people experienced when Jesus cast out an evil spirit in the first chapter (1:25–27) of the gospel.[54] In that first encounter the demon addressed Jesus as "Jesus the Nazarene." We should not be surprised when the angel in today's scene tells the women that he is aware that they seek "Jesus the Nazarene." "This makes the reader certain that the same person who at the beginning of the Gospel manifested his power over evil is the one in whom God now manifests His power over death. From beginning to end Satan has been defeated by Jesus the Nazarene."[55]

The angel tells the women that Jesus "is not here." Mark highlights Jesus' absence. This is understandable in light of the community's experience of the absent Christ as they awaited the parousia.

Jesus' divinity could not be recognized throughout the gospel because he had yet to suffer and die. Recognition could only come through his death and glorification. Now the angel stands ready to proclaim him so all will understand—he is the "one who was crucified." And further, the

---

[48]Ibid., 12.
[49]*BSM*, 397.
[50]Ibid.

[51]*MARK*, 242.
[52]*BSM*, 398.
[53]Ibid.
[54]*RCE*, 14.
[55]Ibid.

"one who was crucified" has similarly been raised from the dead. He was gone from the tomb. The absence of Jesus' body alone would not necessarily have led to the supposition that Jesus had been raised from the dead. It was the appearance of the heavenly manifestation that affirmed definitively for the women that he had indeed been raised.

Mark's intention is not simply to reveal the resurrection in these eight verses. The women are given a mission, all is not finished, Jesus is not yet finished with his disciples. Jesus prophesied that upon his death all would be scattered—and indeed that is true enough. His disciples resembled scattered and lost sheep who did not know where to find their next meal, master, or fold. Lost—they are simply lost. However, Jesus' prophecy upheld a beacon of hope. He promised that after the resurrection he would go back into Galilee before his disciples (14:28). The angel remembers Jesus' promise and tells the women to go back to Peter and tell him and the disciples that Jesus would be going before them in Galilee. His promise to them would them be fulfilled. No matter how bleak or sinful things may have appeared; no matter that Peter not only denied Jesus but cursed him; no matter that a potential disciple fled naked to abandon the Master; no matter that the entire world left Jesus to endure alone to the end; the gravity of it all could still be resurrected. Life could rise like a phoenix from the ashes of death and darkness. The disciples were to go back to the beginning—to the origin of their ministry in Galilee. They were to go back to their original calling; they were to remember all that Jesus taught them and they were to recall their ministry of healing, reconciliation, love, and restoration. They are not to be lost or forsaken forever.

Even though the women are instructed to go to Peter and the others, Mark is still very much focused on the women. We cannot help but be surprised by their reaction to such "Good News." Fear strangled them; trembling had a choke hold on their resolve and they told no one of their encounter. They refused to follow through with the angel's command to them.

They are simply afraid. So far discipleship has not cost them much. Unlike those who were intimate with Christ and failed, the women were not as tested as they. This is their moment of testing, and they, like the other disciples, fail. Throughout the entire gospel Mark reminds his readers how there were so many who simply could not understand and who did not want to hear a message of suffering. The spiritual high was grand enough, but start waving images of cross, nails, blood, and torture before them, and the spiritual realities are not as attractive.

Even though it may have appeared that the women were passive spectators to the events, they are no longer passive. Now they are engaged. Now they meet their moment of trial. "Here, although they have received the revelation of the risen Lord and an angelic commission to proclaim him, they fail."[56] We have still another group of disciples who knew the Lord personally and yet, when push came to shove, they missed the mark. They, like the disciples, stand as hope for the rest of the world of all generations who have failed when tested to accept or reject Jesus Christ and his message of salvation. All is not lost.

The poor women were afraid. What is the saying, "Perfect love casts out all fear?" Their Master loved with perfect love. Here is someone who demonstrated the most perfect love one can show for another, yet the witnesses, the women, were afraid. They certainly did not rise to the occasion. "This uncomplimentary portrait is in harmony with Mark's somber insistence that none can escape suffering in the following of Jesus."[57]

Mark's community was living in the postresurrection church. It would certainly be easy enough to understand the disciples' rejection of Jesus in the face of his Passion, but what about those who failed after the resurrection? Christians who rejected Christ after his resurrection were not tested as the disciples had been. They were privy to the truth, they were heirs to the resurrection, yet they failed as well. The women stand as a reminder and consolation to all those Christians who were persecuted after the resurrection and buckled under the pressure. "There is a parallel between them and the women who appear on the scene only after the crucifixion and observe his death without having become involved even in his burial. Like the women they are well-inclined, but after

---

[56]Ibid., 16.
[57]Ibid.

they hear the proclamation of the resurrection and receive a commission to proclaim what has happened to Jesus, they too can fail if they become afraid."[58]

Mark's message is clear. Not even the resurrection will guarantee that a person will remain steadfast. Every person's faith must be tested if enduring faith in the resurrection is to exist in followers of Christ. Belief in the risen Christ is wonderful. However, if we gloss over Jesus Christ crucified, the resurrection has no meaning. Mark minces no words. This is not an easy gospel. It is not easy even to its conclusion. Discipleship is sobering, serious business, and one is not to approach it lightly.

When Jesus and his disciples traveled to Jerusalem, he told them all the events that were about to transpire. He tried to warn them. He asserted that he would be delivered up, he would be tortured, he would suffer and die, but on the third day he would be raised up. His words were not the words of a delusional madman after all. Everything he said took place. It all happened as he said it would. Jesus will now go to them and do what he promised he would do. The one who healed, reconciled, and restored people to God and the community would now go to them, and from their scattered condition, he would unite them, strengthen them, and restore them again as community. God would open their eyes that had before been blinded by their false expectations, and they would "see Nazarene raised from the dead, the victor over crucifixion whom they had commented themselves to follow."[59]

Other commentators share opposing views on some of the issues mentioned above. Some commentators believe that Mark mentions Galilee as a symbolic reference. Wilfrid Harrington suggests that Galilee is the place where the barriers of exclusivity were torn down and where the gentile mission began.[60] Raymond Brown, as noted above, asserts that Mark had no such symbolic intention in mind other than to perhaps recall the words and mission of Christ that began in Galilee.

Harrington also paints a more positive portrayal of the women. He insists that the women had been followers of Jesus all along. They had followed him all the way to the cross, even though it was "from afar." However, they are the ones to whom the message was entrusted. They followed Jesus to the cross. The chosen Twelve fled and hid; they abandoned Jesus. The women were never ashamed of Jesus; they remained faithful to the end. How does one get past the gospel's insistence that they, too, failed? They were given a mission and they did not follow through out of fear. Harrington refers back to 10:32. Jesus was going up to Jerusalem and his disciples were filled with fear and awe as well. They still forged on at that point, however. "So with the women who had come to the tomb to honor the one who was dead. They find themselves faced with the awesome truth of the Living One. They are in the grip of trembling and 'ecstasy.' "[61] They leave in fear and trembling, in the same type of fear that had gripped not only the disciples but Moses and Paul as well. "The fearful and resplendent presence of the living God is now seen as never before in the crucified Messiah's victory over death."[62] According to this commentator, the women did not fail. The gospel stands as witness to that truth. Someone told Peter and the others. Who, if not the women? Harrington posits an interesting reflection in regard to the "problem or failure of the women." "Much less interest, let it be said, has been attached to the disturbing fact that it is women who were 'apostles to the apostles.' "[63]

Mark leaves his reader with a sense that the rest of the story has yet to be written—an incompleteness. In a sense, isn't that true? The story has yet to be written on the heart of every follower of Christ who walks in the footsteps of the Master. The complete and total picture Mark has given is the theology he intended to teach his audience. Jesus Christ is the Son of God, the Suffering Servant foretold by the prophet Isaiah. He is the Son who suffered, died, and rose again from the dead. He is the One who was victorious over death and now sits at his rightful place on the throne of

---

[58]Ibid., 17.
[59]*RCE*, 15.
[60]*MARK*, 242.

[61]Ibid., 243.
[62]Donald Senior, C.P., *The Passion of Jesus in the Gospel of Mark*, vol. 2, *The Passion Series* (Wilmington, Del.: M. Glazier, 1984), 137. In *MARK*, 243.
[63]*MARK*, 244.

glory, at God's right hand. The rest of the story will come to fulfillment when Jesus returns to gather the elect from the four corners of the world.

The incompleteness in Mark's story is an incompleteness that rests within the community. Jesus is hidden, his resurrected presence is hidden. The community, through the Spirit of God, encounters Christ's presence in his absences as they await his return. The Lord must still remain hidden until he returns; then when we all see him, we will truly know him. Perhaps the words, "they did not tell anyone," are a reference to the messianic secret. The Lord must remain obscured from view until he returns to gather his own. We do not know the hour, but we approach with with fear and trembling, awe and astonishment.

Ched Myers offers a summary of the resurrection account and in so doing reveals Mark's genius.[64] Today's pericope reveals that finally the tables have turned; there is a reversal of fortune. Things are not as they used to appear. First, the young man chastises the women. He knows that they seek Jesus. Throughout the entire gospel we encounter people who seek Jesus, but who in the end betray him—family, friends, community, and authorities. They come seeking the Nazarene, but Jesus is no longer just the Nazarene. Now he is the crucified one—"this is the proper confession of the 'transformed disciple.'"[65] Jesus had the last word after all. He is nowhere to be found. He is not where Joseph laid him and the authorities did not have the power over him that they thought they had. He is, after all, risen! The word used is also reminiscent of healing. Through his resurrection Jesus is liberated from the chains of oppression. A tremendous reversal has occurred. No one had the control over him that they thought they had—not even death.

There are more reversals. The man tells the women to go to Peter and the others and tell them to go to Galilee where they will see him just as Jesus promised. Those exegetes who associate this with a postresurrection appearance to the Twelve apostles, thereby affirming the apostolic

resurrection tradition, have missed something, insists Myers.[66] Myers maintains that Mark is merely opening a door that earlier had appeared to be permanently closed—a "reopening of the 'closed' discipleship story."[67] The community self-destructed in two stages. The disciples fled and Peter denied the Lord, not only denied him, but cursed him as well. Mark resurrects the community similarly. The women were to tell the disciples and Peter. The community will be restored and with it the journey of discipleship. Disciples were to once again take to the road, for the Lord was going before them.

There is now a new journey. The disciples followed Jesus to Jerusalem. Now, in this new journey they will again follow the Lord back to Galilee. "They will see him." This future verb form has been translated by some exegetes to mean that Galilee will be the place where the parousia will occur, especially in light of Jesus' prophecy of the coming of the Human One (Son of Man). Other commentators believe that it is a reference to the risen Jesus' postresurrection appearances. Myers insists that Mark has not moved beyond his own story world. The future locus of events is the same as the past. Galilee is where the disciples were initially called and where they responded to that call. It is where the disciples were "called, named, sent on mission and taught by Jesus. In other words, the disciple/reader is being told that the narrative, which appeared to have ended, is beginning again. The story is circular!"[68]

The disciples had hoped for a triumphant, exalted community. That was never Christ's intention. The rebels hoped for a restoration of the Davidic kingdom. It was never in the plan. Mark's reader feared a tragic failure, ending in total defeat in the narrative. It never happened. Defeat was reversed and turned into victory. The reversal of gargantuan proportions is nothing less than the restoration and "regeneration of the messianic mission."[69]

Those who have eyes to see will see Jesus going before them into Galilee. If we have the faith to experience the advent of the Human One (Son of

[64]*BSM*, 398.
[65]Ibid.

[66]Ibid.
[67]Ibid.
[68]Ibid., 399.
[69]Ibid.

Man) we will follow him as he leads the way. The young man presents the church with a final invitation to discipleship. "He evokes both hope and terror. Hope, in that he who once joined in the naked shame of abandonment (14:51f.) now stands in new attire; terror, in that his new clothes are that of a martyr figure."[70]

There is an inherent invitation to the reader/disciple. Is the reader/disciple ready to undergo similar transformation? When faced with the decision to follow Christ in our own hour of Passion, will we prefer the road of abandonment and rejection, leave our clothes by the wayside, and rush off naked in another direction? Or are we willing to allow Christ to transform us anew and clothe us with a new robe of righteousness? Mark's realism and his genius are striking as the curtain begins to drop. Rather than closure there is ambiguity.

Almost as soon as they enter the tomb, the women flee from it. They are "traumatized" (*tromos*) and "ecstatic" (*ekstasis*), a logical condition of anyone who has just encountered someone they thought was dead. Mark stops us dead in our tracks and we are told that the women remained silent. They refused the young man's exhortation and they told no one. Throughout the narrative people were exhorted to be silent. Now that they are urged to speak and tell the Good News, they are silent. What is going on? "We suddenly freeze in our readerly tracks. After the promise of a new beginning, is this the final betrayal?"[71]

Why are we surprised that the women are afraid? Strong men before them experienced great fear. They walked the journey too; they heard firsthand stories of storm-tossed seas, posttransfiguration reflections, prophecies of crucifixion and the journey to Jerusalem. Who among us would not be afraid? Now add to the mix the real horror of Jesus' execution and most of us would be running for the hills. They, after all, were present at the crucifixion. And is not the Passion scene the most difficult of all?

In it the martyr-figure beckons the disciple to take up the journey afresh, to return to the beginning of the story for a new read-

ing-enactment. The young man's invitation ought to provoke trepidation to us, if we take it seriously. As Bonhoeffer paraphrased Mark 8:34 in *Cost of Discipleship* (1953), "When Christ calls a person, He bids them to come and die."[72]

Perhaps the reader is purposefully left confused. We do not know completely what Jesus' resurrection means, but we have followed his story. We do know, however, where it leads and we must cling to what we know. Jesus continues to go before us, to lead us and invite us to embrace the way of the cross. Perhaps Mark's point is that we do not always know the outcome—it is not always a tragedy, nor is it always a victory, but it is always a challenge to begin again and follow the Lord anew. It always involves a response.

Myers reminds us that from the very beginning the church found it difficult to accept Mark's version of the story. There are some very disturbing things about it. The apostles do not come off as heroes; they are not even very good role models. What is most disconcerting about Mark is that he does not give us a happy ending. There have been unsuccessful attempts to write a more acceptable ending into the Markan account. Myers insists that that is nothing more than our refusal to let Mark speak the word he intended to speak. Mark intended for his reader to wrestle with the ending. We are to grapple with the issue of whether the women overcame their fear (by extension, will we overcome *our* fear?) in order to share the Good News, the new beginning in Galilee. Myers insists that to write a neatly packaged ending would be an invitation for the reader to be a passive spectator, not an active agent, impacted by the text. Without tension at the end, the reader would have no need to respond. "As it stands the discipleship narrative can truly resume only if the reader takes up the practice of the messianic vocation, which response is made possible by the fact that Jesus continues to 'go before us.'"[73] Commitment and response are essential if we are to make any sense out of Mark's gospel.

The Jesus of Mark provides very few answers, especially if we are asking the wrong

---

[70]Ibid.
[71]Ibid.

[72]Ibid., 401.
[73]Ibid.

questions. But as a questioner himself, he compels us to reveal where we stand. If we wish to respond, he offers us only a cross and companionship on the way. If we cannot respond, neither can he. In this case, the story as a whole—just like the episode with the chief priests (11:33)—truly ends in a draw of noncommitment.[74]

Questions for Mystagogical Reflection: How does Mark's account of the resurrection story invite greater participation in the paschal mystery of Christ? How do you feel about Mark's somber approach to the story? Does it put a damper on your Easter joy or is there a deeper message to be learned? How do you feel about the women who failed in their task to go and tell the Good News? How do you relate to them? Is there an experience in your life that identifies with their experience? Imagine how they must have felt. Can you relate to their feelings of probable failure? In what way is this gospel a challenge to you and in what way is there a basic message of hope? How is this story relevant in our contemporary world? What would Mark say the "Good News" is for our modern society? How does this Easter gospel story invite transformation in your life? In the life of your community?

F. SERVICE OF BAPTISM

Following the liturgy of the word is the liturgy of baptism. If there are candidates for baptism, they (the elect) process to the font, singing the Litany of the Saints. The elect and the faithful are in solidarity with the saints of old who went before us and the saints of today who walk with us.

The virgin water is blessed as the candle is plunged three times deeply into it. The intimate union is not to be missed. Water is blessed while remembering past images of God's action through the use of water. We remember the purifying floodwaters, the liberating Red Sea, and the salvation afforded by the water and blood from Jesus' side on the cross. We recall Jesus' mandate to the twelve to go out and baptize in the name of the Father, Son, and Holy Spirit. The blessing of water helps us remember (*anamnesis*) and bring into the present all that God has done throughout human history. We stand with God and the communion of saints as we participate in the ancient and always new and unfolding human and heavenly drama.

Blessing of the Water

Father, you give us grace through sacramental
    signs,
which tell us of the wonders of your unseen
    power.
In baptism we use your gift of water,
which you have made a rich symbol
of the grace you give us in this sacrament.
At the very dawn of creation
your Spirit breathed on the waters,
making them the wellspring of all holiness.
The waters of the great flood
you made a sign of the waters of baptism,
that make an end of sin and a new beginning of
    goodness.
Through the waters of the Red Sea
you led Israel out of slavery,
to be an image of God's holy people,
set free from sin by baptism.
In the waters of the Jordan
your Son was baptized by John
and anointed with the Spirit.
Your Son willed that water and blood
should flow from his side
as he hung upon the cross.
After his resurrection he told his disciples:
"Go out and teach all nations,
baptizing them in the name of the Father
and of the Son and of the Holy Spirit."
Father, look now with love upon your Church,
and unseal for her the fountain of baptism.
By the power of the Holy Spirit
give to the water of this font
the grace of your Son.
You created man in your own likeness:
cleanse him from sin in a new birth of innocence
by water and the Spirit.
We ask you, Father, with your Son,
to send the Holy Spirit upon the waters of this
    font.
May all who are buried with Christ
in the death of baptism
rise also with him to newness of life.
We ask this through Christ our Lord.[75]

---

[74]Ibid., 343.

[75]Easter Vigil: "Blessing of Water," *The Sacramentary*.

Through our profession of the baptismal promises, we renew the promises made for us at baptism. We agree to continue the process of daily death and resurrection. The elect enter the font of death and resurrection and become the living witness of all that we have shared and heard up to this point. Water soaked and Spirit filled, they take their place in the assembly of believers and await the moment at which the trumpets of heaven announce the culmination of their baptismal journey. They are ushered along with the church triumphant to the banquet table of the Lord. Eucharist—not baptism—is the goal of initiation.

Water-soaked and oil slathered, the newly baptized are presented with the baptismal candle. Through baptism we are called out of darkness to live in the light; we become children of the Light. The Easter candle is a sign of the sacramental presence of Christ, the Light of the World. The fire is a symbol of the transforming energy of the Holy Spirit. Elijah prayed and the fire came down from heaven upon his sacrifice at Mount Carmel. This was a foreshadowing of the Spirit who causes transformation. St. John the Baptist said of Jesus that he would baptize with the Holy Spirit and fire. Jesus would cause great transformation and *metanoia* in his followers. Tongues of fire rested on the disciples at Pentecost. Thus, the symbol of fire has been retained as "one of the most expressive images of the Spirit's actions."[76]

As a sign of their new status, of the fact that they are made a new creation, neophytes put on the white garment. In scripture whenever a garment was placed on an individual it was a sign that a new status had been conferred upon that person. The new status for neophytes is that of newly baptized, confirmed children of the Light who await the culmination of their journey as fully initiated members of the community through participation in the eucharist.

Symbol of Water

"Water can cause destruction as well as life and cleansing, lending itself as a symbol of God's judgment as well as of life and forgiveness."[77] The symbol of water speaks to us of multifaceted realities.

Natural Sign

In our natural lives, the experience of water is cleansing, soothing, and thirst quenching. It can be plentiful or in short supply. Water can be smooth and flowing as well as crushingly powerful. It is life-giving and death-dealing. We cannot live without it, and we cannot live in it. The properties of water speak to us of hidden realities. Water reminds us of how God acts and who God is. Like water, God is soothing and God's power is mighty. Immersion in water results in deep cleansing. Immersion in God's love causes deep, interior cleansing. Water is for the body what God is for the soul.

There is another facet to the many dimensions of water's inner realities. Water can be devastating. One can die in water. One is also born in water. No one can control the furious flow of water; no one can control the acts of God. When water is absent, there is thirst. When God is absent, there is parched thirst.

Biblical Sign

God is present in the biblical signs of water. Water is cited in scripture more than any other natural resource. The authors of biblical texts lived in a dry desert land. They were exposed to the continuous shortage of water. They were naturally preoccupied with finding it and the necessity for it. It is no wonder that our biblical texts use water as the revealer of the "God of Mystery who is its source and faithful dispenser."[78]

At creation, God hovered over the waters; the generative power of the Holy Spirit unleashed God's power and action into the lives of human beings. The great flood of Genesis purged the earth of sin. God's judgment came upon the earth and water

---

[76]Cf. St. John of the Cross, *The Living Flame of Love,* in *The Collected Works of St. John of the Cross,* trans. K. Kavanaugh, O.C.D., and O. Rodriguez, O.C.D. (Washington DC: Institute of Carmelite Studies, 1979), 577 ff.

[77]Joseph F. Grassi, "Water," in *CPDBT,* 1060.
[78]Kathleen Hughes, R.S.C.J., "Water: Pastoral Liturgical Tradition," in *CPDBT,* 1062.

purified the human race. "God overcame the primeval waters over the earth (Gen 1:1–10). He unleashed the deluge as a punishment for sin and then brought it to an end, saving Noah, the Hebrew ancestor."[79] God led the Israelites through the Red Sea, drowning Pharaoh in the process. The Israelites were afforded safe passage through the sea to the promised land and, after crossing the hazardous Jordan, were made citizens of a new land.

In scripture, water is a sign of God's providential care. It can be abundantly showered down, or withheld because of sin (Deut 11:14–17). Water, then, is a source of death and of life. As a sign of life it is a sign of God's creative presence.

In scripture water is also a sign of purification. It was used for purification baths before celebrating community rituals. (However, repentance was still necessary for complete forgiveness.) Water is a symbol of the transforming action of the Holy Spirit. The Vigil reading from Ezekiel recalls the power of the Spirit to create transformed minds and hearts.

Water also has a role in the New Testament. Mark uses the image very little. Matthew exhorts everyone to go and baptize all nations. Matthew relates this baptism to the baptism of Jesus in the Jordan. Matthew sees water as a sign of incorporation into Jesus' own baptism. The Acts of the Apostles makes frequent reference to the waters of baptism. Water is a sign of the Holy Spirit. The gospel of John makes abundant use of the symbol of water. The water of Cana represented a repudiation of the old purification rites. The Samaritan woman was offered the new water of Jesus' Spirit. Water was curative in the story of the man born blind from birth who washed in the pool of Siloam. Jesus washed the feet of his disciples as a sign of love, service, and forgiveness. Water and blood came forth from Jesus' side on the cross. This sign was understood as the advent of the Holy Spirit upon the church. The water was a sign of baptism and the blood was the sign of eucharist. (See "Sixth Sunday of Easter.")

Questions: Do the uses of water in scripture have anything to do with your life today? How might contemporary communities relate to the symbolism of water? What does it teach about God, Christ, Spirit, church, or yourself?

Ecclesial Signs

The church's theology of water is many-layered. Even though it is understood that ordinary water may be used for baptisms in an emergency situation, it was always also understood that the water used in baptism must first be consecrated before it can have an initiatory effect. "Not all waters have a curative power; only that water has it which has the grace of Christ.... The water does not heal unless the Spirit descends and consecrates the water."[80]

When the water is blessed at the Easter Vigil, there are two elements to the blessing. The saving action of God in salvation history is remembered, and through the epicletic action the Holy Spirit is invoked to come upon the waters. The Easter candle in plunged into the water as a sign of the power and presence of the Risen Christ. It is also a sign of the Holy Spirit coming upon the water. Cyril of Jerusalem insisted that all baptismal waters are effective because of the action of Christ going down into the Jordan for his own baptism.

When the early Christians invoked the Trinity upon any of the sacramental symbols, God became (becomes) present in the symbol. Bread becomes the Body of Christ; water and oil is the Spirit. The Trinity is present in all of the sacraments. Ancient theologians expressed the doctrine of the Spirit's presence in the water by reflecting on the font. "Theodore [of Mopsuestia] saw the font as a womb into which the candidate descended to receive second birth from the Holy Spirit, whose presence impregnates the water. St. Leo the Great compared the Spirit's action of filling the font with his other action of filling the womb of Our Lady."[81] Through the sign of water we are baptized priests, prophets, and rulers; we become adopted children of God and our sins are washed away. (See also "Baptism": Doctrinal Appendix.)

---

[79]Grassi, "Water," in *CPDBT*, 1060.

[80]Ambrose, Si. 15. Cf. *The Baptismal Homilies of Theodore of Mopsuestia*, 3.9; E. C. Whitaker, *Documents of the Baptismal Liturgy*, 2nd ed. (London, 1970), p. 7, in *AIRI*, 24.

[81]Ibid.

Questions: Does the church's theology of water have any-thing to do with our lives today? What does it teach us about God, Christ, Spirit, ourselves? What is the challenge? What is the response?

Liturgical Sign

In tracing the roots of baptism's earliest liturgical practice, it appears as if the candidate bent low in humble acceptance, just below the surface of the water, while the bishop pushed on his head. Later archaeological evidence suggests a different practice. Fonts have been discovered that were too small for an adult immersion. The water barely came to the knees of the candidates and had to be poured over their heads. The earliest form of the rite was Trinitarian. The candidate for baptism was plunged three times into the water while the three persons of the Trinity were invoked.

St. Paul understood the immersion as death to sin and incorporation into Christ's death and resurrection. The old person was buried and the font's waters gave birth to the new person in Christ. Ambrose thus made allusion to a tomb-shaped font. Archaeological evidence, however, points to an octagonal-shaped construction. It is believed that running water fed some of those fonts and that some were even heated.

Two different formulas for baptism were in use at the same time in different locations around the fourth century. In Antioch the formula was Trinitarian: "I baptize you in the name of the Father...," etc. In Jerusalem and Milan the formulas for baptism centered around the profession of faith. "St. Ambrose describes the ceremonies as follows: You were asked: 'Do you believe in God, the Father Almighty?' You replied: 'I believe,' as you were immersed. The ceremony continues with similar acts of faith in the Son and the Holy Spirit."[82] There is further evidence that the Trinitarian model spoken of by Jesus in Matthew's gospel was not strictly adhered to in every place. All of the church Fathers connected baptism with Jesus' baptism in the Jordan.

Liturgy expresses in ritual action the natural, biblical, and ecclesial signs of God's presence through the symbol of water. The waters of baptism are blessed at the Easter Vigil. Through the ritual wa-

---

[82]S 2.20; cf. Cyril, MC 2.4, in *AIRI*, 26.

ters of baptism the neophyte is purified, justified, sanctified, and incorporated into the Body of Christ, the paschal mystery, the communion of saints. Water is used in the rite of sprinkling to remind us of our baptism and thereby recommit us to its call. The casket is blessed with holy water as a reminder that baptism is a share in the eternal life of Christ. People bless themselves with holy water as a sign of their incorporation into the Body of Christ. Water is used in the multiple blessings provided by the church for its ongoing life in Christ such as the dedications of churches, blessings of homes, seminaries, and religious houses, boats, fields, buildings, schools, animals, etc. (Please refer to the RCIA: General Introduction, # 1, 2, Introduction to the Rite of Baptism, and the *Catechism of the Catholic Church*, #694 for further elaboration.)

Questions: Have you ever had a conscious experience of water in the liturgy? How were you impacted? How did it touch you? How does the experience of water call us to transformation as a community?

Symbol of Oil

Once baptized, the new Christian is permanently configured to Christ through the chrism oil of confirmation. Confirmation confers the gift of the Holy Spirit, not the gifts *of* the Spirit. The form of the ritual is "Be sealed with the Holy Spirit." The substance is oil. The baptized person is sealed with the Holy Spirit through the signing with oil.
In antiquity, the seal had the same function that a person's signature has today. A seal formed in wax identified the author of a document. Soldiers were tattooed with the seal of their division. The seal was a sign of ownership, much like a brand on cattle. Confirmation seals the Christian to Christ. The Christian is branded to Christ, marked permanently with the sign of salvation, the cross of Jesus Christ.

Natural Sign

How does oil express the inexpressible? Oil is difficult to rub off, stains clothing when spilled, and can only be rubbed in. Oil has healing, soothing, medicinal qualities. Oil is necessary for life. It is used in cooking, for energy, for lubrication, and for protection from the elements. Oil is a precious commodity; wars are fought over its control. Oil is the agent that holds things together, that unifies the ingredients in a recipe. All those aspects found in the natural world can be used to express the reality of the Spirit.

Our natural experience of oil reminds us of the Spirit. The Spirit stays with us. The Spirit heals and is a soothing, calming presence. The Spirit is balm for our wounded soul and strength in times of need. The Spirit is the unifier that holds God's people together. The Spirit is our life force. Oil expresses the ineffable reality of the Spirit. The Spirit strengthens us when we must lay down our lives for the sake of this precious new commodity: life in Christ.

In the movie, *Lorenzo's Oil,* a young boy discovers that he has a horribly debilitating disease that, without a certain kind of oil in his system, will kill him. The movie begins with a scene from the mother's experience of the Easter Vigil. The Easter candle processes majestically through the church as the boy's mother is observed wrestling with the demon of anger and grief. She will not accept the prognosis that doctors have given her son. The Easter Vigil connection in the movie subliminally suggests that her quest for the holy oil of life is initiated by the Spirit of God, present in the pillar candle of fire leading her through the dangerous journey inaugurated that night. She leaves the Easter scene with firm resolve and burning determination. Nothing will deter her or her husband. The Spirit is in command and they forge onward. They will find the oil her son, Lorenzo, needs for life. They completely give up their lives for their son.

Through years of tortuous struggle, research, and rejection, they literally lose everything. When scientists rebuff them, they will not take *no* for an answer. Their arduous journey of the cross finally leads them to a cure. It is a simple derivative of the natural, everyday substance found in all kitchens: olive oil.

Lorenzo's family laid down their lives for their son. They loved him unconditionally and completely; they loved him against all odds. They saved their boy's life and the lives of many other children with the same disease. Their selfless act of love resulted in love for others. They "put on Christ" and became Christ for many other suffering children. The oil of chrism is the Spirit's necessary oil. We should be willing to lose all in our quest for it.

The oil of chrism is the necessary oil for the soul. It seals us to Christ. It makes us in his image. We are branded with the sign of his cross. The oil of the Spirit gives us the strength to carry the cross and to bear witness to Christ in our lives.

Questions: What is your experience of oil in everyday life? How might oil remind you of God, the Holy Spirit?

Biblical Signs

Throughout the Hebrew scriptures (Old Testament), oil was used for celebrating and greeting, as well as for preparing a body for burial. Sirach mentions that oil, water, fire, and bread are necessary for life. Oil was used for hygiene and cosmetic purposes and for the healing of wounds. Oil poured on the head of a person signified a changed reality. It meant the person was assigned to a new office. Kings were consecrated to office. Samuel anointed Saul and David for kingly service (1 Sam). It was assumed that God performed the anointing for a special purpose or mission. "So God had brought this person to a new state in life which demanded respect and protection."[83] Prophets were anointed into prophetic service. Elijah anointed Elisha (1 Kgs 19:16). Anointing with oil summons the prophet to hear God's word and sends the prophet to confess it. Priests were anointed or consecrated into God's service. Priestly anointing assumed that the anointed assume "a new role and the imposition of responsibility for effecting and preserving holiness for Israel."[84]

Sacred objects were anointed in scripture. Some oils were reserved for just such anointings (Ex 30:22–33). The tabernacle, the ark, the basin used in the purification rites, the table used for the bread of presence, the menorah, the incense altar, and the liturgical vestments were all anointed with oil.

In the New Testament, the anointings reserved for kings were now assigned to Christ. In the Mary Magdalene incident (Lk 7:50), Jesus connected the anointing of his feet with the forgiveness of sins. The anointing of Jesus by the woman was perceived as an act of anointing in preparation for Jesus' burial. "Matthew shows no interest in naming a motive [for the anointing]. Presumably he,

---

[83]John C. Endres, S.J., "Anointing," in *CPDBT*, 28.
[84]Ibid., 29.

like his readers, ancient and modern, regarded anointing as simply an act of love."[85] Also, since Jesus was anointed by God, this anointing was similarly connected to his consecration as messiah by God. The word *messiah* means anointed of God.

Jesus was anointed prophet by the Holy Spirit. Jesus' ministry of the word and of healing was anointed by God. The letter to the Hebrews asserts that Jesus was anointed high priest by God. Paul's second letter to the Corinthians refers to the Christian as anointed of God. Christ lives and works within the lives of Christians. John later takes up the clarion call and asserts that Christian anointing is realized as the guiding, teaching, and protecting Spirit of God (1 Jn 2:27).

Jesus and the apostles anointed and healed the sick. There are clear directions given in the letter of James for healing the sick; they are to be anointed with oil. As a result, they are healed, sanctified, and forgiven.

Questions: How does your natural experience of oil resonate with scripture's use of oil? Were there any new insights in examining the biblical uses of oil? What does it mean that "oil poured on the heads of a person signified a changed reality"? How can you apply that to your experience of the sacraments of the church? What does oil teach you about God, Christ, Spirit, church, yourself? How do the biblical signs speak to your community?

Ecclesial Sign

The church teaches that oil signifies the conferral of the Holy Spirit. We are sealed with the Spirit at confirmation. Oil configures us to Christ. Oil literally bonds or adheres us to the person of Jesus Christ. Jesus is taken into ourselves. We "put on" Christ. We are branded with Christ himself. We bear the likeness of Christ. We take on Christ's image. We live as Christ would live in the world. The conferral of the Spirit in the oil of confirmation immerses us in the paschal mystery of Christ. We die and rise with Christ. Not only do we plunge into the waters of death and resurrection, but we literally take that death and resurrection into ourselves. We die and rise with the power and strength of the Holy Spirit. The oil of confirmation has an

initiatory character; it completes baptism and leads to eucharist. The oil seals us to the mission of Christ and strengthens our priestly, prophetic, and royal role. "By signing us with the gift of the Spirit, confirmation makes us more completely the image of the Lord and fills us with the Holy Spirit, so that we may be witness to him before all the world and work to bring the Body of Christ to its fullness as soon as possible" (RCIA, #2).

(Please refer to "Apostolic Constitution of the Sacrament of Confirmation" and the "Introduction" of the Rite of Confirmation, and the *Catechism of the Catholic Church*, #695.)

Questions: What does the church's use of oil have to do with your community? How does it affect your life? What does it mean that oil seals us to the mission of Christ and strengthens our priestly, prophetic, and royalty role in the mission of Christ? How does the oil of confirmation signify Christ's life? How does the sign of oil relate to your everyday life? What is the challenge?

Liturgical Signs

An ancient practice that has been retained in the modern rite is the three anointings with oil at different stages in the initiation process. The first anointing is a pre-baptismal anointing with the oil of catechumens. The second anointing is post-baptismal and is with chrism. The third anointing is also with chrism and is a sign of the gift of the Holy Spirit.[86] The anointing with the oil of catechumens is understood as a prayer for the candidate to be released from the power of Satan. The candidates also ask for the strength to endure the great contest ahead of them as they prepare for baptism. In the United States this anointing takes place during the period of the catechumenate. In the early church the candidate was rubbed with oil over his entire body, very much like the practice of the wrestler preparing for his match. St. Ambrose reminded the candidates: "You were rubbed with oil like an athlete, Christ's athlete, as though in preparation for an earthly wrestling-match, and you agreed to take on your opponent" (S 1.4).[87] The intention of the anointing is explicitly clear in the *Apostolic Tradition*, where it is ex-

---

[85] *MI*, 293.

[86] *AIRI*, 22.
[87] Ibid.

plained as the oil of exorcism: "Let all evil spirits depart from you."[88] Cyril paints a different picture. He refers to it as a share in the fullness of Christ. He used the symbolism of the olive tree. The anointing imbues a share in the life of Christ, the true olive. As an exorcism, the oil represents a deterrent to the devil and the removal of sin.[89]

The second anointing mentioned above immediately follows baptism. Jesus Christ was anointed by the Holy Spirit to fulfill his messianic, royal destiny. Baptism was understood by some of the church Fathers as participation in that mission. The ritual anointing emerged as a sign of participation and immersion into Christ's messianic mission. Oil was poured over the heads of the newly baptized and allowed to drip down, reminiscent of the oil that dripped down the beard of Aaron. The pouring of this oil was very much in the tradition of anointing reserved for kings. Ambrose described the anointing as a sign of eternal life and as a sign of the baptized person's share in the messianic mission of Christ in which they are anointed priest, prophet, and king. Theodore posited another view of the anointing. He explained it as a sign of ownership. Those so anointed were inducted as soldiers in Christ's service. He also referred to the newly anointed as branded "sheep of Christ."[90]

The second of the three anointings (the first post-baptismal messianic anointing) is only used when confirmation does not immediately follow baptism, but is deferred to a later date (as is the case in infant baptisms in the West). Obviously the anointing of confirmation takes its place, but what is lost is the language that attests to the newly baptized's new role as priest, prophet, and king.

There were two types of oil used in the ancient liturgical rites—the oil of exorcism and the oil of thanksgiving. The oil of exorcism (oil of catechumens) was used in the first, pre-baptismal anointing. The oil of thanksgiving was used for the two post-baptismal anointings. The latter was laced with a perfume called balsam and was called chrism or *myron*.

There were different interpretations of the significance of chrism in the early church. St. Ambrose described the perfumed chrism as the lure of Christ. "We shall run following the perfume of your robes."[91] Other Fathers referred to the chrism as a sign of a person's understanding of the gospel. John Chrysostom distinguished the two oils by using the image of athlete and bride. The first, pre-baptismal oil is for the athlete; the post-baptismal oil is for the bride. The image of branding as a sign of ownership led to the use of the word *seal* in reference to the signation with oil.

The church uses oil in various ways in its life and ministry. Oils are blessed at the Chrism Mass for use in ministry throughout the diocese. The catechumens are blessed with the oil of catechumens. Oil is used in the dedication of a church. Oil is also used in the sacramental life of the church. Infants are anointed at baptism with the oil of catechumens and chrism. The Spirit is given through the ritual anointing with oil at confirmation. Oil is used in the anointing of the sick and the dying. Priests are anointed for priestly service at their ordination.

Questions: Have you ever experienced the use of oil in liturgy? If so, what do you remember? What did it teach you about God, Spirit, Christ, church, community? What is the challenge for the community?

Symbol of Laying on of Hands

The power of the Holy Spirit is unleashed in the church today by the laying on of hands. The laying on of hands is a sign of the action of the Holy Spirit. It confers the gift of the Spirit in all sacraments.

Natural Sign

The hand can be an instrument of love or an instrument of hate. The touch of a hand can bring comfort and healing in a time of stress. The handshake can express friendship and the hand around another can impart guidance and care. Holding hands is a sign of love. For a child, the hand is a

---

[88]*Apostolic Tradition*, xxi.10, in *AIRI*, 22.
[89]Ibid.
[90]*Ad Senarium*, 6; Whitaker, p. 157 in *AIRI*, 28.

---

[91]M 29, translating a text probably based on the LXX version of Cant 1.4, in *AIRI*, 29.

powerful instrument of protection or discipline. The hand used in massage is healing and curative. People clap their hands when happy or excited.

Questions: Do you remember a time when the sense of touch had a particular impact on you? How did it speak to you?

Biblical Sign

According to Dennis Sweetland, the hand has many uses throughout scripture.[92] The hand usually is a sign of God's power. "They assured Joshua, 'The Lord has delivered all this land into our power'" (Jos 2:24). Power is used as a metaphorical substitution for hand. The word *hand* is used over two hundred times in the Hebrew scriptures. When the right hand is mentioned, it usually refers to a place of honor. When the right hand of God is mentioned, it is usually intended to denote incredible, unusual power. "Your right hand, O Lord, magnificent in power...has shattered the enemy" (Ex 15:6).

The imposition of hands was used ritually in the Old Testament as well as in the New Testament. Hands were extended over offerings in response to the laws of sacrifice (Ex 29:10, Lev 1:4, 4:4, 24, 29, 33, 8:14). When hands were extended over a scapegoat, the guilt was transferred to the animal. The action usually had a direct relation to the acceptability of the sacrifice and the one offering the sacrifice. If the sacrifice was acceptable and pleasing, then the one offering was also acceptable. The sign of hands was intended to set things apart for a sacred purpose.

The laying on of hands is also used in scripture as a gesture of blessing. Hands outstretched over an assembly bless the entire group (Lev 9:22). The same gesture is also understood as a means of consigning power to another person, providing the one doing the consigning has the rightful authority to confer this power. Leaders conferred leadership to others through the action of laying on of hands (Num 27:23).

In the New Testament, the hand was understood in the same way as it was in the Hebrew scriptures.

---

[92]Dennis M. Sweetland, "Hand," in *CPDBT*, 405-407.

Hand was understood as power. The hand of God was not, however, a common New Testament image unless it was referring to an actual Old Testament use of the term (Lk 1:66). The hand was used to heal. Jesus was asked to heal Jairus's daughter by laying his hands on her. The Holy Spirit was conferred at baptism through the laying on of hands (Acts 8:17–19; 19:6). The laying on of hands was also a sign of mission. The apostles laid hands on the seven and they were assigned a special service (Acts 6:6). The laying on of hands was also associated with installation in some office, either as presbyter or apostle (2 Tim 1:6 [See also "Fifth Sunday of Easter: First Reading"]).

Questions: Does the scriptural use of the sign of laying on of hands have anything to do with the life of your community? What does it teach you about God, Christ, the church, or yourself? What are you called to do as a response?

Ecclesial Sign

Traditional theology regarding the laying on of hands is multi-layered. The gesture is believed to be the origin of the sacrament of confirmation. According to Paul VI *(Divinae consortium naturae)*, confirmation (imposition of hands) continues the grace of Pentecost. The action of laying on of hands is the conferral of the Spirit in each of the sacraments. The imposition of hands is used in all the sacraments: baptism, confirmation, eucharist (epiclesis in the eucharistic prayer), healing, penance, marriage, and ordination. The gesture has the same meaning and usage in the church today as it did in the Old and New Testament: it is a sign of power, installation of office, ministry, transfer of authority, healing, and blessing. The laying on of hands is a powerful symbol of the ongoing ministry of Jesus Christ through the power of the Holy Spirit in the church.

Questions: Does Catholic tradition's use of the gesture of laying on hands have anything to do with the life of your community? With your life? What does it say to you about God, God's Spirit, Christ, the church, and yourself?

Liturgical Sign

Every sacrament exercises the epicletic action of calling down the Spirit of God to bless, sanctify, transform, and effect the desired grace. Hands are laid on the elect as they go down into the waters of baptism and are chrismated with the oil of the Holy Spirit, the chrism of salvation. Hands are extended over the gifts of bread and wine as a sign of the Spirit's role in transforming the elements into Christ's Body and Blood. The community is blessed through the laying on of hands at the end of the liturgy. The presider/celebrant extends his hands over the assembly before sending them out to do the work of liturgy in the world. The sacred hand of the Spirit is imposed on the head of those seeking ordination, healing, and forgiveness in the sacraments of orders, anointing the sick, and sacrament of penance. The marriage couple join hands as they enter their solemn covenant and the community extends hands in a gesture of peace and unity at liturgical gatherings. Catechumens experience the hand's ministerial touch frequently throughout the catechumenate through the rituals of acceptance, blessings, anointing, exorcism, and various rites.

Questions: Have you ever experienced the sign of the Spirit at liturgy through the laying on of hands? Describe the experience. How did the experience speak to you? What did it teach you about God, Christ, the Spirit, the church, or yourself? What are the implications? How is the community challenged? What are you and the community called to do in response?

Symbol of the Garment

The white garment is placed on the neophyte after baptism as a sign of his or her new status: a fully initiated member of the Body of Christ.

Natural Sign

The contemporary adage, "clothing makes the person," is usually a very consumer-oriented idea. When people have no clothes they find it difficult to compete in this consumer-oriented world. Clothes are a sign of status and wealth. In our everyday lives, new clothes have the effect of making us feel like new people. Persons in certain professions are identified by their clothing: judges, nurses, doctors, clergy, police, etc.

Biblical Sign

In the Old Testament, Isaiah 1:18 proclaims that Yahweh "has clothed me with the garment of sal-

vation, and with the robe of gladness he has covered me." The garment represents a new status, a change from a condition previously held. Before they were unsaved; through Yahweh they were now saved and covered with joy. Yahweh's joy covered them completely. The garment represented new life as a saved person. The garment was also a sign of divine royalty. Isaiah portrays the Lord sitting on a lofty throne with the train of his garment filling the temple (6:1). Job insisted that he wore his honesty like a garment (29:14). The garment throughout the Hebrew scriptures was a symbol for a person's interior nature—the inner life. Both Isaiah (51:6) and the author of Hebrews (1:11) use the imagery of the garment to reflect on the transitory nature of life. This life and its earthly concerns will wear out like a garment. Baruch uses the image as a sign of penitence and trust in Yahweh, the Eternal God. "I have taken off the garment of peace and have put on the sackcloth for my prayer of supplication, and while I live I will cry out to the Eternal God" (Bar 4:20, NAB).

In scripture, clothing was a sign of office. Prophets such as Elijah and John the Baptist wore hair garments as a sign of their prophetic ministry (Zech 13:4). As Elijah passed on his prophetic ministry to Elisha, he gave him his cloak. "Clothes are an extension of the person; Elisha is thus assuming Elijah's identity."[93] The ceremonial robe is placed on the prodigal son upon his return as a sign of his father's forgiveness. The garment in this case is a sign of God's mercy and forgiveness of sin. When the garment is placed on the neophytes, we affirm that they are new creations and are clothed in Christ. St. Paul used the expression "putting on Christ" to describe what baptism accomplishes. According to Brendan Byrne, S.J., Paul's expression conjured images from Greek drama. Actors were so completely enveloped in the costume of their character that the audience could see only the character and not the original identity of the actor. Thus, when we observe the newly-baptized, all we are to see is Christ. They have been "clothed in him."

Ecclesial Sign

The white garment is a sign of incorporation into the paschal mystery of Christ through baptism.

---

[93]Jerome T. Walsh and Christopher T. Begg, "1–2 Kings," in *NJBC*, 175.

The white garment is a sign that the newly baptized have put on Christ. They have risen with Christ through the waters of baptism. The clothing with the baptismal garment signifies the new dignity that is theirs.

Liturgical Sign

The neophyte puts on the white garment at baptism. Baptized infants also put on white baptismal garments. Many children who receive their first communion wear a white garment. Some people misunderstand the symbolism of the white communion dress, assuming that it signifies being a bride of Christ. However, since eucharist completes baptism, the white garment of eucharist is the baptismal garment, not a bridal dress. The pall placed on the coffin at funerals is a sign of the baptismal garment and the prescribed garment for liturgical functions is an alb ("General Instruction of the Roman Missal," #80, c), again reminiscent of the baptismal garment.

In the very earliest baptismal rites the neophytes were baptized with no clothes on. They were anointed with the oil of the Spirit over their entire bodies; their godparent then helped them don the garment of new life in Christ. The garment signified their incorporation into the paschal mystery and the innocence that was theirs as newborn babes in the Christian life.

St. John Chrysostom alludes to the garment as a uniform, an outward sign of interior reality. The neophytes have put on Christ—they have taken Christ within themselves.

> Men who have undertaken temporal duties often wear on their clothes an imperial badge as a sign to the public of their trustworthiness. They would not permit themselves to do anything unworthy of their uniform; and even if they attempted it, there are many people to stop them. If others wish to harm them, the clothes they wear afford sufficient protection. Now the neophytes carry Christ himself, not on their clothes, but dwelling in their souls with his Father, and the Holy Spirit has descended on them there. They are even more obliged,

> then, to prove themselves reliable, and show everyone by their scrupulous conduct, and careful lives that they wear the imperial badge.[94]

The early Fathers used other images to portray the significance of the white garment. The garment was compared to the shining garment of Christ at his transfiguration, to the wedding garment, and to the fleece of the Lamb of God.[95]

It was a custom in the West for the neophytes to wear their baptismal garment through the octave of Easter, following which they took their place among the assembled faithful. In addition to wearing his baptismal garment, Emperor Constantine also draped his throne in white. In some places white linen was placed on the head of the newly baptized as a sign of their liberation from slavery. Augustine writes: "Today is called the octave of infants. The veils are due to be removed from their heads and this is a sign of freedom.... Today, as you see, our infants mingle with the faithful and fly as it were from the nest."[96]

G. LITURGY OF THE EUCHARIST

There is not much that sets the Easter Vigil's liturgy of the eucharist apart from every other eucharist celebrated throughout the year. However, it is the night, different from all other nights, when new Christians are born and old Christians are renewed, new fire replaces the old light, new water is blessed, and the newly consecrated bread serves as the new leaven for the renewed missionary activity of the entire church. Our senses are attuned, as on no other night, to the words of the eucharistic prayer,

> Father, all powerful and ever-living God,
> we do well always and everywhere to give you thanks
> through Jesus Christ our Lord.

---

[94]St. John Chrysostom, *Baptismal Instructions,* ed. by P. W. Harkins, Ancient Christian Writers, v. 31 (Mahwah: Paulist Press, 1963), in *AIRI,* 32.

[95]Ibid.

[96]*Sermon 376, Patrologia Latina,* 39, ed, J.-P. Migne, in *AIRI,* 34.

We praise you with greater joy than ever on
this Easter night,
when Christ became our paschal sacrifice.[97]

On this Easter night, the trumpets should resound as neophytes triumphantly process to the table for the first time. It is the culmination of their journey. The ritual moment of baptism is not the crowning moment of their experience; it is the gateway. The crowning moment occurs at the table of unity and full participation in the paschal mystery. From the very beginning, the journey of the neophytes has been to the table. All believers come to the table to be nourished by Christ's Body and Blood in order to go out and live their lives in the world. We pour ourselves out for others; we become bread in the world so we can come back to the table again and again, depleted and in need of Easter filling. Every celebration of eucharist is an Easter filling.

Bread and Wine

Bread, food for our bodies, and wine, drink of refreshment, celebration, and merriment—are the stuff of life. These symbols assume a new reality in the paschal celebration of eucharist. They are not only reminders of physical nourishment, they become the very sustenance of the soul. We bring our gifts of bread and wine, made by human hands, and we ask God to bless them and make them holy. We ask that the Holy Spirit change these elements into the Body and Blood of Jesus Christ. We believe it happens every time the church gathers to tell the story and pray the blessing prayers of thanks and praise. Bread is and was a sign of God's providence and protection throughout scripture. It was a sign of nourishment, freedom from hunger, and satisfaction of the soul's longing for God. It is a sign of our very sustenance. Thus, bread broken and shared is a sign that we place our lives completely in God's care. The wine, as symbol of Jesus' blood, is a sign of his life force poured out for humanity in atonement for sin. (Refer to the exegesis for Holy Thursday for further elaboration of the biblical symbol of blood.)

We become the bread we receive. We allow ourselves to be poured out as a libation. Christ's broken body was given up; his blood was poured out for the entire world. This happens every time we take the bread, bless it, break it, and share it. Thus, we too become broken, blessed, and shared.

Symbol of Bread

The sign of bread is at the heart of our identity. We are a eucharistic people. Baptism and confirmation lead us to the table and incorporation into Christ's Body and Blood. We consume the Body of Christ and, in so doing, we become the Body of Christ. Each time the Bread of Life is broken, and the Cup of Blood is shared, we become new creations. We take, bless, break, and share Christ's Body. In the taking, blessing, breaking, and sharing, we too are taken by God, blessed and made holy, broken for one another to share ourselves for others in the world. It is through the eucharist that we fully live the paschal mystery of Christ.

Natural Sign

Bread is the staff of life. Bread offers nourishment. Bread comes in many varieties: muffins, buns, pita, rolls, biscuits, leavened and unleavened loaves. With bread we are nourished; without bread we go hungry. Bread gives us strength for living. It is filled with the necessary nutrients for life. "Bread builds strong bodies twelve ways." Bread is a complement to every meal. Bread and water are all that is needed for life.

Questions: Have you ever had an experience of bread that spoke to you of something other than simply food? What did it mean to you?

Biblical Signs

Bread in the Bible was considered a general term for food.[98] "Bread" is referred to 234 times in the Old and New Testaments. When God judged the people for their sins, it was understood that he withheld the "staff of life" (Lev 26:26). Bread is used to name certain human conditions: "bread of tears," "bread of wickedness," "daily bread," etc.

---

[97]Eucharistic Prayer: "Preface for Easter I, P 21," *The Sacramentary.*

[98]John F. Craghan, "Bread," in *CPDBT,* 109.

In the Hebrew scriptures, bread was a sign of hospitality. Melchizedek offered bread to Abraham and Abraham offered bread to strangers as a sign of hospitality. Shared bread suggested a relationship. The meal covenant bond was so strong that it was considered very serious to turn against someone with whom one had eaten. David tricked the enemies of his son, Absolom, into eating a meal with him so they would not carry out their plot to kill him. Contractual agreements between parties were ratified through the ritual of breaking bread. Israel commits itself to the Lord through the communal meal of Passover (Ex 24: 9–11).

The bread of exodus was unleavened bread (Ex 23:18, 34:25). Only unleavened bread was allowed in Israel's ritual worship. Anything but unleavened wheat bread was deemed impure. Bread was a sign of trust and a sign of God's providential care. God provided manna in the desert for the sojourners. Israel's part of the agreement with Yahweh was to trust him implicitly to care for them. Because God's part was to provide, God provided manna.

On every sabbath, twelve cakes of flour were placed on a table in the holy of holies as a sign of the covenant God had made with the twelve tribes of Israel (Lv 24: 5–9). The book of the prophet Isaiah used the image of banquet to refer to the eschatological day of the Lord, the end of the world. Jesus also referred to the banquet as a metaphor for the end of his earthly reign. Bread is an important symbol for Jesus, a sign of covenant and community (Lk 14:15).

Jesus multiplies the loaves and in doing so demonstrates, in action, the univerality of his messianic mission. Jesus came to save all people.

The Jews celebrated a ritual blessing to accompany every human endeavor throughout the day. Blessings sanctified all of life and were understood to make the recipients and the actions holy. So, too, the early Christians gathered to give thanks and praise to God (to bless God) for the wonders of creation and for God's action in salvation history. They gathered for the breaking of the bread, and in so doing they gathered to worship God. Those first Christians translated the Hebrew word *blessing* into the Greek word *eucharist*. It is clear that the eucharist was understood as ritual celebration.

The eucharist they celebrated has its origins in the Jewish table blessing. Jewish families gathered at mealtime to give thanks and praise to their Creator. "Here the prayer of blessing took the form of a ritual, celebrated in bread as grace before meals, and in wine as grace after meals."[99] The father of the household led the prayer and the rest of the family responded to the prayers. In official gatherings the rabbi assumed the role of father. "These then were the rituals out of which the Lord formed his eucharist."[100] Raymond Maloney makes the interesting observation that Jesus used the rituals of the Jewish family meal, not the elaborate rituals of the Temple, to form his new community's worship.

The biblical genesis of the eucharistic meal is found in the institution narratives of the Last Supper as related in the gospels. However, those texts are more liturgical than historical accounts. The Last Supper account resembles the Jewish retelling of the exodus event at Passover—a liturgical celebration. The evangelists were not concerned with providing an historical sketch of the events on Holy Thursday. The biblical texts reflect the eucharistic faith of the first Christian community. So we must look to faith, rather than to the recorded words and actions of Jesus, in order to understand our eucharistic theology. "Our theology of the eucharist has to take its stand on the faith of the church, indwelt by the Holy Spirit, as we find it in those early texts, rather than in any historical reconstruction of the institution event, for about the latter, little agreement is possible."[101]

While not intentionally historical, the gospel traditions do provide the basis for what is generally considered historical about the narratives. Of this we can be sure: the institution of the eucharist originated at the Last Supper. There was a celebration with bread and wine that was integrally connected to the death and resurrection of Christ. "The setting [of the Last Supper] was significant—the lamb had served year after year to prefigure the great expectation."[102] Jesus was the new paschal lamb. Bread and wine eucharist would sus-

---

[99]Ibid.
[100]Raymond Maloney, S.J., "Eucharist," in *NDT*, 343.
[101]Ibid.
[102]*MRR*, 7.

tain and nourish until Christ's return. The final age had arrived. All would feast on the Lamb of God who takes away the sins of the world.

The biblical-liturgical tradition of first century Israel helps us to understand the implications of Jesus' actions at that first eucharistic supper. Luke and Paul both refer to corporate memory in the liturgical action: "Do this in memory of me." It is important to understand what that meant for the participants of the meal and what we inherited as a result. When Jews gathered to remember the action of God in salvation history, their recollections actualized the benefits of grace for each generation. For example, when they gathered for Passover and ate ritual foods, when they drank from the ritual cups of wine and recalled how their ancestors were delivered from slavery in Egypt, they believed that the liberation won for their ancestors was a grace actualized (made present and real) for every community of people— past, present and future. It is called *anamnesis*, a remembering that makes present and real what is remembered. When Jesus said "Do this in memory of me," he was, in effect, saying: "Every time you gather to remember this story and do the ritual actions that accompany it, it will become real and present to you. I will become present. You will participate in the new exodus, my liberating and salvific life, death and resurrection." According to Joseph Jungman: "If the whole celebration is not only the sign of Christ's death and resurrection but its living memorial . . . , [then] these gifts are not only the signs of Christ's body and blood but . . . in some mysterious way, they are indeed what Christ says they are: his very body and his very blood. . . . In the new Law the offerings of bread, wine, incense, beasts [Old Testament sacrifices] have all been replaced and fulfilled by the body and blood of Christ offered on the cross."[103] This is the context in which the eucharist of the first church was celebrated and understood—as a living memorial (see 1 Cor 10:16–17; 11:27–32 and Jn 6:51–58).

Paul details our Christian theology of eucharist in his letter to the Corinthians proclaimed at the Holy Thursday liturgy. Even though we are diverse, with many and varied gifts, eucharist unites

us and makes us one body in Christ. Eucharist is a sign of unity. It is also a sign of sharing. Eucharist demands that we share with those who are in need. (See also "Feast of Corpus Christi.")

The synoptic traditions equate the broken bread of eucharist with Jesus, the suffering messiah (Mt 26:28). Bread becomes a sign of Christ's paschal mystery. The covenant meal of eucharist replaces the old covenant meal of Passover. Jesus is the New Passover; his meal is the new covenant meal. Jesus is the Bread of Presence. No one who eats Jesus' bread will ever know hunger again.

Blood in the synoptics is interpreted as a sign that Christ shed his blood for the sins of the world. Blood is associated with the forgiveness of sins (Mt 24:27–28, Mk 14:24, Lk 22:20). The Old Testament concept of blood as expiation is carried over in the sacrifice of the cup. John equates blood with the giving of eternal life (6:53–56).

Questions: What do the uses of bread and wine in scripture have to do with the life of your community? What does it mean that bread represents the universality of Jesus' mission? How does it speak to the life of your community? How is the eucharist a sign of unity? What does it mean to you in practical terms? How does the broken bread of the eucharist reveal the suffering Messiah? What do the biblical signs of bread and wine teach you about God, Christ, Spirit, church, or yourself?

Ecclesial Signs

The meal of the Last Supper was unleavened bread. However, Christians of the early centuries did not assign special significance to the unleavened nature of the bread. They no doubt used leavened bread brought from home and presented along with their offerings for the needy. The ritual action of breaking bread was the eucharistic worship of the early church. There is a detailed description of the ritual in a second-century document, the *Didache*. Early Christians understood eucharist to be a corporate sharing in the risen Christ as experienced in the breaking of the bread. This sharing unified them into one people. Raymond Maloney offers this definition of eucharist: "The eucharist is a celebration of Christian community as people commemorate in the rituals of bread and cup the key events from which

---

[103]Maloney, *NDT,* 345.

their community draws its life, namely the death and resurrection of the Lord."[104]

Eucharist means *thanksgiving* in Greek. The early Christians gathered for thanks and praise and the breaking of bread. That early eucharistic liturgy evolved from Jewish table prayers of praise and thanks at festive meals. The early Christians gathered in their house churches for the breaking of the bread while still maintaining their ties to the synagogue. Around 100 C.E., there was a break from the synagogue and the ritual meal continued in the house churches. This meal was eschatological. The eucharist was believed to be the final means of bringing members to belief in Christ before his final coming. Thus, baptism was a requisite for eucharist.

Joseph A. Jungman transports us back to the primitive church and its understanding of that first eucharistic meal.

> From the start the basic motif was to observe the memorial of the Lord, the remembrance of his redemptive Passion, in the form of a meal. Therefore, at first, the framework of supper remained in the foreground. The faithful sat at table; under cover of simple nourishment they feasted upon the Body and Blood of him who had laid down his life for us all and who should someday come again to gather his own into his kingdom. The spoken word would slip easily from the recital of the words of institution and the command therein contained into such thoughts of memory and expectation. Union with our Lord in his glory came as strongly into the consciousness as union amongst themselves came visibly to the eye by means of the meal…. The meal was not an ordinary meal but a sacred banquet, not only hallowed and inspired by the memory which gave it value and which in its course was sacramentalized, but also borne Godwards by the word of the prayer that was added to it. For if, in primitive Christian culture, every meal imported not only various blessings but the prayer of thanks as well, it was never truer of this meal.

> The mind of man not blinded by pride will be turned toward God by even a natural meal. Nowhere is it more plainly and visibly seen that man is a receiver, than when he takes nourishment to keep his life powers together. Therefore a meal has always been the incentive to acknowledge one's own creation by means of [a] prayer of thanks which is bound up with the meal.[105]

The early liturgy consisted of two parts. The word of God was proclaimed: this consisted of the Hebrew scriptures and memoirs of the apostles. A homily was given based on the readings, and prayers of intercession were offered. The second part of the liturgy included the prayers of thanks and praise over the elements of bread and wine. The Body and Blood of Christ were then shared in communion. Very early (ca. 115), Ignatius of Antioch wrote of eucharist as recalling the passion and death of Jesus; it was offered as strength in times of persecution.

By the third century the liturgy had become more formalized with the established orders of bishop, priest, and deacon. The *Apostolic Tradition*, by Hippolytus of Rome, describes the liturgy in detail. The Tradition's prayer of thanks is the origin of the Second Eucharistic Prayer in today's Roman Missal. The *anaphora* (eucharistic prayer) remembers God's saving deeds since the creation of the world, culminating in the death and resurrection of Christ (*anamnesis*) and the calling down of the Holy Spirit to transform the gifts of bread and wine into the Body and Blood of Christ (*epiclesis*). This action is performed for the unity of the church because of its participation in sharing the Body and Blood of Jesus.

Later in the patristic period, there emerged a more sacrificial understanding of eucharistic bread and wine. The prayers over the elements were referred to as offerings rather than as thanksgiving prayers. The bread was still leavened, and beautifully adorned loaves (such as a braided loaf in the shape of a crown of thorns) were baked by skilled bakers. The Arian heresy was plaguing the church at the time and scholars believe that the

---

[104]Ibid., 343.

[105]*MRR*, 21.

special breads emerged at around the same time that theology was stressing the divinity of Christ.

During this same period (fourth to seventh centuries), beginning with Constantine's edict of Milan (315) legalizing Christianity, the liturgy changed to reflect the situation at hand. Christianity became the religion of the Empire. Worship moved from house churches to basilicas, the civic auditoriums large enough to hold the influx of people. It was now advantageous to become a Christian. The catechumenate declined and quality control for converts was minimal. Motivation was questionable. One had to be Christian in order to secure the best employment. The liturgy became more formalized. The hierarchy assumed religious and civic roles of leadership (stoles, miters, and special vestments derived from these roles). The liturgy still maintained the two parts of word and sacrament, but embellishments were added for greater participation of the assembly: processions, litanies, chants, incense, etc.

The churches of the East and the West were established, each adopting its own style of worship. The metaphors of previous times became literalisms of this time. Eucharist was sacralized to such an extent that the meal aspect was difficult to detect. However, the eucharistic action of offering thanks and praise was understood as the "sacrifical action of the priestly community by virtue of their baptism."[106] Augustine asserted that eucharist was the offering of the church to the Father.

During the Middle Ages, the people received communion very infrequently. In order to further distinguish eucharistic bread from real bread, the church mandated that eucharistic bread be unleavened and then reduced it to a coin-shaped size, normally consumed by the priest (smaller varieties were used for the people). The Council of Florence in 1439 acknowledged the right of the Eastern church to use leavened bread while the Roman Church maintained its previous mandate.

In the next period (eighth to sixteenth centuries), the laity became less involved and were reduced to being spectators. Latin was established as the language of liturgy (only the clergy understood

---

Latin). The Eastern church translated the prayers of the liturgy into the vernacular, but Rome maintained Latin as its official liturgical language. The mass was explained as an allegory on the life of Christ. The eucharist was defined as the real Body and Blood of Christ in which the priest broke the body and the people crushed it with their teeth. The Fourth Lateran Council (1215) and Thomas Aquinas refined that theology with terms such as "transubstantiation."

The sacrifical aspect of the mass increased and centered on the re-creation of the sacrifice of Christ on the cross. Because of the penitential overtones and the people's sense of unworthiness, the reception of communion severely declined. Receiving from the cup was reserved for the clergy only. Leaders of the Reformation spoke out against such abuses.

The Council of Trent sought to reestablish the teaching authority of the church and thus affirmed most practices while abolishing the more obvious abuses. The next four hundred years would see little change.

The Second Vatican Council retrieved the church's earlier biblical and patristic heritage. The meal aspect of eucharist was recovered and the role of the church was strengthened. The primary signs of God's presence in the liturgy were set forth in priest, sacrament, word, and church. "Christ is present in the sacrifice of the Mass, not only in the person of his minister... but especially in the eucharistic elements... in the sacraments. ... He is present in his word.... He is present when the Church prays and sings" (CSL, 7).

The church teaches that eucharist completes initiation. The goal of initation is not baptism; it is eucharist. Augustine called eucharist the repeatable sacrament of initiation because it has the power to forgive sins, just as baptism forgives sins. Eucharist is our participation in the paschal mystery of Christ. We are incorporated into his death and resurrection. It is a sign of unity and of charity. We are to share what we have received. We are to become that which we have shared. Eucharist calls us to be bread for the world: the hungry, the suffering, the oppressed. Eucharist strengthens us to take up the cross and

---

[106]Mark R. Francis, C.S.V., "Eucharist," in *CPDBT*, 277.

live the gospel. In the eucharist, we offer our praise and thanks to God for all his great saving acts since the creation of the world. Eucharist is the way we are church; it is our ongoing participation in Jesus' life. We come together as God's people to offer praise and thanks, to share the story of salvation and Christ's covenant meal. Eucharist commits us to the poor.

Questions: How does the church's teaching on the eucharist impact the life of your community? In what way is the eucharist "the repeatable sacrament of initiation"? How does it commit us to the poor? Does it have anything to do with your everyday life? What does it teach you about God, Christ, Holy Spirit, church, or yourself?

Liturgical Sign

The *Constitution on the Sacred Liturgy* (CSL) asserted that the eucharist is the action of the entire church and that "the liturgy is the summit toward which the activity of Church is directed; at the same time it is the fount from which all the Church's power flows..." (#10). "The Church earnestly desires that all the faithful be led to full, conscious, and active participation in liturgical celebrations called for by the very nature of the liturgy. Such participation by the Christian people as a 'chosen priesthood, a holy nation, God's own people' (1 Pet. 2:9; see 2:4–5) is their right and duty by reason of their baptism" (#14). "Every liturgical celebration is a sacred action...surpassing all others; no action of the Church can equal its effectiveness by the same title and to the same degree" (CSL, #7).

From all this, it can be concluded that the celebration of the eucharist is the greatest endeavor of the church. Its celebration deserves our greatest attention. The symbols of the liturgy must be robust and reflect the reality they effect. Real bread, quality wine, full water immersion, abundantly slathered oil, a worthy book, a cross, a real garment, a huge fire and a large Easter candle: these are our primary symbols. We must give them the opportunity to speak to us. Most have heard the quip that it takes more faith to believe that the wafer-like hosts are bread than it does to believe in the real presence of Jesus Christ in the elements.

The bread must be made from wheat and must have been baked recently, according to the long standing tradition of the Latin Church, it must be unleavened. The nature of the sign demands that the material for the eucharistic celebration truly have the appearance of food. Accordingly, even though unleavened and baked in the traditional shape, the eucharistic bread should be made in such a way that in a Mass with a congregation the priest is able actually to break the host into parts and distribute them at least to some of the faithful.
...The action of the breaking the bread, the simple term for the eucharist in apostolic times, will more clearly bring out the force and meaning of the sign of the unity of all in the one bread and of their charity, since the one bread is being distributed among the members of one family. ("General Instruction of the Roman Missal" [GIRM], 282, 283)

"Holy Communion has a more complete form as a sign when it is received under both kinds. For in this manner of reception a fuller light shines on the sign of the eucharistic banquet. Moreover, there is clearer expression of that will by which the new and everlasting covenant is ratified in the blood of the Lord and of the relationship of the eucharistic banquet to the eschatological banquet in the Father's kingdom" (GIRM, #240). "The act of drinking the consecrated wine, the Blood of Christ, strengthens the faith of communicants in the sacrificial nature of the Mass. Communion under both kinds can therefore manifest more fully the nature of the Mass both as a sacrifice and as a sacred banquet, ritually expressing that 'the sacrifice and the sacred Meal belong to the same mystery, to such an extent that they are linked to one another by a very close theological and sacramental bond'[107] ("Directory for the Celebration of Communion under Both Kinds," #19).

On this night of new fire, water, oil, and bread, we encounter the risen Christ anew. We are renewed as we go forth with Easter joy. The liturgy calls us to be world changers, to offer our lives for the sake of the

---

[107]Congregation for Divine Worship, *Actio Pastoralis,* "Instruction on Masses for Special Gatherings" (May 15, 1969), 5.

world. There is an ancient symbol of eucharist that speaks of the mystery we just celebrated. A mother pelican is pictured with droplets of blood dripping from her breast. It was believed that in time of famine, the mother pelican would scratch her breast until droplets of blood dripped into her starving babies' anxiously waiting beaks. Her babies fed off of her freely offered blood. We go forth this Easter night willing and strengthened to offer our droplets of love in the service of God's people.

Questions: Have you had a memorable experience of Christ in the eucharist? Describe your communal experience of eucharist. Does it reflect the theology just expressed? Where is there need for growth? What is the challenge of the church's teaching on the eucharist? How are you and your community called to respond?

Conversation with the Liturgy and the Scriptures

Test your original understanding in dialogue with the text.

Were there any new insights, anything you had not considered before in relation to the entire celebration of the Easter Vigil? How does your original understanding of this liturgy compare with what we just shared? How does this liturgy speak to your life?

Sharing Life Experience

Participants share an experience from their lives that connects with the biblical interpretation just shared.

Thank God for the Easter Vigil. It is a sign of hope. When parishes struggle in the process of dying and rising through the year, we are offered the opportunity to cast off the old and become a new community in Christ. One year, the pastor stood before us and asked us to stand during his homily and repeatedly sing the refrain: "And God saw that it was good!" He asked us if we really believed the power in those words. He repeatedly affirmed that if we truly believed in our own goodness we could transform the world. We know our sinful natures. It is very difficult to see our own goodness. But tonight's liturgy is a testament to the creative ongoing infusion of goodness in our lives.

It is the annual commitment to stay in the struggle to live the call of our baptism. It is a reminder that

we are called to die and to rise. We are to eliminate injustice and become the eucharist. Our parish has had many opportunities over the years to die and rise. Sometimes we stay in death by our own choosing and other times we rise triumphant to new life. When we continue to reach out to the lonely, the sick, the sorrowing, and the poor, we die to our own selfish concerns and live in the resurrection of Jesus Christ. We should rejoice when people get angry that we feed the hungry, offer shelter to the homeless, give blankets to those on the streets, and preach the seamless garment of life. When Jesus made similar choices, he was sent straight to the cross. We are told that we should rejoice when we are persecuted for the sake of the gospel. That is what it means to live the paschal mystery, to be a resurrection people. We have a long way to go, but the Spirit of God continues to lead us in the struggle of death and resurrection. This is the night we take our annual pledge. We recommit ourselves to our covenant with God. The Easter Vigil brings us to our senses, shakes the dust off our feet and the sleep out of our eyes, and tells us to wake up and get on with the business of being God's people, created in the image and likeness of none other than God alone. Washed, anointed, and filled, we are fortified for another year of allowing the spiritually and physically hungry to feed from the satiated Body of Christ. Next year we will return, depleted, ready to be filled again.

All share their life experience.

In what way has this liturgy expressed creation, covenant, church, death, and resurrection? How are those images relevant to our community's life today? In what way is our community challenged by this liturgy? What is our collective and personal response to all of the above questions? Do we still feel the same way about this liturgy and these scriptures as we did when we began?

The gospel demands a response.

What am I /we/community/parish called to do in response to the Easter Vigil?

DOCTRINAL ISSUES

What church truth/teaching/doctrinal issue could be drawn from the gospel for the Easter Vigil?

Participants suggest possible doctrinal themes that flow from the readings.

Possible Doctrinal Themes

Resurrection, paschal mystery, baptism/confirmation, eucharist; symbols: community, fire/light, water, oil, garment, bread and wine, cross

Present the doctrinal material at this time.

1. The facilitator gives input on a particular doctrinal issue of his/her prior choosing. OR
2. The group chooses a doctrinal issue from the list they created. They read together from the Doctrinal Appendix.

(The doctrinal issues are found in the Doctrinal Appendix in the back of this workbook. If you are choosing an issue from this resource, please refer to it now.)

Reflection questions centered around the chosen doctrinal theme can be found at the end of each topic in the Doctrinal Appendix. The questions are based on the five-step reflection process. If you choose a topic not included in the Doctrinal Appendix, craft your own questions according to the same five-step process.

Following the reflection questions you will be reminded to return to chapter 7, "Preparing the Catechetical Session," to assist you in crafting your own session.

Closing Prayer

God, the all-powerful Father of our Lord Jesus
      Christ,
has given us a new birth by water and the Holy
      Spirit,
and forgiven all our sins.
May he also keep us faithful to our Lord Jesus
      Christ
for ever and ever.[108]

---

[108]Service of Baptism: "Concluding Prayer," *RCIA*.

EASTER SUNDAY

Environment

The dark days of purple give way to festive joy as Easter days of white adorn our environments. Your catechetical space might include the draping of cross and book in an elegant, well-chosen, white material. As a reminder of the paschal candle, you might want to replenish your formerly consumed candle with a new (perhaps decorated) candle. An Easter lily or other spring flowers could adorn your space. The ancient icon of the resurrection called *Anastasis* would be a wonderful addition to your Easter environment.[1] The icon is a representation of Christ standing on top of the cross that crushes the evil of hell. Christ takes our first parents by the hand and escorts them out of their graves. "Amazing! Here the departure from the tomb is not that of Jesus but of all humanity."[2]

INTRODUCTORY RITES

Opening Song (or Entrance Antiphon)

Song: Jesus Christ Is Risen Today

The Lord has indeed risen, alleluia. Glory and kingship be his for ever and ever. (Lk 24:34; see Rev 1:6)[3]

Opening Prayer

The facilitator of the session may lead the prayer. Others in the group may be asked to proclaim the readings.

Let us pray
[on this Easter morning for the life
that never again shall see darkness]

Pause for silent prayer.

---

[1] Icons are symbols that draw us into the sacred presence. They help make present what they portray. There are companies that produce icons for purchase by catalogue. One such company is Monastery Icons, Rt. 1, Box 75, Geneva, NE 68361.

[2] *TCY,* 130.

[3] Easter Sunday: "Entrance Antiphon," *The Sacramentary.*

God our Father, creator of all,
today is the day of Easter joy.
This is the morning on which the Lord appeared
   to men
who had begun to lose hope
and opened their eyes to what the scriptures
   foretold:
that first he must die, and then he would rise
and ascend into his Father's glorious presence.
May the risen Lord
breathe on our minds and open our eyes
that we may know him in the breaking of the
   bread,
and follow him in his risen life.
Grant this through Christ our Lord.[4]

LITURGY OF THE WORD

Let us listen to God's word.

The readings are proclaimed.

First Reading
Acts 10:34, 37–43

Overview of the Acts of the Apostles: The Acts of the Apostles was the second volume written by Luke, the evangelist (the gospel of Luke was the first). The original Greek title was "Acts of Apostles, not Acts of the Apostles; the meaning is somewhat indefinite, but it is not limited to the Twelve."[5] The book is intended not as a history, but rather as a record of the church's growth through the power of the Holy Spirit. Luke wrote two gospels: the gospel of the Son and the gospel of the Spirit. The gospel of Luke was the former and the Acts of the Apostles the latter. Luke portrays the spread of the church to the gentile world and considers it complete once the mission extends to Rome. It is believed that Luke wrote his book from oral, rather than written, tradition.

---

[4] Easter Sunday: "Alternative Opening Prayer," *The Sacramentary.*

[5] *DB,* 9.

Irenaeus named Luke the author of Acts and further asserted that it was written in Rome sometime after the death of Paul. Eusebius claimed that it was written during Paul's Roman imprisonment. There is similarity in the structure of Luke and Acts. In Luke, there is movement from Galilee to Jerusalem. In Acts, there is movement from Jerusalem to Rome. The Acts of the Apostles places Rome at the center of the known world. It ends in Rome because the incredible has happened and the "gospel has become a world gospel."[6] It was believed to have been composed between 70–90 C.E.

The Old Testament writers did not record their salvation history in order to chronicle the events that took place. Their primary concern was to interpret that history. Luke inherited that same tradition. Acts is considered the second volume of a two-part work by Luke the evangelist. Rather than writing a detailed history of the growth of the early church, Luke has another agenda in mind. He writes to interpret three major events that caused tension in the missionary communities. The first key event was the destruction of Jerusalem. According to Luke, the destruction of Jerusalem did not signal God's abandonment of his promises to the people. Salvation history proves his point. God did not abandon Israel during the Babylonian exile. God's fidelity is constant. Luke stresses the faithfulness of God as evidenced in the resurrection of Jesus. God did not abandon Jesus but raised him to new life.

Luke's purpose is also to demonstrate that community life is in the hands of God. All things happen according to the will of God. It is God's will that the mission of Jesus go forth to the gentiles. It is God's will that Paul, the scoundrel persecutor that had wreaked so much havoc in their lives, be converted to Christ and chosen to take the word of God out to the nations.

A second event plaguing the early church was the "difficulty of mission."[7] Even though some Jews were converted to Jesus, many were not. For them, Jesus was not the fulfillment of Old Testament prophecy. This was very hard on the missionaries. There was a strong temptation to believe that

Jesus abandoned them—that he was no longer with them. A primary issue for Luke was to assure the church that the Spirit of Jesus was alive and well in the community and that the church would spread according to God's plan.

Luke provides the church with the apologetics needed for dealing with the Jews. The apostles appointed by Jesus continue to be in solidarity with him. They are representative of the patriarchs who led the twelve tribes of Israel. The apostles continue in the same tradition for the restoration of Israel. They will win converts to Jesus Christ.

Paul preaches to pagan and Jew alike and not without considerable difficulty. Both Jesus and Paul fulfill the prophetic destiny [see gospel exegesis—Third Sunday of Easter] and do not abandon their mission in the face of difficulties. They serve as models for the burgeoning church.

The third event that concerns Luke is the persecution of the church by the pagans and the Jews. The Acts of the Apostles is a word of consolation for the persecuted church. The way of the church is the way of the cross. Luke assures his readers that persecution is transitory. God will rescue God's people from the clutches of such persecution. Many will be led to Jesus because of the persecution they are willing to endure.

Luke writes to interpret the past history of the people. Only then will they understand what is going on in their present. Only then will Christians know how to face what is ahead for them.

The Acts of the Apostles also depicts the lives of the early saints—Peter, Paul, Barnabas, Stephen, etc. Such a chronicle is called hagiography. Hagiography honors the saints by extolling their wondrous deeds while on earth. Acts demonstrates how Paul and the others patterned their lives after Jesus, the martyred Son of God. In solidarity with the living Christ, they are Spirit-filled as they go forth spreading his mission. Those first saints are models for other Christians to emulate and follow.

Luke insists that the Spirit-filled church could only advance through the life and example of Spirit-filled Christians. The church needs missionaries.

[6]Ibid., 12.

[7]*IA*, 12.

They are empowered by the Spirit of Christ that is present in the church. Missionary life was not a "Jesus and me" affair. The Spirit was not given for the edification of one individual, but to build up the church. The church, in turn, is to use the gifts of the Spirit to reach out and help others. This is one of Luke's primary and essential themes.

While the church can expect persecution, it will be strengthened through the Spirit and through prayer. Prayer is essential; it is through prayer that the church will know and respond to the will of God. The missionary church experienced difficulty maintaining continuity with the past and at the same time remaining open to the movement of the Spirit in the present. What about adherence to the Law? Should pagan converts be subject to Jewish law? These questions caused great tension in a church that was adding gentile converts to its membership. The first converts were Jewish. What does it mean to be Jewish now? How were they to respond to the movement of the church into metropolitan centers such as Antioch? Should they still preach the gospel of the poor to a culture that cares not a fig for the poor? These were difficult questions midst difficult circumstances.

Luke seeks to uphold a vision of church—an ideal. He challenges those first communities to strive for the ideal. Luke's ideal community is one in which all things are shared in common, the poor are cared for, and bread is broken in worship of the God of infinite love and mercy.

Luke upholds the same image of God as he portrayed in his first gospel. God is all-loving, all-merciful, and all-forgiving. God is constant. God is faithful to God's promises. God is in covenant relationship with God's people. God will not disappoint. God walks with us into our future.

Luke employed a common literary tool used by Greco-Roman historians in which the characters enacted and spoke the historical commentary and analysis they wished to convey. In the Acts of the Apostles, the speeches of the characters interpret and analyze the events of Luke's first volume, the gospel according to Luke.

Peter's speech is a primary piece of the Christian kerygma (proclamation). The Acts of the Apostles was a catechetical tool for early believers. The characters in the text set forth the Christian creed. Peter's speech today is considered the earliest formulation of that creed. Peter and his apostles were the first witnesses. They were the first to confess their faith and were charged with passing on the faith to the world. Every believer was and is to witness to that faith. Today's speech by Peter follows very early christological patterns. Reginald Fuller notes three: 1. Salvation was offered through the scandalous death and subsequent resurrection of Jesus and Israel rejected that salvation. 2. Jesus was vindicated through the resurrection while his religious peers rejected him. 3. The apostles are the first witnesses from his earthly ministry through the post-resurrection appearances.[8]

Peter's Credo is the living faith of the first Christian community passed on to succeeding generations of the church through its living tradition. The roots of Peter's confession can be found in the Apostles' Creed.[9]

On this Easter Sunday, Peter's speech in the Acts of the Apostles contains within it not only the Christian kerygma, but a challenge to the Jewish Christian community. Peter's confession about Christ would have upset long-held religious views. God was demanding the unthinkable of good, law-abiding Jews. This whole section of chapter ten is about God removing obstacles to the gentile mission. Not only was Peter's confession for all people, including the gentiles, but it paved the way for Jewish Christians to consider their gentile counterparts worthy of association.

In order to understand this, it is important to consider the reading within the context of its setting. An angel appeared to Cornelius and told him that God favored him because he was an upright man. He was then instructed to go and seek out Peter in Joppa. Cornelius was a pagan, a God-fearing centurion. He was a holy man as is evidenced by his constant prayer and almsgiving. Meanwhile, Peter had a vision of his own. He was hungry. God dropped four-legged animals and reptiles from the sky and declared them no longer unclean. Cornelius's baptism by Peter and Peter's vision are

---

[8] *PNL*, 23.
[9] *DL* (III), 68.

the catalyst for a significant turning point in the early church.

Cornelius went to Peter's house and was invited to stay. Peter was still reeling from his vision and what it meant. Peter already knew of the universality of Jesus' mission. Jesus had commissioned the apostles to go and baptize *all nations*. However, prior to this time, the mission to the gentiles had not advanced much in the Jerusalem church. There were missionary successes, but not much was happening in Jerusalem.

Jesus' plan for the gentile mission had not taken root in Jerusalem. Why? The apostles did not have to go "to all nations" to find gentiles. They lived in their own backyards. Evangelization to the gentiles had not yet begun.

This reading is not about affirming the gentile mission. It is about clearing away the obstacles to it. Up to this point, the obstacle had been so great that it would have taken nothing less than a vision from God to overcome it. By law, gentiles were unclean pagans. A committed, communal relationship assumed reciprocal hospitality. If gentiles were converted, they would be initiated into the New Covenant. Thus, Jewish Christians and gentile Christians would have in common a covenantal relationship in which both parties shared reciprocal hospitality. In other words, there would necessarily be shared *agape,* communal meals. The obstacle for Jewish Christians was: How could they share meals with the unclean? It was forbidden by God. "Nevertheless he [Peter] is the one who takes the new step that requires the Jerusalem church to re-examine its relation to Gentiles. It is not enough that Peter takes the new step. The Jerusalem church must be convinced of its rightness."[10] God was lifting the status of *unclean* off of the backs of the gentiles, thus paving the way for a Jewish/gentile Christianity. Communal relationship between Jews and Christians was now possible.

In today's pericope, Peter confesses the Jesus story to Cornelius and friends to affirm that "God sent good news to the people of Israel about the peace now available through their Messiah, and this Messiah is Lord of all, offering peace to all. Peter re-

views the Jesus story as told in Luke in order to say to Cornelius that this story is a word of salvation for him also."[11]

Peter's address to the new converts is indicative of the method used for evangelizing gentiles. Methods used for evangelizing Jews would include blaming the Jewish leaders for Jesus' death and using the Hebrew scriptures as a proof text for Jesus' life. Methods of evangelization for gentiles involved the proclamation of Jesus' life and work and the witness of the apostles to back up his claims.

In today's text, Peter confesses the Christians' story (the agenda of every Easter Christian) and asserts the universal message of God's salvation.[12] In other words, Peter demonstrates the inclusivity of God, and paves the way for disciples to move beyond religious fundamentalism and centuries-old prejudices. Only the Spirit could accomplish such a major shift.

Questions for mystagogical reflection: What does this reading have to do with Easter? How is this a word for our community? What are the implications for our community during this season that immerses us in the paschal mystery and Christian witness? What does this reading teach us about God, Christ, Spirit, church, ourselves? How might our community be called to respond? How does this reading challenge us to live the paschal mystery?

Responsorial Psalm
Psalm 118:1–2, 16–17, 22–23

Of all the psalms, Psalm 118 was one of the first that was used to refer to the death and resurrection of Christ. Psalm 118 is an individual song of thanks. "The stone which the builders rejected" (v. 22) was probably an ancient proverb. "A piece of stone judged unworthy of a position of prominence in the structure by the 'experts' has become the most prominent."[13] This line was a metaphor that the early church used to help explain Israel's rejection of its own people. "This is

---

[10]*NULA* (II), 143.

[11]Ibid., 142.

[12]*LY,* 83.

[13]John S. Kselman, S.S. and Michael L. Barre, S.S., "Psalms," in *NJBC,* 547.

the day the Lord has made" (v. 24) referred to the day in which Yahweh acted to save his people. The resurrection was just such a day.

Second Reading
Alternative 1: Colossians 3:1–4

Paul's letter to the Colossians is written in the midst of turmoil. Gnosticism is threatening the church. According to gnosticism, spirit is good and matter is evil. Thus, the only way to attain God is through special knowledge (knowledge that only the elite can obtain); those without this knowledge are trapped in their human, evil bodies. There were two extreme responses to gnosticism: excessive spiritual exercises and extreme attempts to wear down the evil body. Both point to the denigration of Christian redemption through Christ. "If you have been raised in Christ" is a literary phrase. "It means if (and of course you are)."[14] The word, *raised*, is literally translated *co-raised*. We were raised with Christ and given a share in his life. Because we have been given a share in Christ's divine life, we are called to live the redemption that was won for us. Thus, we are called to a higher moral standard.

Reginald Fuller suggests that the letter to the Colossians takes the Romans exhortation from last night's vigil one step further. Romans tells us "that we died with Christ." Colossians is more optimistic and is cause for Easter rejoicing. In this letter Paul maintains that we die *and rise* with Christ. However, this death and resurrection carries with it the responsibility to live the moral life and be aware of the "hidden reality which is not fully revealed until Christ's second coming."[15]

Questions for mystagogical reflection: How is our community dying and rising with Christ (living the paschal mystery)? Do we live the challenge of the gospel? Do we respond in love to our brothers and sisters around the world? Do we live the moral responsibility to care for one another, especially those who cannot care for themselves? Where is there death? Where is there resurrection? What are we called to do about it as a community? How are we called to respond?

---

[14]*PNL,* 24
[15]Ibid.

Second Reading
Alternative 2: 1 Corinthians 5:6–8

Prior to Passover, Jewish women spent many hours removing every particle of leaven from their homes. Leaven was used in a figurative sense in the early church. Leaven was considered an impurity and was a metaphor for sin. A very little leaven impacted the entire batch of dough. Unleavened bread was a sign of purity.

"Do you not know that a little yeast has its effects all through the dough?" (v. 5). The opening line of today's pericope is actually a proverb. "Jesus used it to teach that if the kingdom had modest beginnings, it contains the seeds of great growth."[16] Leaven was also used to symbolize corruption. It is this last reference that Paul uses here. Paul exhorts the reader to get rid of all the old yeast so a new batch can grow. Last night at the Easter Vigil, the neophytes put on the new person of Christ. The old yeast was washed away in the waters of baptism, a new batch was begun, and new life began.

Paul speaks this word to the Corinthians in response to the case of a man who was guilty of incest. He had had relations with his father's wife, which was considered an abomination. Paul was more disconcerted over the community's lack of response than he was about the sin of the man. Paul exhorts the community to rid itself of the sinful leaven. He challenges the community to rid itself of such sin. Easter people are to cast off the darkness of sin and live in the light of the resurrection. Like the Jewish women of old, who swept their houses before Passover looking for the tiniest morsel of leaven, we too are to sweep the houses of our heart to rid them of the leaven of corruption. In so doing, we will then live as unleavened bread, in the resurrection of purity and holiness. Christians are to live and preach the truth and to call one another to holiness. This call to holiness has its basis in living the moral life. "These passages resound to the great Pauline intuition that we are not saved because of our works but neither are we saved without our works.... Moral and ascetic commitment is not the *cause* of salvation; it does, however, have to be the *effect* of

---

[16]*DL* (III), 71.

it."[17] The Christian community and individual are to seek out the leaven of sin through purification from the old yeast in order to live in the resurrection of new, Easter life.

This is the first time that Christian Passover is mentioned and it refers to two different Passovers. One Passover is that already accomplished through Christ's sacrifice of his life on Calvary. The other is the Christian Passover: the passage of the person from death to life, sin to purity. The verb used in reference to Jesus' Passover is in the past tense. Jesus' Passover is already a reality. The Christian need only accept it, "believe it and celebrate it."[18] The verbs that refer to the Christian Passover, on the other hand, infer that the action is still in process. "The verbs in this case are in the imperative: 'purify yourselves, let us celebrate.'"[19]

Questions for mystagogical reflection: Christians are called to be a eucharistic people. In what way is your community like the leavened bread of the Pharisees? How have you grown in the image of unleavened bread—the eucharist? How has your community grown in holiness through the lenten season? What are you called to do in response to this reading?

Gospel
John 20:1–9

Mary Magdalene finds Jesus' tomb empty and runs to tell Peter and the others.

Sequence

To the Paschal Victim let Christians offer a sacrifice of praise.

The lamb redeemed the sheep. Christ, sinless, reconciled sinners to the Father.

Death and life were locked together in a unique struggle. Life's captain died; now he reigns, never more to die.

Tell us, Mary, What did you see on the way?

---

[17]*ME*, 85.
[18]Ibid., 92.
[19]Ibid.

"I saw the tomb of the now living Christ. I saw the glory of Christ, now risen.

"I saw angels who gave witness; the cloths too which once had covered head and limbs.

"Christ my hope has arisen. He will go before his own into Galilee."

We know that Christ has indeed risen from the dead. Do you, conqueror and king, have mercy on us. Amen. Alleluia.

STEP 1
NAMING ONE'S EXPERIENCE

What were your first impressions? What was your first response? What grabbed your attention? How did you feel?

Each person names his or her initial impression. Statements should be brief. No reasons should be given at this time. All simply listen without agreeing or disagreeing.

STEP 2
UNDERSTANDING

In a brief statement, what do you think the readings are trying to convey?

STEP 3
INPUT FROM VISION/STORY/TRADITION

Liturgical Context

The Beginning of the Easter Season

The Easter Vigil is the primary ritual celebration of the Easter event. Easter Sunday is considered the first Sunday of Easter, and the next Sunday the Second Sunday of Easter. There are no special rituals for Easter Sunday other than to revisit the rituals initiated at the Easter Vigil the night before. On Easter Sunday we renew our baptismal promises, sprinkle the community with the newly blessed water of baptism, and continue the jubilant celebration in word, symbol, ritual, and song.

Penitence is over and now begin the seven weeks of meditation on the awesome implications of the paschal mystery.

> He has made us pass:
> from slavery to freedom,
> from sadness to joy,
> from mourning to the feast,
> from darkness to the light,
> from slavery to redemption.
> Therefore we say before him: Alleluia![20]

The Easter season is not a time for giving an historical representation of the chronology of events in Jesus' post-resurrection life. It is, rather, intended to give sufficient time to uncover, unpack, and reflect on the paschal mystery in order to allow all of its dimensions to impact and affect the Christian life. It is a time for the entire church, neophyte and faithful, to reflect upon the Easter gospels, to live their paschal commitment with renewed vigor, and to process in joy to the Easter table. Eucharist, as the living presence of the risen Christ, is our prime focus. The eucharists of the Easter season help us remember and bring into the present the Christ who appeared on the road to Emmaus in the breaking of the bread, the Christ who appeared to believers to dispel the doubts of Thomas, and the Shepherd Christ who lays down his life for the church. Jesus appears to the apostles in the Easter season in the form of a meal. "The roots of the Christian Eucharist lie not only in the last supper, but in the meals which the Risen One celebrated with his disciples in the Easter season."[21]

Through the eucharist, we fully live the paschal mystery. St. Augustine asserted that we are to become that which we eat: the Body of Christ. During the Easter season we enter the mystery unfolding in our lives. (One meaning of the word mystery is "that which is unfolding in our midst.") We are challenged from the opening moments of the liturgy (Opening Prayer) to reflect on the mystery we celebrate with enthusiastic joy:

> God our Father, creator of all,
> today is the day of Easter joy.
> This is the morning on which the Lord appeared to men

who had begun to lose hope
and opened their eyes to what the scriptures foretold:
that first he must die, and then he would rise
and ascend into his Father's glorious presence.
May the risen Lord
breathe on our minds and open our eyes
that we may know him in the breaking of bread. . . .[22]

The liturgies of Easter demand mystagogical reflection (*breathe on our minds and open our eyes*) not only for the neophytes, but for the faithful as well. They ask: What does it mean to live the *unfolding mysteries* of our sacramental life? What does it mean to be people of the water, light, word, cross, garment, oil, bread, and wine? This is not just the task of the newly baptized Catholic Christian. It is the task of the entire church. Just as the lenten church entered the womb of penitence, so too the Easter church enters into the new birth of mystagogical reflection.

The neophytes are a sign of the new life of Easter. As they begin the period of mystagogia, they are a symbol of Easter life. They sit in our midst, perhaps vested in their baptismal garments, and are a living sign of the unfolding mystery of Christ's death and resurrection. These new Christians, who died to the old leaven and rose again to the new leaven of Christ in the eucharist (alternative second reading), remind us that we are to continue in the struggle between life and death. Eucharist strengthens us for the struggle.

The neophytes spend the weeks of Easter growing in the paschal mystery through meditation on the gospel (RCIA, #244).

> How do these Easter scriptures help me experience the risen Christ in my daily effort to die and rise with Christ?

Through sharing in the eucharist and doing works of charity, neophytes grow in the newness of the life they have just received.

> How am I growing through my participation in the eucharist and the giving of myself in the spiritual and corporal works of

---

[20]*Pesachim* 10.5; and Melito of Sardis, *On Pascha* 68 (Sources Chretiennes 123, p. 96, Paris: 1942), in *ME*, 91, #2.
[21]*PNL*, 23.

---

[22]Easter Sunday: "Opening Prayer," *The Sacramentary.*

mercy? How does the eucharist enlighten my understanding of the Scriptures? (RCIA, #246)

Are these not questions we should all be asking if we wish to grow in the Christian life? Is this not the agenda of the Easter Vigil and the entire Easter season?

For the neophyte, the period of mystagogia is a time for unpacking the sacramental mysteries experienced in baptism, confirmation, and eucharist at the Easter Vigil and eucharist during the masses of the Easter season. It is a time to delve deeply into the symbols of the Vigil, to name the experience, and to discover the meaning and the challenge for the Christian life. Easter, then, is a time to lavishly feast and crack open the symbols of bread, wine, oil, water, garment, cross, and light.

The season is a single period of celebration, culminating with the feast of the Holy Spirit given to the church on Pentecost. The *Great Fifty Days of Easter* give ample time and expression to the mystery of Christ's death, ascension, and resurrection. We meditate on what it means to be Easter people. During these fifty days the church commemorates the fruits of Jesus' death and resurrection just as Israel celebrated the first fruit of the harvest during its fifty-day Pentecost feast. Today begins a fifty-day meditation on the wonders of Jesus' saving event and the life and witness of the early church.[23]

The Easter Sunday Liturgy

The readings today are the same for all three cycles. The mass is filled with the joy of the resurrection. It begins in exultation with the words: "The Lord has risen indeed, Alleluia!" Today's opening prayer is an adaptation from the old Gelasian Sacramentary. "*Deus, qui hodierna die,*" the original Latin beginning words, highlight the understanding of *day* in the liturgical sense. The concept of *this day* (also in the responsorial psalm) is important to all liturgical celebration, as it is truly on this Easter day (Easter Vigil and entire season)

that we especially remember the saving event of Jesus' *pasch*. After our forty days of prayer, fasting, and almsgiving, we rise to new life with Christ. The prayers of the liturgy (Opening Prayer—"may we rise again"—and the second reading from Colossians 3: "You have been raised in company with Christ") remind us that through the liturgy we commemorate and share in Jesus' death and resurrection. The responsorial psalm, Psalm 118, is a fitting song of praise to ring in this feast of victory. The second song devoted to the joy of Easter faith is the Easter Sequence: *Victimae Paschali Laudes* ("Praises to the Paschal Victim").[24]

This is the only time of the year when the church experiences the life of the early church through the readings of the Acts of the Apostles. The Acts of the Apostles reads like an adventure-filled novel and is enacted in every community that strives to live the Easter kerygma. In the first reading from Acts, Peter confesses faith in the death and resurrection of Christ. Both choices for the second reading take us to the next step: our moral response. How will we behave, act, and live as people who are incorporated into Jesus' death and resurrection? The gospel from John is the story of the first Christian witness of the resurrection. The Beloved Disciple witnessed to the resurrection without seeing the event himself. Easter is a call for all people to believe without seeing and to go and witness it to the world.

The first Easter preface also refers to "this day" and stresses the victory of Jesus through the sacrifice of his death. The passover images from the Easter Vigil are strong in the preface and remind us that it is "the true Lamb who took away the sins of the world," who offered us redemption and forgiveness of sins.

The church is so insistent on the primacy of the Easter Vigil that it instructs its priests to preach on the unity of the redemptive paschal mystery and on the primacy of the Easter Vigil in the liturgical

---

[23]Please refer to the Easter season overview for a brief history of the Easter Sunday celebration. The gospel from the Easter Vigil is also an option for Easter Sunday morning. Afternoon masses on Easter Sunday may use Luke 13–35.

[24]On Easter Sunday the sequence is sung after the second reading and before the gospel. There are presently only four assigned sequences for the liturgy: Easter Sunday—*Victimae Paschali Laudes* ("Praises to the Paschal Victim"), Pentecost—*Veni Sancte Spiritus* ("Come, Holy Spirit"), Corpus Christi—*Lauda Sion* ("Praise Zion"), Feast of Our Lady of Sorrows—*Stabat Mater* ("The Mother Stood").

year on Easter Sunday.[25] Since many people do not attend the Easter Vigil, the church wishes that we be brought into the annual remembrance of Christ's saving event so explicitly encountered in the Vigil liturgy.

The Easter Vigil and Easter Sunday end with the solemn blessing. This solemn blessing asserts an important sacramental reality. The last part of the blessing reminds us of what it is we are to keep in mind at every liturgy. We feast at this banquet, while awaiting the final, glorious banquet with Christ in the hereafter.

The Triduum is brought to a close with the celebration of vespers on Easter Sunday night.

Gospel Exegesis

The facilitator gives input regarding what critical biblical scholarship has to say about this text. The input includes insights as to how people would have heard the gospel in Jesus' time.

Mary Magdalene enters the tomb, finds it empty, and runs to tell Peter that the Lord's body has been stolen. There is not a hint that she suspects Jesus was raised from the dead. Peter and the Beloved Disciple come to the tomb. The Beloved Disciple enters, sees the burial cloths, and believes. Peter does not believe, but his lack of faith is explained away as lack of understanding: he does not yet understand the scripture in relation to this event.

The two men are needed at the tomb because two witnesses are required to authenticate an event. Women were not acceptable witnesses. Thus, John "places the discovery of the empty tomb by men alongside its discovery by a woman or women. The one confirms the testimony of the other."[26] The cloths were perceived as proof of the resurrection. No one would steal a body by first unwrapping it. Even though grave robbing was a common problem, and even if the disciples had stolen the body (as they were accused of doing), no one would have unwrapped the body. The wrappings left on the floor seemed to suggest a new reality. The per-

son inside those cloths had simply dematerialized, leaving the cloths in place as if his body had simply vanished. "His corpse has not been resuscitated; he has been transformed from mortal to immortal."[27]

Raymond Brown offers a different perspective regarding Jesus' burial wrappings. He suggests that they reflect typical Johannine symbolism. Lazarus came forth from the tomb bound from head to foot. Jesus also was bound from head to foot—just as Lazarus was bound. Lazarus was merely resuscitated, however. He would die again—a natural death in which he would be wrapped for burial a second and final time. The wrappings left by Jesus served as a reminder to the disciples that Jesus would never die again; he rose to eternal life. The disciples did not understand the meaning and implications of the resurrection. They would only come to understand when the scriptures were explained to them.[28]

This story does not set out to prove the resurrection. The New Testament had no need to prove it. This is more a story of faith. There was nothing that could be proved from the evidence of the empty tomb and the left-behind burial cloths. None of it made any sense until Jesus began to appear to the disciples after the resurrection.

The Beloved Disciple enters the tomb and believes without seeing. The Disciple is both an authentic witness of the resurrection event and a model believer for all those generations of people who will also believe without seeing Jesus.

The tomb is no proof of the resurrection. Mary Magdalene did not run off to tell Peter that Jesus was raised from the dead. She thought someone had stolen his body! The entire resurrection account is intended to prove that this man Jesus, whom they knew well, died on a cross and was raised from the dead. Without the cross there was no resurrection. Without the resurrection there was no gospel, no two-thousand year history. The resurrection was understood in the New Testament as the "climactic achievement in the saving deeds of God."[29] Yet John's gospel does not place

---

[25]*LY*, 83–84.
[26]*RJ*, 249.

[27]Ibid., 250.
[28]*RCE*, 69.
[29]*DOB*, 733.

350

the full meaning of Easter at the tomb. Jesus' mission is completed only when he returns to his Father in glory and the Spirit is sent upon the earth. Thus we must look at Easter Sunday with an eye toward Ascension and Pentecost.

Jesus' life and death were redemptive because they were a sign of victory over death. It takes great faith to believe in the resurrection. The disciples did not believe in the resurrection until the risen Lord himself appeared to them. They would not understand the scriptures in regard to his resurrection until Jesus' glorification. The resurrection had to be accepted on faith and on the word of Christian witnesses. The same is true today. During the Easter season the church enters into Jesus' dying and rising, the paschal mystery. We are to give Christian witness to the saving deeds of the Lord. Are we unbelieving, yet chosen for God's mission, like Peter? Or are we like the Beloved Disciple, who believes without seeing for himself and yet cannot contain the power of what he did not see?

Proclaim the gospel again.

Sometimes we gain new insights when we hear the text after the interpretation has been given. Someone from the group proclaims the gospel a second time.

STEP 4
TESTING

Conversation with the Liturgy and the Scriptures

Test your original understanding in dialogue with the text.

(You might consider breaking into smaller groups.)

Are there any new or renewed insights in today's readings or liturgy? How does your original understanding of Easter, the gospel, readings and themes, compare with what was just shared? How does this story speak to your life?

Sharing Life Experience

Participants share an experience from their lives that connects with the biblical interpretation just shared.

I am reminded of so many stories of death and resurrection, not only in my own life, but in the life of our friends (who are like family), and in the life of our parish community. I am reminded of our dearest friend who, at age forty-five, was involved in a life-and-death struggle because his five-year-old's mumps had ended up in the lungs. I remember our prayerful vigil as we stood the death watch in the early morning hours, praying that God would heal him. Like Lazarus, Dan was resuscitated. I also remember the time four months later when my husband's ruptured appendix put him at that same door. There was the same vigil, prayer, and death watch. And again, like Lazarus and Dan, Bob was resuscitated. But I also remember nineteen-year-old Adam, my son's best friend, who was killed in a car accident. I remember Jackie, a forty-year-old friend in the parish who died unexpectedly. I also remember the mother who never recovered from the death of her young daughter fifteen years ago. In addition, this past summer she lost her husband and almost lost her will to live. I remember the pain we felt when a young man took his own life. God did not, like Lazarus, resuscitate them. Our hope sustains us, however, as we envision them ushered to the exalted throne of the Savior, where weeping and tears are no more. We know the power of the resurrection when we see our community being the loving presence of Christ to those who suffer.

Death and resurrection—resurrection and death. In the midst of our joy and sorrow the Spirit of God is present. Jesus reigns from his throne, but not like some lofty, aloof, disinterested ruler. He resides in glory so that his resurrected presence, the Holy Spirit, might stand with us at our vigils and death watches, lament with us in our grief, and sing with us in our joy.

When a baby in our midst suffers from a rare disease that threatens his year-old life and our catechumens ask why God permits such suffering, we are brought to this day, this Easter day. It is this special day that gives us hope in the worst of circumstances and allows us to celebrate in the most graced of circumstances. Suffering and death are mysteries, the depths of which we will never fully plumb. Yet, this day is the day that gives us hope. Death is never final—no matter how hopeless things appear to be, death will not have the last word. This is why Jesus reigns triumphant. He paid the price and today we reap the benefits. This is our Easter faith. We are called to be the weeping, consoling Christ with those who mourn. We are to stand the vigils and keep the watches, and in so doing offer Easter joy to a suffering world. Easter calls us to live the paschal mystery—to embrace death and resurrection. When we lay down our lives for the world's suffering, the poor, and the lost and alienated, this is the day that reminds us that we will take them up again—we will be raised! It is our hope; it is our common calling!

All share their life experience.

What was John's message to the early Christian community in the first reading? What was he trying to tell his community? What does he have to say to our community and to me today? How are we challenged to be re-created (*biblical theme of creation*), to enter more fully into relationship with God (*covenant*), to live in Christian community (*community*), and to die and rise (*exodus*)? In what way have I/we known death/resurrection in my/our experience and understanding of this gospel? How is God speaking to us as a community and how are we challenged? What is our collective and personal response to all of the above questions?

STEP 5
DECISION

The gospel demands a response.

In what concrete way does this liturgy call our parish to action in the church, parish, neighborhood, or world? Has this conversation with the exegesis of this Easter liturgy changed or stretched my personal attitudes? What is one specific action I/we will take this week as a response to what was learned and shared today?

DOCTRINAL ISSUES

What church truth/teaching/doctrinal issue could be drawn from the gospel for Easter Sunday?

Participants suggest possible doctrinal themes that flow from the readings.

Possible Doctrinal Themes

Paschal mystery, resurrection, eucharist, baptism, confirmation, symbols: bread, water, oil, Christian witness

Present the doctrinal material at this time.

1. The facilitator gives input on a particular doctrinal issue of his/her prior choosing. OR
2. The group chooses a doctrinal issue from the list they created. They read together from the Doctrinal Appendix.

(The doctrinal issues are found in the Doctrinal Appendix in the back of this workbook. If you are choosing an issue from this resource, please refer to it now.)

Reflection questions centered around the chosen doctrinal theme can be found at the end of each topic in the Doctrinal Appendix. The questions are based on the five-step reflection process. If you choose a topic not included in the Doctrinal Appendix, craft your own questions according to the same five-step process.

Following the reflection questions you will be reminded to return to chapter 7, "Preparing the Catechetical Session," to assist you in crafting your own session.

Closing Prayer

May almighty God bless you on this solemn feast of Easter, and may he protect you against all sin.
  Response: Amen.

Through the resurrection of his Son,
God has granted us healing.
May he fulfill his promises,
and bless you with eternal life.
  Response: Amen.

You have mourned for Christ's sufferings;
now you celebrate the joy of his resurrection.
May you come with joy to the feast which
lasts forever.
  Response: Amen.[30]

---

[30]Easter Sunday, "Solemn Blessing," *The Sacramentary.*

SECOND SUNDAY OF EASTER

Environment

Refer to Easter Sunday.

INTRODUCTORY RITES

Entrance Antiphon (or Opening Song)

Like newborn children you should thirst for milk,
on which your spirit can grow to strength, alleluia.
(1 Pt 2:2)[1]

Opening Prayer

*The facilitator of the session may lead the prayer. Others
in the group may be asked to proclaim the readings.*

Rite of Sprinkling

Dear friends,
this water will be used
to remind us of our baptism.
Let us ask God to bless it
and keep us faithful
to the Spirit he has given us.
Lord God almighty,
hear the prayers of your people:
we celebrate our creation and redemption.
Hear our prayers and bless + this water
which gives fruitfulness to the fields,
and refreshment and cleansing to man.
You chose water to show your goodness
when you led your people to freedom
through the Red Sea
and satisfied their thirst in the desert
with water from the rock.
Water was the symbol used by the prophets
to foretell your new covenant with man.
You made the water of baptism holy
by Christ's baptism in the Jordan:
by it you give us a new birth
and renew us in holiness.
May this water remind us of our baptism,
and let us share the joy

of all who have been baptized at Easter.
We ask this through Christ our Lord.
(When salt is mixed with the holy water:)
Almighty God,
we ask you to bless + this salt
as once you blessed the salt scattered over the
    water
by the prophet Elisha.
Wherever this salt and water are sprinkled,
drive away the power of evil,
and protect us always
by the presence of your Holy Spirit.
Grant this through Christ our Lord.
(After the sprinkling:)
May almighty God cleanse us of our sins,
and through the eucharist we celebrate
make us worthy to sit at his table
in his heavenly kingdom.[2]

LITURGY OF THE WORD

The readings are proclaimed.

First Reading[3]
Acts 4:32–35

*(Refer to Easter Sunday for an overview of the Acts of the
Apostles.)*

Today's Pericope: In the Acts of the Apostles Luke
depicts a community that goes about the business
of proclaiming the one who came to proclaim the
kingdom. Followers of Christ became a community. Acts is a saga of their lives and mission. This
section of the Acts of the Apostles, part of the sec-

---

[1]Second Sunday of Easter: "Entrance Antiphon," *The
Sacramentary.*

[2]"Rite of Blessing and Sprinkling Holy Water," *The Sacramentary.*

[3]The exegesis for the first and second readings may or
may not be the focus of your group's reflection, as there may
only be time to give adequate attention to the gospel, your
primary concern. However, the exegesis is included here in
order to provide a thorough investigation of the entire liturgy
of the Word as there may be parts (or all) that would be essential to the direction you wish to take with your particular ministry group.

ond "summary," addresses the community's possession of goods and property. The summaries of Acts demonstrate how the Christian community was indeed growing in the life of their risen Lord and growing together as a community. The summaries held up an ideal. "Highly idealized and idyllic presentations, the summaries featured the community as a closely knit group that shared goods and talents in common, gathered around the Twelve for liturgical and catechetical nourishment, and steadily increased in number."[4]

Today's pericope is an example of just how radical a Christian community is called to become. The narrator in today's pericope also addresses the theme of unity. This theme is expressed through the way in which the community's goods are distributed.[5] This is a recurring theme in Acts, as it already surfaced in the discussion of the community's life in chapter 2. The apostles have direct involvement in distributing the goods of the community. When property is sold the apostles divide the proceeds. The apostles administer the needs of the entire community. They realize in chapter 7, however, that there is a breakdown in the system so they enlist the aid of the seven to assist them in their task of management of their community's affairs. It is a shared responsibility. There is not an attempt to suggest that only the Twelve could administer the necessary provisions for the community. In actuality it was far too massive a responsibility for them. Tannehill suggests that it is probably very significant that Paul, Stephen, Philip, and Barnabas are given direct responsibility for the distribution of resources even though they are primarily preachers of the Word.[6] Thus, it is important to note that "the leading preachers gave active support to this important feature of the church's life."[7]

The Spirit inspired the speaking in verse 31 of today's pericope as evidenced by the emphasis on Jesus' resurrection (33). Their preaching fits a previous narrative, including the Pentecost speech in which Jesus was referred to as the originator of life and the one whom God raised to life from death. In this Temple speech the apostles made particular reference to the resurrection, which raised the angst of the Sadducees and authorities in the Temple. The apostles would not yield to their threats or be thwarted in their preaching ministry. They continued "with renewed power the proclamation that provoked their opponents."[8]

While the exhortation to share all things in common is presented as an ideal to be achieved, it is not necessarily a legal obligation. Luke demonstrates this principle with two examples. In later verses he tells the story of the Levite who sold his property and gave all the proceeds to the apostles to distribute as they deemed necessary. The second example Luke presented was that of Ananias and Sapphira. They also sold property but they only gave a portion to the apostles, claiming that they had in fact given the entire proceeds. Their gift was an abomination because they lied to God. The sin was not against the community but against God. The harsh punishment they received (they both fell down and died) was a result of their own greed as they were not obliged to sell their property and give the money to the community. They were free to do whatever they wanted with the money. To give of one's possessions and wealth to the Church has always been and always is a free decision on the part of the giver. The Spirit of God may etch the responsibility on a person's heart, but with that the Spirit will give the strength to joyfully carry out the responsibility.

Another challenge inherent in Luke's perspective is the right attitude toward goods and money. Money has the potential to create barriers. God blesses humanity with the resources necessary for a full and significant life to be enjoyed by all. "No one is the proprietor, in the strict sense, even of his or her legitimately owned goods, but merely their manager."[9]

The Book of Acts is a reminder that as brothers and sisters we are in solidarity with one another—rich and poor alike are created equally in the eyes of God. The surplus of the rich is intended to alleviate the suffering of the less advantaged. The

[4]*WWC*, 167.
[5]*NULA* (II), 77.
[6]Ibid.
[7]Ibid., 78.

[8]Ibid.
[9]*DL* (III), 97.

community of today's reading could boast that there was no one among them who suffered for lack of the necessary provisions of life. "A community would not be worthy of the name if some of its members lived in plenty while others lacked necessities."[10] Christians are to demonstrate their faith in the living Christ and one way to do that is through a proper attitude toward wealth and the riches of this world. The community in Acts gives us an example of what the world would be like if we truly shared our resources in common. The sharing of our resources is not done out of a sense of obligatory justice but it is done because of our love for God and our faith in the resurrected living Christ. Communal living (*koinonia*) flowed out of a deep, abiding relationship with the risen Christ, and through Christ with the Father. They could do no less than share themselves with others—it was a "natural consequence of their unity of heart and purpose."[11] Biblical justice (*hesed*) demands that we act justly and righteously toward one another because it is what God wants of us. When we love God with our entire hearts, evidence of that love will pour out in our behavior toward others. Those who are less fortunate will be cared for. In other words, we will behave justly toward our brothers and sisters out of our love for God—because God wills it. (Refer to the Glossary for more information on biblical justice.) Reginald Fuller insists that this early Christian communism was not based on an economic doctrine but on Christian agape.[12]

Questions for Mystagogical Reflection: In what way does this reading from the Acts of the Apostles invite participation in the paschal mystery of Christ? In what way might this reading challenge contemporary communities? How might an ancient community that shared all things in common have something to speak to our modern-day experience? How could that ancient experience ever work today? If not taken literally, what might we do to embrace the spirit of Luke's intention in writing the summaries in the first place? How does this reading invite us into the cycle of death and resurrection? How does this reading invite transformation in me? Where are the areas of my life that need to be challenged by this scripture?

---

[10]Ibid.
[11]*WWC*, 167.
[12]*PL*, 258.

Responsorial Psalm
Psalm 118:2–4, 13–15, 22–24

Psalm 118 is perhaps the oldest Old Testament scripture appropriated by the Christian community in reference to the death and resurrection of Christ. Christ is the stone once rejected, but who now is the cornerstone. It is a typical "no-yes" pattern used in scripture. "[T]he death of Jesus as Israel's (and all humanity's) no to Jesus, and the resurrection as God's vindication of him, his yes to all that Jesus had said and done and suffered during his earthly life."[13]

Second Reading
1 John 5:1–6

(Please refer to the Feast of the Holy Family for an overview of the Johannine letters.)

Today's Pericope: John's community experienced intense conflicts and struggles, even within their own group. There were two conflicting interpretations of the Christ-event as described in the fourth gospel. There were two factions within the Johannine group, each with differing views. One group eventually broke away from the Johannine community. The points of disagreement centered around the exceptional role of Jesus, the moral responsibility of the Christian community, the role of the Spirit, and eschatology. Those who eventually broke away did not believe in the incarnation of Christ or in the ethical demands of caring for one another. John insisted that to love God and hate one's neighbor is incongruent, an impossibility. Anyone who says otherwise is a liar. The "Antichrists" did boast of a relationship with God, but that was as far as it went. The secessionists were referred to as Antichrists and the letters were intended to help the rest of the community recognize their false teaching.

The author of today's reading exhorts the community members to remain steadfast in their baptismal profession and to live the imperatives of the commandment to love God and one another. Today's reading is connected to the paschal theme of baptism. "Jesus is Christ (Messiah)" is the baptismal profession of faith. Through baptism we be-

---

[13]Ibid.

come God's children. As God's children we can do no less than love God with our whole heart, soul, and being and to extend that love to one another.

Typical of the Johannine school the author adds another theme. Baptism empowers the baptized to overcome the world. "World" for John is the unbelieving world that is against God and that resides in the darkness of sin and death. John boldly asserts that Christian faith has the power to overcome such opposition. The faith John refers to is a deep relationship with the living God; it is not a set of precepts, but a living, loving relationship— "not a dogmatic system but an existential trust in Jesus Christ as the Son of God, the revelation of God's saving love."[14] The victory over faithlessness is found when one embraces the salvation wrought by God through his Son, Jesus Christ.

John drives his point home with greater force in the final paragraph of today's reading when he speaks of the Spirit, water, and blood. There is a polemic argument being made here against those who insist that Jesus came only through water (a reference to Jesus' baptism), not through water and blood. Blood was a reference to his crucifixion. There were false teachers around at the time of the writing of this letter who asserted that Christ was baptized, but not crucified. Gnostics of the day asserted that Christ was nothing more than a mere mortal, and that the divine Christ came down upon him at his baptism and left him again before he was crucified. The secessionists did not accept the truth and reality of Jesus Christ. They did not accept that Christ is the eternal Word of God; thus, their professed faith in him was nothing more than hypocrisy. Further proof of their hypocrisy was their behavior and lack of love shown toward one another. The heretics left the community, thereby affirming the conclusion that they really did not love God after all, and thus were not begotten of God.

John insists that a true believer is in command of this world, that is, in command of the unbelievers of this world. Christ was born of water and the Spirit; Christ is a martyr for the world. Thus Christians can be confident that they, too, as God's children, can endure and conquer all adversity.

---

[14]Ibid., 2.

Questions for Mystagogical Reflection: How does John's letter invite deeper participation in the paschal mystery of Christ? What does it mean to you that Christ was of water and blood? How does that truth speak to the church in this Easter season? How does John's intention in writing this letter speak to the church today? What forces of heresy do we have to counter in our modern culture? What seemed to be the greatest issue for the Johannine community? How does this letter challenge your parish community today? Where is the good news? How does it invite change in your life?

The gospel is proclaimed.

Gospel[15]
John 20:19–31. Eight days later Jesus came and stood in their midst.

STEP 1
NAMING ONE'S EXPERIENCE

What were your first impressions? What was your first response to the gospel (or the other readings)?[16] What captured your attention?

Each person names his or her initial impression. Statements should be brief. No reasons should be given at this time. All simply listen without agreeing or disagreeing.

STEP 2
UNDERSTANDING

In a brief statement, explain what you think this gospel is trying to convey.

---

[15]The gospel exegesis is provided later in this session so that it may be presented in the proper sequence where it occurs in the adult five-step reflection process. The exegesis is provided for the first and second readings for your information and edification and for you to use at your discretion. Once again, the gospel is the primary source of reflection. If there is time for reflection on the other readings, all the better.

[16]The primary focus of reflection is the gospel. However, often the other readings demand attention and must be brought into the dialogue.

Liturgical Context[17]

The liturgies of the Sundays of Easter are centered around the unity of the paschal mystery: the death, resurrection, and ascension of Jesus and the sending of the Spirit. This fourfold reality is the focus of mystagogical reflection during the Easter season.

The readings of the Easter liturgies are chosen to reflect the spirit and heart of the season.

> The first reading is from the Acts of the Apostles, arranged in a three-year cycle of parallel and progressive selections. Thus the life, growth, and witness of the early Church are presented every year.

> The selections from the writings of the apostles are year A, First Letter of Peter; year B, First Letter of John; year C, the Book of Revelation. These texts seem most appropriate to the spirit of the Easter season, a spirit of joyful faith and confident hope.[18]

The gospel for the second Sunday of Easter every year is the same and the first two readings vary according to the cycle. Today's gospel relates the only official appearance of the risen Christ to the apostles. Today's pericope is also the conclusion of the gospel of John, "written so that we might believe and, through faith, that we might have eternal life" (20:31).[19]

John's intention in the final chapters of his gospel is to define paschal faith. He wants his readers to understand that even if seeing is believing, not seeing and believing opens a person to a myriad of hidden truths. Those of us left to live the paschal faith in the messianic age are called to be-lieve with new eyes. The early disciples had to move from their actual experience of the human Jesus, to radical faith in the resurrected, glorified Jesus, who now lives in the presence of the Spirit in the church.

During Easter we are reminded that we have died with Christ and rise again to new life with him through our baptism. We are sprinkled with the waters of baptism in order to remember and call forward our own baptism. We are reminded that through baptism we participate in Jesus' paschal mystery.

In the opening prayer of today's liturgy (the closing prayers for this session), we ask to share God's mercy and life. Christians wash away sins in the water of baptism, are given new birth in the Holy Spirit, and are redeemed by the blood of Christ. Our primary focus during the Easter season is to immerse ourselves in the paschal mystery. The opening prayer reflects this paschal faith and life.

> Let us pray
> (for a deeper awareness of our Christian
>   baptism)
> God of mercy,
> you wash away our sins in water,
> you give us new birth in the Spirit,
> and redeem us in the blood of Christ.
> As we celebrate Christ's resurrection
> increase our awareness of these blessings,
> and renew your gift of life within us.[20]

We are called to be Easter people—people of the Word and people of the eucharist. The disciples in today's reading from the Acts of the Apostles are the epitome of Easter faith. They gathered to pray, to worship, to listen to the apostles' instruction, and to break the Bread of Life. They lived their Easter faith—they were a new creation in Christ and many were added to their number through the example of their lives. They were living their baptismal faith. We are those people.

> Lord,
> through faith and baptism
> we have become a new creation.

---

[17]The scriptures in the Lectionary, the seasons of the year, and the ritual prayers of the mass are interrelated and form the basis for liturgical catechesis. The *liturgical context* attempts to explore and clarify the themes and this interrelatedness.

[18]Lectionary: Introduction, Ch. 2, #IV, 14, #1, p. 13.

[19]*DL* (III), 84.

---

[20]Second Sunday of Easter: "Opening Prayer," *The Sacramentary.*

Accept the offerings of your people
(and of those born again in baptism)
and bring us to eternal happiness.[21]

During Easter we meditate on what it means to be that new creation—to live paschal faith. Through baptism we died to sin and have been resurrected to new life. There are implications. Christian living brings hardships and trials. Today's reading from the first letter to Peter alludes to it. Paschal faith requires that we believe in Christ simply on his word and invitation. Paschal faith demands that we confess that faith, even if it leads to the cross, *especially* if it leads to the cross. Paschal faith also demands that we lay down our lives for one another. Neophytes (as well as the faithful) are to be strengthened by the eucharist they celebrate and they, in turn, are to become the eucharist they receive.

Thus, the period of mystagogy necessarily includes meditation on the Easter gospels and living the charity demanded by the gospel. Easter is the time for neophyte and faithful to celebrate the saving deeds of God in the midst of the Christian community. How has God called our community to transformative faith and life? Easter is the time to witness to God's marvelous deeds. How are we telling our corporate and personal stories of death and resurrection?

The Easter sacraments, especially the eucharist, are the way in which we fully participate in Jesus' paschal mystery. Jesus appears to his disciples on the first day of the week. It is the day in which Christians gather to experience Jesus in the eucharist—both his real presence and his concealed presence. John's community was struggling with what it meant to live as Easter people in the reality of Christ's non-immanent return. They, too, celebrated the presence of Jesus in the eucharist: not only bread eucharist, but the eucharist of service (foot washing). Just as Christ beckoned Thomas to embrace a committed faith, eucharist is our similar invitation. "May the Easter sacraments we have received live forever in our minds and hearts" (prayer after communion). Jesus is both hidden and present in the eucharist. Like Thomas, we are

called to choose. When we fully commit, we are able to come before Christ in the eucharist and profess, "My Lord and My God!" Eucharist strengthens our doubting faith and helps us believe without seeing.

Today's gospel has a eucharistic theme. The double appearance of the risen Christ on the first day of the week has liturgical overtones. The first day of the week is the day Christians gather to celebrate the eucharist, the ultimate celebration of Christ's presence during his absence. "'He comes' in the midst of his own, but under signs that both reveal and conceal him. Only faith can perceive his presence."[22]

Gospel Exegesis

The facilitator provides input from critical biblical scholarship on this text. This input includes insights as to how people would have heard the gospel in Jesus' time.

Today's two post-resurrection appearances of Jesus are read every year throughout all three cycles. Jesus offers his peace, faith, the gift of the Holy Spirit, and a lasting legacy of his merciful forgiveness. He appears first on Easter night, and then a week later. Luke did not relate Jesus' resurrection, ascension, and Pentecost as a one-time event. He extended it over a period of time in order to lead and guide his community to a deeper faith. John's portrayal is probably more accurate: Jesus bestowed the Spirit and commissioned his disciples on the same day. According to Charles Talbert, one purpose of this resurrection account is to show that Jesus is alive and to offer further instructions to the disciples.[23]

A few verses before this pericope, Jesus encountered Mary Magdalene standing beside the tomb. She did not recognize him at first glance. We are led to understand that something has changed; Jesus is different. "In his new identity, Jesus is no longer subject to the constraints of space and time."[24] Today's gospel continues to portray Jesus in his new, altered state. He appears in the midst of the Twelve. There is no question that it is Jesus;

[21]Second Sunday of Easter: "Prayer Over the Gifts," *The Sacramentary.*

[22]*DL* (III), 90.
[23]*RJ*, 253.
[24]*JGNP,* 71.

he identifies himself by showing his hands and his side. His body is still real, though changed. Mary Magdalene in earlier verses was told not to touch him. Jesus passed through his shroud and through doors, but he could still be seen with the human eye. Talbert asserts that Jesus continues in his incarnation even after the resurrection, albeit in a different corporeal form.[25] "The incarnation did not cease with the cross and the tomb; it continues even now in transcendental glory."[26]

Jesus first greets the disciples with peace (he offers it twice). He then offers them the gift of his Spirit; he commissions them and sends them out to forgive sins. The commission to forgive sins has its implications in the Christian community. Charles Talbert suggests that the forgiveness of sins implies that if disciples forgive the sins of other disciples against them, the community will remain intact. If those sins are not forgiven, then community peace and harmony will be disrupted.[27] The Holy Spirit is therefore given in order to help Christians live the peace Christ bestowed upon them and to empower them for their mission to the world. (Later theologians used the forgiveness text as the primary source for the church's understanding of the sacrament of penance or reconciliation.) The power to forgive one another will be given by the Holy Spirit.

In the same gospel, Jesus appears again, eight days later. This time Thomas is present. Jesus miraculously materializes through the doors. Thomas was given the opportunity to touch Jesus' wounds so he would believe. Thomas needed to be assured that the appearance was indeed the human Jesus he knew.

Thomas's scene is regarded by some scholars as the culminating scene of John's entire gospel. It brings closure and satisfaction. John began his gospel by stating the purpose for its writing: to proclaim Jesus, the incarnate Word of God. All the events of the gospel lead to this point. Thomas, upon seeing Jesus' wounds, acclaims him Lord and God. "Jesus is described as being of the essence of God at the outset of the Gospel, and then, fully twenty chapters later, one of his disci-

ples comes to believe in him fully and affirms him loftily as 'my Lord and my God.'"[28] The last phrase of this gospel is the summary of the purpose of the work: 1. that people may believe in him, and 2. that they may have life.

John strongly connects belief with eternal life. "Yet the consequence of believing is itself of extreme importance for John; this consequence is that his readers have eternal life. The one purpose thus involves the other, for to have eternal life cannot be separated from believing."[29]

Jesus' greeting of peace is significant. Israel believed that the advent of the messianic era would be accompanied by the reign of peace, evidenced by people living in reciprocal covenant relationship with God and one another. Jesus manifested his messianic reign by offering the Holy Spirit to accomplish and realize harmony and peace among God's people. Thus, Jesus' salutation—"Peace!"—functioned as realized eschatology. That is, the promised, future reign of God was at hand in the presence of the Holy Spirit of God. The Spirit who was manifest, dynamic, and active in all of God's acts of salvation is the Spirit offered to the disciples on the day of this gospel event. The same Spirit who presided over the stirring waters at creation is the same Spirit who goes with the disciples in their work of healing the sick, forgiving sins, and announcing the messianic reign of God.

John's agenda was to connect the human Jesus with the divine Jesus. He wanted his readers to fully realize that the Jesus who walked the earth was the Jesus who reigned prior to his earthly life in union with his Father and the Spirit. Plagued by the influence of gnosticism, some in the Johannine church preferred to center on Jesus, the divine-man, wonder-worker, to the exclusion of Jesus, the crucified Lord who was raised and glorified. John's Jesus shows his wounds to Thomas in order to remind the community that Jesus' exalted status has its roots in his humiliating death.

The post-resurrection appearances also serve to strengthen the community in the Lord's absence until he returns in glory for a second time. Jesus'

[25] *RJ*, 253.
[26] *TI*, 382.
[27] *RJ*, 255.

[28] *JGNP*, 72.
[29] Ibid.

healing and forgiving mission will continue until he comes again.

Today's gospel also stresses the journey of faith. Thomas reminds us that doubt sometimes is a precursor of committed faith. Thomas struggled, and in his struggle he embraced a deeper, lasting faith. He did not come to belief because he touched the Lord's wounds. Faith was prompted by Jesus' invitation.

Easter reminds us to persevere in our faith in the Risen One, even though we have not put our hands into his wounds. Today's gospel is a challenge to live in the presence of the abiding Spirit, to forgive one another and to promote the reign of God.

Proclaim the gospel again.

Sometimes we gain new insights when we hear the text after the interpretation is given. Someone from the group proclaims the gospel a second time.

STEP 4
TESTING

Conversation with the Liturgy and the Scriptures

Test your original understanding in dialogue with the text.

(You might consider breaking into smaller groups.)

Now that you've heard the exegesis, were there any new insights? How do you feel about it? How does your original understanding of this gospel compare with what we just shared? How does this story speak to your life?

Sharing Life Experience

Participants share an experience from their lives that connects with the biblical interpretation just presented.

> *Today's Easter readings shout to us about life in the community. We are to forgive one another. We are to preserve unity. We are to share our resources with one another. Our faith in Christ will be evidenced by*

the way we love (or do not love) in the Christian community and in the world. The greatest disgrace in the early Christian community as far as Paul and Luke were concerned was disharmony. Luke insisted that living the paschal life in the midst of the community is witness to the world. Radical Christian behavior calls attention to itself. The world notices when people behave as if "two or more are gathered in his name." What would happen in our world today if we really lived the example of the first reading? CNN would be pounding at our doors to see if we were for real. I attended a conference many years ago and was impressed by one of the parishes in attendance. Their mission was to live in accord with today's first reading from the Acts of the Apostles. No one in the parish ever lacked for any necessary thing—medical needs, food, shelter—all of it was secured by the parish, when the person or family was in need. Mortgages were paid, food purchased, doctor bills were covered when a member of the community was experiencing hard times. Anyone with a need was taken care of by the parish at large. That meant, of course, that the parish looked quite different than most parishes today. There were no paid staff—none. If this were to become widespread practice I would shudder to think how my husband and I would support our family as we both work for the Church. However, the idea is tantalizing. I would like to talk to them now that it is fifteen years later and see how it is working. I do not even remember what state they were from, but I remember how impressed I was with their efforts. While Luke was positing an ideal, there is no doubt so much more we could do to work toward that ideal. I often dream of a church in which unity, sharing, and agape love are the charisms most observed and admired by the outside world. The lack of unity in the wider church today is scandalous.

I recently received a call from an out-of-state friend who was very depressed because of the tremendous discord in her parish. The community is divided by animosities, stubborn pride, and the lack of respect for one another. When I hear stories like that I thank God for my parish community. We are not perfect; we have had our days of struggle in the past, but there is an incredible sense of love and respect for the members of the community. The first thing people notice when they come to the parish is the warmth and the hospitality of our members. We are as diverse as any parish, yet there seems to be a place for everyone.

One of my pastor's greatest gifts is his ability to meet people where they are and to encourage honest, forthright communication and dialogue. He has fostered an atmosphere of common ground and consequently we do not seem to be pulled apart by destroying factions within the community.

Jesus asked his father that "they all may be one." When I invite discord through gossip; when I approach everything that happens in our parish with a suspicious eye (much like the doubting Thomas); when I shut myself off to the movement of the Spirit in my community in often the most surprising places, I tear down rather than build up the people of God. Jesus extended peace and forgiveness. When I let the sun go down on my angers, hurts, and jealousies, I give fertile ground to the destructive forces that divide us.

The Easter paschal life demands that we die and rise. It insists that we profess our faith like the Easter women of the gospels and pray that our doubting, contrary spirits be challenged. Jesus extended peace and forgiveness. I must extend it not only to my parish community, but to my family community as well. When I am in right relationship with my God and living the peace envisioned at the creation of the world, then I will love God with my whole heart. I am to love my neighbors as much as I love myself. There will be evidence of that love from the way I live and minister to the world community. Do I build up or tear down? Do I reach out to the poor, the oppressed, and the marginalized? Today's liturgy demands that I offer shalom peace not only to the communities in which I live but to the global community as well. It is because of the cross and resurrection that I am so empowered.

What was John's message to his community? How does it relate to your community and to you today? Who do you relate to the most in today's gospel? What are the times in your life when you are most like Thomas—Mary Magdalene—the women of the gospels—the apostles—Jesus? How might today's liturgy invite re-creation within yourself and your community (biblical theme of creation)? In what way does today's liturgy express our covenant with God? What are the implications of that covenant? In what way does today's liturgy speak to your community specifically? How does today's liturgy speak to the wider world community? In what way do today's readings invite us to embrace the paschal mystery? What new insight do you take with you as a result of your sharing?

STEP 5
DECISION

The gospel demands a response.

In what concrete way might your parish be invited to respond? Are there any attitudes or behaviors you would like to change as a result of today's conversation? What is one concrete action you will take this week in response to the liturgy today?

In many parishes the Easter season unfortunately ends on the second Sunday of Easter. There are fifty days of feasting in the Easter season. How is your parish feasting? We need to remind ourselves that the entire season *is Easter*. That is why they are called the Sundays of Easter—not after Easter. Are there opportunities offered in your parish for sharing Easter faith? What are the stories of death and resurrection in your community in the past year? Is there any forum for sharing those stories? Have your outreach efforts subsided simply because the season of prayer, fasting, and almsgiving is ended? What are the ongoing structures in your community that promote the *peace* Jesus demands in today's gospel?

Christian Initiation: The liturgy of mystagogia is the Sunday eucharist. The purpose of the Easter season homilies is to crack open the mystery of Easter and the paschal mystery for the entire community. We are all to be engaged in mystagogical reflection—not just the neophytes. The neophytes meet weekly until Pentecost to break open the symbols of the vigil. Thereafter they meet monthly until the anniversary of their initiation. Neophytes continue to be a symbol of Easter life in our midst. Are they included in the prayers of the faithful? Perhaps throughout the Easter season they might wear their baptismal gown and carry their baptismal candle in procession. A special place might be reserved for them in the assembly. What opportunities do you offer them to witness to their faith? Perhaps they might dress the altar and process with the bread and wine, the offering, and the gifts for the poor. Perhaps all who celebrated a sacrament of initiation this year (first communion, confirmation, baptism) might carry their baptismal candle or wear their baptismal garment during mass. (The white communion dress has its roots in the baptismal garment. First communicants are not "brides of Christ.")

DOCTRINAL ISSUES

What Church truth/teaching/doctrinal issue could be drawn from the gospel for the second Sunday of Easter?

Participants suggest possible doctrinal themes that flow from the readings.

Possible Doctrinal Themes

Paschal mystery; baptism; Christology; resurrection; two great commandments—love of God and neighbor; social teaching; justice; faith; symbols of Easter—water, blood; eucharist; moral and ethical teaching; discipleship

Present the doctrinal material at this time.

1. The facilitator gives input on a particular doctrinal issue of his or her prior choosing. OR
2. The group chooses a doctrinal issue from the list they created. They read together from the Doctrinal Appendix or other appropriate, official Church documents and the works of respected theologians.

(Many doctrinal issues are found in the Doctrinal Appendix at the back of this workbook. If you are choosing an issue from this resource, please refer to it now.)

Reflection questions centered around the chosen doctrinal theme can be found at the end of each topic in the Doctrinal Appendix. The questions are based on the five-step reflection process. If you choose a topic not included in the Doctrinal Appendix, craft your own questions according to the same five-step process.

Following the reflection questions you will be reminded to return to chapter 7, "Preparing the Catechetical Session," to assist you in crafting your own session.

Closing Prayer

Let us pray
[as Christians thirsting for the risen life].
Heavenly Father and God of mercy,
we no longer look for Jesus among the dead,
for he is alive and has become the Lord of life.
From the waters of death you raise us with him
and renew your gift of life within us.
Increase in our minds and hearts
the risen life we share with Christ
and help us to grow as your people
toward the fullness of eternal life with you.
Grant this through Christ our Lord.[30]

OR

Let us pray
for a deeper awareness of our Christian baptism

Pause.

God of mercy,
you wash away our sins in water,
you give us new birth in the Spirit,
and redeem us in the blood of Christ.
As we celebrate Christ's resurrection
increase our awareness of these blessings,
and renew your gift of life within us.
We ask this through our Lord
Jesus Christ, your Son,
who lives and reigns with you and the Holy Spirit,
one God for ever and ever.[31]

---

[30]Second Sunday of Easter: "Alternative Opening Prayer," *The Sacramentary.*

[31]Second Sunday of Easter: "Opening Prayer," *The Sacramentary.*

THIRD SUNDAY OF EASTER

Environment

Refer to Easter Sunday.

INTRODUCTORY RITES

Entrance Antiphon (or Opening Song)

Let all the earth cry out to God with joy; glory of his name; proclaim his glorious praise, alleluia. (Ps 66:1–2)[1]

Opening Prayer

The facilitator of the session may lead the prayer. Others in the group may be asked to proclaim the readings.

Let us pray
(in confident peace and Easter hope)

Pause for silent prayer.

Father in heaven, author of all truth,
a people once in darkness has listened to your
    Word
and followed your Son as he rose from the tomb.
Hear the prayer of this newborn people
and strengthen your church to answer your call.
May we rise and come forth into the light of day
to stand in your presence until eternity dawns.
We ask this through Christ our Lord.[2]

LITURGY OF THE WORD

The readings are proclaimed.

First Reading
Acts 3:13–15, 17–19

(Refer to Easter Sunday for an overview of the Acts of the Apostles.)

---

[1]Third Sunday of Easter: "Entrance Antiphon," *The Sacramentary.*

[2]Third Sunday of Easter: "Opening Prayer," *The Sacramentary.*

Today's Pericope: Few exegetes would claim that these are the actual words used by Peter in those early days of the Christian community. Luke uses the speeches in his narrative to posit his theology. They also reflect early Christology as well. Jesus is referred to as "Holy and Righteous." This designation is a reference to Jesus' earthly life and ministry. He is the righteous servant of God. The title "Author of life" is a very ancient Christological term. The etymology of the word *author* comes from the Greek that means "captain" or "leader." Jesus is the new leader, the new captain of life's vessel, who leads the people, just like Moses led the people out of the desert into the Promised Land. Jesus is the new leader/liberator who leads people out of bondage into a new promised land, the messianic reign of God.

Today's reading from Acts follows a typical pattern used by Luke throughout the book. Luke relates a miraculous action, then follows it with a speech. People were attracted to Peter and John because of the mighty deeds they were able to accomplish. It was/is no small feat to cure a lame person. Peter used the event to turn everyone's attention to the power of God.

In the discourse that followed the miraculous cure, Peter preached that the wondrous event was prophesied in scriptures and was the fulfillment of God's plan of salvation. As far as Luke was concerned the miracle was a wonderful vehicle to call people's attention to the marvels of God. However, he considered preaching the Christian kerygma to be of far greater value than the miracles. The miracles point to the one who is the object of the message.

The preaching insists that people turn toward God, that they be totally converted to God. It is the heart of the kerygma. Peter's power to heal does not come from within himself. It comes from the living Christ who empowers him to heal in his name.

Jesus is God's vindicated servant, who sits at the right hand of God. The power to heal is further testimony of God's vindication of Jesus. Jesus was faithful to the end. He was a faithful servant who suffered according to God's holy will. Jesus' resurrection and ascension into glory are proof that sinful people put Jesus to death; that he suffered a martyr's death; and that it was in accord with God's plan of salvation for the entire world. Human beings may have rejected him, but God never rejected him. God upholds his servant and he now sits at God's right hand. Jesus' resurrection is proof that he is truly the Savior of the world. Evidence of Jesus' saving power is found in the miraculous works that continue in his name.

Luke makes the authority and the claim about Jesus as official and important as he can by identifying God as the God of Abraham, the God of Isaac, the God of Jacob, and the God of all our ancestors. It is this very same God who has moved all of salvation history to this moment. Jesus' resurrection was planned by God since the very beginning. It is the fulfillment of God's plan of salvation since the creation of the world. Jesus is the fulfillment of the liberation foreshadowed at the exodus-event. Jesus' death and resurrection now liberate the world from the ravages of sin and death. Peter calls Jesus servant, the Suffering Servant of Isaiah's "Song of the Suffering Servant." Jesus is the one who was foretold in the scriptures. He now sits at God's right hand in glory.

Luke makes excuses for those who put Jesus to death in verse 17. He insists that they did not know any better. They were ignorant of the truth. Those who witness the miracles before them, who see the works performed by the apostles, however, and have heard their preaching can no longer claim ignorance. Peter's preaching mission was one of invitation and exhortation. He invited sinners to repent, believe the good news of Jesus, and make a decision to become disciples of Christ.

Woe be to them who have seen and heard yet have not believed. In other words, there will be no excuse for those who have experienced the power of the risen Christ and still refuse to embrace him as their Lord. By their rejection they condemn themselves. It is on their own heads.

Questions for Mystagogical Reflection: *Have you ever experienced the liberating power of the risen Christ? The healing power of the risen Christ? In what way does this reading invite fuller participation in the paschal mystery of Christ? How does this reading invite transformation in you? In the community?*

Responsorial Psalm
Psalm 4:2, 4, 7–8, 9

Today's psalm is a lament. It is the prayer of a faithful Israelite who calls out for deliverance from his enemies and who is vindicated. Once vindicated, the person is free to sleep peacefully. Obvious connections with Jesus' death and resurrection can be made. Jesus is the Suffering Servant who cried out to the Lord and was delivered from his enemies and ultimately from death itself—the greatest enemy of all time.

Second Reading
1 John 2:1–5

(Please refer to the Feast of the Holy Family for an overview of the Johannine letters.)

Today's Pericope: Many of the Johannine letters were written in response to the Christological debates that were taking place during the time of their writing. (See exegesis for last week's second reading.) The Gnostics believed that good Christians were sinless. Yet no one can argue that sin still exists in the Christian community and that one does not have to go far to find it. However, the power of the resurrection lies in the fact that we have an advocate that pleads our case before God, who intercedes for us before the throne of glory. God was not an angry God who needed to be appeased. Rather, Christ willingly offered the benefits of his death, thereby wiping away and cleansing us of our sins. Christ acts as our advocate before God. He pleads our case.

The author of 1 John called Jesus an "offering" (v. 2) for our sin and that of all the world. The Greek term for *offering* is *hilasmos* and is more properly translated as *expiation* or, as C.H. Dodd has preferred, "disinfection." Even those who *know* God can sin; and knowledge, even absolute knowledge cannot atone for sin. For that reason, sinners need Christ to disinfect them from the taint of sin; by his sacrifice the union between God and those who would know him is restored and strengthened.[3]

The Gnostics believed that since they already "knew" God, there was no need to look at their behavior. They were indifferent and did not see any positive value or salvific value attached to the way one lived (or did not live) the moral life. Their behavior was not necessarily scandalous; they simply saw no connection between salvation and ethical living. They believed that they were already in the ultimate state of union with God, which circumvented the need to observe the commandments. There was no need to ask forgiveness for sin, as they were sinless. They believed that their relationship with Christ earned them the right to be excused from any moral and ethical responsibility.

"Knowing" God has always inferred living in right relationship with God. Right relationship insists that we love God with our entire beings and that our love for God will be evidenced by the way we live the great commandments. Is there evidence of our love for God in the way in which we love others (or do not)? The ancient Semitic understanding of "knowing" was not as we might interpret it today. It is not an intellectual knowing. Knowing involved the entire person—sharing God's life. Sharing in God's life assumes that we follow God's will. It is God's will that we lead moral, ethical lives and that those lives be evidenced by behavior.

Questions for Mystagogical Reflection: In what way does this pericope invite us to enter more fully into the death and resurrection of Jesus? Can you relate to the scriptural understanding of "knowing" God? In what way do you "know" God today? If you were charged with "knowing" God, would there be enough evidence to convict you? How is this reading relevant in today's contemporary church? How does this reading invite change in your life?

The gospel is proclaimed.

Gospel
Luke 24:35–48. Thus it was written that Christ would suffer and rise from the dead on the last day.

---

[3] *WWC*, 170.

STEP 1
NAMING ONE'S EXPERIENCE

What were your first impressions? What was your first response to the gospel (or the other readings)? What captured your attention?

Each person names his or her initial impression. Statements should be brief. No reasons should be given at this time. All simply listen without agreeing or disagreeing.

STEP 2
UNDERSTANDING

In a brief statement, explain what you think this gospel is trying to convey.

STEP 3
INPUT FROM VISION/STORY/TRADITION

Liturgical Context

It is worthy to note that Luke uses the entire twenty-fourth chapter to uncover, break open, and shed light on the mystery of Jesus' Passion, death, and resurrection. Luke's agenda is the agenda of the entire Church during the Easter season. Each year the Church takes time out during the Easter season to reflect on the paschal mystery—to engage in mystagogical reflection. The homilies of the Easter season are intended to crack open that mystery and help the faithful reflect on their own experiences of death and resurrection in light of the Jesus-event.

By sharing the story of Christ and interpreting it in their lives; by offering their fish so the Lord could eat and share his life and word with them, the disciples' eyes were opened. They were transformed. Luke sets forth a pattern of conversion for all of us. The gospel for today's liturgy picks up where the Emmaus story left off. The disciples were engaged in mystagogical reflection on their experience of the risen Lord in the their midst. They had returned to the Jerusalem community and were sharing the Emmaus experience when the Lord appeared to them again and extended peace. Once again Jesus shared a meal with them. Always the postresurrection Christ was present to them as nourishment. It is no accident that his death and resurrection is a remembering that makes the paschal mystery present. We cannot reflect on the paschal mystery without reflecting on the eucharist. Eucharist is our ongoing way of participating in the events of Calvary, the resurrection, and all of Jesus' postresurrection appearances. It is all part of his paschal mystery. We cannot embrace the message of Christ without embracing it all. When we eat the Bread of Life each Sunday we consume the Christ who died, but also the Christ who rose again as well as the Christ who ate and celebrated his way through Galilee with his friends, even after his death—the Christ of abundant life. Eucharist is our celebration and participation in the presence of Christ while he is still absent.

How privileged we are to have been given such food. St. Catherine of Sienna remarked how truly blessed we are that our Lord should love us so much that he gives himself to us as food. Thus, we experience the postresurrection appearances of Christ every time we gather for eucharist. We experience Christ walking along the road and offering us nourishment in the form of fish, conversation, and the offering of "Shalom" every time we gather for Sunday liturgy.

The episode on the road to Emmaus and subsequently in Jerusalem after Emmaus provides the church with a model for what takes place in the catechumenate and in many small Christian communities. Questions are asked, hospitality is extended, stories are told, scripture is shared and interpreted, and peace is offered. Discussion and dialogue invite conversion and transformation. The life of Christ as it is celebrated and proclaimed throughout the liturgical year in the scriptures is the primary formation of catechumens. From that Word flows the primary truths of our faith. The lesson of Emmaus and the post-Emmaus appearance of Christ are important in their formation, for it is through dialogue and reflection on that Word and making it operative in their lives that the catechumens' hearts are opened to recognize and encounter Christ in the breaking of the bread at Easter.

Luke presented the church with a foundational understanding of the eucharist. The eucharist is intimately connected with the paschal mystery of Christ. Eucharist is a remembering, an anamnesis, that brings the Passion-event into the present and makes it real. "It [the liturgy] is concerned with past events, the saving work of Christ, but it is not concerned with them *as past*. It seeks to bring about an encounter between the worshipers and the saving mystery. If an event is to be experienced, it has to be experienced *as present*."[4] When preaching an Ascension homily, St. Leo the Great avowed that Christ's visible suffering and death have become manifest in the sacraments. Our sacraments remember and make present Jesus' life, mission, death, resurrection, ascension into glory, and his sending of the Spirit to the church. Why? So the church of every generation might meet and encounter the risen Christ as they worship. "By the liturgical mystery we are actualizing the past event, making it present so that the saving power of Christ can be made available to the worshiper in the here and now."[5]

Today's pericope cleverly shows us the intimate connection between the liturgy of the Word and the liturgy of the eucharist. On the road to Emmaus the Word prepared the hearts of the disciples to recognize Jesus in the breaking of the bread. "Word and sacrament are not only not mutually exclusive, they are in fact complementary. Augustine's adage still holds: *accedit verbum ad elementum et fit sacramentum* (the word is spoken upon the human reality and it becomes a sacrament) (*In Joann. Ev.* Tr. 80, 3)."[6] The Word proclaimed in liturgy is Christ himself who speaks to us (*Constitution on the Sacred Liturgy, #10*). His self-gift opens our hearts and our eyes to encounter him in the eucharist.

In today's liturgy Jesus shared a eucharistic meal with his disciples on the road. There is evidence in ancient drawings and artwork that fish may have been part of an early eucharistic meal. Jesus multiplied and distributed the fish and the loaves in his earthly life; now he shares another postresurrec-

---

[4]J. D. Chrighton, "A Theology of Worship," *SL*, 14.
[5]Ibid., 15.
[6]Kathleen Cannon, O.P., "Theology of the Word," *NDSW*, 1330.

tion eucharistic meal of fish with his disciples for a second time. It is significant that Jesus asked them to feed him. Perhaps it was a symbolic way to remind the disciples that the ball was now in their court. They were to do what Jesus did. They were to go out and feed others.

In connection with the meal, Jesus taught them the scriptures. He reminds them that what they have experienced is part of the fulfillment of salvation history as foretold in the scriptures. He opened their minds to make the scriptures come alive—to understand them. The liturgy of the Word is intended to prepare us for full participation in the liturgy of the eucharist. Yet, in today's gospel the meal came first. Perhaps the reality is not an either/or proposition—yes, Word prepares for and leads to eucharist. However, today we are provided with an example where Word and eucharist are a circular reality. Yes, the Word prepares our hearts to receive Christ in the eucharist. But also, the eucharist strengthens us and nourishes us so our hearts can be receptive to hear and listen to the Word of God and make it operative in our lives. Both feed and nourish the spirit so we can go out and feed others.

Jesus opened the eyes of his disciples when he shared the scriptures with them. The alternative opening prayer for today's liturgy affirms those who were once in darkness, but because they listened to the Word they followed Christ as he rose from the tomb. The *Word* (Christ) strengthens and empowers Christians to stand firm in the faith and be faithful to God's call. We will then share in the joy of the resurrection that is ours because God has made us his sons and daughters (opening prayer). It is our Easter faith.

The center of today's liturgy is the paschal mystery. It is the central reality of every liturgy, every sacrament, and particularly of the Easter season. The gospel portrays disciples who lost all hope in the mission of Christ. Jesus appeared to them in his risen state but they were unable to recognize him until he took the bread, blessed it, broke it, and gave it to his friends, and in today's gospel, when he shared a meal of fish with them and when he showed them the reality of his human form. Those ritual actions took them back in time and transported their remembering into the present. They

bore the imprint of their Master. The sacrifice of Calvary was an integral part of the remembering. We participate in the mystery of Easter every time we take, bless, break, and share the Body of Christ. We then are taken, blessed, broken, shared, and poured out for the world just as Jesus was and continues to be in his living memorial. Today's liturgy offers consolation to those who have lost all hope, who have forgotten the touch of the Master's hand, and who have given up on life. It is often difficult to believe in the promise of God when our lives are besieged by pain, sorrow, and disappointment. The disciples on the road to the nations are a sign of hope for us. When all seems lost and our dreams are dashed, Christ is there to give us the gift of himself and to offer us Easter joy and to send us out to share it.

This is the *One* of whom we speak today:

> Let me tell you how I came to know him.
> I had heard many speak of him, but had paid
>   no attention.
> Each day he sent me presents, and I never
>   thanked him.
> Often he seemed to want my friendship, but I
>   ignored him.
> I was homeless and miserable and hungry;
> every moment I was in peril:
> he offered me shelter, comfort, food; he
>   guarded me from all danger:
> but I was always ungrateful.
> Finally he met me on the road, and with tears
>   in his eyes,
> he entreated me, saying: "Come and dwell
>   with me."
> Let me tell you how he treats me now:
> He provides all my needs,
> He gives me more than I dare ask;
> He anticipates all my desires,
> He urges me to ask for more;
> He never reminds me of my past ingratitude.
> Never does he reproach me for my past foolishness....
> Let me tell you what I think of him:
> He is as good as he is great,
> He loves me with a love both ardent and true,
> He is as bounteous with promises as faithful to
>   keeping them;
> He is as jealous of my affection as worthy of retaining it.

In everything, I am his debtor, but he wants me to call him "My Friend."[7]

Today's liturgy invites us to see Christ as "Friend"—the One who loved us *unto death*. He is the One who gives us the precious gift of his life. We are to see him with Easter eyes of faith and conform our lives to his as we become immersed in his paschal life. "May we rise and come forth into the light of day to stand in your presence until eternity dawns" (alternative opening prayer).

Gospel Exegesis

The facilitator provides input from critical biblical scholarship on this text. This input includes insights as to how people would have heard the gospel in Jesus' time.

Today's gospel takes us to the tenth and last meal of Luke's story on the genesis of the eucharist. Jesus insisted before he died that he would not eat again until the reign of God had come to fulfillment. Now is the time of fulfillment. Jesus died and rose again, thus inaugurating the new age.

In the story of Emmaus in verses prior to today's pericope (refer to the third Sunday of Easter, Cycle A), Jesus gradually revealed his resurrected presence to his disciples as he shared the scriptures with them and in the breaking of the bread. The community gathered in the house of two disciples and they broke bread and shared reflection on the Word. This is Christian community at its best. "Community faith sharing, an integral aspect of Christian *koinonia*, is absolutely basic for the life of the church."[8]

Today's gospel forms the conclusion to the gospel. It is the last event on the journey that began in 9:51 and was to culminate at the Lord's ascension into glory. Luke's intention is to remind his reader/disciples how the Lord will continue his presence in the community now that he is gone. Of the ten meals Jesus shared with his friends, seven of them were celebrated on the journey. Four of them were eaten on the way to Jerusalem and the Passover (Jesus' last meal) and to the cross. There would be two postresurrection meals.

Today's story continues the Emmaus story. After Emmaus the disciples returned to Jerusalem. There is no longer a focus on individual disciples. Today's pericope is in the context of the gathered community. The segment begins with the disciples engaging in mystagogical reflection on the Emmaus-event. The disciples have now returned to the wider assembled community. Jesus enters the midst of the community and greets them with peace. The corollary of this gospel is John 20:19–23, in which Jesus stands in the midst of the disciples and says, "Peace be with you." Luke's disciples are awestruck. They believe they have seen a spirit. Both Luke and John make the point that Jesus has to show them his hands and feet for them to believe it is Jesus' risen body.

Jesus reminds them of what he taught them while he was still on earth—that they would have a mission to all the nations. He also promised that he was going to send them the promise of the Father. Before he died he bestowed the Father's promise on them and then he ascended into heaven. Luke's missionary theme is repentance, forgiveness of sin, and the gift of the Spirit.[9] The disciples are to go forward and preach that message. It is possible that this second postresurrection meal story is an early form of a eucharistic liturgy. Jesus greeted them with peace; they shared a meal; there was a proclamation and teaching of the Word and a final blessing of the community.

When Jesus stood in their midst he offered the worshiping community an offering of peace. For Luke, this extension of peace is important. At Jesus' birth the angels announced peace on earth. When Jesus made his triumphant entry into Jerusalem the people blessed him and announced the arrival of God's peace. Jesus Christ crucified and now risen stands in their midst and offers them peace.

When Jesus sent the seventy-two out he told them to offer peace to every house they entered. Peace would be evident where peace existed. Peace is the offering of a people on a mission, a people gathered for prayer, and a people gathered to share the Lord's Supper. Peace is the effect of God's grace, the self-revelation of God. Peace— that is, God's grace—was extended to anyone who was a recipient of the greeting of peace.

---

[7] R. H. Benson, *L'Amitié de Jésus Christ* (Paris: Perrin, 1923), XI–XII, in *DL* (III), 137.

[8] *DKG*, 174.

[9] Ibid., 177.

The people were startled and terrified. This is the same reaction they experienced when the women related the events at the tomb. Jesus asks them why they are disturbed. The only other time the verb *tarasso* is used in Luke's gospel is when the angel announced the birth of John the Baptist to Zechariah—there is a connection. He, too, struggled with doubt and disbelief. Jesus asked them the source of their fear and then invited them to look at his hands and feet. Luke informed his readers in verse 34 that following the Emmaus-event the disciples were willing and ready to accept the witness of the resurrection. Yet in spite of the happenings at Emmaus, the disciples, when confronted with the risen Christ once again, are initially filled with fear and unfortunately then continue to disbelieve. His bodily presence was real. Luke makes no mention of the actual wounds. John is the only gospel that gives us more detail. It is from John that we know that Jesus was nailed to the cross. The other evangelists merely related the fact of his crucifixion—not the details. John has told us how Jesus was attached to the cross.[10] However, even the witness of his hands and feet did not cement the disciples' faith in what they had experienced. We are told their disbelief still kept them from joy. It was almost too good to be true. "Dare we believe?" This continued disbelief (not only here, but also when they encountered the women) is a sobering reminder to the reader/disciple that even when one sees the risen Christ in person blindness to God's power can and does still exist. Contact with Jesus' physical bodily presence was not enough to fully convince them. Then what did? "Additional steps beyond a physical appearance were necessary to reach full faith. These include the meal with the risen Jesus and especially his instruction about how the events they have experienced fit God's purpose."[11]

Jesus had a very important message that he was compelled to drive home if they were to fully embrace the truth of his passing. Jesus must now share the same message with the disciples in Jerusalem that he had shared with the disciples in Emmaus. Jesus' life, mission, death, and resurrection were part of God's plan of salvation for the world. It was foretold in the scriptures long ago.

The fact that Jesus died and rose again from the dead for the forgiveness of sins had to be etched on their hearts. They could not go forward if they did not accept the paschal mystery. Only after the disciples believe that Jesus had to suffer and die would they be able to accept and understand the mission they were about to undertake. Thus, the mission of Jesus is not yet complete. It continues in the mission to all the nations. In Luke's act 2 he will take up that mission. We will have a front row seat to the expansion of Christianity in the Acts of the Apostles. The Acts of the Apostles is Luke's log of the disciples' mission to all the nations.

Jesus invited them to touch his hands and feet to prove that he was truly of human flesh and bone. Flesh and bone is a biblical reference to "bone of my bone and flesh of my flesh" in Genesis 2:23. It suggests that Jesus was not only human but that he shared a common humanity, indicating kinship. "In the story of Emmaus, the risen Lord was really present to them in and through a stranger on the church's journey. The presence was real, but in symbol or sacrament, to use today's terminology. The same can be said of the present story. The risen Lord is really present among the community. He is present in the assembly of a community of real flesh and blood."[12]

Jesus demonstrated his presence in absence as he shared the meal with them. The purpose of Jesus eating the meal with his disciples was to make them eyewitnesses to the resurrection. The disciples were over their fright. "The Emmaus story emphasized the elusiveness and indirection of Jesus' presence: Jesus could appear as stranger without being recognized. This story emphasizes the other side: he is not a ghost, but a real person: 'It is truly myself!' "[13] They are overcome with joy once they realize what is really taking place, yet still they forget the customary gestures of hospitality. They forget to offer him food. He has to ask for something to eat. Jesus served the disciples at the Last Supper. Now he asks to be served. They offered him their meal of baked fish, recalling the feeding of the multitudes with bread and fish. Jesus was acting as a model for the future mission. He was following the instructions that he gave to the seventy-two as he sent them out.

---

[10]Ibid., 180.
[11]*NULA* (I), 23.

[12]*DKG*, 180.
[13]Luke Johnson, *GL*, 405.

"After greeting them with peace (see 10:5), Jesus accepted what they offered him (see 10:7–8), a piece of baked or broiled fish, and he ate it in their presence."[14]

The meal in today's gospel prepares the disciples to understand the discourse Jesus had shared with them while he was living—what the mission to all the nations meant. He reminded them of the words he shared with them while alive—that everything that had been prophesied about him in the scriptures had to be fulfilled. Jesus was present to the disciples, but not in the same way as when he was alive. This was a new presence. If Jesus appeared to them as he always had there would have been no need for them to make closer inspection of his hands and feet. Something was different. "Before he was with them as a historical figure. Now he was with them in sign and symbol, that is sacrament."[15] Luke informs his readers that Jesus taught them the meaning of the words about him while he was still with them. Luke Johnson posits a reason: "the oddness of this last phrase indicates that Jesus is truly 'present' to them and also that he is not 'with them' in the same way he was before the resurrection."[16]

Jesus addresses the scriptures that had prophesied about him, the major books of the Hebrew scriptures—the Law, the Prophets, and the Writings. The messianic age has arrived as foretold in the scriptures. Jesus is the fulfillment of God's plan of salvation. God's plan would go forward. Jesus suffered, died, rose again, and ascended to glory as part of God's plan of salvation. Jesus presented his own catechism on the paschal mystery. He refreshed their memories and renewed with them what he taught them when he walked with them on the journey. Jesus explained his Passion, death, and resurrection. Now they could understand. Whenever Jesus tried to prepare them about things to come throughout his earthly ministry, they simply could not understand. At Emmaus they came to gradual understanding and only after they encountered his sacramental presence in the breaking of the bread. Now their understanding comes full circle.

Disciples of the fully revealed Lord of Glory now are commissioned to go out and preach the same message of repentance that Jesus preached to them. Nothing less than complete conversion was required of the disciples. They are now to go out and invite all the nations into that same relationship with the Christ. Jesus is now more than prophet. He is Lord of the universe. And the disciples are witnesses to his glory. They must, they can do no less, than go out and share the incredible good news with the world.

Jesus declared them witnesses of these events, with firsthand, on-the-job experience. Who but they were best equipped to go out and spread the kerygma of Christ? As witnesses they were given the grace and responsibility of sharing what they "knew" of the Christ with all the nations. "One might be called a witness by accident, but to be a witness one had to be called."[17]

Jesus wanted to remind the disciples that from now on the place where they would experience this same presence would be in the community gathering for breaking of bread—eucharist. When they gather to break bread and to share the scriptures they will encounter Jesus truly present in their midst. They will remember and in the remembering it will a present reality for them and for all generations to come. Jesus blessed them with the same blessing given to Abraham, who was promised that his descendants would be as numerous as the stars in the skies. The apostles were to go out with the blessing of the Father, but not until they were anointed with the power of God's Spirit. The Spirit would take up where Jesus left off and lead them out to the nations. During Jesus' earthly life he was restricted by the confines of location. He could not go out to all the world. His resurrection changed all that; the bonds of confinement were broken. Through the ministry entrusted to the apostles the reign of God will now go forward to all the earth. The good news can be proclaimed to every person in every language.

Let the words of Jean Corbon serve as summary of today's liturgy:

> He, the Lamb of God is present; he comes into our world, but so many images hide

---

[14]Ibid.

[15]*DKG*, 182.

[16]*GL*, 402.

---

[17]*DKG*, 184.

him from us still and the darkness of deceit turns us away from him. Then the Paraclete, the new precursor of Jesus' coming in glory, will purify our vision with his silent light; he will bring us from our carnal views to the pure knowledge of faith. The Holy Spirit brings Christ as the fullness of time and gives us participation in him. He transfigures us by first enlightening the eyes of our hearts. We then become, even more than the disciples at Emmaus, contemporary with the hour of Jesus. This is the Today of liturgy.

Having awakened us to the unmerited gift of faith, the Holy Spirit can penetrate with his life giving light the deformed image that is the human being and transfigure it. He can reach into our darkness where death is entrenched. If the light gives us a participation in itself by becoming our faith, it does so in order that we may offer our whole being to it and become increasingly light. This energy, we sense, reaches into the very depths of our mortal condition; it is the energy proper to the last times, the energy by which the Holy Spirit seeks to transform us into the glorious body of the Lord.

Finally, if we are given the gift of "believing in his name" and if we have received "power to become children of God" (Jn 1:12), it is in order that he may send us into this world as he himself was sent by the Father. The Spirit gives us a new birth in order that his glory may be manifested to others through us and that they in turn may be transformed into the body of the Lord. This final extension of the life-giving light is intended to communicate the reality that is the body of Christ and introduce into communion with it the scattered children of God. In this energy the Spirit and the Church are bound together in the closest possible synergy because they entrust themselves to one another in a single mission of love.[18]

---

[18] *TWOW*, 67.

Proclaim the gospel again.

Sometimes we gain new insights when we hear the text after the interpretation is given. Someone from the group proclaims the gospel a second time.

STEP 4
TESTING

Conversation with the Liturgy and the Scriptures

Test your original understanding in dialogue with the text.

(You might consider breaking into smaller groups.)

Now that you've heard the exegesis, were there any new insights? How do you feel about it? How does your original understanding of this gospel compare with what we just shared? How does this story speak to your life?

Sharing Life Experience

Participants share an experience from their lives that connects with the biblical interpretation just presented.

> I am awed by the truth of today's gospel. I have had the privilege of traveling to various parts of the country to share whatever piece of the kerygma I am invited to share. It is always a humbling experience for me. Seldom do I not encounter the incredible, all-abiding peace of God in the Christian community. I am particularly impressed by people of goodwill who come together, not always on the same page or with the same agenda, but who can enter into relationship and dialogue and keep the unity and peace of the Christian community intact. I have heard experiences of people where that is anything but true. However, I am thankful that as yet I have encountered the Shalom of God wherever I have gone.

> Today's gospel is a reminder for me that I am called to be a witness to the resurrected presence of God around the world. That means that I am called to spread the good news. That good news begins at home. Week after week I am touched by the people in our catechumenate who break open the mystery of their lives and God's action in their lives. They are nourishment for

us. Their unconditional, fresh, and lively faith is a sign of hope for us all. They are a reminder that my relationship with God is to be renewed and refreshed. That renewal takes place at the Sunday banquet table every week. When I experience the faces in our community that I know bear much to live the eucharist I am strengthened to continue. I remember a comment by someone in the initiation process a few years ago. She was remarking how eager she was to be baptized at the Easter Vigil. Her language, however, reflected hunger. "I didn't know I could be so hungry. There is a pit in my heart, a hunger so deep, that nothing but the Bread of Life can fill it. I think I should starve if it does not come soon." When was the last time I approached the table with that hunger? Jesus sat down with his friends. He allowed them to feed him. That means that it is our turn to go out and host the great banquet.

The mission we are to proclaim is the mission of God's incredible mercy and forgiveness of our sins. Our church teaches that the eucharist forgives sins. How many of us believe that? I do. I remember one Sunday morning, I was angry with the world. I was particularly angry with a member of my family. I approached the liturgy so out of sorts that I would have rather been sitting on the beach across the way than celebrating anything with these happy people. The friendliness and hospitality of the community were obnoxious to me. I was not only angry about a situation on the home front, I wanted to extend it to my parish community. And while I was at it, why not throw in the world? Watch out anyone who dare step in my path.

By the time the liturgy began, my anger had quickly progressed from family, to church, and was well on its way past the world. Like a demon perched on the parapet of my spirit, my anger started to accelerate and all my unresolved anger came crashing to the fore. Remember that incident in 1990? I am still angry over that one! Now God was the object of my wrath. (I find it interesting that I do not even remember why I was so angry in the first place!) How could I pray? How could I celebrate the living presence of Christ in the midst of the community? I could not. I resolved to simply endure until the time when I could leave and nurse the raging fires that by this time were way out of control within the tinderbox of my emotions.

And then the prayer of the community began. It was difficult to remain passive. My shoes are still an inch shorter from digging them into the carpet of my stubborn will. Yet ever so gently I felt a nudge. The sung prayer of the community softened the way. It seemed that the community had never sung so energetically than it had on that morning. They nearly carried me away with the promise of God's unconditional love and forgiveness. "Who was looking for forgiveness anyway?"

Like the disciples, I remained in my unbelief. Until the Word. I heard words such as stony hearts, forgive one another as I have forgiven you; forgive seventy times seven. All the images of forgiveness I had ever heard came crashing into my consciousness. I asked myself: "What will it take for you to listen?" My stubbornness was melting away. It was time to receive Christ in the eucharist. I had already partaken of him in the community and in the Word of God. Now it was time to be healed. Yet I knew that unless I reconciled in my heart I could not go forward. I looked over to the object of my wrath. He was not even aware that this melodrama was going on inside of me. Pride is the last sin to fall, however. I was reveling in the smoldering embers of my misplaced anger. Do I really want to let go of this? I am sure there is more mileage to be had. Of course I had to let go. I had to leave my gifts at the altar and reconcile. Before I moved to the table I extended peace and together we were served at the Lord's Table.

I have no doubt that the presence of Christ in the community, in the Word, and in the sacrament strengthened me to let go of my rage. No doubt I would have sooner or later come to it on my own. There was something so sacramental about my experience, however. It was a moment of encounter. I was invited to see just how ridiculous I had been. But I also learned a powerful lesson.

If I had not eventually been opened to reconciliation there is no way in the world I could have gone forward to the Table. There is such a truism that our love for God is intimately connected to our love for one another. That momentary fractured relationship I was experiencing filtered over into my relationship with God. I never realized before that time how intimately connected both relationships are. I could offer peace to no one, not even God.

The prayer of God's people prompted me to ask myself: "How can I stay in this overblown anger when I just celebrated the life, death, and resurrection of someone who loved us so much?" My anger was certainly not huge in proportion to the sins in the world. However, my refusal to reconcile, to offer love, at least to offer communication was a sin against love. I had to be shaken into consciousness. Part of my mission that day was to look at the areas of stupid, built-up annoyances and address them with the person in question. The issue that morning wasn't even the real issue. Like life, it was the culmination of a lot of little annoyances that I ignored until something inside said, "Tilt, enough already."

Had I not been willing to reconcile I would have been little use to God or his universal mission. Someone recently said that the primary mission of Christ is reconciliation of all people. I have reflected on that statement a great deal. If all people would reconcile with God, one another, and the earth, we would live in peaceful harmony. Our mission is to promote that reconciliation. When I am willing to die to myself and enter into that mission I am living today's gospel. When I refuse, I remain in the disbelief of the disciples and am no good for anyone's mission—let alone the greatest mission on earth.

What was Luke trying to teach his community? How is there any relevance for today's Church in today's gospel? In what way do you relate to the disciples in today's gospel? To Jesus? Have you ever experienced a time of great misunderstanding, only to later come to full understanding? What did you learn from the experience? How does today's liturgy invite you to more deeply participate in the paschal mystery of Christ? In what way does this gospel challenge your community today? In what way has this conversation with the scriptures for today's liturgy invited change in your life? In what way are the biblical themes of covenant, exodus, creation, and community evident in today's readings? Do you still feel the same way about this text as when you began? Has your original understanding been stretched, challenged, or affirmed?

STEP 5
DECISION

The gospel demands a response.

In what concrete way might your parish be invited to respond? Are there any attitudes or behaviors you would like to change as a result of today's conversation? What one concrete action will you take this week in response to the liturgy today?

Pastoral Considerations: The community's response to today's gospel is simple. We either go out and proclaim the good news or we are concerned with in-house agendas. One way to check ourselves is to ask if there are smoldering fires within the community that need to be put out. Is the mission of peace and reconciliation lived at the parish level? Does our community realize that it has a responsibility to offer it on a global level as well? If we look at our parish life and do not see much extension of Christ's mission in the world, then we need to spend more time with today's liturgy. If your parish were charged with spreading the universal message of Christ's death and resurrection, the way of suffering and new life to the world, would there be enough evidence to convict you?

Hospitality is a key issue in today's gospel. Perhaps this would be a good time to look at that issue in your parish community. In what ways are you a hospitable people? Is everyone in your community invited to the meal? Who are invited but ignored? Who are the outsiders? Who would not get invited? How do you welcome newcomers? Does your Sunday worship reflect a welcoming community? How are children welcomed in your parish? Are they a nuisance to endure, or do they have an honored place at the Table? How are the handicapped welcomed? The poor? The marginalized? Is cultural diversity recognized and celebrated, or is it something to be endured? Where is transformation needed in your parish? What needs to happen to change that? The mission begins at home—sometimes the most difficult place to begin.

Christian Initiation: Mystagogia continues. The neophytes have a visible place in the assembly. They break open the riches of the Easter symbols. They, along with all the faithful, explore the paschal mystery in light of their experience of the sacraments. They put their sacramental life into practice. Catechumens who are still in process continue to be dismissed to reflect on the Word of God. Perhaps there are people in the inquiry ready to celebrate a rite of acceptance/welcome and move to the catechumenate. Perhaps there are candidates for full communion ready to be received. The Easter season is a wonderful time to celebrate the initiation sacraments.

DOCTRINAL ISSUES

What Church truth/teaching/doctrinal issue could be drawn from the gospel for the third Sunday of Easter?

Participants suggest possible doctrinal themes that flow from the readings.

Possible Doctrinal Themes

Paschal mystery; eucharist; reconciling mission of Christ; ecumenism; soteriology; evangelization; faith; Christ present in the liturgy—community, Word, sacrament, presider; sacraments; discipleship; sacramentality; grace

Present the doctrinal material at this time.

1. The facilitator gives input on a particular doctrinal issue of his or her prior choosing. OR
2. The group chooses a doctrinal issue from the list they created. They read together from the Doctrinal Appendix or other appropriate, official Church documents and the works of respected theologians.

(Many doctrinal issues are found in the Doctrinal Appendix at the back of this workbook. If you are choosing an issue from this resource, please refer to it now.)

Reflection questions centered around the chosen doctrinal theme can be found at the end of each topic in the Doctrinal Appendix. The questions are based on the five-step reflection process. If you choose a topic not included in the Doctrinal Appendix, craft your own questions according to the same five-step process.

Following the reflection questions you will be reminded to return to chapter 7, "Preparing the Catechetical Session," to assist you in crafting your own session.

Closing Prayer

Deacon: Bow your head and pray for God's blessing.

Priest: Through the resurrection of his Son, God has redeemed you and made you his children.
May he bless you with joy.

Response: Amen.

The Redeemer has given you lasting freedom.
May you inherit his everlasting life.

Response: Amen.

By faith you rose with him in baptism.
May your lives be holy,
so that you will be united with him for ever.

Response: Amen.

May almighty God bless you,
the Father, and the Son, and the Holy Spirit.

Response: Amen.[19]

---

[19]"Solemn Blessing or Prayer Over the People—Third Sunday of Easter," *The Sacramentary.*

FOURTH SUNDAY OF EASTER

Environment

Perhaps an icon of Christ, the Good Shepherd, might be added to your catechetical space.

INTRODUCTORY RITES

Entrance Antiphon (or Opening Song)

The earth is full of the goodness of the Lord; by the word of the Lord the heavens were made, alleluia. (Ps 32:5–6)[1]

Opening Prayer

The facilitator of the session may lead the prayer. Others in the group may be asked to proclaim the readings.

Let us pray
(to God our helper in time of distress)

Pause for silent prayer.

God and Father of our Lord Jesus Christ,
though your people walk in the valley of darkness,
no evil should they fear;
for they follow in faith the call of the shepherd
whom you have sent for their hope and strength.
Attune our minds to the sound of his voice,
lead our steps in the path he has shown,
that we may know the strength of his outstretched
     arm
and enjoy the light of your presence for ever.
We ask this in the name of Jesus the Lord.[2]

LITURGY OF THE WORD

The readings are proclaimed.

First Reading
Acts 4:8–12

---

[1] Fourth Sunday of Easter: "Entrance Antiphon," *The Sacramentary.*

[2] Fourth Sunday of Easter: "Opening Prayer," *The Sacramentary.*

(Refer to Easter Sunday for an overview of the Acts of the Apostles.)

Today's Pericope: Peter's speech is addressed to the leaders of the people and the elders. Chapter 4 of Acts is closely parallel to the Passion story. In verse 7, prior to today's pericope, Peter is asked by the Temple authorities where the source of his authority was derived. Where did he get his power to perform the miraculous healing of the lame man? Peter answered by insisting that the "stone scorned by the builders has become head of the corner" (Acts 4:11).[3] Peter was repeating a phrase used by Jesus (Lk 20:17). Jesus used this quotation as an accusation against the authorities, chastising them for plotting to kill the world's greatest messenger. The stone image, then, recalls the fact that Jesus was rejected and then vindicated by his death and resurrection. Peter uses the image that Jesus himself used. The people in both the gospel of Luke and in Acts prevent the authorities from taking action against Jesus at that time and against the apostles in Acts. The people's response served only to delay the inevitable death and resurrection of Jesus—not prevent it.

The conflicts in chapter 4 parallel the conflicts Jesus experienced. Luke masterfully shows that the conflicts are still alive and well. The church is facing the same difficulties Jesus experienced— "the conflict over Jerusalem's Messiah has not been resolved."[4] Chapter 4 plainly illustrates that the conflict has simply entered a new phase, with the apostles serving as Jesus' witnesses.

The apostles pick up where Jesus left off. They have the honor of pointing out the blindness of those who refuse to accept Jesus as Messiah and Lord. Their role is to call the people and the rulers of Jerusalem to repent and believe the good news. Now, as apostles, they too have the opportunity to show that given a second chance they will not fail Christ. They will be faithful. There is a stark difference in their behavior from the first ar-

---

[3] *NULA* (II), 69.

[4] Ibid.

rest scene with Jesus as there is in this interrogation scene with the rulers. It "highlights the difference in the behavior of the apostles before and after the resurrection and sending of the Spirit."[5] No more will Peter deny the Lord; this time he will go to prison. This time Peter will stand firm and speak with boldness before these very powerful authorities. It is the boldness of John and Peter that makes the rulers recognize that they had been disciples of Jesus—the very thing Peter denied in his darkest hour.

The apostles are now seeing the fulfillment of Jesus' promises to them. Jesus prophesied that the opposition would hand the apostles over and that they would be thrown in prison because of Jesus' name. This would lead, promised Jesus, to their witnessing to the truth. Today Peter witnesses before the religious court. Jesus' promise that they were not to fear for the Holy Spirit would direct their words is also fulfilled in today's gospel.

Luke's comparison of the events of chapters 4 and 5 of Acts and the Passion narrative serves to demonstrate how radically the apostles had been transformed. Before fear ruled their behavior, now courage. They boldly proclaimed Christ crucified and risen and in the process they too entered the cycle of dying and rising. Only the power of the risen Christ and his Spirit could wrought such a profound change in the lives of the apostles.

Questions for Mystagogical Reflection: Have you ever had an experience in which you had to stand up with boldness and integrity for a principle? Can you relate to the incredible transformation that is evident in the apostles in today's reading? Have you ever experienced such a dramatic change? Explain. How does this reading invite you into the paschal mystery—the cycle of death and resurrection? Reflect for a moment on what it would be like to be dragged before a court to defend your faith. Knowing yourself, how might you respond? How would you like to respond? What would need to happen for you to respond the way you would like to respond?

Responsorial Psalm
Psalm 118:1, 8–9, 21–23, 26, 28, 29

Psalm 118 is a psalm that appears frequently throughout the Easter season. This psalm refers directly to the stone the builders rejected, attested by Peter in the first reading.

This psalm was used in the Old Testament for the annual enthronement festival in Israel. When the king approached his throne with great pomp and circumstance in this enthronement ritual, it seemed as if a new and beautiful stone was added to the cornice of the Temple, a stone that had not been beautified by the original builders. The enthronement and exaltation of Jesus at God's right hand is the eschatological fulfillment of the enthronement liturgy of ancient Israel. Jesus is the cornerstone of the messianic community of the new age.[6]

Second Reading
1 John 3:1–2

(Refer to the Feast of the Holy Family for an overview of the First Letter to John.)

Today's Pericope: This passage from John's first letter is the most eloquent expression of God's love for humanity to be found in all of scripture. It professes how great God's love for human beings is— so great that we were given the gift of the incarnation. God loved us so much that he sent a part of Godself in the form of human flesh and blood. God gave us his Son.

God's love is so great that all who believe can call themselves children of God. Believers are children of God who enjoy God's presence now in this realm, but also look forward to the future reign that is yet to be revealed.

All will know that believers are God's children by the suffering and persecution they will experience for the sake of the gospel. Nonbelievers ("the world") rejected Christ. Those who follow Christ and are his disciples will experience the same fate that Christ endured. To be a child of God in the Christian sense is a present and future reality. Christians live in the reign of God right now (realized eschatology) as they await the reign of God to come in the future (future eschatology). The author of John promises the disciples that if they

---

[5]Ibid.

[6]*PL*, 263.

persevere to the end, they will see the future glory of God; they will see God as he really is.

Throughout the centuries, the precise meaning of this promise has been debated. Athanasius saw no problem speaking of a future deification (*theopoiesisthai*) of the believer, but Thomas Aquinas preferred to emphasize the aspect of the beatific vision, i.e. seeing God in his essence. For the author's first century contemporaries and for his 20th century readers, his words offer hope for an eternal future with the Father and the Son who had made us heirs of light and life.[7]

Questions for Mystagogical Reflection: Can you honestly say you have experienced the depths of God's love expressed in John's first letter? Is there an experience in your life that could attest to such love? What does love of God and for God mean to you? How does this reading invite participation in the paschal mystery of Christ?

The gospel is proclaimed.

Gospel
John 10:11–18. The Good Shepherd lays down his life for his sheep.

STEP 1
NAMING ONE'S EXPERIENCE

What were your first impressions? What was your first response to the gospel (or the other readings)? What captured your attention?

Each person names his or her initial impression. Statements should be brief. No reasons should be given at this time. All simply listen without agreeing or disagreeing.

STEP 2
UNDERSTANDING

In a brief statement, explain what you think this gospel is trying to convey.

---

[7] *WWC*, 173.

STEP 3
INPUT FROM VISION/STORY/TRADITION

Liturgical Context[8]

Good Shepherd Sunday helps us focus our attention on our Shepherd, Jesus, and his sheep, the church. We ask for the strength to follow the Shepherd to the end and our glorification in Christ: "give us new strength from the courage of Christ our shepherd, and lead us to join the saints in heaven" (Opening Prayer). The shepherd motif is carried throughout the liturgy. It appears again in an adapted form in the Prayer After Communion: "Father, eternal shepherd, watch over the flock redeemed by the blood of Christ. . . ." Note that, in this instance, the title of "shepherd" is used in reference to the Father. Chapter 10 of John's gospel contains Jesus' series of parables of the Good Shepherd. The whole section is read over the three year cycle, beginning in Cycle A. While not stated in today's section of the chapter (it is directly stated in years B and C), Jesus strongly asserts that he and his Father are one. When Christ protects, it is with the power and protection of the Father because they are one. John asserts that there is "one flock, one shepherd."

We who gather for eucharist, are in communion with one another. We are all a part of the same flock. We, the church, a sacrament of Christ,[9] have been redeemed by his blood. We are in the process of transformation. We are to persevere in our response to God's redeeming work within us: "may the continuing work of our redeemer bring us eternal joy" (Prayer Over the Gifts).

The image of Jesus as shepherd and the church as lamb offers hope to the suffering of the world. "Because Jesus was victorious in his death, by the sacrifice of his own body and blood, so will his

---

[8] The scriptures in the Lectionary, the seasons of the year, and the ritual prayers of the mass are interrelated and form the basis for liturgical catechesis. The *liturgical context* attempts to explore and clarify the themes and this interrelatedness.

[9] "By her relationship with Christ, the Church is a kind of sacrament or sign of intimate union with God, and of the unity of all mankind." (*Dogmatic Constitution on the Church [Lumen Gentium]*, #1).

faithful followers share in that ultimate victory over evil and death."[10]

In this paschal season we are reminded that there is another gate to enter. Jesus is the gate for us, but he himself passed through a gate—death to glory. It is to this gate he leads us.

> Jesus has passed the gate of death to enter into glory: "God has made him Lord and Messiah." To proclaim his resurrection is to recognize that he is the guide in whose footsteps we must follow in order to have life, and to have it more fully. He marches at the head of the ransomed people, leading them on the road of their paschal exodus.[11]

The custom of focusing on the Good Shepherd during the Easter season is a very ancient practice. During the seventh century, the passage, "I am the good shepherd..." (Jn 10:14–16) was read on the Second Sunday of Easter. There is evidence that proclamation of the Good Shepherd scriptures dates as far back as Pope Gregory (590–603 C.E.), and perhaps even as far back as the fifth century with Pope Leo the Great (440–461 C.E.). Pope Leo intimately connected the sheep to the Good Shepherd as he proclaimed the reading on the Wednesday before Easter. What happened to the sheep, happened to the shepherd, and vice versa. Christ and his people shared a mutual life. When people enter the waters of baptism, die to the old self, and are born again to the new, true conversion and transformation take place and they are incorporated into Jesus' paschal mystery. "For these newly baptized creatures are filled and fed by their Shepherd—since to participate in Christ's body and blood is to become, in fact, what we consume (St. Leo)."[12]

Later in the patristic period, the image of Christ as the Good Shepherd was appropriated as an image to describe leadership in the church. Christ who nourished and safeguarded his flock became a metaphor for those who would shepherd the people in his church. The word *pastor* was derived

from this image. Gregory the Great formulated a working pastoral theology. Gregory, like those before him, connected the shepherd to Christ's passion and cross. Gregory insisted that pastors must not please people at the expense of the truth; they must bear the pain of those they serve in self-sacrificing love.

The Second Vatican Council drew on the patristic formulations as it developed a theology of pastoral ministry.

> In the Constitution on the Church, no. 6, the Johannine images of flock and Shepherd are invoked to support the view that the Church is a communion born of Christ's sacrifice on the cross, enlivened by the Spirit, and nourished by the paschal sacraments. Similarly, the council's documents on the Bishop's Pastoral Office in the Church, nos. 2, 16, and on the Life and Ministry of Priests, no. 3, interpret ordained ministry by reference to Christ the shepherd, who freely surrendered his own life that others might live.[13]

Gospel Exegesis

The facilitator provides input from critical biblical scholarship on this text. This input includes insights as to how people would have heard the gospel in Jesus' time.

Scholars surmise that the discourse of the Good Shepherd is the combining of two separate parables. It is believed that they became intertwined in the process of oral transmission. The two original parables are probably authentic parables of Jesus. The two parables center around the same images and pastoral setting: shepherd, sheep, sheep gate, thieves, and marauders. There are two distinct focuses, however. The first parable centers around a sheepfold in which two people—a shepherd and a thief—try to enter. The second parable is concerned with the relationship between the shepherd and his sheep and between the shepherd and the stranger. In putting the two parables together John allegorically interprets Jesus as the gate and the shepherd. Today's pericope centers around the second parable.

---

[10]Carol Osiek, R.S.C.J., and Ronald D. Witherup, S.S., "Shepherd," in *CPDBT,* 907–909.

[11]*DL* (III), 139.

[12]Nathan D. Mitchell, "Shepherd," in *CPDBT,* 909–911.

---

[13]Ibid., 911.

Imagine the scene. It is first-century Palestine. Each day the shepherd would take his flock out into the desert for the day's grazing only to return to the sheepfold, a common enclosure with a low stone wall and a gated entrance. At day's end the shepherds would bring their sheep to the fold to keep them safe from the dangers of the night—wolves and thieves. Each night a shepherd was designated to lie down in front of the sheep gate so no one could enter without having to pass him first. He was the protector of the flock—with his very life if need be. After all the sheep were safely inside the yard, the shepherds would return to their nomadic tents. In the morning they would return to the fold again, each whistling or calling out the names of their sheep. The sheep instinctively knew the sound of their shepherd's voice. They would not respond when anyone other than their shepherd called out their names. One would assume that the morning gathering would be mass chaos and confusion. Not so—the sheep knew the sound of their shepherd's voice and instinctively followed him. The shepherd led the way out to safely graze in the pasture and the sheep always followed their shepherd.

Jesus is the model Good Shepherd. He cares for his sheep; they know his voice and respond to his voice. There is ownership. Jesus knows his sheep; he knows them by name. He is in loving relationship with them, which is why he is willing to lay down his life for them. Jesus, the Good Shepherd, lays down in front of the sheep gate and protects the sheep with his life. John's image of the Good Shepherd is a metaphor for the sacrifice of Christ on the cross. Christ laid down his life to offer safety and salvation to the sheep/disciples who follow him, those who know his voice and trust him unto death.

Jesus offered his life—he died—in order to rise again and thus save his sheep. Jesus' resurrection completes his death. As far as the fourth gospel is concerned, Jesus' death, resurrection, and ascension into glory is but one action of salvation. In John's Passion narrative Jesus is in control of the situation. He is aware of his preexistence, and the events at hand are completely under the power of his masterful hand. No one takes from Jesus what he freely chooses to give. Pilate was a fool to think Jesus was under his control: "You would have no power over me if it were not given to you from above," asserts Jesus to the Roman inquisitor. The same theme continues in today's gospel. "This is why Father loves me, because I lay down my life in order to take it up again. No one takes it from me, but I lay it down on my own" (v. 17). Jesus *chooses* to offer his life. He is in control. John's high Christology continues throughout the gospel. Whereas earlier Christology asserted that God raised Jesus from the dead, John in his more developed high Christology understood God and Jesus to share equally in the same power.[14] "That this death is not defeat but victory, and entirely voluntary, is made clear as Jesus says, 'I lay down my life in order to take it up again' (v. 17–18). This shepherd is no ordinary protector of his people, but one who will bring eternal life (v. 28)."[15]

Today's gospel is a challenge to Israel's religious leadership. Jesus takes up the clarion call in chapter 10, immediately following the Good Shepherd Discourse. The Pharisees were blind to the truth right under their noses, yet the faithful sheep who knew the sound of their master's voice were not blind. They followed the Master wherever he bid them go. The Pharisees, on the other hand, were like the man in today's parable—a hired man who does not care for the sheep. He leaves them unattended so the wolf is free to come and snatch them away.

The Pharisees were highly regarded religious leaders. Everyone looked up to them for their meticulous observance of the Law. Jesus knew their core; he knew the deception that lurked behind their façade of piety. They were like the hired hand who cared nothing for the sheep. A hired hand's only concern is self-interest. Love is not the motivation of the hired hand. The hired hand cares more about shepherding himself than he does about the sheep. "The salary may be money, honors, feeling like the center of a small world. Only by pretending to be shepherds can some people attain social consideration effortlessly, something they would have a hard time attaining by any other means. However, such motives do not create strong bonds; they are shepherding themselves, not the sheep. They look after their own interests and prestige, not the people they claim to serve."[16]

---

[14] Ibid., 174.

[15] Carolyn Osiek, R.S.C.J., and Ronald D. Witherup, S.S., "Shepherd—New Testament," *CPDBT*, 908.

[16] *SWTLY*, 97.

Verses 11 and 12 of today's gospel refer directly to Ezekiel 34. No doubt John's Jesus hearkened back to Ezekiel's admonishment of the false shepherds of Israel. Jesus is the fulfillment of Ezekiel's promise that God would remove the scattered flock from the care of the false shepherd and provide a safe pasture for them. "Jesus is like one of the family who depend on the sheep for their livelihood. Jesus is the model, caring shepherd who truly tends his sheep."[17] Jesus invites us to be in solidarity with him and with all his sheep—especially those sheep who cannot care for themselves, the poor, the marginalized, the oppressed, those whose wool has long lost its luster and is past the stage of bringing a premium price. Jesus shepherds them all—and expects no less from the rest of his sheep. His judgment is harsh on anyone who refuses to listen.

Jesus' challenge of the Pharisees asks the inherent question: "Will they recognize the shepherd's voice or not?" Jesus cannot prove his authority, but those who hear his voice and accept it know that it is the voice of God. John no doubt had his own circumstances in mind when he combined the parables of Jesus into an allegory of his own weaving. Jesus struggled with the Pharisees; John's community struggled with the Jewish leaders of their day.

In the preceding chapter of John's gospel, Jesus confronted the Pharisees in the story of the man born blind. He challenged their blindness. In the parable of the Good Shepherd, the reader is aware that the Pharisees still lurk in the shadows and stand in sharp contrast to the Shepherd of the flock. Jesus, the Good Shepherd, cares for his flock while the Pharisees care only for themselves. Like the blind man in the previous chapter, the flock recognizes Jesus for who he is—the Son of Man, guardian of the flock. The parable of the Good Shepherd is relevant teaching not only for communities of Jesus' day, but also communities of the 1990s as well as communities of the new millennium.

John draws from the figure of shepherd found in the Old Testament and in the Synoptic tradition. By the time John was writing, other New Testament writers were using "shepherd" as a term for human pastors of the church. John uses the shepherd motif in relation to Jesus and Jesus alone—only Jesus is the model shepherd.

A common theme in the Synoptic gospels is the failure of onlookers to understand Jesus' message. He usually applied several variations on the point he was trying to make: 1. Jesus is the shepherd who guards the gate to the enclosure. He will designate who enters and who does not. "The only authentic pastors are those admitted by Jesus (of whom Peter will be a chief example for the redactor in ch. 21)."[18] The Pharisees, who cannot accept Jesus and seek to come in some other way, are the thieves. 2. Only through Jesus, the gate, will the sheep *go out to* or *come in from* the pasture. "Those who come through this gate will have life (Jesus is the water of life, the bread of life, the gate of life)."[19]

Jesus is the model Good Shepherd. He cares for his sheep; they know his voice and respond to his voice. There is ownership. Contrast that with the Pharisees, who are merely hired workers who come in to shear the sheep and care nothing for their welfare. Jesus knows his sheep. He is in loving relationship with them, which is why he is willing to lay down his life for them. "In the last analysis, both identifications of Jesus—gate and shepherd—make the same point. The risen Christ is the One who nourishes his people in his word and sacraments, giving them life and enabling them to have it abundantly."[20]

Through baptism we are incorporated into Christ Jesus. Jesus knows each of us by name and invites us in through the gate. He loves us so intimately that he is willing to lay down his life to keep us from becoming prey to wolves and marauders.

Jesus also offers a model of authentic Christian leadership. Rather than indulging in self-serving interests, we are to take the time to learn the names of our sheep and to become the guardian of the gate that keeps them safe from the dangers of the night.

---

[17]Carolyn Osiek, R.S.C.J., and Ronald D. Witherup, S.S., "Shepherd—New Testament," CPDBT, 908.

[18]*GEJ*, 58.
[19]Ibid., 59.
[20]*PL*, 81.

"The shepherd,
with his familiar voice, cried:
'A new earth!'

He has crossed the ravines of death,
we leap toward the source of living water.

Shepherd who frees us
eternal love!

The lost sheep,
I go to seek out.

The sick sheep,
I carry in my arms.

The scattered sheep,
I gather around me.

The sheep of my flock,
I lead to my mountain."[21]

Proclaim the gospel again.

Sometimes we gain new insights when we hear the text after the interpretation is given. Someone from the group proclaims the gospel a second time.

STEP 4
TESTING

Conversation with the Liturgy and the Scriptures

Test your original understanding in dialogue with the text.

(You might consider breaking into smaller groups.)

Now that you've heard the exegesis, were there any new insights? How do you feel about it? How does your original understanding of this gospel compare with what we just shared? How does this story speak to your life?

---

[21]Commission Francophone Cistercienne, *Tropaire pour les dimanches*, Le L'ivre d'Heures d'En Calcat (Dourgne: 1980), 36 (Fische de chant I LH 175), in *DL* (III), 146.

Sharing Life Experience

Participants share an experience from their lives that connects with the biblical interpretation just presented.

> *If I did not have Jesus as my Shepherd I would be lost in a briar patch, unable or perhaps refusing to move to safety. I shudder to think what life would be like were it not for the great Shepherd who places his body in harm's way so that I might enjoy the pasture's safe enclosure.*

> *Woe be to me should I ever fall into the category of hired hand. It is my fervent wish that I never stoop so low. However, I am very aware that self-denial is our most dangerous companion. I want to shepherd God's people not for self-interest, but out of genuine love. It is my heart's desire. However, sometimes my actions do not match my desire; but on the other hand, sometimes my feelings do not match my decision.*

> *To shepherd as Jesus shepherds is a decision. Such a decision does not always bring about nice, "wooly" feelings. Sometimes it is not fun, it is costly, it hurts and there is little reward (the shepherds' union insists that the pay is out of this world!). Imagine a night of using your body as a human shield on the stony, scorpion-infested ground! Imagine hanging from a cross!*

> *Sometimes I look out at my community and I am filled with the deepest love and compassion for them—all of them, especially the ones who complain the most, those who ache from years of treks through dry desert pastures, who have lost their way, whose children have lost their way—who have known disappointment in themselves, their family, and sometimes even in other shepherds. And saddest of all, those who have lost faith in the fold's safe enclosure that was to keep them safe in the first place. The Church is a fold filled with broken, bruised, and lame sheep in spite of the great shepherding we have received. The Good Shepherd promised to lead us. He did not promise to keep every briar patch out of our way. In those moments of compassion I am aware of a deep, abiding love that exists within me for the people of God.*

> *On the other hand, there are times when I feel nothing. There are no feelings whatsoever to match the decision I make every day to continue to do the best I*

can to lead people to Christ. When life brews its pot of sheep dip, I am forced to make a decision. Will I continue to be baptized in its pot, or will I lag behind, hoping not to be noticed, and silently slip away in the night? Who cares about all those other sheep anyway? Of course, the slipping away leads to being lost, which ultimately leads to being found, which also leads me right back to the fold. Isn't God's mercy awesome?

Metaphors aside, we are blessed as a Christian community to have examples in our midst of people who imitate the Shepherd's example and heroically follow in his steps. We can look to the great saints, the Mother Teresas, the St. Peters, the Archbishop Romeros, but it is my strong belief that we do not have to look much past our own parish to find such heroes and heroines of faith.

One such person comes to mind. A woman who has known suffering in her own life. She knows the great love of God because God has raised her from the pit and offered her incredible new life. She has much to share about the cycle of death and resurrection.

This woman of great faith quietly and unobtrusively reached out to one of God's very lost sheep. A homeless, mentally ill woman arrived on our doorstep. For weeks she was a visitor to our grounds. Many of us talked about what we should do. The woman of great faith responded, embraced her, and invited her into her home. She worked diligently to get the necessary provisions for her to be on the road to wholeness and a life off the streets.

This woman of great faith brought this young woman into her home and by her very action brought her into a safe enclosure and placed herself as guard over its gate. One need only look into the woman's eyes to see the great miracle that has been accomplished in her life. She has been given a new lease. She is on medication, appropriate agencies have been secured to give her the care she needs, and she has had the experience of a loving family to nurture her. When I see her worshiping with this family in our Sunday assembly, I am thankful and privileged to know this great woman of faith. She is a Good Shepherdess, to be sure!

What was John trying to tell his community? Describe the ways in which you have been a faithful

sheep. Is there any way you might relate to the hired hand? Have you ever known any "hired hands"? Have you ever been invited to imitate the Good Shepherd? Explain. How does this gospel invite you to more fully participate in the paschal mystery of Christ? How might this Word be a challenge to your community? How might this liturgy invite you to change? In what way does this gospel challenge your community today? In what way has this conversation with the scriptures for today's liturgy invited change in your life? In what way are the biblical themes of covenant, exodus, creation, and community evident in today's readings? Do you still feel the same way about this text as when you began? Has your original understanding been stretched, challenged, or affirmed?

STEP 5
DECISION

The gospel demands a response.

In what concrete way might your parish be invited to respond? Are there any attitudes or behaviors you would like to change as a result of today's conversation? What one concrete action will you take this week in response to the liturgy today?

Pastoral Considerations: Who are the sheep most in need of your parish's care and concern at this time? In what way has your parish fallen short of the example raised by Christ, the Good Shepherd, in today's gospel? It is usually extremely evident if one were to take the time to honestly reflect.

Christian Initiation: Neophytes continue to be a symbol of new life in our assemblies. When they continue to don their baptismal garment and carry their baptismal candle in procession they are a reminder to all of us that we are all baptized into the death and resurrection of Jesus Christ. Is there anyone in your process ready to celebrate any of the rites? Easter is a wonderful time to celebrate a rite of full communion in the Catholic Church, rite of acceptance/welcome, and so on. Perhaps today would be a good time to forgo extended catechesis so you can mentor your catechumens and go with them to minister to God's sheep in the world. What might that look like?

DOCTRINAL ISSUES

What Church truth/teaching/doctrinal issue could be drawn from the gospel for the fourth Sunday of Easter?

Participants suggest possible doctrinal themes that flow from the readings.

Possible Doctrinal Themes

Jesus, the Good Shepherd; Christology; paschal mystery; initiation sacraments of baptism, confirmation, and eucharist; symbols of the Easter Vigil; sacramentality; love of God; faith; discipleship; grace; soteriology

Present the doctrinal material at this time.

1. The facilitator gives input on a particular doctrinal issue of his or her prior choosing. OR
2. The group chooses a doctrinal issue from the list they created. They read together from the Doctrinal Appendix or other appropriate, official Church documents and the works of respected theologians.

(Many doctrinal issues are found in the Doctrinal Appendix at the back of this workbook. If you are choosing an issue from this resource, please refer to it now.)

Reflection questions centered around the chosen doctrinal theme can be found at the end of each topic in the Doctrinal Appendix. The questions are based on the five-step reflection process. If you choose a topic not included in the Doctrinal Appendix, craft your own questions according to the same five-step process.

Following the reflection questions you will be reminded to return to chapter 7, "Preparing the Catechetical Session," to assist you in crafting your own session.

Closing Prayer

Let us pray.
Father, eternal shepherd,
watch over the flock redeemed by the blood of
    Christ

and lead us to the promised land.
Grant this through Christ our Lord.[22]

---

[22]Fourth Sunday of Easter: "Prayer after Communion," *The Sacramentary.*

FIFTH SUNDAY OF EASTER

INTRODUCTORY RITES

Entrance Antiphon (or Opening Song)

Sing to the Lord a new song, for he has done marvelous deeds; he has revealed to the nations his saving power, alleluia. (Ps 97:1–2)[1]

Opening Prayer

The facilitator of the session may lead the prayer. Others in the group may be asked to proclaim the readings.

Let us pray
(in the freedom of the sons of God)

Pause for silent prayer.

Father of our Lord Jesus Christ,
you have revealed to the nations your saving
    power
and filled all ages with the words of a new song.
Hear the echo of this hymn.
Give us voice to sing your praise
throughout this season of joy.
We ask this through Christ our Lord.[2]

LITURGY OF THE WORD

The readings are proclaimed.

First Reading[3]
Acts 9:26–31

---

[1]Fifth Sunday of Easter: "Entrance Antiphon," *The Sacramentary.*

[2]Fifth Sunday of Easter: "Alternative Opening Prayer," *The Sacramentary.*

[3]The exegesis for the first and second readings may or may not be the focus of your group's reflection, as there may only be time to give adequate attention to the gospel, your primary concern. However, the exegesis is included here in order to provide a thorough investigation of the entire liturgy of the word as there may be parts (or all) that would be essential to the direction you wish to take with your particular ministry group.

(Refer to Easter Sunday for an overview of the Acts of the Apostles.)

Today's Pericope: When Saul arrived in Jerusalem he tried to join the Christian community, but the people were understandably fearful of him. His reputation was difficult to overcome. Reports of his newfound discipleship were dubious. Saul? The persecutor's persecutor? Hardly! Luke uses the disbelief of the community to stress just how radical Saul's transformation is. The "Lord's work is revealed through events that overthrow human expectations."[4] People simply are not prepared to deal with God's unfathomable plans. As always, Luke presents God as the ultimate Surprise Artist! The "church has difficulty keeping up with such a God."[5] Saul, the master tormentor, will prove to be a master disciple. He will become a prime example of what it means to endure great suffering for the sake of the gospel. He who was the great persecutor will himself become greatly persecuted for the mission of Christ. His powerful mission of preaching will result in adversity, suffering, imprisonment, and ultimately martyrdom for the kingdom.

Saul's moment of conversion on that Damascus road will result in one of the greatest missionaries who ever lived! His missionary thrust will be to Jews and gentiles alike, but his work with the gentiles is a matter of history and is responsible for the rapid spread of the church in the Hellenized world.

Saul stayed in Damascus after his encounter with the exalted Messiah and began to preach in the synagogues. Barnabas introduces Saul to the Jerusalem community and can personally attest to Saul's missionary activities in Damascus. "When Saul goes to Jerusalem, he is a preacher with a record in Damascus to which Barnabas can point."[6] Saul left Damascus only when it became too dangerous for him to remain.

---

[4]*NULA* (II), 117.

[5]Ibid.

[6]Ibid., 122.

Saul's mission in Jerusalem was no different than his mission in Damascus—he did not skip a beat. He continued to preach, and as he preached, plots to kill him followed him wherever he went. The plots were always discovered and other Christians interceded to help Saul escape. Saul used the same boldness to preach Jesus Christ, Lord and Messiah, in Jerusalem as he did in Damascus.

Paul's missionary activities in Damascus and Jerusalem are indications that the Lord's prophecy about Saul is indeed being fulfilled. He will suffer much for professing the name of Jesus Christ. The sequence of preaching, danger, and escape will continue throughout Saul's tour of duty for the Lord.

The Jerusalem church is incredulous. They are not willing to immediately embrace Saul as one of their own. Barnabas serves as Saul's advocate as he testifies to his great works in Damascus. Barnabas is referred to as "son of encouragement" and later will be called a good man who is filled with the Spirit of God and with faith. Barnabas will earn these accolades because of his ability to discover the action of God in the most unexpected places. He will discover the new and surprising works of God in the lives of gentiles in Antioch. He is open enough to see God's grace operative in the most unexpected people. This openness is what characterizes his action of introducing Saul to the community in Jerusalem. Saul needed someone to testify on his behalf. Barnabas is willing to assume that role. Barnabas tells Saul's story to the gathered community and later Peter will also pass the same story on to others.

The telling of the story changes hearts. The story of Saul's conversion experience on the Damascus road in which he personally encountered the Lord as well as his subsequent ministry of preaching has a powerful impact on those who hear it. "The change in Saul is traced back to the Lord, a Lord whose surprising power is already known to the apostles, and the authenticity of the encounter is supported by Saul's subsequent behavior. Thus Barnabas helps the leaders of the church to recognize the unexpected work of the Lord and to accept Saul, not only as a Christian but also as a partner in mission, who accompanies

the apostles and begins to preach in Jerusalem as he had in Damascus."[7]

Barnabas attests that Saul "saw the Lord." This is an important testimony. Saul did not see a brilliant light, but the Lord himself. This makes Saul a firsthand eyewitness of Jesus, the risen and exalted Lord and Messiah.

Saul is sent to Tarsus to continue his preaching mission. The final verse in today's pericope is a summary statement of the church's state of affairs in light of all the unfolding events. It describes a church on the move, growing and expanding as the mission goes forward in Galilee, Judea, and Samaria. Luke describes a church at peace. This peace is a result of persecution that began with Stephen's death and that now is coming to an end as a result of Saul's conversion. Everyone is amazed by the power of the Word to go forward in spite of resistance. The church is experiencing a new momentum of growth and expansion. There is understandable excitement in the air.

Questions for Mystagogical Reflection: *Put yourself in the place of those gathered in Jerusalem. Can you relate to their suspicions? How might that situation have any relevance today? In what way can you relate to Saul's conversion? How might you relate to Barnabas? Have you ever been placed in a situation in which you had to speak for another? What was that like? In what way does this reading invite participation in the paschal mystery? What is the challenge inherent in the reading and how does it invite transformation in the believer? In you?*

Responsorial Psalm
Psalm 22:26–27, 28, 30, 31–32

Psalm 22 is best known as the Passion psalm. Reginald Fuller maintains that it is both a Passion and resurrection psalm. The first twenty-one verses refer to the righteous Suffering Servant. Verses 22–31 refer to the Servant's vindication. When the Passover of the Lord was celebrated as one feast, the entire psalm was sung at one time. The tone changed dramatically, however, when the vindica-

---

[7]Ibid., 123.

tion/resurrection theme of the psalm began. The Easter portion of this psalm, which is proclaimed today, speaks of the vindication of the Servant that occurs in his suffering.

Second Reading
1 John 3:18–24

(Refer to the Feast of the Holy Family for an overview of the First Letter of John.)

Today's Pericope: Scholars suggest that this section of John's first letter is very difficult to summarize. It has been suggested that perhaps the author was pulling together various notes that he had not taken the time to develop fully. However, there are some emerging themes. Christians will be assured of their good standing as long as they follow the imperative to love one another. If we question whether we love as we should, we should be confident that the Lord knows us better than we know ourselves. Those who are confident of their standing are free to live the Christian life of prayer and faithfulness to God's will and will follow the Lord's commands. There are two primary concerns that should be the agenda of every Christian. Christians are to love the Lord and have complete faith in him and they are to love one another. Evidence of our relationship with God, God's indwelling within us, will be the way in which we follow the Lord's commands and ultimately God's Spirit *will dwell* in the righteous.

The themes of today's reading make particular sense in light of the author's agenda. There was a great concern to counter the heresies of the secessionists who claimed that behavior had absolutely nothing to do with one's relationship with God. John insists that they are sorely mistaken.

Questions for Mystagogical Reflection: *If you were charged with having an intimate relationship with God, what evidence would your accusers find to convict you? How do you relate to the command to love in this reading? How does this reading invite you into the cycle of death and resurrection? In what way does this reading challenge you? The church? What does this reading challenge you to do this week?*

The gospel is proclaimed.

Gospel[8]
John 15:1–8. Whoever remains in me and I in him will bear much fruit.

STEP 1
NAMING ONE'S EXPERIENCE

What were your first impressions? What was your first response to the gospel (or the other readings)?[9] What captured your attention?

Each person names his or her initial impression. Statements should be brief. No reasons should be given at this time. All simply listen without agreeing or disagreeing.

STEP 2
UNDERSTANDING

In a brief statement, explain what you think this gospel is trying to convey.

STEP 3
INPUT FROM VISION/STORY/TRADITION

Liturgical Context[10]

Today's liturgy is an invitation to enter into the abiding love and presence of Christ, to allow ourselves to be pruned and to suffer as Christ suffered for the sake of the gospel—a theme also

---

[8]The gospel exegesis is provided later in this session so that it may be presented in the proper sequence where it occurs in the adult five-step reflection process. The exegesis is provided for the first and second readings for your information and edification, and for you to use at your discretion. Once again, the gospel is the primary source of reflection. If there is time for reflection on the other readings, all the better.

[9]The primary focus of reflection is the gospel. However, often the other readings demand attention and must be brought into the dialogue.

[10]The scriptures in the Lectionary, the seasons of the year, and the ritual prayers of the mass are interrelated and form the basis for liturgical catechesis. The *liturgical context* attempts to explore and clarify the themes and this interrelatedness.

picked up by the first reading. It is an invitation to commit more fully to the paschal mystery with the assurance that God's love will sustain us. The readings are rooted in self-sacrificing love. All of our work is to flow from the example of Christ. We are to lay down our lives for the reign of God and for one another. We are to persevere in promoting the gospel of Christ, and we are to be agents of Christ's love to all of God's people. The alternative opening prayer calls for the joy necessary to sing praise to Christ; in other words, to proclaim his mighty deeds to all people. The gospel promises such joy when we live according to the will of God.

The liturgy today is a reminder of what it costs to live the Christian life. Without the Pauls and Barnabases of this world the church remains stagnant. Is there still evidence of such heroes of faith today?

Both the first and second readings today demand that we take seriously the commitment to spread the gospel and to live according to the command of love. Jesus has given us the example of true love and invites us to follow his example. If we live in love we will face opposition. Today's liturgy asks us if we are willing to continue to enter into the death and resurrection of Jesus. Today's liturgy invites our communities to seriously ask ourselves if we reflect the love Jesus asks of us in today's readings. Could nonbelievers say of us: "See how much they love one another"? And even more important, could they say, "See how much they love us"? Are our communities comprised of living stones or unmovable slabs of granite?

John's gospel today is the most profound expression of God's love for his people. Jesus is the only way home. To "remain in God and God in us" Jesus grafts us to himself. Jesus reveals God; the Church reveals Jesus. Jesus desires nothing more than we be united in him as he is with the Father. We experience this love in the community, in the liturgy, in the sacraments, and ultimately in the eucharist. Love forgives a multitude of sins. We need to examine where love is lacking in our parishes.

The gospel brings us back to reality. Jesus is the sacrament of God. He is the real, tangible, touchable expression of the Father's love for us. Only through Jesus can we begin to imagine how deeply we are loved. If we lose our way, we need only look to him, for we are attached to the trunk of his mighty tree. He will never cut us off completely. He will prune away the excess debris, but he prunes us so we can grow and bear fruit. The opening prayer reminds us: "You redeem us and make us your children in Christ. Give us true freedom and bring us to the inheritance you promised." Today's gospel leaves us with that same promise. We will be given the blessings we need to go out and bear fruit—to be the disciples that Paul shows us how to be. The prayer over the gifts offers us a wonderful summary statement of today's gospel: "by this holy exchange you share with us your divine life. Grant that everything we do may be directed by the knowledge of your truth."[11] The eucharist grafts us to the vine, as intimately attached to Christ, the vine, we share his divine life. We can do no less than act in accord with our status as divine children of God.

> "In these Easter days,
> Lord God,
> your vine receives new sap.
> Hold the branches to the vine:
> thus will charity make us live
> one for another
> in the one who died and rose for us,
> Jesus, the Christ our Lord."[12]

Gospel Exegesis

The facilitator provides input from critical biblical scholarship on this text. This input includes insights as to how people would have heard the gospel in Jesus' time.

The vineyard metaphor is a typical Hebrew scripture metaphor for Israel. When Israel was unfaithful it was compared to a barren, unproductive vine. John's gospel often contains two levels of meaning—the meaning attached to the events at the time of Christ, and the meaning assigned by a community fifty years later. In an original setting

---

[11]Fifth Sunday of Easter: "Prayer Over the Gifts," *The Sacramentary*.

[12]Commission Francophone Cistercienne, *Priéres au fil des heures*, Vivante liturgie 99 (Paris: Publications de Saint-André—Centurion, 1982), 101.

the metaphor of unproductive branches may have been a reference to Judas; in the Johannine setting fifty or sixty years later they were probably a reference to the Gnostic heretics. It is also possible that the vine and branches image was a message to all the Jews who refused to accept Jesus and who rejected the disciples of Christ. They (the Jews) believed themselves to be the true vine. "Josephus in his Antiquities (XV, 11:13) described the Jerusalem temple as decorated with a vine and branches motif. Archaeologists and numismologists have dated the special coinage of the Jewish war (66–70 C.E.), minted with a vine and branches design. After the destruction of the temple, those who assembled in Jamnia to preserve Judaism from further destruction called themselves the 'vineyard.'"[13] John's Jesus is the true vine, not Israel. Jesus superseded Israel—its worship and its Law.

The vine and branches metaphor describes the relationship between Jesus and his followers. Thus, the vine was Jesus and the branches that bore no fruit were people who refused to believe in Christ and his mission. God, the Vinedresser, in this scenario is the one who excises and throws the unproductive branches into the fire (judgment). The pruned branches represent the remaining disciples who will experience persecution, but who will be stronger and who will adhere more permanently to the vine.

"I am the vine" probably derives from language used in the Bread of Life Discourse, "I am the Bread of Life." Eucharistic overtones are obvious. The association of the branches with the community of believers is probably derived from Paul's theology of the church as the Body of Christ. Those who reject Jesus also reject the eucharistic body of believers.

In addition to eucharistic overtones there are also images of baptism. Like the pruning by the Vinedresser, baptism cleanses people of sin and conforms them permanently and securely to the vine, Jesus Christ. Persecution strengthens the believer to adhere more closely to Christ. The pruning enables the Christian to remain faithful to Christ, thereby sharing Christ's eternal life. Those who

have cut themselves off from God's unmerited, completely gratuitous love and grace through Christ have chosen to be cut away, thereby throwing themselves into the fires of judgment. No one can earn God's grace—it is freely given—but Christians can do no less than live grace-filled lives in accord with God's will. Righteous behavior flows directly from the free gift of God's self.

The phrase, "Remain in me, as I remain in you," in other translations reads, "Abide in me, as I abide in you." The more accurate sense of the original text, however, comes from the verb, "to stay." This is an important phrase in the fourth gospel. The Johannine author uses it sixty-seven times, forty occurrences found in John's gospel. It is only found fifty-one times in all other three Synoptic traditions put together. Sometimes it is used in the normal sense, such as to live, or to stay. However, most of the time John uses it in a very profound theological sense. When John uses the phrase it is a signal to pay attention—something very significant is happening in the salvation history of humankind. God is truly dwelling within the hearts of his believers in a new way. "To abide in" also means "to stay with." It is a divine presence. In chapter 6 John insists that the eucharist is this same kind of "staying with," or "abiding." The eucharist is "the means of this mutual and life-giving indwelling."[14] John begins the gospel by foreshadowing the type of "abiding with" or "staying with" God intends for human beings. When Jesus called the first disciples he asked them what they were seeking. Their response was, "to stay." They/humanity desire the wondrous experience of God's deep, abiding presence. "To stay" implies that the disciples should come to see the place where the Father lives—the place where the Father dwells with Jesus and Jesus dwells with the Father. Jesus desired that these new disciples come and experience the essence of what it truly means to be Christian. Without the indwelling of God, the Christian life is empty—it is rubbish. It is an invitation to come and see through eyes of faith where Jesus really abides and then take up residence in the same place.

Ultimately the discipleship Jesus speaks of in today's gospel is an invitation to be grafted to

---

[13] WWC, 176.

[14] JHW, 44.

Jesus at the vine and at our very core. The Synoptic gospels invited disciples to leave everything to follow Christ—jobs, family, possessions. John has a different vision. John insists that discipleship involves the total gift of one's self and "the abandonment of one's prior faith commitments."[15]

As Christians the Johannine disciples were unique. They were no longer part of the Jewish tradition. Christianity involved a radical choice and the choice was initiated by invitation. "Jesus' question ('What do you seek?') initiates the invitation; his 'come and see' brings it to fulfillment."[16]

The first seventeen verses of chapter 15 are intended to remind the community that Jesus is the source of their existence. They are also a part of Jesus' second farewell address in which he prepares the disciples for his absence. Whenever Jesus proclaims "I am" in the fourth gospel, John is theologizing about Jesus' role in salvation history. As the true vine he is the source of life for all the branches. The branches can only bear fruit through the power of God. Bearing fruit can mean winning believers to Christ or it can mean demonstrating great love to members of the community. Probably in today's gospel the more probable meaning is the latter. However, unless Jesus abides in his disciples such bearing of fruit is simply impossible.

The pericope ends in a promise that hearkens back to the covenant between God and Israel expressed in Deuteronomy. God entered into a covenant of love with the people. God's election of Israel was freely offered because of God's love. God keeps the covenant with those who live according to God's will. The terms of the covenant/agreement between God and Israel are that the Lord God will love his people, take care of them, protect them from famine, disease, and their enemies. Such are the benefits for God's people when they enter into steadfast, covenant love. The promises God offers in today's reading remind the disciples that this loving relationship with Jesus and the Father will result in benefits for the disciples. God will answer their prayers; they will bear fruit and live in joy.[17]

Gustavo Gutierrez reminds us that the vineyard is indeed a reference to the people of Israel as mentioned above.[18] John now is portraying the new, true people of God—Jesus and his followers. They are in solidarity, a total bond of love. The love Jesus presents is rooted in service and humility. The love we share with Christ cleanses us—it also strengthens the bond between the community and Jesus. The covenant God made with Israel now extends to the Christian fellowship. The implications of the covenant can never be forgotten. God promised to love and care for Israel. In response the people would love the Lord their God with their entire personhood and as a sign of that love they will love one another, evidenced by the way they care for God's *anawim*—widows, orphans, oppressed, marginalized, and the poor.

We do not become pruned overnight. It is a process. The pruning often takes place one branch at a time. It is often very painful, but with patience it bears much fruit. Our love cannot simply turn inward to God's indwelling. Love of God must also result in external manifestation. Love finds expression through action. "Loving God means entering fearlessly into the lives of our neighbors regardless of the difficulties which this may bring about."[19]

John's catechism on God's love and the relationship of the Christian to Christ, the true vine, continues to present disciples with an invitation to love as we are loved. Our love will be rooted in selfless action—just as Christ's love was so rooted. The artistry of Catherine of Sienna's poetry captures the essence of today's gospel and invites the imagination into serious reflection, and ultimately, action.

> High eternal Trinity!
> O trinity, eternal Godhead!
> Love!
> We are trees of death
> and you are the tree of life.
> O eternal Godhead!
> What a wonder,
> in your light,
> to see your creature as a pure tree,
> a tree you drew out of yourself,

---

[15]Ibid., 45.
[16]Ibid.
[17]*RJ*, 214.

[18]*SWTLY*, 100.
[19]Ibid., 101.

supreme purity,
in pure innocence!
You planted it and fused it
into the humanity you had formed
from the earth's clay.
You made this tree free.
You gave it branches:
the soul's powers
of memory,
understanding,
and will.
With what fruit did you endow the memory?
With the fruit of holding.
And understanding?
With the fruit of discerning.
And the will?
With the fruit of loving.
O tree
set in purity
by the one who planted you!
Once we have been engrafted unto you,
the branches you gave our tree
begin to produce their fruit.
Our memory is filled
with the continual recollection of your
        blessings.
Our understanding gazes into you
to know perfectly your truth
and your will.
And our will chooses to love and follow
what our understanding has seen and known.
So each branch offers its fruit to the others.
You made us into trees of life again
when we were trees of death
by engrafting yourself, life,
into us.
Eternal Truth,
take those you have given me
to love with a special love:
join and engraft them into yourself
so that they may bring forth the fruit of life.[20]

Proclaim the gospel again.

Sometimes we gain new insights when we hear the text
after the interpretation is given. Someone from the group
proclaims the gospel a second time.

_____

[20] RF, 108.

STEP 4
TESTING

Conversation with the Liturgy and the Scriptures

_Test your original understanding in dialogue with the
text._

(You might consider breaking into smaller groups.)

Now that you've heard the exegesis, were there
any new insights? How do you feel about it? How
does your original understanding of this gospel
compare with what we just shared? How does this
story speak to your life?

Sharing Life Experience

_Participants share an experience from their lives that
connects with the biblical interpretation just presented._

> _Today's gospel reminds us that we are grafted to
> Christ, that our relationship with him is so close
> that there is nothing to separate us. We are a branch
> on the Great Vine. We will be pruned if we are to
> grow stronger on the Vine, but we will never be cut
> away and thrown in the fire unless by a total act of
> will._
>
> _In looking back on my life I sometimes have to
> chuckle at the way God accomplished his pruning.
> God is the Master Pruner. Many years ago when my
> life as a disciple was in its infancy stage, it seemed
> very often as if chaos was the order of the day. One
> year we celebrated family reunions at the cemetery
> seven different times. Every attempt to do things on
> our own ended in failure. Just when we thought we
> had things "under control" all hell broke loose and
> we were wrong. Just when we thought we had the
> Christian life figured out, the bottom would fall out
> and we would discover we knew nothing!_
>
> _There was the time we were part of a group that
> sponsored a religious event requiring that we rent a
> large auditorium. We were certain it would be a
> huge success. We were confident that we were doing
> exactly what God wanted us to do! Perhaps we
> were—God needed another teachable moment! The
> event was a huge failure. Few people came to the
> event in spite of our best efforts._

There was another time we were involved in an important evangelization effort. It was a brand-new program that generated much enthusiasm. The bishop of the diocese in which we lived was behind the project. It had the potential to touch many people. The program was developed by outsiders who came to promote this wonderful new program. So many people were involved; it was exciting to be part of it. After months and months of work, everything began to disintegrate. The person who was responsible for developing the program left town with the lion's share of the money collected for the project. We were horror-stricken! "Hello, God! Are you there?!"

We learned so many things in those days! We learned that we are a sinful church and that we desperately need God's mercy to remain grafted to the true vine. God's message was simple. "Will you let me be God? Will you allow me to prune you into the tree I want you to become?" So often I said, "Are you kidding? What is it about NO you do not understand?" Yet in looking back on those days they were incredibly formative and they were exciting. They taught us the meaning of trust. They taught us patience. They taught us that no matter what, God will always be with us. God will be with us in all of life's difficulties. God will especially be with us when we suffer for promoting the gospel.

God used the circumstances of our lives to create in us a tremendous love and compassion for poor, frustrated, broken, and hurting people and those who are unable to make sense out of life. The events of our lives were the training ground for a life of discipleship. Today it seems a normal part of life to receive a call from John, the homeless man who last week asked us to bail him out of jail for the crime of sitting in front of our local grocery store.

I sometimes long for those early days—they were exciting. Each weekend we packed our children in the car and trekked off with other families to plant tomato fields in order to feed the poor in South America. We were part of a community called the "Community of the Cross." We were given many opportunities to reflect on what it means to be committed to the cross of Christ. We are no longer part of that community, but there are still many opportunities to reflect on that mystery. Times have changed, the crosses are different, life has settled down. The middle school and teenage years with our children

demanded that they do. But pruning never ends. There have been continued and many experiences to allow the grace of God to prune us into the people God wants us to become. We have been pruned in the context of parish, family, and self. I still cannot enthusiastically say to God, "Bring on the pruning sheers, Lord." But every time I look back, I am aware of the growth and I know that I am loved.

Sometimes our efforts to live the gospel and to love as Jesus invites us to love will bring opposition and hostility. I remember a time when I gave a homeless person some money to get some food. Someone approached me and chastised me for giving money to this person. The person in question proceeded to tell me that the homeless are worthless and that many of them should be eliminated (only his language was a bit more violent).

I believe that my desire to give to this man was rooted in my love for God. I know it was. I will admit that I do not work in the ministry day in and day out so I do not begin to know the sociology involved in the problem of homelessness. It is a complex problem. I do know this much. In that situation, at that time, it was my job to respond to a human need.

It was very uncomfortable to be so chastised. I would have preferred praise. But today's gospel is a reminder that the Christian life brings the cross. Paul was not deterred in the face of opposition. Even though I am tempted to avoid it, it is part of my Christian commitment. I am confident that God will continue to strengthen (prune) me so I can live the life of love today's gospel invites.

What was John trying to tell his community? In what way does this gospel invite Christians to enter more deeply into the Easter cycle of death and resurrection? What does it mean to you personally that Jesus is the vine and you are the branches? How do you feel about being pruned? Have you ever felt that you were pruned by the Vinedresser? What did you learn from the experience? Who in today's world might represent those who were cut away and thrown into the fire? How does this gospel invite transformation in your life? In what way does this gospel challenge your community today? In what way has this conversation with the scriptures for today's liturgy invited change in your life? In what way are the biblical themes of covenant, exodus, creation, and community evident in today's readings? Do you still feel the same way about this text as when you began? Has your original understanding been stretched, challenged, or affirmed?

STEP 5
DECISION

The gospel demands a response.

In what concrete way might your parish be invited to respond? Are there any attitudes or behaviors you would like to change as a result of today's conversation? What one concrete action will you take this week in response to the liturgy today?

Pastoral Considerations: In what way is your community living the implications of the first reading? How is your parish engaged in evangelization—dangerous evangelization, at that? Perhaps this gospel would be a good opportunity to reflect on the way in which your community lives the command to live as Jesus loves—with a self-sacrificing love. How long would your list be, if you were to name the ways?

Christian Initiation: Mystagogia continues to be a visible symbol in the community. The catechumens still in process continue to be dismissed to break open the Word. Is there anyone ready to celebrate a rite of acceptance, welcome, or full communion in the Catholic Church? In what way do you continue to invite people to "come and see" and to "stay with the Lord"? Easter season would be a wonderful time for a big evangelization effort and to invite people into your inquiry process.

DOCTRINAL ISSUES

What Church truth/teaching/doctrinal issue could be drawn from the gospel for the fifth Sunday of Easter?

Participants suggest possible doctrinal themes that flow from the readings.

Possible Doctrinal Themes

Symbol of cross; paschal mystery; love of God; paschal love; Christology; prayer; baptism; eucharist; mystery of church; service and servanthood; evangelization

Present the doctrinal material at this time.

1. The facilitator gives input on a particular doctrinal issue of his or her prior choosing. OR
2. The group chooses a doctrinal issue from the list they created. They read together from the Doctrinal Appendix or other appropriate, official Church documents and the works of respected theologians.

(Many doctrinal issues are found in the Doctrinal Appendix at the back of this workbook. If you are choosing an issue from this resource, please refer to it now.)

Reflection questions centered around the chosen doctrinal theme can be found at the end of each topic in the Doctrinal Appendix. The questions are based on the five-step reflection process. If you choose a topic not included in the Doctrinal Appendix, craft your own questions according to the same five-step process.

Following the reflection questions you will be reminded to return to chapter 7, "Preparing the Catechetical Session," to assist you in crafting your own session.

Closing Prayer

God our Father,
look upon us with love.
You redeem us and make us your children in
    Christ.
Give us true freedom
and bring us to the inheritance you promised.
We ask this through our Lord Jesus Christ, your
    Son,
who lives and reigns with you and the Holy Spirit,
one God, for ever and ever.[21]

---

[21]Fifth Sunday of Easter: "Opening Prayer," *The Sacramentary.*

Sixth Sunday of Easter

INTRODUCTORY RITES

Entrance Antiphon (or Opening Song)

Speak out with a voice of joy: let it be heard to the ends of the earth: The Lord has set his people free, alleluia. (see Is 48:20)[1]

Opening Prayer

The facilitator of the session may lead the prayer. Others in the group may be asked to proclaim the readings.

Let us pray
(that we may practice in our lives
the faith we profess)

Pause for silent prayer.

Ever-living God,
help us to celebrate our joy
in the resurrection of the Lord
and to express in our lives
the love we celebrate.
Grant this through our Lord Jesus Christ, your Son,
who lives and reigns with you and the Holy Spirit,
one God, for ever and ever.[2]

LITURGY OF THE WORD

The readings are proclaimed.

First Reading
Acts 10:25–26, 34–35, 44–48

(Refer to Easter Sunday for an overview of the Acts of the Apostles.)

Today's Pericope: Cornelius is a figure of great importance in the Acts of the Apostles. His appearance is a turning point in the mission of the church. Luke went to great lengths to stress this importance. The Cornelius affair was repeated in verse 11 and referenced again at the Council of Jerusalem in chapter 15. The conversion of Cornelius signals a major missionary effort to the gentiles, even though the mission had already begun through the efforts of Hellenist Jewish Christians. Luke had a theological purpose in making Peter instrumental in the mission to the gentiles. As far as Luke was concerned all the growth and development of the early Christian community flowed from Jerusalem, and Peter was the recognized leader of the Jerusalem church. Thus, Luke gives Peter the credit for bringing Cornelius into the fold of believing Christians.

Today's reading is cut from a longer section. The way it is pieced together in this pericope it looks as though Peter's words are responsible for the sending of the Spirit. When taken as a whole, together with Peter's sermon, this is not the case, however. The Spirit comes upon those whom God chooses—it is God's initiative. Raymond Brown asserts: "Because there are heavenly revelations both to Cornelius and Peter, readers are meant to recognize that what occurs here is uniquely God's will. Such an emphasis was probably necessary because of the controversial nature of the two issues involved: Are Christians bound by the Jewish rules for kosher foods? Should the Gentiles be received without first becoming Jews?"[3]

The last question prompts serious reflection for Christians today. Jesus did not solve the dilemma of whether gentile Christians should become Jews. Raymond Brown reminds us: "There are those today on both extremes of the ecclesiastical spectrum (ultraliberal, ultraconservative) who think they can appeal to the words or deeds of Jesus to solve any question in the church (parochial, diocesan or universal). If Jesus did not solve the most fundamental question of the Christian mission, we may well doubt that his recorded words solve most of our subsequent debated problems in

[1]Sixth Sunday of Easter: "Entrance Antiphon," *The Sacramentary.*

[2]Sixth Sunday of Easter: "Opening Prayer," *The Sacramentary.*

[3]*OCSP*, 60.

the church."[4] In the tenth chapter of Acts Peter allows Cornelius to be baptized because the Holy Spirit came upon him. "In other words we have another instance of Christians facing an unforseen problem and solving it, not by appealing to a previous blueprint for the church, but by insight (gained from the Holy Spirit) as to what Christ wanted for the church."[5] Today's reading perfectly expresses one of Luke's primary concerns: "the universality of the church and the equality of all its members in Christ."[6] In the opening verse of today's reading, Cornelius falls at the feet of Peter. Peter bids him rise, stressing that he (Peter) is only human. This is Luke's way of stressing the humanity of the church and that to be Jewish is not better than being gentile. It is also a lesson in servanthood. Peter recognized himself as no greater than even the most humble servant in his midst.

Luke's agenda of universality was difficult to promulgate. Tensions and prejudices ran deep and were difficult to overcome. The Council of Jerusalem and the debates with the Judaizers demonstrate that universality was a principle which caused serious tension in the church.

Another major theme of Luke is that the Holy Spirit is the engineer behind the Christian movement. It is not surprising therefore that the Holy Spirit descended upon Cornelius and his household before they were baptized. There is a theology being expressed here. This coming of the Spirit on the house of Cornelius is God's way of uniting Christians and gentiles, whether they liked it or not. How could anyone argue with God's intention? What greater approbation could anything receive than the authority of Almighty God? Peter responded to divine initiative. He baptized non-Jewish persons into the fold of Christian believers.

Why, then, did Cornelius need to be baptized since he was already baptized by the Holy Spirit? "What would have been the status of converts who had received the Spirit but who had not yet been baptized? The best answer to this question is that the Spirit has, in this unique instance, gone beyond the confines of the Church and bestowed its blessing on outsiders. They are then brought into the circle of the people of God through baptism. Normally one is brought into the Church and there receives the Spirit."[7]

A new missionary stage was inaugurated with the baptism of Cornelius. Through the ascension of Jesus disciples were empowered to proclaim the good news to Jerusalem, Judea, and Samaria, then all the earth. The Cornelius saga situates this mission to preach "to all nations" within the heart of the church and makes the universal mission part and parcel of the Christian tradition. To be Christian is to be inclusive of all people.

No obstacles were to be placed in the path of people coming to faith in Christ—not prejudice, not cult. Religious rituals would no longer be seen as a barrier. Circumcision was no longer a requirement. God was doing something new. The veil had been torn and obstacles removed. The final obstacle, Jesus' body, had ascended to the throne of glory and now all people are universally invited with no exceptions.

Luke's theology is quite sophisticated. He demonstrates how people who are open and receptive to the will of God can and must respond to the divine prompting of God's Spirit. Those same receptive individuals respond even when they do not fully understand. This receptivity leads to openness to other people with mutually shared vision.[8] This vision opens people up to one another, to other ideologies, and to other cultures. Receptivity of this nature leads people to accept other people's experiences of God, even when different from one's own.

The single most significant result of the resurrection was the sending of the Holy Spirit to all believers. The Church does not just celebrate the sending of the Spirit on Pentecost. It is an integral part of the whole paschal mystery. The entire fifty days of Easter celebrates the sending of the Spirit, just as the Jewish feast of Pentecost celebrates the enjoyment of fruits of the Promised Land.[9] Today's Pentecost on the house of Cornelius is one more facet to the mystery of the sending of the Spirit.

---

[4]Ibid., 62.
[5]Ibid.
[6]*WWC*, 176.

[7]*PL*, 269.
[8]*NULA* (II), 131.
[9]*PL*, 268.

Questions for Mystagogical Reflection: Put yourself in Peter's shoes. Do you think you would have made the same decision he did in regard to Cornelius? Are you similarly open to seeing the work of the Spirit in your life and in the lives of others? Explain. In what way has the Spirit of God worked in your life in a surprising way? In what way is this reading a challenge to the contemporary church? In what way does the church live according to the example in today's reading? Where is growth needed? In what way does this reading invite you to enter more deeply into the paschal mystery?

Responsorial Psalm
Psalm 98:1, 2–3, 3–4

Psalm 98 was an enthronement psalm celebrating Yahweh's victory. This was symbolized by the enthronement liturgy in which Israel's king was ceremoniously crowned. It is used in the Easter season as a reminder that Jesus is enthroned and was victorious over sin and death through the power of the resurrection.

Second Reading
1 John 4:7–10

(Refer to the Feast of the Holy Family for an overview of the First Letter of John.)

Today's Pericope: The author of the first letter of John is returning to a favorite theme he commonly used as a polemic against his Gnostic friends—love of one another is the sure test of a person's love for God. In other words, behavior matters. It is through love of others that a person really "knows" God. This love of one another is possible because God is love.

Probably the most quoted truism in the scriptures, "God is love," has also been the most misused. It is not a creedal statement or a philosophical principle. The statement "God is love" flows from the proclamation of a gospel in which God's love is recognized and experienced in the awesome, incredible sacrifice of God's Son through a horrible death, only to be raised from that death to resurrected and exalted life. Too often that phrase gets relegated to meaningless fluff. Few stop to think of what it really means and how we "know" that love. "God is love" is the profession of faith of those who know firsthand and have experienced

what God's love truly means. God's love is known through the sacrifice and death of someone so dear that the earth cried out in wailing and lament. We know God's love because of the incarnation and atonement.

"Knowing God" in the scriptural sense assumed that there was an intimate relationship with the living God. The secessionist members of the Johannine community minimized the importance of the incarnation and the responsibility to live ethical lives. The author of John's letter understood intimately that love comes directly from God—that love is the essence of God. Thus, in order to love God, one must be begotten of God. Only like can know like, so in order to "know" God one must be a child of God. To be begotten of God is to live in God's love that ultimately leads to righteous living. The Gnostics claimed to have a special knowledge of God that only they possessed. The author insists that true "knowledge" of God flows out of loving relationship with God and one another.

Questions for Mystagogical Reflection: In what way do you "know" God in this biblical understanding of knowing? In what way have you experienced the reality that God is love? How is the division between the Johannine community and the secessionist members of that community relevant today? What does their situation have to teach us? In what way does this reading invite you into the cycle of death and resurrection?

The gospel is proclaimed.

Gospel
John 15:1–17. No one has greater love than this: to lay down one's life for his friends.

Step 1
Naming One's Experience

What were your first impressions? What was your first response to the gospel (or the other readings)? What captured your attention?

Each person names his or her initial impression. Statements should be brief. No reasons should be given at this time. All simply listen without agreeing or disagreeing.

In a brief statement, explain what you think this gospel is trying to convey.

Liturgical Context

Today's liturgy is a blending of Easter themes—baptism, paschal mystery, death, resurrection, and Holy Spirit. Baptism features strongly in the first reading. The issue of baptism by the Holy Spirit places this liturgy squarely in the midst of the initiatory life of the church. Through the sacrament of baptism, we are given the gift of the Spirit. When the early Christians gathered and the bishop prayed the prayer of blessing over the Easter waters, they believed that the Trinity became present in the water. Through the calling down of the Holy Spirit upon the sacred chrism, it transcends from mere ointment to Jesus' "grace which through the presence of the Holy Spirit instills his divinity into us."[10] Through baptism, the Father calls us, we die with Jesus, and we are sealed with the Holy Spirit.[11] "Theodore saw the font as womb into which the candidate descended to receive second birth from the Holy Spirit, whose presence impregnates the water."[12] Jesus' promise to send his Holy Spirit is made real through baptism and the sacraments. All of the readings today punctuate the fulfillment of Jesus' promise to his disciples. We see the effects of his word in the ministry of the apostles and those first early communities.

John's gospel exhorts us to follow the great commandment of love. Our Easter faith empowers us to experience what the opening prayer asks of the Father: "help us to celebrate our joy in the resurrection of the Lord and to express in our lives the love we celebrate." Through the eucharist we actu-

alize and make tangible the indwelling Spirit. We are thus empowered to go out and live the law of love, to evangelize and give witness to the saving power of God. "Strengthen us by this Easter sacrament; may we feel its saving power in our lives" (prayer after communion).

The Lord asks us to be with our brothers and sisters in the world. When we receive the Spirit of God we become defenders of God's people. We become God's advocates for those who cannot defend themselves in a hostile world. "In his surrender, Jesus gave us life. This gift from the Lord should make us respect and welcome our neighbors with their needs, their suffering, and their life projects.... We cannot, therefore, allow people to set themselves up as masters of the lives of others. The right to life is the primary right of the human person."[13]

We are given a glimpse of how John understands love in today's second reading. It is not simply a nice feeling or an intellectual knowledge. Love is rooted in action, and as we can see from today's gospel, it is a love that leads to the offering of one's life for another. Pure love ultimately means the sacrifice of self. Dietrich Bonhoeffer, the German theologian who was killed in the Nazi concentration camps, expressed it with his life. His legacy and wisdom live on.

> When a man really gives up trying to make something out of himself—a saint or a converted sinner or a churchman (a so-called clerical somebody), a righteous or unrighteous man.... When in the fullness of tasks, questions, successes or ill-haps, experiences and perplexities, a man throws himself into the arms of God ... then he awakes with Christ in Gethsemane. That is faith, that is metanoia and it is thus that he becomes a man and a Christian. How can a man wax arrogant if in *a this-sided life* he shares in the suffering of God?[14]

G. Leibholz, when writing about Bonhoeffer, wrote: "To Bonhoeffer Christianity was not the

[10]Edward Yarnold, S.J., *AIRI*, 23–24.

[11]Ibid.

[12]Ibid., 24.

[13]*SWTLY*, 104.

[14]Dietrich Bonhoeffer, *Das Zeugnis eines Boten*, ed. by Visser 't Hooft, Geneva, 1945, 46–47.

concern of the believing pious soul who shuts himself up and keeps himself within the bounds of the sacramental sphere. No, according to him Christianity has its place in this world and the Church as the Body of Christ and the fellowship in him can only be the visible church. Man must follow him who has passed through this world as the living, dying and the risen Lord. Therefore, wherever it pleases God to put man in this world, the Christian must be ready for martyrdom and death. It is only this way that man learns faith."[15]

The season of Easter is an extended meditation on the paschal mystery. It is the time in which the entire church is to engage in mystagogical reflection. Today's liturgy takes us right into the heart of Easter's purpose.

Gospel Exegesis

The facilitator provides input from critical biblical scholarship on this text. This input includes insights as to how people would have heard the gospel in Jesus' time.

John the evangelist loves the word "love." In eight verses he used it eight times. Emotions had little to do with "love" in the ancient Mediterranean world, however. Loving had more to do with attachment to a group than it did with warm feelings. When Joshua exhorted the people to love the Lord he added that they should also "hold fast" to him (Jos 22:5). Solomon clung to his wives in love (1 Kgs 11:2). A husband and wife leave their parents and "cling" to each other—they become one flesh. The husband clings now to his wife, even though he still lives in his father's house. This "leaving his father and mother" assumes a detachment from his parents and a new attachment to his wife. The image of vine and branches from last week's gospel best expresses the meaning of love. The branches (Christians) are attached to the vine (Jesus).

How is this *love as attachment* theme played out in the gospel? God so loved the world (God was so attached to human beings) that he sent his Son. God is intimately attached to the Son. Jesus was incredulous when the Pharisees insisted that God

was their Father. How could God be their Father when they persisted in rejecting Jesus, who comes from the Father? "Rephrased, Jesus' objection is that if his opponents were attached to him who came from God it would be clear that they are indeed attached to the Father. But since they are not attached to Jesus, they cannot be attached to the Father."[16] Jesus' entire ministry centered around inviting people to become attached intimately to God, just like the branches are attached to the vine.

To be elected of God in Israel presupposed deep relationship with God. This relationship is authenticated by righteous behavior. One of the reasons the prophets had to repeat the message of faithfulness to the commandments ad nauseam was because the people did not hear it, get it, or live it! "Each prophet challenged the people to 'keep' the covenant to 'obey' the commandments to 'perform deeds of justice and charity', because this was not the normal cultural script."[17] Jesus constantly repeated his instruction to observe the great commandments because of his great love. He so dearly wanted people to embrace his/God's love for them. Yet like Israel, so many did not get, hear it, or live it!

In antiquity the primary disposition of women was "doing." Thus, Jesus extolled Mary's orientation of "being" and challenged Martha's orientation toward "doing." The male orientation, on the other hand, was that of "being." Jesus' primary audience in chapter 15 was probably male. Thus, in this case Jesus was challenging the male orientation toward "being." Jesus teased the imagination to look at things from new perspectives. He presented a new and transformed way of looking at the world and at God. Jesus demanded that the disciples move out of the mold of "being" and embrace the way of doing. He called the disciples to action—to keep the commandments, to *really* keep the commandments, not just give lip service, but heartfelt observance.

Today's gospel pericope takes the argument posed by the First Letter of John to the next level. Jesus demonstrates how far love of God is to go. There is

---

[15] G. Leibholz in *The Cost of Discipleship* by Dietrich Bonhoeffer (New York: Collier Books, Macmillan, 1963).

[16] *CWJB*, 83.
[17] Ibid., 83–84.

no greater love, insists John's Jesus, than to lay down one's life for a friend.[18] Thus, for those who say behavior means nothing (the Gnostics), the evangelist tells them that they are wrong. Behavior not only means something, but the ultimate act of love exists in the offering of one's life for the sake of love. Jesus' death on the cross is the primary example of this love. However, evidence of his love has earlier origins. Jesus' incarnation "brings into the picture an earlier act of love: the divine self-giving in becoming one of us."[19] Raymond Brown uses the word *earlier* from a human perspective since the entire action of God's gift of the Son is considered one divine action.[20] Some theologians, while reflecting on the awesome, incredible intensity of Christ's love demonstrated in the incarnation, have wondered if that love alone would have been enough to bring about the salvation of the world. So great and intense is the love of Christ, that perhaps it would have been enough—even without the crucifixion. It is an interesting reflection, but the fact remains that God chose Christ's selfless act of sacrifice as the means of redemption.

Brown describes the origin of love spoken of in today's gospel. He affirms that Jesus and the Father love one another. The Sonship of Jesus means more than divine identity. The most intense human love known, for example, the love parents have for their children, is but a minuscule shadow of the love Jesus shares with his Father. We try to compare heavenly realities according to the things we experience on earth. Jesus, on the other hand, knew heaven. He tried to find things on earth he could use to explain the realities of heaven. "[H]eaven was to him more real or true than earth, and God's love was the standard by which our love was to be measured."[21]

The message is clear—if human beings could only fathom the love Jesus and his Father share, and in turn love with that kind of love, they would never know loneliness again. They would be bound to one another just as the Father and the Son are bound to each other. This kind of binding would offer the believer a kinship unlike any they had ever known as a Jew, Samaritan, or Gentile believer. "[F]or the very existence of followers of Jesus who love one another with the love by which he loved us constitutes a revelation of the Father and the Son, a revelation that gives life."[22]

In Jesus' farewell address to his disciples at the Last Supper, Jesus describes to them the way in which he will continue to offer his self-gift to the world—his unconditional, unmerited, gratuitous love and presence after his death, resurrection, and ascension. Jesus tells them that he will send his Spirit to continue his mission in the world. In this section of chapter 15 Jesus describes what true friendship means. In chapter 14 John explains the special way in which Jesus will continue his presence in the community of believers. We hear of the love that Jesus has for his disciples; how the disciples will be rewarded for such love, and how they will experience opposition in the world.[23] Today we hear to what depths love is expected to go. Love continues to shake hands with the cross as the ultimate expression of God's love.

In the face of such love, Christians are to keep the commandments. Jesus exhorted his followers to follow the two great commandments. Disciples must love the Lord their God with their entire body, soul, and spirit—with the totality of themselves. They are to love one another, as Jesus himself loved—unto death. This love will be evident by the way in which it is poured out to God's *anawim*—the poor, marginalized, and oppressed—and to all people. It is a tall order, but Christians will be empowered through the power of Jesus and the Holy Spirit. Love will win over death. The poor will be cared for, animosity will cease, and where two or more are gathered in Jesus' name, the reign of God will be realized.

---

[18]It is important to note that according to the Johannine community "friends" were believers of Christ. There was so much tension between Christians and the Jews and Christians and the Gnostics, that the gospel was written as a polemic to the issues faced by the Christian community. Thus, "friend" does not mean outsiders. Friends refers to brother and sister Christians. In Matthew's gospel the imperative to love extends toward enemies. Since that is not John's agenda, it is not specifically mentioned. The primary concerns of the Johannine community were issues of tension just mentioned.

[19]*JTE*, 24.

[20]Ibid.

[21]*CWJB*, 82.

---

[22]Ibid., 83.

[23]Pheme Perkins, "The Gospel According to John," *NJBC*, 975.

In Jesus' second farewell address his compassion and love for his disciples capture our hearts and take residence there. He knows they will feel lost and abandoned. He knows they will long for his comforting presence and to return to the "way things used to be." He knows they will be lonely and bewildered. Jesus prepares the disciples for his absence by assuring them of his indwelling in the midst of his absence. This indwelling is the love shared between Father and Son offered to believers. He promises to dwell in the hearts of all believers. He promises to send his Spirit to dwell within. Then they will fully appreciate and know that Jesus and the Father are one.[24] His return hinges on their fidelity to the commandments—Jesus' commandments, the great commandments.

John expresses a theology of church and friendship—an ecclesiology. To be grafted to Jesus brings untold joy, but it also carries a responsibility. When love is given, love must be shared. God offered the greatest gift of love to human beings that could ever be offered. Human response in kind is to offer the gift of faithfulness as well as the supreme gift of one's self. This selfless act of love was possible with Christ because the Father dwelt within him. It is possible in the Christian because Christ and the Father dwell within each Christian. We know that Jesus and his Father shared mutual indwelling because of the love Jesus had for his Father, evidenced by the faithfulness and obedience to his will. This obedience is rooted in the two great commandments and obedience and faithfulness are possible only when the believer lives them. Believers can be confident that God through Jesus will continue to dwell within them by their faithfulness to the covenant.

The invitation to offer one's life in self-sacrifice is one of the most distinguishing differences between Judaism and Christianity. Nowhere in Judaism is there such an exhortation to offer one's life in sacrifice. It is the hallmark of Christianity—the ultimate invitation and challenge. The willingness to offer one's life for others is central to the paschal mystery. We join Christ in the sacrifice of his life for the sins of the world.

Jesus' own action of self-sacrifice forged a new community and those who belong to this new community are called his friends. At every eucharistic banquet we remember and make present this sacrifice of love. We remember that Jesus gathered with his "friends" and for all generations continues to gather with his friends. This friendship is rooted in reciprocal, covenant love.

To be Christian only required one credential—faith in the Risen One and a commitment to love. There were no more barriers. The old designation of chosen people was resurrected to include Jews, gentiles, and all believers. The obstacles are gone; there are no more elites. Jesus' community is inclusive. All are invited; all are called friends. Abraham and Moses were both called friends of God. God spoke to them and related to them in intimacy. "By making his followers friends, first of himself and then of the Father, Jesus performed in the same manner as did divine wisdom: 'In each generation, she passes into holy souls and makes of them the beloved (*philai*, friends) of God (Wisdom 7:27).'"[25]

Today's gospel is a strong word of encouragement to martyrs and disciples of all ages who suffer and struggle to live the gospel and the command to love selflessly. John's insight provides Christians with the ongoing inspiration needed to endure in the face of persecution, suffering, and pain.

In the ancient world there were varied meanings attached to human suffering. There was a sense that trials and hardships were beneficial to human beings, that suffering was somehow part of God's divine plan. "It was regarded as a means to human betterment."[26] Jews and pagans referred to suffering in varying, but common ways. Suffering was regarded as discipline, purification, refinement, and education. The Jewish perspective of suffering was rooted in monotheism. Pagan understanding was rooted in pantheism. "Jews regarded a relationship with a personal God as the end of human existence and obedience to God as the supreme virtue; pagans saw virtue as an end in itself."[27] Jews believed that suffering was useful to correct misguided direction in human life. Pagans believed that adversity and pain helped to develop and strengthen the individual.

---

[24] *GEJ*, 77.

[25] *WWC*, 178.
[26] *LTS*, 91.
[27] Ibid.

Early Christianity appropriated the Jewish and pagan notions of suffering and situated them within the context of the Christian experience. Christians believe that suffering embodies divine education, correction for misdirection, and suffering as refinement of a person's strength and stamina. For the Christian, suffering is the classroom in which a person learns obedience to God. Jesus more deeply embraced the will of God as he passed through suffering.

Suffering heightens our ability to look within our lives and discern the state of our relationship with God and to assess where growth is needed. Suffering often situates the teachable moment. "Suffering is the arena in which the Christian can be 1) disciplined, in the sense of training that develops strength; 2) refined, in the sense of the smelting process's use of fire to purify precious metals; and 3) educated in the sense of learning the right way to live. Looked at in this way, suffering and adversity as divine education are not only compatible with God's loving nature but also inherent in Christian existence." (*LTS,* 90).

Thus, suffering has the potential to bring about good—to offer positive benefits. Jesus takes the principle a step further in today's gospel. He insists that if we suffer for others, if we lay down our lives for others, there would not only be positive benefits, but our action would be redemptive. There is no greater love that anyone could ever show toward another human being.

It has been suggested by some scholars that an underlying perspective–a subtext for John's gospel—is persecution. Looking at today's gospel from the vantage point of a church under siege provides a whole new perspective on the meaning of today's pericope. In early pagan documents written around A.D. 110 there is mention of a new Christian movement. These documents have shed much light on Christian practice, loyalties, and attitudes and the way they were regarded by Roman officials. Persecution against the Christians probably resulted from pagans who spread rumors against the Christians for economic reasons. Sales in the sacrifice of animals used in pagan sacrifices soared as the Christian persecutions increased and Christianity became an illegal religion. Even Pliny, a prosecutor of Christians, concluded that Christians were not guilty of regular crimes—they were simply guilty of professing the name of Christ and paying homage to him—*accusatio nominis,* an "accusation of the name." It is not certain when (or for certain if) widespread persecution began. A letter signed by Gaius Plinius Caecilius Secundus, commonly known as Pliny the younger and an emissary of the emperor Trajan, indicates that persecution did indeed take place.

> For the moment this is the line I have taken with all persons brought before me on the charge of being Christians. I have asked them in person if they are Christians; and if they admit it, I repeat the question a second time and a third time, with a warning of the punishment awaiting them. If they persist, I order them to be led away for execution. . . . For a great many individuals of every age and class, both men and women, are being brought to trial, and this is likely to continue. It is not only the towns, but villages and rural districts too which are infected through contact with this wretched cult (*Letters* X. 96, 3, 9).[28]

Throughout John's gospel Jesus' sovereignty as Lord is acclaimed. There were others who coveted that same sovereign title. The emperors of the first century professed their own divine sovereignty and status. Is it any wonder that Christians were so suspect and found themselves in harm's way when they hailed as king and Lord someone other than the emperor? "Within a context of Roman imperial claims and within context in which some members of John's audience may have been under the threat of denunciation and trial, the evangelist's emphatic upholding of Christ's sovereignty beyond any sovereign entity of 'the world' could only inspire a renewed dedication of commitment to Jesus. It was, of course, Jesus and not Nero or any other emperor who was truly the *Savior of the world.* It was, of course, Jesus and not Domitian or any other emperor who was truly *Lord and God.* No Roman emperor of any age, but only Jesus shows the way to the Father and the life that is everlasting."[29]

A community under siege would have taken great solace in a Jesus who stood victorious before his

---

[28]*JGNP,* 20.
[29]Ibid., 55.

human court, stating that it had no power over him. A community under siege would need the power of the Holy Spirit as Paraclete, Counselor, and "Defense Attorney." A community under siege would need the Spirit to help them stand firm in their testimony to Jesus over and against the evil one.

How does a Christian community become ready to face arrest and persecution? The farewell discourse of John's gospel provides wonderful material for support, encouragement, prayer, and strength as a community looks down the proverbial barrel of the gun into the onslaught of torture and persecution. Since the crime was allegiance to Christ, where to go for strength but to the Christology of the Johannine community? The fourth gospel's insistence that Jesus is Lord over all the powers of the earth, including the power of death, would be most assuring when facing death and persecution. Who to call on but the Christ who stood in the very place where the church now stands? Where does the church now stand? The church now stands as a "friend of Jesus" as opposed to a "friend of Caesar" (sound familiar?). "In encouraging one another, might not Christians familiar with John's Gospel have framed their encouragement in terms: Better to be the friend of Jesus than the friend of Pliny Caesar? Better to lay down one's life as a friend of Jesus than to compromise with Pliny for 'friendship' with Trajan."[30] Persecuted Christans could not find better encouragement and support for enduring through persecutions than the words and images of Jesus in his farewell address to his disciples.

Persecution forces decision. Will Christians remain steadfast in their profession of faith in Christ? Will they stand firm in the face of persecution and torture? What matters most to the community is that members have the courage to face the trials ahead, that they give faithful witness to Christ, and that they express the incredible love already grafted to their entire being through the love of Christ by laying down their lives for him and for one another. Preparation for the time of testing is crucial. Preparing for siege is therefore time to call in the troops, to regroup, to close the ranks, and to strengthen one another for the ordeal ahead.[31] "This very image of the community gathered together in love and intimacy during a time of persecution is in fact almost the very image provided in John's description of Jesus' presence with his disciples under the circumstances of his approaching 'hour.' "[32]

Jesus not only talked the talk, he walked the walk all the way to the cross. He showed the church with the example of his life what lay ahead for them. He offered the ultimate gift of love to his friends—everyone who called on him in faith—and in the process he saved the world. The ordeal that faced the Johannine community would be faced with Christ leading them every step of the way. They too would be called to lay down their lives out of love, but never could there be so great a sacrifice. Jesus' final words to his friends promise that when he returns to his Father they will be given the Holy Spirit who will be their strength. The Paraclete/Advocate/Defense Attorney will assist them in their "hour." They will have the strength to act in love because God and the Father dwells within them—they are grafted to the Divine Branch. They will remain steadfast.

The gospel is simple but it is not easy. "There is a legend recorded by Saint Jerome that when John was an old man, when he could no longer compose a sermon, he said over and over again, 'Little children, love one another.' When people kept asking him why he always repeated the same words, he answered, 'If you do that, you do enough.' "[33] What is enough? To love unto death, that is enough! To love as a martyr loves with all that implies.

View from a Martyr's Grave

He gave them food, they called him Saint Francis.
When he asked, "Why are they hungry?"
...then he was Marxist.
He was the Pied Piper of children, they called him a lover
Till he empowered their parents....

---

[30] Ibid., 65.

[31] Next week's gospel expresses a strong *us versus them* mentality that at first glance (at least for modern readers) appears so antithetical to the gospel. However, in light of the persecution context of the gospel it is most understandable.

[32] *JGNP*, 65.

[33] *RJE*, 87.

He was the worst kind of traitor.
A man in good standing, he was polite and political,
Till he discovered the poor; they branded him radical.
He spoke without fear from the streets and the pulpit,
"Justice, not charity, our God demands it!"
The Kingdom of God belongs to just such as these....
The poor, the oppressed, those brought to their knees.
So listen, you rich, you powerful,
you hidden evil powers,
We stand in the midst of the God of this hour.
You may pierce my hands, put a crown on my head,
You can send flying bullets with blood flowing red.
But God will be heard in the cries of the poor.
You may run, you may hide, you may feel quite secure.
All who will listen, I give my command, Now is the time,
You, be my hand....
That will summon the poets, give sweat to the plow,
Suck blood from the martyrs,
Who cry, "Listen to us now.
We spoke with our lives, we shout from our graves....
Listen people, hear us,
You're not free ... you are slaves
To the riches that bind,
the greed that rots the soul,
To death-dealing power,
To lives heartless and cold."
Turn not a deaf ear when rumors start to roam
About a God who is angry, is weeping, who moans ...
For a people in silent pain, for a world in grave danger,
For the weak, the powerless, the lost, and the stranger.
Take heart, O Hopeful, for all is not lost,
There is time, it is now,
But great is the cost.
You must work, you must build,
You must fight and demand more,
For now it is *their* banquet,
You must stand with the poor![34]

_____

[34] Mary Birmingham, 1995.

Proclaim the gospel again.

Sometimes we gain new insights when we hear the text after the interpretation is given. Someone from the group proclaims the gospel a second time.

STEP 4
TESTING

Conversation with the Liturgy and the Scriptures

Test your original understanding in dialogue with the text.

(You might consider breaking into smaller groups.)

Now that you've heard the exegesis, were there any new insights? How do you feel about it? How does your original understanding of this gospel compare with what we just shared? How does this story speak to your life?

Sharing Life Experience

Participants share an experience from their lives that connects with the biblical interpretation just presented.

> *I love movies. I am particularly fascinated by movies that touch the spiritual imagination through the world of symbol. There are not many such movies, but when one comes on the scene I am enthralled. One of my favorites is "The Spitfire Grill." Another is called "The Mighty." They are both quite paschal in nature. In "The Spitfire Grill" a victim's compassionate love for another ultimately led to suspicion and her death. Her death did not end in tragedy but was the source of life for the entire community and invited its transformation. Ultimately it is the Christ story played out in a twentieth-century setting—in the life of a very ordinary person. It is also today's gospel played out in twentieth-century narrative. The Christlike figure in this movie is a young disadvantaged, abused sixteen-year-old woman parolee who served time for stabbing her father who had repeatedly raped her throughout her life. She was recuperating from the loss of her father's baby in utero, killed by him in one of his drunken fits of rage. She felt nothing but guilt for the sin of killing her father and the inability to protect her baby. But she was determined in the midst of this brokenness to forge a*

new life and to reach out to the God who intimately knew her suffering and pain. She chose Gilead, a place of peace and solace in the scriptures, as her place of new life and refuge. This very glum place was anything but peaceful and idyllic, however.

This young woman chose to reach out and love another broken, human being—someone who had long ago given up on not only love, but life as well. She chose to offer hope when everyone around her had given in to cynicism and hopelessness. She was a beacon of light in the midst of gloom and despair. Her love was contagious. She upset the status quo and threatened the pride and position of another character in the drama and as a result a plot against her was put in motion. In the end she paid for her love with her life.

Most of us are not given such dramatic opportunities to live today's gospel. We all know the stories of great heroes of faith such as Maximilian Kolbe, Mother Teresa, and Archbishop Romero. We can, however, die in small ways every time we stand up for the gospel. When we choose to love rather than hate, when we refuse to give in to petty jealousies, useless animosities, and power plays that serve no one but human gods, when we stand up for truth and justice and in the process get labeled a freak or "off the edge," when we are willing to put others first, then we truly live today's gospel.

I think of the people who stand in protest over the schools of death such as the "School of the Americas," the ones who stand in picket lines of any sort—at abortion clinics, nuclear waste sites, and so on. I think of the people who are willing to risk speaking up when the needs of the poor are not met through demeaning legislation. I think of those who speak out against unpopular issues such as the death penalty and those who refuse to be swayed by what is politically correct or incorrect. I think of the missionaries in every country who risk life and limb to minister to the world's poor. I think of all those people who are willing to lay down their lives for others. I think of the people in parishes who sacrifice their lives every day to care for others.

There is the young woman whose husband is a paraplegic and who selflessly and lovingly has given her entire life to care for him. There are the spouses who care for their Alzheimer-afflicted spouses. There is a woman in our parish who spends a few hours every Sunday morning with an Alzheimer patient so her husband can get some needed relief and come to mass. There is another woman who spends hours every day ministering to the needs of people in the parish in one way or another. There is another woman who lovingly gave every bit of her seventy-five-year-old energy to care for her 101-year-old mother with the greatest tenderness I have ever seen given to another human being. She chose to be her sole care so she could love the mother who gave her so much love. There is the young man who had a lucrative job as an engineer, who chose to lay down his life and give it all up so he could develop a water treatment plant for the Third World. It has not been easy. He does not always have enough to pay his bills, but over thirty thousand people in the Third World have clean drinking water because of him. I feel honored to know him. There are the many single mothers in our parish who try so desperately to provide a nurturing home for their children, who fall exhausted into bed every night, who minister to their children and still seem to have time to give to the community. There is the man who refused to sign off on a shipment of steel that was going to an airline factory and in the process lost his job. There is my friend and my husband who spend the cold nights of winter on the floor next to our city's homeless. The list is endless. So are the invitations.

Dying also involves faith-filled, trusting endurance. I cannot help but connect this gospel with the events of this past weekend. Tonight the nation mourns the death of John F. Kennedy Jr.—a very good man, and his lovely wife and her sister. We grieve with and for the family. Here is a family who has known incredible suffering, death, and tragedy but who has refused to give in to despair. Faith is their anchor and in spite of their human failings they are an example of how adversity has the power to strengthen. Their faith in the midst of this tragedy is an example that the power of death will not have the last word and that endurance comes through testing by fire. They could write the modern-day Book of Job. Job, too, was wealthy. His wealth meant nothing when faced with the ultimate test of his life. His primary concern in the midst of his tragedies was his relationship with God. He refused to believe that God had abandoned him. We as a nation ask God how one family could be asked to endure so much. There are no answers. If it were my family I would have a difficult time working through my anger. I would hear St. Theresa's words echo in my ear all too frequently, "Lord, if this *is how you treat your friends, no wonder you have so few." Yet all I ever hear every time this family experiences another tragedy is an expression of faith in God.*

Those who stand before the world and attest to their faith in God as their strength live the imperatives of today's gospel. They have learned what it means to die so we might all live. Their faith is a form of dying and it is a sign of hope for the world. Who knows how many people might remember this family's example of faith (perhaps it is only a decision to trust) and turn to God in a desperate moment to find strength and solace in the midst of tragedy?

Today's gospel is the heart of all scripture—it could be a summary of everything contained within its pages. If we get today's gospel and live by it, we get it all. It is the heart of paschal faith.

What was John trying to tell his community? Have you ever had an experience in which you were invited to "die for a friend," if even in a very small way? In what way does today's gospel invite you to embrace the paschal mystery? In what way does it invite change in your thinking and/or your behavior? In what way have you grown in your love (love as described in today's gospel) for God and one another? In what concrete way does this gospel and liturgy invite you to enter more deeply into the paschal mystery of Christ? In what way does this gospel challenge your community today? In what way has this conversation with the scriptures for today's liturgy invited change in your life? In what way are the biblical themes of covenant, exodus, creation, and community evident in today's readings? Do you still feel the same way about this text as when you began? Has your original understanding been stretched, challenged, or affirmed?

STEP 5
DECISION

The gospel demands a response.

In what concrete way might your parish be invited to respond? Are there any attitudes or behaviors you would like to change as a result of today's conversation? What one concrete action will you take this week in response to the liturgy today?

Pastoral Considerations: In what way might your parish grow in its responsibility to evangelize as Peter and the early church evangelized in today's first reading? Perhaps this would be a good time for your parish to participate in an effort to evangelize your neighborhoods, to invite those without a church family to "come and see." What strategies might you consider? Who are the people in your community in need of the love expressed in the gospel? Who are the marginalized members of your community? Who are the favored members of your community? Who are the ignored members of your community? How does your parish extend hospitality?

Christian Initiation: This would be a most appropriate day to celebrate a rite of full communion for baptized Christians in another ecclesial tradition. This would also be a marvelous day to celebrate infant baptisms. The initiation themes are very strong in today's liturgy. It might also be fitting to celebrate a rite of acceptance or a rite of welcome. Neophytes continue to be a visible presence in the Sunday assembly, and they continue to meet to break open the symbols of the Vigil. Catechumens continue to be dismissed to further reflect on Word and tradition.

DOCTRINAL ISSUES

What Church truth/teaching/doctrinal issue could be drawn from the gospel for the sixth Sunday of Easter?

Participants suggest possible doctrinal themes that flow from the readings.

Possible Doctrinal Themes

Love of God; faith, hope, and love; evangelization; ecumenism; paschal mystery; mystery of suffering; moral living; the great commandments; justice; baptism; sacraments

Present the doctrinal material at this time.

1. The facilitator gives input on a particular doctrinal issue of his or her prior choosing. OR
2. The group chooses a doctrinal issue from the list they created. They read together from the Doctrinal Appendix or other appropriate, offi-

cial Church documents and the works of respected theologians.

(Many doctrinal issues are found in the Doctrinal Appendix at the back of this workbook. If you are choosing an issue from this resource, please refer to it now.)

Reflection questions centered around the chosen doctrinal theme can be found at the end of each topic in the Doctrinal Appendix. The questions are based on the five-step reflection process. If you choose a topic not included in the Doctrinal Appendix, craft your own questions according to the same five-step process.

Following the reflection questions you will be reminded to return to chapter 7, "Preparing the Catechetical Session," to assist you in crafting your own session.

Closing Prayer

Through the resurrection of his Son,
God has redeemed you and made you his children.
May he bless you with joy. Amen.
The Redeemer has given you lasting freedom.
May you inherit his everlasting life. Amen.
By faith you rose with him in baptism.
May your lives be holy,
so that you will be united with him for ever.
    Amen.[35]

---

[35]Sixth Sunday of Easter: "Solemn Blessing," *The Sacramentary*.

ASCENSION

Environment

The Easter environment continues. Perhaps an icon of the ascension may be added.

INTRODUCTORY RITES

Opening Song (or Entrance Antiphon)

Men of Galilee, why do you stand looking in the sky? The Lord will return, just as you have seen him ascend, alleluia. (Acts 1:11)[1]

Opening Prayer

The facilitator of the session may lead the prayer. Others in the group may be asked to proclaim the readings.

Let us pray
[that the risen Christ
will lead us to eternal life]

> *Pause for silent prayer.*

God our Father,
make us joyful in the ascension of your Son Jesus
    Christ.
May we follow him into the new creation,
for his ascension is our glory and hope.
We ask this through our Lord Jesus Christ, your
    Son,
who lives and reigns with you and the Holy Spirit,
one God, for ever and ever.[2]

LITURGY OF THE WORD

Let us listen to God's word.

The readings are proclaimed.

First Reading
Acts 1:1–11

The narrative of Christ's ascension in the Acts of the Apostles is concerned with the mission of the church and the future coming of Christ. Both the end of Luke's gospel and the beginning of the Acts of the Apostles deal with the commissioning of new members to promote the new reign of God. The commissioning of the chief characters highlights the central purpose of the entire narrative, which is concerned with rooting the events of the story in the divine purpose of God and Jesus' command.[3]

In this pericope Jesus reminds his hearers that not only did he promise the Spirit, but so did his Father. John the Baptist also prophesied regarding the sending of the Spirit. Jesus thus relates the prophetic utterances of two prophets: himself and the Baptist.

The Pentecost event is foreshadowed in verses 4 and 5. Even though the power of the Spirit is poured out at Pentecost, these early verses attest that the Spirit's role is more than just one of extending power. The Spirit has something to do with the essence of God. The connection of the Spirit with the essence of God as Father suggests that the Spirit's presence is a powerful experience of God's grace.[4] Even though Pentecost is anticipated, there is a sense throughout Acts that the conferral of the Spirit is not just a one-time event, but is the active movement of the Spirit in the ongoing life of the church.

The forty-day resurrection period is a time to teach the disciples about the reign of God (v. 3) that finds complete fulfillment in Jesus Christ. The number forty is symbolic and represents a sufficient period of time to prepare those who witnessed the Easter event for the mission of the church. This pericope sets the stage for the entire missionary thrust of the volume. God's reign is synonymous with the reign of Christ.

There is concern in verse 6 over God's intention for the salvation of Israel. Where was Israel's place in what God was doing in Christ? There is hope

---

[1]Ascension: "Entrance Antiphon," *The Sacramentary.*
[2]Ascension: "Opening Prayer," *The Sacramentary.*

[3]*NULA* (II), 12.
[4]Ibid., 13.

that Christ will deliver Israel, but there is also concern and question. Hope is not dead in spite of Israel's rejection of Jesus. Acts highlights the drama of a people turning away from the messianic fulfillment that was theirs for the taking. However, this rejection is still fraught with the future hope of restoration. All is not lost for Israel.

The evangelists are commissioned to further the mission of Christ and to go out to the ends of the earth with the Good News, again proving that God's mission is to the whole world.

The scene ends with the Galileans being chided for looking upward, when their gaze should be toward the missionary activities they have been commissioned to pursue. The chastisement of the angels is a call to action. Servants of the master are called to go out and gather in new members. They will one day be held accountable for their successes and failures.

The reader is made aware that the action of God throughout Acts is prompted by God's direction, not by human desires. Jesus' exalted reign has a future dimension. He will one day return as divine judge. Thus, the church waits in hope for the future day when Christ will return in his exalted state to judge and to bring the faithful home to share his heavenly reality.

Responsorial Psalm
Psalm 47:1–2, 5–8

This psalm is an enthronement psalm. It celebrates the hypothetical annual feast that enthroned an earthly king as a sign of Yahweh's reign over his people. The church appropriated this psalm to its celebration of the ascension of Christ. Jesus is enthroned in heaven with Yahweh, the supreme ruler over all creation.

Second Reading
Ephesians 1:17–23

(Refer to the fifteenth Sunday in Ordinary Time for an overview of the Book of Ephesians.)

Today's Pericope: Most scholars believe that the letter to the Ephesians was written by a devotee of Paul's. It begins with a hymn that is reminiscent of

an ancient liturgy's opening prayer of thanksgiving. The first section of this reading is a prayer for the church to grow in wisdom and knowledge through the power of the risen and ascended Christ. Knowledge of God fills us with God's illumination. We can scarcely take in the brilliance of God's light within us. The rest of the pericope highlights the exalted, glorified Christ. Christ is Lord over his own faithful as well as over the world, which does not yet recognize him. We, like the small child who recognizes the voice of his or her parents, recognize the voice and the light of our heavenly Father. The missionary thrust of the church is to bring the world to knowledge of Christ and his saving works. It is up to the church, the Body of Christ, to help others recognize the voice and the light of God.

OR

Optional Second Reading for Cycle B
Ephesians 4:1–13

Today's Pericope: The image of Paul as prisoner is recalled to attest to his preaching authority. Christ's resurrection and exaltation created a new humanity. The unity of this new humanity is evidenced by the unity of the church. This new humanity is lived in the Christian community and the unity of the community is nurtured by the virtues of humility, patience, and long-suffering.

The reading from Ephesians is inspired by Colossians 3:15, in which the church is referred to as one body. This one body in Christ, the Christian community, must be characterized by unity and that unity must permeate and reflect all of Christian life.

Christ is Lord of all the earth. All heavenly powers are subject to Christ because he now sits on the throne of glory. Christians enter into Christ's life through baptism, which is incorporation into the one body in Christ. Christians profess one faith and one baptism, which is another expression of unity—the unity of belief. For the author of Ephesians, to have unity in faith is the same as having unity of belief.[5] Unity of belief presupposes that all members of the community believe and accept

---

[5]Paul J. Kobelski, "Ephesians," *NJBC*, 889.

the teachings of Christ. Postapostolic, institutional Christianity understands faith as the acceptance of apostolic authority in the face of false teaching.

The author professes ultimate faith in the one God who is all in all. The transcendent God is in all things and through all things. God permeates human experience, God permeates the cosmos, God permeates the Christian community. This same God gifts the Church. This same God strengthens the community to become one body in Christ. The diversity of the community is set within the context of the Church's unity.

Jesus ascended into glory so he could bestow gifts on the Church. The reference to the lower regions is either a reference to the abode of the dead (Hades) or to the incarnation in which Christ came to earth, referred to as the lower region. The latter reflects the author's common cosmology in which he asserts that all nonhuman beings reside in the heavenly regions. Thus, the heights constitute the upper region and the earth is the lower region. In that context Christ's *descent* would be a reference to Christ taking human form on the earth—the incarnation.

The author returns to his understanding of ecclesiology. The "gifts" given to the church are understood in terms of church offices. The first gifts were apostles and prophets who were part of the church's past history and its present foundation. The next gifts given to the church are preachers of the word, shepherds and teachers—roles that played prominently at the time of this letter's writing. This is the only place in the New Testament where the word *shepherd* is a reference to a church official. The above-named offices contribute to the life and ongoing mission of the church. These gifts are given so the church may grow and mature into adulthood and such adulthood is measured by the extent to which the Church is incorporated into the life of Christ.

Questions for Mystagogical Reflection: What does it mean to you that the community is to live in unity? What gifts have you experienced in your parish community that build up the reign of God? In what ways over the years have you observed your community growing into adult maturity? In what way does this reading invite conversion and participation in the paschal mystery?

OR

Optional Second Reading for Cycle C
Hebrews 9:24–28, 10:19–23

(Refer to the twenty-seventh Sunday in Ordinary Time for an overview of the Letter to the Hebrews.)

Today's Pericope: In today's pericope the author of Hebrews continues to expound on the contrast between the priesthood of Jesus and the Levitical priesthood. Some of the same arguments made last week are repeated in today's reading. The Levitical priest performs his work in a physical space—the temporal sanctuary. Jesus' locus is the heavenly sanctuary—God's presence. The Levitical priest must repeat sacrifices. Jesus' sacrifice is once and for all. The Levitical priest offers blood from creatures. Jesus offered his own blood.

The author alludes to the Day of Atonement. On the day of the celebration the priest would exit the sanctuary after completing his priestly duties in the Temple. He would then announce to the people that the work of atonement had been accomplished. The author contrasted the priest's function on the Day of Atonement with the second coming of Jesus that will signal the completion of his priestly mission. The hallmark of Jesus' priestly service is the intercession he makes to God on behalf of the human race.

The next section of today's reading jumps to chapter 10, which reminds Christians that because of Christ's suffering on the cross and his subsequent death—through the blood of Christ—human beings are assured of a place at the throne of God. Jesus' sacrifice elevated humanity and made human beings heirs of eternal life.

Christ's flesh, like the veil to the Holy of Holies, was an obstacle to heaven's entrance. Jesus had to enter into glory and move beyond his fleshy existence in order to remove the obstacle. Thus, the resurrection and ascension of his body into glory removed the veil. Christ's ascension into glory removed all the obstacles that prevent access to God and eternal life. Jesus' earthly body was carnate and of this world. However, the resurrection transformed his body into a spiritual, heavenly body.

The veil may also be an allusion to the tearing of the Temple veil at the death of Jesus.

Christ's sacrifice cleansed and purified the human race. The Jewish rites of purification with water only produced external cleanliness. Those who have been cleansed and washed clean with the blood of Christ are purified within—their conscience is cleaned and purified. "Washed clean with water" is an obvious allusion to baptism. The author reminds readers to remain steadfast in their baptismal confession of Christ. Professing faith in Christ and living according to that confession will never disappoint because Christ is worthy of our trust.

Questions for Mystagogical Reflection: In what way have you experienced being washed clean with water? Have you ever been called on to make a profession of faith in Christ? Explain. What would you like to say to Christ for offering us the sacrifice of his life? How has that personally touched your life?

The gospel is proclaimed.

Gospel
Mark 16:9–20. The Lord Jesus was taken up into heaven and took the seat at the right hand of God.

STEP 1
NAMING ONE'S EXPERIENCE

What were your first impressions? What was your first response to the gospel (or the other readings)? What captured your attention?

Each person names his or her initial impression. Statements should be brief. No reasons should be given at this time. All simply listen without agreeing or disagreeing.

STEP 2
UNDERSTANDING

In a brief statement, explain what you think this gospel is trying to convey.

STEP 3
INPUT FROM VISION/STORY/TRADITION

Liturgical Context

"Let us remind ourselves once more that if we are to be true to the perspective of the New Testament and the early liturgy we should not think of the Ascension Day as a historical commemoration."[6] The ascension of Jesus is an integral piece of the resurrection. The feast of the Ascension is not the commemoration of the historical ascending of Jesus into heaven, but rather it celebrates the glorification of Christ as a result of the resurrection. Jesus rose from the dead on the third day. He went immediately to the Father. His post-resurrection appearances flowed from his heavenly, glorious existence. Even though Luke and John seem to posit the ascension and resurrection separately, they are not regarded as two successive events. They are regarded separately in order to appropriately contemplate the dimension of each reality. Luke places the ascension on Easter Sunday night or the next day. John places the event after the appearance to Mary Magdalene. The Acts of the Apostles places the event forty days after the resurrection. (However, "forty" is "symbolic of the time of revelation, and there may be no intention to suggest the ascension actually 'occurred' on the fortieth day."[7]) It is obvious in the post-resurrection Emmaus account that Jesus was understood to have come from his realm of glory before the final ascension.

The New Testament gives us three different narratives of the ascension of Christ that describe Jesus' final withdrawal of his physical presence from his disciples. The ascension is an expression of Jesus' risen state that celebrates his victory and points toward Pentecost and the second coming.[8]

The passion, death, resurrection, and ascension were always considered a single entity. This reality is the fullness of the paschal mystery. In the first Christian centuries, ascension was not celebrated as a separate feast. By the end of the fourth century, there is evidence of a separate feast. The

---

[6] *PNL*, 33.
[7] Ibid., 34.
[8] M. Dennis Hamm, S.J., "Ascension," in *CPDBT*, 52.

Apostolic Constitution (380 C.E.) describes a celebration that took place forty days after Easter. The pilgrim Egeria (384 C.E.) reported a celebration of the ascension and the sending of the Spirit on the fiftieth day after Easter. St. John Chrysostom asserted that even though there were two separate celebrations (Pentecost and Ascension), they nevertheless were "two facets of the same reality."[9]

By 388 C.E., St. Gregory Nyssa preached a sermon on the feast of the Ascension that did not look toward Pentecost. The fifth century entertained a celebration of ascension forty days after Easter, followed by a fast, thus the term, "the great forty day pascha." As a result of these shifts, the celebration of Easter as a fifty-day feast diminished and was replaced by historicization of the Easter event.

The "General Norms for the Liturgical Year and the Calendar" (#7) restored a non-literal understanding to the feast, stressing the connection between the passion, resurrection, ascension, and sending of the Spirit. The feast is a solemnity and in places where it is not designated as a holy day of obligation, it is to be moved to the next Sunday. The feast still is celebrated forty days after Easter in order to give it the proper focus for contemplation. There is no intention of making an historical connection.

The ascension was understood as symbolizing Christ's exaltation as well as the exaltation of those who believe in Christ. One scholar refers to the ascension as a metaphor that reflects an ancient belief in the divine destiny of Jesus. The theology of ascension includes Jesus' relationship to his church, his supremacy over the created universe, the sending of his Holy Spirit, his role as revealer, his heavenly priesthood, and the expectation of his return.[10]

No human being dares presume the right to live in heaven's exalted glory. Only unique chosen ones such as Enoch and Elijah were "taken up" to God. By affirming that Jesus is exalted and sits at his Father's right hand, the New Testament asserts that Jesus' death and resurrection transported him to an entirely new mode of existence with God. The resurrection symbolizes Jesus' victory over death. The ascension symbolizes Jesus' divinely controlled destiny.

The ascension narratives explain why the post-resurrection appearances of the risen Christ ended. Jesus entered into a new kind of existence in heaven. Scripture understood heaven as symbolic of God's mysterious inaccessibility as well as God's abiding presence. In his absence, Jesus is profoundly present. Jesus, now with God, is present to the world as God is present to the world.

Jesus is understood as the Lord of the universe. The ascension reveals Jesus' status as Lord and Christ. Since he ascended into heaven, he demonstrated control over the created order of the universe. Thus, Jesus is its master.

Jesus' ascension served as prelude to the sending of his Spirit. In the Acts of the Apostles, Jesus was reported to have ascended the mountain (symbol of heaven) where he "poured out his Spirit." The Spirit would be the *One* who would continue the work of Christ's new Covenant.

Jesus, now in heaven, is able to reveal the things of God as well as exercise his role as intercessor and high priest (letter to the Hebrews). The ascension of Jesus guarantees that Jesus will return again. It is because Jesus ascended to his Father that he became the Son of Man who will accomplish the completion of God's ultimate plan of salvation for the world. Jesus' ascension reminds us that we will one day share his heavenly home. We are on a journey to our ultimate destiny.

The entrance antiphon of this liturgy emphasizes Jesus' return. The communion antiphon highlights his presence within the community: "Father, in this eucharist we touch the divine life you give to the world. Help us to follow Christ with love to eternal life where he is Lord for ever and ever." The opening prayer reminds us that Christ is indeed exalted and, as his followers, we share in his exaltation.

Gospel Exegesis

The facilitator provides input from critical biblical scholarship on this text. This input includes insights as to how people would have heard the gospel in Jesus' time.

---

[9]Edward Foley, O.F.M.Cap., "Ascension," in *CPDBT*, 52.
[10]Lionel Swain, "Ascension of Christ," in *NDT*, 63.

Many scholars believe that Mark intended to finish the gospel at verse 8 of this chapter. However, early Christians were troubled by his brusque ending to the gospel. There have been attempts to finish it for the evangelist. Three different endings to Mark's gospel have been preserved. In older Greek manuscripts verses 9–20 (today's begins at verse 15) do not exist. The literary style and language used by the author are not consistent with Mark. It was probably composed in the second century. The verses are nevertheless part of the official Roman canon.[11] One reason early redactors felt the need to rescue Mark's rather abrupt ending is because, unlike the other gospels, Mark does not include postresurrection appearances of Christ to round off his story. This appended ending is comprised of material from the other gospel traditions.

The author of this section stresses the importance of Jesus' resurrection. It is central to the Christian tradition. Jesus shows himself as a living person before he is taken up into heaven. The commission to go out and preach the good news is probably a reference to Matthew 28:18–19. The "signs" the author speaks of are a reference to the signs/miracles in the synoptic gospels and in the Acts of the Apostles. One piece of information that is particular to this text, however, is the verse which affirms that believers possess the ability to drink poison without fear of harm.

The author speaks of the "Lord Jesus," a designation used only by Luke in the Acts of the Apostles. The story of the Lord's ascension uses language that hearkens back to the Elijah story in the Hebrew scriptures. The only Old Testament tradition that is a type for the ascension can be found in the Elijah and Enoch tradition. In the Book of Genesis, Enoch walked with God and after three hundred plus years he was no longer here—he was gone from the earth. Sirach later interpreted this to mean that Enoch was taken up in bodily form. Chapter 11 of the Letter to the Hebrews referred to it as "bypassing death." Elijah is similarly taken into heaven. Elisha asks for a double portion of Elijah's spirit before he is taken up (thus taking him away from Elisha). Elijah promised Elisha that if he (Elisha) were to see Elijah taken up, then his wish would be granted. A fiery chariot appeared and Elijah was taken in a whirlwind. Elisha thereupon strikes the Jordan, the water parts, and the prophets observe that Elijah's spirit comes to rest on Elisha. Both Enoch and Elijah experienced a transfer of the human body to another realm. They both were referred to in the passive and neither of them died before they were taken up.

Jesus' ascension differs in that it is part of his resurrection. The ascension is an image used to denote the final removal of Jesus' physical presence from earth and from the midst of the disciples. Jesus' resurrection is not just transfer to a different realm, it is a new reality—a sharing in divine glory. Jesus' postresurrection appearances come out of the context of his divine glory that he had already experienced at his resurrection.[12]

The last verse refers to the church, which Christ sent out to carry on the missionary work of God's reign. The "good news" for Mark is not a set of doctrinal dogmas and precepts, but an intense deep relationship with the Lord. The disciples are to go out and introduce the person of Jesus to the world. Jesus set the example for this evangelization in his earthly ministry. He went before his disciples, healing, teaching, and preaching. His disciples are to do likewise. Now that he is gone Jesus reaffirms the commission and the authority he gave to the disciples to follow in his footsteps. It is through Jesus' resurrected and exalted glory that the new missionaries were empowered to work the miracles which revealed Christ and his gospel.

The pericope attests that Christ was "taken up into heaven." The New Testament often uses the divine passive—"he was lifted up," "Christ was raised," and today, Christ "*was* taken up into heaven." The reason the divine passive is used is to demonstrate that Christ was raised, not by his own power, but by the power of God.

The fact that later redactors felt compelled to add a more complete ending to Mark's gospel must

---

[11] *MARK,* 245.

[12] Edward Foley, "Ascension," *CPDBT,* 51.

not lull the reader into a sense of passivity. It is very easy to get caught up in the theology of the resurrection and ascension and forget the reality of it—the incredible implications. Jesus went to his death for the sins of the world. Jesus sent his apostles out on the mission. Throughout the entire gospel Mark's Jesus reminded his disciples that mission meant opposition and death. The commission to go out is not a "pie in the sky" enjoinder to go out and engage in neighborhood coffee klatches (unless, of course, they be attended by people who have yet to hear the message of Jesus Christ crucified and risen). It is an invitation to go out and tell the story, and in the telling be willing to die, if necessary. Our "going out" is to be bolstered by the hope that no matter what opposition we face, we are empowered by the Christ who now sits at the throne of glory, and who has left the midnight door unlocked for us should our mission bring us prematurely home to our eternal abode.

Mark seems to have purposefully refused to allow his readers to become passive spectators of the greatest human/divine drama in history. That is why he left us with so many unanswered questions after verse 8. Mark insists that new missionaries write the ending. Even though today's verses are later additions, it is no doubt significant that the proclamation of Jesus' ascension is accompanied by the proclamation of mission. Mark's Jesus sounded the same clarion call all through Galilee, on the way to Jerusalem, and back to Galilee again—the mission is an invitation to die for the kingdom. We die because we have the promise of resurrection. We have the promise of resurrection because Jesus sits at the right hand of God in glory.

The empty tomb means the story of biblical radicalism can continue in the living and dying of disciples of all ages. The resurrection represents the apocalyptic hope that the blood of the martyrs will be vindicated and the pain of the world healed, and confirms the call to historical insomnia.

Proclaim the gospel again.

Sometimes we gain new insights when we hear the text after the interpretation is given. Someone from the group proclaims the gospel a second time.

Conversation with the Liturgy and the Scriptures

Test your original understanding in dialogue with the text.

(You might consider breaking into smaller groups.)

Now that you've heard the exegesis, were there any new insights? How do you feel about it? How does your original understanding of this gospel compare with what we just shared? How does this story speak to your life?

Sharing Life Experience

Participants share an experience from their lives that connects with the biblical interpretation just presented.

> *Today's liturgy reminds me of the true cost of discipleship. We may never have to test it like people in other parts of the world have to test it, but we must be ready, and we must stand in solidarity with those who do.*

> *Jesus' ascension is a reminder that we are promsed the gift of eternal life. It is a joyful message, but it is a sobering one as well. The proclamation of Jesus' ascension is accompanied with the commissioning of the disciples. We know where the mission leads. My experience of mission tells me that it sometimes leads to opposition and hardship, but it is nothing, absolutely nothing, in comparison with the opposition disciples experience in other parts of the world.*

> *In 1986 in Guatemala, forces entered an Indian village and found a family gathered around a Bible. Such behavior was considered procommunist and antigovernment. The forces in charge dragged the family out in the town square and charged them— "If by tomorrow night you have not delivered up the catechists responsible for this Bible (where there were Bibles, catechists were not far behind), then we will kill all eighteen hundred men, women, and children in this village. And by the way, it will be your job to kill the catechists." The village assembled after their tormentors left. All agreed that they would rather die than to kill their beloved catechists. In an act of pure, self-sacrificng love, the catechists would not hear of*

412

it. There were only five of them; they insisted that they give up their lives for the village ("for the many"). They knew they would be going home to sit at the God's right hand. "We willingly give our lives. You must carry out their orders." That night the entire village processed to the village cemetery and in a very bloody sacrifice, the catechists gave up their lives.

When in our lives will we ever face such horror? Probably never (history teaches that we should never say never). However, the horror is getting closer and closer to our borders as similar atrocities are beginning to emerge in Mexico right now. When will we stand up with our brothers and sisters? When will we demand that our complicity in such horror cease? (The School of the Americas is responsible for training the henchmen in both of those countries.)

The implications of mission do not necessarily invite us to catch the next flight to Guatemala or Mexico. But it does challenge us to take the unwatered-down version of the gospel out into the world in which we live. If people are uncomfortable with the gospel, good, they need to be. The role of the missionary is to comfort the afflicted, but also to afflict the comfortable. When we do that, opposition will come creeping out of the woodwork faster than cockroaches at the local landfill.

My response is to pray, to live the gospel with integrity, and to stop wasting time with petty divisions and insignificant issues that have little to do with living the paschal mystery. Today's gospel promises me eternal life. My job in this world is to live the mission. I hope that I have the strength to take it to the lengths that my brothers and sisters from the south have been forced to do. They are our martyrs. I look to them for hope.

What was Mark trying to tell his community? Imagine yourself present to the events described in today's gospel. What would you be feeling? What would it cost you? In what way does today's gospel invite you into the cycle of death and resurrection—the paschal mystery? In what way does today's gospel invite transformation in your life? In what way does this gospel challenge your community today? In what way has this conversation with the scriptures for today's liturgy invited change in your life? In what way are the biblical themes of covenant, exodus, creation, and community evident in today's readings? Do you still feel the same way about this text as when you began? Has your original understanding been stretched, challenged, or affirmed?

STEP 5
DECISION

The gospel demands a response.

In what concrete way might your parish be invited to respond? Are there any attitudes or behaviors you would like to change as a result of today's conversation? What one concrete action will you take this week in response to the liturgy today?

DOCTRINAL ISSUES

What Church truth/teaching/doctrinal issue could be drawn from the gospel for the the Ascension of the Lord?

Participants suggest possible doctrinal themes that flow from the readings.

Possible Doctrinal Themes

Ascension; Christology; mission; justice; resurrection; paschal mystery; discipleship; conversion; soteriology

Present the doctrinal material at this time.

1. The facilitator gives input on a particular doctrinal issue of his or her prior choosing. OR
2. The group chooses a doctrinal issue from the list they created. They read together from the Doctrinal Appendix or other appropriate, official Church documents and the works of respected theologians.

(Many doctrinal issues are found in the Doctrinal Appendix at the back of this workbook. If you are choosing an issue from this resource, please refer to it now.)

Reflection questions centered around the chosen doctrinal theme can be found at the end of each topic in the Doctrinal Appendix. The questions are based on the five-step reflection process. If you choose a topic not included in the Doctrinal Appendix, craft your own questions according to the same five-step process.

Following the reflection questions you will be reminded to return to chapter 7, "Preparing the Catechetical Session," to assist you in crafting your own session.

Closing Prayer

Father, all powerful and ever living God,
we do well always and everywhere to give you
    thanks
through Jesus Christ our Lord.
In his risen body he plainly showed himself to his
    disciples
and was taken up to heaven in their sight
to claim for us a share in his divine life.
And so with all the choirs of angels in heaven
we proclaim your glory
and join in their unending hymn of praise.
Holy, holy, holy Lord, God of power and might,
heaven and earth are full of your glory.
Hosanna in the highest.
Blessed is he who comes in the name of the Lord.
Hosanna in the highest.[13]

OR

May almighty God bless you on this day
when his only Son ascended into heaven
to prepare a place for you.
    Amen.

After his resurrection,
Christ was seen by his disciples.
When he appears as judge
may you be pleasing forever in his sight.
    Amen.

You believe that Jesus has taken his seat in majesty
at the right hand of the Father.
May you have the joy of experiencing
that he is also with you to the end of time,
according to his promise.
    Amen.[14]

---

[13]Ascension, "Preface," (P27), *The Sacramentary*.
[14]Ascension: "Solemn Blessing," *The Sacramentary*.

SEVENTH SUNDAY OF EASTER

INTRODUCTORY RITES

Entrance Antiphon (or Opening Song)

Lord, hear my voice when I call to you. My heart has prompted me to seek your face. I seek it, Lord; do not hide from me, alleluia. (Ps 26:7–9)[1]

Opening Prayer

The facilitator of the session may lead the prayer. Others in the group may be asked to proclaim the readings.

Let us pray
(to our Father who has raised us to life in Christ)

Pause for silent prayer.

Eternal Father,
reaching from end to end of the universe,
and ordering all things with your mighty arm:
for you, time is the unfolding of truth that already
   is,
the unveiling of beauty that is yet to be.
Your Son has saved us in history
by rising from the dead,
so that transcending time he might free us from
   death.
May his presence among us
lead to the vision of unlimited truth
and unfold the beauty of your love.
We ask this in the name of Jesus the Lord.[2]

LITURGY OF THE WORD

The readings are proclaimed.

First Reading
Acts 1:15–17, 20c–26

(Refer to Easter Sunday for an overview of the Acts of the Apostles.)

Today's Pericope: The time frame of today's reading from the Acts of the Apostles reflects the twelve-day interval between Jesus' ascension and Pentecost. This was a time of preparation for the new church and a new member is added to the Twelve. Luke divided the "moments" of Jesus' death into individual pieces—the Passion and death, resurrection, ascension and exaltation, and the sending of the Spirit—in order to facilitate comprehension.[3]

Today's pericope is a combination of an older tradition and the author's new perspective. That is not to say, it is not historical. The apostles were reduced to eleven with the defection of Judas. A replacement had to be found among the five hundred who had witnessed Christ's life, mission, resurrection, and postresurrection appearances. Psalm 69 was used as an apologetic to explain the betrayal by Judas. Luke put all the elements of the then known tradition together to express his theology of apostleship.[4]

The original role of the Twelve differed from that of the apostolate. Jesus commissioned the Twelve "as a sign of the eschatological community, the new Israel, which was to be the outcome of his work. As recipients of the second resurrection appearance after Peter, they became the foundation of the eschatological community. The choice of the twelfth man would have preserved this eschatological significance."[5] The twelve apostles were a symbolic representation of the twelve patriarchal leaders of the twelve tribes of Israel. Jesus called them together and formed them in unity for a purpose. These were the new leaders of the messianic era, the new eschatological age. Luke's Peter definitely determines the qualifications for being listed among the Twelve. Witness to a postresurrection appearance and participation in the earthly ministry of Jesus from the time of the Baptist until Jesus' ascension was the prerequisite for being numbered among the Twelve. The apos-

---

[1]Seventh Sunday of Easter: "Entrance Antiphon," *The Sacramentary.*

[2]Seventh Sunday of Easter: "Opening Prayer," *The Sacramentary.*

---

[3]*WWC,* 179.

[4]*PL,* 274.

[5]Ibid.

tles were the bridge between the earthly ministry of Christ and the new eschatological, messianic reign of God in which the church carried on the mission of Christ. The church is responsible for narrowing the understanding of apostle to just the Twelve. Luke and the early church understood the term to be mutually independent. Originally the term was used as a reference for more than simply the Twelve.

The gentile roots of the word *apostle* come from naval parlance. Apostle was a naval fleet or army sent to settle or colonize a new area. Jewish roots of the word meant ambassador or emissary (*sheluhim*). The *sheluhim* were sent out by the rabbis with the same power to preach as the rabbis who sent them out. The *sheluhim* were vested to go out through the laying on of hands and were thus considered the perfect representatives of the ones who sent them. Moses, Elijah, and Ezekiel were considered *sheluhim.*

Paul probably understood his mission within the context of the *sheluhim* tradition. He was a *sheluhim* mandated by God to go out and witness to Christ.

The church eventually understood *apostle* to mean one of the Twelve. The theology of the Twelve was such that they were the "transmitters and guarantors of the word, the Spirit and the authority of Jesus."[6] Paul bristled over the fact that according to the criteria for membership, the "Twelve" did not include him. The community did not fully accept him as apostle in the beginning because of that same criteria. However, who, if not Paul, was an apostle of the Lord?

The organized body of apostles were empowered by the Holy Spirit. They determined policy for the church and designated others to assume roles of leadership. They also stood watch over the deposit of faith, the teaching authority of the emerging church.

Luke used the psalms to authenticate the theology and the action posited in today's reading. The appointment of Mathias was understood like the life and mission of Christ was understood—as part of

God's preordained plan of salvation for the world. This same plan—God's will—is evident in the mission of the church just as it was in the mission of Christ.

The choice of the new apostles was understood as God's initiative. The casting of lots was not seen as some holy gamble, but as the means by which God exercised his free choice of their new delegate, the choice between Joseph and Mathias. Peter's prayer stressed God's election in the choice.

Peter takes a center-stage role and assumes responsibility for the appointment of the new apostle. Peter's words show that something has changed. "Peter is now an interpreter of Scripture and God's purpose for the church."[7] Even before his preaching mission begins Peter emerges as one who knew "what was necessary to fulfill the Scriptures."[8] Jesus had interpreted the scriptures to the community while he was with them and in his postresurrection appearances. Now Peter assumes Jesus' role. His speech is evidence that the minds of the disciples had been opened by the risen Lord. Now that their eyes were opened, they could understand all the events they witnessed as fulfillment of scripture—even the betrayal and defection by Judas. Restoring the Twelve is an important step as the new church prepares to witness to Israel. "Choosing a twelfth member of this core group of witnesses implies acceptance of Jesus' commission to be his witnesses in the new situation following his death and resurrection. This is an act of faith in Jesus and a first step in obedience to his new call. The community responds by doing as Peter recommends. Peter's faith inspires the faith of the others."[9]

Responsorial Psalm
Psalm 103:1–2, 11, 12, 19–20

Today's psalm is a thanksgiving psalm and is chosen particularly in thanksgiving for Christ's ascension into glory.

Second Reading
1 John 4:11–16

---

[6] *WWC*, 274.

[7] *NULA* (II), 20.
[8] Ibid.
[9] Ibid., 21.

(Refer to the Feast of the Holy Family for an overview of the First Letter of John.)

Today's Pericope: Today's reading from John picks up the same theme as last week's reading. God dwells within the human person. People are to love one another because God is the source of all love. Ethical behavior flows from a deep personal relationship with God. God dwells within the hearts of the faithful and the love of God is fully realized through the saving event of the cross. Even though the theme is repetitious, in typical Johannine fashion, a new point is nevertheless made. Further proof or evidence of the indwelling of God in the human person is the confession of Jesus as Christ, Savior and Lord—as God's Son.

The secessionists of John's community placed little importance on the incarnation of Christ or his redemptive sacrificial action of salvation. The Gnostics placed little emphasis on the role of Jesus. They believed they could maintain a relationship with God without the intervention of Christ. In response the Johannine author cries, "Absurd!" For the Johannine community, relationship with God presupposed immersion into the life, death, resurrection, and ascension into glory of Jesus and the belief in his eternal preexistence.

Love, not intellectual knowledge, is the most direct avenue to God. The intellect certainly plays a part in one's relationship with God, but love is the primary vehicle for our close encounter with the divine. Such love requires the self-gift of the entire person into the loving care of God—body, soul, and spirit.

The gospel is proclaimed.

Gospel
John 17:11b–19. That they may be one just as we are one!

STEP 1
NAMING ONE'S EXPERIENCE

What were your first impressions? What was your first response to the gospel (or the other readings)? What captured your attention?

Each person names his or her initial impression. Statements should be brief. No reasons should be given at this time. All simply listen without agreeing or disagreeing.

STEP 2
UNDERSTANDING

In a brief statement, explain what you think this gospel is trying to convey.

STEP 3
INPUT FROM VISION/STORY/TRADITION

Liturgical Context

Today's first reading situates the time as the twelve-day interval between ascension and Pentecost. It appropriately breaks the "consecutive order in which the excerpts from Acts have been read during the Easter season."[10] Karl Barth once referred to the period between the ascension and Pentecost as a "significant pause." "It is a pause between the actions of God, a pause in which all the community can do is wait and pray. It may seem paradoxical, but although the Spirit came, in Johannine language, 'to abide with you [the community] for ever,' the Church nevertheless has to pray constantly, *Veni, Creator Spiritus.* The gift of the Spirit is never an assured possession but has to be constantly sought anew in prayer."[11]

Jesus' prayer looks toward absence. He prays for his disciples and asks that God continue to give them the good care he has given them while on earth. Today's opening prayer reiterates that promise and reminds us that Christ now lives in glory and promises to be with the church until the end of time. That promise is fulfilled at Pentecost.

John gives us a glimpse of Jesus' intimate relationship with his Father and invites us to enter into that intimacy with them. Disciples are invited into the mystery of intimate union with God in heaven. From that intimate union flows the unity of the

---

[10]*PL*, 274.
[11]Ibid., 93.

Church. The communion antiphon reminds us of Jesus' prayer for his disciples: "that his believers may become one as he is one with the Father, alleluia" (Jn 17:22). Jesus prayed for the unity of the church. The Spirit is the tangible presence of Christ who strengthens the church to work for the unity that Christ envisioned.

While we wait for the Spirit's action in our lives we are to pray without ceasing. The Spirit is not God's agent to answer our every manipulative request. The Holy Spirit is the gratuitous, unmerited gift of God's love and action in our lives. In response we are called to constant prayer and to self-sacrificing discipleship. We are given the bold reminder that to be a follower of Christ we must be willing to lay down our lives (1 Pt). Incorporation into the Body of Christ is also incorporation into the paschal mystery. We wait in awe for the coming of the Spirit at Pentecost and every day of our lives.

Our Church is a Church at prayer. Prayer is central to our existence. We are a Church that prays liturgically, eucharistically, communally, spontaneously, and individually. The Church has given us a rich prayer tradition and heritage. One need look no further than the *Book of Blessings* or the Masses and Prayers for Various Needs and Occasions (*The Sacramentary*) to find beautifully composed prayers for almost every human circumstance one can imagine. When commissioned to continue the mission of Christ we also commit to pray with and for his people. Our tradition provides a rich tradition from which to draw.

Gospel Exegesis

The facilitator provides input from critical biblical scholarship on this text. This input includes insights as to how people would have heard the gospel in Jesus' time.

In John's first chapter Jesus came as an empowering and revealing presence who set out to form a new community. Throughout the rest of the chapters and for the rest of his ministry Jesus set the stage for a new and different type of worship. He privately predicted what the future would hold for the disciples and while in their midst he taught them. In Jesus' farewell speeches he turns to prayer—prayer for himself and for his disciples.[12]

---

[12]*RJ*, 223.

Farewell addresses in antiquity often closed with a prayer. Abraham prayed that God would protect Jacob and protect, bless, and sanctify him to lead the people who belong to God. Today's farewell address follows the typical pattern used in all such addresses. He ends the discourse with a prayer of petition and intercession.

John's Jesus is a person of prayer. Jesus' prayers during his farewell address show that he predicted that he will one day intercede for his disciples after the resurrection. Other instances of Jesus at prayer are in the context of his earthly ministry. Two such instances show that Jesus' prayer was immediately answered—Lazarus was raised from the dead in chapter 11 and a voice from heaven is heard as a response in chapter 12. Those two answered prayers, along with the community's experience of the Holy Spirit that Jesus promised to send in chapter 14, allow the disciples to know and be assured that the prayers he utters in today's gospel will also be answered. Hearers of the fourth gospel can be assured that Martha's words ring true: "I know that whatever you ask from God, God will give you" (11:22). "It is the earthly Jesus who prays in John 17, but his intercession for disciples in vv. 9–24 prefigures his heavenly intercession."[13]

Charles Talbert reminds us that John's seventeenth chapter is divided into three parts. Jesus prays for himself (vv. 1–8); he prays for his disciples (vv. 9–24); and he summarizes his ministry and reaffirms his commitment to his mission.[14] Today Jesus prays for his disciples who accompanied him on his earthly ministry. "Since Jesus is going to the Father, the Father needs to look after his own, the disciples, who remain in the world."[15] He prays for the unity of the disciples, which is rooted in the reality that they belong to the Father. Jesus prays that the Father will take over Jesus' role as caretaker of the disciples now that he is going to the Father. Jesus has done an admirable job with the disciples. Only Judas, the son of perdition, was lost. Perdition can mean a person's character or destiny. In Judas's case, it was probably a reference to both meanings.

---

[13]Ibid., 224.

[14]Ibid.

[15]Ibid., 226.

Jesus prays that they be given the strength to cope with the world—the powers of opposition that are hostile to Christ and his followers. "This request is not that the disciples be in the world but not of it, but rather that while they are in the world they be protected from the evil one."[16] Today Jesus prays not only for his immediate disciples, but for all who would follow in his and their footsteps. Jesus' answer to coping is prayer. Jesus looked up to heaven and prayed. His prayer is an example of all religious prayer—communication with God in the hopes of obtaining certain results. Jesus prayed to his Holy Father. His prayer reflected solidarity and attachment between Father and Son (see last week's gospel exegesis for further elaboration on the meaning and implication of attachment). Jesus' attachment to his Father is also reflected in his willingness to be totally obedient to his will. What is the essence of Jesus' prayer? He asks God to protect the disciples in this world of hostility and from the evil one. He also asks that they be rooted in the truth, that they may be made holy in the truth revealed by God through Christ.

Prayer for protection flowed out of the cultural experience of Jesus' day. The ancient Mediterranean world was a group-oriented society. Protection existed within the community or clan. No one could be expected to "take on" forces by themselves. Trials, hardships, and adversity in antiquity were the problems of the entire group, not just the individual. What happened to one happened to all. There was no life outside the clan. Protection came from the group and not just the individual.[17] There were two groups represented in Jesus' dialogue today, the world group and the Jesus group. The group comprised of those who were of the "world" was hostile to the group that was comprised of Jesus' followers. Jesus' group already suffered a loss because the evil one is the champion of the other side. Thus, the only way to win out over a powerful enemy is to enlist the aid of an even more powerful advocate. Who is more powerful than Jesus' own heavenly, powerful Father?

Jesus prayed that his disciples be consecrated (sanctified) in the truth. To "sanctify" means to set something aside for a holy purpose, or to set a

person aside for a sacred calling. Jesus prays for his disciples as those whom he commissioned to go out and continue his work in the world by preaching the Word and revealing the Father's self-love. Also, the Hebrew scriptures insisted that persons sanctify themselves, that is, they were to separate themselves from things that were considered unholy. Disciples belong to the household of God. They are therefore to become holy by removing themselves from those forces that are opposed to God.

Disciples are to become holy in God's truth that is God's Word. For John, Jesus is the Word as well as the truth. Thus, disciples are to remove themselves from all that which is opposed to Jesus and attach themselves ever more strongly to him. The disciples have been prepared by the Lord himself to go out and proclaim mission. Bolstered by the Word and truth that is Jesus and strengthened by his prayer, the disciples stand ready to go out to proclaim the mission.

The prayer of sanctification also prays that the disciples be set apart for the service of God, in service of the truth and the Word. Jesus was consecrated and sent by the Father into the world. Jesus thus consecrates himself, that is, he agrees with the Father's decision about him, so that, like himself, his disciples may be set apart for the service of the truth/Word.[18] The disciples not only need God's general care but they need God all the more now that Jesus, who took care of them in the past, is leaving them and going to the Father.

Another interpretation of Jesus' sanctification flows from the context of Jesus' farewell address. It was given on the night before he died. His sanctification could also refer to his immanent death. Within the context of consecration (meaning setting aside for a sacred purpose or a person for a sacred calling), Jesus prays here as the high priest who sets aside, who offers himself in sacrifice. This prayer has thus been aptly termed the priestly prayer of Jesus. Jesus offers himself in sacrifice so his disciples may be similarly consecrated in God's revealing Word—God's message of love for the world.

Ultimately Jesus prays for the same unity that he enjoys in his relationship with the Father. This

---

[16]Ibid., 227.
[17]*CWJB*, 86.

[18]*RJ*, 228.

unity will be a source of belief for others. When people see the unity of the Christian community they will be attracted to become part of it. Thus, the unity of the community is evangelistic in nature. Disunity in the human community is due to a spiritual cause—human pride and the evil powers that resist unity. Thus, if the cause of disunity is spiritual in nature, there is a spiritual cure as well. That cure takes place through participation in the love that the Father and Son share and which together they share with believers.

The unity of the Christian community is evangelistic in nature because it provides an alternative society, a different way to live. In this new society the message of God's messianic reign is proclaimed, lived, and realized. This new society invited people out of the world as they knew it and into Christ's messianic community. This did not simply happen by words—the community lived what it preached. St. Francis used to say to the brothers: "Preach the gospel, brothers, and if you must, use words!" The Johannine community knew what it meant to be unified because they knew what it mean to "be" a Christian community—they lived it. "The Johannine Community confronted the world not merely with a doctrine or a creed but, as all sectarian groups do, with an alternative society, a counterculture, in which the message of the messiahship of Jesus was realized. It sought to draw people out of the world and into the messianic community, and it did this not only by its words but by being that community."[19]

Last week we discussed the possibility that persecution of the community was an issue which was always just below the surface for the community. As background for this next section read last week's portion of the gospel exegesis starting with: "It has been suggested by some scholars that an underlying perspective—a subtext for John's gospel—is persecution."

Jesus' disciples would have to face persecution, but they were confident that Jesus would return for them. The persecution the church had to face—the evil—was not just persecution and death at the hands of the Roman court, but almost worse was the betrayal and apostasy of their own commu-

nity members. What could be worse than to watch their former Christian brothers and sisters walk with abandon to the pagan statuary to prostrate themselves in worship or to watch them casually acknowledge the emperor as Lord? They could not help but wonder why these evils descended upon them. What did it all mean?

Jesus' final address assures them and tells them why. Satan still roams and rules this world. Jesus assures them, however, that Satan will be no more victorious over the disciples than he was over Jesus. They have nothing to fear. Judas did betray the Lord; Peter did deny him. Satan, while he seemed to be in control, had no control over the situation. Events happened the way they did in order for the scriptures to be fulfilled. If Jesus could pass through the trials of evil, betrayal, and denial, do not the disciples facing persecution know that they, too, will be victorious as Jesus was victorious? Jesus passed to a new life. And besides, did he not promise the Holy Spirit to assist them as they faced temptation? Jesus' prayer is not that the disciples be taken out of this world, but that they be protected from the evil one. Jesus may be returning to the Father, but the disciples will be remaining in the world. Since Satan is the ruler of the world, they will have to contend with the presence and power of evil. This is serious business. Jesus prays that the disciples will be safeguarded from the sway of Satan's wiles.

The Holy Spirit will help believers prepare their testimony before the court. They will know what to say when face to face with Pliny and his henchmen. They will remain faithful to the end. Not to worry. "Jesus' disciples, his friends, are thus not left to their own resources. In a mysterious manner, not fully explained, the Holy Spirit will be present to them as a kind of 'defense attorney' to help them maintain and confess their belief."[20] The evil ruler will be judged for the pain inflicted on the world—this also Jesus promises his friends.

The language of today's gospel seems very biased toward an us versus them mentality. This is quite disturbing to contemporary readers. Jesus' gospel is so inclusive, yet we come to this portion of the gospel and it seems as if everyone out there is "the world," and only this small Johannine community

---

[19]David Rensburger, *Johannine Faith and Liberating Community* (Philadelphia: Westminster, 1988), 147, in *RJ*, 229.

[20]*JGNP*, 67.

is a "friend of Jesus." This is only understandable in light of the issues of persecution that may have undergirded this text.

> Yet clearly to prepare for such a momentous step, if there is time to prepare, it is to the interest of the community's members to draw together for intense mutual encouragement. In other circumstances Christians can easily be imagined evangelizing in public places of towns and cities. With the advent of persecution, though, there is almost inevitably a need for a closing of the ranks in an effort to defend against this threat and to withstand it.[21]

For those who face betrayal, apostasy, torture, persecution, and death for the sake of the name must cling to the sovereignty of the Lord Jesus Christ. The only one who speaks the final, definitive word is Christ. No informer, betrayer, or torturer will ever have the last word. Jesus sent his disciples into the world with the assurance that he has overcome it, no matter what the believer must face. Disciples know that they will receive the reward of eternal life. There is nothing to fear.

Jesus prays for disciples of all ages. He prays that we be strengthened and delivered from temptation. He prays that we may all be one. He showed us how to live. He insisted that only through love is God and Spirit fully expressed in our lives. We cannot know God and Jesus and be attached to them without allowing that love to extend out to others—a self-sacrificing love. Yet who is it we are to love? We cannot look at John's or any other gospel without reflecting on the inclusive nature of his signs and his mission. Jesus is our Messiah and Liberator. He saves us in our time of need. His Spirit gives us the words to say when we face the courts of human judgment. He frees us to live for God. He promises that we will perform even greater signs than he. Jesus promised to send the Spirit once he returned to the Father. That same Spirit prompts Christians to do the works, to love, as Jesus challenges us to do. Who benefits? Who must benefit? God insists that the poor, oppressed, persecuted, disenfranchised, and marginalized are the ones who are to benefit from this love. Let us listen to the words of challenge by liberation theologian, Jose Miranda:

Remember, though, that Jesus' miracles were not simply what we call "good deeds"; they were messianic "good works." They implied a terrifyingly revolutionary thesis that this world of contempt and oppression can be changed into a world of complete selflessness and unrestricted mutual assistance. Jesus created an intolerable situation; his behavior and his words were a constant goad to "the world"; they inescapably demanded a collective decision. The "good works" of the Messiah did not consist in giving what was left over, in distributing the surplus of a civilization that in itself remains untouched by the distribution. They were not good works of supererogation (act of doing more than what is required or expected). Had they been no more than that, Christ would not have been afraid nor would he have died as he did.[22]

If we cannot accept the Messiah, defender of the poor and marginalized, then we cannot accept the Christ of today's gospel, for not one of his own did he lose. He protects us all. How dare we not offer the same care to all God's people—especially those God cares so desperately about, the *anawim* of God?

Proclaim the gospel again.

Sometimes we gain new insights when we hear the text after the interpretation is given. Someone from the group proclaims the gospel a second time.

STEP 4
TESTING

Conversation with the Liturgy and the Scriptures

Test your original understanding in dialogue with the text.

(You might consider breaking into smaller groups.)

Now that you've heard the exegesis, were there any new insights? How do you feel about it? How

---

[21]Ibid., 65.

[22]Jose Porfirio Miranda, *Being and the Messiah: The Message of Saint John* (Maryknoll: Orbis, 1977), 108.

does your original understanding of this gospel compare with what we just shared? How does this story speak to your life?

Sharing Life Experience

Participants share an experience from their lives that connects with the biblical interpretation just presented.

> The heart of today's gospel is the prayer of Jesus. Believers will not be able to withstand persecution without the intercession of their Lord and Messiah. Jesus prays that we be protected from the evil one. Prayer is central to our lives. It was central to Jesus' life. Without prayer our lives have no meaning and substance. Prayer is the way in which we nurture the love God has for us and remain attached to the vine.

> There is continuous prayer going on in my spirit. I have only been awakened to its voice in recent years. When I take the time to yield to its song within me, I am led into an imaginative intimacy with my Lord and God who is my life, my stronghold, my God, my all. There is nothing in my life and the life of my family that has not been bolstered, supported, and strengthened by prayer.

> We offered thanks at the foot of our son's bed the night he returned home to us alive, while his friend was dead blocks away in the hospital. We summoned the heavens for a healing when my husband was critically ill, and he was healed. Also when our best friend lay dying in the hospital, we prayed and he was healed. We prayed through our grief at the loss of my parents. We prayed through every teenage mishap, frustration, and disappointment. We continue to storm the heavens asking for the gift of a new grandchild to be born to would-be, hope filled parents. We pray that God protect, guide, and lead our son on his unusual, unconventional, and spiritual path to God. We thank God for his presence, nurturing, compassion, testing, and mercy as we continue to grow in our love for him one day at a time. I thank him for being present to a very small child in an intense time of need and leading her safely through very dangerous waters to new adult life.

> Our parish is extremely committed to our communal prayer, primarily the Sunday liturgy. We truly understand it to be the font from which our life as people and parish flows. As a community we have prayed for wisdom, endurance, and forgiveness during a parish crisis. We pray that God leads our ministry and that we do his bidding rather than our own. We pray for the poor and the suffering in our midst and ask God to show us the way to minister to them. We pray before we begin any new endeavor, asking God to bless it or show us alternative ways. We ask that our intentions be purified so that we be better servants of the Lord. Our parish staff spends a good deal of time in prayer each week. Our parish has a thriving community of praise in which all the elderly and shut-ins of the parish intercede for the needs of the parish and the world. The last time I heard there were over two hundred people committed to this ministry of prayer. They not only pray, but they offer the struggles of their aging conditions and their suffering for the needs of those for whom they pray. Our parish has a chapel in which multiple people are on their knees twenty-four hours a day in prayer for their own needs, the needs of the parish, the Church, and the world. Prayer is the hallmark of our community. Our pastor has been a wonderful example because his ministry as shepherd is also rooted in prayer. Do we ever say enough about prayer? Liturgical, private, spontaneous, conversational, or devotional—no matter how we pray, it is all an invitation to be intimate with God. That intimacy will strengthen us to be effective witnesses. Even our prayer is a witness to God. See how they love one another—see how they pray! Without prayer our good works have the potential to become idolatry. Jesus always points the way for us. He tells us what to do, but more than that, he shows us. Jesus always turns to his Father in prayer.

> Three weeks ago a woman who always sits in the front row at one of our evening liturgies told me that her husband was facing serious surgery. It was believed they may have to amputate a limb because of a very serious condition. She and I stopped for a moment on our way out of mass and the two of us prayed a very simple prayer, right then and there, on our way out of church. We asked that he be healed and enjoy a speedy recovery. Last week she reported that when the doctors took her husband in to do the surgery, he was completely healed. The problem was gone. All he could say in response is, "It is a miracle of God." We marveled as we thanked God together. God still heals his people.

> That is not to say that every prayer is answered in the way we would want. Our parish desperately

prayed for the recovery of our precious little Jarrod. Yet every prayer is answered. God is always with us. Of this I can truly testify: God has been with us in every sorrowful, joyful, frustrating, blissful moment of our lives. I may not be dragged before courts, but one way or another I am constantly called upon to witness to Christ. Through prayer and trust in Jesus who has grafted me and attached me permanently to his side, I am confident that I will withstand the test. Prayer is my constant companion and my shield in the time of need. I hope to strengthen its power in my life and yield to its constant beckoning.

What was John trying to tell his community? How does Jesus' prayer for unity speak to you at this time in your life? If this is a word to strengthen disciples for mission and to prepare them for Jesus' absence, how might it be relevant for you today? Put yourself in the place of the persecuted Johannine community. What in today's gospel would give you consolation? How might you relate to the issue of persecution described in today's exegesis? Have you ever experienced persecution of any sort? How did you respond? Imagine facing death for professing the name of Jesus. Have you ever thought about that before? Are you aware that there are people in different parts of the world who face such persecution each day? How does that make you feel? What would you like to do about it? What does today's gospel have to say to those people? How does today's gospel invite you into deeper relationship with God? How does it invite deeper participation in the paschal mystery? How does this gospel invite transformation in you? How might this liturgy speak to your community? In what way does this gospel challenge your community today? In what way has this conversation with the scriptures for today's liturgy invited change in your life? In what way are the biblical themes of covenant, exodus, creation, and community evident in today's readings? Do you still feel the same way about this text as when you began? Has your original understanding been stretched, challenged, or affirmed?

STEP 5
DECISION

The gospel demands a response.

In what concrete way might your parish be invited to respond? Are there any attitudes or behaviors you would like to change as a result of today's conversation? What one concrete action will you take this week in response to the liturgy today?

Christian Initiation: Next week is Pentecost. Perhaps all those who celebrated a sacrament of initiation last year might be recognized and blessed at the Sunday liturgies (baptism, confirmation, or eucharist). Today would be an appropriate day to celebrate a rite of full communion into the Catholic Church, provided that you have candidates ready and prepared. This would also be an appropriate time to celebrate a rite of welcome or acceptance. The neophytes continue to be a visible presence in your assembly.

DOCTRINAL ISSUES

What Church truth/teaching/doctrinal issue could be drawn from the gospel for the seventh Sunday of Easter?

Participants suggest possible doctrinal themes that flow from the readings.

Possible Doctrinal Themes

Prayer; evangelization; ecumenism; mystery of suffering; redemption; paschal mystery; Jesus Christ; soteriology; discipleship; conversion; baptismal call of priest, prophet and king

Present the doctrinal material at this time.

1. The facilitator gives input on a particular doctrinal issue of his or her prior choosing. OR
2. The group chooses a doctrinal issue from the list they created. They read together from the Doctrinal Appendix or other appropriate, official Church documents and the works of respected theologians.

(Many doctrinal issues are found in the Doctrinal Appendix at the back of this workbook. If you are choosing an issue from this resource, please refer to it now.)

Reflection questions centered around the chosen doctrinal theme can be found at the end of each topic in the Doctrinal Appendix. The questions are based on the five-step reflection process. If you choose a topic not included in the Doctrinal Appendix, craft your own questions according to the same five-step process.

Following the reflection questions you will be reminded to return to chapter 7, "Preparing the Catechetical Session," to assist you in crafting your own session.

Closing Prayer

Father, all powerful and ever-living God,
we do well always and everywhere to give you
    thanks
through Jesus Christ our Lord.
We praise you with greater joy than ever in this
    Easter season,
when Christ became our paschal sacrifice.
He is still our priest,
our advocate who always pleads our cause.
Christ is the victim who dies no more,
the Lamb, once slain, who lives for ever.
The joy of the resurrection renews the whole
    world,
while the choirs of angels sing for ever to your
    glory.[23]

---

[23]"Preface, Easter III," *The Sacramentary*.

PENTECOST SUNDAY

Environment

The feast of Pentecost has always been associated with the first gathering of the harvest. The fifty days of spring were an anxious time of waiting for the fruits to ripen. The Jewish feast of Pentecost, "The Feast of Weeks—Shavuot," was a time of gathering the grain harvest.

Strawberries, cherries, and apricots are associated with the feast as these are usually the first ripened fruits of summer. Easter pastels should turn to vibrant shades of reds. Since the liturgical color of Pentecost is red, the catechetical environment should be draped in abundant shades of red. One is hampered only by a limited imagination. The image of the dove, while not directly associated with Pentecost, is associated with the coming of the Spirit upon Christ at his baptism. Icons have used the image of a firebird with vibrant feathers as a symbol of Pentecost. The symbol of the phoenix rising up out of the ashes has been a traditional symbol of the resurrection. Perhaps one of these images might be incorporated into a Pentecost environment.

INTRODUCTORY RITES

Opening Song (or Entrance Antiphon)

Song: Veni Creator Spiritus

The Spirit of the Lord fills the whole world. It holds all things together and knows every word spoken by man, alleluia. (Wis 1:7)[1]

Opening Prayer

The facilitator of the session may lead the prayer. Others in the group may be asked to proclaim the readings.

Let us pray
[in the Spirit who dwells within us]

Pause for silent prayer.

---

[1]Pentecost Sunday: "Entrance Antiphon," *The Sacramentary.*

Father of light, from whom every good gift
    comes,
send your Spirit into our lives
with the power of a mighty wind
and by the flame of your wisdom
open the horizons of our minds.
Loosen our tongues to sing your praise
in words beyond the power of speech,
for without your Spirit
man could never raise his voice in words of
    peace
or announce the truth that Jesus is Lord,
who lives and reigns with you and the Holy
    Spirit,
one God, for ever and ever.[2]

LITURGY OF THE WORD

There are two liturgies of Pentecost: the vigil mass and the mass during the day. The vigil mass is not widely celebrated since the mass during the day is usually chosen for the Saturday evening liturgy prior to Pentecost Sunday. However, exegesis is provided for both the vigil and the mass during the day. Readings from both liturgies together form the fullness of truth inherent in the feast of Pentecost.[3]

Let us listen to God's word.

The readings are proclaimed.

READINGS FROM THE VIGIL OF PENTECOST

Vigil First Readings
Genesis 11:1–9, Tower of Babel, or
Exodus 19:3–8, 16–20, Giving of the law and the
    manifestation at Mount Sinai, or

---

[2]Pentecost, Mass During the Day: "Alternative Opening Prayer," *The Sacramentary.*

[3]The second reading and the gospel for the vigil mass are always the same: Romans 8:22–27 and John 7:37–39. The first reading is chosen from among four possibilities: Genesis 11:1–9; Exodus 19:3–8, 16–20; Ezekiel 37:1–14; Joel 3:1–5.

Ezekiel 37:1–14, Ezekiel and his vision of the dry
bones, or
Joel 3:1–5, prophecy about the outpouring of the
Holy Spirit

The Tower of Babel

The author of Luke-Acts no doubt made a connection between the sending of the Spirit and the story of the Tower of Babel. At Babel the people were following their own whimsical designs. They wanted to establish a permanent settlement, achieve their own prestige. Their human designs were thwarted and they were dispersed as a people. They were in disarray and they no longer understood one another's language. Pentecost answers the tragedy of Babel. Pentecost gathers and unites God's dispersed people. The preaching in tongues at the Pentecost event was understood as the restoration of the human race. People were able to understand one another in their own languages. Unity was again possible. People would be able to understand the gospel in their own language. The ravages of sin had been broken through the power of the Spirit.

Manifestation at Sinai

In the manifestation of God at Mount Sinai, God was present and spoke in majesty, in mystery, and in great Cecil B. DeMille fashion, midst thunder, lightning, and clouds. God is both accessible and inaccessible. Sinai was connected to Pentecost in the symbolism of the tongues of fire and the rushing wind. God is still both present and absent; we are still in relationship as Creator and creature. Yet, Christ is the ongoing presence of God in the community of his new covenant.

Ezekiel's Dry Bones

Israel had sinned. They were dispersed. They saw their captivity as a result of their sin. All was lost. There was no hope. They could do nothing on their own power. Ezekiel rose up as prophet in their midst and offered encouragement in their desperate situation.

God, through his prophet, sends down the Holy Spirit (an epiclesis) and breathes new life into the dry, dead bones. The Spirit breathes new life and gives new hope. The dry bones of Ezekiel summarize the entire drama of salvation history. When

we lose our way (as we have and we will), God has been and will be there to breathe new life into what is dead, lost, and forgotten. Pentecost is the restoration and ongoing life of that same Spirit in the life of the community.

Prophecy of Joel

Peter quotes Joel in his speech at Pentecost. Joel was referring to the outpouring of the Spirit upon Israel. Usually it was understood that the Spirit was poured down upon a charismatic leader, a prophet, or particularly the messiah. However, Joel's vision extended beyond that narrow understanding. It was inclusive of the entire community. The community was to be empowered by the Spirit and would know the law in their hearts. Knowing the law would give them knowledge of God. In the community of the messianic age, the Spirit would come upon not just the leaders, but the entire community.

Responsorial Psalm
Psalm 104:1–2, 24, 27–28, 29, 30, 35

This is a psalm in praise of the God of creation. The understanding of Spirit throughout the Wisdom tradition is that the Spirit of God participated in the creation of the world. The New Testament tradition centers on the work of the Spirit in the messianic age. In the Hebrew Scriptures, says Reginald Fuller, "'renewal' by the Spirit probably refers to the renewal of nature at springtime."[4] However, Christianity expanded the notion of renewal to mean the renewal of creation in the messianic age, beginning first with the church, the people of God.

Vigil Second Reading
Romans 8:22–27

Paul's letter to the Romans picks up the theme of the Spirit at work in the universe. It is not just the Christian community that is renewed by the Spirit; the entire cosmos is renewed. Paul is concerned about the bondage of sin that traps people and keeps them enslaved to sin. On their own power, people can do nothing. Paul knows this principle from personal experience. He understands that we are still in the flesh and, as long as we are, the battle will continue and we will not achieve our destiny.

---

[4]*PNL*, 38.

However, in spite of our innermost groaning, we do have the Spirit of God to renew and lead us to this ultimate destiny. The Spirit will help us withstand the suffering in our lives and persevere courageously. The Spirit uplifts all creation as we strive to live in accord with the will of God.

Vigil Gospel

The Jewish feast of Booths was a feast of great rejoicing over the end of the harvest. During the feast, the people erected and spent seven days living in tents (*sukkoth*). Later, this celebration was combined with a memorial of certain aspects of the Passover. The priests would go to the pool of Siloam ("the one who has been sent"); they would draw water in a golden pitcher, ceremoniously process into the temple, and then pour out the water at the corner of the altar. The water was reminiscent of the water that Moses caused to spring up from the desert and the water of Ezekiel's vision that flowed from under the temple. These were purifying waters that watered the whole country and purified the waters of the Dead Sea. "I will sprinkle clean water upon you to cleanse you from all your impurities, and from all your idols I will cleanse you. I will give you a new heart and place a new spirit within you, taking from your bodies your stony hearts and giving you natural hearts. I will put my spirit within you and make you live by my statutes, careful to observe my decrees. You shall live in the land I gave your fathers; you shall be my people and I will be your God" (Ez 36:25–28).

The feast of Booths was a celebration of all the mighty things God has accomplished, the new "Exodus of joy and glory, the definitive purification of the people, the coming of the Messiah, the effusion of God's Spirit and its manifestation on the last day."[5] This was a great feast of rejoicing that ended on the eighth day. It was on this eighth day that Jesus pronounced what was in this gospel.

"Let any one who thirsts come to me and drink." It is Jesus who now offers the life-giving waters of refreshment. All the hopes and dreams embodied in the great feast are now to be found in Jesus. The life-giving water was a sign of the Spirit who came in the sign of water at the Red Sea, the water

from the rock in the desert, Ezekiel's spring, the water promised to the Samaritan woman by Jesus, and water flowing from the side of Christ. The Spirit is given at baptism and confirmation and continues to be poured out on the church as it gathers to offer perfect worship in spirit and truth in the sacred liturgy.

A constant theme in the farewell discourses is that Jesus suffered, died, and rose again in order to send his Spirit to those who believe. In John's gospel, the water and blood that poured from Jesus' side at the crucifixion was a sign of the coming of the Holy Spirit upon the church. Blood and water, then, became the symbolic sign of Christ's fulfilled promise to those who believe. The coming of the Spirit to the gathered twelve at Pentecost was the actual event: the conferral of the Holy Spirit upon the church.

READINGS FROM THE MASS DURING THE DAY ON PENTECOST SUNDAY

First Reading
Acts 2:1–11

The actual historical event of the sending of the Spirit is not what is at issue in today's readings. In this reading, the Spirit comes at Pentecost; in the gospel it happens on Easter Sunday. The *when* is not important. This appearance denotes the establishment of the church as larger than just the twelve. It is also the beginning of the church's mission: the Christian kerygma.

The Pentecost account is told in a way that reminds the reader of the giving of the law on Mount Sinai. The new *Twelve*, like the twelve tribes of Israel, gather together for the event. There is a sound from heaven that fills the *whole* house, just as there was a thunderous noise from God on Mount Sinai that shook the *whole* mountain. The fire of Pentecost is reminiscent of the fire at Sinai—both evoking the manifestation or theophany of God. The tongues of fire are symbolic of the presence of God that will manifest itself in human language, the "prophetic ministry of the disciples (tongues)."[6] Jesus mediates God's word to his people. The Holy

---

[5]*DL* (III), 265.

[6]M. Dennis Hamm, S.J., "Pentecost-New Testament," in *CPDBT,* 715.

Spirit will empower God's people with a new evangelical strength. The apostles will go out and spread the word among the nations.

By naming all the places of origin of those present, the Acts of the Apostles is positing a very powerful eschatology. Pentecost is the fulfillment of the promises made to Israel. All are now living in the eschatological age. This is the final gathering of Israel. The gift of Pentecost is first intended for the Jews and then for all the nations on earth. As said earlier, this pericope is understood as an answer to Babel. The people of Babel, filled with self-importance and sin, are scattered in confusion. They do not understand one another. In contrast, this reading highlights the gathering of a people, who now, under the power of the Spirit, are able to communicate. Formed as a repentant and reconciled new community, they now are able to understand one another, each in their own native language—under God's initiative, not their own.

Questions for Mystagogical Reflection: Has your community ever had an experience in which the Spirit of God brought understanding out of confusion? How are you personally challenged by the reading from Acts? Does your baptismal commitment have anything to do with today's liturgy? What might be going on in the world, in the church, or in your life that is in need of the Spirit today?

Responsorial Psalm
(same as vigil)

Second Reading
1 Corinthians 12:3–7, 12–13

One of the effects of gnosticism on Paul's community was that they treated those who did not have all the special gifts of the Spirit as somehow *less than.* Glossalalia (speaking in tongues) was just one such instance. Those who did not speak in tongues were considered inferior. This caused division within the community.

Paul puts priorities in the right place. He definitively asserts that to be in the Spirit means one confesses Jesus as Lord. He is referring here to the earthly, crucified Lord. The gnostic Corinthians regarded the death of Jesus as a past, forgotten reality and were more interested in an ethereal, intangible Jesus. Paul grounds them in the reality of the cross.

All the gifts of the spirit are for the uplifting of the Body. One gift is not to be stressed over another. All are to be used with prudence and balance for the good of the community, not for self-edification. Through baptism, the church is one Body. Through eucharist, all are "to drink of the one Spirit." There is to be no divisiveness. All gifts are to be used for the common good, to uplift and nourish the entire Body. Reginald Fuller notes that this letter was possibly written for the paschal feast.

Questions for Mystagogical Reflection: How does this reading challenge our community today? Is there any evidence of using gifts for personal gain rather than for the common good? How are we personally challenged by this reading? What does this reading have to say about our status as baptized, fully initiated people in the Body of Christ?

OR

Optional Second Reading for Cycle B
Galatians 5:16–25

(Refer to the Feast of Mary Mother of God for an overview of the Letter to the Galatians.)

Today's Pericope: Paul writes his letter to the Galatians to convince his readers of the error of their ways. He seeks to convince them to return to his earlier teaching. In the opening section of the letter he openly states the issues. He then proceeds to defend his authority—how he came to faith in Christ, how he became an apostle to the gentiles, how he developed his relationship with the Jerusalem community, how he defended a Torah-free gospel, how he challenged Peter as he defended that gospel, and how he was rejected by the Antioch community.

The letter goes on to make the case against his opponents, citing examples from Christian experience, scriptures, and the Law. In this section of Paul's letter he exhorts community members to be faithful to his gospel, to the Christian life, and to life in the Spirit. The latter exhortation is the theme in today's pericope. The Spirit of God is more powerful to lead and strengthen God's people than blind obedience to the Torah.[7]

Paul speaks to them more affectionately in this

_____
[7] *GWT*, 51–52.

section of his letter. He reminds his readers that freedom from the Law does not mean that one is free to behave selfishly. Paul insists that love and service toward one another are crucial. Paul reminds his readers that before Christ we were slaves to this world and to the legalistic demands of the Law. Jesus was obedient to God's will and was ultimately pleasing to God. He died and was raised again, and by his resurrection God annulled the Torah. Through Christ we now enjoy a new freedom—a freedom for God, a freedom to love and to serve. What is important is that faith prompts action rooted in love.

How does one offer this service? Paul exhorts the people to conduct themselves according to the Spirit. It is God's Spirit that leads and directs all Christian activity. We serve others through the fruit of the Spirit, not by deeds of the flesh. Even though Christians are in union with Christ and his Spirit they still struggle with the "flesh" (a symbol of human opposition to God).[8] Flesh is anything willful, self-dependent, weak, sinful, or unredeemed. Spirit is that part of the human core which is goodness—the part of the human soul that responds to God's Spirit. Through the power of the indwelling Spirit Christians have the necessary means to fight the influences of the flesh. Paul insists that right action is important. Good deeds are essential to the Christian life. Good deeds are rooted in love and are lived out through a life of constant, continuous service—service that is a way of life, not a fleeting, momentary philanthropic action. Christians should avoid the laundry list of "flesh" concerns (actions that should be avoided). The lifestyle of Christians should never be filled with such things. What should fill the life of the Christian are concerns of God and the fruit of the Spirit—love/ *agape* and all its characteristics. The lists that Paul creates are intended to demonstrate how a Christian should act in the world and toward other believers. Through faith and baptism Christians have been crucified with Christ. They have died not only to the law but also to the "self"(that is, to the earthly tendency to sin). Now Christians are free to walk righteously with God and love with paschal love.

Questions for Mystagogical Reflection: In what way have you ever called upon the indwelling Spirit in combating the influences of flesh as described in this reading? Why do you suppose "good deeds" are essential to the Christian life? In what way have you ever died to yourself? What does that mean to you? What does it mean in light of Paul's meaning of the word "flesh"? Have you ever been the recipient of the agape love that Paul affirms in this reading? Where in this reading is there good news for the church? How does this reading invite participation in the paschal mystery of Christ?

OR

Optional Second Reading for Cycle C
Romans 8:8–17

(Refer to the fourth Sunday of Advent for an overview to the Letter to the Romans.)

Today's Pericope: Paul's letter to the Romans typifies a refined, systematic articulation of Pauline theology. It is considered his greatest theological masterpiece.

Paul insists that God freely *forgives and forgets* people's sins; they are not held against them. Each sinner is welcomed into God's loving arms as a parent would forgive a precious, wayward child. The child is treated as if she or he had never strayed in the first place. The Law can never replace the peace, freedom, and relief that only God can give. With the Law, human beings work out their own salvation. With Christ, it is already won for those who accept it. Prior to Christ, the Law was a necessary guide. But now, the guide is Christ. We are set free from sin by Jesus' saving action. Jesus' death/resurrection signaled the way for the Spirit to reign in the hearts of humankind.

Paul offers us the greatest gift: to see ourselves as God sees us—loved and forgiven. The Law does not give us freedom; only Christ gives us freedom. This does not mean that we are no longer bound to an ethical code. Law will always serve as a reminder of our obligations and responsibilities to God, the world, other people, and ourselves. Paul insists that the Law does not "capture the will of God."[9] Jesus did not come to create a new set of rigid codes that would replace the old set of rigid

---

[8]Joseph A. Fitzmyer, S.J., "The Letter to the Galatians," *NJBC*, 789.

[9]*GAP*, 97.

codes. Jesus did not denigrate the Law; he simply wished to restore its spirit.

Jesus came to *show us how to live.* Discipleship consists in living in the pattern of Christ, to do what he did. Thus, Christians are freed from rigid observance of the Law. They are, instead, guided by a new motivator—the Spirit of God. When led by the Spirit, Christians participate in a mature, love-based faith. It is a faith based on biblical justice (*hesed*): a reciprocal, covenant relationship with God that is active and alive and produces every good action because of the demands of love. Loving God with heart, mind, and soul is synonymous with extending that same love to all of God's creation. It is a higher law—one that is not self-determined, but rather Spirit-provoked.

Human nature is flawed simply because of the sinful, human condition—no one is exempt. However, we must never forget the power and affirmation of our Genesis origins: God created men and women in God's image and saw that "it was good." Thus, we have the ultimate disposition and created potential to be elevated to the divine status that is our birthright since the beginning of the world. Yet we are nevertheless born into a sinful world and are thus subject to sin. It is simply (or not so simply) the way it is. We are human beings and so we are sinners. The indwelling of the Spirit prompts, nudges, and leads us ever so gently—and sometimes not so gently—toward the created grace that is our destiny. The Spirit gives human beings the possibility of being free from sin. Humanity is to cooperate with the work of creation taking place within each of us. It is not automatic. The Spirit provides the yeast and, out of love, we become one complete loaf, ready to be broken and shared.

We are new creations in Christ to the extent that we cooperate with the generating work of the Spirit within us. When we live the cycle of death and resurrection and when we lay down our lives for others, we become that which we were created to be. "Paul shows how theology and morality are intimately connected. When we speak of 'Christian being,' we are led to discerning what is 'Christian acting.' "[10]

---

[10]*DL* (II), 129.

One result of living in the Spirit is that we become true children of God. The Spirit does not place us back in the realm of fear, not even holy fear. The Spirit reminds us that we belong to God—we are God's children. We, like Jesus, call him "Abba" or "Daddy," so intimate is our relationship intended to be. We are never to lose sight of the two-edged sword associated with this relationship, however. The fact that we are God's precious children also means that we are heirs of Christ's suffering. We suffer with Christ so we may be exalted with him. The suffering pales in comparison to the joy that awaits us.

Questions for Mystagogical Reflection: Do you believe that you are truly loved and forgiven? What does it mean to you that God loves you unconditionally, that there is nothing you can do to merit God's love? Have you ever personally experienced such love? What does it mean to you that you are freed from the Law? What are you freed to do and how do you concretely respond to that gift of freedom? In what way does this reading invite you to enter more deeply into the cycle of death and resurrection?

Sequence

Come, Holy Spirit, and from heaven direct on man the rays of your light. Come, Father of the poor; come, giver of God's gifts; come, light of men's hearts.

Kindly Paraclete, in your gracious visits to man's soul, you bring relief and consolation. If it is weary with toil, you bring it ease; in the heat of temptation, your grace cools it; if sorrowful, your words console it.

Light most blessed, shine on the hearts of your faithful—even into their darkest corners; for without your aid man can do nothing good, and everything is sinful.

Wash clean the sinful soul, rain down your grace on the parched soul and heal the injured soul. Soften the hard heart, cherish and warm the ice-cold heart, and give direction to the wayward.

Give your seven holy gifts to your faithful, for their trust is in you. Give them reward for their virtuous acts; give them a death that ensures salvation; give them unending bliss. Amen. Alleluia.[11]

Today and on Easter Sunday the sequence is sung. The sequence is a hymn that is sung after the second reading and before the gospel. The Alleluia is prefaced by the sequence. The Veni Creator was written by Stephen Langton, the Archbishop of Canterbury (d. 1228), says Joseph A. Jungman, S.J. All of the attributes of the Spirit's presence, such as light, comfort, consolation, guidance, healing, refreshment, forgiveness, warmth, and joy are poetically set forth in the sequence assigned to Pentecost Sunday. There are presently only four assigned sequences for the liturgy: Easter Sunday–*Victimae Paschali Laudes* ("Praises to the Paschal Victim"), Pentecost–*Veni Sancte Spiritus* ("Come, Holy Spirit"), Corpus Christi–*Lauda Sion* ("Praise Zion"), Feast of Our Lady of Sorrows–*Stabat Mater* ("The Mother Stood").

Gospel for Cycles A, B, and C
John 20:19–23. Jesus passed through the locked doors, stood in the presence of his disciples, and offered his peace and the Holy Spirit.

OR

Optional Gospel for Cycle B
John 15:26–27; 16:12–15. The Spirit of truth will guide you all to truth.

OR

Optional Gospel for Cycle C
John 14:15–16, 23b–26. The Holy Spirit will teach you everything.

STEP 1
NAMING ONE'S EXPERIENCE

What were your first impressions? What was your first response? What grabbed your attention? How did you feel?

Each person names his or her initial impression. Statements should be brief. No reasons should be given at this time. All simply listen without agreeing or disagreeing.

---

[11]Pentecost Sunday: "Sequence," *The Lectionary.*

STEP 2
UNDERSTANDING

In a brief statement, what do you think this gospel is trying to convey?

STEP 3
INPUT FROM VISION/STORY/TRADITION

Liturgical Context

Pentecost is the grand finale to the extended celebration of the Lord's resurrection that takes place during the seven weeks of Easter. It is the day the church celebrates the gift of the Holy Spirit. By the first century, the feast also had "an historical association with the law given on Mount Sinai as well as the covenant with Noah and Abraham."[12] Pentecost ushers in the new covenant, the good news that was foretold by the prophets. Pentecost is the final manifestation of God that gave birth to the church. "It appears on the fiftieth day, when the Spirit was poured out on the first Christian community, giving it the strength and confidence to testify publicly to the resurrection."[13] The paschal celebration of redemption through Christ took place over the fifty days of Easter and was understood to include the "victorious passion and death, his resurrection and ascension, and the sending of the Spirit upon the Church."[14] Thus, Easter was not just a celebration of the resurrection of Christ, but it was an extension of his ministry through the Spirit to the Church: "... Pascha was a total celebration of our redemption...."[15]

When the Easter Vigil became the prime locus for initiation, Pentecost also was used as an occasion for the celebration of baptism. This is the source of the term "Whit Sunday," which referred to the white garments worn by the newly baptized neophytes.

Refer to the overview of the Easter season for further historical background regarding the feast.

---

[12]John F. Baldovin, S.J., "Pentecost," in *NDT,* 755.
[13]*DL* (III), 293–294.
[14]*OLY,* 57.
[15]Ibid.

Its origins, briefly, lie in the connection to the Jewish feast of gathering in the grain harvest that was inaugurated at Passover. In later Jewish history, the feast was associated with Israel's salvation history including the giving of the law at Sinai and the forming of Israel into a people. The Christian appropriation of the feast included the gift of the Spirit in place of the grain harvest and the law. The forming of Israel as a people was adapted in the Christian understanding to refer to the forming of a people in the new covenant.

In the early church there was no sense that the celebration of the Easter season included three separate feasts within the season. Resurrection, Ascension, and Pentecost were considered one great joyful feast that celebrated Christ's victory over death. "The early community did not share the tendency of later periods to divide this fifty-day feast into three feasts, each with its own season. Until the end of the second century, notices about Christians celebrating Pentecost refer to their keeping of the Jewish agricultural festival (e.g., *Epistula Apostolorum* 17)."[16]

Tertullian is the first to give evidence of a Christian rendering of the feast. It is noted as a fifty-day period of festival and as a "feast day appropriate to baptism."[17] As the feast evolved and in places where it was celebrated on Sunday, the feast of Pentecost was counted from Easter day itself, thus making Pentecost the eighth Sunday after Easter Sunday.

Edward Foley maintains that it was Origen (254) who asserted: "If a man is able to say truthfully 'we are risen with Christ,' and also that 'he raised us up and made us sit with him in the heavenly places of Christ,' he is always living in the days of Pentecost... [and] he becomes worthy also of some share in the fiery tongue given by God" (*Contra Celsum*).

The first four centuries understood Ascension and Pentecost to be intimately connected: "Ascension is the triumphant completion of Christ's earthly ministry, with the missionary outpouring of the Holy Spirit as the unavoidable result. Thus they were celebrated on the same day."[18] This tradition comes from John 20 where the resurrection, the sending of the Spirit, and the end of Jesus' earthly mission all took place on the same day.

By the fourth century, the unitive dimension to the fifty days of Easter waned in the Roman church as Ascension and Pentecost were regarded as distinct festivals. Adolf Adam reminds us that the East always regarded Pentecost as the close of the Easter season. The Roman liturgy, on the other hand, "made this day an independent entity and thus a more or less isolated feast of the sending of the Holy Spirit."[19] Foley suggests that the reason for this might be due to the Council of Constantinople that occurred around the same time. The Council definitively asserted the divinity of the Holy Spirit. This shift may have resulted in taking a primarily christological feast and turning it into a feast celebrating the Holy Spirit.

Liturgical renewal restored Pentecost to its unity with Easter and reaffirmed the close connection between the Resurrection, Ascension, and the sending of the Spirit. The "General Norms for the Liturgical Year and the Calendar" states: "The fifty days from Easter Sunday to Pentecost are celebrated in joyful exultation as one feast day, or better as one 'great Sunday'" (#22). Even though the unity was restored, there is nevertheless still a tendency to focus primarily on the Holy Spirit rather than on the Easter mystery. However, today's preface strongly adheres to the proper connection between Resurrection, Ascension, and Pentecost.

> Today you sent the Holy Spirit
> on those marked out to be your children
> by sharing the life of your only Son,
> and so you brought the paschal mystery to
>   its completion.
> Today we celebrate the great beginning of
>   your church
> when the Holy Spirit made known to all
>   peoples the one true God,
> and created from the many languages of
>   man
> one voice to profess one faith.

---

[16]Edward Foley, O.F.M.Cap., "Pentecost-Pastoral Liturgical Tradition," in *CPDBT,* 717.

[17]Ibid.

---

[18]Ibid.

[19]*LY,* 89–90.

The joy of the resurrection renews the
   whole world,
   while the choirs of heaven sing for ever to
   your glory. . . .[20]

Pentecost brings the great Fifty Days of Easter to a close. The paschal candle is removed and placed by the font and there is great rejoicing and merriment. Perhaps parishes might consider gathering in a place where the entire parish could assemble for one large annual liturgy that celebrates their identity as church.

Christian Initiation: This is, perhaps, a day in which those who were not baptized at the Easter Vigil could be baptized.

During the seven weeks of Easter, the newly baptized gathered with the assembly for the masses of the Easter season. They entered into mystagogical reflection on the mysteries of the Easter season and the sacraments. They were fed at the table, they took their place with the people of God at the banquet table, and they continued to ask their questions. Their questions flowed from their experience as fully initiated members of the Roman Catholic Church.

The Rite of Christian Initiation calls the seven weeks of Easter the period of mystagogia or post-baptismal catechesis. During the seven weeks, the neophytes engage in an intense time of post-baptismal reflection. It culminates today on the feast of Pentecost. Paragraph #249 of the RCIA suggests that "some sort of celebration should be held at the end of the Easter season near Pentecost Sunday; festivities keeping with local custom may accompany the occasion." The formation of the neophyte continues to take place in the midst of the celebrating assembly with monthly gatherings for the first full year following baptism at the vigil. At the end of the year, on the anniversary of their baptism, "the neophytes should be brought together in order to give thanks to God, to share with one another their spiritual experiences, and to renew their commitment."

Pentecost was inaugurated in the first Christian community, but its power is ongoing for all generations. Pentecost celebrates the perpetual gift of

the Spirit to build the Body of Christ. Pentecost celebrates within the community that which takes place in the individual through baptism and eucharist. The Spirit who breathes transforming life into the church is given at baptism and continues to be manifest through the ongoing celebration of eucharist. It is the same Spirit who challenges, teaches, seals us permanently to Christ, and leads us forward in holiness to the new Jerusalem, the holy, eternal city. Pentecost celebrates the reign of God *now and not yet;* it is a present and future reality. The Spirit of Pentecost continues the work of Christ on earth as we are formed and prepared for the great day of his return. Pentecost is the ongoing renewal of our participation in Christ's new covenant. The liturgy of Pentecost calls us to worship in spirit and in truth. We are strengthened for mission to the world's poor, oppressed, and spiritually hungry.

Perhaps Pentecost is a day on which all those who have celebrated an initiation sacrament during the year, such as infants, neophytes, first communicants, those who were confirmed or received into full communion could gather to be a visible sign in the assembly. Perhaps all those mentioned might don their baptismal garments and gather in the midst of the community as a visible sign of Christ's resurrection and the new life of the church as we bring this season to a close.

The Johannine perspective on the mystery of Pentecost and the Holy Spirit.

Reading the Christ-event from the perspective of Luke makes for wonderful drama. Luke breaks the event of Christ's death, resurrection, ascension, and sending of the Spirit into separate units spread out over fifty days. This makes the story far more understandable. It allows the reader to reflect on each aspect of the divine mystery. However, Johannine representation of the paschal mystery is probably more accurate. John melds the Christ-event into one action. John's Jesus gives the gift of his Holy Spirit on the same day of his resurrection. The single most significant result of the resurrection was the sending of the Holy Spirit to all believers. The Church does not just celebrate the sending of the Spirit on Pentecost. It is an integral part of the whole paschal mystery. The entire fifty days of Easter celebrates the sending of the Spirit, just as the Jewish feast of Pentecost cele-

---

[20]Pentecost Sunday: "Preface," *The Sacramentary.*

brates the enjoyment of fruits of the Promised Land.[21]

The mystery of the Easter-event is complex. Lest we be tempted into a literalist hearing of the paschal mystery Raymond Brown reminds us of some very poignant inconsistencies in scripture's rendition of the resurrection and the sending of the Spirit.[22] In one divine action, which extends beyond earthly time as we know it, Jesus is victorious over death, rises from the tomb, returns to his Father, and sends the Spirit to believers. The first disciples understood these events as spread out over time. The tomb was empty on Sunday morning; the risen Christ appeared to them on that Sunday or later; when the appearances ended they realized that Jesus was now permanently with God and that the Spirit had indeed come upon them. However, God's perspective of the timelessness of the action has also been woven into the narratives of the New Testament. The literalist might have a difficult time reconciling the sometimes blatant and opposing differences recorded by various accounts. Hebrews 9:11–28 records that Jesus ascended directly from the cross with his blood into heaven. On Good Friday, from the cross itself, Luke 23:43 records the dying Jesus assuring the good thief that "this day you will be with me in paradise." On Easter Sunday morning in John 20:17 Jesus says that he is ascending to his Father, yet that evening he appears to the disciples. Luke 24:51 records Jesus ascending on Easter Sunday night and Acts 1:3 insists that the same event takes place forty days later. "Now in all these accounts the same basic action of going to God's presence, terminating Jesus' existence on earth, is involved; but it is described in different ways with different theological nuances."[23]

The same situation occurs when it comes to Jesus Christ crucified and risen sending the gift of his Spirit. The event surpasses time, insists Brown, and is described in different moments in the various New Testament narratives. In the Gospel of John, Jesus is already triumphant as he is raised on the cross. He fulfills his God-ordained mission before he dies and he gives over his Spirit to the disciples at the foot of the cross.[24] The sign of his Spirit is manifest in the blood and water that flowed from his side. However, John's gospel also reports that Jesus appeared to his disciples on Easter Sunday night and said, "Receive the Holy Spirit." The Acts of the Apostles records Jesus' Spirit descending on the church fifty days after Easter. Thus, throughout the season of Easter, even before the Spirit "officially?" came upon the church at Pentecost, we have been celebrating the Holy Spirit active in the life of the Christian community. "The Church need not wait until the feast of Pentecost when it will solemnly celebrate that gift. Theologically it knows that the gift of the Spirit is part of an Easter mystery that goes beyond time."[25]

Many of the passages of John's Gospel "seem to belong to a liturgical setting; one often has the impression that it contains material which John first preached in a liturgy."[26] The gospel appointed for all three cycles, John 20:19–23, portrays Jesus appearing in the midst of his fear-stricken disciples announcing the messianic salutation, "Peace be with you." He showed them his hands and his side in order to make the connection between his resurrected presence in their midst and the earthly friend and teacher they knew and loved. This was also the Johannine way of reminding the Gnostics that Jesus' earthly life and sacrifice were not irrelevant and were indeed intimately connected to his Spirit. There is a direct link between Jesus' death, his resurrection, and the sending of the Holy Spirit—they are one divine action of God, ordained since the beginning of the world.

Jesus offered them peace. In itself this might not be any more significant than the obvious desire to quell their fears and to offer them the customary form of greeting one's friends. However, perhaps there is something more lurking beneath every reassuring word of this salutation. This is a greeting given by the Risen Lord, whose death and resurrection and ascension into glory inaugurated the long-awaited, messianic reign of God—the *Day of the Lord*. The Hebrew scriptures which foretold the coming of the Messiah prophesied that the Day of the Lord would usher in a reign of peace and a return to the *shalom* peace of Eden. At the dawn of creation the human family lived in perfect harmony. This was God's intention for the human

[21] *PL*, 268.
[22] *OSCP*, 4, 5.
[23] Ibid., 5.
[24] Ibid.

[25] Ibid., 6.
[26] *DL* (III), 277.

race—that the lamb would lie down with the lion and that all living creatures would live in harmony. It is perhaps significant that Jesus' greeting of peace is accompanied by a teaching on forgiveness.

If the messianic reign of God is a restoration of paradise and if the kingdom of God is to be the restoration of Eden as it was originally intended by God, then Jesus is the one who established that reign on earth by his death, resurrection, and sending of the Spirit. Thus, Jesus' offer of peace is not just any peace, it is the peace of Eden returning to the new Jerusalem. It is the peace which reestablishes harmony that was always intended by God until sin entered the world.

Jesus' salutation of peace is an affirmation that indeed the long-awaited messianic reign of God was in their midst. God's plan of salvation and restoration had been accomplished. Now the lion and lamb recline peacefully, side by side at the same feast. Wherever the reign of God is proclaimed, whenever believers gather in the name of the Risen one, the peace of Eden is restored. All, then, are living in the messianic reign of God—the eschatological promise of *shalom* in the here and now as they await the final glory at the consummation of the world. Now that Christ has atoned for human sin through his victory over death and as he sits on the throne of glory, sins have been forgiven, and that power continues through the ministry he passed on to his church.

The New Testament authors understood the Spirit as a mighty wind that prompted the apostles to preach at Pentecost, the source of the charisms given to the church and a force that groans within the human heart. The Greek word *pneuma* influenced their understanding. However, the Johannine community described the Spirit in very unique terms—Paraclete, Spirit, and Spirit of Truth.[27] John's Gospel is the only source of the word Paraclete (*Parakletos*).[28] The Greek meaning of the word is "one called alongside," particularly one called to help out in a legal situation—a prosecuting attorney. Jesus was going to die on the cross. The world judged him guilty. The Spirit's role as prosecutor is to enter the theater of con-

flict and prove Jesus' innocence. The Paraclete would thus reverse the sentence passed on Jesus by convicting the world (for John *the world* constituted those who opposed Jesus). Jesus was sinless, but those who judged him were the guilty ones. Jesus is truly righteous before God as he is the one who now sits at the right hand of glory.

Job had a similar Paraclete. Job knew that he would go to his death judged guilty because of all the suffering heaped upon him. However, he knows that his vindicator is alive—the angel who will stand on his grave and announce to all the world that he was indeed innocent. Jesus' angel/Paraclete is the Holy Spirit.[29]

In his role as one who walks alongside, the Paraclete has another function. He walks alongside those who need a comforter. The Spirit comforts the afflicted; the Spirit is the great Consoler or Comforter. When Jesus was preparing his disciples for his absence he wanted to assure them that they would never be alone. He assured them that he would send the Paraclete—that they would have one who would walk alongside them to uphold them in their loneliness, their fear, when they faced persecution and when the journey became too long for them. Thus, the primary force in the Christian life is the Spirit/Paraclete. The Spirit dwells within every believer to guide and lead everyone to the truth. The Spirit teaches the believer the way to live. The Gnostic secessionists in the Johannine community prompted the community to seriously reflect on the role of the Spirit in the life of God's people. The secessionists believed that they alone were privy to the Spirit's direction. The Johannine community exhorted themselves to test the Spirit to see if it was of God. The opposition insisted that they alone had the power to test the Spirit. This issue is what finally led to the emergence of human shepherds in the Johannine community (Jn 21:15–17).

Raymond Brown offers some interesting observations in relation to the fourth gospel that shed further light on the Johannine theology of Spirit.[30] At the time of the fourth gospel's composition, all the eyewitnesses to the Jesus-event were gone. They had been the link between the earthly Jesus and

---

[27] *RJE*, 90.

[28] The word *Paraclete* is masculine, which requires masculine pronouns, asserts Raymond Brown (*RJE*, 90).

---

[29] Ibid., 91.

[30] Ibid.

the risen Christ. In addition, John the *Beloved Disciple* also died. He was the ultimate eyewitness and he was one of them—a member of the Johannine community. He died before the final edition of the fourth gospel was completed. The community wondered how they would ever survive without their actual link to Jesus of Nazareth.

The Holy Spirit as Paraclete was the answer to their concerns. If the *Beloved Disciple* bore witness to Christ it could not have been solely on his own remembrances. There were many people who walked with Jesus day in and day out and still did not understand him. It was the Spirit of the risen Christ given to the church after Jesus returned to the throne of glory, after he had been exalted, that reminded the community of what Jesus was trying to teach them. Through the Spirit's power and intervention, the disciples finally understood all that had been revealed to them by the Master. They witnessed to Christ because the Paraclete opened their eyes to the fullness of his revelation.

Those who were beloved disciples of the "Beloved Disciple" committed to written form all they had learned in the "Johannine school." The result? The fourth gospel. The gospel insists that the Spirit continues to be active and to guide the church of all generations.

Another issue in the writing of John's Gospel is the realization that Jesus' return was not as imminent as once thought. All the expected times of his return had come and gone. The realization had set in that the day or hour was certainly not known or imminent. The Johannine community believed it would take place before the death of John, their own *Beloved Disciple*. But now that he, too, was gone, those hopes were dashed.

The Johannine community did not lose faith in the second coming, but they realized that many of the elements promised were already in place and activated (realized eschatology). They were already a part of Christian life, for example, "judgment, divine sonship and eternal life.. And so, in a very real way, Jesus actually had come back during the lifetime of his companions, for he had come in and through the Paraclete."[31] Thus, Jesus is present in the community, in the

---

[31]Ibid., 96.

hearts of all believers through the indwelling of the Holy Spirit.

Gospel Exegesis

The facilitator gives input regarding what critical biblical scholarship has to say about this text. The input includes insights as to how people would have heard the gospel in Jesus' time.

Gospel for Cycles A, B, and C
John 20:19–23

(*Please refer to "The Johannine perspective on the mystery of Pentecost and the Holy Spirit" above.*)

John uses the event of Jesus' appearance to his disciples in Jerusalem to demonstrate that Jesus was fulfilling his promise to return in the hour of his exaltation/glorification. In John's gospel, Jesus gives the Holy Spirit on Easter Sunday. Reginald Fuller suggests that perhaps all of Jesus' post-resurrection appearances were associated with the gift of the Holy Spirit. Today is the day that the church is empowered for mission. It is given the Spirit to live out the Christian story.

The mission in today's story, however, has more to do with the forgiveness of sins. Catholic and high Anglican tradition traditionally associated this with the conferral of the sacrament of penance. However, in the New Testament understanding, the forgiveness of sin is always associated with baptism. It is not surprising that the command to forgive sins is associated with a missionary emphasis. Baptism was withheld for those who did not believe after hearing the good news. Pentecost was a day for baptisms in the early church. It is fitting that this gospel's baptismal mandate be given on a day that was often devoted to the celebration of baptism.

Pheme Perkins suggests that since John uses "only the general expression, 'disciples,' the commissioning in these verses may be intended to apply to the believing community as a whole, not to some specific group within that community such as the 'Twelve.' This 'power' of forgiveness is probably expressed in the bestowing of the Spirit on those who believe as a result of the disciples' 'mission' and who join the community, rather than in a process of dealing with Christians who have committed sins (as in Mt

18:19)."[32] Jesus insists that this is possible because of the gift of the Spirit. If people forgive each others' sins, then there will be no "obstacles to community oneness. If they continue to hold on to the sins against them . . . the sins remain as obstacles to community harmony."[33] The Holy Spirit, thus, is not only given to empower them for mission, but to enable them to live in harmony with one another. Jesus gives the Spirit to fulfill the promise that all would be one in him. This oneness is accomplished through the forgiving of one another. The sins that are to be forgiven are post-baptismal sins of Christians committed against one another. Many though we are, through the power of the Holy Spirit we are called to be one in Christ.

John posits this event on Easter Sunday as a foundational document. Through it he hopes to remind his progressive community that the Christian life is lived only through the cross and resurrection of Christ. John believes that it is essential to identify the Christ who appeared after Easter as the earthly one who suffered and who promised to return. Today's gospel is a reminder that Jesus' journey to Jerusalem took him eventually to Golgotha before the subsequent resurrection of Easter morn. We, too, are to walk the same journey to Jerusalem, strengthened and supported by the risen presence of Christ in the Holy Spirit.

Optional Gospel for Cycle B
John 15:26–27; 16:12–15

(Please refer to "The Johannine perspective on the mystery of Pentecost and the Holy Spirit" above.)

Jesus is preparing his disciples for his absence. This is part of his farewell address. One can almost hear the compassion and love for his disciples in his voice. He knows what lies ahead. They do not understand. He knows the ordeal that he is about to endure, but even more the ordeal *they* are about to endure. He desperately wants to give them something they will remember, something that will remind them to listen with new ears. The time of understanding has yet to arrive. It will come soon enough. Now is the time for preparation.

In earlier verses the disciples are warned that persecution can be expected. Refer to the gospel exegesis of the sixth and seventh Sundays of Easter for an explanation of the strong persecution context of the farewell discourse. It sheds an entirely new light on the Johannine understanding of Jesus' words in the farewell address. The Spirit/Advocate will testify on behalf of Jesus and ultimately convict the world of the crime of his death. Both the Spirit and the witnesses will give testimony to Christ.

The Spirit now takes a front and center role in John's sixteenth chapter. At the beginning of the ministry Jesus' absence and the subsequent persecutions facing the church were not immanent. There was no need to talk about it at that juncture. However, now that the specter was just around the corner the time had arrived. The topic caused untold grief for the disciples.

Jesus insists that their grief is unnecessary because once he departs, then and only then will they be gifted with the Spirit/Paraclete. The void created by the absence of Jesus will be replaced with the abundance created by the presence of the Spirit. The presence of the Spirit will be proof that those who refused to believe were of the world, and thus were sinners. The Spirit's presence proves that Jesus did indeed have to be glorified and return to the Father's right hand and that the spirit of evil had indeed been defeated.

But the Spirit will accomplish even greater deeds. The Spirit will guide the church. The Spirit will speak to the disciples what the Spirit hears from the Son, and what the Son in turn hears from the Father. Jesus continues to speak to the disciples/church through the Spirit. Thus, Jesus must leave and it is cause for rejoicing. Unless Jesus leaves them, the Spirit will not be able to come.

The Spirit is sent by Jesus after he is exalted. It is in the disciples' best interest that Jesus go to his Father. There are great benefits for the church involved. The Paraclete/Prosecutor will convict the world. The world is guilty of the sin of unbelief; Jesus is vindicated because of righteousness; thus the world is convicted of convicting him. The Paraclete will also judge the ruler of this world.[34] The

---

[32] Pheme Perkins, "The Gospel According to John," in *NJBC*, 984.

[33] *RJ*, 255.

[34] Ibid., 218.

conviction of Christ will be overturned and he will be vindicated.

God has given all things to Jesus and the Spirit in turn receives those same things from Jesus' bounty. The Spirit is the agent of the Son. The Spirit's role, then, is subordinate to Christ's role. The Spirit did not come to offer a new revelation beyond that of Christ. The Spirit clarifies the revelation already given by Christ. The Spirit will also explain the events of the past and point to the things of the future. The Spirit will assume the prophetic role. "He will take what belongs to the past, Jesus' revelation on earth and interpret it for a new situation. He will also declare the future as it must be in light of what God has revealed in Jesus Christ."[35] This would give credence to the Johannine community to discern which spirits are false and which Spirit is authentic.

Optional Gospel for Cycle C
John 14:15–16; 23b–26

(Please refer to "The Johannine perspective on the mystery of Pentecost and the Holy Spirit" above.)

Jesus now begins to speak to his disciples, his dearest friends. Jesus' absence is the context for this entire section of John's gospel. Jesus' leaving prompts the reiteration of one very important commandment. Everyone is to love one another. The disciples are troubled by the dialogue. The gravity of the situation is beginning to dawn on them. Jesus insists that faith will be their strength and that he must go in order to prepare a place for them. Even though this sounds like a proclamation of the second coming, the Johannine church sees it differently. They know they still have access to Christ through the Paraclete, the Holy Spirit.

Jesus assures them that the love they share will prompt the Father to send the Paraclete, the Spirit of Truth who will remain with them forever. This is the way Jesus will never leave them, through the presence of his Spirit. Now instead of "a place out there" where Jesus is going to prepare, the place he is going to prepare is none other than the human heart of believers. This is where the Paraclete will dwell.

They will soon know a new presence. The Paraclete will take up residence in their hearts. They will not experience Jesus' absence for very long. John says "very soon" the Paraclete will come. The disciples, who loved so well, will know a new love, the love of God for Jesus, and the love of Jesus for God. The love of God through Jesus will be poured out on believers through the Spirit. In verse 22 the disciples ask Jesus why he does not reveal himself to the world. Jesus' answer is found in verses 23 and 24 and it is merely a restatement of what he taught them before. God and Jesus will come and dwell within those who love. For John, this is the parousia—the indwelling of the Holy Spirit. For John this coming is the coming of the Paraclete who will convict the world but also instruct and enlighten the hearts of believers.

The Johannine community was confident that the Spirit lived in the community. The Spirit of Christ was present to reveal and interpret all that Christ had taught them. Christ returned, all right, and his return placed him squarely at the heart of the community. The Holy Spirit is the Christ who returned after his glorification. Those who wait in fear and trepidation for the Lord to come and swoop them away in the clouds have no place in the Johannine community. The Johannine community is to live in peace, confident that Christ is exalted. "The prediction of Christ's imminent departure is matched by his promises for the disciples' future, a fact that ought to bring consolation to the disciples."[36]

Proclaim the gospel again.

Sometimes we gain new insights when we hear the text after the interpretation has been given. Someone from the group proclaims the gospel a second time.

STEP 4
TESTING

Conversation with the Liturgy and the Scriptures

Test your original understanding in dialogue with the text.

---

[35]Ibid., 219.

[36]Ibid., 210.

(You might consider breaking into smaller groups.)

Now that you've heard the exegesis, were there any new insights? How do you feel about it? How does your original understanding of this gospel compare with what we just shared? How does this story speak to your life?

Sharing Life Experience

Participants share an experience from their lives that connects with the biblical interpretation just presented.

There are so many things going on in today's liturgy. There is celebration of the many gifts, though one Body. There is celebration of being in community, of being church, the people of God. There is a call to mission and to forgiveness. There is a singleness of purpose in those who were empowered to understand the Word of God though they each spoke a different language. There is the ultimate celebration of Christ's Passion, death, resurrection, ascension, and the sending of the Spirit, culminating in the Pentecost event. One experience does not quite express the many dimensions of this liturgy.

I am filled with deep emotion as I write my last personal reflection for this three-year project. It is no coincidence that the very last word I will write is written on the Feast of the Spirit of Jesus Christ. Jesus announced "Peace" to his friends. This three-year labor has been a labor of shalom peace in my life. I am honored and humbled to have spent the past three years exploring the heart of our tradition, liturgy, and scriptures. It has been a life-changing experience. As I have grappled and wrestled with some of the incredible insights, insights I had never before considered, I was invited by God's Spirit to enter deeply into a journey of conversion.

The "peace" I have been given is the resolve to respond to the Word as the gospel challenges us to respond, albeit ever so imperfectly. My relationships on the home front have grown, strengthened, and shalom peace is stronger. I know I have changed. I have discovered a more compassionate face of God. I have discovered a God who will go to any lengths to show us how much we are loved. I have discovered a God who seeks to break down any and all barriers that keep people from a deep, abiding relationship with him. I have had my faith reaffirmed in the power of God's Word to transform the life of the

Church. I also believe that what the scriptures "really proclaim" is often the best kept secret on the face of the earth. Ours is a liberating God! Ours is a God who desires our hearts and nothing else. Our God is a God who is passionate about those he loves. Our God waits patiently, and then waits some more, and will never, ever give up on us. Our God creates less laws for us than we create for ourselves. Our God desperately wants us to follow two very simple rules. God commands, God demands only one thing—LOVE, LOVE, and more LOVE! Not the mushy sentimental stuff we see slathered over every soap opera, but a love born of deep compassion. If we love God like God loves us, like we are called to love him, the rest is simple. We will do no less than LOVE as he taught us to LOVE. Forgiveness will be a moot point because it will go without saying.

I used to muse, "If the messianic reign is the restoration of the peace of Eden, how do we explain the fact that we are not at peace, we are often still at war, and very often with ourselves?" The Lion not only does not lie down with the lamb, he devours it! Then the realization came to me. When the Lion devours the Lamb, that Lion is of the world—at least he is acting like he is of the world (those forces opposed to the messianic reign of Christ). However, when two or more are gathered honestly, with upright hearts in the name of the Lord Jesus Christ, when they live according to the covenant and biblical justice, then everything Christ promised about the messianic reign is right and true. We are living in it! Then and only then are we living in peace. Then and only then has the shalom of Eden returned.

When I am not reconciled with my brothers and sisters I am not living the shalom peace of Eden—I am not living in the Spirit-filled messianic reign of God. Thus, I can do no less than reconcile. If I truly believe what I profess I would move heaven and earth to live according to the love I have been given.

Writing these pages has more than once had an impact on my life, my behavior, and my attitudes. So often I have been forced to change the way I live and the way I think. For example, after doing the exegesis for the parable of the prodigal son I had to take a serious look at the way I loved, or failed to love my teenage (growing toward adulthood) children. Could I love with the humiliating kind of love demonstrated by the Father? Before I was not, but now, could I really do no less? It was time to seri-

ously reassess. With the help and power of the Holy Spirit who opens our eyes to such things, I was able to begin an entirely new way of relating to my children. Another example, after spending time with Job and all his commiserations, I was able to minister (in probably the most effective way I had ever ministered to anyone) to someone who had nearly given up on God. I have become a stronger voice for justice. There are many ways God has turned my apple cart on its end and invited me to consider a new world view.

However, it is also through the power of the Holy Spirit and close encounter with the three-year Cycle of the Lord's Paschal Mystery that I know there are many places in my life where only the surface has been scratched. I have been forced to look at the areas of denial, arrogance, pride, and idolatry that lie just beneath the surface of my consciousness. The Spirit of God continues to challenge me and invite me into deep transformation and conversion.

A Word about Community. *We often say Pentecost is the birthday of the church. The birthday of the church is really Calvary, when the blood of eucharist and water of baptism flowing from the side of Christ make it possible for the Church to draw life from the Spirit's power. The entire Easter-event is the birthday of the Church. We have had a fifty-day celebration!*

Every scripture is first a word to the community. This three-year project has given me the opportunity to watch a community at close range, to live or not live the liturgies we celebrate. I often ask myself what I have learned. I have learned that the parish is where the paschal mystery finds the greatest expression in the Church. The parish is where we so often see the cycle of death and resurrection played out in lives of people of faith. The parish is the place where the best and the worst of us are discovered. The parish is where I so often see the two greatest commandments lived to the fullest possible potential. So many parish saints dot these pages and they, as well as any who went before them, belong in our annual litany to their memory. Their faces and stories have inspired every page.

Parish is where the Spirit of God dances the dance of life and kicks the rest of us out onto the dance floor. "You will dance," the Spirit gently and sometimes not so gently cajoles. The dance, I have dis-

covered, is the most important part. It is not the end of the dance, but the dance itself. The end of the dance will come soon enough and we will see the Lord face to face, as the story goes. But the dance itself is the holy encounter. It is filled with swift turns, sore and blistered feet, dizziness from moving too fast, weariness from moving too slowly, confusion from dancing out of step, and imbalance from dancing out of rhythm. But it is also a dance of peace, for when we dance in step with the Spirit Dancer, his guidance is so effortless, her touch so light, and their coercion ever so gentle. But it is nevertheless the Spirit Dancer who ever so graces us with gazelle-like presence.

Confidently we allow ourselves to be glided across the splintered floor, only slightly aware of its slivers, knowing that there was one who went before us who knows well the legacy of splintered hands and feet. So on this Pentecost feast, let the song ring in our hearts, but let us not just sing it, let us live it. "Dance, dance wherever you may be. I am the Lord of the dance," said he. "And I lead you all wherever you may be and I'll lead you all in the dance," says he.

Questions for Mystagogical Reflection

What was John's intention in his telling of this event in the postresurrection appearance of Jesus? What might the Spirit be creating or re-creating in us through this liturgy (creation)? In what way does this liturgy point to God's promise to be with us (covenant)? In what way does this gospel invite us to die and rise (exodus)? How does this liturgy speak to our community? In what way is our community challenged? Do we still feel the same way about these scriptures and this feast as we did when we began? Has our original understanding been stretched, challenged, or affirmed?

Optional Gospels for Cycles B and C: Put yourself in the disciples' place as they are listening to Jesus. What would be your thoughts and feelings? How might that be relevant today? Have you ever had the experience of a force outside yourself bringing clarity out of a difficult situation? Describe. In what way might you relate to the Holy Spirit as described in the gospel? How does this gospel invite deeper immersion in the paschal mystery? In what way does this gospel invite transformation in your life, in the life of the community?

The gospel demands a response.

What are the contemporary implications of the scriptures in today's liturgy? In what concrete way does this gospel call our parish to action in the Church, parish, neighborhood, or world? Has our conversation with these scriptures and this liturgy changed or stretched my/our personal attitudes? What am I/we/our community/our parish called to do in response? What is one concrete action we will take this week in response to what we have learned and shared today?

DOCTRINAL ISSUES

What Church truth/teaching/doctrinal issue could be drawn from the gospel for the Feast of Pentecost?

Participants suggest possible doctrinal themes that flow from the readings.

Possible Doctrinal Themes

Holy Spirit; mystery of the Church; resurrection/ascension/Pentecost; paschal mystery; ministry in the Church; sacraments; symbols of the Church; evangelization; prayer; Jesus Christ; salvation, laying on of hands

Present the doctrinal material at this time.

1. The facilitator gives input on a particular doctrinal issue of his/her prior choosing. OR
2. The group chooses a doctrinal issue from the list they created. They read together from the Doctrinal Appendix or other appropriate, official Church documents and the works of respected theologians.

(Many doctrinal issues are found in the Doctrinal Appendix at the back of this workbook. If you are choosing an issue from this resource, please refer to it now.)

Reflection questions centered around the chosen doctrinal theme can be found at the end of each topic in the Doctrinal Appendix. The questions are based on the five-step reflection process. If you choose a topic not included in the Doctrinal Appendix, craft your own questions according to the same five-step process.

Following the reflection questions you will be reminded to return to chapter 7, "Preparing the Catechetical Session," to assist you in crafting your own session.

Closing Prayer

(This day) the Father of light
has enlightened the minds of the disciples
by the outpouring of the Holy Spirit.
May he bless you
and give you the gifts of the Spirit for ever.
    (Amen.)

May that fire which hovered over the disciples
as tongues of flame
burn out all evil from your hearts
and make them glow with pure light.
    (Amen.)

God inspired speech in different tongues
to proclaim one faith.
May he strengthen your faith
and fulfill your hope of seeing him face to face.
    (Amen.)[37]

---

[37]Pentecost: "Solemn Blessing," *The Sacramentary.*

ORDINARY TIME

ORDINARY TIME: AN OVERVIEW

The word *ordinary* in Ordinary Time is not to be confused with *ordinary* as in lackluster, boring, or routine. *Ordinary* in this instance refers to ordinal (counted time). Each Sunday is designated a number that is counted from Sunday to Sunday. The liturgical color of Ordinary Time is green.

Ordinary Time's primary focus is the feast of Sunday.[1] Each Sunday is an Easter celebration of sorts. We remember and celebrate the life, death, and resurrection of Jesus. Each Sunday the paschal mystery is revealed in its fullness. During Ordinary Time there is no highlighted, singular aspect to the remembered story of Christ as in the other seasons. Rather, all the many facets of Christ's mystery are unfolded on these thirty-three to thirty-four Sundays of the year.[2]

> Ordinary Time begins on Monday after the Sunday following 6 January and continues until Tuesday before Ash Wednesday inclusive. It begins again on Monday after Pentecost and ends before evening prayer I of the First Sunday of Advent. (GNLY, #44)

The Ordinary Time cycle is often delineated in bite-sized chunks corresponding to the time of the year. Thus, winter Ordinary Time covers the block of time immediately following Christmas. The Second Sunday in Ordinary Time begins Ordinary Time and it falls after the feast of the Baptism of the Lord. Winter Ordinary Time extends to the lenten season. Summer Ordinary Time begins after the feast of Pentecost on the feast of the Trinity. Following Trinity and Corpus Christi, the counted Sundays begin again where they ended before Lent began. Autumn Ordinary Time begins around the 23rd or 24th Sunday and continues until the season of Advent.

SUNDAYS OF CYCLE A

Much of Mark's gospel is proclaimed on the Sundays and weekdays of Ordinary Time. (Refer to chapter 9, Overview of Mark's Gospel.) Most of the gospel of Mark is read from the beginning of Jesus' public ministry through the teaching on the coming of the Son of Man. Mark is the shortest gospel, however. There is not enough material to stretch over all the Sundays of Ordinary Time. For this reason, the reading of Mark is interrupted through the seventeenth through the twenty-first Sundays of the year. John's version of the feeding of the multitudes and the subsequent discourse on the Bread of Life is inserted for these five weeks. The reading of Mark begins again on the twenty-second Sunday.

The first readings chosen for Ordinary Time are taken from nineteen of the forty-eight books of the Bible: Genesis, Exodus, Leviticus, Numbers, Deuteronomy, Joshua, 1 Samuel, 1 Kings, 2 Kings, Job, Proverbs, Wisdom, Isaiah, Jeremiah, Ezekiel, Daniel, Hosea, Amos, and Jonah. The second readings are extracted from three of Paul's letters —1 Corinthians, 2 Corinthians, Ephesians—and Hebrews. The proclamation of Mark's gospel begins on the third Sunday in Ordinary Time as a selection from John's gospel is chosen for the second Sunday of every year. The "Introduction to the Lectionary" explains: "On the Second Sunday of Ordinary Time the gospel continues to center on the manifestation of the Lord.... Beginning with the Third Sunday, there is a semicontinuous reading of the Synoptic Gospels. This reading is arranged in such a way that as the Lord's life and preaching unfold, the teaching proper to each of these gospels is presented."[3]

The meaning of each gospel for a given Sunday corresponds to the flow and the movement of the liturgical cycle. For example, after the feast of Epiphany, at the transition between the Christmas

---

[1]See Chapter 8 regarding liturgical time and the liturgical calendar. The understanding and celebration of Sunday are covered extensively.

[2]*GNLY*, #43, in *TLD*.

[3]"Introduction to the Lectionary," #105, in *TLD*.

season and the beginnings of Ordinary Time, the church centers on the beginnings of Christ's preaching ministry. This connects well to the first Sunday of Ordinary Time, the solemnity of the Baptism of the Lord, with its stories of "the first events in which he manifests himself."[4] By the same token, the theme of "last things, *eschatology*" naturally coincides with the readings and liturgies of the end of the liturgical cycle. The beginning of the year reflects beginnings and the end of the year reflects endings.

The first readings are chosen to bring unity to the Old and the New Testaments by their connection to the gospel. There is no logical order given for the readings from the Hebrew scriptures (Old Testament) other than their connection with the gospel.

Paul's and James's letters are read semicontinuously. Peter and John are read during the Easter and Christmas seasons. The letters are distributed over the three-year cycle.

On the solemnities of the Lord during Ordinary Time (Holy Trinity, Corpus Christi, and Sacred Heart), the readings are chosen to highlight the central theme of the solemnity. Some call these feasts "idea feasts," as they do not celebrate an event of Jesus' life, but rather a creed in regard to the mystery of Christ.

All of the Sundays, feasts, and solemnities of the sacred liturgy celebrate the mystery of redemption through Jesus Christ. In his encyclical, *Mediator Dei*, Pius XII asserted:

> In the sacred Liturgy, the whole of Christ is proposed to us in all the circumstances of His life, as the Word of Eternal Father, as born of the Virgin Mother of God, as He Who teaches us truth, heals the sick, consoles the afflicted, Who endures suffering and Who dies; finally, as He Who rose triumphantly from the dead and Who, reigning in the glory of heaven sends us the Holy Paraclete and Who abides in His Church forever: "Jesus Christ, yesterday and today; and the same forever." (#163)

---

[4]Ibid.

WEEKDAYS OF THE LITURGICAL YEAR

The first nine weeks of weekday readings proclaim the first twelve chapters of Mark's gospel.[5] The readings from Matthew and Luke consist of all material not contained in Mark. The first readings of the weekday masses rotate between sections from the Old and New Testament. During a period of weeks the first reading is taken from the Old Testament; another block of weeks will center on the New Testament. The number of weeks depends on the length of the specific book being read. There are large sections of the New Testament readings proclaimed so that the fullness of the apostles' teaching may be provided. The Old Testament readings are limited and very select. The passage chosen reflects the character of the book from which it was taken.[6]

Just as Mark redacted the story of Jesus according to his community's needs, so too the church, through the chosen texts of the Lectionary, determines the scriptural texts that best reflect our Christian faith as celebrated in the context of the liturgical cycle. There is no attempt made to render an historical, chronological depiction of the life of Christ from his birth to his death and resurrection. Rather, the intent is to reveal the entire mystery of Christ. In the last analysis, every liturgical feast celebrates the paschal mystery of Christ, who empties himself, sacrifices himself in obedience, and is present and active in his community of believers. Herein lies the beauty, depth and intensity of this extended season we call Ordinary Time. Far from being *ordinary*, it is imbued with passion—the passion of a people in covenant, radical relationship with the Christ of the gospels, the Christ of the eternal universe! No Sunday is routine, humdrum, or subservient and antithetical to the major seasons of the year. Each Sunday, solemnity, and feast is *manifestation* in itself!

CHRISTIAN INITIATION

A thorough explanation of the ongoing process of Christian initiation is placed in the overview of Ordinary Time since initiation is the normative

---

[5]There is one exception. Two passages from the sixth chapter of Mark are read in other cycles and thus are not read in those first nine weeks.

[6]"Introduction to the Lectionary," #105–110, in *TLD*.

way a parish lives as *church.* It is part of the ongoing life of a parish. Since Ordinary Time is where the church spends thirty-four weeks of the year, this is an appropriate place to digress and include an examination of an initiation process that is fluid and continually celebrated in the midst of the Christian community throughout the weeks of the liturgical cycle. With the exception of the initiation rituals of Lent and Easter, most of the rites of initiation are celebrated on the Sundays of Ordinary Time. There is a comprehensive explanation of the rites of Lent and Easter such as election, scrutinies, and Christian initiation in the chapters that deal with Lent and Easter.

THE YEAR-ROUND CATECHUMENATE

Operating Assumptions

The Spirit is not a respecter of time. The Spirit moves where the Spirit wills. How do we welcome people who inquire at inopportune times, times that do not fit our neatly packaged school calendar models? Each journey is unique.

Formation for the catechumen consists of living and experiencing the life, death, and resurrection of Jesus as it unfolds in one complete liturgical cycle. Thus, a candidate who enters the precatechumenate in September, celebrates the Rite of Acceptance in December, and is initiated at the Easter Vigil in April, is in the catechumenate stage for only four or five months. Such a person is formed by less than half of Christ's complete story of redemption!

In an ongoing model, the process is suited to the needs of each individual. The process takes into account the movement of God's grace and the circumstances of time and place of each person's faith journey (RCIA, #5). Realizing that God deals with us as individuals, an ongoing model is crafted in such a way that each person moves through the process when he or she is ready, not when it is convenient to the parish structure.

Thus, there is no official beginning or "start-up" time in an ongoing process. It is continuous. Once the four periods of the catechumenate are in progress, each period continues forever. There is no beginning or ending.

The catechumenate is an extended period during which the candidates are given suitable pastoral formation and guidance, aimed at training them in the Christian life. . . . A suitable catechesis is provided, planned to be gradual and complete in its coverage, accommodated to the liturgical year. . . . (RCIA, #74)

The duration of the catechumenate will depend on the grace of God and on various circumstances. . . . The time spent in the catechumenate should be long enough, several years—if necessary—for the conversion and faith of the catechumens to become strong. By their formation in the entire Christian life and a sufficiently prolonged probation the catechumens are properly initiated into the mysteries of salvation and the practice of an evangelical way of life. (RCIA, #76)

The period of the catechumenate, beginning at acceptance into the order of catechumens and including both the catechumenate proper and the period of purification and enlightenment after election or the enrollment of names, should extend for at least one year of formation, instruction, and probation. Ordinarily this period should go from at least the Easter season of one year until the next; preferably it should begin before Lent in one year and extend until Easter of the following year. (National Statutes of the RCIA, #6)

. . . It [the catechumenate] should extend over a substantial and appropriate period of time. The rites prior to sacramental initiation should not be unduly compressed, much less celebrated on a single occasion. (National Statutes of the RCIA, #20)

It is clearly the vision of the Rite that the catechumenate proper extend for one full year in order for the catechumens to experience the paschal mystery as it unfolds in one complete liturgical cycle.

FINAL REFLECTIONS

When do inquirers enter the precatechumenate?

Whenever they come seeking.

447

How long does the precatechumenate last?

As long as it needs to.

How do we know when people are ready to move to the catechumenate?

When they demonstrate initial stirring of faith, a spirit of repentance, the *beginnings* of the spiritual life, including calling on God in prayer, initial conversion, the intention to change their lives and a sense of church. (RCIA, #42)

When is the Rite of Acceptance celebrated?

The Rite of Acceptance is celebrated whenever there are people ready to move to the catechumentate, the next stage. This works out to be approximately four times a year, but preferably not during Lent and Advent.

Entry into the catechumenate is marked by the Rite of Acceptance.

The Rite of Acceptance celebrates what people experienced in the inquiry and foreshadows what they will experience in the catechumenate.

When are baptized Christians received into full communion with the Catholic Church?

Whenever they are ready.

For an illustration of how this might be implemented in a parish setting, see *Word & Worship Workbook for Year C,* pages 331–338.

LITURGICAL PRAYER

Liturgical prayer is the official, communal, public prayer of the church. It is the primary way we should begin all our Catholic/Christian gatherings and mark all major life experiences and transitions. Liturgical prayer is different from other prayer forms such as private prayers, devotions, spontaneous prayer, or prayer services crafted in a catechetical resource. Our church enjoys a vast repertoire of liturgical prayer. As stated in the introductory section of this book, catechesis has the responsibility of forming children and adults in the liturgical life of the church. This does not simply mean the eucharistic liturgy of the church.

Since liturgy forms children and adults in their Catholic Christian faith, we must be attentive to all the church's liturgical prayer. This prayer constitutes the way we live our Catholic life on a routine, day-to-day, week-to-week basis. Thus, this section on liturgical prayer is placed in the overview of Ordinary Time as liturgical prayer is the normative way we are to pray as community throughout the year, not only seasonally, but throughout the days and weeks of the year. Suggestions for use of this vast repertoire will be included in the weekly sessions.

The treasury that comprises the church's liturgical prayer includes:

Eucharistic liturgy

Liturgy of the hours

Liturgy of the word

Rite of Penance:
Sacramental celebrations of the sacrament of reconciliation, including three revised liturgical celebrations:
a) Rite of Reconciliation of Individual Penitents
b) Rite of Reconciliation of Several Penitents with Individual Confession and Absolution
c) Rite of Reconciliation of Several Penitents with General Absolution

Non-sacramental Celebrations

Penitential celebrations are gatherings of the people of God to hear the proclamation of God's word. This invites them to conversion and renewal of life and announces our freedom from sin through the death and resurrection of Christ. (Rite of Penance, #36)

It is desirable to arrange such services especially for these purposes:
– to foster the spirit of penance within the community;
– to help the faithful to prepare for confession that can be made individually later at a convenient time;
– to help children gradually form their conscience about sin in human life and about freedom from sin through Christ;
– to help catechumens during their conversion. (Rite of Penance, #37)

Within the Rite of Penance there are various models for these non-sacramental liturgical celebrations that should be adapted to the specific conditions and needs of each community.

I. Penitential Celebrations during Lent
II. Penitential Celebrations during Advent
III. Common Penitential Celebrations
IV. For Children
V. For Youth

We are a people in need of continuous reconciliation and healing. The rite provides a fount of grace to heal and reconcile as we struggle with abuse, sin, pain, and broken relationships. We should celebrate reconciliation on a continuing basis in sacramental and non-sacramental celebrations. Non-sacramental celebrations do not require a priest and may be presided over by a lay minister.

Book of Blessings

The following is a sample list of blessings from the *Book of Blessings* that might be appropriately celebrated throughout the liturgical cycle.

Order for the Blessing of Children
Order of Blessing of the Sick
Order for the Blessing of a Person Suffering from Addiction
Order for Blessing of a Victim of Crime or Oppression
Orders for Blessings that Pertain to Catechesis and to Communal Prayer
Order for the Blessing of Animals
Order for the Blessing of Students and Teachers
Order for the Blessing of Seeds at Planting Time
Order for the Blessing on the Occasion of Thanksgiving for the Harvest
Order for the Blessing before or after Meals
Order for the Blessing of an Advent Wreath
Order for the Blessing of a Christmas Manger or Nativity Scene
Order for the Blessing of a Christmas Tree
Order for the Blessing of Throats on the Feast of Saint Blase
Order for the Blessing and Distribution of Ashes
Order for the Blessing of Food for Thanksgiving Day
Order for the Blessing of Readers
Order for the Blessing of Altar Servers, Sacristans, Musicians, and Ushers
Order for a Blessing in Thanksgiving

Order for a Blessing to be Used in Various Circumstances

Other Liturgical Celebrations

Celebration of the Triduum

Holy Communion and Worship of the Eucharist outside Mass
– Rite of Eucharistic Exposition and Benediction
– Eucharistic Processions
Rite of Baptism for Children—celebrated in the parish
Rite of Confirmation—celebrated in the parish
Rite of Marriage—celebrated in the parish
Rite of Ordination
Pastoral Care of the Sick: Rites of Anointing and Viaticum
– Visits to a sick child
– Anointing of the Sick
– Celebration of Viaticum
Order of Christian Funerals

Catholic Household Blessings and Prayers—a vast repertoire of liturgical prayers for use in the home—for every occasion.[7]

Feasts and Events of Note Throughout the Year

The following is a compilation of some of the events and feasts of note that occur throughout the year. While they will not be addressed in full in this resource, they are nevertheless part of our Christian/Catholic/social life and are worthy of mention in our catechetical ministry.

January. January 1—New Year's Day. (Mary, Mother of God and Epiphany, Baptism of the Lord are covered during the Christmas season.) January 4—Memorial of St. Elizabeth Ann Seton (religious founder from the U.S.A., 1774–1821). January 5—Memorial of St. John Neuman (bishop, religious, missionary—U.S.A., 1811–1860). January 18–25 is the Christian Unity Octave in which eight days are set aside for special prayer for the unity of Christians. There are prayers in the *Book of Blessings* for

---

[7]This section on liturgical prayer was taken from Sister Linda Gaupin's course, "Catechesis and Liturgy 106," Diocese of Orlando, Orlando, Florida, 1996.

use at ecumenical gatherings. The church prays for the unity of Christians throughout the year, but sets aside the octave for special remembrance and prayers. January 25—Conversion of Paul. Third Monday in January—Martin Luther King, Jr. Day. January 26—Sts. Timothy and Titus. January 28—Thomas Aquinas.

February. February 25—Feast of the Presentation of the Lord (Candlemas, the day on which enough candles for the entire year are blessed). February 3—St. Blase (Order for Blessing Throats, *Book of Blessings*); February 12—birth of Abraham Lincoln. February 22—The Feast of the Chair of Peter, birth of George Washington. President's Day—third Monday in February.

March. First Friday in March—World Day of Prayer. March 8—International Women's Day. March 19—Solemnity of St. Joseph. March 24—Anniversary of the death of Oscar Arnulfo Romero. March 25—Solemnity of the Annunciation of the Lord.

April. April 1—April Fools' Day. April 22—Earth Day. April 25—Feast of St. Mark the evangelist.

May. Second Sunday in May—Mother's Day. Last Monday in May—Memorial Day (U.S.A.). Monday on or before May 24—Victoria Day (Canada). May 3—Feast of Sts. Philip and James, apostles. May 14—St. Matthias, apostle. May 15—St. Isidore the Farmer (a good day to bless gardens and fields—check Catholic Household Blessings and *Book of Blessings* for an appropriate blessing). May 31—Feast of the Visit of the Virgin Mary to Elizabeth.

June. Third Sunday in June—Father's Day. June 3—Anniversary of the death of Pope John XXIII. June 24—Solemnity of the Birth of John the Baptist. June 29—Solemnity of Sts. Peter and Paul.

July. July 1—Canada Day. July 3—St. Thomas, apostle. July 4—Independence Day (U.S.A.). July 16—Our Lady of Mount Carmel. July 22—St. Mary Magdalene. July 25—Feast of St. James, apostle.

August. August 6—Feast of the Transfiguration of the Lord. August 10—Feast of St. Lawrence, deacon, martyr. August 15—Solemnity of the Assumption of the Virgin Mary into Heaven. August 22—

The Queenship of the Virgin Mary (octave[8] of Assumption).

September. First Monday in September—Labor Day. September 8—Feast of the Birth of the Virgin Mary. September 14—Feast of the Holy Cross. September 15—Our Lady of Sorrows. September 21—Feast of St. Matthew, apostle and evangelist. September 29—Sts. Michael, Gabriel, and Raphael, archangels.

October. Second Monday in October—Thanksgiving Day (Canada). October 4—St. Francis of Assisi, patron saint of ecologists and all environmentalists. October 18—Feast of St. Luke the evangelist. October 28—Feast of Sts. Simon and Jude.

November. First Tuesday after the first Monday in November—Election Day (U.S.A.). Fourth Thursday in November—Thanksgiving Day (U.S.A.). November 1—All Saints, solemnity. November 2—All Souls. November 9—Feast of Dedication of the Lateran Basilica in Rome (reminds us of our history as a people; this church thinks of itself as the parish for the entire world as it is the cathedral of Rome, home to the bishop of Rome—the pope). November 11—Veterans Day (U.S.A.); Remembrance Day (Canada). November 21—Memorial of the Presentation of Mary. November 29—Anniversary of the death of Dorothy Day. November 30—Feast of St. Andrew the apostle.

December. December 1—Anniversary of the day Rosa Parks kept her bus seat. December 8—Solemnity of the Immaculate Conception of the Virgin Mary. December 10—International Human Rights Day. December 12—Feast of Our Lady of Guadalupe. December 25—Solemnity of the Birth of our Lord. Octave of Christmas begins. December 26—Feast of St. Stephen, first martyr. December 27—Feast of St. John the apostle, evangelist. December 28—Feast of the Holy Innocents.

---

[8]"In church tradition, an octave represents eternity.... Seven days make a normal, run of the mill week. But add an eighth day and you've got something special. You've got a week that ends and begins on the same day. In the early church, they thought that eight days was a symbol of perfection and of heaven." Mary Ellyn Hynes, *Companion to the Calendar* (Chicago: Liturgy Training Publications, 1993), 126.

SECOND SUNDAY IN ORDINARY TIME

Environment

The season of Ordinary Time is thirty-three to thirty-four weeks long, interrupted by the Lent/Easter season. The liturgical color of the season is green. The catechetical environment may simply include a candle, green cloth, and plants. The early days of Ordinary Time center on the beginning of Jesus' ministry. Perhaps an icon reflecting one of these early scenes could be incorporated into the catechetical environment. Ordinary Time spans thirty-four weeks and might naturally be divided into segments by the natural rhythm of the winter, spring, summer, and fall seasons. Thus, in order to provide variation in the environment, images from the seasons (or recurrent themes that occur in those seasons) might be incorporated into the catechetical setting.

INTRODUCTORY RITES

Entrance Antiphon (or Opening Song)

May all the earth give you worship and praise and break into song to your name, O God, Most high. (Ps 65:4)[1]

Opening Prayer

The facilitator of the session may lead the prayer. Others in the group may be asked to proclaim the readings.

Let us pray
to our Father for the gift of peace.

Pause for silent prayer.

Father of heaven and earth,
hear our prayers,
and show us the way to peace
   in the world.
Grant this through our Lord Jesus Christ, your
   Son,

who lives and reigns with you
   and the Holy Spirit,
one God for ever and ever.[2]

LITURGY OF THE WORD

The readings are proclaimed.

First Reading[3]
1 Samuel 3:3–10, 19

Overview of the Books of Samuel: From the time of Joshua, Israel was governed by a loose tribal confederacy. The Books of Samuel signal the move to one central government that reached its pinnacle in the reigns of David and Solomon. The major figure during this time of political change was Samuel, a late-eleventh-century B.C.E. prophetic, religious, and political voice of the times.[4] The books span events from Samuel's childhood years and his prophetic call through the life and reign of David and the succession of his sons. The reign of David was remembered as Israel's golden years. Israel prospered and developed into a great nation.

Prior to the establishment of David's reign, Israel was suspicious of the monarchy system. The Books of Samuel reflect those suspicions. Many people preferred the tribal system over the monarchy. They feared a government with too much centralized power. The Books of Samuel reflect this sensitive tension.

Yet the monarchy was born with the anointing of Saul by Samuel. Saul did not fare well, however.

---

[1]Second Sunday in Ordinary Time: "Entrance Antiphon," *The Sacramentary.*

[2]Second Sunday in Ordinary Time: "Opening Prayer," *The Sacramentary.*

[3]The exegesis for the first and second readings may or may not be the focus of your group's reflection, as there may only be time to give adequate attention to the gospel, your primary concern. However, the exegesis is included here in order to provide a thorough investigation of the entire liturgy of the Word as there may be parts (or all) that would be essential to the direction you wish to take with your particular ministry group.

[4]*ROT,* 228.

His moody, irrational, temperamental behavior as well as his lack of organizational skills became his undoing.[5] He turned against his young aide, David, a brilliant warrior and a highly charismatic personality. Saul was no match for this rising star. David outmaneuvered Saul, rose to power, and continued his brilliant military campaign.

In addition to his military conquests, David unified and consolidated the nation and established the newly conquered city of Jerusalem as the capital. Since the city was situated on the border between the northern tribes of Israel and the southern tribes of Judah, the neutrality of the site made it acceptable to all. David's reign would be remembered as Israel's greatest moment.

The high point of the Books of Samuel can be found in Yahweh's promise to David that his reign would last forever. Israel would remember this promise as a sign of God's protection during future difficult times.

Today's Pericope: The child Samuel was dedicated to the service of the sanctuary. One night he woke up thinking that he heard a voice call out to him. He thought it was Eli, the priest in charge of the sanctuary. Samuel called out twice in response to the voice he heard. After the third time, Eli realized that the voice Samuel heard was God's.

Samuel's call is reminiscent of every prophetic vocation in the scriptures. God called and the prophet responded. The invitation to the prophetic life was extended to the prophet in complete freedom. The initiative was always God's. Great biblical figures such as Moses, Jeremiah, Mary, and Paul were called in a similar fashion. Manifestations such as that experienced by Samuel were deeply and personally intimate and reached the very depths of the heart.

In today's story, the wise Eli understood that the voice Samuel heard might just be the voice of God trying to break into his consciousness. After Samuel called to Eli a second time, Eli told him to respond to the Lord should he call again and say, "Speak, Lord, your servant is listening." Eli thus exhorted Samuel to be open to the voice of God.

He did not discourage Samuel or deny his experience. Rather, Eli encouraged him to listen with patience for the God who would reveal his will in due time.

The call of the *child* Samuel is reminiscent of others God used in the salvation history of the world—the weak, the lowly, the poor, and other insignificant ones. The task is always out of proportion to the chosen one's capability—and always he or she objects, citing his or her deficiencies. For example, Moses complained to God that he had a speech impediment. God said not to worry—he would make it easy—Moses would only have to know four words: *set my people free!* The prophet could hardly wallow in his own self-importance! God even put the words in his mouth! God chooses the weakest and the smallest to confound the strongest and the largest! God will be God!

The crux of the story is that Samuel said, "I am listening, Lord. Whatever you ask, I will do." There was no blueprint, no plan, and no glimpse of the future. He was simply invited and in humble submission said yes. Samuel is a model for every disciple called into the Lord's service. He also mirrors every believer who is invited into intimate relationship with a God who desires to communicate Godself to his children.

Reginald Fuller suggests that Samuel serves as a type of Jesus' baptism. Even though John's gospel does not relate Jesus' baptism, it is perhaps alluded to in the profession of faith by John in today's gospel. John was probably able to attest to Christ as the "Lamb of God" because of the heavenly voice who proclaimed him "Son" at his baptism. Samuel foreshadowed Jesus' submission to his Father's will. Samuel listened and responded to the Word of God. Many times John's gospel tells how Jesus responded to the will of his Father.[6] Today Samuel points us to Christ.

Responsorial Psalm
Psalm 40:2, 4, 7–8, 8–9, 10

Today's psalm affirms the typology asserted by Fuller in the exegesis of the first reading. In the

---

[5] Ibid., 229.

[6] *PL*, 289.

letter to the Hebrews, Jesus is the one who utters the words of this psalm. "Here am I, Lord, I come to do your will" is the sacrificial stance and attitude of Christ's entire life and death. It was the response to the total incarnation event—his birth, life, Passion, death, resurrection, and sending of the Spirit.

Second Reading
1 Corinthians 6:13–15, 17–20

Overview of the Books of 1 and 2 Corinthians:
Corinth was a Greek city that was demolished in 146 B.C. and restored a century later. The diversity of Corinth was most apparent in the disparity between the very wealthy and the very poor. Most of those on the lower end of society's ladder were slaves. Corinth was an intellectual center that played host to many aberrant religious philosophies and doctrines. Paul preached and ministered in Corinth for about eighteen months on his second journey beginning in the fall of A.D. 51. His third missionary journey to Corinth occurred in the spring of A.D. 54.

Paul became aware of troubles in Corinth. First Corinthians is a response to those concerns. This letter did not produce the desired result, so Paul sent Timothy to Corinth. He was also unsuccessful. Paul followed up with a visit of his own, but to no avail. Second Corinthians was written as a response to Paul's visit. Both letters were probably written in A.D. 57, 1 Corinthians in the spring; 2 Corinthians in the fall.

The letters were written as a response to Hellenism. "All we know about Corinth leads us to believe that there was scarcely a more unlikely place in the entire Roman world for the gospel to find a favorable reception."[7] Paul's letters not only reflect that the Corinthian community did indeed accept the gospel, but they also demonstrate his affection for the community in spite of their faults.

The moral problems inherent in the Corinthian community had to do with their recent conversion from paganism. Paul's community was under a great deal of pressure because of the temptations and lures of the culture's religious and intellectual oddities. People were succumbing to pagan influences. The concerns of morality centered around the community's attitude toward sex, toward the eating of meat sacrificed to idols, and around the appropriate celebration of the eucharist. There was also a problem distinguishing spiritual gifts from the phenomena associated with certain cults and their practices. The Greek-influenced Corinth experienced difficulty in accepting the teaching of the resurrection of the body. Gnosticism was also a concern addressed and refuted by Paul. Gnosticism claimed a special knowledge of God that only a few were privileged enough to experience. Gnosticism was a serious problem in the Corinthian community. One of the effects of gnosticism on Paul's community was that they treated those who did not have all the special gifts of the Spirit as somehow "less than." Glossolalia (speaking in tongues) was just one such instance. Those who did not speak in tongues were considered inferior. This caused division within the community. Second Corinthians addresses the community's difficulty in accepting the apostleship of Paul.

The Corinthians, like their ancient counterparts, were beginning to take God's gifts and promise of salvation for granted. Paul put priorities in the right place. He definitively asserts that to be in the Spirit means one confesses Jesus as Lord—the earthly, crucified Lord. The gnostic Corinthians regarded the death of Jesus as a past, forgotten reality and were more intent on centering in on the ethereal, intangible Jesus. Paul grounds them in the reality of the cross.

All the gifts of the Spirit are for the uplifting of the Body. One gift is not to be stressed over another. All are to be used with prudence and balance for the good of the community, not for self-edification. Through baptism, the church is one Body. Through the eucharist, all are "to drink of the one Spirit." There is not to be divisiveness. All gifts are to be used for the common good, to uplift and nourish the entire Body. Fuller notes that 1 Corinthians was possibly written for the paschal feast.[8]

---

[7] *DB*, 150.

[8] *PL*, 289–290.

Scholars maintain that the brilliance of Paul in these letters shines forth in his synthesis and application of belief and doctrine. Paul cleverly uses doctrine to address the everyday life and problems of Christians.

Today's Pericope: Paul challenges the illicit sexual behavior of someone in the community. He is actually more angry with the community for its failure to discipline the offending party. Paul railed against the popular gnostic attitude that "anything goes." Gnostics felt they were not subject to the disciplines of this world. They believed that their bodies were not subject to the confines of the earthly plane. They saw themselves only as spiritual beings.

Paul argues that the human person is both body and spirit and that both are under the authority of Christ. For the first time Paul makes reference to the church as the Body of Christ. Since the church is the Body of Christ, everyone is under his authority and dominion. Thus, as one who belongs to Christ the believer has no right to profane what belongs to him.

Another image Paul uses is that of temple. He asserts that the body is the temple of the Holy Spirit. As such, it may not be profaned by sexual immorality. It is home to God's own Spirit living within. Some scholars suggest that Paul may have been writing in response to the Corinthian participation in temple prostitution. This makes the image of body as temple all the more understandable and profound.

The gospel is proclaimed.

Gospel[9]
John 1:35–42. "They saw where Jesus lived and they stayed with him."[10]

---

[9]The gospel exegesis is provided later in this session so that it may be presented in the proper sequence where it occurs in the adult five-step reflection process. The exegesis is provided for the first and second readings for your information and edification, and for you to use at your discretion. Once again, the gospel is the primary source of reflection. If there is time for reflection on the other readings, all the better.

[10]*LM*, 66.

STEP 1
NAMING ONE'S EXPERIENCE

What were your first impressions? What was your first response to the gospel (or the other readings)?[11] What captured your attention?

Each person names his or her initial impression. Statements should be brief. No reasons should be given at this time. All simply listen without agreeing or disagreeing.

STEP 2
UNDERSTANDING

In a brief statement, explain what you think this gospel is trying to convey.

STEP 3
INPUT FROM VISION/STORY/TRADITION

Liturgical Context[12]

Today begins the season of Ordinary Time. At the end of each liturgical season, the readings are eschatological in nature and the gospels focus on the end of Jesus' life and ministry. At the beginning of the new liturgical cycle, the focus is on the beginning of Jesus' ministry. Thus, the opening scene in today's gospel begins the Sundays in Ordinary Time with John and two of his disciples in Bethany. John sees Jesus walk by and professes him as the "Lamb of God." Peter and Andrew thus begin to follow Jesus, who simply extends the invitation, "Come and see." Similarly, today's first reading from Samuel foreshadows the gospel with the story of Samuel, who was also called by God and subsequently responded in obedience.

---

[11]The primary focus of reflection is the gospel. However, often the other readings demand attention and must be brought into the dialogue.

[12]The scriptures in the Lectionary, the seasons of the year, and the ritual prayers of the mass are interrelated and form the basis for liturgical catechesis. The *liturgical context* attempts to explore and clarify the themes and this interrelatedness.

Mark's gospel is read continuously throughout the liturgical year. This Sunday's theme of "invitation and call" from John's gospel coupled with Mark's theme of "repentance and the universal message of salvation" next week form an internal unity between the second and third Sundays in Ordinary Time. A new sequence begins on the fourth Sunday.

On the second Sunday in Ordinary Time each year the gospel is from John rather than from one of the evangelists, Matthew (Cycle A), Mark (Cycle B), or Luke (Cycle C). Mark will be read on the following consecutive Sundays. The reason John's gospel is used each year is to place the first Sunday in Ordinary Time in continuity with the feasts of manifestation—Epiphany and Baptism of the Lord.[13]

The symbolism surrounding John's title for Jesus, "Lamb of God," should be remembered in every fractioning rite of the eucharistic liturgy in which we profess that the bread we break is Jesus, "the Lamb of God who takes away the sins of the world." There is a reference to Jesus, the "Lamb of God," in three places in the eucharistic liturgy—the Gloria, the fractioning rite or breaking of bread, and the prayer before the communion procession.

In the East, the breaking of the bread is a symbol of the Lord's Passion and death. Thus, the Greek fathers referred to the eucharistic bread as *lamb*. The Latin fathers of the West used the word *hostia*—sacrificial gift. During the late seventh century, the two complementary images merged when the "Lamb of God" became part of the Roman liturgy. It was sung as a litany that accompanied the entire action of the breaking of the bread. In the eleventh and twelfth centuries it was mandated that only unleavened bread be used. As a result, the meaning of the fractioning rite was diminished and the litany was reduced to just three invocations. Later it accompanied the kiss of peace and was separated from the breaking of the bread; hence the genesis of the invocation, "grant us peace."

In the prayer before communion, the priest elevates the eucharistic bread and cup and says, "This

is the Lamb of God who takes away the sins of the world. Happy are those who are called to his supper." This proclamation professes the presence of Christ in the eucharist as well as the sacrificial offering. The phrase *behold the Lamb of God* from the sixteenth century was changed in the Reformed liturgy to *this is the Lamb of God*.[14] The change was intended to place less emphasis on gazing upon the sacred species in spiritual communion and more emphasis on "partaking in Christ our Passover sacrifice."[15]

It was the Spirit of God who made it possible for John to recognize Jesus as Messiah. It is that same Spirit who makes it possible for us to recognize Jesus in the assembly of believers, in the breaking of the bread, and in all of our sacramental signs and symbols.

Gospel Exegesis

The facilitator provides input from critical biblical scholarship on this text. This input includes insights as to how people would have heard the gospel in Jesus' time.

Matthew, Mark, and Luke tell us that the first disciples were called in the context of Jesus' Galilean ministry. They also set the stage for Jesus' public ministry by announcing that John prepared the way for him through his ministry of preaching. John the evangelist gives us more specifics. The "Fourth Gospel insists more than the others on the testimony given to Jesus by a deliberately self-effacing John."[16]

John is the only one to inform us that the first disciples were followers of the Baptist. They begin to follow Jesus at the Jordan River. The details, though sparse, are revealing. The hour was four in the afternoon. We all remember the hour of the day when the life-changing events of our lives take place. The announcement of the hour subtly alludes to personal involvement in the events by those recording them. It is like saying, "I should know about this. I was there." Yet John's primary intention is to mark the moment with exclamation points. From the very beginning of Jesus' ministry,

---

[13]*DL* (IV), 21.

[14]Joyce A. Zimmerman, C.P.P.S., "Lamb of God," *CPDBT*, 531–533.

[15]Ibid., 533.

[16]*DL* (V), 17.

in one declaration, the reader is given a summary of the entire gospel. The Christian creed is opened before us in the proclamation of John the Baptist, "Look, there is the Lamb of God."

John often referred to Israel's premier event, the exodus. Today's reference to the "Lamb of God" catapults the disciples back to the exodus' ritual remembrance—the paschal lamb of the Passover meal. The lamb was sacrificed just as Jesus was sacrificed on the cross. The lamb is consumed in the Passover supper just as Jesus' body was consumed at the Last Supper. The lamb also refers to the lamb of the "Suffering Servant" fame (Is 49:3) "who will bear the sins of others and justify them. From the first pages of his gospel, the evangelist insists on Christ's redemptive mission."[17] Isaiah's imagery paints the portrait of lamb as a "figure of innocence (Is 53:7), as one who needs care and nurturing (Is 40:11), and as a sign of gentle and serene peace (Is 11:6) and prosperity (Is 65:25)."[18]

The term *Lamb of God*, was used by the Christian community as a title for the dead and risen Christ. It was a term pregnant with meaning. It embodied prophetic fulfillment of the new covenant, the paschal mystery of Christ. Jesus was the new Lamb whose blood was shed for the people. With the shedding of his blood he inaugurated the new covenant. John brilliantly proclaimed the Christian paschal faith from Jesus' first public appearance.[19]

Before we are even introduced to Mark's perspective of the good news, John "tells us the rest of the story." "Believe it," insists John. John is the last of Israel's prophets. Thus, the reader is not to miss the point. Israel itself heralds the burgeoning ministry of Jesus. The Hebrew scriptures foretold Christ the new paschal Lamb and the *One* who would establish the new covenant.

Today's pericope contains even more important Christian kerygma—the call of the disciples and their response in faith. Andrew and another un-named disciple recognize Jesus as "Teacher." On the next day, Peter is brought to Christ, the Messiah. The day after that (not included in this peri-

cope), Philip and Nathanael come to Jesus believing that he is a great prophet like Moses, the Son of God, and the King of Israel. Raymond Brown suggests that this is a technique used by the evangelist to show the gradual way in which the disciples came to awareness of who Christ really was. They moved from Teacher, to Messiah, and ultimately to Son of God and King.[20] The synoptic evangelists portrayed this coming to awareness as an ongoing development throughout Jesus' public ministry.

John the evangelist uses this event to situate Peter's profession of faith and his subsequent change of name. The synoptics place this incident much later in the Jesus story. Brown asserts that this also reflects a Johannine tendency to "present the whole truth about Jesus in each episode."[21]

Today's gospel is an icon of vocation. The primary question for a prospective follower is, "What do you seek?" It is followed by the invitation or the command to "come and see." John's definition of "seeing" follows the proverbial adage—it is "believing." The one who comes and believes, according to Brown, becomes the "new Israel: people seeing God."[22]

Another profound theology undergirds this text. Jesus asks the disciples what they are looking for. He is not asking for information. Rather, he touches the desire deep within their being. All of salvation history can be summarized in this event: God seeks out the human heart. We can seek all we want, but unless God finds us, we are still lost. God seeks us. "The soul seeks the Word, but it does so because the Word has been seeking the soul."[23]

The disciples answer correctly. They ask Jesus where he is staying. They call him "Teacher," and ask him, in essence, where they can go to learn from him. Where is Jesus' school? They followed Jesus in order to learn from him. They leave John to follow the "Lamb of God." Jesus invited them to

---

[17]*SWTLY*, 125.

[18]Joyce A. Zimmerman, C.P.P.S., *CPDBT*, 531.

[19]*DL* (V), 18.

[20]*GEJ*, 27.

[21]Ibid.

[22]Ibid.

[23]St. Bernard (1090–1153), *Sermon 84 sur le Cantique des Cantiques*, 3, in *Invit'es aux noces*, trans. and ed. P.-Y. Emery (Paris: Descl'ee, 1979) 162, in *DL* (V), 18.

come and follow him. Jesus was willing to show them and to teach them. They showed by their actions that they were serious. They sealed their decision to follow Christ by going with him wherever he went. Their response was their action. They went with him and stayed with him that day.

Jesus aroused desire within the disciples on this fateful day. He was not asking for information when he posed the question to them. He was extending a gratuitous invitation. All of salvation history can be summarized as the process in which God is in constant search of human beings. God is the initiator. But the invitation must be accepted in faith and in freedom. It is an invitation to respond. We are told what that response involves: action. Today's gospel is pregnant with action words—*see, stay, hear, believe, come, watch.* "These verbs evoke the acts which lead from one's initial discovery of the Lord to the resolute commitment to follow him in order to be near him and live in intimate union with him."[24] Ultimately, today's gospel is a call to intimate union with God in Christ. It is a celebration of God's election. We cannot boast of the call. We can only accept it and act on it. Like the call of Samuel, the call from God is not always evident at first. It is only through repeated prodding that we come to recognize the authentic voice of God. Often our friends are the channels of that recognition. Andrew and the disciple followed Jesus because of the testimony of John. Peter left all to follow the Lord because of the testimony of his friends, Andrew and the other disciple. Very often our conversion is the result of the stories, faith, and good news shared by other friends of the Lord. It behooves us never to miss an opportunity to echo the voice and the face of Christ to all we encounter. We are the hands, feet, and mouthpiece of Christ. Our faith is watered and nurtured when it is shared. Today's Alternative Opening Prayer echoes the theme of today's gospel. We profess that God orders all of life according to God's will. God is the active agent in life. Not even our worst sin will frustrate God's will. It will go forward in spite of us. We pray that we might be faithful to God when God calls so that God's truth may reign in our hearts and bring about God's peace in the world.

---

[24]*DL* (V), 19.

Proclaim the gospel again.

Sometimes we gain new insights when we hear the text after the interpretation is given. Someone from the group proclaims the gospel a second time.

STEP 4
TESTING

Conversation with the Liturgy and the Scriptures

Test your original understanding in dialogue with the text.

(You might consider breaking into smaller groups.)

Now that you've heard the exegesis, were there any new insights? How do you feel about it? How does your original understanding of this gospel compare with what we just shared? How does this story speak to your life?

Sharing Life Experience

Participants share an experience from their lives that connects with the biblical interpretation just presented.

> *We evangelize by the way we live our lives as well as by our intentional efforts. In my childhood family experience my father and mother were like the Baptist, Andrew, and the other disciples in today's gospel. Their efforts were both unconscious and intentional. Their faith life was very important to them. They passed it on to me and to my sisters. Their lives were centered in their church community. Every Sunday my father took me, my mother, and my sisters by the hand and expressed his love for us in the midst of the worshiping assembly. A wink, a loving pinch, a daddy thumb pressed into a child's thumb, a husband's hand cupped around a wife's hand are the memories that warm and kindle my fires of spiritual nostalgia. Worship always was synonymous with the expressive love of our father.*

> *Dad and Mother were faithful to a life of service and prayer. They broke their lives open not only for us, but also for their parish community as well. Their lives were rooted in prayer. My father kept a holy hour every Wednesday night for twenty years.*

My mother prayed throughout the day and night and offered her life of physical suffering for the world. She is the least judgmental person I have ever known. When someone behaved abominably it simply meant that the poor person must have had a terrible day, week, year, or upbringing.

My sisters and I were certain of our parents' love for us. We were raised in a cocoon of intimate, unconditional love. My mother railed against racism when it was not fashionable or politically correct to do so. My father wore his love of the Lord on his sleeve and shared it with everyone he knew. He always insisted that God was "his buddy" and his "co-pilot." The memory of his simple faith continues to nurture and strengthen me when I find my life becoming too complicated.

They have both been dead for nearly twenty years, yet their legacy remains with me and leads me closer to the living Christ who invites me into intimate relationship with him. Today's gospel is about faith, discipleship, evangelization, and conversion. The seeds of all those realities were lived in the day-to-day reality of my family experience. Our lives were not perfect. There was sorrow, illness, and strife. But my parents taught me from a very early age what it means to live the paschal mystery. I cannot count the times I was invited to offer up the difficult moments of life for the suffering of the world. My poor mother struggled for every breath for many years. Every day was an opportunity for her to live her paschal faith.

For their love, their lives, and their example, I thank God. They are a reminder that we often reveal God (or not) by our very simple responses to life situations as well as by the way we live (or don't live) the Christian life. We are called to invite others by the example of our lives, but we are also called to intentionally go out like Andrew and shout the good news to the world. Perhaps we might even hook a Peter or two in the process!

What was John trying to tell his community? In what way does this gospel challenge your community today? In what way have you encountered the "Lamb of God" of today's gospel? Have you ever gone out to tell another about the great deeds of the Lord? What was it like? If not, why not? What keeps us from seizing the opportunities to bring people to Christ? In what way does this liturgy invite you into a deeper relationship with Christ? In what way has this conversation with the scriptures for today's liturgy invited change in your life? In what way are the biblical themes of covenant, exodus, creation, and community evident in today's readings? Do you still feel the same way about this text as when you began? Has your original understanding been stretched, challenged, or affirmed?

STEP 5
DECISION

The gospel demands a response.

In what concrete way might your parish be invited to respond? Are there any attitudes or behaviors you would like to change as a result of today's conversation? What is one concrete action you will take this week in response to the liturgy today?

Pastoral Considerations: In what way is your parish an evangelizing community? Today would be a good time to reflect on what that means and to discern ways that you might grow more fully into that reality. How do you welcome new people? In what way does your parish create an environment that bespeaks the "come and see" invitation in today's gospel? In what way do you empower parishioners to share the good news in their wider community?

Christian Initiation: Since the scriptures speak of the call of the first disciples, today would be an excellent occasion to celebrate a rite of acceptance or welcome. It might also be an appropriate time to celebrate an anointing of catechumens. The undergirding paschal theme of the gospel reminds us that the Christian life is an invitation to live the paschal mystery. Catechumens would certainly benefit from the grace and strength bestowed by the celebration of this sacramental. Perhaps this would be a good time to remind the community of their role in the initiation of adults (RCIA 9). It would also be an excellent time to invite people in your parish and wider community to "come and see."

DOCTRINAL ISSUES

What Church truth/teaching/doctrinal issue could be drawn from the gospel for the second Sunday in Ordinary Time?

Participants suggest possible doctrinal themes that flow from the readings.

Possible Doctrinal Themes

Conversion; paschal mystery; Christology; discipleship; Lamb of God; soteriology; ministry; mission; reign of God; evangelization

Present the doctrinal material at this time.

1. The facilitator gives input on a particular doctrinal issue of his or her prior choosing. OR
2. The group chooses a doctrinal issue from the list they created. They read together from the Doctrinal Appendix or other appropriate, official Church documents and the works of respected theologians.

(Many doctrinal issues are found in the Doctrinal Appendix at the back of this workbook. If you are choosing an issue from this resource, please refer to it now.)

Reflection questions centered around the chosen doctrinal theme can be found at the end of each topic in the Doctrinal Appendix. The questions are based on the five-step reflection process. If you choose a topic not included in the Doctrinal Appendix, craft your own questions according to the same five-step process.

Following the reflection questions you will be reminded to return to chapter 7, "Preparing the Catechetical Session," to assist you in crafting your own session.

Closing Prayer

Let us pray for the gift of peace.

Pause for silent prayer.

Almighty and ever-present Father,
your watchful care reaches from end to end
and orders all things in such power
that even the tensions and the tragedies of sin
cannot frustrate your loving plans.
Help us to embrace your will,
give us the strength to follow your call,
so that your truth may live in our hearts
and reflect peace to those who believe in your love.
We ask this in the name of Jesus the Lord.[25]

---

[25]Second Sunday in Ordinary Time: "Alternative Opening Prayer," *The Sacramentary.*

Third Sunday in Ordinary Time

Environment

Refer to Second Sunday in Ordinary Time.

INTRODUCTORY RITES

Entrance Antiphon (or Other Appropriate Psalm or Song)

Sing a new song to the Lord! Sing to the Lord, all the earth. Truth and beauty surround him, he lives in holiness and glory. (Ps 95:1, 6)[1]

Opening Prayer

The facilitator of the session may lead the prayer. Others in the group may be asked to proclaim the readings.

Let us pray

Pause for silent prayer.

All-powerful and ever-living God,
direct your love that is within us,
that our efforts in the name of your Son
may bring mankind to unity and peace.
We ask this through our Lord
      Jesus Christ, your Son,
who lives and reigns with you and the Holy Spirit,
one God, for ever and ever.[2]

LITURGY OF THE WORD

The readings are proclaimed.

First Reading
Jonah 3:1–5, 10

Overview of the Book of Jonah: The Book of Jonah is considered to be a prophetic book. There are no oracles, however. It is a book *about* the prophet Jonah, in which the author creatively weaves humor and surprise into his literary work.

The Word of the Lord came to Jonah. Instead of going to Nineveh, where the Lord commanded him to go, he did an about-face and fled in the opposite direction. While at sea, a raging storm threatened him and his shipmates. Unsuspecting Jonah slept through it all, however. The shipmates blamed him for the evil imposed on them by the angry sea. Jonah offered himself as a sacrifice to appease the angry Yahweh and was subsequently swallowed by a huge fish. While sitting in the whale's belly, Jonah sang hymns of thanks and praise. It took God three days to grant Jonah his aquatic reprieve.

The story humorously spins a yarn and makes a point in the process. God called Jonah. Jonah ran the other way and ended up in the belly of a big fish. God told Jonah where to go and what to do. Jonah refused to obey God and was subsequently swallowed alive by his own refusal. He was given a second chance and accepted Yahweh's mission. He went to Nineveh. Note the irony in the story. Jonah prophesied to the people and they obeyed. Yahweh spoke to Jonah and he refused to obey. He was incredulous that God should care about gentiles. God refused to let Jonah off the hook. He would fulfill the mission God intended for him. In today's story Jonah fulfills his preaching mission to the Ninevites.

Not included in today's pericope, however, is the fact that Jonah was not willing to extend the same courtesy to Nineveh that God extended to him. Jonah was sent as God's prophet to announce salvation and mercy to a pagan nation. The people listened and accepted. Jonah was angry that God granted mercy to the Ninevites.

According to Lawrence Boadt, the book addresses two major issues: the relation of Israel and Yahweh to other nations and the meaning of divine justice.[3] The reluctant prophet Jonah was sent to proclaim

---

[1] Third Sunday in Ordinary Time: "Entrance Antiphon," *The Sacramentary.*

[2] Third Sunday in Ordinary Time: "Opening Prayer," *The Sacramentary.*

[3] *ROT*, 469.

460

God's universal salvific will to all the nations. In the process human beings were taught a powerful lesson. God's mercy far surpasses God's judgments, "and his plan will not be thwarted even by the negative 'righteousness' of his prophet."[4]

In Luke's gospel Jesus likened his ministry to Jonah's with the exception that his (Jesus') ministry included the establishment of God's reign. Matthew's typology compared the three-day entombment in the fish's belly to Jesus' death and resurrection. For today's pericope, Luke's is the most appropriate interpretation. The story of Jonah in today's reading foreshadows the gospel as both Jonah and Jesus preached to the kingdoms.[5]

Responsorial Psalm
Psalm 25:4–5b, 6, 7b–9

Today's psalm asks that God teach the sinner how to live uprightly. It is an invitation to repent. According to Reginald Fuller, both Jesus and Jonah preached a message of repentance. Repentance requires a response—obedience to the will of God. Thus, the upright are to live according to the will of God.

Second Reading
1 Corinthians 7:29–31

(Refer to second Sunday in Ordinary Time for an overview of 1 Corinthians.)

Today's Pericope: Chapter 7 in Paul's first letter to the Corinthians deals with the issue of sex and marriage. Paul addresses the issue by expressing his beliefs about the world in light of what he believes to be the immanent return of Christ. Paul insists that Christians must detach themselves from the concerns of the world.

Since the world still awaits the parousia there is a temptation to dismiss Paul's exhortation as irrelevant. Reginald Fuller cautions against such an attitude. He maintains that the "form of this world is passing away. All its structures and relationships are provisional and must not be treated as if they were ultimates . . . because of the Christ-event, the kingdom of God has become a present reality awaiting

its consummation."[6] This world is transitory. We are to seek the reign of God above all else—nothing is to get in the way of our relationship with God as we wait in hope for Christ's return.

Gospel
Mark 1:14–20. Repent and believe the good news.

STEP 1
NAMING ONE'S EXPERIENCE

What were your first impressions? What was your first response to the gospel (or the other readings)?[7] What captured your attention?

Each person names his or her initial impression. Statements should be brief. No reasons should be given at this time. All simply listen without agreeing or disagreeing.

STEP 2
UNDERSTANDING

In a brief statement, explain what you think this gospel is trying to convey.

STEP 3
INPUT FROM VISION/STORY/TRADITION

Liturgical Context

Today Mark's gospel gives us a front row seat at the opening scene of Jesus' Galilean ministry and the subsequent call of his first four disciples. Jesus' ministry begins with the arrest of the one who announced his coming—John the Baptist. Last week it was the Baptist who helped the disciples recognize the "Lamb of God." Thus, last week and this week possess an internal unity.

---

[4] Ibid.
[5] *PL*, 292.

[6] Ibid., 292.
[7] The primary focus of reflection is the gospel. However, often the other readings demand attention and must be brought into the dialogue.

Jesus preached the reign of God and announced the good news to all who would listen. Today's gospel announces that John the Baptist's ministry is officially ended. Jesus begins his Galilean ministry and assumes John's mission of conversion and repentance. Jesus also chooses his first disciples. Mark reveals a radical theology of kingdom and discipleship in today's very brief gospel passage.

Today's Opening Prayer asks that God infuse us with the love we need so that our discipleship efforts bring unity and peace to the world. As the saying goes, "if you want peace, work for justice," today's liturgy is a reminder that the call of Christ is universal and is extended to all people. When there are suffering, marginalized people, disciples are called to action. All members of God's reign are equal. Disciples are to work for the peace and unity of the *entire* world. This liturgy (and every liturgy) carries with it a challenge to preach the good news to all people without exception. Jesus invites us to leave everything to follow him—even our comfortable structures. Today's liturgy professes that truth in triplicate. Jonah knew well what was being asked of him. Paul insisted that disciples were to detach from worldly concerns and the gospel demonstrates that Jesus asks no less than *everything* of would-be disciples.

Gospel Exegesis

The facilitator provides input from critical biblical scholarship on this text. This input includes insights as to how people would have heard the gospel in Jesus' time.

In the first thirteen verses of chapter 1, Mark sets forth the Christology that is the cornerstone of his entire gospel. Mark proclaims that Jesus is the Son of God who is engaged in a committed struggle with the power of evil. This is the lens through which we are to read the rest of the story. It is also the starting point for understanding Jesus' burgeoning preaching ministry. Mark takes us to the cross in the opening scene of the gospel, and it remains an ever-present shadow throughout the entire narrative. The gospel pericope opens with the arrest of the Baptist. From the very beginning John reminds us of the suffering Messiah. He foreshadows the cross to come and the implications of committed discipleship.

Mark subtly paints an obscure portrait of the gospel's major antagonists, the religious authorities, by establishing a contrast between Jerusalem, their religious center, and Galilee, the center of Jesus' ministry. Galilee is where he preached, healed, and inaugurated the reign of God. Jerusalem, on the other hand, is the place where Christ was crucified. Earlier in Mark's gospel it was announced that Jesus was from Nazareth in Galilee. Ched Myers suggests that there is another reason for the Galilee connection. "One would expect the hero to be credentialed through miraculous origins or a solid genealogy (something Matthew and Luke cannot resist). Mark, however, stresses Jesus' obscure origins, 'from Nazareth,' tantamount to introducing him as 'Jesus from Nowheresville.'"[8] The reader is reminded from the outset that Jesus' origins are humble. He is not the powerful political Messiah expected by an oppressed Israel.

The mission of Christ is circular. It begins in Galilee, the place of preaching and healing; it sets out on the road to Jerusalem, the place of struggle, Passion, and death; and it returns "only to open again to eschatological hope in Galilee."[9] Jesus is the fulfillment of the scriptures. Jesus is God's agent. Jesus is the one who came to establish the final age—the reign of God—both the present age and the age to come. Mark insists that his readers believe the good news of salvation realized in the life and mission of Jesus, the Christ.

The term *kingdom of God* functions like a symbol in the gospel. It embodies Israel's hope for the messianic reign. It includes Israel's understanding of itself as the people of God in relationship with the God who is an active agent in their history. The term also was understood as God's final act in history.

Mark insists that the reign Jesus came to establish is different than the one expected by Israel. Israel understood themselves in exclusive terms—as the only ones entitled to God's salvific action. Jesus radically challenged their narrow self-awareness. He included *all people* in his invitation to God's eschatological reign. Jesus proclaimed

---

[8] *BSM*, 128.
[9] *MK*, 12.

God's action in history both now and in the future. He invited sinners to repent and he confronted evil in all its dimensions. Jesus, completely obedient and faithful to his Father's will, came to invite others into that same intimate relationship with his Father.

Jesus calls the first disciples in today's gospel. His call echoes a famous Old Testament one—the call of Elisha by Elijah. Elisha left all behind to follow Yahweh. Similarly, the disciples left all to follow Jesus. They "followed after" (*akolouthein*) him. They became his disciples. They were transformed into a new reality. They would now become fishers of people.

Two sets of brothers were called. The first set highlighted the disciples' immediate response; the second set, the "completeness of their renunciation."[10] The manner in which Jesus called his disciples was radical. Typically, disciples sought out a rabbi, walked with him, and studied the Torah under his tutelage. When they learned all they could from the rabbi, they ventured off on their own to become rabbis in their own right. In this case, however, Jesus sought out the disciples. To onlookers Jesus and his disciples resembled a typical rabbinic group, but the relationship Jesus established with his disciples was different from the outset. Jesus' disciples never left him; they remained disciples.

> Normally the student sought the teacher and followed only for as long as it took to attain rabbinic status himself. The call of Jesus, however, is absolute, disrupting the lives of potential recruits, promising them only a "school" from which there is no graduation. This "first" call to discipleship in Mark is an urgent, uncompromising invitation to "break with business as usual." The world is coming to an end, for those who choose to follow. The kingdom has dawned, and it is identified with the discipleship adventure.[11]

Mark insists that we take note of this Galilean discipleship community. The call of Simon is in-

tended to remind us that there is something radically different about the discipleship Jesus is suggesting. Ched Myers turns the "grand old tradition" on its proverbial overturned apple-cart in his interpretation of "fishers of men" found in this gospel. He insists that we have misinterpreted that phrase throughout history. Traditional interpretation of "fishers of men" asserts that Jesus established the disciples as the first evangelists with the mission of bringing new disciples into the fold—the saving of souls. Myers suggests a radically different approach: "the image is carefully chosen from Jeremiah 16:16, where it is used as a symbol of Yahweh's censure of Israel. Elsewhere the 'hooking of fish' is a euphemism for judgment upon the rich (Am 4:2) and powerful (Ez 29:4). Taking this mandate for his own, Jesus is inviting common folk to join him in his struggle to overturn the existing order of power and privilege."[12]

The fishing industry of antiquity was comprised of an artisan class. Fishermen were capable of hiring day laborers. Thus, they were not poverty-stricken people. They were probably the middle class of Jesus' day. The entire family and cultural social structure were centered around the workplace. When Jesus asked the disciples to leave everything to follow him, he was asking them to abandon their entire economic and social life. Some scholars insist that this reflects Jesus' eschatological belief that the world was soon coming to an end—the final age was upon them. Thus, they need not be concerned or responsible for the world they left behind. Since we in the "real world" know that the parousia is not immanent it lets the enlightened among us "off the hook." Myers insists that such a position is "another case of bourgeois hermeneutics."[13] The radical paradigm for conversion is thus missed and we run the risk of trivializing the gospel Christ intended. "The point here is that following Jesus requires not just the assent of the heart, but a fundamental reordering of socio-economic relationships."[14] Disciples cannot remain unchanged in the face of the demands of the gospel. In the reign Jesus came to establish there is no dominant social order—all people are equal. Disciples cannot remain passive in the

---

[10]Ibid., 15.
[11]*BSM*, 133.

[12]Ibid.
[13]Ibid., 132.
[14]Ibid., 133.

midst of structures that oppress, dominate, marginalize, and keep people in poverty. Later in Mark's gospel we learn that the rich have a very difficult time accepting this imperative of the good news. "Mark will have a great deal to say about concrete social and economic responsibility within the new order of the discipleship community. This is not a call 'out' of the world, but into an alternative social practice."[15] Jesus invites disciples to live a radical Christian life.

Mark illustrates the essence of discipleship. Discipleship demands a response, a response made in freedom. There was nothing extraordinary about those who were called. They were not particularly brilliant. They were not moral giants. They were ordinary people. The initiative was Jesus'; he did the choosing. It was a free, gratuitous choice. The disciples did nothing to merit Jesus' choice of them. The disciples' choice consisted in either accepting or rejecting the kingdom and the self-gift Christ was offering. It is the same choice faced by every would-be disciple of all ages.

Proclaim the gospel again.

Sometimes we gain new insights when we hear the text after the interpretation is given. Someone from the group proclaims the gospel a second time.

STEP 4
TESTING

Conversation with the Liturgy and the Scriptures

Test your original understanding in dialogue with the text.

(You might consider breaking into smaller groups.)

Now that you've heard the exegesis, were there any new insights? How do you feel about it? How does your original understanding of this gospel compare with what we just shared? How does this story speak to your life?

---

[15]Ibid.

Sharing Life Experience

Participants share an experience from their lives that connects with the biblical interpretation just presented.

Jesus invites people to change their lives, to live the good news, and to leave all to follow him. There have been many times in my life when I heard that call and responded like the disciples in today's gospel; there were other times when I heard the call and ignored it like Jonah in the first reading. Early in our active Christian life, our family committed to go wherever God might ask us to go. That willingness led us to Florida and to incredible years of Christian family and parish life and ministry. God multiplied our willingness in unimaginable ways.

There have been other times when God asked me to reach out in faith and in repentance to take the initiative to heal wounds of division. It was a very difficult request and one that I agreed to do only reluctantly and with dragging feet. There were many invitations and many refusals. I always had something better to do than humble myself in the sight of God and risk vulnerability. There was always an excuse—I needed to press my shoelaces, or replace the grout on my kitchen floor, or whatever! Whenever I responded in obedience, however, God blessed my willingness. On two occasions that I can remember I was asked to stay with a situation, to work toward healing and reconciliation. I felt the situations were injurious to my wounded pride. Yet I marvel at how God truly knows what is best for our sinful souls. Both situations resulted in a long-term call to loving friendship and intimate relationship that continues to bear fruit.

The call to discipleship is not a one-time wake-up call. It is a daily commitment that asks that we be willing to give everything. Discipleship insists that we be willing to risk, to step out when asked, to embrace the cross, and to make everything in our lives secondary to living the gospel of Jesus. Just last week I was complaining that something I was involved in that truly had God's stamp of approval was not bringing me the rewards I had hoped to see. The dialogue that ensued between God and my spoiled-child self resulted in the awareness that all God asks of me is faithfulness—the desired or expected results are up to God. I will continue to respond in obedience to God's will one day at a time, sometimes one minute at a time (complaints and arguments notwithstanding).

What was Mark trying to tell his community? In what way does this gospel challenge your community today? In what concrete way does this gospel challenge you to leave everything to follow Christ? What does that mean in your everyday life? How do you feel about Ched Myers' caution about trivializing or explaining away the radical demands of the gospel? In what way does this gospel invite the community out of complacency? In what way has this conversation with the scriptures for today's liturgy invited change in your life? In what way do the readings in today's liturgy express God's covenant relationship with us? In what way is the creative action of God expressed? How is this liturgy a word to God's people? Do you still feel the same way about this text as when you began? Has your original understanding been stretched, challenged, or affirmed?

STEP 5
DECISION

The gospel demands a response.

In what concrete way might your parish be invited to respond? Are there any attitudes or behaviors you would like to change as a result of today's conversation? What is one concrete action you will take this week in response to the liturgy today?

Pastoral Considerations: The prayer for unity and peace is especially poignant in the month of January as this is the month set aside to pray for Christian unity. In what way does your parish work for Christian unity? What might you do this year to promote unity? In what way is your parish cooperating in Christ's mission to establish the reign of God in the world? How do you reach out to the poor in your midst and the poor in the world? How do you challenge oppressive structures in society? How does your parish deal with issues of division within your own parish community? Is cultural diversity respected, tolerated, or, worse, not tolerated?

Christian Initiation: With the obvious themes of discipleship inherent in today's liturgy, one cannot imagine a better time to celebrate a rite of acceptance or welcome. A rite of reception into full communion of the Catholic Church would also be appropriate. Perhaps today would be a good time to remind the parish community of their own responsibility in the initiation of Christians. If conversion and discipleship are important messages in today's liturgy, part of the responsibility of discipleship consists in bringing others to Christ. Perhaps a word about #9 in the RCIA would be appropriate today. Christian initiation is the responsibility of all the baptized.

DOCTRINAL ISSUES

What Church truth/teaching/doctrinal issue could be drawn from the gospel for the third Sunday in Ordinary Time?

Participants suggest possible doctrinal themes that flow from the readings.

Possible Doctrinal Themes

Discipleship; conversion; evangelization; universal mission of Christ; paschal mystery

Present the doctrinal material at this time.

1. The facilitator gives input on a particular doctrinal issue of his or her prior choosing. OR
2. The group chooses a doctrinal issue from the list they created. They read together from the Doctrinal Appendix or other appropriate, official Church documents and the works of respected theologians.

(Many doctrinal issues are found in the Doctrinal Appendix at the back of this workbook. If you are choosing an issue from this resource, please refer to it now.)

Reflection questions centered around the chosen doctrinal theme can be found at the end of each topic in the Doctrinal Appendix. The questions are based on the five-step reflection process. If you choose a topic not included in the Doctrinal Appendix, craft your own questions according to the same five-step process.

Following the reflection questions you will be reminded to return to chapter 7, "Preparing the Catechetical Session," to assist you in crafting your own session.

Closing Prayer

God, all-powerful Father,
may the new life you give us increase our love
and keep us in the joy of your kingdom.
We ask this in the name of Jesus the Lord.[16]

---

[16]Third Sunday in Ordinary Time: "Prayer after Communion," *The Sacramentary.*

FOURTH SUNDAY IN ORDINARY TIME

Environment

Refer to the second Sunday in Ordinary Time.

INTRODUCTORY RITES

Entrance Antiphon (or Opening Song)

Save us, Lord our God, and gather us together from the nations, that we may proclaim your holy name and glory in your praise. (Ps 105:47)[1]

Opening Prayer

The facilitator of the session may lead the prayer. Others in the group may be asked to proclaim the readings.

Let us pray

> *Pause for silent prayer.*

Father in heaven,
from the days of Abraham and Moses
until this gathering of your Church in prayer,
you have formed a people in the image of your
     Son.
Bless this people with the gift of your kingdom.
May we serve you with our every desire
and show love for one another
even as you have loved us.
Grant this through Christ, our Lord.
one God, for ever and ever.[2]

LITURGY OF THE WORD

The readings are proclaimed.

First Reading
Deuteronomy 18:15–20

---

[1]Fourth Sunday in Ordinary Time: "Entrance Antiphon," *The Sacramentary.*

[2]Fourth Sunday in Ordinary Time: "Alternative Opening Prayer," *The Sacramentary.*

Overview of the Book of Deuteronomy: The Book of Deuteronomy is in the form of an address. The author writes in the voice of Moses, who is giving a final speech to the people before they cross over the Jordan into the promised land. It is his farewell address to the Israelites whom he led out of Egypt's bondage through the Sinai desert. Moses delivered God's covenant to Israel and on numerous occasions he saved the people from God's wrath, which they deserved because of their infidelity.

Deuteronomy does not fit with the other four books of the Pentateuch. Unlike the short stories and incidents of Genesis and Exodus, Deuteronomy contains long speeches and sermons. Deuteronomy was not written at the same time as the other books, but was a much later reflection on the ancient history of Moses and the people of Israel. The book demands that the people return to their covenant relationship with God. It places the exhortations in the mouth of Moses himself. (A common ancient practice involved placing words and exhortations in the mouth of an ancient respected leader in order to bring that leader's authority to bear on the writer's material.) The purpose of the book was to exhort the people to return to covenant living experienced under the leadership of Moses.

The book is divided into sections: a long preface, a restatement of the old covenant laws, a section containing the teaching of Moses, and his final blessing and death scene. The heart of Deuteronomy is the section containing the law code. It is similar to the law code of Exodus and is therefore referred to as the second (deutero) law.

The second law code was written at a much later date, however. The situations in Deuteronomy reflect a nation that had grown since the days of the exodus. A nation of small farmers had developed into a land of populated cities (evident during the later reign of the kings). There is also evidence in the book that a long time had passed since the liberation from Egypt. The book looks back and remembers the exodus and the covenant as completed events in the history of Israel.

One of the primary focuses of Deuteronomy is to look back on the covenant with a mind and a heart to return to it in faithfulness. The book exhorts the people to become more faithful than their ancestors had been in following the law. There is a constant call to reform, to return to the covenant made with God. The election of Israel by God is an example of the special relationship that existed between God and the people of Israel. The book uses language reminiscent of that used in treaties between nations to describe the covenant between God and the people.

The central theme of the law was true worship, which consists of worship of the one God, Creator of heaven and earth. The people were to reject all pagan idols. The relationship between God and Israel was summed up in the Shema, Israel's prayer, the heart and the creed of Judaism. "Hear, O Israel, the Lord our God is one Lord, and you shall love the Lord your God with all your heart and with all your soul and with all your strength" (Dt 6:4–5). Those words were never to be forgotten. They were to be handed on to their children, talked about in the house, bound on the hands and the forehead, and written on the doorpost. In other words: "It was never to be forgotten!"

The theology of Deuteronomy also extolls a single sanctuary in a place appointed by God (Jerusalem was the implied place). It also upholds the importance of the right use of the land. Faithfulness and obedience to God will ensure a prosperous land. Disobedience and unfaithfulness will result in loss of the land, exile, and destruction. Sin leads to a curse. A curse ensures failure in war, failed crops, and failure in preserving the one nation. If Israel fails to live the imperatives of justice, they will lose their right to the land. Their society will fail. Deuteronomy looks back at the history of Israel and explains it in terms of fidelity and infidelity to the covenant.

Today's Pericope: Later in Israel's history this text was understood to prefigure the final prophet that God would send before the end of the world, referred to by scholars as the "eschatological prophet."[3] Jesus understood his own role in similar terms. He professed that he was the "last messenger

before its [the world's] consummation."[4] The early church interpreted the Christ event in terms of the eschatological prophetic mission of Moses. Like Moses, who taught with authority and led the people out of bondage, Jesus was the new Moses who taught with God's authority and ushered in the new and ultimate liberation for God's people. Today's reading was chosen for its connection to the gospel's allusion to Jesus' authoritative teaching.

Responsorial Psalm
Psalm 95:1–2, 6–9

Today's psalm is a call to worship and an admonition against neglecting God's Word. The refrain warns the listener to pay attention to the prophet like Moses.

Second Reading
1 Corinthians 7:32–35

(Refer to second Sunday in Ordinary Time for overview of Paul's letter to the Corinthians.)

Today's Pericope: Paul believed that marriage was a lawful and acceptable state of life. He possessed a bias in favor of celibacy, however, and recommended it for both men and women. Paul believed that the celibate state kept men and women from becoming distracted from serving the Lord. Paul insisted that the celibate life is to be freely chosen, "without restraints." Thus, he made no hard and fast rules around such issues.

The context for chapter 7 is to be understood in light of what was going on in the Corinthian community. Some Corinthians believed they were already in the last age and thus were living as mystical, spiritual beings, not subject to physical death. It was their belief that all those who were presently living would not have to endure the pain of death. They would live forever. Obviously, there would be no need to continue the species as those who were alive would continue to live. It did not take a gargantuan leap to move to the next line of reasoning. Since there was no need for procreation, there was obviously no need for the sexual relations necessary for procreation to continue. Those who followed this belief system sought to impose

---

[3]*PL*, 294.

[4]Ibid., 295.

their own brand of sexual asceticism on the entire community. They insisted that sexual relations were totally unnecessary, and thereby should be avoided—even in marriage. New marriages were frowned upon and there were even attempts to break up existing marriages.[5]

In a city that was known for its sexual freedom, this new imposed sexual asceticism was fertile soil for the germination of sexual strain and tension. In chapter 7 Paul addressed the sexual transgressions that he believed would be the logical result of rigidly imposed sexual mores.

Paul is somewhat sympathetic to the Corinthians. Yet he upheld the virtue of praising God with our bodies. He maintained that even the sexual life should be a means of praise and worship of God. This would not have set well with the Corinthians who believed matter (body) to be evil and spirit to be good. While not exactly exalting the married state, however, Paul exercised pastoral and practical sensitivity.

What is striking in this chapter is Paul's belief in the mutuality of men and women. In the culture of Paul's day, women were to please and cater to men. It is quite remarkable that Paul insisted that each partner was to give to the other partner their conjugal rights (vv. 2–4, not in today's pericope). Totally out of character in light of the prevailing culture, Paul was concerned about the balance of rights between husband and wife.

Paul also defied a Graeco-Roman and Jewish principle which asserted the unacceptableness of those who engaged in sexual relations as unfit for religious duties.[6] On this Paul was clear. Lawful, married sexual relations in no way prohibited a person from coming to God in prayer. The abstinence Paul encouraged in this chapter is simply a matter of convenience. While celibacy is no doubt a charism given to some, it is not intended for everyone. "But he recognizes that other Christians have gifts in other directions. However appropriate it may be in terms of the New Age, perpetual abstinence is not for them."[7]

What should jump off the Corinthian pages for contemporary readers is Paul's obvious affirmation of the human dignity of every person—men and women. What was good for women was good for men. What was expected of women was expected of men. Neither men nor women enjoyed superior status—both enjoyed equality. In verses 10 and 11 we are surprised to discover that women as well as men were allowed to take the initiative in seeking a divorce. This is contrary to customary Jewish practice. Paul seemed to go out of his way to express the rights of men and women in equal terms. It is Paul's way of putting Galatians 3:28 into concrete terms: there is neither male nor female, Jew nor Greek, slave nor free person. Brendan Byrne maintains that for Paul it is a question of human dignity: "the wife has equal rights and responsibilities and equal voice in the decisions that regulate marriage."[8]

More than once in chapter 7 Paul asserted that the celibate state is preferable. His position did not stem from a belief that sexual relations were evil. On the contrary, he was so certain that the Lord's return was imminent that it made no sense to him to spend the remaining years attending to earthly familial relationships. Marriage is imbued with present-day concerns. When the end is so near, would it not be better to spend the remaining days in preparation? This is the prism through which we are to view Paul's treatise on marriage and surrounding themes.

In today's pericope, there is further evidence of the chapter's theme of mutuality. Both husband and wife are to "please" their spouse. While acknowledging that Paul considered marriage an earthly concern, it is encouraging to know that he nevertheless possessed a healthy vision of it. Husbands and wives were to cherish and give pleasure to one another. "Although he ranks this among 'worldly concerns', it at least suggests a view of marriage as a union of sensitive friendship and respectful equality."[9]

Ultimately, Paul's primary concern was for Christians to wait upon the Lord. His intention was not to give his readers a theological discourse on the

---

[5] *PCW*, 18.
[6] Ibid., 21.
[7] Ibid.

[8] Ibid., 23.
[9] Ibid., 25.

sacramentality of marriage. His urgency stemmed from what he believed to be the immediate proximity of the great eschaton. Christians were to be single-hearted and keep their eyes and their hearts focused on the Lord.

Gospel
Mark 1:21–28. This is a new kind of teaching that speaks with authority.

STEP 1
NAMING ONE'S EXPERIENCE

What were your first impressions? What was your first response to the gospel (or the other readings)?[10] What captured your attention?

Each person names his or her initial impression. Statements should be brief. No reasons should be given at this time. All simply listen without agreeing or disagreeing.

STEP 2
UNDERSTANDING

In a brief statement, explain what you think this gospel is trying to convey.

STEP 3
INPUT FROM VISION/STORY/TRADITION

Liturgical Context

There is a unity between the fourth through the sixth Sundays in Ordinary Time. Jesus begins his ministry in Capernaum with his teaching and deliverance mission on this fourth Sunday. On the fifth and sixth Sundays, Jesus' ministry of healing and deliverance proceeds in full force.

The Entrance Antiphon serves as a summary statement for today's liturgy. What better prayer than

---

[10]The primary focus of reflection is the gospel. However, often the other readings demand attention and must be brought into the dialogue.

to ask for God's saving power so that we (unlike the demons in today's gospel) may proclaim and worship the holy name of Jesus?

The church of Jesus' time listened and observed in amazement. Today's Opening Prayer asks that we be formed in Jesus' likeness. We believe that we have been created in the image and likeness of God. Jesus paid the price for our lives with his very life. It is because of his incarnation that we enjoy the status of divine. We stand with Christ and embrace our own created dignity. We are made in his image—thus we should not only be in awe of Christ, but also in awe of the great gift of life and humanity we have been given. In today's gospel Jesus paved the way for the establishment of his reign. Today's Opening Prayer is a reminder that we are the recipients of his sacrifice and that we have the responsibility to promote it in our everyday lives.

> To the extent that we allow him [Jesus] to shine through us, he calls human beings where they are, that is, still in darkness, and leads them from light to light.
>
> Because he, only Friend of human beings, understands them, he is able to lay hold of them and set them free. Jesus is neither demagogue or dogmatician; he is the pure light of the Father's glory. He speaks to us with "authority" and not as a commentator; the truth of what he says reflects what is, and simple, upright hearts are able to see this. He is the only truly human being, because he knows in his flesh both the struggles sinners have and the freedom to live divinely as a human being. That is why our words, which are the sacrament of his mystery, are neither discourse about God nor moral code for human beings, but the revelation that these human beings are loved and called to become God because the Father has first loved them and because his Son has become one of them. The word we proclaim will be all the truer to the extent that it has first transformed us by divinizing us.[11]

---

[11]*TWOW*, 180–181.

Exorcism is a ritual prayer of deliverance from evil prayed for the unbaptized. Exorcism prayers are included in the rite of baptism of children, the minor rites of the catechumenate, the rite of anointing of catechumens, and the scrutinies of the Lenten season (third, fourth, and fifth Sundays of Lent, Cycle A).

The children's exorcism prayer acknowledges the power of Jesus to cast out the power of evil and to rescue us from its grip—sin. The prayer asks that the children be delivered from the effects of original sin and the power of darkness. The prayer remembers Christ's ministry of liberation from evil (evidenced in today's gospel) and asks that we be delivered from such evil.

In the scrutinies, the Church prays for the elect, and asks that God free the elect from bondage and the power of evil and to send the Holy Spirit to incorporate them more fully into the living presence of Christ, the people of God.

Exorcism was a common practice in the early church. It was often used in response to mental illness as well as encounters with Satan. Exorcisms today focus on the power to resist the power of evil rather than on demon possession. However, there is an infrequently used rite specifically for cases of demon possession. The bishop may delegate a priest to celebrate the rite.

Any talk of exorcism without the proclamation and exaltation of Christ, the Victor and Liberator, is not true to the heart of the paschal mystery. Christ came to crush the power of evil. And so he did. He continues that mission in the lives of his followers. Ultimately, there is no power greater than the healing, liberating power of Jesus Christ.

Gospel Exegesis

The facilitator provides input from critical biblical scholarship on this text. This input includes insights as to how people would have heard the gospel in Jesus' time.

Prior to today's pericope Jesus called and gathered his first disciples. His mission was off and running. This section in Mark's gospel is intended to paint the picture of the early days of Jesus' ministry. His authority is established and to prove it

Jesus heals and casts out demons. There are two parts to this episode. Jesus captures his spellbound audience, who marvel at his teaching power and authority. He then instills "holy awe" in them as he casts out an evil spirit.

Mark establishes the playing field and players from the very beginning of his story. From the outset, Mark's readers are aware that Jesus' authority comes from God himself. This is God's Son. Throughout Mark's gospel Jesus' exorcisms play a significant role. They depict the ultimate struggle between good and evil. Christ has come to wage that battle and will win.

Jesus begins his ministry in Capernaum, a little village located on the Sea of Galilee. He entered the synagogue and began to preach. What was different? Why did he captivate his listeners? They were used to preachers who knew the scriptures. What was different about Jesus? What made them "spellbound"? He spoke with a novel assurance and authority. A prophet was truly in their midst. They were not used to Jesus' liberating good news. Legalism was their daily fare, not liberation.

John Pilch offers another perspective. When Jesus began to preach in the synagogue, he was not acting in accord with his status as artisan. Tension mounted. Who does this artisan think he is? Who gave him the authority? Isn't he the carpenter from Nazareth? The audience was not so alarmed over the demons since they were a common, expected reality; they were more alarmed over Jesus' behavior.[12]

Evil spirits were believed to be more powerful than human beings, but not more powerful than God. Spirits could wreak havoc in a person's life. Spirits could bring about good fortune or incredibly bad, disruptive fortune. It was believed that in order to gain control over an evil spirit all one had to do was to call out its true identity and it would magically disappear. The demon tried to use that trick to gain control over Jesus. Jesus, however, prevailed.

The people now are truly dumbfounded. In a surprising turn of events, Jesus displayed mastery

---

[12] *CWJB*, 29.

over the spirit. The irony is not to be missed—the demon is the only one with no illusions when it comes to Jesus. He knows only too well who Jesus really is. There are only three occasions in Mark's entire gospel in which the characters address Jesus by name: twice the demons address him in order to gain control over him and once blind Bartimaeus seeks healing for his blindness.

Illness was understood to be part of a violent, evil world. Illness, especially mental illness, was understood in terms of demonic possession. Modern Western society has a difficult time relating to this story. Western understanding of science and technology seems to fly in the face of the ancient and contemporary Middle Eastern understanding of evil spirits. Such cultures believe in the presence of both good and evil spirits.

The man shrieked in a loud voice—he shouted at Jesus. He arrogantly tried to exercise magic control over Jesus by calling out his yet to be revealed, God-given identity. Throughout the gospel the demons commonly know who Jesus is when people do not. They know Jesus comes from God. They understand that he has come to destroy the power of evil.

Jesus demands that the demon be silenced. His command cannot be ignored. On Jesus' word alone violent eruptions occur. In fits of rage and desperation the demon thrashes and clutches his poor victim before surrendering to the Gentle Authority before him. From the outset of his ministry, Jesus offers compassion and liberation to people gripped in the throes of unforgiving, unrelenting bondage and oppression.

Needless to say, the onlookers were amazed, awestruck, and in wonder, a common state for all those people in Mark's gospel who encountered this compassionate healer who taught with new authority. One can almost hear the hushed undertones spreading throughout the region. "Did you hear about this Jesus? Just who is he? Where did he get his power? He obviously has power over the spirits, but where does his power come from? Could it be from God? Perhaps his source is other evil spirits? What does it all mean?" The people are amazed and astonished and Jesus' fame (honor) spread throughout the land. Amazement and astonishment are common tools used by Mark to stress Jesus' true identity.

From the very beginning we are to know who it is we are dealing with in these stories. This is not some fly-by-night miracle worker. This is not just some new "prophet-come-lately." This is *God's own Son*. There is to be no mistake. We, the readers, are to continue reading, knowing the rest of the story.

Scripture scholar Ched Myers offers a thought-provoking insight into this gospel pericope (albeit the entire gospel). Jesus left the temptation scene in the desert to confront the world. His first confrontation takes place in Capernaum. "This is a story of engagement with the world, not flight from it."[13]

Myers suggests that the unclean spirit Jesus cast out "obliquely symbolized the scribal class."[14] Jesus' ministry fearlessly sets out from the beginning to challenge the religious political order that oppressed and burdened the people.

Myers maintains that there is more to this story than meets the eye. Miracle workers and healers were plentiful in the ancient Graeco-Roman world. There was nothing new about healing and exorcism. Why would Jesus be in so much trouble with the authorities from the outset of his ministry for offering healing and liberation to people who were in such tormented bondage? Other healers operated freely and without scrutiny. Why was Jesus so controversial? Myers maintains that biblical scholarship has always explained it away as a tragic misunderstanding. "This is social and historical nonsense: healers and magicians abounded and practiced freely in the Hellenized antiquity, but Jesus encounters official hostility almost from the outset."[15] Very early in Mark's gospel (ch. 3) Jesus is politically accused of his healings and exorcisms. Myers insists that there has to be more to these stories than once assumed.

Mark begins the story by placing Jesus in the heart of the Jewish social order—the synagogue (sacred

---

[13]*BSM*, 135.
[14]Ibid., 138.
[15]Ibid., 141.

space). The story takes place on the Sabbath (sacred time). We are immediately alerted to the conflict. Jesus was teaching them and *they* were amazed. *They* constituted the synagogue audience. "[T]hey distinguish Jesus' teaching as (*hos*) one having *authority*, not as (*kai ouch hos*) the scribes (1:22)."[16] In other words, the community compared Jesus' new authority with the lack of authority they observed in the scribes. To add insult to injury, the community's amazement over Jesus' new authority (read—surpassing that of the scribes) is reiterated at the end of the scene. The beginning scene and the ending scene thus frame the exorcism, alerting the reader that the exorcism has something to do with the struggle between the authority of Jesus and that of the scribes.

Jesus entered the sacred space that belonged to the scribes. He entered their world and immediately faced opposition in the symbolic encounter with the demon. One translation of the demon's question to Jesus is, "What do we have in common? And why do you meddle with us?"[17] There is an implicit agenda. Jesus is a hostile intruder who is threatening the sacred space already controlled by the scribal aristocracy.

Myers affirms that Mark uses amazement as a constant reaction to Jesus' teaching, but he adds a dimension to their amazement—"a kind of panic associated with the disruption of the assumed order of things."[18]

Myers strongly criticizes attempts to explain this miracle away as a cure of epilepsy or mental illness. Manipulation of the spirit world was a common occurrence in antiquity. The details of this cure are not at issue. What is at issue is what the cure meant and what it symbolized. The demon represents the authority of the scribes, who in turn represent the authority of the Jewish order. This scene sets the conflict that will continue—Jesus' authority versus scribal authority.

Exorcism is a hallmark of Jesus' mission. He will pass this ministry on to his disciples, who will in turn pass it on to the church. Even though Jesus' disciples do not yet know who Jesus really is, the demons know only too well.

Returning to the question of why Jesus' healing activity brought down the religious and political powers upon him, more insight might be gleaned by examining the symbolic world set up by Mark throughout the gospel text. In Mark's gospel Jesus violates every social and religious boundary established by Jewish law. Jesus blatantly disregards the law when it comes to the needs of human beings. He defiles the ritual purity codes that maintain the status quo of who is in and who is out. People who are part of a society often understand the ordering of that society to be natural and unquestionably ordained by God.[19] Thus, anything unclean must be avoided and cast out. The barriers to such things must be guarded.

In Jesus' world, holiness and purity were synonymous. To risk purity contamination was to risk the way things were ordered by God. In Mark's gospel, the human body was a primary place where purity and unclean found a symbolic home. The body was understood as a place for either the clean or the unclean to inhabit. "It is frequently noted that Jesus cast out demons, as in the Capernaum synagogue (1:21–28), as if they are being evicted from a dwelling they have made their home: 'Come out of him!'"[20] When Jesus initiated the liberation of people who were inhabited by the unclean, he stepped over a boundary—he crossed a forbidden gate. This is what brought down the anger of the religious authorities. It was an issue of power and control. Such things were in *their* domain.

Jesus' *new authority* was frightening to some, amazing to some, and a threat to some. Where would we have stood? Gustavo Gutierrez presents us with the gospel's challenge. "To a mentality closed to change, new is synonymous with false. But the mes-

---

[16]Ibid.

[17]Ibid., 142.

[18]Ibid.

[19]For example, a young man tells the story of growing up in New Orleans during segregation days. He never gave the issue a second thought. It was just the way things were—and were meant to be. It was almost as if God had planned it that way, it was so normal. It was not until he saw a black woman bodily beaten and thrown off a bus, that he began to question that social ordering.

[20]*NS*, 69.

sage to love is always new because it calls us to abandon the way of selfishness and of formalism and to take the path of generosity and consistency."[21]

Proclaim the gospel again.

Sometimes we gain new insights when we hear the text after the interpretation is given. Someone from the group proclaims the gospel a second time.

STEP 4
TESTING

Conversation with the Liturgy and the Scriptures

Test your original understanding in dialogue with the text.

(You might consider breaking into smaller groups.)

Now that you've heard the exegesis, were there any new insights? How do you feel about it? How does your original understanding of this gospel compare with what we just shared? How does this story speak to your life?

Sharing Life Experience

Participants share an experience from their lives that connects with the biblical interpretation just presented.

Today's liturgy invites me to ask myself: "Have I ever been a recipient of God's liberating, transforming deliverance and healing power?" I cannot answer that question without turning to the single most healing event in my life.

I know only too well the power of Christ to exorcise the destructive demons that distort truth and kill the spirit. As an adult survivor of abuse I have been delivered and made whole by the power of Jesus' name. The demons that shouted accusing words of shame have been silenced. The voices that remain are but faint whispers shouting from the depths of the deafening abyss. By his divine authority Jesus stilled their raucous denunciations. It is the sacrament of Christ, the people of God, and my family who have

taught me what it means to be a child of God, created in the Divine Image. Throughout the healing journey I clung to the still, small voice: "By my life, cross, and resurrection I have elevated you to the status of divine." How can a divine child of God be damaged goods? The divine edict of Genesis is my creed: "And God saw that I was good." Unfortunately, the evil events of life have the power to perpetuate further evil. Christ does not remove us out of harm's way on this earthly sojourn, but he parts the waters and goes before us. He becomes Compassion. Yet in the early days of remembrance my rage bellowed, "Where were you, Lord, when this child of God needed you most?"

Today's liturgy exalts the true identity of Jesus. This one gospel obliquely tells the entire story of salvation history. God has been in relationship with human beings since the beginning of the world. In the beginning God created men and women in the Divine Image. Christ was present at creation and from the very beginning was destined to save the world from the tyranny of death, destruction, and the demonic. Today's gospel quickens the fulfillment of Jesus' divine destiny—the cross. Christ has come to do what Christ was sent by his Father to do—to be God's Compassion through the sacrifice of the cross. Even the demons know the cosmic battle they face. The Jesus of today's gospel invites me to enter into that sacrifice and in the process find true healing and liberation.

My journey and continued invitation toward wholeness is best expressed by the meditations of Jean Corbon in his work, Wellspring of Worship:

"Where are you Lord? How long will you delay?" The cross of his Son is the place from which he seems the most absent but in which he in fact gives himself completely. The place where his Christ is crucified is the place where his compassion is poured out, for it is the place where human beings are most deeply wounded by death. People today are surprised at the deep silence of God, probably because the power of death has thrown aside its mask; but who is willing to enter into the silence of the compassion of Jesus, to follow him that far? It is only a stone's throw between the slumber of the disciples and the agony of their Lord: to cross that space is to enter into the struggle of prayer, intercession and compassion.

---

[21] *SWTLY*, 127.

When we enter into the depths of the Name of the holy Lord Jesus, our whole being is in a state of epiclesis,[22] and the Spirit Comforter pours himself out through us into the hearts of our suffering brothers and sisters. How does the Father of the Poor make himself a Comforter? Certainly not with empty words and barren emotions as we do! He who is the silence of the Word and the power at work in his resurrection restores to the hearts of the poor the power to live and the joy that no one can take away. He possesses the secret of that compassion by which the poor in turn become an altar of salvation for their brothers and sisters. For to suffer with, to be powerless, is to share in the weakness of God on the cross. We must believe and enter into this kenosis of the Word and his Spirit, into this kenosis of the Church that becomes ours through compassion. Without it there is no communion or community, no resurrection or liberation. Instead of bemoaning the sufferings inflicted on us by others, let us learn to suffer with them; the "groaning of the Spirit" in them and in us will become a spring of life. "The glory of God is living human beings," says St. Irenaeus; his radiant love makes them live.[23]

I can do no less than be amazed at the power of Jesus' name in today's gospel, in today's liturgy, and in my life.

What was Mark trying to tell his community? In what way does this gospel challenge your community today? Since we are unaccustomed to the phenomenon of demon possession in our contemporary society, how is this gospel a relevant word for your community and for you? What is your experience of the power of evil? Has it touched your life? Have you ever experienced the liberating power of God in your life? In the life of your community? In what way has this conversation with the scriptures for today's liturgy invited change in your life? In what way are the biblical themes of covenant, exodus, creation, and community evident in today's readings? Do you still feel the same

way about this text as when you began? Has your original understanding been stretched, challenged, or affirmed?

STEP 5
DECISION

The gospel demands a response.

In what concrete way might your parish be invited to respond? Are there any attitudes or behaviors you would like to change as a result of today's conversation? What is one concrete action you will take this week in response to the liturgy today?

Pastoral Considerations: In light of the fact that it is probably January, or in close proximity to it, and January is the month set aside to pray for Christian unity, today's liturgy is a clarion call to stand with Christ in unity with all Christians in his mission of healing, deliverance, and reconciliation.

Is there unity in your parish? What are the areas most in need of healing and reconciliation? Is there unity between the multicultural communities in your parish? When was the last time you addressed issues of evangelization and ecumenism?

Christian Initiation: This would be a good time to celebrate the minor exorcisms and to make the appropriate connections with the healing, liberating mission of Christ in our everyday lives. The minor rite of exorcism is intended to strengthen the catechumens in their daily efforts to avoid the power of sin in their lives and to live the Christian way of life. This would also be an appropriate time to celebrate a rite of anointing of catechumens. When was the last time you apprenticed your catechumens and candidates in the ministry of evangelization?

DOCTRINAL ISSUES

What Church truth/teaching/doctrinal issue could be drawn from the gospel for the fourth Sunday in Ordinary Time?

Participants suggest possible doctrinal themes that flow from the readings.

---

[22]Epiclesis is the invocation, the calling down of the Holy Spirit to sanctify, change, transform, and make new.
[23]*TWOW*, 174–175.

Possible Doctrinal Themes

Jesus Christ, Teacher; Jesus Christ, Son of God; Jesus Christ, Healer and Deliverer; sacraments of healing and reconciliation; evangelization; ecumenism; conversion; paschal mystery, salvation history; human dignity

Present the doctrinal material at this time.

1. The facilitator gives input on a particular doctrinal issue of his or her prior choosing. OR
2. The group chooses a doctrinal issue from the list they created. They read together from the Doctrinal Appendix or other appropriate, official Church documents and the works of respected theologians.

(Many doctrinal issues are found in the Doctrinal Appendix at the back of this workbook. If you are choosing an issue from this resource, please refer to it now.)

Reflection questions centered around the chosen doctrinal theme can be found at the end of each topic in the Doctrinal Appendix. The questions are based on the five-step reflection process. If you choose a topic not included in the Doctrinal Appendix, craft your own questions according to the same five-step process.

Following the reflection questions you will be reminded to return to chapter 7, "Preparing the Catechetical Session," to assist you in crafting your own session.

Closing Prayer

Almighty and eternal God,
you gather the scattered sheep
and watch over those you have gathered.
Look kindly on all who follow Jesus, your Son.
You have marked them with the seal of one
    baptism,
now make them one in the fullness of faith
and unite them in the bond of love.
We ask this through Christ, our Lord.[24]

---

[24]"Third Week in January: Week of Christian Unity," *Household Blessings and Prayers.* [USCC, NCCB].

FIFTH SUNDAY IN ORDINARY TIME

Environment

Refer to the second Sunday in Ordinary Time.

INTRODUCTORY RITES

Entrance Antiphon (or Opening Song)

Come, let us worship the Lord. Let us bow down in the presence of our maker, the Lord our God. (Ps 94:6–7)[1]

Opening Prayer

The facilitator of the session may lead the prayer. Others in the group may be asked to proclaim the readings.

Let us pray
[with reverence in the presence of the living God]

Pause for silent prayer.

In faith and love we ask you, Father,
to watch over your family gathered here.
In your mercy and loving kindness
no thought of ours is left unguarded,
no tear unheeded, no joy unnoticed.
Through the prayer of Jesus
may the blessings promised to the poor in spirit
lead us to the treasures of your heavenly
  kingdom.
We ask this in the name of Jesus the Lord.[2]

LITURGY OF THE WORD

The readings are proclaimed.

First Reading
Job 7:1–4, 6–7

---

[1] Fifth Sunday in Ordinary Time: "Entrance Antiphon," *The Sacramentary.*

[2] Fifth Sunday in Ordinary Time, "Alternative Opening Prayer," *The Sacramentary.*

Overview of the Book of Job: The Book of Job is one of the unique treasures of the ancient literary world. It is rarely used in the Lectionary. The Book of Job is part of the third group of books in the Hebrew Scriptures called the "Writings." The primary theme of the Book of Job is suffering—the plight of the sufferer and the mystery of suffering. The literary form consists of prose and poetry. The prose depicts a long-suffering, persevering Job in the face of suffering and persecution. The poetry bespeaks Job's frustration and anger with God over his condition.

Job was considered one of the great heroes in ancient biblical literature. He was a righteous man. Job's fine qualities are extolled throughout the prose section of the text. God and Satan engage in conversation. God affirms his servant Job. Satan agrees with God's assessment of Job but questions Job's motivations. Satan unleashes menace upon Job—his suffering becomes unendurable.

The narrator continues to insist that Job is righteous. The antagonists in the plot (Job's three friends), however, arrive on the scene and set out to disprove God's assessment of Job. As Job's "friends" accelerate their charges against him, Job becomes more persistent in his charges against God. He is frustrated with God's injustice toward him.

God seems to be in a defensive game of cat and mouse with Satan at Job's expense. We can all sympathize—Job seems to be justified in his anger against God. Satan's power was unleashed against Job simply to prove that he would remain righteous. Underneath the story, however, is the strong undercurrent that God is Job's biggest fan. He has no doubt about Job's commitment and perseverance.

One unfortunate theme that emerged out of the wisdom tradition is that prosperity is a sign of righteousness before God: do good and God will reward you. This assertion challenges human integrity. Job nips that theme in the bud. He will not be lured into giving up his personal integrity—not even by God. His response before God is not dependent on the favors God will bestow on him.

Things begin to deteriorate. Job's wife adds salt to the wound. She tells him that he would be better off if he would curse God and then die. This is a turning point in the story. The reader becomes aware that the end of the rope has arrived. There is nowhere to go now but to the depths of depression and ultimately suicide.

Job spews forth his pent-up feelings; yet he still does not curse God. He curses instead the day he was born. Life is meaningless. He questions why he was born in the first place. Job embodies the fullness of human suffering and pain.

Job longs for answers to his plight. He plumbs the depths of human suffering. He demands that his anguish not be ignored, sugar-coated, or relativized in the process. "Utterly senseless suffering is terrifying, since it strikes at the heart of our human need for some sense of order…Job is ready to listen to doctrine—if it is honest. But where is honesty, when anguish is ignored?"[3]

Job dares to challenge God. How does a person challenge One so powerful? The arguments intensify. Job begins to yield to his friends' supposition: if God is just, how then could God's actions against Job be unjust? The wisdom tradition rears its head again. Since suffering is a result of sin and since God's justice is not open to question, then those who suffer must be sinners. Job will have none of it. He knows his own heart. He knows that he is not a sinner. His integrity will not allow him to capitulate. The problem is God's. God will simply have to readjust his own position. If God's justice is responsible for this human misery, then God's justice is open to challenge. "If theology is being formulated to distort human life, then theology must be refashioned."[4]

Job's primary virtue is not patience. Anthony Campbell insists that Job is anything but patient. Job's poetry reveals a man of passion. "It is his total passion for human integrity. Job stands by the

truth of his own experience and will let nothing be used to distort the reality of that experience."[5]

Job is in a deep abyss. He knows he is innocent. God is responsible. Job seeks an answer. Is God just like his friends? God answers. No. God is not like his accusing friends. God has compassion for those who suffer. In verse 12 Job remembers the love and care God has shown to him.

Job's friends insist that since God is compassionate, God will demonstrate that compassion as long as Job repents for his sins. Job will not capitulate: if righteousness is all that is required for God to act, then God should have acted long ago. Job is already righteous. Job concludes that his friends defend God with lies and deception. Job is an innocent sufferer who is beguiled by a faulty theology that insists on his guilt.

Job has his day in court with God and is silent in the face of it. God speaks to him. God vindicates Job and accuses his friends. God never was Job's enemy as Job had thought. Job's opinion of God was wrong—God was not against him. God reminds Job that his suffering is part of the human condition—it is a mystery. Human suffering is a mystery. Job changes his opinion that God is his enemy. God chastises Job's friends for insisting that Job's suffering is the result of God's punishment for sin. Job was honorable in his defense of human integrity and human dignity.

The ending of the book seems to betray the intent of the entire story. Job's friends enjoined him to turn away from his sins and humble himself before God, and God would reward him. It seems as if that is exactly what happened. Yet we know that God insisted that Job's friends were wrong.

The Book of Job does not give an explanation for suffering. It points to an answer. The book points to the reality that both beauty and violence coexist in God's creation. Those who see with eyes of faith possess the ability to see the goodness of God's creation, and the goodness in human love and human life even in the midst of life's tragedies and misery.[6] Suffering might overwhelm that abil-

[3]*SCOTL*, 463.
[4]Ibid., 465.

[5]Ibid.
[6]Ibid., 481

ity at times, but it is there. Once we see that good-ness, no matter what happens to us, we can find meaning in the midst of life's worst calamities. Such goodness begets hope.

Job's friends insisted that human suffering is to be understood in terms of punishment and purifica-tion—and they were wrong. Job insisted that it was a result of God's malice. He was wrong. So, if it is not sin or God's wrath, what is it? Human beings are free of guilt and God is ultimately compassion-ate; thus, no one is responsible for suffering. It just is. It is a mystery. There is an invitation inherent in the mystery, however. We are invited to reflect upon the incredible tenacity of the human spirit to endure and persevere, and upon the incredible love of God, "which must suffer and grieve with us in our hurt and misery, but which—as we can say to each other—say also to us: 'you are precious in my eyes, and honored, and I love you.'"[7]

Today's Pericope: Job reflects on the misery of human life in light of the accusations and theolo-gizing of his three friends. This pericope's connec-tion with the gospel is probably to be observed in the contrast between the mystery of human suffer-ing and the healing ministry of Jesus highlighted in today's gospel.

Responsorial Psalm
Psalm 147:1–6

This psalm is a hymn of praise probably set in the context of the return of the exiles from Babylon and the rebuilding of Jerusalem.

Second Reading
1 Corinthians 9:16–19, 22–23

Some commentators suggest that since chapter 9 does not begin with the customary words, "Now concerning . . . ," it does not deal with the issues that were raised by the Corinthian community. It is suggested that this chapter might be part of a dif-ferent letter in which Paul defends his apostleship.

At issue is the criticism leveled against Paul for not allowing his newly converted Christians to help support him in his preaching ministry. Paul's op-ponents suggest that his refusal is a sign that he is not confident of his own apostolic authority. Paul insists that he indeed has a right to ask for sup-port, but that he chooses not to for specific rea-sons. False teachers converged on Corinth and sponged off the community and nearly converted the community to their way of believing. Paul does not want to be identified as a similar itinerant preacher. He is afraid that the Corinthians will misconstrue the gospel. Paul preached Jesus Christ crucified. He did not want anything to get in the way of the message he preached.

The gospel is proclaimed.

Gospel
Mark 1:29–39. He cured many who suffered from diseases of one kind or another.

STEP 1
NAMING ONE'S EXPERIENCE

What were your first impressions? What was your first response to the gospel (or the other read-ings)?[8] What captured your attention?

Each person names his or her initial impression. State-ments should be brief. No reasons should be given at this time. All simply listen without agreeing or disagreeing.

STEP 2
UNDERSTANDING

In a brief statement, explain what you think this gospel is trying to convey.

STEP 3
INPUT FROM VISION/STORY/TRADITION

Liturgical Context

The fifth Sunday in Ordinary Time is the second Sunday in a three-part sequence. A headline for

---

[7]Ibid., 485.

[8]The primary focus of reflection is the gospel. However, often the other readings demand attention and must be brought into the dialogue.

themes Sundays might read, "A day in the life of Jesus—teacher and healer." "Here we have a general presentation, a sort of summary of the activities that typically filled Jesus' days: prayer, teaching, and healing."[9] Last week's gospel was a pronouncement and a demonstration of Jesus' authority. He possessed the power to cast out demons. Today, his authority and power are observed in his ability to heal sickness.

While there is certainly redemptive value in finding meaning in the midst of our suffering and illness, today's first reading and gospel speak in exclamation points to the reality that God has compassion for human suffering. Jesus extended that compassion to those who were in need of healing. As the gospel exegesis suggests, people were always healed in one way or another. Obviously, not every person who came to Jesus was cured, but all who accepted him and entered into relationship with him were healed (see the distinction below).

The Church continues this ministry of healing in charitable and sacramental ways. Through the ministries of pastoral care for the sick, the hospitalized, the aged, and so on, the healing compassion of Christ is extended to God's people. The sacramental means of healing is experienced through the sacraments of the Church—eucharist, penance, and anointing of the sick, but most especially in the anointing of the sick. In every liturgy we pray for the needs of God's people. We pray for those who are sick and we acknowledge the healing power of the eucharist as we affirm: "Lord, I am not worthy to receive you, but only say the word and I shall be healed."

Both opening prayers ask that God watch over and protect us. They affirm that God is the source of all compassion, and therefore should be the source of our trust.

Gospel Exegesis

The facilitator provides input from critical biblical scholarship on this text. This input includes insights as to how people would have heard the gospel in Jesus' time.

We are still in the first week of Jesus' very busy ministry. Last week he expelled a demon and his authority was confirmed. Today Jesus heals Peter's mother-in-law and others in the vicinity. There is a close connection between Jesus' power to cast out demons and his ability to heal sickness. Jesus understands sickness to be the result of demonic activity. In Luke's gospel Jesus "rebuked" the fever. Healing and exorcism are signs of salvation.[10] In some languages the root of the word salvation (*soter*) means whole, not divided, disrupted, or disintegrated. Healing restores that which was not whole before. Healing restores original harmony. Salvation restores life and implies victory over death. In the New Testament scriptures salvation implies deliverance of human beings from all forms of evil: sickness, mental illness, the demonic, and death.[11]

John Pilch offers interesting insight into the ancient understanding of healing. Drawing upon contemporary medical anthropology, he defines the difference between disease and illness, curing and healing.

> They [medical anthropologists] distinguish between disease as a biomedical malfunction that afflicts an organism, and illness as disvalued human life. Curing is aimed at disease; it is a rare occurrence. Healing is aimed at illness; it occurs infallibly all the time for all people. Everyone works out a new meaning in life no matter what the predicament.[12]

Jesus' miracles were significant for his community because they were a sign that Jesus possessed God-given power. They were also a sign of God's reign, redemption, and the arrival of the fullness of time. Jesus' ability to heal was a living sign that the reign of God had arrived. The words used, "he raised her up," is also translated, "he raised her from the dead." Jesus' action in this earthly life foreshadows the resurrection we will all share.[13] We are healed and delivered from the ravages of sin and subsequently invited into ministry.

---

[9]*DL* (V), 33.

[10]*MK*, 19.
[11]Lucien J. Richard, O.M.I., "Healing," *NDSW*, 520.
[12]*TCWJ*, 31.
[13]Ibid., 20.

Not only does Jesus heal and restore the sick to the community, he also invites and empowers ministry. Some exegetes suggest that the etymology of the word, "to wait on them," derives from the same word used for official ministry in the community. Wilfrid Harrington suggests that this story "is a symbolic portrayal of the believer; one who has been prostrate beneath the power of sin but now, raised up by the Lord, is called upon to serve him" (v. 31). Thus, Peter's mother-in-law, a woman, after being touched by the healing power of Jesus, is healed of her sickness, restored to her family and community, and empowered to serve. Our first-glance assumption places her back in the kitchen. The gospel invites us to consider a broader vision.

Jesus' healing power was not only an historical reality—people were healed, meaning was renewed in their lives, and they were restored to community—but it was also symbolic action. Jesus' healing miracles spoke to the religious and political conditions of the day; but they spoke in action, not words. To the Hebrew mind-set, miracles were not "proofs" of God's sovereignty. God created the world and could intervene in it if God so chose. God's lordship over the world is not proven through miracles; miracles simply recognize the lordship that is already present. God's sovereignty over the world is proven by the way in which God controls the destinies of nations—especially Israel. The true miracle of the exodus was not that God parted the waters of the Red Sea, but that God freed the people out of bondage to pharaoh, thereby bringing Egypt to its knees. Similarly, the miracles of Jesus prove his lordship (the *authority* referred to in last week's gospel) because they challenge the religious and political powers and structures that oppress, exclude, and enslave.

Jesus begins his mission by reaching out to the untouchables of Israel and in the end he ultimately extends it to the untouchables of the world—the gentile nations. Jesus' healing ministry reaches out to the "unclean"—those who are ritually impure—people with blood flow, lepers, skin disorders of all kinds—the sick. He includes all who have been shut out by institutional boundaries of exclusion. Throughout Mark's gospel there are gates that have to be toppled in order to touch and heal people. In today's gospel the people

flock to Jesus as soon as the observance of the Sabbath is over. At times even the Sabbath is a barrier to God's compassion and healing and thus becomes a gate that must be crossed. The entire gospel reveals a tension in which structures, systems, and people seek to prevent access to Jesus. Doorways are blocked, Jesus is deterred from entering towns. Access and entrances serve to maintain the status quo—to keep people in, to keep people out, to prevent life. Thus, when access is denied, so is the potential for Jesus to heal, reconcile, and save.

Thus, the sick in Mark's gospel also serve as a symbolic reference to the wider issue of social exclusion. Jesus breaks through the barriers. "In the symbolic order of Judaism, illness was associated with impurity or sin, a state that meant exclusion from full status in the body politic."[14] Rather than Jesus becoming unclean by his association with unclean, he brought wholeness, healing, and purity to all he touched. "He became sin"—he entered their world and brought the wholeness and holiness of himself to transform what and whom he touched. He restored people to the community. He not only healed and liberated, he broke the barriers of exclusion and welcomed people into space that was previously unaccessible to them. Consider a modern-day corollary. What would be the response if a modern prophet were to take a homeless, AIDS-infected schizophrenic by the hand and escort him or her as an honored, front row guest to the installation of a newly elected pope, bishop, or government leader? Is it any wonder that Jesus met with resistance almost from the outset of his ministry? "Jesus' opponents are shown to be defending a social system that preserves itself by prevention mechanisms. Jesus, by contrast, is the advocate of open gates. His power opposes his opponents' impotence."[15]

Jesus' ministry of healing resonates with Jesus' constant emphasis on compassion. The root of the word *compassion* means to be deeply moved at the core of one's being. Jesus was deeply moved at the core of his being when he encountered those who were in need of healing. Jesus was so concerned with restoring people to health and wholeness

---

[14]*BSM*, 145.

[15]*NS*, 75.

that he broke the law—he healed on the Sabbath, he welcomed outcasts, and he cast out the forces that he believed were responsible for illness in the first place. Jesus never glorified sickness. He always set out to heal it and he empowered others to continue his healing mission.

From a historical point of view, Jesus stood in the tradition of Jewish charismatic healers. Touching is a very important aspect of Jesus' ministry of healing. In fact, in the Hebrew Scripture the language of the senses is used to express God's compassion. God is the one who sees our afflictions, who hears our cries, and feels our pain. The ministry of Jesus represents God as salvific God, a God of life.[16]

Proclaim the gospel again.

Sometimes we gain new insights when we hear the text after the interpretation is given. Someone from the group proclaims the gospel a second time.

STEP 4
TESTING

Conversation with the Liturgy and the Scriptures

Test your original understanding in dialogue with the text.

(You might consider breaking into smaller groups.)

Now that you've heard the exegesis, were there any new insights? How do you feel about it? How does your original understanding of this gospel compare with what we just shared? How does this story speak to your life?

Sharing Life Experience

Participants share an experience from their lives that connects with the biblical interpretation just presented.

I cannot consider the healing stories of Jesus without thinking of the healing story of one very special fam-

---

[16]"Healing," *NDSW*, 520.

ily in our parish. I have written about them before. This is the first time, however, that I have written about them since young baby Jarrod died.

Jarrod was afflicted with an extremely rare disease. Only two other children in the United States are afflicted with it. We stormed the heavens for a cure. We demanded, pleaded, cried, bargained, and ultimately submitted. Why wouldn't God cure Jarrod? Who would not want to alleviate this baby's suffering? Surely it was God's will.

Pious platitudes about suffering and the will of God simply were out of place in the face of such suffering. What our community gleaned from the long-suffering of this family was a glimpse into the power of God to sustain us even in the worst tragedies of life. The hope we tasted from their cup is not born of human design.

God did not physically cure Jarrod, but he completely healed him, his family, and the entire community. The "Jarrod event" taught us all about the power of self-sacrificing love. Jarrod's parents gave up their lives as they ministered to their dying son. Their ordeal would have broken the back of the world's staunchest stoic. Who among us could watch a precious little child struggle for every breath of air and enter in and out of consciousness day after day, week after week, and month after month? Who among us could have withstood the all-night vigils, night after night, week after week, and month after month? Yet this family endured with a strength born of nothing but divine compassion. As life continued to fade from his body, the family affirmed the great gift of life all the more.

A week before Jarrod died, both Jarrod and his new baby brother were brought before our community. We baptized baby brother and we blessed and anointed Jarrod, not knowing that it would be the last time we would be graced with his sacramental presence.

Jarrod died peacefully in his sleep. Even though his Mommy and Daddy, Grandma and Grandpa, and family were broken vessels of grief in those hours of acute loss, they were also vessels of hope for the rest of us. We were buoyed by their faith and they in turn were upheld, strengthened, and uplifted by the community that walked with them every step of the way. The compassion of God was embodied in the commu-

nity who prayed with them, wept by their side, fed them, mowed their lawn, held their hands, and prayerfully vigiled in the church, throughout the dark hours of the night, in the presence of his tiny little body, in anticipation of the funeral liturgy the next day. This special family is a living witness to the Church's teaching that the people of God are the living presence of Christ in our midst.

Jarrod was not cured, but he was healed. Does that minimize the power of God to cure? No. There are no answers for the reason that some people experience physical healing and others do not. Ultimately, it is a mystery. While this is the most painful ordeal this family has yet to experience in life, their faith-filled hearts helped them pass through it without being crushed in the process. Like Job, their integrity is intact. Their suffering was and is real, and they took it where it needed to go—to God. Every question that Job asked God, they echoed in triplicate.

In the end, the truth of the Book of Job is an anchor for us all. Life and death coexist at the banquet table of life. Suffering is part of the human condition. It is a mystery. God did not cause this baby's illness, suffering, and ultimate death. But God was with his family in it. The healing ministry of Christ washed over them through it all.

Jesus healed them from the influences that would tell them to give up and lose hope. He in turn strengthened their faith, their relationship with God, one another, and the community. He gifted them with insight regarding the meaning of life and death.

Jesus ultimately healed Jarrod; he now enjoys perfect union with God. What more can we say? At Jarrod's funeral, our pastor reminded us that the funeral liturgy celebrates and remembers the great deeds of the deceased's "well-lived" Christian life. "What a marvel," he reminded us, "that this little eighteen-month-old boy, in his very brief life, evangelized, testified, and gave witness to the healing power of God's love, mercy, and healing that is freely given to each and every one of us."

Jesus not only healed Jarrod, his parents, and his family, he empowered them to serve. He gave Jarrod's mother and father the strength to stand before our community at his funeral and testify to the marvels of God and the wonders of Christ's presence in our community. Like Peter's mother-in-law, they were healed; they still grieve, but in their brokenness, they in turn set out to serve the rest of us. I have been forever touched and fed by the great gift of wisdom, life, and presence tasted at the banquet of Jarrod's life, death, and resurrection into eternal life.

My sincere hope is that every family in the parish, especially those families on the margins, would find the same loving support of our community should tragedy and illness befall them.

What was Mark trying to tell his community? In what way does this gospel challenge your community today? What structures keep people excluded today? Who are the "untouchables" in today's world? In what way does this conversation with this liturgy's scriptures invite a new outlook or transformed attitude? In what way are the biblical themes of covenant, exodus, creation, and community evident in today's readings? Do you still feel the same way about this text as when you began? Has your original understanding been stretched, challenged, or affirmed?

STEP 5
DECISION

The gospel demands a response.

In what concrete way might your parish be invited to respond? Are there any attitudes or behaviors you would like to change as a result of today's conversation? What is one concrete action you will take this week in response to the liturgy today?

Pastoral Considerations: When was the last time your parish gathered together to pray for healing? Do you celebrate a communal anointing of the sick at least once or twice a year? Do you gather periodically the rest of the year to pray with those who are sick? Who are the sick in your midst that might not be welcomed? What might you do to reach out to them?

Christian Initiation: Today would be an appropriate time to celebrate the anointing of catechumens or a minor exorcism. It would also be important to spend time in prayer for the sick friends and relatives of those in the catechumenate. Are there any baptized candidates ready to celebrate full communion in the Catholic Church? Are there any inquirers ready to celebrate a rite of acceptance/welcome?

DOCTRINAL ISSUES

What Church truth/teaching/doctrinal issue could be drawn from the gospel for the fifth Sunday in Ordinary Time?

Participants suggest possible doctrinal themes that flow from the readings.

Possible Doctrinal Themes

Mystery of suffering; paschal mystery; healing; sacrament of anointing; salvation; reign of God; social justice; sacraments; Christology; ministry of healing

Present the doctrinal material at this time.

1. The facilitator gives input on a particular doctrinal issue of his or her prior choosing. OR
2. The group chooses a doctrinal issue from the list they created. They read together from the Doctrinal Appendix or other appropriate, official Church documents and the works of respected theologians.

(Many doctrinal issues are found in the Doctrinal Appendix at the back of this workbook. If you are choosing an issue from this resource, please refer to it now.)

Reflection questions centered around the chosen doctrinal theme can be found at the end of each topic in the Doctrinal Appendix. The questions are based on the five-step reflection process. If you choose a topic not included in the Doctrinal Appendix, craft your own questions according to the same five-step process.

Following the reflection questions you will be reminded to return to chapter 7, "Preparing the Catechetical Session," to assist you in crafting your own session.

Closing Prayer

Let us pray
[that God will watch over us and protect us]

Pause for silent prayer.

Father,
watch over your family
and keep us safe in your care,
for all our hope is in you.
Grant this through our Lord,
Jesus Christ, your Son,
who lives and reigns with you and the Holy Spirit,
one God for ever and ever.[17]

---

[17]Fifth Sunday in Ordinary Time, "Opening Prayer," *The Sacramentary.*

SIXTH SUNDAY IN ORDINARY TIME

INTRODUCTORY RITES

Entrance Antiphon (or Opening Song)

Lord, be my rock of safety, the stronghold that saves me. For the honor of your name, lead me and guide me. (Ps 30:34)[1]

Opening Prayer

The facilitator of the session may lead the prayer. Others in the group may be asked to proclaim the readings.

Let us pray

    Pause for silent prayer.

God, our Father,
you have promised to remain
    for ever
with those who do what is just and right.
Help us to live in your presence.
We ask this through our Lord
    Jesus Christ, your Son,
who lives and reigns with you and
    the Holy Spirit,
one God, for ever and ever.[2]

LITURGY OF THE WORD

The readings are proclaimed.

First Reading
Leviticus 13:1–2, 44–46

Overview of the Book of Leviticus: The Book of Leviticus, one of the books of the Pentateuch and the legal code book of priestly regulations for the priests who served at the Temple in Jerusalem, speaks to us from antiquity about the religious life and the practices of ancient Israel. It is assumed that a large agricultural community supplied the necessary sacrifices and offerings used for festivals and feasts. Leviticus was compiled by the Priestly authors around the sixth century B.C.E. Much of the material in the book centers around appropriate behavior for worship. Included in the book is a listing of sacrifices to be performed, foods to abstain from, and the narrative story explaining how Moses was the originator of the liturgical practice.

The first part of Leviticus includes the ordination of priests (chs. 1–7), the sacrifices (chs. 8–10), foods that are taboo (chs. 11–15), and the liturgy of atonement (ch. 16). The final liturgy of atonement is the climax of the first part of the book. Once a year the high priest placed the sins of Israel on the head of a goat[3] and then sent the goat out into the desert to die as a sign of God's forgiving nature. God always is eager to wipe out the sins of humanity.

The taboo laws demonstrate that worship of God extended into everyday life. The restrictions on certain foods were probably a result of medical concerns of contamination. Some scholars suggest that perhaps the fear of trichinosis is responsible for the prohibition against pork.

In addition to the concerns about contamination, there does seem to be an inherent order to the prohibition of foods. It appears to be based on Genesis 1 and the order in which God created living things: plants are in the ground, birds are in the air; fish swim, and animals graze. Foods that are taboo do not fall into the natural order of creation such as birds that do not fly, fish without fins and scales, and animals that do not graze. "It teaches us that the basic outlook of Israel toward food was not just to gain nourishment but to reflect God's goodness in creation."[4]

The last part of Leviticus contains the "Holiness Code." The Holiness Code is a special set of laws

---

[1]Sixth Sunday in Ordinary Time: "Entrance Antiphon," *The Sacramentary.*

[2]Sixth Sunday in Ordinary Time: "Opening Prayer," *The Sacramentary.*

[3]The term *scapegoat* originates from this ritual practice.

[4]Lawrence Boadt, *ROT*, 189.

that highlight the holiness of God. The laws demand that the Levites act holy like God is holy and refrain from "profane behavior unworthy of their special calling."[5] The code highlights Israel's relationship with Yahweh and contains regulations concerning sex, marriage, touching blood, violating moral commandments, upholding justice, and observing feast days. The concluding chapter in Leviticus concerns the repayment of vows.[6]

The Holiness Code is concerned with the meaning, the implications, and the foundation of worship and daily conduct and how both are connected. The laws are kept because God is holy. "The deep reason why we must conform to the Lord's commands is best expressed with the utmost clarity."[7] God's transcendence is emphatically heralded throughout the scriptures, yet at the same time God is also known to be intimately involved in human history. While expressing God's Other-ness and God's transcendence, the Bible uniquely extols God's nearness. God does not direct human events as a "sidewalk supervisor," but is intimately involved in human affairs. God entered into a covenant relationship with human beings and is partner with them in their unfolding history. God is not completely hidden in a crowd of unknowing, but allows himself to be known and to be seen. Human beings can know God because God has revealed God's name—people may call God "You." God allows human beings to share in his holiness. God is not stingy; God does not keep his holiness to himself.

God is near at God's own initiative—because God desires to be in relationship with humanity. The Holiness Code reveals the face of God: who God is, how God acts, and how God expects those in relationship with him to act. Human beings are to love because God is holy and God loves.

Today's Pericope: The quarantine of victims of skin disorders such as leprosy, evident in today's reading, is probably a result of the highly contagious nature of skin rashes. Even though such diseases were deemed contagious, it was also believed that such conditions rendered a person spiritually un-

clean as well. Spiritually unclean persons were unfit for community worship. The afflicted persons were to follow the established rules concerning them. They were to present themselves to the priest who alone was to determine the nature and extent of their condition. As a minister of the Torah, he would determine how long their necessary quarantine would last. After the determined amount of time, the afflicted person was to return to the priest in order to be declared ritually clean again. This second visit is the setting of today's gospel.

Responsorial Psalm
Psalm 32:1–2, 5, 11

Psalm 32 is one of the seven traditional penitential psalms. Paul used this psalm in his argument about justification. Reginald Fuller suggests that this psalm was chosen for today's readings because leprosy is understood as a symbol of human sin. "Just as the leper reports to the priest, so the sinner comes and confesses to Yahweh (second stanza) and receives forgiveness from him (first stanza)."[8]

Second Reading
1 Corinthians 10:31–11:1

The issue in the Corinthian community in today's reading had to do with the meat that was purchased from the butcher that had been previously sacrificed to idols. The question concerned whether it was acceptable for Christians to eat such meat. In the final analysis, the fully formed Corinthian Christians knew that idols did not exist, so there really was no problem in eating the meat in question. However, Paul exhorted the Corinthians not to make things difficult for their weaker, more scrupulous brothers and sisters or to give opportunity to the pagans to embarrass them for eating such meat. In the interest of not causing undue scandal, Paul initiated guidelines to deal with the problem.

Certainly the food itself has no effect on a person's holiness or lack thereof. What matters ultimately is the impact one's behavior has on other people. Thus, Paul insisted that nothing be done

---

[5] Ibid., 190.
[6] Ibid., 188–190.
[7] *DL* (IV), 63.

[8] *PL*, 300.

to cause scandal or to give offense. The Corinthian believers were to give glory to God in all things.

Paul encouraged the community to imitate him, who in turn imitated Christ. In essence, he exhorted them to follow the way of the cross—self-sacrifice for the sake of others. "Paul reproduces the same pattern of self-emptying, humiliation and suffering. His whole life as an apostle is thus an epiphany of Christ."[9]

Gospel

Mark 1:40–45. He sent the leper from him and he was cured.

STEP 1
NAMING ONE'S EXPERIENCE

What were your first impressions? What was your first response to the gospel (or the other readings)?[10] What captured your attention?

Each person names his or her initial impression. Statements should be brief. No reasons should be given at this time. All simply listen without agreeing or disagreeing.

STEP 2
UNDERSTANDING

In a brief statement, explain what you think this gospel is trying to convey.

STEP 3
INPUT FROM VISION/STORY/TRADITION

Liturgical Context

A lot has happened in Jesus' burgeoning ministry that began on his first day in Capernaum leading to the cure of the leper in today's gospel. Thus,

---

[9]Ibid., 301.

[10]The primary focus of reflection is the gospel. However, often the other readings demand attention and must be brought into the dialogue.

the fourth, fifth, and sixth Sundays of Ordinary Time in Year B form a tightly knit sequence. Ultimately the three Sundays taken together ask one major question: "Just who is this Jesus who teaches with authority, who makes the demons obey, and who cures lepers?" When we gather for liturgy we profess the rest of the story. We answer that question. We know who Jesus is—he is the Son of God, the one who came into the world to heal our sickness, to restore us to life, to die for our sins, and to take upon himself the burden of all his children. We can do no less than love Christ with our entire being and go out and serve his people—the command inherent in every gathering of the Christian assembly.

The leper knows only too well what today's Entrance Antiphon professes: God is our only rock of safety. The Opening Prayer reminds us of the ethical imperative found hidden in the verses of today's gospel. We are reminded of the allusion to the stern warning Malachi gave to the sons of Levi who were unjust in their dealings with God's anawim. In the Opening Prayer we ask God to strengthen us to be just and right in all our actions. Hidden within that prayer, we might add: "Lest God's judgment be heaped on our heads for doing to the poor and the marginalized what Malachi chastised Israel's priests for doing."

Perhaps inherent in today's liturgy is also a reminder that we are not only to be agents of Christ's healing, but that we are to strive diligently to break down the barriers of exclusion that keep people from seeking the wholeness Christ desires for them.

Gospel Exegesis

The facilitator provides input from critical biblical scholarship on this text. The input includes insights as to how people would have heard the gospel in Jesus' time.

The healing story in today's gospel parallels a common motif found in most healing stories. The condition is diagnosed and a request for healing is sought. A leper seeks healing. Jesus cured the leper by word and touch. Jesus commanded a response. The leper was to go and present himself to the high priest, who would confirm the healing and subsequently restore the leper to the community (according to the prescriptions of the law; see exegesis for first reading).

The last part of this threefold pattern catapults the imagination into a common Markan construct—the messianic secret. The leper was told to keep quiet—not to tell anyone about his healing. Last week Jesus told the demon to be quiet. He seems to have a vested interest in the silence of his characters. Yet this week the leper cannot contain himself, and like a lit torch on an oil spill, spreads the news to all who will listen. The news will not be contained.

Mark uses the messianic secret to downplay the tendency to see Jesus as simply another wonderworker. The messianic secret is also used as an attempt to deter or delay the inevitable misunderstanding of Jesus and to foreshadow his future cross and glory. Why do the characters in Mark's drama constantly disobey Jesus' command to secrecy? Why does Jesus continue to enjoin a command he knows will be broken? Theologically Mark intends the reader to understand that while the messiahship of Christ cannot be prematurely revealed since it can only be understood in the context of Christ crucified and resurrected, it is nevertheless a mystery that cannot be suppressed—it *will* go forward; it *will* be revealed. The mystery will be revealed in its fullness in the post-Easter reflections of the community. Today's leper hints to that day and points us in its direction.

In 1868 a scientific discovery shed light on this gospel in a significant way. The cause of leprosy was discovered. Leprosy, also known as Hansen's disease, is not a highly contagious disease. Significant in today's gospel is the fact that this disease is not highly communicable. Research has proven that spouses do not always catch this condition from their infected spouses. Unless scriptures are referring to a disease that is not leprosy, it was not a disease that could be passed on to others. Thus, the quarantine imposed by the disease had little to do with the nature of the disease, and everything to do with a pervasive cultural perspective. Dirt, not contagion, was the issue.

Israel worshiped and praised Yahweh, the Holy One of Israel. Anything or anyone that possessed a blemish or imperfection was not capable of God's

holiness and thus was considered dirty and unclean. The blemished entity needed to be excluded from the community in order not to pollute it. Infected persons were thus excluded from the community until the danger of pollution subsided. "None of these can approach the Lord. Leviticus commands that the person afflicted with 'biblical leprosy' must 'live alone; his dwelling shall be outside the camp'" (Lv 13:46).[11] For the people of biblical antiquity, to permanently live outside the community was a death sentence, akin to fish seeking residence on dry land. Without family, society, and relationships, they were subject to death by seclusion.

Jesus used a command known in theological parlance as the divine passive—"be made clean." That is, he acknowledged God as the one responsible for the healing without having to use God's name. "Jesus willed it; God cleanses the leper."[12] What is significant to first-century listeners is the fact that Jesus touched the leper. He broke the barriers of exclusion and restored the unclean to the community.

Ched Myers invites us to consider another scenario in this one-act healing drama. He insists that the healing of the leper is an event that has been widely misunderstood by most commentators. Even though most English translations of this story seem to give the impression that Jesus commanded the leper to willingly submit to the priestly purity code, the Greek rendering is not so quick to give the same impression. The point and the tone of the story have all too often been missed. Commentators have interpreted this vignette to be Jesus' way of affirming the Mosaic Law. If this is what is going on in the story, there would be no cause for controversy—why would Jesus have to go into hiding for his healing action? He was, after all, upholding the Mosaic Law by his enjoinder to the leper. There is more to this story than what first meets the eye.

The leper approached Jesus. He was well aware that his action of approaching Jesus, a nonpriest, was a violation of the purity code. Thus, he gave Jesus an opportunity to refuse. His hidden agenda

---

[11] *CWJB*, 35.
[12] Ibid.

almost jumps off the page. He seems to say, "You could heal me if you dared to heal me." Jesus takes the dare. Mark lets us in on Jesus' strong emotion and response to the leper, expressed in the original Greek—Jesus is angry (*origeistheis*, 1:41). "Then, after the declaration of wholeness has been delivered, Jesus, 'snorting with indignation' (*embrimesamenos*), dispatches the man *back* to the priests (the probable meaning of *exebalen*). How are we to make sense of these strong emotions? They only make sense if the man had *already been to the priests*, who for some reason had rejected his petition."[13]

Jesus decides to take up the cause and demands that the leper say nothing to anyone. He tells the leper to return to "*them*" once again. "The cleansed leper's task is not to publicize a miracle but to help confront an ideological system: the change in object (from 'priest' to 'them') suggests a protest against the entire purity apparatus, which the priests control. The leper is to go back to make the prescribed offering in order to 'witness against them' (*eis marturion autois*). This is a technical phrase in the Gospel for testimony before hostile audiences."[14]

Jesus is angry with a religious system that victimizes its weakest members. Not only are ill persons considered outcasts in the eyes of their neighbors and country-folk, but to add insult to injury, they are also forced to make a payment in order to be restored to the community they never should have been excluded from in the first place. Myers suggests that this might be a repeated attempt by Mark to give commentary regarding the oracle of Malachi already cited in verse 2. Malachi's oracle promises that Yahweh will "cleanse" the sons of the Levi (the priests) until they bring their offering under the Lord's own justice. Speaking to the priests (the sons of Levi), Malachi warns that Yahweh will "witness against" anyone who oppresses the poor, broken, and marginalized.

We are not to miss the subtlety: "This oracle too, was being fulfilled in their hearing." Jesus brings the judgment and the cleansing of Yahweh to bear on the sons of Levi—the priestly system, the ritual purity code that oppressed and kept people bound and excluded.

Something goes awry for Jesus, however. His plan misfires. Instead of carrying out his appointed task, the leper ignores his assignment and tells all and Jesus is forced into hiding. Some interpretations of this story have translated this as Jesus' desire to hold his popularity at bay. Not so, insists Myers—it is just the opposite. "Jesus is now a marked man, considered unclean in the city due to his contact with the leper. This first symbolic action of healing thus sets the tone for Jesus' campaign: liberation provokes conflict."[15]

Is it not, also, the paradigm of the cross?

Proclaim the gospel again.

Sometimes we gain new insights when we hear the text after the interpretation is given. Someone from the group proclaims the gospel a second time.

STEP 4
TESTING

Conversation with the Liturgy and the Scriptures

Test your original understanding in dialogue with the text.

(You might consider breaking into smaller groups.)

Now that you've heard the exegesis, were there any new insights? How do you feel about it? How does your original understanding of this gospel compare with what we just shared? How does this story speak to your life?

Sharing Life Experience

Participants share an experience from their lives that connects with the biblical interpretation just presented.

> *Today's story reminds me of days we recently spent with the missionaries who came to our parish to thank us personally for building and supporting*

---

[13] *BSM*, 153.
[14] Ibid.

[15] Ibid., 154–155.

their clinic in Peru. They shared with us how simple items we take for granted in the ministrations of health and the medicinal arts are pure luxury in their poor, underdeveloped country. While healing their not-so-uncommon ailments would require a quick trip to the doctor for us, for people in the Third World, things are not so easy. Yet, with simple, appropriate medicines healing would certainly be facilitated. Government corruption and greed make it very difficult to ensure that those medicines are obtained, however, and when they are obtained, they are far more costly than they are here.

The reason the clinic was built in the first place was because of the courage and tenacity of a group of sisters from Ireland. Sister Mary and her friends worked in the government's health clinic and faced daily frustration with a system that kept the poor from receiving the care they deserved as children of God. In the healing example of Jesus, Sister Mary and her friends not only extended the healing touch of Christ to those they served, but they took drastic steps to change a system that victimized them even more than the poverty in which they lived. With the help of our community, they opened two clinics. Their effort was not without conflict. They were bombed and the clinic was nearly put out of business. Self-sacrificing love brought conflict into their lives. Yet they did not back down in the face of such terrorism.

The message for me in this is that I am called not just to extend myself as Christ to others in healing love, but I am also called to go to the source of people's pain and be a history changer when and where I am able. When anyone attempts to change a system, it always rattles a cage at some level of power and control. Yet, the reign Jesus came to establish was never intended to be a cushy resort—from the beginning it was to be a hospital for sinners.

The visitation by our missionary friends from the south left me humbled and powerless. How can I offer Christ's healing love as they offered it, as it was offered in today's gospel? The first place is to determine for my life just who the lepers are in my midst. How do I exclude them and how do I continue to support structures that exclude them? Am I willing to risk confrontation and challenge exclusive barriers? Am I part of the problem or the solution? I am called to have the courage of Christ. Yet, like Christ,

I know I have to risk becoming a marked person. Isn't that the challenge of the cross?

What was Mark trying to tell his community? In what way does this gospel challenge your community today? In what way do you and your community offer Christ's healing love found in today's gospel to the lepers in your midst? Who are the lepers in your midst? Who do you personally exclude with your attitudes? In what way has this conversation with the scriptures for today's liturgy invited change in your life? In what way are the biblical themes of covenant, exodus, creation, and community evident in today's readings? Do you still feel the same way about this text as when you began? Has your original understanding been stretched, challenged, or affirmed?

STEP 5
DECISION

The gospel demands a response.

In what concrete way might your parish be invited to respond? Are there any attitudes or behaviors you would like to change as a result of today's conversation? What is one concrete action you will take this week in response to the liturgy today?

Pastoral Considerations: It might be an appropriate time for your parish to enter into dialogue regarding the hidden lepers in our world, in our civic community, and in our church. What would happen if they were named and efforts were made to restore them to the communities from which they are excluded? What would it cost your community? Perhaps now would be an excellent time to explore the church's social teaching and how it might challenge your parish to be more radically the hands and feet of Christ to the world's outcasts. It is easy to extend healing love to "all the beautiful people." What about all the "not-so-beautiful" ones? Sadly, this is a place where Christians are sometimes more evangelized by nationalism than we are by the gospel.

Perhaps there are groups within the parish that look upon one another in a leprous fashion. Where might such leprous attitudes lurk? How does your community deal with multicultural issues? How are the people on the fringes of your community treated?

In your sacramental preparation programs, is the attitude conveyed that sacraments have to be earned? Are you implying by your practices the same stringent ritual purity codes that faced the leper in today's gospel? Perhaps serious reflection needs to be given to #36 in the *National Catechetical Directory*:

> From its earliest days the Church has recognized that liturgy and catechesis support each other. Prayer and the sacraments call for informed participants; fruitful participation in catechesis calls for the spiritual enrichment that comes from liturgical participation.
>
> While every liturgical celebration has educative and formative value, liturgy should not be treated as subservient to catechesis. On the contrary, catechesis should "promote an active, conscious, genuine participation in the liturgy of the Church, not merely by explaining the meaning of the ceremonies, but also by forming the minds of the faithful for prayer, for thanksgiving, for repentance, for praying with confidence, for a community spirit, and for understanding correctly the meaning of the creeds. (GCD 25)."

Sacramental catechesis has traditionally been of two kinds: preparation for the initial celebration of the sacraments and continued enrichment following their first reception. The first is elementary or general in nature; it aims to introduce catechumens to the teaching of scripture and the creed. The second reflects on the Christian mysteries and explores their consequences for Christian witness. Preparatory sacramental catechesis can be for a specified period of time—some weeks or months; the catechesis which follows is a lifelong matter.[16]

---

[16]*NCD*, 36.

If our attention is placed more on what "we" are doing in the sacramental celebration, and less upon what God is doing in us, we have missed something very important in the way we prepare people for the sacraments. Perhaps we are using our sacramental programs as a means to further supplant their religious education instead of helping them to fully, vibrantly, encounter the sacramental mystery and reflect upon it and the implications for life. If the sacramental rite, complete with scriptures, symbols, gestures, and ritual prayers, is not the springboard and the context for what we do to prepare people for the sacraments, we need to take a serious look at our practice. The Church has already given us a model for liturgy and conversion based on sacramental preparation. It is called the Rite of Christian Initiation of Adults. It has everything to teach us about the way in which we prepare people for all the sacraments.

Very often our sick and homebound, our elderly and young, the addicted and those who have been the victims of crime or oppression are made to feel like society's lepers. They are made to feel like they are a burden on others. The Church in its great compassion desires that we reach out in the name of Jesus and minister to the sick and brokenhearted. Perhaps this would be a good time to consider how your parish might celebrate "Orders for Blessing of the Sick" (for Adults and for Children); "Order for the Blessing of a Person Suffering from Addiction or from Substance Abuse"; or "Order for the Blessing of a Victim of Crime or Oppression," all found in the *Book of Blessings*. Is there a need in your community to celebrate any of these blessings? What might be the appropriate context and setting?

Christian Initiation: Is there anyone ready to celebrate a rite of full communion in the Catholic Church? Remember that the minor exorcisms and blessings are intended to be used in your sessions with catechumens and candidates. Perhaps one of the above-mentioned blessings might be incorporated in your session this week if there is a need within your given catechumenal community. Perhaps catechesis this week might simply be to go out and consciously and actively respond in some way to the "lepers" in your community.

DOCTRINAL ISSUES

What Church truth/teaching/doctrinal issue could be drawn from the gospel for the sixth Sunday in Ordinary Time?

Participants suggest possible doctrinal themes that flow from the readings.

Possible Doctrinal Themes

Healing; God's love; Jesus Christ; social justice; kingdom of God; dignity of the human person; grace; signs of the kingdom of God; miracles; sign of touch; laying on of hands; sacraments of the anointing of the sick and reconciliation; the Law

Present the doctrinal material at this time.

1. The facilitator gives input on a particular doctrinal issue of his or her prior choosing. OR
2. The group chooses a doctrinal issue from the list they created. They read together from the Doctrinal Appendix or other appropriate, official Church documents and the works of respected theologians.

(Many doctrinal issues are found in the Doctrinal Appendix at the back of this workbook. If you are choosing an issue from this resource, please refer to it now.)

Reflection questions centered around the chosen doctrinal theme can be found at the end of each topic in the Doctrinal Appendix. The questions are based on the five-step reflection process. If you choose a topic not included in the Doctrinal Appendix, craft your own questions according to the same five-step process.

Following the reflection questions you will be reminded to return to chapter 7, "Preparing the Catechetical Session," to assist you in crafting your own session.

Closing Prayer

Lord, we make this offering in obedience to your
    word.
May it cleanse and renew us,
and lead us to our eternal reward.
We ask this in the name of Jesus the Lord.

Let us pray.

Pause for silent prayer.

Lord,
you give us food from heaven.
May we always hunger
for the bread of life.
Grant this through Christ, our Lord.[17]

---

[17]Sixth Sunday in Ordinary Time: "Prayer Over the Gifts and Prayer After Communion," *The Sacramentary.*

492

SEVENTH SUNDAY IN ORDINARY TIME

INTRODUCTORY RITES

Entrance Antiphon (or Opening Song)

The Lord has been my strength; he has led me into freedom. He saved me because he loved me. (Ps 17:19–20)[1]

Opening Prayer

The facilitator of the session may lead the prayer. Others in the group may be asked to proclaim the readings.

Let us pray
that the peace of Christ find welcome in the world

> *Pause for silent prayer.*

Father in heaven,
form in us the likeness of your Son
and deepen his life within us.
Send us as witnesses of gospel joy
into a world of fragile peace and
broken promises.
Touch the hearts of all men with your love
that they in turn may love one another
We ask this through Christ, our Lord.[2]

LITURGY OF THE WORD

The readings are proclaimed.

First Reading
Isaiah 43:18–19, 21–22, 24–25

(See first Sunday of Advent for overview of the Book of Isaiah.)

Today's Pericope: The oracle by the prophet of Second Isaiah was prompted by the culminating crisis event of his day. The Babylonian exile, which the people believed was God's punishment for their sins, was soon coming to an end. The exiles would be returning to Israel. This return of the exiles from Babylon to Israel was understood as a "second exodus."

The "things of long ago" in today's pericope refers to the first exodus. Israel proclaimed and professed a "God who saves." This proclamation was rooted in their corporate memory of the liberation from bondage in Egypt. God gathered and formed this new people under the leadership of Moses. He led them through the desert and formed them in the Law and the worship that would be pleasing to Yahweh.

The "new thing" God is doing in today's reading is nothing less than the creative power of God at work. "Each step of the history of salvation is a new creation at God's initiative."[3]

The author of Second Isaiah insists that the new exodus, the return from exile, is now to be etched in Israel's new corporate memory. The hallmark of Israel's new liturgy would be the confession of sin. The apparent gratuitous mercy of Yahweh is evident in the final verse of today's reading. Yes, we are to remember and confess our sins, but we are not to lose sight of the overarching reality of God's mercy. God forgives our sins. God does not remember them. They are wiped out. This is great news!

Christians understand this new exodus in terms of the Christ event. Through the passage of Christ from death to resurrected life, the sins of the world are obliterated.

Responsorial Psalm
Psalm 41:2–3, 4–5, 13–14

While the psalm has little application to the theme of the first exodus evident in the first reading, it is a most appropriate choice for the theme

---

[1] Seventh Sunday in Ordinary Time: "Entrance Antiphon," *The Sacramentary.*

[2] Seventh Sunday in Ordinary Time: "Opening Prayer," *The Sacramentary.*

[3] *DL* (V), 61.

of healing in the gospel. This is a psalm of thanksgiving for the restoration of health after illness. Like the paralytic who is completely dependent on the mercy of God, so is the sinner just as dependent on that same mercy. "It thus prepares our minds to focus upon the plight of the paralytic, and therefore upon our own plight as sinners."[4]

Second Reading
2 Corinthians 1:18–22

(See second Sunday in Ordinary Time for an overview of 2 Corinthians.)

Today's Pericope: Some scholars believe that the second letter to the Corinthians was one of many letters written to the Corinthian community in response to various spiritual crisis situations. This letter is believed to have been written after the resolution of the crisis and restoration of harmony. During the controversies, Paul visited the community but his mission failed. He was unable to effectively work things out. He planned a second visit, but postponed it in hopes that Titus might have more success than he did. As a result, Paul was accused of instability. Paul calmly explained his actions by insisting that they were consistent with the way he always behaved. Paul always said "Yes" to the gospel of Christ. Even though Paul tried to be all things to all people, he never did so at the expense of the gospel. Paul insisted that his actions were rooted in God's will and the proclamation of the gospel. This was his best defense. Paul put his money where his mouth was and lived the gospel he preached. Every Christian is to do no less. The gospel affirmed and empowered Paul just as it affirms and empowers every Christian at the moment of his or her sacramental initiation. "In this, God has established and commissioned us, put his seal upon us, and given us his Spirit as a down payment (*arrhabon*; RSV: 'guarantee') of our final salvation."[5]

The gospel is proclaimed.

Gospel
Mark 2:1–12

---

[4]*PL*, 303.
[5]Ibid., 303–304.

STEP 1
NAMING ONE'S EXPERIENCE

What were your first impressions? What was your first response to the gospel (or the other readings)? What captured your attention?

Each person names his or her initial impression. Statements should be brief. No reasons should be given at this time. All simply listen without agreeing or disagreeing.

STEP 2
UNDERSTANDING

In a brief statement, explain what you think this gospel is trying to convey.

STEP 3
INPUT FROM VISION/STORY/TRADITION

Liturgical Context

The next four Sundays of the liturgical cycle form a sequence that begins "at home" in Capernaum. It begins at Simon's house and ends four Sundays later at an unknown house. Mark's style is so engaging that he forces the reader to become intimately involved. Observer and reader are forced to take a stand.

For the next four Sundays Jesus becomes embroiled in controversy. He is accused of blasphemy (seventh Sunday). He is accused of a lackadaisical attitude toward traditional religious practices such as fasting (eighth Sunday). He stands charged with violating the Sabbath (ninth Sunday). His family questions his sanity and certain scribes suggest that he is demon-possessed (tenth Sunday). The observer and reader are forced to choose. Just who is this man? Will you, or won't you, believe in his authority? Is he, or is he not, the Son of God? The bottom line for Jesus in these weeks is a timeless message for all ages. Does your life reflect your worship? Do you live what you believe?

The implications for worship then and today are clear. Does your worship of God reflect your behavior toward your neighbor? Actions speak louder than words and empty praise. Praise and worship are to result in changed behavior and a response of love toward all of God's creatures.

The words of the Entrance Antiphon echo a summary statement that could be made for today's liturgy. The paralytic, his friends, and all recipients of God's incredible healing love would do well to shout and proclaim the God who has been our strength and who leads us to freedom. Jesus heals and he cures. Above all, he restores us to life.

If we are truly willing to be transformed by today's liturgy we will allow the gospel to take root in us. We will live the hope expressed in the Opening Prayer. We will allow Christ to dwell within us and we will go out into the world of broken promises, a world that excludes, communities that exclude, and we will be agents of Christ's healing, reconciling, and welcoming love. Today's liturgy serves as a clarion call for such loving action.

Today also begins the proclamation of Paul's Second Letter to the Corinthians. It will be read from the seventh Sunday through the fourteenth Sunday in Ordinary Time.

Gospel Exegesis

The facilitator provides input from critical biblical scholarship on this text. This input includes insights as to how people would have heard the gospel in Jesus' time.

There is more going on in this story than meets the eye. At first glance it would appear as if this story (vv. 1–5a and 11–12) is the same healing of the paralytic found in John 5 and Acts 9. Sandwiched between those verses, however, is the theme of remission of sins (vv. 5b–10). Herein lies the source of controversy. Mark uses a healing miracle to underscore Jesus' power to forgive sins. The "good news" of early Christianity was dependent on the understanding that Jesus possessed the authority to forgive sins.

Jesus' ministry of reconciliation was a present, ongoing reality. Herein lies the bone of contention. Jewish belief insisted that forgiveness of sins was something to be hoped for in the future heavenly kingdom. Furthermore, the power and the prerogative to forgive sins belonged to Yahweh alone.

Jesus arrived on the scene and, in his own name, claimed God's power to forgive in the here and now. Why would anyone be surprised over the rancor of the scribes? Jesus claimed and assumed for himself God's divine power and authority. To the Jewish leaders, this was blasphemy. The reader is given a foretaste of Jesus' trial, in which the charge of blasphemy will be leveled against him.

The scribes simply do not see Christ as the fulfillment of messianic prophecy. They fail to see what is happening under their antagonistic noses. The reign of God, evidenced by the remission of sins, was being established in their midst yet they were blind to it.

The fact that Mark inserted this issue in the midst of this healing story is an indication that Mark's own community was struggling with their Jewish neighbors over this same controversial issue. Jesus' power to forgive sins is a sign of the eschatological reign of God established in their midst, the fulfillment realized in the death and resurrection of Christ. It is only through the eyes of faith that believers can understand the fullness of God's power and authority in and through Jesus Christ. Furthermore, when believers live the gospel and embrace the paschal mystery of Christ, they too share in the healing and forgiving ministry of Jesus.

Thus, this gospel event also underscored and gave credence to the church's claim that it had been given the authority of Jesus to continue his ministry of reconciliation. The Jewish community simply could not reconcile such a claim. Tension was fierce.

In today's story a group of people brought the paralytic to Jesus for healing. People of the ancient world were bound to one another by bonds of loyalty. The word "faith" in today's pericope is better translated "loyalty." Loyalty of this ancient sort meant that people stood by one another through thick and thin. Jesus was moved by the loyalty of this group, which so tenaciously sought the healing of their friend. This loyal group would not be deterred from their appointed task, no matter what the danger to themselves. They would seek Christ so their paralytic friend might be restored.

Through laborious effort, the friends of the paralytic man lowered him through the roof so Jesus could minister to him. The paralytic did not ask for healing. His friends did the bidding for him. The paralytic's friends are the ones who moved Jesus to compassion. Their faith, solidarity, and creativity were enough to catch Jesus' attention. As a result, Jesus healed and cured the man who was presented to him.

In the Books of Leviticus and Deuteronomy the physical condition of the paralytic disallowed him from offering the bread of God. People with such maladies were, in essence, excluded from the community. The social consequence was far worse than the condition itself. Jesus' healing of the paralytic raised another issue for the onlookers and readers. Jesus forgave the man the debt code he was subject to as a result of his condition. It was believed that lack of bodily wholeness was the result of the person's sin, or if inherited at birth, the sins of his or her parents. As a maimed individual, the man was denied access to the communal life of Israel. Jesus forgave his debt and restored his full personhood. He restored the paralytic to wholeness.

Jesus was posing the ultimate questions to his onlookers. Which was more difficult—to completely heal the paralytic or to forgive his sins and thus restore him to the community? "In today's episode, Jesus phrased it thus: 'Which is easier to say to the paralytic, Your sins are forgiven' [repairing the social condition], or to say 'Rise, take up your mat and walk' [repairing the physical condition; v. 9]? Clearly his culture sees restoration to normal function as easier to achieve than restoring someone to full membership in the community."[6]

In antiquity restoring someone to health following illness was considered a cure. When meaning was restored to the life of the afflicted one, his or her family, and the community, it was considered a healing. Complete cures are rare, healing is plentiful. Everyone is the beneficiary of God's merciful healing.

In this case, Jesus healed and cured the paralytic. First, Jesus healed him, restoring him to the community and helping him find meaning for his life. Jesus offered the hand of reconciliation through the forgiveness of the man's sins and invited the healed man into intimate relationship. Jesus called him "son," thereby restoring him to his proper status in Jesus' family-like community. Jesus also cured the man by removing his physical condition.

Jesus healed and cured the man and the crowd was moved to glorify and praise God. The scribes were no doubt perturbed because Jesus took it upon himself to act on behalf of God. Where did he get such authority? Who did he think he was anyway? Only God forgives sins; only God can remit debt. The scribes were not pretending to uphold God's sovereignty in this exchange with Jesus. They were angry over their own loss of power. As agents of the Torah, they were the brokers of debt reduction. Therefore, much was at stake. They were not about to lose their religious control over the people so they leveled the worst charge against Jesus. They accused him of blasphemy.

In Matthew's and Luke's version of this story the paralytic is on a "bed" rather than a "mat." Mark's paralytic is on a mat, which alerts the reader to his social status. The fact that he is lowered on a mat indicates that the paralytic man is poor. The word used for mat indicates a poor man's mattress or perhaps a soldier's bed roll. In this ancient group-centered culture, the health and well-being of rich and poor alike is the concern of all the members of the community. Yet Mark shows special concern for the poor throughout the gospel. They are always a presence throughout Jesus' ministry. They are usually the ones who were considered outcasts and sinners. The poor were considered part of Jesus' own community. They were never openly chastised or given any special instructions or conditions. They were generally alienated from the religious leadership and thus were strongly aligned with Jesus in his struggles with the Jewish authorities.[7] The poor had a special place in Jesus' heart and in his work.

Mark demands that all disciples take a stand. Reader and onlooker are challenged to choose.

---

[6] CWJB, 38.

[7] BSM, 158.

Who is this man and from where does his power flow? Will we stand with the scribes, those in power, and those who cling to formalism, or will we stand with the poor, disenfranchised, and powerless who know only too well who this Christ really is?

Mark introduced the apocalyptic term "Son of Man" from the Book of Daniel in today's gospel. In the prophetic work of Daniel, the Son of Man enjoys special power over all creation and will one day come to judge the world—saint and sinner alike. Believers, readers, and onlookers are forced to decide. Is this the One? Is Jesus the Son of Man who will come to judge the world? We are given plenty of evidence, but the decision is forged in freedom in the heart of every believer.

Proclaim the gospel again.

Sometimes we gain new insights when we hear the text after the interpretation is given. Someone from the group proclaims the gospel a second time.

STEP 4
TESTING

Conversation with the Liturgy and the Scriptures

Test your original understanding in dialogue with the text.

(You might consider breaking into smaller groups.)

Now that you've heard the exegesis, were there any new insights? How do you feel about it? How does your original understanding of this gospel compare with what we just shared? How does this story speak to your life?

Sharing Life Experience

Participants share an experience from their lives that connects with the biblical interpretation just presented.

> *Jesus healed the paralytic and restored him to the community. He broke the chains of oppressive authority and healed and cured the paralytic. What does that have to say to me, today?*

I have experienced much healing in my life. We prayed for my parents to be cured. They were not cured, but they were healed. We were all healed. My family was bound closer together through the death and dying process of my mother, who died on Easter Sunday, and my father, who died on Easter Monday two years later. Both of them were healed in the midst of their process of dying. They found tremendous meaning for their lives. They shared love and reconciliation, and bid their final farewells to their daughters whom they adored.

The paralytic who was lowered by friends through the roof so Jesus would heal him reminds me of two other significant events in our lives. In these two events the community lowered the mat, upheld in prayer, and summoned the heavens not just for healing but for a cure. Our best friend was at death's door. The father of young children, he was dying of chicken pox that he contracted from his five-year-old. The chicken pox lodged in his lungs and he was given a 20 percent chance of survival. We kept vigil, we prayed, we camped out in the waiting room of intensive care. All of us experienced the healing power of Christ present in the midst of a loyal, praying community. Our friend was healed and he was cured. He was restored to complete health.

Four months later we kept the same vigil with my husband, whose appendix burst and caused the onset of peritonitis. Again, the outcome was touch and go. We prayed for a cure, the community rallied. Not only was my husband cured, but again we were all healed. Our wonder at the power of God at work in the community was once again renewed.

We have often reflected on what it must be like for those who suffer similar situations but who have no one to stand with them, watch with them, or pray with them. Jesus restored people to the community. He restored people to wholeness.

I am reminded of a funeral many years ago of a young man who died from AIDS. He was not cured, but the entire family experienced the healing love of God. Christ was so present to their pain. The way in which the parents of this young man responded to their son and to who he was reminds me of Jesus in today's gospel. They went out of their way to make sure that everyone knew how much they loved and accepted their son and they demon-

strated that acceptance in word and deed. They opened their arms and their hearts, and the entire funeral experience was for his friends. Our culture would tell us to shun the dying young man. Some in the church would shake their heads and look upon him as an outcast. (Someone recently told me the story of a mother who bemoaned the fact that her daughter was sleeping with men for money and her son was a homosexual. She blatantly announced at a church meeting that she was certain that her daughter was saved but that her son was damned to eternal hellfire.)

Yet Michael's parents loved unconditionally and, like Jesus, restored him to the life of the community even in the midst of his death. They were proud parents as they brought their son to the church for the last time for his funeral liturgy. They testified to the presence of Christ in their son. They shared with us his zest for life and his love of people. Their love reconciled him to the community. There was no shame. Their love and acceptance had restorative power.

The message today for me and for the community is a reminder that we are all beneficiaries of God's healing, restorative, and transforming love. The power of that love demands that we tear down structures that are barriers to healing and wholeness in the lives of all humanity. When we participate in structures that exclude people from our communities in any way, we are not living the spirit of today's gospel. To be an agent of Christ's healing means that I must reach out to the poor and disenfranchised and extend Christ's compassion to them just as we extended it at the bedside of our dear, dying friend.

What was Mark trying to tell his community? In what way does this gospel challenge your community today? In what way has this conversation with the scriptures for today's liturgy invited change in your life? How might you relate the paralytic's situation to today's world? Who are the people that are excluded from communities because of some condition? What does this gospel have to say to them and to your response to them? Is there anything in this gospel exegesis that your community especially needs to hear at this time? In what way are the biblical themes of covenant, exodus, creation, and community evident in today's readings? Do you still feel the same way about this text as when you began? Has your original understanding been stretched, challenged, or affirmed?

STEP 5
DECISION

The gospel demands a response.

In what concrete ways might your parish be invited to respond? Are there any attitudes or behaviors you would like to change as a result of today's conversation? What one concrete action will you take this week in response to the liturgy today?

Pastoral Considerations: Who are the paralytics in your community? Who are the ones that are excluded in any way from full life and wholeness in your community? What might you do to welcome them and restore them to wholeness like Jesus did in today's gospel? Today's liturgy is a reminder to us that part of our ministry to God's people is to offer the sacraments of healing and reconciliation to our communities on a regular basis. How often do we provide opportunity for our communities to gather to pray for healing? How often do our communities come together to celebrate the sacrament of reconciliation? Does it occur only once or twice a year? Perhaps there is need for more frequent celebrations of the sacrament of reconciliation. Perhaps your community might gather every month, or every other month, to pray for healing for the sick members of the community. A couple of times a year the sacrament of the anointing of the sick should be celebrated in the parish. The *Book of Blessings* contains blessing prayers for many of life's hurtful, needful situations. Today's liturgy is an invitation to use the gifts and charisms that have been given to us to build up and restore the Body of Christ.

Christian Initiation: If there anyone ready to celebrate a rite of full communion in the Catholic Church, or a rite of acceptance or welcome? Lent is fast approaching. Has your catechumenal community been diligent in its ministry of discernment for those who will be celebrating the rite of election and subsequently initiated at the Easter Vigil? This should be an ongoing endeavor that should be coming to some closure at this time.

DOCTRINAL ISSUES

What Church truth/teaching/doctrinal issue could be drawn from the gospel for the seventh Sunday of Ordinary Time?

Participants suggest possible doctrinal themes that flow from the readings.

Possible Doctrinal Themes

Jesus Christ—Son of Man; Jesus Christ—Messiah; healing ministry of Christ; forgiveness of sins; sacrament of anointing of the sick; sacrament of reconciliation; social justice; reign of God

Present the doctrinal material at this time.

1. The facilitator gives input on a particular doctrinal issue of his or her prior choosing. OR
2. The group chooses a doctrinal issue from the list they created. They read together from the Doctrinal Appendix or other appropriate, official Church documents and the works of respected theologians.

(Many doctrinal issues are found in the Doctrinal Appendix at the back of this workbook. If you are choosing an issue from this resource, please refer to it now.)

Reflection questions centered around the chosen doctrinal theme can be found at the end of each topic in the Doctrinal Appendix. The questions are based on the five-step reflection process. If you choose a topic not included in the Doctrinal Appendix, craft your own questions according to the same five-step process.

Following the reflection questions you will be reminded to return to chapter 7, "Preparing the Catechetical Session," to assist you in crafting your own session.

Closing Prayer

Lord and God,
you know the secrets of our hearts
and reward us for the good we do.
Look kindly on the efforts and the progress of
   your servants.
Strengthen them on their way,
increase their faith,
and accept their repentance.
Open to them your goodness and justice
and lead them to share in your sacraments on
   earth,
until they finally enjoy your presence in heaven.
We ask this through Christ our Lord.[8]

---

[8]RCIA 94, "Prayers of Exorcism—F."

499

EIGHTH SUNDAY IN ORDINARY TIME

Environment

It is now summer Ordinary Time. Your catechetical environment might include the colors of and images of spring and early summer harvest. If at all possible, include fresh flowers and plants in the catechetical environment along with candle, Lectionary, and cross.

INTRODUCTORY RITES

Entrance Antiphon (or Opening Song)

The Lord has been my strength; he has led me into freedom. He saved me because he loves me. (Ps 17:19–20)[1]

Opening Prayer

The facilitator of the session may lead the prayer. Others in the group may be asked to proclaim the readings.

Let us pray
that the peace of Christ may find welcome in the world

> *Pause for silent prayer.*

Father in heaven,
form us in the likeness of your Son
and deepen his life within us.
Send us as a witness of gospel joy
into a world of fragile peace and broken promises.
Touch the hearts of all men with your love
that they in turn may love one another.
We ask this through Christ our Lord.[2]

LITURGY OF THE WORD

The readings are proclaimed.

---

[1]Eighth Sunday in Ordinary Time: "Entrance Antiphon," *The Sacramentary.*

[2]Eighth Sunday in Ordinary Time: "Opening Prayer," *The Sacramentary.*

First Reading
Hosea 2:16–17, 21–22

Overview of the Book of Hosea: Hosea was a prophet who preached in the northern kingdom of Israel. His prophetic ministry extended from about 786 to 746 B.C. (around the time of the fall of the northern kingdom). Hosea possessed a passion for the precepts of the covenant. The early chapters of the book seem to suggest that Hosea was in a marriage that caused him great grief. His wife was unfaithful. He used this painful situation to highlight how the covenant and the unconditional love of God for Israel were impacted by Israel's infidelity and sinfulness.

The book is divided into three sections. Section one (chs. 1–3), the prelude to the book, describes the broken marriage covenant between God and God's people. Section two (chs. 4–13) is a compilation of Hosea's oracles. Section three (ch. 14) proclaims a postjudgment vision of hope.

Hosea's message is one of justice and judgment. He denounced oppression of the poor and infidelity to the commandments. He demanded a return to a covenant relationship with God. Hosea portrays a God who is sorrowful over the sins of the people and who mourns over their need for correction and discipline. The prophet upholds fidelity, love, compassion, and a personal relationship with God. He denounces the pious churchgoer who worships God while continuing to live a vain, sinful life. Hosea insists that corporate amnesia and rebellion are the causes of the broken covenant. People forgot God's benevolent action in their history and chose instead to live reckless, materialistic, idol-worshiping lives. Hosea regards their rebellion as stupid. He continues to hold out the promise of hope and God's compassion. God's love is radical, personal, and unending. Israel's wanton hubris in the days prior to the fall stands in stark contrast to the God who is welcoming and forgiving. It is never too late to turn away from sin and toward God's love.

Today's Pericope: The relationship between God and the human family often reads like a modern-day soap opera. If one were to stop watching for a week, a month, a year, or years, it does not take much to "catch up" on events, because the plot is always the same—people struggle to live their love relationships, they sometimes fail, they sometimes succeed. The game of life, however, goes on and on. The history of God's relationship with humanity is similar. God invites people into faithful, covenant love. People sometimes respond, and sometimes they do not. People sometimes love God in return, and sometimes they turn away from God and worship other gods. Ultimately God never gives up on people, and for the most part, people try to stay "in the game of life" in relationship (or not) with their God.

God is all-mighty, all-powerful, and all-loving. At God's bidding, people are called into a contractual, covenant relationship with God. No other religion knows a deity such as this. God knows the power of his all-consuming love, and that it has the power to lure the sinner back into God's forgiving embrace. The marriage metaphor is an apt description of God's relationship with human beings. Marriage is based on a contractual, covenant, unbreakable love relationship between two people. The Book of Hosea and today's reading draw heavily on this metaphor to give insight into this love relationship. God is not a bridegroom in denial. He knows well the unfaithfulness of his people and is distressed and wounded by them. They left his embrace in the desert and prostituted themselves to other gods that offered empty promises. Hosea draws from his own human experience to get inside the heart of how God must feel when his people are unfaithful. Yet God will romance his people back into the safety and intimacy of the marriage he shares with his people. God will never give up on us.

The reading from Hosea was chosen for its connection with today's gospel, which also employs the marriage metaphor.

Responsorial Psalm
Psalm 103:1–2, 3–4, 8, 10, 12–13

Today's psalm is one of the most familiar psalms of thanksgiving in the entire psalter. The psalmist's hymn of thanks because of an answered prayer (perhaps healing from sickness) became a prayer of praise for the entire community. He understands his experience of healing to be an image of the restoration of God's people, Israel, throughout salvation history. The psalm expresses thanks for God's mercy and kindness manifested particularly in the forgiveness of sins.[3]

Second Reading
2 Corinthians 3:1–6

(Refer to second Sunday in Ordinary Time for overview of Paul's letter to the Corinthians.)

Today's Pericope: Paul's letter is sometimes referred to as the first apology. Paul visited Corinth. After his visit, he received word that false teachers had arrived on the scene. They tried to discredit Paul and his work. They suggested that he did not have the appropriate credentials to do the ministry he claimed to do in the name of Christ. It was customary in antiquity for traveling preachers to take with them letters of recommendation attesting to the preachers' accomplishments. The letter would contain testimonials of miracles, healing, ecstasies, and spiritual phenomena that would suggest the success of the preacher's ministry. The false teachers intimated that since Paul did not have such letters, his authority and ministry were not to be trusted and carried no weight.

Paul defended his ministry and unveiled the arrogance of his antagonists. Paul insisted that proof of the efficacy of his ministry lie not in letters of recommendation, but in the very people he ministered to. The people were living letters, living witnesses and testimonials to the authority and power of Paul's ministry—and ultimately to the redeeming power of the risen Christ. Paul introduced them to the living Christ. "All will recognize these Christians as a letter which Christ has composed and published, using Paul as his instrument."[4] What further recommendation was needed?

Paul reminded his readers that even though the Law was inspired by the Spirit and written on stone, it was nevertheless inanimate. The Corinthian con-

[3] *PL*, 305–306.
[4] *SEPC*, 43.

verts, on the other hand, were living beings whose very lives proclaimed the gospel of Christ. They were literary masterpieces who revealed Christ through the power of the Spirit. They were the only letters of recommendation needed.

Christians of all generations are to be such masterpieces. "It is the duty of every Christian to remember that his life should be an epistle 'known and read of all men,' so sincere, so true, so honest, that in it all men will see the handiwork, the touch, the impress of the Spirit of the living God, witnessing to the glory and grace of Christ."[5]

The gospel is proclaimed.

Gospel
Mark 2:18–22

STEP 1
NAMING ONE'S EXPERIENCE

What were your first impressions? What was your first response to the gospel (or the other readings)? What captured your attention?

Each person names his or her initial impression. Statements should be brief. No reasons should be given at this time. All simply listen without agreeing or disagreeing.

STEP 2
UNDERSTANDING

In a brief statement, explain what you think this gospel is trying to convey.

STEP 3
INPUT FROM VISION/STORY/TRADITION

Liturgical Context

Today's gospel and liturgy comprise the second part of a four-part sequence (refer to the seventh

---
[5]Ibid., 44.

Sunday in Ordinary Time, Liturgical Context). Tension continues to mount in Jesus' ministry. Onlookers and readers are faced with the decision: Will I accept Jesus' authority? Will I accept the reign he came to establish? It is a time of decision.

Every liturgy is an opportunity and a time of decision. Every liturgy invites the participants to accept the living Word of God and be changed by it. Every liturgy invites God's people to be transformed and to live in the newly established reign of Christ.

We are there and it is now when we proclaim Mark's gospel that invites his ancient readers to decide and to choose. Is this the Son of God? Where will we stand?

The Entrance Antiphon for today's liturgy asserts the power of the Lord to save and to strengthen his people. This was certainly an expectation of the Messiah. Today's gospel is an affirmation that Jesus is the "One Who Is to Come." He is the One Who Saves.

As the wedding feast is a symbol of joy in the scriptures and as Christ referred to himself today as the "Bridegroom," the opening prayer quite powerfully echoes Jesus' theme in the gospel. This is not a time for sorrow. We are to pray that God will send us out in the world with gospel joy to witness to the power of Christ and to gather all people in love to his loving embrace.

The Great Bridegroom desires nothing less than the offering of our entire beings. We are to rejoice in the intimacy that Jesus suggests in today's gospel. We are not to fast in the presence of the Bridegroom, because fasting is for mourning and anticipation. We can do no less than feast when in his presence. Eucharist is that feast for us. The liturgy is that bountiful cup that pours out the bridal feast upon souls hungering for freedom to love. St. Augustine eloquently reflects our hunger for God and where we find satisfaction for that hunger.

> It is with doubtful knowledge, Lord, but with utter certainty that I love you. You have stricken my heart with your word and I have loved You. And indeed heaven and

earth and all that is in them tell me wherever I look that I should love You....

But what is it that I love when I love you? Not the beauty of any bodily thing, nor the order of seasons, not the brightness of light that rejoices the eye, nor the sweet melodies of all songs, nor the sweet fragrance of flowers and ointments and spices: not manna nor honey, not the limbs that carnal love embraces. None of these things do I love in loving my God. Yet in a sense I do love light and melody and fragrance and food and embrace when I love my God—the light and the voice and the fragrance and the food and the embrace in the soul, when the light shines upon my soul which no place can contain, that voice sounds which no time can take from me, I breathe that fragrance which no wind scatters, I eat the food which is not lessened by eating, and I lie in the embrace which satiety never comes to sunder. This it is that I love, when I love my God.[6]

Jesus addresses the issue of fasting in today's gospel. Fasting is a discipline rooted in biblical tradition. Jesus does not set out to abolish the tradition of fasting known by his contemporaries. He did not come to abolish the Law; he came to fulfill it. Jesus simply breathed new life and meaning into the understanding of it.

Fasting was intended as prayer and supplication in anticipation of the coming Messiah. "All forms of fasting, all ascetical and penitential practices that the Church continues to observe, all states of life, the liturgy itself, have in common this qualification, this fundamental dimension: the active expectation of the Lord who has come and is coming."[7]

Gospel Exegesis

The facilitator provides input from critical biblical scholarship on this text. The input includes insights as to how people would have heard the gospel in Jesus' time.

---

[6]*CONF.* 10.6
[7]*DL* (V), 77.

Mark cleverly couches the theme of today's gospel in a dialogue of Jesus in which the point of the story is not really the point of the story. Jesus addresses the issue of fasting, which was a common religious practice. Jesus was not suggesting a halt to this asceticism but simply a reorientation in focus. Why and for what purpose did he take on this issue? Fasting is not the underlying issue of this dialogue.

In earlier exchanges Jesus challenged the priestly scribes and the way in which they regulated the debt code, thereby oppressing and controlling the people's access to the Temple and to the community. The Pharisees were another matter. Pharisaic Judaism was a lay movement whose sole project was to regulate the religious life and pastor the people of God. The Sadducees were a sect comprised primarily of chief priests and the aristocracy. They believed that holiness was an essential ingredient in the preservation of the nation of Israel. They enjoined strict purity regulations on those serving at the Temple. Lesser priests were required to observe the same strict codes when they gave their two-week tour of duty each year at the Temple. Sadducees believed that the average Israelite need only observe the strict codes when they entered the Court of the Israelites to offer their sacrifices. The Sadducees stood guard over everything and everyone that entered the Temple in order to ensure the preservation of holiness.

The Pharisees were a sect devoted to studying the written Law. They passed down the oral tradition and interpreted it for the people. They taught the people how to apply the Law to their everyday experience. The Pharisees embraced all the holiness laws in relation to the Temple. They took the laws a step further than the Sadducees, however. They insisted that the ritual purity codes apply to Israelites at all times, not just when they entered the Temple. Pharisees believed that every Israelite was also a priest. Since every priest was enjoined to keep free from defilement, so, too, were all Israelites to remain from such defilement. Therefore, all Israelites were to keep the purity regulations. Since priests were required to ritually wash their hands before meals so as not to become defiled, so, therefore must all Jews do the same before every meal, for the same reason. In this way they would remain untainted by contact with something or someone that might be unclean. This was intended as a protection from unsuspected contact with an unclean gentile.

Most Israelites were peasants—simple, ordinary folk. They followed the codes when they went to the Temple for festivals. Few of them had the time, money, or energy to carry them out the way the Pharisees insisted they be observed. Other Sabbath and Temple rules were ignored by the Jews as well. Tithes were often ignored and many Jews had contact with the gentiles in the marketplace. Thus, the Pharisees considered anyone who ignored the ritual codes to be "sinners."[8]

Lest we be too critical of these codes, they did serve Judaism well. They helped keep Judaism from being absorbed into the dominant Greek culture of the day. "By keeping themselves separate from the Gentiles, the Jews maintained their beliefs and practices. At the same time, they sought to be an example of purity for the nations. The Jewish nation hoped that eventually the gentile nations would be drawn to Jerusalem as the place of justice and true worship."[9]

Jesus challenged the very codes intended to bind the nation together. Mark's gospel constantly paints the picture of the Jewish nation and Jesus who challenges it. Jesus is the holy one; he was proclaimed so at his baptism. Throughout Jesus' ministry he moved into the sphere of the unholy ("he became sin"). He literally "took it on." Jesus risked ritual defilement. "Through the agency of the Holy Spirit upon Jesus, God enters the arena of impurity without regard to the risk of defilement."[10]

How might a contemporary reader begin to understand the purity codes when they are so foreign to our understanding? Cultural anthropologist Mary Douglas sheds light on the concept. She maintains that purity has to do with the proper order of things—a place for everything and everything in its place in the order of creation. The culture establishes boundaries for itself. Things that do not fit are out of place and out of order; they

are polluted. Dirt is out of place because it is not where it belongs—in the soil. Israel classified people, animals, things, and objects in terms of holiness. Purity implies order and a proper, rightful place for things. Impurity or pollution implies that something does not belong—is out of order and has no place. By keeping the purity codes people cooperated with the harmony of creation and participated in the experience of order for their own lives.

There are two concepts embedded within the notion of holiness—wholeness and set-apartness. Everything must be completely whole within its own classification. For example, human beings are not to have deformities and animals may not be tainted with blemishes. People with deformities were not allowed in the Temple; animals with blemishes were not fit as sacrifices. Fish, cattle, and doves were considered clean and would not pollute the people who consumed them. They were considered normal. Eels, pigs, and ostriches were not considered normal. Such animals, when eaten, polluted those who consumed them.

Gentiles were considered unclean because they did not fit in the Jewish system. Things that were in their place were considered holy; if out of place, they were unholy. For example, things that belonged in the body were holy as long as they were in the body. When they were no longer in the body, they were defiled. The spilling or display of blood, spit, and semen was therefore considered unclean. Thus, menstruating women were believed to be defiled and in turn defiled anyone who came in contact with them. Lepers were unclean because the boils on their bodies were in danger of bursting, thereby spilling an unclean liquid (pus). Certain places were considered holy and could be entered only by those so designated. Gentiles were put to death for entering the Holy of Holies and women were only allowed in the place designated for them.

The authorities supported this purity code system of the Jewish nation. Jesus clashed with it. He constantly crossed boundaries and borders, and entered the world of the unclean. He touched unholy people, places, and things. Jesus sought to break through the limiting boundaries in order to bring the outcast within its borders. Jesus and his

---

[8]*MAM*, 148.
[9]Ibid., 149.
[10]Ibid.

followers desired to bring the reign of God to those who previously had no access.[11]

Jesus challenged the promulgation of codes that placed some of God's people within the system and some outside the system. The Pharisees set themselves up as regulators of religious practice and table fellowship—an integral part of Israel's social life. Jesus challenged any and all obstacles put in the path of people's quest for and approach to God.[12]

In verse 16 (not in this pericope), Mark strangely introduces the Pharisees as "scribes of the Pharisees." He links the Pharisees with his earlier antagonists, the priests and the scribes. Mark's literary device lumps all the antagonists in one basket—scribes, priests, Pharisees—all are in the same ruling classes and all oppose Jesus' establishment of the kingdom. Mark postulates a couched accusation that the people they served were not the Pharisees' first priority. Mark implies that they were more concerned with regulating the laws of table fellowship and religious piety in order to secure and maintain their own dominant status. By determining who could dine at table and who could be excluded, the Pharisees exerted power and lorded it over the people they pretended to shepherd. Jesus would have none of it. He saw through their hypocrisy.

Thus, in today's pericope, Jesus defends the fact that his disciples do not follow the recognized fast days like the disciples of the Pharisees and of John. The Law only required fasting on the Day of Atonement. The primary theme of Hebraic fasting was "self-humiliation." It was a public practice. People fasted in front of God and God's people. The purpose of fasting was to challenge others into action. "The one fasting is begging for assistance from others without ever saying so explicitly in words. Fasting speaks louder than words."[13] Fasting on the Day of Atonement was for the purpose of moving God to forgive the sins of those who fasted. Pharisees went far beyond the prescriptions of the Law. They fasted on Mondays and Thursdays as well as on days that commemorated

historical events. Sometimes when they fasted the Pharisees put on an ostentatious show by donning makeup in order to look haggard from their rigorous asceticism.

Jesus' response regarding the issue of fasting draws on apocalyptic metaphors—"Bridegroom" and "on that day." Both are images of the messianic reign and the last days. Both images point the reader to Mark's main theme—the Passion and death of Christ, which ultimately ushers in the messianic age. The wedding banquet was an image used to depict joy in the messianic age. Nowhere in scripture is the Messiah referred to as a bridegroom. However, Yahweh was referred to as a *husband* to his covenant people. When Jesus referred to himself as a Bridegroom he put himself on a par with Yahweh.[14] Thus, the wedding banquet and Bridegroom represent joy and fasting represents sorrow. Feasting joy is the order of the day; soon enough sorrow will come—Jesus will die and the Bridegroom will leave.

Jesus posits an apocalyptic dualism in his reference to the two ages. The phrase, "new (*kainos*) age," referred to in the gospel is a reference to the "making of all things new" that will occur in the last age. It is an eschatological term. Jesus intends to show the sharp contrast between the kingdom he came to establish and its social order versus the hypocritical "cosmetic social piety of the Pharisaic holiness code."[15] Mark is challenging his young eschatological Christian community not to be impressed or lured by a false piety that may look worthy and progressive, but which in fact is no different than other oppressive legalistic structures that continue to oppress the people of God. "To do so would jeopardize the messianic project, represented by images of a 'worst tear.' And 'the wine and skins will both be lost.' The 'new wine' will later be revealed by Mark as the genuine social practice of nonviolent love."[16]

The tension Mark creates is between those who are able to read the sign of the times and recognize the "Bridegroom," and those who find his behavior scandalous. The Jesus movement cannot be

---

[11]Ibid., 151–152.

[12]*BSM*, 158.

[13]*CWJB*, 41.

[14]*MK*, 34

[15]*BSM*, 159.

[16]Ibid.

boxed in by the restraints of old Judaism. The ultimate question is raised for readers and onlookers—"Is this really the Bridegroom?" "If we are truly in the last age, are we still to fast?"

The pericope also provides evidence of tension between two groups of people. It refers to the "disciples of the Pharisees." The Pharisees did not have disciples. John the Baptist did. There was sometimes tension between the followers of John the Baptist and the followers of Jesus. Some of John's followers believed that John was the Messiah. The gospel is clear. Jesus' followers are no longer to follow John's vision. John's followers fasted. John fasted so the people would pay attention to his warnings that the coming reign was upon them. John is now considered part of the "old religion," the old garment and old wineskins. Jesus set out on his own after John was placed in prison. The hallmark of Jesus' ministry was the healing power of God. This convinced Jesus that the kingdom of God had already arrived—"indeed God is already rescuing his people. If this is so, there is no need for self-humiliation to persuade God to act."[17] Mark insists that the new religion of Christianity is not something that can be superimposed on the old religion of Judaism. It is independent of it. "The new spirit is not a piece added to the old nor a new element poured into the old: it [Christianity] is a vivifying force which transforms the abiding teaching of the old revelation."[18]

Today's gospel is not a sermon on the merits of fasting. Mark's concern is eschatological. Today's pericope is a commentary or a midrash on Jesus, the Messiah, the *One Who Has Come*, the One who established the last age—the eschatological kingdom of God on earth. Jesus ushers in the new reign and a new vision and with it sharp conflict between himself and the religious authorities. We are to stay tuned for further conflict as the plot thickens.

Proclaim the gospel again.

Sometimes we gain new insights when we hear the text after the interpretation is given. Someone from the group proclaims the gospel a second time.

---

[17] *CWJB*, 41.
[18] *MK*, 35.

Conversation with the Liturgy and the Scriptures

Test your original understanding in dialogue with the text.

(You might consider breaking into smaller groups.)

Now that you've heard the exegesis, were there any new insights? How do you feel about it? How does your original understanding of this gospel compare with what we just shared? How does this story speak to your life?

Sharing Life Experience

Participants share an experience from their lives that connects with the biblical interpretation just presented.

> *Mark's Jesus cuts to the heart of the matter and invites readers ancient and contemporary to cut away the trappings of our false selves and look straight into our hearts. He looks hypocrisy in the eye and names conscious and unconscious motives in the lives of people of power in order to cut away obstacles that keep people from having access to God.*

> *As a person in ministry I often ask myself if we are not sometimes guilty of replacing wornout legalisms of the past with legalisms dressed up in more progressive, rubrical attire. Day in and day out I meet people who come to our doors honestly seeking the living God and yet have to face obstacles put in their way by the very people whose job it is to assist them in their search. People do not often fit into our neat and tidy programs because they come to us with histories of pain and brokenness. How we deal with those realities requires the wisdom of Solomon and the patience of Job. Sometimes our sacramental programs are extremely Jansenistic. In the interest of providing good catechesis we sometimes insist that the free gift of grace somehow has to be earned. Someone told me the story of a mother who went to her parish seeking first communion for her mentally challenged teenage son. Her child expressed a desire to receive communion. He was quite certain that Jesus was present in the elements of bread and wine. However, he was not capable of any academic proficiency. This young man was*

promised that if he would memorize the Lord's Prayer, the Hail Mary, and other key prayers he would be allowed to receive communion. When this mentally challenged young man arrived for his test, he fumbled and failed his oral quiz. He was instructed to go back and do a better job of memorization on the prayers he failed to recite. He was then told to come back next year and add the Creed to the list of things to memorize. If he passed his test the following year, he would be allowed to receive Holy Communion. Need we ask what Christ's response would have been to this young man? We already know. "Bring the children to me and do not hinder them."

If someone's life does not fit the demands of our structured programs, we often shut the door on them and ask them to come back tomorrow when their lives are ready for our programs. Christ invited everyone to the feast. No one was excluded. We have been given the sacred trust of discernment when it comes to access to the sacramental life of the church. We are bound by the tradition of our own ecclesial community. Such discernment carries with it, however, a tremendous sense of responsibility and an absolute exercise of humility. Jesus plucks the demon of hypocrisy from our hearts and demands that our motives be pure and not driven by unconscious motives of greed, pride, and control. Jesus questioned the motives of his contemporaries, the Pharisees. In the process, he questions us as well.

Over and over again I have seen the fruits of a loving, unconditional pastoral response to people who come seeking the living God, yet who come with grave, pressing needs. One situation stands out in my memory. Many years ago a woman came with a devastating, lifelong debilitating disease. All of her life she required constant, costly medical attention in order to stay alive. Many years before she found the love of her life and entered into a committed relationship with this young man. They were never able to legally marry because she would lose her medical care if she were to do so. Thus, this man and woman built a life and together they parented two lovely children. After a few years, God exploded into their lives. They began their quest for Christ, for community, and, above all, for the Lord's table.

Here is where our community entered the picture. Officially we could do nothing for this couple. They still could not get legally married as they did not

have the financial ability to pay for her excessive medical bills in light of her increasing failing health. Here was a family hungering for the ministry of the Church, yet it seemed as if we were powerless. How would Jesus have responded to this family? We know he railed against unjust structures and systems that bound and oppressed people. We also know that Jesus railed against obstacles and undue burdens placed on people in their quest for God. Jesus consistently and creatively offered the gift of life to those who came to him in faith, while also upholding the spirit of the Law. That same challenge exists for us today.

Solutions to this situation are not grist for this public forum. Pastorally working with this family instead of turning them away with no options was certainly in keeping with the spirit of today's gospel. New wine was poured into old wineskins that perhaps would have required that this family seek Christ in some other ecclesial tradition, when indeed their hearts belonged to ours. As we celebrated the funeral liturgy of this woman a year later, I pondered the good fruit of drinking new wine with this special family and I was very thankful and awed by the work of God in their lives.

What was Mark trying to tell his community? In what way does this gospel challenge your community today? How might the issue of fasting and its underlying agenda have anything to do with our contemporary communities? How might the tension between followers of Jesus and John speak to our contemporary communities today? In what way has this conversation with the scriptures for today's liturgy invited change in your life? In what way are the biblical themes of covenant, exodus, creation, and community evident in today's readings? Do you still feel the same way about this text as when you began? Has your original understanding been stretched, challenged, or affirmed?

STEP 5
DECISION

The gospel demands a response.

In what concrete way might your parish be invited to respond? Are there any attitudes or behaviors you would like to change as a result of today's conversation? What one concrete action will you take this week in response to the liturgy today?

Christian Initiation: Is there anyone ready to celebrate rites—acceptance, welcome, anointing of catechumens, reception into full communion of the Catholic Church?

DOCTRINAL ISSUES

What Church truth/teaching/doctrinal issue could be drawn from the gospel for the eighth Sunday in Ordinary Time?

Participants suggest possible doctrinal themes that flow from the readings.

Possible Doctrinal Themes

God's covenant relationship with humanity; reign of God; messianic reign; Jesus Christ; salvation history; eschatology; disciplines of prayer, fasting, and almsgiving; sacrament of marriage

Present the doctrinal material at this time.

1. The facilitator gives input on a particular doctrinal issue of his or her prior choosing. OR
2. The group chooses a doctrinal issue from the list they created. They read together from the Doctrinal Appendix or other appropriate, official Church documents and the works of respected theologians.

(Many doctrinal issues are found in the Doctrinal Appendix at the back of this workbook. If you are choosing an issue from this resource, please refer to it now.)

Reflection questions centered around the chosen doctrinal theme can be found at the end of each topic in the Doctrinal Appendix. The questions are based on the five-step reflection process. If you choose a topic not included in the Doctrinal Appendix, craft your own questions according to the same five-step process.

Following the reflection questions you will be reminded to return to chapter 7, "Preparing the Catechetical Session," to assist you in crafting your own session.

Closing Prayer

Lord,
you care for your people even when they stray.
Grant us a complete change of heart,
so that we may follow you with greater fidelity.
Grant this through Christ, our Lord.[19]

---

[19]"Prayers Over the People," #6, *The Sacramentary.*

NINTH SUNDAY IN ORDINARY TIME

Environment

See the eighth Sunday in Ordinary Time.

INTRODUCTORY RITES

Entrance Antiphon (or Opening Song)

O look at me and be merciful, for I am wretched and alone. See my hardship and my poverty, and pardon all my sins. (Ps 24:16, 18)[1]

Opening Prayer

The facilitator of the session may lead the prayer. Others in the group may be asked to proclaim the readings.

Let us pray

> *Pause for silent prayer.*

Father,
your love never fails.
Hear our call.
Keep us from danger
and provide for all our needs.
Grant this through our Lord
Jesus Christ, your Son,
who lives and reigns with you and the Holy Spirit,
one God for ever and ever.[2]

LITURGY OF THE WORD

The readings are proclaimed.

First Reading
Deuteronomy 5:12–15

Overview of the Book of Deuteronomy: The Book of Deuteronomy is in the form of an address. It is written as Moses' last speech to the people before they cross over the Jordan into the promised land. It is his farewell address to the Israel he led out of the bondage of Egypt through the Sinai desert. Moses delivered God's covenant to them. He also saved them from God's wrath due to their infidelity on numerous occasions.

Deuteronomy is different from the four other books of the Pentateuch. It contains long speeches and sermons, unlike Genesis and Exodus, which contain short stories and incidents. Deuteronomy was not written at the same time as the other books, but was a much later reflection of the ancient history of Moses and the people of Israel. The book demands that the people return to their covenant relationship with God. It places the exhortations in the mouth of Moses himself. (A common ancient practice involved placing words and exhortations in the mouth of an ancient, respected leader in order to bring that leader's authority to bear on the writer's material.) The purpose of the book was to exhort the people to return to the covenant living experienced under the leadership of Moses.

The book is divided into sections: a long preface, a restatement of the old covenant laws, and a final section containing the teaching of Moses and his blessing and death scene. The heart of Deuteronomy is the section containing the law code of Exodus and is therefore referred to as the second (deutero) law.

The second law code was written at a much later date, however. The situations in Deuteronomy reflect a nation that had grown since the days of exodus. A nation of small farmers had developed into a land of populated cities (evident during the later reign of the kings). There is also evidence in the book that a long time had passed since the liberation from Egypt. The book looks back and remembers the exodus and the covenant as completed events in the history of Israel.

One of the primary focuses of Deuteronomy is to look back on the covenant with a mind and a heart to return to it in faithfulness. The book ex-

---

[1] Ninth Sunday in Ordinary Time: "Entrance Antiphon," *The Sacramentary.*

[2] Ninth Sunday in Ordinary Time: "Opening Prayer," *The Sacramentary.*

horts the people to become more faithful than their ancestors had been in following the Law. There is a constant call to reform, to return to the covenant made with God. The election of Israel by God is an example of the special relationship that existed between God and the people of Israel. The book uses language reminiscent of language used in treaties between nations to describe the covenant between God and the people.

The central theme of the Law was the true worship of the one God, Creator of heaven and earth. The people were to reject all pagan idols. The relationship between God and Israel was summed up in the Shema—Israel's prayer—the heart and the creed of Judaism. "Hear, O Israel, the Lord our God is one Lord, and you shall love the Lord your God with all your heart and with all your soul and with all your strength" (Dt 6:4–5). Those words were to be handed on to their children, talked about in the house, bound on the hands and the forehead, and written on the doorpost. In other words, never to be forgotten!

The theology of Deuteronomy also extolls a single sanctuary in a place appointed by God (Jerusalem being the implied place). In addition, it upholds the importance of the right use of the land. Faithfulness and obedience to God will ensure a prosperous land. Disobedience and unfaithfulness will result in loss of the land, exile, and destruction. Sin leads to a curse. A curse ensures failure in war, in agriculture, and in preserving the one nation. If Israel fails to live the imperatives of justice, they will lose their right to the land. Their society will fail. Deuteronomy looks back at the history of Israel and explains it in terms of fidelity and infidelity to the covenant.

Today's Pericope: The Jewish feast of Sabbath celebrates incorporation in the community. Faithful observance was enjoined upon all Jewish people. The heart of Sabbath observance is the spirituality that undergirds it. One of the most uncompromising rules of Sabbath is the observation of the day of rest. This not only calls to mind the day Yahweh rested from the labors of creation, but also the liberation from slavery in Egypt.

Jesus was not reacting to the Sabbath rule of rest, but to the many oppressive statutes that had been added to the Law over the centuries. Jesus constantly challenged oppressive regulations that imposed undue burdens on people. The Sabbath is a day in which human beings honor their Creator. Approaching its observance requires pure intentions and proper motives. Overzealous additions to the Law and insistence on scrupulous adherence have the danger of reducing it to mere legalism, thereby overshadowing its spirit. The Sabbath is a spiritual matter. Observance is an act of faith in the God who is in covenant relationship with God's people.

God rested upon completion of his act of creation. God's people are to do likewise. They are to imitate their Creator and rest. Their rest is an act of worship. The Sabbath is a reminder that without God all human endeavor is useless. It is also an offering of one's life and work to God. The day is spent reflecting on the Law, the word of the prophets, God's greatness, God's benevolence in their lives, praying for God's intervention and for the coming of the kingdom.

The Sabbath remembers Israel's ultimate event of liberation—deliverance out of Egypt's slavery. Through the exodus event, God entered into a special relationship with Israel. In a supreme act of love, Yahweh gave Israel the Law, freedom from bondage, and the promise of a new land free from oppression and tyranny. Israel never enjoyed a day of rest as slaves in Egypt. They endured harsh, violent labor. A day of rest recalled (anamnesis) the rest they never enjoyed as slaves, but now as free people were to enjoy in complete freedom. The day of rest invited the recollection (anamnesis) that all life belongs to God and that material concerns are subordinate to one's relationship with God.

The day of rest also was not only enjoined upon Jews, but also upon all who were considered outside the loop of insiders. Slaves, foreigners, women, and beasts of burden were also to enjoy the Sabbath rest. This precept was intended to recall (anamnesis) the biblical justice established at the creation of the world. God created the world and entered into relationship with all God created. God willed that all creation live in perfect harmony and solidarity with all living things. Sabbath observance is a celebration and anamnesis of that harmony and solidarity. All creation takes time out to praise its Creator. St. Augustine reflects this in his *Confessions*:

And, what is this God? I asked the earth and it answered: "I am not He"; and all things that are in the earth made the same confession. I asked the sea and the deeps and the creeping things, and they answered: "We are not your God; seek higher." I asked the winds that blow, and the whole air with all that is in it answered: "Anaximenes (a philosopher) was wrong; I am not God." I asked the heavens, the sun, the moon, the stars, and they answered: "Neither are we God whom you seek." And I said to all the things that throng about the gateways of the senses: "Tell me of my God, since you are not He. Tell me something of Him." And they cried out in a loud voice: "He made us.'[3]

Today's first reading is chosen for its connection with the gospel. Jesus is in a heated debate with the religious authorities over issues surrounding the Sabbath.

Responsorial Psalm
Psalm 81:3–4, 5–6, 6–8, 10–11

The Feast of Tabernacles and the Passover were two yearly feasts that commemorated the exodus event. Today's psalm was appointed for liturgical use at the Feast of Tabernacles, thus its choice for today's liturgy. It is a perfect complement to the first reading.[4]

Second Reading
2 Corinthians 4:6–11

(See second Sunday in Ordinary Time for an overview of 2 Corinthians.)

Today's Pericope: Last week Paul (like Jesus today) was engaged in heated debate. Paul argued over his authority to preach the gospel. Paul did not point to miraculous signs to prove his authenticity, but rather to his ministry and ultimately to its fruit—the lives of the community he served. The Corinthian disciples of Christ who were living the gospel were all the proof he needed.

---

[3] *CONF.* 10.6
[4] *PL,* 308.

The gospel received in faith will be a light in the world by those who receive it. Christ, the Light who dispels the darkness, will manifest himself to those with hearts opened to receive it. Paul's conversion was a manifestation of the light of Christ, who manifested himself to Paul on the road to Damascus. Paul could either accept or reject the light that was piercing through to him midst the darkness. Paul accepted it and the rest is history.

Paul makes no mistake in today's reading. The manifestation of Christ's light is given to frail human persons. Rather than boasting of showy miracles, Paul instead brags about his weakness and the suffering he has endured. It is far more spectacular that Christ is revealed in the midst of human weakness and frailty. Paul's opponents boasted of miracles, great oratories, ecstasies, and credentials of great divine power. Paul insists that it is in the paradox of suffering that Christ is revealed. Paul insists that the miracles of Jesus are not his great claim to fame. The hallmark of Christ's life is his Passion and death. Herein lies the cause for boasting and rejoicing—certainly a stumbling block for those seeking flashy signs and showy miracles.

All but the cross of Christ stands in the shadows when it comes to the power of the Christ event. The cross proudly steps into the spotlight on the front and center stage of salvation history.

The gospel is proclaimed.

Gospel
Mark 2:23–3:6 or 23–28

STEP 1
NAMING ONE'S EXPERIENCE

What were your first impressions? What was your first response to the gospel (or the other readings)? What captured your attention?

Each person names his or her initial impression. Statements should be brief. No reasons should be given at this time. All simply listen without agreeing or disagreeing.

STEP 2
UNDERSTANDING

In a brief statement, explain what you think this gospel is trying to convey.

STEP 3
INPUT FROM VISION/STORY/TRADITION

Liturgical Context

The gospels for the seventh through the tenth Sundays in Ordinary Time form a compact unit. See the seventh Sunday in Ordinary Time, Liturgical Context, for an explanation of this four-part sequence.

Today we are reminded that Jesus calls us to embrace the spirit of the Law, not the letter of the Law. There is no inherent license to use this phrase as a sign that we are to frivolously pick and choose which laws we will observe and which laws we will break depending on the mood of the day. It is obvious that Jesus takes the Sabbath seriously. It is Jesus, the Messiah, who gives the authority to break the rules. It is not done at the initiative of the disciples.

Today's gospel reminds us that Jesus heard the pleas of suffering people and let no obstacles get in the way of answering those pleas. Today's Entrance Antiphon and the Opening Prayer reflect the longing of the human heart in the midst of sorrow, pain, and ambiguity. We can be thankful that Jesus did not allow the Law to keep him from touching people who needed healing.

The following essay on the Law is worthy of our reflection. "The law has its own uses in the ordering of the human community and in the discipline of the individual. But it is not an instrument of salvation, ultimately considered. Ultimately every fact of experience proves the simple gospel affirmations about the supremacy of grace to be true. We need both the power and the pardon of divine grace. We are not free to do good by our own resources. . . . The contradiction between man and God cannot be healed by any human contrivance. If the attempt is made, religion produces not the fruits of the spirit—not love, joy, and peace—but a frantic self-righteousness and a confusing self deception" (Reinhold Niebuhr).[5]

Gospel Exegesis

The facilitator provides input regarding critical biblical scholarship on this text. The input includes insights as to how people would have heard the gospel in Jesus' time.

The form of this story is one of pronouncement with its inherent threefold structure: setting, action, and pronouncement. The setting is the stroll through the grainfields by the disciples, the subsequent picking of grain on the Sabbath, and a healing story on the Sabbath— both are an infringement of Sabbath law. The action is the angst of the Pharisees over the disciples' violation. The pronouncement is Jesus' defense of their action, citing an event in which David ate the Temple showbread when fleeing from Saul.

It is suggested that the original pronouncement in this passage was authentically proclaimed by Jesus himself. He did not claim to be the Son of God or the Messiah. He simply compared his situation to one in the Old Testament. Both situations (David's and Jesus') were emergencies in which the rules logically needed to be amended. "David was in flight from Saul; in Jesus' ministry the kingdom of God is breaking through."[6] In both cases the rule of law must give way to the emergency: "in case of need law had to give way to human concern."[7] Undergirding this dialogue is the assumption that someone greater than David was in their midst. Jesus exercised his right as a *king* to violate the Law when necessity demanded. David secured bread for his soldiers on the move. Jesus secured grain for his soldiers on the way. "The point would seem to be that the disciples have a right to commandeer grain, because they too are on a campaign with Jesus, who will later be revealed as superior to David."[8]

[5] *RF*, 112.
[6] *PL*, 309.
[7] *MK*, 35.
[8] *BSM*, 160.

Some scholars suggest that the saying, "The Sabbath was made for man, not the man for Sabbath," is straight from Jesus' own mouth. They maintain that it has no connection to anything Jewish and that it would have been radical even for the early emerging church. Another point of view is that the saying does indeed have close connections to a rabbinical wisdom saying: "The Sabbath is delivered unto you, and ye are not delivered to the Sabbath" (*Mekilta* on Ex 31:14). This meant that the Sabbath was created for human beings, but not for them to become a slave to it. Matthew and Luke omit the phrase altogether. Fuller cautions us not to take license with the saying and view the phrase in purely humanistic terms. It does not mean that all institutions can be lackadaisically observed or broken. There is an evangelical message inherent in the phrase. Judaism believed that the Sabbath was an eschatological sign of the salvation God intends for the human race. Now that Jesus is the embodiment of that salvation, the sign pointing to it must take a back seat. Why does someone need a sign to point to something that is right in front of them? The phrase is Jesus' own pronouncement of the coming of the eschatological reign of God.

There is difficulty with the phrase, "so the Son of man is lord even of the Sabbath." Scholars believe that Christ would not have given himself the title, "Son of Man," except in a figurative way. He did refer to the coming of the Son of Man in glory and he obliquely linked himself with that figure, but he did not explicitly call himself by that title. It is suggested, therefore, that Mark added this phrase as a commentary on this entire vignette. He makes a convincing point. "Mark asserts that not only has the Human One expropriated authority over the debt code, but the Sabbath as well."[9] Mark wants to make sure that no one misinterprets Jesus' comments about the Sabbath in a self-serving, "anything goes" manner. He wants to make sure the reader understands the eschatological meaning of the exchange. The disciples are free to break the Law because they were given permission from a higher authority than the Law— the long-awaited messianic authority of Jesus, the Christ. The disciples did not have the authority to take such matters into their own hands.

Last week's gospel addressed the issue of ritual purity. Today's gospel is a continuation of that theme. The avoidance of unclean foods, things, and people was a safeguard against the pollution of the nation. The Jewish nation must remain free from the polluting effects of persons, places, and things that do not conform, that defile and threaten the safety of their well-established boundaries. The religious authorities cooperate with this system devised to protect Israel from outside influence and ultimately contamination and dilution of their nation, religious practices, and customs. The antagonists in Mark's story are enmeshed in this system throughout the gospel. They guard the Temple from unclean people and blemished animals. They protect the body from unholy foods, they protect the community from unholy people and things, and today they protect the Sabbath from defilement.

Something else is developing in this story that speaks to the larger cultural issue of honor. So far Jesus is winning every round with his opponents. This will have serious consequences. Honor was an important value in this ancient Mediterranean community. The Pharisees were no less gluttonous for their share than the average citizen. The Pharisees were self-appointed champions of the Law. They tabulated 613 commands that a good observant Jew must observe. They were proud of their own efforts at observance. They were the paragons of exemplary behavior.

The Pharisees challenged Jesus' observance of the Sabbath. Yet they who knew the Law so well were upended by the Law they claimed to champion so earnestly. Something very curious is going on here. Jesus tells a story from the Hebrew Scriptures that he could be quite sure the Pharisees knew well. It is the story of David, who entered the Temple and ate the bread reserved only for priests. David seemingly broke an important law. Jesus recounts this event as taking place when "Abiathar" was the high priest. Something is wrong, however. The recorded event comes from 1 Samuel 21:1–6, in which Ahimelech is the high priest, not Abiathar. Abiathar comes on the scene much later in David's career.[10] So what is going

9 *BSM*, 160.

10 Wilfrid Harrington suggests another explanation for the mistake. "Mark names Abiathar the high priest. This is

on? Why was the mistake made? Who made it? Why didn't Matthew correct it since he used Mark's version of the gospel as his primary source? Later scribes also failed to correct the mistake when they transcribed the account of the incident. The mistake was left as is. Why?

Obviously, the joke is on the Pharisees. The Pharisees would have relished catching Jesus in his scriptural faux pax. "Did Jesus make the mistake? If he did, someone among these scholars should and would have pounced on it. No one did! If Jesus made the mistake intentionally, then the report indicates that he had the last laugh at these experts. Perhaps Mark didn't record that part of the exchange in which Jesus revealed how he tripped them up at their own game. No matter. The Scripture-savvy reader knows that Jesus has beaten these Scripture experts at their own game."[11]

Jesus was playing with fire in his dealings with the religious authorities. Honor was a life-and-death matter. It is beyond our Western imaginations to understand the importance of honor and shame in cultures both ancient and modern. Honor was defended at all cost and shame was similarly avoided. Those who were responsible for bringing shame to another could expect serious consequences. Jesus was a master at exposing his opponents, thereby bringing shame down upon their heads. This was no doubt a contributing factor in his sentence of death.

There is another issue to consider in the examination of today's gospel and that is the perspective of Mark's community. The Sabbath was a source of tension for early Christian communities. Observance of the Sabbath often put Christians at odds with their Jewish neighbors. Very early in the development of the church, the community started to ignore the Sabbath in deference to observing the day of the resurrection—the Lord's Day. This was the beginning of the schism between Chris-

tianity and Judaism. Christians insisted that the Lord's saving act on the cross and his resurrection from the dead "set the sabbath free; and their distinctive observance was traced back to his authority."[12] Perhaps today's gospel contains hints of apologetic motives; Mark may have used this story to encourage and teach his community about the new and renewed understanding of Sabbath in light of the Christ event.

In regard to the healing of the man with the withered hand, Jesus once again is catapulted into conflict with the Pharisees. Jesus entered the synagogue under the close scrutiny of his adversaries. He was approached by a man with a withered hand. The Law prohibited healing on the Sabbath, unless the afflicted person was in danger of death. Jesus challenged their interpretation of the Law, insisting that it is always lawful to do something good and save a life.[13] Jesus exposed the Pharisees' interpretation of the Law as void of compassion. He subsequently healed the man. To say that Jesus sparked the ire and angst of his adversaries is an understatement. The Pharisees went away to plot his destruction. It is only chapter 2 and Mark already plots the course toward the pivotal theme of his gospel: the conflict between Jesus and the authorities is "to the death."[14]

Gustavo Gutierrez reminds us that a major point in today's gospel is that hunger takes priority over ritual prohibitions. Laws are to serve human need and human life. Where there is hunger, human life hangs in the balance. Today's reading from Deuteronomy serves as a reminder that the Sabbath, the day of rest, and all other laws were given so that human beings would be given the opportunity to acknowledge their dependence on God as the source of all life. "However, we must not forget the reason for this rule: the liberation from the slavery endured in Egypt (v. 15). In our surprise, we might wonder what one thing has to do with the other. The fact is that religious precepts cannot be new and subtle forms of slavery. On the contrary. They have to lead us to be free, free to love, as Paul would say."[15]

---

incorrect; the high priest in question was Abiathar's father, Ahimelech (1 Sam 21:1). The fact of the matter seems to be that, while the biblical background is 1 Sam 21:1–6, the immediate source is a haggadic development of the passage. And it may well be that, in a free version of the Old Testament story, Abiathar, the priest and associate of David, had replaced the lesser known Ahimelech" (*MK*, 36).

[11]*CWJB*, 44.

[12]*MK*, 36.
[13]*CM*, 72.
[14]Ibid.
[15]*SWTLY*, 156.

Proclaim the gospel again.

Sometimes we gain new insights when we hear the text after the interpretation is given. Someone from the group proclaims the gospel a second time.

STEP 4
TESTING

Conversation with the Liturgy and the Scriptures

Test your original understanding in dialogue with the text.

(You might consider breaking into smaller groups.)

Now that you've heard the exegesis, were there any new insights? How do you feel about it? How does your original understanding of this gospel compare with what we just shared? How does this story speak to your life?

Sharing Life Experience

Participants share an experience from their lives that connects with the biblical interpretation just presented.

> *I am humbled by today's gospel and amazed at the ways in which God uses the events of my very ordinary life to teach me, humble me, and challenge me to embrace a new, transformed worldview. As I write this reflection, it is Sunday evening; I have just spent the day celebrating liturgy with my community. I am awed by an experience that took place at our early morning liturgy. It was a liturgy like every Sunday liturgy—nothing particularly unusual about it—yet what a manifestation! As we stood for the prayers of the faithful, a young man came forward. Rain-soaked and somewhat disheveled, he walked up the steps toward the altar. Time seemed to stand still. There was an air of absurdity about it all. The lector continued to intercede on our behalf—just like the lector does every week. The presider, cantor (me), and assembly stood fixated on the lector, desperately trying to ignore the human drama unfolding before our eyes. We were transfixed. None of us moved. Everything in me screamed, "Go to him." But I stood motionless, feet firmly cemented in the moment.*

> *This young man fell to his knees, dropped his head to the floor, and sobbed to the very depths of his being. His sobs came from broken dreams, hopeless causes, and the powerlessness of human misery. He raised his body but an inch or two and extended his hands in begging supplication toward the cross we venerate week after week. What a parable in action before our lethargic eyes! It was for just such as these that Christ came to hang upon that cross we venerate. Still none of us moved.*

> *The image of the man sparked a memory in me. What was it? The face, the pose, the stance, the misery—it was so familiar. Where had I seen this before? I remembered a work of art—a beggar, tattered and ragged, pleading for mercy before Christ, the compassionate healer of broken souls. The prayer of the psalmist in the Entrance Antiphon was the obvious prayer of the broken human form that loomed before us. "O look at me and be merciful, for I am wretched and alone. See my hardship and my poverty, and pardon all my sins" (Ps 24:16, 18). Through his sobs I heard the unspoken words, "Heal me Lord, help me, Lord; I am alone; I am broken; I am hopeless." At the very end of this passion scene his entire being seemed to scream in silence, "I am sorry, Lord—forgive me, forgive me, forgive me." As quietly and unobtrusively as he entered our sacred space, so did he exit.*

> *I stared into nothingness as incredulity over my/our lack of response to this Christ in our midst crept under my skin. None of us moved or responded. My mind raced as he stood before us. Everything in me wanted to go to him, put my arms around him, and be Christ to his suffering. But I could not move; or is the truth really that I would not move? Convention suggested that if we ignored the situation it would go away.*

> *What kept us from offering compassion to this man? Surprise? Yes. The abnormality of the situation? Probably. Disruption of the liturgy? Most assuredly. The fact that the man was sick, poor, or homeless? Maybe—I would hope not—but maybe. In our Sabbath celebration, in this twentieth-century day, we failed to heal the man with a withered spirit—and it happened in our very own synagogue.*

> *What if we had responded? Who knows what kind of healing and new life we could have offered this*

stranger in our midst? But most important, who knows what kind of healing and new life he would have given us? Perhaps we needed him more than we will ever know.

Jesus invites us to break away from slavery to any boundaries, conventions, ritual practices, rules, and regulations that keep us from becoming our true, authentic selves and that keep us from loving with the compassion of Christ.

We did not need a homily today. The man was our gospel, our homily, and our challenge. He was the suffering Christ in the midst of the assembly. I was reminded of all those disciples who remained silent and walked away from their Lord in the face of his suffering. Their lack was just as human as the suffering before them. Jesus came for the broken, the oppressed, the unclean, the outcast, the sick, the crazy—all those who fit outside our human-made boundaries. Will we ever learn? Like the disciples, perhaps next time we will respond differently.

What was Mark's message for his community? How do Jesus' actions in today's gospel have anything to do with the everyday lives of the people in your community or with you? Does Jesus' challenge of the ritual purity codes and Sabbath regulations have any relevance for us today? What does this have to do with your life in the marketplace, in your home, and in the world? In what way does this gospel challenge your community today? In what way has this conversation with the scriptures for today's liturgy invited change in your life? In what way are the biblical themes of covenant, exodus, creation, and community evident in today's readings? Do you still feel the same way about this text as when you began? Has your original understanding been stretched, challenged, or affirmed?

STEP 5
DECISION

The gospel demands a response.

In what concrete way might your parish be invited to respond? Are there any attitudes or behaviors you would like to change as a result of today's conversation? What one concrete action will you take this week in response to the liturgy today?

Pastoral Considerations: There is a great liturgical lesson for all of us to learn today. As Catholics we come together each week to celebrate the Lord's paschal mystery. We are given regulations that govern the celebration. To some, those rules and regulations seem arbitrary and meaningless and therefore they either omit or add things to the liturgy according to their own interests. While the Roman Missal does enjoin on those who prepare the ritual celebration to select and arrange various components of available liturgical options, nowhere is there an explicit or implicit license to "do whatever one wants to do" to make the ritual more meaningful. Adding a decade of the rosary or the clown ministry to the liturgy might be meaningful to some, but it is not part of the Roman rite and does not express what we are there to do—celebrate the paschal mystery of Christ and feast on the Lord's presence in assembly, word, and eucharist. Every text, every gesture, every action is undergirded by a rich heritage and interpretation that expresses who we are as church and what we are to become. If our liturgies are not meaningful, then we are not making the primary symbols of the liturgy speak the way they are intended to speak. They are not "robust." (See Easter Vigil's explanation of the symbols of the Church.) It is not the fault of the liturgy, but of those responsible for crafting and celebrating it.

Our liturgy expresses what we believe and who we are as the people of God, *lex orandi, lex credeni*—from the rule of prayer, flows the rule of belief. We had better be very careful about changing what we pray, what we do, and how we move and respond to one another in the liturgy, as we may be tampering with the very precious sense of our core identity. The question must be posed: Are we forming people in the image of Christ in the context of the Roman Catholic Church, or are we forming people in our own image? It behooves every person responsible for preparing liturgical celebrations to know exactly what the ritual prayers, actions, and gestures express before changing them. The *General Instruction to the Roman Missal* must be the guide and constant companion of all who wish to know what we are to do and, for the most part, why we are to do it that way (what the action expresses). This is not to suggest a legalistic approach to the liturgy. It is simply to suggest that we know what we are doing, do it well, and do it according to the principles that define us as the Body of

Christ so that we might enter into the spirit of the action with "full, conscious, and active participation." The disciples had Jesus in their midst to suggest a meaning of the Sabbath that transcended their understanding. We rely on a biblical, ecclesial, and liturgical tradition to help us in that endeavor. We had better be careful when we take such matters into our own hands.

When all is said and done, however, the liturgy serves the people, the people do not exist for the liturgy. If our concern for rubrics transcends our concern for people, we are living the letter of the Law, but are we living its spirit? Therefore, let us ask ourselves: In what way do our liturgical and sacramental practices create obstacles for people who seek the living God? It is a critical question worthy of our serious reflection.

Christian Initiation: Today's liturgy is an invitation to ask if your initiation process places undue burdens on those seeking initiation. Do your programs exist to serve the people's needs, or must they fit into your neatly packaged program? How does your parish respond to people who come to you at times other than your predetermined start-up times? How does your parish respond to people who are already baptized and catechized? Do you treat them the same as unbaptized, uncatechized people? The RCIA demands the same freedom from unnecessary burdens that Jesus demands in today's gospel. Familiarity with the paragraphs of the RCIA, including the National Statutes, regarding our response to baptized, unbaptized, catechized, and uncatechized folks is extremely important. If today's liturgy is taken seriously and after serious reflection on the rite, it is altogether possible that your parish might be challenged to take a serious look at the way it initiates new members. Perhaps today's liturgy might serve as the catalyst to take the first step toward beginning a continuous, year-round catechumenate.

DOCTRINAL ISSUES

What Church truth/teaching/doctrinal issue could be drawn from the gospel for the ninth Sunday in Ordinary Time?

Participants suggest possible doctrinal themes that flow from the readings.

Possible Doctrinal Themes

The Law—spirit versus letter; scripture and tradition; morality; moral decision making; Jesus, Son of God and Messiah; commandments; social justice; covenant; the Lord's Day—Sunday

Present the doctrinal material at this time.

1. The facilitator gives input on a particular doctrinal issue of his or her prior choosing. OR
2. The group chooses a doctrinal issue from the list they created. They read together from the Doctrinal Appendix or other appropriate, official Church documents and the works of respected theologians.

(Many doctrinal issues are found in the Doctrinal Appendix at the back of this workbook. If you are choosing an issue from this resource, please refer to it now.)

Reflection questions centered around the chosen doctrinal theme can be found at the end of each topic in the Doctrinal Appendix. The questions are based on the five-step reflection process. If you choose a topic not included in the Doctrinal Appendix, craft your own questions according to the same five-step process.

Following the reflection questions you will be reminded to return to chapter 7, "Preparing the Catechetical Session," to assist you in crafting your own session.

Closing Prayer

Let us pray
for the confidence born of faith.
God our Father,
teach us to cherish the gifts that surround us.
Increase our faith in you
and bring our trust to its promised fulfillment
in the joy of your kingdom.
Grant this through Christ our Lord.[16]

---

[16]Ninth Sunday in Ordinary Time, "Alternative Opening Prayer," *The Sacramentary.*

TENTH SUNDAY IN ORDINARY TIME

INTRODUCTORY RITES

Entrance Antiphon (or Opening Song)

The Lord is my Light and my salvation. Who shall frighten me? The Lord is the defender of my life. Who shall make me tremble? (Ps 26:1–2)[1]

Opening Prayer

Let us pray
to our Father who calls us to freedom
in Jesus his Son

Pause for silent prayer.

Father in heaven,
words cannot measure the boundaries of love
for those born to new life in Christ Jesus.
Raise us beyond the limits this world imposes,
so that we may be free to love as Christ teaches
and find joy in your glory.
We ask this through Christ our Lord.[2]

LITURGY OF THE WORD

The readings are proclaimed.

First Reading
Genesis 3:9–15

Overview of the Book of Genesis: Genesis, from the Greek "genesis," means beginning or origin. Genesis is the first book in the Bible and the first book of the Pentateuch (the first five books of the Bible). The Book of Genesis spans a vast period of time—from the creation of the world to about 1500 B.C. The writers were hardly concerned about (or aware of) the world's 2 million year history, or the inherent details. What concerned the authors of Genesis was to record the religious sig-

nificance of the events of human history from the very beginning. The authors were also concerned with helping Israel remember its past, and thus to reflect on and understand how they were formed as "a people." A small portion of the book is devoted to the origins of creation and the rest is concerned with the life, deeds, and stories of the patriarchs. Israel believed that God was in a special, covenant relationship with them as a people. Israel believed that when God chose Abraham and the patriarchs he was choosing an "historical people for the realization of his purposes. . . . In Israelite tradition these patriarchs were presented as the first to hear Yahweh's promises for the future."[3] God's dealings with the patriarchs were understood as the covenant God made with Israel as a people.

Genesis is not understood as the history of the nation—which began with the liberation of Israel in the exodus event. Genesis is a "pre-history, a collection of remembrances and theological reflections that help throw light on the exodus."[4] God acted mightily in the exodus event. Genesis seeks to show that God was in relationship with Israel as a people and had planned for the momentous exodus from the very beginning of the world.

Scholars define four different traditions or sources that were responsible for the first books of the Bible. Some of the traditions were older than others. Two sources were named for the way the writer referred to God. The Yahwist ("J") source, believed to be the oldest (ca. 10th century B.C.), referred to God as Yahweh. The Elohist ("E") source (ca. 9th century B.C.) referred to God as Elohim. Originally it was believed that there were only two sources, the Yahwist and Elohist. Although the Books of Genesis and Exodus contain passages that refer to God as Elohim, they clearly were written by two separate authors. This led to the belief in a third source that also referred to God as Elohim, but contained overtones that reflected a priestly focus (interest in rituals, geneal-

---

[1] Tenth Sunday in Ordinary Time: "Entrance Antiphon," *The Sacramentary.*

[2] Tenth Sunday in Ordinary Time: "Opening Prayer," *The Sacramentary.*

---

[3] *PAI,* 55.
[4] *ROT,* 110.

ogy, laws, and liturgical concerns). This source is referred to as the Priestly ("P") source. A fourth and independent source is the Deuteronomic ("D") source. It is believed that the unique and distinctive Book of Deuteronomy, noted for long speeches and sermons, was written by an author other than the Yahwist, Elohist, or Priestly writers. Biblical scholarship usually refers to the four traditions by the abbreviations, J, E, P, and D.

The Yahwist tradition forms the "heart" of the first books of the Bible. The Yahwist is primarily concerned with the continuous story of God's action in salvation history. As artisan and theologian, the Yahwist wove together stories, songs, and poems that had been handed down in the life of the community. He was a master storyteller. The Yahwist has God engaged in grand dialogue with those in the stories and even with himself, thus illustrating that God orders and is in charge of all human events. There is a quality of the modern epic inherent in the Yahwist tradition. "The Yahwist created more than a story of Israel's past; he created a theology and a purpose that explained the religious faith and special spirit of the nation. It became the foundation for Israel's future meditation upon Yahweh's love."[5]

The Yahwist tradition is also the dominant tradition in the Book of Genesis. The Yahwist is the only source that tells the story of the fall of humanity and the parallel story of the tower of Babel. The flood, believed to be of Priestly origin, most probably served the same theological purpose as the story of the fall. Some stories were recorded by more than one tradition. One such story was the covenant of Abraham.

Genesis introduces the prehistory of Israel, beginning with the origins of the human race, the subsequent fall and alienation from God, "followed by his [man's] progressive degeneration."[6] Genesis begins Israel's understanding of promise and covenant with the emergence of Abraham. At first it appears that the promise simply involves new land and multiple descendants. It was the Abraham covenant, however, that eventually gave birth to Israel's messianic hope.

Today's Pericope: There were two trees in the garden that were not intended for human purposes—the tree of life and the tree of the knowledge of good and evil. God ultimately removed Adam and Eve from the garden as the temptation associated with the tree of life still loomed and was a dangerous threat to the couple. Should they eat from the tree, they would live forever, thus making them gods. The story's main thrust, however, is not the tree of life, it is the tree of the knowledge of good and evil.

When opposites appear together in scripture it is known as a merism. The opposites represent the totality of something—good and evil encompassed knowledge of all things. To "know" something meant to be in relationship with that which was known. Knowledge was not simply understood in intellectual terms—it was also relational. Eating the fruit of the tree of knowledge of good and evil (totality) allowed the one who ate the fruit to possess special mastery over life and a special independence and autonomy. This was quite inappropriate for the creature who was fashioned from the dust of the earth. It would allow humans beings to transcend their humanity—they would become immortal.

The garden was understood as God-space, God's locale. It encompassed the "totality of the world."[7] The humans, made from the dust of the earth, were to till the garden—to be caretakers. However, there was a limit placed on humanity's ability to master the environment—they were to avoid eating the tree of the knowledge of good and evil. To eat of the tree meant death. "To die" meant to be cut off from covenant relationship with God. The man and the woman would be exiled, not killed.

Christian wisdom taught that God's original intention was for men and women to live forever. Death was understood as a result of sin. Only gods were immortal. Thus, God's original intention for human beings was divinity. The advent of Christ restored God's original intention for humanity. The incarnation elevated human beings to the status of divine intended for them at the

[5]Ibid., 101.
[6]*DOB*, 302.

[7]Richard J. Clifford and Roland E. Murphy, O. Carm., *NJBC*, 12.

creation of the world, but lost through sin and death. Christ's ransom for sin restored humanity's divine nature.

Adam and Eve ate the fruit of the tree of knowledge of good and evil. They entered into relationship (knowledge) with the totality of the world—good and evil. There was no knowledge of evil prior to their action. For the first time they were aware of their nakedness. For the first time they knew shame. Once they possessed knowledge of evil, they entered into experiential relationship with it. The serpent tempted the couple to become like *divine beings* (another word for God). In their divine state they would possess knowledge of the totality of all things.

The author of Genesis did not identify the serpent with Satan. The serpent was simply a symbol for temptation. Satan became associated with the serpent much later in Judaism and even later in Christian theology. The serpent/Satan link is the reason this reading was chosen for proclamation; it is connected with the Beelzebub fracas in the gospel.

Adam and Eve ate from the forbidden tree and were awakened to their lost innocence. Their action was not hidden from the One who knows all things. The man blamed the woman and the woman blamed the snake. All were held accountable. Punishment was exacted according to the order of the sins. The snake was cursed to a life of eating dirt, crawling on the ground, and being feared and hated. Forever, it would be the enemy of the descendants of Eve. Women were afflicted with the pain of childbirth—a symbol of the loss of ease with oneself and the environment. Women were created equal to men at the creation of the world; they would now become subordinate. "Woman's original equality with her 'correspondent,' the man, is part of the loss, suggesting that the subordinate place of woman in Israelite society was not intended by God, but is rather a result of human sin."[8] The man's punishment is the climax of God's action. The man was not cursed, but his mastery over the earth would be forever cursed. Bringing forth fruit from the land would require strenuous, hard work. Survival would depend on tilling the earth, but sustenance would be procured midst labor, weed, and thorn.

There is incredible hope in this story of God's covenant and mercy. Punishment was not to have the final word. *God* would have the last word. In a very obscure but significant move, Adam gave Eve a new name. Conferral of a new name in scripture signifies a change in direction or in the essence of the person. Eve would now be called *mother of the living*. The sin would not alter God's intention that human beings have dominion over the earth or that they would bear fruit. God also put clothes on the couple—another sign of reconciliation. God covered their shame. He protected them from further disaster by removing them from the temptation to eat from the tree of life. Then God sent them out into the world to fend for themselves.[9] Prophetic eschatology understood the messianic reign to be the restoration of the lost paradise. The tree of life was a symbol of that promise. It would "furnish men with nourishment and restorative power."[10] Christ recalls the promise of Eden and insisted that those who remained steadfast would eat from the tree of life in the new Eden—the reign of God.

The purpose of the Genesis myth is twofold. It gives the listener insight into the insidious nature of temptation. It explains the etiology of the world—its origins. It is also an explanation of why things are the way they are in the world—why the serpent crawls on its belly, why man must toil, why woman must suffer in childbirth, and why human beings know shame and must wear clothes. The Book of Wisdom associated the serpent with the devil. However, there is no basis in fact for the later developments (serpent/Satan connection) of this text. The bottom line of Genesis in its original setting is quite simple—evil will not defeat humanity. Human beings will ultimately win. Christians understand the fulfillment of that to be embodied in the Christ event. We look to our origins with eyes of faith, realizing that seeds of the redemption won for humanity were present from the very beginning.

Due to the later Christological understanding of this text, today's first reading became known as

[8] Ibid.

[9] *NJBC*, 12–13.
[10] *DBT*, 612.

the *protoevangelium*—it was the first proclamation of the gospel in the Bible.[11]

Responsorial Psalm
Psalm 130:1–2, 3–4, 5–6, 7–8

This psalm is the lament of an individual as he reflects on sin and death. It begins from an individual's perspective and shifts to the communal. It is ultimately the cry of God's people for redemption from exile. Today's psalm is a plea for salvation for all peoples of the world.

Second Reading
2 Corinthians 4:13–5:1

Today's Pericope: The backdrop for today's reading is Paul's defense of his apostleship (the object of discussion for the past few Sundays). Unlike his accusers, Paul has no showy credentials of divine power to flash in the face of his antagonists. Paul has only his faith. His faith is rooted in the paschal mystery—Christ crucified and risen. Paul's frustrations and sufferings are not in vain, however. They have been grist for growth. God's outpouring of grace resulted in more and more people coming to faith in the message of the gospel.

In today's pericope Paul continues his sermon on the mystery of suffering begun earlier in the chapter. Paul assures disciples that because of Christ's resurrection, all will one day share in his rising. Christ won that right for all people. Paul hints that he believes that Christ will return in his (Paul's) lifetime, but he never emphatically declares that to be so. Paul does insist that if Christ were to return during his lifetime, he would be dramatically transfigured. Similarly, if Christ returns after his death, he would be raised from the dead. Paul's blessed hope became the professed and proclaimed hope of all subsequent Christian generations. Paul pronounces such hope for the benefit of his readers in hopes that they will share the good news with others. In that way, an increasing number of people will be led to give God glory, praise, and thanks.

Thus, bolstered by God's grace and the hope that all Christians profess, no one is to lose heart. Bod-

ies may decay, but the spirit is stronger than ever. The pain of suffering pales in comparison to the glory that awaits. The suffering of the present moment is transitory. When weighed against eternity, it is but a fleeting reality. The suffering of today is light when compared to the incredible joy and glory of eternity—that which is not seen.

Paul reveals the power and wisdom behind his steadfast endurance in the midst of his own persecutions, imprisonment, and suffering. The more his human frailty came to the fore, the more he relied on the power of God. Paul understood his sufferings as an opportunity to share in the suffering of Christ, thereby participating in the glory to come. "[H]e knew that for one whose gaze was fixed upon Christ, the very sufferings of the present were producing a blessedness which would abide forever."[12]

Paul's divine nature is in the process of renewal and purification as he awaits the ultimate resurrection of his mortal body. There is no hidden dualism going on here—the earthly reality versus a spiritual one. Both realities exist in the same plane. "The things that are eternal are partly future (the glorious resurrection life) and partly present (the inner transformation that is already taking place)."[13]

The gospel is proclaimed.

Gospel
Mark 3:20–35

STEP 1
NAMING ONE'S EXPERIENCE

What were your first impressions? What was your first response to the gospel (or the other readings)? What captured your attention?

Each person names his or her initial impression. Statements should be brief. No reasons should be given at this time. All simply listen without agreeing or disagreeing.

---

[11]*PL*, 311.

[12]*SEPC*, 57.
[13]*PL*, 312.

In a brief statement, explain what you think this gospel is trying to convey.

Liturgical Context[14]

In the liturgies of the past four weeks we have stood in the midst of the Christian assembly and asked the ultimate question: Just who is this Christ? He is not a Christ whose essence can be captured in theology books, but rather in a person-to-person encounter. Christ is known (according to the first reading's understanding of knowledge) through personal relationship. We can only answer the question of Jesus' identity through an unfolding relationship with him. When we live our lives in companionship with the Spirit of the risen Christ in our midst, we come to know Jesus, Messiah, and the One foretold from of old with complete and utter certainty.

Today's Entrance Antiphon sums up the heart of today's gospel. Jesus is the Stronger One who rescues us from all that we fear. Jesus is the one who defends us from the grip of the strong man. Is it no wonder we tremble in awe? Wouldn't it be incredibly awesome if our assemblies really believed in the marrow of our bones that Christ is the defender of our lives, and so we have nothing to fear? We would worship differently and we would live stress-free lives. The purpose of liturgy is to help us believe and live that truth. Christ fills us, nourishes us, and rescues us from fear week after week, until we return next week to be replenished again.

The opening prayer echoes the desire of Jesus in today's gospel. He desires freedom for his own.

---

[14]The scriptures in the Lectionary, the seasons of the year, and the ritual prayers of the mass are interrelated and form the basis for liturgical catechesis. The *liturgical context* attempts to explore and clarify the themes and this interrelatedness.

Jesus was and is willing to engage the strong man in order to rescue us from the power of evil. His death and resurrection freed the world to love. This liturgy can be summed up in the psalm proclaimed in the Communion Rite:

> "I can rely on the Lord; I can always turn
> to him for shelter.
> It was he who gave me my freedom.
> My God you are always there to help me."[15]

Gospel Exegesis

The facilitator provides input from critical biblical scholarship on this text. The input includes insights as to how people would have heard the gospel in Jesus' time.

Something quite significant is going on in today's gospel. We notice a storytelling technique commonly used by Mark. It is a technique known as intercalation or "sandwiching." Mark introduces an event that requires time for its completion. He then interrupts the scene with other situations—the meat between the bread. He closes the section by returning to the original event. The first side of the sandwich begins with the scene in which Jesus' family thinks he has gone mad. They want to take him away. Not only had he stopped eating, but his life had taken a questionable turn. The time it takes to move from Nazareth to Jesus' new home in Capernaum is earmarked by the arrival of the scribes (the meat). The scribes enter the scene with their own accusations. "The relatives' objection 'He is beside himself' is matched by the scribes' 'He is possessed by Beelzebub,' the one expressing radical misunderstanding and the other antagonistic disbelief."[16] The other piece of bread that forms the sandwich shows the return of Jesus' mother and brothers. By that time, however, Jesus had already established a new family—the kingdom of God. The followers of Christ are his new family.

Thus, we see Jesus in conflict with his own cultural environment. His family thinks he has gone mad and we witness the replacement of Jesus' natural family with a new family. Earlier in the gospel,

---

[15]Tenth Sunday in Ordinary Time, "Communion Rite (Psalm 17:3)," *The Sacramentary.*
[16]*CGOS,* 45.

Jesus chose the twelve apostles. He entered into a deep, close, and personal relationship with them. He appointed them to preach, to cast out demons, and to go out into the world.

We have spent the past couple of Sundays listening to the conflicts between Jesus and the authorities. In contrast to the enthusiasm and adulation of the people, the scribes and Pharisees reject him. The evil spirits display more wisdom than their counterparts in the religious leadership. The spirits discern Jesus' identity. The religious authorities are blind to it. In a few verses prior to today's pericope, Mark draws the line and Jesus steps over it. Jesus segues from the old Israel to the establishment of the new Israel—the reign of God.

There are three themes in today's gospel: Jesus' family's fear; cooperation with Satan; Jesus' new and true family. Not only do the scribes and Pharisees reject him and miss his mission, so does Jesus' family. Only those who accept Jesus and do the will of God are Jesus' real family. Those who accuse Jesus of demon possession are guilty of an unforgivable sin. Mark ponders the mystery of the universe in his query about why people prefer the darkness over the light.

The Greek word for family used in this text has multiple meanings. It can mean family, friends, neighbors, or relatives. Most scholars believe the latter designation is the most accurate. It is widely accepted that Jesus' own relatives rejected him. They come to seize him and take him home. They show no support or empathy for Jesus' mission. They are unimpressed and incredulous. They question his sanity and assume that he is possessed by demons.

There are only two situations in the gospel in which Jesus' family comes into the picture. Today's gospel is one of those instances. Jesus' family comes to take him home; they think he is demented and they are mortified by his behavior. His family problems frame a section of the gospel riddled with irony. In this segment, Jesus' family requests that he return home. In the next scene in which his family appears (6:1–6), Jesus is refused refuge. "They reject him in response to what they fear of his rejection of them. In bringing the good news to Nazareth he has the temerity to imply that they are in need of it. Yet he is one of their own, a local product. Apparently the upbringing he received at their hands does not seem adequate to him. He has been listening to other mentors, other 'parents.' As one result of the consolidation of his movement, he is in effect cut loose from his home moorings."[17]

For the first time in the gospel we are introduced to the scribes in Jerusalem—the first official Jewish reaction to Jesus. Also on the front and center stage is the devil, a word derived from the god Baal "*Zabul (Prince).*" Jesus is accused of demon possession (Beelzebub) and that his exorcisms are demon-driven and -initiated. The Pharisees rest their case. Jesus was doing the devil's bidding. Jesus ate with sinners, he crashed through the boundaries of ritual purity by eating with sinners, and he openly flaunted his disregard for Sabbath observance. No way could this man be sent by God!

Satan is God's nemesis. The demons under Satan's dominion were called "unclean spirits." Before Jesus established God's reign, Satan was in control of the house. With the advent of God's reign, God leaves his lofty throne and takes on Satan on his own turf. Mark relates the eschatological battle. God broke through the boundaries between heaven and earth and engaged the evil one.

God sent his Spirit upon Jesus at his baptism. Jesus then engaged Satan in the desert in a contest of wills. Today, God binds Satan and ransacks his house. When the scribes accused Jesus of being Satan's agent, he cleverly retorted with a response that should have been as obvious as the noses on their antagonistic faces. Throughout Jesus' ministry he cast demons out of people. Jesus' repartee was dripping with irony. If he was sent to do Satan's bidding, why in the world would he cast out the very one for whom he was sent and for whom he was working? The assumption went beyond absurdity. If such a thing were so, there would be significant evidence of civil war in Satan's realm and there was no such evidence. "[T]he breakup of Satan's domain should be evident if the charge of the scribes were true. There

_____
[17]*NS,* 53.

ought to be unmistakable signs of the havoc of this alleged civil war.[18] Jesus emphasized his point further using the metaphor of the strong man. Should someone rob the house of a strong man, he would first have to overwhelm the man. Wilfrid Harrington suggests that Jesus' statement is allegorical; it is drawn from the saying in Isaiah 49:24–25, which asks if prey can be taken from the powerful or if prisoners of a taskmaster could be rescued. The Lord God responds that prisoners of the powerful and prey of the taskmaster would be taken and rescued and that God would contend with those who contend with them.[19] God will save their children. The bottom line for Mark is clear. Satan may be the strong man, but Jesus is the Stronger One. Jesus is outfitted with God's power and might. The exorcisms performed by Christ are all the proof needed that God has broken down the doors of Satan's house and is liberating those held captive to his evil machinations and power. Blasphemy against the Holy Spirit, the charge leveled by Jesus in response to the ludicrous accusation against him, is intended to bring home a powerful, unmistakable message. Anyone who suggests that the work and ministry of Jesus are the work of Satan blasphemes against the Holy Spirit as it is none other than God's Spirit who drives and initiates the powerful, liberating mission of the Christ. Such a sin is unforgivable and puts the guilty party's eternal soul in jeopardy. Such a charge is a denial of the advent of God's reign and thus puts the offender outside the reign. It is a refusal of the salvation offered by God through the action of Christ.

The rabbis of Jesus' time insisted that some sins are forgiven by God in this life, others are forgiven in the afterlife, and, due to the gravity of some sins, they are ultimately never forgiven. Jesus refutes their supposition. He insists that God's mercy is always available to those who repent, no matter the gravity. The implications of the sin against the Holy Spirit is that those who insist that Jesus' mission of light is really the work of darkness close themselves off to seeing the light when it shines brilliantly in their faces. They do not see the need to repent, and thus are cut off from God's forgiveness. They refuse the salvation that is freely offered to them—they cut themselves off from the saving, merciful power of God's love.

God reclaims his people as God's own. God delivers the people from unclean spirits. God's work is holy as it offers new life and conquers the destruction of Satan. Those who accept Jesus are the new insiders. Those who reject him find themselves on the outside looking in.

The new boundaries Jesus establishes have nothing to do with ritual purity. People are divided over their acceptance of Christ and their adherence to the gospel. "God is spreading holiness throughout the earth. Followers are also to spread out in order to tell others the good news. They are not to avoid people or animals or things that are considered unclean by society."[20]

Today's pericope ends with Jesus' sad pronouncement that his own relatives did not accept him or understand his mission. Those who listen to Jesus and become his followers assume the role of Jesus' new family. Jesus insists that a person's family relationships are not to take precedence over one's relationship with God. Those who follow Christ are following God's will for the people. They belong to a new family—the family of God. The way one learns the will of God is by following and learning from the Master, Jesus, the Christ, Messiah and Savior of the world.

Ched Myers offers political insight into the events in today's pericope. He maintains that Jesus' ministry has come to a climax. He is at the point at which he must "face the consequences of his campaign."[21] As noted above, Jesus' family thinks he has gone too far and must be stopped. In antiquity, the family determined a person's identity, his or her personality, and his or her future goals. The family was in complete control of the person's life. Kinship was the heart of the society. Jesus not only took on the scribal authorities, but he also challenged the social order of Palestinian society. Jesus' rift with his family becomes mutual as evidenced in verse 33. He refused to see them. If they could not accept his mission, he would not accept their "kindredness." They were no doubt

---

[18]*MK*, 46.
[19]Ibid.

[20]*MAM*, 156–157.
[21]*BSM*, 164.

embarrassed. Jesus' behavior would have been a reflection upon them. All would ask, "Where did the family go wrong?" Today we might all be tempted to sympathize with the family. Perhaps it would be the response of every family whose son or daughter entered the world of political or religious dissidents. Yet Jesus was challenging the kindred system as it stood in order to establish a new one—this new family system would be based on devoted obedience to God—not the family.

Nevertheless, the pleading, coaxing, and interference by Jesus' family were too late. Official investigators entered the picture; they pressed charges against Jesus. Jesus' family thinks he is demented and the authorities think he is demon-possessed.

Anthropological studies have noted that it was a common practice in traditional societies that exorcists who asserted an optimistic, dynamic, but especially revolutionary posture would be accused of demon possession. When the ruling, oppressive class suspected that opponents were challenging their power and control, they would discredit them by associating them with evil spirits. The implications of Jesus' ministry were clear. Since the scribes believed that they were the only representatives of God, Jesus' contrary message could only mean that he was a representative of Satan.

Myers suggests that the "house of Satan" also has indirect reference to the doctrine of the scribal system, the Davidic state, its politics and its religious center, the Temple (v. 25). The very foundations of Israel are in crisis. Jesus confronts the crisis later in his ministry. Their house cannot stand and Jesus highlighted that fact later in the gospel when he refused to be associated with the kingdom of David (12:35). When Jesus later confronted the Temple itself, he exorcised it of those who *divided* or thwarted it from its purpose—a house of prayer. Jesus proclaimed that Israel with its present Temple center will not stand. The Lord of the House will come to reclaim his kingdom. Thus, it is Jesus' responsibility to rid the house of Satan of its oppressive religious rule, and bring it all to an end. Today Jesus waged ideological war with the scribes and the religious establishment.

In verse 27 of today's pericope the parable of the strong man points to an interesting inference. No one can enter the strong man's house to rob him of his *goods*. The word *goods* had multiple meanings—it could mean utensils of any sort—utensils used in agriculture, in the home, utensils of war or peace, and could refer to either the secular or the sacred. The word is used only one other time in Mark's gospel (11:16); it refers to the vessels used in Temple worship, the vessels Jesus banned. Also, the word *binding* possessed other meanings and references in Mark. It was used in reference to the demon in chapter 5, whom no one was strong enough to exorcise. Myers reminds us that it was also used in reference to the imprisonment of John, Jesus, and Barabbas. Thus, today's parable by Jesus sheds light on and explains later events in the story.

What, then, is going on? Mark implies that Jesus is the "stronger one" heralded by John whose mission it was to overthrow the reign of the strong man (the scribal system identified as the demon in 1:24) and steal his vessels for worship. In other words, to establish a new worship. Is it no wonder they plotted against him? He must be stopped—their power, control, religious structure depended on it. To add insult to injury, Jesus also defied the ritual codes that were policed by the scribes and offered the people of God blanket pardon. "How dare he? Who does he think he is anyway?" There is one critical exception to the pardon: all will be forgiven except the sin of mistaking the work of the Spirit for the work of Satan. As Juan Luis Segundo puts it:

> The blasphemy resulting from bad apologetics will always be pardonable. . . . What is not pardonable is using theology to turn real human liberation into something odious. The real sin against the Holy Spirit is refusing to recognize, with "theological" joy, some concrete liberation that is taking place before one's very eyes.[22]

Jesus, in his usual clever form, turned the dialogue on its end and placed it squarely in the lap of his antagonists. They were the ones who could not see. They were the ones who were aligned with the house of Satan—not Jesus: "it is they who are aligned against God's purposes. To be captive to

---

[22]*BSM*, 167.

the way things are, to resist criticism and change, to brutally suppress efforts at humanization—is to be bypassed by the grace of God."[23]

Proclaim the gospel again.

Sometimes we gain new insights when we hear the text after the interpretation is given. Someone from the group proclaims the gospel a second time.

STEP 4
TESTING

Conversation with the Liturgy and the Scriptures

Test your original understanding in dialogue with the text.

(You might consider breaking into smaller groups.)

Now that you've heard the exegesis, were there any new insights? How do you feel about it? How does your original understanding of this gospel compare with what we just shared? How does this story speak to your life?

Sharing Life Experience

Participants share an experience from their lives that connects with the biblical interpretation just presented.

> *Once again Jesus announces the arrival of his reign. How in the world might today's gospel speak to me or to our modern communities? We certainly do not live in the world of spirits as did our ancient counterparts. How is this a relevant word for us today? The bottom line is that we are not to miss what God is doing in and through us, around and beyond us, in our very midst and under our often disbelieving noses. We had also best observe caution when labeling anything contrary to the Spirit of God, when evidence of God's Spirit is unmistakable.*

> *Someone close to my sister was captured by God, turned inside out, and became a radically new person. The change was so complete and radical, and the language this person adopted to explain the expe-*

---

[23]Ibid.

rience was so foreign that it seemed as if this person might also need the same kind of intervention that Jesus' family attempted. What were the symptoms of this radical new life? This person exuded a radical, unconditional love like no one had ever before observed—and he lived it no matter what the temptation to do otherwise. He refused to get caught up in petty human annoyances. He refused to judge another human being, no matter what they were guilty of doing. He insisted that everyone embrace the divinity promised at the creation of the world. He prayed that everyone would be awakened to the Christ within. This man brutally and honestly named what he believed to be the human and religious obstacles to finding and experiencing the God within. What he was doing was very reminiscent of Jesus' continuous confrontation with the scribes and Pharisees. It was difficult to argue with his assessments. There was no way to rattle this person or persuade him to alter the course God had planned for him. He understood his mission to be that of disciple and evangelist of God's love. He was to go out into the world, no matter where that might take him, and offer love to those who were not yet awakened to the Christ within. His language sounded very New Age and countercultural, but his faith was firmly rooted in God and in Christ. He would not, could not, waver from his understanding of the truth.

In the face of such love, everyone was taken aback, puzzled, and thought perhaps that something was mentally wrong. Upon professional examination, however, nothing conclusive was determined.

It is easy to identify with Jesus' family. We are not accustomed to knowing someone who has so completely given her or his life over to God's service that he or she is completely outside the bounds of what is considered conventional or normal.

This person indeed appeared to be extremely countercultural. He seemed to be choosing a life that was completely out of the realm of what middle America would consider normal. The more people tried to persuade him of the error of his thinking, the more certain he was of God's action in his life, and more important, of the voice of God that was insisting obedience to his call.

What was clear to everyone close to him, however, is the one truth that no one could question. This person had a huge impact on everyone he met. He manifested God's love to everyone—a piercing, unconditional love. He loved with a love that could only have originated from the heart of the God he intimately knew and spent hour upon hour loving. No matter how much he was challenged, judged, misunderstood, or denied, this person remained steadfast to what he staked his life on—the power of God's love and presence in his life and in the lives of others. He knew *that love in ways so intimate that I could only hope to one day have that same knowledge.*

Whether his fervor is born of flawed thinking, illness, or the like, only time will tell. This man's incredible intimacy with God has touched everyone. It flowed out from him to others in his life. The God within this man is real.

Reflecting upon all this with the person in question was quite humorous. He was reminded of today's gospel in Mark. The young man was teased that he was in good company—Jesus' family thought he was a little unbalanced too.

Today's gospel is a reminder to me that sometimes the manifestation of God comes in surprising, unexpected ways. We can get so caught up in the expected and the conventional that we fail to see God breaking through in ways we never imagined.

It is a caution to us as church that we not hold our institution so sacrosanct that we refuse to see God working in places other than expected sacred spaces. The church in today's gospel ultimately found themselves at odds with God's plan of salvation. Do we as church act in a similar fashion? The only unforgivable act according to this gospel is to be so blind to what God wants that we fail to be open to the action of the Spirit and the need for our own repentance when it comes to such issues.

I think of all the outcasts that Jesus invited into his house. This gospel is a stern warning that there are to be no outsiders for purposes of our own domination and control. I recently experienced the pastoral and loving response to someone that resulted in inclusion in the Church and ultimately our community. Under some parish circumstances, this person never would have been treated so pastorally. The fruits of this loving response are everywhere. This family is now living an intimate, ongoing relation-

ship with the God they encountered in our community. They are engaged in fruitful, loving ministry. They are being the hands and feet of Christ in innumerable ways. The Stronger One came knocking on their door, rescued them from the strong man, and escorted them into a new and exciting life—the reign of God—and made it possible for them to enter the reign of God in new and exciting ways.

What was Mark trying to tell his community? How might this gospel have relevance for your life? What structures in your life might be obstacles to your relationship with God? Is there any *strong man* in your life or in the life of your community that needs to be rescued by the Stronger hand of Christ? In what way does this gospel challenge your community today? In what way has this conversation with the scriptures for today's liturgy invited change in your life? In what way are the biblical themes of covenant, exodus, creation, and community evident in today's readings? Do you still feel the same way about this text as when you began? Has your original understanding been stretched, challenged, or affirmed?

STEP 5
DECISION

The gospel demands a response.

In what concrete way might your parish be invited to respond? Are there any attitudes or behaviors you would like to change as a result of today's conversation? What one concrete action will you take this week in response to the liturgy today?

Pastoral Considerations: What obstacles does your community put in the path of people who are honestly trying to seek God? Do any of your parish policies have the effect of the strong man? That is, what policies and practices do you insist upon that keep people from experiencing the power of the Spirit in their lives? What countercultural liberating things are taking place in our Church today that we need to affirm as the work of the Spirit?

Christian Initiation: Many people who enter the initiation process find that it strains their family relationships. This gospel might surface some of those tensions. Perhaps it would be a good time to celebrate a rite of anointing of catechumens. It is a ritual prayer for strength as the catechumens continue on their journey. Are you remembering the minor rites? If there are baptized people in your process, please adapt the blessings in order to respect their status as already sacramentally one with us through baptism.

DOCTRINAL ISSUES

What Church truth/teaching/doctrinal issue could be drawn from the gospel for the tenth Sunday in Ordinary Time?

Participants suggest possible doctrinal themes that flow from the readings.

Possible Doctrinal Themes

Jesus Christ; reign of God; Holy Spirit; conversion; family of God, people of God; paschal mystery; freedom from Satan's power; grace and sin; the fall of humanity

Present the doctrinal material at this time.

1. The facilitator gives input on a particular doctrinal issue of his or her prior choosing. OR
2. The group chooses a doctrinal issue from the list they created. They read together from the Doctrinal Appendix or other appropriate, official Church documents and the works of respected theologians.

(Many doctrinal issues are found in the Doctrinal Appendix at the back of this workbook. If you are choosing an issue from this resource, please refer to it now.)

Reflection questions centered around the chosen doctrinal theme can be found at the end of each topic in the Doctrinal Appendix. The questions are based on the five-step reflection process. If you choose a topic not included in the Doctrinal Appendix, craft your own questions according to the same five-step process.

Following the reflection questions you will be reminded to return to chapter 7, "Preparing the Catechetical Session," to assist you in crafting your own session.

Closing Prayer

I can rely on the Lord; I can always turn to him for
    shelter.
It was he who gave me my freedom.
My God you are always there to help me.[24]

---

[24]Tenth Sunday in Ordinary Time, "Communion Rite (Psalm 17:3)," *The Sacramentary.*

ELEVENTH SUNDAY IN ORDINARY TIME

INTRODUCTORY RITES

Entrance Antiphon (or Opening Song)

Lord, hear my voice when I call to you. You are my help; do not cast me off, do not desert me, my Savior God. (Ps 26:7, 9)[1]

Opening Prayer

The facilitator of the session may lead the prayer. Others in the group may be asked to proclaim the readings.

Let us pray
for the grace to follow Christ more closely

Pause for silent prayer.

Almighty God,
our hope and our strength,
without you we falter.
Help us to follow Christ
and to live according to your will.
We ask this through our Lord
Jesus Christ, your Son,
who lives with you and the Holy Spirit,
one God for ever and ever.[2]

LITURGY OF THE WORD

The readings are proclaimed.

First Reading
Ezekiel 17:22–24

Overview of the Book of Ezekiel: Ezekiel brings a message of judgment and hope. Ezekiel is considered third in a line of the great writing prophets: Isaiah, Jeremiah, Ezekiel. Ezekiel was a priest and a prophet who was deported to Babylon along with the other inhabitants of Judah (ca. 597–538).

The prophetic ministry of Ezekiel was a testament to the awesome faithfulness and power of Yahweh. Only Yahweh possessed the power to bring life out of the ashes of despair and failure. Israel understood its tribulations and exile as punishment for its sinfulness. The people of Israel believed that God had punished their disobedience and unfaithfulness by inflicting political disaster.[3] The exile was God's divine retribution and only God could breathe life into their hopeless situation. Ezekiel boldly asserted that even though the signs of God's covenant with Israel (promised land, Temple, Davidic monarchy) appeared to be dead and gone, Yahweh was still sovereign and in control of their history.

The exile plays a great role in the corporate memory of this people; it is remembered as Israel's time of tribulation. Yahweh punished Israel for its sins. Yet, in spite of Israel's unfaithfulness, Yahweh was steadfast in his love for it. Yahweh never broke the covenant, but rather, in his power and love, stood with Israel to deliver it in its great time of distress.

Ezekiel vehemently professed God to be the sole agent in Israel's liberation. God spoke the word and caused it to be, so that all would know: "I am the Lord." Ezekiel puts these words in the mouth of the Great Author of Life at least eighty-six times throughout the book.

The great age of Israel had collapsed. The people were forced into an alien land (Babylon) without the support of their religious structures to sustain them. Ezekiel was a revolutionary. He demanded that Israel engage in reform that would see them through their faith-shattering trials.

Ezekiel forged a bold new path in prophetic prophecy. His language and style were like no other prophet's before him. One of Ezekiel's favorite techniques was to shock his constituents out of their complacency by using abnormal words and by doing strange things. Ezekiel used radical

---

[1] Eleventh Sunday in Ordinary Time: "Entrance Antiphon," *The Sacramentary.*

[2] Eleventh Sunday in Ordinary Time: "Opening Prayer," *The Sacramentary.*

---

[3] Boadt, Lawrence, C.S.P., "Ezekiel," *NJBC.*

means because the times in which he lived required a radical response. The literary text reads like an oratory which suggests that an oral tradition preceded its writing. Ezekiel's message was clear: trust Yahweh, return to the corporate memory and celebration of God's previous saving actions. Worship and observe the Law, and faith will be strengthened. Since Ezekiel stressed the Torah as central to his message, he is often called the "father of modern Judaism."

Ezekiel lived up to his name—God strengthens. Ezekiel was an ambassador of God's strength during a very dark period in Israel's history. Ezekiel laid bare the sins of his people, and then offered them hope and consolation when the weight of awareness came crashing down upon them.

Today's Pericope: Today's reading is taken from the concluding verses of this chapter. Ezekiel understood Judah's future within two separate contexts—the immediate restoration following the exile and the future establishment of the messianic reign.

Ezekiel used the image of Yahweh as the divine lumberjack who chopped off the top of a tree in order to replant it in Jerusalem. The chopped tree top grew to great heights. It grew into a great and mighty cedar with looming branches and plentiful fruit. Ezekiel was not trying to impress students with his scientific prowess; his biology was inaccurate. His concern was spiritual. The treetop represented the remnant of Israel. God would reform his people. He would re-create his people from this sheared-off portion of the great cedar.

The image used today recalls the promise made to David. The re-created remnant was likened to God's promise regarding the Davidic dynasty—the shoot of Jesse. The root of Jesse was the sprout that would give birth to the messianic reign of God. Ezekiel's tree spread out in all directions, thus enabling birds of every kind (people) to find refuge in its massive, protective messianic branches. Ezekiel insists that the fate of Judah was under the control of Yahweh. God would govern and control its destiny. In other words, both the exile and the restoration of the people in Israel were part of God's divine plan of salvation. Nothing happened to Israel by accident. God ordained

it all. The reading from Ezekiel was chosen for the gospel's allusion to the nesting birds in the mustard shrub, a direct reference to the nesting birds and the cedar of this reading. Both are signs of the messianic reign of God.

Responsorial Psalm
Psalm 92:2–3, 13–14, 15–16

Second Reading
2 Corinthians 5:6–10

Today's Pericope: Paul was a passionate apostle. It was Paul's faith that captured the imaginations of believers since the earliest days of Christianity. There was nothing eloquent about Paul. He was not sophisticated; he often approached situations like the proverbial bull in a china closet. What was the magnetism? Paul's faith. Paul was not concerned with the details and events of Jesus' life. He left that up to others, or at least to the oral tradition. It is odd that he does not recount any of Jesus' miracles. Paul did not know the historical Christ. Paul had only one concern—the intimate, personal, living relationship with the risen Christ. That is the Christ he knew well. His claim to apostleship was real and personal contact with the risen Christ. Paul could do no less than shout his faith and revelation from the rooftops. Even when it would have been safer to remain silent, Paul could not. His assurance in the resurrection of Christ and ultimately in his own salvation compelled him to proclaim the message of Christ to all who would listen.

Paul taught his followers that Greek dualism had no place in Christianity. God created the totality of the human person. All is good—body and soul. Greek dualism asserted that the body is evil and the spirit is good. Paul said, "Nonsense!" The body is created by God and is destined for risen life in Christ. Paul extended his belief in the goodness of the body to his theology of suffering. Paul believed that suffering endured for the sake of the gospel was redemptive. The Greek culture around him subjected the body to all forms of purgation to rid it of impurities. Paul believed that deep within the human body resides divinity and eternity. Paul's suffering was willingly and joyfully endured. Such suffering afforded him the opportunity to share in the paschal mystery of Jesus.

Paul was able to rejoice in the midst of suffering because he was able to look forward to the day he would be united with Christ in resurrected glory. Suffering endured on this plane of existence was merely preparation for eternal life in the hereafter.

The gospel is proclaimed.

Gospel
Mark 4:26–34

STEP 1
NAMING ONE'S EXPERIENCE

What were your first impressions? What was your first response to the gospel (or the other readings)? What captured your attention?

Each person names his or her initial impression. Statements should be brief. No reasons should be given at this time. All simply listen without agreeing or disagreeing.

STEP 2
UNDERSTANDING

In a brief statement, explain what you think this gospel is trying to convey.

STEP 3
INPUT FROM VISION/STORY/TRADITION

Liturgical Context

Liturgies of the past week have concentrated on the Jesus who expels demons, the Jesus who was rejected by his family, the Jesus who established a new family, and a Jesus in deep trouble with the authorities. Jesus' trial has already begun. Evidence is being gathered. Witnesses are taking sides. People are deciding where they will stand. Everyone is answering the question: Who is this Jesus anyway? The authorities believe he is a blasphemer and a violator of the Law. The reader begins to understand the implications of Jesus' conflict. We are given a greater appreciation of the

evidence stacking up against the Lord. We are brought into the inner circle and are invited to realize the gravity of Jesus' situation. We see the case for his Passion and death beginning very early in his ministry and very early in Mark's gospel.

The eleventh and twelfth Sundays in Ordinary Time form a mini sequence in which we reflect upon the teaching authority of Jesus. He manifests his wisdom, power, and authority by the way he instructs the crowds. We are given an intimate glimpse of the reign Christ came to establish.

The Entrance Antiphon speaks of the assurance of the kingdom portrayed in today's gospel. We ask God not to desert us—we are assured that God will not desert us. God will give us safe sanctuary. God will allow us to rest within the branches of his secure providence. The farmer that went out to sow the seeds was completely dependent on the grace of God for the harvest. The Opening Prayer recognizes that God is our source. We are reminded that without Christ we will falter. Without Christ there will be no harvest. We are completely dependent on God's grace. We must have hope that God will give us the strength we need to follow Christ and do the will of God.

Gospel Exegesis

The facilitator provides input from critical biblical scholarship on this text. This input includes insights as to how people would have heard the gospel in Jesus' time.

Jesus was the proverbial storyteller. He especially loved using parables. In antiquity the parable was used as a tool to compare one thing to something else. Jesus revealed the face of God by comparing God's essence or his behavior to something that was familiar to people in their culture. John Pilch reminds us that the parable is difficult to understand because it not only relates how things are similar, but also how they are different. "In other words, God is similar to, yet different from, whatever is presented as the point of comparison."[4] Pilch reminds us that when Jesus refers to the kingdom he is not referring to a place, but to a person. That person is God. When the reign of God is compared to something, what is ultimately being

---

[4] *CWJB*, 97.

asserted is that this is what "happens when God is totally in charge of life."[5] It is important to understand an ancient Mediterranean principle that all goods are limited in quantity and number and are already allocated. Anyone who suddenly turned up with more goods was considered a thief. "One peasant's gain was considered another peasant's loss."[6] In the story of the woman with the lost coin we are told that she hosted a party due to her precious find. She wanted everyone to know that she did not steal the coin or find a coin that belonged to someone else. The party cost her more money than the coin she found, thus emphasizing her point. Peasants considered some things to be beyond human control, and thus belonging to God's prerogative. A good harvest, good livestock, good crops, and children were considered to be an addition to limited goods—they were grace. In limited goods cultures it was expected that surprise windfalls be shared with others. Those who did not were considered greedy.

In the first parable today the man does nothing but plant the seed. Perhaps he was lazy. He failed to weed, hoe, or fertilize. He planted it and left it. The rest was left up to God. When it comes to God's reign, a similar outcome can be expected. If humans trust in God, God will do the necessary tilling, watering, nurturing, and harvesting. God will provide over and above the limited goods already distributed—abundance.

While Ezekiel was botanically incorrect, Mark, on the other hand, is precise in his description of the mustard seed. It does not grow into a tree, it grows into a shrub. It can be a very large shrub, capable of providing shelter for birds, but it is nevertheless a shrub. The listener is invited to choose. Will the new kingdom be small and insignificant? Will the new kingdom be opened to a select few, or will it be small like a shrub, but large in stature? Will the new kingdom be inclusive of all people seeking refuge within the shade of its shrubs? The followers of Christ are asked to decide.

The mustard seed was used for the seasoning of food and for medicinal purposes. It was believed in antiquity that the mustard seed cured nearly all

that ailed a person. It is possible that the reign of God and its associations with the mustard seed also drew upon the medicinal properties of the mustard seed.

Mark is the only evangelist to tell the story of the sower who went out into the field day after day. The origin of the parable is not certain. Wilfrid Harrington maintains that its point is the contrast between the sower who went out every day and the certain harvest that was beyond his control.[7] The earth produces and the sower can do nothing about it. It will take place without his intervention. The sower goes about his daily business unaware of the seed's activity or growth until the seed grows to maturity and the harvest is ready. The farmer is thus ready to harvest the ripened grain. The parable alludes to Joel's eschatological exhortation that the sickle must be taken to the ready harvest. It is a parable about the final judgment and the coming of God's reign. God causes the growth of his people and God will harvest them.

Scholars suggest that perhaps this parable was Jesus' response to those who demanded a more forceful establishment of the kingdom or for those disciples who were discouraged at the rate at which the kingdom was proceeding (or not proceeding). Mark stresses that the disciples' responsibility in the kingdom was to plant and water the seed, but it was God's responsibility to nurture it and bring it to fruition.

The parable of the mustard seed offers a similar contrast. The reign of God grows from very humble beginnings into something mighty. The mustard seed is the smallest of seeds yet it grows into a mighty tree. The reign of God begins in the smallest, most insignificant ways, yet through the intervention of God's providence grows into something of great significance. The disciples certainly needed the hope offered by today's parable. Jesus was rejected by his family, he was cast out of the cities, and he was in trouble with the authorities. One would think that hopes of the kingdom had all but vanished. Today's message reminds the disciples not to give up. They were to have hope. The seeds of the kingdom were being sown and would be harvested on some future day.

---

[5] Ibid.
[6] Ibid., 98.

---

[7] *MK*, 62.

There is a great paradox in today's parable. "The way of the sower will subsequently be revealed as the way of non-violence: servanthood become leadership, suffering become triumph, death become life. The lesson of the 'unknowing farmer' is that the means of the kingdom must never be compromised by attempting to manipulate the ends."[8]

According to some authors, the small mustard seed has the potential to grow to unimaginable heights. In the Book of Daniel and today's first reading from Ezekiel the image of the tree is a sign of the great kingdom and its protection of the inhabitants of the kingdom. Harrington maintains that Mark is referring to the gentiles in this passage.[9] All the nations of the world will be brought under the care and protection of the reign of God. Ched Myers insists that the "disproportion between the seed and the mature plant is meant to instill courage and hope in the small and fragile discipleship community for its struggle against the entrenched powers."[10]

Jesus' parable proclaims a marvelous and obvious truth. His small band of disciples, as insignificant as they felt themselves to be, would one day grow into a mighty kingdom. This growth would be initiated by God. God planted the seed and would harvest it in due time. Since it is God's work, it will always be a surprise to human beings. The kingdom cannot be predicted by looking to its origins. It can only be predicted by looking at God's power. Jesus invites the disciples to be patient.

Bernard Brandon Bailey offers another perspective for our consideration. The mustard plant was a common plant that grew and rapidly spread. It grew to about four feet in height. Farmers were forced to control the sowing of the seeds, however. There is a rabbinic principle that underlies this parable. It is the principle of diverse kinds. The rule of diverse kinds intended to bring order and harmony to the world; like things were to be together with like things. This helped to protect the distinctions between the sacred and the unholy. "These early prohibitions have as their purpose maintaining the order of creation (Gen. 1:11–12,

21, 24–25.). Order presents holiness, and disorder uncleanliness."[11]

The mustard seed was not to be commingled with other plants. The mustard plant is an annual. The seed germinates as soon as it is planted so it grows very quickly. It is very difficult to control once it has grown to a certain height and it is difficult to keep pruned. The ancient listeners would have perked their ears when Jesus began his parable about the mustard seed. They immediately would want to know where and how it was going to be planted. Immediately the hearer would ask: Is the planting of this seed associated with a blessing or with a violation of law? Is it clean or unclean? Was it planted inside or outside the garden? Was it planted in a place that would automatically contaminate it?

In the reading from Ezekiel the messianic reign was to grow into a mighty cedar of Lebanon. In today's gospel the messianic reign was to grow into an insignificant shrub that offered shelter and nesting for the birds. The metaphors of both readings are somewhat opposed to each other. The mustard seed is minuscule compared to the hugeness of the cedar—the kingdom. "Jesus' parable stays with the kingdom of insignificance."[12] In the original telling of this parable the mustard seed becomes a shrub. As the oral tradition developed, however, there were more allusions to the cedar of Lebanon, and the mustard seed becomes a tree. Mark's parable alludes to the cedar with its reference to the nesting birds, but the seed still becomes a shrub, not a tree. Bailey reminds us that the listener would have been surprised by the contrast. The parable begins with hints of the unclean with a reference to where the seed was planted. Since the seed did not become a tree, it will not meet great expectations. In spite of the threat of uncleanness and insignificance, however, birds still find shelter within the mustard shrub's branches. One cannot miss the implication or the "recognition that God's mighty works are among the unclean and insignificant."[13]

There is a political reading of this text, also worthy of consideration. The image of the tree had another meaning in later chapters of Ezekiel. The

[8]*BSM*, 181.
[9]*MK*, 62.
[10]*BSM*, 179.

[11]*HTP*, 382.
[12]Ibid., 387.
[13]Ibid.

tree metaphor was used as a polemic against the oppressive political power of Egypt. The tree represented the toppling of imperial power—"upon its ruin will dwell all the birds of the air" (31:2). Mark was quite aware of this reference when writing his gospel. He certainly had images of the Roman Empire and its domination of Israel, which did not fare well under Rome's domination. How in the world would this significant band of Jesus' followers fare? It was an absurdity to consider the idea of this small troupe toppling the tall tree of imperial Rome. Mark truly believed that God was capable of such an absurdity.

Mark reminded his readers that Jesus spoke in parables to the crowd, but he offered special instruction to his disciples. Pilch offers insight into this strange phenomenon. Why did Jesus speak in veiled language to some? Pilch insists that it is connected to the honor and shame code of the ancient Mediterranean culture. It was unthinkable and a transgression against honor for outsiders to learn anything damaging about insiders.[14] Thus families maintained strict secrecy. However, secrets were treated suspiciously by the people. Secrets suggested that someone was plotting against them. This created a quandary. Jesus taught the crowds in parables. They (the crowds) were the outsiders. The parables meant one thing to the crowds and another thing to Jesus' disciples. Mark's readers are invited to decide. Should they settle for the meaning given to the crowds, or do they dare seek after the deeper meaning given to the disciples?

Proclaim the gospel again.

Sometimes we gain new insights when we hear the text after the interpretation is given. Someone from the group proclaims the gospel a second time.

STEP 4
TESTING

Conversation with the Liturgy and the Scriptures

Test your original understanding in dialogue with the text.

---

[14]*CWJ*, 99.

(You might consider breaking into smaller groups.)

Now that you've heard the exegesis, were there any new insights? How do you feel about it? How does your original understanding of this gospel compare with what we just shared? How does this story speak to your life?

Sharing Life Experience

Participants share an experience from their lives that connects with the biblical interpretation just presented.

> The reign of God comes crashing in from very insignificant beginnings. I am reminded of the many ways God's reign is manifested in our community. I remember how our initiation process has grown from very worthy, but humble beginnings. It is amazing to see what God has done in people's lives. We are constantly amazed at the action of God in people who share their lives with us in the initiation process.

> God has given us the opportunity to realize that the RCIA works the way it is intended to work. We jumped into the deep waters and made the move from a nine-month model in which everyone began the process in September and was either baptized at the Easter Vigil or received into full communion— all were treated the same, baptized and unbaptized. We moved to a continuous, year-round model, in which each person was treated according to the action of God in his or her life with no set timetable. The baptized are baptized at the Easter Vigil or when special circumstances dictate and the baptized are brought into full communion whenever they are ready (as the rite intends). The task seemed insurmountable. There were times in the early days that we were very discouraged. There were times we could not see the forest for the trees (no pun intended). God, however, has blessed us, and watered, nurtured, and harvested our efforts. There were times all we could do was trust that God was guiding and leading us. The result—God has blessed this ministry. Many people have come forth to share their gifts in this ministry. There are four teams (eleven people) of inquiry catechists (one team works with children), nine catechumenate catechists (two people work with children), and two mystagogy catechists. There is an abundance of excellent catechists, sponsors, hospitality ministers, and incredi-

ble catechumens and candidates who continue to teach us and invite us to examine our relationship with God. Our parish embraces and welcomes the catechumens and candidates enthusiastically. Week after week people in the pews reach out their hands to those being dismissed to further reflect on God's Word.

We are still quite insignificant in the grand scheme of things, however. God's work goes on in similar fashion all over the world and in many and powerful ways. But in our insignificance it is amazing to reflect upon God's work in our parish. We do not have a perfect initiation process or a perfect parish—no one does. There is no such thing.

What we are blessed with, however, is a parish that lives in the reality of God's kingdom. Seeds of life and faith are sown everywhere. God waters and harvests the seeds and we see incredible life. It is very exciting for those of us in initiation ministry to see catechumens, candidates, and neophytes actively and powerfully engaged in ministry.

I often hear of communities that are riddled with strife and controversy. We have had our share of similar problems, but Christ has walked with us and has invited us to reconcile and to live in his Spirit. In spite of our failings, the reign of God thrives in our parish community. The elderly, the poor, the sick, the homeless, families, and many others are served by the ministry of God's people. Many people find refuge in the branches of God's reign that reside within the boundaries of our parish community.

Lest we become too proud, we do need to take a serious look at the question of the unclean and the outcasts. Even though we make great efforts to serve the poor and marginalized, there is room for improvement. The reign of God was first given to the lowly. How are the lowly welcomed in our parish? We do our best, but I am sure there are areas where improvement is needed. I am reminded of a sacramental preparation meeting in which a mother and her daughter were completely ignored by all the other families—they resembled the marginalized of Jesus' gospel. They were not treated badly, they were simply ignored. The day that no one is ignored or treated as "less than" is the day we truly live within the promise of today's gospel. We still have a long way to go.

What was Mark trying to tell his community? How is the kingdom of God evident in your parish? How do you relate to the mustard seed parable in your own life? How does it speak to your relationship with God? What is the "good news" in today's gospel? In what way does this gospel challenge your community today? In what way has this conversation with the scriptures for today's liturgy invited change in your life? In what way are the biblical themes of covenant, exodus, creation, and community evident in today's readings? Do you still feel the same way about this text as when you began? Has your original understanding been stretched, challenged, or affirmed?

STEP 5
DECISION

The gospel demands a response.

In what concrete way might your parish be invited to respond? Are there any attitudes or behaviors you would like to change as a result of today's conversation? What one concrete action will you take this week in response to the liturgy today?

DOCTRINAL ISSUES

What Church truth/teaching/doctrinal issue could be drawn from the gospel for the eleventh Sunday in Ordinary Time?

Participants suggest possible doctrinal themes that flow from the readings.

Possible Doctrinal Themes

Hope; reign of God; faith; conversion; discipleship; Jesus Christ; mystery of suffering; paschal mystery; evangelization

Present the doctrinal material at this time.

1. The facilitator gives input on a particular doctrinal issue of his or her prior choosing. OR
2. The group chooses a doctrinal issue from the list they created. They read together from the Doctrinal Appendix or other appropriate, offi-

cial Church documents and the works of respected theologians.

(Many doctrinal issues are found in the Doctrinal Appendix at the back of this workbook. If you are choosing an issue from this resource, please refer to it now.)

Reflection questions centered around the chosen doctrinal theme can be found at the end of each topic in the Doctrinal Appendix. The questions are based on the five-step reflection process. If you choose a topic not included in the Doctrinal Appendix, craft your own questions according to the same five-step process.

Following the reflection questions you will be reminded to return to chapter 7, "Preparing the Catechetical Session," to assist you in crafting your own session.

Closing Prayer

Let us pray
[to the Father whose love gives us strength to follow his Son]

> *Pause for silent prayer.*

God our Father,
we rejoice in the faith that draws us together,
aware that selfishness can drive us apart.
Let your encouragement be our constant
    strength.
Keep us one in the love that has sealed our lives,
help us to live as one family
the gospel we profess.
We ask this through Christ our Lord.[15]

---

[15]Eleventh Sunday in Ordinary Time, "Alternative Opening Prayer," *The Sacramentary.*

TWELFTH SUNDAY IN ORDINARY TIME

INTRODUCTORY RITES

Entrance Antiphon (or Opening Song)

Lord, hear my voice when I call to you. You are my help; do not cast me off, do not desert me, my Savior God. (Ps 26:7, 9)[1]

Opening Prayer

The facilitator of the session may lead the prayer. Others in the group may be asked to proclaim the readings.

Let us pray
that we might grow in the love of God

Pause for silent prayer.

Father,
guide and protector of your people,
grant us an unfailing respect for your name,
and keep us always in your love.
Grant this through our Lord
Jesus Christ, your Son,
who lives with you and the Holy Spirit,
one God for ever and ever.[2]

LITURGY OF THE WORD

The readings are proclaimed.

First Reading
Job 36:1, 8–11

(See the fifth Sunday in Ordinary Time for an overview of the Book of Job.)

Today's Pericope: Job was a wealthy landowner with a large family, who enjoyed great prosperity and many blessings. The blessings were a sign that he was a just and good man in the sight of God. Then God unleashed Satan and Job's life was turned up-side down. Job was certain that God had cursed him. The people around him believed that Job was responsible for his own misfortunes. Trials, tragedies, and tribulations were looked upon as punishment for sin. His friends wasted no time reminding Job of that fact. Today's scene opens immediately after Job's friends have had their way with him. They argued, cajoled, blamed, and tried to explain why Job was faced with such calamity in his life. Job was not satisfied. He insisted that he was righteous before God. He wanted answers. Why must he suffer like this? Why was he subject to this suffering?

God finally steps in "out of a whirlwind." Clouds, tempests, whirlwinds, smoke, fire—all are Old Testament symbols that shout to Israel, "I am in this place!" Scripture often portrays God appearing to frightened human beings who find themselves in a storm at sea. Only God has the power to withstand the raging water, calm frightened people from its deafening roar, and save those who are dragged under by its powerful current. In antiquity people believed all sorts of wild tales about the sea. It was a dangerous place from which many people did not return after a dangerous voyage. Those who were saved from treacherous experiences related tales of sea monsters and other frightening phenomena. The sea was believed to be the abode of evil spirits bent on destroying human beings at the first opportunity. The Bible insists that God is master of the waters. God controlled the flood; God parted the waters for people to pass through and then ordered their return. God sent a whale to rescue Jonah from the frightening waters and deposit him on land. The sea may be powerful, but God is more powerful.

In today's reading Job experiences a theophany—God becomes present to him. In one of the most beautiful dialogues in all of scripture, God answers Job. God asserts his transcendence. God insists that human beings simply do not have the ability to fathom God's ways, which are beyond human comprehension. Job was not with God at the creation of the world. He does not know the way God

---

[1]Twelfth Sunday in Ordinary Time: "Entrance Antiphon," *The Sacramentary.*

[2]Twelfth Sunday in Ordinary Time: "Opening Prayer," *The Sacramentary.*

thinks or the way God acts. God's ways are unfathomable. God created the heavens and the earth and the sea and all that is in the sea. God is sovereign over all of creation. God is especially sovereign over the waters—which is why this text was chosen. It prepares the reader for the gospel and Jesus' calming of the sea. Just as God/Jesus/Spirit was sovereign at the creation of the world and ultimately the waters, so too is Jesus sovereign when he stills those same waters in the event recalled in today's gospel.

Responsorial Psalm
Psalm 107:23–24, 25–26, 28–29, 30–31

Today's psalm resonates with both the first reading and the gospel. The psalm speaks of four groups of people that should thank Yahweh. The psalm was chosen because of the fourth group, which was exhorted to thank God for rescuing them from a storm at sea. It is believed that verse 29 inspired the written text of today's gospel.

Second Reading
2 Corinthians 5:14–17

(Refer to the second Sunday in Ordinary Time for an overview of 1 and 2 Corinthians.)

Today's Pericope: For the past few weeks, liturgical assemblies have been inside spectators at Paul's defense of his apostolic authority and mission. Today the battle continues. Paul contrasts the impetus that drives his ministry versus the flashy credentials of the false teachers who took Corinth by storm and captured the imaginations of the people. Paul's defense causes curiosity even among some of his friends. In today's dialogue Paul reaches the high point of his defense—he reveals the secret of his life.[3] The love of Christ has made him a new creation. Paul tries to convince his audience of the driving force behind his ministry.

Love is the driving motivator—the incredible, passionate love of Christ, who demonstrated that love through his death upon the cross. Thus, Paul's own ministry is patterned after the example of Christ who died for all. The cross of Christ

is what drives Paul's apostolic ministry. No longer does Paul live for himself; he now lives for the crucified and risen Christ. Christ's death has made a greater life possible. Everyone who follows Jesus' example and dies to the old self, rises to a new, more abundant life. Those who die to self and live for others are heirs to the new, resurrected life of Christ. Paul insists that this is what his friends may say to those who think Paul is insane and insincere.

Paul hopes that all will trust his sincerity and vouch for him as a true minister of Christ. In previous verses he reminded his readers that his motives had already been judged by God, and he hoped that they, too, might understand his honest intentions in similar fashion. Even though this sounds like conceit and self-recommendation, Charles Erdman suggests otherwise. He maintains that Paul is not indulging in self-praise—his enemies do enough of that already. Paul is simply affording his friends the basis for defending him against his opponents.[4]

Paul's opponents accused him of mental imbalance as well as insincerity. Paul defends his seeming "imbalance" as nothing more than his enthusiasm and love for God. Paul's love for Christ and Christ's love for Paul are so all-encompassing that Paul can do no less than go selflessly forward with one purpose—"the ceaseless service of Christ."[5]

Paul is not concerned with the details of Christ's humanity. His focus is the glorified and risen Christ; it is the risen Christ who occupies Paul's thoughts and heart. Paul is so radically transformed by his experience of Christ risen that old behaviors have melted into a new outlook, perspective, and way to live. Everything that was part of the former world before Christ is insignificant in comparison. The old rites, the old way of behaving, the old weaknesses, "the old pride and conceit, the old hypocrisies and sins"[6] have given way to a new, transformed outlook and way of living. "'The love of Christ,' believed, accepted, appreciated, appropriated, is the supreme motive in the transformation of human life and character.

---

[3] *SEPC,* 62.

[4] Ibid.
[5] Ibid., 63.
[6] Ibid., 64.

It may be regarded as the essence of Christian experience."[7]

The itinerant false teachers claimed that Jesus was no more than a wonder worker or a divine man. Paul challenged their narrow identification of Christ and labeled it mere "human judgment." He insisted that the power of Christ is to be found in his resurrection—not his humanity. It is not through the beauty, biography, teaching, or behavior of the earthly Christ that we are transformed, even though such things are necessary and vital to our formation. It is the risen, ascended, and glorified Christ, who sits on the throne of heaven, who has the power to transfigure and transform us. It is because of Christ's incarnation, death, resurrection, ascension, and glorification that we are elevated to the status of divine, which was intended for us at the creation of the world. It is only through that event that we become new creations in Christ.

The gospel is proclaimed.

Gospel
Mark 4:35–41. Jesus calms the sea.

STEP 1
NAMING ONE'S EXPERIENCE

What were your first impressions? What was your first response to the gospel (or the other readings)? What captured your attention?

Each person names his or her initial impression. Statements should be brief. No reasons should be given at this time. All simply listen without agreeing or disagreeing.

STEP 2
UNDERSTANDING

In a brief statement, explain what you think this gospel is trying to convey.

---

[7]Ibid.

STEP 3
INPUT FROM VISION/STORY/TRADITION

Liturgical Context

Today's gospel is part of a two-part sequence. Refer to last week for more information. The boat is a symbol often used for the Church. We, the Church, are tossed in the turbulent sea of life and we forget that the One who captains the boat is none other than the One who stills the storm with a gesture of his hand. If we think our world is upside down, we have sympathetic company in communities of old that struggled with the same discouragements. During St. Augustine's life the world and the Church were in disarray—just as they appear to be today. The Church was plagued with heresies that threatened to undermine its very core and the world that Augustine knew was threatened with invasion. Things seemed tenuous at best. Augustine's exhortation to the Church is as relevant today as it was then. Let us listen.

> Why therefore be disturbed? Your heart is agitated by the tribulations of the world, as the boat in which Jesus Christ was asleep. Here is, foolish man, the true cause of your heart's dismay. This boat in which Jesus Christ is sleeping is your heart in which faith is slumbering. What news do you hear, O Christian, what news do you hear?

> Since the beginning of the influence of the Christian religion of the world, the world has been prey to those devastations; it has been nearing its end. Did not your Lord predict this ruin of the world? You used to believe these predictions when they were made, and now that they are fulfilled, you are disturbed? The storm is brewing in your heart, watch out for the shipwreck, awaken Jesus Christ....

> Jesus Christ dwells in you through faith. Faith present in your heart is Jesus Christ present. Watchful faith is Jesus Christ watching. Sleeping faith is Jesus Christ asleep. Therefore, wake him up, arouse

yourself and make this prayer,
"Teacher, . . . we are perishing."[8]

Every Sunday we bring our lives to the Sunday celebration of the eucharist. We find ourselves in the storm-tossed sea of life, and we bring those turbulences to the celebration of the Lord's Passion, death, and resurrection. Through the Sunday scriptures we hear the living presence of Christ in the stories of those who have gone before us and have faced similar rough seas and were sustained by God's saving power. As we offer our prayers of intercession for the world and for one another we are reminded that only in Christ will we find the peace to sustain us in difficult times. We bring all our travails and the travails of the world to the Lord's banquet table to be broken and poured on in union with the broken body of Christ and blood that was poured out for us all. The liturgy helps us navigate life's vessel through both the turbulent and the calm seas of life.

What sustains us in today's liturgy is the assurance that no matter what this life brings us, no matter what we have to endure, we are not alone. We are gifted with the presence of the Christ, who is in control of our destinies. We are not to fear—we are not alone!

The eleventh and twelfth Sundays in Ordinary Time serve as a brief course on faith and trust for all disciples. Since Mark's gospel moves us ever closer to the Passion of Christ, we must take time out now and remind ourselves of our anchor. Steadfast faith and earnest trust will see us through the most turbulent seas we might encounter.

If the liturgy were to manifest a single theme (which it does not), it would be embodied in today's Entrance Antiphon. God alone is our strength and only in God will we ever know the security for which we long. The antiphon acknowledges our complete dependence on God for all that we need. What better prayer to prepare our hearts to listen to the "Sleeping Christ" of today's gospel. We are reminded in today's alternative opening prayer, "God, ever close to us, we rejoice

to call you Father. From this world's uncertainty we look to your covenant." Only God can save us from the unknown and the fearful.

Gospel Exegesis

The facilitator provides input from critical biblical scholarship on this text. This input includes insights as to how people would have heard the gospel in Jesus' time.

Chapter 4 of Mark's gospel changes the locus of the story. We move from the land and "the way" (on the way to Jerusalem and, ultimately, the cross) to the sea. The word *sea* is used three times and the word *boat* is used once. The sea becomes a primary setting for Mark 4 through 8:21. When Mark's gospel returns to "the way," there is also a transition in the story.

At first sight it appears that this gospel pericope is a testament to Jesus' awesome power over the elements and an obvious proclamation of Christ's divine nature. While this is certainly true, there is more going on beneath the surface of this text than readily meets the eye. Deeper meaning is to be found in the narrative style Mark uses to tell the story. Sandwiched into the text are details and biblical references that reveal more about the heart of Mark's homily.

The sea is a force no human being has the power to control. The text reveals a sleeping, unaffected Christ—asleep, no less, on the tossing, turning, savagely rolling stern of the ship. Who could really sleep in the midst of such violent turbulence? Jesus could, and did! Picture the scene. Aquatic hell has broken loose on the deck of the ship. All hands scream violently to be heard above the wild roar of crashing waves. Fear has all but taken over. The disciples are frantic. They can hardly believe that Jesus is sleeping through the commotion. Surely he *could* do something if only he *would*. And yet, much like Rip Van Winkle, Jesus is not roused in spite of the unfolding events around him. This absurd scene is Mark's way of arousing his audience out of their own complacent sleep in order to catch the dichotomy of the situation.

The disciples are in fear and terror, afraid for their lives. Trust is the furthest thing from their frantic minds. Contrast that with a dozing, peace-

[8]St. Augustine, *Sermons*, 81:8, in *Oeuvres complètes*, vol. 16 (Paris: Vivés, 1871), 581, in *DL* (V), 112.

ful Jesus, unaffected by the titanic tragedy unfolding around him. Mark is hardly concerned with the outlandishness of the scene he has painted. It is his way of theologizing with an exclamation point! The peaceful, assured Christ does not waver in the face of terror, death, and destruction. There will be another time that we will encounter this same scene—the confident, trusting, single-minded Christ versus the terrified disciples in disarray. That scene will be Jesus' arrest, trial, Passion, and death.

The meaning of Jesus' slumber is also hinted at in allusions to the story of Jonah in the belly of the sea monster (1:4–15). It is believed that the Jonah story influenced Mark's rendition of today's gospel. In Matthew's gospel, Jesus compared his coming death and subsequent stay in the tomb to Jonah's sojourn in the belly of the whale. Jesus' slumber and the allusion to Jonah reveal Mark's powerful theology—Jesus is victorious over the powers of death, destruction, and evil. The ancients believed that the deep abyss of the sea was the abode of sinister, evil powers. Jesus is victorious "over everything evoked by a stormy sea: the demons' attacks and death."[9]

What language does Jesus use to calm the storm? The same language he used to cast out demons—the language of power and authority. He rebuked the waves and they obeyed him, just like the demons. It is as if we have a front row seat to another exorcism. Jesus sent the evil, destructive powers back to the abyss from which they came, forbidding them their appetite of havoc, fear, and destruction.

Jesus then addresses the disciples. Where is your faith? Have you not witnessed enough to know that with me you are safe from the power of death and evil? Why were you so afraid? It is easy for armchair sympathizers to identify with the disciples. Who would not be afraid in the face of such terror? Their whining has a familiar ring to it, however. We know that they have had this struggle before and will have it again. They were sluggish in coming to faith in Christ in the first place. They will complain like spoiled children after his death. Their hopes will be dashed—they thought he was

the one who would save Israel. In their minds, all was lost. The portrait of downcast, depressed, fearful disciples is a picture not uncommon in the gospels.

As always, Jesus' calming, healing touch elicited wonder and amazement in their ranks. We hear the familiar question that Mark loves to pose. Who is this person who makes the sea obey him? Mark did not tell this miracle story to ensure a ringside seat at the event for future generations. The issue for Mark is not the miracle itself, but what the miracle meant.

Mark was speaking to his post-Easter community: "Mark has painted an episode in the life of Jesus in colors of early Christianity."[10] Mark's community (and all subsequent communities) was experiencing its own turbulent tempest. Fear, uncertainty, skepticism were in danger of shaking the foundation of the emerging church. "Where was Jesus now? Why had he not returned? He promised he would return. Here we are, enduring all kinds of tempestuous hell for the sake of the *One Who Calms the Seas*, and where is he? Asleep in the boat? Certainly he is not here as he promised he would be!" Mark picks up his community by its doubting bootstraps and shakes it out of its dripping fear and skepticism. He cautions believers of all ages not to lose heart when the storms of life crash upon them suddenly. They know this Christ—the Christ whom even the winds obey. There is nothing to fear. Believers beware! Remain steadfast in your faith.

The scene elicits biblical remembrances for both the author of the story and for the readers. They are reminded of a psalm from the Hebrew Bible, in the form of the Septuagint:

> Some who went off to sea in ships,
> plied their trade on the deep waters.
> They saw the works of the Lord,
> the wonders of God in the deep.
> He spoke and roused a storm wind;
> it tossed the waves on high.
> They rose up to the heavens, sank to the
>   depths;
> their hearts trembled at the danger.

---

[9]*DL* (V), 112.

[10]*MK*, 66.

They reeled, staggered like drunkards;
their skill was of no avail.
In their distress they cried out to the Lord,
who brought them out of their peril.
Hushed the storm to a murmur;
the waves of the sea were stilled.
They rejoiced that their sea grew calm,
that God brought them to the harbor they
longed for.
Let them thank the Lord for such
kindness,
such wondrous deeds for mere mortal.
Let them praise him in the assembly of the
people,
give thanks in the council of the elders.
(Ps 112:23–32, NAB)

Today's gospel is filled with powerful biblical images. Mark is the first writer to refer to a fresh body of water as a *sea* rather than its appropriate designation of *lake*. The intention is to make connections between the Hebrew Bible's use of *sea* and Mark's reference to *sea*. Control of the sea and the calming of storms are signs of divine power throughout scripture. The calming of storms is a sign of God's care and protection. Peaceful and untroubled sleep is a sign of perfect trust in God. Wilfrid Harrington reminds us that Mark's story is a miracle story with a catechetical point. "By his tranquil sleep, his reproach, and his stilling of the storm, Jesus exhorts his disciples to have trust in him at all times and in all circumstances."[11]

The power of Christ is the power of God. Mark professes this reality in miracle, story, image, and imagination. "The power of Jesus the Christ is the power of God. All these affirmations are shown, not told."[12] No one answers the disciples' question. The reader then and the reader today are left to answer it.

Generations have asked the question. Did this really happen the way the text insists it happened? The story evokes so many biblical images. Is this perhaps a midrash on the origin of Christ's power using the biblical images mentioned above? Harrington addresses the issue: "Evidently it is not easy to establish what really happened on the lake;

the story has been much embellished. Though, in Mark, the passage stands as a miracle story, it is by no means certain that the basic incident was a miracle in the strict sense. Rather, we seem to have a combination of circumstances in which the disciples, and Jesus himself, perceived a message, one which had the impact of revelation. It is also to be noted that our passage offers certain close contacts with the narrative of the walking on the waters (6:45–52); and it, too, raises the question of what really happened."[13]

Raymond Brown also addresses the same subject. He reminds us that the worldview of ancient Palestine was far different from ours. Nearly half of Mark's account of Jesus' public ministry deals with miracles. He refers to them as *dynameis* (acts of power). He did not use the Greek word that means *wondrous* as does the English word *miracle*. "Many modern scholars dismiss completely the historicity of the miraculous; others are willing to accept the healing of Jesus, because they can be related to the coming of the kingdom as a manifestation of God's mercy, but reject the historicity of 'nature' miracles such as the calming of the storm in Mark 4:35–41 (Twelfth Sunday). However, that distinction finds no support in an OT background where God manifests power over all creation. Just as sickness and affliction reflect the kingdom of evil, so also does a dangerous storm; accordingly, Jesus rebukes the wind and the sea in 4:39 just as he does a demon in 1:25. (Lest one think this picture impossibly naive, one should note that when a storm causes death and destruction today, people wonder why God has allowed this; they do not vent their anger on a high/low pressure system.) The victory of Jesus over the storm is seen as the action of the stronger one (3:27), whom even the wind and the sea obey."[14]

John Pilch gives us another lens from which to view this text. He asserts that the honor and shame code would have been the primary theme for ancient readers of this story. The honor and shame code insisted that individuals face any situation with brave resolution and undaunted by fear. Yet what does this story reveal? Jesus cruises off with his disciples like any other day and a violent storm comes out of nowhere (as is often the case

---

[11]*MK,* 65.
[12]*MAM,* 38.

[13]*MK,* 66.
[14]*CGOS,* 47–48.

on the Sea of Galilee). Storms of that nature were not an uncommon occurrence. The disciples were fishermen and were well aware of the moody disposition of the lake. Yet they behaved like cowards. Shame would be dripping out of their pores along with water from their sea-drenched bodies if anyone were to find out how abominably they behaved. Jesus seems to add insult to injury and asks them why they were so afraid.

Pilch insists that Jesus' calming of the sea would not have surprised ancient listeners. Rabbinic tradition spoke of saints who had challenged God to make it rain or stop raining. Therefore, it was not Jesus' power that attracted the attention of the audience—it was the "honor status that derived from his power."[15]

The peasants believed that there was a certain hierarchy of spirits. Spirits were capable of doing things humans could not. Some spirits were more powerful than others, and it was important to know the rank of the spirits in order to give them the proper honor they were due.

The disciples, therefore, were not asking about Jesus' identity, but were trying to see what rank they should give him in the order of spirits. What kind of honor and respect did he deserve in their code of honor and shame? Jesus is not only more powerful than human beings, he is more powerful than the wind and the sea! Jesus was more powerful than his birth status would allow. This caused consternation among his contemporaries. His power had to come from somewhere! Where? The disciples' question about Jesus was in relation to the source of his power. As we have seen repeatedly, the disciples believe that Jesus' power comes from God. The scribes and Pharisees believe that demons are the source of his power (see last week's gospel).

Pilch insists that the Greek and Hebrew translation of the word *faith* is "personal loyalty" or "personal commitment."[16] Jesus rebuked the disciples for their breach of loyalty. Their "fear of death shook their loyalty to him."[17] This would happen again at his trial and execution.

---

[15]*CWJB*, 101.
[16]Ibid., 102.
[17]Ibid.

Reflection on the gospel would not be complete without turning our attention to those who live in fear because of the very conditions in which they live—the poor, the lonely, the brokenhearted, the abused, the disenfranchised, the oppressed, the sick, the homeless, and all those who have no one to speak for them. They live in a sinking boat every day of their lives. We might easily brush off their plight by saying, "The poor you will always have with you." Jesus certainly did not tell the disciples to help themselves since there are plenty of other shipwrecked people in the world. No—he calmed their storm. Their boat was sinking. The world's poor are in a sinking boat every day. If the Church is to be the vessel of hope in a sinking ocean of despair, then we may not look upon these people's plight as "none of our business." Gustavo Gutierrez reminds us: "[S]ome find reasons not to see reality as it is; in this way they try to escape from the commitments that a truly evangelical attitude demands. They are afraid of losing their present security—or their privileges—and they refuse to assume total responsibility to the Lord's will. Today's text reminds all of us that fear in the presence of the challenges of the gospel hides something very grave: a lack of faith."[18]

Proclaim the gospel again.

Sometimes we gain new insights when we hear the text after the interpretation is given. Someone from the group proclaims the gospel a second time.

STEP 4
TESTING

Conversation with the Liturgy and the Scriptures

Test your original understanding in dialogue with the text.

(You might consider breaking into smaller groups.)

Now that you've heard the exegesis, were there any new insights? How do you feel about it? How does your original understanding of this gospel

---

[18]*SWTLY*, 170.

compare with what we just shared? How does this story speak to your life?

Sharing Life Experience

Participants share an experience from their lives that connects with the biblical interpretation just presented.

I cannot reflect on today's gospel without thinking of the young family in the parish who recently lost their baby boy to a horrible disease shared by only five other children in the world. I have written about this tragedy many times, but it continues to be foremost in my reflections on the awesome power of God. These devoted parents watched their baby gasp for air, lapse into unconsciousness, only to be revived again, and totter on the edge of death day after storm-tossed day. They begged, "Are you asleep? Where are you?" God slowly led them through the valley of death to the peace that only God could give. This family taught our community how the gift of faith and the power of trust can transform storm-tossed despair into the calm gift of peace in the midst of excruciating troubled waters. At the baby's funeral our pastor read from the mother's journal, her written sojourn of the months they vigiled by their dying son. It is a testament to the innocent faith of a young family that moved from the fear described in today's gospel to a trust born of nothing more than the sleeping, ever-trusting presence of Christ in their midst. We have encouraged the baby's mother to one day share her diary with the world. The parents knew that Christ was with them. With every passing day hope was born anew. They knew that no matter what, they would not be thrown out of the boat. They knew that even in the midst of their sorrow, there could be the most mysterious joy budding forth out of the ashes of despair. One week before we buried baby Jarrod, we baptized his brand-new healthy, disease-free baby brother—in itself an astounding miracle of God.

So, let the skeptics come! Are there miracles? Did Christ still the storm at sea? I will not join the ranks of skeptics. We have been privy to the most sacramental encounter one could ever witness. We watched a family journey through the abyss with faith, confidence, and an assurance that God was leading the way. We watched a family lose a precious child and then stand before our community to thank us and encourage us in our sorrow over their loss. We watched a community lift up and embrace a family in their deepest need, and we watched the new gift of healthy, budding life come to this family in the throes of death. Death would not have the last word.

So, yes, there are miracles—miracles of the most stupendous order! Whether the calming of a sea or a storm-tossed life, the miracle is no lesser or greater. Both point to the incredible, awesome presence and power of God in and through Jesus Christ.

In this "show me" world that hungers for the spiritual, today's gospel stands as a clarion call to look at the ways Christ gifts us with sacrament and steadies the vessels of our lives with an even hand. The Church must not forget that Christ is there to calm the waters even midst the turbulence found within our own communities. The disciples' rhetorical question was not answered because the answer was left to be worked out in their/our lives. Who is this Christ that the winds and the sea obey? He is the Christ who walks with us in our darkest, most troubling hours. Is there any miracle greater than that? We can do no less than follow the example of Christ. We, the people of God, are to calm whatever tempests we have the power to calm with the gift of our presence, our time, our talent, and our treasure.

What was Mark trying to tell his community? Where are the storms in the Church today? In our parish? In the wider Church? In the global Church? In what way might we relate to Mark's community? How does it make you feel that Jesus slept through the storm? In what way have you or your community acted like the disciples in today's gospel? In what way might you relate to the shame/honor issues described in the exegesis? Is there any corollary in our contemporary society? How might this gospel serve as a challenge for your community? In what way has this conversation with the scriptures for today's liturgy invited change in your life? In what way are the biblical themes of covenant, exodus, creation, and community evident in today's readings? Do you still feel the same way about this text as when you began? Has your original understanding been stretched, challenged, or affirmed?

STEP 5
DECISION

The gospel demands a response.

In what concrete way might your parish be invited to respond? Are there any attitudes or behaviors you would like to change as a result of today's conversation? What one concrete action will you take this week in response to the liturgy today?

Christian Initiation: This might be a good time to celebrate a rite of anointing of catechumens. This gospel might surface areas of great struggle and turbulence in the life of catechumens and candidates. It might be an opportune time to celebrate a rite of anointing, an exorcism, and, most assuredly, the blessing. Are there any candidates ready to come into full communion in the Catholic Church? When was the last time you invited the catechumens and candidates to accompany parishioners as they serve in various ministries?

DOCTRINAL ISSUES

What Church truth/teaching/doctrinal issue could be drawn from the gospel for the twelfth Sunday in Ordinary Time?

Participants suggest possible doctrinal themes that flow from the readings.

Possible Doctrinal Themes

Faith; hope; Jesus Christ, fully human, fully divine; paschal mystery; miracles and signs, manifestation; conversion, service/ministry

Present the doctrinal material at this time.

1. The facilitator gives input on a particular doctrinal issue of his or her prior choosing. OR
2. The group chooses a doctrinal issue from the list they created. They read together from the Doctrinal Appendix or other appropriate, official Church documents and the works of respected theologians.

(Many doctrinal issues are found in the Doctrinal Appendix at the back of this workbook. If you are choosing an issue from this resource, please refer to it now.)

Reflection questions centered around the chosen doctrinal theme can be found at the end of each topic in the Doctrinal Appendix. The questions are based on the five-step reflection process. If you choose a topic not included in the Doctrinal Appendix, craft your own questions according to the same five-step process.

Following the reflection questions you will be reminded to return to chapter 7, "Preparing the Catechetical Session," to assist you in crafting your own session.

Closing Prayer

Let us pray
to God whose fatherly love keeps us safe

> *Pause for silent prayer.*

God of the universe,
we worship you as Lord.
God ever close to us,
we rejoice to call you Father.
From this world's uncertainty we look to your
    covenant.
Keep us one in your peace, secure in your love.
We ask this through Christ our Lord.[19]

---

[19]Twelfth Sunday in Ordinary Time, "Alternative Opening Prayer," *The Sacramentary.*

THIRTEENTH SUNDAY IN ORDINARY TIME

INTRODUCTORY RITES

Entrance Antiphon (or Opening Song)

All nations clap your hands. Shout with a voice of joy to God. (Ps 46:2)[1]

Opening Prayer

The facilitator of the session may lead the prayer. Others in the group may be asked to proclaim the readings.

Let us pray
that Christ may be our light

Pause for silent prayer.

Father,
you call your children
to walk in the light of Christ.
Free us from darkness
and keep us in the radiance of your truth.
We ask this through our Lord
Jesus Christ, your Son,
who lives and reigns with you and the Holy
 Spirit,
one God, for ever and ever.[2]

LITURGY OF THE WORD

The readings are proclaimed.

First Reading
Wisdom 1:13–15; 2:23–24

Overview of the Book of Wisdom. "The book of Wisdom is known only in Greek and may be the last book of the Old Testament to be written."[3] The book draws upon the philosophical material of Philo of Alexandria and other Jewish authors living in the Hellenized city of Alexandria in the first century before Jesus was born. It employs the oratorical techniques of the period. The following overview is based on the observations of Lawrence Boadt in his book, *Reading the Old Testament*. He divides the book into four sections. First, 1:1 through 6:21, in which the wisdom and justice of God afford victory and immortality to the righteous. Second, 6:22 through 11:1, which includes Solomon's praise of wisdom as something that is beyond compare. Third, 11:2 through 19:5, which reviews salvation history up to the exodus to show that God was always merciful to Israel. Fourth, 19:6 on, which concludes with a psalm praising wisdom.[4]

The first ten chapters extol the wisdom in creation as coming from God. God gifted Israel with God's revelation. God punishes sinners and rewards the righteous. The book is intended to encourage believers living in Egypt to hold fast to their faith in spite of the other pressures and temptations inherent in living in a pagan land. The book reminds the reader of God's benevolence during the exodus and stresses the idiocy of choosing pagan idols over the Law.

There are two prominent themes in the Book of Wisdom that are noteworthy: salvation history is the lens through which one learns wisdom and the immortality of the soul is the just reward for those who live the righteous life. The Book of Wisdom reveals the struggle of people who try to preserve the values of their tradition in the midst of competing philosophical and contemporary pressures.

Even though the Law and Prophets were given far more attention than the books of Wisdom, the Wisdom tradition endured far longer and was the heart of Jewish life. The prophets Amos, Hosea, Isaiah, and Jeremiah drew heavily on the Wisdom tradition in their preaching. The Wisdom tradition borrowed insights from other cultural and philosophical systems and applied them to Jewish teaching.

---

[1] Thirteenth Sunday in Ordinary Time: "Entrance Antiphon," *The Sacramentary.*
[2] Thirteenth Sunday in Ordinary Time: "Opening Prayer," *The Sacramentary.*
[3] *ROT*, 488.

[4] Ibid.

Roland Murphy asserts that the Wisdom sages were "relentless in pressing home their insights into life: the rewards of justice, the value of diligence and self-control, and so forth. It is said that they were in pursuit of the order that governed the world, but it can be equally maintained that they pressed against the mysteries of creation."[5]

Today's Pericope: In today's gospel Jesus is victorious over the power of death when he heals Jairus's daughter. Today's first reading reaches into the archives of Old Testament thought to support the theology posited in the gospel. Today's pericope from Wisdom grapples with the question of death and the precarious nature of human existence. Why do human beings want to live forever? Surely God would want the same for his children, wouldn't he? God wants life, not death, is the operating assumption of the author. Death is not normal. God did not create the phenomenon. (Reginald Fuller reminds his readers: "Protestants can be assured that although this reading comes from one of the 'apocryphal' books, the doctrine it asserts is an interpretation of Gen 1–3, consonant with Paul's teaching.")[6]

The Book of Genesis asserts that God made the heavens and the earth and God made them "good." According to Genesis 1, men and women were created immortal—they were not supposed to know death. Genesis 3, however, insists that humans are mortal. The Book of Wisdom assumes the Genesis 1 posture of immortality. If humans beings are created in God's image, it follows that they are immortal. Paul embraces this same notion. The reality is, however, that death did arrive on the human scene. Who was responsible? None other than the devil himself. Satan was responsible for tempting the couple to disobey God and thus forfeit their immortality. God's plan was interrupted by human sin. Christ would one day restore the original harmony intended for the human race. Satan will not seduce the Christ. The Messiah would one day resist temptation and redeem the human race by the sacrifice of his life.

For the first time in biblical literature, the serpent of Genesis is equated with the devil in verse 24 of today's reading. The author of the Wisdom passage seems to speak of death as if it were not a biological certainty. The death referred to in this reading, however, is a moral or spiritual death. The meaning of biological death takes on spiritual significance. "[I]t is the ultimate sign of human beings' alienation from God. . . . It is death in this sense—not physical death *per se*, as Christians still have to die—that Christ overcomes by his death on the cross."[7]

Responsorial Psalm
Psalm 30:2, 3, 5–6, 11, 12, 13

Today's psalm is traditionally a psalm of national thanksgiving. It recalls what was considered "death" in the desecration of the temple by Antiochus Epiphanies during the Jewish war. This psalm was originally connected to the restoration of the temple during the time of the Maccabees. In the context of today's liturgy, however, the psalm is used as a prayer of praise for the victory of Christ over death. It points to today's gospel.

Second Reading
2 Corinthians 8:7, 9, 13–15

(Refer to the second Sunday in Ordinary Time for an overview of 1 and 2 Corinthians.)

Today's Pericope: Two years prior to Paul's Corinthian letter, he attended an apostolic meeting in Jerusalem in which he agreed to take up a collection for the church in that city. The Jerusalem church was struggling financially. Paul was faithful to his promise and invited the Corinthians to participate in the fund-raising effort.

Paul then became embroiled in controversy over the false prophets who challenged his ministry. The collection idea was squashed for a time in order to deal with other things that were going on in the community such as Paul's impetuous, ill-fated trip to Corinth and the visit to Corinth by his envoy Titus.

Paul resumed his fund-raising effort and tried to convince the Corinthians to be generous. He in-

---

[5] *CPDBT*, 1085.
[6] *PL*, 319.

[7] Ibid., 320.

sisted that the reason for giving is rooted in the incredible self-gift of Jesus Christ and his incarnation. The Corinthians were invited to pour themselves (and their pockets) out just like Christ poured himself out for us. "Meditation on this mystery of the self-abasement of God's Son very early on led the disciples to the way of voluntary abnegation and poverty. All are not called to go that far; and those who by vocation live in poverty, on account of Christ and their brothers and sisters, are careful not to condemn others who have not made the same choice . But they do not fail to remind people that no one can be reconciled to the blatant inequalities between humans, many of whom are hungry while others are surfeited."[8] Paul reminds his community that they have a responsibility to their needy brothers and sisters in Jerusalem. "The surplus of the ones must compensate for the want of others."[9] Every Christian community has a responsibility to reach out beyond their own borders and extend the gift of faith to others. Christians are to be in solidarity with other Christians who are in need.

The only justification for the responsibility to provide for their needy brothers and sisters lies in Jesus Christ himself. He is the only reason a person needs. One can do no less in light of the ultimate sacrifice of the cross.

The gospel is proclaimed.

Gospel
Mark 5:21–43. Jesus heals Jairus's daughter.

STEP 1
NAMING ONE'S EXPERIENCE

What were your first impressions? What was your first response to the gospel (or the other readings)? What captured your attention?

Each person names his or her initial impression. Statements should be brief. No reasons should be given at this time. All simply listen without agreeing or disagreeing.

---

[8]*DL* (V), 121.
[9]Ibid.

STEP 2
UNDERSTANDING

In a brief statement, explain what you think this gospel is trying to convey.

STEP 3
INPUT FROM VISION/STORY/TRADITION

Liturgical Context

Today's liturgy continues the question that has been looming large in every liturgy of the Ordinary Time cycle. "Just who is this Jesus?" We have grown in a more profound understanding of that question. Satan trembles in his midst; even the elements bow in submission to him.

Last week we observed the foreshadowing of Christ's paschal mystery—his Passover from death to risen life. Asleep in the ship's womb of death, he awakens to the assurance of new life (risen life to come). Last week's story introduces the gospels for the thirteenth and fourteenth Sundays. Faith is the key to belief, life, and salvation through Christ (today's gospel). Without faith Jesus cannot exercise his power (next week's gospel).

The Entrance Antiphon voices our deepest emotions in the face of the gift of faith. We can do no less than rejoice, clap our hands, and sing praise to the living God. The opening prayer invites us to walk as the children of light we are called to be. We might superimpose the word *life* and be reminded that today's gospel invites us to embrace Jesus' passion for the fullness of life. We ask to be delivered from the darkness of death. Implicit is the prayer that we be given faith like that of the woman who merely hoped to touch Jesus' garment in order to be healed. She sought healing. She was healed and thereby included in the community from which she had been excluded. As children of the light we can do no less than work to include in our communities all those who are excluded.

Gustavo Gutierrez offers an interesting footnote on this liturgy. He reminds us that Jesus told the girl to get up—to rise. He then ordered that she be given something to eat. Gutierrez insists that this is part of every person's right to life. "Today the friends of death (Wis 1:16) would deny that right to many people in the world. The texts of this Sunday remind us of the will for life that Jesus announces. Thus, before the needy who are suffering, Paul asks the Christians of Corinth to share what they have. With tact he tells them that he is not giving them a command, he is simply suggesting a concrete gesture to prove 'the genuineness of their love' (2 Cor 8:8). This sharing with those in need will bring about a fair balance (v. 14). This is what Jesus has done for the sick woman and for Jairus' daughter."[10]

Gospel Exegesis

The facilitator provides input from critical biblical scholarship on this text. This input includes insights as to how people would have heard the gospel in Jesus' time.

Today's gospel includes the interweaving of two stories of healing. We are alerted immediately that there is a teaching element to these stories. The site alone sparks our interest. Whenever crowds are gathered by the sea, it is a teachable moment. The stories are connected and we are to be alerted to their connection by the use of the number twelve. The girl is twelve years old and the woman was plagued with her malady for twelve years. An official of the synagogue approached Jesus and implored him to heal his critically ill daughter. Jesus went with the man and an abrupt interruption of the scene ensued: Jesus is mobbed and approached by a woman who had been hemorrhaging for years. Jesus becomes aware that healing power went out from him. The woman acknowledges that she was the recipient of that power. We observe a common Markan technique of sandwiching one story in the middle of another. Jesus affirms the woman's faith when we are catapulted back to the original healing scene.

Jesus is surrounded by throngs at the lakefront setting. Someone from the official's house arrives on the scene and informs everyone that Jairus's daughter is dead. Jairus was the director of worship in the synagogue (an ancient liturgist). In his

desperation over the fate of his daughter, he defies the norms of convention and falls at the feet of Jesus. Later it is announced that Jesus is too late. The girl is dead. The healing of the dead girl and the hemorrhaging woman is accomplished by Jesus through physical contact. Jairus asks Jesus to lay hands on his daughter so she may be made well and live. (The catechetical translation, according to Wilfrid Harrington is better elucidated, "so she may be saved and have eternal life.")

It is easy to sympathize with the afflicted woman. She suffered with her menstrual bleeding condition for over twelve years. Her ailment excluded her from the community. Anyone who came in contact with her was rendered ritually unclean and required to undergo ritual purification. She heard "reports about" Jesus' power to heal and sought him out for that healing. The phrase "reports about" usually referred to a postresurrection profession of faith in Christ. Mark's community would have read it in that context. There are resurrection images running throughout this story such as the theme of victory over death won by Jesus through the Easter event.

The woman tried to fade into the crowd and surreptitiously pass by Jesus in hopes of touching his garment. She knew she was putting others in jeopardy by her mere presence. Yet Jesus was aware that power had gone from him. He sought her out and told her that her faith had saved her. Faith and salvation were consonant ideas.

The healing of Jairus's daughter is connected to theology of the resurrection. The same language ("arise") is used in reference to Jesus' resurrection. It would not go unnoticed by the early Christian that the three disciples who were privy to the miracle were none other than the same disciples who were present at the transfiguration, Gethsemane, and the Mount of Olives. Mark lets us know in no uncertain terms that an epiphany is going on here—the epiphany of Jesus. There is revelation taking place in this story—Jesus' true nature is being revealed. "For Mark and his readers Jesus is the Son of God already mediating the power of his resurrection; he is Lord, the source of saving power (v. 30). And the narrative is a lesson of salvation by faith."[11]

---

[10]*SWTLY*, 174–175.

[11]*MK*, 75.

The catechesis inherent in this gospel is that faith is dependent on a personal relationship with Jesus. The invitation to Jairus and ultimately to all of us is to believe in Jesus' ultimate power and identity, in spite of temptation and evidence to the contrary. Jairus was confident that Jesus could heal his daughter before death ensued. He was asked to stretch, however. Will you take your belief another step? Will you believe that Jesus has the power to transcend life and death—to raise someone from the dead? The moral of the story is "faith in Jesus can transform life and is a victory over death."[12] This faith must be pursued. Intimate, close, personal dialogue with the Christ nurtures that faith. The woman sought after Jesus. He in turn healed her and called her "daughter." He knew what was in her heart. It took great faith to do what she did—to risk. Christians are to seek him out. They are to humbly seek healing, wholeness, and the salvation he comes to offer.

The crowd gathered around Jesus, by the sea, is comprised mostly of the poor class of the day. The two main characters in this saga are from opposite classes. Shame and honor codes require different treatment of both. Jairus, a ruling class personage, approached Jesus as an equal. The man was the head not only of his family, but of a social group (leader of the synagogue). The man falls at Jesus' feet, "a proper granting of honor prior to asking a favor."[13]

Contrast Jairus with the woman, an unclean, lower-class personage. The woman is nameless— she has no status. She represents the status-less crowd. No one comes forward to defend her. Mark makes no bones about the serious nature of her poverty and illness. She has been suffering terribly for many years. She has been treated poorly by doctors and has spent all her income trying to get well, but to no avail. She is an outcast's outcast.

Ancient medicine in no way resembled medicine today. Some have complained that Mark gives physicians a bad name in today's gospel. We absolutely have to put our modern-day concepts of healing on the back burner when we approach this story. There were two kinds of healers—pro-

fessional doctors and folk healers. Prior to her encounter with Jesus, the woman had relied on professional doctors, and depleted all her resources doing so. Doctors hesitated to treat some patients for if the patient died, they could be put to death along with the patient. They often chose the path of philosophical reflection.

The physicians of Jesus' day were not highly regarded. God was considered the Great Healer, thus the people of that era were suspicious of doctors. Folk healers, on the other hand, employed a more "hands on" approach to healing. They risked contact with the patient. Many thought that Jesus was a folk healer. "In the gospel reports, people definitely identified Jesus as a folk healer, specifically a spirit-filled prophet who could still storms, conquer malevolent spirits, and restore people to their rightful and proper place in community."[14]

Curing was understood as the complete eradication of illness. Healing restored meaning to life. In every situation Jesus encountered, people were healed. Cures were rare; healing was a forgone conclusion. Healing gives meaning to life and restores people to wholeness and integration in the community.

The restoration of the woman is dramatic. According to the levirate law, she was permanently segregated from the community. Her blood disorder demanded it. She was not permitted to contaminate the community. Adding insult to injury, she was further abused by the very system that should have helped her—the medical community. In antiquity the poor who were in dire need of medical attention were often taken advantage of. The woman had spent everything she had, and had nothing to show for her efforts. Jesus, the Great Physician, will cure her and charge her nothing.

Jesus violates the purity code and his own purity by touching her, just as he did in the healing of the leper. Her healing signified restoration to physical wholeness as well as social wholeness. The healing restored her to the community.

Jesus was on a mission to lay hands on the daughter of Jairus, who fell at Jesus' feet pleading for in-

---

[12]Ibid., 76.
[13]*BSM*, 200.

[14]*CWJB*, 104.

tervention and healing. Jairus came to Jesus out of a privileged social class that rejected him—not as a member of that class, but as an individual in great need. Jairus's plea was interrupted by an outcast woman who touched Jesus and subsequently fell at Jesus' knees to pay him homage. She intruded into the space of someone more important than she according to the social status scale. According to the culture, the official deserved greater attention and higher priority. "From the bottom of the honor scale she intrudes upon the daughter of someone on the top of the honor scale—but by the story's *conclusion, she* herself has become the 'daughter' at the center of the story."[15] Jesus elevated the woman to a status greater than Jesus' male disciples because she had faith greater than theirs. He reversed her status, and thereby her dignity.

The scene returns to its original course. Jesus continues on his first mission—to heal Jairus's daughter. When everyone arrives on the scene, Mark lets the reader in on the quality of faith of those in the household. They are sarcastic and disgusted that the healing party arrived too late. The official mourning had already commenced. Mark highlights their disbelief (contrast that with the woman of great faith). Jesus throws everyone out of the house (the literal translation). The reader is alerted that something noteworthy is about to take place by virtue of the entourage he takes with him into the house—the three disciples. Perhaps a little angered, Jesus dismisses everyone but the parents of the girl and the disciples. He completes his mission, takes the girl by the hand, and restores her to life. The erudite symbolism of the moment is irresistible. The number twelve is of great significance.

The girl was dead; those around her knew she was dead. Things appeared hopeless for her—she was now cut off from life. Jesus does not challenge their supposition. He simply insists that God will raise her from death. He then takes her by the hand and raises her to life. The implication? The girl represents the twelve tribes of Israel. Mark's Jesus believes he is presiding at the collapse of the social order determined by Jairus's Judaism. The twelve-year-old daughter of privilege was dead.

The woman with no privilege suffered for twelve years not only with the physical ailment, but with the effects of exclusive purity codes. She took the initiative to restore her status. She reached out to gain access. She sought freedom. Jesus responded to her initiative. Israel need only embrace the reign of God in their midst, thereby tearing down the walls of social and religious status. In the reign of God, all are welcome. "This alone will liberate the lowly outcast and snatch the 'noble' from death. Mark's narrative of symbolic action thus achieves the same effect as Matthew's blunt announcement to the Jewish leaders that 'tax collectors and prostitutes are making their way into the kingdom of God before you' (Mt 21:31)—and with equal shock value"![16]

This gospel is also a reminder for disciples not to be stopped dead in their tracks when all seems lost. Jesus did not listen to the naysayers or the despair mongers; he offered life to the girl when life seemed gone. The disciples are to remember this when it appears as if Jesus and his kingdom are dead.

Both healing episodes are intended to proclaim the arrival of God's salvation through Christ. The events prefigure the salvation that Christ will offer through his own death and resurrection. Jesus commands that people keep secret about the incident. In so doing Mark is making the theological assertion that the significance of the rising cannot be fully appreciated. It will become apparent only at a later time. "It is only at the resurrection that the veil of secrecy over Jesus will be lifted (see Mark 9:9), and therefore it is only then that Jesus will be seen as victor over death."[17] The healing of the girl prefigured Jesus' victory over physical death. The healing of the bleeding woman prefigures Christ's death in terms of the cleansing of sin.

Proclaim the gospel again.

Sometimes we gain new insights when we hear the text after the interpretation is given. Someone from the group proclaims the gospel a second time.

---

[15]*BSM*, 201.

[16]Ibid., 203.
[17]*PL*, 321.

Conversation with the Liturgy and the Scriptures

Test your original understanding in dialogue with the text.

(You might consider breaking into smaller groups.)

Now that you've heard the exegesis, were there any new insights? How do you feel about it? How does your original understanding of this gospel compare with what we just shared? How does this story speak to your life?

Sharing Life Experience

Participants share an experience from their lives that connects with the biblical interpretation just presented.

> Our staff recently had a discussion about the disease of poverty. We talked about ways we might make a difference in the lives of those in our parish who live on the edge. One family came to mind. Their situation seemed chronic. We wanted to help them, not just put a Band-Aid on the situation, but really help. In our zeal we thought it might be helpful to get a few people together to help them with some of the core issues—not necessarily or only money issues, but parenting, cleanliness, and the like. We reached out to them, hoping to remedy their situation. Even though they had constantly sought the help of the parish, they were now underwhelmed with our overtures. They did not want that kind of help.

> The mother wryly reminded us that such help was hardly what they needed, as they were being evicted out of their home in less than four days. Mother, father, and four children were going to be on the street. Our overtures meant little.

> Their situation seemed hopeless. They did not need philosophical advice such as was offered by the medical community to the hemorrhaging woman. That woman needed concrete help. She needed to be reinstated in the community. She needed her condition to cease. She needed freedom. Jesus did not offer her advice on why she had this condition, or possible reme-

> dies to try to fix it. He addressed the problem head on and remedied it.

> This family needed help that reached to the very core of their family life. But their immediate need was a home and a place to live. Our parish administrator jumped on the situation and after a couple of days found public housing for the family. They were provided with a nicely furnished place that they could afford—a place much more conducive to their family situation. Without the advocacy of our administrator, they would not have had success in finding a place. All their own efforts failed. The appropriate officials responded to our parish administrator in all earnestness. He did not encounter the response the family was given: "Sorry, we do not have any place at this time—we cannot help you." Options were explored, investigated, and "no" was not an option.

> I know I am being simplistic when it comes to a complex problem. Yes, the family needed long-term help. They needed our community. The woman in the gospel was excluded from the community because of her condition. Jesus restored her to full life in the community. In a sense, our family in question was also excluded—psychologically excluded—from our community. It is the kind of unconscious exclusion that invites people to ignore, or at least fail to see, people who do not fit our stereotype of what people in our middle-class communities should look like. I would hope that I am not blind to such people. But the reality is, I probably am. I do not want to be—I try not to be. This gospel invites me to ask myself: Do I go out of my way to reach out to the marginalized in my own community?

> I thought my efforts to help the family constituted reaching out. Perhaps it was to give myself the self-satisfaction of philanthropic activities. I was the one in control when I approached that family. Little time was spent asking them what they wanted or needed. I was in a position of power. It was only after the encounter that I realized the aphrodisiac that it offered. It felt good to be in a position to fix someone else. (Would that I could "fix" myself!) I was the determinant of what they needed. How arrogant! I remember a line from the movie Nell. The psychiatrist was being chastised for taking advantage of this poor young woman who had been raised by a grandmother but had never had any

other human contact. The doctor was accused of taking advantage of the woman for the sake of medical research. He reminded his accuser that there is no such thing as a purely philanthropic action. He insisted that even Mother Teresa got something in return for her care of the poor: she saved her soul. Her motives were selfish—they guaranteed her salvation. While the doctor's observation was harsh, it nevertheless serves as a reminder that motives require constant discernment and purification. Paul reminded the Corinthian community that they should support the Jerusalem church because of the gift of Christ's sacrifice. When approached with that attitude—our responsibility to our brothers and sisters—it is difficult to have obtuse motives.

Now that I have sufficiently bashed myself over the head with heaping helpings of well-deserved guilt, it is time to get over it. I know my intentions were good in helping that family. I learned a powerful lesson, however. The woman with the hemorrhage had a right to full inclusion in the community. She was an equal of every person in that crowd—including influential Jairus. She possessed the right to life and dignity. Our family in question possess the same rights. I unconsciously did not respect their dignity. My eyes will be more attuned to the ways I participate in attitudes and actions that foster exclusivity. I trust I will respond more appropriately in the future. At least I hope I will.

What was Mark trying to tell his community? Who in our present world might relate to the plight of the hemorrhaging woman? How would you feel? Imagine you are Jairus, a wealthy person who was on a desperate mission to seek healing for your daughter. Imagine further that you are detained by the interruption of a lower-class, outcast woman. What would go on in your head? What would be your primary challenge? Is that challenge unrealistic? How might this speak to your community? In what way does this gospel challenge your community today? In what way has this conversation with the scriptures for today's liturgy invited change in your life? In what way are the biblical themes of covenant, exodus, creation, and community evident in today's readings? Do you still feel the same way about this text as when you began? Has your original understanding been stretched, challenged, or affirmed?

STEP 5
DECISION

The gospel demands a response.

In what concrete way might your parish be invited to respond? Are there any attitudes or behaviors you would like to change as a result of today's conversation? What one concrete action will you take this week in response to the liturgy today?

Pastoral Considerations: This liturgy invites an open dialogue about issues of inclusion and exclusion. Who are the people in your parish who might feel excluded? Who are the unspoken outcasts in your parish, your civic community, the world? Who might resonate with the medical issues alluded to in this gospel? How might this gospel invite us to work for patient rights, medical coverage for all, and equal opportunity for health care?

Some people might complain that such issues are political and therefore have no place in church concerns. They are right and they are wrong. The issues are indeed political. The American bishops, in their document on political responsibility, however, remind us that the gospel calls us to be political—not partisan. In what way can the Church, your parish, be a voice to help people in powerless medical situations?

DOCTRINAL ISSUES

What Church truth/teaching/doctrinal issue could be drawn from the gospel for the thirteenth Sunday in Ordinary Time?

Participants suggest possible doctrinal themes that flow from the readings.

Possible Doctrinal Themes
Resurrection; cross as cleansing of sin; eternal life; death; paschal mystery; healing; eschatology; dignity of human person rooted in creation; social teaching; stewardship; justice; reign of God

Present the doctrinal material at this time.

1. The facilitator gives input on a particular doctrinal issue of his or her prior choosing. OR
2. The group chooses a doctrinal issue from the list they created. They read together from the Doctrinal Appendix or other appropriate, official Church documents and the works of respected theologians.

(Many doctrinal issues are found in the Doctrinal Appendix at the back of this workbook. If you are choosing an issue from this resource, please refer to it now.)

Reflection questions centered around the chosen doctrinal theme can be found at the end of each topic in the Doctrinal Appendix. The questions are based on the five-step reflection process. If you choose a topic not included in the Doctrinal Appendix, craft your own questions according to the same five-step process.

Following the reflection questions you will be reminded to return to chapter 7, "Preparing the Catechetical Session," to assist you in crafting your own session.

Closing Prayer

Prayer After Anointing of the Sick

Let us pray,
Lord Jesus Christ, our Redeemer,
by the power of the Holy Spirit,
ease the sufferings of our sick brother (sister)
and make him (her) well again in mind and body.
In your loving kindness forgive his (her) sins
and grant him (her) full health
so that he (she) may be restored to your service.
You are Lord for ever and ever.[18]

---

[18]Anointing and Care of the Sick: "Prayer After Anointing," *RCC,* 603.

FOURTEENTH SUNDAY IN ORDINARY TIME

INTRODUCTORY RITES

Entrance Antiphon (or Opening Song)

Within your temple, we ponder your loving kindness, O God. As your name, so also your praise reaches to the ends of the earth; your right hand is filled with justice. (Ps 47:10–11)[1]

Opening Prayer

The facilitator of the session may lead the prayer. Others in the group may be asked to proclaim the readings.

Let us pray
for greater willingness
to serve God and our fellow man

    Pause for silent prayer.

Father,
in the rising of your Son
death gives birth to new life.
The sufferings he endured restored hope to a
    fallen world.
Let sin never ensnare us
with empty promises of passing joy.
Make us one with you always,
so that our joy may be holy,
and our love may give life.
We ask this through Christ, our Lord.[2]

LITURGY OF THE WORD

The readings are proclaimed.

First Reading
Ezekiel 2:2–5

(Refer to the eleventh Sunday in Ordinary Time for an overview of the Book of Ezekiel.)

---

[1]Fourteenth Sunday in Ordinary Time: "Entrance Antiphon," *The Sacramentary.*

[2]Fourteenth Sunday in Ordinary Time: "Alternative Opening Prayer," *The Sacramentary.*

Today's Pericope: Today's reading from Ezekiel was chosen for its connection to the gospel. Ezekiel was a prophet who was sent to speak God's Word to the people. He was warned that he would be rejected. In similar fashion, Jesus was rejected by his own people.

Today's reading comes from the first section in Ezekiel that deals with his call. Ezekiel marks a transition in the prophetic tradition. Prior to Ezekiel, prophets avoided using the word *Spirit.* It was too closely associated with the worship of Baal and ecstatic prophecy. Ezekiel reintroduced the concept. Time purified it of the negative connotations. Starting with Ezekiel, Israel's prophets would consider themselves empowered by the Spirit. The same connotation of Spirit would continue in the New Testament. The term *Son of man* is not a messianic title. It simply refers to "man." "It denotes a man in contrast to God, the human bearer of the divine message."[3]

Prophets are often sent on their mission with their feet kicking and dragging. Who willingly wants to go somewhere where persecution and rejection are waiting? Ezekiel was warned that his mission was nearly impossible. He was given a vision of what was ahead. God promised that he would give Ezekiel the words he needed to use. To stress the point, God ordered Ezekiel to eat a scroll on which was written the words God wanted Ezekiel to speak to the people. Ezekiel proceeded as commanded and proclaimed God's message in all its brutal honesty. Obviously, the people were not standing in line to hear it.

God knows that his Word will eventually come to fruition. God does not give up; he sends his prophets to speak to the people. God sends a message of mercy, healing, and reconciliation.

Responsorial Psalm
Psalm 123:1–4

---

[3]*PL*, 322.

No one is sure what situation provides the context for today's psalm. What we do know is that it is the community's cry for help. One member of the community prays on behalf of all the people. The connection of the psalm with the first reading is obscure. Reginald Fuller suggests that the connection might be found in the final stanza of the psalm. It resembles the lament of a prophet whose message was rejected and who received animosity from those who heard the message.[4]

Second Reading
2 Corinthians 12:7–10

(Refer to the second Sunday in Ordinary Time for an overview of 1 and 2 Corinthians.)

Today's Pericope: Paul feels he must boast. For the past weeks we have walked with Paul through his troubles with the Corinthian community. He has had to defend himself against the accusations leveled at him by his enemies, who challenged his apostleship and who jeopardized the community. Paul takes this opportunity to sing his own praises—to give a chronology of the labors, sufferings, trials, and tribulations he endured that attest to his apostleship. This part of the letter is a testament to his career as an apostle. In today's pericope Paul's boasting is in regard to spiritual experiences he encountered. He connected this experience to the physical suffering he has endured. Paul insists that his boasting resides in his weakness, as it is only in weakness that Christ is made manifest.

Paul has nothing of his own to boast about except his suffering, weakness, and hardship. He can only glory in the grace that God has bestowed on him. He will not boast of any of his own achievements, successes, or labors. He would not be a fool if he were to boast, however, for he would be merely speaking the truth. Yet he will refrain from boasting as the boasting is deserving only of the Lord.

Such is Paul's theological backdrop for today's verses. So that he not be filled with pride due to the honor of witnessing something so speechlessly grand, Paul was given a thorn in the flesh. Thus, a messenger of Satan brought an affliction to Paul.

Many have assumed it to be a moral temptation or a spiritual weakness. There is no way to know for sure, but Charles Erdman maintains that it was a "physical disease, humiliating, agonizing, incurable, so terrible, indeed, that it could be described as devilish, literally, 'an angel of Satan sent to deal blow after blow upon the body of the sufferer.'"[5] Paul likened the pain to a stake (translation of thorn), perhaps the kind used to impale bodies of imprisoned captives. There is no way to know for sure what Paul's thorn was. Erdman suggests that perhaps it was providential that the thorn was never named. The unnamed thorn bears within it the seeds of every person's most dreaded pain.

Paul begged that the thorn be removed. God answered his prayer by providing the necessary strength and grace to endure the pain and by stating the inherent divine plan in the decision. God's answer was to be effective for all of Paul's life. God's grace would be sufficient. Inherent in God's promise is the strength to patiently endure suffering; God's revelation and plan will be contained in the midst of such suffering. While the pain is not removed, Jesus is present and revealed in the midst of it. God had great plans for Paul and his divine will would be accomplished through him. Through Paul's weakness, witness was given to the world of Christ's power. Others would be invited to trust God as Paul trusted him.

Paul then glories in his weakness. His suffering was unavoidable, and therefore would be used for the honor and glory of God. He would glory in his weakness in hopes that the power of Jesus himself rest upon him, that God would spread a tabernacle over him. "The power of the living Christ overshadowed and rested upon the human sufferer like a tent, or as the cloud of glory rested upon the Tabernacle of Israel."[6]

The ageless theology of Paul's heartfelt, self-revealing analysis of his situation serves as a promise to all sufferers in the world. It is appropriate that Christians pray for relief from pain and expect God to answer their prayers, with the understanding that such relief is not always possi-

---

[4]Ibid.

[5]*SEPC*, 123.
[6]Ibid., 125.

ble and the specific request may be denied. It therefore becomes an opportunity for divine grace to enter, transform, provide abiding peace and good, and manifest to others God's incredible love and power. Paul realized a powerful truth that he invites us all to learn. God can accomplish the greatest works in and through us when we willingly submit in the midst of weakness to God's providence in our lives. It is at such times when we have the potential to become great, effective disciples.

The gospel is proclaimed.

Gospel

Mark 6:1–6. Jesus, the prophet, was rejected by his own friends and relatives.

STEP 1
NAMING ONE'S EXPERIENCE

What were your first impressions? What was your first response to the gospel (or the other readings)? What captured your attention?

Each person names his or her initial impression. Statements should be brief. No reasons should be given at this time. All simply listen without agreeing or disagreeing.

STEP 2
UNDERSTANDING

In a brief statement, explain what you think this gospel is trying to convey.

STEP 3
INPUT FROM VISION/STORY/TRADITION

Liturgical Context

Today's gospel is the second in a two-part series that began last week. The catechesis of last week's gospel reminds the believer that faith is the key to salvation. This week we learn that without faith, Christ is powerless to accomplish his mission in our lives. Today's gospel asks us the same question asked of Nazareth: Will we have the faith to see the works of Christ in places we would never expect—in our own families, in our friends, in our communities? Are we numbed to the reign of God in our midst? Or are we tuned in to the ever fresh presence of the Spirit of God at work in our lives and in the life of the community? Jesus invites a choice. There was a choice then; there is now. Nazareth almost stepped over the line into the world of belief. Will we have the requisite faith?

> On only two occasions does the Gospel tell us that Jesus was astonished at anything. In both cases, it is about faith. The first episode is when Jesus comes back to Nazareth.... "He was amazed at their lack of faith."...
>
> The second episode is at Capernaum. The Roman centurion implores the cure of his paralyzed servant. "I will come and cure him," Jesus says. The centurion protests, "I am not worthy to have you enter under my roof; only say the word and my servant will be healed." Having heard the centurion, Jesus "was amazed." He cures the servant from afar and he declares that even in Israel he has not found such faith (Matt 8:5–13).
>
> The orthodoxy of Nazareth is not the living faith, the faith that saves. If such a faith had animated them, the people in Nazareth would have opened their hearts to Jesus. But they are content with a correct and sterile belief. Their hearts remain closed.
>
> We know nothing of what exactly the centurion believed. About Jesus he did not know what it has been given us to know. But he opens his heart to Jesus. He feels that in him there is a Savior and a Lord.
>
> Jesus sees what is in us. Does he find in us the centurion's faith or the incredulity of the Nazareth townsfolk? By what is Jesus

going to be amazed: by our faith or by our lack of it?[7]

Fortified by the faith Jesus hoped to find in Nazareth we can do no less than open our liturgy with the heartfelt acclamation of faith in the living God apparent in the Entrance Antiphon. "Within your temple, we ponder your loving kindness, O God. As your name, so also your praise reaches to the ends of the earth; your right hand is filled with justice" (Ps 47:10–11).[8]

Today's liturgy is a reminder to approach the liturgy not like the Nazarenes, but like the centurion whom we quote in every eucharistic liturgy— "say but the word and we shall be healed." Today's liturgy is a challenge to avoid being lulled by the familiar into a boredom that forgets the awesome presence of Christ in our midst—Christ in our assembly, in the Word, in the eucharist, and in the presider/celebrant (Constitution on the Sacred Liturgy). Jesus was present in the flesh in Nazareth—they refused the Christ they could see. Might we be accused of the same when we refuse to acknowledge the Christ who is present in one another, in the living proclamation of the Word, and in our eucharistic feast? Might that also be true when we bury our noses in missalettes when the living Word of God is proclaimed? Should Christ walk into our "Sabbath Day synagogue" on a given Sunday, and we were given an advance copy of his teaching, would we read along, or would we be amazed at his wisdom, hang on his every word and engage in faith-filled, full, conscious, and active participation? We are challenged to keep our faith ever fresh and ever alive. Familiarity breeds contempt. It happened in Nazareth; it can happen in Cocoa Beach, Chicago, San Diego, New York, and Juneau.

Gospel Exegesis

The facilitator provides input from critical biblical scholarship on this text. This input includes insights as to how people would have heard the gospel in Jesus' time.

Imagine the scene. It is the Sabbath. All are in the synagogue, including Jesus' friends, co-workers, neighbors, and relatives. Jesus begins to teach them. Wow! Local boy returns home. All had heard rumors about what he had been doing throughout Galilee. They were curious and incredulous. They were indeed amazed by his wisdom, but could not help asking: "Where did that come from? He grew up with us—attended the same schools and received the same religious instruction. If he had enrolled in the school of a special master word would have somehow gotten back to us—word like that travels. Besides, that would have brought honor on this little hamlet of ours. What is going on here? Just who is this fellow?" The motive behind their questions is not belief in Jesus, however. They are driven by unbelief. "What do you mean he performs miracles? Isn't this the same fellow that did carpentry work in town? Isn't he Mary's boy?"

Mark strategically places this story within his gospel account. It is laden with meaning and significance. Mark is writing for the benefit of his community. Gentiles were being added to the church in growing numbers. The Christian movement emerged out of Judaism. The first converts were Jewish, yet there was great consternation in the Jewish community regarding Christianity. For the most part, they rejected it. Mark continues a pattern that began when Jesus started his ministry in Capernaum. Mark continues to raise and answer the question: Just who is this Jesus? He leaves it up to his readers to decide. He gives enough hints, however!

So far in Mark's gospel Jesus has already encountered opposition from the authorities and was misunderstood by his family. Today he is rejected by them. Jesus is coming to the end of his Galilean ministry. His own friends, neighbors, and citizens of Nazareth are asked to decide: Who is this Jesus? They all reject him. Their rejection foreshadows rejection by the Jewish nation. We learn in John's gospel that those who rejected Jesus were already closed off to God's revelation in their lives before Jesus ever appeared on the scene.

Jesus' disciples accompanied him on his official visit to Nazareth. Mark places Jesus in a role of authority—Jesus is teaching in the synagogue on the

---

[7]Un moine de l'Eglise d'Orient, *Jésus: Simples regards sur le Christ* (Chevetogne, 1062) 41–42, in *DL* (V), 133.

[8]Fourteenth Sunday in Ordinary Time: "Entrance Antiphon," *The Sacramentary*.

occasion of the Sabbath, and all are amazed (a typical pattern for Mark). Yet a quorum certainly was "not impressed." Disdain by the majority prevailed. The people were awed by the where and the what of Jesus' message. They wondered where his message came from and what its nature was. They had heard about his mighty works from others—they just could not believe someone so great could be one of their own. It was tantamount to belief in their own mediocrity (I once heard someone refer to it as the Nazareth syndrome). How could one so great come from a place like Nazareth?

After a brief flirtation with admiration for Jesus, the situation turns hostile. Wilfrid Harrington asserts that the Greek word for carpenter (*tekton*) refers to woodcutter, stonecutter, or metalcutter. The only time the term *son of Mary* appears in the New Testament is in this passage. It was not the custom of the day to refer to a man by his mother's name, which leads to one supposition that Mary was a widow. Some scholars suggest that referring to Jesus in this manner was a derogatory comment. Thus, the Nazarenes were nastily questioning Jesus' legitimacy.[9]

Brothers and sisters are referred to in verse 3. Harrington posits three commonly held ancient views regarding this verse. Helvidius insisted that they were Jesus' blood brothers and sisters. Epiphanius maintained that they were the children of Joseph and a former wife. Jerome insisted that they were Jesus' cousins. Belief in the perpetual virginity of Mary does not allow for the first view. The second view sounds like someone's interesting conjecture. The third has more basis in fact since the term *brother* was a broad-based, inclusive designation for brothers and cousins in the Hebrew Scriptures. Further support for the latter position is that two of the brothers mentioned are mentioned elsewhere (15:40) as the sons of a different Mary.

The only offense the Nazarenes took toward Jesus was that he was one of them. The word used to describe the offense they took, *skandalon*, became a term associated with the obstacle people encountered that prevented them from faith in Christ.

Jesus himself proclaims his own role as prophet. We are told that Jesus could not perform mighty works in that place. Luke soft-pedaled the comment and Matthew omitted it altogether. Mark insists that the prerequisite for Christ to perform miracles was prior faith in him. "Jesus always demanded faith in himself before he worked a miracle: because a miracle is a sign that of the kingdom and without faith would lack significance."[10] The Nazarenes' lack of faith meant that the opportunity for a miracle was closed to them. A few believed, however, and were opened to Jesus' power.

The people in Nazareth were amazed by Jesus' wisdom and they had heard of his power. They were even on the verge of coming to awareness. What prevented it? They could not accept that the Messiah and Lord could come from origins so humble. Would we not have the same difficulty today? All one needs to do is imagine the parish carpenter announcing that he was the one who would usher in the long-awaited kingdom. It is not difficult to sympathize with the Nazarenes. Their serious flaw was refusal to believe that one so great could come from among those who were so wretched.

It is important to note that the response to Jesus is not unlike the response to all biblical prophets. It is no wonder Jesus could not perform miracles for his own people. If he had, they would not have believed in him anyway. They would have explained it away. He was one of them, after all. Jesus' inability to perform miracles in Nazareth foreshadows the final refusal of his mission by Israel. Mark paints a message in stark colors for his early community. If you are dismayed over the disbelief of the Jewish authorities and community, and the persecution you are enduring for being a Christian, you are in good company. Jesus experienced the same thing before you. He was just as incredulous over Nazareth's lack of faith.

Jesus does not take the rejection to heart. In later verses we note that his response is to heal whomever is faith-filled enough to accept it, to move on to a different place, and to commission and send out the Twelve to continue his mission.

---

[9]*MK*, 77–78.

[10]*MK*, 78.

John Pilch insists that we see the honor and shame code of the ancient Mediterranean world in full swing in today's gospel. A person's claim to honor is determined by the origin of his birth. It is called ascribed honor. When the names of the relatives are identified, readers are informed of Jesus' place of honor—his ascribed honor. We are given a hint of scandal when Jesus is referred to as the son of Mary. Since, as noted before, a male is designated as son of the father, the reader is alerted to a confusion about the father. Luke removes the confusion and the hint of scandal by identifying Jesus as Joseph's son.[11]

We are given another clue about Jesus' status by the text's reminder that he is a carpenter, an artisan—his father's profession. It was expected that sons would follow in their father's footsteps. People were to remain in their inherited status. Children were not to improve their lot—they were not to rise to a higher status than their parents.

Any qualified person was permitted to teach in the synagogue. The people were so amazed at Jesus' wisdom that they almost were ready to grant him a higher level of honor. The crowd stops dead in its tracks and refuses to bestow the honor. Jesus was an artisan, one who worked with wood and stone. Wood was scarce, stone was plentiful. Most carpenters were required to travel to nearby cities to find work. The artisans put their family's honor in jeopardy when they left the women and children unattended. Thus, they were negatively regarded as people unconcerned about the requirements of honor.

Jesus takes the offensive and delivers a barb of his own. When he becomes aware that the crowd will not bestow appropriate honor upon him, he quotes a proverb to the ones who want to shame him. He shames them before they can deliver the blow to him. "His point is that outsiders are better able to determine the honor rating of a prophet, one who speaks the will of God for the here and now, than insiders, the people who should know him best."[12] Jesus' own community was on a path of self-destruction—they precluded themselves from the experience of God's salvation and kingdom.

Jesus was making a name for himself. He was a scandal to the townsfolk. Jesus breaks with cultural, binding ties to kinship. "He must concede that he is a 'prophet without honor,' stripped of status and robbed of clan identity. Disowned, Jesus withdraws and takes up again his itinerant mission to the village circuit."[13]

Proclaim the gospel again.

Sometimes we gain new insights when we hear the text after the interpretation is given. Someone from the group proclaims the gospel a second time.

STEP 4
TESTING

Conversation with the Liturgy and the Scriptures

Test your original understanding in dialogue with the text.

(You might consider breaking into smaller groups.)

Now that you've heard the exegesis, were there any new insights? How do you feel about it? How does your original understanding of this gospel compare with what we just shared? How does this story speak to your life?

Sharing Life Experience

Participants share an experience from their lives that connects with the biblical interpretation just presented.

> *Every person in full-time ministry can relate to today's gospel. Any situation that challenges the status quo in any given situation brings resistance. Even though the challenge of today's liturgy is to be open to the ever new and constantly revealing presence of Christ in our midst, it is nevertheless a challenge. The Church has had many such opportunities thrust upon it since the advent of the Second Vatican Council. For some people it has been upsetting.*
>
> *Anyone who is charged with initiating change in a situation can find solace in today's gospel. The role*

---

[11] *CWJB*, 107.
[12] Ibid., 107–108.

---

[13] *BSM*, 212.

of liturgist by its very nature is a prophetic role. The person responsible for preparing the community's ritual prayer often faces the stinging rebuke of well-intentioned people who bemoan the loss of the liturgy they once knew and held so dear and to which they would like to return. Implementing the directives in the "General Instruction of the Roman Missal," incorporating vibrant and robust symbols and music that will appeal to diverse styles and tastes, sometimes brings consternation to individuals or certain groups. It would often be easier if an expert from somewhere else were to come into our parishes and insist that "this is how things are to be done." Even though I long ago crossed that painful bridge, memories of such encounters come to mind every time this gospel is proclaimed in the assembly. Jesus reminds us to forge ahead when it comes to what we believe is the will of God.

Jesus was tough on his own people and no doubt with good reason. Since I am not in a place where I can sit in judgment, I am unable to draw the same conclusion he did about his townsfolk. Change is difficult and there has been a lot of it when it comes to people's communal prayer. Some of the changes have not been implemented well. Some have taken a long time to implement and some have been implemented without proper catechesis. People's frustration is understandable. I do not, therefore, assume the "Nazareth syndrome" is necessarily in force when there is opposition to change. I have been challenged by faith-filled people. They have been opportunities for growth for all involved. However, I do recoil in the face of bad temper and poor manners. Rejection is never easy.

There is a very real human principle at work in today's gospel that we see in parish life all the time. I would venture a guess that it is not restricted to parish life, but can be found in the business world as well. We often become starstruck by people of wisdom from other places, and fail to see those people right under our noses. We often fail to see Christ's prophets who live and work side by side with us. We often fail to see the gifts within our own communities; nor do we lift them up for the good of the community.

There is an elderly woman in our parish who has carried a burden for the rights and inclusion of women for many years. It is a torch upon her heart. She is sometimes not taken seriously by her contemporaries. I am struck by the power of her message.

There is no question that it comes directly from God. She has experienced rejection and a great deal of suffering for the burden she carries. However, her persistence has resulted in more attention given (albeit imperfect attention) to the concerns she raises. She has been an inspiration to me. She reminds me not to give up when I am called to speak an unpopular word. Every parish has similar prophets, but we often fail to see them or, even worse, we get tired of hearing the same message. Yet that same message gets shouted and proclaimed because, like Nazareth, we did not get it the first time.

What was Mark trying to tell his community? In what way does this gospel challenge your community today? In what way might your parish relate to the Nazareth community? In what concrete way might this gospel relate to your everyday life? Who are the people of wisdom in your life that you refuse to hear? In what way has this conversation with the scriptures for today's liturgy invited change in your life? In what way are the biblical themes of covenant, exodus, creation, and community evident in today's readings? Do you still feel the same way about this text as when you began? Has your original understanding been stretched, challenged, or affirmed?

STEP 5
DECISION

The gospel demands a response.

In what concrete way might your parish be invited to respond? Are there any attitudes or behaviors you would like to change as a result of today's conversation? What one concrete action will you take this week in response to the liturgy today?

Pastoral Considerations: Are there prophetic voices in your community that have been silenced?

Christian Initiation: This might be a good time to reflect on the cost of discipleship. Are your catechumens and candidates facing rejection in their lives for the choice they have made to follow Christ? It might be an opportune time to celebrate an exorcism for catechumens or a rite of anointing. Is anyone in your process ready to celebrate rites—rite of welcome, rite of acceptance, full communion in the Catholic Church? Are there baptized candidates ready to celebrate the sacrament of reconciliation? The rite of penance suggests that they be prepared for the sacrament and draw upon its strength in the midst of their journey to full communion.

DOCTRINAL ISSUES

What Church truth/teaching/doctrinal issue could be drawn from the gospel for the fourteenth Sunday in Ordinary Time?

Participants suggest possible doctrinal themes that flow from the readings.

Possible Doctrinal Themes

Faith; Christology; paschal mystery; discipleship; prophets; baptismal anointing—priest, prophet, and king; conversion; mystery of suffering (second reading)

Present the doctrinal material at this time.

1. The facilitator gives input on a particular doctrinal issue of his or her prior choosing. OR
2. The group chooses a doctrinal issue from the list they created. They read together from the Doctrinal Appendix or other appropriate, official Church documents and the works of respected theologians.

(Many doctrinal issues are found in the Doctrinal Appendix at the back of this workbook. If you are choosing an issue from this resource, please refer to it now.)

Reflection questions centered around the chosen doctrinal theme can be found at the end of each topic in the Doctrinal Appendix. The questions are based on the five-step reflection process. If you choose a topic not included in the Doctrinal Appendix, craft your own questions according to the same five-step process.

Following the reflection questions you will be reminded to return to chapter 7, "Preparing the Catechetical Session," to assist you in crafting your own session.

Closing Prayer

Lord,
may we never fail to praise you
for the fullness of life and salvation
you give us in the eucharist.
We ask this through Christ.[14]

---

[14]Fourteenth Sunday in Ordinary Time: "Prayer After Communion," *The Sacramentary.*

FIFTEENTH SUNDAY IN ORDINARY TIME

INTRODUCTORY RITES

Entrance Antiphon (or Opening Song)

In my justice I shall see your face, O Lord; when your glory appears, my joy will be full. (Ps 16:15)[1]

Opening Prayer

The facilitator of the session may lead the prayer. Others in the group may be asked to proclaim the readings.

Let us pray
to be faithful to the light we have received,
to the name we bear

> *Pause for silent prayer.*

Father,
let the light of your truth
guide us to your kingdom
through a world filled with lights
contrary to your own.
Christian is the name and the gospel we glory
    in.
May your love make us what you have called us to
    be.
We ask this through Christ, our Lord.[2]

LITURGY OF THE WORD

The readings are proclaimed.

First Reading
Amos 7:12–15

Overview of the Book of Amos: The Book of Amos was probably written by the prophet's disciples after his death so that his prophetic utterances would be remembered. There were portions of the book that he probably helped compile. Amos's spoken word came first. He was terse and to the point. His words carried great weight and meaning. It is often suggested that the Book of Amos was written around 722 B.C.E., probably in the Southern Kingdom after the fall of the Northern Kingdom.

It is believed that Amos prophesied during the reigns of Uzziah and Jeroboam II. It was a time of prosperity. The economy was good and the political condition was stable. Religious and social debauchery, however, was rampant. People ignored their covenant with God. The nation was basking in the victory against the Arameans. While Assyria still posed a threat, they were blind to it. Instead, the rich enjoyed their opulence.

Amos came from the eastern Judean village of Tekoa. He spent most of his time with shepherds in the region. Amos was by profession a dresser of sycamore trees. By puncturing their figlike fruit, he improved the quality of their taste. Amos lived outdoors, and used images and metaphors from nature for the spiritual life. Amos left the south and headed to the Northern Kingdom to prophecy to them about their immediate need for divine correction.

There are three major sections to the Book of Amos. Chapters 1–2 contain prophecies against neighboring nations as well as a word against Israel. The second portion of the book (chs. 3–6) refers to the spiritual, social, and religious degeneration of Israel. The third section (chs. 7–9) depicts Amos's five visions, the story of his argument with Amaziah, and other utterances.

In the first section, Amos rails against the sins of first the farthest-away areas of the kingdom. He then cleverly levels his attack against the sins of Judah, his own Southern Kingdom; then he centers his attack on Israel itself. "Israel is judged for exploitation of the poor (2:6), immorality (2:7), senseless forms of worship (2:8), and silencing Yahweh's prophets (2:12)."[3] Amos demanded that God come down upon Israel in judgment. The

---

[1]Fifteenth Sunday in Ordinary Time: "Entrance Antiphon," *The Sacramentary.*

[2]Fifteenth Sunday in Ordinary Time: "Alternative Opening Prayer," *The Sacramentary.*

[3]*PAI*, 267.

strength Israel enjoyed under Jeroboam II was swiftly coming to an end.

The second section of the book is concerned with justifying why Israel was to be judged and punished. God's vengeance was to be hurled against a people who had failed to meet their social and religious obligations.

The third section deals with Amos's prophetic oracles and visions. The prophet railed against the meaningless sacrifices and public rituals that were being conducted while the poor remained downtrodden. The people, in their own self-righteousness, believed that they were in good standing with Yahweh. They believed the Day of the Lord would find them ready to receive the light of Yahweh. Amos assured them that they would find only darkness. The Day of the Lord was believed to be a time when Yahweh would once again crash into Israel's history and intervene on its behalf. Amos was incredulous. How could they expect the Day of the Lord to take place when their lives did not reflect their covenant responsibilities?

Amos denounces the rich who exploit and take advantage of the poor. The merchants considered the Sabbath an intrusion into their questionable business transactions. The rich of Amos's day lived lavishly while the poor languished. Amos challenged the people of the Northern Kingdom to change their ways, as God's judgment was imminent.

During Amos's prophetic ministry, the Hebrew mind-set was that covenant relationship with God presupposed care for the poor and oppressed. Such care was a sign of good discipleship. Evidence of that discipleship could be observed in the way resources were used to build God's kingdom.

As a messenger of God, the prophet was to communicate God's desires for his people. Two methods of persuasion used by prophets were *criticism* and efforts to *energize the people*. Prophets would chastise the people for straying away from God and from the covenant. Departure included worshiping other gods, abuse and injustice toward the poor, excessive self-reliance, mistreatment of one another, and exploiting the poor. Such misdeeds would raise the ire of God and bring condemna-

tion. Prophets would insist on repentance. Israel would repent; God would forgive and restore.

In their role as energizers, prophets were charged with laying before the people new possibilities and dreams. They would tell of the future restoration of the peace and harmony of Eden—a new heaven and a new earth. They would promise the re-creation of humanity. The energizing and criticizing of the prophets were directed toward the structures of their time—political, religious, and economic. The prophet remembers God's works of salvation. "The prophet presents a vision of the future as motivation for present action."[4]

Today's Pericope: Today's reading was chosen to accompany the gospel's proclamation of the mission of the Twelve. Both Amos and the Twelve were sent to God's people—Amos to the Northern Kingdom, the apostles to Galilee.

Reginald Fuller asserts that today's reading places before us two opposite notions of religion. One notion is represented by Amaziah's way of thinking, the other by Amos. Amaziah, the priest of Bethel, believed that religion existed to support the state, nationalism, and the status quo.[5] Bethel was the royal sanctuary, similar to a modern-day national cathedral. Amaziah understood his role as that of a court prophet—one who foretold "smooth sailing" for the royal house. During the time of Amos there was an organization of prophets. They were attached to the king and his court. They were charged with prophesying for the kingdom. It was not in their best interest to be bearers of questionable news—good news was the order of the day. Amaziah's attitude about religion would have been shared by the other court prophets. Amos, however, was not a member of the guild of court prophets. He operated independently. He was sent by God to challenge and chastise the king and his court for their acts of injustice and malice toward God's people.

Today's text is part of a section containing visions of projected destruction for Israel. Amos was loyal to Yahweh alone. He denounced the king and warned that God would seek requital. Amos challenged the political structures of his day. He knew

---

[4] *CPDBT*, 785.
[5] *PL*, 325.

what he was about and what he was to do. He was not to be deterred. He would stay the course—proclaim God's Word to the people, no matter how unpopular or unpatriotic it may be, even if it meant castigating the king.

Amaziah called Amos a visionary. Amos denounced that negative designation as well as the designation of prophet. He did not want to be put in the same basket as the other avaricious prophets whose primary concerns were personal gain and advancement. Unlike the others, Amos did not seek after his role as prophet. Amos was a simple shepherd. God sought Amos and commissioned him prophet of the Lord. "For that reason he was not tempted by a conflict of interest as was perhaps the priest and royal advisor Amaziah. After all, a pessimistic and nay-saying employee would not be kept for long on the royal payroll."[6]

Responsorial Psalm
Psalm 85:9–10, 11–12, 13–14

The psalm is generally appropriate for any occasion and enjoys no particular connection with any of the readings today.

Second Reading
Ephesians 1:3–14

Overview of Paul's Letter to the Ephesians: The letter to the Ephesians is directly related to the letter to the Colossians. Duling and Perrin attest that Ephesians quotes and develops the themes found in the letter to the Colossians. Nearly a third of the words from Colossians appear in Ephesians.[7]

There is a question as to the Pauline authorship of both letters. Those who insist that Paul was the author say that it is highly probable that one man could have written the letters in a short amount of time, thus their similarity. Those who argue that Paul did not write the letters suggest that both (Colossians and Ephesians) were reiterations of Paul's previous writings. Those former letters were probably used as a reference for the writing of Colossians and Ephesians. Those who do not believe that Paul wrote Ephesians also point to the many words (40) that are not found elsewhere in

Paul's other letters, but are instead found in later Christian literature.

Another reason scholars deny Pauline authorship lies in the differences between Paul's usual theology and the theology inherent in this letter. In the letter to the Ephesians, the author refers to the "holy apostles" as having special insight. Duling and Perrin suggest that "Paul never distinguishes apostles in this way and never regards them as 'holy' in a way other Christians are not."[8] Ephesians uses the word *church* exclusively as a term for the universal church (resonant with the theme of the "Great Church" of later centuries). Paul used the word to mean local community as well.

The letter to the Ephesians is also not a letter in the usual Pauline form. Usually Paul wrote in response to problems or an occasion in his life. The letter is certainly different from Paul's other letters. Whether it be the work of a calmer, more reflective imprisoned Paul or the brilliant work of a later disciple of Paul who was eager to make his master's ideas known, what is certain is the plentiful adherents to both sides of the controversy.

As far as the context of the letters goes, Paul had established a mission in Ephesus and Colossae ten years earlier on his third missionary tour. Ephesus was his headquarters. The letters to the Colossians and Ephesians are known as the "Captivity Epistles" because they were written from his jail cell. Paul had left Corinth for Jerusalem. He was constantly in trouble with his pursuers, the Jewish authorities. They accused him of defacing the Temple and he was subsequently thrown in prison. He spent three years in prison in Jerusalem and Caesarea.

A great concern for Paul in Ephesus and Colossae was dilution of the gospel due to the influence of gnosticism. Paul was concerned with promoting an authentic gospel, not one made of people's own agendas and exclusive concerns. Even though Paul passionately preached the universality of the Christ-event, he was appalled at the way in which the gnostics distorted his teaching and in the process diluted the Christ-event. They relegated the person of Christ to the realm of angelic being or a heavenly body. Paul would have none of it.

---

[6] *WWC*, 213.
[7] *NTI*, 220.

[8] Ibid.

"Christ is no mere angel or semi-god. He is the very image of the invisible God, a window through which men can finally see without distortion God as he really is."[9] To reduce Christ to a mere heavenly body was to deny his role as Savior of the world. The letter to the Ephesians addresses and refutes this gnosticism.

Today's Pericope: The letter's style more appropriately follows that of paranesis, rather than epistle (see glossary). It is a collection of prayers and preaching. Today's pericope is probably an ancient liturgical hymn used in the baptismal liturgy. The prayer is based on Jewish blessing prayers. The letter is a general discourse on the Christian understanding of salvation history. God has been in relationship with human beings since the beginning of the world, brought his plan to fulfillment through Jesus Christ, and continues his plan in the life of the Church. The letter begins in the language of liturgy, with a long thanksgiving. It is lyrical and sounds very much like the eucharistic prayer of the liturgy.

The author of Ephesians understood Christ as the source and summit of all life and creation. His Christology asserts the role of Christ as mediator with God. God so blessed the world with his Son that human beings can do no less than praise him and live in harmony and love. The letter proclaims the redemption won for the human race *in Christ*, through Christ's saving, paschal action.

The translated word for redemption implies liberation from slavery. The same word was used in the Septuagint in reference to the exodus event and the freedom from slavery that was wrought by it. Jesus Christ, crucified, his blood poured out for all, won liberation for all people for all time. The people have been freed from the everlasting tyranny of sin and death. The gates of heaven were opened, and Christians (those *in Christ*) were privy to the eschatological Day of the Lord, the messianic age, the *kairos of Christ*.[10] *Kairos* is time in terms of event—the momentous, stupendous events of God. *Chronos* is measured time such as minutes, hours, or seasons. Christians are beneficiaries of the *kairos* of Christ in which he suffered,

---

[9] *GAP*, 113.
[10] *WWC*, 213.

died, rose again, and ascended to his throne in glory. As a result of the Christ-event, all things will be re-created. The *kairos* of Christ, the paschal mystery, unites all people in and through him and brings us together as adopted children of God.

The gospel is proclaimed.

Gospel
Mark 6:7–13. Jesus sends out the Twelve.

STEP 1
NAMING ONE'S EXPERIENCE

What were your first impressions? What was your first response to the gospel (or the other readings)? What captured your attention?

Each person names his or her initial impression. Statements should be brief. No reasons should be given at this time. All simply listen without agreeing or disagreeing.

STEP 2
UNDERSTANDING

In a brief statement, explain what you think this gospel is trying to convey.

STEP 3
INPUT FROM VISION/STORY/TRADITION

Liturgical Context

There is an internal unity between the fifteenth and the sixteenth Sundays in Ordinary Time. Jesus sends the Twelve out on the mission this week, and he gives them instructions for their journey. Next week they return to report to Jesus on the success of their mission—what they did and what they taught. These two weeks comprise a sequence before the liturgy moves to Mark's chapter 6, the "Discourse on the Bread of Life," which will take place in the gospels of the seventeenth through the twenty-first Sundays.

The mission of the Twelve, under the direct supervision of Jesus, foreshadows the same mission that every believer would embark on for all generations to come. The first reading demonstrates that the evangelizing mission set forth in today's gospel is part of God's plan of salvation for the world since the very earliest times. Today also begins the continuous reading from Paul's letter to the Ephesians. Both opening prayers for today's liturgy remind us that Christ is the light and the glory that we take with us on the mission inaugurated by Christ.

Hospitality is an important issue in today's gospel. It continues to be an important issue today. Ancient cultures believed that the extension of hospitality, especially to strangers, was a religious act. Hospitality and biblical faith went hand in hand—not to offer it was considered an abomination. It was a sacred duty. Hospitality was a very important responsibility for Israel. The people knew well what it meant to be a stranger in a foreign land. Hospitality was a way for them to extend God's mercy to others. Divine hospitality was a common metaphor for God's protection and care for Israel. The New Testament extends this hospitality a step further by insisting that the poor, oppressed, outcast, and marginalized are to be recipients of hospitality. Offering such hospitality is the same as offering it to Christ himself. It was understood that even the smallest act of hospitality to one of God's messengers, apostles, prophets, God's people, the lowly, would be richly rewarded. It was understood that hospitality is a sign that the kingdom of God has arrived. It is a witness of God's love. Lack of hospitality brought serious implications. There was nothing more important than to welcome a stranger in the name of the Lord. In the Old Testament, extending hospitality especially to strangers was a religious act. The New Testament continues the Jewish reverence for hospitality through the constant attention to welcoming the poor and the outcast. To extend hospitality is a moral imperative because in receiving the poor and the outcast, one receives Christ.

Concern for hospitality is a primary virtue in Christianity and also in later monastic spirituality.

The same concern for hospitality is continued in the Church today and is a primary concern of those preparing for worship. The introductory rites of the mass are the embodiment of the Church's imperative to offer hospitality. This is a communal religion. Implications of hospitality require us to ask how we offer hospitality to children, strangers, the indigent, lonely, elderly, deaf, the sick, the lonely.

There are many issues in today's gospel that speak to our sacramental, liturgical, and ministerial life. Within this gospel are the roots of our sacramental healing and liberation mission. The disciples are given Jesus' authority to expel demons; they are given oil to use in their miraculous ministry of healing. They paved the way for the mission that continues today.

This gospel carries the seeds of the healing sacraments of the Church. Jesus sent the disciples with oil. Oil was commonly used in the treatment of medical conditions, thus it was appropriately associated with Jesus' miraculous healing mission. Jesus used the things of ordinary life and common experience to demonstrate God's incredible power—water, mud, spittle, bread, wine. James attests to the use of oil in the healing ministry continued in the early church, probably as a result of this gospel passage. Oil continues to be used in the sacramental ministry in the Church today. Oil is one of the Church's nine dominant symbols. (For greater elaboration on the symbol of oil, refer to "Easter Vigil: Symbol of Oil.")

In the gospel we are reminded that Jesus gave the disciples authority over unclean spirits. Jesus' life, death, and resurrection were definitive victories over the power of Satan and evil. It is comforting to know that we have been given Jesus' authority to deal with those forces of evil that plague us throughout life. We sometimes reduce the power of evil to nothing more than interior demons in need of the latest psychology or the Satan beast that seeks the destruction of global powers. While both may be true, we thereby avoid the realization that evil is real. Jesus engaged in battle with the power of evil and won. While an overemphasis on evil gives the "devil more due" than he deserves, to ignore it altogether is absurd. The following reflection is worthy of our attention:

Today we speak a lot about the "power" of the ministers. It is curious: the only power given to ministers in Mark is one we do not exercise, that of driving out demons. This conception of the missionary's task, according to Mark, is in conformity with that of the Acts of the Apostles or Paul's letters. Paul had the certitude that he worked miracles on his way by preaching the gospel. We, for our part, have difficulty seeing things this way. Miracles make us uncomfortable.... Our attitude is in contrast with the attitude of the sects that make abundant use of miracles. When we read the gospel, we feel estranged and we ask: By any chance are the sects closer to the gospel than we are? Do they not represent a reaction aimed at reestablishing a balance which we ourselves have lost?

We get the impression that what, in Mark, formed a beautiful unity is now scattered: there are specialists in preaching and specialists in miracles—a loss for all concerned. A yen for miracles can be unwholesome (John will be very reticent on this point.) But on the other hand, perhaps we are not attentive enough to the fact that the preaching of the gospel must have repercussions on human equilibrium. I know that we have replaced the healing of the sick with the will to create a world more just and kinder to one's brothers and sisters. It is, no doubt, legitimate to seek for signs of the coming of the kingdom into our world in the improvement of human life. But under the condition that we not forget the potency of the gospel: it is a power of action against the reign of evil.[11]

The Church takes the battle with evil seriously. One need look no further than the rites of initiation to encounter the liberation ministry of Christ that continues today. The RCIA provides for minor exorcisms to be celebrated with catechumens throughout their journey in order to strengthen them against the power of evil in their everyday lives. The exorcisms of the scrutinies celebrate that ultimate liberation won for us through the power of the risen Christ. The eucharist strengthens us in our struggle with evil.

Evil exists. We have been given the grace and the tools to overcome it. Christ overcame it once and for all time. We have nothing to fear.

Gospel Exegesis

The facilitator provides input from critical biblical scholarship on this text. This input includes insights as to how people would have heard the gospel in Jesus' time.

Mark's gospel has embarked on a new theme, starting with today's reading from chapter 6. Mark 6:6 through 8:30 is devoted to Jesus and his teaching, training, formation, and frustration with the disciples. Jesus sends the Twelve out on a mission of healing and reconciliation, yet there are still episodes that reveal Jesus' consternation over the disciples' lack of understanding. Another major theme for Mark is the emergence of the gentile mission.

Jesus has been rejected by his own family and friends. His attention turns to his chosen ambassadors—the Twelve. He has been teaching and forming them in his mission. Now it was time to test their preaching skills. Even though presented as a trial run, the directions given to the Twelve on their maiden voyage were intended as a blueprint for *all* future missionary activities. While we are given the plan, we are told nothing of its execution. The focus is not on the execution of the mission, but on Jesus' instructions to the Twelve. There is no sense that the orders Jesus set before the apostles were intended for this particular mission—"they are for 'the way' (*eis hodon*)—that is, paradigmatic of discipleship lifestyle."[12] The significance of this text lies in the exhortation to rely completely on hospitality as they go forth on "the way." The only time Mark refers to the Twelve as apostles is in verse 30, upon their return from the mission. On this mission they were allowed sandals and staff—the means of travel. In Mark's gospel, sandals were a metaphor for discipleship (their use forbidden by Matthew, and Luke omitting the

[11]J. Delorme, "Lecture de l'Evangile selon saint Marc, *Cahiers Evangile*, 1/2 (1972), 55–56, in *DL* (V), 143.

[12]*BSM*, 213.

reference to them altogether). Means of survival such as food, lodging, money, and clothing were dependent on the hospitality of others. "In other words, they, like Jesus, who has just been renounced in his own 'home,' are to take on the status of sojourner in the land."[13]

Matthew and Luke relate this event through the prism of kingdom—they went out preaching the reign of God. That is hardly Mark's perspective. According to Mark, the disciples do not yet understand what the reign of God is really about. How can they preach what they do not yet understand? Their message was the same as John's—"Repent! Repent! Repent!"

John the Baptist is alluded to in the mission of repentance. Mark wants to make sure that the implications of the mission are not forgotten. John hints about what lies ahead for every disciple, most especially, what lies ahead for Jesus. The mission is directly related to the fate of Jesus. The formation of the community has only begun. They are being apprenticed in phase one of the mission. Phase two has yet to be revealed. Today we are given hints. Phase two is the mission of the cross. The mission (of repentance—like John the Baptist's mission of repentance) leads to the end usually reserved for prophets—death. The mission—the kingdom—will eventually clash with the political and religious powers. Just like John. It is a subtlety not to be missed. Mark leads us into the conflicts, struggles, frustrations, humanity, and tragedy of the community and "its struggle to understand and truly embrace the mission with which it is *already* engaged."[14]

According to the traditional Jewish custom of sending people out in pairs to announce an important message, the apostles were sent out two by two. They were to take nothing with them but were to depend on the hospitality of all they met. They were to stay in the first welcoming household they encountered. They were not to move elsewhere for more plush accommodations. They were to shake the dust from their feet in places where they encountered rejection, just as all Jewish people were to do when they returned from pagan lands. The implication? Those who rejected them were no better than heathens and pagans! It is possible that this was the early Christian community's means of establishing a network of safe houses around the district for purposes of shelter on missionary ventures.

Mark intentionally charged the disciples with a message of repentance. Like the Baptist, they prepared the way for Jesus' own proclamation. Jesus would announce his own kingdom. It is also possible that Mark wishes to make the distinction between the preaching of the disciples before and after the Easter event. Their mission included the authority to continue Jesus' ministry of healing and exorcism.

John Pilch provides a cultural context for today's reading based on the honor and shame code of early Palestine. Jesus sent the Twelve out with the authority to control demons. This was not a lateral promotion; it catapulted them a rung or two up the honor ladder.[15]

In antiquity there was a strong belief in spirits. Spirits were believed to have enjoyed their own honor status and hierarchy. There were five levels of order. The highest order of spirit was "'our' God, the second level was 'other gods,' sons of god or archangels."[16] Lower on the totem pole and the third level of order included the less powerful spirits such as angels, spirits, and demons. Human beings were even lower, the fourth level, and other created beings, lower yet. Jesus elevated the disciples from level four to level three by giving them authority over unclean spirits. Greek terminology referred to "demons" and Semitic language used "unclean spirits," but both meant the same thing. Jesus healed a man with an unclean spirit who was referred to as a demoniac in the man's pagan homeland.

What we refer to as exorcism, the New Testament called authority and power. Exorcism was not a word used in the New Testament. Jesus had authority over spirits. His power to expel demons was similarly a sign of his authority. He passes that authority on to the Twelve in today's reading.

---

[13]Ibid.
[14]Ibid.

[15]*CWJB*, 108–109.
[16]Ibid., 109.

Travel was dangerous in Jesus' day. Marauders waited in the bushes to ambush lone travelers. It is no wonder that Jesus sent the disciples out in pairs. They probably joined other groups of travelers. It was not uncommon to depend on the hospitality of strangers when traveling. Hospitality was a sacred act. Not to extend hospitality was considered an abomination before God.

Pilch makes a distinction, however. Hospitality was something offered to strangers. Relatives and friends were recipients of steadfast lovingkindness. There were three steps. The stranger would be given protection by a host for a period of time, thus becoming a temporary guest, and eventually leaving as either friend or enemy. Both options were possible. The host provided food, lodging, and protection from other villagers who were fearful that the stranger was up to no good. It was a serious breach of honor not to extend hospitality.[17]

Jesus exhorted the disciples to hurl a major insult to the transgressor. "It effectively writes these people out of the human community. The gesture implied total rejection, hostility, and unwillingness to be touched by anything the others have touched."[18]

Ched Myers posits an interesting observation when he compares Jesus' nonviolent band of spiritual subversives with other typical types of subversive movements. Jesus' disciples were subject to the social and political attitudes of the community to which they were sent. Those attitudes would determine how they were, or were not, received. Subversives, such modern-day guerrillas, must operate under covert circumstances. Christians, when well received, stayed put, became publicly involved, and were willing to establish a base operation from that place. Military subversives seize what they want and what they need by force. Christians were dependent on the mercy of others and Jesus forbade retaliation in the face of rejection. They were in no position to force their opinions on anyone.[19]

Ultimately the instructions of Jesus are still operative. Disciples are still to go out in a spirit of poverty. Two tunics are a sign of wealth. We are to go out as beggars in solidarity with the beggars of the world. Disciples are to take only what is essential to their mission. The Christian kerygma must go forth. It will not go forth, however, from a position of power, wealth, and prestige. It will only go forward in humility and in poverty. Missionaries and disciples must depend on the gracious hospitality of the recipients, not on the social status they bring to the encounter.

The same prophetic call exists today. We are to announce to the world the message of the prophets. Where there is injustice the prophet is to scream from the highest parapet. Amos had no problem taking his place among the prophetic greats. The disciples were to go out and do the same. And so are we, relying on the power of God to sustain us.

Gustavo Gutierrez reminds us: "The mission we receive comes from an election 'before the foundation of the world' (Eph 1:4). Being children of God is a grace as well as a responsibility for which we will have to account before God. Only a profound sense of God, the rejection of every social or economic privilege, an authentic personal poverty, a 'nonprofessional' practice of our evangelizing role will enable us to give testimony leading to conversion (Mk 6:12)."[20]

Proclaim the gospel again.

Sometimes we gain new insights when we hear the text after the interpretation is given. Someone from the group proclaims the gospel a second time.

STEP 4
TESTING

Conversation with the Liturgy and the Scriptures

Test your original understanding in dialogue with the text.

(You might consider breaking into smaller groups.)

---

[17]Ibid., 110–111.
[18]Ibid., 111.
[19]*BSM*, 213.

[20]*SWTLY*, 183.

Now that you've heard the exegesis, were there any new insights? How do you feel about it? How does your original understanding of this gospel compare with what we just shared? How does this story speak to your life?

Sharing Life Experience

Participants share an experience from their lives that connects with the biblical interpretation just presented.

I recently shared in an experiment of this gospel. Our parish initiated an evangelization effort similar to the one described in today's gospel. We prayed this scripture before we were sent forth, blessed by our Sunday assembly. Our pastor, staff, catechumens, candidates, and sponsors set out on a Sunday afternoon to go door to door to invite people to visit our parish family. I was amazed at how frightening it was. I thought myself to be a very hospitable, open, friendly person. I was surprised at how shy I became as we knocked on that first door. I realized how turned off our culture is to such endeavors. We experienced both hospitality and rebuke. Some found the experience incredibly wonderful; others found it disheartening at best. I was struck by two particular situations.

Our staff went out on a trial run to a poor area before the Sunday event. We went to nicer neighborhoods on the Sunday we were dismissed from the assembly. It just so happened that the houses my partner and I were assigned to were not paragons of hospitality. One lady was a fairly new member of the parish and expressed her displeasure that we were doing such a thing. "It is not our job to be going door to door like the Mormons!" She was embarrassed for us. Some people wished us well. Others told us they resented religion on their front doorstep. Others related pain and hurt at the hand of the Church and promised to give things a second look. A few expressed the desire to "Come and See!"

The experience certainly did not bring in the hoards. But it did awaken the neighborhoods to the presence of the Christian community. Perhaps when the moment comes, some people will remember those overtures and come knocking at our doors. There were some remarkable "success" stories. There were a few alienated Catholics who were reconciled to the Church and have returned. A couple of people expressed interest in finding a church home.

I mentioned the rebuke at one of the houses. I am struck by a contrasting incident in the poor neighborhood. We knocked on the door to a tiny apartment. It took a while, but shortly we were met by two young men. They enthusiastically invited us in—almost too enthusiastically. At first glance I was frightened. The only piece of furniture in the house was a tattered sofa.

We gave our rehearsed piece of welcome. Both young men were touched. One of the men started to tell us his story. He asked us if we thought God could heal him. He was a drug addict and could not get clean. He had been in jail and treatment programs and had completely given up hope. "Can Jesus help? I have tried everything else." We invited him to come and assured him that we would do anything we could to help him. We have not heard from him; we are still hoping that we will. Perhaps it is time to go back and invite once again.

I was so touched by the encounter. We were offered more welcome and hospitality in that house than anywhere we went. Two young teens, without families, marginalized—one a drug addict, the other trying to help his friends. They certainly were not people who could win friends or influence anyone. Of all the houses, that would have been the place, according to Jesus' instructions, where we would have lodged for the night. We offered the compassion and invitation of Jesus. Perhaps they will one day accept the invitation. Maybe I need to return so they can once again offer it to me.

This gospel reminds me of all the traveling I do around the country and the many wonderful people who have extended hospitality to me on those journeys. I leave each place amazed by the incredible love and hospitality of God's people. They are the compassion of Christ. Even though friends for just a short time, they will never be strangers.

What was Mark trying to tell his community? What do you suppose was going through the minds of the disciples as Jesus was giving them instructions? Is there any relevance for today? How would the mission as described in today's gospel be received in your neighborhood? Jesus gave the disciples the authority over unclean spirits. How does that speak to you today? What are the implications? In what way does this gospel challenge your community today? In what way has this conversation with the scriptures for today's liturgy invited change in your life? In what way are the biblical themes of covenant, exodus, creation, and community evident in today's readings? Do you still feel the same way about this text as when you began? Has your original understanding been stretched, challenged, or affirmed?

STEP 5
DECISION

The gospel demands a response.

In what concrete way might your parish be invited to respond? Are there any attitudes or behaviors you would like to change as a result of today's conversation? What one concrete action will you take this week in response to the liturgy today?

Pastoral Considerations: Perhaps this would be a good time for your parish to participate in evangelization efforts. Have you ever considered organizing a door-to-door effort to welcome people to your parish?

Christian Initiation: This would be an appropriate occasion to celebrate the minor rite of exorcism as part of your gathering this week. This might be a good opportunity to welcome people into your inquiry. Are there any people ready to celebrate a rite of acceptance, welcome, or full communion in the Catholic Church?

DOCTRINAL ISSUES

What Church truth/teaching/doctrinal issue could be drawn from the gospel for the fifteenth Sunday in Ordinary Time?

Participants suggest possible doctrinal themes that flow from the readings.

Possible Doctrinal Themes

Call of discipleship; baptismal call—priest, prophet, king; hospitality; mission of Christ; sacra-

ments; sacramentality, symbols; symbol of oil; evangelization; sacraments of healing

Present the doctrinal material at this time.

1. The facilitator gives input on a particular doctrinal issue of his or her prior choosing. OR
2. The group chooses a doctrinal issue from the list they created. They read together from the Doctrinal Appendix or other appropriate, official Church documents and the works of respected theologians.

(Many doctrinal issues are found in the Doctrinal Appendix at the back of this workbook. If you are choosing an issue from this resource, please refer to it now.)

Reflection questions centered around the chosen doctrinal theme can be found at the end of each topic in the Doctrinal Appendix. The questions are based on the five-step reflection process. If you choose a topic not included in the Doctrinal Appendix, craft your own questions according to the same five-step process.

Following the reflection questions you will be reminded to return to chapter 7, "Preparing the Catechetical Session," to assist you in crafting your own session.

Closing Prayer

Blessing of Missionaries within Celebration of Word

Prayer of Blessing

We bless you, O God, and we praise your name.
In your merciful providence you sent your Son
    into the world
to free us from the bondage of sin by his own
    blood
and to enrich us with the gifts of the Holy Spirit.
Before he returned, triumphant over death, to
    you, Father,
he sent his apostles, the bearers of his love and
    power,
to proclaim the Gospel of life to all peoples
and in the waters of baptism to cleanse those who
    believe.

Lord, look kindly on your servants:
we send them forth as messengers of salvation and
     peace,
marked with the sign of the cross.
Guide their steps with your mighty arm
and with the power of your grace strengthen them
     in spirit,
so that they will not falter through weariness.
Make their words the echo of Christ's voice,
so that those who hear them
may be drawn to obey the Gospel.
Fill the hearts of your missionaries with the Holy
     Spirit,
so that, becoming all things to all people,
they may lead many to you, the Father of all,
to sing your praises in your holy Church.
We ask this through Christ our Lord.[21]

---

[21]Blessing of Missionaries with Celebration of Word:
"Prayer of Blessing," *BB*, 198.

Sixteenth Sunday in Ordinary Time

INTRODUCTORY RITES

Entrance Antiphon (or Opening Song)

God himself is my help. The Lord upholds my life. I will offer you a willing sacrifice; I will praise your name, O Lord, for its goodness. (Ps 53:6, 8)[1]

Opening Prayer

The facilitator of the session may lead the prayer. Others in the group may be asked to proclaim the readings.

Let us pray
to be kept faithful in the service of God

Pause for silent prayer.

Lord,
be merciful to your people.
Fill us with your gifts
and make us always eager to serve you
in faith, hope, and love.
Grant this through our Lord,
Jesus Christ, your Son,
who lives and reigns with you and
the Holy Spirit,
one God, for ever and ever.[2]

LITURGY OF THE WORD

The readings are proclaimed.

First Reading
Jeremiah 23:1–6.

Overview of the Book of Jeremiah: During a period in which Jeremiah was in hiding (ca. 604 B.C.), he dictated to his secretary Baruch a summary of what he had preached during his prophetic ministry. Jeremiah preached in the Southern Kingdom under the rule of King Jehoiakim. The king

burned Jeremiah's first manuscript. Jeremiah had Baruch compile a second manuscript. Scholars suggest that chapters 1–20 and 25 of the Book of Jeremiah is the bulk of that second manuscript.

There is very little chronological order in the book. This is often confusing. The siege of Jerusalem, which occurred around 588–587 B.C.E., is mentioned in chapter 21 and events that took place in 604 are mentioned in chapter 25. The reason for this, scholars suggest, is that rather than try to put the vast collection of different types of prophetic material in some kind of reasonable chronological order, the author chose instead to arrange it thematically.

Jeremiah speaks out against the kings of Israel. He puts Israel on trial and charges Israel with crimes against God. He pronounces God's judgment against Israel. Jeremiah claims to speak as one sent by God—God's messenger. The prophet understood his role as one of messenger sent by God to announce judgment on Israel for infidelity to the covenant. Israel failed to live up to moral imperatives of the covenant.

Others could claim to be God's messengers, but only one *truly* sent by God could speak God's Word. A prophet who asserted that he was God's messenger, but in reality was not sent by God, was considered a false prophet. Prophets therefore had to make a strong case and authenticate that they were truly sent by God. Jeremiah, Isaiah, and Ezekiel all testified that their prophetic mission was directly commissioned and sanctioned by God. There is no doubt about their divine commission when one considers how their extremely unpopular message has withstood the test of time.

When Israel failed to live the commandments— the love of God and love of neighbor— they failed to live up to the covenant. It is usually sins against the two great commandments that make up the primary agenda of the prophets. When the people worshiped false idols and failed to take care of the poor and oppressed, the prophet was sent to

---

[1]Sixteenth Sunday in Ordinary Time: "Entrance Antiphon," *The Sacramentary.*

[2]Sixteenth Sunday in Ordinary Time: "Opening Prayer," *The Sacramentary.*

speak God's word of judgment. Prophets behaved like prosecuting attorneys when speaking about God's anguish over Israel's failure to be faithful to the covenant. When speaking for the people, they took the role of defense attorneys. The prophet's concern was to reconcile and help Israel understand and appreciate their unique, special relationship with God. Jeremiah had a burning passion for God and an abiding love for God's people.

Today's Pericope: Today's reading was chosen for its connection to verses in the gospel that tell of Jesus' compassion toward the crowds, who "were like sheep without a shepherd." The image of shepherd was closely related to the image of king in ancient Israel. David was a shepherd boy who became the great king of a united Israel.

> In all peoples whose origins are pastoral and nomadic, shepherds are important personages. Usually they are heads of families who work at their tasks with the help of their sons and daughters. If they must have recourse to strangers, these must be trustworthy persons because they are charged with an important responsibility. As a consequence, among those people, in the Ancient East in general and among the Hebrews in particular, the image of shepherd is naturally used to designate the chiefs, the kings, and even God.[3]

Israel's later history was plagued with kings who abused their role as shepherd. Jeremiah remembered Israel's recent history up to the time of the captivity and railed against those leaders who misused their power and failed to shepherd their people. Jeremiah hurled a very serious accusation against the shepherds. They failed to take care of God's people. God promises retribution to those who squander the ones entrusted to their care. God will personally take care of the neglected and misgoverned flock.

Full expression of this neglect is the historical reality of the exile. The sheep were scattered across the land—the people were exiled. As with all of salvation history, religious significance was given to a real historical situation.

The religious meaning of the exile was a typical motif for Israel. Israel sinned and was unfaithful to the covenant. As a result, they were scattered and sent into exile. Israel repented, God was merciful, and Israel was restored. Israel put its trust in something other than God, and as a result, was exiled. The religious leaders—the shepherds—failed to call the people to accountability for their sins. The exile served as a natural corrective. It was an opportunity for Israel to own their failings and to realize that salvation is possible only through the mediation of God. God therefore restored the exiles, who were to live in faithfulness to the covenant.

Jeremiah brings his condemnation of the shepherds to a close with a promise that a "righteous shoot" would survive. This righteous shoot would be a future righteous king who would one day shepherd Israel in all its glory. The righteous shoot would be an ideal king. Jeremiah's promise bespeaks the restoration of the Davidic monarchy, which he hoped would return following the exile.[4] While this obviously did not take place, Jeremiah's promise carried within it the seeds of Israel's messianic expectations. We live in the fulfillment of Jeremiah's promise. We live in the eschatological reign of the ideal king—the true Shepherd of Israel, Jesus Christ.

Responsorial Psalm
Psalm 23:1–3, 3–4, 5, 6

There is an obvious connection among the psalm, the first reading, and the gospel. Yahweh is portrayed as Shepherd but also as a host of a great banquet in the Temple. It was believed that the king of Israel was the incarnation of God's shepherding and care. Christianity assigns that role to Jesus. Jesus is the true Shepherd. Jesus alone is the incarnation of God. He will lead the people through this earthly reign to their ultimate destiny—eternal life. They will then feast at the eschatological banquet of heaven.

Second Reading
Ephesians 2:13–18

(See the fifteenth Sunday in Ordinary Time for an overview of Paul's letter to the Ephesians.)

---

[3]*DL* (V), 147.

[4]*PL*, 328–329.

Today's Pericope: The Deutero-Pauline writer reflects the life and mission of the apostle. Jews and gentiles were gathered into one family in Christ. Through the sacrifice of Jesus on the cross, the Law was both fulfilled and abolished and the way of salvation was guaranteed.

Christians observe the Law now, not because of some moral demand, but out of incredible love for Christ. They can do no less in light of his ultimate sacrifice. "It is the blood of Christ, shed in violent and undeserved death, that destroyed everything that functioned in our world to separate us from one another."[5] We are saved by the grace of God. Salvation cannot be earned. All people have access to this salvation. It is God's free, unmerited grace offered to all human beings.

Paul preached a unified Body of Christ. As far as he was concerned, the alienation between the Jews and the gentiles was the antithesis of the gospel. Paul probably did not live to see the realization of the unity he preached, and its lack was cause of great pain and consternation. He longed to see the day when Jew and gentile would gather in heartfelt unity around one banquet table. All were given access to that table through the sacrifice of the cross. The word *access* in biblical language was a liturgical reference. It referred to common worship—through the sacrifice of Christ all gained praise-filled access to the throne of God. "Our author knows about the grievous historical division of humanity into Jew and Gentile—one group far from God and the other God's chosen people—but chooses to develop instead the good news that unity has been achieved in and through Jesus Christ.... The author shows us as we should be, or better, as we really are because of God's gift in Christ. In Christ we are a forgiven church. In Christ we are a resurrected and glorified people. In Christ we are one."[6]

The gospel is proclaimed.

Gospel
Mark 6:30–34. The apostles return and Jesus takes them to a deserted place to rest for a while.

---
[5]*LPT*, 99.
[6]Ibid., 98.

What were your first impressions? What was your first response to the gospel (or the other readings)? What captured your attention?

Each person names his or her initial impression. Statements should be brief. No reasons should be given at this time. All simply listen without agreeing or disagreeing.

STEP 2
UNDERSTANDING

In a brief statement, explain what you think this gospel is trying to convey.

STEP 3
INPUT FROM VISION/STORY/TRADITION

Liturgical Context

The fifteenth and sixteenth Sundays in Ordinary Time form an internal unity. The gospel for both Sundays deals with the mission that Jesus entrusted to the Twelve.[7] Today's liturgy is a sober reminder that God takes the role of pastor and shepherd very seriously. Jeremiah does not beat around the bush. There are serious consequences for failing in that sacred trust. Jesus the Good Shepherd will gather all people into one family through the sacrifice of the cross (second reading) and will lead and teach those who were neglected by those who were responsible for that role (gospel).

Mark emphasizes Jesus' teaching role. That role continues today in the liturgy. Jesus the Shepherd continues to teach his flock in the liturgy of the Word. Similarly, Jesus the Good Shepherd continues to feed his flock at the great banquet table (psalm) in the liturgy of the eucharist.

---
[7]*DL* (V), 136.

Today's gospel seems to suggest reflection on the balance between contemplation and action. Jesus provided the disciples with a pattern for ministry. We are called to ministry by virtue of our baptism, confirmation, and eucharist. Nourished by Word and bread, the liturgy sends us forth to minister to the world. Our ministry is empowered by the living Word of God, by the eucharist, by prayer and ongoing intimacy with God who leads us on a journey that is often fraught with danger. Jesus shows us the way in today's gospel. He invites balance between prayer and action.

> Thus in and through solitude we do not move away from people. On the contrary. We move closer to them through compassionate ministry.
>
> In a world that victimizes us by its compulsions, we are called to solitude where we can struggle against our anger and greed and let our new self be born in the loving encounter with Jesus Christ. It is in this solitude that we become compassionate people, deeply aware of our solidarity in brokenness with all humanity and ready to reach out to anyone in need.
>
> The end of Anthony's story shows him, after years of compassionate ministry, returning to solitude to be totally absorbed in direct communion with God. . . . It is therefore to solitude that we must return, not alone, but with all those we embrace through our ministry. This return continues until the time when the same Lord who sent us into the world calls us back to be with him in a never-ending communion.[8]

Today's proclamation of the gospel omits key passages in Mark's sixth chapter. We do not hear the story of the feeding of the five thousand or Jesus' walking on water. For the next five Sundays we stop and our attention turns to the proclamation of John's gospel. Ray Brown sheds light on the reason. "Indeed Markan brevity presents a liturgical problem, for this shortest gospel does not provide enough pericopes or segments to cover all the

Sundays in Ordinary Time. To meet that problem, in mid-summer the Lectionary interrupts its reading of Mark at 6:34 (the beginning of the brief first account of the multiplication of the loaves) and substitutes for five Sundays (17th through 21st) the much longer Johannine account of the multiplication—a disputable decision."[9]

Gospel Exegesis

The facilitator provides input from critical biblical scholarship on this text. This input includes insights as to how people would have heard the gospel in Jesus' time.

The Twelve return from their missionary jaunt and for the first time (only in Mark) they are called "apostles" (emissaries, envoys). Jesus sent them out with a specific mission. "On their ministry to Israel, the twelve stand out as Jesus' messengers, or ambassadors: Receiving them is tantamount to receiving Jesus himself (9:37)."[10] That mission was to expel demons, heal the sick, and proclaim Jesus' message. They were charged with the responsibility to be good and faithful stewards of that message and report to Jesus about the efficacy of their mission. They not only were sent, but they were held accountable for their efforts.

Jesus announces that he wishes to be alone with the apostles. This desire leads them to the ultimate place where Jesus will multiply the loaves. Even though they were called "apostles," their true apostolic mission will not begin until commanded so by the risen Christ.

Tired from their missionary activities, the disciples needed to rest from their labors. The real significance in this pericope lies in the fact that Jesus wanted them to be "by themselves" (*kat idian*). This is a Greek expression that occurs seven times in Mark (4:34; 6:31, 32; 7:33; 9:2, 28; 13:3) and usually occurs in a passage intended to instruct (especially the disciples).[11]

There may have been another reason Jesus wished to be alone with the Twelve. Herod had just murdered John the Baptist. After the miracle stories in

---

[8]Henry J. M. Nouwen, *The Way of the Heart: Desert Spirituality and Contemporary Ministry* (New York: Seabury, 1981), 39–40 in *DL* (V), 154.

[9]*CGOS*, 41, n. 35

[10]*CM*, 95.

[11]*MK*, 87.

chapter 5 and the execution of John, there is a definite transition in Mark's gospel. The focus is more on the Twelve and less on the crowds. Jesus goes off to teach them because he wishes to impart special revelation. It turns out at this juncture that the special revelation is the feeding of the multitudes.

Today begins the story of the feeding of the five thousand. The pericope for today's liturgy stops short of the feeding, however. "People were coming and going in great numbers, and they had no opportunity to even eat. So they [Jesus and the disciples] went off in the boat by themselves to a desert place."[12] The disciples were tired and hungry. Jesus was concerned for their welfare and takes them off to be alone with him for a while, to a quiet place where he can teach them following the feeding of the crowds. Jesus models for them the pattern of healthy ministry: ministry to the multitudes, followed by solitude and spiritual refilling by quiet prayer and intimacy with God. Jesus regularly followed his own plan. Thoreau once said that he went to the forest to be alone in order to reflect on the meaning of life so that at the end of his life he would not discover that he lived his life not having lived at all. It is often in the silence that God speaks to us, teaches us, and lays our path before us.

Jesus and company could not get away from the crowds—they arrived in town before them. When Jesus encountered the crowds, he was moved to pity, a pity understood in the Scriptures to come from deep within the heart and soul of an individual. It is a compassion born out of sorrow for the suffering of others. It is a compassion that demands action; "the pity mentioned in the Scriptures is an extremely deep feeling and an attitude of active benevolence that impels us to do everything possible to relieve the sufferers by total commitment of ourselves. Pity characterizes God: we appeal to it when we are in distress and when we seek pardon for our sins. It impels Jesus to heal the sick, to multiply the loaves for the crowd that has nothing to eat (Mark 8:2)."[13] Compassion was a feminine value—the Hebrew word for the pity described in this text is "womb." When people are

hurting and hungry, disciples of Christ are to extend the compassion of God and one's very life—balanced, of course, with appropriate doses of much needed solitude, contemplation, and prayer.

The way this story is presented in the Lectionary serves as a reminder that even though we read certain verses of the gospel on a given Sunday, it is important not to read them in a vacuum, but in the context of the whole from which they came. This gospel begins the story of the great miraculous feeding of the multitudes. Today, however, they are not fed with bread; they are fed with Christ's Word. Bread follows. Before they are given the bread of sustenance, Jesus taught them. Obviously their greatest hunger was spiritual. Every word that comes forth from the mouth of Jesus is food for the soul. (The Johannine discourse on the bread of life refers to Jesus' teaching as "bread.") They were nourished at the table of God's Word before they were nourished at the table of God's bread. The liturgical connections are not to be missed.

Wilfrid Harrington insists that Mark cannot be understood without taking a serious look at the way in which he arranged the text. Jesus feeds five thousand in chapter 6. He feeds four thousand in chapter 8. Jesus crosses the lake in chapter 6. Jesus crosses the lake again in chapter 8. Jesus is embroiled in controversy with the Pharisees in chapter 7, and again in chapter 8. In chapter 7 Jesus insists that only the children of Israel are entitled to bread. Jesus insists that he is the One Loaf for both Jews and gentiles in chapter 8. Jesus heals a deaf mute in chapter 7 and a blind man in chapter 8.[14]

The first feeding takes place in Galilee and the primary recipients are Jewish. The number twelve in the feeding story conjures images of the twelve tribes of Israel—the chosen people. The second feeding takes place in Decapolis and gentiles are similarly fed. Both feeding events prefigure the eucharistic banquet in which all people are invited to partake of the One Loaf.

The feeding stories frame an important event: the gentiles are called to salvation. Jesus insists that the real criterion of purity is not whether one is

---

[12]*Lectionary for Mass, Sixteenth Sunday in Ordinary Time (2nd typ. ed.)*

[13]*DL* (V), 152.

---

[14]*MK*, 88.

Jew or gentile, but what resides in a person's heart. Righteousness is a matter of conscience and the intention to live an upright, moral life. The story of the woman who was willing to accept the crumbs that fell from Israel's table demonstrated that if Jesus was willing to include gentiles in the salvific meal, who are others to refuse such inclusion? Jesus healed the deaf mute citizen of Decapolis—a gentile. The subtle implication is not to be missed. The "gentiles, once deaf and dumb toward God, are now made capable of hearing God and/or rendering him homage. And so they can participate in the eucharistic meal. The second multiplication of loaves is a sign for gentiles."[15]

Having examined the arrangement of Mark's stories and the purpose of those arrangements, our attention turns to today's gospel. We have been given the lens from which to view this gospel and the gospels of coming weeks.

All four gospels relate the multiplication of the loaves. Matthew and Mark relate two separate feeding events. Some scholars suggest that the two events are simply variants of the same event.[16] John seems to have redacted his account from an independent source—similar to Matthew's and Mark's second story.

Early Christian catechesis underscored the connection of multiplication of the loaves with the eucharist. The wording and gestures of the Last Supper and Mark's and Matthew's feeding narratives are closely analogous. The feeding of the multitudes inaugurates the Bread of Life discourse. Thus, this event was not only remembered as an awesome demonstration of Jesus' miraculous power, but also because it was so explicitly eucharistic.

The "where" of this event is also significant—the desert. It recalls another significant feeding story that took place in the desert—manna in the wilderness, the bread from heaven. "Jesus is the Good Shepherd of Ezekiel who feeds his sheep."[17] He feeds them in the desert with the new manna, the new bread from heaven. Elisha miraculously

fed 120 men with only twenty barley loaves. Jesus' accomplishment was far more spectacular—five loaves feeds five thousand.

In today's pericope Jesus uses messianic language to describe the event at hand. He took his disciples off to a deserted place to "rest." Rest was always understood in biblical parlance to mean God's "blessing which God as shepherd would bestow upon his faithful."[18] When Israel arrived in the promised land after a forty-year trek in the desert it was considered a well deserved *rest*. There is also a Wisdom connotation to the word *rest*. Sirach spoke of a disciple of wisdom who found rest with Lady Wisdom following his toil and labors (Sir 6:28; 51:27). In early Christianity Jesus was understood as the incarnation of wisdom. Is it any wonder he offered *rest/wisdom* to his messengers after their missionary sojourn? Their rest was not a break *from* something; it was a break *for* something. They were given rest in order to be taught by their Master.

Jesus is the Shepherd who shepherds the people who have no shepherd—those people referred to in Numbers 27:17 and 1 Kings 22:17. Jesus alludes to himself as the messianic shepherd foretold by Ezekiel. "The substance of this miracle is that Jesus feeds five thousand men, manifesting himself not only as the authoritative Son of God but also as Israel's Shepherd King."[19]

If Jesus is the Shepherd, what do we know about sheep? They are extremely defenseless, dull-witted animals. They will stay in one place and die rather than make attempts to save themselves. When lost in the wilderness, they will lay down and die rather than try to find their way. They must be driven. They will not see to their own needs. They cannot take care of themselves. "Shepherdless sheep were a frequent motif in the Old Testament signifying the needs of the people for leadership, security, sustenance and healing."[20] Moses prayed that after he was gone God would raise up a leader who would not leave his sheep without a shepherd. Jesus is the new Moses. He is the Shepherd who drives the sheep, who provides for their every need because they cannot take care of them-

---

[15]Ibid., 89.

[16]Ibid.

[17]Ibid., 90.

[18]*WWC*, 216.

[19]*CM*, 98.

[20]*WWC*, 216.

selves. The "sheep" that comprised Jesus' multitudes were probably the poor peasants, the "people of the land." Jesus had compassion for them because no one else in the world cared. The religious and political powers cared little for their welfare. Jesus the Good Shepherd was concerned for their temporal as well as their spiritual needs. Like a mother sheep, Jesus, moved by compassion, fed the lambs from the table of his Word and teaching authority—there they would find hope and encouragement.

The crowd was so captivated by Jesus' teaching that they gave no thought to their own welfare. They had no food or provisions and it was getting late. They were, after all, in a deserted place far away from relatives. Jesus knew these sheep probably did not provide or even think of their provisional needs before setting out and, as the compassionate Good Shepherd, realized that he must provide for their every need. Thus, Jesus also fed the lambs food—the bread of life, the manna from heaven.

In Mark's gospel there are two prominent signs that the messianic age had indeed arrived—the banquet and the ministry of healing and exorcism. Jesus was known for his penchant for parties. In Luke's gospel Jesus feasted his way through Galilee. We often find Jesus eating or feasting at someone's house. He frequently used Israel's messianic metaphor of banquet in relation to his pronouncement of the reign of God. It was an identifying characteristic of Jesus to be concerned with feeding people. It was so common to Jesus' experience that it was carried over in the early Christian community. The banquet meals that evolved into eucharist had their origins in Jesus. The banquet was for Jesus a sign of the establishment of God's reign on earth.

The feeding stories are part of that tradition. Richard Horsley insists that the feeding stories in Mark's gospel are "to be understood as portrayals of how God was finally feeding the people with miraculous abundance despite appearances of paucity."[21]

_____
[21]Richard Horsley, *Jesus and the Spiral of Violence: Popular Jewish Resistance in Roman Palestine* (San Francisco: Harper and Row, 1987), 179.

In today's pericope we have evidence of both signs. The disciples just returned from their missionary activities with stories of their successes—they healed and expelled demons. People's lives were restored through Jesus' ministry of healing and liberation. The establishment of God's reign is the embodiment of God's shepherding, compassionate care of his people. People were healed, restored, and fed off the loaves of Jesus' messianic teaching.

Proclaim the gospel again.

Sometimes we gain new insights when we hear the text after the interpretation is given. Someone from the group proclaims the gospel a second time.

STEP 4
TESTING

Conversation with the Liturgy and the Scriptures

Test your original understanding in dialogue with the text.

(You might consider breaking into smaller groups.)

Now that you've heard the exegesis, were there any new insights? How do you feel about it? How does your original understanding of this gospel compare with what we just shared? How does this story speak to your life?

Sharing Life Experience

Participants share an experience from their lives that connects with the biblical interpretation just presented.

> *I am often aware of how the rigors of ministry can be very demanding and tiring. After a Sunday morning of liturgies, celebrating the Word of God and reflecting on that Word with catechumens, I come home exhilarated but exhausted. After a full week's work I am ready at the end of the week to do nothing but veg-out. Yet I am amazed how the celebration of Christ present in the proclamation of the Word and in the eucharist can provide new energy and readiness to face each new week with renewed*

enthusiasm. This ministry may be demanding, but it is never boring.

I find it amazing that the rest the apostles were given was to hear the living Word of God proclaimed and to observe Jesus wondrously feeding the multitudes. It is a reminder that we do need to carve out time for our personal prayer and our communion with God—it empowers us. But the liturgy also empowers and enlivens us with the energy to go out again. It is the age-old tension between contemplation and action. Just when I think I can't go another day, I am touched by the faith of someone who goes to heroic efforts to live the gospel. I am energized to go out again.

There is a woman in our parish who is dying. She is not long for this world. She is in pain. Yet today she called asking for articles on a justice project that she wants to send to her daughter so her parish might become involved in the same project. She dragged herself out of her deathbed to come and worship with our community—to be a light of love and hope for us all. How can I become tired or stagnant with faith like that around me?

When I hear of the great and mighty deeds of God, I am once again strengthened to go out and be Christ's light in the world. Last week I spoke to an inquirer who shared how he had never been a churchgoer. His father had recently died. The reason he decided to come and inquire is that he could not believe the untiring, selfless way in which his father's community not only reached out to his father when he was alive, but also the way in which they responded to his family when his father died. This community's self-sacrificing love was a sign and symbol of the love God has for each and every one of us. That community "shepherded" that man and his family. As a result, he was led to our community. He felt invited to "come and see" what our Christian community could offer because of the untiring efforts of God's people in another place. It just so happened that the other community in question was a Baptist church. I was humbled that he should come to us after experiencing Christ the Shepherd in the midst of our Baptist brothers and sisters.

Today's gospel also reminds me of the value of finding quiet time to be alone with God. As a mother of four children and a full-time liturgist, musician, and director of initiation, I know how difficult that is. I have found over the years that mothers have to be creative in stealing those sacred moments. It is amazing the solitude one can find in the shower, driving the car, while grocery shopping, and in all the other not-so-mundane tasks associated with the everyday duties of family life.

The invitation in today's gospel is to find balance in our baptismal life. Prayer, worship, liturgy—it strengthens, nourishes, and empowers us to go out and be the missionaries we are called to be. When we take the appropriate rest that Jesus showed us we must have, we discover that we cannot go on our own steam, but only on the steam that comes straight from the mouth of God. God's Word can provide us with the rest we need. In this crazed go-go-go society in which we live, if ever afforded the luxury, we must, like the apostles and Jesus, steal away to the nearest shore in order to encounter the God who lives within and who resides in all of creation, but most especially in the solitude of our hearts.

What was Mark trying to tell his community? In what way does this gospel challenge your community today? In what way is your community called to go to a deserted place and rest for a while with the Lord? What would your response be if you had just returned from a long missionary jaunt and had to face the crowds? How does this relate to your work life, your family life, your ministry life? How does this scripture invite transformation in the life of the community, in your life? In what way are the biblical themes of covenant, exodus, creation, and community evident in today's readings? Do you still feel the same way about this text as when you began? Has your original understanding been stretched, challenged, or affirmed?

STEP 5
DECISION

The gospel demands a response.

In what concrete way might your parish be invited to respond? Are there any attitudes or behaviors you would like to change as a result of today's conversation? What one concrete action will you take this week in response to the liturgy today?

Christian Initiation: Perhaps this would be a good time to set aside an evening for quiet, prayerful retreat for catechumens, candidates, sponsors, and the faithful. Is anyone ready to celebrate a rite of acceptance or welcome? Many people celebrate that rite because of the efforts of those who are just like the apostles in today's gospel—they were evangelized. When was the last time you and the catechumens and candidates engaged in evangelization efforts? Perhaps this would be a good time to extend an invitation to "come and see" in your community.

DOCTRINAL ISSUES

What Church truth/teaching/doctrinal issue could be drawn from the gospel for the sixteenth Sunday in Ordinary Time?

Participants suggest possible doctrinal themes that flow from the readings.

Possible Doctrinal Themes

Prayer–action–contemplation; evangelization, reign of God; Jesus, the Good Shepherd; healing and exorcism; eucharist; liturgy of the Word; ministry; call of baptism

Present the doctrinal material at this time.

1. The facilitator gives input on a particular doctrinal issue of his or her prior choosing. OR
2. The group chooses a doctrinal issue from the list they created. They read together from the Doctrinal Appendix or other appropriate, official Church documents and the works of respected theologians.

(Many doctrinal issues are found in the Doctrinal Appendix at the back of this workbook. If you are choosing an issue from this resource, please refer to it now.)

Reflection questions centered around the chosen doctrinal theme can be found at the end of each topic in the Doctrinal Appendix. The questions are based on the five-step reflection process. If you choose a topic not included in the Doctrinal Appendix, craft your own questions according to the same five-step process.

Following the reflection questions you will be reminded to return to chapter 7, "Preparing the Catechetical Session," to assist you in crafting your own session.

Closing Prayer

Let us pray
that God will continue to bless us with his compassion and love

Pause for silent prayer.

Father,
let the gift of your life
continue to grow in us,
drawing us from death to faith, hope and love.
Keep us alive in Christ Jesus.
Keep us watchful in prayer
and true to his teaching
till your glory is revealed in us.
Grant this through Christ our Lord.[22]

---

[22]Sixteenth Sunday in Ordinary Time, "Alternative Opening Prayer," *The Sacramentary.*

Seventeenth Sunday in Ordinary Time

Environment

Perhaps today would be an opportune time to include stalks of wheat, a loaf of bread, or an icon of the Last Supper or the feeding of the multitudes.

INTRODUCTORY RITES

Entrance Antiphon (or Opening Song)

God is in his holy dwelling; he will give a home to the lonely, he gives power and strength to his people. (Ps 67:6–7, 36)[1]

Opening Prayer

The facilitator of the session may lead the prayer. Others in the group may be asked to proclaim the readings.

Let us pray
that we will make good use of the gifts that God has given us

Pause for silent prayer.

God our Father and protector,
without you nothing is holy,
nothing has value.
Guide us to everlasting life
by helping us to use wisely
the blessings you have given to the world.
We ask this through our Lord
Jesus Christ, your Son,
who lives and reigns with you and the Holy Spirit,
one God, for ever and ever.[2]

LITURGY OF THE WORD

The readings are proclaimed.

First Reading
2 Kings 4:42–44

---

[1]Seventeenth Sunday in Ordinary Time: "Entrance Antiphon," *The Sacramentary.*

[2]Seventeenth Sunday in Ordinary Time: "Opening Prayer," *The Sacramentary.*

Overview of the Two Books of Kings: The history of Israel between King David's death and the Babylonian exile (586 B.C.) is encapsulated in the Books of Kings. The books relate the history of a people in relationship with their God. The reader is given a panoramic view of the Davidic dynasty, the relationship between the Northern and Southern Kingdoms of Israel, and the religious judgment of a people. This era also gave rise to the prophetic tradition. The role of prophet was to serve as Israel's conscience. "[T]he prophets contributed a powerful new factor to Israel's idea of itself, namely the conviction that they are not God's people unless they are *morally* upright. From the prophets on, Israel considers the *ethical* dimension to be as important as the *worship* of Yahweh's name in cult."[3]

The first eleven chapters unfold the story of the Davidic monarchy through the reign of Solomon. From that point, the chapters are concerned with the kings that followed in both the Northern and Southern Kingdoms. Enough information was given in the two books that a fairly accurate history of Israel's monarchy has been sculpted from it.

The kings are judged according to their faithfulness to Yahweh. The northern kings are severely and negatively judged. None of them found favor with God. The authors of the work were writing in retrospect from a much later time and from a Southern Kingdom perspective. It was generally believed that the catalyst for idolatry, rejection of Yahweh and the Temple, and the ultimate fall of Israel to Assyria was the schism of the northern tribes following Solomon's death.[4]

The southern kings did not fare much better in the analysis of the authors. They were all judged according to the high standard set by the greatest king of all time in their estimation—King David. Only three southern kings were favorably perceived—Asa, Hezekiah, and Josiah.

---

[3]*ROT,* 307.
[4]Ibid., 296.

The history portrayed in the Books of Kings shows that Judah, the Southern Kingdom, was far more stable than the north. The monarchy was passed down through intermarriage between sensible and honorable royal families. The north, on the other hand, went through its kings rather quickly. In half the amount of time detailed by the writers, Israel endured nineteen different kings. Throughout northern history, the prophets and tribal leaders were at war with the kings. The reign of Israel lasted about two hundred years contrasted with Judah, which endured for at least double that amount.

King Omri came to power in the north about fifty years after Solomon died. He established Samaria as the new capital. Omri sought to strengthen Israel by making an alliance with the Phoenician kingdom in Lebanon on their northern border. Omri's son, Ahab, married the king of Tyre's daughter, Jezebel, in order to unite the kingdoms. The result of that union began the ultimate demise of Omri's dynasty thirty years later. Jezebel worshiped the pagan god Baal. She brought her own prophets into Israel and established temples to Baal. This raised the angst of Israel's prophets, which led ultimately to fierce battles between the religious establishment and the monarchy.

The two legendary prophets of this historical theater were Elijah and Elisha. The Books of Kings chronicle their heroic prophetic efforts. They left no written words, but like all legendary heroes, much that was written about them was the stuff of epic cinema. Historians take great pains to sort out the exaggerated recount of their deeds from the actual deeds. Often the exaggerations served as an exclamation point to the extraordinary greatness of the prophets. Later prophets never spoke of miracles in conjunction with their prophetic ministry. Yet Elijah and Elisha did have a powerful prophetic and healing ministry that had a huge impact on the corporate memory of the people of that age.

The purpose of the Books of Kings was to portray the history of a nation gone awry and the subsequent consequences of that unfaithfulness. Throughout the wars and devastation one thing was certain: God was always in control. The stories of Elijah and Elisha reminded readers that even in the midst of desperation God continued to raise up prophets like Moses who would mediate God's relationship with the people. Elijah, like Moses, went up to Mount Sinai to encounter God and Elisha parted the Jordan, provided water and bread for those in need, and turned water into blood. The similarities between the two prophets and Moses are not to be missed. The two prophets continued the mission of Moses to uphold the covenant of Sinai to a recalcitrant people.

The ultimate theme of Kings was concerned with the degree of faithfulness of the kings, not with their deeds. The author makes the point that infidelity to the covenant resulted in serious, disastrous consequences. The kings failed miserably to live up to the covenant. They lapsed into idolatry. God warned the people through the prophets, but they did not listen. The authors of Kings, also the authors of Joshua, Judges, and Samuel, supported the premise of Deuteronomy that the blessing of promised land belonged only to those faithful to the Lord's command. Thus, failure to live by the covenant resulted in the loss of the promised land—both the north and the south eventually lost their land.

Today's Pericope: The Lectionary has chosen this episode in the Elisha tradition to accompany the feeding of the multitudes by Jesus in today's gospel. One key factor in this reading is the underlying fact that bread is multiplied to be shared with many. "Bread plays so many roles! We have learned to recognize, in it, an instrument of the human community, because of the bread we break together. We have learned to recognize, in it, the image of nobility of work, because of the bread we earn by the sweat of our brow. We have learned to recognize, in it, the essential vehicle of pity, because of the bread we distribute in times of want. The taste of shared bread is without compare."[5]

The genesis of today's reading has its roots in the liturgy of the Temple. Barley loaves were used in the Temple offering. The man who brought the bread to Elisha as "firstfruit" also has a liturgical significance. By rights the man should have taken the ritual bread to the Gilgal sanctuary, which had

---

[5] A. de Saint-Exupery, *Pilote de guerre*, Paris: Gallimard, 1942, 200. In *DL* (V), 158.

been turned into a shrine to Baal. He chose, instead, to take the bread to Elisha as a sign that he would not worship idols but would remain true to the one Lord and God.

In the Bible, bread was understood as a sign of God's gift to strengthen human beings. It was also a sign of hospitality, wisdom, intelligence, peace, and life. The bread that feeds the many, the poor, and those in want was an eschatological sign of the reign of God. God will one day satisfy every human hunger.

Today's reading is understood as a literary prototype for the miraculous feedings of the New Testament. There is a similar pattern. Food is brought to the holy man. The quantity of the food is determined. Objection is raised that the quantity is insufficient. The holy man ignores the inadequacy and demands that the food be distributed anyway. The hunger of the crowd is satiated and there are leftovers.[6]

Responsorial Psalm
Psalm 145:10–11, 15–16, 17–18

Psalm 145 is frequently used as a responsorial psalm. This is the first time, however, that these particular verses have been used. The refrain exalts the theme of both the first reading and the gospel.

Second Reading
Ephesians 4:1–6

(See the fifteenth Sunday in Ordinary Time for an overview of Paul's letter to the Ephesians.)

Today's Pericope: It is generally believed that the letter to the Ephesians was written by a second-generation student of Paul. There is a clear pattern. According to Reginald Fuller, chapters 1 through 3 are concerned with doctrinal issues. Chapters 4 through 6 are parenetical—they are concerned with ethical issues. Today's reading begins the parenesis.[7]

The doctrine of part 1 of the letter asserts that the one body of Christ was comprised of Jew and gen-

tile. The parenesis of the second part of the letter insists that all members must strive for that unity. The exhortation is based on firm theology. Readers are invited to live what they already are—"one body, one Spirit, one hope, one Lord, one faith, one baptism, one God and Father of all Christians."[8] The letter was an invitation to readers to more fully live their reality, to grow into their baptismal identity.

Today's reading exalts evangelical attitudes and behaviors—humility, patience, forgiveness, and love. Paul's letter exhorts the reader to live the covenant of love—love of God, self, and others. Baptized Christians can do no less than live the above-mentioned virtues when they are faithful to the gospel.

Today's reading was probably part of a baptismal liturgy. The profession of faith contained in the text is a call to unity, not only to an ancient church struggling with issues of inclusion, exclusion, division, and rancor, but also to a modern church struggling with the same thing. It is a call to strive for unity when there is danger of rupture. Since we are all brothers and sisters who share the same Father, we dare not behave with malice toward one another. There is no room for such behavior in the Christian community.

The gospel is proclaimed.

Gospel
John 6:1–15. Jesus fed the multitudes as much as they wanted.

STEP 1
NAMING ONE'S EXPERIENCE

What were your first impressions? What was your first response to the gospel (or the other readings)? What captured your attention?

Each person names his or her initial impression. Statements should be brief. No reasons should be given at this time. All simply listen without agreeing or disagreeing.

---

[6] *PNL*, 330.
[7] Ibid.

---

[8] Ibid.

In a brief statement, explain what you think this gospel is trying to convey.

Liturgical Context

For the next five Sundays we leave Mark and enter the world of John. Today's liturgy relates the story of the miraculous feeding of the multitudes. The four remaining Sundays concentrate on the Discourse on the Bread of Life. This inclusion of the feeding story in John takes the place of the first multiplication story in Mark. The Old Testament texts for the next five Sundays reveal and point to the theology of John's sixth chapter.

There is a definite break in movement in the story line we have been following. Mark's gospel is fluid. The characters have been on the move. We now come to a brief, abrupt halt. We are invited to remain in place for a while. We will stay in Capernaum and reflect on the Discourse of these weeks. It seems as if this is a message we have heard before. The repetition almost suggests that we did not "get it" the first time around. However, John's intent is to invite us to reflect on Jesus, the Bread of Life, and to enter into his mystery in our lives. The liturgy gives us a taste, whets our appetite, and, for the next five weeks, invites us to take this reflection beyond the confines and limitations of the liturgy and spend time in prayer and contemplation on the theology of the next five gospels in Ordinary Time.

One cannot consider the readings of today and not think of the Lord's hand that feeds and sustains his people. Since we are the hands and feet of Christ, we cannot look at this text without considering our responsibility to address world hunger and issues of poverty.

The second reading invites a discussion on Christian unity—a hotly debated topic in the present-day church (as it was when it was written).

The heart of our eucharistic theology is proclaimed in today's gospel. In addition to the Old Testament typology, allusions to eucharist form the primary thread running through the seams of this gospel. Interestingly, John omits the institution narrative in his account of the Last Supper. His eucharistic theology is heralded in chapter 6 of the gospel. Today's pericope reads like an ancient liturgy. Jesus took the bread and gave God thanks. Jesus himself distributed the bread to the crowd. This happens only in John's gospel. The event alludes to sacramental eucharist and is a Last Supper-type meal. Only in John's gospel does Jesus command that the fragments be gathered into baskets. A later liturgical document, the *Didache*, referred to broken fragments of eucharistic bread (*klasma*)—the same word used for the fragments gathered in today's pericope. Eucharistic bread was also understood as an eschatological gathering (*synagein*—the same word used in today's gospel for the gathering of leftover morsels of bread) of the Church itself. "Later in chapter six, when Jesus declares himself to be bread and food for all, it becomes clear that all will be gathered (*synagein*) when he is fragmented (*klasma*) and broken upon the cross."[9]

The ritual prayers of the liturgy support the themes of today's readings. The opening prayer asks that we be good stewards of the gifts that God has given us. We are reminded that nothing without God has any value for our lives. We ask that God guide us to our ultimate destination and help us use the gifts that have been given to us in service of God's reign. The alternative opening prayer picks up a consonant theme in that it asks God to help us cherish the gifts that have been given to us. We ask that we be given the wisdom to see the reign of God as a pearl of great price in the first place. The prayer takes it a step further, however, and asks for the strength and the grace to extend what we have been given to others (becoming eucharist for others). Always the liturgy reminds us of the ethical imperatives of the gospel. It is not a "Jesus and me" affair. Our faith is rooted in living in community and responding to the needs of a broken world. The Entrance Antiphon sets the tone, reminding us of all we need to know. God is in his holy dwelling. That dwelling is the reign of God, here and now and

---

[9] *WWC*, 218.

not yet. God always reaches out to the lonely—to anyone in need of God's compassion. God strengthens us to do as God does—comfort the lonely. The reign of God, the pearl of great price, cannot be hoarded. It must be shared, just as the Bread of Life was shared in today's gospel. This is the bottom line of today's liturgy, the response in faith to every liturgy. "Eucharist commits us to the poor," affirms the Catholic Catechism (1397). Eucharist empowers us to live in God's reign as God would have us live. Thus, there is always a commitment and a responsibility.

Is the way of justice and love so smooth? Certainly the image of the reign of God as a banquet is often tried and tested, purified even, when we see hatred and injustice living side by side with those who celebrate liturgy every Sunday and claim to be disciples of Jesus Christ. Perceptive people grow disillusioned by institutional violence and benign indifference. At that moment one must be just with one's own consciousness and one's own conscience. It is then that one learns the meaning of honesty and truth, that one learns how to respond to the presence of God's Spirit in the human heart calling for a deeper entry into the paschal mystery of Jesus Christ in order to share in the transformation of the world. The meaning of the banquet is transposed to a level where hope for the future becomes the great source of nourishment that one offers to others.[10]

Gospel Exegesis

The facilitator provides input from critical biblical scholarship on this text. This input includes insights as to how people would have heard the gospel in Jesus' time.

It is widely believed that John did not draw his account of the feeding of the multitudes from Mark, Matthew, and Luke, but from an independent source. John's version of the story includes ancient elements as well as his own creative input. John Pilch suggests that one ancient, original segment is "Jesus' question to Philip: 'How are we to

buy bread, so that these people may eat?' That Jesus' apparent ignorance about this was embarrassing to the early Christians is evident in the editorial comment that follows: 'he said this to test him, for he himself knew what he would do.'"[11] One Johannine creative addition can be found in verses 11–12. It is obvious that John's eucharistic connotations are drawn from synoptic accounts of the institution of the eucharist, "a tradition not included in John's passion story."[12]

The gospel of John, the gospel of "signs," recounts a supernatural manifestation of God's power. Raymond Brown defines a sign as a prodigious act with strong symbolic potential that depicts Jesus' message of salvation.[13] Through symbol and allusion, the signs in John's gospel point to the supernatural reality inherent in the sign—a reality not readily observable. (See glossary: *signs/miracles*.) John's gospel recounts only seven signs. They were understood as revelatory and as moments of encounter. Signs were manifestations of God and opportunities to encounter the living Christ. The signs themselves were secondary. The challenge of the sign was to invite people to go deeper, to see beyond it, to come to belief in the person the sign revealed—Jesus Christ.

The feeding of the multitudes holds an exalted place in all the gospels. John adds the Discourse of Jesus to his account of the event. Theology is gradually revealed by Jesus as the Discourse is proclaimed. "Jesus is revealed as bread and bread-giver for the life of the world."[14]

The observer is invited to enter the world of detail when attempting to understand today's signs. Meaning is lurking within the details of the event itself. Jesus crossed the Sea of Galilee. Jesus began his ministry in Galilee. He inaugurated his first among many signs at the wedding feast of Cana. The intended beneficiaries were a "select few" of preinvited guests. The first sign took place in a small, confined area. Today's sign took place on a mountain in the midst of a crowd who followed Jesus because of the spreading news of his healing ministry. Mountains were places of manifestation

---

[10] R. Kevin Seasoltz, O.S.B., "Liturgy and Social Consciousness," *TDJR*, 47.

[11] *CWJB*, 115.
[12] Ibid.
[13] *GAJ*, 527–530.
[14] *WWC*, 218.

and God's authority. Perhaps the mountain setting is an allusion to the Sermon on the Mount. Perhaps John was alerting readers to another momentous discourse similar to the Beatitudes. John wants his readers to know that this is a sign of the highest order. Joseph Grassi suggests that the two fish and five loaves, which add up to a total of seven, possibly indicate the centrality and importance of this sign among all of the signs in John's gospel. Seven is the number indicating completeness.[15]

Often in John's gospel John uses an earlier event to shed light on a later event. For example, Jesus raised Lazarus from the dead. This could only be possible because of the death, resurrection, and ascension of the One who is the source of all life. Thus, the Lazarus sign revealed the meaning of the resurrection that would come later. The sign of the loaves, expressed as real food and bread from heaven, can only be understood after Jesus is raised from the dead.

We are also told that Passover is near. Part of John's underlying theology was to demonstrate that Jesus himself replaced the traditional feasts and symbols of Judaism. Jesus is the new Passover. The text alludes to all the events in Israel's history that formed them as a people: Sinai and the desert sojourn. One cannot miss the similarities between Philip's response to Jesus and Moses' response to God in the wilderness. Readers are immediately transported to the imaginative world in which bread falls from heaven and feeds the hungry masses in the desert. Jesus is the new manna, the new bread come down from heaven, the new Bread of Life. In the desert, however, the people were fed "enough." On the grassy knoll they were fed their fill with an abundance left over.

The allusion to Passover also touches the corporate memory of that fateful night. Jesus knew his hour had come to pass from death into the loving embrace of his Father. Jesus' sign also had something to teach about death to life and the movement from slavery to freedom.

Jesus loved those he invited into his reign. He gave them a sign of that love during a meal. Jesus raised his eyes toward the multitudes and asked

where he could buy enough food for them to eat. This sign of bread was a demonstration of his great love, care, and concern for his followers. Moses also interceded on behalf of the people who were hungry.

The situation is dire. There are no logical solutions. Even if they had the wages of two hundred days' work, it would not be enough to feed all these people. Andrew mentions the meager supplies of a young boy. Barley cakes and fish—could an amount so small feed so many? This is the bread used in the offering. Barley is a hearty grain. It survives extreme weather conditions such as heat and drought. It matures in less time than other grains. The feast of Passover coincided with the barley feast, so it is no surprise that barley cakes take a star role in this drama.

Barley was also the staple of the poor. Messianic prophecy refers to the messianic age as a time of prosperity, abundance, and justice for God's *anawim*, the poor. "Significantly, Jesus' action feeds with banquet-like portions the poor ones who have come to him."[16]

Putting ourselves in the imaginative world of the story helps us more fully appreciate and understand it. Things that hold no meaning for our modern culture possess very explicit meaning in another age and time. Modern scholarship helps us get inside the everyday life of those cultures. John Pilch asserts that the Greek word for "fish" comes from "another word that means 'food that is cooked and eaten with bread.'"[17] It is possible that the fish referred to in the text was a common variety of processed food—fish that was either pickled, cured, salted, or dried to preserve it for travel (i.e., a boxed lunch—the forerunner of luncheon meat). No doubt the young boy's fish was of the processed variety. The fish (*ichtys*) was also an acronym for *Jesus Christ Savior, Son of God*, and a symbol used in the early church to identify Christians.

Jesus asked Philip how they were going to feed the crowds. Scholars have often wondered why Jesus singled out Philip. According to Pilch, the answer

---

[15] *LAF*, 87.

[16] *WWC*, 218.
[17] *CWJB*, 116.

is obvious. In Luke's version of the story the feeding takes place in Bethsaida. Philip is from the fishing village of Bethsaida. It is logical that Jesus ask the hometown boy where to find the necessary resources to feed the people. Philip, however, has no solutions. He is a pragmatist and realizes that it would take two-thirds of a year's salary to feed so large a crowd. He only supports the hopelessness of the situation.

Jesus seized the opportunity to demonstrate God's power and performed a sign. Taking the paltry fruits of human hands, Jesus was ready to act. He invited the people to recline (reclining was the posture of learner and disciple). There was "plenty of grass for them to find a place." John is not known for creating idyllic scenery. It is probable that the allusion to grass is an attempt to highlight the contrast between the "thorns and thistles" that appeared after Adam's sin and the Eden-like grassy knoll present in the messianic reign.

Jesus then takes, gives thanks, and shares the bread and fish with the people. One cannot miss the language of the institution narrative of the Last Supper. Even the closing remarks carry special significance.

The apostles filled twelve baskets with the remaining fragments of bread. Five thousand took their reclining seat on that grassy knoll, underscoring the overwhelming nature of Jesus' multiplication of the bread and fish. The fragments were then gathered into a basket, symbolic of the gathering of the fragmented Christian communities that would one day be gathered into one basket to celebrate with Christ presiding at one heavenly eucharistic table. Abundant bread will never cease. It will continue to feed the Church until the end of time. Never will the cupboard be bare; God's people are promised a never-exhausted table of plenty.

Like water raging through a broken levy, fever-pitch excitement grew in the crowd. Who is this man who feeds the crowds? Surely, he is the one for whom they had longed. Could he really be the long-awaited Prophet? Jesus retreated from the crowd lest they crown him king on the spot. Earthly royal courts were not in the divinely ordained game plan.

The sign of abundant bread did not point to Jesus' earthly kingship. The sign had another purpose. Jesus refused to allow his miracle to feed the whirlwind messianic fervor of his day. He would wait for normalcy to return before explaining the sign's significance. The discourse of the next Sundays provides that explanation.

In John's story everyone has a place at the banquet. All are fed. Not only are they fed, but there is plenty left over—enough to fill twelve baskets. The number "twelve" always signals the corporate memory—twelve tribes of Israel, twelve apostles, *all the people*. Yet they still do not get it. The people misread the signs. Understanding will come slowly and gradually. Jesus must lay low and wait for the opportune moment. Jesus' presence is felt in his absence through the sign of bread. He withdraws from the crowds, but they are left with the taste and the memory of his bread of presence. "Remaining are Jesus' loving gesture in sharing the bread and our mission continues that gesture throughout history with all people. The twelve baskets set on the grass are calling us to continue Jesus' deed."[18]

Elisha fed one hundred men. Jesus, atop a mountain perch, his throne of authority, fed the hungry five thousand who followed him to a desert place. Then he taught them. Even though John draws obvious parallels among Jesus, Moses, and manna, today's gospel is not a repetition of a former time, a former place, or former prophets. It is clear that God is initiating something brand-new. God sent Jesus to gather the nations into one body and one Spirit without the intervention or meddling of earthly kings.

Jesus fled from the crowd. He would not be bound or limited by mere human power. The genesis of Jesus' power was divine. Everything was in God's hands. God would determine the fateful hour when earthly powers would unleash their fury and nail Jesus to his earthly throne of glory—the cross (a stumbling block even to some of his firsthand witnesses). Jesus reminds readers ancient and contemporary that God's ways are not our ways. God's strength is shown in weakness. Hoards are fed from crumbs. Life emerges from ashes. Kings are

[18]*SWTLY*, 192.

overshadowed by paupers and power and glory are born of failure. No wonder the crowds were looking for a different kind of Messiah.

Jesus knew that he was going to perform a sign for all to witness, yet he still addressed Philip. It was a test—not only for Philip, but for every person in every generation. The test asks the question: "Do you have confidence in Jesus' power to provide?"

> Having followed him without food
> the multitude was hungry
> He took pity on them
> > I was there and you too
> > When he shared with us
> > The two fish and the five loaves
> > He gave thanks
> No one was forgotten
> Everyone received from his hand
> What they wanted
> > When all were satisfied
> > Twelve baskets were filled
> > With the remaining bread
> > So that nothing be wasted
> This remnant that is the whole Thing
> Is broken for us every day
> Unceasingly undivided
> > Formerly as today
> > We forget as soon as we have eaten
> > > our fill
> > And ceasing to believe in him
> We demand signs.[19]

Proclaim the gospel again.

Sometimes we gain new insights when we hear the text after the interpretation is given. Someone from the group proclaims the gospel a second time.

Step 4
Testing

Conversation with the Liturgy and the Scriptures

Test your original understanding in dialogue with the text.

---

[19]P. Emmanuel, *Evangélaire*, Livre de vie 93, Paris: Seuill, 1969, 99. In *DL* (V), 164.

(You might consider breaking into smaller groups.)

Now that you've heard the exegesis, were there any new insights? How do you feel about it? How does your original understanding of this gospel compare with what we just shared? How does this story speak to your life?

Sharing Life Experience

Participants share an experience from their lives that connects with the biblical interpretation just presented.

> *I am reminded of the many stories people have shared with me of times when their best-intentioned efforts to be eucharist for someone did not result in joy and happiness. Not every selfless act of eucharist leads to happily ever after in this life. It leads to happily ever eternally. Jesus' selfless action led him to the cross. With eyes of faith we are nourished, strengthened, and healed by the Bread of Life, who fills every need.*

> *Today's gospel conjures memories of my own history. I have been fed, nurtured, strengthened, and comforted by the Christ who gifts us with the bread of presence. I am reminded of a time when a friend and I sat at our font's edge late one night to ritualize the letting go of a broken relationship. Christ was present to us in the intimate encounter between friends. I remember deathbed vigils in which the only consolation was hope in the Christ who heals, is present in our tragedies, and promises an afterlife reunion with our loved ones. I remember times of doubt, disillusionment, failures, and regret—times that I wanted to run, but the gentle hand of Presence tugged at my shirttails and refused to let go. I remember times I longed for a Messiah that really did teach a prosperity, rather than a just gospel. Riches were much more appealing than rags.*

> *The Christ of John's gospel reminds us that he is our Source, our Provider, our Nourishment. Jesus serves us—what a powerful image. Through all my life events one message resounded—no matter what, we were not alone, even in the midst of failures and hardships. Today's gospel invites me to be the bread of presence to others who are suffering. Recently I was working with parents preparing their children for first communion. I became aware of the spiritual hunger we all possess. I so desperately wanted to con-*

vey the love that Christ has for them, a love especially manifest in the eucharist. I shared with them how Catherine of Sienna was so captivated by the Christ who offers himself to us as food that she asked and answered her own question. "What would possess you to offer yourself to us as food? I know, you are madly in love with us." I wondered what it would take to help these parents really own that reality. I felt so frustrated. Jesus must have known such frustration. How many ways can we say it? How many ways can we demonstrate it? How many stories do we have to tell before people really own the fact that when bread is taken, blessed, broken, and shared, we too are taken, blessed, broken, and shared—the love Jesus has for us, the relationship he invites, is real and it is rooted in love. We can do no less than share it with others. I am Christian today because of the bread of love, encouragement, hope, courage, and presence that others have shared with me. I can do no less than share it with others.

What was John's theology? What are some elements in today's gospel that are unique to John? Why do you think he included them? In what way might this gospel invite your community to grow? In what way might you relate to Jesus' need to withdraw from the crowd? How might your community react in a similar situation? How would you answer the question posed to Philip? In what way might this liturgy invite change in your life? In what way are the biblical themes of covenant, exodus, creation, and community evident in today's readings? Do you still feel the same way about this text as when you began? Has your original understanding been stretched, challenged, or affirmed?

STEP 5
DECISION

The gospel demands a response.

In what concrete way might your parish be invited to respond? Are there any attitudes or behaviors you would like to change as a result of today's conversation? What one concrete action will you take this week in response to the liturgy today?

Pastoral Considerations: How does your community feed the multitudes? Who are you not feeding?

Who is hungry in your midst? Perhaps this would be a wonderful time for your community to reflect on what it means to be a eucharistic community. How is your community eucharist in your parish, civic, and world community?

Christian Initiation: This would be a most appropriate occasion to celebrate a rite of full communion in the Catholic Church. Are there any candidates ready to be received?

DOCTRINAL ISSUES

What Church truth/teaching/doctrinal issue could be drawn from the gospel for the seventeenth Sunday in Ordinary Time?

Participants suggest possible doctrinal themes that flow from the readings.

Possible Doctrinal Themes

Eucharist; Jesus, the Bread of Life; symbol of bread; Jesus the Teacher; paschal mystery; mystery of suffering; love of God; conversion; faith; discipleship; eschatological reign of God; messianic reign; justice; social teaching

Present the doctrinal material at this time.

1. The facilitator gives input on a particular doctrinal issue of his or her prior choosing. OR
2. The group chooses a doctrinal issue from the list they created. They read together from the Doctrinal Appendix or other appropriate, official Church documents and the works of respected theologians.

(Many doctrinal issues are found in the Doctrinal Appendix at the back of this workbook. If you are choosing an issue from this resource, please refer to it now.)

Reflection questions centered around the chosen doctrinal theme can be found at the end of each topic in the Doctrinal Appendix. The questions are based on the five-step reflection process. If you choose a topic not included in the Doctrinal Appendix, craft your own questions according to the same five-step process.

Following the reflection questions you will be reminded to return to chapter 7, "Preparing the Catechetical Session," to assist you in crafting your own session.

Closing Prayer

Let us pray
for the faith to recognize God's presence in our world

Pause for silent prayer.

God our Father,
open our eyes to see your hand at work
in the splendor of creation,
in the beauty of human life.
Touched by your hand our world is holy.
Help us to cherish the gifts that surround us,
to share your blessings with our brothers and
 sisters,
and to experience the joy of life in your presence.
We ask this through Christ our Lord.[20]

---

[20]Seventeenth Sunday in Ordinary Time, "Alternative Opening Prayer," *The Sacramentary.*

EIGHTEENTH SUNDAY IN ORDINARY TIME

INTRODUCTORY RITES

Entrance Antiphon (or Opening Song)

God come to my help. Lord, quickly give me assistance. You are the one who helps me and sets me free: Lord, do not be long in coming. (Ps 69:2, 6)[1]

Opening Prayer

The facilitator of the session may lead the prayer. Others in the group may be asked to proclaim the readings.

Let us pray
to the Father whose kindness never fails

Pause for silent prayer.

God our Father,
gifts without measure flow from your goodness
to bring us your peace.
Our life is your gift.
Guide our life's journey,
for only your love makes us whole.
Keep us strong in your love.
We ask this through Christ our Lord.[2]

LITURGY OF THE WORD

The readings are proclaimed.

First Reading
Exodus 16:2–4, 12–15

Overview of the Book of Exodus: The exodus-event is at the heart of Israel's identity. God was not a disinterested, aloof deity, but a God who was involved in the history and the lives of the people. God delivered Israel from bondage. Yahweh and the exodus were inseparable realities for the people of Israel. It was the exodus experience that inaugurated Israel's role as God's people. Upon receiving the covenant at Sinai, they entered into an unbreakable bond with Yahweh. Thus, the exodus not only identified Yahweh as their involved God, but it identified Israel as the people of their involved God. The Book of Exodus is a chronicle of that twofold reality. It captures and records Israel's roots. It is not intended as a biographical sketch and history of the people (although much of their history is indeed included in the book). It is the story of a people in relationship with their God. It is a story of sin and grace, bondage and deliverance. The exodus-event, then and now, was the axis upon which Israel's history spun, just as the cross is the axis upon which Christianity revolves. While there is no certain date for the book, most scholars place it around the thirteenth century B.C.

The Book of Exodus contains a myriad of biblical literary styles, from legendary embellishment to liturgical formulas, covenant codes, and song writing. The multiple styles are a testament to the creativity used by biblical authors to record and remember their central event. The book is influenced by the authorship of three different theologians at work in the creation of the text. The Yahwist, the Eloist, and the Priestly writers, each writing at a different time, posited their own perspective of events. Often they do not mesh and at times they even conflict with each other. As readers we are not to attempt to harmonize the accounts, but simply to acknowledge that all three contributed their interpretation of events. They remembered and judged the past from the perspective of the present while looking ahead to the future. Each writer possessed his own bias. The story of the exodus is Israel's premier story of deliverance from bondage. Christians believe that the exodus prefigures the liberation won by Christ, and his Passover from death on the cross to new life in the resurrection.

Today's Pericope: Today's account of the manna from heaven is one of two accounts provided in scripture of the same event. In the Book of Numbers the manna was sent first, and then because of the people's complaining, Yahweh gave them

---

[1]Eighteenth Sunday in Ordinary Time: "Entrance Antiphon," *The Sacramentary.*

[2]Eighteenth Sunday in Ordinary Time: "Opening Prayer," *The Sacramentary.*

quail to satisfy them. In this account from Exodus, the emphasis is on the manna. Manna was a sweet substance excreted from insects that lived in the Sinai desert. "Manna is the natural secretion of two species of scale insects or plant lice called the *Trebutina mannipara* and *Najacoccus serpentius*. The infestation of these insects results in the sweet secretion on the leaves of the tamarisk shrub during the months of May and June in the central Sinai. As the substance drops from the leaves to earth, it cools in the night air and becomes firm. If allowed to remain on the ground, the substance soon melts but if gathered early (before 8:30 A.M.) before the sun parches the desert, it provides a tasty nourishing feast."[3] Even today the inhabitants of the desert gather and eat the tasty delicacy. Scholars are uncertain as to where the word *manna* comes from, but believe that roots can be found from the word meaning, *what is this?—man hu.* Quail are migratory birds that often fall from exhaustion on their flight over the desert. Both phenomena were regarded as gifts from God and a sign of his providential care and a means of the people's sustenance.

No doubt the environment of the desert left a lot to be desired. The more plentiful resources of Egypt started to look attractive. The provisions at hand were not what the people were accustomed to, but it is doubtful that the Israelites were really *starving*. Yet still they grumbled. Their memory of God's saving act of liberation was short-lived. A common theme in the wilderness stories is Israel's incessant grumbling. It was sign and symptom of a serious flaw—the people's lack of faith and trust in Yahweh. However, God is great in mercy and slow to anger so when Moses intervened, Yahweh responded.

Responsorial Psalm
Psalm 78:3, 4bcd, 23–25, 54–55

The psalm picks up the theme of the first reading. The motif of "bread from heaven" is found in the refrain. The psalm recounts salvation history from the time of Jacob to the time of David. Today's section centers on the wilderness period. "The bread from heaven becomes the 'bread of the angels,' a further step on the road to its typo-

logical interpretation of the messianic banquet and the Eucharist."[4]

Second Reading
Ephesians 4:17, 20–24

(Refer to the fifteenth Sunday in Ordinary Time for an overview of Paul's letter to the Ephesians.)

Today's Pericope: Today's material is an exhortation to the people (the letter is a parenesis, which is in and of itself an exhortation—an ethical imperative) that is the thrust of the entire letter. It is probably part of an early catechism. Human beings must continually struggle to become the persons they already are. This tension comes from the fact that the freedom given to human beings by God, which is their right and dignity as children of God, has been tarnished by sin. Even though God created men and women in his image, unlike God human beings are capable of sin and do not always live up to their created goodness. They do have the freedom for good, however. They have the freedom to choose to turn away from sin—a metanoia—and to turn toward God. Human beings have the freedom to respond to God's grace. One-time conversion is not enough. It is an ongoing process that requires diligence if we are to grow in our relationship with and conformity to the person of Jesus Christ.

The intended recipients of the letter's exhortation are Christians who are in danger of slipping back into their pagan ways. The gospel of Christ is the lamp that lights the way. It is the sure way to hold fast to Christian principles. Christ and the gospel must be the lens from which we view all our earthly decisions. Human beings are not able to serve both pagan idols and Christ. No matter how attractive the idol, whether ancient or contemporary, they ultimately fail to satisfy. Idols may tease us, but we must remain steadfast and not be seduced by them. Christians are to allow themselves to be taken over by Christ—to allow our old natures to be made new in Christ. Christians are citizens of a new world order. It takes time and effort to learn what it means to live as such a citizen. In order to allow our old natures to be transformed in Christ, it takes a willing heart and spirit.

---

[3] *WWC,* 219.

[4] *PL,* 332.

The gospel is proclaimed.

Gospel
John 6:24–35. Those who come to Jesus will never be hungry. Those who believe in him will never thirst.

STEP 1
NAMING ONE'S EXPERIENCE

What were your first impressions? What was your first response to the gospel (or the other readings)? What captured your attention?

Each person names his or her initial impression. Statements should be brief. No reasons should be given at this time. All simply listen without agreeing or disagreeing.

STEP 2
UNDERSTANDING

In a brief statement, explain what you think this gospel is trying to convey.

STEP 3
INPUT FROM VISION/STORY/TRADITION

Liturgical Context

Last week we left Mark in order to spend time in reflection with John's Jesus and the Bread of Life Discourse. Today begins the Discourse and the explanation of the feeding of the multitudes that was proclaimed last Sunday. The three remaining Sundays continue the Discourse. We leave Mark for a few Sundays to reflect with John. The Old Testament texts for these Sundays reveal and point to the theology of John's sixth chapter.

Today's opening prayer reminds us that the gift of life itself comes from God. That life is nourished by Jesus, the Bread of Life, who gives us eternal food—food that satisfies. Gifts without measure flow from God's goodness, and the ultimate gift to us is the gift of his Son, Jesus. The prayer after

communion reminds us again that this gift of love is ultimately given to us in the sacrament in which Jesus continues to give us his presence in absence in the gift of eucharist.

Ninth-century abbot and mystic Symeon speaks to us in poetry of the ineffable mystery of Christ who is present in our sacramental symbols.

> "You Oh Christ, are the kingdom of heaven; You the land promised to the gentle; You the grazing lands of paradise; You, the hall of the celestial banquet; You the ineffable marriage chamber; You, the table set for all.
> You, the bread of life; You the unheard of drink;
> You, both urn for the water and the life giving water;
> You, moreover, the inextinguishable lamp for each one of the saints;
> You, the garment and the crown and the one who distributes crowns;
> You the joy and the rest; You, the delight and glory;
> You, the gaiety; You the mirth;
> and Your grace, grace of the Spirit of all sanctity, will shine like the sun in all the saints; and You, inaccessible sun, will shine in their midst and all will shine brightly, to the degree of their faith, their asceticism, their hope and their love, their purification and their illumination by your Spirit"
> (Symeon, *Hymns of Love Divine*, 949–1022, abbot at Constantinople and mystic).[5]

Gospel Exegesis

The facilitator provides input from critical biblical scholarship on this text. This input includes insights as to how people would have heard the gospel in Jesus' time.

Manna, the bread of angels, the bread from heaven, became associated with Jewish eschatological messianic hope. There was an expectation of the renewal of the manna from heaven. 2 Baruch 29:3, 8, puts it:

---

[5]*RF*, 123.

And it shall come to pass when all is accomplished . . . that the Messiah shall then begin to be revealed. And it shall come to pass at that self same time that the treasury of manna shall again descend from on high, and they will eat of it in those years, because these are they who have come to the consummation of time.[6]

Messianic hopes centered around the return of a Moses-like prophet. Moses, the first prophet, interceded on the people's behalf and they were fed. Messianic hopes centered on One who would come to feed them in similar fashion. Jewish tradition considered Moses both prophet and king. John makes the same association with Christ—Messiah, King, Prophet. In last week's gospel the people confessed him as prophet. Their attempt to make him king was a logical extension of their confession.

After Jesus fed the people he withdrew to the hills by himself. The people misunderstood and thus acted incorrectly and impulsively to Jesus' sign in their midst. So he retreated first to the hill country and then across the lake. While both Mark and Matthew treat the sea rescue as miraculous, John does not. The Greek rendering of the text places Jesus walking beside the sea. The text functions as an explanation as to how Jesus arrived on the other side of the lake. "[T]he narrative implies that while the disciples toiled at their oars through the storm, Jesus made his way up the coast toward Capernaum where they sighted him walking along the shore."[7] People missed the sign. They thought Jesus' miracle signaled the arrival of a great prophet like Moses. "Thus some people may have thought of Jesus as a miracle and sign worker like Moses who gave them 'wonder-bread' (Exodus 16:1–31)."[8] Jesus reminds them that Moses did not give true heavenly bread. Only the Son of Man has the power to give such bread. The obvious next question for the people is addressed in next week's gospel. If Jesus gives them bread as the Son of Man, how is it that the Son of Man has earthly parents, is a human being? It made no sense to them. Here is where the great split began in Jesus'

ministry. This was simply too much for some people to handle, as we will see next week.

After Jesus performs the great sign of multiplication of loaves, the people go looking for him. They get in their boats at Tiberius and cross the lake to Capernaum. They find him. For John, there are two kinds of "finding." One is authentic and one is not. The latter is based on inappropriate motives. The people have no idea how Jesus got away from them in the first place. They ask Jesus how he got there. Jesus does not answer them. It is more important to know why *they* are there. Jesus knows their hearts and responds to them. A dialogue ensues. Jesus reminds them that their search is not for spiritual things, but is a direct result of being fed. Jesus exhorts them to work for whatever will bring eternal life. What kind of work is Jesus talking about? The work of God—lives lived in conformity with God's will—actions that please God. "What pleases God in the Fourth Gospel is to believe in the one whom he has sent (3:17, 34)."[9] Faith is the expected response to God's awesome power and works. However, God never forces the issue. God always holds out the hand of invitation, which is often rejected by willful and sinful human beings.

It was common practice that a true prophet would lend credibility to himself and his announcement by demonstrating a sign. The people want Jesus to show them Moses' sign—manna, bread come down from heaven. They want a return to manna. Lest we forget, this is one and the same audience who, on the day before, were beneficiaries of Jesus' multiplication of the loaves and fishes. Were they asleep? "Present day miracles regularly appear less awesome and less convincing than those of the past, amplified, as they are, by imagination."[10] They failed to see the spiritual reality in Jesus' sign.

Jesus, the Teacher, reminded them that it was not Moses who fed the people manna in the wilderness. God was and *is* the One who rained down the bread from heaven. Heavenly bread comes from a heavenly source. The gift of manna continues through Christ. Jesus not only gave the bread

---

[6]*RJ*, 132.
[7]Ibid., 133.
[8]*LAF*, 87.

[9]Ibid., 134.
[10]*DL* (V), 171.

of life—Jesus *is* the Bread of Life. "One final point. Unlike Mark, who has seventeen miracle stories, John has seven (2:1–11; 4:46–54; 5:1–15; 6:1–15; 6:16–21; 9:1–41; 11:1–44), which he calls 'signs.' While relatively few in number, these signs fit into John's theology of Jesus as the giver of life, whose seventh and therefore perfect sign is raising a person from the dead."[11] The feeding of the multitudes reminds us that Jesus is the ultimate giver of the only life that matters. Jesus is the one who feeds our spirits. He is our nourishment.

A primary theme of today's gospel is faith. Faith in the Old Testament was centered on the reliability of God. Assurance of reliability was later appropriated by Christians in the New Testament to Jesus Christ. John uses the phrase "believing in Jesus" thirty-four times. Believing has everything to do with seeing and knowing. Jesus is the revelation of God. This is the faith of believers. In John's gospel a believer is not only to see and to know, but he or she must also act. Believers must testify to what they have seen and heard. All of the heroes of John's gospel—the man born blind, the Samaritan woman, the Beloved Disciple—all confessed faith in Jesus and publicly acknowledged and testified to that faith. John is insistent that faith must not be rooted in miracles and signs. They simply point to the glory of God. Faith must be rooted in experience; experience must lead to testimony. John wants his readers to take note—"believing in Jesus" is the Christian's primary concern.

In the Hebrew mind-set faith is an act of heart and soul—not necessarily the intellect. To our modern culture faith often refers to matters of the mind—belief in certain dogmas, or belief in one who possesses authority (i.e., doctor, clergy, etc.). In Middle Eastern thought faith has more to do with loyalty, commitment, and solidarity.

Jesus tries to move the people from mere desire for things bound to this earth, from physical needs, to things that will last eternally—things of God, that which pleases God. Jesus is asking for their loyalty, commitment, and solidarity with God and the One whom God sent—Jesus himself. Whoever "believes into" Christ will never be hungry again. John Pilch provides synonyms for "be-

lieves into": abide with, follow, love, keep the words of, receive, have, and see.[12] Faith demands relationship, commitment, and solidarity with Jesus, the one who feeds us with himself.

Proclaim the gospel again.

Sometimes we gain new insights when we hear the text after the interpretation is given. Someone from the group proclaims the gospel a second time.

STEP 4
TESTING

Conversation with the Liturgy and the Scriptures

Test your original understanding in dialogue with the text.

(You might consider breaking into smaller groups.)

Now that you've heard the exegesis, were there any new insights? How do you feel about it? How does your original understanding of this gospel compare with what we just shared? How does this story speak to your life?

Sharing Life Experience

Participants share an experience from their lives that connects with the biblical interpretation just presented.

> *Our community stormed the heavens for the healing of one of our children. The bread we sought was full healing and restoration. It was difficult for many of us to reconcile what we perceived to be God's refusal to answer our prayer. Yet the truest miracle or sign was the faith and reflection on God's incredible love, God's presence in the midst of tragedy, and God's desire to feed us with bread of hope and trust. It invited a new and deeper faith. We all were seeking tangible signs. We wanted healing. We wept and grumbled when healing did not take place.*

> *In the beginning we were sure we would receive the miracle we prayed for. We were confident that God would act. Slowly God reached out to us and re-*

---

[11] *JMUG*, 45.

[12] *CWJB*, 120.

vealed himself to us. Today's gospel serves as a wonderful summary of what God revealed. We see with earthly vision. We wanted healing. Our hearts were breaking. The child would ultimately know perfect healing. The grieving family and friends were the ones who now needed healing. What became so incredibly evident through the sojourn of one of our members is that God's ways are not ours. We were all called to trust that the living God was with the family and with our community. The life and death of this little child was catalyst for many people to grow in faith. Obviously, God did not snatch this child away as a means to bring people to faith. However, the love of God in the midst of the tragedy, shown through the faith of the family and the love and support of the community, invited people to reflect on the meaning for their lives and ultimately grow in their relationship with God. The family has many stories to tell of how this little one in his short year and a half of life was an evangelist in his own right.

So often I come to God with my request for manna. I want my adult children to follow the script I wrote for them; I want things in my life to work out the way I planned. I want answers to all my prayers. I become immersed in earthly realities and fail to see what God is trying to do in the midst of my life. If I would focus on Christ, the true Bread of Life, fear and worry would be obliterated from my vocabulary.

What was John trying to teach his community? How is this a word for your parish as a whole? In what way does your community ask for signs like the crowd in today's gospel asked for signs? In what way does this gospel speak to what is going on in your life right now? In what way has this conversation with the scriptures for today's liturgy invited change in your life? In what way are the biblical themes of covenant, exodus, creation, and community evident in today's readings? Do you still feel the same way about this text as when you began? Has your original understanding been stretched, challenged, or affirmed?

STEP 5
DECISION

The gospel demands a response.

In what concrete way might your parish be invited to respond? Are there any attitudes or behaviors you would like to change as a result of today's conversation? What one concrete action will you take this week in response to the liturgy today?

Pastoral Considerations: Is there any project in your parish that is hampered by your community's lack of faith or failure to see the work of Christ within it? What gifts, manna, miracles are right under your noses, yet you fail to see them? Do you listen more to those who seek signs or to those who desire to celebrate the signs that have already been given?

DOCTRINAL ISSUES

What Church truth/teaching/doctrinal issue could be drawn from the gospel for the eighteenth Sunday in Ordinary Time?

Participants suggest possible doctrinal themes that flow from the readings.

Possible Doctrinal Themes

Conversion; eucharist; faith; love of God; Jesus, the Bread of Life; hope and trust; Jesus, the Messiah; eschatological reign of God; true discipleship; Christology

Present the doctrinal material at this time.

1. The facilitator gives input on a particular doctrinal issue of his or her prior choosing. OR
2. The group chooses a doctrinal issue from the list they created. They read together from the Doctrinal Appendix or other appropriate, official Church documents and the works of respected theologians.

(Many doctrinal issues are found in the Doctrinal Appendix at the back of this workbook. If you are choosing an issue from this resource, please refer to it now.)

Reflection questions centered around the chosen doctrinal theme can be found at the end of each topic in the Doctrinal Appendix. The questions are based on the five-step reflection process. If you choose a topic not included in the Doctrinal Appendix, craft your own questions according to the same five-step process.

Following the reflection questions you will be reminded to return to chapter 7, "Preparing the Catechetical Session," to assist you in crafting your own session.

Closing Prayer

Let us pray.
Lord,
you give us the strength of new life
by the gift of the eucharist.
Protect us with your love
and prepare us for eternal redemption.
We ask this through Christ our Lord.[13]

---

[13]Eighteenth Sunday in Ordinary Time, "Prayer After Communion," *The Sacramentary.*

Nineteenth Sunday in Ordinary Time

INTRODUCTORY RITES

Entrance Antiphon (or Opening Song)

Lord, be true to your covenant, forget not the life of your poor ones for ever. Rise up, O God, and defend your cause; do not ignore the shouts of your enemies. (Ps 73:20, 19, 22, 23)[1]

Opening Prayer

The facilitator of the session may lead the prayer. Others in the group may be asked to proclaim the readings.

Let us pray
that through us others may find the way to life in Christ.

Pause for silent prayer.

Father,
we come, reborn in the Spirit,
to celebrate our sonship in the Lord
Jesus Christ.
Touch our hearts,
help them grow toward the life you have
     promised.
Touch our lives,
make them signs of your love for all men.
Grant this through Christ, our Lord.[2]

LITURGY OF THE WORD

The readings are proclaimed.

First Reading
1 Kings 19:4–8

(Please refer to the seventeenth Sunday in Ordinary Time for an overview of the Books of Kings.)

---

[1]Nineteenth Sunday in Ordinary Time: "Entrance Antiphon," *The Sacramentary.*

[2]Nineteenth Sunday in Ordinary Time: "Opening Prayer," *The Sacramentary.*

Today's Pericope: King Omri came to power about fifty years after Solomon died. Omri sought to strengthen Israel by making an alliance with the Phoenician kingdom in Lebanon on their northern border. Omri's son, Ahab, married the king of Tyre's daughter, Jezebel, in order to unite the kingdoms. Jezebel worshiped the pagan god, Baal, the personification of natural forces. She brought her own prophets into Israel and established temples to the deities.

Elijah was enraged by the pagan worship. The covenant was in jeopardy. The people flirted with the pagan gods and wavered in their faithfulness to Yahweh. Elijah fearlessly went on the offensive and attacked Israel's apostasy. He interceded to God to end the drought. He was confident that Ahab would return to the worship of Yahweh once the pagan gods, who supposedly boasted mastery of the elements, were exposed as nothing more than inanimate nonentities.

Jezebel's prophets were put to the sword. She lashed out in fury and in retaliation, vowing to do to Elijah what had been done to her prophets. Elijah was forced to flee to the Negeb desert. After a day's run in the desert, Elijah was exhausted. He could go no farther. In despair he sat down under a broom tree and prayed for death. He fell asleep and was subsequently visited by an angel (a manifestation of God). The angel told Elijah to get up and eat the hearth cake and drink the jug of water provided for him. Elijah went back to sleep. Once again the angel returned and ordered Elijah to get up and eat lest the difficult journey be too long for him. The angel of the Lord, God's messenger, ordered him to go on—to continue his journey. This time there was no question—God was speaking. Elijah was not to give up. He was to continue the journey fortified by the food provided by the Lord's angel. He walked forty days and forty nights to the mountain of God, Horeb. Horeb was the name given in some traditions to Mount Sinai, the mountain of the covenant. Mountains traditionally are places of revelation and encounter with God. Elijah journeyed to the mountain of encounter.

Elijah was beaten down by his mission. The angel appeared and offered him nourishment to go on—bread of strength and bread of God's presence. Elijah cried out like Moses, "This is enough." It is the cry of all great prophets who feel the burden of responsibility placed on them by Yahweh. The bread given to Elijah strengthened him for his forty-day journey to his encounter with God. The number forty conjures images of the forty-year desert sojourn and Jesus' forty-day fast in the desert, after which the angels ministered to him. Elijah reminds all who sojourn through this life that when the mission and the journey become too difficult and we become discouraged, we are given the bread of presence to strengthen and to keep us going. That promise continues for us in the bread of eucharist.

Responsorial Psalm
Psalm 34:2–3, 4–5, 6–7, 8–9

Classified as both a Wisdom psalm and a psalm of praise, today's responsorial psalm was used in the early church to accompany the reception of communion. It appropriately connects to the first reading and the gospel.[3]

Second Reading
Ephesians 4:30–5:2

(Please refer to the fifteenth Sunday in Ordinary Time for an overview of Paul's letter to the Ephesians.)

Today's Pericope: Christians are sealed with the Spirit of God. Paul exhorts believers to rid themselves of everything that saddens the Holy Spirit. To break the seal by attitudes or behaviors not in conformity with righteousness is to break one's relationship with God. Christians are graced by Christ to love. Selfless love comes from Christ. Christians are to love as Christ loved—a universal and timeless exhortation. "Therefore there are no need for codes, lists of duties to fulfill and faults to avoid."[4] If one loves as Christ loves, worry about such codes is a waste of time. Those who love as Christ loves will live in conformity with God's will, provided, of course, they grow in their relationship with God. There is an inherent responsibility

---

[3]*PL*, 335.
[4]*DL* (V), 176.

to form a good conscience and to situate discernment within the people of God—the Church—since human judgment can be flawed by sin. The Spirit has gifted the Church with various charisms and ministries—apostles, teachers, prophets—to facilitate truthful and Spirit-filled discernment.

The gospel is proclaimed.

Gospel
John 6:41–51. Jesus said, "I am the living bread come down from heaven."

STEP 1
NAMING ONE'S EXPERIENCE

What were your first impressions? What was your first response to the gospel (or the other readings)? What captured your attention?

Each person names his or her initial impression. Statements should be brief. No reasons should be given at this time. All simply listen without agreeing or disagreeing.

STEP 2
UNDERSTANDING

In a brief statement, explain what you think this gospel is trying to convey.

STEP 3
INPUT FROM VISION/STORY/TRADITION

Liturgical Context

Jesus' Bread of Life Discourse continues today. The Discourse serves as Jesus' exegesis of his multiplication of the loaves and fishes and subsequent feeding of the five thousand. We take time out from Mark for these few weeks to enter into dialogue with Jesus about the meaning of his signs, and what it means for us that Jesus is our "Bread of Life."

Underneath Jesus' sign is his incredible, passionate love for us. We see evidence of that love in the Elijah story. God simply would not allow Elijah to give up on life, so he gave him bread of presence. Jesus wants the same thing for his followers. He wants to communicate his incredible love for us. He was frustrated when his followers didn't understand.

The opening prayer resonates with that same theme. We are reminded that we are God's very own children—we are God's sons and daughters. We celebrate that truth when we gather for worship. We ask that our lives be touched in such a way that love will flow from us to others. St. Paul reminds us that if we love as Christ loves, that will happen automatically.

Gospel Exegesis

The facilitator provides input from critical biblical scholarship on this text. This input includes insights as to how people would have heard the gospel in Jesus' time.

The Discourse follows a pattern similar to the one Jesus used in the parables. He makes a pronouncement or a statement that is metaphorical or connected to an Old Testament symbol. The people do not understand what is really meant by his words so he explains. People are still in a quandary after his explanation, or they object vociferously to what he has to say. New questions are asked. Nothing deters Jesus from proclaiming the good news. People are moved to decide. Today's gospel signals a definite moment of decision. Jesus' teaching was difficult and shocking to many of his listeners. Their suppositions about matters of faith were turned upside down. They were asked to see with new vision. Who is this man anyway? By what right does he come turning over our sacred apple carts? He is only the carpenter's son, for heaven's sake! Enough is enough! How can this mere carpenter claim to be bread sent from heaven? If he really is the Son of Man—a being of divine or heavenly origin—how is it that his human roots are so ev'dent? The people were incredulous and many disciples defected—this was the proverbial back-breaking straw.

The people's reaction is emotionally charged. We know this person—how dare he claim to come from God! (It is easy to put ourselves in their shoes. Would we look similarly upon him if times were reversed?) Ultimately, this is the moment of decision. From now on, people will have to accept the pronouncement of Jesus on mere faith. Belief in Jesus as Son of God would require a radical new confession for his followers. "Now the power of faith is derived neither from evidence nor from the logical and necessary conclusion of reasoning nor from irrefutable proofs nor from the persuasive and irresistible force of words and miracles."[5]

Jesus knows how difficult the invitation is. He reminds his listeners that faith must come from the Father. It is pure gift. It is not a gift that is given to some to the exclusion of others. Faith is sister to love—to believe and to love belong in the same family. The gift of faith must be freely received as it is freely offered. Faith can be analyzed after it has been received and embraced, but it must be seized by the one receiving. "To believe is to allow oneself to be drawn—captured—by him who alone is infinitely worthy of love."[6]

Jesus tells the crowd to stop murmuring. His Father will not force anyone into relationship. Those who have been captured by Divine Love simply cannot understand when others are not so captured—it is inconceivable to them. We all know what it is like to commend someone we respect, love, and admire to someone who does not share our opinion. It is like speaking to a brick wall. We are never quite sure what it will take to melt the preconceived notions, reserves, barriers, and obstacles. People are invited to embrace Christ through the witness and testimony of others. Deep, abiding faith takes place, however, when those same people are seized by the gripping love of the One who was sent.

Faith is not simply belief in what Christ taught, it is relationship. It is ongoing, life-giving, conversational relationship. Faith in Christ is participation in his life, strengthened and empowered by the food he gives us. In the desert the Israelites were given food to sustain them on their way. The manna in the desert was perishable, however. The manna disappeared and the people died. The new food that Christ offers is the food of his own body—it is not perishable. Jesus' bread will never die and those who eat it will live forever.

---

[5] *DL* (V), 177.
[6] Ibid., 178.

The bread of Christ is the bread that answers the question for us: "What happens when all is lost?" Jesus gives us himself as food. Catherine of Sienna tells us it is because Christ is a mad lover—so much so, that he gives himself to us as food.

The first part of the Discourse identifies the giver of the bread, the Father. This part of the Discourse identifies the bread. The bread is Christ—"I am the bread of life." The term *bread of life* was a commonly known phrase that meant "bread which yields eternal life."[7] John's Jesus not only gives the bread of eternal life, he *is* the bread of eternal life. This type of language is not foreign to Jewish thought. Moses was often referred to as the bread that was given for the people to eat—divine nourishment given by God to Israel. "That the giver and the gift fit are identical means that one does not receive something from Jesus without receiving Jesus himself."[8]

Jesus insists that only he has seen the Father. The people have seen Jesus but have refused to believe in him. The inherent message in the text is that people are responsible for their failure to believe. It is an act of will to believe or not to believe. However, Jesus reminds his listeners that in order to come to faith in him a person must be drawn by the Father. It is God's initiative. The grace is available for all. People are given the invitation; it is up to them to respond. Even though the Father invites, it does not preclude individual responsibility. Those who do respond are promised eternal life. Similarly, John makes it clear that the promise of eternal life does not mean that eternal life is an absolute certainty—it can be lost.

When Jesus begins a statement, "I am . . . ," he is saying something about his relationship with human beings. The statements are not intended to teach us about his essence, but to "reflect his dealing with humans. In each of these seven sayings ['I am the bread of life,' 'I am the resurrection and the life,' 'I am the Good Shepherd,' 'I am the true vine,' 'I am the light of the world,' 'I am the way, the truth, and the life,' 'I am the door of the sheep'] what Christ does for human beings is identified with a metaphor. If Jesus is the bread

of life, then what he does is to nourish us with himself."[9]

In the ancient world the shame and honor system was so deeply embedded in the consciousness of the people that it dictated the attitudes and behaviors of the entire culture. Honor dictated that people remain in the social status into which they were born. People were not to attempt to better themselves or move up the social class ladder. It was considered divisive to attempt to improve one's birth status. The knee jerk reaction of the people to the things Jesus said about himself is not surprising. They were impressed by his teaching, but he stepped over the line. The people "murmur"—the same word used for what the Israelites did in their desert wanderings. Earlier in chapter 6 (last week's gospel) the people posited their interpretation of the desert manna in Exodus 16. Jesus corrected their interpretation and reminded them that it was not Moses who gave the bread, it was God—the heavenly Father.

The people are cynical about Jesus' doctrinal assertion. They lash out at him for stepping outside the bounds of his social status. The tone of the dialogue is derogatory. The dialogue would more appropriately be translated, "Is this fellow . . . ?" or "Isn't this chap . . . ?" The people know full well who Jesus is and where he came from—they know his parents, they know his birth status. For Jesus to make the claim that he, above all people, has "come down from heaven" was considered audacity at its worst, and "threatening to an established and well-ordered community. How dare Jesus claim more honor than he deserves?"[10]

There are two levels of interpretation going on in today's reading: the perspective of Jesus' contemporary community and the perspective of John's community over a half century later. Some parts of the gospel text include the thoughtful reflection of a community that has had considerable time to make the connections between what Jesus said and what they now understand in light of living the Christian kerygma for many decades. "The Church reminds Bible readers to distinguish the meaning a passage might have had in Jesus' life-

---

[7] *RJ*, 136.
[8] Ibid.

[9] Ibid., 137.
[10] *CWJB*, 122.

time from the meaning it could have had at the time of the evangelist's."[11] For example, verses 6:35–50 probably reflect Jesus' lifetime. John Pilch reminds us that there is no mention of eating bread until verse 51.[12] In the Old Testament God's instruction to the people was often referred to as bread. Jesus alludes to this understanding when he loosely refers to Isaiah 54:13: "They shall all be taught by God." In Jesus' day the people would have heard and understood his words in a metaphorical sense—bread as teaching. The "instruction Jesus gives about the Father is life-yielding bread for those who believe in him whom God has sent."[13]

Eating the bread, the idea that begins to emerge in verse 51 and following, is probably the interpretation of the Christian community read back into the historical life of Jesus—it is "likely the product of early Christian insight, now placed on the lips of Jesus."[14]

In the final verse of today's pericope, Jesus tells his audience that he is the living bread come down from heaven, and that all who eat his bread will live forever and that it is life for the world. Bread is therefore Christological, eucharistic, and eschatological. Jesus is the new food of the messianic age.

> Its language [v. 51] is understandable in light of a saying of R. Hillel, son of Gamaliel III: "There shall be no Messiah for Israel, because they have already eaten him in the days of Hezekiah" (b. Sanhedrin 99a). Just as one may devour books, drink in a lecture, swallow a story, stomach a lie, and eat one's own words, so one may eat the living bread, Jesus, the incarnate Word.[15]

The word *bread* carried within its essence many layers of meaning in the Old Testament. It is a symbol of hospitality. When bread is shared between host and guest, a special relationship is forged. Be-

---

[11] Ibid., 123.
[12] Ibid., 122.
[13] Ibid., 123.
[14] Ibid.
[15] *RJ*, 138.

trayal of the host violates the sacredness of the relationship implied in the sharing of bread[16]—"Even my friend who had my trust and partook of my bread has raised his heel against me" (Ps 41:10). Covenants were sealed through the communal meal in which bread always played an important role. Through the sharing of the community meal Israel committed itself to the Lord.

Bread enjoyed rich liturgical usage in the Old Testament. Bread was a sign of Israel's fidelity to Yahweh as well as the terms of the covenant between Yahweh and the people of God. Jesus becomes the new bread of the new covenant. Jesus identifies himself as the Bread of Life. Included in that title are all the images, metaphors, and symbols associated with bread and its religious significance. Those who accept Jesus as this new bread will never hunger again. The Jews only knew perishable manna. The manna of Christ not only is imperishable, but those who eat this bread will live forever. "For John the symbol of bread is Christologically central to the entire mystery of Jesus."[17]

Proclaim the gospel again.

Sometimes we gain new insights when we hear the text after the interpretation is given. Someone from the group proclaims the gospel a second time.

STEP 4
TESTING

Conversation with the Liturgy and the Scriptures

Test your original understanding in dialogue with the text.

(You might consider breaking into smaller groups.)

Now that you've heard the exegesis, were there any new insights? How do you feel about it? How does your original understanding of this gospel compare with what we just shared? How does this story speak to your life?

---

[16] John F. Craghan, *CPDBT*, 109.
[17] Ibid., 111.

Sharing Life Experience

Participants share an experience from their lives that connects with the biblical interpretation just presented.

Sometimes we become so accustomed to the precious gift we celebrate every week that we never stop to consider what would happen if we lost the gift of the eucharist. I once heard someone posit an analysis that suggests that even if we were to allow for married priests, for the return of the priests that left, and even if we were to allow deacons and women to become priests, the shortage is so exponentially in motion that the day is coming when there will not be enough ordained priests, thereby putting the celebration of eucharist in jeopardy. Whether this is true remains to be seen. However, the reflection it prompted and continues to prompt is sobering. I ask myself, "Would we as a people really miss it?" I would certainly hope the answer to that would be a resounding, "Would we miss water, would we miss the air we breathe? Of course, we would miss it!"

In my own experience eucharist is the power that drives my life. I am able to live my life as priest, prophet, and king because of the nourishment of Christ as food in the eucharist. No matter what life brings, eucharist sustains me in the midst of it. Eucharist draws us as community and it is because of the eucharist that I cannot stay in my petty animosities or my grievous hatreds. Eucharist commits me to the poor, the brokenhearted, the marginalized, and the oppressed around the world. Eucharist demands that I strive for unity and live in harmony. Eucharist insists that I speak and live a just life. If I eat Christ as food, as the food that never stops nourishing, then I must act like Christ. Eucharist makes that possible. I get so frustrated when people say that liturgy has nothing to do with their lives, that it is empty and boring. I know we have a long way to go in all our parishes to allow the symbols of our faith to speak the way they are intended to speak, but if ever there was a place that helped bring meaning into people's everyday lives it is the liturgy. Over the years I have witnessed story after story of people who have suffered, grieved, and endured unimaginable losses, but who have found strength in the eucharist and in a community that lives the eucharist.

I will never forget one particular experience of eucharist. It was a workshop and I was a team member. We had spent the week together sharing life and sharing stories of faith. I was caught off guard and in the process so thankful for the robust symbols of our faith. When it was my turn to receive from the cup, I approached as I do every week. It was a large cup and the crimson red wine, turned precious blood, poignantly stood out as if suspended momentarily in time. As the life-giving liquid from the clear glass goblet came closer to my lips, I was struck by the paschal feast we are so privileged to celebrate. This blood poured out carried within it every story of brokenness that we shared together that week as well as the brokenness of all the people in the world. Jesus' blood, the blood of the new covenant, the promise that he will always be with us in the form of food—bread and wine—and will never allow us to go hungry again or be deprived of his presence in the midst of his absence. Today's gospel has awesome implications for us. Jesus is the food who will never disappoint. Jesus is the food who will never give up on us, even when the entire world gives up. Jesus is the food who will always promise us a place to call home and a family to call brother, sister, mother, father, and friend. Jesus is the food who invites us as equal guests to the same banquet feast. Jesus is the food who invites the pauper to dine with a higher place of honor than the king. And Jesus is the food who demands that we love as he loved—and that we eat with those he loved, the outcasts, the unclean, the beggars, and the prostitutes. Jesus is the food who insists that I discern who I have placed in those categories, seek them out, and break the bread of life with them. Jesus is the food to whom the world, if it were awakened, would come crawling on its knees to feast from his leftover crumbs.

What was John trying to tell his community? Have you ever had an experience in which you tried to witness to something wonderful God has done in your life, only to encounter a deaf ear in response? Imagine how it must have been for Jesus to want everyone to accept the good news he was offering, only to have the people murmur? Where might your community have stood had they been present to hear Jesus' discourse? How is this gospel a challenge for your community today? In what way has this conversation with the scriptures for today's liturgy invited change in you? Can you or your community relate in any way to Elijah in the first reading? In what way are the biblical themes of covenant, exodus, creation, and community evident in today's readings? Do you still feel the same way about this text as when you began? Has your original understanding been stretched, challenged, or affirmed?

STEP 5
DECISION

The gospel demands a response.

In what concrete way might your parish be invited to respond? Are there any attitudes or behaviors you would like to change as a result of today's conversation? What one concrete action will you take this week in response to the liturgy today?

Pastoral Considerations: Is your parish a place that offers the Bread of Life to all who come? Are all invited as equal participants? Who are not invited? Who would be offered a back row seat at your banquet table? Who would think they were not even invited in the first place? Perhaps it is time for all our parishes to ask those questions, be prepared for the answers, and act accordingly. That alone could change the world.

Christian Initiation: Are there any candidates for confirmation and eucharist ready to complete their initiation? Today would be a most appropriate occasion to celebrate a rite of full communion in the Catholic Church. Eucharist calls us to mission. Perhaps this week would be a good time to invite catechumens to participate in serving the local soup kitchen, visiting the sick, imprisoned, or nursing home residents, or assisting at the homeless shelter and then gathering to reflect on the experience—these are some of the ways in which we live the eucharist.

DOCTRINAL ISSUES

What Church truth/teaching/doctrinal issue could be drawn from the gospel for the nineteenth Sunday in Ordinary Time?

Participants suggest possible doctrinal themes that flow from the readings.

Possible Doctrinal Themes

Eucharist; morality; moral decision making; Jesus Christ, the Bread of Life; conversion; faith; symbol of bread (see Easter Vigil, symbol of bread); discipleship

Present the doctrinal material at this time.

1. The facilitator gives input on a particular doctrinal issue of his or her prior choosing. OR
2. The group chooses a doctrinal issue from the list they created. They read together from the Doctrinal Appendix or other appropriate, official Church documents and the works of respected theologians.

(Many doctrinal issues are found in the Doctrinal Appendix at the back of this workbook. If you are choosing an issue from this resource, please refer to it now.)

Reflection questions centered around the chosen doctrinal theme can be found at the end of each topic in the Doctrinal Appendix. The questions are based on the five-step reflection process. If you choose a topic not included in the Doctrinal Appendix, craft your own questions according to the same five-step process.

Following the reflection questions you will be reminded to return to chapter 7, "Preparing the Catechetical Session," to assist you in crafting your own session.

Closing Prayer

Let us pray.
Lord,
may the Eucharist you give us
bring us to salvation
and keep us faithful to the light of your truth.
We ask this in the name of Jesus the Lord.[18]

---

[18]Nineteenth Sunday in Ordinary Time, "Prayer After Communion," *The Sacramentary.*

Twentieth Sunday in Ordinary Time

INTRODUCTORY RITES

Entrance Antiphon (or Opening Song)

God, our protector, keep us in mind; always give strength to your people. For if we can be with you even one day, it is better than a thousand without you. (Ps 83:10–11)[1]

Opening Prayer

The facilitator of the session may lead the prayer. Others in the group may be asked to proclaim the reading.

Let us pray
with humility and persistence

Pause for silent prayer.

Almighty God, ever loving Father,
your care extends beyond the boundaries of race
    and nation
to the hearts of all who live.
May the walls, which prejudice raises between us,
crumble beneath the shadow of your outstretched
    arm.
We ask this through Christ, our Lord.[2]

LITURGY OF THE WORD

The readings are proclaimed.

First Reading[3]
Proverbs 9:1–6

---

[1]Twentieth Sunday in Ordinary Time: "Opening Prayer," *The Sacramentary.*

[2]Twentieth Sunday in Ordinary Time, "Opening Prayer," *The Sacramentary.*

[3]The exegesis for the first and second readings may or may not be the focus of your group's reflection, as there may only be time to give adequate attention to the gospel, your primary concern. However, the exegesis is included here in order to provide a thorough investigation of the entire liturgy of the Word as there may be parts (or all) that would be essential to the direction you wish to take with your particular ministry group.

Overview of the Book of Proverbs: The Book of Proverbs was written around the ninth or tenth century B.C.E. It was a compilation of wise sayings and poetry. Solomon was remembered for his unparalleled wisdom; he was therefore considered the founder of the Wisdom tradition. He was believed to have written the Book of Proverbs, The Song of Songs and Ecclesiastes, and the Book of Wisdom (the last book of the Old Testament written).

The themes inherent in the collection of sayings in the Book of Proverbs date back to the Sumerians in 3000 B.C.E., so it is possible that the sayings could have been gathered together during Solomon's time and put in one collection. However, chapters 25–29 were not written until two centuries after Solomon's death during the reign of King Hezekiah.

The only organized section of the book is chapters 1–9, in which there is a planned section of short proverbs mixed in with long instructions. Those first chapters serve as a prologue to the entire collection and they describe wisdom as a way of life. The Book of Proverbs was a treasured source of practical wisdom to assist people in finding meaning for their lives.[4] The purpose of the proverbs was to guide people as they struggled to live a well-ordered life. Overall, the book exalts Yahweh, the living God and Master who orders the universe and everything in it and has complete power over it.

The proverbs are concerned with the issues of relationships—parents, children, husbands, wives, and friends. They are concerned with the difference between the righteous and the unrighteous. They uphold the virtues of honesty, generosity, justice, and integrity. The proverbs extol the need to discipline one's passions and sexual appetites. They encourage the appropriate use of speech—when to speak and when to be silent. They insist upon good stewardship of resources, such as wealth and the land. They describe the proper attitude one is to display toward one's superiors and they exalt the "value of wisdom over foolish

---

[4]*ROT*, 480.

and careless behavior."[5] The prominent literary form of the "proverb or *mashal*, [is] a pithy saying based on comparison. Often the saying was expressed in a hidden manner that necessarily provoked from its reader (or hearer) a certain intellectual effort in order to penetrate its true meaning. *Mashal* also means 'to rule,' hence proverbs were regarded as having value for governing human behavior."[6] The Book of Proverbs is considered canonical by Roman Catholics, but deuterocanonical by Protestants and Jews (both positions a result of the Jamnia decision, A.D. 100).

Today's Pericope: Today's pericope is set in the context of wisdom and its contrast with foolishness. Wisdom is personified as lady and foolishness as harlot. Both lady and harlot have prepared a home and a feast; both lady and harlot extend invitations to the feast. However, the feast of the lady is rich fare—food that provides life. The harlot's meal of stolen bread and water offers nothing but death. Herein is the comparison and its inherent lesson. Wisdom is a life-giving feast, foolishness is death-dealing, meager rations. Obviously, a wise person will choose the lady over the harlot.

There is an invitation in today's sapiential saying, "Come." It is an invitation to anyone who lacks wisdom, "judgment, discernment, clear-sighted-ness in the management of their lives, an easy prey for folly and its allurements."[7] Such people are in dire need of the practical art of living, not flowery oratories or illusive theories. They need to digest the food of practical wisdom.

"Drink of the wine I have mixed" refers to the mixing of wines in order to embellish the taste of the delectable victuals. There are eschatological overtones for the Israelite listener. The festive fare and banquet is reminiscent of the advent of the Messiah prophesied in Isaiah's eschatological banquet (Is 25:6; 55:1–5). The New Testament appropriated the banquet metaphor and assigned it to represent the messianic reign of God in Christ. Jesus Christ, host of the wedding banquet, invited all people to the festive feast, gathering all together in the last eschatological age.

Wisdom's banquet anticipates the bread and wine of Christ's—his own body and blood—which become humanity's perfect, ultimate wisdom and teaching. The connection with today's gospel is obvious.

Responsorial Psalm
Psalm 34:2–3, 4–5, 6–7

Last Sunday's responsorial psalm employed different verses of this same psalm but both last week and this week's appointed psalm employ the same refrain. This is a Wisdom psalm. The last verses most appropriately connect with the first reading.

Second Reading
Ephesians 5:15–20

(Please refer to the fifteenth Sunday in Ordinary Time for an overview of Ephesians.)

Today's Pericope: While it is not certain that today's reading was chosen for its appropriate connection with the Wisdom themes of today's liturgy, the pericope from Ephesians also addresses the contrast between wisdom and folly. Folly involves not seizing the opportunity to make the most of each day. It also involves engaging in drunkenness and debauchery. There are eschatological overtones in today's parenesis. Humanity is in the last age, which is under the dominion of evil powers. However, their days are numbered and their time is short. The evil is in the process of being overthrown—thus, people are to live as children of the new, last age. The author of Ephesians contrasts drunkenness from wine with Pentecostal ecstatic joy of hymns, psalms, and songs of praise.

The exhortation against drunkenness is as timely today as it was then. It is often true that crisis invites denial. Drink and drugs perpetuate the denial that keeps people from dealing with the crisis of their lives. Then and now people evade the truth by losing themselves in mind-altering substances. The author exhorts his community to keep clear heads as they journey through their dangerous age—a timeless word for all generations.

Today's pericope is also believed to be part of a household code (*Haustafel*). Such codes were often begun with an enjoinder to execute one's duties toward God (Jewish code) or to the gods (pagan codes).

---

[5]Ibid., 481.
[6]*WWC*, 223.
[7]*DL* (V), 182.

The gospel is proclaimed.

Gospel[8]

John 6:51–58. Jesus' flesh is true bread and his blood true wine.

STEP 1
NAMING ONE'S EXPERIENCE

What were your first impressions? What was your first response to the gospel (or the other readings)?[9] What captured your attention?

Each person names his or her initial impression. Statements should be brief. No reasons should be given at this time. All simply listen without agreeing or disagreeing.

STEP 2
UNDERSTANDING

In a brief statement, explain what you think this gospel is trying to convey.

STEP 3
INPUT FROM VISION/STORY/TRADITION

Liturgical Context[10]

Wisdom plays a major role in today's liturgy. The author of Ephesians in today's second reading ex-

---

[8]The gospel exegesis is provided later in this session so that it may be presented in the proper sequence where it occurs in the adult five-step reflection process. The exegesis is provided for the first and second readings for your information and edification, and for you to use at your discretion. Once again, the gospel is the primary source of reflection. If there is time for reflection on the other readings, all the better.

[9]The primary focus of reflection is the gospel. However, often the other readings demand attention and must be brought into the dialogue.

[10]The scriptures in the Lectionary, the seasons of the year, and the ritual prayers of the mass are interrelated and form the basis for liturgical catechesis. The liturgical context attempts to explore and clarify the themes and this interrelatedness.

horts his community to live wisely in a dangerous age. Wisdom is the banquet from which we all should feast. Today's first reading from Proverbs is quoted in the liturgy for the Solemnity of the Body and Blood of Christ. It is used in reference to the eucharist, "the table to which the Lord himself invites us, welcomes us, and gives us his very self to us as food."[11] In today's gospel Jesus reminds us that he is the Bread of Life and that the food he gives will allow those who eat to live forever. Thus, we continue the proclamation of Jesus' Discourse on the Bread of Life, a brief detour from Mark's gospel for these few weeks.

Today's Entrance Antiphon asks that God, our protector, give us strength. Today's liturgy reminds us that we are given that strength through the eucharist. It is through the eucharist, the Bread of Presence, that Christ continues to be present and in our midst.

The outstretched arm of Christ suggested in the opening prayer for today's liturgy is offered to us in the eucharist and in the gathering of the eucharistic assembly. We are reminded that we are united in Christ and thus may not allow disunity and prejudice to divide us. Eucharist commits us to one another. It also commits us to the poor.

Gospel Exegesis

The facilitator provides input from critical biblical scholarship on this text. This input includes insights as to how people would have heard the gospel in Jesus' time.

Continuing the exegesis from last week, Jesus referred to himself as the bread come down from heaven. The Jews were incredulous and began to murmur. So begins today's gospel. They cannot imagine how Jesus could possibly give his flesh to eat. *How* is the key word; it begins the next dialogue, the heart of which is eucharist. Charles Talbert suggests that the language of eating flesh and drinking blood was not literal.[12] Both early Christianity and Judaism prohibited the drinking of blood. However, eating Jesus' flesh and drinking his blood was used by the time of John's gospel as a reference to participation in the eucharist. There is a definite progression from Christology

---

[11]*DL* (V), 182.

[12]*RJ*, 138.

to eucharist. For the Johannine community the eucharist is the continuation of the incarnation of Jesus. "Whoever eats my flesh and drinks my blood remains in me and I in him"—verses 53 and 54 are language of intermingling, which ultimately bespeaks personal intimacy. Those who partake of the eucharist enter into personal relationship with Jesus. Christ has life within himself as does the Father, who passed on this life to the Son. Thus, anyone who eats the eucharistic banquet has the same life that Jesus has within himself. Those who eat will have life—the fullness of a life in personal relationship with Christ.

John's gospel does not relate the institution of the eucharist at the Last Supper. The ultimate eucharistic narrative in John's gospel occurs in 6:53–58, in the middle of Jesus' Galilean ministry, not at the end of his life. This eucharistic theme runs concurrently in a highly Christological section of John's gospel. The incarnation of Christ having just been broken open, John situates the Johannine community's understanding of eucharist.

Charles Talbert describes three views of the Supper in the New Testament.[13] According to Paul's letter to the Corinthians, Mark, Luke, and Matthew there is evidence that the meal is understood as a memorial of Jesus' death as a covenant sacrifice. A second view, posited by Luke–Acts, is that of an extension of the mealtimes Jesus shared during his life and after his resurrection, an anticipation of the messianic banquet. The third view, and the view espoused by the Johannine community, understands the meal as a ritual continuation of the incarnation of Christ through the elements of bread and wine.

It is logical to place the meal at the end of Jesus' life, when it is understood as covenant sacrifice. Further, it is also logical to place the ritual language of breaking bread in the postresurrection appearance at Emmaus if one's perspective of eucharist is that of shared meal with the risen Lord. It also makes perfect sense to situate the eucharistic narratives within the Galilean ministry of Christ, in which the nourishing dimensions of Jesus as Bread of Life are proclaimed. This is especially poignant in light of the perspective of eu-

charist as a ritual continuation of the incarnation of Christ through the eucharistic elements. John understands Jesus' death as the reason this cultic extension of the incarnation continues. Eucharist is the consumption of Jesus, the incarnate, divine Son of God.

An interesting analysis of the signs in John's gospel helps to shed further light on Jesus' multiplication of the loaves and fishes. Joseph Grassi points to the commonly held belief that the first twelve chapters of John's gospel are referred to as the "Book of Signs."[14] There are seven signs in these chapters: (1) wedding feast of Cana, (2) raising of the official's dying son, (3) healing of the paralytic on the Sabbath, (4) multiplications of the loaves and fishes, (5) Jesus walking on water, (6) healing of a blind man on the Sabbath, (7) raising of Lazarus. If we refer to the definition of *sign* given by Raymond Brown as an extraordinary act with strong symbolic potential that depicts Jesus' message of salvation,[15] Jesus walking on the water simply does not fit that description. The event may depict his divine power, but in and of itself it is not a message of salvation. Rather, it is more than likely connected to the multiplication of the loaves as a possible symbolic reference to Passover (parting of the waters). Nowhere in the story of Jesus walking on water is the word *sign* used as it is in the other signs. If Jesus' ambulatory stroll across the lake does not constitute a sign, then John leaves us with only six signs, which is highly improbable. Six is a sign of incompleteness (as the six jars of water at Cana demonstrate). Seven, on the other hand, constitutes totality. We are to ask, "Where, then, is the seventh sign?" We are told in chapter 12 that even though Jesus performed many signs for the people they still did not believe in him. Perhaps another sign was needed for belief to occur. We are told in the last chapter of John's gospel that all these signs took place so all may come to believe in Jesus as the Christ and Son of God.[16] They needed another sign to accept so great a revelation. The seventh sign is Jesus' death and the water and blood that flowed from his side. The sign was so powerfully etched in the evangelist's memory that he claimed himself an eyewitness to the event so all who

[13]Ibid., 140.

[14]*LAF*, 83–84.
[15]*GAJ*, 527–530.
[16]Ibid.

heard would be converted. Thus, the first six signs are completed by the seventh sign, the culmination of which is Jesus' Passover from death to life. "[T]he Passover connections are so strong in Jesus' death that the writer presumed his readers surely know that all the Passover's meaning came to a climax with the 'sign of the blood' of the Passover lamb: 'The blood shall be a sign for you, upon the houses where you are: and when I see the blood, I will pass over you, and no plague shall fall upon you to destroy you' (Exod 12:13)."[17]

We come to a crisis of major proportions in Jesus' ministry. People are horrified at the thought of Jesus' exhortation to eat his body and drink his blood. Jesus insists that the only way to understand is to reflect on his death, resurrection, and ascension. All the signs help shed light on Jesus' difficult saying that we are to eat his flesh and drink his blood. The multiplication of the loaves and fishes is intimately connected to the seventh sign—Jesus' Passover. Examination of three signs begins to solve the questions. Only three signs deal with blood—the first sign, the blood of the grape at Cana; the fourth sign, drinking Jesus' blood; and the seventh sign, blood flowing from the side of Jesus. All three signs have to do with obedience. Jesus obeyed his Father and drank the sour wine from the cross, the disciples were enjoined to accept Jesus' difficult word about eating flesh and drinking blood, and the waiters obeyed Jesus and new wine flowed. Remember, the people misunderstood Jesus' sign and thought perhaps he was a great Moses-like leader. People were skeptical that someone who claimed to be a divine being, the Son of Man, could come from very familiar human origins. At first glance it would appear that today's dialogue reflects an early church argument about the meaning of eucharist.[18] Perhaps there is far more going on, however.

Eating flesh and drinking blood refers to Jesus' humanity as well as to his death. In later verses in chapter 6 Jesus reminds the disciples that this very difficult teaching can only be understood when Jesus returns to his throne of glory, when he ascends into heaven. The sign raises questions about Jesus' divinity. Jesus was not a wonder-worker. He

was divine. If he is divine, then how can he also be human? It was a tremendous stumbling block for his followers.

Jesus' death on the cross provides further clues regarding the meaning of the sign of the loaves and fishes which, in turn, points to a theology of Jesus' humanity and his divinity. The Jews complained that Jesus referred to himself as "bread come down from heaven." The witnesses to Jesus' death, Mary and the Beloved Disciple, were also witnesses to the fact that Jesus seemed to know the exact moment he was going to die. After he drank the sour wine, he bowed his head and proclaimed, "It is finished." Then he died. In chapter 10 Jesus insisted that no one would take his life away from him—he would give it by choice. He has the power to give it or take it up again. Jesus' death transcends the human. Human beings cannot choose the moment of death at will. The Prologue of John's gospel asserts that the Word became flesh by choice. Now the Word dies the same way. There is divinity within Jesus that gives credence to his ability to give heavenly bread.

Why eat his flesh and drink his blood? What does that imply? Jesus died a horrendous, human death. His mother wept. A lance was thrust into his side. Water and blood flowed—a guarantee of death. This only tells us that he died. It tells us nothing about the reason we are to eat his flesh and drink his blood. We are given clues when we are told that Jesus "bowed his head and gave up his spirit"—literally, he died. However, symbolically those words perhaps refer to Jesus' gift of the Holy Spirit to humankind.

The issue of blood and water from the side of Jesus holds tremendous significance for the author of the fourth gospel. Even though he does not directly tell us that, he would not have gone to such lengths to provide us with an eyewitness were it not so.

The water that flowed from the side of Jesus was a sign of the Spirit. As a result of Jesus' bloody sacrifice, and upon Jesus' ascension into glory, the Spirit would be sent as gift for all the world. In the fourth sign Jesus referred to eating his flesh and drinking his blood as spirit and life and that it could only be understood after his glorification. The water from Jesus' side was a sign to the wit-

[17]Ibid., 85.
[18]Ibid., 87.

nesses that Jesus had indeed ascended to his Father's throne and that the Spirit had been sent.

Even though Jesus' flesh and blood are understood as the spirit and life that would flow when the Son of Man was glorified, thereby sending the Spirit into the world, it does not tell us why we are to eat his flesh and blood. We need look no further than to the paschal lamb for an answer. Eating the flesh of the paschal lamb and taking upon themselves the blood of the lamb (a sign of the blood sprinkled on the doorposts as a deterrent to the angel of death) was primary to the Passover supper. The fourth evangelist understands Jesus as the new paschal lamb, whose flesh is to be eaten and whose blood is to be drunk, giving life.

The allusions to Passover in the Passion narratives are so strong that to miss them would be to miss the nose on the front of one's face. Jews would not enter Pilate's headquarters lest they become defiled before *Passover*. Jesus was led away at the hour the paschal lambs were to be slaughtered in preparation for *Passover*. The mention of hyssop and basin were *Passover* images—blood was sprinkled on the houses by hyssop in a basin.[19] The Jews wanted to remove Jesus' body from the cross because it was *Passover*. At the beginning and at the end of Jesus' ministry he was referred to as "Lamb of God."

All ritual sacrifices and meals were to be executed out of obedience to God. Thus, the Passover meal was a ritual meal celebrated in obedience to Yahweh. John reminds us that Jesus was obedient up until the moment he drew his last breath. Jesus alludes to Psalm 69:22 when, from the cross he cries out, "I thirst." The psalmist refers to bitter wine given for his thirst. Jesus consumes the bitter wine as his last act of obedience before he hands over his spirit. "The 'good wine' will be made possible through obedience to Jesus' word, just as he obeyed his Father right to the end by accepting the 'bitter wine.'"[20]

Another allusion to the paschal lamb occurs when Jesus' bones were not broken by the soldier, just as the Israelites were to not to break the bones of the

paschal lambs (Ex 12:46). Exodus also enjoined the people to eat the *flesh* that night. The blood of the Passover was a sign for the Israelites. Jesus' blood flowing from his side was a sign for those who witnessed it. For there to be a valid sacrifice, Jewish law required that blood had to *flow*. Blood sacrifice was also necessary for purification from sin.

Thus, in obedience to his Father, Jesus himself drank the bitter wine, thus making his own flowing blood a sacrifice for all, a prayer of forgiveness, and a sign of life—just as the blood of the paschal lamb was a sign of life for the Israelites.

The ritual requirements of the Passover and the author's allusion to Jesus within the context of Passover reveal the meaning of Jesus' command to eat his flesh and drink his blood. Jesus' flesh and blood are understood as spirit and life for the believer.

For John, drinking the bitter wine of the cross, Jesus' final act of obedience, is a reminder to the community that they must "participate in Jesus' hour and its meaning if they wish to receive the choice wine and Spirit made available by his death."[21] Drinking from the cup was primary. Perhaps it was understood that the cup also included the flesh as was posited by Leviticus 17:11— "The life of the flesh is in the blood." John's primary theme is that in obedience to Jesus' command, and in imitation of him, we are to drink the cup of his blood, thereby participating in his sacrifice.

Thus, Jesus, the new paschal lamb, as evidenced by the water and blood flowing from his side, takes away the sins of the world. We are to eat this Lamb if we want to participate in the Spirit and have abundant life.

Even though there is a temptation to see an "institution narrative" in today's verses of the gospel, there is instead a theology of Jesus as the "new paschal lamb whose flesh is to be eaten and whose blood brings life to believers."[22] Such life demands that we do what Jesus did for the remission of sins so that his abundant Spirit may be poured out on

---

[19]Ibid., 92.
[20]Ibid., 93.

[21]Ibid., 97.
[22]Ibid.

the face of the earth. If we are to share his life, then we must also share the responsibility. Can we drink from his cup? Dare we drink from it?

Proclaim the gospel again.

Sometimes we gain new insights when we hear the text after the interpretation is given. Someone from the group proclaims the gospel a second time.

STEP 4
TESTING

Conversation with the Liturgy and the Scriptures

Test your original understanding in dialogue with the text.

(You might consider breaking into smaller groups.)

Now that you've heard the exegesis, were there any new insights? How do you feel about it? How does your original understanding of this gospel compare with what we just shared? How does this story speak to your life?

Sharing Life Experience

Participants share an experience from their lives that connects with the biblical interpretation just presented.

When the topic of living the paschal mystery comes up, my thoughts always turn to the question: Do I ever even come close to living its implications? The bottom line of today's gospel for me is simple: Jesus asks us if we are willing to drink the bitter wine, so that the new wine of the Spirit may flow and give life to others. If it is willingness he asks for, then I would certainly hope that I am willing. Willingness must lead to action, and that is where I falter. How in the world could any cup that I might drink even compare to the sacrifice of Christ? When I began to reflect on the implications of this gospel for my own life, I had to ask myself, "Just how have you, or better yet, have you, ever had to drink the bitter wine of poured-out blood so others may live?" There are so many heroes and heroines I can point to that do just that every day of their lives. I look at the Archbishop Romeros, the women of San Salvador, the missionar-

ies in dangerous lands, those who have given their lives in the service of others. There is nothing I can point to that even comes close to their example. So again my question returns, "How is this gospel relevant in my own life?" In small ways I am invited to live this gospel in my family life when I try to put the needs of others in my family before my own needs. I fall short so much of the time that I dare not hold that up as any example. In fact, this gospel is a constant challenge to me to practice drinking the bitter cup more often in small ways so that I will be up to the challenge when the moments for heroic demonstrations come my way.

Yet my reflection on the implications of this gospel would not be stilled—"I have been walking this Christian road for many years. Surely I have had opportunities to drink the bitter wine so new life might flow." I have not been called to the front lines of dangerous missionary living, but I have been called to live the prophetic life demanded at my baptism, which insists that I share the good news wherever and whenever I am called. This has sometimes not been met with eager and enthusiastic response, to be sure. I have also, on occasion been asked to respond to a human need when I would rather collapse in an easy chair and veg my brain on meaningless chatter from the electronic drug that is perched on its throne in the midst of my living room. In those ways I have had occasion to drink bitter wine. But what has it really cost me?

When have my actions, my dying, been a cause and a source of life for others? I had to ponder that one for a while. One thing stands out for me. As a child I endured a very painful experience. As an adult I have encountered the broken body of Christ, and the effervescent flow of his blood, which has flowed over me, within me. Yet in spite of the healing I have encountered, what is healing if it is not shared? Every time I have been in a situation where I felt compelled to share that childhood brokenness, the Pandoras that have come crashing out of the box have been so powerful and the results so incredible, that there was no question that the bitter gall of vulnerability was indeed the intended choicest wine to be served on that particular day's platter. Life flowed from its cup to other wounded spirits.

One time in particular stands out. I shared my experience and affirmed that the Spirit of God had *taken over that chapter in my life and now I am healed and am on the way to continued, ongoing wholeness. When I made the announcement, I wished I hadn't. "No one needs to know that part of me. It is secret, you know." I felt incredibly vulnerable. If I could have taken back the words, I would have. I was angry with God. "You led me here, didn't you?" Yet the results were staggering. Out of a crowd of one hundred people a minimum of six came up to me to share their story. Three of them had never told another human being and the secret was destroying their lives. Some of the people were prompted for the first time in their lives to seek healing.*

I have always found in ministry that the extent to which I am willing to live the paschal mystery is the extent to which I am an effective minister of God. When we break open the joys and struggles of our lives with others, we find strength to endure. Herein lies the incredible success of all the twelve-step programs out there today. There is sometimes more honest, life-giving spirituality to be found in those rooms than in many of our church communities. None of us may be called to the front lines or to actual crosses where the only fare served is bitter gall, but we are all called to share the vulnerable parts of ourselves and to lay down our lives in the small ways so that when the large ones come our way, we will not shy away from them. When we eat the flesh of Christ and drink his blood we are not only nourished and strengthened to live the implications of his ritual meal, we also commit to it. I wonder how many of us are aware of that as we take that weekly pilgrim walk to his table?

What was Jesus trying to teach his followers? What was John trying to teach his community? In what way does this gospel challenge your community today? Has your community ever had the opportunity to live the implications of eucharist set forth in today's gospel? In what ways have you ever been invited to drink bitter wine so the Spirit of Life might flow out to others? In what way has this conversation with the scriptures for today's liturgy invited change in your life? In what way are the biblical themes of covenant, exodus, creation, and community evident in today's readings? Do you still feel the same way about this text as when you began? Has your original understanding been stretched, challenged, or affirmed?

The gospel demands a response.

In what concrete way might your parish be invited to respond? Are there any attitudes or behaviors you would like to change as a result of today's conversation? What one concrete action will you take this week in response to the liturgy today?

Pastoral Considerations: When was the last time your community reflected on the implications of eucharist that it is in the taking, blessing, breaking, and sharing that we are taken, blessed, broken, and shared for others? We could change the face of parish life were we to spend considerable time reflecting on that reality.

Christian Initiation: All these Sundays would be wonderful opportunities to celebrate a rite of full communion in the Catholic Church, or the rite of acceptance. We are initiated into a eucharistic community with all the implications set forth in today's gospel. Remember to celebrate the minor rites with catechumens—they foreshadow the eucharist they will one day celebrate.

DOCTRINAL ISSUES

What Church truth/teaching/doctrinal issue could be drawn from the gospel for the twentieth Sunday in Ordinary Time?

Participants suggest possible doctrinal themes that flow from the readings.

Possible Doctrinal Themes

Paschal mystery; eucharist; symbols of bread/flesh and wine/blood (see Easter Vigil symbols of bread and wine); Holy Spirit; genesis of Church at Calvary with the sign of water (baptism) and blood (eucharist) flowing from the side of Christ; cost of discipleship; conversion; mystery of suffering.

Present the doctrinal material at this time.

1. The facilitator gives input on a particular doctrinal issue of his or her prior choosing. OR

2. The group chooses a doctrinal issue from the list they created. They read together from the Doctrinal Appendix or other appropriate, official Church documents and the works of respected theologians.

(Many doctrinal issues are found in the Doctrinal Appendix at the back of this workbook. If you are choosing an issue from this resource, please refer to it now.)

Reflection questions centered around the chosen doctrinal theme can be found at the end of each topic in the Doctrinal Appendix. The questions are based on the five-step reflection process. If you choose a topic not included in the Doctrinal Appendix, craft your own questions according to the same five-step process.

Following the reflection questions you will be reminded to return to chapter 7, "Preparing the Catechetical Session," to assist you in crafting your own session.

Closing Prayer

Save us, Lord our God,
and gather us together from the nations,
that we may proclaim your holy name and glory in
　　your praise.[23]

---

[23]Psalm 105:47, *NAB.*

Twenty-First Sunday in Ordinary Time

INTRODUCTORY RITES

Entrance Antiphon (or Opening Song)

Listen Lord and answer me. Save your servant who trusts in you. I call to you all day long, have mercy on me, O Lord. (Ps 85:1–3)[1]

Opening Prayer

The facilitator of the session may lead the prayer. Others in the group may be asked to proclaim the readings.

Let us pray
with minds fixed on eternal truth.

Pause for silent prayer.

Lord our God,
all truth is from you,
and you alone bring oneness of heart.
Give your people the joy
of hearing your word in every sound
and of longing for your presence more than life it-
     self.
May all the attractions of a changing world
serve only to bring us
the peace of your kingdom which this world does
     not give.
Grant this through Christ our Lord.[2]

LITURGY OF THE WORD

The readings are proclaimed.

First Reading
Joshua 24:1–2a, 15–17, 18b

Overview of the Book of Joshua: The Book of Joshua begins a new section of scripture often referred to as the "Historical Books." These books constitute the first compilation of the history of Israel from the time of Moses through the Babylonian exile. The Historical Books include Joshua, Judges, 1 and 2 Samuel, and 1 and 2 Kings. These works bear the mark of seventh- and eighth-century B.C.E. prophetic thought. Some scholars believe that the writers of Deuteronomy also penned the Historical Books, which is why they are sometimes referred to as Deuteronomic History.[3] There is much debate about the entitlement of Israel's bragging rights regarding its military conquest of the land. Israel was, in fact, able to conquer only a portion of the land. However, their grandiose overexaggeration was a result of the spiritual significance they placed on the victories they were able to accomplish.

There are two major sections in the Book of Joshua. Chapters 2–12 describe Israel's conquest of the land under the leadership of Joshua. Chapters 13 and following describe how Joshua apportioned the land among the tribes once the conquest was complete. Chapter 1 and the epilogue provide the theological underpinnings for Israel's great conquest—they describe the religious significance of the event. The first nine chapters of the Book of Joshua relate the epic of the Israelites as they conquered the land of Canaan. The chronicle depicts Joshua being victorious after only three military conquests, portraying a spectacular, miraculous, undefeated Israel. The story seems to suggest that the Israelites conquered every nation in their path. Chapters 13–22 describe the division of the land. When the boasting is stripped away, the facts of the chronicle make it all too clear that there were many walled Canaanite cities that were impregnable. The victories were extolled, but the realities of the conquest fell short of the idealized account.

However, the purpose of the book was not to provide a detailed history. It was intended to show

---

[1]Twenty-First Sunday in Ordinary Time: "Entrance Antiphon," *The Sacramentary.*

[2]Twenty-First Sunday in Ordinary Time: "Opening Prayer," *The Sacramentary.*

[3]The Greek Septuagint includes 1 and 2 Chronicles, Ezra, Nehemiah, Ruth, Esther, Judith, Tobit, and 1 and 2 Maccabees in the Historical Books.

that Israel marched forward armed with the power of God. Religious history, pregnant with meaning, was at the heart of the narrative. This small, ragtag military band accomplished great victories only because they were sustained and empowered by the Holy One of Israel. Only Yahweh could have accomplished the successes that did take place. Israel laid claim to all of the land (not just the land they conquered) because God was the one who helped them secure it in the first place. Thus, it was God's intention that they have dominion over it. Salvation history exalts the God who strengthened Israel in all its endeavors—deliverance from slavery and conquest of the Canaanite land. The Israelites gave Yahweh complete credit and honor for their achievements. In antiquity one method of honoring the God who led them in battle was to slay every man, woman, and child left in the conquered cities as a sign that Israel trusted God alone and desired no spoils of war for itself. This horrible practice was called the "ban," or *herem* in Hebrew. The ancients did not regard this as the brutal atrocity that would so offend sensibilities today. The survival of the nation was far more important than the welfare of individuals.[4]

Today's Pericope: Today's pericope is part of the epilogue of the Book of Joshua. The intention of this chapter is to give spiritual significance to the history described in the first chapters of the book. Scholars consider this a very important piece of Old Testament tradition. It is part of an ancient liturgy in which the covenant at Shechem between the people of Shechem and the Israelite invaders is renewed. The inhabitants of Shechem worshiped a god called El-berith. The Israelites worshiped Yahweh. The covenant agreement reached by both groups was to worship the one God, Yahweh. The liturgy in this pericope remembers and celebrates the agreement made by the two groups of people.

This reading is chosen for the parallel with the gospel in that both pericopes concern a choice. The people of Shechem and Israel chose to worship and serve the one God together. The disciples make a similar choice—"Master, to whom shall we go?"

Responsorial Psalm
Psalm 34:2–3, 16–17, 18–19, 20–21

Even though the refrain and the first stanza are the same as last week's psalm refrain, a new theme has emerged—"God's vindication of the righteous sufferer. The goodness of the Lord that we taste and see in the Eucharist is the goodness manifested in the suffering and vindication of Jesus, the righteous servant of God."[5]

Second Reading
Ephesians 5:21–32

(Please refer to the fifteenth Sunday in Ordinary Time for an overview of Paul's Letter to the Ephesians.)

Today's Pericope: Today's reading marks the beginning of the household code found in the Letter to the Ephesians. This code is a major part of the parenesis (moral exhortation) found in the second portion of the letter.

The code concerns the issue of being subject to others. Christianity adopted it from Hellenized Jews, who in turn adopted it from the Stoics. The household code determined the behavior of husbands, wives, children, slaves, masters, and parents. Christianity made the household code its own by adding the phrase "in the Lord" to the commands. However, in this case Christianity takes it a step further. Ephesians sets forth the parable that compares marriage to the relationship between Christ and the church. The author of Ephesians developed his theology. He begins with Genesis and its pronouncement of the unity of husband and wife in marriage. The church is described in the language of the purity code found in Leviticus. The command toward a person's neighbor found in Leviticus 19 provides the basis for verse 27 in today's reading. An early Christian profession of faith is found in verse 25 and a liturgical baptismal prayer is evident in verse 26. Paul combines two themes—the unity of husband and wife, and the ecclesiology of the church—its relationship to Christ. The author of Ephesians compares the duties of the wife to the relationship of the church to Christ. "As a result, the marriage relationship is transformed from one

[4]*ROT,* 196–198.

[5]*PL,* 339.

in which the wife is simply subjected to the husband without qualification into one in which the husband is to devote himself unreservedly to the love of his wife. Thus, the household code is turned upside down—the emphasis rests no longer on the duty of the wife to the husband but on the husband's love for his wife."[6] (See liturgical context.)

The basic message of the code is of great importance. It insists that order is needed for a family to run well and smoothly. By his emphasis on love, the author of Ephesians insists that something more is required of families than simply the rote following of code. Love is at the heart of all family relationships. There should be something unique and special about the Christian family. The code in scripture and its appearance in the proclamation of Sunday liturgy is a reminder that God cares about the family and that it is a primary concern of the church. "The well-being of families who belong to the church is important for the well-being of the church itself."[7]

This discourse shocks modern listeners as cultural norms today suggest equality between spouses rather than subordination. It is important to note that the reading does not "amount to an ideological canonization of the submission of woman to man, as if this were a 'natural law,' so that the eventual emancipation would be 'against nature.'"[8] The author of Ephesians wants to show Christian women of his day that they must live their lives according to the heart of the gospel imperative to love. The submission that Paul demands of the wives has nothing to do with subjection to authoritarian power. "Husbands are not the lords of their wives; this title belongs to Christ alone. Husbands must behave toward their wives as Christ behaves toward the Church."[9]

The gospel is proclaimed.

Gospel
John 6:60–69. Lord, to whom shall we go? You have the words of eternal life.

---

[6]Ibid., 340–341.
[7]*PTE*, 83.
[8]*DL* (V), 193.
[9]Ibid., 194.

STEP 1
NAMING ONE'S EXPERIENCE

What were your first impressions? What was your first response to the gospel (or the other readings)? What captured your attention?

Each person names his or her initial impression. Statements should be brief. No reasons should be given at this time. All simply listen without agreeing or disagreeing.

STEP 2
UNDERSTANDING

In a brief statement, explain what you think this gospel is trying to convey.

STEP 3
INPUT FROM VISION/STORY/TRADITION

Liturgical Context

The second reading today (as well as the reading from Colossians on the Feast of the Holy Family) causes much angst when read in the Christian assembly. Raymond Collins places the issue in its proper context.

> [T]he liturgical reading of these passages has provoked so much discussion, confusion and consternation that the bishops of the United States have petitioned Roman authorities for permission to substitute a shorter reading from Ephesians 5:25–33 on the twenty-first Sunday of the year.

> At the same time, the bishops asked that a shortened reading of Colossians 3:12–17 be allowed as a pastoral option on the solemnity of the Holy Family. This reading from the epistle to the Colossians on the solemnity of the Holy Family is not quite as problematic as it once was. The second edition of the editio typica of the Order of Readings

for Mass now provides for different readings from the apostolic writings when the solemnity of the Holy Family is celebrated in years B and C."[10]

Raymond Collins suggests that to omit the problematic verses does not erase them from one's consciousness.[11] He maintains that both readings from Colossians and Ephesians are taken from what is known as a household code. The structure focuses on what is to be considered order in a first-century Palestinian household. There were three types of relationships in the ancient household: husband/wife, parent/child, master/slave. The code addresses those in the household who are considered socially inferior. They are enjoined to obey those who are their superiors. The rest of the text concerns those who are socially privileged. They were to treat their "inferiors" with appropriate behavior—with love and fairness. The fact that the enjoinder upon slaves toward their masters is not included in the Lectionary text for either the Feast of the Holy Family or the twenty-first Sunday of the year is an automatic reminder to readers that the social conditions that prompted such texts in the first place no longer hold and are no longer appropriate for public proclamation.

The household codes draw from a very ancient literary form dating back to Aristotle. Greek Stoic and Cynic philosophers employed similar moral exhortations. Hellenized Judaism embraced the code as a model of moral exhortation and Christianity similarly adopted it. The code was considered a model for a well-ordered household. The codes had another purpose in the Christian economy.

Christians were accused of upsetting the social order of the community. They refused to worship divinized emperors. On the home front, women, children, and slaves became Christians, which automatically led to suspicions about Christianity—even to persecution. It was believed that Christianity upset social and domestic harmony.[12] Establishment of the household code was a way of saying to the neighbors that indeed Christian

people accepted contemporary family values in vogue at the time.

Collins insists that we should not omit the reading of these texts in the liturgy. We should read them with the understanding that the exhortation was a socially conditioned formulation. Families exist in the cultural milieu of their time and place. The household code was an affirmation that God cares about the harmony of "family life as it is actually lived."[13] "One cannot make any given society's family structures the norm for all families of all times and places. We can, however, affirm that God is not indifferent to family life, as it is actually structured within any given society. That the New Testament's household codes point to an historically and socially conditioned structure of the family is not a liability; it is an asset, because it points to God's concern for the real family rather than for an ideal or abstract family."[14]

The real-life situation that prompted the household code is both our strength and our liability. As a strength we are reminded that we must live the Christian life within the context of our lived experience, our culturally conditioned experience. The liability exists when we try to make the mores of an earlier period of time become the norms for the social relationships of the present time. No one should ever teach that wives should be submissive [the recently published Lectionary uses the word "subordinate" rather than "submission" in the Colossians reading for the Feast of the Holy Family] to their husbands. "Such submission is no longer acceptable; indeed, in our times, it may well be antithetical to the gospel itself."[15]

Today's gospel is an opportunity for us to reflect on the eucharistic liturgy. What do we celebrate and profess? This gospel reminds us that the mass is both sacrifice and meal. We feast on the Bread of Life and we share in the sacrifice of Calvary. We remember (anamnesis) that Jesus suffered, died, and rose from the dead. We remember that Jesus allowed his body to be broken and his blood poured out for the sins of the world. Through the sacrifice of eucharist we make present that reality

---

[10]*PTE*, 79.
[11]Ibid.
[12]Ibid.

[13]Ibid., 82.
[14]Ibid.
[15]Ibid., 84.

in our midst. We feast on Jesus' broken body and we drink from the cup of his blood and in so doing participate in his sacrifice. We allow ourselves to be taken, blessed, broken, and poured out for others as Christ poured himself out for us.

Today's alternative opening prayer so resonates with the gospel that one could almost see in it a theme for the entire liturgy. We pray that our minds be fixed on Christ, the only eternal truth. We acknowledge that truth comes from God alone, and only God gifts us with the heart to acknowledge that truth with singlemindedness. We pray that we hear the Word of God and long for his presence more than life itself. Jesus reminds us in the gospel that he is the Bread from heaven and that he should be the only object of our hunger.

Jesus offers himself to us as eucharist and as the eternal, nourishing Bread of Wisdom. Eucharist is the ongoing sacrament of salvation and participation in the life of Christ. We live the imperative of today's gospel when we gather for liturgy and consciously participate in the life and death of Christ that is remembered and made present in the eucharistic liturgy. The communion antiphon draws from the scripture of last Sunday's liturgy and from Jesus' discourse on the Bread of Life that we have celebrated over the past weeks. "The Lord says: The man who eats my flesh and drinks my blood will live for ever; I shall raise him to life on the last day" (Jn 6:55). Eucharistic Prayer IV aptly summarizes the heart of Jesus' challenge to us in the gospel. We are reminded that it is through the power of God's goodness that we are blessed and made holy. We are reminded that God did not abandon us in our sinfulness, but offered us hope in the salvation that Jesus won for us. Jesus continues to invite us into covenant relationship, which is the bottom line of today's gospel.

Gospel Exegesis

The facilitator provides input from critical biblical scholarship on this text. This input includes insights as to how people would have heard the gospel in Jesus' time.

Up to this point the disciples have been missing from the discussions with Jesus regarding his unusual Bread of Life Discourse. Many disciples are filled with angst over his command to eat his flesh and drink his blood. They believe it is a difficult

saying. They offer mixed reviews to Jesus' pronouncement and wait to formulate their final decision regarding whether they continue to follow him. Today is the moment of decision for many. Some disciples decide that Jesus is hopeless. They see nothing in him worth following any longer; they lose faith in him. They are not ready to make the commitment to put their faith in this man and his strange teaching. They do not trust themselves to let go and believe what their hearts once nearly dared to embrace.

To believe in Christ disciples must look beyond the absurdity of the cross and put their total faith in him. It would be the same for us today if Jesus were tried and put to death in an electric chair and we were called upon to attest to our faith in him as Christ. The faith required of disciples leads the believer to gaze upon Christ hanging from the cross and attest that he is indeed the Son of God! This same profession of faith takes place in every Sunday assembly when in the breaking of bread we remember and make present the sacrifice of the cross and celebrate its power in our lives. Christ gave us his broken body and poured out his blood so we may live. We participate in this mystery every time we gather for eucharist. We are given his broken body and his blood poured out as a living memorial of his presence in our lives.

Jesus reminded his listeners that some will fall away. Jesus reads the human heart. Some would betray their Lord. God provides the necessary grace for believers to turn to God in sorrow and in humility when there is temptation to turn away. There must be receptivity to God's grace and mercy, however.

The disciples are asked if they, too, plan to leave their Master. Peter responds with incredulity. "Where would we go, Lord? You and you alone have the words of life." Once they know the truth, how could they go elsewhere to find it? The disciples profess faith in Jesus, the Christ, Son of God and Messiah. Conversion is a prelude to profession of faith and complete belief and trust in Jesus Christ.

According to Charles Talbert, there are three basic understandings of the Lord's Supper in the New Testament.[16] In 1 Corinthians, Mark's 14th

_____

[16]*RJ*, 140.

620

chapter, Luke's 22nd chapter, and the 26th chapter of Matthew, the meal is understood as a memorial of Jesus' death as a covenant sacrifice. Luke–Acts posits an understanding of the Supper as a continuation of the mealtimes Jesus celebrated with his friends during his life and after the resurrection, anticipating the messianic banquet. The third understanding is that of cultic or ritual extension of the incarnation of Jesus in which the bread and wine function as Jesus' nourishing, life-giving body and blood. John's gospel embraces this third understanding.[17]

If the understanding of the Supper is that of memorial of Jesus' death (first understanding), it is no wonder that it is situated in the final week of Jesus' life. If the understanding of Supper is an extension of Jesus' mealtimes (second understanding), it is logically placed after Jesus rose from the dead. If the Supper is understood as a ritual expression of Jesus' incarnation, it is logical to place it in the middle of Jesus' ministry after he expounds on the life-giving, nourishing dimensions of his life and ministry. John asserts that Jesus' death made this ritual extension of his life possible.

In verse 59 Jesus reminds the listener that his words caused great anxiety for some of his followers. The incarnate Christ and the eucharistic expression of the incarnation that offers nourishment and life was a scandal to some of his disciples. Jesus prophetically read their hearts and knew that some would leave him.

Jesus reminds the listeners that his words are Spirit and Life. The manna given to their ancestors by Moses was an earthly reality. It belonged to the things of this world. It was a temporary solution to a pressing human need. There was no use for the manna beyond its actual purpose. Jesus' words, however, put the believer in touch with the spiritual reality of God's Spirit, the source of all life. The incarnation and the gift of eucharist put the believer in touch with the Holy Spirit.[18] The Spirit is given only because the Son of God ascended to the throne of the Father. The Jews questioned Jesus' divine genesis. It is obvious from today's text that some of Jesus' fol-

lowers questioned him similarly. "If those who had witnessed his words and works did not believe he 'came from heaven,' then how could they ever accept his return to the Father in glory?!"[19]

Jesus invited his disciples to accept the truth of who he was on faith. He was not going to offer any miraculous signs to prove it to them. This time they would be called upon to exercise the gift of faith given to them by God. Faith alone would be necessary in order to recognize Jesus' words as spirit and life.[20] According to Hebrew theology, the law—Torah—was believed to communicate life to the people of God. Jesus was inviting his disciples to place in him the trust that had once been placed in the Torah. Only with eyes of faith would they be able to accept the truth of his identity and mission—his incarnation, redemption, ascension, and glorification. Today's pericope is part of the conclusion to the Discourse on the Bread of Life. There seems to be a contradiction in this section. Verses 51–59 assert that one must eat Jesus' flesh and drink his blood if one is to have eternal life. Now, in verse 63, he tells us that flesh is of no avail. It is important to remember that flesh in this verse does not refer to eucharistic flesh, but to the natural principle in human beings that is incapable of giving everlasting life. "Spirit" refers to the "life-giving Spirit that will be given as a result of the ascension of the Son of man to where he was before (v. 62)."[21] Ultimately, then, today's passage is not referring to the reception of Christ in the sacrament of his body and blood, but rather the reception and revelation of Christ as the embodiment of heavenly wisdom, bread from heaven.[22]

Reginald Fuller insists that it is Jesus' claim that he is the revelation of God, not the eucharistic teaching, which is the difficult saying that causes dismay for so many. However, the Twelve do accept his teaching and the section concludes with the profession of faith by their leader, Peter.

When Jesus asked his disciples if they would also betray him, Peter insists that the Twelve would

---

[17]Ibid.

[18]Ibid., 141.

[19]WWC, 227.

[20]Ibid.

[21]PL, 341.

[22]Ibid.

never leave him. Peter insisted that no matter what, they had made a commitment to Jesus and would ultimately remain loyal to him. Peter called Jesus the "Holy One of God," using a phrase from the Hebrew scriptures that identified people who were consecrated to God. Jesus knew better than to believe that others would not betray him. According to John Pilch, most Mediterranean people would know better.[23] Jesus and his disciples were a small faction group. Loyalty would be strong between the leader and the members he recruited. However, loyalty between members of the group would be weak. The members of the faction would not be in strong relationship with other members of the group. Sometimes they would care very little for the others in their faction. We remember that James and John, the sons of Zebedee, went to Jesus privately to secure a higher place of honor than the others.

Jesus knew there would be a betrayer. Some disciples would have difficulty accepting the incarnation and the eucharist. The evangelist suggests that their faith was shallow; they were not called by God and were not considered among the disciples of the Lord. Faith, loyalty, and commitment are gifts from God that must be accepted and acted upon. Talbert suggests that perhaps this perspective is a result of the recent history in John's community in which some fell away from Christ because of their theological difficulties with the incarnation and the eucharist. They refrained from partaking of eucharist because they could not accept it as the flesh of the Lord who suffered for the sins of all. The gospel leaves all the readers with a question: "Will we also leave, or will we remain with Christ? Will we accept his incarnation and eucharist, or will we, like Judas, betray him, or like Peter, abandon him?" There is an inherent challenge.[24]

Proclaim the gospel again.

Sometimes we gain new insights when we hear the text after the interpretation is given. Someone from the group proclaims the gospel a second time.

---

[23]*CWJB*, 128.
[24]*RJ*, 140.

Conversation with the Liturgy and the Scriptures

Test your original understanding in dialogue with the text.

(You might consider breaking into smaller groups.)

Now that you've heard the exegesis, were there any new insights? How do you feel about it? How does your original understanding of this gospel compare with what we just shared? How does this story speak to your life?

Sharing Life Experience

Participants share an experience from their lives that connects with the biblical interpretation just presented.

> *My gaze is glued to the television as I reflect on this gospel for the twenty-first Sunday in Ordinary Time. We are in the middle of the conflict in Kosovo, a war in which those intimately involved must indeed ask themselves about the existence of God when atrocities and inhumanity so reflect the horror of this conflict.[25] My heart also aches in solidarity with the parents of those teenagers in Littleton, Colorado, who were gunned down yesterday in their school library. I remember what it is like to be the parent of a teenager whose life was spared, when my son's best friend was killed in a car accident. The gratitude for the life of my son was so bittersweet in comparison to the grief we felt over the loss of his friend and the loss his family had to endure. Gratitude and grief—what strange bedfellows! Life is a mystery. We never know what life will bring. Our way is not always paved*

---

[25]I was struck by the comments of a Nazi concentration camp survivor when asked if she questioned the existence of God because of her experience. She responded that it was her faith in God that helped her endure the ordeal. As far as doubting the existence of God because of humanity's propensity for horror and atrocity, she attested to the contrary. She mused that God must look at us from the heavenly throne and wonder why in the world he created us in the first place—"What is this creature that is capable of so much death and destruction?" Why should God be blamed for humanity's participation in evil?

with rose petals. We truly have nowhere to go except into the loving arms of Christ. He is our only bread. I simply do not understand how people endure the trials of life without faith.

People ask, "What has gone wrong in our world?" Hope seems to have taken a back seat to rage, disillusionment, anger, and dysfunction. What would possess two young people to embrace the ideology of a madman and shoot and kill with the glee of a lunatic? As a people we spend little time reflecting on the meaning of life. Young people often fall prey to sick philosophies because they have not been introduced to the only truth that matters.

Many disciples were introduced to Jesus, the Bread from heaven, the only source of life and hope, yet they were unable to embrace his love and make it a part of their lives. The invitation is there for all of us. Jesus is the only source of life in a world that has seriously tilted off the edge. Our equilibrium is teetering on the edge and we wonder about our future. Jesus offers us hope. He offers us himself. In the midst of the horror of yesterday there are multiple stories of miracles, and of heroic, selfless actions that not only attest to the presence of Christ, but scream to us that in the midst of chaos and hopelessness, Christ is our only hope. Life does not always make sense. Jesus walks with us and invites us to find meaning in our lives by entering into deep, trusting, and personal relationship with him. Like Peter, today's gospel is an invitation to forsake everything that would get in the way of our relationship with Christ. Like Peter, we must respond, "Yes, Lord, I will make mistakes, I will not always follow you the best way I can, but where else will I go? You alone offer meaning for my life, especially when life seems so absurd." Does it take tragedy for us to realize that Jesus is our only source? Sometimes even tragedy fails to convict. I am thankful that Christ continues to invite me to ingest his life-giving wisdom and Spirit. Come, O Spirit of God, and breathe new life on the face of the earth. Our children need to be delivered from its madness—only God's Spirit can so deliver us.

What was John trying to tell his community? In what way do you relate to Peter who was asked by the Lord if he too was going to desert Jesus and his mission? In what way have you responded to Jesus' invitation? In what way have you fallen short? In what way does this gospel challenge your community today? In what way has this conversation with the scriptures for today's liturgy invited change in your life? In what way are the biblical themes of covenant, exodus, creation, and community evident in today's readings? Do you still feel the same way about this text as when you began? Has your original understanding been stretched, challenged, or affirmed?

STEP 5
DECISION

The gospel demands a response.

In what concrete way might your parish be invited to respond? Are there any attitudes or behaviors you would like to change as a result of today's conversation? What one concrete action will you take this week in response to the liturgy today?

Pastoral Considerations: Jesus' discourse on the Bread of Life in John's gospel proclaimed over these past weeks provides an opportunity for parishes to reflect on their parish liturgy. Does your parish liturgy reflect the Church's teaching that it is the source and summit of all we do and the font from which our power flows? Perhaps now is a good time to assess the liturgy in your parish. Are the symbols of the liturgy robust? What about the liturgical ministries in your parish—proclamation of the Word, preaching, presiding, music, hospitality? Is renewal and change needed? What first steps need to be taken?

Christian Initiation: Is there anyone in your process ready to celebrate any of the rites of initiation, such as rite of welcome, rite of acceptance, rite of full communion in the Catholic Church, anointing of catechumens?

DOCTRINAL ISSUES

What Church truth/teaching/doctrinal issue could be drawn from the gospel for the twenty-first Sunday in Ordinary Time?

Participants suggest possible doctrinal themes that flow from the readings.

Possible Doctrinal Themes

Jesus Christ, the Bread of Life; conversion; discipleship; eucharist; liturgy; Word of God; paschal mystery; salvation; reign of God; morality; law

Present the doctrinal material at this time.
1. The facilitator gives input on a particular doctrinal issue of his or her prior choosing. OR
2. The group chooses a doctrinal issue from the list they created. They read together from the Doctrinal Appendix or other appropriate, official Church documents and the works of respected theologians.

(Many doctrinal issues are found in the Doctrinal Appendix at the back of this workbook. If you are choosing an issue from this resource, please refer to it now.)

Reflection questions centered around the chosen doctrinal theme can be found at the end of each topic in the Doctrinal Appendix. The questions are based on the five-step reflection process. If you choose a topic not included in the Doctrinal Appendix, craft your own questions according to the same five-step process.

Following the reflection questions you will be reminded to return to chapter 7, "Preparing the Catechetical Session," to assist you in crafting your own session.

Closing Prayer

Father in heaven,
it is right that we should give you thanks and
   glory.
Source of life and goodness, you have created all
   things,
to fill your creatures with every blessing
and lead all men to the joyful vision of your
   light. . . .
Even when man disobeyed you and lost your
   friendship
you did not abandon him to the power of death,
but helped all men to seek and find you.
Again and again you offered a covenant to man,

and through the prophets taught him to hope for
   salvation.
Father, you so loved the world
that in the fullness of time you sent your
only Son to be our Savior.[26]

---

[26]"Eucharistic Prayer IV," *The Sacramentary.*

624

Twenty-Second Sunday in Ordinary Time

Environment

Fall is the time of harvest. Since we are tuned in to our culture's natural rhythm of the seasons, fall is also a time for new beginnings that coincide with the beginning of the academic year. "For the church the harvest is an intense spiritual image of the paschal mystery. . . . The liturgist Pius Parsch wrote:

> The autumn of the church year is devoted to preparation for the end of life and the second coming of Christ. Now we more readily see the truth: Advent is really a continuation of the church's autumn season, her preparation for the Savior's return.
>
> Without overemphasizing the imagery, we might say that the weeks between Pentecost and Advent are a gradually intensifying ingathering, a process that echoes the harvest and that is compelled in the liturgy (and in the agricultural cycle) at Christmas and Epiphany, at the turning of the year.[1]

The natural harvest symbols of autumn—squash, gourds, pumpkins, cornucopias, grapevines, bundled grains and grasses, corn shocks, dried flowers, vegetables, cattails, leaves, acorns, fall flowers, fruits and vegetables, honeycombs and honey—are easily incorporated into the catechetical environment. The green of ordinary time might be laced with the deep tones of red, purple, yellow, gold, and brown. Tasteful art and icons of the prominent saints and fall feasts that appear during this season might be incorporated throughout autumn, such as Blessed Virgin Mary (August 15), John the Baptist (August 29), Holy Cross (September 14), Michael, Gabriel, and Raphael, Archangels (September 29), and All Saints, All Souls (November 1, 2).

INTRODUCTORY RITES

Entrance Antiphon (or Opening Song)

Lord, you are just, and the judgments you make are right. Show mercy when you judge me, your servant. (Ps 118:137, 124)[2]

Opening Prayer

The facilitator of the session may lead the prayer. Others in the group may be asked to proclaim the readings.

Let us pray
to God who forgives all who call upon him

Pause for silent prayer.

Lord God of power and might,
nothing is good which is against your will,
and all is of value which comes from your hand.
Place in our hearts a desire to please you
and fill our minds with insight into love,
so that every thought may grow in wisdom
and all our efforts may be filled with your peace.
We ask this through Christ our Lord.[3]

LITURGY OF THE WORD

The readings are proclaimed.

First Reading
Deuteronomy 4:1–2, 6–8

(Please refer to the fourth Sunday in Ordinary Time for an overview of Deuteronomy.)

Today's Pericope: Today's reading comes from the prologue to the Deuteronomy code. A common feature in ancient legal codes was to enjoin people not to add or subtract anything from the code.

---

[1]Peter Mazar, *CY*, 176.

[2]Twenty-Second Sunday in Ordinary Time: "Entrance Antiphon," *The Sacramentary*.

[3]Twenty-Second Sunday in Ordinary Time: "Opening Prayer," *The Sacramentary*.

The first five books of the Bible—the Pentateuch, the Law, the Torah, constitutes the Law of the covenant, the Law of Moses. It was considered a national treasure. The Law was understood as a living reality that embodied the relationship between God and his created beings. The Torah was considered God's blessing, as it gave the people an identity. The Law is intimately tied to the possession of the land, which in turn was the vehicle for making Israel a great nation. The people of Israel could do no less then follow the statutes given to them by their God who cared deeply for them. Observance of the Law was a reciprocal act of love on the part of Israel. It was also a response of trust in the God who is author of all life and who prepares the way for his people.

The Law sets forth a relationship between the Lawgiver and those who follow the Law. Believers will not add or subtract from the Law because God ordained the Law in the first place. When people follow the Law with a steadfast heart, they grow in holiness. To follow the Law is to recognize that we are evolving and developing creatures of the most High God. We are in relationship with our Maker whose will continually unfolds in the lives of people. The Law assists people in living life according to the will of God. The Law invites humble, steadfast observance. Those who follow the Law with humble and contrite hearts set forth an example for all to follow. They witness to the God who is in relationship with his children.

The author of Deuteronomy insists that there are four motivations for following the Law—life, land, wisdom, and a close relationship with God. It was believed that those who lived outside the Law were flirting with death. To follow the Law was intimately tied with possession of the land. Wisdom is obtained through faithful observance of the Law. Perhaps this is the genesis of the eventual association of wisdom with the Law in later scriptures.

"The Law is the pride of God's people and is the ground for its responsibility."[4] Today's reading reminds the people how fortunate they are to have been given the Law. This reading was chosen for the comparison made between God's Law and human law, which is the theme of the gospel.

---

[4]*DL* (V), 202.

Responsorial Psalm
Psalm 15:2–5

Today's psalm is known as an entry psalm, a psalm sung upon entry into the Temple. The psalm exalts the qualities God deems worthy of the pilgrim—justice, sincerity, and integrity.[5]

Second Reading
James 1:17–18, 21b–22, 27

Overview of the Letter of James: For the next five weeks we will hear from the Letter of James, which is known as one of the seven "Catholic" letters or "general" epistles as they are not addressed to a specific church or community. The letter is addressed completely to the issue of moral exhortation. The writing is similar to the Wisdom writings of the Old Testament. The author has also drawn from the Greek Stoic philosophical tradition. There appears to be remnants of a liturgy and of a baptismal creed. The letter's style is that of Jewish-Hellenistic exhortation. The author of the letter is Jewish, judging from the familiarity with the Wisdom tradition of the Old Testament and from the concrete patterns of thought (unlike Greek abstract thought.) It is obvious that the author of James was very involved in the life and theologies of the early Christian community. It is apparent to scholars that the letter was written for Jewish Christians.

Some scholars suggest that James is James, the leader of the church in Jerusalem. There is no proof for this assertion, but there is nothing to refute it either. Other scholars believe that James was a pseudonym, or that the author writes as an interpreter of James.

James pays very little attention to the person of Jesus in his writing. Jesus is named only a few times. It is suggested that if the author were an apostle or a relative of Jesus this would be highly unlikely. The original Greek writing is so refined that it is doubtful that a first-century Palestinian would have had such mastery of the Greek language. Thus, it is doubtful that the letter could have been penned by Jesus' "brethren" or an apostle. There is much debate concerning the date of authorship. Some place the date as early as the year 57 and others as late as the latter part

---

[5]*PL*, 342.

of the first century and the first part of the second century.[6]

Reginald Fuller suggests that it was probably a Hellenistic Jewish document that contained twelve exhortations based on the twelve patriarchs in Genesis 49. It was appropriated by Christianity during the time after Paul by a Hellenized Jewish Christian teacher. The letter draws from the Wisdom tradition.

Today's Pericope: Today's reading is taken from the second exhortation. The author Christianized this portion of the original letter by adding the baptismal reference. The gospel is to be received "anew and made the basis for Christian action."[7] The author of James insists that true believers and authentic religion demand moral obedience. He illustrates what he means. He insists that liturgy must lead to a life of moral obedience and cannot be a substitute for it.[8]

The gospel is proclaimed.

Gospel
Mark 7:1–8, 14–15, 21–23. You disregard God's commandment, but cling to human traditions.

STEP 1
NAMING ONE'S EXPERIENCE

What were your first impressions? What was your first response to the gospel (or the other readings)? What captured your attention?

Each person names his or her initial impression. Statements should be brief. No reasons should be given at this time. All simply listen without agreeing or disagreeing.

STEP 2
UNDERSTANDING

In a brief statement, explain what you think this gospel is trying to convey.

---

[6]*DOB*, 412–413.
[7]*PL*, 343.
[8]Ibid.

STEP 3
INPUT FROM VISION/STORY/TRADITION

Liturgical Context

For the past five Sundays we interrupted the reading of Mark's gospel and diverted our attention to the gospel of John and Jesus' feeding of the multitudes and subsequent Discourse on the Bread of Life. We resume our reading of Mark and will continue it through the thirty-third Sunday. The shift is not abrupt, however, as we pick up where Mark left off. We read John's version of the feeding of the multitudes and now we resume the reading of Mark that follows his version of the same story. For the next two Sundays we hear the story of Jesus' altercation with some Pharisees over the issue of ritual purity and the story of the healing of the deaf-mute. The two events are related. Today the topic is the correct practice and observance of the Law that witnesses to the people before God. The topic for next Sunday asserts that Jesus is the one who fulfills what was foretold—the day the Lord would come to heal and save the people.

The Letter of James will be read through the twenty-sixth Sunday of the year. A primary theme emerges in these two Sundays that form a unit. We are to act on God's Word. Baptism healed our deafness. We are to open our ears to the teaching of God and put it into practice in our lives.

Gospel Exegesis

The facilitator provides input from critical biblical scholarship on this text. This input includes insights as to how people would have heard the gospel in Jesus' time.

In an honor-based culture conflict is a given. Jesus' reputation was growing. This was a threat to the scribes and Pharisees. They were the ones who dictated religious observance. Jesus was a threat to their religious superiority. They constantly spied on him to keep abreast of his teaching and his impact on the community. Today's dialogue follows the form of "challenge and riposte." In a shame-based culture underneath every question lies the possibility of being shamed. "Every question is a challenge, if for no other reason than that the addressed might not know the answer and be shamed or forced to lie."[9]

This conflict erupted because Jesus' disciples did not observe the ritual washing of the hands before meals. This did not go unnoticed by the Pharisees, which led to the confrontation in today's gospel. Jesus employed a common form of riposte. He followed their challenge with an insult. He called the Pharisees "hypocrites" (Greek, *actor*). John Pilch puts words in Jesus' mouth in order to suggest the implications of his charge: "You actors! Scripture may be the lines you quote, but it is not the script by which you live!"[10] The Pharisees believed that the disciples' infraction was against the *Halakah*, the oral teaching of the elders. Jesus responded to their charges. He looked beyond the actual issue at hand regarding specific ritual purity and addressed the heart of the matter. He used Isaiah 29:13 as an indictment against the Pharisees. It was an imaginative ancient Mediterranean who could respond to a challenge on the spot by quoting from Tradition itself. Jesus must have impressed his antagonists. He compared the "precepts of men" and the "traditions of men" in the Isaiah account to the oral tradition promulgated by the Pharisees. Isaiah denounced "the hypocrisy of sham religion devoid of inner conviction."[11]

Jesus accused the Pharisees of placing the oral law, their own law, the law of tradition, above the Law of God, or at the very least on the same level with the Law of God. As far as Jesus was concerned, the *Halakah* had the propensity to be at odds with God's Law. Love was often sacrificed in deference to ritual purity. The Pharisees insisted that the oral law was as binding on individuals as the Torah. These oral interpretations from former prominent rabbis were eventually gathered together into a collection in the second century known as the Mishnah and the Talmud.

The cultural context of this scene is important to consider. The Pharisees (urban dwellers) enjoined the people to follow strict religious washing practices. They insisted that country peasants as well as city folk follow the urban traditions they set forth. Country people and road travelers would have a difficult time following such strict religious practices. Water was not readily available in the arid countryside. Also, fishermen found it difficult to avoid contact with dead things. They often were forced to touch dead animals, fish, and other things considered to cause pollution. They would, therefore, be constantly decontaminating themselves from their contact with dead things. In response, and in order to live within the confines of their real lived experience, the peasants adapted their own "Little Tradition" from the "Great Tradition."[12] Jesus supported this approach and sided with the peasants. He took his challenge a step further, however, by castigating the Pharisees for placing their law on a higher plane than the Law of Moses.

Clean and unclean were the issues that lay at the heart of ritual purification. Jesus insisted that a person has more opportunity to be unclean in one's heart through evil actions than one does from some external action such as ritual uncleanliness. Jesus' castigation of the ritual purity code made it abundantly clear to Christians that the "tradition of the elders" was no longer binding on new Christians. Christians were not bound by Jewish religious observances.[13] The Pharisees went so far overboard in their insistence on rigid observance of the oral tradition that it became a terrible burden in the lives of first-century peasant Palestinians. Scribes were the only ones who possessed the slightest hope of remembering all the commands—it was their job, after all. The peasants ("people of the land") were ignorant when it came to the excessive commands of the oral law. They were too busy trying to make a living for themselves and their families. Jesus challenged the proscriptions of the oral law and the unnecessary burden it placed on simple folk. He challenged the Pharisees with the very scriptures they touted. Isaiah had long ago challenged similar practices and attitudes. He accused the leaders of replacing the Law of God with mere human precepts. Jesus shouted a hearty "Amen!" to Isaiah's charge and applied it to his present situation.

Legal determinations regarding ritual cleanliness or uncleanliness have nothing to do with the state

---

[9] *CWJB*, 131.
[10] Ibid.
[11] *RM*, 104.

[12] *CWJB*, 130–131.
[13] *MARK*, 98.

of one's intentions or what is in a person's heart. Ritual purity does not free a person from sin or exact a clean heart from the observer of cultic purity. Jesus came to establish something new. The old order passed away, and Jesus came to replace the need for archaic formulations that have little to do with the purity of one's soul. He replaced it with the freedom to love.

There are three parts to today's gospel—ritual purification, corban, and defilement. Jewish ritual defilement became an issue in the Jewish Christian community. Official Judaism ("scribes who had come from Jerusalem") was aghast over the disdain of ritual purity codes. The inclusion of gentiles in the Christian community created a tension. Should they be forced to follow Jewish ritual practices? The Torah proscribed that only priests ritually wash their hands before meals. The Pharisees extended that law to include everyone.

Corban. Jesus critiqued the excessive legalism with a concrete example. Obsessive concern over vows lead to a direct violation of the Law of God. With a lilt of ironic sarcasm, Jesus implied that the Pharisees regarded their own oral tradition more highly than the commandments of God. "Corban" referred to an offering or a gift offered to God. The vow in question is one of dedication. A child is required by God's Law to care for his aging parents. However, if that same child vowed (corban) that money that was intended for the support of his parents was to go instead to the Temple treasury, that person's vow would be binding. Even though the parents possessed a God-given right by Law to be cared for, this "solemn duty, enjoined by the Law, was set aside."[14] The Law of God (in this case, the commandment to honor one's father and mother) was repealed in favor of the oral law. "Such financial ostracism and the resultant impoverishment of the elderly in the community was in effect a nullification of the will of God."[15] Jesus cited this example, but reminded the Pharisees that it is only one of many such circumstances in which the Pharisees usurped the commands of God. Corban is also an instance in which the religious leaders oppressed the poor. In the case of corban,

oppression was perpetrated in the name of God. Jesus denounced such practices throughout his ministry.

Defilement. Jesus answered the Pharisees' original question as to why his disciples did not observe the ritual washing of the hands. He used a parable to answer their question and then explained the parable for the benefit of his followers. "Jesus' statement about defiling and non-defiling foods is a 'parable.' He meant what he said but also intended something other and something more."[16] Jesus insisted that clean and unclean have more to do with a person's heart than with any external condition. The heart is the source of a person's moral response to God. People are clean or not clean according to the extent to which they are faithful to God, not according to ritual adherence to a human-made law.

Jesus had great compassion for those who followed him. He taught them many things. When he enjoined them to "listen," he was in essence preparing them for the mysterious nature of his teaching. He insisted that holiness is an issue of ethics. Sins of the tongue defile. However, something extremely noteworthy was taking place in this dialogue that would have raised the eyebrows of every observant Jew in the gathered crowd. Jesus insisted that the distinctions between clean and unclean, sacred and secular, in no way separated a person from contact or relationship with God. Jesus' words have "no parallel in Judaism for it denies a basic principle of Jewish religion and sets aside a large area of Mosaic Torah. It is a flat denial that any external things of circumstances can separate a man from God (cf. Rom 8:38–39). We can only be separated from God by our own attitude and behavior."[17]

Jesus withdrew from the crowds, as he often does in Mark's gospel, in order to explain his mysterious teaching to his disciples. Jesus was incredulous over their lack of understanding. He asserted that food cannot defile a person. The food is eaten and eventually dispelled from the body. It has nothing to do with a person's heart.

---

[14] Ibid., 100.
[15] *BSM*, 222.

[16] *CWJB*, 132.
[17] *MARK*, 101.

A common technique used throughout the Markan account of Jesus was the use of parable to teach an important lesson. Wilfrid Harrington defines Mark's use of parable as "an enigmatic saying requiring an explanation."[18] Gentile Christians would have found this event in Jesus' life to be extremely significant. It represented the overturning of the entire Jewish system of ritual purity, particularly ritual purity codes associated with the distinction between foods. Verse 19 solidifies this new teaching.

In verses 20–23 Jesus continued his explanation. He named particular vices, a common practice in Hellenized philosophical circles. The first six vices listed are listed in the plural in the original Greek. They are evil actions—sexual violations, thefts, murders, adulteries, acts of lust and coveting, general evil and wickedness. The next five vices were also listed—licentiousness, envy, blasphemy, arrogance, and folly, the stupidity of someone who lacks moral discernment. Jesus insisted that all these things reside in a person's heart. These are the things that defile, not the refusal to follow some arbitrary ritual purity code. Jesus' words were revolutionary. It is no wonder that the authorities plotted against him. He was a danger to the religious status quo.

Jesus was upsetting the power apple carts of scribes and Pharisees who lorded their teaching and authority over the people. The issue ultimately boils down to "the maintenance of strict group boundaries."[19] The Pharisees believed that purity codes safeguarded ethnic and national identity. Jesus repudiated their exclusive restrictions by attacking the practices at the core—the theology that underpins them in the first place.

Jesus began his dialogue not by attacking the specific code, but the oral tradition itself. He ended with denouncing the kosher regulations. Probably the reality of the situation was that priests and only an extremist sect of Pharisees (*haverim*) observed the strict regulations. It is possible that this sect of Pharisees was challenging the Christian community to observe their own superpiety as a sign of holiness.

Another interesting observance can be made about this exchange. In 7:4 the marketplace is mentioned. Immediately this places the exchange in the realm of economic concerns. Later in chapter 12 Mark refers to the marketplace as the public place of scribal piety that oppresses the poor.[20] Galilean peasants were at odds with the Pharisees over their control of the production and distribution of the foods for the purpose of maintaining ritual purity and the prevention of ritual contamination. Mark constantly reminds us that Jesus challenged the religious and political establishment of his day—any institution that placed undue burdens on the shoulders of God's poor and simple folks.

Mark twice tells us that the disciples were eating bread. We are to take note and make the comparison with the feeding of the people in the wilderness. Mark prepares the readers for the wilderness feeding of the gentiles highlighted in the story of the Syro-Phoenician woman. It is possible that the Pharisees were leveling an indictment against the disciples for eating with gentile Christians and eating ritually unclean foods—rendering them unclean.

Mark's Jesus not only attacked the purity code, but the authority of the Pharisees as well. Jesus was not the only one who attacked the Pharisees' interpretation of Law, the oral tradition. As noted before, the Pharisees arrogantly put their interpretation on the same par with the Torah. They intimated that both the Torah and the oral tradition emanated from Mount Sinai itself. Other groups, such as the priestly group called Sadducees, had a vested interest in challenging the oral law, as it called their own authority into question. Jesus was not concerned with the issues of the other groups, however. What was novel to Jesus' challenge were his reasons for the challenge in the first place. Jesus denounced the Pharisees who placed human law above God's Law and he accused them of being alienated from God in their own hearts.[21] The Isaiah passage was a denouncement of leaders who were steeped in blindness and unable to read God's Word. Mark used the prophet Isaiah to intensify the attack on the religious authorities.

---

[18]Ibid., 102.

[19]*BSM*, 218.

[20]Ibid., 219.

[21]Ibid., 221.

Gustavo Gutierrez reminds us that Phariseeism is a risk for every believer.[22] Every time we reduce the scriptures to a compilation of do's and don'ts we run the risk of reducing them to a code book to be observed rather than a relationship that needs to be lived. The next step in Phariseeism is to judge others who do not follow the rules as well as good "Pharisees" who do follow them. The logical result of such judgments is exclusion based on personal piety. Those who do not follow the rules are "out" and those who follow them are "in." Like Jesus, Guitierrez reminds us that it is the heart that determines righteousness and the heart that leads to righteous action based on love.

> Often the poor consider themselves "sinners" because they live in a complex and confused world without being able to follow what Jesus calls "human precepts" (v. 6) in agreement with Isaiah. These norms characterize Christians who are arrogant, devoid of compassion, people whose hands are clean because they have no hands, as the poet Peguy used to say. True cleanliness consists in putting the word of God into practice (Dt. 4:1; Jas. 1:22). It demands of us concrete gestures toward others: caring for orphans and widows (v. 27); visiting the victims of poverty, exploitation, and oblivion; opting for a just and human order and against what causes deaths, "disappearances"[23] and sufferings.[24]

Proclaim the gospel again.

Sometimes we gain new insights when we hear the text after the interpretation is given. Someone from the group proclaims the gospel a second time.

STEP 4
TESTING

Conversation with the Liturgy and the Scriptures

Test your original understanding in dialogue with the text.

---

[22]*SWTLY*, 214.

[23]This is a reference to the assassinations by the terrorists of Sender Lameness in August 1991.

[24]Ibid., 214.

(You might consider breaking into smaller groups.)

Now that you've heard the exegesis, were there any new insights? How do you feel about it? How does your original understanding of this gospel compare with what we just shared? How does this story speak to your life?

Sharing Life Experience

Participants share an experience from their lives that connects with the biblical interpretation just presented.

> Today's gospel is extremely relevant to what is taking place in our contemporary Church communities. Holy wars are being raged. Movements are afoot whose sole reason for existence is to serve as policing organizations for those who commit various infractions against Church law. Perhaps it is a backlash response to a world disillusioned by disrespect for law on any level. Laws are necessary in any well-ordered society or community. Laws are not bad. Overemphasis on the law is bad. When the law no longer serves people, it becomes an end unto itself.

> Those who long for a return to times in which black was black and white was white (there never really was such a time, but nostalgia has a way of romanticizing things that never happened) believe that Catholics no longer follow the teaching of the Church. My personal bias is that the best kept secret on the face of earth is what the Church really teaches. It is good news and it supports the revelation of Christ in our midst. There are those who look to old catechisms to support their position that we no longer teach the "truth." A mother who home-schools her children because the Church no longer teaches "truth" put her child in our sacramental process for confirmation. This process is a conversion-based one that invites full and conscious participation in the celebration of the sacrament of confirmation in which the Spirit of God is conferred and the person bears the seal, the character of Christ, and thus is empowered to more powerfully live as a Christian in the world. This parent was disconcerted because of the absence of language of former times—"sanctifying grace, actual grace, etc." "Why are you not teaching our children those important concepts?" The children are being taught those concepts, perhaps not using the same language of old, but existentially, they are taught. However, what is more im-

portant is the attempt to form our children in the faith, life, and liturgy of the Church and help them grow in their relationship with God. Is that not what today's gospel is all about?

There are multiple challenges in this gospel. First, I am to guard against the yeast of the Pharisees in which I set myself apart from everyone else and assume that I am the only guardian of the truth. When I set myself up as the only interpreter of God's Law, I come dangerously close to being the object of Jesus' denouncement in today's gospel. Interpretation of scripture takes place within the discerning confines of community—the teaching authority of the Church, the sensus fidelium, and the work of respected scholars. A rigid fundamentalist understanding does not serve me or the Church. I have a responsibility to be in dialogue with sound scholarship and the teaching authority within a community context. Scripture invites relationship. Second, when I become rigidly legalistic I am subject to forgetting the heart of the Law, thereby ignoring my relationship with God in deference to the Law itself. Third, when I set myself up as the only one who possesses the "truth," I consciously and unconsciously set myself apart from others. I thereby believe I possess a special piety and holiness that those who do not believe the way I believe do not possess. In so doing, I perpetuate and participate in exclusive behavior that Jesus railed against. Fourth, I may not judge the spirituality of others—that responsibility belongs to God.

This scripture invites me to enter more deeply into a personal relationship with God, which further prompts me to live an upright, moral life—not rooted in law, but in love.

What was Mark trying to tell his community? In what way does today's gospel speak to what is going on in the church—universal, diocesan, parish? In what way do you relate to the Pharisees, the disciples who are criticized by the Pharisees, the crowd, Jesus? In what way does this gospel challenge your community today? In what way has this conversation with the scriptures for today's liturgy invited change in your life? In what way are the biblical themes of covenant, exodus, creation, and community evident in today's readings? Do you still feel the same way about this text as when you began? Has your original understanding been stretched, challenged, or affirmed?

The gospel demands a response.

In what concrete way might your parish be invited to respond? Are there any attitudes or behaviors you would like to change as a result of today's conversation? What one concrete action will you take this week in response to the liturgy today?

Pastoral Considerations: Is there an attitude of religious superiority lurking within the confines of your parish community? What needs to happen in order to address the situations? Are there people in your parish who have set themselves apart as judge and jury of others? Who are the victims of Phariseeism in your own community?

Christian Initiation: Perhaps this would be a good time to concretely live the heart of God's Law—love. Rather than gather for extended catechesis this week perhaps it would be appropriate to go out in the community and live the command of love—visit the sick, serve the poor, and so on.

DOCTRINAL ISSUES

What Church truth/teaching/doctrinal issue could be drawn from the gospel for the twenty-second Sunday in Ordinary Time?

Participants suggest possible doctrinal themes that flow from the readings.

Possible Doctrinal Themes

Word of God—scripture—liturgy of the Word; commandments; morality; conversion, discipleship, Church—people of God, shepherd, pilgrim; Church structure; social teaching; commandment justice—hierarchy

Present the doctrinal material at this time.

1. The facilitator gives input on a particular doctrinal issue of his or her prior choosing. OR
2. The group chooses a doctrinal issue from the list they created. They read together from the

Doctrinal Appendix or other appropriate, official Church documents and the works of respected theologians.

(Many doctrinal issues are found in the Doctrinal Appendix at the back of this workbook. If you are choosing an issue from this resource, please refer to it now.)

Reflection questions centered around the chosen doctrinal theme can be found at the end of each topic in the Doctrinal Appendix. The questions are based on the five-step reflection process. If you choose a topic not included in the Doctrinal Appendix, craft your own questions according to the same five-step process.

Following the reflection questions you will be reminded to return to chapter 7, "Preparing the Catechetical Session," to assist you in crafting your own session.

Closing Prayer

Happy are the peacemakers: they shall be called
    sons of God.
Happy are those who suffer persecution for justice' sake;
the kingdom of heaven is theirs. (Mt 5:9–10)[25]

---

[25]Twenty-Second Sunday in Ordinary Time, "Communion Rite," *The Sacramentary.*

TWENTY-THIRD SUNDAY IN ORDINARY TIME

Environment

See the twenty-second Sunday in Ordinary Time.

INTRODUCTORY RITES

Entrance Antiphon (or Opening Song)

Lord, you are just, and the judgments you make are right. Show mercy when you judge me, your servant. (Ps 118:137, 124)[1]

Opening Prayer

The facilitator of the session may lead the prayer. Others in the group may be asked to proclaim the readings.

Let us pray
to our just and merciful God

Pause for silent prayer.

Lord our God,
in you justice and mercy meet.
With unparalleled love you have saved us from
    death
and drawn us into the circle of your life.
Open our eyes to the wonders this life sets before
    us,
that we may serve you free from fear
and address you as God our Father.
We ask this in the name of Jesus the Lord.[2]

LITURGY OF THE WORD

The readings are proclaimed.

First Reading
Isaiah 35:4–7a

---

[1]Twenty-Third Sunday in Ordinary Time: "Entrance Antiphon," *The Sacramentary.*
[2]Twenty-Third Sunday in Ordinary Time: "Opening Prayer," *The Sacramentary.*

(Please refer to the first Sunday of Advent for an overview of the Book of Isaiah.)

Today's Pericope: Even though this passage occurs in the preexilic section of Isaiah, First Isaiah, it is nevertheless in the spirit of Second Isaiah, the postexilic portion of the book. Today's reading is chosen for the verses that speak of the miraculous healing that will occur following the return from exile (vv. 5, 6). The underlying theology of Second Isaiah asserted that the return from exile was God's final act of salvation. Christianity logically appropriated these texts and understood them within the context of the Christ-event. They believed that the words from Isaiah prophetically foretold the healing wrought by Jesus Christ, Messiah and Savior of the world. Mark had this in mind in his use of the word *mogilalon, with difficulty of speech,* in his recounting of Jesus' healing of the deaf-mute. The same Greek word is used in verse 6 of today's reading in the original Septuagint in reference to the word "dumb," making this a most appropriate choice of texts to accompany the gospel reading.

Responsorial Psalm
Psalm 146:7–10

Today's psalm extols the magnificent healing power of the almighty God. Yahweh is particularly praised for his power to heal the blind. Even though the healing of deaf-mutes is not explicitly mentioned, it is, of course, implied.

Second Reading
James 2:1–5

(Please refer to the twenty-first Sunday in Ordinary Time for an overview of the Letter of James.)

Today's Pericope: Beginning last Sunday, the exhortations in the Letter of James are based on the twelve patriarchs of Israel. Today's exhortation is based on the name Judah (Lord of glory—Gn 49:8–12).[3]

---

[3]*PL*, 343.

The moral imperative concerns proper treatment of the poor—Yahweh insists that the poor be cared for.

The Old Testament deals far more with issues of justice than does the New Testament. The New Testament consisted primarily of poor, powerless peasants subject to an imperial ruling power. There is less exhortation to care for the poor since the intended or implied audience of the New Testament was the poor. However, the Letter to James was written for an audience both rich and poor. Concern for the poor is an immediate issue for James. "The wealthy members of the community possessed no real political power so there is little suggestion of a real social ethic."[4] The implication of this letter is not that the New Testament has no concern for such issues, but rather "It all depends on the conditions under which the Church has to operate, and these vary in time and place."[5] However, care for the poor is a given. Every good Jew would have been raised on the pablum that connects care for the poor with the covenant between God and human beings. The covenant that God entered into with human beings at the creation of the world intended that in return for God entering into relationship with humanity and agreeing to care for human beings, human beings in turn would agree to care for those who could not care for themselves—widows, orphans, the poor (hesed—the heart of biblical justice). Every New Testament Christian would be aware of this covenant agreement.

James' parenesis is based on the inherent truth of the gospel. Wealthier members should care for poor members because baptism affords the poor a primary place in the reign of God—they will inherit the kingdom.

The poor are to be treated with the same deference given to the rich, particularly in liturgical celebrations. All give God the same honor and glory. No one is to be exalted above the others based on status of wealth. Unfair and inappropriate biases have no place in the reign of God—no partiality is to be shown according to any type of human established norms. James is demanding concrete behavior. This is not a pious platitude; James demands explicit, constant action. Lest his readers miss the point, James gives a concrete example. The poor person is not to be ignored or treated as a second-class citizen in the assembly of the Lord.

> The way we behave toward others during the liturgy, especially toward the poor, is, therefore an excellent mirror of our heart and mind set. If, at church, we judge according to false values, what of our daily lives? A liturgical assembly offering the same spectacle as a worldly gathering in which the poor, the lowly, do not have a place, while the rich and powerful are honored, causes harm to the true nature of the church, a community of brothers and sisters in which there is no longer any difference between slave and freeborn, employer and employee, rich and poor, man and woman. It is not enough to know and say it: we must show it. The behavior of the assembled community must confirm the variety of witness given, in daily life by scattered Christians.[6]

The gospel is proclaimed.

Gospel
Mark 7:31–37. Jesus heals the deaf-mute.

STEP 1
NAMING ONE'S EXPERIENCE

What were your first impressions? What was your first response to the gospel (or the other readings)? What captured your attention?

Each person names his or her initial impression. Statements should be brief. No reasons should be given at this time. All simply listen without agreeing or disagreeing.

STEP 2
UNDERSTANDING

In a brief statement, explain what you think this gospel is trying to convey.

---

[4] Ibid., 346.
[5] Ibid.
[6] *DL* (V), 212.

Liturgical Context

Even though today's gospel thematically asserts the healing power of Christ and the inclusion of all people in the eschatological reign of God, a primary theme of the kingdom and a theme in today's second reading is care for the poor. We cannot ignore the poor and think we are living committed Christian lives.

In his Lenten message to the world on February 17, 1998, Pope John Paul II echoed the sentiments of today's readings. He exhorted people to enter the desert of solitude in order to acknowledge their inadequacy before God, thereby becoming more sensitive to the presence of the poor.

> This year I wish to propose for reflection by the faithful words inspired by the Gospel of Matthew: "Come, O blessed of my Father, for I was poor, marginalized and you welcomed me!" (Cf. Mt 25:34–36.)

> Poverty has different meanings. The first which comes to mind is the absence of sufficient material means. This poverty, which for many of our brothers crosses the line to misery, is a scandal. It assumes a multiplicity of forms and is found linked to various painful phenomena: the lack of necessary means of survival and primary health care; the absence of home or its inadequacy and the consequent abnormal situations; the marginalization of the weakest from society and unemployed from the productive sector; the loneliness of those having no one to count on; the condition of international refugees and those who suffer war and its cruelties; the inequality of salaries; the absence of a family and the grace consequences which derive from this such as drugs and violence. The individual is humiliated by the lack of these necessities of life. It is a tragedy before which those who have the possibility to intervene cannot in conscience remain indifferent. . . . The church continually

combats all forms of poverty because, as mother, she is concerned that each and every person be able to live fully in dignity as a child of God.[7]

Jesus was the champion of the poor and downtrodden. Our liturgy insists we reach out to the poor and suffering. The Catholic Catechism insists that "Eucharist commits us to the poor" (#1397). Let us be reminded:

> Jesus is poor. He is infinitely and rigorously poor. Poor with an absolute poverty. The Prince of poverty, the Lord of perfect poverty. Poor with the poor, having come for the poor, speaking to the poor, giving to the poor, working for the poor. Poor among the poor, destitute among the destitute, beggar among beggars. The poor one of eternal poverty. The poor one, happy and rich, who accepts poverty, wants it, espouses it, sings it. The beggar who gives alms. The naked one who covers the naked, the hungry one who nourishes others. The miraculous and supernatural poor one who transforms the rich into as many poor and the poor into as many truly rich.[8]

Today's liturgy is a stark reminder of the incredible compassion Jesus had for suffering people. Jesus invited his disciples into the heart of his compassion. He challenged his followers to act as compassionately as he acted. Healing is a sign of God's incredible love and compassion for his people. It is also a sign of the messianic reign of God and Jesus' incredible charismatic power. Jesus was a healer in the tradition of healers of his time. Jesus, however, mediated the power and compassion of his Father in heaven. His healing was a sign of salvation. Jesus' compassion moved him to the core of his being. Jesus is a living sign and symbol of God's compassion in the midst of a broken people. Jesus sent his disciples out to continue his mission of healing and restoration.

---

[7]Pope John Paul II, "John Paul II/1998 Lenten Message, Welcoming the Poor: Reuniting Hope," February 17, 1998, in *Origins*, April 1998, 604–605.

[8]G. Papini, *Mammon* (Paris: Payot, 1922), quoted in *Lectures pour chaque jour de l'année: Prière du Temps présent*, coedition (Paris, 1974), 480, in *DL* (V), 212–213.

Jesus viewed illness as a destructive force. "Any attitude which glorifies sickness is alien to Jesus' attitude."[9] Jesus wanted health for his people. Health is defined by the World Health Organization as a "state of complete physical, mental and social well being and not merely the absence of disease or infirmity."[10] Health implies wholeness. Our Christian faith demands that we look at health through the eyes of faith. We are to understand that it involves the total well-being of all people. It is thus difficult to separate any discussion of healing from the issues of healing and health care for the poor peoples of the world. In a just society, the health care concerns of all of its people must be a concern for all of its members.

Healing restores the unity of that which was disrupted. Jesus not only healed, but he restored people to full life in the community—he restored the people to wholeness. Healing is intimately connected to salvation. The words for salvation and healing are interchangeable—*whole, not yet split.* Healing in the context of salvation implies victory over death. Salvation/healing in the New Testament included healing from sickness, mental illness, the demonic, and death. Reconciliation involved the healing of fractured relationships.

Jesus' ministry of healing continues in the Church through its mission to offer care for the sick and suffering of the world. It also continues in sacramental ways through the eucharist, penance, and anointing of the sick. The new rite of anointing is intended to help us "understand human sickness in the context of the whole mystery of salvation."[11] Physical health goes hand in hand with a healthy soul. Ultimately, full restoration of health will only take place in the reign of God yet to come.

Suffering is a fact of this life—it is paschal in nature. There is an inherent invitation in the midst of suffering to join our suffering to the suffering of Christ. Not all are physically healed, but all who ask are spiritually healed. The Church's ministry of healing is a sign of our great celebration of life and the victory of life over death, symbolized ultimately in the resurrection of Jesus.

We petition our just and merciful God in today's opening prayer of the liturgy. We acknowledge him as the source of all mercy and the font from which true justice flows. We celebrate the life that is offered to us. We are reminded that true healing resides in intimate close relationship with God. The communion antiphon reminds us that the true source of our healing is Jesus, who offers himself to us as food.

Gospel Exegesis

The facilitator provides input from critical biblical scholarship on this text. This input includes insights as to how people would have heard the gospel in Jesus' time.

Today's story takes place in the region of the gentiles—Decapolis. In a previous healing story in Mark's gospel, Jesus healed the girl and delivered her from an unclean spirit. His miracle signaled an overture toward the gentiles. We have been carefully led into Jesus' conflict with the authorities. In the first part of this chapter we were led into the conflict over "eating with sinners" (last week's gospel). Mark opens the door to the world outside the accepted boundaries—"outside the Judean social universe, the unclean gentiles."[12] Today Jesus delivers the man from a spirit but he also fully restores him with all his senses intact to the community. In addition to Jesus' healing there is an expressed theology in the event itself. Jesus healed the gentile, which symbolically represented the inclusion of the gentiles in the mission of Christ. They were now ready to hear and speak the message of Christ. They are capable of entering into relationship with God and worship him. The gentiles now stand ready to inherit the reign of God and eternal salvation.

Since Mark's geography makes absolutely no practical sense, the reader is to assume that the stated itinerary of Jesus has a theological intent. Mark sets up the global, unified nature of the region of Galilee—Galilee is the place of the gentiles. Galilee is the place where gentiles were invited into the household of God, where salvation came to their house. Galilee is the locus of the gospel and the mission of Jesus. Galilee is where the Word was first preached, where disciples were called, where crowds gathered to listen to Jesus,

[9] Lucien J. Richard, OMI, "Healing," *CPDBT*, 521.
[10] Ibid.
[11] Ibid., 522.

[12] *NS*, 74.

where unity between divided regions was established, where the Lord will return.

In the exegesis for the first reading, it was noted that the word *mogilalon* was used both in this instance only and in the instances of the first reading. "The evangelist is pointing to the Jewish hope to open blind eyes and release dumb lips."[13]

We immediately are invited into the world of symbol when Jesus takes the man aside privately. This is a common technique employed by Mark to alert the readers that an epiphany or a manifestation is about to take place. God's saving power was about to be revealed. Both Greek and Hebrew healers used spittle when healing. This was not uncommon. Even the emperor Vespasian was recorded as healing a person using spittle. However, there is a sacramental nature to the action. "Jesus' use of these tradition gestures was purely sacramental, i.e., they were not the means of the healing in themselves but merely the outward, visible signs of his messianic power. For humans whose perception is sensible, the gestures (like other sacraments) were vehicles that communicated the intangible, otherwise invisible and ineffable activity of God in Christ."[14] Jesus looked up to heaven—we are allowed into Jesus' intimate relationship with his Father. Jesus sighed—we are allowed into Jesus' heart, his compassion for those who suffer. Jesus shouts "ephphatha!", that is, "be opened!" Both this action and the saliva became part of the baptism at a very early date.

Jesus enjoined silence upon the witnesses. Yet, Jesus' action alone shouts to the rooftops by the very nature of the action. Jesus' sacramental action resounds with the good news. All are astonished at Jesus' miracle. Mark underlines this astonishment in exclamation points! This is indeed an astonishing, significant miracle. Mark asserts that even the deaf hear and the blind see. This is no doubt an allusion to the pericope in Isaiah that attests to the arrival of the messianic age—the day of salvation. Jesus ushered in the day of the Lord, the long-awaited day. His action is truly good news—yes, for the recipient of his healing power, but ultimately for the whole world, especially for the gentiles. "In these words of Isaiah nearly all

the healings of Jesus are mentioned. Against this backdrop they are to be seen as the signs of the new age: which for Isaiah himself, his audience and first readers is the time when YHWH will lead the exiles from Babylon back to Palestine, and for the readers of Mark is the time of God's kingdom which has come in Jesus."[15]

Jesus followed the ordinary routine of healers in the ancient world. Jesus laid his hands on the recipient of his power—the normal means to extend therapeutic advantages on the one seeking healing. Jesus also healed through the touch of his garments or through his word alone. He used spittle, a common ward against evil spirits or persons who cast the "evil eye" upon another. Spit was considered the antidote or the deactivating power to the evil eye cast upon its victim. Ancient healers used this technique to ward off evil spirits.[16]

Mark used the actual Aramaic word Jesus spoke to cast out the spirit. It was believed that the word itself contained power. To translate the word into another language robbed the word of its power—hence, for all generations the actual "ephphatha" is used in the proclamation of this text. Mark affirms Jesus as a traditional healer par excellence.

Jesus did not want anyone to tell of this marvelous event. Former scholars referred to this as the messianic secret. Modern scholars suggest the need for further examination as the text is incredibly complex. First, the people of that time had no sense of who the Messiah was going to be or if they should be looking for him in their midst. There were varied expectations of what the Messiah was going to be about. No one would be rushing to tell others that this Jesus was indeed the Messiah. They were not all that sure what that meant. In the honor-based culture, all persons were to stay within their own status—they were not allowed to rise above their birth status. Jesus challenged the cultural norms of his day—he stepped out of his birth status, thus posing a threat to the cultural status quo. In order to maintain his honor, Jesus had a vested interest in keeping the event as quiet as he could—"he must do his utmost to keep this potentially damaging informa-

---

[13]*MARK*, 107.
[14]*WWC*, 231.

[15]*RM*, 115.
[16]*CWJB*, 132–135.

tion hidden from public awareness."[17] Secrecy was in the best interest of protecting his family's honor. Jesus restored the man to life in the community—for the ancients this was the first and primary meaning assigned to the art of healing.

Since we are still in the region of the gentiles, and a gentile is the recipient of Jesus' healing and liberating power, we are reminded that this healing has many symbolic factors present. There is the issue of clean and unclean. As a gentile, the person was considered unclean in the first place. Jesus' mission to the gentiles restored them to fullness in the community of God, thereby ridding them of the designation unclean. Healing for Jesus always included full restoration in the community, wholeness. Healing included the need to find meaning in one's life. The man was healed in order to hear the Word of God and proclaim it to others. This was the implication of Jesus' mission to the gentiles. Jesus demonstrated his power over evil and the spirit world. A person such as Jesus is a most welcome healer in a world where people felt themselves battered by demons of the spirit world, at the mercy of evil spirits whose sole purpose of existence was to create havoc in the lives of people. Jesus' mastery over the world of spirits was a sure sign that the reign of God had indeed arrived.[18] People in antiquity lost hope and meaning in life when they were faced with catastrophic illness. Jesus restored that hope and gave them the means to fullness of life. It is interesting to note that even though the people in Mark's gospel called him "teacher," Mark placed Jesus in the constant role of teacher and healer. Matthew paints a portrait of Jesus that differs from Mark's. For Matthew, Jesus' healing miracles are a sign of his superiority over the elements of nature—his power and mastery. Luke understands the healing authority of Jesus as one that leads to renewed insight on the part of the one healed. Jesus bestowed sight on the blind—beyond the physical healing of blindness the reader is to understand healing as the ability to see what God is doing in one's life. John portrays the healing ministry of Jesus as one in which the healer helps people find meaning in their lives and in their relationship with God.

---

[17]Ibid., 135.
[18]John J. Pilch, *CPDBT*, 418–420.

Proclaim the gospel again.

Sometimes we gain new insights when we hear the text after the interpretation is given. Someone from the group proclaims the gospel a second time.

STEP 4
TESTING

Conversation with the Liturgy and the Scriptures

Test your original understanding in dialogue with the text.

(You might consider breaking into smaller groups.)

Now that you've heard the exegesis, were there any new insights? How do you feel about it? How does your original understanding of this gospel compare with what we just shared? How does this story speak to your life?

Sharing Life Experience

Participants share an experience from their lives that connects with the biblical interpretation just presented.

> *Someone came to me during a workshop I was doing in a large metropolitan city and told me about a parish near them that was celebrating a milestone event of some sort. There was not room in the main hall for all the guests. The VIPs and the major contributors of the parish were treated to an indoor seat with a fancy menu; ordinary parishioners were relegated to an outdoor tent with a menu that was far less lavish than the one for those who feasted inside. Often our actions, even though unconscious, speak loudly to us of the secular statuses that define our communities. Our self-made boundaries are often so silent and insidious that it takes an astute eye to see them in the first place, and then ask for a communal response to address them.*

> *Today's gospel addresses two issues—inclusion of the unclean and the healing power of God. Jesus invites the gentile man into the fullness of community life and he restores him to health—he delivers him from his inability to hear or speak the good news.*

> *The way in which we/I continue this mission of Christ is to extend his compassion to others so af-*

flicted. One cannot address the healing mission of Christ as evident in this gospel without addressing the social responsibility attached to it. James sets the stage for this dialogue and we have a responsibility to continue it. There is an inherent option for the poor that runs throughout the scriptures. James names it upfront. We cannot ignore it. There is no greater need for us to address the issues of the poor than when it comes to health care related issues. As Church we are called to mediate the healing of Christ to a sick world. Part of that responsibility includes working for the equitable care of all people when it comes to health-related issues. Malnutrition, inadequate health care, excessive expenses for routine procedures, and scarcity of common medicines are not just the problem of the Third World; they are our problem. When any brother or sister is denied proper health care, a member of our family is denied. Our pastor just returned from a visit to our sister parish in Peru. We have built two clinics, and are presently building a church. He was so saddened one afternoon as they were walking through town and a grieving mother and father were carrying a handmade casket crafted for an infant. Those traveling with my pastor knew the story of that family. They insisted that the death of that little girl was completely unnecessary. In the United States it would never have happened. They were unable to secure the necessary (what in this country we would consider routine) treatment for the condition the child contracted. The child died. How utterly senseless! Yet there are those, even Christians, no less, who assert that we have no business meddling in such things as government controls of such issues. They regard such issues as political and not in the domain of Christians.

I often feel powerless in my armchair ministry and wonder if I should leave what I am presently doing to go work in a Third World environment. As I have yet to purchase such a ticket, I am presently content to do what I can and to proclaim the scriptures' option for the poor, oppressed, and broken wherever I can. However, I honor the saints, the men and women who have given their lives to such incredible pursuits.

As a Christian I am challenged to move out of my complacent role of sideline politician and become an active voice for the powerless. Some people suggest that such issues are not our responsibility. Would

they be our responsibility if one of our own babies were unable to secure the care needed for a common, easily treated condition? Today's gospel demands that we "sigh" as Jesus sighed and offer his compassion to those who suffer. Today's gospel asks me to ask the question of myself and my community. Whom do I exclude? What artificial barriers do I erect when it comes to God's people? Does the social standing of some folks prompt me to treat them differently? In what way am I deaf and mute to the needs of a broken, isolated world?

What was Mark trying to tell his community? What needs to be healed in you so that you may more powerfully proclaim the message of Christ? In what way are you deaf and mute? In what way is your community deaf and mute? In what way does this gospel challenge your community today? In what way has this conversation with the scriptures for today's liturgy invited change in your life? In what way are the biblical themes of covenant, exodus, creation, and community evident in today's readings? Do you still feel the same way about this text as when you began? Has your original understanding been stretched, challenged, or affirmed?

STEP 5
DECISION

The gospel demands a response.

In what concrete way might your parish be invited to respond? Are there any attitudes or behaviors you would like to change as a result of today's conversation? What one concrete action will you take this week in response to the liturgy today?

Pastoral Considerations: Perhaps this liturgy gospel might serve as the catalyst for your parish to address issues of exclusion, healing, and health care. In your parish, who is treated to places of greater honor than others? Who is treated like the poor in today's letter from James? What needs to happen to change that situation? Is your liturgy a place where everyone is treated with partiality? Are children, the elderly, the disabled, minorities treated as second-class citizens? Are the healing needs of your community being met? Perhaps now is the time to consider celebrating the sacrament of the sick a few times during the year, and perhaps gathering to pray for healing on a regular basis. Perhaps this would be a good time to bless all the people involved in health care ministries. Is there a respite ministry in your parish? How do family members who care for chronically ill relatives find the needed relief from round-the-clock care of their loved ones? Is your parish involved in any outreach that addresses the health and welfare of God's people, locally and globally?

Christian Initiation: Perhaps this would be a good time to celebrate the anointing of catechumens. It is intended as a blessing for catechumens to strengthen them from the onslaught of evil in their lives so they may more fully walk the journey before them. Is there anyone ready to celebrate the rite of acceptance or welcome, rite of full communion in the Catholic Church? Perhaps this would be a good week to take catechumens to visit the sick or a nursing home.

DOCTRINAL ISSUES

What Church truth/teaching/doctrinal issue could be drawn from the gospel for the twenty-third Sunday in Ordinary Time?

Participants suggest possible doctrinal themes that flow from the readings.

Possible Doctrinal Themes

Healing; Jesus' ministry of healing and deliverance; reign of God; social justice; ministry; ministry of the Word; sacraments of healing and reconciliation

Present the doctrinal material at this time.

1. The facilitator gives input on a particular doctrinal issue of his or her prior choosing. OR
2. The group chooses a doctrinal issue from the list they created. They read together from the Doctrinal Appendix or other appropriate, official Church documents and the works of respected theologians.

(Many doctrinal issues are found in the Doctrinal Appendix at the back of this workbook. If you are choosing an issue from this resource, please refer to it now.)

Reflection questions centered around the chosen doctrinal theme can be found at the end of each topic in the Doctrinal Appendix. The questions are based on the five-step reflection process. If you choose a topic not included in the Doctrinal Appendix, craft your own questions according to the same five-step process.

Following the reflection questions you will be reminded to return to chapter 7, "Preparing the Catechetical Session," to assist you in crafting your own session.

Closing Prayer

Lord,
your word and your sacrament
give us food and life.
May this gift of your Son
lead us to share his life for ever.
We ask this through Christ our Lord.[19]

_____

[19]Twenty-Third Sunday in Ordinary Time, "Prayer After Communion," *The Sacramentary*.

Twenty-Fourth Sunday in Ordinary Time

Environment

See the twenty-second Sunday in Ordinary Time.

INTRODUCTORY RITES

Entrance Antiphon (or Opening Song)

Give peace, Lord, to those who wait for you and your prophets will proclaim you as you deserve. Hear the prayers of your servant and of your people Israel. (Sir 36:18)[1]

Opening Prayer

The facilitator of the session may lead the prayer. Others in the group may be asked to proclaim the readings.

Let us pray
that God will keep us faithful in his service.

Pause for silent prayer.

Almighty God,
our creator and guide,
may we serve you with all our heart
and know your forgiveness in our lives.
We ask this through our Lord Jesus Christ, your
    Son,
who lives and reigns with you and the Holy Spirit,
one God, for ever and ever.
one God, for ever and ever.[2]

LITURGY OF THE WORD

The readings are proclaimed.

First Reading
Isaiah 50:5–9

[1] Twenty-Fourth Sunday in Ordinary Time: "Entrance Antiphon," *The Sacramentary.*

[2] Twenty-Fourth Sunday in Ordinary Time: "Opening Prayer," *The Sacramentary.*

(See the first Sunday of Advent for an overview of the Book of Isaiah.)

Today's Pericope: Today's passage from Isaiah is chosen because it parallels the gospel's prediction of the Passion in which Jesus asserts the certainty of his vindication. This passage is also the appointed reading for Palm or Passion Sunday. This is the third servant song from Second Isaiah. The backdrop for today's reading is the exile. People are still in the throes of captivity yet reject the prophet's message of hope. The people are doubtful of the future promise that Isaiah foretells. Isaiah insists that the day of restoration will take place. The exile continues and the people are weary of his Pollyanna predictions of a positive outcome. The prophet will not be stopped, however. God gave him a word to speak, and speak it he will—no matter what the personal consequences. He has complete faith and trust that God will accomplish what God said God would do. God would prove him right.

Early Christianity found it easy to see in the four suffering servant songs of Isaiah the foreshadowing or a *type* of the Messiah. They saw the life, death, resurrection, and mission of Christ embodied in those texts. In today's text the servant speaks—with serenity and dignity. His oppressors tortured his body, but his spirit remains strong, untouched by his captors' torturous machinations. The servant remains calm, nonviolent, and steadfast in the face of such adversity because of his trust in God. God strengthened him to endure. God revealed his plan to the servant. The servant is confident that God is accomplishing his plan of salvation in the midst of this terror. Such trust always results in the strength to endure. Through human weakness the strength of God abides.

Jesus' Passion and death are the result of living a righteous, obedient life in submission to his Father's will. Jesus, too, is confident of vindication. Even though the people reject Jesus as they rejected the prophet in Isaiah, in the end, he too would be vindicated. Early Christianity understood the servant songs to be fulfilled in the person of Jesus Christ.

Responsorial Psalm
Psalm 116:1–6, 8–9

Today's psalm's theme is death and resurrection. God vindicates his servant. When the gospel insists that the Son of Man *must* suffer, it was the same as saying *according to the scriptures—so the scriptures might be fulfilled.* The psalms such as this and scriptures that speak of the suffering servant point to and find their fulfillment in the person of Jesus Christ.

Second Reading
James 2:14–18

Refer to the twenty-second Sunday in Ordinary Time for an overview of the Letter of James.

Today's Pericope: Today's letter deals with the issue and the relationship between faith and works. The issue of faith and works caused hot debate in the early Christian community. There were those who believed that strict adherence to the Law to the devaluation of faith was the means of salvation. Others believed that works were secondary. James' letter is catechetical. He does not offer theology. Rather, he posits an example. If someone is naked and hungry and the only response given by a Christian is to offer encouragement but no concrete help, there is no value in that. It increases the suffering of the afflicted one and creates understandable resentment. Those who have faith but do not exercise their faith in a concrete response of love really have no faith at all—it is empty. People will be judged according to the way in which they loved and cared for God's people.

James' letter is not a contradiction to Paul's teaching on faith and works. Paul addressed people who believed they were saved on their own merit, by the way in which they observed the Law. Paul insisted that salvation is a gratuitous, unmerited gift from God. We share that gift through faith in Jesus Christ. Both scripture and tradition attest to the unification of faith and works. "Faith without works is spineless."[3] We do not have the luxury of

---
[3]*DL* (V), 223.

listening to the Word and then doing nothing. To be Christian means to act upon the Word as our response in love.

The gospel is proclaimed.

Gospel
Mark 8:27–35. Whoever wishes to follow me must deny himself, take up his cross, and follow me.

STEP 1
NAMING ONE'S EXPERIENCE

What were your first impressions? What was your first response to the gospel (or the other readings)? What captured your attention?

Each person names his or her initial impression. Statements should be brief. No reasons should be given at this time. All simply listen without agreeing or disagreeing.

STEP 2
UNDERSTANDING

In a brief statement, explain what you think this gospel is trying to convey.

STEP 3
INPUT FROM VISION/STORY/TRADITION

Liturgical Context

The twenty-fourth Sunday in Ordinary Time through the twenty-sixth Sunday in Ordinary Time begins a new sequence. Jesus' disciples, while confessing him as Messiah, still have notions of an earthly, royal ruler who will restore the Davidic kingdom. It will be a while before they fully accept the concept of Messiah as suffering servant. Still in a fog of misunderstanding, the disciples in next Sunday's gospel vie for a place of prominence in this new earthly kingdom once the Lord assumes his royal throne. In the gospel for the twenty-sixth Sunday, Jesus makes it clear that in the reign he came to establish there would be no reserved places—no one would enjoy special status. Those who furthered the kingdom would be disciples, but those who caused others to stumble would be severely judged.

Today's gospel finds Jesus predicting his Passion and death. The cross takes center stage, its ominous presence standing in the shadow of the conversation between Jesus and Peter. Today's gospel reminds us of the principal theology that supports every liturgy and every sacramental celebration. When the church gathers the paschal mystery is remembered and becomes present. The sacrifice of Jesus is at the heart of every liturgy. (Refer to the Easter Vigil, symbol of the cross and the Doctrinal Appendix, paschal mystery.) The cross of today's gospel is not just the cross of daily tribulations—it is the cross of martyrdom. When exhorted to take up our cross, the gospel invites us to suffer for the sake of the gospel. Jean Corbon poetically reminds us of the implications:

> [T]he mission of the word reaches its completion in martyrdom, the supreme form of witness. The form which martyrdom takes is unimportant; the important thing is that the mission of the Church would no longer be the mission of Christ and the Holy Spirit if it did not reach this climax. "What does it matter to you? You are to follow me" (Jn 21:22). We can be witnesses of him whom we have heard, whom our eyes have seen and our hands have touched, only if his fire purifies us until we are wholly conformed to him. From the epiclesis of our baptism to the epiclesis of our Eucharists the same fire is at work in us in order that life may do its work in our brothers and sisters. If our mission does not encounter opposition, we are false prophets. Though we are sent to be with human beings, we cannot be like them; we can truly be with and for them only if we are, like Christ, "a sign that is opposed" (Lk 2:34) and that reveals the secrets of hearts. Tribulation—suffered because we are Christians (1 Pt 4:16)—is the seal upon the ministry of the word, its completion in the silence of the love that gives life after having first given the "imperishable seed" of life (1 Pt 1:23). The mission begun in the liturgy of the

Church is thus brought to completion in the eternal liturgy. In martyrdom compassion reaches the utmost limits of love.[4]

Ultimately today's liturgy is an exhortation to proclaim Jesus Christ, crucified and risen from the dead. We are empowered to proclaim that message through our hope and faith in Christ. The alternative opening prayer acknowledges our need before God, who is the source of our peace. We are reminded that there is no greater vocation than to serve Christ and his people. The communion antiphon serves as a punctuation to the scriptures today. We are reminded that every participation in the Lord's Supper—feasting on his bread of life and drinking from his precious blood—is participation in his life. We enter the mystery that Jesus foretells in today's gospel.

Gospel Exegesis

The facilitator provides input from critical biblical scholarship on this text. This input includes insights as to how people would have heard the gospel in Jesus' time.

A socio-political interpretation of today's text. An interesting point of departure for analyzing this text is to consider the implied reader of Mark's gospel. Robert Beck offers interesting insight into the socio-political conditions that are the context for this pericope.[5] A socio-political interpretation of the gospel provides a worthwhile backdrop for understanding what is taking place in its story world. Thus, before delving into the narrative itself, a fascinating historical diversion is in order. Beck reminds us that our understanding of the implied reader of this gospel is faulty at best. We draw from the known empirical evidence of the first-century Mediterranean sociological world. We cannot interpret today's gospel without an appreciation for some very important concepts prevalent in Mark's world at the time of this writing. An examination of the terms *popular messiah, servant (slave), cross,* and *ransom* will help explain what drives some of the dialogue in today's gospel, albeit the entire gospel of Mark.

By the time Mark wrote this gospel, the Messiah question had already been bantered around.

---

[4]*TWW*, 181–182.
[5]*NS*, 97–100.

Mark's community had already been interpreting and redacting the Christ-event. Their interpretation would be laced with a common understanding of contemporary realities. Messiahs were not uncommon in first-century Palestine. The Essenes prayed and hoped for the emergence of the long-awaited Davidic Messiah. However, dotting the landscape were "political messiahs" who were engaged in serious acts of revolt against the imperial ruling power of Rome and the wealthy Jewish class that supported Roman rule.

Jesus was born into turbulent times. Around the time of his birth, the city of Sephorris, a few miles north of Nazareth (where it is believed that Jesus probably worked as a young carpenter), was burned and the citizens sold into slavery around the year 4 B.C.E. due to an uprising that originated there. For a century before and following the birth of Jesus, unrest and civil disorder was the rule rather than the exception. Jesus was born and raised in this climate of political unrest and social disharmony. To assume that he was unaffected by the conditions which surrounded him would be absurd. Jesus and Mark would be all too aware of the existence of popular messiahs and the role they played in the cultural scene of Jesus' day. Furthermore, it is believed that this gospel was written during the time of the great Jewish revolt—again a lens through which we must consider these texts. In the latter part of Mark's gospel the reader is warned against the leaven of false messiahs—that is, the popular messiahs who came brandishing a message contrary to the mission of Christ. There is to be no mistake. Jesus is not the Messiah of their common experience. He is a new Messiah with a radical new message.

The Jesus movement follows a similar path to other popular Messiah movements, however. It begins as a "grassroots" movement among peasant folk in Galilee. It eventually moves to Jerusalem, the center of political life and upheaval. Jesus is tried and convicted, charged with being both Messiah and bandit. The narrator and the high priest claim Jesus as messiah. For the high priest it is mockery. The narrator knows it is truth.

There is clear evidence in today's gospel that Peter brings his cultural understanding of "Messiah" to bear on his response to Jesus. Perhaps he was caught up in the whirlwind revolutionary po-litical excitement. It would appear at first glance that Jesus' confrontational episodes very clearly resemble the resistance movements of his day. Jesus did not shy away from confrontation. He walked headlong into it. However, there is something uniquely different about the "Jesus movement." Jesus chose a path of nonviolence from the very beginning of his ministry. Jesus chose the role of servant.

The first reading is the lens through which we are to view the resistance movement of Jesus—the new Messiah. The *servant* motif in Israel's consciousness arose out of a cultural situation in which an entire people were exiled—they were extracted from their homeland. They experienced humiliation, defeat, and political subjection. The elite class was sold into Babylonian slavery. They became slaves of their captors. It is probable that the term *servant* has its root in the word *slave*, drawn from the experience of the exile.

What is at stake in a military conquest of this magnitude is the people's belief in God. The god of the conquering nation (Marduk) was obviously more powerful than the god of the defeated nation. God was the author of Israel's entire reality. Now the God they knew was defeated. Along with the defeat was the defeat of their entire reality. What was Israel's precaptivity reality? God was the answer to every problem. What was to be their reality now in light of the captivity? Isaiah passionately set out to give them a new worldview—a new reality. The prophet drew from their past reality to formulate a new one, however.

The prophet did not insist that strength is the only power there is. Isaiah implanted a new metaphor in their consciousness for understanding power—servant. The "slave of Yahweh" is truly powerless on one level. But within that powerlessness emerges a new kind of power. It is a power that belongs to the powerless. In any society, power is ordered through a set of relationships. It is agreed that some people will be on the top of society's ladder, and ultimately some will be on the bottom. However, everyone ultimately agrees with the arrangement. Essentially those on the bottom of society's ladder agree with the evident fact that those on the top do indeed possess power over them. Additionally, anyone who benefits from the powerful class has no reason to question their power. When everyone agrees to the structure, status quo is maintained. The powerful remain powerful, the powerless remain powerless.

Something changes, however, when those on the bottom no longer agree that others have power over them. When they choose a path of nonviolent resistance, power takes on new meaning. It can make the powerless become more powerful. Strength is found in weakness. Isaiah's suffering servant would be restored with a new form of power—power in weakness.

How did first-century Palestinians (the locus of Mark's gospel) understand the role of slave? Slaves commonly donned the demeanor of dullness and total deference to their master in order to supplant the master's feelings of superiority. Such a posture made life easier for the slave. It guarded against the master's annoyance with the slave, thereby avoiding charges of insubordination and subsequent recriminations. The slave maintained this charade in order to make life easier. The slave, while appearing dull-witted and a nonperson to the master, possessed a different reality, known only to herself or himself and to other slaves. This is probably the perspective of servant/slave that the listeners to Mark's gospel would have brought to their hearing of the servant/slave motif in the scriptures. Israel's history of slavery and subjugation would have to be implanted in their consciousness.

Furthermore, servant/slave would be the antithesis of the popular messiah of Jesus' day. The popular messiah envisioned power as the violent overthrow of the ruling power. The slave/servant image envisioned power in different terms, an internal source, a power that comes from within, a power not readily observable by those in power, but nevertheless present—nonviolent resistance.

The *cross* could not, would not have been spiritualized as it later was and as it is today. Mark's listeners would have possessed only one image of the cross. It was an abhorrent, subhuman form of execution. Mark's readers would have understood the cross as a symbol of execution—a deterrent to anyone who considered revolt. The cross was reserved for nonpersons—slaves, prisoners of war, and political dissidents. It was a public, extremely humiliating form of execution. It was a public symbol of the consequences of rebellion. It was a constant, gruesome reminder that those in power dealt severely with dissidents.

In chapter 10 Mark links slave with *ransom*. Ransom was the price needed to repossess indentured slaves, to purchase their freedom. Jesus shows us the way of the servant and in so doing reminds us that the suffering servant transforms and leads people to freedom, to liberation. Jesus ransoms all those subjected to tyranny of any sort.

Jesus' servanthood also led him to substitute his life for others. In today's gospel, Jesus attests that "whoever loses his life for my sake and that of the gospel will save it" (v. 35). In chapter 10, this losing of life to gain a life is expanded—it is for the benefit of others. Jesus took the place of Barabbas, the place of the socially punished.[6] Jesus took upon himself the violence due to others and responded with nonviolence. "The nonviolent actor's motivation is not to be a victim but to be a conspicuous noncombatant."[7] The nonviolent posture is an invitation to the perpetrator not to strike out in violence. It is an invitation not to strike at the person in question, but also to future victims of the same violence. In a sense, this nonviolent action is a form of ransom. By taking this posture of nonviolence Jesus ransomed future victims from the same violence. Jesus' cross, in this context, represents a servant's—not a victim's—response to oppression. Jesus maintained his internal, spiritual power through resistance, but he also demonstrated a nonviolent response in the face of cruel violence. Therefore, to "gain one's self means to put one's self at risk, but to risk one's self in order to interrupt the flow of violence in its cycles is to ransom others."[8]

Both the servant and messianic themes are threads that run through the plot that Mark crafts. It is highly possible that the disciples failed to understand Jesus' messianic mission because it possessed no resemblance to common popular messianic movements. Once awareness dawned, however, Jesus earnestly taught them the differ-

---

6. Ibid., 102.
7. Ibid., 103.
8. Ibid., 102.

ence. Jesus used the image of servant to show them the difference between their expectations of Messiah and his.

When Mark addressed his disciples he was also addressing his reader (a common technique of Mark's). Today's dialogue hearkens back to a more ancient dialogue between God and Moses at the site of the burning bush. Why are we catapulted back to that mountain epiphany? Perhaps it is an allusion to Moses' commission by Yahweh to go back to Egypt and liberate the Israelites and the inauguration of Jesus' journey to Jerusalem and the liberation that will be won by his sacrifice. More probably, however, the dialogue is Christological. Jesus, like Yahweh in his exchange with Moses, revealed, "I am." This is Jesus' divine self-revelation.

As mentioned above, Peter answered the question with a politically charged response. "Jesus is not simply a great prophet; he is a royal figure who will restore the political fortunes of Israel. The revolution, Peter is saying, is at hand."[9] We have already discussed Jesus' response—he silences Peter. He silences him with the same word used to silence the demons and the raging elements of nature. Jesus thus sets the stage for the accusation hurled against Peter—in his mistaken notions, he aligned himself with Satan.

Jesus is now on his way to Jerusalem. There is something apocalyptic about his mission. It is necessary that the events of suffering unfold, because in God's eschatological plan of salvation, this is to be the fate of servant and prophet. Jesus called himself the "Human One" rather than Messiah in his response to Peter. The "Human One" is one who challenges the authority of the scribes and Pharisees. (T)his apocalyptic persona is taken from Daniel:

> I saw in the night visions: behold, with the clouds of heaven there came one like a Human One; and he came to the Ancient of Days and was presented before him. And to him was given dominion and glory and kingdoms, that all peoples, nations and languages should serve him (Dn 7:13).

The "Human One" who also appears in the Book of Ezra represents "true 'human' government as opposed to the brutality of the 'beasts' in the visions."[10] Mark is drawing on the Daniel of old as a statement of political resistance to oppression by Hellenistic rulers.

Jesus foretells his execution at the hands of a new ruling authority—the high priests, elders, and scribes—the Jerusalem establishment. Mark's Jesus challenges common eschatological theology. Peter thinks *messiah* means political victory and the restoration of Israel's national honor. Jesus parabolically overturns that faulty theological apple cart. "Human One"—*Messiah*—must mean suffering. It is absolutely inevitable. The "Human One" cannot challenge structures that keep some people on the top of society's ladder and some on the bottom without angering the people on top. Jesus challenged the authority of the religious leaders when he attacked Sabbath observance and the ritual purity laws.

Jesus openly (*parresia*—meaning frankly or boldly) asserted his identity. Now is the time for stark reality. No illusions here. "Peter's fantasy of power must be censured by clear-eyed realism."[11] Jesus rebuked Peter and called him Satan. We are reminded of the parable of the sower, and in this dialogue we observe the parable enacted. The sower sows the Word and Satan comes to take away the Word that was sown. Mark used the parable to alert his reader to the obstacles that true disciples will encounter along *the way*. The parable unfolds as live drama in the exchange between Jesus and Peter. Jesus explained the Word to them and Satan came to snatch it away.

Mark's catechism defines the call of discipleship. Disciples are to deny themselves. Disciples are to take up their crosses. Disciples are to follow Jesus. Jesus' invitation to take up the cross was a clear indication that discipleship involved challenging those in power in defense of the gospel. We cannot ignore the imperative behind this text. When called on to defend Christ, wherever that may be, whether a political or religious court, no matter what court, disciples are to walk boldly to the cross

---

[9] *BSM*, 242.

[10] Ibid., 243.
[11] Ibid., 244.

and all its inherent meanings—humiliation, and ultimate degradation. "Self-denial" for the readers of Mark did not mean the privatized, spiritualized asceticism of modern Christianity. Self-denial meant that when people stood before the court and faced their inquisitor, they risked their very lives by the answer they would give. Ched Myers insists that it is at this point that Mark introduces the central paradox of the entire gospel.[12] The only control a ruling power has over the populace is punishment by death; fear of this threat keeps the status quo in order. Fear of death is the control used by those in power to remain powerful. The rich become wealthier and the poor remain subjected to oppression and powerlessness. When disciples rebuke such fear and live fully in the reign of God at the risk of their very lives, they "contribute to shattering the powers' reign of death in history."[13]

A literary interpretation of today's text. The sixty-four thousand dollar question of Mark's gospel then is, "Just who is this Jesus, the carpenter's son?" Crowds were following him. He was a charismatic teacher. He performed great miracles. The religious leaders rejected him outright and were becoming increasingly suspicious of him. Followers were beginning to wonder if he was an Elijah-type prophet. His own disciples were certainly impressed and awed, but even they did not fully understand him or who he was. Interestingly and ironically, the only ones who knew the identity of this incredible human being for sure were the evil spirits.

We are at a threshold moment in today's gospel. The disciples finally acknowledge Jesus as the Messiah. Today brings the first part of the gospel to a close and transitions the reader into the next section. In the first section Jesus' secret identity is slowly revealed. Jesus taught by example, not by overt teaching. The next section deals with the fulfillment of God's plan that the Son of Man must be handed over to suffer, die, and accomplish God's grand design. The second act of this divine drama answers the questions posed in the first section. Who is this Jesus? Jesus answered, but his answer is unacceptable and completely unimagin-

able for his disciples. A suffering, tortured Messiah? Never.

Peter's confession of Jesus as Messiah is critical. Jesus predicts his Passion as a response to Peter's confession. Jesus' pronouncement throws his trusted disciple for a proverbial loop. This is not what Peter expected. Jesus has knocked Peter's equilibrium off its center with this new and unexpected revelation.

For the first time, Jesus openly and plainly revealed his identity. Up until now he kept that revelation secret. Now he professed it clearly and plainly. This denotes a definite shift; 8:31 illustrates the beginning of a new journey for Jesus and his disciples. Today begins the arduous road toward Jerusalem that ultimately ends with the women at the tomb.

Peter's objection revealed his incredulity at the prospect of a different type of Messiah than he expected. He dared to rebuke the Lord. Even though Peter claimed Jesus as Messiah, he had no concept of what that meant. Perhaps he was stuck in the image of political messiah mentioned above. One can almost hear him, "Jesus, I did not sign on for this, you have to be joking—not this— no, never!" Even though Peter and the disciples acknowledged Jesus as Messiah and, as a result, Jesus subsequently deemed them a special group of people set apart from other people, Jesus now chastised Peter and scolded him. Jesus rebuked him by telling him that his thinking was no different than the thinking of other human beings— even those who oppose him. "Peter, and all like him who stand 'on the side of men,' stand opposed to God's saving purpose and align themselves with Satan."[14]

The purpose of this pericope is to reflect the historical situation of Mark's community, the church—not Jesus' ministry. Jesus' first question deals with the historical situation at the time: "Who do our neighbors and country folks say that I am?" However, the second question, the use of the title "Christ" has early Christian overtones and "the prediction of the passion is cast in language of the early Church (vv. 29, 31). Peter's reaction

---

[12]Ibid., 247.
[13]Ibid.

[14]*MARK*, 122.

and the sharp correction of it (vv. 32–33) have much to do with an understanding of christology."[15]

Historically Jesus and Peter have a conversation and Peter makes a profession of faith. On a symbolic, theological level, Jesus is catechizing the church and Peter represents all followers of Christ who profess faith in him, but whose interpretation is incorrect. Jesus' intended audience is the "multitude" who represent all the people who need to hear his teaching. This is a catechetical moment in the life of an early community that tries to reflect upon the meaning of the risen Lord in their midst.

Mark, the teacher, comes to the fore in this passage. Nowhere else in the gospel does Mark more clearly posit his Christology than in this text. Many of the people in Mark's community professed a watered-down misunderstanding of Jesus. Mark corrects their theology. He insists that there is no way to experience resurrection without the Passion and the cross. The road to Calvary continues to be paved with broken and bruised disciples. Mark reminds his community that to be Christian, to profess Christ, one must be willing to enter into and live the life of servant. The Christian must be willing to die. In his Letter to the Romans Paul reminded us that we are baptized into Christ's death—into his paschal mystery.

The event (Jesus' dialogue with Peter) surrounding the theology Mark presents in today's gospel is authentic. The dialogue between Peter and Jesus and the subsequent charge that Peter is Satan is no doubt historical. Mark's theologizing of the event, however, is for the benefit of his community. Mark is clear—the Christ-event is not a glorified account of a brilliant, successful prophetic career. The Messiah was rejected, he suffered, he died. Yes, he rose from the dead, but suffering is the hallmark of this man's earthly sojourn. There were to be no illusions.

Peter speaks in the voice of all people from all generations when he refused to accept the road Jesus insisted he must take. Jesus reminded him that his thinking was like that of other "human be-

ings." Who among us would automatically gravitate toward a suffering, rejected Messiah over a glorious, triumphant, victorious, just, and exalted earthly ruler of the people? No one walks willingly or headlong into the world of suffering. Jesus' words to Peter continue to be a challenge to all people. Human beings have a way to twist them into *not* meaning what Jesus clearly intended them to mean. One need only observe many well-intentioned religious groups today who preach the gospel of prosperity. Their creed becomes: "Just love the Lord and give to our cause, and God will reward you and give you anything you ask. You want riches? You will have riches. You want healing? You will be healed." Often religious movements shy away from the cross and its implications, just as do the people within those movements. Peter is a prototype for all people of every generation.

Even though Jesus scolded Peter, it was not enough to bring about change in him. Peter would once again fall short. He would deny the Lord. Peter would deny him, the apostles abandon him, and so would the church again and again throughout the centuries.

The church is built on the rock of Golgotha; its genesis flows from the side of Christ. The church began with a leader who was not triumphant in any earthly sense of the word. Jesus was overcome; he failed—at least through the eyes those who think like "human beings" think.

Mark's Jesus tells us that after three days he will rise again. In no way is this a means to minimize the agony that preceded his death. "That word of victory for the Son of Man over death is a promise of victory for the oppressed, the vanquished, the silent in death—the forgotten. It is a word of warning against our human way of exalting the victorious and triumphant. Through the suffering Messiah victory is possessed by the vanquished; through the dead Messiah life is possessed by the dead. He and his way are the sole guarantee of our victory and our life."[16]

Proclaim the gospel again.

---
[15]Ibid.

---
[16]Ibid., 122.

Sometimes we gain new insights when we hear the text after the interpretation is given. Someone from the group proclaims the gospel a second time.

STEP 4

TESTING

Conversation with the Liturgy and the Scriptures

Test your original understanding in dialogue with the text.

(You might consider breaking into smaller groups.)

Now that you've heard the exegesis, were there any new insights? How do you feel about it? How does your original understanding of this gospel compare with what we just shared? How does this story speak to your life?

Sharing Life Experience

Participants share an experience from their lives that connects with the biblical interpretation just presented.

> *I cannot help but note the irony in our president's exhortation against violence in the aftermath of the student killings in Littleton, while at the same time dropping bombs on our "enemy." It rings very hollow. Today's gospel reminds us that violence begets violence. Jesus shows us a new way, that there is power in our powerlessness. I am reminded of a friend who was in a very tense, challenging situation. Most people would have been severely threatened by this situation. It challenged him and his relationship with God. His response reminds me of the exhortation of Jesus in this gospel. Many people would have responded to a similar situation with justifiable anger, maybe even violent rage. This person chose the path of Christ. He did not deny the cross that lie before him. He walked right into it with love. He respectfully allowed the events to unfold. He calmly and nonviolently addressed the situation in terms of his responsibility to follow Christ. There was strength in his humility. This person understands his life as servant. He chooses not to be the slave of anyone else's expectations. He will follow the path God has ordained for him even if it leads to suffering and misunderstanding.*

> *I hope I can learn from his example. I hope I have the necessary faith and trust to live the imperative of today's gospel. Jesus is asking for both. He invites us to assume a nonviolent approach to life no matter where that leads us.*

> *Today's gospel also reminds me of the young girl who was asked if she believed in Jesus as she stared down the sawed-off shotgun of two very ill young boys in Colorado. Would "no" have spared her life? Who knows? She stood firm in her faith in Christ. She answered "yes." She stood before the ultimate courtroom. Death stared her in the face. Her response triggered the blast that killed her. However, her witness (root word—martyr) stands as a beacon. How could a young girl stand before this mock court and risk everything? Would I? Or would I, like Peter, deny him too? Perhaps faith is easy enough—but do I have enough trust? Someone gave the analogy that faith is like the person watching a tightrope walker balance a wheelbarrow across the high wire. The observer can certainly have faith that the artist knows what he is doing and can accomplish his feat. Trust, on the other hand, is getting inside the wheelbarrow. Today's gospel invites the latter. I hope I am up for the challenge. I hope that I can and will carry the cross of nonviolence so others can be ransomed when I am called on to do so. That is the invitation of every liturgy and the empowerment it offers.*

What was Mark trying to tell his community? How do you feel about the social conditions that serve as a backdrop for this gospel? Does it have any bearing on your life? Have you ever had the opportunity to assume a posture of nonviolence? In what way does this gospel challenge your community today? In what way has this conversation with the scriptures for today's liturgy invited change in your life? In what way are the biblical themes of covenant, exodus, creation, and community evident in today's readings? Do you still feel the same way about this text as when you began? Has your original understanding been stretched, challenged, or affirmed?

STEP 5

DECISION

The gospel demands a response.

In what concrete way might your parish be invited to respond? Are there any attitudes or behaviors you would like to change as a result of today's conversation? What one concrete action will you take this week in response to the liturgy today?

Pastoral Considerations: What would it mean for you to embrace a posture of nonviolence in all your dealings? Perhaps today's gospel is an invitation to your community to study the issue of nonviolence and the challenges it presents in our complicated world.

Christian Initiation: With the emphasis on the call of discipleship involving taking up one's cross and following Christ, today would be a very appropriate Sunday to celebrate a rite of acceptance.

DOCTRINAL ISSUES

What Church truth/teaching/doctrinal issue could be drawn from the gospel for the twenty-fourth Sunday in Ordinary Time?

Participants suggest possible doctrinal themes that flow from the readings.

Possible Doctrinal Themes

Paschal mystery; cross; mystery of suffering; nonviolence; humility; conversion; servanthood; discipleship; reign of God; Christology; ministry; martyrdom; Christian witness

Present the doctrinal material at this time.

1. The facilitator gives input on a particular doctrinal issue of his or her prior choosing. OR
2. The group chooses a doctrinal issue from the list they created. They read together from the Doctrinal Appendix or other appropriate, official Church documents and the works of respected theologians.

(Many doctrinal issues are found in the Doctrinal Appendix at the back of this workbook. If you are choosing an issue from this resource, please refer to it now.)

Reflection questions centered around the chosen doctrinal theme can be found at the end of each topic in the Doctrinal Appendix. The questions are based on the five-step reflection process. If you choose a topic not included in the Doctrinal Appendix, craft your own questions according to the same five-step process.

Following the reflection questions you will be reminded to return to chapter 7, "Preparing the Catechetical Session," to assist you in crafting your own session.

Closing Prayer

Let us pray
for the peace which is born of faith and hope

　　Pause for silent prayer

Father in heaven, Creator of all,
look down upon your people in their moments of
　　need,
for you alone are the source of our peace.
Bring us to the dignity which distinguishes the
　　poor in spirit
and show us how great is the call to serve,
that we may share in the peace of Christ
who offered his life in the service of all.
We ask this through Christ our Lord.[17]

---

[17]Twenty-Fourth Sunday in Ordinary Time, "Alternative Opening Prayer," *The Sacramentary.*

Twenty-Fifth Sunday in Ordinary Time

Environment

See the twenty-second Sunday in Ordinary Time.

INTRODUCTORY RITES

Entrance Antiphon (or Opening Song)

Lord, you are just, and the judgments you make are right. Show mercy when you judge me, your servant. (Ps 118:137, 124)[1]

Opening Prayer

The facilitator of the session may lead the prayer. Others in the group may be asked to proclaim the readings.

Let us pray
that we will grow in the love of God and of one another

Pause for silent prayer.

Father, guide us, as you guide creation
according to your law of love.
May we love one another
and come to perfection
in the eternal life prepared for us.
Grant this through our Lord, Jesus Christ, your
    Son,
who lives and reigns with you and the Holy
    Spirit,
one God for ever and ever.[2]

LITURGY OF THE WORD

The readings are proclaimed.

First Reading
Wisdom 2:12, 17–20

(Please refer to the thirteenth Sunday in Ordinary Time for an overview of the Book of Wisdom.)

Today's Pericope: The person in this reading is closely related to the just one in the psalms who is vindicated by God. There are also similarities with the Suffering Servant of Isaiah (last week's first reading).

The reading illustrates the life of the righteous person, which stands in stark contrast to the life of rebellious people. The rebellious are probably the apostate Jews of Alexandria. The lawless, unruly, and godless people seek to destroy the righteous. Some people not only cower in the face of goodness, they try to destroy it. True goodness in such a case is a reminder of the lack of goodness in those who resent it. The evildoers seek to damage the reputation of those they castigate.

The sage in this reading lays bare the dishonest motives of such people. He uncovers the sinister way in which the unrighteous try to make their case by citing their honorable intentions, while in fact their intentions are anything but honorable. The sage insists that the maltreated righteous find strength through patient endurance. The unrighteous end up indicting themselves.

This scripture is a type of the future Christ and a prophecy of the Passion of Jesus. Christ is obviously the falsely maligned righteous one in the reading. This pericope is appointed to accompany Mark's second Passion prediction.

Responsorial Psalm
Psalm 54:3–8

Today's psalm is a good companion to the reading from Wisdom. The person in the psalm is confident of God's intervention and vindication in the face of persecution and oppression.

Second Reading
James 3:16–4:3

(Please refer to the twenty-first Sunday in Ordinary Time for an overview to the Letter of James.)

---

[1]Twenty-Fifth Sunday in Ordinary Time: "Entrance Antiphon," *The Sacramentary.*

[2]Twenty-Fifth Sunday in Ordinary Time: "Opening Prayer," *The Sacramentary.*

Today's Pericope: James compares true wisdom with false wisdom. The letter corresponds to the twelve patriarchs. Today's letter is part of the seventh exhortation. Leah represents false and earthly wisdom; Rachel is true, heaven-borne wisdom. Wisdom is the virtue that helps us cherish the things of value in everyday life. James addresses the issue of Christian wisdom. Christianity does not have the market cornered on wisdom. There is much to learn from people of other faith traditions. People in all religious traditions seek the wisdom of God and believe that the wisdom they possess comes from God.[3] Christians are not to think that they must reinvent the wheel when it comes to wisdom. We are to benefit from the wisdom, experience, and prayers of others.

James addresses the issue of discord within the community and the issue of peace. Peace resides in the human heart, where wars are also waged. Peaceful people embody the peace they possess. Peaceful, nonviolent people and nonviolent communities are an example to the world that peace is possible when it is a priority and when communities work for it. True wisdom begets peace; false wisdom begets false wisdom. Some people in the early Christian community believed they possessed a special gnosis—knowledge—that set them apart from everyone else. James exposed them as frauds. They did not possess wisdom; they were filled with pride and arrogance. Their wisdom was of this world, not of heaven. True wisdom exists in the hearts of compassionate people who put their love into action.

Finally, James reminds us of the power of prayer. He insists that we do not have what we need because we do not ask. Prayer is the way we learn the will of God and conform our will to God's will. Prayer invites conversion and a transformed will.

The gospel is proclaimed.

Gospel
Mark 9:30–37. Whoever wishes to be first in the reign of God shall be last and servant of all.

---

[3]*DL* (V), 213.

STEP 1
NAMING ONE'S EXPERIENCE

What were your first impressions? What was your first response to the gospel (or the other readings)? What captured your attention?

Each person names his or her initial impression. Statements should be brief. No reasons should be given at this time. All simply listen without agreeing or disagreeing.

STEP 2
UNDERSTANDING

In a brief statement, explain what you think this gospel is trying to convey.

STEP 3
INPUT FROM VISION/STORY/TRADITION

Liturgical Context

Today's gospel is the second in a three-part sequence that began last week. Today Jesus predicts his pending Passion and death for the second time, and he teaches his disciples the meaning of *servant.* His teaching extends beyond the life and situation of the disciples and reaches out to the entire Church. We are all servants of Christ and servants in his household. All are equal in the household of God. St. Augustine puts this in proper perspective:

> If I am afraid of what I am for you, I am consoled by what you are for me. For you, I am a bishop; with you I am a Christian. The former title is that of the dignity I am invested with; the latter reminds me of the grace I received; the former is rife with dangers for me; the latter spells salvation and safety for me.... Seeing that I am entrusted with such important, numerous and varied duties, help me with your prayers and your obedience; ask that I be affected less by the honor of giv-

ing you orders than by happiness of serving you.[4]

Today's opening prayer serves as an apt theme for today's liturgy. It puts love at the heart of the question. Without love, servanthood is impossible. We ask that our love for God and one another grows and that we come to perfection in the life Christ prepared for us. We will be unable to endure the cross Christ asks of us if we do not grow in the love he gives us. The opening prayer affirms the same theme. Love is the only means to live just and upright lives. When we follow the way of the Lord and the will of God in love, we live in the perfection of justice we seek in our prayer. Only then will we understand and live the life of a true servant of Christ.

Today's liturgy is an invitation inward and outward. We are to look within and root out our hidden lust for power and prestige, and we are to go out beyond ourselves and live Jesus' command to serve the least in his reign. Gustavo Gutierrez challenges our darkest inner selves: "They [the disciples] have actually understood that the Lord is advocating a transformation of the religious order. What is grave is that even in that realm, ambition for prestige and power can exist. It is not necessary to believe in a temporal kingdom to fall into this attitude. We see that daily in our midst. The pursuit of honors, the desire to be the center of decisions, self-complacency in the authority entrusted to us, all these temptations which are found in the church itself. It is a major perversion of the message of the Lord reminding us once again that the mark of disciples consists in being 'the last and the servant of all.'"[5]

Gospel Exegesis

The facilitator provides input from critical biblical scholarship on this text. This input includes insights as to how people would have heard the gospel in Jesus' time.

The second part of Mark's gospel is the locus and crux of Mark's theology. He frames the theology with three predictions of the Passion, followed by the misunderstanding of the disciples. Jesus

stressed the implications of what it means to be a disciple—it means following Christ and modeling our lives after his. Christians are to follow Jesus' way. A primary motif in this section is the phrase, "on the way"; it is repeated frequently. Jesus restored the sight of Bartimaeus and he followed Jesus "on the way." "On the way" today, the disciples asked who was greatest. Jesus continued "on the way" to Jerusalem and brought his disciples with him.

Earlier in Mark's gospel, Jesus and his disciples descended the Mount of Transfiguration. The disciples were confused and afraid. Jesus predicted his Passion for a second time. Jesus, Son of God, Son of Man, was moving toward his death and resurrection. He bound the disciples to secrecy over these awe-inspiring, astonishing realities. Jesus used these encounters with his disciples to teach them about the mystery of life and death.[6]

The disciples were still clouded by confusion, however. They were still thinking like human beings, rather than with the wisdom of God. They simply could not fathom the need for suffering. They also failed to understand Jesus' self-revelation. They were imbued with the fear of God, religious fear, a fear they frequently experienced when face to face with the revelation of Christ and his mission.

Mark's honesty is commendable. He did not try to romanticize the memory of the disciples as later evangelists did. He painted a truthful picture—human warts and all. Later evangelists watered down Mark's harsh portrait. The picture painted in today's gospel is shocking to our sensibilities. Jesus was trying to tell his friends about his impending death, and all they could talk about was who was greatest among them. "Jesus has death on his mind; the disciples glory."[7]

Jesus and his disciples were on their way through Galilee; they reached Capernaum.[8] Once inside the house in Capernaum, Jesus began to teach

---

[4]St. Augustine, "Sermon 340," 1–2 *Oeuvres complètes*, vol. 19 (Paris: Vivés, 1873), 120–121, in *DL* (V), 234.

[5]*SWTLY*, 227.

[6]*MARK*, 142.

[7]*MAM*, 69.

[8]Jesus took his disciples to Capernaum. This geographical locus is significant. Capernaum was the center of Jesus' ministry in the first part of the gospel and the place where his ministry began.

them. Frustration filled the air. Like a low-lying cloud, denial hovered over their consciousnesses. The disciples did not want to hear Jesus' repeated reminders that he must suffer. They did not seem to absorb the implications of what Jesus was trying to teach them—what awaited their Master in Jerusalem. Instead of facing the truth of Jesus' mission, they engaged in petty, jealous banter over the issue of seniority within their own ranks.

Jesus used this teachable moment to express his theology regarding the "dignity of service."[9] The last among you is the greatest. The word for *servant* (*talya*) is interchangeable with *child*. Thus the child of verses 36–37 is connected to the servant of verse 35. The word *receives* is the same word used for *welcomes* in 6:11. It means *taking care of the weaker members of the community*—those who are in most need of being served. *The child who is received in Jesus' name* is a child who belongs to Jesus. The child is Jesus' child, just as those who are baptized also become Jesus' own. The implications? Disciples are the presence of Christ to others and Jesus is the presence of the Father for the disciples. A stranger meets Christ in the heart of every believer. Herein lies the dignity of Christian service—it is rooted in the presence of Christ and his Father.

Ched Myers suggests that this section of Mark's gospel continues the theme of nonviolence.[10] What are the implications of Jesus' journey to Jerusalem? What does a discipleship of the cross really mean? "A discipleship of the cross makes far more difficult demands: the application of nonviolence to every sphere of life. As Ghandi put it, 'If one does not practice nonviolence in one's personal relations with others and hopes to use it in bigger affairs, one is vastly mistaken' (1948: I, 187). Genuine revolutionary transformation occurs from the 'bottom up.'"[11]

The first section of Mark laid bare a new vision—a new social order based on reconciliation and economic justice. This vision was revealed by the symbolic action of miracles in the first part of Mark's gospel. In this new section Jesus used the art of teaching to inaugurate this new social order. What did he teach? The way of the cross involves resistance to political oppression and a new way of relating—servanthood. Nonviolence forces serious reflection on the issues of life and death. Jesus insisted that the mystery before them (the mystery of the cross) carries within it the seeds of a new way of existence, which in time will mature.

The disciples are twice told that Jesus will be killed. They do not understand. Mark makes sure his reader understands the connection between the disciples' failure to fathom and accept the political inevitability of Jesus' execution and the consequences of their failure, their betrayal, particularly Peter's betrayal.

Jesus laid bare their intentions and unmasked the truth of their hearts. What really drove the disciples was their lust for power. They were not only confused about Jesus' mission, they thwarted it. The greatest–least riposte between the disciples served as the greatest irony to illustrate the point. An argument over honor broke out in the ranks—"I'm the greatest in the Lord's community," "No, *I'm* the greatest!" In the honor/shame culture of the Mediterranean world it would be common for such an argument to break out over who held the highest place of honor in an organized group like Jesus'. Jesus tackled the problem head on. His direct challenge to them shamed them. Jesus did not stop there, however; he went even further. When he told them to welcome children, the lowest creatures in the culture, the cultural response would have been, "What on earth for?" Hospitality was offered to strangers in hostile foreign lands, not to children. People would have laughed at such a suggestion. In a shame-based culture the recipients of hospitality are to broadcast the magnanimous charity of those who offered hospitality to everyone they encountered. Children could hardly be counted on to reciprocate in such a manner. No one would pay any attention to them if they did. "Jesus teaches that life is full of surprises. True honor can be found in the most unlikely places."[12]

Mark used Jesus' exchange with the disciples to teach his readers. "Jesus sat down to teach

[9]*MARK*, 144.
[10]*BSM*, 257.
[11]Ibid.

[12]*CWJB*, 141.

them"—in other words, "Pay attention, folks! An important revelation is about to take place!" Jesus began his discourse on the theology of *servant.* The way of nonviolence is to pay close attention to the dynamics of power and privilege among family, friends, and neighbors. Jesus laid bare the seeds of violence within their own community. Those who vie for power with family and friends follow the way of violence and are no better than those who live their lives by it. Disciples must be willing to accept the subversive life. That is, they must be willing to upset the status quo and power structure and put themselves at risk for the sake of others. However, one prepares for this subversive life by daily attention to a nonviolent way of life within the Christian community.

Jesus used a parable in action, a concrete, living example to show the disciples how willing they should be to live the life of servant and of nonviolence. Jesus demonstrated what his teaching about *the least, the greatest,* and *servant* meant. He used a child to illustrate his point. Children were at the bottom of society's social ladder. Childhood was a time of great danger. Thirty percent of live births ended in death. Disease and lack of hygiene caused 60 percent of children to die by the age of 16. Children in antiquity were the last to be considered for anything. "Thomas Aquinas taught that in a raging fire a husband was obliged to save his father first, then his mother, next his wife, and last of all his young child."[13] In time of famine children were the last to be fed. In some cultures today, this is still the norm. Children possessed no rights and absolutely no status. They were on a par with slaves. Children received no recognition whatsoever until young adulthood, at which time they became free persons. Jesus called attention to a group who in reality was considered a nongroup, nonpersons. To suggest they become living, viable members of the community would have upset the status quo, a subversive action met with suspicion by society and its structures of authority. "Who does this upstart think he is to change a social order that has always served us well?"

Jesus turned the hearer's world upside down by his simple act of using the children. His action suggested a major reversal—the overthrow of a cultural norm, a "radical status-reversal of the kingdom."[14] Even though they had absolutely no place in society and were considered the lowest of the low, children were nevertheless loved and cherished. Children were loved because they were a symbol of family continuity. They were the promise of security for parents. Women who did not bear a child were not accepted in the patriarchal family setting. Disciples would still have been insulted by Jesus' comparison of them to a child, however. They certainly would not want to be compared with a group who were ignored and considered nonexistent by the rest of the culture. They would have regarded Jesus' exhortation to become like a little child and to welcome the child an absurdity.

Jesus twice warned the disciples of the betrayal, death, and resurrection he was about to endure. Death and resurrection? What could he have been talking about? They would understand betrayal all too well. Betrayal was common in this Mediterranean shame-based culture. Honor would have dictated that someone intervene and thwart betrayal whenever possible. However, when all attempts failed, the honorable thing to do in an honor- and shame-based society was to die with dignity. The disciples would have a clear concept of betrayal. Resurrection, however, was another matter. They were in uncharted waters and dared not ask too many questions.

Mark used the Passion predictions to posit his Christology. The three predictions frame all the material of chapters 8 through 10. They are so boldly proclaimed that the reader can hardly miss the impact they have on the rest of the narrative. Yet even though the reader is privy to Mark's Christology, the characters in the story are blind to it. No matter how bold the proclamation, the disciples miss it altogether. The reader, however, cannot help but be "educated by these signposts to future moments in the narrative."[15]

Mark emphasized the cross—not Jesus' miracles—as the means by which the world was purged of sin. False teachers were professing Jesus as a won-

---

[13]Ibid., 139.

[14]*BSM,* 261.
[15]*MAM,* 60.

der worker. They were also claiming special privilege, suggesting that Jesus passed his special wonder-working power on to them. Mark nips that idiocy in the bud. Jesus predicted his Passion and death three times. There is only one way to follow Christ—the cross. Mark situated the content of Jesus' teaching parallel to the place where it was taught—"on the way." "The message is about Jesus' way of life and the way of life of whoever wishes to follow him. The way taken by Jesus and the disciples is at the same time a way of learning, first and foremost for those who together with Jesus are on the way to Jerusalem, but also for readers, who through the words of Mark are able to join them."[16]

Proclaim the gospel again.

Sometimes we gain new insights when we hear the text after the interpretation is given. Someone from the group proclaims the gospel a second time.

STEP 4
TESTING

Conversation with the Liturgy and the Scriptures

Test your original understanding in dialogue with the text.

(You might consider breaking into smaller groups.)

Now that you've heard the exegesis, were there any new insights? How do you feel about it? How does your original understanding of this gospel compare with what we just shared? How does this story speak to your life?

Sharing Life Experience

Participants share an experience from their lives that connects with the biblical interpretation just presented.

> *It is so easy to become filled with self-importance and forget who the Lord is. Sometimes my darkest inner self perches my own ego on that throne. Today's*

liturgy is a challenge of the highest order. What comes to mind as I reflect on this gospel is every "little child" in our community—all the silent, marginalized, insignificant persons who are nameless faces in every Sunday assembly. Do I give each and every one of them the same consideration I would give to a visible, active (perhaps powerful and influential) member of our community?

I am thinking about a homeless woman who presently is taking up "secret" residence during the day in our church. She sleeps in her car, she slips into our restroom to attend to daily hygiene, she eats at the local soup kitchen. Recently, she asked to become a member of the choir and I heartily accepted her request. The other night, however, she sat in the back of the church throughout choir rehearsal. When I approached her and asked her if she would like to come up and join us, she declined.

I later felt that I should have spent a little more time asking how she was; if I could help her further; if she needed someone to talk to. But once again I missed that moment of epiphany. If a regular parishioner had been sitting in that pew, seemingly distressed, I would have spent far more time and energy ministering to his or her needs.

The challenge to my servanthood is inviting me to ask other questions. If we can build two clinics in Peru, a school in Haiti, a church in our sister parish, homes in Appalachia, then what prevents us from helping this lone woman get a new start in life?[17] Why is it sometimes easier to help those unknown faces from far away than to respond to broken and abused people right under our noses? Judgments abound. I do not even know the woman and already I have assumed that she is either an addict or mentally ill—and today that could spell danger. Yet there are people who are willing to take that risk for the sake of the cross. Right now I have an extra bedroom. Should I open my home to her? What is her story? Would we be taking on more than we are prepared to handle? At the very least I know I am called to get to know her better. I am called to be her

---

[16]*RM,* 127.

---

[17]Since this woman just recently came to our attention, we have not addressed her need, so to say that we will not respond to her is certainly premature. I have every confidence that we will do something to help her.

servant and welcome that "little child" in Jesus' name.

The disciples were concerned with power and prestige. It is easy to get caught up with the roles we play, whether in the world or in a parish setting. Parishes have much to learn from today's gospel. When we seek the counsel of parishioners, do we always go to the powerful, wealthy, influential people, or do we actively seek out those who might have another word to teach us—the poor and disenfranchised members, those who are often voiceless? Do we live parish life as if every person were equal in the reign of God? Even in our ministry to the poor it is often difficult to rise above the tendency to unconsciously exalt ourselves for being such wonderful servants of the Lord for helping these lowly creatures. We need instead to see that it is a privilege to help God's children attain the dignity that is theirs simply because they are children of God. We/I have a long way to go.

Many poor, transient people come to our parish seeking assistance. Each one has a story of brokenness. Each story is unique, but in a sense, they are all the same. Their brokenness has given birth to serious dysfunction. It is all too easy to approach them with an expectation of dysfunction rather than to see the dignity of the human person that God sees. I try to see with the eyes of God. Sometimes I am able to have such vision. Other times I am absolutely blind and get caught up in my own self-importance and busyness. Perhaps their presence is a reminder to us all that we are one serious catastrophe away from walking in their shoes. We have no way of knowing how life's tragedies will impact our lives. Today's gospel invites me to ask: "Am I willing to put them in the place of 'greatness' and myself in the place of 'last-ness'? Would I be willing to usher them to a reserved place of honor within our Sunday assembly?" My Christian reflection wants me to say, "Of course." My honest reflection says that I probably would not. The gospel's message is simple—but it is not easy. I have a long way to go for the perfection of Christ to become complete in me.

What was Mark trying to tell his community? How does today's gospel speak to concrete situations in your community? Put yourself and your community in the place of the characters in this story. In what way do you relate to the disciples and their argument over who is the least and greatest? How do you relate to Jesus' challenge to welcome the children? Who are the "children" in your midst? How does Jesus' message of nonviolence relate to your life? How might you live its imperative in your sphere of life—family, coworkers, and friends? In what way does this gospel challenge your community today? In what way has this conversation with the scriptures for today's liturgy invited change in your life? In what way are the biblical themes of covenant, exodus, creation, and community evident in today's readings? Do you still feel the same way about this text as when you began? Has your original understanding been stretched, challenged, or affirmed?

STEP 5
DECISION

The gospel demands a response.

What is one concrete action you will take this week in response to the liturgy today?

Pastoral Considerations: The challenge for any parish community that wishes to take this gospel seriously is to ask itself: In our parish, who are "the least"? "the greatest"? "the children?" Where does our parish fall short of Jesus' teaching and moral imperative in today's gospel? These are difficult, upsetting, and history-changing questions to ask. People on the top have a vested interest in not wanting them answered; people on the bottom do not trust that you want to ask them in the first place. It requires great courage to ask such questions. Jesus asked them and we know what happened to him.

Perhaps today would be an apt occasion to bless those servants of the Lord who minister to "the children" in our world—those the world would judge "the least."

Christian Initiation: Today's gospel would be an opportune time to replace extended catechesis with an experience of service and mission. There is no better way to absorb today's gospel than by "doing it."

DOCTRINAL ISSUES

What Church truth/teaching/doctrinal issue could be drawn from the gospel for the twenty-fifth Sunday in Ordinary Time?

Participants suggest possible doctrinal themes that flow from the readings.

Possible Doctrinal Themes

Service; servanthood; ministry; nonviolence; cross; mystery of suffering; paschal mystery; discipleship; conversion; social teaching

Present the doctrinal material at this time.

1. The facilitator gives input on a particular doctrinal issue of his or her prior choosing. OR
2. The group chooses a doctrinal issue from the list they created. They read together from the Doctrinal Appendix or other appropriate, official Church documents and the works of respected theologians.

(Many doctrinal issues are found in the Doctrinal Appendix at the back of this workbook. If you are choosing an issue from this resource, please refer to it now.)

Reflection questions centered around the chosen doctrinal theme can be found at the end of each topic in the Doctrinal Appendix. The questions are based on the five-step reflection process. If you choose a topic not included in the Doctrinal Appendix, craft your own questions according to the same five-step process.

Following the reflection questions you will be reminded to return to chapter 7, "Preparing the Catechetical Session," to assist you in crafting your own session.

Closing Prayer

Let us pray
to the Lord who is a God of love to all peoples.

Pause for silent prayer.

Father in heaven,
the perfection of justice is found in your love
and all mankind is in need of your law.
Help us to find this love in each other
that justice may be attained
through obedience to your law.
We ask this through Christ, our Lord.[18]

---

[18]Twenty-Fifth Sunday in Ordinary Time: "Alternative Opening Prayer," *The Sacramentary.*

TWENTY-SIXTH SUNDAY IN ORDINARY TIME

Environment

See the twenty-second Sunday in Ordinary Time.

INTRODUCTORY RITES

Entrance Antiphon (or Opening Song)

O Lord, you had just cause to judge men as you did: because we sinned against you and disobeyed your will. But now show us your greatness of heart, and treat us with your unbounded kindness. (Dn 3:31, 29, 20, 43, 42)[1]

Opening Prayer

The facilitator of the session may lead the prayer. Others in the group may be asked to proclaim the readings.

Let us pray
for God's forgiveness and for the happiness it brings

Pause for silent prayer.

Father,
you show your almighty power
in your mercy and forgiveness.
Continue to fill us with your gifts of love.
Help us to hurry toward the eternal life you
    promise
and come to share in the joys of your kingdom.
Grant this through our Lord Jesus Christ, your
    Son,
who lives and reigns with you and the Holy
    Spirit,
one God, for ever and ever.[2]

LITURGY OF THE WORD

The readings are proclaimed.

---

[1]Twenty-Sixth Sunday in Ordinary Time: "Entrance Antiphon," *The Sacramentary.*

[2]Twenty-Sixth Sunday in Ordinary Time: "Opening Prayer," *The Sacramentary.*

First Reading
Numbers 11:25–29

Overview of the Book of Numbers: The name "Numbers" comes from the description of the census in chapter 1. The laws contained in the Book of Numbers are directed to a people on a journey through the promised land. The material in the Book of Numbers extends over multiple centuries and comes from various ancient biblical sources. The narrative portion of Numbers belongs to an earlier period, while the laws were written during a later time in Israel's history. A portion of Numbers parallels the story of Exodus, especially stories of the grumbling, rebellious Israelites in the desert. "The incidents in Exodus stress the patience of Yahweh, who always listens to Israel's needs and intervenes to help. Numbers 11–21, on the other hand, stresses that the people's constant rebellion led Yahweh to punish them time and again. But each time Moses intervenes and begs for the sake of the people, and God softens his anger and turns back his punishments or heals the victims."[3]

Later biblical authors of Numbers looked back on the rebellion and failures of their ancestors and believed that the trials and hardship they endured were God's punishment for rebellious behavior. "They could look back on the centuries of injustice, disobedience, and false worship, the condemnations of the prophets, the failures of the kings, and know that the loss of their freedom and land in exile had been richly deserved. God cannot be pushed too far without asserting his own justice and honor. Yet even at a late hour, he could turn from his anger and spare them, if they would only turn to him."[4] It was a constant theme for Israel: Israel sinned; God punished; Israel repented; God forgave and restored.

It is at the end of Numbers that leadership of Israel is passed on to Joshua at the death of Moses and Israel begins its conquest of the promised land.

---

[3]Lawrence Boadt, *ROT,* 192.

[4]Ibid., 193.

Today's Pericope: In today's reading Moses appointed seventy elders to join him in leading the people. The meandering people of the desert periodically stopped and pitched their tents. The "meeting tent" was erected a distance from the main camp. Yahweh gave Moses directions and answered his questions in this tent. God's presence was made visible and manifest by a cloud that rested in front of the entrance to the tent. Yahweh instructed Moses to appoint the seventy elders to help him guide, direct, and lead the people of Israel. A special ceremony of investiture was celebrated in which God's Spirit was invoked and came to rest on the elders. They were obviously endowed with a temporary, charismatic gift of prophecy. Two elders, not present for the Spirit-filled manifestation, were bestowed with a belated exhibition of the same gift of prophecy.

Medad and Eldad were not official members of the seventy. They did not share in legitimate succession. Joshua urged Moses to stop the men from exercising the ministry they were unauthorized to perform. Joshua was probably afraid that the action of the two would put Moses' authority in jeopardy.[5] "[T]he Spirit cannot be confined to regularly appointed offices. Its freedom to blow where it wills is a pointer to the day when the whole people of God will prophecy—an aspiration that Christian faith can see fulfilled at Pentecost."[6]

Religious structures that are created by human hands are subject to the will of God. God's gifts are for the benefit of the community—they serve the community—not the individual who received the gift. No one is rendered *less than* by the distribution of God's gifts among many.

Responsorial Psalm
Psalm 19:8, 10, 12–14

This psalm is used at the Easter Vigil and on the third Sunday in Ordinary Time, Cycle C. It is a prayer that the supplicant be cleansed of secret faults, especially the sin of pride. The connection to the first reading is unclear. Perhaps it is an exhortation to all people not to allow the sin of pride to get in the way of God's saving deeds.

Second Reading
James 5:1–6

(Refer to the twenty-second Sunday in Ordinary Time for an overview of the Letter of James.)

Today's Pericope: Today's reading from the Letter of James is the tenth in his series of exhortations and it is based on the patriarch's name, Asher (Gn 49:20). The letter warns the rich employer not to oppress his employee. James's parenesis is a teaching on social justice. James insists that God has heard the pleas of the oppressed whose cries have reached all the way to "the Lord of hosts" (an Old Testament allusion to Yahweh, who cared for the rights of the poor and oppressed).[7]

Concerned with Jesus' immanent return, James was bent on preparing his community. "Concern yourselves with things that really matter—plan for the eternal, long haul." James exhorted his community to worry about primary eschatological concerns, not wealth and possessions. Unlike his biblical counterparts, both ancient and contemporary, James upheld the poor and castigated the rich.

James preached a just word in the assembly of believers and in so doing challenges assemblies of all ages to listen to a similar word. Lust for riches is an obstacle to living in the reign of God *now and not yet*. This is word to the complacent rich who are so absorbed in the concerns of their fortune that they fail to pay attention to what really matters—their relationship with God and to the rest of the world. Wealth has the propensity to foster inattention to the needs of others. There is a tendency to become "less concerned with God's judgment and insensitive to the values of the gospel. Poverty, on the other hand, was not a good in itself, but seemed to foster reliance on God and a realization of responsibility for other community and society members."[8]

While riches in and of themselves are not evil, they become evil when only a select few are able to enjoy their fruits. When there are starving, oppressed people in the world that have no benefit

---

[5]*DL* (V), 236.
[6]*PL*, 352.

[7]Ibid.
[8]*WWC*, 237.

from such riches, then riches are evil. James castigates employers who do not give a just wage after a hard day's work in the fields. He reminds employers that another Harvester is coming who will expect payment in full. They had better be prepared. The Harvester will judge those who neglect the cries of the poor and oppressed.

The gospel is proclaimed.

Gospel

Mark 9:38–43, 45, 47–48. If anyone causes the "little ones" who believe in Jesus to stumble, it would be better for him if he were thrown into the sea.

STEP 1
NAMING ONE'S EXPERIENCE

What were your first impressions? What was your first response to the gospel (or the other readings)? What captured your attention?

Each person names his or her initial impression. Statements should be brief. No reasons should be given at this time. All simply listen without agreeing or disagreeing.

STEP 2
UNDERSTANDING

In a brief statement, explain what you think this gospel is trying to convey.

STEP 3
INPUT FROM VISION/STORY/TRADITION

Liturgical Context

Today's liturgy is the third in a three-part, unified sequence. In today's gospel Jesus challenges his disciples' penchant for power and control. John, vividly revealing his intolerance, insists that a non-Christian exorcist who cast out demons in Jesus' name be silenced. Jesus chastised John's insolence by reminding him that anyone who is for Jesus is not against him. It is a reminder to all Christians to be open to God's Spirit working in surprising

ways. It is a sobering reflection that invites us to welcome all who offer God's compassion to others, even nonbelievers. They are, according to today's gospel, somehow united with us. It is a powerful message of ecumenism.

We are reminded in today's Entrance Antiphon that God judges us—and has every reason to judge us. We are consoled in our sinfulness that God shows us greatness of heart and unbounded kindness. When we behave like John in today's gospel, this is a most assuring word. It is a message we are not to miss. The opening prayer echoes it again—only through God's mercy and forgiveness will we know happiness. We are challenged by God's Word, but in the challenge we are constantly given the hope of his mercy.

The gospel's exhortation to "receive" the "little ones" leads us to James's Letter. The "little ones" are the poor and oppressed. It is a strong, clear exhortation that we simply cannot ignore if we wish to follow the teaching of Christ. The gospel's teaching regarding the poor is not an option. It lies at the heart of the kerygma. In the spirit of James's Letter the church fathers admonish us:

> "If everyone kept only what is necessary for ordinary needs and left the surplus to the poor, wealth and poverty would be abolished.... Are you not a thief? The bread you store belongs to the hungry. The cloak kept in your closet belongs to those who lack clothing. The money you keep hidden away belongs to the needy. Thus you oppress as many people as you are in a position to help."[9]

Gospel Exegesis

The facilitator provides input from critical biblical scholarship on this text. This input includes insights as to how people would have heard the gospel in Jesus' time.

A strong belief in an overactive spirit world prevailed in first-century Palestine. The spirits had the power to create havoc in the lives of the people. A non-Christian exorcist invoked the power of

---

[9] St. Basil (329–379), *Homélie 6 contre la richesse*, 7, in A. Hamman, *Riches et pauvres dans l'Eglise ancienne*, Lectures chrétiennes 6 (Paris: Grassat, 1962), 76, in *DL* (V), 238.

Jesus' name and successfully cast out a demon in today's gospel. We are made privy to John's intolerance. The exorcist in question, even though not a follower of Jesus, was aware of the power Jesus possessed. He was not against Jesus, he was for him. The results speak for themselves. The man cast out demons in the power of Jesus' name and they were gone. The exorcist acknowledged Jesus' power and the results were clear—a "mighty work" was accomplished. The bottom line? Anyone who acts justly and accomplishes a good and mighty work in the name of Jesus cannot be against him—she or he is indeed aligned with him. "In a Christian setting the statement means that one is a member of Jesus' church as long as one does not categorically separate oneself from him."[10]

This is the first time in all of the Synoptic Gospels in which John takes a stand alone. In Luke's gospel John and his brother James show similar intolerance when they want to rain fire upon the Samaritan village that refused hospitality to them. John's attempt to construct a power-based barrier around who is authorized to extend Jesus' ministry of compassion is met with swift denunciation by Jesus. John "equates exorcism with the accrual of status and power, and wishes to maintain a monopoly over it."[11] This is laughable in light of the disciples' own inability to perform exorcisms in verses 14–29. Their intolerance is also in direct violation to the exhortation to "receive" in verse 37. Jesus demands inclusivity, not exclusivity. One can almost hear the childish complaint, "They are not on our team, so why should they have the same power you gave to us?" "John's censure is based on the fact that the stranger 'was not following us.' The disciples want to be followed, not followers. Never was a 'royal we' less appropriate!"[12]

Rather than openly chastise the petty intolerance, Jesus chose to use it as a teachable moment. He gave three reasons why the exorcist should not be stopped. The first and obvious reason: anyone who performs powerful works in Jesus' name cannot at the same time speak badly of him. The second reason is not only obvious, it is a truism: anyone who is not against him is for him. Ironically, Peter and the disciples would certainly consider themselves

among those who are "for him." However, who, but they, turned against him in the end?

The third reason is the most important, judging by the tone, the accompanying *Amen* saying, and the use of the word *Messiah*. Jesus is not only willing to accept the hospitality of strangers, but even the simplest acts of kindness have redemptive value. John is concerned with the threatened roles of power whereas Jesus cares only that his ministry of love, mercy, and compassion continue. He welcomes anyone who offers similar works of mercy and justice.[13] There is no place for attitudes of "holier than thou" in the service of God's people. Such attitudes are unacceptable and, above all, delusional. Disciples of the Lord are not the only ones who share in his ministry of healing and liberation. Christians are to support all efforts to extend compassion and redemptive love to others—whether or not the genesis is Christian. Similarly, anyone who offers mercy to Christians is rewarded in the reign of God.

Karl Rahner's designation of the "anonymous Christian" is certainly affirmed by this gospel. One's life is the testament by which the person is judged. "[I]t is practice, 'not the right name,' that is recognized in the kingdom."[14] Every action taken in the name of Christ, every kindness shown to a disciple of Jesus will not go unnoticed or unrewarded by God. The "reward" is the gratuitous, totally unmerited gift of God.

Jesus' teaching is also an admonishment to anyone attempting to erect exclusive boundaries around the community of faith. One surefire way to subvert the lust to control a group is to make sure the definition of *belonging* is inclusive and adaptable. Jesus cements his argument by showing the disciples how just as an *outsider* might generate life and healing, an *insider* is capable of serious betrayal.

Jesus once again stood up against the ritual purity laws of his day. He insisted that anyone who caused "a little one" to stumble had best cut off his hand and throw it into the fire. We are horrified by the thought of losing one's hand, the disability, the pain, and so on. For a first-century lis-

[10]*MARK*, 146.
[11]*BSM*, 261
[12]Ibid.

[13]Ibid., 262.
[14]Ibid.

tener such an action would illicit a similar response, but there would be another more pressing issue: to have a hand removed would also make them unacceptable in the eyes of God and thereby cut off from the community—it would have rendered them ritually impure. Things that were not whole were also not ritually pure. Those with deformities were considered unclean. "In the same way, the Markan Jesus gives place to moral behavior over against physical wholeness. Mark shows through the many healings that it is God's will to make people whole. Yet rather than cause someone else to sin, it is better to cut off one's own hands and be thrown into Gehenna (9:42–49). Thus, physical wholeness is not a criterion for being acceptable to God; it is what comes out of the heart."[15] That which comes from a person's heart is to be a source of life, not death.

Mark also alerts us to conflict within the community. He returns to the theme of least/greatest (last week's gospel)—"the little ones who believe in me." The word *scandalize* in Mark's gospel usually refers to causing to stumble or rejection of the kingdom. It is difficult to believe that such scandals might arise from within the community. But Jesus makes it clear that they do indeed arise from within. It is better for the offender to die than to cause such scandal. He will repeat this in reference to the betrayal by Judas.

Verse 43 mentions Gehenna, probably in reference to the constant embers of the burning trash dump outside the walls of the city of Jerusalem. The second reference in verse 48, however, refers to eschatological judgment. Ched Myers insists that the traditional interpretation of the sayings concerning the hand, foot, and eye misses the point.[16] Traditional interpretation draws from the Jewish understanding of the eye, hand, and foot as the "sites" of aggressive acts. Thus, the eye, hand, and foot are the means by which a person sins or causes another to sin.

There is something else going on here. In first-century Palestine (as well as in many modern Muslim courts) punishment meted out by secular justice demanded that the body part used in the commission of a crime be amputated. It was considered a *liberalization* of the death penalty. The hand was amputated for crimes of theft, fraud, and forgery. The foot was amputated for crimes of robbery and repeated thefts, and in the case of fugitive slaves. The eye was removed for crimes of adultery and sexual misconduct. Mark, all too aware of the secular form of justice, was alluding to it, and in so doing, suggesting leniency when it came to disciplining errant members of the community. Mark thus rejected any form of justice that favored execution of informants and defectors in order to protect the safety of the community. "Mark's exhortations call for the expulsion (but not execution) of the informer/apostate, for the sake of the 'whole body.'"[17] Myers insists that his interpretation makes more sense due to the phrase in verse 49 which asserts that everyone in the community must be seasoned with salt and fire. Salt and fire were used to close and heal a wound after amputation.

Mark continues his teaching of nonviolence. The way of the kingdom is a way that fosters peace, unity, reconciliation, and conflict management and resolution within the messianic community. He also insists that any boundaries of social exclusivity be breached and that good outsiders be welcomed and recalcitrant insiders be expelled, always with the possibility of forgiveness, reconciliation, and restoration within the community.

Proclaim the gospel again.

Sometimes we gain new insights when we hear the text after the interpretation is given. Someone from the group proclaims the gospel a second time.

STEP 4
TESTING

Conversation with the Liturgy and the Scriptures

Test your original understanding in dialogue with the text.

(You might consider breaking into smaller groups.)

---

[15] *MAM,* 158.
[16] *BSM,* 263.

[17] Ibid.

Now that you've heard the exegesis, were there any new insights? How do you feel about it? How does your original understanding of this gospel compare with what we just shared? How does this story speak to your life?

Sharing Life Experience

Participants share an experience from their lives that connects with the biblical interpretation just presented.

I am reminded of the woman who felt guilty because she could not participate in mystagogia. She was a single mother. She needed to spend every hour she could with her child. The only time the group met was when she volunteered two hours a week in a spousal abuse center. Her catechist very wisely informed her that she was already living mystagogia. Sometimes we think that things have to be generated from within the Church for them to be Christian or holy. We fail to see that even secular efforts to offer compassion are "rewarded" by God. Today's gospel reminds us that we are to accept all acts of kindness from "outsiders"; that they are, in essence, "with us."

Often we experience more betrayal at the hands of insiders than we do at the hands of outsiders. It is that betrayal which stings the most. Somehow Christians are supposed to know better. Yet, if today's gospel teaches us anything, it is a reminder that we are not immune from becoming outsiders by our actions. The most hurtful experiences in ministry have been the result of encounters with "good Christians" who through gossip, backbiting, and petty annoyances have caused hurt in the lives of other Christians. Those who think they have the only "truth" and lash out at others who do not share the same "truth" live in the mirror image of John's intolerance in today's gospel.

John is a prototype for many of us in parish life today. How many times have I unconsciously approached an idea or a newcomer with suspicious eyes because the idea or the person might just threaten my own position of power—real or imagined—in the community? It is so human. And because it is such obnoxious behavior, we do not want to acknowledge it—so we deny it. My prayer is that I resist such temptations. I usually feel such feelings in my gut, however, and denial is difficult. I am usually forced to make a decision. I usually decide to walk through my feelings of inadequacy and be open to what is

presented (at least I hope that I do). There are no doubt times when I have chosen to give in to those feelings and in so doing became an obstacle in God's creative action.

This gospel particularly touches me on the home front. Someone close to me has an incredibly intimate relationship with God. However, it is not the relationship I would have chosen. (How arrogant of me!) I am struck by this person's wisdom, gleaned in less than traditional means, yet nevertheless incredible wisdom. My inclination is to be suspicious, yet I cannot deny the truth in what I see. Today's gospel reminds me that God's actions do not always follow the course we/I assume they will follow. God can and will choose whomever God wishes and in any way he chooses to manifest love to his children. I had better get out of the way and let God be God.

Today's gospel is also an exhortation against triumphalism. It is very easy to get stuck in a mode that says, "We have the whole truth and nothing but the truth." I/we can be very smug about our tradition and think we are the only game in town. I thank God for the RCIA because it, above all other things, constantly challenges me to exorcise that attitude. Not only does the RITE constantly challenge against such attitudes, but I am also awed by the people who come to our doors with a faith life and relationship with God, born in other traditions, which make my own faith seem small and insignificant.

In reflecting on the gospels for these weeks I am struck by Jesus' understanding of the human heart. He had no degrees in psychology, but his understanding of the human psyche is beyond measure. He constantly challenges me to move out of my petty intolerance, my blindness, and my denial.

What was Mark trying to tell his community? If you were to put yourself in the story, how would you relate to John? To the exorcist? To Jesus? Are there people in your community who have been similarly invited into inactivity because they do not possess the appropriate authority (power) to act? In what way is this a relevant word for today's parishes? In what way does this gospel challenge your community today? In what way has this conversation with the scriptures for today's liturgy invited change in your life? In what way are the biblical themes of covenant, exodus, creation, and community evident in today's readings? Do you still feel the same way about this text as when you began? Has your original understanding been stretched, challenged, or affirmed?

STEP 5
DECISION

The gospel demands a response.

In what concrete way might your parish be invited to respond? Are there any attitudes or behaviors you would like to change as a result of today's conversation? What one concrete action will you take this week in response to the liturgy today?

Pastoral Considerations: Continue the dialogue from last week.

Christian Initiation: Is anyone ready to celebrate a rite of acceptance or rite of welcome? This would be an appropriate Sunday to celebrate a rite of full communion.

DOCTRINAL ISSUES

What Church truth/teaching/doctrinal issue could be drawn from the gospel for the twenty-sixth Sunday in Ordinary Time?

Participants suggest possible doctrinal themes that flow from the readings.

Possible Doctrinal Themes

Ecumenism; nonviolence; social justice; Vatican II teaching on non-Christians; Christian community; reconciliation; peace and unity; conversion; discipleship; moral teaching; parochialism

Present the doctrinal material at this time.

1. The facilitator gives input on a particular doctrinal issue of his or her prior choosing. OR
2. The group chooses a doctrinal issue from the list they created. They read together from the Doctrinal Appendix or other appropriate, official Church documents and the works of respected theologians.

(Many doctrinal issues are found in the Doctrinal Appendix at the back of this workbook. If you are choosing an issue from this resource, please refer to it now.)

Reflection questions centered around the chosen doctrinal theme can be found at the end of each topic in the Doctrinal Appendix. The questions are based on the five-step reflection process. If you choose a topic not included in the Doctrinal Appendix, craft your own questions according to the same five-step process.

Following the reflection questions you will be reminded to return to chapter 7, "Preparing the Catechetical Session," to assist you in crafting your own session.

Closing Prayer

Lord, may this eucharist
in which we proclaim the death of Christ
bring us salvation
and make us one with him in glory,
for he is Lord for ever and ever.[18]

---

[18]Twenty-Sixth Sunday in Ordinary Time, "Prayer After Communion," *The Sacramentary.*

Twenty-Seventh Sunday in Ordinary Time

Environment

See the twenty-second Sunday in Ordinary Time.

INTRODUCTORY RITES

Entrance Antiphon (or Opening Song)

O Lord, you have given everything its place in the world, and no one can make it otherwise. For it is your creation, the heavens and the earth and the stars: you are the Lord of all. (Est 13:9, 10–11)[1]

Opening Prayer

The facilitator of the session may lead the prayer. Others in the group may be asked to proclaim the readings.

Let us pray
before the face of God in trusting faith

Pause for silent prayer.

Almighty and eternal God,
Father of the world to come,
your goodness is beyond what our spirit can touch
and your strength is more than the mind can bear.
Lead us to seek beyond our reach
and give us the courage to stand before your
    truth.
We ask this through Christ our Lord.[2]

LITURGY OF THE WORD

The readings are proclaimed.

First Reading
Genesis 2:18–24

(Refer to the tenth Sunday in Ordinary Time for an overview of Genesis.)

Today's Pericope: Today's reading from Genesis is from an earlier tradition—the Yahwist (J) account of the creation story. The later creation tradition is from the Priestly (P) source in Genesis 1. The priestly tradition places the creation of man and woman at the culmination of God's creative work. The Yahwist places it at the heart, at the center. In the priestly story people are created after the animals in both sexes. In the Yahwist account man (male) is created first and "he made woman from man's flesh and human community was created."[3] Animals are then created and "man" names them, thus giving him dominion over them (naming something indicates control over the thing named). Woman is created from the rib of the man. The etymology of the word *rib* is uncertain. However, its meaning professes the "common humanity of man and woman."[4]

The New Testament authors (of Corinthians, Colossians, and Timothy) used the J tradition rather than the Priestly tradition to support the subordinate role of women in the complementarity of men and women—not the subordination of one over the other. The story of the rib is etiological. It is intended to answer the question of why the man leaves his parents and marries a woman. "It is because man and woman share a common humanity and are complementary to each other, and therefore neither is complete without the other."[5] In the Hebrew mind-set "one flesh" means far more than physical union. It involves the totality of the person in contrast to God—the goodness and the flaws. Flesh includes the physical and the spiritual totality of human nature.

Responsorial Psalm
Psalm 128:1–6

Today's psalm paints an idealistic portrait of family life in Israel. The theology that underpins the psalm comes from Deuteronomy. Faithful adherence to the Torah will result in happiness and

[1]Twenty-Seventh Sunday in Ordinary Time: "Entrance Antiphon," *The Sacramentary.*

[2]Twenty-Seventh Sunday in Ordinary Time: "Alternative Opening Prayer," *The Sacramentary.*

[3]*ROT,* 118.
[4]*PL,* 354.
[5]Ibid.

prosperity. Ultimately, virtue is the foundation of family life. The psalm is an appropriate complement to the Genesis story of the beginning of the institution of marriage.

Second Reading
Hebrews 2:9–11

Overview of the Letter to the Hebrews: The identity of this epistle's author is not known. The Letter to the Hebrews and 1 John are the only books of the New Testament that do not begin with an introduction naming the writer. Paul was given credit for authorship as early as the second century. Clement of Alexandria ascribed to the view of Pantaenus in believing that Paul wrote this letter in Hebrew for the Hebrew-speaking community and that Luke later translated it into Greek. Others accepted that assumption. Origen, however, was quick to point out that there existed a sharp contrast between Paul's known writings and this letter. He did, however, accept Pauline authorship only in a wide, general sense. Origen maintained that the theology and thoughts were Paul's but the writing was done by someone who knew the mind and heart of Paul—but it was not Paul. He had not a clue who that might be, however. By as late as the fourth century, the West had accepted Pauline authorship and declared the book canonical.[6] It would not be until the fifteenth century that the genesis of this letter would be once again called into question. In 1516 Erasmus raised the red flag of doubt. He was the first to do so after the book was placed in the official canon. Today, however, scholars, "almost without exception,"[7] do not ascribe to the belief that Paul is either the direct or indirect author of this work. The contrast between Paul and this author is too great. There are not only differences in style and vocabulary, but also in structure. "The divergences from Paul in vocabulary, style, sentence structure, and patterns of thought are more numerous and more notable than the resemblances."[8]

It is believed that the author was well versed in Hellenistic thought. Evidence of this assertion is the writer's use of dualistic constructs such as his consistent use of the difference between earthly and heavenly realities. Earthly realities were "merely a shadow" of the heavenly realities.[9] Elevating the heavenly realm and denigrating the earthly plane of existence are Platonic in origin, similar to the philosophy of the Jewish Hellenist, Philo of Alexandria. Some scholars suggest that the author of the epistle may have been a student of Philo who eventually converted to Christianity. This is perhaps one of the reasons the Letter to the Hebrews is very similar to the writings of Philo.

A primary motif for this author is the historical reality of the redemptive work of Christ and his eschatological fulfillment. Its primary theme is the priesthood of Christ ("the centrality of Christ precisely as priest is not a characteristic Pauline idea").[10] Jesus is not only the eternal preexistent Son of God, he is also high priest. The letter attests to Jesus' humanity, which is the means by which Jesus is in solidarity with the human race and therefore the perfect and only mediator. Jesus' death is akin to sacrifice. Novel to this epistle is the doctrine which asserts that more than Jesus' resurrection was required to assure salvation for the world; it was his ascension into glory. Jesus had to return to take his rightful place on the throne with the Father. This is the means by which human beings gain access to heaven's portals. The epistle also insists that the sacrifice of Jesus superseded the old covenant made with Israel.

The readers are exhorted not to forswear their Christian tradition. Some believe the intended audience was gentile. Others believe it was Jewish. If gentile, why would there be need to alert them to the inefficacy and danger of Old Testament sacrifice? It would not have been part of their consciousness or observance in the first place. They were not formed in the old covenant. The exhortation more logically could be understood as addressing Jewish Christians rather than gentile Christians. "We would date it about 85 and regard it as written to Greek-speaking Jewish Christians in Italy (probably Rome)."[11] The letter is considered a letter of exhortation because it was a warning

---

[6]M. Bourke Myles, "The Epistle to the Hebrews," *NJBC*, 920.

[7]Ibid.

[8]*DOB*, 349.

[9]M. Bourke Myles, "The Epistle to the Hebrews," *NJBC*, 921.

[10]*DOB*, 349.

[11]*PL*, 354.

against apostasy. It was a word exhorting Christians who had not grown to maturity in their Christian faith not to forsake Christ.

The letter compared the church to the wandering people of God in the desert. Just like Israel wandered in the desert before their entry into the promised land, Christians exist in a desert-like experience until Christ returns. The community exists in an "in between" time—"between the Christ event and the parousia."[12] Israel grew lackadaisical about God in the desert and they were ultimately punished. Imagine what will happen to those who are beneficiaries of the incredible gift of salvation offered by the priesthood of Christ and still turn away from it! Seriously consider the implications of forsaking their heritage! Such was the letter's word of urgent exhortation.

Today's Pericope: In this pericope and the pericopes for the next two Sundays the author crafts his argument for the eschatological high priesthood of Jesus. Even though Jesus is not from the tribe of Levi, he nevertheless holds the necessary qualifications to assume the role of high priest. Jesus shares our humanity and in so doing, in solidarity with us, calls us brothers and sisters. In tandem with the profession of Jesus' humanity, the author posits Jesus' other reality—as the preexistent Son of God who was present at the creation of the world—who in fact ordained it!

Christ was made "perfect" through his suffering and death. Reginald Fuller maintains that perfect, in this sense, means to accomplish a goal or to fulfill a destiny.[13] To define the word in the moral sense would mean that he was not morally perfect from the very beginning.

Through Jesus' suffering and death he accomplished the destiny for which he was sent—the salvation of the human race. In so doing, he became our high priest. As high priest he pleaded for our lives before the Father. In order to effectively do so, he had to have firsthand experience of our limitations and human infirmities.

The gospel is proclaimed.

---

[12]Ibid., 344.

[13]Ibid., 355.

Gospel
Mark 10:2–16. The Pharisees ask Jesus a question about divorce.

STEP 1
NAMING ONE'S EXPERIENCE

What were your first impressions? What was your first response to the gospel (or the other readings)? What captured your attention?

Each person names his or her initial impression. Statements should be brief. No reasons should be given at this time. All simply listen without agreeing or disagreeing.

STEP 2
UNDERSTANDING

In a brief statement, explain what you think this gospel is trying to convey.

STEP 3
INPUT FROM VISION/STORY/TRADITION

Liturgical Context

The gospel readings for this Sunday and next Sunday (a compact unit) take place between Jesus' second and third Passion predictions. Jesus continues his march toward Jerusalem. Along the way he is approached by Pharisees who question him about the laws surrounding divorce. Jesus refuses to be sidetracked in a legalistic debate. He hearkens back to the will of God. Divorce is not the issue—marriage is the issue. God's intention for marriage is based on creation. God created men and women to live in loving, covenantal love. Jesus also continues his message of nonviolence and receptivity to the kingdom in his welcoming of the children. Healthy family life is important in the reign of God.

The pericope involving the children is believed to have something to do with the question of infant baptism in the first century. Tertullian records the use of this passage as a defense of the practice of infant baptism. The word *hinder* was commonly used in a baptismal context and referred to the inquiry involving whether anything hindered the candidates from becoming baptized Christians. It is possible that there are roots of a baptismal formula inherent in this passage.

Jesus' teaching in the gospel is echoed in the liturgical prayers of the Wedding Mass:

Opening Prayer:

> Father, you have made the bond of marriage a
>   holy mystery,
> a symbol of Christ's love for his Church.
> Hear our prayers for N. and N.
> With faith in you and in each other
> they pledge their love today.
> May their lives bear witness
> to the reality of that love...."[14]

OR

Alternative Opening Prayer:

> Father,
> when you created mankind
> you willed that man and wife should be one.
> Bind N. and N.
> in the loving union of marriage
> and make their love fruitful
> so that they may be living witnesses
> to your divine love in the world....[15]

Nuptial Blessing

> My dear friends, let us turn to the Lord and
>   pray
> that he will bless with his grace this woman (or
>   N.)
> Now married in Christ to this man (or N.)
> and that (through the sacrament of the body
>   and blood of Christ)
> he will unite in love the couple he has joined
>   in this holy bond.

> Father,
> by your power you have made everything out
>   of nothing.
> In the beginning you created the universe
> and made mankind in your own likeness.
> You gave man the constant help of woman
> so that man and woman should no longer be
>   two, but one flesh,
> and you teach us that what you have united
> may never be divided.
> Father,
> by your plan man and woman are united,
> and married life has been established
> as the one blessing that was not forfeited by
>   original sin
> or washed away in the flood.
> Look with love upon this woman, your daughter,
> now joined to her husband in marriage.
> She asks your blessing.
> Give her the grace of love and peace.
> May she always follow the example of the holy
>   women
> whose praises are sung in the scriptures.
> May her husband put his trust in her
> and recognize that she is his equal
> and the heir with him to the life of grace.
> May he always honor her and love her
> as Christ loves his bride the Church.
> Father,
> keep them always true to your commandments.
> Keep them faithful in marriage
> and let them be living examples of Christian
>   life.
> Give them the strength which comes from the
>   gospel
> so that they may be witnesses of Christ to others.
> [Bless them with children
> and help them to be good parents.
> May they live to see their children's children.]
> And, after a happy old age,
> grant them the fullness of life with the saints
> in the kingdom of heaven.
> We ask this through Christ our Lord.[16]

Today also begins the proclamation of the Letter to the Hebrews. We will read this in the liturgical

---

[14]Wedding Mass, "Opening Prayer," *The Sacramentary*.

[15]Wedding Mass, "Alternative Opening Prayer," *The Sacramentary*.

---

[16]Wedding Mass, "Nuptial Blessing," *The Sacramentary*.

assembly over the next six weeks. These readings have no connection with the first reading and the gospel. They were chosen for the Lectionary because they shed light on the mystery of salvation, which is celebrated in every eucharistic liturgy, the source and summit of our lives.

We are reminded in today's opening prayer that only through God are we forgiven and offered the peace we need to live the way of salvation. Forgiveness is at the heart of marriage—without it, Jesus' insistence on the indissolubility of marriage is impossible. The alternative opening prayer reminds us that all the strength we need to live the truth of the gospel is freely given to us by God. The eucharist nourishes and strengthens us to live the life of love, forgiveness, and reconciliation we are called to live.

Gospel Exegesis

The facilitator provides input from critical biblical scholarship on this text. This input includes insights as to how people would have heard the gospel in Jesus' time.

According to form-critical analysis it would appear that Jesus' teaching is a two-part catechism—a section about marriage and a section on the family.[17] Prompted by a question about divorce, Jesus posits his creation-based theology of marriage. While there is much debate over Jesus' teaching regarding divorce, theologians for the most part agree that Jesus' intention was to restore marriage to the way God intended it to be since the dawn of creation—as a community of love between two partners transcending even the physical union. It is a covenant of love in which lovers desire only what is good for the beloved. It is why men and women leave their parents and cling to one another in lifelong committed love. "Jesus prohibited divorce under the assumption that the marriage involved is a real marriage."[18] Underlying the text is not what constitutes the conditions for divorce, but what an ideal marriage should be. It is love based on the two great commandments—the same love that should guide the entire church. The antidote to broken relationships is ideally forgiveness, reconciliation, and the rekindling of flames of love

that lie smoldering in the ashes of disappointment, resentment, and deep woundedness. Often, however, the ideal falls short and we are faced with the realism of fractures so deep that they are irreparable—thus divorce.

Mark geographically alerts his readers that his drama is heating up—tension is mounting. Jesus proceeds southward to Jerusalem to face his enemies. The drama builds, the reader is aware that Jesus stands on the precipice of mounting conflict. Will he take a wrong step? Jesus enters into conflict with the Pharisees, very much like the confrontation in Mark 7:1. Jesus actively pursues his teaching mission as he moves closer to his destination. His teaching today about marriage and divorce constitutes a radical challenge for his followers. It is an absolute word yet exceptions to Jesus' hard and fast teaching do appear in later New Testament sources (Mt 5:32; 19:9; 1 Cor 7:10–16).

The Pharisees ask Jesus about the controversial subject of divorce.[19] Debate over the legal ramifications of divorce was nothing new to people in charge of legislating such matters. The Torah did not explicitly spell out rules for divorce. The only legislation there was (other than the prohibition of a divorced couple to remarry each other found in Dt 24:1–4) was the allowance of a husband to divorce his wife for a scandalous act. Custom was simply taken for granted. There were no divorce courts to settle such disputes. All that was required was for the husband to produce a "writ of divorce" and present it to his wife. Even though a husband was allowed to divorce his wife, she was left with no recourse on her own behalf.

It is possible that the Pharisees simply wanted to hear Jesus' "spin" on a debate that had been going on for quite some time—the Hillel–Shammai debate over divorce. Hillel was a Jewish lawyer who lived between 50 B.C.E. and 20 C.E. He moved from Babylon and started a Pharisaic rabbinic school. He became known as a tolerant, loving person. His popularity grew rapidly. Hillel, a transplant from Babylon and the exile, was not formed in the temple cult. The temple, therefore, did not hold the same importance as it did for his counterpart,

---

[17]*PL*, 355.

[18]*MARK*, 151.

[19]It is possible that the Pharisees initiated the topic of divorce in hopes of baiting Jesus into a conflict with the Herodian family, which was no stranger to divorce.

Shammai, also a Pharisaic rabbi. Hillel's influence is responsible for the Pharisaic movement continuing after the destruction of the temple. Hillel's interpretation of the scriptures helped bring them into the sphere of everyday life rather than to be solely connected to the temple and its worship. Shammai, on the other hand, was a conservative, rigid interpreter of the law. His influence did not continue after the Jewish War.

The argument between the two centered on the one proscription in the law. Deuteronomy 24:1–4 states that a man may divorce his wife for scandalous behavior, an indecent action, and so on. Shammai interpreted this as adultery. A woman would have to be guilty of adultery for a man to divorce her and expel her from their home. Hillel avowed a broad interpretation to the law. A man could divorce his wife for transgressions such as poor culinary skills, publicly speaking to another man, complaining about her in-laws in front of her husband, and on and on.

Jesus refused to be caught up in petty squabbles over the reasons divorce is allowed. He moved the conversation beyond loopholes to the heart of the divorce question. The question is not a question of divorce—it is a question of marriage and what it means.

The Pharisees insisted that Deuteronomy, albeit Moses, allowed divorce. They were correct. Jesus did not challenge their assertion. He simply insisted that the reason Moses allowed divorce in the first place was because of the willfulness of the people—their hardness of heart. The people were unteachable and could not accept God's moral authority or God's intention for humanity since the creation of the world. The text in Deuteronomy was not the formulation of a law, it was a concession to it because of the hubris of the people. Divorce was a concession to human weakness as far as Jesus was concerned.[20] Jesus insisted that God's intention for husband and wife as they stood before each other on creation's stage was unity, love, and complementarity—wholeness, one flesh, the total union of body, soul, and spirit. God's intention was for perfect harmony between husband and wife and for a lasting, unbreakable covenant. This covenant is unbreakable because God joined the two and because the two are formed into one totality. Jesus acknowledged the Mosaic concessions due to sin. "Since sin in principle is done away with in Christ, a reversion to the condition before the fall, where divorce was unknown, becomes feasible."[21]

When alone and in private (designated by the abrupt use of the words *in house*—a place of private instruction of the disciples), Jesus elaborated on his teaching to his disciples. He insisted that marriage after divorce constituted adultery because the first bond was still in place—it was never broken. Jesus went beyond Jewish law by suggesting that even a man would be guilty of adultery against his wife. Scholars suggest that in this instance Mark was pastorally addressing the cultural situation in which Roman law permitted wives to divorce their husbands, thus adapting to the experience and needs of gentile Christians.

There was no provision in Jewish law making it unlawful for a man to commit adultery against his wife. Adultery was understood as the sexual liaison between a married woman and another man—not her husband. "Thus, whereas a woman could commit adultery against her husband, a man could not commit adultery against his own wife, but only against another married man."[22] In Jewish law a woman was not allowed to divorce her husband.[23]

In light of our contemporary experience of "fast foods," "fast marriages," and "fast divorces," Jesus' teaching about divorce is hard to swallow and we try to wiggle out of its clarity. There is very little wiggling room, however. Jesus is clear. He not only transcended Jewish law, but also the contemporary thinking of his day. He was emphatic and his teaching crystal clear: God's intention for marriage has its roots in creation. Two become one flesh; the marriage bond is a lasting covenant; it is a relationship of love and complementarity. It is not to be broken; it is to flourish in mutual love. To break the covenant is a breach of God's design of creation. Jesus' teaching about divorce is af-

---

[20]Daniel J. Harrington, S.J., "The Gospel According to Mark," *NJBC*, 617.

[21]*PL*, 356.

[22]*MARK*, 153.

[23]Daniel Harrington submits that there were some examples of Jewish women who divorced their husbands.

firmed throughout the New Testament (1 Cor 7:10; Mt 19:3–9; 5:31–32; Lk 16:16).

It is no wonder that Jesus referred to creation theology in his teaching about marriage. At the creation of the world God created men and women, and then placed them in the garden, where all things existed in perfect harmony. God created man and woman, entered into covenant with them, and placed them in this paradise. In response to the gratuitous gift of life and God's providence, human beings were not only to love God with their entire heart, mind, and soul, they were to love and care for one another, especially those who could not care for themselves. God gave people dominion over creation—they were to be stewards of that creation. In the perfect world God created, God's intention for marriage was harmony, mutual love, and complementarity. The advent of the Messiah meant the restoration of the perfect harmony of Eden. In the new reign of God, the eschatological, messianic reign, Jesus restores the harmony of Eden. In the reign Jesus came to establish, when believers embrace the cross and live the gospel, the lion and lamb lie down together in peace, and husband and wife live in covenant, indissoluble love. In Jesus' eschatological reign, could it be any other way?

Some scholars suggest that the reason for the absolute nature of Jesus' teaching is the urgency of his message. Jesus believed the parousia was immanent. If so, divorce is hardly an issue worth splitting hairs over. Eschatological concerns are all that matter—promoting the reign of God, preparation for the Lord's return and the parousia. Obviously Jesus' return was not immanent. Disciples had to face the reality of living in the tension of the kingdom of God *now and not yet.* "It is clear that when the Church came to treat Jesus' eschatological enunciation of the absolute prohibition of divorce as a community law, it was compelled to adapt and even modify its absolute character in various ways."[24] The struggling New Testament communities acknowledged their propensity to sin. While delivered from sin's everlasting effects, people were not immune from it and its effects in this world. Once again, as in Deuteronomy, concessions were obviously made. "The point is not

that the particular concessions made in the New Testament, and these only, are valid for all time, but that the New Testament grants to the Church the authority to make concessions that are pastorally necessary, while at the same time keeping Jesus' absolute prohibition before men and women and making clear that nothing short of radical obedience is sinful in the eyes of God, and therefore in need of forgiveness."[25] This is probably why evidence of exceptions and concessions appear in Matthew's gospel written in the latter part of the century.

Jesus' prohibition against divorce is found in more traditions than almost any other saying. Paul professed it in 1 Corinthians 7:10. It is found in today's pericope from Mark and its corollary in Matthew 19:3–9 and the Q source (5:31–32/Lk 16:18). The Q source contained the most definitive, absolute prohibition.[26] Paul, Mark, and Matthew adapt the command in different ways. Paul permits the concession of allowing remarriage for a Christian if divorced by a non-Christian spouse (Pauline Privilege). Matthew adds an exception to today's commands—divorce is allowed in the case of the wife's unchastity.

A rather thought-provoking, unconventional exegesis of this text is presented by Ched Myers. He insists that Jesus is challenging the way in which social practice surrounding divorce is legitimated. Marriage was not simply between husband and wife. Families were wed in this patriarchal arrangement. Myers insists that Jesus' argument is that divorce is necessary because of the male obstinacy, the patriarchal attitudes and practices. God, however, did not intend the patriarchal system. He intended mutuality. Woman is not given over to the control of man to continue his lineage. Man is the one that leaves his patriarchal family and the two become one *sarx*—that is, they are created *equal.* This was revolutionary thinking to those listening. Myers insists that verse 9 is not an absolute prohibition against divorce (it would, after all, overturn the Mosaic law). He maintains that the term for divorce (*apoluse*) was dropped in favor of a term that means to separate (*chorizeto*). Jesus' strong assertion is a criticism of the patriar-

[24]*PL*, 356.

[25]Ibid.
[26]Ibid., 355.

chal system that undermines the unity and equality intended by God at the creation of the world. This equality is particularly articulated in the marriage covenant in Genesis. In Jesus' "aside" with his disciples he gives further explanation. He acknowledges the reality of divorce (as does 1 Cor 7:10), but forbids remarriage—*separation.* Jesus is careful to maintain equality. A man cannot divorce his wife and marry someone else without committing adultery against her. Jewish law allows for a man to commit adultery against another married man, but not his wife. Jesus' injunction also allowed for the woman to divorce (as in Roman law). Jewish law (as mentioned earlier) forbade the woman to initiate divorce.

Divorce is a profound spiritual, mental, and psychological tearing apart of the "one flesh." Myers concludes:

> The teaching acknowledges, however, that divorce is a reality, within which the fundamental issue of justice must not be lost. *Both* parties must have the right to take initiative, and both must accept the responsibilities and limitations involved in the death of a marriage. Again Mark refuses to overlook the *actual* relations of power, no matter how "sacred" the institution. The "least" in this concrete case is the woman, and Mark is making it clear to his community that she can be protected only if she is no longer treated as object, but as equal subject, in situations of conflict resolution.[27]

Following Jesus' teaching on divorce, he addressed the issue of children. It is a proclamation of the reign of God and a message of receptivity. The reign of God must be received in simplicity, just as little children would receive it. Jesus sent the disciples out on their mission of evangelization "as children." Those who rejected them were to experience the fallout of dusty, shaking feet as a witness against them. The children now stand ready to similarly witness against those who refuse the new social change that Jesus insists is the hallmark of his kingdom. Jesus gives complete and full access to all who receive him in faith. There is

tension surrounding the presentation of the children to Jesus. Because they were low-status members of the society, the disciples tried to deter them from approaching. Jesus was annoyed. He opened his arms and welcomed the children. This revolutionary stance turned more than one eyebrow askance and scandalized more than one self-righteous proponent of the status quo. Jesus offers the children free access and threatens to deny access to those who would deter them.

Jesus' catechism of nonviolence continues in this exchange over the children. Children are statusless. Jesus reversed their status. Once again the "last" have been elevated to "first." Jesus simply will not tolerate exclusivity—something the disciples, on the other hand, continue to promote. Children take their new, rightful places in the inner circle. No longer do they exist on the dangerous periphery. In Mark's gospel children usually are found in the seat reserved for "victim." They usually number among the sick and oppressed.

Children have no expectations; they receive in simplicity. This is the posture of all seekers of the kingdom. It is pure gift and is to be received with gratitude and receptivity. Jesus laid hands on the children. He blessed them, and in so doing elevated their status of nonentity to full membership in the community—members who are to be received by all. This is how the church is to treat its children—*all* of them. Mark insists that a posture of nonviolent living has its genesis in the home itself. "Could it be that the discourse of Mark is arguing that if we are to forge a non-violent way of life, we must weed out the structures and practices of violence at their roots? That the validity of nonviolence must pertain to the most basic building block of human social existence: the family?"[28]

Proclaim the gospel again.

Sometimes we gain new insights when we hear the text after the interpretation is given. Someone from the group proclaims the gospel a second time.

---

[27] *BSM,* 266.

[28] Ibid., 268.

Conversation with the Liturgy and the Scriptures

Test your original understanding in dialogue with the text.

(You might consider breaking into smaller groups.)

Now that you've heard the exegesis, were there any new insights? How do you feel about it? How does your original understanding of this gospel compare with what we just shared? How does this story speak to your life?

Sharing Life Experience

Participants share an experience from their lives that connects with the biblical interpretation just presented.

Today's gospel reminds me of four different marriages of people I know. Two were ravaged by separation, pain, and the tearing of "one flesh," but were eventually reunited. Two marriages ended in total separation, the death of the relationship—divorce. For some mysterious reason, the first two were eventually reconciled and the torn flesh returned to wholeness—life, harmony, and mutuality returned; broken, fractured spirits were restored. God healed their marriages. Like the children, however, there had to be receptivity and a willingness to forgive and allow God to restore the covenant. Those who love them consider it a miracle and feel honored to have witnessed the restoration of what God intended to remain indissoluble from the beginning. The marriages in question were indeed an example of what Jesus taught his disciples. Marriage is intended by God to last forever. Human limitations got in the way, and there was a temporary separation.

How does that fit with the experience of the two other couples who were unable to mend the fracture? In both relationships one of the spouses enjoyed a deep, personal relationship with God. Their constant prayer was for the healing of the marriage. Yet healing never took place. In its place was the death of a relationship—divorce. In both cases, one of the parties was simply incapable of entering into the community of covenant love envisioned by God at the creation of the world. Their own human story and the human condition placed such limitations on the relationship that the marriage never stood a chance of succeeding from the beginning. The hallmark of the brokenness in both cases is the refusal (or more aptly, the inability) of one of the parties to offer the free, unconditional gift of self to the other. What seems obvious in today's gospel is that Jesus indeed upheld an ideal. When both parties are capable of the ideal, when both parties are capable of reconciliation, when both parties are open to the healing hand of God, living in a mutual covenant of love is possible. When one or both of the parties is not, the former is impossible.

In a free act of gratuitous mercy, God postponed the immanent parousia expected by Jesus and his contemporaries. Perhaps an extension of that love is evidenced in the Church's pastoral response to situations like the ones I just described. Concessions have been made because we are fallible, sinful people.

One thing I have learned after thirty wonderful years of marriage is that it must be rooted in self-sacrificing love and that it is a daily decision. There are wonderful, awe-inspiring times, times of bliss and exaltation, times etched in joyful perpetuity. But there are also times when KP duty in the foreign legion looks far more attractive. But isn't that the way life is? Isn't that the paschal mystery, and where sacrament strengthens and fortifies? The image of the status-less child also bears light on the implications of marriage. If the child continues Jesus' theme of nonviolence, and the least/greatest exchange, then do we not sometimes encounter the "least of these" snoring loudly on the pillow adjacent to ours? And do we not automatically assume that the role of greatest belongs to none other than the self-righteous "moi"? Jesus' message of inclusivity begins at home.

At my daughter's wedding one of the other young husbands teasingly reminded our new son-in-law, "There is only one thing you have to remember to have a happy marriage—she's always right and you're always wrong!" I think I have heard that cute little joke multiple times since then and in many different contexts. What a revelation! Is that really the posture we as women want to project? I know I am profoundly guilty of the attitude. In discussing this with my friends, we discovered that this posture of control is something we share in common. It is insid-

ious and it is lethal. It certainly does not promote mutuality. It upsets the equality intended for marriage by God. Perhaps it is woman's inherited unconscious rebellion for the centuries of domination. It is, however, just as destructive and sometimes just as controlling. Today's gospel is a wake-up call for me to love as Jesus loves me—unconditionally and without reservation. It is also an invitation to live the radical reign he came to establish. Obviously that begins at home. If I fail to love those I am committed to love, just as Jesus loves me, how can I hope to promote the reign of God? Who would listen? Who would believe that it is worth possessing in the first place? What evidence could I produce?

What was Mark trying to tell his community? How do you feel about the absolute nature of Jesus' teaching on divorce? What does that say to our present experience of marriage, divorce, and annulment? What would it take for couples to realize the ideal he sets forth? In what way does this gospel challenge your community today? In what way has this conversation with the scriptures for today's liturgy invited change in your life? In what way are the biblical themes of covenant, exodus, creation, and community evident in today's readings? Do you still feel the same way about this text as when you began? Has your original understanding been stretched, challenged, or affirmed?

STEP 5
DECISION

The gospel demands a response.

In what concrete way might your parish be invited to respond? Are there any attitudes or behaviors you would like to change as a result of today's conversation? What one concrete action will you take this week in response to the liturgy today?

Pastoral Considerations: Are there any structures in your parish for promoting family life issues, marriages, parenting, issues concerning children? The *Book of Blessings* contains blessings for marriages, anniversaries, families, and children. How might they be effectively used in your parish? Is there a forum for raising issues of family violence, abuse, addictions, or major dysfunction?

Christian Initiation: Perhaps this would be an appropriate time to celebrate a rite of anointing of catechumens. It is a rite that celebrates God's strength for the journey—obviously something sorely needed if one is to live the challenge of today's gospel. A nonsacramental penitential celebration would also be most appropriate in light of the reconciliation themes present in today's liturgy. The blessings and minor exorcisms are intended for use in your gatherings with catechumens.

DOCTRINAL ISSUES

What Church truth/teaching/doctrinal issue could be drawn from the gospel for the twenty-seventh Sunday in Ordinary Time?

Participants suggest possible doctrinal themes that flow from the readings.

Possible Doctrinal Themes

Marriage; kingdom of God; creation; morality; social justice; reconciliation; commandments; two great commandments; messianic reign; Christian family; church—the people of God; paschal mystery; baptism

Present the doctrinal material at this time.

1. The facilitator gives input on a particular doctrinal issue of his or her prior choosing. OR
2. The group chooses a doctrinal issue from the list they created. They read together from the Doctrinal Appendix or other appropriate, official Church documents and the works of respected theologians.

(Many doctrinal issues are found in the Doctrinal Appendix at the back of this workbook. If you are choosing an issue from this resource, please refer to it now.)

Reflection questions centered around the chosen doctrinal theme can be found at the end of each topic in the Doctrinal Appendix. The questions are based on the five-step reflection process. If you choose a topic not included in the Doctrinal Appendix, craft your own questions according to the same five-step process.

Following the reflection questions you will be reminded to return to chapter 7, "Preparing the Catechetical Session," to assist you in crafting your own session.

Closing Prayer

Father, all-powerful and ever-living God,
we do well always and everywhere to give you
    thanks.
You created man in love to share your divine life.
We see his high destiny in the love of husband and
    wife,
which bears the imprint of your own divine love.

Love is man's origin,
love is his constant calling,
love is his fulfillment in heaven.
The love of man and woman
is made holy in the sacrament of marriage,
and becomes the mirror of your everlasting love.
Through Christ the choirs of angels
and all the saints
praise and worship your glory.
May our voices blend with theirs
as we join in their unending hymn of praise.[29]

---

[29]"Preface, Marriage III," *The Sacramentary.*

TWENTY-EIGHTH SUNDAY IN ORDINARY TIME

Environment

See the twenty-second Sunday in Ordinary Time.

INTRODUCTORY RITES

Entrance Antiphon (or Opening Song)

If you, O Lord, laid bare our guilt, who could endure it? But you are forgiving, God of Israel. (Ps 129:3–4)[1]

Opening Prayer

The facilitator of the session may lead the prayer. Others in the group may be asked to proclaim the readings.

Let us pray
in quiet for the grace of sincerity

    Pause for silent prayer.

Father in heaven,
the hand of your loving kindness
powerfully yet gently guides all the moments of
    our day.
Go before us in our pilgrimage of life,
anticipate our needs and prevent our falling.
Send your Spirit to unite us in faith,
that sharing in your service,
we may rejoice in your presence.
We ask this through Christ our Lord.[2]

LITURGY OF THE WORD

The readings are proclaimed.

First Reading
Wisdom 7:7–11

---

[1]Twenty-Eighth Sunday in Ordinary Time: "Entrance Antiphon," *The Sacramentary.*

[2]Twenty-Eighth Sunday in Ordinary Time: "Opening Prayer," *The Sacramentary.*

(Please refer to the thirteenth Sunday in Ordinary Time for an overview of the Book of Wisdom.)

Today's Pericope: Solomon prayed for wisdom, and wisdom was lavishly showered upon him, much to his great joy. He desired it above all else—above wealth, riches, power, prestige, health, and light. Wisdom always exists—it never ends. The sage of this piece of Wisdom literature is writing in a center of Hellenistic culture that is greatly influenced by Jewish thinking. After serious reflection on the scriptures and on life experiences, the sage concludes that only through wisdom is the world led on the right path. Human beings are to seek wisdom above all else—it is to be the object of their desire and their prayers. Wisdom will guide a well-ordered life. Wisdom is a free gift from God. It is one of God's characteristics. Wisdom discerns what is good and what is evil. God's prophets are imbued with wisdom. Wisdom is characteristic of the messianic reign. The comparison between wisdom and wealth is common through all the Wisdom literature of the scriptures. Today's pericope is chosen to accompany the story of the rich young man.

Responsorial Psalm
Psalm 90:12–17

Today's psalm is influenced by the Wisdom literature, which is why it was Solomon's prayer in the first reading.

Second Reading
Hebrews 4:12–13

(Please refer to the twenty-seventh Sunday in Ordinary Time for an overview of the Letter to the Hebrews.)

Today's Pericope: Today's passage is a hymn to God's Word. One certain way to know the will of God is through God's Word. The author of Hebrews draws from Jeremiah 31, which promises the new covenant. One sign of the covenant will be an interior knowledge of what is pleasing to

God. Jesus possessed this interior knowledge. Jesus knew the mind, heart, and the will of his Father through intimate communication with him. Jesus grew in awareness of God's will not only for himself, but also for the people of God. Jesus' response to God's will was a life of faithfulness.

The Word comforts those who turn to its counsel. Like a sword it penetrates the dark recesses of the human soul. It pierces the lies and the denial and exposes them to the truth. The Word judges the heart. The word *judge* originates from the Greek word *kritikis*, the origin of the word *crisis*. "Crisis time means a time for judgment, for decision."[3] The Word of God uncovers the hidden secrets and questionable motives in our hearts and invites transformation. Jesus' life and mission were strengthened and fortified by intimacy with God's Word.

God's Word negotiates human affairs and salvation history. The Word accomplishes what it professes. The Word of God is alive and in the New Testament is understood as the gospel of Jesus Christ.[4] It is a living Word generated from the creative hand of God. God's Word will go forward; it cannot be silenced or stopped. God spoke a generative word and life came into being.

The intended audience of the Letter to the Hebrews was in danger of falling away through lackadaisical attention to its faith (likened to the wandering Israelites in the desert). The people are admonished to take heed. The gospel is serious business and demands constant attention. Failure to grow in the faith is subject to judgment just as rejection of the faith is similarly judged.

The gospel is proclaimed.

Gospel
Mark 10:17–30. Jesus said, "Sell all you have and follow me."

---

[3]*CEH*, 109.

[4]In the Old Testament the Word was understood as Israel's salvation history and the Word of God spoken by the prophets.

STEP 1
NAMING ONE'S EXPERIENCE

What were your first impressions? What was your first response to the gospel (or the other readings)? What captured your attention?

Each person names his or her initial impression. Statements should be brief. No reasons should be given at this time. All simply listen without agreeing or disagreeing.

STEP 2
UNDERSTANDING

In a brief statement, explain what you think this gospel is trying to convey.

STEP 3
INPUT FROM VISION/STORY/TRADITION

Liturgical Context

Today's gospel continues Mark's catechism of the kingdom of God. It continues the question asked in earlier chapters of Mark's gospel concerning who is the least and the greatest in the reign of God. Today Jesus tells the rich man what is expected of him if he wants to be a follower. The rich man cannot accept Jesus' teaching. We are vicariously asked the same question. How would we respond to Jesus' request that we sell everything we have, give it to the poor, and leave all to follow him? The liturgy invites serious reflection and it invites action.

Today's opening prayer prays that God's love be the foundation of our lives and the catalyst for loving others. We pray that our love for God be expressed in eagerness to love others. Concrete expression of that love is evidenced by the way we take care of those who are considered last in the eyes of the world—the poor and disenfranchised. The alternative opening prayer asks that the Spirit unite us in faith so we may be joyful in God's presence as we share in his service. The Communion Antiphon concretely supports the gospel's theme:

"The rich want and go hungry, but nothing shall be lacking to those who fear the Lord (Ps 33:11)."[5]

We are not to forget that Jesus is on the way to Jerusalem when he presents this teaching to his disciples. The gospel is simple, but it is not easy. Jesus does not seem to be making polite suggestions. They are commands. If we say we want to be disciples, then this is what we must do. Jesus not only was teaching his disciples *on the way*, but he was showing them *the way*, and leading them toward it. Jesus was trying to reorient their lives to God's will.

Ultimately, every eucharist we celebrate commits us to the poor and invites the same radical response insisted by Jesus in today's gospel:

> "This eucharist is the sign of your abundant life
> and the unity of all men in your love.
> May it keep us aware of our Christian duty
> to give our brothers a just share in what is ours...."[6]

Gospel Exegesis

The facilitator provides input from critical biblical scholarship on this text. This input includes insights as to how people would have heard the gospel in Jesus' time.

Jesus is still on the way to Jerusalem. In today's gospel Jesus invites a would-be disciple to participate in his reign. When awareness of what it would cost him became all too clear, he was unable to commit. The man was a wealthy, large landowner. We are not informed of this fact until after he has turned away from Jesus' invitation to follow him. Today's gospel is a pronouncement story. Jesus pronounces the arrival of the messianic reign of God. Mark uses three stories in chapter 10 to illustrate Jesus' catechism on wealth and the reign of God: the story of the rich man (vv. 17–22), Jesus teaching his disciples (vv. 23–27), and the teaching regarding the rewards

of giving up riches (vv. 28–31). Mark's theology asserts that wealth is a potential obstacle to the kingdom and that rewards associated with the kingdom far outweigh the sacrifices.

The story begins. A man approaches Jesus. We are not aware he is wealthy. He asks Jesus, "What must I do to obtain *eternal life* (a synonym for the kingdom of God)"? The man calls Jesus "good master." Jesus becomes testy. He insists that no one is good but God. This implied distance between Jesus and God is not faithful to the gospel tradition. Therefore, Jesus' comments probably constituted his annoyance at the man's unrestrained, impetuous address. It also could have been a literary device used by Mark to proclaim Jesus as Son of God. Jesus answers the man's question by listing the second part of the Ten Commandments, the section that deals with relationships between people. Jesus looked at the man and loved him, a response to the man's earnest faithfulness in following the law.

Jesus challenges the man, however. He tells him to go and sell what he has and give it to the poor. Judaism understood wealth as a sign of God's favor. Those who were wealthy were obligated to care for the poor. Some scholars suggest that Jesus' intention was not to formulate a general Christian principle for believers to emulate.[7] Rather, he was addressing this man specifically; he was challenging him to move outside the realm of his comfort zone, the basis of his security. It was an invitation to put his trust and his security in a radically new place—in Jesus—not in his amassed fortune. Jesus invited the man to rely completely on God.

The rich man was faced with a choice (as is the reader and every disciple who confronts the gospel of Jesus). Jesus' call to discipleship was too difficult for the man. Mark no doubt was posing the same question to his readers: "Is Jesus' question too difficult for you, too?"

Another Markan device comes into play at this point in the story: Jesus teaches the crowds, then afterward he teaches the disciples in private. Jesus

---

[5]Twenty-Eighth Sunday in Ordinary Time: "Communion Rite," *The Sacramentary*.

[6]Masses and Prayers for Various Needs and Occasions: In Time of Famine or for Those Who Suffer From Famine, "Prayer Over the Gifts," *The Sacramentary*.

---

[7]See below for Ched Myers's refutation of that suggestion. He insists that Jesus is indeed formulating a new radical Christian principle.

discusses the rich man's decision with his disciples. They are amazed by Jesus' teaching. He overturned a deeply held conviction in their Jewish tradition. Jesus upended the belief that riches are a sign of divine favor. Just in case they missed the point, Jesus shocked them into understanding. It would be easier for a camel to pass through the eye of a needle, than for a rich person to enter the kingdom—in other words, very close to impossible! Some manuscripts substituted the word *kamilon/rope* for the word *kamelon/camel*. A medieval interpretation suggested that in Jerusalem there was a low gate through which a camel could bend low and enter. These interpretations were nothing more than attempts to soften the impact of Jesus' teaching. Just as there was little wiggle room last week for Jesus' absolute teaching on marriage and divorce, there is similarly little wiggle room in this instance. Jesus was saying that it is almost impossible for a rich person to enter the kingdom of God.

No wonder the disciples were incredulous. Who, then, could be saved? Jesus reminded them that with God all things are possible—salvation is only through God. Human beings do not have the power to secure their own salvation, even if they renounce all their wealth. God is the only broker of salvation.

There is an unspoken question on the part of disciples. "What about those who have accepted the challenge of discipleship? What is their reward?" Jesus promises them rewards not only in the eschatological reign of God *not yet*, but also in the eschatological reign of God *now*. Disciples who renounce their possessions will be blessed with rich communal fellowship. Mark adds his own catechism to the equation. Faithful disciples can also expect persecution and suffering. Jesus' hopeful theme of last/first and least/greatest returns and with it the gospel's primary message. The establishment of the reign of God ushers in the great reversal: those who are first will be last, the poor will enter before the rich, and the powerless before the powerful. The expected takes a back seat to the unexpected and words like *surprise, awe,* and *wonder* are the street signs that mark every intersection. The "new heavens and the new earth" is paved with adjectives that describe the magnificent power of God.

There is another, less conventional perspective to consider in this gospel. Scripture scholar Ched Myers pulls no punches as he invites his reader to consider a different hearing of this text: "One hardly need emphasize that this text, which is so crucial to the community ideology of Mark, has been notoriously mishandled by those whose self-interest lies in soft-peddling its criticism of wealth."[8]

Myers concurs with what was suggested above. We are not told until after the exchange with Jesus that the man is a wealthy landowner. We are alerted that an extraordinary exchange is about to take place.

The salutation, *good teacher*, is a rare greeting in Jewish literature. It was probably intended as flattery. In this shame- and honor-based culture, when a man flatters another man, there is an expectation that the flattery will be reciprocated. Jesus did not reciprocate. Instead, he insulted the man—he addressed the man with no title at all!

Theologians have struggled with the Christological implications of Jesus' self-abasement in verse 18. Christology is not even an issue, insists Myers, when Jesus' comment ("only God is good") is understood as a rebuff to the man who is merely setting himself up for a compliment. There is only One who is good (and deserving of a compliment), and that is God.

The key to this story is the use of the term *eternal life*. Jesus' answer to the man who asks him how to "get it" is to recite the Decalogue. In last week's gospel Jesus insisted that parts of the Torah were given as concessions due to people's hardness of heart. Is he now trying to reaffirm the authority of the Torah? No. There is something far more clever going on—more ideological apple carts are being upended. A closer inspection of the list that Jesus cites reveals that one of his commands— "You shall not defraud" (*me apostereses*)—is not even part of the Decalogue. Matthew and Luke's version of the story drops it altogether.

The command not to defraud is clearly an exhortation against economic exploitation. When the

---

[8] *BSM*, 272.

Greek Bible uses the verb it means the act of keeping back the wages of an employee.[9] The first-century reader is alerted that Jesus is not simply speaking to the failure of one individual in this story—"judgment is being passed upon the wealthy class."[10]

Jesus' rebuff to the man that "only God is good" apparently went right over his head. His answer to Jesus was that he certainly is good—in fact, so good that he is blameless before the law. He kept it all. The arrogance of the man is blatant. In the Talmud it is said that Abraham, Moses, and Aaron kept the entire law. In essence, the man was comparing himself to Abraham, Moses, and Aaron!

The story also presents the reader with an interesting aside for the benefit of catechesis. We are told that Jesus *loved* (*agapaō*) the man. It is the only time in Mark's gospel we are told that Jesus loved someone. The only other time this same word *love* is used is in a later, similar confrontation with a scribe (Mk 12:28–34) in which Jesus is asked which commandment is the most important. Jesus tells the scribe that the greatest command is love (*agapaō*)—love of God and love of neighbor. Mark's catechism, therefore, while obscure, is nevertheless poignant. It also sets the stage for the confrontation in chapter 12. While Jesus may be reciting the commandments of the law to the rich man in today's gospel, he is *practicing* the greatest commandment—the command to love.

Myers also suggests that there might be another possible reason we are told Jesus loved the rich man. This could also be a homily or a midrash on the parable of the sower: love of wealth strangles the word, making it fruitless. Jesus contrasts his love for the man with excessive love for one's possessions.

Landowners were the most politically powerful, wealthy class of people who very often oppressed the poor. When the man realized that the call of discipleship meant that he must relinquish his power and give up his wealth he went away *gloomily* (a reference to Ez 27:35, in which Ezekiel brings judgment against the rich and powerful). Mark in-

fers that the man's wealth is a result of defrauding the poor. He was hardly blameless before the law! His sin required that he make restitution. "For Mark, the law is kept only through concrete acts of justice, not the facade of piety."[11]

Jesus took his disciples off to the side to explain the meaning of what had just taken place in his exchange with the rich man. Jesus uses sarcastic humor to underscore his unmistakable point. "Mark's stinging sarcasm is perhaps more recognizable in F. Beuchner's contemporary paraphrase: for wealthy North Americans it is harder to enter the kingdom 'than for Nelson Rockefeller to get through the night deposit slot of the First National City Bank' (1977:63)!"[12]

Last week, Jesus' catechism of the kingdom (least/greatest) centered around the family system. Today's gospel centers around the economic system. The disciples are simply incredulous. If pious, wealthy people at the top of the social class cannot be saved, then who in the world can be saved? Jesus' teaching betrays the prevailing ideology mentioned above that wealth was a sign of God's blessings. Jesus reverses the economic status quo by insisting that the only way for the rich to enter the kingdom is to redistribute their wealth among the poor and break down the barriers of class discrimination. The disciples wonder how this class reversal could ever really happen. Jesus insists that with God all things are possible.

The third question hangs in the air like a cliff-hanger anticipating the story's final conclusion. What about the man's question: "What must be done to gain eternal life?" Peter insists that while the rich man failed to accept the demands of discipleship, they (the disciples), on the other hand, did not fail. They did forsake all—wives, property, possessions—to follow the gospel. Jesus does not agree or disagree with Peter. Rather, he continues the theme inherent in the parable of the sower. Even though there are many obstacles to *the way*, the kingdom, such as Satan, the fear of persecution, and love of wealth, the good soil will nevertheless yield a good harvest. Forfeited homes, lands, and family—things considered more impor-

[9]Ibid.
[10]Ibid., 273.

[11]Ibid., 274.
[12]Ibid., 275.

tant than life itself—will be returned in this life-time a hundredfold. In this new reversal, the new messianic kingdom, the last will be first and the rich will redistribute their wealth with the poor, and a new economic order will be established. "The miracle of multiplication through sharing implied in the wilderness feedings is thus enacted in the new economic practice of the community."[13]

Mark tempers the hope of this new order with stark reality. It will definitely be opposed! There will be persecution! For those at the top of the social structure who do not see with eyes of faith, there is much to lose. What will they choose: power and wealth or eternal life? Gustavo Guitier-rez tells us: "But giving up his possessions proves to be too much for the man. Like many of us, he prefers to live his faith resigned to comfortable mediocrity (v. 22). He does believe but not that much. We profess our faith in God although we refuse to put God's will into practice. Jesus takes advantage of the opportunity to make things very clear to his disciples: attachment to money and to the power it provides is a major obstacle to entering the kingdom (v. 23). . . . The Lord reminds us that our capacity to believe in God alone is a grace (v. 27)."[14]

Proclaim the gospel again.

Sometimes we gain new insights when we hear the text after the interpretation is given. Someone from the group proclaims the gospel a second time.

STEP 4
TESTING

Conversation with the Liturgy and the Scriptures

Test your original understanding in dialogue with the text.

(You might consider breaking into smaller groups.)

Now that you've heard the exegesis, were there any new insights? How do you feel about it? How

[13]Ibid., 276.
[14]*SWTLY*, 241.

does your original understanding of this gospel compare with what we just shared? How does this story speak to your life?

Sharing Life Experience

Participants share an experience from their lives that connects with the biblical interpretation just presented.

> *A few years ago our son went to our sister diocese in the Dominican Republic. It was a month-long immersion experience into the life of the people. He was not there to help them—he was there to live with them, to experience their lives.*
>
> *Their abject poverty is the result of massive debt and interest owed by their country to First World lending institutions. The family my son lived with saved for a month in order to buy a chicken so he could have protein during his brief stay with them. They taught him the meaning of true poverty—poverty of body and poverty of spirit. They were starving, but in their hunger they knew true joy in the Lord and they trusted in his providence. My son came home believing that we in this country are the ones who are really poor. His Dominican Republic friends possess a wealth we will never understand.*
>
> *The experience transformed my son—and us. We raised our children with a consciousness for the poor. It has always been a thread that runs through the faith life of our family. However, our son Rob challenged us with questions that even today, six years later, continue to hover over us.*
>
> *I still struggle with the questions he hurled at us. Today's gospel is one of those teachings, which taken at face value, is extremely difficult to accept. Does Jesus really mean that the rich have no possibility of salvation? No doubt he meant that without major conversion of heart it is extremely difficult.*
>
> *We are part of middle-class America. By the world's standards we are wealthy. The idealism of youth and his newfound passion prompted my son to confront "our wealth" and the entire way we live our lives—from the way we use water to the purchases we made for our house. "You don't need such and such—you could sell it and give the money to the poor." "Do you know what my friends in the Dominican Republic would say if they saw you let an*

extra drop of water run down the sink? Do you know how far they have to walk for a bucket of filthy water?" He was a proverbial thorn in the flesh. He challenged me for the excesses of modern living and I reminded him that he could feed an entire village for a week on the money he and his friends spend on beer, cokes, and fast food in one night! We were at an ideological standoff. How do we enflesh this gospel in the context of our daily, family life?

While in principle we accept the teaching of Jesus, we have a long way to go to live it. Memories of those conversations continue to linger in the air. If I embrace Ched Myers's interpretation I have to accept this gospel at face value—I am called to redistribute my wealth, give it all to the poor and rely completely on the Lord. There have been times in our lives that we have come close to living that imperative. There have been other times that we have not. Thank God it still depends on God's gratuitous grace!

Even though the gospel calls for action, it also calls for attitudinal change. The gospel insists that my security is not in possessions, but in the Lord. I constantly try to live that imperative, as in all of the difficult kingdom sayings. This is not an easy one, however. I honestly have to admit that I love my home and my possessions. Do I love them more than the Lord? No. Could I give them up for the sake of the gospel? I hope I would say, "Of course, in a flash!" The attitudinal change also requires detachment from this world's goods and the realization that a preferential option for the poor is not really an option—it is a command. My attitudinal change must be accompanied by just action. I am to give to the poor not just because I am called to act in charity, but also because they deserve it. They are children of God, and I have the responsibility to help them live up to their dignity as God's children. What's mine really is theirs too! I constantly struggle to determine what that means in my everyday life—and I fall so short. However, I take hope in Jesus' words of consolation. It is grace—and God is the broker of salvation, not I!

I am thankful that I live in a parish that is committed to the world's poor. While there is always room for growth, we try to live Jesus' exhortation in today's gospel (albeit imperfectly!). While we have built schools in Haiti, clinics and churches in Peru, churches in the Dominican Republic, and water treatment facilities in the Third World, and donated over a million dollars to the world's poor in the last ten years, I believe the question still remains for us: does our parish truly embrace a preferential option for the poor with all that entails? We have a long way to go, but we are trying. Again, with God, nothing is impossible; with his grace, all things are possible.

What was Mark trying to tell his community? Do you find this saying of Jesus just a little too difficult for twentieth-century living? Do you suppose the gospel really means what it says? How does today's gospel speak to the way I live my life? In what way does this gospel challenge your community today? In what way has this conversation with the scriptures for today's liturgy invited change in your life? In what way are the biblical themes of covenant, exodus, creation, and community evident in today's readings? Do you still feel the same way about this text as when you began? Has your original understanding been stretched, challenged, or affirmed?

STEP 5
DECISION

The gospel demands a response.

In what concrete way might your parish be invited to respond? Are there any attitudes or behaviors you would like to change as a result of today's conversation? What one concrete action will you take this week in response to the liturgy today?

Pastoral Considerations: Perhaps this would be a good time to reflect on the Bishops Document, *Communities of Salt and Light: Reflection on the Social Mission of the Parish* (Washington, NCCB). It explicitly addresses the issue of parish responsibility to the poor. In what way does your parish uphold a preferential option for the poor? In what way do you fall short?

Christian Initiation: This would be an opportune time to ask parishioners who are involved in social outreach to invite catechumens and candidates to go with them as they minister to the poor (St. Vincent de Paul, Meal on Wheels, homeless ministry, and so on).

DOCTRINAL ISSUES

What Church truth/teaching/doctrinal issue could be drawn from the gospel for the twenty-eighth Sunday in Ordinary Time?

Participants suggest possible doctrinal themes that flow from the readings.

Possible Doctrinal Themes

Justice; preferential option for the poor; moral teaching; morality; kingdom of God; faith and trust; commandments; Beatitudes

Present the doctrinal material at this time.

1. The facilitator gives input on a particular doctrinal issue of his or her prior choosing. OR
2. The group chooses a doctrinal issue from the list they created. They read together from the Doctrinal Appendix or other appropriate, official Church documents and the works of respected theologians.

(Many doctrinal issues are found in the Doctrinal Appendix at the back of this workbook. If you are choosing an issue from this resource, please refer to it now.)

Reflection questions centered around the chosen doctrinal theme can be found at the end of each topic in the Doctrinal Appendix. The questions are based on the five-step reflection process. If you choose a topic not included in the Doctrinal Appendix, craft your own questions according to the same five-step process.

Following the reflection questions you will be reminded to return to chapter 7, "Preparing the Catechetical Session," to assist you in crafting your own session.

Closing Prayer

Let us pray,
that God will help us love one another

Lord,
our helper and our guide,
make your love the foundation of our lives.

May our love for you express itself
in our eagerness to do good for others.
Grant this through our Lord
Jesus Christ, your Son,
who lives and reigns with you and the Holy Spirit,
one God for ever and ever.

Twenty-Ninth Sunday in Ordinary Time

INTRODUCTORY RITES

Entrance Antiphon (or Opening Song)

I call upon you, God, for you will answer me; bend your ear and hear my prayer. Guard me as the pupil of your eye; hide me in the shade of your wings. (Ps 16:6, 8)[1]

Opening Prayer

The facilitator of the session may lead the prayer. Others in the group may be asked to proclaim the readings.

Let us pray
to the Lord who bends close to hear our prayer

Pause for silent prayer.

Lord our God, Father of all,
you guard us under the shadow of your wings
and search into the depths of our hearts.
Remove the blindness that cannot know you
and relieve the fear that would hide us from your
　　sight.
We ask this through Christ our Lord.[2]

LITURGY OF THE WORD

The readings are proclaimed.

First Reading
Isaiah 53:10–11

(Please refer to the first Sunday of Advent for an overview of the Book of the Prophet Isaiah.)

Today's Pericope: The fourth Servant Song of Isaiah was written during the Babylonian exile. Israel was awaiting deliverance. Jerusalem had yet to be reconstructed.[3] Deutero-Isaiah grieved over the situation of those in captivity. The intention of Deutero-Isaiah was to offer a word of hope and consolation. In preexilic times the people enjoyed extravagant prosperity, leading to excessive greed and materialism. Captivity changed the people. Deutero-Isaiah insisted that they were "dazed, discouraged, and destitute, severely tempted to apostasy."[4] The prophet wanted to console the people, not chastise them. His goal was to strengthen their faith as they awaited deliverance.

The early Christian community believed that Jesus Christ was the Suffering Servant of the first reading. They believed that Deutero-Isaiah was heralding and foretelling the Passion and death of Christ and the inauguration of the messianic age. Jewish scholars are not certain who the Suffering Servant of Isaiah was. Christians proclaim with faithful assurance: it was Christ, the One who suffered for the many, the One who bore our infirmities. Jewish scholars maintain that the "many" referred to gentiles. It is not certain whether Jesus saw himself as the servant of this Isaian passage. But there is evidence in the scriptures that he embraced Isaiah's servant image as a metaphor for his own mission.

The Servant Songs of Isaiah set the stage for understanding the pasche of Jesus. Jesus, Servant of God, who by all appearances was reduced to nothing, was exalted and raised up by the living God. Like Isaiah's Suffering Servant, Jesus was also vindicated. The passage ends on a note of peace and hope and helps form our understanding and theology of the cross: "Jesus' suffering was innocent, vicarious and redemptive; it is for all people inclusively; the righteous sufferer is finally vindicated."[5]

Today's pericope was chosen because of the word *many*. The self-sacrifice of the Suffering Servant resulted in the righteousness of the "many." In later Judaism the "many" was understood to mean "all"—everyone, all the nations, all people. The Suffering Servant would save all people

---

[1]Twenty-Ninth Sunday in Ordinary Time: "Entrance Antiphon," *The Sacramentary.*

[2]Twenty-Ninth Sunday in Ordinary Time: "Opening Prayer," *The Sacramentary.*

[3]Carroll Stuhlmueller, C.P., "Deutero-Isaiah and Trito-Isaiah," *NJBC,* 329.

[4]Ibid., 330.

[5]*PNL,* 19.

from all nations—his mission would be universal. Rabbinic commentary interpreted the servant to be a reference to Israel, not the Messiah. Christianity believed otherwise. Today's selection portrays the universal nature of Jesus' redemptive work of salvation.

Responsorial Psalm
Psalm 33:4–5, 18–19, 22

Today's psalm is a song of praise suitable for any occasion.

Second Reading
Hebrews 4:14–16

(Refer to the twenty-seventh Sunday in Ordinary Time for an overview of the Letter to the Hebrews.)

Today's Pericope: Today's reading centers on the humanity of Christ. Jesus is certainly qualified to be high priest as he is fully human. He is able to sympathize with human beings because he understands their weakness. Jesus has walked the road of human experience. He was tempted in every way that human beings are tempted. He knows the temptations that human beings face every day. He was similarly tempted, yet he was sinless.

Reginald Fuller raises the question: Did that mean Jesus was tempted in every way?[6] Was he tempted sexually? Fuller reminds us that the gospel writers had no way of knowing the inner life of the Lord. The evangelists showed absolutely no interest in the psychological experience of Jesus. Nevertheless, it was very clear that early Christian tradition insisted that Jesus was sinless. "No one ever examined every overt act that our Lord did and concluded that he was sinless."[7]

The meaning of Jesus' sinlessness is best grasped by examining the temptation stories in the gospels. The theme of each temptation story was Jesus' role in the fulfillment of salvation history— his role as Messiah. Jesus was tempted to abandon that role and move in a different direction than the one ordained by God. The "sinlessness" referred to in the scriptures is primarily understood in terms of complete and total faithfulness and commitment to God's will for the salvation of the world, and the role he would play in that unfolding, salvific drama. The other human temptations that our modern world is wont to investigate simply were not concerns for the New Testament writers.

The gospel is proclaimed.

Gospel
Mark 10:35–45. The Son of Man came to give his life as a ransom for many.

STEP 1
NAMING ONE'S EXPERIENCE

What were your first impressions? What was your first response to the gospel (or the other readings)? What captured your attention?

Each person names his or her initial impression. Statements should be brief. No reasons should be given at this time. All simply listen without agreeing or disagreeing.

STEP 2
UNDERSTANDING

In a brief statement, explain what you think this gospel is trying to convey.

STEP 3
INPUT FROM VISION/STORY/TRADITION

Liturgical Context

Jesus predicted his own Passion three times. The predictions set the stage for Jesus' entry into Jerusalem. Following the third prediction and before Jesus' entry into Jerusalem, Mark inserted the gospel stories we read on the twenty-ninth and the thirtieth Sundays in Ordinary Time. Thus, the readings for this Sunday and next Sunday share an internal unity. Jesus spends time with the disciples before he moves toward the fulfillment of his mis-

---

[6]*PL*, 360.
[7]Ibid.

sion in Jerusalem. Jesus tries to prepare his disciples for the ordeal ahead. He tells them what is in store for him in Jerusalem—arrest, indictment, death sentence, then resurrection. They are understandably afraid. James and John misunderstand. They mistakenly believe that Jesus is ready to establish his earthly reign. In this Sunday's gospel Jesus insists that the disciples understand and embrace the truth. Next Sunday the blind Bartimaeus has his sight restored. The gospels for both Sundays remind us that through the gift of faith God provides believers with the necessary sight to understand the paschal mystery.

Today's disciples continue to misunderstand Jesus' mission. The opening prayer asks that God remove our blindness and fear—the antitheses of true servanthood. The alternative opening prayer reminds us that God is our source of power, not illusive positions of honor. God is our inspiration, not lofty dreams of political superiority. Only God gifts us with the necessary strength and joy to live Jesus' command to serve. The liturgy heralds Jesus Christ, true Servant of the Lord, and invites us to become the servants he invites us to become in today's gospel.

Gospel Exegesis

The facilitator provides input from critical biblical scholarship on this text. This input includes insights as to how people would have heard the gospel in Jesus' time.

Stark ambition was running through the veins of James and John when they approached Jesus with their question. Perhaps mixed in with ambition was the desire to do an end run around the other disciples and beat them to the punch before they would ask Jesus the same question they were about to ask. Jesus retorts with a question of his own. "Do you know what you are asking? Can you drink the cup that I will drink? Are you ready to face the humiliation, the suffering, and the death that I am about to endure? If it is power you seek, this is the power I give—the powerlessness of the cross."

The power of the risen Christ will eventually break through their delusions of grandeur and they, too, will one day follow the same path as their Lord and Master. But for now they are steeped in delusions of power, honor, and prestige.

Jesus insists that their request is not his to give—it can only be granted by God and God has no favorites. The other disciples, also deluded by their own misinterpretations, are jealous and angry with their comrades for their backdoor negotiations. Jesus returns to a previous teachable moment and repeats his teaching on true greatness. Jesus affirmed his own role as servant—he was a servant willing to lay down his life in order to deliver people from sin and bondage. In the reign Jesus came to establish, those who want to lead will serve; they will lay down their lives for those they serve. Those who vie for positions of power serve only themselves, and not the reign of God. There is no place in Jesus' kingdom for self-serving, power-hungry "want-to-be" rulers. In Matthew's version of this story, the disciples' obnoxious behavior is toned down by suggesting that the question originated with their ambitious mother (20:20–21). Luke omits the event altogether.

The disciples brusquely ask for the highest place of honor when Jesus achieves his victory (glory). Mark's interpretation of glory is eschatological—the fulfillment of God's reign at the parousia. Misunderstanding guided their ambitious entreaty. They professed Jesus as Messiah; they were in on the ground floor of some grand design and they knew it—they wanted and deserved to make the most of it. This story is another case in which Mark underscores the disciples' incredulous lack of understanding of Jesus and his mission. If they really knew what they were asking, would they have asked it? The portrait of disciple that Mark paints makes that highly doubtful. Jesus responds by asking if they were ready to drink from the same cup from which he was ready to drink. Jesus' allusion to *cup* has its genesis in the Old Testament, where it is a symbol of joy (Pss 22:5; 115:4) and suffering (Ps 74:9; Is 51:17–22; Jer 32:1; Ez 33:31–34).[8]

This gospel focuses on Jesus' messianic suffering. The baptism Jesus speaks of in this pericope is immersion in the waters of adversity and tribulation. This baptism will drown Jesus in the floodwaters of pain, torture, and death. "If it is greatness you desire, then dive into these waters. If you seek a place at my right hand in glory, then plunge in

_____

[8]*MARK*, 166.

with both feet into the waters of affliction. Take this bath if you dare; this is what true leadership entails. Follow your Master down this road and through these waters if it is glory you seek." The brothers insist that they can indeed follow him into those waters. Through the strength and power of the risen Christ, they will eventually do just that. But not right now.

The disciples' request for a seat of priority in Jesus' kingdom is met with Jesus' insistence that such places of authority can only be given by God. In the reign of God, all things are under God's dominion. "The appointment of places in the kingdom is at the Father's disposition only; discipleship does not entitle one to receive a special reward or to make any demand. As in 13:32 Jesus' words imply a subordination to the Father."[9]

Jesus presents his catechism on leadership. In God's reign there is a need for leaders, but there is no place for blind ambition. The hallmark of true leadership is service. Mark slowly awakens the reader to the disciples' crass pettiness. They position themselves for places of honor and power in Jesus' "kingdom" while Jesus talks to them about his pending suffering and death. In the midst of their negotiations none of the disciples think to offer him support or encouragement for the ordeal of his life they were about to witness. The epitome of selfishness!

The statement regarding those who use power to "lord it over" people is perhaps a reference to the illusive nature of earthly power. Those in authority believe they hold the cards of power, but they are, in truth, blindly ignorant. The real source of power and authority is God, and *only God* has the power to topple that house of cards and to send it crashing to the ground. Any structure or organization that rules like an authoritarian monarchy rather than with *diakonia* (service) is antithetical to the gospel. Yet from the very beginning the church has struggled to live the imperative of this gospel. Jesus' words are crystal clear and yet we find them very difficult to follow. He not only speaks to us in words, he taught us with the example of his life. Jesus challenged his disciples then and now to lead through loving service. The love

and service Jesus demands are intended to help people live up to their full human potential and to free them from any form of oppression that enslaves them. Ostentatious, pompous, and showy authority has no place in God's reign.

Jesus further explains the service he offers to the human race. The word used is *ransom*—an allusion to Isaiah 53:10–11. Originally the word was used in a commercial sense. Ransom was the price paid to recover a pawned object, to redeem a pledge, or to free a slave.[10] The Septuagint often referred to God who ransomed—acquired, purchased, and bought his people. The way the word is used in this setting, however, is Hebrew in origin. It means an offering for sin, an atonement offering.[11] "By laying down his life for a mankind enslaved to sin, Jesus fulfills the saying about the Servant in Isaiah 53:10–11. Jesus has paid the universal debt: he has given his life to redeem all others. But this is metaphor, not crude commerce."[12]

In first-century Palestine groups similar to Jesus' organized group of disciples were common. Such groups were called factions and consisted primarily of a leader and his disciples. Members of factions were closely committed to the leader, but not to each other. The exchange that took place in today's gospel between James, John, and Jesus would have been customary in a shame- and honor-based culture. Two blood brothers would have no compunction vying for a higher position of honor than the other members of the faction. In an honor/shame society, achieving honor is the highest priority. James and John ask for a personal favor from Jesus in order to upgrade their position of honor within the community. The leader of the faction is in a position to favor the members with special perks and, in so doing, upgrade their place of honor within the group.

Jesus' reply to the disciples' question affirms the honor that is already his. Jesus already possesses honor through participation in his own cup of suffering. John Pilch maintains there is another meaning to Jesus' reference to the "cup" and that

---

[9]Ibid., 167.

[10]Ibid., 169.

[11]Ched Myers offers a different interpretation of the word. See below.

[12]Ibid.

it is based on an ancient Mediterranean custom.[13] The head of each household fills the cup of everyone at the table. Everyone is expected to receive the cup offered by the head of the family. Theology was formulated by comparing the action of God to the behavior of human beings. Thus, "the cup came to represent the lot in life which God has assigned for each person (see Pss 11:6; 16:5; 23:5; etc.)."[14] Jesus accepts the plan God designed for him, the cup God prepared for him, thereby achieving the honor determined by God. The brothers are confident that they can do likewise. Jesus reminds them that God is the patron and he is God's intermediary. Jesus is the agent who will introduce people to the patron, but only the patron (God) can determine each person's place of honor.

Jesus suggests a new way of relating in the reign of God. Once again he calls for a major status reversal. People in power positions should behave like the deacons that serve at ceremonial meals—like slaves. Why? Because they have been given an example by the Son of Man, who gave his life in ransom so that people would be set free. Pilch posits an interesting reflection. When two countries are at war, the only way one hostage is acceptable to a warring party is if that hostage is a person of power and authority, such as a king. They would gladly kill the king and give the peasants their freedom. It is far more prestigious to hold a king hostage and subsequently kill him, than it is a large horde of peasants. An illustration of this principle is found in the game of chess. When the king is captured, the game is over—even if all the other game pieces are still on the board. Jesus certainly qualifies as the prized hostage king. As hostage he is willing to give his life in ransom for the nations of peasants who would be freed by his self-sacrificing act of love.

Ched Myers's political reading of Mark's Gospel invites us to reflect more deeply upon the next step in Jesus' mission—the way.[15] For the past few weeks we have been concerned with Jesus' catechism concerning who is the least and the greatest in the reign of God. Jesus applied it to life in society, life in the family, and life in the community. A

transition has now taken place in the narrative and we move from the least/greatest motif to the teaching of Jesus "on the way to Jerusalem."

Mark tells us in verse 32 (not in today's reading) that Jesus was *going ahead of them*—a foreshadowing of the postresurrection scene in which the disciples are told that Jesus is not dead, but *going ahead* of them into Galilee, and they respond with fear. We are to remember that *fear* at the end of the story as it is a "constitutive element of 'following.' "[16] Mark prepares us for Jerusalem and all that awaits Jesus there. Jesus predicted his Passion in graphic detail, and today's gospel illustrates in bold colors the extent of the disciples' gross misunderstanding. The incredibly naive James and John still translate Jesus' *glory* to refer to some idealized, romanticized messianic coup. They are thinking in political terms. Their leader will be victorious and they will have seats of authority in his new regime. Beads of exasperated sweat must have formed on Jesus' brow alongside droplets of disappointment and discouragement. They begin to form similarly on the brows of frustrated readers. Are they really that thick-headed? Is anyone really that dull-witted? Jesus tries to reach them again. Leadership has nothing to do with coveted seats of power and authority. True leaders must follow the way of nonviolence and accept the consequences. The leaders God will appoint to places of honor will be leaders "who are 'prepared' not to dominate but to serve and to suffer at Jesus' side."[17]

The other disciples are angry at the maneuvering of James and John, which alerts the reader that the whole community is now involved in the struggle over power. Politics are politics—so what else is new? Even in Jesus' little society, it is politics as usual! Jesus' dripping sarcasm flows over the disciples as they posture themselves like panting dogs awaiting every little morsel of power and prestige that might inadvertently fall from their Master's table. He reminds them that in his community there will be no leaders of the ilk they all know only too well. "You know, the ones who 'lord it over' everyone, the 'great ones,' the 'so-called rulers of the nations'—the ones who will ultimately put me to death?" Jesus names the "so-called

---

[13]*CWJB*, 152.
[14]Ibid.
[15]*BSM*, 277–282.

---

[16]Ibid., 277.
[17]Ibid.

rulers" who will ultimately take his life. They are the perfect example of what Jesus taught the disciples *not* to be—they dominate those they serve. Jesus returns to the Zebedees' original question by alluding to the messianic psalm. The question by James and John was an allusion to Psalm 110:1— "The lord said to my lord, 'Sit at my right hand.'" Jesus responds with an allusion to Psalm 110:2— "Dominate in the midst of your foes." The rulers dominate their foes. Jesus insists this is not the way of true leadership. Jesus also begins to hint that this psalm has been grossly misunderstood (Mark will cite it two more times: 12:36 and 14:62). "Dominate in the midst of your foes" was a psalm text that supported a then popular, albeit mistaken, vision of the messianic kingdom. The hoped-for messianic reign is not the Davidic restoration of Israel that involved the military overthrow of the political ruling system. Verse 43 is nothing more than dry sarcasm—"Of course, none of these things is happening among you!" In other words, if it is happening to you, you had better reconsider and change your course of action. This is not the way it will be in the reign of God.

Again, Jesus is emphatic! If it is greatness you desire, then be a servant, a slave. *Slave* was a euphemism for the political vocation of martyrdom. Mark's theology runs throughout this discourse. Jesus is the Holy One who lived the life of nonviolence, who has come to serve, to give his life— refusing to save it—and to ransom it. Myers insists that the word *ransom* is a reference to *slave*. It was the price required to reclaim captives or purchase freedom for indentured servants.[18] Jesus ransomed the captives and in the process won their freedom, their liberation. Rather than a developed theology of atonement as mentioned above, Myers favors the position that the purpose of the use of the word *ransom* is to show that the death of Jesus is in accord with the scriptures. If you want to be a leader, then practice the way of nonviolence. Nonviolence cannot be taught by word of mouth. Gandhi insisted that nonviolence can only be taught by people who live it with little or no regard for its consequences.

Gustavo Gutierrez reminds us that "serving implies initiative and creativity, knowledge and ef-

forts to build a human, just and loving world. What the gospel rejects is power as domination, the desire to be recognized as 'leaders.' It does not reject power that is understood as effective solidarity. In our own days, the hunger which two-thirds of humanity are experiencing and the constant violation of human rights by authoritarian governments, make it urgent for us to place what we are and what we have at the service of the marginalized and to transform today's injustice and exclusion of the many."[19]

Proclaim the gospel again.

Sometimes we gain new insights when we hear the text after the interpretation is given. Someone from the group proclaims the gospel a second time.

STEP 4
TESTING

Conversation with the Liturgy and the Scriptures

Test your original understanding in dialogue with the text.

(You might consider breaking into smaller groups.)

Now that you've heard the exegesis, were there any new insights? How do you feel about it? How does your original understanding of this gospel compare with what we just shared? How does this story speak to your life?

Sharing Life Experience

Participants share an experience from their lives that connects with the biblical interpretation just presented.

> *This gospel invites me to ask, "Who do I know that embodies the kind of servanthood Jesus asks for in today's gospel?" I think of a couple in our parish who are seriously ill. The precious wife of the blessed pair is clinging to life. In her last labors of life, she still thinks of others. Her pain is secondary to the needs of everyone in the community she prays for. Every day of her life and throughout the day, this*

---

[18]Ibid., 279.

[19]*SWTLY*, 246.

special lady has a list of people she remembers and for whom she storms the heavens. No matter how sick she is, they come first. I feel very honored, as my children are on her list. She is one "suffering servant who gives her life for the many" that I will sorely miss when the time comes for her to enter her eternal reward. I am confident that her intercession will continue beyond the grave, and I am grateful for her life.

I think of all those wonderful, silent disciples in our parish who in so many quiet ways reach out in love to people in need. I think of those who work in the cold night ministry and those who work with the poor. I think of people such as a young doctor in our parish who has given so much of his time, energy, efforts, and finances to begin a crisis pregnancy center to reach out in love—not judgment—to those contemplating abortion. I think of the great heroes and heroines who work with young children, with middle-school children, and with teens. Their reward in heaven will be great—because it is sometimes very difficult to measure their rewards in earthly realities.

I think of a special lady in our parish who agreed to take in two special needs children because the love of God compelled her to do no less. I think about how her act of love has rewarded her so greatly. She seeks no position of power; she is simply grateful to the God who has now blessed her with a new young family in her middle-aged years. She was just informed that these two precious bundles of joy (one child is blind because of prior abuse) could now be adopted. She sees no great service in her action. She sees it first as a response to the love of God and then as an incredible blessing from the God who loves her. Never mind that the financial burden will be heavier and the concerns of raising children with their background more difficult. Her act of quiet love and service has helped her ransom those children and, in the process, she and they have been abundantly blessed.

Today's gospel reminds me of my husband, who continues to love and support me no matter how hectic life becomes. I think of the selfless way he is always available to anyone who needs him. I think of the way he loves me unconditionally—even when it is a challenging, tricky venture! I think of the way he always stops to talk to the homeless guys, how he knows them by name, how he respects their dignity and their personhood. We cannot go for a walk in which we do not stop along the way to talk to his friends. I am humbled by his example.

And, finally, today's gospel reminds me of our community, which struggles to move beyond its own selfish concerns and share what we have with the world's poor—and not because of some kind of exalted ego trip, but because our people are committed to living the gospel in every way we are called to live it, from giving to the poor, to building schools and clinics in Third World countries, to reaching out to those in need and in pain in our midst. I am confident that as we open ourselves to the teaching of the gospel, we will continue to learn what a true servant community is called to be. I am in a good place to learn such things and I am thankful.

This gospel also reminds me of all those who are more interested in the power of their office, the prestige of their positions, the accolades on their wall, the degrees in their hip pockets, and the respect of their peers than they are about the marginalized, disenfranchised members of our communities. And if those shoes fit my servant feet, then I had better wear them when they fit. On the other hand, I think of all the people who face ridicule and rejection for their belief in the gospel—those who fight for the rights of others, and those who take issue with a culture of violence and seek to change it. I hope that when I try those shoes on, they fit better than the other pair.

What was Mark trying to tell his community? Put yourself in the place of James and John. In what way can you relate to their request of Jesus? Can you think of any modern-day corollaries? Now put yourself in the place of Jesus. How must he have felt because of their request? How does Jesus' teaching about servanthood challenge you? In what way have you lived the message of this gospel? Where is there need for growth? In what way does this gospel challenge your community today? In what way has this conversation with the scriptures for today's liturgy invited change in your life? In what way are the biblical themes of covenant, exodus, creation, and community evident in today's readings? Do you still feel the same way about this text as when you began? Has your original understanding been stretched, challenged, or affirmed?

STEP 5
DECISION

The gospel demands a response.

In what concrete way might your parish be invited to respond? Are there any attitudes or behaviors you would like to change as a result of today's conversation? What one concrete action will you take this week in response to the liturgy today?

Pastoral Considerations: When was the last time your parish reflected on what it means to be "servant church"? Is your parish a servant like Jesus, or is it a parish that "lords it over others"? Do parishes today have the courage to honestly answer that question? We could change the world if we did! Name concrete ways your parish serves like Christ served. Name ways that it is the antithesis of that service. Name one or two ways you can grow more fully in the image of servant portrayed by Jesus in today's gospel.

Christian Initiation: These weeks would be an excellent time to go with your catechumens to reach out to the highways and byways—to discover firsthand the implications of true servanthood. Are there soup kitchens in your area? See if they would allow you to come and serve a meal for them. Are there efforts in your wider community to help the homeless? Drug addicts? Alcoholics? AIDS patients? Is there a St. Vincent de Paul society in your parish? Perhaps your catechumens could go on a call with the ministers.

If you do go out on such a mission, you might begin by gathering for prayer first. There are blessings in the *Book of Blessings* provided for such occasions. Also, do not forget to reflect on the experience when you meet again afterward. What are the pitfalls? Where is there temptation to be like James and John in today's gospel?

With the emphasis on what it means to be a true servant, today would be an opportune time to celebrate a rite of acceptance or a rite of welcome. Is there anyone ready to be received into full communion in the Catholic Church? Are you remembering to use the minor rites in the catechumenate?

DOCTRINAL ISSUES

What Church truth/teaching/doctrinal issue could be drawn from the gospel for the twenty-ninth Sunday in Ordinary Time?

Participants suggest possible doctrinal themes that flow from the readings.

Possible Doctrinal Themes

Service; discipleship; nonviolence; way of the cross; social justice; reign of God; paschal mystery; Christology; salvation; soteriology

Present the doctrinal material at this time.

1. The facilitator gives input on a particular doctrinal issue of his or her prior choosing. OR
2. The group chooses a doctrinal issue from the list they created. They read together from the Doctrinal Appendix or other appropriate, official Church documents and the works of respected theologians.

(Many doctrinal issues are found in the Doctrinal Appendix at the back of this workbook. If you are choosing an issue from this resource, please refer to it now.)

Reflection questions centered around the chosen doctrinal theme can be found at the end of each topic in the Doctrinal Appendix. The questions are based on the five-step reflection process. If you choose a topic not included in the Doctrinal Appendix, craft your own questions according to the same five-step process.

Following the reflection questions you will be reminded to return to chapter 7, "Preparing the Catechetical Session," to assist you in crafting your own session.

Closing Prayer

Let us pray
for the gift of simplicity and joy
in our service of God and man

Pause for silent prayer.

Almighty and ever-living God,
our source of power and inspiration,
give us strength and joy
in serving you as followers of Christ,
who lives and reigns with you and the Holy Spirit,
one God, for ever and ever.[20]

[20]Twenty-Ninth Sunday in Ordinary Time: "Opening Prayer," *The Sacramentary*.

THIRTIETH SUNDAY IN ORDINARY TIME

INTRODUCTORY RITES

Entrance Antiphon (or Opening Song)

Let hearts rejoice who search for the Lord. Seek the Lord and his strength, seek always the face of the Lord. (Ps 104:3–4)[1]

Opening Prayer

The facilitator of the session may lead the prayer. Others in the group may be asked to proclaim the readings.

Let us pray
in humble hope for salvation

Pause for silent prayer.

Praised be you, God and Father of our
    Lord Jesus Christ.
There is no power for good
which does not come from your covenant,
and no promise to hope in,
that your love has not offered.
Strengthen our faith to accept your covenant
and give us the love to carry out your command.
We ask this through Christ our Lord.[2]

LITURGY OF THE WORD

The readings are proclaimed.

First Reading[3]
Jeremiah 31:7–9

---

[1] Thirtieth Sunday in Ordinary Time: "Entrance Antiphon," *The Sacramentary*.

[2] Thirtieth Sunday in Ordinary Time: "Opening Prayer," *The Sacramentary*.

[3] The exegesis for the first and second readings may or may not be the focus of your group's reflection, as there may only be time to give adequate attention to the gospel, your primary concern. However, the exegesis is included here in order to provide a thorough investigation of the entire Liturgy of the Word as there may be parts (or all) that would be essential to the direction you wish to take with your particular ministry group.

(Please refer to the sixteenth Sunday in Ordinary Time for an overview of the Book of the Prophet Jeremiah.)

Today's Pericope: Today's pericope is taken from the second in a series of poems dedicated to the return from Babylonian captivity. Reginald Fuller maintains that they are very much in the style of Deutero-Isaiah.[4] It is believed that perhaps they were crafted in the Deutero-Isaiah school and inserted into the Jeremiah prophecies in order to lessen his engrossment with the fall of Judah (the Southern Kingdom) and Israel's acclimation to captivity.

God is so happy to restore his people that he wants it shouted to all the nations. God speaks about his children like parents speak about the achievements of their favorite child—the most important of all people. It was with great reluctance that God punished them in the first place. It was out of love that he chastised them. He hoped against hope that they would turn away from their sins. *Now* is the day of salvation; *now* God will forgive and restore them. It is a momentous occasion, as are all such occasions of God's reversal. It will be looked upon as a new exodus. In this new exodus, the people will be led safely back to their land. In this new exodus, the tribes of the north and south will be reunited and division will cease. All people will benefit from God's new salvation, especially the weaker members of the community.

Jeremiah's message is one of hope. Today's hymn is reminiscent of the same hymn of return found in Isaiah 35. It extols the return of the weaker members of the community—nursing mothers, the blind, and the lame—the purpose of which is to emphasize that the return is a result of God's complete and unmerited grace. The choice of this text is obviously because it mentions healing of the blind, a companion text for the gospel's proclamation of the healing of Bartimaeus.

Responsorial Psalm
Psalm 126:1–6

---

[4] *PL*, 362.

Today's psalm celebrates the contrast between joy and sorrow. It is a most appropriate psalm to accompany today's first reading, as it also extols the return from Babylonian captivity.

Second Reading
Hebrews 5:1–6

(Refer to the twenty-seventh Sunday in Ordinary Time for an overview of the Letter to the Hebrews.)

Today's Pericope: The author of Hebrews has painstakingly been making his case. We have watched it unfold over the past weeks. Jesus is truly qualified for the role of high priesthood. Today he spells it out. Jesus has been appointed for the role by God. God chose Jesus to act on behalf of humanity before God to offer sacrifices for sins. Jesus obviously demonstrated compassion for the ignorant and the wayward.

Priests in the Old Testament tradition were divinely elected for the purpose of priestly service. Their election came in the form of belonging to the priestly lineage. Today, election comes in the form of the call of the Church represented by the bishop who shepherds the local community. Jesus' election as high priest, however, comes from God, the One who said to him, "You are my son; this day I have begotten you."

The priesthood of Melchizedek is remembered as having something to do with the priesthood of Jesus. Melchizedek is mentioned only once in the Old Testament. He is quite mysterious. He is the "king of Salem [king of peace] and priest of the Most High." He brought bread and wine to Abraham and he blessed him. Nothing is known of his parents, his family, or his lineage—he has no history. Scripture is virtually silent about this king and priest. Rabbinic exegetes believed that Melchizedek was eternal. Judaism believed that anything that was not in the Torah did not exist—thus he transcended history. He was a figure of Christ. Jesus is not bound to history and is thus priest forever.

In the ancient world people offered sacrifices to appease the myriad of pagan gods, some of which were angry and vengeful. The gifts of sacrifice were offered in hopes that the wrath of the gods would not come crashing down upon the people.

Israel's understanding of sacrifice was different, however. Israel's God was *One*, holy, mighty, and transcendent. Israel praised God's goodness, mercy, and compassion. Thus, they offered sacrifice in praise of God's mercy and compassion and, ultimately, God's greatness and holiness. The sacrifices of Israel were sacramental in nature—they were outward signs that expressed an internal reality. Sacrifices were representative of repentant, faith-filled, trusting, and grateful hearts. Sacrifices were offered in praise and thanksgiving to God and for atonement for sin and failure before God.

Priests offered sacrifices for the people. They offered sacrifice for the sins of the people. However, they offered sacrifice only for the people of Israel. Jesus' sacrifice extended beyond the borders of Israel to include all humanity. He became the sacrifice that atoned for *all* sin. Jesus' incarnation made him the representative of every human being. Jesus walked with human beings in their joy, sorrow, and pain. Thus, the Letter to the Hebrews points out that Jesus was both sacrifice and priest. No longer was there need for grain, cereal, or animal offerings. Jesus is the one and only offering before God. Jesus knows us in our human weakness; he walked with us in it. He represents us before the throne of glory as the true high priest.

In the later section of the reading, the author of Hebrews addresses the issue of God's appointment. The author quotes the coronation psalm (2:7): "You are my son: this day I have begotten you." At his resurrection, God appointed Jesus as Son and high priest. Even though the author's use of Psalm 2 might seem to suggest that Jesus was bestowed with divinity at his resurrection, such an assumption would be heresy. The author of Hebrews was approaching his argument from a Hebrew context. Psalm 2 was used in the celebration of the coronation of a king. At his coronation Jesus functioned like a king—he functioned as the Son of God. Thus, it is at his resurrection and ascension that Jesus "embarks upon his messianic functions, which include that of high priest."[5] His priesthood "flowed not only from the sacrifice of his passion and cross but also from his exaltation in glory whereby his priesthood was both divinely proclaimed and perfected."[6]

---

[5] Ibid.
[6] *WWC*, 247.

The gospel is proclaimed.

Gospel[7]
Mark 10:46–52. Jesus heals blind Bartimaeus and he becomes a disciple on the way.

STEP 1
NAMING ONE'S EXPERIENCE

What were your first impressions? What was your first response to the gospel (or the other readings)?[8] What captured your attention?

Each person names his or her initial impression. Statements should be brief. No reasons should be given at this time. All simply listen without agreeing or disagreeing.

STEP 2
UNDERSTANDING

In a brief statement, explain what you think this gospel is trying to convey.

STEP 3
INPUT FROM VISION/STORY/TRADITION

Liturgical Context[9]

See last week's liturgical context for the connection between the twenty-ninth Sunday and the

thirtieth Sunday in Ordinary Time and the sequence they form.

For the past few weeks, we have had a front row seat to witness the effects of blindness at its delusional worst. We have examined the blindness of the disciples. In the process, we could not help but examine our own blindness. We may not point a finger at the disciples without remembering that four are pointed at ourselves. Spiritual blindness is difficult to heal. We are seldom aware of it in ourselves. Recently there was a fascinating true story on television. It was the story of a man who was blind from early childhood and through some marvel of modern science had his sight restored. Rather than be an instant, wonderful thing, it was extremely difficult. The man had to learn everything from scratch. He had never known perception or color. There was so much sensory stimuli that he was bombarded. He had to learn to trust what he was seeing. The story is a metaphor for the Christian life. Often we are steeped in spiritual blindness and have been that way for so long, that even when our eyes are opened to the truth, we have to learn to trust the new truth we have been given. We have to become comfortable with right vision—we have lived with our blind delusions for so long that we are not sure that we can believe what we think we see. For example, people who have been racist all their lives, and then have their eyes opened to the evil of racism, may need time to become comfortable with their newfound truth. They may need to "practice" not being racist, since racism is all they have known. They may have to practice "seeing." Maybe this is why living the Christian life is called a discipline. We have to "practice" the discipline of living righteous, moral lives.

We practice seeing when we open ourselves to voices of discernment around us. Today's liturgy is an invitation to open our eyes to the areas of blindness in our lives. The disciples not only were blind, but they were also blind to their blindness. They did not have a clue. Yet they are a sign of hope for us. If they, who walked daily with the Lord, could miss it, is it no wonder that so many continue to miss it today? The challenge of today's liturgy is to seek healing for our blindness and to be open to the surprising ways we will find it. Then we are to go out like the blind Bartimaeus and follow Jesus to the cross, evangelizing as we go.

---

[7]The gospel exegesis is provided later in this session so that it may be presented in the proper sequence where it occurs in the adult five-step reflection process. The exegesis is provided for the first and second readings for your information and edification, and for you to use at your discretion. Once again, the gospel is the primary source of reflection. If there is time for reflection on the other readings, all the better.

[8]The primary focus of reflection is the gospel. However, often the other readings demand attention and must be brought into the dialogue.

[9]The scriptures in the Lectionary, the seasons of the year, and the ritual prayers of the mass are interrelated and form the basis for liturgical catechesis. The *liturgical context* attempts to explore and clarify the themes and this interrelatedness.

The Entrance Antiphon reminds us to rejoice as we seek the Lord. We are reminded to pray for the Lord's strength. If we are to live today's gospel, we must turn daily to the Lord, confident that he *will* hear our prayer. Bartimaeus knew the source of his salvation. Today's opening prayer asks us to pray in humble hope for the salvation he received in faith. We are reminded that our power to do good comes only from God. We ask for the strength to live the covenant and to love according to its promise. Bartimaeus offered a similar prayer and left everything behind to follow the Lord in response. Could we do the same?

The preface that is included as a closing prayer for today's session speaks to us of the compassion Bartimaeus encountered when he came face to face with *Love* in today's gospel.

Gospel Exegesis

The facilitator provides input from critical biblical scholarship on this text. This input includes insights as to how people would have heard the gospel in Jesus' time.

Up to this point in Mark's narrative, the ones who know the truth of who Jesus really is are the demons and the evil spirits. The disciples were the ones who walked with Jesus and should have known the truth, but even they were blind to it. They simply had no comprehension of the nature of Jesus' mission or what his messiahship was all about. Today, however, as Jesus and company approach the outskirts of Jerusalem in a town called Jericho, someone does recognize Jesus' true identity. Bartimaeus, the blind son of Timaeus, acknowledges Jesus as Son of David.

Today's story functions as the second in a pair of bookends that define the way to Jerusalem. The first bookend, the healing of a blind man, occurs at the beginning of Jesus' excursion toward Jerusalem. The other bookend (the healing of blind Bartimaeus) occurs at the end of the journey to Jerusalem. Sandwiched between these bookends are variations on the theme of "the disciples' blindness on the way." The disciples were given opportunity to see, but they were blind to the mission of Jesus.

Today we are presented with a new model of faith. This new disciple, even in the midst of discourage-ment, answers the call of faith and follows the Lord. Bartimaeus acknowledges Jesus as "Son of David"—the title set aside for the Messiah. Jesus does not silence him; instead, he restores his sight. There is no longer need for secrecy as the days are soon approaching when the true mission of Jesus will become all too apparent.

As stated before, the inauguration of the journey toward Jerusalem began with the healing of the blind man. Mark sets up the expectation that the journey will be a source of healing for the disciples' blindness. "The blind man whom he then cures resembles the disciples and is at the same time their counterpart. The story makes one expect that Jesus will sooner or later heal their blindness too, but this expectation is not realized within the story itself. There is only the promise, at the very end of the book, that they will see in the future (16:7)."[10] Mark, however, puts vision in the eyes of the blind Bartimaeus. He is the one who really sees—he becomes the true follower and disciple of Christ, the one with eyes of faith. Bartimaeus displays the courage of true discipleship. It is he who recognizes Jesus as Son of David, acknowledges his identity and his mission, and follows him to Jerusalem.

Pilgrims who were on their way to Jerusalem for the celebration of important festivals frequently stopped in Jericho (about fifteen miles northeast of Jerusalem) to rest before their final leg of the journey. We can almost picture the hordes converging on Jericho and feel the mounting tension. Our hair stands on end as we think of the events about to take place in Jerusalem and the ambush that awaits Jesus once they arrive in the city for Passover. We are afraid for him. Another disciple, this time a true believer with full awareness, joins Jesus' entourage as they head for the Holy City.

Matthew's version of this story includes two blind people. Luke's version of the story takes place before they arrive in Jericho so he can include the story of Zacchaeus and the parable of the pounds. Mark's version of the story gives the blind man a name, which seems to suggest that Bartimaeus was known among the early Christians as someone who was healed of blindness by the Lord.

------

[10]*RM*, 23.

Bartimaeus refers to Jesus as the Son of David. This is clearly a messianic title. He recognizes Jesus as the heir to the promise made to David through the prophet Nathaniel (2 Sm 7:12–16). It is obvious that Mark affirms Jesus as the realization of the eschatological expectations associated with David. "Mark's characterization of the Son of David is radically different from that found, for example, in Psalms of Solomon 17. There the Son of David is made out to be a warrior king, who will place his royal authority in the service of political and military struggle in order to vindicate Israel and crush its Gentile enemies. Here, by contrast, Jesus wields his Davidic authority in order to have mercy on one who is afflicted (10:47–48, 52), to heal and in this fashion to 'save' (10:52)."[11] The blind man asks for mercy—he asks Jesus to restore his sight. It was believed that a hallmark of the messianic reign would be the restoration of sight for the blind. The crowds, however, try to silence the man. Irony pours its brew of contrast over the unsuspecting characters in the scene. Before, Jesus was the one who silenced those who attempted to acknowledge his messiahship. Now it is the crowd who silences the man who seeks healing from Jesus. Jesus allows the proclamation to go forward, however. With all Jesus' talk and admonition to the disciples about the suffering he was about to endure, there was no longer concern that his messiahship would be misunderstood in militaristic terms. Today's story signals a reversal in the messianic secret motif. We will see it again when Jesus triumphantly enters Jerusalem and when the centurion proclaims him Messiah at the foot of the cross.

Jesus tells Bartimaeus to ask his question. Jesus told James and John to do the same last week. The contrast is clear. James and John hope to enjoy material benefits and the promise of power, prestige, and glory. Bartimaeus simply asks for healing from the One *he knows can give it.* He knows his own powerlessness and he knows who stands before him. He humbly acknowledges Jesus as the one who has the power and authority to heal him. Jesus is awed by his faith. "'Faith' is confident trust in God and in the healing power of Jesus."[12]

Bartimaeus's faith and healing are also his salvation. His faith saved him. The healing of blind Bartimaeus is intimately tied to his salvation. Bartimaeus responded in faith by following Jesus on the way to Jerusalem—he followed Jesus as a true disciple, without fear.

As noted before, Jericho was the last stop before the final leg of the pilgrim's journey into Jerusalem. At the skirts of this suburb would be a throng of beggars waiting to receive their hoped-for alms from the purses of generous pilgrims as they passed by en route to the city. It is here Jesus meets the blind beggar, Bartimaeus.

This story is generally interpreted as a story about discipleship as discussed in the previous paragraphs. However, Ched Myers, as usual, raises our consciousness to other, less conspicuous concerns inherent in the gospel—the political and social ramifications apparent in the text.[13]

Bartimaeus represents a contrast—the difference between the discipleship he displays and the nondiscipleship of the rich man. The story of Bartimaeus and the rich man corresponds to two other stories in the gospel—the healing of the hemorrhaging woman and the synagogue ruler. There is an implied class contrast in each set of stories. In both sets of stories there is (1) interference by the observing crowd, (2) a comment by Jesus regarding the faith of the one who is healed (both use the same language—*hē pistis sou sesōken se*—refer to 5:34 and 10:52), and (3) a ritually unclean person in the story—the hemorrhaging woman in the one set and Bartimaeus, "whose name in Hebrew could mean 'son of the unclean' in the other."[14]

Bartimaeus encounters Jesus "on the way." So did the rich man. The rich man could not let go of his material possessions. Bartimaeus throws away his garment, his only means of support. Beggars spread out their garments on the ground, which were used for gathering alms. The one who belonged to the higher social class rejected a direct invitation from the Lord. The one at the bottom of society's social order did not even wait for the invitation in the first place.

[11]*COMG*, 107.
[12]*MARK*, 171.

[13]*BSM*, 282.
[14]Ibid.

He jumped up, gave up all, and was ready to follow Jesus "on the way."

Often it is the poor and insignificant ones who are the first to recognize the work of Christ. "Acknowledging Jesus as the Christ comes from the insignificant people of society, from those who are by the roadside, from people that some try to silence."[15] Bartimaeus was able to see what others could not. When he called out, "Jesus, Son of David," he anticipated the enthusiastic welcome given to Jesus by the crowd in Jerusalem—the welcome that ultimately got the attention of the authorities and was one of the causes of Jesus' arrest.

The reader, then and now, is not to miss the point of the exchange on the eve of the consummation of Jesus' mission. "The poor join in the final assault on the dominant ideological order, and the rich have walked downcast away. The first have become last and the last first."[16] Through repeated attempts by the crowd to stop or silence Bartimaeus, he will not be thwarted. In the midst of formidable odds, the least "have been healed because they have taken the initiative of faith."[17]

Mark offers a stark contrast between the faith of Bartimaeus and the blind ambition of the disciples. The latter wanted status and prestige; the former simply wanted vision. Jesus cannot give the first, but he only too happily granted the second. Bartimaeus is told to take courage, the same thing the disciples were told when earlier crossing the sea. The beggar goes forth with courage. There is a message of hope for both ancient and contemporary audiences. "Only if the disciples/reader struggles against the internal demons that render us deaf and mute, only if we renounce our thirst for power—in a word, only if we recognize our blindness and seek true vision—then can the discipleship adventure carry on."[18]

Proclaim the gospel again.

Sometimes we gain new insights when we hear the text after the interpretation is given. Someone from the group proclaims the gospel a second time.

---

[15]*SWTLY*, 250
[16]*BSM*, 282.
[17]Ibid.
[18]Ibid.

Conversation with the Liturgy and the Scriptures

Test your original understanding in dialogue with the text.

(You might consider breaking into smaller groups.)

Now that you've heard the exegesis, were there any new insights? How do you feel about it? How does your original understanding of this gospel compare with what we just shared? How does this story speak to your life?

Sharing Life Experience

Participants share an experience from their lives that connects with the biblical interpretation just presented.

> *Today's gospel reminds me of those times that I arrogantly believe that I know the whole truth and yet, like James and John in last week's gospel, I find that I am, in truth, really blind. I think of the times in my family experience when I believed I was the righteous one when, in fact, I discovered that the one who was truly righteous was the one who silently suffered at my arrogant hand. Those times are legion as I honestly look back over my life. I think of the way in which I, as a wife, often think that it is my husband's responsibility to make me happy, and conversely and unfortunately think that he is the one to blame when I am not. Like James and John, I often act as if I am the only one with the authority to sit on the throne of power and am blind to the true authority that exists in the people I love who, through their loving acts of service, own the right to really sit on that throne. Bartimaeus simply wanted vision— no trappings. Today's gospel is a challenge to me to look at the blind spots, to open them to scrutiny, to have the courage to ask the appropriate questions. James and John asked inappropriate questions and perhaps I often succumb to the same temptation. Is it vision I seek, or false ego needs? Bartimaeus wanted what was essential and trusted that Jesus would give it to him and followed him to the end of the earth—or more aptly, to the cross—to get it.*

> *From a communal perspective, today's gospel reminds me of the way in which the church is called to*

live the challenge of this gospel. There are two approaches the church can take. We can approach Jesus like James and John, or we can approach him like Bartimaeus. We know who was first in the eyes of Jesus. However, we often live by the standards set forth by the world and alternately we know how the world would judge first-ness. I look at the concerns of our rather affluent parish and then I compare that with the concerns of a parish in the Third World. In many ways they are the same—or at least they should be. We are called to be disciples of Jesus, to live his mission, to promote the reign of God. We are called to give what we have—to throw out our garment, our means of support, and trust that we will be given what we need to promote the reign of God.

Our parish makes a strong effort to live the challenge of the gospel. I do not need to extol the giving patterns of our community. The people in our parish are extremely generous. Large sums of money are given to the poor. Is there room for growth? Of course. There always is. I am sure that our attitudes are always in need of scrutiny and renewed vision. If we see our giving as "charity" rather than as what "rightfully belongs to those who have not had the opportunity to live according to their dignity as God's children," then we need an attitude adjustment. I believe for the most part we understand that we have a responsibility to the world's poor.

I am most impressed, however, with our sister parish in Peru, which, in the midst of its own abject poverty, tithes 10 percent of its income to an even poorer parish in Africa and sends missionaries to help them. They truly live the spirit of today's gospel. They are the living incarnation of the healed, blind Bartimaeus. They know that everything they have flows from the grace of God. They receive in graciousness and in turn cast their garments to the wind and follow the Lord in faith. I am sure the 10 percent they send to Africa is an incredible hardship for them, yet they humbly wish to follow the Lord in faith. Like Bartimaeus, they have true vision. They know their poverty before God and are blessed by the abundance they have been given. They trust in God's providence—and look how God blessed them. God sent them us! (We are similarly blessed, by the way!) Our parish has built two clinics in their parish and is in the process of helping them build a new church. Our association in the Lord continues.

What was Mark trying to tell his community? In what way do you relate to the blindness of James and John in last week's gospel and how do you relate to the vision of Bartimaeus? Where are the blind spots in your life? Have you ever experienced vision that invited you to follow Jesus more closely? In what way does this gospel challenge your community today? In what way has this conversation with the scriptures for today's liturgy invited change in your life? In what way are the biblical themes of covenant, exodus, creation, and community evident in today's readings? Do you still feel the same way about this text as when you began? Has your original understanding been stretched, challenged, or affirmed?

STEP 5
DECISION

The gospel demands a response.

In what concrete way might your parish be invited to respond? Are there any attitudes or behaviors you would like to change as a result of today's conversation? What one concrete action will you take this week in response to the liturgy today?

DOCTRINAL ISSUES

What Church truth/teaching/doctrinal issue could be drawn from the gospel for the thirtieth Sunday in Ordinary Time?

Participants suggest possible doctrinal themes that flow from the readings.

Possible Doctrinal Themes

Conversion; the mission and reign of Christ; the ministry of healing; discipleship; Christology; social justice; salvation; soteriology

Present the doctrinal material at this time.

1. The facilitator gives input on a particular doctrinal issue of his or her prior choosing. OR
2. The group chooses a doctrinal issue from the list they created. They read together from the Doctrinal Appendix or other appropriate, offi-

cial Church documents and the works of respected theologians.

(Many doctrinal issues are found in the Doctrinal
Appendix at the back of this workbook. If you are
choosing an issue from this resource, please refer
to it now.)

Reflection questions centered around the chosen
doctrinal theme can be found at the end of each
topic in the Doctrinal Appendix. The questions
are based on the five-step reflection process. If you
choose a topic not included in the Doctrinal Appendix, craft your own questions according to the
same five-step process.

Following the reflection questions you will be reminded to return to chapter 7, "Preparing the
Catechetical Session," to assist you in crafting your
own session.

Closing Prayer

It is truly right to give you thanks,
it is fitting that we offer you praise,
Father of mercy, faithful God.
You sent Jesus Christ your Son among us
as redeemer and Lord.
He was moved with compassion
for the poor and the powerless,
for the sick and the sinner;
he made himself neighbor to the oppressed.
By his words and actions
he proclaimed to the world
that you care for us
as a father cares for his children.
And so, with all the angels and saints
we sing the joyful hymn of praise.[19]

---

[19]Eucharistic Prayer for Masses for Various Needs and
Occasions: "Preface—Jesus the Compassion of God," *The
Sacramentary.*

Thirty-First Sunday in Ordinary Time

INTRODUCTORY RITES

Entrance Antiphon (or Opening Song)

Do not abandon me, Lord. My God, do not go away from me! Hurry to help me, Lord, my savior. (Ps 37:22–23)[1]

Opening Prayer

The facilitator of the session may lead the prayer. Others in the group may be asked to proclaim the readings.

Let us pray
that our lives will reflect our faith

> *Pause for silent prayer.*

God of power and mercy,
only with your help can we offer you fitting service
    and praise.
May we live the faith we profess
and trust your promise of eternal life.
Grant this through our Lord
Jesus Christ, your Son,
who lives and reigns with you and the Holy
    Spirit,
one God, for ever and ever.[2]

LITURGY OF THE WORD

The readings are proclaimed.

First Reading
Deuteronomy 6:2–6

(Please refer to the fourth Sunday in Ordinary Time for an overview of the Book of Deuteronomy.)

Today's Pericope: Today's reading is etched on the heart of every good Jewish person. It should be etched on the hearts of *all* people. It is a foundational creedal formula known as the *Sh'ma Israel (Hear O Israel!)*. It is a profound expression of faith. If someone were to ask Jewish people what they believed as Jews, they would recite the Shema. Devout Jews wore this prayer in phylacteries, or prayer containers attached to their wrist and forehead. Every home had a mezuzah mounted on its doorframe. The Shema was prayed every morning and evening. It is a summation of Judaism. The Shema professes belief in a monotheistic God. It was Israel's daily prayer. "God is to be loved in response to his prior revelation of himself as the one God."[3] God's self-revelation took place through the exodus-event, and as far as the author is concerned continues in the constant availability of his presence in the one central sanctuary. The Shema also affirms belief in the God who is active in the history of people and who is in relationship with people. The prayer describes the response owed to Yahweh in the face of such incredible, gratuitous covenantal love. "You shall love the Lord your God with all your heart, all your soul and all your strength"—with every fiber of your being. Jewish thought is not dualistic, unlike its Greek counterpart. Heart, soul, and strength are not individual entities—they form the totality of the human person. Body and soul are one. In Judaism Greek dualism does not exist. Body and spirit are one—not divided. Matter is not evil. Hebrew thought upholds and exalts the unity of body and soul.

God loves Israel completely and unconditionally. Therefore, such love should prompt a response from Israel. Hence the great commandment found in today's reading and elaborated in the gospel by Jesus. To love with heart, soul, and strength means the "total love of God with one's deepest life (soul), all of its rational choices and commitments (heart). And with one's external achievements and possessions (strength)."[4] Response to God's love also assumes a social ethic.

---

[1]Thirty-First Sunday in Ordinary Time: "Entrance Antiphon," *The Sacramentary.*

[2]Thirty-First Sunday in Ordinary Time: "Opening Prayer," *The Sacramentary.*

[3]*PL,* 364.

[4]Anthony J. Tombasco, "Love," *CPDBT,* 568.

Love for God demands that it be extended to those in need—especially the poor and oppressed.

Thus, the stage of this love drama is set for us. The people stand on the threshold to the Promised Land. It is enjoined upon them to keep their side of the covenant with God. This is where today's text begins. Deuteronomy is a summation of Israel's salvation history.

In the first part of today's pericope the author establishes the requirements necessary for God to act and fulfill his part of the covenant that will ultimately establish the people in the land. The second part of the pericope professes and proclaims the one God who stands alone above all other gods—who is, in deed and in fact, the only God. Originally this text was a polemic against the Canaanite baals and the myriad of other pagan gods. The Shema was a radical profession of faith in the One God and a commitment to respond by offering nothing less than a people's entire peoplehood, their entire being, their political, spiritual, psychological, and theological selves.

Responsorial Psalm
Psalm 18:2–4, 47, 51

Today's psalm is one of the royal psalms probably going back to the time of David. It is a prayer of thanks for victory after battle and is a wonderful response to the Shema.

Second Reading
Hebrews 7:23–28

(Refer to the twenty-seventh Sunday in Ordinary Time for an overview of the Letter to the Hebrews.)

Today's Pericope: The author of Hebrews has been carefully making his case. Jesus is certainly qualified to be high priest. He now moves to the primary theology of his letter. He compares Jesus' high priesthood to the Levitical priesthood, the priesthood of the old covenant. His polemic insists that Jesus is superior to them—point by point, in all ways, he is superior. The comparison is succinct. There are many Levitical priests. Jesus is only one. The Levitical priesthood is transitory

and temporal. Jesus' priesthood is eternal. Levitical priests are subject to death. Jesus is alive forever. The Levitical priest was a sinner and had to offer sacrifice not only for others, but for himself as well. Jesus, on the other hand, was sinless and thus did not need to offer sacrifice for himself. The Levitical priest was required to offer repeated sacrifices. Jesus offered the one sacrifice—once and for all people, for all time. Levitical priests were appointed by the law. Jesus was appointed by an oath that superseded the Law.

Melchizedek was considered an ideal king and an eternal priest. Even Abraham affirmed his superiority. Since his ancestry, like Jesus' ancestry, is clouded in mystery, he was considered a type for Jesus, the eternal king, the priest above all other priests. Jesus was not born into the priesthood nor was he appointed to it by any human person or institution, nor does it seem, was Melchizedek. Jesus was appointed and ordained to it by God—according to the order of Melchizedek. Jesus' priesthood in essence rendered the priesthood of the covenant passé, outmoded, and obsolete. Jesus' one sacrifice was enough to render all other sacrifices unnecessary. "Jesus is the establishment of a new and more effective priesthood . . . which replaces the Levitical, Aaronic priesthood."[5]

The gospel is proclaimed.

Gospel
Mark 12:28b–34. Jesus tells the scribes that the Shema is the first commandment.

STEP 1
NAMING ONE'S EXPERIENCE

What were your first impressions? What was your first response to the gospel (or the other readings)? What captured your attention?

Each person names his or her initial impression. Statements should be brief. No reasons should be given at this time. All simply listen without agreeing or disagreeing.

---

[5]Michael G. Witczak, S.J., "Melchizedek," *CPDBT*, 608.

STEP 2
UNDERSTANDING

In a brief statement, explain what you think this gospel is trying to convey.

STEP 3
INPUT FROM VISION/STORY/TRADITION

Liturgical Context

Jesus has entered Jerusalem. The liturgy takes us with him—in the liturgy's anamnesis we remember these events and, in the remembering, we are there and it is now. This week a scribe questions Jesus about which is the greatest commandment. Jesus answers by citing the Shema and adds his own elaboration. Jesus places love of neighbor on a par with love of God. This is revolutionary. Love of neighbor flows out of our love for God. Neighbor is not simply the one who lives with us or who worships next to us in the Sunday assembly. Neighbor is anyone who might need our help—*anyone*! Especially those who need our help the most. "The help that is needed may not always, or even usually, be ministering to physical needs; more frequently it will have to do with welcoming the other into our love, with bringing the other into the community."[6]

Today's alternative opening prayer asks that through faith we be given the strength to live the demands of love. The demands of love are borne out in our response to the human family. Let us not forget that every liturgy is an invitation and a command to love. We are sent out into the world to become what we have received. We receive the sacrament of love in the eucharist, the memorial of Jesus' sacrifice for us, and in response we are to go out and live as Jesus lived. The catechism reminds us that eucharist commits us to the poor. Today's liturgy reads like a summary statement of the entire Christian ethos. To live as Christ commands us to live we must love as he loved us—with a self-sacrificing love. We cannot love God without it spilling over into our relationship with others.

---

[6]Joseph Jensen, O.S.B., "Neighbor," *CPDBT*, 675.

Gospel Exegesis

The facilitator provides input from critical biblical scholarship on this text. This input includes insights as to how people would have heard the gospel in Jesus' time.

Mark's narrative, like all good narrative, is resplendent with adversaries and supporters. Jesus' supporters are with him from the very beginning of his ministry. Throughout the story we are introduced to the scribes—doctors of the law. They are not scholars in the modern sense; they have no formal education. The oral tradition was passed on to them and they were to pass it on to others. Their mission was to promote the Torah and the life applications that flowed from it. They were the religious leaders of the day. They interpreted the Torah in order to regulate day-to-day behavior. They were also charged with the duty of teaching younger students and were involved in the courts of justice.

They were headquartered in Jerusalem even though they looked upon the priests in Jerusalem with disdain. Most of the scribes held to Pharisaic theology. Mark usually includes them in the narrative along with the Pharisees, the chief priests, and the elders. With the exception of today's gospel, they are always adversaries. The scriptures are often painted with a bias, however. No doubt the scribes of ancient Palestine have been stereotyped to such a degree that we should be somewhat suspicious of believing the evangelist's portrait of them. It is probably a tainted caricature.

Today's gospel is another pronouncement story. Jesus answers a question posed to him by the scribe: "Which commandment is the most important?" It was a common question posed by rabbis of each generation in hopes of finding a concise formula of the Law to pass on to believers and to formulate one, succinct basic truth on which the Law was built. It was an honest question coming from an honest person in search of an answer—so Jesus answered his question by reciting the Shema. Instead of giving him one command, Jesus cites two. He joins Leviticus 19:18 to the Shema cited in the first reading today. Some scholars maintain that Jesus was the first to put the two love commands—love of God and love of neighbor—together. However, he was not the first. Intertestamental literature from about 100 B.C. shows examples of the two laws placed together. The Testament of Issachar asserted: "Love the Lord and love your neighbor." The Testament of Dan insisted: "Love the Lord throughout all your life, and one another with a true heart." What is remarkable in Jesus' statement of the Law, however, is that he took one law considered to be a great law, and put it together with another considered to be a lesser law and in so doing, placed equal importance on both.[7] He also expanded Israel's exclusive and nationalistic notion of neighbor. When Israel referred to neighbor they meant their own countryfolk. Jesus' understanding of neighbor meant "everyone"—all people, people from all places, no boundaries. Jesus insists that love of neighbor flows out of a person's love for God, and evidence of our love for God can be found in the way we love our neighbor. Our love for God is empty if we fail to love our neighbor.

Jesus' love for God led him to offer his life for the people of the world. His love for God and his faithfulness led him to accomplish the purpose for which God sent him. Jesus was sent by God to fulfill God's plan of salvation for all people. Jesus offered himself in ransom for the many.

Loving with one's whole heart is another way of saying that love cannot be measured. We are to give it all—our entire capacity to love. Love and legalism cannot stand side by side. Legalism sets limits on love. "Love is incompatible with a legalism that sets limits, that specifies what one should do and should avoid."[8] It would be difficult to argue with Jesus, however. How could anyone find fault with naming the Shema as the first command? All Jews would agree that unreserved and unabashed love of God is the heart of the Law. Jesus' expansion of the command to love God was a reminder that love of neighbor is on a par with love of God—"it is as worthy an obligation as the love of God."[9]

The scribe's surprising answer, unique to Mark, agrees with Jesus' answer and insists that love of God and neighbor supersedes all forms of extravagant cultic worship. Jesus tells the scribe that he is close to the reign of God. His heart is in alignment with God's purpose. Jesus' response to the scribe is an invitation and the reader is left with the hope that the scribe will respond favorably to it. The scribe asked no more questions. No one lasted long in a debate with Jesus. Encounters with Jesus demanded a swift decision—Acceptance or Rejection. Jesus awarded the scribe with a public mark of honor, which had to impress the status-conscious audience.

In the ancient Mediterranean world, *to love God* meant that people attached themselves solely to God and to God's purpose. That included attaching oneself to the group that most clearly supported the same goal—the group that attached itself solely around Yahweh, the One God. *Loving one's neighbor as one's self* meant that the object of that love was to be treated as if they were family.

Today's story is unique not only for the reason stated above, but for other reasons as well. It is the climax to a series of Jesus' debates in the Temple. As mentioned above, it is the only time Jesus has an encounter with a scribe that is not antagonistic. The theme of the encounter deals with a primary ideological question—the greatest commandment.[10] This is the last encounter with his opponents before he is arrested and prosecuted by them—"and in it he silences them once and for all."[11]

We immediately expect a confrontation. The scribe is a member of the opposing group, Jesus' antagonists. There is clever literary interest raised. We also expect that the comment made to Jesus—"Well done, teacher, you have answered forthrightly"—is insincere flattery.

We know that the scribe has heard Jesus before and has heard him in debate. In verse 28 we are reminded that the scribe saw Jesus answering well. This may be a literary device used to alert the reader that the scribe may just be a prospective disciple—perhaps one who is neither deaf nor blind. We are led to believe that Jesus is impressed with the scribe. However, Ched Myers reminds us that Jesus' sympathetic tone is illusive—it paves

[7] *WWC*, 250.
[8] *MARK*, 189.
[9] *WWC*, 250.

[10] *BSM*, 317.
[11] Ibid.

the way for Jesus' eventual condemnation of the scribal class in verse 38.[12] Contrary to the exegesis given in the preceding paragraphs, Myers insists that Jesus' final comments are not condemnation, but neither are they an invitation to discipleship.

The scribe's question is grist for typical rabbinic dialogue. It could be honest. However, it could also have been an attempt to coax Jesus into revealing his political commitments. Jesus is quite orthodox, however; he cites the Shema. He does add his own twist by inserting the command from Leviticus to love one's neighbor. He then insists that there are no other commands greater than these. Jesus' answer is startling—no one has ever put the two commands together for the purpose of summarizing the entire Law. Mark's theology adroitly shouts between the lines—*heaven must be wedded to earth, love of God cannot exist in a vacuum. Love of neighbor flows from that love.*

The Leviticus citation is of primary interest in Myers's exegesis of the text. In Leviticus love of neighbor is synonymous with nonexploitation. "The verse Jesus cites is the culmination to a litany of commands prohibiting the *oppression and exploitation of Israel's weak and poor* (Lv 19:9–17), including:

1. Leave your field for the sojourner to glean (vv. 9f.);
2. Do not steal, deal falsely, or profane God (vv. 11f.);
3. Do not oppress the neighbor, exploit employees, or discriminate against the disabled (vv. 13f.);
4. Do no injustice or show partiality in judgment, or slander or witness against the neighbor (vv. 15f.)"[13]

However, Mark's position throughout the narrative is that it is precisely the ruling class, especially the scribes, who are the worst offenders of these laws.

The scribe agrees with Jesus and reinforces it by asserting the importance of obedience over cultic worship. The scribe will give Jesus this much—he is *thoughtful*, insists Jesus. However, the word *thoughtful* used in the narrative is derived from the adjec-

tive describing *the mind*. The scribe has intellectually agreed with Jesus. The story tells us that the scribe is "not far" from God's reign. There is no direct invitation from Jesus to follow him. Myers insists that "not far" implies that orthodoxy is not enough.[14] More than intellectual assent is required. There must be observable, direct action—justice toward one's neighbor must be practiced.

"Mark *appears* to reject the possibility of scribal discipleship. Why? Because however aware of biblical imperatives they might be, they are by definition committed to a *system* that oppresses. To repudiate that system would be to stop being a scribe within it."[15] It is easier for the scribe to say the right things; it is quite another thing to put them into practice.

Mark then proclaims Jesus' victory. After this encounter no one dared challenge Jesus again. No one was a match for him. He expelled people with commercial interests from the Temple. In the face of confrontation he demonstrated cleverness and great rhetorical skill. He challenged anyone who in any way was responsible for or was part of the system based on privilege and exploitation. Ultimately, Jesus is the champion of all people, especially the underdogs. Through the sacrifice of his life Jesus demonstrates the power of love. Jesus taught that loving God means loving the people God loves and considering important the people God considers important. The weakest, lowest members of society always have that distinction.

Proclaim the gospel again.

Sometimes we gain new insights when we hear the text after the interpretation is given. Someone from the group proclaims the gospel a second time.

STEP 4
TESTING

Conversation with the Liturgy and the Scriptures

Test your original understanding in dialogue with the text.

---

[12]Ibid.
[13]Ibid.

[14]Ibid., 318.
[15]Ibid.

(You might consider breaking into smaller groups.)

Now that you've heard the exegesis, were there any new insights? How do you feel about it? How does your original understanding of this gospel compare with what we just shared? How does this story speak to your life?

Sharing Life Experience

Participants share an experience from their lives that connects with the biblical interpretation just presented.

In my many years as a Christian, I have watched many people try to live the Christian life. I have met not many, but a few, who appear to love God, who are daily communicants, yet who return to their nasty false selves once they exit the doors of the church each day. Bitterness and anger are written all over their faces and I wonder what has hurt them. Their speech and their attitudes are laced with vitriolic sarcasm. They often tear down rather than build up. I often wonder how they can see Jesus in the eucharist when they can be so hateful and fail to see Jesus in their brothers and sisters or spouses. I feel sad for them.

I see others who touch everyone with their incredible love. They have time for everyone. No matter what, they stop and share a word of encouragement. Their love of God flows out into love of others. They are the ones who minister to the needy—whether it be the needy poor or the needy grieving. Compassion seems to ooze from them. I see self-sacrificing love—love that goes the extra mile, love that stops everything to help someone in need.

I most especially think of the people who reach out to those the world considers unlovable. I think of the people who minister in prisons and who reach out to AIDS victims. I think of a priest friend who has worked in a prison for many years and offers the face of Christ to the broken humanity that passes through those walls. No doubt he has experienced love in return, but it must take an incredible amount of self-sacrifice to give so much to those who are so alienated from the world. He is someone who has balanced his love of God with love for his neighbor. In his case, his neighbors just happen to be convicts. In the same vein, I think also of those who minister to the homeless and who try to respect them as children of God—not the undeserving poor.

I think about those who suffer from times when it seems that love has failed, such as when a person's relative was so depressed that it resulted in a suicide that also claimed the lives of the children. In those times we ask, Where was love then? Did we fail our loved one? Could we have loved them more? Where was God's love for them? Wasn't it big enough? Love is a mystery that we cannot always fathom. Even though we are called to practice it, it does not always fix everything. "If I would just love her enough" is not always the recipe for making a marriage work in the real world.

Love often gets reduced to pious platitudes and warm fuzzy feelings, but it is often difficult and it is always a mystery. Love can be painful. I think of the beautiful woman I know who struggles to love a relative who hates her. In the midst of constant barbs and nastiness, she tries to reach out in love. She cannot change her relative, but she tries, with the help of God, to change herself. And she has changed. I have witnessed the change.

I think of the wonderful man who is a father to a special needs young adult. He longed to "feel" God's love on a feeling, emotional level. He was Catholic all his life; he did all the right things, but he longed to "feel" the consolation of God. He knew he loved God, but he longed for the "feeling" of God's love in return. It was exciting to watch the "a-ha's" of awareness flood over him as he came to the realization that the "feeling of God's love" he longed for had been present to him all his life. It was manifest through the love of his family, the community, and most especially the precious love of his child. The man's love of God was evident in the love and constant care he showered on his child. We all felt that we were privileged to preside at a most intimate manifestation of God's love and God's presence. We are called to love God with our being, but we must not forget that God loves us passionately as well. Catherine of Sienna insists that God is a mad lover, God loves us so much! The Shema assumes and celebrates that love!

Sometimes love is not returned. It is often rejected altogether. When that happens, it is devastating and nearly breaks the human spirit. Sometimes love is tough. Jesus gives us an example as to how far love can stretch us. It is easy to love our friends, but what about our enemies? That is not always so easy.

It is sometimes difficult to love people who do not share our politics, our religious beliefs, or our attitudes toward others. We become suspicious of those who are different from ourselves.

We might be tempted to dismiss today's gospel as an easy one—one that does not require much effort. After all, who doesn't love? When we look more deeply into who Jesus was asking us to love, the commitment is not quite as easy as it appeared at first glance. The test of whether we are truly living the mandate of today's gospel is to ask how we reach out to those people we really do not like very much. I cannot remember the last time I did that. Perhaps it is time. Also, when was the last time I reached out to those the world considers unlovable? There is much to think about and much to do.

What was Mark trying to tell his community? What does this gospel teach us about love? Who are we to love? How are we to love? Describe your love for God. Now describe your love for neighbor—especially the neighbor envisioned by Jesus in today's gospel. How does this gospel invite you to live differently? In what way does this gospel challenge your community today? In what way has this conversation with the scriptures for today's liturgy invited change in your life? In what way are the biblical themes of covenant, exodus, creation, and community evident in today's readings? Do you still feel the same way about this text as when you began? Has your original understanding been stretched, challenged, or affirmed?

STEP 5
DECISION

The gospel demands a response.

In what concrete way might your parish be invited to respond? Are there any attitudes or behaviors you would like to change as a result of today's conversation? What one concrete action will you take this week in response to the liturgy today?

Pastoral Considerations: In what way does your parish fall short in its mandate to love? Who in your parish is in most need of the love Christ demands in today's gospel? What are the obstacles to

offering the love of Christ? What needs to happen to overcome them? Is there anyone in your parish or your civic community who is exploited? How might you help them? What about the multicultural issues in your parish? Is there unity or is there division? Who is excluded in any way in your community, either intentionally or unintentionally?

Christian Initiation: Are there any people ready to celebrate the rite of acceptance or welcome as this liturgical year draws to a close? What is going on in your catechumenate that might warrant the celebration of the anointing of catechumens?

DOCTRINAL ISSUES

What Church truth/teaching/doctrinal issue could be drawn from the gospel for the thirty-first Sunday in Ordinary Time?

Participants suggest possible doctrinal themes that flow from the readings.

Possible Doctrinal Themes

Love; charity; justice; two great commandments; morality; commandments; Beatitudes; virtues of faith, hope, and love; service; conversion; discipleship.

Present the doctrinal material at this time.

1. The facilitator gives input on a particular doctrinal issue of his or her prior choosing. OR
2. The group chooses a doctrinal issue from the list they created. They read together from the Doctrinal Appendix or other appropriate, official Church documents and the works of respected theologians.

(Many doctrinal issues are found in the Doctrinal Appendix at the back of this workbook. If you are choosing an issue from this resource, please refer to it now.)

Reflection questions centered around the chosen doctrinal theme can be found at the end of each topic in the Doctrinal Appendix. The questions are based on the five-step reflection process. If you choose a topic not included in the Doctrinal Appendix, craft your own questions according to the same five-step process.

Following the reflection questions you will be reminded to return to chapter 7, "Preparing the Catechetical Session," to assist you in crafting your own session.

Closing Prayer

Let us pray
in the presence of God, the source of every good

Pause for silent prayer.

Father in heaven, God of power and Lord of
    mercy,
from whose fullness we have received,
direct our steps in our everyday efforts.
May the changing moods of the human heart
and the limits which our failings impose on hope
never blind us to you, source of every good.
Faith gives us the promise of peace
and makes known the demands of love.
Remove the selfishness that blurs the vision of
    faith.[16]

---

[16]Thirty-First Sunday in Ordinary Time: "Alternative Opening Prayer," *The Sacramentary.*

Thirty-Second Sunday in Ordinary Time

Environment

This Sunday falls in or around the month of November. During November we remember the dead. Some parishes display a special book of the dead in which the names of the deceased are written and displayed near the baptismal font. The Church remembers its deceased members in prayer especially during this month. While not wishing to duplicate the book of the dead used in the worship space, it still might be worthwhile to find a way to imaginatively and creatively remember the deceased relatives of those in the catechetical group. Perhaps the names could be written in calligraphy on parchment paper, or pictures of the deceased might be gathered into an album and then placed in the late autumn catechetical environment. Small votive candles in dark red, green, or amber holders might be placed throughout the environment. Perhaps the catechetical environment might include late fall flowers (fresh or dried) or a cornucopia filled with the late fall harvest of corn, squash, dried grasses, and gourds.

Icons that reflect an eschatological theme might also be used during these last days. Another possibility is to place a grapevine wreath adorned with produce, wheat stalks, or dried grasses in the environment. It may then be used later to craft an Advent wreath. There are multiple sizes available. "A wreath is more than a decoration. It is an emblem of royalty, of victory, of God's reign, of the wedding band we wear to remember our fidelity to Christ."[1]

INTRODUCTORY RITES

Entrance Antiphon (or Opening Song)

Let my prayer come before you, Lord; listen and answer me. (Ps 87:3)[2]

Opening Prayer

The facilitator of the session may lead the prayer. Others in the group may be asked to proclaim the readings.

Let us pray
for health of mind and body

Pause for silent prayer.

God of power and mercy,
protect us from all harm.
Give us freedom of spirit
and health in mind and body
to do your work on earth.
We ask this through our Lord
Jesus Christ, your Son,
who lives and reigns with you and
the Holy Spirit,
one God for ever and ever.[3]

LITURGY OF THE WORD

The readings are proclaimed.

First Reading
1 Kings 17:10–16

(Please refer to the seventeenth Sunday in Ordinary Time for an overview of the Books of Kings.)

Today's story comes from the Elijah cycle in the Books of Kings. The Elijah and the Elisha tradition contains stories of the multiplication of food. They are remembered in the New Testament as a type for the multiplication of the loaves. Elijah was in conflict with King Ahab and his wife Jezebel. Ahab allowed his foreign wife to bring her pagan worship of Baal with her into Israel. Jezebel's prophets sought to destroy the prophets of Yahweh. Elijah informed King Ahab that a drought would come upon the land as punishment for his actions. Elijah took refuge near a stream and God

---

[1] Peter Mazur, *CY*, 191.

[2] Thirty-Second Sunday in Ordinary Time: "Entrance Antiphon," *The Sacramentary*.

[3] Thirty-Second Sunday in Ordinary Time: "Opening Prayer," *The Sacramentary*.

provided bread and meat in the morning and meat in the evening. The streams ran dry because of the drought. Yahweh told Elijah to go to the widow of Zarephath—she would see to his needs.

The widow lived near Sidon, the home of Jezebel's father—who, incidentally, despised Elijah. It was also the pagan home of Baal. Baal was the god of nature. It was believed that Baal had dominion over the land and power over the elements—rain, thunder, and lightning. Yahweh's power over the rain extended even to the land where Baal supposedly had dominion. Yet Baal proved powerless in the face of Yahweh's transcendent might. Not only did the drought extend to the land of Baal, but all those favored by Yahweh were protected and provisions were made for them, just as manna (cakes made with oil, Nm 11:8) was provided in the desert.

Today's pericope is a story of faith. Elijah proceeded headlong into a place of danger simply on the Word of the Lord. How could it be that the pagan woman of Zarephath could be convinced to help him? Only by the power of Yahweh!

Upon arrival in the city, Elijah saw the woman gathering wood. He assumed it was the widow as she was still wearing mourning clothes. Elijah asked for a drink—a common way to initiate a conversation. In a desert climate no one is refused a drink. This safe exchange was a way for people to size up one another. Elijah wasted no time. He immediately asked for more than water. He asked the woman to give him bread as well. She told Elijah that she was on her way to cook the last of her rations and then she and her son would die together.

Elijah would not be deterred. God told him the woman would help him—Elijah believed the Lord. Her destitution would not be a detriment. God would provide the resources the woman needed to accomplish her mission of hospitality. Elijah informed her that God would not allow her to die as a result of the famine and drought. The woman believed God's Word. God's Word was accomplished. The woman and her son were provided with bread and oil for a year.

This pagan woman had no reason to believe in the word of a stranger. Even more extraordinary was the fact that this stranger was a prophet of God—an enemy of her god. She risked everything she had, her life and her son's life, on the word of this stranger. Most scholars insist that the point of this story is faith.

The story is an illustration of the power of God's Word. As God's agent, the prophet spoke that Word and the Word was fulfilled. The story was also a polemic against all the Canaanite gods of fertility and nature. Elijah, prophet of the Lord, spoke the Lord's Word and famine came over the land. The woman's life and the life of her son were in jeopardy because of the famine. God's Word, however, was sufficient to provide for the woman and her son. Elijah promised that her jar of flour would not go empty and that she would have enough oil to carry her through the famine.

To a people in the throes of Babylonian captivity, this was a story of hope and consolation. This story, and others like it, served as encouragement to those who believed in a surviving, remnant people who would be reestablished on the land, the moral ineptitude of the kings notwithstanding.

The woman trusted in the Word of the prophet—she put her faith in Yahweh and as a result God provided for all her needs. She is an icon of faith and trust. Unlike the corrupt kings of Israel, this lowly woman trusted God to provide all her needs.

The story of the widow from Zarephath was chosen for its similarity to the story of the widow in today's gospel. Today we are given the image of two widows, lowly in the eyes of the world, but not in the eyes of God. God shows special care for widows and orphans. They own a piece of God's heart. God's compassion and mercy flow out to them in abundance. It is they, not the rebel kings, who show God the reverence due him—they put their faith and trust in God. God works wondrous deeds in a pagan land—a sign of the universal nature of God's mission of salvation.

Responsorial Psalm
Psalm 146:7–10

In today's Hallel psalm, God is praised for his compassionate care of those in need. Widows are included among those in need of God's mercy.

Second Reading
Hebrews 9:24–28

(Refer to the twenty-seventh Sunday in Ordinary Time for an overview of the Letter to the Hebrews.)

Today's Pericope: In today's pericope the author of Hebrews continues to expound on the contrast between the priesthood of Jesus and the Levitical priesthood. Some of the same arguments made last week are repeated in today's reading. The Levitical priest performs his work in a physical space—the temporal sanctuary. Jesus' locus is the heavenly sanctuary—God's presence. The Levitical priest must repeat sacrifices. Jesus' sacrifice is once and for all. The Levitical priest offers blood from creatures. Jesus offered his own blood.

The author alludes to the Day of Atonement. On the day of the celebration the priest would exit the sanctuary after completing his priestly duties in the temple. He would then announce to the people that the work of atonement had been accomplished. The author contrasts the priest's function on the Day of Atonement with the second coming of Jesus, which will signal the completion of his priestly mission. The hallmark of Jesus' priestly service is the intercession he makes to God on behalf of the human race.

The gospel is proclaimed.

Gospel
Mark 12:38–44. The widow put in more than anyone else.

STEP 1
NAMING ONE'S EXPERIENCE

What were your first impressions? What was your first response to the gospel (or the other readings)? What captured your attention?

Each person names his or her initial impression. Statements should be brief. No reasons should be given at this time. All simply listen without agreeing or disagreeing.

STEP 2
UNDERSTANDING

In a brief statement, explain what you think this gospel is trying to convey.

STEP 3
INPUT FROM VISION/STORY/TRADITION

Liturgical Context

The end of the liturgical year is just around the corner, and with it comes a focused attention on the end of times while the beginning of the year dovetails from reflection on ending things to new beginnings. Both the ending and the beginning express our constant hope and the hope we celebrate at every liturgical gathering: "Lord Jesus, come again in glory!"

Jesus is in Jerusalem. We know what happens in Jerusalem. His teaching reflects a more urgent tone. His time with the disciples is getting shorter and there is much they still do not understand. One day they will, however. For now, Jesus continues his catechism on discipleship. He challenges those who would put themselves first in the reign of God and he upholds the rights of the poor. He demonstrates what it means to live the Christian life. It means that we must give ourselves completely to God—just as he gave himself for the sake of the world. Gregory Nazianzus spoke of the implications of Christ's sacrifice:

> Become like Christ, since Christ has become like us. Become gods for him since he became human for us. He has become inferior to make us superior; he has become poor to enrich us by his poverty; he has taken the condition of a slave to procure freedom for us; he has come on earth to bring us to heaven; he has been tempted to see us triumph; he has been dishonored to cover us in glory; he has died to save us; he has ascended to heaven to draw us to himself, we who lie prostrate because of falling into sin. Give all, offer

all, to him who has given himself for us as a prize and a ransom. We will give nothing as great as ourselves if we have grown by the nature of this mystery and have become for him all which he has become for us. (Gregory Nazianzus, 329–89, bishop, Cappadocian theologian)[4]

In the reading from the Letter to the Hebrews the author continues to compare Jesus' priesthood with the Levitical priesthood.

In the alternative opening prayer for today's liturgy, we remember God, who is just and merciful. We ask that we be shielded from the distortion of pride—a prayer that should have been etched on the hearts of the scribes Jesus refers to in today's gospel. We further ask to conform our lives to the will of God so that we may become better servants. These past weeks Jesus reminds his disciples what it means to be a good disciple—those who desire greatness should serve those the world considers the least, even poor widows!

Gospel Exegesis

The facilitator provides input from critical biblical scholarship on this text. This input includes insights as to how people would have heard the gospel in Jesus' time.

The gospels for the preceding weeks have reminded us that Jesus' break with the scribes is now complete. The crowds are still fervent supporters in spite of the antagonistic break with his opponents. Mark wants to make sure his readers realize that the break is with Judaism, not with the Jewish people.

Jesus assumes a formal role as teacher. The debates are over. Jesus now addresses the "great crowd" and they gladly hear him. He no longer engages those who would entrap him. Rather than entering into conflict with his opponents who ask him questions, Jesus now reverses the process and asks questions of the crowds, thereby teaching them. Mark's Christology is picking up momentum. In verses 35–37, prior to today's pericope, the title *Son of David* comes to the fore again. Jesus asks the people how it is possible that

he could be both the "son" of David and the "lord" of David. The question is an opportunity for Mark to posit his Christology. "The Messiah is the 'son' of David because he is descended from David; by the same token, the Messiah is also the 'lord' of David because, as the Son of God, he is of higher station and authority than David."[5] Mark has been leading up to this theology throughout the gospel. Jesus is not only the Messiah, he is also the Son of David. Both are correct designations. He is a descendant of David and he is the one who was sent by God to fulfill all the eschatological expectations associated with David. However, Jesus does not engage in military conflict; instead, his Davidic authority is exercised in love and mercy—*to heal and to save*. In spite of the public proclamation of Jesus as Son of David and Messiah, even in spite of Bartimaeus's bold proclamation, the messianic secret is still intact because no one as yet could begin to fathom the cross that lies ahead. Thus, while all the above-mentioned titles are correct, they are nevertheless insufficient.

Jesus exercised his role as Son of David when he healed and saved the blind Bartimaeus. He exercised his role as the Son of God when he saved the human race from the ravages of sin by his sacrifice on the cross. Even though Jesus allows his identity to go forward as the promised messianic Son of David, the one whose reign would inaugurate healing and freedom from oppression, the messianic secret is still intact. Jesus' identity as Son of God will not be fully understood until after Calvary and the resurrection.

Jesus is in Jerusalem; his life and mission are coming to fulfillment. As insiders to Mark's purpose, we are given a lens through which to view the stories and events that take place in Jerusalem. Jesus is the eschatological Son of David with all the meaning (except militaristic) attached to that title. More than that, however, he is the Son of God, who saves the entire world from sin. This is the Jesus who lays bare the hypocrisy of the scribes and exalts the integrity of the poor widow.

The scribes. People deferred to the scribes because of their status as learned theologians. They invited

---

[4]*RF*, 136.

[5]*COMG*, 112–113.

and enjoyed the special attention. The Talmud insisted that when two people met in public, the person learned in the Law should be greeted by the other person first.[6] No one knew the Law better than the scribes—they fed off the honor due them. They wore distinguishing attire and strictly observed the Law. Special seats in the synagogue were reserved for them—facing the people, directly in front of the sacred scrolls. They put on a showy display of piety and verbose prayer. It was no secret that they treated the poor and the marginalized unfavorably. The scriptures are filled with condemnation for greedy, exploitive people in leadership. Judaism did not look kindly on unscrupulous scribes.[7] However, Mark's difficulties with the scribes probably reflect the church's tension with official Judaism. (Matthew addresses the same issue in chapter 23.)

Widows. Women were entirely dependent on their fathers or their husbands. Their status was on a par with slaves and children. A widow with no father or male to take care of her was among the most vulnerable in the society. Thus, the Law was very insistent that widows' rights be preserved. Widows enjoyed God's special favor. Woe be to anyone who treated them badly! One definition of the unrighteous was someone who had disdain for orphans, widows, and strangers. (See Ps 146:6.)

Orphans were often named in tandem with their mothers because when the father was absent and there was no male protector, they were as vulnerable as the widow. A widow who never bore a son was expected to claim her right to marry her husband's brother. Any children from that union would bear the name of the mother's first dead husband (Levirate Law—Dt 25:5–10, Mk 12:18–27). The surviving brother's refusal brought great shame upon him. Widows were very special people deserving of protection. We see God's compassion for widows evident in Jesus' response to the widow in today's gospel.[8]

The widow in today's gospel. The story of the widow follows on the heels of Jesus' chastisement of the scribes. She is no doubt set apart as a contrast to

their false piety. She is an example of true Jewish piety. She is a symbol of the common people, the peasant community. The split Jesus makes is with the leaders of Judaism, not with the people.

The woman comes forward to place her money in the "treasury." This is probably a reference to the thirteen trumpet-shaped containers placed in the court of the Temple. The coins she deposited were the smallest Roman coin in circulation (half a penny—*quadron*). It is an incredibly insignificant sum. The woman deposited two coins. This would have captured the audience's interest. She not only gave one coin, she gave two—she could have kept one for herself. Mark used a common literary device *(he summoned the disciples to him)* for alerting the readers that something significant was either taking place or being taught.

Jesus' words about the woman were not words of praise; they were words of lament. The poor woman gave out of her poverty. The wealthy were generous in their giving, but the woman gave everything she had—her entire subsistence. She gave it all to God, trusting God's providence completely. She held nothing back. She gave everything—her livelihood and, most important, her security. Jesus' teaching to the disciples is now complete. He finished his catechism on discipleship, bringing his ministry to a proper close. The story of the widow is an apt transition to events that are now ready to step out of the shadows. Also, what a wonderful way to segue into the story of another who would give everything—not just his security, but everything, his entire life! This is the discipleship of the new covenant.

Ched Myers offers a contrasting perspective to this gospel. Traditional exegesis (presented in the preceding paragraphs) interprets this gospel as a contrast between the hypocrisy of the scribes and the woman's true piety. Myers insists that "bourgeois scholarship, oblivious to Mark's critique of the political economy of the temple, portrays the common theme as contrast between the religious hypocrisy of the scribes and the genuine piety of the poor woman."[9] Myers insists that recent scholarship challenges former interpretations.

[6] *CWJB*, 160.
[7] *MARK*, 192.
[8] Carolyn Osiek, R.S.C.J., "Widows," *CPDBT*, 1072–1073.
[9] *BSM*, 320.

Jesus warns the *crowd*—(*crowd/blepete*, a word used when referring to the Pharisees and Herodians and their hypocritical practice). He levels a charge against them. They love to prance in long robes, to be greeted in public, to be given front row seats in the synagogue, and to be ushered to the first couch at dinners. Mark accuses the scribes of seeking positions of status, power, and prestige (all values with the highest priority in an honor-based culture) at every level of social life. This behavior is the antithesis of Jesus' insistence that the last will be first and the first will be the servant of all. Jesus dismissed the entire scribal class as unfit for discipleship.

The condemnation becomes more intense. "They devour the houses of widows and as a pretext, recite lengthy prayers" (v. 40). The scribes have become wealthy off the backs of poor widows. There are two possible interpretations of this text. First, women were not trusted to take care of their husbands' estate. It was customary for scribes to assume the role of trustee for the widow's estate in the event of her husband's death. If a scribe could not be trusted, then who could? Their public piety and long prayers were certainly enough evidence to attest to their trustworthiness. Right? *Wrong!* As trustees, the scribes were entitled to compensation from the estate. The system was notorious for greed, embezzlement, and abuse. Scripture may demand that widows and orphans be cared for, but practice was another matter altogether. Widows and orphans were exploited while the scribal class feathered their own corrupt nests.

The second possible interpretation—the place where scribes recited their long prayers was the Temple; the taxes and donations levied by the Temple were an excessive burden for the poor. Jesus illustrates his disgust for the way in which the poor were given limited access to the place of prayer by calling attention to the poor widow. Myers suggests this is probably the more accurate of the two interpretations.

Regardless of which position is the correct one, the bottom line is the same. Scribal piety is a cover for opportunism and exploitation of the poor.[10] Mark holds the scribal class responsible for such

abuses and insists that they will be subject to severe judgment.

The story tells us that Jesus *sat down* in front of the treasury. The reader is alerted that this is a moment of judgment. "This stage direction is proleptic of judgment, for Jesus will shortly 'face' the temple mount in order to predict its demise (13:3)."[11] Jesus observed "how the crowd put money in the treasury" (v. 41). He scrutinized (*etheōrei*) the situation. As mentioned above, we are alerted that a significant teaching is about to take place as he called his disciples to him. "The temple has robbed this woman of her very means of livelihood" (12:44). "Like the scribal class, it no longer protects widows, but exploits them. As if in disgust, Jesus 'exits' the temple—for the final time" (13:1a).[12]

John Pilch presents another interesting interpretation of this text. This vignette is not to be understood as a story about the superior piety of the poor. He insists that in the honor and shame culture of the Mediterranean world there was an obligation to maintain one's birth status. No one was to purposefully jeopardize or lessen it. If the woman donated her entire livelihood it would have been considered shameful behavior—she deliberately made her status worse than it was.

Earlier in the gospel Jesus taught that it was wrong to jeopardize support for one's parents by donating to the Temple (*corban*). It would be doubly wrong for a poor person to give everything she had to the Temple, thereby increasing her poverty. How could Jesus praise such behavior? Rather than praise, Jesus lamented her behavior. The religious leaders taught her sacrificial giving. She obeyed. However, they promised to help the poor with the donations given to the Temple treasury—they had a responsibility to help the poor. Temple funds were used to feed the greed of those in charge, not the poor. Money was spent on "conspicuous consumption instead: long robes and banquets. This is how they 'devoured the estates of widows.' "[13]

---

[10]Ibid., 321.

[11]Ibid.
[12]Ibid., 322.
[13]*CWJB*, 162.

Proclaim the gospel again.

Sometimes we gain new insights when we hear the text after the interpretation is given. Someone from the group proclaims the gospel a second time.

STEP 4
TESTING

Conversation with the Liturgy and the Scriptures

Test your original understanding in dialogue with the text.

(You might consider breaking into smaller groups.)

Now that you've heard the exegesis, were there any new insights? How do you feel about it? How does your original understanding of this gospel compare with what we just shared? How does this story speak to your life?

Sharing Life Experience

Participants share an experience from their lives that connects with the biblical interpretation just presented.

Today's gospel reminds me of the ways in which the poor are exploited in the world and in the church. We often embrace an attitude that insists that if the poor would just work harder, they would not be in such dire straits. While there is no doubt some truth to any statement, it is false to assume that the poor are poor because they refuse to work. The system keeps them poor. Years ago our family was working with the poor in an urban parish. We were driving from a suburb to an inner-city parish. We decided to look into moving into a poor inner-city neighborhood in the parish. Our investigation began in earnest. Our good intentions were thwarted at every turn. We looked at many rat-infested, dilapidated houses in the inner city. In the end we decided against the move. We could not afford to move. We were paying far less rent for a nice house in the suburbs than what we would have to pay in the inner-city neighborhood. We could not afford to move into the city, nor would it have been good stewardship of the resources we were given. The reason the rent was so high was because it was offered on a weekly basis—

an attractive option for the poor who are often paid by the week. The very people who need a break are exploited at every turn of the road.

Parishes are also guilty of exploitation. Some parishes publish the giving history of their parishioners in hopes of shaming people into better stewardship. As we know from today's gospel, the dollar a week of Mrs. So and So may represent the greatest sacrifice in the entire parish. One parish took people off the parish roster if after one year they failed to donate anything to the parish. They were no longer considered members of that community. No questions were asked; they were simply expunged. That same parish donates nothing to the world's poor.

Our parish is very generous to the poor. I am honored to be in a parish that tithes, and that supports multiple projects for the poor in this country and in the Third World. Do we always exercise an option for the poor, however? Probably not. Our first question is not, "How does this decision impact the poor in our parish, community, and world?" We have a long way to go before we get to that point in our justice consciousness. I am confident that we are on the way, however.

While the Catholic Church gives more than any other institution to the world's poor, we still have much room for growth. When our corporate efforts to pass on the gospel and the tradition to our children generation after generation evolve into an institution that serves only the more affluent members of our communities, we need to take a serious look at our practice and our mission. I am proud that 30 percent of our elementary schoolchildren are subsidized by the parish, but at the same time I am saddened that in some places Catholic education has become something that is nearly priced out of the pocketbooks of the struggling middle class and the poor. For example, three of our children are eighteen months apart in age. Catholic high school education was not a possibility for us. When tuitions average between $4,000 and $5,000 a year for Catholic high school education, $10,000 to $15,000 a year in school tuition is more than even the most frugal family can afford to pay for education. While there are no easy answers to these very complex questions, today's gospel is an invitation to begin to at least stay with the questions, to grapple with them and to seek "just" solutions.

Today's gospel, whether it is a gospel challenging scribal greed and status seeking or whether it is a proclamation in praise of faith, it makes no difference. It all boils down to the same issue. What are my priorities? Where does my security lie? How do materialism and greed have a foothold in my life? If my relationship with God is not my first concern, what is? Am I willing to give my life, my all, for Jesus Christ and the gospel?

When I believe that the plight of the poor is "their problem," then I fail to live the discipleship Jesus asks of me in today's gospel. Today's gospel is a reminder to us as church and as individuals that it is not "their problem." It is "our problem." If I truly have faith, then I will respond to the gospel. When I/we place complete trust in God and his providential care, I/we will let go of the fear that says "there will not be enough for me/us." When I/we share out of my/our poverty—physical and spiritual—I/we will have more than I/we need.

What was Mark trying to tell his community? What way, if any, do you relate to the widow, the scribes, Jesus? Who are the poor widows in your parish, your workplace, your home? Who are the scribes in your parish, your workplace, your home? Are you in a position to initiate change? What are the obstacles? In what way does this gospel challenge your community today? In what way has this conversation with the scriptures for today's liturgy invited change in your life? In what way are the biblical themes of covenant, exodus, creation, and community evident in today's readings? Do you still feel the same way about this text as when you began? Has your original understanding been stretched, challenged, or affirmed?

STEP 5
DECISION

The gospel demands a response.

In what concrete way might your parish be invited to respond? Are there any attitudes or behaviors you would like to change as a result of today's conversation? What one concrete action will you take this week in response to the liturgy today?

DOCTRINAL ISSUES

What Church truth/teaching/doctrinal issue could be drawn from the gospel for the thirty-second Sunday in Ordinary Time?

Participants suggest possible doctrinal themes that flow from the readings.

Possible Doctrinal Themes

Preferential option for the poor; justice; morality; faith; discipleship; paschal mystery; social sin; stewardship

Present the doctrinal material at this time.

1. The facilitator gives input on a particular doctrinal issue of his or her prior choosing. OR
2. The group chooses a doctrinal issue from the list they created. They read together from the Doctrinal Appendix or other appropriate, official Church documents and the works of respected theologians.

(Many doctrinal issues are found in the Doctrinal Appendix at the back of this workbook. If you are choosing an issue from this resource, please refer to it now.)

Reflection questions centered around the chosen doctrinal theme can be found at the end of each topic in the Doctrinal Appendix. The questions are based on the five-step reflection process. If you choose a topic not included in the Doctrinal Appendix, craft your own questions according to the same five-step process.

Following the reflection questions you will be reminded to return to chapter 7, "Preparing the Catechetical Session," to assist you in crafting your own session.

Closing Prayer

Let us pray
that our prayer rise like incense
in the presence of God

Pause for silent prayer.

Almighty Father,
strong is your justice and great is your mercy.
Protect us in the burdens and challenges of life.
Shield our minds from the distortion of pride
and enfold our desire with the beauty of truth.
Help us to become more aware of your loving
    design
so that we may more willingly give our lives in ser-
    vice to all.
We ask this through Christ our Lord.[14]

[14]Thirty-Second Sunday in Ordinary Time: "Alternative
Opening Prayer," *The Sacramentary*.

THIRTY-THIRD SUNDAY IN ORDINARY TIME

Environment

Please refer to the thirty-second Sunday in Ordinary Time.

INTRODUCTORY RITES

Entrance Antiphon (or Opening Song)

The Lord says: my plans for you are peace and not disaster; when you call to me, I will listen to you, and I will bring you back to the place from which I exiled you. (Jer 29:11, 12, 14)[1]

Opening Prayer

The facilitator of the session may lead the prayer. Others in the group may be asked to proclaim the readings.

Let us pray
that God will help us to be faithful

Pause for silent prayer.

Father of all that is good,
keep us faithful in serving you,
for to serve you is our lasting joy.
We ask this through our Lord
Jesus Christ, your Son,
who lives and reigns with you and
the Holy Spirit,
one God, for ever and ever.[2]

LITURGY OF THE WORD

The readings are proclaimed.

First Reading
Daniel 12:1–3

Overview of the Book of the Prophet Daniel: The title of this book of the Bible is named after the protagonist of the book, not the author. The locus of Daniel is the New Babylonian Empire of the sixth century B.C. The name *Daniel* means "my judge is God," or "God has judged." The Daniel of this book is not the Daniel mentioned in other biblical books, such as the Daniel of Ezekiel, Ezra, and Nehemiah fame.

The Book of Daniel is naturally divided into two equal parts. Chapters 1–6 include stories about Daniel and three companions at the Babylonian royal court.[3] The six other chapters (7–12) consist of Daniel's four visions. The vivid, symbolic images of Daniel's visions portray the four kingdoms of Jewish occupation from the time of the Babylonian conquest of Judea until the future establishment of God's kingdom. The Greek version of the book contains further elaborations—"two additions in chapter three and three stories of Daniel's exploits with Susanna, the priests of Bel, and the Dragon (chaps. 13–14)."[4]

Two centuries before the writing of Daniel, Assyria added Israel (the Northern Kingdom) to its vast empire, thereby making it Assyria's vassal state. At the end of the seventh century Cyaxares, the king of the Medes, joined forces with the Babylonians and conquered Nineveh and the Assyrian Empire. Babylonian Nebuchadnezzar occupied most of the Assyrian territory and extended it even farther by his conquest of Judah, the Southern Kingdom. Over the years Nebuchadnezzar's successors allowed Babylonian power to decline until the Persian king, Cyrus the Great, conquered Babylon in 539 B.C. From that point on the region was ruled by successors of Cyrus. The only noteworthy Persian kings after Cyrus were Darius I and Alexander the Great (331). Alexander placed the ancient Near East under Greek control. Thus, the Greek dynasty of Ptolemies ruled Palestine during the third century and the capital was Alexandria in Egypt. In the second century the Seleucid dynasty was in control and the capital was Antioch in Syria. (See the following list of kings, rulers, and dynasties.)

[1]Thirty-Third Sunday in Ordinary Time: "Entrance Antiphon," *The Sacramentary.*

[2]Thirty-Third Sunday in Ordinary Time: "Opening Prayer," *The Sacramentary.*

[3]Louis F. Hartman, C.SS.R., revised by Alexander A. DiLella, O.F.M., "Daniel," *NJBC,* 406–407.

[4]Ibid., 407.

The Book of Daniel was written from the context of the historical situation of the time. During the reign of Nebuchadnezzar many of the people of Israel were exiled to Babylon (ca. 598–582). Cyrus allowed the exiles to return to their homeland in 539. The Jews were granted religious freedom and limited political autonomy under the Persian and Ptolemaic dynasties. The Seleucid ruler, Antiochus IV Epiphanes, on the other hand, attempted to force Hellenization upon the Jews for sociopolitical reasons. He insisted that the Jews abandon their former religion and worship the pagan gods of the kingdom. The Jews revolted (see Maccabees 1–2).

Kings and Rulers of the Ancient Near East

Kings of the Neo-Babylonian Empire
(605–539 B.C.E.)
Nebuchadnezzar, Evil-merodach, Neriglissar, Labashi-marduk, Nabonidus

Kings of the Persian Empire
(550–331 B.C.E.)
Cyrus, Cambyses, Darius I, Xerxes I, Artaxerxes I, Serxes II, Darius II, Artaxerxes II, Artaxerxes III, Arses, Darius III

Greek Rulers
(336–309)
Alexander the Great, Philip Arrhidaeus, Alexander IV

Ptolemaic Dynasty
(323–146 B.C.E.)
Ptolemy I Soter, Ptolemy II, Philadelphus, Ptolemy III Euergetes, Ptolemy IV, Philopator, Ptolemy V Ephiphanes, Ptolemy VI, Philometor

Seleucid Dynasty
(312–164)
Seleucus I Nicator, Antiochus I Soter, Antiochus II Theos, Seleucus II Callinicus, Seleucus III Soter, Antiochus III the Great, Seleucus IV, Philopator, Antiochus IV Epiphanes (175–164). Forced Hellenization took place under Antiochus IV Epiphanes.[5]

The conflict between the Jewish religion and the paganism of the foreign ruling power is the backdrop for the Book of Daniel and its primary theme. Daniel maintains that God is in control of the situation and that Israel's wisdom far surpasses pagan philosophy.[6] God will manifest his universal power and authority over all the kings of the earth until such time as God's reign will be established permanently on the earth.

The literary genre used by the author to make his point is haggadic and apocalyptic. The apocalyptic literature is observable in the mysterious visions and revelations of chapters 7–12. The theme of the visions centers around the eschatological establishment of God's messianic kingdom. The book alludes to an unknown ancient historical character who received the revelations. Daniel writes in typical apocalyptic style about events that are already part of Israel's past history, but he writes about them as if they have yet to occur— they are written as future events. The apocalyptist then predicts the events of the final days: "resurrection and the last judgment, the cosmic consummation."[7] Even though the text refers to events that have already taken place, it is still considered a form of prophecy because it offers an interpretation of past events through the eyes of God.

The haggadic literature is found in chapters 1–6 and 13–14. Haggadic literature gets its name and its origin from the Hebrew word *haggadah*, which means a "setting forth," a "narrative"—a "story" whose purpose is to teach a moral lesson and which has little to do with historical fact. A story can be an elaboration and embellishment of an actual historical event; in such a case it is called an haggadic midrash. A haggadah can also be a story with absolutely no historical basis whatsoever. It is difficult to determine how much of a haggadah is historical and how much is elaboration and embellishment.

The stories about Daniel are haggadic. They cannot be taken as strict history, yet it is possible that historical data are contained within them. However, since the purpose of the stories is not history telling, one cannot conclude definitively that

---

[5]Ibid.

[6]Ibid.
[7]*PL*, 368.

Daniel is an historical character or whether he is simply a person of legend—a creation of Jewish folklore.[8] The author's intent is not to satisfy twentieth-century Western curiosity and fascination with issues of inerrancy. The author's haggadic stories are simply for the purpose of conveying a spiritual message.

Prior to advanced biblical scholarship, it was believed that the first six chapters of Daniel were historical, that Daniel was the author, and that the latter chapters contained biblical prophecy. Few scholars would defend that position today. The author's belief in angels, his apocalyptic leanings, and his belief in the resurrection of the dead date the writing of this book to a time much later than the Babylonian captivity. Besides, the details of the exile are sketchy at best. Details of the Seleucid dynasty are quite clear, however, and therefore date the writing of this text to the period of the Hellenistic age, probably shortly before the death of Antiochus Epiphanes in 164 B.C.

While it is not certain, there is broad agreement that the Book of Daniel may have been written by several authors who shared the same religious views, spirit, and purpose. The book's purpose was to encourage the Jews to remain faithful to Judaism during a time when pagan Hellenism was spreading rapidly and during a time of religious persecution at the hands of Antiochus Epiphanes. They were encouraged to remain faithful to the teaching of Moses and to resist the new religion being forced upon them. Daniel exalts the superiority of Yahweh's wisdom over the wisdom of the pagans. He also wants to assure the people that God will rescue his faithful ones from the clutches of their persecutors. There is an enduring, ageless message in the Book of Daniel: "God is the master of history, who uses the rise and fall of nations as preparatory steps in the establishment of his universal reign over all people."[9] Daniel is the first book to mention the angel, Michael, whose name means "who is like God." Michael is designated God's servant. Michael is ready because now is the hour that God wants to conquer evil in what will prove to be a very difficult conquest. Everyone's righteous deeds will be recorded in a book—

everyone, no matter what their nationality. What will happen to those who die before the final battle? They will have died without the joy of experiencing the complete victory over evil. Both the enemy and the righteous are subject to the same fate—both will die. Daniel insists that the righteous will rise after death; they will be rewarded for their heroic efforts. Unlike their wicked companions in death, the death of the righteous will not be eternal. What will be the fate of our dead heroes in faith before that final, cosmic battle? Description transcends human language but the righteous dead will enjoy a new world of light emanating from the Source of all Light; "they will have a share in the nature of God."[10]

Today's Pericope: Today's reading is a transition text before the proclamation of the cosmic end of the age. God's deliverance comes to bear in the form of resurrection. Daniel 12 is the earliest recorded belief in the resurrection in the Old Testament. After the resurrection the just will be separated from the unjust. The just will enjoy eternal reward while the unjust will live in eternal shame and condemnation.

Resurrection living involves radical change—the resurrected will shine like the stars. Jesus insisted that resurrected life will be similar to that of the angels. Paul insists that the resurrected will don a heavenly body.[11] Resurrection is not understood as life as usual *somewhere else*; it is new, transformed life, completely different than *life here*. It is a new, transcendent form of existence.

Responsorial Psalm
Psalm 16:5, 8–11

Today's psalm is a prayer of trust in Yahweh, who delivers people from death and destruction. In its original form it is not apocalyptic; it is a prayer for deliverance from immanent death. This psalm will later be appropriated by the early church as an apologetic for the death and resurrection of Jesus. The Christian meaning deepens the psalm's original meaning. It is a general prayer of hope in the resurrection.

---

[8]*NJBC*, 407.
[9]Ibid.

[10]*DL* (V), 302.
[11]*PL*, 368.

Second Reading
Hebrews 10:11–14, 18

(Please refer to the twenty-sixth Sunday in Ordinary Time for an overview of the Letter to the Hebrews.)

Today's Pericope: Today's pericope brings the theological theme to a conclusion in the continued comparison between Jesus' priesthood and the Levitical priesthood. Last week's reading compared the yearly offering by the high priest on the Day of Atonement with Jesus' once and for all offering on Calvary. Today the comparison is between the daily offering by the ordinary priests and Jesus' sacrifice.

The author of Hebrews seeks to demonstrate that Israel's sacrificial system became obsolete with the once and for all sacrifice of Christ. The Book of Leviticus prescribed five types of sacrifice.[12] (1) *Holocaust (that which rises or ascends).* The holocaust offering involved the complete burning of the offering on the altar. Holocausts were offered each day in atonement for individual sin and in praise of God. (2) *Cereal offerings.* These were offerings made by the priest on the altar and were grain or cereal and oil and incense. Part of the sacrifice was burned and the rest was consumed by the priest and his family. (3) *Peace offerings.* There were three types of peace offerings. First, an animal was offered in *thanksgiving* to God. Second, the *votive* offering was offered as a response to a vow of obligation. Third, a *free will* offering was offered as a spontaneous gift. It was not to be completely burned but shared by the one offering the gift and his family in God's presence. Through the peace offering it was believed that the relationship between God and the offerer was rendered harmonious. Some scholars refer to the peace offering as a communion sacrifice. (4) *Sin offering.* The sin offering was offered as atonement for an ethical or physical uncleanness. If people came in contact or touched something unclean, if they contracted a disease or sinned against the Law, it was required they seek atonement. The sin offering consisted of burning the fat of an animal, sprinkling its blood on the altar, and burning the rest of the offering outside the temple. The poor were allowed to sacrifice a dove instead of an animal. In light of Israel's system of sacrifice it is no wonder that the author of Hebrews insists that Jesus' once and for all sacrifice rendered the sacrifices obsolete. "In the one unique and irrepeatable sacrifice of Jesus, perfect praise has been given to God (holocaust), absolute and intimate union has been achieved (peace offering), and sin with its guilt has been expiated (sin, guilt offerings). (5) *Guilt offering.* A male ram was usually offered in guilt offerings—the prescribed sacrifice for very serious sin. Because of his perfect sacrificial act, Christ is now seated in glory at the right hand of God, waiting until his enemies are placed beneath his feet (v. 14)."[13]

The image of Jesus *sitting* refers to Christ on his throne. Jesus is raised from the dead and has ascended to the throne of glory. His intended purpose has been accomplished. Jesus can now sit on his throne and wait for the full effects of his saving action to be fulfilled at the parousia. Jesus' priesthood continues in the Christian community, however. The reference to *standing* perhaps refers to the intercession that Christ continues to make on our behalf in the presence of God.[14]

The word *perfection* does not refer to moral perfection. It means that all those who follow Christ and are heirs to the paschal mystery are fully initiated into his life. While on earth they are honored to be present at the banquet in which heaven is wedded to earth. By participation in the divine liturgy Christians achieve their destiny by anticipating it in the eucharistic feast.

Jesus' sacrifice was once and for all people. It cannot be repeated. However, he does continue in his role as priest in the presence of God by offering intercession on our behalf.

The gospel is proclaimed.

Gospel
Mark 13:24–32. Jesus will gather the elect from the four winds.

---

[12] *WWC,* 254.

[13] Ibid., 254.
[14] *PL,* 369.

What were your first impressions? What was your first response to the gospel (or the other readings)? What captured your attention?

Each person names his or her initial impression. Statements should be brief. No reasons should be given at this time. All simply listen without agreeing or disagreeing.

STEP 2
UNDERSTANDING

In a brief statement, explain what you think this gospel is trying to convey.

STEP 3
INPUT FROM VISION/STORY/TRADITION

Liturgical Context

Every eucharistic liturgy is eschatological. We feast at the eucharistic banquet in communion with the saints in heaven as we await the eternal banquet. Every memorial acclamation professes our common hope:

> Dying you destroyed our death,
> rising you restored our life.
> Lord Jesus come in glory.[15]

At the end of every liturgical year the Church preoccupies itself with things concerning finitude—the end of creation and the end of history. We also begin each liturgical cycle with the same reflection. Thus, the liturgy for today and next Sunday invites us to consider the mystery of eternity by reflecting on what we celebrate in faith. God created the heavens and the earth and saw that it was good. All creation will be transformed by the Holy Spirit. Jesus will return in glory and those whose hearts are grounded in love will live with him for all eternity—"this future is decided in the

present."[16] We do not know the day or the hour—it is shrouded in secrecy. We simply must be ready. One way to wait out our days is through our participation in and celebration of the liturgy. The poetic words of Jean Corbon express our belief and celebration of these end times in which we live.

The river of life, rising from the throne of God and of the Lamb (Rev 22:1), flowed hidden in the passage of the time of the promises and God's patience. But "when the completion of the time came" (Gal 4:4) that is, when the incarnation occurred, the river entered into our world and assumed our flesh. In the "hour" of the cross and the resurrection it sprang forth from the incorruptible and life-giving body of Christ. From that moment on it has been and is liturgy. A new period thus began within "the present time" in which after its decisive defeat death carries on its war on all fronts but in which, at the same time, the Passage of the Lord continues to penetrate the depths of humanity and history. We are in the last times....

...Jesus died once and for all, and that event now lives on through all of history and sustains it. But when in his humanity he takes his place beside the Father and from there pours out the life-giving gift of the Spirit, he does not cease to manifest and carry out the liturgy. There is but a single Passover or Passage but its mighty energy is displayed in a continual ascension and Pentecost....

...What, then, is this "work" by which the conqueror of death pours out his life in abundance? What is this energy with which the Father and the risen Son henceforth "still go on working" (Jn 5:17)? It is the fontal liturgy in which the life-giving humanity of the incarnate Word joins with the Father to send forth the river of life; it is the heavenly liturgy. In the words of the Letter to the Hebrews, "the principal point of all that we have said is that we

---

[15]"Memorial Acclamation," *The Sacramentary.*

[16]*DL* (V), 298.

have a high priest [who] ... has taken his seat at the right hand of the throne of divine Majesty in heaven, and ... is the minister of the divine sanctuary and of the true Tent which the Lord, and not any man, set up" (Heb 8:1–2). This liturgy is eternal (inasmuch as the body of Christ remains incorruptible) and will not pass away; on the contrary, it is this liturgy that "causes" the present world "to pass" into the glory of the Father in an ever more efficacious great Pasch.[17]

We continue to celebrate and make present Christ's Passover from death to life and to the throne of God. We continue to celebrate the eschatological banquet and remember that in this liturgy we profess our faith that Christ has died, he is risen, and he will come again to gather all the nations in glory. It is in these last times we live; it is in these last times we celebrate; it is in these last times that we wait in hope for the coming of our Savior. It is in these last times that we eat bread and drink from the cup as we wait in hope for his coming in glory.

Gospel Exegesis

The facilitator provides input from critical biblical scholarship on this text. This input includes insights as to how people would have heard the gospel in Jesus' time.

Today's gospel is an example of the way in which a particular passage might be interpreted and viewed through various and multiple lenses. The value in this is that it gives a community the opportunity to dialogue with the perspective that best suits its needs at a given time.

Wilfrid Harrington. Today's reading is part of a larger section toward the end of Mark's gospel that seeks to prepare the disciples for Jesus' absence. This section utilizes the literary form of a farewell discourse. This common literary form occurred in the Old Testament as a last will and testament of great figures such as Moses, Joshua, and David, as well as of Jesus and Paul in the New Testament.

This section also utilizes the literary form known as apocalypse. There are features of the apocalypse that make it distinctively Christian. The text insists that there is a positive value in suffering persecution for the sake of Christ. Those who suffer persecution for the sake of the gospel give witness to Jesus. Jesus is also exalted as the one who saves the world from sin and vindicates believers.[18]

Mark draws from Old Testament prophetic imagery. His description of the parousia is taken directly from Jewish apocalyptic literature concerning the *Day of the Lord.* Mark prepares his audience—all is ready, now the Son of Man can appear. The Son of Man has shown his authority to the world. For Mark's purposes, the paschal mystery has already been accomplished. The Son of Man suffered, died, and rose from the dead for the salvation of humanity. It is the same Son of Man who will be finally manifested to all the world at his second coming—the parousia. *He will be seen,* that is, he will be fully revealed—there will be no mistaking his identity. All people will recognize him in all his glory. This is the promise Christians cling to as they wait for his return. It is this hope that sustains believers until the parousia. Mark urges watchfulness and readiness. The suffering Christ will "rejoice in his glorious coming."[19]

The Son of Man will return to gather all people to himself. He will not come in judgment; he will come to gather his elect. Mark insists that the time is drawing near, yet he insists that the intervening time is not to be wasted—there is no room for lethargy within the ranks of disciples.

As a testament to the nearness of the parousia, Mark's Jesus gives us the parable of the fig tree. When should we expect Jesus' return? The fig tree gives us a hint. Most of the trees in Palestine are evergreens. The fig tree is used to illustrate Jesus' point. Buds appear on the fig tree when winter is over and summer is near. When will it be summer? When Christians witness the destruction of the Temple they will know that the end is fast approaching.

Mark insisted that the end would come in his lifetime—the Day of the Lord was, in fact, very near.

---

[17]*TWOW,* 35, 37–38.

[18]*MARK,* 194.
[19]Ibid., 205.

Mark leaves no "wiggle" room. As far as he is concerned, the parousia will take place soon—he will witness it firsthand. His generation will not completely perish before the arrival of the Son of Man.

Mark looks to the authority of Jesus himself, insisting that the gospel is a testament to the truth. Mark does not specify a timetable. No one knows it—not even Jesus. Only the Father knows it. However, of this Mark is certain: it will take place in his lifetime or within his generation.

The parousia obviously did not take place when Mark insisted it would. What does this mean? Perhaps it is a sign of God's continued mercy for the human race. However, there is a timeless, unchangeable truth in Mark's proclamation of the parousia. Jesus' death and resurrection inaugurated the messianic age. All that is left to complete God's plan of salvation is the final consummation. Wilfrid Harrington maintains that the "parousia" is an apocalyptic symbol.[20] It is a sign that God's plan is complete and circular. God began the salvation of the world through the sending of the Son. God will complete the salvation drama when the Son returns within the context of the final, cosmic battle that will draw human history to its ultimate conclusion.

Two thousand years later, we find it difficult to relate to the "nearness" theme Mark espouses. However, what is as fresh today as it was for Mark is the truth of the Christ-event: Jesus was victorious over sin and death. God's plan for the salvation of the world was accomplished through the Son. Nearness might not be as far from our consciousness as we might expect when we realize that each one of us will be facing the parousia when we experience our own passing from this world. Thus, we are challenged to take heed and not become complacent or sleepy, but to be watchful and alert.

Bernard B. Bailey. Bernard B. Bailey suggests that the parable is really a catechism about the *time process* and about the *reign of God.*[21] Time disappears in this parable. The parable segues from budding to summer harvest. All come together in the present. Now is the end. We are in it. All that is left to come is *now—now* is the age of the fig tree; there is not an apocalyptic future. "There is no future over-abundant fig tree, but in its very ordinariness there is only this tree."[22] The fig tree becomes a metaphor for the reign of God—present here and now.

Ched Myers. It is probable that no other chapter has attracted as much attention from biblical exegetes as Mark 13. It is often referred to as the "Little Apocalypse." Mark's text reads like underground political literature reminiscent of apocalyptic literature[23] written during times of persecution, such as Daniel (first reading) and Revelation. Mark seems to be positing a midrash on the Book of Daniel, chapters 7, 9, and 11. He is also presenting a moral exhortation for the community using both apocalyptic and traditional primitive catechetical material. Such literature drew from other biblical sources and apocalypses and was used as a critique against current ruling powers. Apocalyptic literature often functioned like an editorial page. It was "a popular vehicle for interpretation of current events during the Hellenistic era."[24] Some scholars suggest that chapter 13 functions in the aforementioned capacity. The use of the apocalyptic form was something Mark's community would recognize and understand. He used a genre that already had a history of speaking to the issue of political resistance under Hellenism.

This part of Mark's narrative is intimately connected to the political situation that was taking place at the time of its writing. The political situation in Galilee between A.D. 68 and 70 was tenuous,

[20]Ibid., 207.
[21]Ibid., 342.

[22]Ibid.

[23]Apocalyptic literature is not intended to tempt the believer with the promise of eternity. The purpose of apocalyptic literature is to reinforce that victory will be difficult—human beings and tribulation are partners in the unfolding drama of salvation history. Apocalyptic literature seeks to offer hope amid travail. Mature faith waits and endures. Believers of Jesus are all too aware of the consequences of human sin. Apocalyptic New Testament literature chronicles humanity's fall while at the same time expressing hope for the fulfillment of God's promise to come and to come soon. In the meantime, however, believers continue to live and act as responsible disciples in the reign of God *now* in hopes that the *not yet* will not delay. We do not presume to know God's timetable. Apocalyptic literature is and has always been a constant and sobering reminder of that truth.

[24]*BSM*, 326.

dangerously close to revolution. An insurrection was in the making that promised to restore Israel and to drive out Roman occupation. Mark's narrative asks the question: Should the Christian community enter the conflict? Jesus speaks a strong, nonviolent word and insists that the community is not to come to the defense of Jerusalem, "warning against the temptation to seize power as a way of overthrowing the powers."[25] Questions abound. Jesus obviously has chosen a nonviolent means to overthrow the structure of power. What does that mean now that pressure is being put on the community to join forces and declare allegiance in the Jewish-Roman war? The situation calls for a sermon and Mark cleverly has inserted it into chapter 13. Almost every biblical commentator would agree that the context for this narrative is the Jewish-Roman war. It is hotly debated whether Jesus' prediction of the destruction of the Temple took place before it actually happened, or if his prediction was read back into the text after the fact.

The gospel was written near A.D. 69. The revolt began in June 66 and spread to the provinces of Idumea, Perea, and Galilee. By November, the Roman legate marched on Jerusalem to put a halt to the insurrection. He held the northern part of the city, but was resisted when he forged an assault on the Temple Mount. Shocked, dismayed, and suffering severe loss of troops, he retreated as the Jewish guerrillas forced him back to the sea. The Jewish rebels won. Word spread like wildfire—Jerusalem was liberated! The oppressors were defeated!

A provisional government was established, but was plagued by internal turmoil. The liberation did not last long. Vespasian converged on Palestine in legion with troops from Egypt and Syria. Six thousand troops trounced through Galilee toward Jerusalem. Heroic guerrilla resistance succumbed in the end, and Galilee, Perea, and western Judea fell to Vespasian. The summer of 68 Vespasian was ready to march on Jerusalem. The siege did not take place, however. Vespasian was summoned back to Rome. Nero was dead. There was political mayhem on the home front and four candidates were trying assume political control. The Zealot movement was given a year and a half to prepare

for the next onslaught. Yahweh twice saved the holy city, but the inevitable was coming.

Vespasian won the political contest on the home front. He sent Titus to finish the job he started in Palestine. In the spring of 70 Titus marched on Jerusalem and after five months the city fell. The city was ransacked and the Temple was burned to the ground. One can be certain that in the year and a half prior to the siege the rebel resistance fighters were calling on all the faithful to join in Israel's last great battle. They would have called on the corporate imagination and conjured images of a return to the Davidic kingdom and inauguration of the messianic age. Anyone who called themselves a *Jew* would simply have to rise up in defense of the holy city.

This is the backdrop for chapter 13. This is also the backdrop for an exegesis of this chapter posited by Ched Myers.[26] He poses a convincing argument about what this chapter intended, what it meant to the listeners, and hopefully what we might draw from it today.

Mark had to speak in veiled language. He could not speak directly in fear of bringing the wrath of both sides down on his community. This chapter is concerned with the political destiny of the disciples. Political persecution is on the horizon. The time has come for disciples to ready themselves to be handed over just as John and Jesus were handed over. Verses 9, 11, and 13 of chapter 13 are stern cautions that the disciple/reader will not escape arrest and persecution.

Zealots were trying to convince the Jewish Christians that they, too, must enter the fight—it was their responsibility. After all, it was obvious that Yahweh had inspired this war and in addition, it was the fulfillment of all their messianic hopes. How was the Christian community to respond in the face of such pressure? No doubt Mark was sympathetic to the issues (political oppression by Rome) behind the Zealots' revolt.

What about Jesus' message of nonviolent resistance? Members of Mark's community may have already been enlisted in the rebel army. The patri-

---

[25]Ibid., 324.

[26]Ibid., 324–353.

otic call was overwhelming. No less overwhelming was the looming, hopeful shadow of the ultimate, hoped-for, prophesied, final battle in which Israel would be vindicated. Only one voice had the authority to resist the allure of the rebel cause—the voice of Christ the teacher. Believers called on the authority of Jesus to help clarify the meaning of their historical moment.

The historian Josephus recorded that the rebels believed they were defending the Temple against desecration and that Yahweh would stand by their side and defend them. Josephus also recorded that there were natural signs that the insurgents interpreted to be further indication that Yahweh was inspiring their cause.

Jesus does speak to the issue of war, but he speaks in direct opposition to the rebel cause. From the Mount of Olives Jesus predicted the destruction of the Temple, not the protection of it. The disciples are thoroughly confused and question Jesus. When will all these things take place? "These things" refer to Jesus' judgment against the Temple. The disciples are incredulous that this bulwark institution would meet its end. Could the Roman siege really topple this ageless institution? Jesus refuses to give them a sign. He insists that heaven will not intervene—they will be taught to "see the signs." They will know how to read the political situation at hand.

Mark's narrative is divided into two sections. The first refers to time, the second refers to "signs" associated with the "end." The *time* referred to in the narrative refers to the time of the war, not the time of the "end." Early in the chapter the disciples are warned to be wary of those who might deceive them, who speak of wars, who proclaim a false messiah. Mark is alluding to the pending Roman conflict.

The second part of the narrative returns to a more traditional form of discourse—the apocalyptic. There are three parts to this second section. Two of them—the cosmic cataclysms and the parable of the fig tree—appear in today's pericope.

The rebels regarded the political and cataclysmic events as a sign that the end of time was fast approaching. Mark insists that they were simply using this as bait to recruit fighters for their mes-

sianic war. Verse 7 of chapter 13 refutes that notion of "the end" by calling it "the beginning": "When you hear of wars and rumors of wars . . . the end is not yet . . . these are only the beginnings of the birth pangs." Mark warns his listeners that no one should act hastily when approached by overzealous recruiters. "These events, insists Mark, do not obligate the faithful Jew to join the revolt; indeed 'it is necessary that they happen' . . . Mark is counter-recruiting, challenging the grounds upon which Jews are being conscripted into the 'final battle.' "[27]

What does this all mean then? Jesus calls the events the "beginning of the sufferings"—an allusion taken from the prophetic tradition. It can mean either the pain of childbirth or death. It is a metaphor intended to prepare the disciples for suffering and tribulation, not for military nationalism or political patriotism.

The rebels preach an "end-times" theology. Mark preaches the paradox of life and death and the response of nonviolence. The community's nonviolent stance against the war will bring down the wrath of local and national Jewish authorities as well as the Roman authorities, perhaps even Caesar.

Many exegetes maintain that Mark believes that the coming events will be the springboard from which to begin the mission of the church to all the nations. In other words, the church will survive to carry on the gentile mission. Myers insists that such an interpretation makes no sense. Furthermore, it is the very interpretation that Mark is trying to avoid. Any suggestion that the disciples would be spared because of their service to Christ was ludicrous to Mark. Were not Elijah and John important in God's overall mission of salvation? They were hardly spared. Therefore, if the disciples were to entertain any notion that their importance to the mission of Christ might somehow provide a ticket of safety through the ensuing tribulations, they were sorely deluded.

Mark's point? Just as the war is not a sign of the end, but of the beginning of suffering, political persecution is similarly not a sign of the end, but the beginning of real discipleship. The community will join ranks with the "hunted." They will

_____

[27]Ibid., 333.

not even be certain of safety and protection within the family or the community. Child may rise against parent and parent against child. The issues at stake in the war were cause for tremendous tension and strife within families and the community. The pressures of the war resulted in serious betrayal on the home front. Rebels were executed by Rome and sympathizers were executed by the Zealots. Those who assume a nonviolent posture and walk the way of the gospel will be persecuted—of this they can be certain. All sides will hate them. Only those who endure to the end will save their lives—those who lose them for the sake of the gospel will save them in the end.

Mark instructs his disciples/readers to flee to the hills when the siege begins—to resist the resistance. They were not to rally to Jerusalem's defense, even if they witnessed the desecration of the Temple. They were to flee to the hills, no matter where they were. This would, of course, be difficult for pregnant women or for people doing work in the fields, or if it were to take place during the winter. This is the typical plight of wartime refugees. The bottom line for Mark is that his community was being called away from Jerusalem. Mark's sermon sets up a contrast between the rebel call to arms against Rome and Jesus' call to discipleship by way of the cross.

The new order. The new order that Jesus inaugurated is both now and not yet. This is why the call to radical discipleship is so urgent. The follower of Christ can participate in the unfinished, genuine struggle for establishment of the reign Jesus envisioned. The rebels simply wanted to superimpose new domination over an old model of domination. Jesus proposed something new altogether—a new order that stood in direct opposition to all forms of domination. "Why not aid and abet the rebel cause? Because it was mere rebellion, the recycling of oppressive power into new hands. To journey deeply into history, to experiment with political practice that will break, not perpetuate the reign of domination in the world—that is the meaning of Mark's final call to 'Watch!' (13:37). It is a call to nonviolent resistance to the powers."[28]

And now is the time. The issue of time in this apocalyptic discourse has little to do with chrono-

logical time. The reference to time is not to be taken literally. It is *kairos* time, not *chronos* time.[29] Mark uses the apocalypse to challenge his disciples/readers to enter into the historical moment. *Kairos* time is now—the time in which the disciples are living the new gospel way of life. Time in the context of this section of Mark's gospel does not necessarily refer to "end time." Mark's term for *time* functions like a symbol. There are many prisms with which to understand the complexity of its meaning. *Time* might refer to the coming of the reign of God and the political struggle that accompanies it. *Time* may also refer to Jesus' or the disciples' suffering and the suffering of the whole world. *Time* could also refer to the final resurrection and the fulfillment of God's reign. History is fluid and open—it is not determined a priori. "Time as metaphor functions precisely to subvert the notion of literal time—thus obviating 'eschatological timetables.' Which is to say that those who see apocalyptic discourse as *deterministic* have not yet understood it."[30]

Mark does not suggest that believers sit back and wait for "these things" to come to pass. He demands that disciples become history changers, that they be proactive in bringing about the reign of God on earth. "Mark advocates neither fatalism or escapism, but a revolutionary commitment to the transformation of history, which always demands vigilance and discernment."[31]

The disciple/reader is to choose between the old and the new orders. This section of Mark's narrative draws from the "combat myth" typically found in apocalyptic literature. One example of the combat myth can be found in the Book of Revelation, with the war between the beast and the lamb. It is a political parody on the emperor Nero. The reader is challenged to make a choice in an actual historical contest. In the Book of Daniel the reader is asked to resist Antiochus—the apocalyptic visions provide support for the basis of their decision. This "combat myth" is evident in today's pericope.

War is immanent. The cosmic lines have been drawn and battle is ready to begin. Mark insists

---

[28]Ibid., 343.

[29]See chapter 8: Time and the Liturgical Calendar.
[30]*BSM*, 340.
[31]Ibid., 341.

that one of the portents in his apocalyptic drama is that the stars will fall—a sign of impending judgment. Mark's "falling stars" was an allusion to the falling of the power structures. How would they fall? Mark returns to the theme of the "Human One coming on the clouds (26)."[32] The fallen power structures will see and recognize the glory of the Christ—the fallen powers will see the glory of the Human One. Ched Myers insists that the "moment" they will see is at the execution of Jesus. Both Roman and Jewish authority are present at Calvary. The light of the sun is darkened. It is at this moment that the kingdom comes in power (see 9:1). Through the offering of his life on the cross, Jesus gathered all people to himself. The cross is the apocalyptic moment referred to in this apocalypse. Christ will gather all those who have endured suffering and resisted the power structure—the elect.

They will be gathered from the *four winds and the ends of the earth*. This is an allusion to other biblical texts that speak of the scattering of God's people and their subsequent return. The gathering will take place from one end of the earth to another—all of creation. Everything will be renewed. The crashing down of oppressive power structures makes way for the new world. All creation will be renewed in the new order established by Christ.

If the life of Jesus is situated in the Calvary-event, how is such a new world vision possible in the midst of such apparent defeat? The new world vision is observed in the regathering of the people. It is observed in discipleship and evangelization that spreads from one end of the globe to the other. This is the new heavens and the new earth—it is a "journey of discipleship, . . . a struggle for justice in the only world there is."[33]

Myers takes us through Mark's last sermon.[34] He insists that Mark exhorts the disciples/readers to learn from the parable (*methete tēn parabolēn*). This is the only time Mark uses the verb *manthanein* from which the word *mathētēs* derives. *Mathētēs* is the word for disciple—"one who learns from practice." Mark is moving his narrative to a conclusion and wraps it up with a very important parable. He

uses an image that was used earlier in the gospel, the fig tree. The use of the fig tree is an allusion to a combat myth in Isaiah 34:4:

> And the heavens will roll up like a scroll,
> and all the stars fall
> as leaves from a vine
> and as leaves fall from a fig tree.

Mark adapts Isaiah to fit his own purposes. The fig tree's leaves are not falling, they are blossoming. Mark takes us back to his teaching about the Temple in chapter 11. One theory suggests that the blossoming of the fig tree in this chapter is a contrast to its withering in chapter 11. The withering of the fig tree was a symbol of the curse of Jerusalem (vis-à-vis the Temple authority). The blossoming of the tree is symbolic of the blessing bestowed on the Christian community. A second theory suggests that rather than contrast, there is instead a continuity between the two trees. The tree in chapter 11 was also blossoming. In fact, it was in full bloom. Jesus cursed a tree in full bloom. We are to listen carefully and learn from both of these parables. What did we learn from the tree in chapter 11? We learned that Jesus was going to disavow the Temple. He proved that he meant what he said through his actions, through his act of overturning the tables in the Temple, when he walked out of the Temple for the last time, and when he predicted its destruction.[35] Thus, the ultimate lesson of the fig tree is not to be missed. Jesus was explicit. The religious world they knew was over. Their present world (religious, social, and political), which centered around the Temple, was coming to an end and Jesus' new world was ready to emerge.

The community stood on the threshold of that moment in history. Jesus insisted that the present generation would not die before all these things came to pass. Myers insists that "these things" was a reference to the incarnation and the "harvest" that would occur at the moment of the cross. Through the offering of his life on the cross, Jesus gathered all people to himself. The cross is the apocalyptic moment alluded to in this cosmic narrative. The present generation would not pass away until the power of the cross would be revealed. Once the

[32] Ibid., 343.
[33] Ibid., 344.
[34] Ibid., 343.

[35] Ibid., 345.

cross is revealed, then and only then will all "these things" be fulfilled—that is, the dominant order will be broken, the Temple state will end, and the power structures will be overthrown.

When will all "these things" take place? It is like the seed in Jesus' seed parables. No one knows for sure, but disciples will know when it happens. At that time they will realize that the cross does not mean defeat, but is a sign of the coming of the Son of Man, the Human One, and the toppling of the powers. "At every point this discourse is clear: the mythic moment is to be identified with the cross. It stands at the center of history, and is for Mark the focus of all true political discernment. Now, at the end of the sermon, he invites his readers to become truly discerning, offering a new metaphor: 'Gethsemane.' "[36]

Through the cross the powers of domination will be defeated. Mark reminds the reader that only Jesus' words *do not pass away*. Jesus' words take us directly to the cross. We may not compromise our truth. Disciples are called to vigilance. "Watch!" is not a call to passive nonaction, waiting for God to intervene and save the day. Jesus rejected the Temple because its system, structure, and leadership oppressed people. Yet, Mark's Jesus posits a new vision—one that will not oppress. There is life after the Temple. "The disciples can still pray, because God does not live in the temple but among those who believe, they need not be anxious when the social world unravels, because Jesus' words do not unravel."[37] Jesus took his way of nonviolence all the way to the cross. Mark's Jesus prepares the disciples to do the same. This, of course, hints that the disciples were not already doing so. Perhaps intimidation ruled the day, and a huge paradigm shift was in order. Image how difficult these issues were for first-century believers. It would be as if Jesus were to arrive on the scene and repudiate the Roman Catholic Church. It was an ideology shift of huge proportions. Mark was adamant, however. What he proposed was not only difficult to comprehend, it was dangerous with war close at hand. It was a shift that would lead them to the cross. It will lead contemporary disciples to the cross, too. Whenever domination is nonviolently resisted, we live the message of this gospel. In a culture of violence, we had better wake up to the example of Jesus. It is time to rediscover his catechism on nonviolence.

Mark knows that . . . having rejected the scribal establishment, the Zealot opposition, and the Hellenistic collaborators, places him virtually alone in the historical moment: "you will be hated by all for the sake of my name" (13:13). So he chooses a metaphor of loneliness, of the trial brought on by the darkness of unknowing: "Gethsemane." Mark calls the discipleship community to live in history with eyes open, to look deep into present events, beyond the conflicting claims of those vying for power. They must search for and attack the very roots of violence and oppression that hold the human story hostage. The coming of the kingdom has nothing to do with triumphalism; it comes from below, in solidarity with the human family in its dark night of suffering. The world is Gethsemane, and we are called to "historical insomnia."[38]

Proclaim the gospel again.

Sometimes we gain new insights when we hear the text after the interpretation is given. Someone from the group proclaims the gospel a second time.

STEP 4
TESTING

Conversation with the Liturgy and the Scriptures

Test your original understanding in dialogue with the text.

(You might consider breaking into smaller groups.)

Now that you've heard the exegesis, were there any new insights? How do you feel about it? How does your original understanding of this gospel compare with what we just shared? How does this story speak to your life?

---

[36]Ibid., 346.
[37]Ibid., 351.

---

[38]Ibid., 353.

Sharing Life Experience

Participants share an experience from their lives that connects with the biblical interpretation just presented.

> The message of end times always comes to bear at this time of year. It goes without saying that we are to be prepared for Christ's return, no matter when that will take place—in history, in the present, upon our death, or at the end of time. The stronger message of this gospel is the exegesis of nonviolence, particularly now—in this historical time. We live in a century of death. I wonder if ever in our history more people have been put to death by violent means than in these past fifty or sixty years? We know of the six million Jews, the million or more Africans, the ethnic cleansings around the world. We live in a culture of violence. We just experienced one case after another of high school shootings. Colorado hangs like a death pall in the air. A black man was recently dragged to his death behind a car in Texas. A homosexual was recently murdered because of his sexuality. Texas subverted a bill that would extend a new law against hate crimes to include crimes against homosexuals. The only conclusion to such idiocy is that hate crimes are bad unless perpetrated against homosexuals.

> We are engaged in a confusing, devastating war. Refugees cry out to the world amid their torture and violence. It prompts us all to ask: "If this is not a just war, then what is?" Yet the message of today's gospel suggests a different perspective. But, what if the other perspective does nothing to stop the violence? And the cycle continues . . . I volley back and forth each day. Yet the bottom line of today's gospel is this: domination begets domination. In the history of the people in the Yugoslavia conflict hatred is rampant on all sides. Victory and overthrow will result in domination no matter who wins. Then what has really been gained? The cycle of violence continues. I do not pretend to know the answer, which certainly demands that I stay with the question. I applaud those people who are doing something about it, such as the relief workers and those who sponsor refugee families.

> It is common for peoples who have been oppressed to oppress others once they gain power and control. Oppression becomes a way of life. The cycle is difficult to break. The only way to break it is through nonvio-lent resistance. When I was in Israel a few years ago I was struck by the complexity of the issues plaguing the Jews and the Palestinians. I know the issues are complex, but as a novice to the area, I was struck by the idiocy of it all. We were told a story by a woman in a cordoned-off Palestinian village. When the Israelis took control of Israel after the war of independence, they converged on one of the cities. With their loudspeakers blaring they ordered every man, woman, and child to leave their homes and move out into the streets. All obeyed. They proceeded to make them all march to a place of reserve many miles away. Many people died on that forced march. The Jews in that instance did what had recently been done to them. It was what they knew. Violence and oppression.

> I know the issue is far more complex. We cannot imagine what it is like to live in a land in which all the guns of the neighboring countries are pointed directly at them. We have little appreciation for what it must be like to know that most of the Mideast would love to see them annihilated. Still—violence gives rise to more violence. There simply has to be another way. Today's gospel gives us a glimpse. We know from others who have practiced its wisdom that it is a way that wields power—nonviolent power. The message of nonviolent resistance speaks volumes to an incredulous world. Why else would Gandhi have received so much attention?

> We are living in a time in which Fundamentalists love to look at the portents in the sky and say the end is near. Y2K looms over us like an atomic bomb ready to drop at the stroke of midnight. Fear is the watchword of the day!

> Mark's message in the face of similar impending disaster is a simple word—it is simple but not easy. We will not be spared the travesties of life. But we are given a way to walk through them. We have been given the "sign of the cross." Whenever we stand against any power of domination—institutional, political, religious—and stand for justice, we can count on the cross. The world cannot tolerate martyrs. In their silence they scream for the world to hear. Their silence indicts the guilty. I think of the martyrs in San Salvador and their silent screams. The world heard. I think of those who sit in prison for just causes—their plight screams for the world to listen. I think of those who are not afraid to shout

injustices from the rooftops even when people in their own communities accuse them of being too political. I think of the people who cast partisanship aside and fight to get rid of assault weapons simply because they promote violence. I think of those who are willing to fight against violence in the home, in our world, and in our entertainment industry. People who serve in shelters that protect people from violence are heroes and heroines. I think of the people who stand in picket lines over against nuclear arms, schools of torture, and the killing of innocent, unborn children. I think of those who fight for the rights of the living. I think of the people who risk violence in the city streets as they reach out and protect the homeless. I think of the woman in a city who started a soup kitchen and was thwarted every step of the way—particularly hurtful was the rejection she encountered by her own church. I think of the scores of catechists in the Third World who have given their lives in the service of the gospel. I think of the people who are fighting for a just end to the war. I think of all those who ever suffered at the hands of any institution for the sake of righteousness.

I am forced to ask myself: "When have I ever faced that kind of suffering and persecution for the sake of the gospel?" There have been small—very small—ways. I would hope that if called upon in a large way I would have the strength to respond. However, whenever I do not give in to violence in my own life, I am living the gospel of nonviolence. When I refuse to support violent structures I am living the gospel of nonviolence. When I stand up for those that have been unjustly treated, I am living the gospel of nonviolence. When I am a voice for justice, I know I am living the gospel of nonviolence. Twice I was called upon to defend a person unjustly treated—once I failed, the other time I responded. The way to live the gospel of nonviolence is to practice it in the little things. I may not own an assault weapon, but there are times when my mouth qualifies. When I do violence to others through my speech I am practicing a gospel of violence.

Many of us are not called out on the front lines, but perhaps in a way we all are. Our front lines may be the home front, the work front, the civic front, or the global front. No matter what front requires our nonviolent resistance, today's gospel does not promise deliverance from the difficulties caused by our resis-

tance. It does offer us the power and glory of the cross, however. When we stand up for another, we might lose our job. When we speak out against government abuse, we may be called a subversive. When we stand in a picket line, we may spend time in jail and we may be called crackpots. But if we are, promises Mark, we are in good company. I want to be in his company.

What was Mark trying to tell his community? How do you feel about the message of the end times? What about Mark's catechism on nonviolence? How does Jesus' teaching on nonviolence have anything to do with your life? In what way do you practice nonviolence? In what way is your behavior the antithesis of nonviolence? In what way does this gospel challenge your community today? In what way has this conversation with the scriptures for today's liturgy invited change in your life? In what way are the biblical themes of covenant, exodus, creation, and community evident in today's readings? Do you still feel the same way about this text as when you began? Has your original understanding been stretched, challenged, or affirmed?

STEP 5
DECISION

The gospel demands a response.

In what concrete way might your parish be invited to respond? Are there any attitudes or behaviors you would like to change as a result of today's conversation? What one concrete action will you take this week in response to the liturgy today?

Pastoral Considerations: What structures exist in your parish that either overtly or inadvertently oppress people? What needs to happen to change the situation?

DOCTRINAL ISSUES

What Church truth/teaching/doctrinal issue could be drawn from the gospel for the thirty-third Sunday in Ordinary Time?

Participants suggest possible doctrinal themes that flow from the readings.

Possible Doctrinal Themes

Nonviolence; parousia; eschatology; soteriology; discipleship; paschal mystery; mystery of suffering; symbol of the cross; conversion

Present the doctrinal material at this time.

1. The facilitator gives input on a particular doctrinal issue of his or her prior choosing. OR
2. The group chooses a doctrinal issue from the list they created. They read together from the Doctrinal Appendix or other appropriate, official Church documents and the works of respected theologians.

(Many doctrinal issues are found in the Doctrinal Appendix at the back of this workbook. If you are choosing an issue from this resource, please refer to it now.)

Reflection questions centered around the chosen doctrinal theme can be found at the end of each topic in the Doctrinal Appendix. The questions are based on the five-step reflection process. If you choose a topic not included in the Doctrinal Appendix, craft your own questions according to the same five-step process.

Following the reflection questions you will be reminded to return to chapter 7, "Preparing the Catechetical Session," to assist you in crafting your own session.

Closing Prayer

Let us pray
with hearts that long for peace

Pause for silent prayer.

Father in heaven,
ever-living source of all that is good,
from the beginning of time you promised man salvation
through the future coming of your Son,
our Lord Jesus Christ.
Help us to drink of his truth

and expand our hearts with the joy of his
        promises,
so that we may serve you in faith and in love
and know for ever the joy of your presence.
We ask this through Christ our Lord.[39]

_____

[39]Thirty-Third Sunday in Ordinary Time: "Alternative Opening Prayer," *The Sacramentary.*

THIRTY-FOURTH OR LAST SUNDAY IN ORDINARY TIME
THE SOLEMNITY OF OUR LORD JESUS CHRIST THE KING

Environment

There need not be a special catechetical environment for this feast. The space should reflect the overall eschatological tone of the past weeks. The liturgical color for this feast is white. An icon of Jesus Christ might be added to the environment, if not already included.

INTRODUCTORY RITES

Entrance Antiphon (or Opening Song)

The Lamb who was slain is worthy to receive strength and divinity, wisdom and power and honor: to him be glory and power for ever. (Rv 5:12, 1–6)[1]

Opening Prayer

The facilitator of the session may lead the prayer. Others in the group may be asked to proclaim the readings.

Let us pray
[that all men will acclaim Jesus as Lord]

    Pause for silent prayer.

Almighty and merciful God,
you break the power of evil
and make all things new
in your Son Jesus Christ, the King
    of the universe.
May all in heaven and earth
    acclaim your glory
and never cease to praise you.
We ask this through our Lord
    Jesus Christ, your Son,
who lives and reigns with you and
    the Holy Spirit,
one God, for ever and ever.[2]

OR:

Let us pray
[that the kingdom of Christ
may live in our hearts and come
to our world]

    Pause for silent prayer.

Father all-powerful, God of love,
you have raised our Lord Jesus Christ
    from death to life,
resplendent in glory as King of creation.
Open our hearts,
free all the world to rejoice in his peace,
to glory in his justice, to live in his love.
Bring all mankind together in
    Jesus Christ your Son,
whose kingdom is with you and
    the Holy Spirit,
one God, for ever and ever.[3]

LITURGY OF THE WORD

The readings are proclaimed.

First Reading
Daniel 7:13–14

(See the thirty-third Sunday in Ordinary Time for an overview of the Book of Daniel.)

Today's Pericope: The choice of the text from Daniel serves the liturgy well. Our attention moves spontaneously to thoughts of Jesus and his royal enthronement in heaven. The author of Daniel used the medium of visions, a common literary technique in ancient literature. The influence of other biblical sources is obvious throughout the text. It was common to speak out about political situations and the hoped-for toppling of the em-

---

[1]Christ the King—Last Sunday in Ordinary Time: "Entrance Antiphon," *The Sacramentary.*

[2]Christ the King—Last Sunday in Ordinary Time: "Opening Prayer," *The Sacramentary.*

[3]Christ the King—Last Sunday in Ordinary Time: "Alternative Opening Prayer," *The Sacramentary.*

pire under the veil of symbolic language. The Book of Daniel employs the mediums mentioned above to do just that.

As mentioned in last week's exegesis, the contemporaries of Daniel were suffering persecution under the domination of Antiochus Epiphanes. They were being forced to abandon Judaism. The author is not in despair; he is hopeful. God will win in the end. God alone has dominion and power. The watchword was *"fear not!"* With God at the helm, who need fear? God reigns over heaven and earth.

Daniel's image: The Son of Man is enthroned in glory on heaven's seat. The term *Son of Man* originally meant human being. Starting with the Book of Daniel, there is a shift in the understanding and significance of the term. The Son of Man is a human person who was also part of the heavenly domain and a "leader and representative of the holy ones of the Almighty."[4] This marked an incredible shift in thinking. "Salvation cannot come from just any human being, however prestigious, but only from the Son of Man: a human being, yes, but one who has an absolutely unique relationship with God, who is entrusted with an incomparable mission and unequaled power."[5] Jesus appropriated the term and applied it to himself. His true identity was beyond that of mere mortal. It could only be seen through the eyes of faith.

Responsorial Psalm
Psalm 93:1, 1–2, 5

Today's psalm is an enthronement psalm and its appointment for today's liturgy is obvious. Originally the enthronement referred to in the psalms was the kingship of Yahweh. There was no intention to foretell the kingly role of Christ. The reign exalted in the psalm is an eternal, everlasting domain. God exercises God's reign through Jesus Christ from the time of Jesus' ascension into heaven. God's reign through Christ continues in "his revelatory and redemptive work."[6]

---

[4] *DL* (V), 310.
[5] Ibid.
[6] *PL*, 373.

Second Reading
Revelation 1:5–8

Overview of the Book of Revelation: The Book of Revelation is of the literary genre known as apocalypse (*Greek: apocalypsis = revelation*). Visions of God's judgment can be found throughout the Book of Revelation. Thus, many people believe that the book is an allegory that predicts the end of the world. However, the images found in Revelation were common to first-century audiences and were of the same genre as other biblical works such as the Book of Daniel, portions of Ezekiel, and Zechariah.

Revelation is in some ways different than the typical Jewish biblical apocalypse. This book has a known author, and it is in the form of a letter addressed to the seven churches in Asia Minor. It is, however, apocalyptic in its eschatology and in its understanding of persecution. Jewish apocalypses were written under the assumed name of a famous person of the past. The Book of Revelation was not written by some ancient writer who foretells the future. John of Patmos is the author of Revelation. He refers to himself as servant, brother, and prophet to the persecuted Christians to whom he writes. He explains that he has been exiled to the island of Patmos. John is historically contemporaneous with the events he writes about. John does not need the authority of some past prophetic hero. He insists that the only authority he needs is the death and resurrection of Jesus Christ, who inaugurated the last days—the messianic age. Jesus is the lens through which martyrs are to understand suffering and persecution. The Christian community became aware that prophecy returned to the community. John is certainly one of the new prophets of the Lord. His work is not only apocalyptic in style, it is also prophetic.

Some people have suggested that John of Patmos is the John of the gospels, Zebedee's son. Others have tried to connect him with John the evangelist, author of the fourth gospel. Both designations are unlikely. Language and style alone prohibit the identification with John the evangelist.

While the use of apocalyptic is obvious, there are other evident forms used in the Book of Revelation—prophetic, liturgical, mythical, and parenetic (see parenesis in glossary). Included in the work are hymns, antiphons, doxologies, acclamations of worth, thanksgivings, *amen* and *halleluia* responses, woes, laments, dirges, and curses. The mythic form is frequently used, as evidenced by the myth of the birth and attempted destruction of the divine child (12:1–6); the sacred marriage (19:6–10, Christ, the Lamb and his bride); victory of the good angel Michael against the dragon and his angels (12:7–9); the divine warrior (martyred lamb who overcomes and rules the universe from a throne); the combat myth and the divine city. The letter form of the book was probably due to the popular influence of Paul's letters to the early churches. The entire book is written in letter form. It begins with an address and ends with a benediction.

John uses imagery found in other biblical sources. The use of visions is common to Daniel and Ezekiel. John draws upon a biblical image used by prophets to denote God's divine council by his reference to the assembly of the gods. A common Old Testament motif was that of the holy war in which God defeats the forces of chaos. Revelation uses the mythic holy war motif in the assault against Satan and his troops. John refers to divine judgment and that it is recorded in a book—a common motif in biblical literature. The mythic city of heaven versus earth is often used in Old Testament apocalypses. Revelation refers to the two cities to draw upon the same image. Another common ancient, mythological theme is the struggle between the chaos monster and the divine child. The use of the cataclysmic forces of nature is a common literary technique used in apocalypses of antiquity. The exodus plagues are alluded to in Revelation and the image of winepress is taken directly from Old Testament prophetic images.[7]

The prophet of Revelation is afforded a special commissioning vision, and many of the visions refer to the heavenly liturgy. Whereas the prophet of the Old Testament might be commissioned in a vision to carry out his work on earth, the prophet of Revelation carries out his work from the heavenly realm.

Revelation is influenced by the "apostolic letters" of the early church. The seven letters written to the churches in Asia Minor follow a common format. There is also a common theme running throughout the letters. Pheme Perkins reminds us that one obvious theme is that Christians are to stand firm in the midst of suffering and persecution.[8] They are also in danger of the loss of initial fervor and of complacency in the midst of prosperity. False teaching was also a concern.

Throughout the Book of Revelation visions are shown to the prophet in heaven. There are seven cycles of these visions, with the contrasting vision of the two cities, Babylon and the heavenly Jerusalem. The visions increase in intensity and within them are woven three woes; the final woe is the seven plagues. Like two bookends framing a library shelf, the epilogue returns to the opening. The epilogue and the opening remind the reader that all that is contained in the book is God's soon-to-be-fulfilled will. All who listen to the words of prophecy will be blessed and Jesus Christ, the ultimate faithful martyr, is the Alpha and the Omega—the beginning and the end of all things.

Using apocalyptic imagery Revelation remembers synoptic allusions to judgment and preparedness. Other New Testament themes include the death, resurrection, ascension, and exaltation of Jesus, and his return to God's throne, from where he rules the nations. Common titles such as Son of Man, Son of God, Son of David, and Lamb of God are used in reference to Jesus.

John refers to contemporary events in his writing. In his letters to the churches, John reports that blood has already been spilled and that Christianity was being threatened. The time was fast approaching (in some places it had already begun) in which the emperor would insist that Christians give allegiance to the Roman gods. Christians will and must refuse; persecution will ensue. These are the conditions that inspire John's apocalyptic vision.

The Roman Empire allowed polytheism as long as it did not disrupt the empire—everyone was to give allegiance to Rome. Citizens were required to

---

[7]*RNT*, 312–313.

[8]Ibid., 316.

acknowledge the gods of Rome, but once they did so they were free to practice their religion. Even though the Jews were monotheistic they were recognized as a legal religion and were given a certain level of autonomy. They were given a special dispensation and were not forced to give allegiance to the Roman gods. Christians were no longer Jews, however, and were thus placed in a position of having to refuse allegiance to the gods. If they refused, they were subject to persecution, torture, or death. They had to be on guard—the moment or hour could come crashing upon them at any time. The moment they lost their protected status within the ranks of a legal religion, they were at risk. When the Christian church broke off ties with Judaism, persecution loomed like a stagnant canvas over the burgeoning church. Some of the emperors demanded that their subjects prove allegiance by paying them homage and worship. Again, Jews were free from such demands. Christians were not so fortunate.

Christians were not only persecuted by Romans, they were also persecuted by Jews. The reference by Paul that he was beaten "forty lashes less one" (2 Cor 11:24) was a Jewish beating. Paul's beating with a rod in 2 Corinthians 11:25 was a Roman beating. However, there is no evidence that there was systematic persecution of Christians by Jews. It was sporadic and spontaneous.[9] Thus, the primary persecutors were Roman.

The author is writing during a time of pending persecution. This somewhat helps date the writing of the text. The book refers to a series of seven kings of Rome. John alludes to the fact that he is living under the reign of the sixth king. If these are references to the six Roman emperors beginning with Augustus and omitting three insignificant kings who reigned only briefly, then Vespasian is the emperor in question (A.D. 70–79). However, Vespasian did not demand that he be worshiped as a god, nor did he persecute Christians in Asia Minor. However, if the text is referring to the kings who were designated gods by the Roman Senate such as Julius Casesar, Augustus, Claudius, Vespasian, and Titus, the sixth king is Domitian. He did demand that worship be given

to him and Christians suffered tremendous persecution under his dominion.

Perrin and Duling suggest that the beast 666 (any first-century reader would have known that 666 was the spelling of *Nero Caesar* in the Semitic alphabet) refers to the name of Nero, who made the Christians the scapegoat responsible for starting the fires of Rome.[10] However, since the Nero affair took place in Rome, not Asia Minor, the reference was probably an allusion to the belief that Nero would come back to life (Nero *redivivus*) and attack from the east. It is possible that Domitian was regarded as the Nero *redivivus*. Most modern scholars believe that Revelation was written during the Domitian persecution (ca. A.D. 95). Revelation 13:17 mentions that no one could buy or sell without the mark of the beast. It is likely that the mark referred to the image of the emperor on the minted coins. Jesus treated the coins in question as unimportant even though there were special coins used in the Temple. Both Peter and Paul instructed Christians to honor the emperor insofar as one would honor a head of state. Revelation insists that those days were over, however. "Christians must resist Satanic divinization of Roman power in all its forms."[11] The Book of Revelation demands a new, rigorous, and costly discipleship.

Other symbols in Revelation are worthy of note. The use of numbers: 4 represents the various parts or divisions of the order of creation; 7 represents completeness, totality, fullness; 12 refers to Israel. The number of the beast refers to the Roman Empire and the imperial line. Colors are used as symbols. White stands for victory, purity, and eschatological happiness; red refers to war and bloodshed; black suggests economic depression; pale refers to death. Horns are a symbol of power and eyes of knowledge. A sharp sword stands for the judging and punishing Word of God.[12]

The Book of Revelation also highlights the separation of Judaism and Christianity. Christianity may have asserted itself as the true Israel with its own right of self-government and Judaism may have

[9]*NTI*, 115.

[10]Ibid.
[11]*RNT*, 325.
[12]*NTI*, 122.

denied the right of this "renegade" sect (Christians) to call themselves Jews. The result was the breaking away of Christianity from Judaism.

Another agenda in the Book of Revelation was the internal tension in the churches of Asia Minor. John was addressing the issue of false teaching and practices that were evident in the churches. John is ultimately speaking to a Christian community in danger of accommodating itself too much to the culture in which it found itself. "Accommodation might be sought by some to avoid persecution. Others appear to have had more secular goals: adaptation to the demands of business associates or social relationships."[13]

Ultimately the Book of Revelation is a book written by a Christian to other Christians. It is not intended to scare outsiders into the membership. Those who proselytize with this book by using fear tactics have completely lost the intent of the book. "John's message is to his fellow Christians. They can repent and recover their former enthusiasm. They can be encouraged to stand fast when confronted by times of suffering. They can be inspired by its visions of heavenly victory with the Lamb."[14]

Like all apocalyptic literature, it seeks to reflect upon the ultimate meaning of life. The Book of Revelation is an example of the human potential for embracing symbol and myth when faced with life's ultimate meaning. Throughout history we note that apocalyptic literature comes to the fore when human beings face the ultimates of life and are required to find meaning in the midst of it. "So in thinking of apocalyptic we have to think of the human mind at a level of ultimacy and at that level turning naturally to the use of myth and symbol. In the case of ancient Jewish and early Christian apocalyptic the ultimacy comes from a total despair in the course of human history and an absolute trust in the purposes of God. The result is the visions and symbols we have been discussing. . . . Early Christian apocalyptic does not challenge us to gather together on a hillside to await the coming of Jesus as Son of Man, or to identify with the Beast; it challenges us to recognize the importance and significance of the myths and symbols it uses so dramatically to express hope in the midst of despair."[15]

Today's Pericope: Today's address is a greeting from Jesus Christ, the Father, and the seven spirits. It is taken from the prologue of the book. Today's text is a wonderful companion to the Feast of Christ the King. It is liturgical in style. The point of today's passage is threefold. First, Jesus loves us—now in the present. Christ's love is extrahistorical. It is eternal and goes beyond the event of redemption. Second, included in the text is the historical event of atonement found in the midst of a creedal statement. Third, redemption results in the establishment of a community that continues the priestly and kingly function of Jesus Christ.

The doxology is followed by a proclamation of the coming of the parousia. Then follows Yahweh's own self-proclamation with assigned titles of Alpha and Omega, God as past, present, and future and God as *Pantocrator* (Greek for *Sabaoth*, "hosts").

Jesus' return to the throne of heaven made him King of the universe—a universe he redeemed. The image reads like a divine liturgy. An elder in the community intones a thanksgiving, an anamnesis. We recall that Jesus loved us and freed us by the shedding of his blood. Through this act of redemption we have been made into a kingdom. We are there and it is now. We remember, and in the remembering it becomes present. The entire gift of salvation history flashes before the stage of our present lives. Jesus gave his life for us and the eternal gift of himself continues from the throne of glory. We are invited to the foot of his throne to live with him eternally—"through him, with him, and in him." In the liturgy of praise we celebrate the heavenly banquet while we feast at the banquet before us. Today's reading from Revelation is reminiscent of a eucharistic prayer. One is almost compelled to rise to one's feet and shout, "Amen," before the heavenly/earthly throne!

The gospel is proclaimed.

---

[13]*RNT*, 327.
[14]Ibid.

---

[15]*NTI*, 123.

Gospel
John 18:33b–37. You say I am a king.

STEP 1
NAMING ONE'S EXPERIENCE

What were your first impressions? What was your first response to the gospel (or the other readings)? What captured your attention?

Each person names his or her initial impression. Statements should be brief. No reasons should be given at this time. All simply listen without agreeing or disagreeing.

STEP 2
UNDERSTANDING

In a brief statement, explain what you think this gospel is trying to convey.

STEP 3
INPUT FROM VISION/STORY/TRADITION

Liturgical Context

This is the final Sunday of the liturgical cycle. In Cycle B the liturgy does not call upon Mark for its profession of Christ as King. Unlike Cycles C and A, this one does not end the year with the synoptic evangelist associated with it. We leave Mark, and John ends the liturgical year for us with a pericope chosen from his Passion narrative. One of the so-called idea feasts, the Feast of Christ the King serves as climactic celebration and a finely tuned blending of the major themes of the gospel.

All four gospels give us a lens with which to view Christ, who came to establish his reign in the hearts of all believers. If Jesus is King, then what is this kingdom he came to establish? Mark insists that the kingdom of God was embodied in the content and purpose of Jesus' parables. The kingdom motivates moral living. Only the child-like can enter the kingdom and the rich will find it difficult. The eucharistic meal anticipates it

and looks forward to it. The kingdom of God is situated primarily in the preaching of Jesus. It is the goal of history and the symbol of everlasting life.[16] Matthew understands the kingdom as a social (not individualistic) reality. "A kingdom is a territory and a people over which a king rules, a society ordered by a king; the kingdom is something one enters (Matt 5:20; 7:21)."[17] The kingdom is an earthly and heavenly political entity—the kingdom of God now and not yet. The kingdom of God respects the created dignity of all persons. The kingdom of God is for all people—it is universal. The kingdom of God belongs to God—it is connected to faith and the spiritual life. Matthew referred to the term fifty-one times, Mark fourteen times, and Luke thirty-nine times. The *reign of God* is a primary theme for Matthew as is the kingship of Christ. Luke connects the kingdom or reign of God to the preaching ministry of Jesus. The kingdom prompts a look to the future reign of God in heaven, but also demands a response of faith in the here and now—the reign requires a present decision of faith. John does not refer to the theme of kingdom. John is more interested in the royalty of Jesus. He replaces the theme of *reign* with the notion of eternal life and the theme of truth—the *reign of God* is realized in the acceptance of truth. These are the biblical lenses through which we continue to celebrate Christ, the universal King of heaven and earth.

Today's solemnity is reminiscent of the Ascension, Epiphany, and Palm Sunday. All celebrate the reign of Christ. Pope Pius XI instituted this feast in his encyclical letter, *Quas primas*, December 11, 1925, in response to the destructive forces of the age. He insisted that the only weapon against such forces and chaos is the acknowledgment of the sovereignty of Christ.

> It is necessary that the royal dignity of Our Lord be recognized and accepted as widely as possible. To this end it seems to Us that nothing else would help so effectively as the institution of a special feast dedicated to Christ our King. The annual

---

[16]Benedict T. Viviano, O.S.P., "Reign of God/Reign of Heaven," *CPDBT*, 820.
[17]Ibid.

celebration of the sacred mysteries is more effective in informing people about the Faith and in bringing them the joys of the spiritual life than the solemn pronouncements of the teaching Church. Documents are often read only by a few learned men; feasts move and teach all the faithful. The former speaks but once; the latter every year and forever. The former bring a saving touch to the intellect; the latter influence not only the mind but the heart and man's whole nature.[18]

At the time when the encyclical was written, the world had experienced the Bolshevik revolution in 1917, the spread of fascism, the loss of the church's political power, and the decadence of the 1920s. However, as cultural conditions changed, so did the focus of this feast. The moving of this feast to the last Sunday of the liturgical cycle placed it center stage in our unfolding eschatological agenda. Thus, today, this feast serves as an appropriate way to remember the Second Coming of Christ. "It is now clearer that the exalted Lord and King is the goal not only of the liturgical year but of our entire earthly pilgrimage. . . . At the end of the liturgical year, then, stands the Lord of Glory."[19]

Adolph Adam suggests that Epiphany is the feast par excellence that remembers the kingship of Christ in the liturgy as expressed in Epiphany's Entrance Antiphon: "The Lord and ruler is coming; kingship is his, and government and power." He quotes W. Durig on the matter:

Only an obscuring of the content of the liturgical feast of Epiphany and an intellectualization of liturgical theology could have led Pius XI in 1925 to introduce a second Feast of Christ the King on the last Sunday of October. This move is typical of the development that modern piety has undergone; this development becomes clear from a comparison of the two feasts. The feast of Christ the King *celebrates the general idea of Christ's kingship; it celebrates a title of honor, a name, a concept* [italics mine]. On the other hand, it is essential to the liturgi-

cal feast of Epiphany that it brings before us, in a concrete way, a royal action of Christ, an event that is an essential part of the process of salvation. On the one hand, then, an idea; on the other, the reality of the mystery of Epiphany which contains in itself the entire mystery of redemption.[20]

Reginald Fuller asserts that the feast duplicates the themes of Ascension Day and provides a distinctive emphasis on social action. According to Fuller, this feast provides the liturgical support for the social teaching of the great papal encyclicals since Leo XIII.

When it was first established as a feast assigned to the last Sunday in October, there was danger of removing the kingship of Christ from its eschatological context. Jesus' enthronement at the Ascension is the inauguration of his eschatological reign, his rule over all until he comes again in glory, and his ongoing defeat of the power of evil. By moving the feast to the last Sunday of the year, this eschatological emphasis was retained.

The events that prompted establishment of the feast had to do with the sixteenth-century anniversary of the Council of Nicea's pronouncement that Christ and the Father are one and the same (consubstantiality), thus providing the basis for his kingly rule. "He [Pius XI] chose this day chiefly in view of the coming feast of all Saints; the feast of Christ the King would exalt 'before all men the glory of Him Who triumphs in His saints and His elect.' "[21] On this feast there was to be a consecration to the heart of Christ, the Redeemer.

In a decree promulgating the *editio typica* of the General Roman Calendar on March 21, 1969, *Anni liturgici ordinatione, #3760,* the Feast of Christ the King was moved to a new day: "The feast of the Baptism of the Lord and Christ the King are to be celebrated on the days newly assigned to them."[22] The revised liturgical calendar reflected the change away from the last Sunday in October.

---

[18]AAS 17 (1925), 593–610; *LY*, 177.

[19]*LY*, 178.

[20]W. Durig, "Epiphanie," in *Ercheinung des Herrn* (Am Tisch des Wortes, Neue 118; Stuttgart, 1971), p. 12, in *LY*, 147.

[21]*LY*, 177.

[22]*DOL*, 1156.

Because of its special importance, the Sunday celebration gives way only to solemnities or feasts of the Lord. The Sundays of the seasons of Advent, Lent and Easter, however, take precedence over all solemnities and feasts of the Lord. Solemnities occurring on these Sundays are observed on the Saturday preceding [#5].

By its nature, Sunday excludes any other celebration's being permanently assigned to that day, with these exceptions: a. Sunday within the octave of Christmas is the feast of the Holy Family; b. Sunday following 6 January is the feast of the Baptism of the Lord; c. Sunday after Pentecost is the solemnity of the Holy Trinity; d. The last Sunday in Ordinary Time is the solemnity of Christ the King.[23]

The liturgy exalts the universal reign of Christ, not just today, but in every celebration of liturgy. Today's Entrance Antiphon asserts Christ's divinely instituted power. Christ, the slain Lamb, is worthy to receive strength and divinity and to him be "glory and power for ever." The opening prayer expresses our confidence in Christ's exaltation and his power to reign over all creation: "You break the power of evil and make all things new." The prayer over the gifts acknowledges the sacrifice of Christ's life on the cross that reconciled the world to the Father and inaugurated Christ's kingship. The preface for today's liturgy makes repeated references to the kingdom established by Christ:

Father, all-powerful and ever-living God,
we do well always and everywhere to give
   you thanks.
You anointed Jesus Christ, your only Son,
   with the oil of gladness,
as the eternal priest and universal king.
As priest he offered his life on the altar of
   the cross
and redeemed the human race
by this one perfect sacrifice of peace.
As king he claims dominion over all creation,
that he may present you, his almighty
   Father,

an eternal and universal kingdom:
a kingdom of truth and life,
a kingdom of holiness and grace,
a kingdom of justice, love, and peace.[24]

The third form of the penitential rite picks up the same theme: "Lord Jesus, you rule over the kingdom of truth and life."

As Ordinary Time comes to a close and Advent begins, both dovetail in focus. Both exalt Christ, who reigns triumphant over the world and will come again in glory. Thus, Advent's *Solemn Blessing Over the People* is included in this session's closing prayer. It echoes today's contemplation on the reign of Christ.

Gospel Exegesis

The facilitator provides input from critical biblical scholarship on this text. This input includes insights as to how people would have heard the gospel in Jesus' time.

For an overall context of John's Passion narrative, please read the gospel exegesis for Good Friday before you begin today's exegesis. Today, Jesus is arraigned before Pilate. It is interesting to note that this is significant for John, whereas Jesus' interrogation before Caiaphas is nearly ignored. Jesus finds himself in a face-to-face struggle with secular, political power. Pilate cross-examines Jesus in order to discover the nature of his subversive actions. Pilate leads the conversation with Jesus to the reason for this arraignment in the first place—Jesus' claim to kingship. If he can prove Jesus guilty on this charge from the outset, he has an open-and-shut case. Subversive action against Caesar is punishable by death. Dialogue ensues. John uses this debate with Pilate to allow the meaning of Jesus' royal status to gracefully and adroitly unfurl.

Pilate cleverly asks Jesus if he is the king of the Jews. Pilate wants to know why the Jewish authorities sent this man to him. Why should he settle their internal disputes? Why should Pilate be put in the position of imposing capital punishment on this man? Pilate senses a hidden agenda but does not know its origin. Jesus does not help Pilate. He

[23]*GNLY*, #6.

[24]Christ the King, "Preface," *The Sacramentary*.

simply retorts with a question of his own. He wants Pilate to define kingship. Pilate has no time or use for rabbinic subtleties. "Answer the question." Jesus not only answers, but the heart of his response provides the substance for today's feast. What does it mean that Jesus is the King of the universe? The question is still food for reflection.

Jesus insists that his kingdom did not come from this world. He has no army to defend him. There is no band of insurgents lying in wait to rescue him. Jesus did not impose his teaching on anyone; people willingly embraced it. James and John were chastised by Jesus when they suggested that fire and brimstone be rained upon the Samaritans. Jesus' message of nonviolence permeated his mission. Jesus preached that those who wanted to be first must be last in his kingdom. He did not come to be served but to serve and to give his life for the many. In that sense of "king," then indeed Jesus was and is king. However, such a kingdom does not belong to this world—at the very least, we have no experience of such a kingdom. Imagine this world if we did!

Jesus' authority was heaven-sent. Jesus came to testify to the truth. Let us examine that word. What is truth? The Hebrew word for truth, 'met, has Semitic origins ('aman) meaning reliable, faithful, constant, certain, secure, permanent, and honest.[25] When we attest to something that we know to be reliable, constant, secure, permanent, and honest in the liturgical assembly, we reach back to our Semitic roots and proclaim a resounding "Amen!" In the Old Testament when anything was associated with something known to be faithful and certain it was referred to as "truth." God is "truth" because God can be counted on to be reliable, certain, and faithful. God created the heavens and the earth in harmonious order. Creation itself is evidence of the God of truth. However, people have not always acknowledged the truth. The scriptures are filled with laments over the fact that Israel failed to listen and respond to truth. Yet God, who is Truth, is constant and faithful.

The Wisdom tradition insists that truth is the ultimate pearl of great price. It should be sought above all else. It is easy to lose sight of truth. Truth must be given a place of honor within a person's heart. Truth was associated with the biblical understanding of justice. Justice had to do with people's relationships with each other. Zechariah tells us: "These are the things you should do; Speak the truth to one another; let there be honesty and peace in the judgments at your gates and let none of you plot evil against another in his heart, nor love a false oath. For all these things I hate, says the Lord" (8:16–17).

God was faithful to the covenant. This faithfulness became associated with divine truth and divine love. Truth was also understood to be synonymous with God's covenant love. God's love is faithful; it is therefore divine truth. Walking in God's truth keeps a person faithful to the covenant. Those who love and trust God live in truth.

In John's gospel God is the ultimate reality and truth. Jesus testifies to the truth today because he heard it from God. Those who accept Jesus accept the truth—they accept and embrace knowledge of God. For John, truth is the revelation that Jesus brings to the world. Love is an imperative if one is to live according to the truth. Truth requires that one live justly in word and deed.

John Pilch asserts that the Passion narrative can be divided into seven separate scenes.[26] The scenes take place outside and inside. The first scene is the mocking of Jesus. His mockers call him the King of the Judeans. Their irony captures the truth (which is often the function of irony in ancient literature). When Jesus faced Pilate, he retorted to Pilate's query with a question. Jesus asked Pilate if he was simply responding to gossip or was he really interested? When Pilate tries to summarize Jesus' words by insisting "So, you say you are a king," Jesus cleverly dodges the trap. "Wait a minute, you said that I am a king." Pilate was certainly of a higher social standing. He did not have to subject himself to Jesus' sarcasm. However, curiosity got the better of Pilate. He intended to find out more about Jesus. Who was he and what was behind his movement?

Jesus insists that his royal identity is separate from any earthly notion of kingship, royalty, and king-

---

[25]Gregory J. Polan, O.S.B., "Truth," *CPDBT*, 1019.

[26]*CWJB*, 166–168.

dom. The charges of insurrection claimed by his antagonists are simply unfounded and ridiculous. Jesus affirmed that his reign originates outside this realm. Not *of* this world, really should be translated, not *from* this world. Truth of his assertion is evidenced by the fact that no one was waiting in the wings armed and ready to defend him.

Jesus' kingdom is described in terms of "truth." John's Jesus does not use the language of kingdom as is found in the synoptic gospels. He uses the language of truth. Jesus came to teach the truth about God. In John's gospel the kingdom theme is replaced by the concept of eternal life.[27] Like the prophets of old, Jesus attested to the will of God in the present. Those who listen to Jesus' teaching follow the will of God. Even though the text seems to suggest that Jesus' reign has nothing to do with this earthly plane of existence, what it means more explicitly is that Jesus' reign does not originate here. We must be careful that we do not reduce Jesus' promise for this world into a "purely heavenly, mystical, and spiritual idea of kingdom." Jesus' reign, Jesus' truth, is a call to prayer and a call to action. Jesus is king or ruler of followers who will live the message he came to preach. Followers of Christ will listen to the truth and respond in justice to the will of God.

Jesus' retort to Pilate posed a veiled challenge. He invited Pilate to listen and respond to the truth. He reminded Pilate that only those who know the truth hear his voice. Jesus presented Pilate with an invitation to accept God's plan of salvation. Pilate evades Jesus' question with a question of his own: "What is truth?" John encapsulates the heart of the entire liturgical cycle. He asks the reader, ancient and contemporary, "Will you respond to the truth of God's will? Or will you, like Pilate, evade the question?"

On June 25 each year the Ethiopian Christian Church venerates Pilate as a saint because he washed his hands of Jesus' blood and declared him innocent. John's gospel was not so forgiving of Pilate. However, John used the exchange with Pilate to an advantage, demonstrating that Jesus is king and that his reign is of divine origin. John placed the guilt for Jesus' death at the doorstep of those who should have recognized the truth when it was in their midst, but failed to do so.

The only way the Jews were able to get the attention of the authorities was to suggest that Jesus posed a political threat. When Jesus insisted that his kingdom was not *of this world*, we must look to the Johannine understanding of that phrase. John made a distinction between the world as the created universe and the world as an environment hostile to the truth of Christ.[28] Jesus probably inferred both meanings in his statement in today's gospel. Jesus and his kingdom have divine genesis—they come from God. Jesus and his kingdom do not originate from human scheming and political machinations; they are ordained by none other than God. Jesus' kingdom is not like the kingdom Pilate has in mind. When Jesus thinks kingdom, it is a far cry from what Pilate understands kingdom to be. In Pilate's world kingdom is domination, privilege, power, and prestige. In Jesus' world kingdom is God's reign—"love, justice and service.... 'For this I came into the world': to inaugurate a world of peace and fellowship, of justice and respect for other people's rights, of love for God and for one another. This is his kingdom which comes into human history, enhancing it and leading it beyond itself, a kingdom which will have no end though it is present as of now; it is not only for the future, 'his dominion is everlasting' (Dn 7:14). It is not limited to the past, to the present, or to the future. In the Lord's Prayer we ask for this kingdom to come in its fullness."[29]

Proclaim the gospel again.

Sometimes we gain new insights when we hear the text after the interpretation is given. Someone from the group proclaims the gospel a second time.

STEP 4
TESTING

Conversation with the Liturgy and the Scriptures

Test your original understanding in dialogue with the text.

---

[27]Benedict T. Viviano, O.P., "Reign of God/Reign of Heaven," *CPDBT*, 821.

[28]*WWC*, 257.
[29]*SWTLY*, 268.

(You might consider breaking into smaller groups.)

Now that you've heard the exegesis, were there any new insights? How do you feel about it? How does your original understanding of this gospel compare with what we just shared? How does this story speak to your life?

Sharing Life Experience

Participants share an experience from their lives that connects with the biblical interpretation just presented.

If there was ever a need for a King, now is the time. The world cries out from the very bowels of its core and begs to find meaning in the midst of chaos and destruction. There are wars and rumors of wars. We are fighting a war—bombs are dropping daily. Genocide is rampant—Bosnia, Albania, Kosovo. Hundreds of thousands are butchered in Africa and the world lends a deaf ear. Young people mow down their friends in our schools over issues as mundane as unrequited love. In some places religious wars are fought—Protestants against Catholics, Serbian Orthodox against Albanian Orthodox. There is misunderstanding and mistrust between ecclesial traditions, and in our own house there is disunity and sometimes downright hatred and antagonism. Our homes are often the theater of serious violence and our relationships lack the intimate love Jesus invites us to share. Do we need a King of the Universe? The answer is obvious. The question is, will we let him in? Pilate washed his hands, turned away, responded to Christ's invitation with evasiveness. The challenge is there for all of us—leaders of nations and leaders of families. Will we let the King of the universe in? Even though the notion of King is foreign to the American consciousness, what is not foreign is the need to have the truth, which is the hallmark of Jesus' royal mission.

This truth is the Word and will of God fully alive in the hearts of those who recognize Jesus as sovereign in their lives. Yes, the world sometimes seems to be teetering on the brink of collapse. I can fall with it, or I can work to be a history changer. On the world level, I can pray for the victims of world violence and genocide. I can be a voice for the just resolution of the conflict. I can speak to genocide and our disregard for life on all levels of human society. I can do what I can do, one day at a time, one person at a time. I can be a person of nonviolence in my deal-

ings with others. I can be the image of Christ and work toward being last rather than first in the reign he came to establish in our midst.

In my church family I am called to be an agent of life rather than death. I must resist attempts to divide and foster mistrust. I must look for areas in which we can come together and celebrate what we hold in common, rather than breed resentment over the areas of disagreement. I am amazed at what happens when people from opposite poles come together and find that there are precious areas of agreement. I recently presented a workshop on the eucharist. I chuckled at the end of the day when two people came to me at different times and thanked me for the perspective they heard which touched on things that were important to them. I was teaching from the General Instruction to the Roman Missal. *Each person heard what I said according to their own biases and perspectives. Yet both were able to celebrate it. It was obvious that both people were coming from entirely different points of view, yet each one was able to take and celebrate the truth of Jesus Christ crucified, risen, and ascended into heaven—our ultimate Truth.*

When two or more are gathered with one heart in the name of Jesus Christ he is present—sacramentally present. He is also sovereign and he is Lord. This feast reminds me that I am never to give in to despair that insists that all is lost. Jesus Christ leads our communities. Jesus Christ leads our families.

On this last Sunday of the yearly cycle I reflect on things past, celebrate the present, and look forward to things in the future. On a very earthly, practical level I cannot consider this feast without taking time to reflect on the power and presence of the risen Christ in my own experience of family. When I consider the struggles of raising a family in today's difficult world, I celebrate the Christ who has been present to us year after year. I am filled with wonder and awe when I contemplate my young adult children. My heart is filled with love and pride. They are precious in my eyes and in the eyes of God. I celebrate their gifts and the way they use them to bring joy and life to others. I look at my youngest daughter who is still in college. I see the joy and peace of Christ shine through her and I know that her love and kindness touch everyone around her—she resonates peace and I am humbled by Christ the King who reigns and has reigned in our lives. I look at my son who has a heart of gold and who is such an agent of hospitality in his everyday life that people love to be around him. I know that Christ walks with him and continues to gift him in his everyday life—even if he is not always conscious of it. I look at my other son, who has given his entire life to God and who truly lives the gospel in ways I never could have imaged for him. I am filled with wonderment over Christ the King who has led and continues to lead our family. I look at my oldest daughter and my new son-in-law. I am thankful for the incredible heart of compassion that I see in both of them. My daughter's sense of family, her faith, her loyalty, and her willingness to always be there no matter what make her the embodiment of the truth spoken of in today's gospel. I could name my children's concrete accomplishments, but in the grand scheme of things they do not really matter. What matters is heart. When I reflect upon the adults our children have become, I know Jesus was present in our lives—that he led us and sustained us. Jesus did indeed lead a husband and wife who very early on wanted nothing more than to lead their children into the reign of God.

When we establish the reign of God in our homes, in our marketplace, and in the world, we are living the message of Jesus in today's gospel—we are living the reality of this feast. We simply must resist the temptation to think that all is lost on the vigil of this new millennium. We have much to celebrate. Despite this past millennium of death and destruction, there is life and goodwill. Christ continues to lead the church, the people of God, through this present age and will lead us in the age and the reign yet to come.

What was John trying to convey in this Passion narrative? How does this gospel speak to the Feast of Christ the King? Where is the relevance for today's world? Put yourself in Pilate's shoes. How does it feel? How would you respond to Pilate's question of Jesus, "What is truth?" How does this gospel challenge your community? How does it challenge you? In what way have you responded to the call of Christ the King in your life? In what way have you fallen short? In what way has this conversation with the scriptures for today's liturgy invited change in your life? In what way are the biblical themes of covenant, exodus, creation, and community evident in today's readings? Do you still feel the same way about this text as when you began? Has your original understanding been stretched, challenged, or affirmed?

STEP 5
DECISION

The gospel demands a response.

In what concrete way might your parish be invited to respond? Are there any attitudes or behaviors you would like to change as a result of today's conversation? What one concrete action will you take this week in response to the liturgy today?

Pastoral Considerations: What is the most pressing need in your community at this time in terms of furthering the reign of Christ in your midst? How are you falling short? Where is the greatest need? Who are the ambassadors of Christ in your midst that you fail to recognize? What needs to happen in order to address these issues?

Christian Initiation: The Feast of Christ the King strongly echoes the fullness of the Easter Vigil. Christ's sovereignty over all creation through his life, death, resurrection, and ascension into heaven, and the coming of his Spirit, finds concrete expression in the passage of the elect through the waters of new birth from death to new life in baptism. The newly baptized died to the old self to rise again with Christ, Lord and Ruler of their lives. Thus, the feast of Christ the King might be an appropriate time to baptize infants and those unable to be baptized at the Easter Vigil.[30] It might also be an occasion to celebrate a rite of acceptance/welcome or a rite of reception into full communion of the Catholic Church, if needed.

---

[30]For example, fully catechized, unbaptized persons (such as spouses who have attended weekly liturgy for years) might fall under this category. Since there would be no need to delay their initiation longer than necessary, they could be initiated on this feast. The Easter Vigil remains the Church's premier time for adults to celebrate baptism, confirmation, and eucharist, however. (See RCIA, Part II: "Christian Initiation of Adults in Exceptional Circumstances.")

DOCTRINAL ISSUES

What Church truth/teaching/doctrinal issue could be drawn from the gospel for the thirty-fourth Sunday in Ordinary Time?

Participants suggest possible doctrinal themes that flow from the readings.

Possible Doctrinal Themes

Christ the King; Christology; eschatology; final judgment; Book of Revelation; reign of God; conversion; heaven; hell; cost of discipleship; evangelization; mission; human dignity of all persons; paschal mystery

Present the doctrinal material at this time.

1. The facilitator gives input on a particular doctrinal issue of his or her prior choosing. OR
2. The group chooses a doctrinal issue from the list they created. They read together from the Doctrinal Appendix or other appropriate, official Church documents and the works of respected theologians.

(Many doctrinal issues are found in the Doctrinal Appendix at the back of this workbook. If you are choosing an issue from this resource, please refer to it now.)

Reflection questions centered around the chosen doctrinal theme can be found at the end of each topic in the Doctrinal Appendix. The questions are based on the five-step reflection process. If you choose a topic not included in the Doctrinal Appendix, craft your own questions according to the same five-step process.

Following the reflection questions you will be reminded to return to chapter 7, "Preparing the Catechetical Session," to assist you in crafting your own session.

Closing Prayer

You believe that the Son of God once came to us; you look for him to come again.
May his coming bring you the light of his holiness and free you with his blessing.
(Amen.)

May God make you steadfast in faith, joyful in hope, and untiring in love all the days of your life.
(Amen.)

You rejoice that our redeemer came to live with us as man.
When he comes again in glory, may he reward you with endless life.
(Amen.)[31]

---

[31]"Advent Solemn Blessing," *The Sacramentary.*

SOLEMNITIES AND FEASTS

SOLEMNITY OF THE MOST HOLY TRINITY

Environment

We have just left the pinnacle season of the church year. One almost needs time to catch one's breath. It almost seems anticlimactic to go from the festive whites and golds of Easter, the red of Pentecost, to the simplicity of green with instant abruptness. But move we must. Trinity Sunday and Corpus Christi give us two opportunities to slowly ease into the ripened green of summer Ordinary Time. We are not, however, to assume that the Easter season is extended for two more weeks. Ordinary Time has definitely begun. The liturgical color of these two solemnities is white, even though Ordinary Time has returned. The profound nature of the two feasts, God's sacramental expression of love, calls for highlighted attention.

Perhaps one way to return to the longest season of the year is to replace any remaining festal flowers of the Easter season with simple green plants. What better plant to begin with on this feast than the shamrock, nature's own hint of the Triune God? Without verbiage, its placement in the catechetical environment is a simple reminder that all creation praises the Creator. Perhaps the stark simplicity of a white cloth adorned with nothing but the shamrock and the nearby enthronement of the scriptures would be all that is needed to capture a sense of the feast and movement into a new season.

INTRODUCTORY RITES

Entrance Antiphon (or Opening Song)

Blessed be God the Father and his only begotten Son and the Holy Spirit: for he has shown that he loves us.[1]

Opening Prayer

The facilitator of the session may lead the prayer. Others in the group may be asked to proclaim the readings.

Let us pray
[to the one God, Father, Son and Spirit,
that our lives may bear witness to our faith]

Pause for silent prayer.

Father,
you sent your Word to bring us truth
and your Spirit to make us holy.
Through them we come to know the mystery of
    your life.
Help us to worship you, One God in three Persons,
by proclaiming and living our faith in you.
We ask this through our Lord Jesus Christ, your Son,
who lives and reigns with you and the Holy Spirit,
one God, for ever and ever.[2]

LITURGY OF THE WORD

The readings are proclaimed.

First Reading
Deuteronomy 4:32–34, 39–40

(Please refer to the fourth Sunday in Ordinary Time for an overview of the Book of Deuteronomy.)

Today's Pericope: Biblical heroes such as Abraham, Jacob, and Moses received revelations from God. Thus, God was not only *One* because of their experience, but God also was in relationship to them as people of God. The people of God came to realize that there was none other than Yahweh alone. God was incredibly near, present, and manifest. God's manifestation was not something Israel earned. It was completely gratuitous. God acted in freedom. God led Israel out of Egypt, formed them as a people, and led them by signs and wonders through the desert. The exodus was the ultimate sign of God's covenant with Israel. Even today we recall that wondrous event and are filled with hope in the God who liberates and sets God's people free.

---

[1]Solemnity of the Most Holy Trinity: "Entrance Antiphon," *The Sacramentary.*

[2]Solemnity of the Most Holy Trinity: "Opening Prayer," *The Sacramentary.*

Through the act of anamnesis we remember the saving action of God. We remember and make present the gratuitous action of God in the salvation of the world. Thus, in times when there is great temptation to forget God, to doubt that God will act, we are to call upon our corporate power of remembering (anamnesis) and remember that God can, does, is, and continues to act in the lives of human beings.

For the ancients, one way of remembering and keeping alive the covenant was to keep the commandments enjoined upon them. Obedience to the will of God "is often the last recourse of humans about to be broken by trials."[3] Only by looking back with a discerning eye on the pages of salvation history can we appreciate the fullness of God's will and action in the lives of a people. It took the discerning eye of the Church to look back upon the Christ-event and fully discern the action of God in Christ through the Holy Spirit willed at the creation of the universe.

God went out of his own transcendence to the world in order to transform the world. God's first act of revelation took place at the creation of the world. The second act of revelation is when God spoke through the flaming bush to Moses and presented him with the Law on Mount Sinai. God claimed and formed a people as they were led by God's hand through the exodus-event. The exodus is a type of the Christ-event. It looked forward to the ultimate eschatological salvation wrought by Christ. God invites the human heart to respond to God's action in faith. It is God's initiative. The response in faith is to live the demands of the covenant.

Responsorial Psalm
Psalm 33:4–5, 6, 9, 18–19, 20, 22

Today's psalm highlights the Hebrew biblical understanding of the Word of the Lord. It is very similar to John's rendering of Logos in the fourth gospel. God spoke the Word and creation was breathed into existence. The creative power of God's Word, ultimately experienced in the Christ, carries within it the seeds of our belief in the Trinity.

Second Reading
Romans 8:14–17

---

[3]*DL* (VII), 18.

(Please refer to the fourth Sunday of Advent for an overview of the Letter to the Romans.)

Today's Pericope: The verses of today's reading from Romans are skipped when the letter is read in the summer cycle of year A. They are most appropriate today. Paul refers to the essence of the Trinity. He speaks of Abba, Father, Jesus Christ with whom we are co-heirs and the Holy Spirit who guides and leads the children of God.[4] The belief in the Triune God is the essence of the Christian experience. Baptism makes us adopted children of Christ. Through the epicletic action of the Holy Spirit in the eucharistic liturgy the Christian invokes the power of the Father. "Abba" was a liturgical expression of worship in the Aramaic-speaking church.

Adoption by Christ is a gratuitous gift of grace—an eschatological gift. It is given to us through the life, death, resurrection, and ascension of Jesus. The Spirit makes it a living reality in our midst. Paul wakes up the believer with a sobering reminder and invitation. The final line of today's reading reminds us that adoption into Christ's life and into life with God in and through the Spirit is a membership into the mystery of Christ's suffering. It is an invitation to live the paschal mystery—to embrace the cross of Christ.

The gospel is proclaimed.

Gospel
Matthew 28:16–20. Go, therefore, and baptize all nations in the name of the Father, and of the Son, and of the Holy Spirit.

STEP 1
NAMING ONE'S EXPERIENCE

What were your first impressions? What was your first response to the gospel (or the other readings)? What captured your attention?

Each person names his or her initial impression. Statements should be brief. No reasons should be given at this time. All simply listen without agreeing or disagreeing.

---

[4]*PL*, 284.

STEP 2
UNDERSTANDING

In a brief statement, explain what you think this gospel is trying to convey.

STEP 3
INPUT FROM VISION/STORY/TRADITION

Liturgical Context

Trinity Sunday is one of the four solemnities of the Lord during Ordinary Time. Since these feasts are dependent upon the celebration of Easter, they are called movable solemnities of Ordinary Time. The solemnities are Trinity Sunday, Corpus Christi, Sacred Heart, and Christ the King.

Adolf Adam calls them feasts of devotion and feasts of ideas. As feasts of devotion they are expressions of piety born in response to an internal or external trial. As idea feasts, each one extols a particular truth or specific aspect of the mystery of Christ. By stressing these truths or mysteries, the Church hoped to renew and strengthen the faith of God's people.

The Arian controversies of the fourth and fifth centuries gave rise to a strong emphasis on and devotion to the Trinity in Spain and Gaul. Arius, a priest in Alexandria who died in 336, denied the divinity of Christ. As a result, faith in God, the Father, Son, and Holy Spirit, and the equality of the three Divine Persons was threatened. The Councils of Nicea and Constantinople (381) condemned the heresy and formulated the Nicene Creed, the profession of faith recited at every Sunday mass.

The heresy had an impact on Catholic faith and life. Preaching sought to strengthen faith in the Church's doctrine regarding the Trinity. The first preface of the Trinity found its way into the liturgy in the 400s as this feast was born out of controversy. The modern preface of the Trinity appeared during the eighth century. By 800 the mass of the Trinity was celebrated as a votive mass for Sundays. All Sunday liturgies became more Trinitarian in focus. By the year 1000, the Feast of the Trinity was celebrated on the Sunday after Pentecost in Frankish and Gallic monasteries. The feast reminds the faithful of what it means when we refer to the Father, Son, and Spirit: We believe in three Divine Persons in one God.

In 1077 Pope Alexander challenged a special feast devoted to just the Trinity. The pope's contention was that Trinity is remembered and celebrated every Sunday, even every day. One hundred years later, Alexander III said the same thing. However, the feast continued to exist. John XXII made it an official feast during the exile in Avignon in 1334. Adam suggests that the placement of this feast on the Sunday after Pentecost served as a mirror to reflect back on the mystery of salvation just culminated with the celebration of Pentecost.

The feast celebrates a lofty, abstract dogma that seems unrelated to our everyday lives. The overall context for approaching this feast, then, is best found in the following exhortation: "The feast is only a feast if we follow the lead of the assigned scriptures and acclaim a God of love, not dissect an arcane theological treatise."[5]

The Solemnity of the Most Holy Trinity is celebrated on the first Sunday after Pentecost. In the Byzantine rite it is celebrated on Pentecost Sunday. The liturgy for Trinity Sunday has assigned to it three different readings and responsorial psalms for the three-year cycle. Cycles A and C draw from John's gospel and Cycle B chooses Matthew to speak to us of the implications of this feast.

Every liturgy is Trinitarian and not necessarily because it always refers to the three Divine Persons. Rather, it is because every liturgy professes the glory of God who, through a history of salvation, redeems the world through Christ and the Spirit. "The Trinitarian character of the Christian liturgy is to be sought and located in the fact that the liturgy, by definition, is the ritual celebration of the events of the economy of redemption and as such is the celebration of the mystery of God."[6] Thus, one might summarize the doctrine of the

---

[5]Bishops Committee on the Liturgy Secretariat, National Conference of Catholic Bishops, *Study Text 9: The Liturgical Year Celebrating the Mystery of Christ and His Saints* (Washington: USCC, 1984), 60.

[6]Catherine Mowry LaCugna, "Trinity and Liturgy," *NDSW*, 1294.

Trinity by stating that it is, in essence, the doctrine of God. Doctrine on the Trinity expresses what it means that God entered human history and saved the world through Christ and the power of the Holy Spirit. God willed that all creation be saved. In theological terms this is referred to as the *economy of salvation*. The incarnation of Christ is the revelation of God, the sacrament of God in our midst, "the visible icon of the invisible God."[7] The Holy Spirit makes us participants in the divine life by restoring human beings in the image and likeness of God (God's intention at the creation of the world). The Spirit transforms us into the image of Jesus Christ by restoring our divine nature. Both the theology of God's plan of salvation for the world and the triune nature of God are considered part of one reality. God, through Christ and the Spirit, gives God's own self to human beings in love—a gratuitous act of selfless love. The goal and fulfillment of God's plan for the salvation of the world are realized in perfect union with God for all eternity—"the eschatological glorification of God."[8]

Liturgy and doctrine are intimately intertwined in relation to our understanding of the Trinity. In light of God's self-gift to the world, the people of God can do no less than give praise and thanks (doxology). Our doxology expresses our creed *(lex orandi, lex credendi)*. In other words, we should be able to tell something about what we believe on the basis of how we pray *(lex supplicandi legem statuat credendi*; the law of prayer founds the law of belief). Thus, the doctrine of the Trinity is the formal statement of what we practice, celebrate, and profess in our public worship. We give praise and thanks to God through Christ in the power of the Holy Spirit. The liturgy, then, is the primary source for our understanding of the Trinity. Similarly, the Christian doctrine of the Trinity should also be the lens, focus, and context through which our reflection on the liturgy should flow. Put simply, Christian faith is Trinitarian faith. "Christian liturgy has a Trinitarian shape. It expresses the inner life of God revealed in Jesus Christ as three persons in one God, as both personal and communal. God's own consciousness revealed in Jesus Christ is both personal and social."[9] The Trinity invites us into relationship, a relationship that is modeled for us by the way in which Father, Son, and Spirit show us how to live in harmonious community.

One cannot go to the scriptures and find a clearly articulated doctrine of the Trinity. It is implicit rather than explicit. However, in both the Old and New Testaments God "is experienced as going forth out of himself (from his 'aseity') in revelation and redemptive action, and also creating in human hearts a believing response to his revelatory and redemptive action."[10] It is interesting to note that the gospel appointed for the Solemnity of the Most Holy Trinity is the same gospel appointed for the Feast of the Ascension of the Lord in Cycle A. The Feast of the Ascension of the Lord celebrates Jesus' return to the throne of glory. Not until Jesus returns to his rightful place at the right hand of the Father are human beings heirs to the promise of eternal life. These two feasts are viewed through a similar prism—both celebrate the action of God in Christ through the Spirit. God willed the salvation of the world by sending his only Son. The Hebrew scriptures herald the God who has revealed God's self to us personally through God's divine action in the world. The human race knows God through the ways in which God has acted in history. The reading from the Book of Deuteronomy heralds the action of God in salvation history. The heart of today's liturgy resides in the statement "God does not prove himself; he shows himself."[11] There is no proof for the existence of the Trinity. We know the Trinity through the action of God in Christ continued in and through the Spirit.

The alleluia verse is one grand summation and doxology in praise of the One, Triune God: "Glory to the Father, the Son and the Holy Spirit: to God who has been given to us." The opening prayer asks that the Father help us pray to the One God in Three Persons by living and proclaiming our faith. "One hears criticism about this feast because it commemorates not an event but a Christian doctrine. However, the opening prayer blends both event and doctrine: Belief in the Trinity leads us to life of the Father by experiencing the truth revealed by Jesus and the holiness of the Spirit."[12]

---

[7]Ibid.

[8]Ibid.

[9]R. Kevin Seasoltz, O.S.B., *TDJR*, 42.

[10]*PL*, 283.

[11]*DL* (VII), 7, 10.

[12]Stephen T. Jarrell, *Guide to the Sacramentary* (Chicago: Liturgical Training Publications, 1983), 74.

All liturgy professes belief in the Triune God. Never is there a liturgical celebration in which the power of the Trinity is not invoked. The Sunday assembly professes faith in the Triune God when it begins every gathering by invoking "The grace of our Lord Jesus Christ and the love of God and the fellowship of the Holy Spirit be with you all."[13] "Celebrated on the Sunday after Pentecost, it [the Feast of the Trinity] is a great doxology to the Father who raised his Son and brought him into the glory where he reigns with the Holy Spirit he has sent to us. When the sequence of the Sundays in Ordinary Time is about to begin, this feast sheds light on the face and true nature of Jesus, the Son of God, who, by his teaching and his acts, reveals the Father and leads humankind to himself in the Spirit."[14]

If we were to say that there is a bottom line in this liturgy, it can be summed up in words of the Entrance Antiphon: Blessed be God the Father and his only begotten Son and the Holy Spirit: *for he has shown that he loves us.*

Every liturgy celebrates the action of the Triune God in time, space, and history. Every liturgy is a celebration of the heavenly liturgy. This feast is a reminder that we continue to "participate in the feast of the eternal liturgy."[15] The liturgy offers us the means to drink deeply from the wellspring of life. To celebrate the liturgy is to enter into the joy of the Father, the only joy that can enable us to share Christ's exultation in the Holy Spirit. The liturgy makes two demands of us. The first is for conversion and faith. We celebrate, remember, and make present the reality of the Lord's coming. All of salvation history—all that went before us in God's plan for the redemption of the world—as well as the liturgy that will go on into eternity is celebrated every time the church gathers. Every liturgy incorporates us into the divine life. We are called to allow the transformative power of the Trinity to radically transform us more fully into the image of Christ. The second demand of the liturgy insists that we lead authentic lives. We cannot be transformed by the Spirit of God in the celebration of the eternal liturgy and not allow the resurrection of Christ to impact the way we live in the world.

How can we be filled with the jubilant wonder and thanksgiving in our celebrations—including those for the dead—if the power of the resurrection does not daily penetrate the depths of our sinfulness and death? How can we share the Father's joy if we are not constantly open to his overwhelming mercy? How can we sing the canticle of the Lamb, the canticle sung by the blood of martyrs and the perseverance of the saints, if we do not pray for our oppressors? And since the only true joy is paschal joy, joy in the life that springs from the victory over death, how can we celebrate the feast that is the liturgy if we have not learned to be "glad of . . . distress for Christ's sake" (2 Cor 12:10) in the details of our everyday lives, as the Father takes delight in his beloved Son (Mt 17:5)? In short, how can we celebrate the liturgy if we do not live it? The converse is also true: we can live it only if we celebrate it.[16]

Gospel Exegesis

The facilitator provides input from critical biblical scholarship on this text. This input includes insights as to how people would have heard the gospel in Jesus' time.

Once in Galilee, the Twelve were summoned to the mountain by Jesus. A treasure house of meaning is implied and assumed by this alpine manifestation. In the Old Testament, mountains were significant places of revelation and encounter with God. It is no accident that the Great Commission should take place on a mountain summit.

Mountains were the site of Jesus' foundational events: "The call of the twelve, prayer, and the transfiguration."[17] Mountains were places of revelation and eschatological authority. The mountain is an intentional motif in Matthew's gospel employed to develop his theological purpose.[18] For Matthew, mountains were used "as eschatological sites where Jesus enters into the full authority of his Sonship, where the eschatological community is gathered, and where the age of fulfillment is in-

---

[13]"Greeting-Order of Mass," *The Sacramentary.*
[14]*DL* (VII), 7.
[15]*TWOW*, 87.

[16]Ibid., 88.
[17]Benedict T. Viviano, O.P., "Mountains," *CPDBT*, 650.
[18]Ibid., 652.

augurated."[19] Such is the setting of today's gospel for the feast that celebrates our foundational faith in the Triune God.

Consider the picture. The reader is taken from Jerusalem to Galilee, where Jesus inaugurated his mission to the world. Before he died, Jesus predicted that he would return to the disciples in Galilee. The angel at the tomb and Jesus himself reiterated the promise. And so he met them on the mountain. It is the mountain of the Sermon and the transfiguration. Moses was given the Law on Mount Sinai. Jesus was transfigured in glory in the presence of his awestruck disciples on this mountain. Jesus interpreted the Law on this mountain. Matthew's cyclical purpose comes full circle. Jesus, who was worshiped by the magi at his birth, now is worshiped by his disciples after his death, in his resurrected glory, on this mountain of holy events.

Raymond Brown reminds us that the disciples were plagued by doubt throughout Jesus' earthly and postresurrection life. Yet such doubt did not deter Jesus from coming close to his disciples to speak to them. They worshiped him; Jesus responded.

Not only did the appearance stories serve an apologetic function to prove that Jesus died and rose again, they also laid the groundwork for the future mission of the church. Disciples were to go and tell what they had seen—they were to proclaim Christ crucified and risen from the dead. Jesus appeared to the apostles to commission them to carry on his work. "The sending is based on Jesus' own status, showing that as Jesus carried on God's work, the apostles carry on Jesus' work. . . . The authority of the church is delegated from Jesus who has been elevated and has authority in heaven and on earth; the mission that flows from it will touch all nations."[20]

With full authority Jesus commissioned the Twelve to go out and continue his mission. Earlier in the gospel, the apostles were instructed not to go to all the nations (Samaritan towns and gentiles). They were to gather the lost sheep of Israel. In Matthew's gospel, Jesus ministered only to Jews. So did the apostles at first. It was not until a few decades later that God's wider plan for the development of the church was understood as outreach beyond their borders—to the gentiles.

Now, with the full authority of his Sonship and Lordship, Jesus commissioned the Twelve to go to *all* nations. Israel is still welcome, but there are no boundaries when it comes to those who are included in the new kingdom. It is from his exalted throne that Jesus will reign until all his enemies have been defeated.

The mission of Jesus is to be accomplished through baptism. By the time Matthew's gospel was written, baptism was in the name of the Father, and of the Son, and of the Holy Spirit whereas, in the Acts of the Apostles and Paul's Letter to the Corinthians baptism was in the name of Jesus. The Trinitarian formula found in Matthew's gospel signals the church's inauguration of the baptismal profession of faith in the Triune God.

The apostles are now commissioned to go forth and teach all that Jesus commanded. Jesus' authority has now been passed on to the church. The final verse of today's gospel echoes the first words ever spoken about Jesus. He is Emmanuel— God is with us. Now in fulfillment, Jesus remains with the Church. God is with God's people.

The ruling powers of the earth tried to stop *God Is With Us* at the birth of Jesus, and then again at his crucifixion. God's plan would not be deterred; it will go forward until the end of time.

Proclaim the gospel again.

Sometimes we gain new insights when we hear the text after the interpretation is given. Someone from the group proclaims the gospel a second time.

STEP 4
TESTING

Conversation with the Liturgy and the Scriptures

Test your original understanding in dialogue with the text.

(You might consider breaking into smaller groups.)

---

[19]T. L. Donaldson, *Jesus on the Mountain*, Sheffield, 1985, 196–197, in *CPDBT*, 652.
[20]*RCE*, 35.

Now that you've heard the exegesis, were there any new insights? How do you feel about it? How does your original understanding of this gospel compare with what we just shared? How does this story speak to your life?

Sharing Life Experience

Participants share an experience from their lives that connects with the biblical interpretation just presented.

> *As I reflect on today's liturgy, two things seem to jump off the pages. God is present in human history—history of the past, the historical present, and the history of the future. In other words, God is involved in human experience. Second, Jesus is the sacramental presence of God in human history and that presence continues in the Body of Christ. On this Feast of the Trinity we are reminded that we are incorporated into the life of the Trinity through baptism and we celebrate the Trinity and the Trinity become manifest every time we gather for liturgy. So, what does that mean? It means everything! God is the center of our lives. God desires to be in relationship with us. God loves us unconditionally. When the world rejects us, God is always faithful. Through baptism we are incorporated into God's life but we are also incorporated into the suffering of Christ. The way this makes sense for my life is to remember the times of intense suffering—the loss of my parents, dealing with difficult life issues—and I know that the Triune God exists. God has always been present and manifest in the moments of greatest darkness and ambiguity. It was not always easy to see—sometimes it was only after the fact. But discernment always makes it possible for me to acknowledge that the darkness of the moment was only sustained by the brilliance of the light that was leading, protecting, and shielding me from the edge of the abyss.*

> *Ultimately God has been manifest to our lives in the love and compassion of other people. I look at all the people God has put in our lives. They have been the manifestation of God—the consoling hand, the listening ear, the strong shoulder to cry on—all have constituted the Body of Christ manifest to our lives. When I open myself to the power of God in my life and receive the grace available to me, I am empowered to live for others. I look at the beautiful woman in our initiation process who, out of her own loneliness and pain, reached out to God and in the process, found a way to offer life to two children the world might have rejected altogether.*

> *In our brokenness God reaches out to make us whole. There is a gift in suffering. It helps me know how incredibly blessed we are to have a Christ who suffered for us. I would not have known the gift of human love and those who have reached out in compassion and I would not have the sensitivity for the suffering people in the world. Even though I rant and rave when the world comes crashing down around me, it is only after the fact that I am able to see it as gift. When I look at the days after we were spared the loss of our son in a car accident, I could hardly reflect on the grace of those days. God was so incredibly present to us. The precious nature of life and the gift of creation were so much in our consciousness. We were gifted with the awareness that this life is fleeting and that we are to love with our deepest capacity to love, to the core of our beings. God's manifested self-gift during that difficult time taught me to love to the fullest each day, in every way I am capable of loving. I will and do fall short, but the gift of God's manifestation is that I am continually renewed.*

> *On this Feast of Trinity, I celebrate God's presence in my life and the way God has led me through the desert of my life's experiences. I remember and I am grateful. I hope my remembering will sustain me through the next dark moments. The purpose of liturgy is to remember and to allow the remembering to change us. The challenge for me and for the community is to be open to live the paschal mystery in my life. In that way I am privileged to share in the mystery of the cross and the redemption of the world. It is awesome. The theology of Trinity may be some lofty doctrinal treatise, but at its core it is the engine that drives the soul of Christians. If I live in and through the gift of Trinity, I am fully alive.*

What was Matthew's concern in today's gospel? How does Matthew's challenge impact the contemporary church? What does it mean to you that we are baptized in the name of the Trinity? What is your experience of *Emmanuel, God Is With Us*? Would you be able to share that experience with others? What is the significance of today's solemnity for your life? The life of the community? In what way do today's readings reflect the four biblical themes of covenant, creation, community, and exodus? In what way does this liturgy invite transformation in your life? Do you still feel the same way about this text as when you began? Has your original understanding been stretched, challenged, or affirmed?

STEP 5
DECISION

The gospel demands a response.

In what concrete way might your parish be invited to respond? Are there any attitudes or behaviors you would like to change as a result of today's conversation? What one concrete action will you take this week in response to the liturgy today?

Christian Initiation: When was the last time you celebrated an anointing of catechumens? Are you attentive to the celebration of the minor rites? Is there anyone in your process ready to celebrate a rite of acceptance or a rite of welcome? Is there anyone in your process ready to come into full communion of the Catholic Church?

DOCTRINAL ISSUES

What Church truth/teaching/doctrinal issue could be drawn from the gospel for the Solemnity of the Most Holy Trinity?

Participants suggest possible doctrinal themes that flow from the readings.

Possible Doctrinal Themes

Trinity; God as Father, Son, and Spirit; economy of salvation; soteriology; paschal mystery; conversion; evangelization; Christology; faith; creed; images of God

Present the doctrinal material at this time.

1. The facilitator gives input on a particular doctrinal issue of his or her prior choosing. OR
2. The group chooses a doctrinal issue from the list they created. They read together from the Doctrinal Appendix or other appropriate, official Church documents and the works of respected theologians.

(Many doctrinal issues are found in the Doctrinal Appendix at the back of this workbook. If you are choosing an issue from this resource, please refer to it now.)

Reflection questions centered around the chosen doctrinal theme can be found at the end of each topic in the Doctrinal Appendix. The questions are based on the five-step reflection process. If you choose a topic not included in the Doctrinal Appendix, craft your own questions according to the same five-step process.

Following the reflection questions you will be reminded to return to chapter 7, "Preparing the Catechetical Session," to assist you in crafting your own session.

Closing Prayer

The Lord be with you.
(And also with you.)

Lift up your hearts.
(We lift them up to the Lord.)

Let us give thanks to the Lord our God.
(It is right to give him thanks and praise.)

Father, all-powerful and ever-living God,
we do well always and everywhere to give you
     thanks.
We joyfully proclaim our faith
in the mystery of your Godhead.
You have revealed your glory
as the glory also of your Son
and of the Holy Spirit:
three Persons equal in majesty,
undivided in splendor,
yet one Lord, one God,
ever to be adored in your everlasting glory.
And so, with all the choirs of angels in heaven
we proclaim your glory
and join in their unending hymn of praise:
Holy, holy, holy Lord, God of power and might,
heaven and earth are full of your glory.
Hosanna in the highest.
Blessed is he who comes in the name of the Lord.
Hosanna in the highest.[21]

---

[21]"Preface—Trinity Sunday," *The Sacramentary.*

SOLEMNITY OF THE BODY AND BLOOD OF CHRIST (CORPUS CHRISTI)

INTRODUCTORY RITES

Entrance Antiphon (or Opening Song)

The Lord fed his people with the finest wheat and honey; their hunger was satisfied. (Ps 80:17)[1]

Opening Prayer

The facilitator of the session may lead the prayer. Others in the group may be asked to proclaim the readings.

Let us pray
[to the Lord who gives himself in the eucharist
that this sacrament may bring us salvation and
    peace]

Pause for silent prayer.

Lord Jesus Christ,
you gave us the eucharist
as the memorial of your suffering and death.
May our worship of this sacrament of your body
    and blood
help us to experience the salvation you won for us
and the peace of the kingdom
where you live with the Father and
    the Holy Spirit,
one God, for ever and ever.[2]

Alternative Opening Prayer

Let us pray
[for the willingness to make present in our world
the love of Christ shown to us in the eucharist]

Pause for silent prayer.

Lord Jesus Christ,
we worship you living among us
in the sacrament of your body and blood.
May we offer to our Father in heaven
a solemn pledge of undivided love.

May we offer to our brothers and sisters
a life poured out in loving service of that kingdom
where you live with the Father and the Holy Spirit,
one God, for ever and ever.[3]

LITURGY OF THE WORD

The readings are proclaimed.

First Reading
Exodus 24:3–8

(Please refer to the eighteenth Sunday in Ordinary Time for an overview of the Book of Exodus.)

Today's Pericope: Today's reading is a reference to the Sinai (Horeb) covenant as understood through the perspective of the Eloist writer. The ratification of the Sinai covenant had serious implications for Israel. It impacted its social, political, and religious life. (See the glossary for a definition of covenant.) The covenant was ratified through an act of sealing. The fact that the covenant was sealed in blood indicated not only that it was an agreement to follow the Law, it was also an agreement to allow it to be the center of life—it was an agreement to share life. (Refer to symbol of blood, Easter Triduum.) Recall that blood was a sign of life force—life was believed to reside in the blood. The ratification by sealing with blood was a sign that the people were willing to enter into covenant—an intimate, binding relationship—with Yahweh. The blood ritual only took place once. It would not be repeated again until the blood sacrifice of Jesus.

The burnt offering mentioned in verse 5 was a holocaust offering. A complete victim was burned on the altar as an offering of worship and adoration. The peace offering was consumed by those hosting the festive meal as a sign of their intimate relationship with one another and with God. Ac-

---

[1]Corpus Christi: "Entrance Antiphon," *The Sacramentary.*
[2]Corpus Christi: "Opening Prayer," *The Sacramentary.*

[3]Corpus Christi: "Alternative Opening Prayer," *The Sacramentary.*

cording to the Book of Deuteronomy, the peace offering was understood as a joyful eating and drinking before the Lord (12:7, 12, 18). The Israelites ratified their covenant relationship with Yahweh and sealed that covenant with a ceremony of blood. The blood spilled at Calvary incorporates people into the life of God. Eucharist continues participation in the cross of Christ.

Responsorial Psalm
Psalm 116:12–13, 15, 16bc–18

The verses of today's psalm are also used on Holy Thursday. The eucharistic cup is the fulfillment of Moses' blood-spilling ritual mentioned in the first reading. When we share the cup we participate in the saving event of Jesus.

Second Reading
Hebrews 9:11–15

(Refer to the twenty-seventh Sunday in Ordinary Time for an overview of the Letter to the Hebrews.)

Today's Pericope: The author of Hebrews defended the perfect priesthood and liturgy of Jesus. He compared the priesthood of Jesus with the Levitical priesthood. The author of Hebrews compared Jesus' saving action with the activities of the high priest on the Feast of Atonement, Yom Kippur. On the Day of Atonement the high priest secured two goats and made a sin offering. The priest also offered a ram in holocaust for the people and a bull for his own sins. The priest confessed his sins and the sins of the people. The blood of the sacrifices was taken to the Holy of Holies and sprinkled on the gold on the ark of the covenant. This blood, a symbol of life, was hoped to be an atonement for sin so God would forgive the sins of the people. God would reconcile the people to himself and to each other. Fast and sabbatical rest were part of the annual celebration.

Jesus is the new high priest of the new covenant he established. Jesus is the holocaust, the sacrifice, the new victim. Jesus offered his sacrifice only once, however. Jesus' sacrifice, unlike the sacrifice of the Day of Atonement, was not an annual sacrifice. Jesus offered his blood once, for all time and for all people. Jesus' life was atonement for the many.

Jesus reconciled people to God. "Moreover, unlike the animal blood and heifer's ashes which were thought to render one ritually pure (Nm 19:9, 14–21), the blood of Jesus wrought a *moral* purification that cleansed the defiled conscience of the believer."[4]

Some translations of verse 11 suggest that Jesus is the high priest of the good things that *have come*. Other translations refer to the things *to come*. The latter translation is preferable on text-critical merits but also theologically. Asserting that Christ is the high priest of the good things to come enunciates Christ's anticipated eschatology. It leaves us open to the final, ultimate consummation Christ will inaugurate and it stresses the continued reminder of this anticipated truth in the eucharist.

The gospel is proclaimed.

Gospel
Mark 14:12–16, 22–26. This is my body. This is my blood.

STEP 1
NAMING ONE'S EXPERIENCE

What were your first impressions? What was your first response to the gospel (or the other readings)? What captured your attention?

Each person names his or her initial impression. Statements should be brief. No reasons should be given at this time. All simply listen without agreeing or disagreeing.

STEP 2
UNDERSTANDING

In a brief statement, explain what you think this gospel is trying to convey.

---

[4] *WWC*, 261.

Liturgical Context

Prior to the ninth century there was no true worship of the eucharist outside of mass. Such worship began in about the eleventh century. It grew in accord with controversies regarding the "real presence" of Jesus in the sacrament. The controversies helped define eucharistic theology: "the Eucharist is really the Body and Blood of Christ, but under the sign—the sacrament—of bread and wine."[5] Controversies over the eucharist gave birth to eucharistic devotion.

The origin of this feast dates back to the twelfth century. During that time there was an "intense cult of the Blessed Sacrament that placed particular emphasis on the real presence of 'Christ whole and entire' in the consecrated bread."[6] This strong emphasis led to the desire *to see*. Thus, in 1220 in Paris, the practice of elevating the host began.

The feast originated largely due to the vision received by an Augustinian nun who saw a shining disk with a dark spot on it. She was told that the spot was there because there was no feast to commemorate the eucharist. Consequently the bishop of Liège introduced the feast into his diocese in 1246. In 1264 Pope Urban IV established the feast for the entire Church. In his presentation intended to explain the reasons for establishing the feast (*Bull Transiturus*—the document establishing the feast), the pope put forth a balanced theology of eucharist as sacrifice and meal. Some believe that Thomas Aquinas wrote the text for the mass and office. The feast did not spread rapidly. However, Pope Clement V reintroduced it at the Council of Vienne in 1311–12.

Traditionally the feast was called "Feast of the Most Holy Body of Christ." The new Roman missal expanded the title to include the fullest understanding of the sacrament and to include the mystery of the "precious blood": "Solemnity of the Most Holy Body and Blood of Christ." However, popular usage has retained the Latin title, "Corpus Christi."

Corpus Christi is a duplication of the feast that already commemorates the sacrament of the eucharist: the day of its institution—Holy Thursday. Both feasts emphasize the redemptive effects of Jesus Christ. However, Adam insists that it is a defensible duplication, as Holy Thursday cannot quite enter into the fullness of festal joy as it is explicitly connected to Good Friday. Thus, a feast dedicated to the expression of joy in the eucharist as the "precious fruit and operative presence of the paschal mystery"[7] is certainly a laudable practice. Every Sunday celebrates the paschal mystery in its entirety in the celebration of eucharist. Notwithstanding, Adam asserts that "the objection of duplication has no place."[8]

St. Thomas Aquinas's influence is evident in the eucharistic theology woven through the presidential prayers of the proper of the mass. In his *Summa*, Thomas examines the importance of the eucharist in terms of past, present, and future. As a past reality it commemorates Jesus' sacrifice of Passion, death, and resurrection. As a present reality it unites us to Christ and one another. As a future reality it anticipates "enjoyment of the divinity."

The liturgy reflects this past, present, and future understanding. The opening prayer touches the past remembrance: "You gave us the eucharist as the memorial of your suffering and death." The prayer over the gifts touches on the present reality: "Lord, may the bread and wine we offer bring your Church the unity and peace they signify." The concluding prayer connects us to the future hope: "May we come to possess it fully in the kingdom."

The Sequence, *Laud, Sion, Salvatorem (Zion, praise your Savior)*, expresses classical eucharistic theology.

Laud, Sion

Zion, praise your Savior. Praise your leader and shepherd in hymns and canticles. Praise him as much as you can, for he is

---

[5]*DL* (VII), 38.
[6]Adolf Adam, *LY*, 169.

[7]Ibid., 171.
[8]Ibid.

beyond all praising and you will never be able to praise him as he merits.

But today a theme worthy of particular praise is put before us—the living and life-giving bread that, without any doubt, was given to the Twelve at the Table during the Holy Supper.

Therefore, let our praise be full and re-sounding and our soul's rejoicing full of delight and beauty, for this is the festival day to commemorate the first institution of this Table.

At this Table of the new King, the new Law's new Pasch puts an end to the old Pasch. The new displaces the old, reality the shadow and light the darkness. Christ wanted what he did at the Supper to be re-peated in his memory.

And so we, in accordance with his holy di-rections, consecrate bread and wine to be salvation's Victim. Christ's followers know by faith that bread is changed into his flesh and wine into his blood.

Man cannot understand this, cannot per-ceive it; but a lively faith affirms that the change, which is outside the natural course of things, takes place. Under the different species, which are now signs only and not their own reality, there lie hid wonderful realities. His body is our food, his blood our drink.

And yet Christ remains entire under each species. The communicant receives the complete Christ—uncut, unbroken, and undivided. Whether one receives or a thousand, the one receives as much as the thousand. Nor is Christ diminished by being received.

The good and the wicked alike receive him, but with the unlike destiny of life or death. To the wicked it is death, but life to the good. See how different is the result, though each receives the same.

Last of all, if the sacrament is broken, have no doubt. Remember there is as much in

a fragment as in an unbroken host. There is no division of the reality, but only a breaking of the sign; nor does the break-ing diminish the condition or size of the One hidden under the sign.

Behold, the bread of angels is become the pilgrim's food; truly it is bread for the sons, and is not to be cast to dogs. It was prefigured in type when Isaac was brought as an offering, when a lamb was appointed for the Pasch, and when manna was given to the Jews of old.

Jesus, Good Shepherd and true Bread, have mercy on us; feed us and guard us. Grant that we find happiness in the land of the living. You know all things, can do all things, and feed us here on earth. Make us your guests in heaven, co-heirs with you and companions of heaven's citi-zens. Amen. Alleluia.

The Earliest Celebration of the Eucharist. Weaving together all the elements of chapters 10 and 11, we are able to "sketch the rite of the Lord's Sup-per as Paul had introduced it at Corinth and as he wished it to be maintained."[9] The Supper should not begin until all are gathered.

It is a real meal, to which the well-off con-tribute food and drink. It opens with the customary Jewish blessing of God over the bread, which is then broken in pieces and distributed to all, probably with the words of interpretation of distribution identifying the bread as the Body of Christ (11:24). By this gathering it is constituted as the eccle-sial Body of Christ (10:17). The meal con-tinues, and at the end "the cup of blessing" is produced and the thanksgiving is said before all drink of it. It would seem that during the thanksgiving the death of the Lord, the risen, victorious, ever-present Lord of the community, is *proclaimed* "until he come" (11:26). The action is not an acted parable that needs no explanation. It needs a verbal proclamation, for which there is no satisfactory antecedent in Jew-ish tradition other than the extended

---

9Jones, "The Eucharist—The New Testament," *SL*, 192.

thanksgiving after the meal, the *birkat ha-mazon*. The content of this thanksgiving and proclamation might have been the re-calling of the wonderful words of God in creation, election, and providence, and now in his Son and all he has done through his death and resurrection. In this way the whole eucharistic action is performed "for my memorial *(anamnesis), because*...you proclaim...." Thus the memorial is raised to God through the thanksgiving of those who are mindful and grateful; and yet men are enjoined to "do this," that they may re-member. "...Until (that goal is reached that) he may come." This phrase seems to be a paraphrase of the Aramaic *Maranatha*, still preserved in the Corinthian liturgy.... The death of the risen Lord is so proclaimed that his return is invoked and anticipated; his *parousia* is both his ex-pected arrival and also in some sense his presence.[10]

In Corinth, the meal came before the celebration of the Word. The father of the house presided over the blessing of the bread and may have al-lowed a guest to pray the thanks over the cup. It appears as if Paul was passing on a tradition that was already established even before his conver-sion; "it is the earliest surviving account of the Last Supper, and there is a *prima facie* case for its authenticity."[11]

The prayer over the cup is based on Jeremiah 31:31–34, in which he authorized the establish-ment of a new covenant, yet provided no way to initiate it. Jesus provided the way—he offered his own blood, just as the first covenant began simi-larly (Ex 24:4–8). However, the thanksgiving over the cup refers specifically to the "cup" with only implicit allusion to its contents in order to respect the Jewish prohibition and abhorrence for drink-ing blood.

The Liturgical Prayers for Corpus Christi. In the rit-ual prayers two images of eucharist emerge. The first is eucharist as Jesus at table with his disciples, feeding the people with the gift of himself (Pref-ace II of Holy Eucharist). The second image is eu-

charist as a gift of adoration and worship ("we worship you living among us in the sacrament of your body and blood"—Alternative Opening Prayer). The first is more communal in nature, the second reflects a posture of private devotion. Both are valid and helpful reflections on the eu-charist, but coming from the context of Sunday worship, the communal image best reflects our Sunday experience and theology of the eucharist. The opening prayer, prayer after communion, and first preface reflect a theme of personal worship, strengthening, and cleansing. The alternative opening prayer begins with our worship of Christ in the sacrament of his Body and Blood, and ends with the prayer that we offer our lives poured out in service of our brothers and sisters. The second preface refers to the feeding of God's people with the gift of Christ in the eucharist. The prayer over the gifts asks that the bread and cup, signs of peace and unity, bring unity and peace to the Church. The second invocation of form C of the penitential rite expresses the fullness of eucharist. "Lord Jesus, you came to gather the nations into the peace of God's kingdom: Lord have mercy. You came in word and sacrament to strengthen us in holiness: Christ have mercy. You will come in glory with salvation for your people: Lord have mercy." Eucharist gathers us as a people in unity and peace. Eucharist strengthens us and makes us holy as we await the day we will feast at the heav-enly banquet.

This feast has moved from a feast of devotion to the blessed sacrament reserved in the tabernacle and presented to the people for adoration to a celebration of eucharist. Observe the preface for Holy Thursday, which reflects that focus:

> Father, all-powerful and ever-living God,
> we do well always and everywhere to give
>   you thanks
> through Jesus Christ our Lord.
> He is the true and eternal priest
> who established this unending sacrifice.
> He offered himself as a victim for our de-
>   liverance
> and taught us to make this offering in his
>   memory.
> As we eat his body which he gave for us,
> we grow in strength.
> As we drink his blood which he poured
>   out for us,

---

[10]Ibid., 192–193.
[11]Ibid., 195.

we are washed clean.
Now, with angels and archangels,
and the whole company of heaven,
we sing the unending hymn of your
    praise.[12]

One distinguishing feature of this feast is the eucharistic procession. During the Middle Ages the procession included tableaus of the Passion and Old Testament figures. During the baroque era, the procession became far more elaborate. It evolved into a public, triumphant procession of thanksgiving. Floats and scenes that had little or nothing to do with the eucharist became part of the procession. During the Enlightenment, this practice all but disappeared.

The procession is considered an exercise of devotion (*pia exercitia*) under the direction of the local ordinary. There has been a recent call for a return to the practice of eucharistic processions, perhaps sparked by the renewed vision of the Vatican Council. The Council affirmed the image of God's people as a pilgrim people who could withstand the dangers of the journey only with the help and assistance of Christ.

> Our contemporaries so often suffer from the randomness of existence. If the Corpus Christi procession were properly conducted in the spirit of the liturgy, it could, more than any other procession, be or become a way of making them aware, by means of a real symbol, that they are not alone as they make their way along the difficult mountain path of life on earth, but rather that in the communion of the Church, which has the eucharistic Lord with her, going before, beside and behind her, they are on the way to eternal union with the Christ of the parousia, when "he comes on that day to be glorified in his saints, and to be marveled at in all who have believed" (2 Thes 1.10).[13]

Ultimately, then, "Corpus Christi retains its theological significance as a celebration of God's gift

of Christ in the Spirit to the church and the world as its food and drink of everlasting life. Moreover, in the celebration of this feast the church as the body of Christ experiences itself called to let the Spirit fashion it more into bread and drink for the world."[14]

Gospel Exegesis

The facilitator provides input from critical biblical scholarship on this text. This input includes insights as to how people would have heard the gospel in Jesus' time.

The exodus and its memorial feast of Passover were and are for the Jewish people what the death and resurrection of Jesus and its memorial feast, the Triduum, are for Christians. It is the hallmark, premier event of God's saving action in the history of a people. Originally Passover was a pastoral feast celebrated prior to the exodus-event. The events of the great liberation out of Egypt and the settlement into the Promised Land forever changed the celebration. It became embedded in the history and remembrance of the event in which Israel was led out of bondage.

Once Israel had settled in Canaan, Passover also became associated with the Feast of Unleavened Bread, an agricultural feast. Passover and the Feast of Unleavened Bread happened at the same time, around the 14th or 15th of Nisan, according to the instructions given in the Book of Numbers. Mark's narrative betrays an ignorance of those dates. Why? Mark acts as if the eating of the Passover lamb and the Feast of Unleavened Bread were taking place on the same day. In actuality, the sacrificing of the lambs for Passover took place on the afternoon of the 14th of Nisan. The Feast of Unleavened Bread began at sundown on the 15th of Nisan. Was Mark's version of events for theological reasons, or was he not aware of Jewish customs?[15]

Mark's version of the Last Supper is situated in the context of the Passion narrative. It takes place at the Passover meal, a detail ignored by Paul. Both Matthew and Mark understand the meal to be intimately connected with the paschal event. Matthew, Mark, and Luke portray a similar com-

---

[12]Preface of Eucharistic Prayer I, *The Sacramentary.*

[13]W. Durig, "Zur Liturgie des Fronleichnamsfeier," in *Am Tisch des Wortes*, Neue Reihe 113 (Stuttgart, 1971), p. 17; in Adolf Adam, *LY*, 169, 170.

---

[14]McDermott, "Feasts of Christ," in *NDSW*, 204.
[15]*WWC*, 262.

posite of events. "On the night before the crucifixion he lays bare his own inner purpose in approaching and accepting death; he makes it into a sacrificial offering, to provide the blood for a new alliance between God and the twelve-fold Israel (cf. Exod. 24.4) and for 'many' (= all, cf. Isa. 53.12) by the twofold sign; by accepting the bread and cup the disciples accept his intention and their own share in it."[16] Verse 25 looks to Jesus' vindication and glorification that will be celebrated in God's reign.

Mark's narrative reflects the experience of his own community, which celebrated the eucharist years after Paul described the earliest liturgy. Mark's version shows a movement away from the particularly Jewish meal dimensions of the Supper, perhaps as a response to the influx of gentiles into the community. The text reveals a liturgical formula and probably reflected the method in which Mark's community of the 60s celebrated eucharist. First Corinthians reveals that Paul's community celebrated the cup and bread earlier in the meal. Mark places it at the end of the meal. Mark's liturgy bears resemblance to the pattern found in the distribution of the loaves' sequences in chapters 6 and 8 of Mark. Bread was *taken*. Prayers of *blessing* and *thanksgiving* were prayed. Bread was *broken*. Bread was shared, *distributed*. The cup was *taken*. Prayers of *blessing* and *thanksgiving* were prayed. The cup was shared and *distributed*. The actions Mark describes are ritual actions and they are liturgical. They reflect a theology of eucharist already present in Mark's community. Jesus drank from what was probably the third cup of the Passover meal. After the Passover meal everyone sang the Hallel psalms and drank from the third cup of wine. Jesus interpreted the sharing of this cup in terms of the Suffering Servant of Israel. In so doing, he presents an exegesis of the reason for his suffering and death. Jesus poured out his blood for the many (Semitic word for *all*). The cup bonds people to participation in Jesus' covenant. The cup most fully expresses the atoning nature of Jesus' sacrifice and our participation in his sacrifice. (Crucial to our understanding of this meal is our understanding of the symbols of bread and wine. Please refer to the Easter Vigil—symbols of bread and wine for further elaboration. Refer also to the liturgical and scriptural exegesis

for Holy Thursday for further insight on the fullness of the eucharist.)

It is obvious from the text that Jesus did not want the location of the celebration of the paschal meal to be revealed ahead of time. It is not sure whether the reason had more to do with ensuring privacy in his last moments with friends, or if it was to keep the place secret so arrest would be delayed. Regardless, Jesus carefully set things in motion and planned the event with every detail in mind. However, the text leaves out meal preparations, which included other key ingredients such as the lamb, herbs, nuts, apple, sauces, and salt water. Even though the meal was closely tied to the Passover meal, there is no mention of other key Passover foods. Obviously Mark was less concerned with the Passover lamb and its association with Passover. He was more concerned with the new Passover of Jesus accomplished through his death and resurrection—the passage from death to life.

Key elements in Jesus' ritual were akin to most household celebrations of his day. Jesus took bread, he blessed it, and he gave thanks. Jesus took the cup and acknowledged that all gifts come from God.[17] It was common to pass around a fragment of bread and a common cup. Up to this point there was nothing unusual in Jesus' actions. What was extremely unusual was the significance he assigned to those actions. Jesus proclaimed that the bread he broke and shared and the cup he passed from one to another was the gift of *his body* and *his blood*, broken and poured out for the sins of the world. The blood of the covenant was an allusion to the sacrifice of his blood on the cross, which would be the sacrifice of atonement for the sins of the world. Jesus proclaimed that he was giving his life so others might share in the new *covenant* he was establishing. Jesus' life blood sealed the covenant.

Mark recounts the event with marked simplicity. The eucharistic liturgy is laid out before the reader in all its simplicity. There are no explanations—the rite is simply defined and expressed. Everything that Jesus said and taught is embodied in the simple words and actions put before us by Mark.

---

[16]Jones, *SL*, 196.

[17]*DL* (VII), 53.

The extreme simplicity of these words and of the gesture that accompanies them mirrors the incomprehensible simplicity of God. What he had first unfolded, in the announcement of the Good News, embracing the multiple aspects of human complexity, Jesus now encloses at the Last Supper, without excluding anything, in a rite that borders on insignificance. For only a sort of insignificance can signify the Abyss of the humility of the Glory. Anything resembling explanation or feeling would obscure God instead of revealing him. At the hour he had most ardently desired, Jesus rigorously refrained from doing. "Body given . . . blood of the Covenant shed for many . . . take . . . eat . . . drink"; nothing more, whatever the differences between the four accounts. There is only the essential. When the essential has the aspect of insignificance, it risks to go unnoticed. There is a drift toward banality. But there are risks also when one claims to highlight the essential by having recourse to pedagogies in which the eminently significant value of the form of insignificance would disappear.[18]

There are eschatological overtones in Mark's version of the meal. Jesus promises to return. Jesus gives his disciples the meal as a perpetual reminder—his presence in the midst of absence. The sacrament of Christ's Body and Blood continues to be the tangible sign of Christ's continued presence in the midst of believers.

The preparations involved in the planning and preparation of the Passover meal are limited to Jesus and his twelve apostles. It was common for the citizens of Jerusalem to accommodate pilgrims in their homes for the celebration of Passover. Jesus tells them that a donkey would be tied and waiting and that a room was secured. They would know which room by virtue of the sign of the man with a water jar. It would have been most peculiar for a man to be carrying a water jar—that was customarily a woman's job. Men carry wine, but not in jars—it was usually transported in wineskins.

Why was this a sign? What was its significance? One conjecture suggests that perhaps the water brought into the house was to be used for the washing of hands, particularly significant in light of the fact that the disciples refrained from such hand washing on other occasions.[19] There is no way to know for sure the significance attached the sign, however.

Jesus does seem to have prior knowledge about the events at hand. He knows that he will be betrayed. He knows who will betray him. The disciples do not yet know who the betrayer will be. Only the reader is privy to that information. "Jesus' foreknowledge gives the impression that by anticipating what is to happen to him he has his future in his own hands to some extent."[20]

Something quite significant takes place at this meal. The previous signs of unleavened bread and wine of Passover are replaced by a new sign. Jesus insists that the new sign is his body in the form of the broken, unleavened bread. The cup of his blood poured out is shared as the sign that seals the new covenant. The bread is the body of the murdered Jesus and the cup is his blood spilled for all. Jesus already foretold the events of his death. Now he gives his disciples a sign. "Thus, Jesus makes clear through a sign what so far he has announced only with words."[21]

Every eucharist is a participation and celebration of the events of Calvary. It is an anamnesis—a remembering that makes present. Mark's community was fully aware of that reality as evidenced by today's text. So are we when we gather for the eucharistic liturgy.

Ched Myers as always sheds interesting, thought-provoking light on the events of the Last Supper.[22] Jesus is aware that he has been betrayed and names the seriousness of the offense. Table fellowship in antiquity was the deepest form of intimate bonding and relationship. Jesus was highlighting the seriousness of the offense by saying that the one who betrayed him was the one who dipped

---

[18] Fr. Varillon, *L'humilité de Dieu* (Paris: Centurion, 1974) 156–157, *DL* (VII), 53–54.

[19] *RM*, 183.
[20] Ibid., 184.
[21] Ibid.
[22] *BSM*, 361–364.

from the same dish—"to participate as an 'agent' represents the deepest violation."[23]

The atmosphere of the meal moves from rumors of betrayal to the deepest intimacy. The meal continues. Mark's recounting of the meal reveals a liturgical formula already in use. It also reveals the blessing of normal table fellowship that was customarily prayed by the head of every household.

> When at the daily meal the *paterfamilias* recites the blessing over the bread ... and breaks it and hands a piece to each member to eat, the meaning of the action is that each of the members is *made a recipient of the blessing by this eating;* the common "Amen" and the common eating of the bread of benediction unite the members into table fellowship. The same is true of the "cup of blessing," which is the cup of wine over which grace has been spoken, when it is in circulation among members: *drinking from it mediates a share in the blessing.*[24]

Mark's breaking and blessing of bread remembers the wilderness feedings as mentioned earlier. There is a difference, however. This time they do not distribute the bread to others—this bread is for them and so is the cup. Along with the bread and cup, however, is the cup of suffering that will also be theirs. They will suffer at the hands of those in power. Earlier allusions to baptism and now eucharist remind Jesus' disciples that both baptism and eucharist are participation in Jesus' suffering—participation in the cross of Christ.

Rather than give a homily based on the grace and benefit of the Passover, Jesus instead assigns new meaning to it. He appropriates the meal in terms of himself and his own mission. Jesus is the "eschatological paschal lamb." Mark makes his final assault on the symbol world of Judaism. Mark does not mention the heart of the Passover meal—the eating of the Passover lamb. Rather, he takes old symbols and assigns new meaning to them. He narrates a new myth—Jesus is the new Passover lamb. Mark also makes another editorial comment re-

garding the ritual purity system of Judaism. "His blood is atonement blood which is 'poured out for many' (14:24); it takes away uncleanness. The final irony is that death, the ultimate pollution, serves as the very source of purity for Jesus' followers."[25]

In verse 25 Jesus turns the feast into a fast. He insists that he will fast from wine until the new day, in which he will drink wine in the new kingdom. The bridegroom now is leaving and the time for fasting has approached. The bridegroom himself announces the fast. One hypothesis suggests that Jesus is following the tradition of Jewish dissent. He abstains and intercedes on behalf of those who persecute him. We will see this prayer again in Gethsemane. Evidence that this is indeed what Jesus is doing can be noted from looking back at the primitive church, which fasted on Passover in intercession for the Jews. The early church document, the *Didache*, reveals this tradition when it enjoined people to fast for those who persecuted them. There is great logic in this hypothesis when one considers the irony. On this great day of celebration, the day that celebrates the liberation of Israel, Jesus called for abstinence rather than for the customary feasting. "The struggle for liberation is not a past memory, but a task that ever binds us to the future."[26]

Myers insists that Mark's rendering of the Last Supper is not a "memorial."[27] Rather than look back, it looks forward. Through the venue of fellowship meal, Jesus invites his disciples into his arrest, torture, and death. In so doing, he invites us all. Mark overturns the highest feast of the old world. In its place Jesus offers his own body—that is, the continued gift and sacrifice of his life for the many. Participation in eucharist commits us to participation in his cross.

Proclaim the gospel again.

Sometimes we gain new insights when we hear the text after the interpretation is given. Someone from the group proclaims the gospel a second time.

---

[23]Ibid., 361.

[24]Joachim Jeremias, *The Eucharistic Words of Jesus,* in *BSM,* 362.

[25]Neyrey, "The Idea of Purity in Mark's Gospel," *Semeia,* 35, pp. 91–127, in *BSM,* 363.

[26]*BSM,* 364.

[27]Ibid.

Conversation with the Liturgy and the Scriptures

Test your original understanding in dialogue with the text.

(You might consider breaking into smaller groups.)

Now that you've heard the exegesis, were there any new insights? How do you feel about it? How does your original understanding of this gospel compare with what we just shared? How does this story speak to your life?

Sharing Life Experience

Participants share an experience from their lives that connects with the biblical interpretation just presented.

A few years ago I attended a workshop in which a national leader suggested that we have not passed on good eucharistic theology to our people. He arrived as pastor in a parish that had not celebrated eucharist in over a year. Every Sunday for over a year, this community celebrated a communion service as the parish priest was incapacitated due to illness. This workshop presenter asserted that the greatest sadness was that it [eucharist] was not even missed. He insisted that we have not taught the heart of our eucharistic theology. People do not realize that it is in the taking, blessing, breaking, and sharing of the Bread of Life that we are taken, blessed, broken, and shared. We are poured out like Christ was poured out for the sins of the world. We most fully realize and celebrate that truth in the liturgy of the eucharist.

We have a place to bring the joys and struggles of our lives. We have a place to bring our brokenness and allow it to have redemptive value—our loneliness, our inconsistencies, our ambiguities—all of them are placed on the altar and allowed to be transformed into gift. The eucharist feeds us for mission. The Catholic catechism tells us that eucharist commits us to the poor. If we go to the table with a "Jesus and me only" perspective, it borders on idolatry. Eucharist commits us to others. I cannot feast on the Body and Blood of Christ and not be aware that I am to go out and feed others similarly.

I am reminded of all the people in our parish who are fed from the Lord's Table and who, in turn, go out and feed others in our community—the poor, the sick, the grieving. I am reminded of Archbishop Romeros and all the saints of the Third World who put their lives on the line. I am particularly reminded of a village in Guatemala in 1986 in which all the village catechists were forced to give their lives for the community, in order to prevent the community from being butchered. They feasted at the Lord's Table and were able in turn to feed others. They fed their people with the sacrifice of their lives. They, and others like them, give fresh meaning to what it means to participate in the cross of Christ.

I certainly have not been called on to sacrifice my life for others. Perhaps eucharist prepares me in the event that should ever happen. There have been small ways, however. Many years ago my husband and I strapped our very young children on our backs and every weekend went out to plant tomatoes so we could send the proceeds to the poor south of our borders. My adult daughter looks back on those days as incredibly formative in her life. There have been many projects over the years, and we have always felt privileged to participate in so radical a way in the life-giving nourishing ministry of Jesus. Eucharist demands that we leave the church each Sunday with a firm resolve to change not only ourselves, but the world as well.

Eucharist reminds me that no matter what suffering I face in my life, it can have redemptive value. Suffering has the potential to offer deep meaning in my life as well as providing the potential to be life-giving for others. It might be something as simple as sharing an experience of pain and allowing another person to realize she or he is not alone in their suffering. I remember an evening of reflection in the parish. I shared an experience in which my family was forced to reflect on the transitory nature of life following a car accident in which my son's life was spared. It was a raw time and the experience was difficult to share. A woman came to me a few weeks later and told me how she went home that night and called a relative with whom she had been estranged for twelve years. She realized how short life is and how foolish she had been. We have no idea how we might be called on to be eucharist for others. Today's liturgy is a reminder of the precious gift we have been given. It also reminds us that in these very difficult times of violence and ambiguity, we have a place where we can discover meaning in the midst of our suffering. I am thankful to be part of a eucharistic community. It is a hopeful place to live.

Can you relate to the paschal nature of the eucharist as suggested by Mark's gospel? What was Mark trying to tell his community? In what way does this gospel challenge your community today? In what way has this conversation with the scriptures for today's liturgy invited change in your life? In what way are the biblical themes of covenant, exodus, creation, and community evident in today's readings? Do you still feel the same way about this text as when you began? Has your original understanding been stretched, challenged, or affirmed?

STEP 5
DECISION

The gospel demands a response.

In what concrete way might your parish be invited to respond? Are there any attitudes or behaviors you would like to change as a result of today's conversation? What one concrete action will you take this week in response to the liturgy today?

Christian Initiation: What a wonderful occasion to celebrate a rite of full communion in the Catholic Church! Christian initiation incorporates a person into the eucharistic assembly. All sacramental catechesis leads to that reality. When was the last time your initiation group participated in a mission-centered activity? The minor rites of the catechumenate foreshadow full participation in the eucharistic assembly through the sacrament of eucharist. Are you celebrating the minor rites with catechumens every time you gather?

DOCTRINAL ISSUES

What Church truth/teaching/doctrinal issue could be drawn from the gospel for the Solemnity of the Most Holy Body and Blood of Christ?

Participants suggest possible doctrinal themes that flow from the readings.

Possible Doctrinal Themes

Corpus Christi; eucharist; symbol of bread and wine; Christology; sacramentality; eucharistic prayer; providence of God; incarnation; paschal mystery; Body of Christ; mystery of suffering; non-violence

Present the doctrinal material at this time.

1. The facilitator gives input on a particular doctrinal issue of his or her prior choosing. OR
2. The group chooses a doctrinal issue from the list they created. They read together from the Doctrinal Appendix or other appropriate, official Church documents and the works of respected theologians.

(Many doctrinal issues are found in the Doctrinal Appendix at the back of this workbook. If you are choosing an issue from this resource, please refer to it now.)

Reflection questions centered around the chosen doctrinal theme can be found at the end of each topic in the Doctrinal Appendix. The questions are based on the five-step reflection process. If you choose a topic not included in the Doctrinal Appendix, craft your own questions according to the same five-step process.

Following the reflection questions you will be reminded to return to chapter 7, "Preparing the Catechetical Session," to assist you in crafting your own session.

Closing Prayer

Father,
you have brought to fulfillment the work of our
    redemption
through the Easter mystery of Christ your Son.
May we who faithfully proclaim his death and res-
    urrection in these sacramental signs
experience the constant growth of your salvation
    in our lives.
We ask this through our Lord Jesus Christ, your

Son, who lives and reigns with you and the
Holy Spirit, one God for ever and ever.[28]

OR

Lord, hear our prayer for your mercy
as we celebrate this memorial of our salvation.
May this sacrament of love be for us
the sign of unity and the bond of charity.[29]

OR

Lord,
may our sharing at this holy table make us holy.
By the body and blood of Christ
join all your people in brotherly love.
Grant this through Christ our Lord.[30]

[28]Votive Masses, Holy Eucharist: "Opening Prayer," *The Sacramentary.*

[29]Votive Masses, Holy Eucharist: "Prayer Over the Gifts," *The Sacramentary.*

[30]Votive Masses, Holy Eucharist: "Prayer After Communion," *The Sacramentary.*

SOLEMNITY OF THE SACRED HEART OF JESUS

INTRODUCTORY RITES

Opening Song (or Entrance Antiphon)

The thoughts of his heart last through every generation, that he will rescue them from death and feed them in time of trouble. (Ps 32:11, 19)[1]

Opening Prayer

The facilitator of the session may lead the prayer. Others in the group may be asked to proclaim the readings.

Let us pray
[that we will respond to the love of Christ]

Pause for silent prayer.

Father,
we rejoice in the gifts of love
we have received from the heart of Jesus your Son.
Open our hearts to share his life
and continue to bless us with his love.
We ask this through our Lord Jesus Christ, your
    Son,
who lives and reigns with you and the Holy Spirit,
one God, for ever and ever.

OR

Father,
we have wounded the heart of Jesus your Son,
but he brings us forgiveness and grace.
Help us prove our grateful love
and make amends for our sins.
We ask this through our Lord Jesus Christ, your
    Son,
who lives and reigns with you and the Holy
    Spirit,
one God for ever and ever.[2]

LITURGY OF THE WORD

Let us listen to God's word.

---

[1]Sacred Heart: "Entrance Antiphon," *The Sacramentary.*
[2]Sacred Heart: "Opening Prayer," *The Sacramentary.*

The readings are proclaimed.

First Reading
Hosea 11:1, 3–4, 8c–9

(Please refer to the eighth Sunday in Ordinary Time for an overview of the Book of Hosea.)

Today's Pericope: For Hosea the marriage contract and conjugal love was a metaphor for Israel and its covenant relationship with Yahweh. As far as Hosea was concerned, Israel's breaking of the covenant was akin to a woman abandoning her marriage vows and selling herself into prostitution. Yahweh, however, was like a faithful, loving husband who continued to invite repentance and restoration to the covenant relationship, which had been severed.

Hosea reminded the people that they must remember the exodus, their founding, premier event—the time when Yahweh tested the people. It was the time of their election. All salvation history that preceded the exodus was intended to prepare the people for it. All salvation history that followed was a result of it. Hosea exalted the mercy of Yahweh, who pursued and educated the people with tenderness. The heart of Yahweh was pierced by the sins of Israel, like a parent who grieves over the loss of a favored child. God loves human beings with a transcendent, all-encompassing love. We cannot begin to fathom it. It is unlike any human love we might experience. Even though human beings are made in the image of God, we cannot begin to plumb the depths of God or God's love for us.

Responsorial Psalm
Isaiah 12:2–6

Isaiah assures us: "You will draw joyfully from the springs of salvation." In the context of this feast, the springs of life-giving water are the blood and water that flow from the pierced side of Christ—a sign of his eternal love.

Second Reading
Ephesians 3:8–12, 14–19

(Please refer to the fifteenth Sunday in Ordinary Time for an overview of the Letter to the Ephesians.)

Today's Pericope: The Letter to the Ephesians is a reminder to the Church of incorporation into the life of Christ through baptism. It is also a proclamation of Christian faith. According to the author of Ephesians, God envisioned the image of Christ in the human person at the creation of the world. Yet God kept God's awesome plan secret. God sent prophets to prepare the way and to announce God's plan in overt and hidden ways. Those who recognized God's work realized that God's Word was accomplished in Christ. Thus with certain faith we are empowered to proclaim the good news with boldness.

We can do no less than worship the God who is praised in heaven. We remember the wonder of God and we give praise and adoration. We are beneficiaries of Christ's ultimate sacrifice. We are one with him through baptism. We are heirs to his death and resurrection. Through Jesus we are new creations. Thus, we are amazed and awestruck over the incredible love of Christ and his unfathomable mystery. Mystery is something we can understand but will never exhaust the depths of meaning contained within it. We may never completely tap the fullness of the mystery of Christ. The way in which we are able to discern his mystery, however, is through the power of the Holy Spirit.

Gospel
Matthew 11:25–30

STEP 1
NAMING ONE'S EXPERIENCE

What were your first impressions? What was your first response? What grabbed your attention? How did you feel?

Each person names his or her initial impression. Statements should be brief. No reasons should be given at this time. All simply listen without agreeing or disagreeing.

STEP 2
UNDERSTANDING

In a brief statement, what do you think this gospel is trying to convey?

STEP 3
INPUT FROM VISION/STORY/TRADITION

Liturgical Context

This feast is celebrated on the third Friday after the feast of Pentecost. Since this feast takes place on a Friday, it is seldom thoroughly treated in catechetical groups. However, it is an important solemnity of the Lord and, as such, is part of the deposit of faith as it is revealed in the unfolding liturgical cycle. While most parishes will not have the luxury of meeting on this day, it would nevertheless be important that this liturgy be addressed in catechetical groups whose formation is centered on breaking open the riches of the liturgical cycle.

The feast of the Sacred Heart is a devotional feast that honors Christ for the love he showers upon humanity. That love is symbolized by his heart. The earliest origins of such a devotion can be traced back to the church Fathers who stressed certain passages in John (7:37, 19:34). Anselm and Bernard of Clairvaux also cited similar passages in the twelfth century, only to be followed by others such as Albert the Great and Bonaventure in the thirteenth century.

According to Adolf Adam, later mystics increased their devotion to the Sacred Heart and by the sixteenth century Jesuits and other groups also promoted the devotion. French Oratorians Pierre Berulle and John Eudes helped move the devotion to official levels. After receiving permission from his bishop, Eudes celebrated the first feast in honor of the Sacred Heart in his community.

Visitation nun Margaret Mary Alacoque had a series of visions encouraging her to work toward establishment of the feast on the Friday after Corpus Christi. She also promoted the observance of Fridays in honor of the Sacred Heart.

Rome did not allow the feast to be officially celebrated for another hundred years. In 1856 Pius IX established the feast as obligatory for the universal church. Pope Leo XIII raised the feast to a higher rank and consecrated the world to the Sacred Heart of Jesus. Pius XI in 1927 elevated it again and, without making it a holy day of obligation, raised it to the same status as Christmas.

In this century, Karl Rahner addressed some objections to the feast when he explained the word "heart" as a primordial concept. Rahner maintained that the word "heart" in scripture and tradition refers to the body and soul, the totality of a person. Thus, the heart of Christ refers to the complete essence of his being.

The text for this mass was compiled by Pius XI in 1928 in collaboration with Benedictine Abbot H. Quentin. An earlier focus for this feast was the passion of Christ and the mysticism of the Song of Solomon. Pius XI emphasized expiation, humanity's need for the love of Christ to redeem sin.

There are two opening prayers—one old, the other new. The new prayer, the first, acknowledges the love we have received through Christ and asks that we continue to be blessed with that love. The second acknowledges human guilt and asks that we worship Christ through the service we offer to our brothers and sisters. Love, then, is not just an internal state of being between Creator and created, but rather is demonstrated and evidenced in love extended to others.

The old concluding prayer, "we have tasted the sweetness of your loving heart," was replaced with "May this sacrament fill us with love. Draw us closer to Christ your Son and help us to recognize him in others." A new preface was assigned to the feast that centers more closely on the scriptures and the theology of the Fathers: "Lifted high on the cross, Christ gave his life for us, so much did he love us. From his wounded side flowed blood and water, and the fountain of sacramental life in the Church. To his open heart the Savior invites all men, to draw water in joy from the springs of salvation."

There are other forms of devotion to the Sacred Heart: the first Fridays of each month and the eve of first Friday. There is also a votive mass for First Fridays approved at the end of the nineteenth century by Leo XIII. When properly explained within its scriptural and historical context, this feast has great pastoral value.

Gospel Exegesis

The facilitator provides input from critical biblical scholarship on this text. This input includes insights as to how people would have heard the text in Jesus' time.

Read the Passion narrative for Good Friday. Blood and water flowed from the side of Christ and the church was born—water, a sign of the Spirit and baptism, and the blood, a sign of eucharist. The Jews asked the authorities to hasten the death of condemned criminals so they could be removed from the cross before the Sabbath. The soldiers complied and broke the legs of the other two men who died with Jesus. When they came to Jesus he was already dead. They thrust a lance into his side and water and blood flowed from his side. The evangelist insisted that the reason for this was so the scriptures would be fulfilled—that none of Jesus' bones would be broken. The paschal lamb of Passover was to be blemish-free and none of its bones were to be broken. Jesus is the new Lamb of the new covenant, the new Passover. As the new Lamb, none of his bones could be broken.

We have been given a mystery of faith. Jesus sacrificed his life out of love for the world. Jesus unleashed his Spirit upon the world as water and blood poured forth from his side. Jesus paid the price for our salvation. He is the source of the fountain that wells up within us. Jesus' heart was pierced and broken for a sinful world. Jesus, the Suffering Servant who gave his life in ransom for the many, invites all people to turn to him and embrace the life won by the sacrifice of his life. This feast invites us to drink deeply from the fountain of life—the waters of baptism that incorporate us into his Passion, death, and resurrection and the cup that unites us to his suffering and the suffering souls of the world.

Proclaim the gospel again.

Sometimes we gain new insights when we hear the text after the interpretation has been given. Someone from the group proclaims the gospel a second time.

Conversation with the Liturgy and the Scriptures

Test your original understanding in dialogue with the text.

(You might consider breaking into smaller groups.)

Now that you've heard the exegesis of this liturgy, were there any new insights? Was there anything you had not considered before? How does your original understanding of this story compare with what was just shared? How does this story speak to your life?

Sharing Life Experience

Participants share an experience from their lives that connects with the biblical interpretation just shared.

I cannot reflect on the love of God and his Sacred Heart that pours out in kenosis for me and for the world without thinking about two people who are the personification of love in our parish. They are beacons of God's light and love. There is never a time of encounter in which the words, "I love you," are not spoken. There is never a time of meeting in which they do not ask about our families, our concerns, and our general well-being. If they even remotely reflect the love God has for us, then God's love for us is beyond mere words. They exude God's presence and their love pours out and impacts the parish in powerful ways. If they promise to pray for someone, that person can be assured that the hounds of heaven are persistently storming the gates of the eternal city until asked to stop. The judge of the "judge and widow fame" of the gospel would run in fear at the sight of these two faithful servants on their knees. My own children know that they have prayer advocates in this holy couple.

When asked who they know that reminds them of God's love, our schoolchildren always point to this incredible couple. They know they are loved and cherished, even if not personally known. These two special people are very sick with life-threatening illnesses as I write this reflection. I sit with tears as I think of the possibility of losing them. Our parish

will grieve tears of unspeakable loss. We have been blessed with the breath of God through the self gift of these two committed disciples of the Lord. On this feast of God's gracious gift of love for humanity, I thank him for the Sacred Heart of his Son, but I also thank him for the sacred hearts of these two faithful children of the covenant. We have been blessed by their lives. (Note: This past week we buried one of them. There are no words to adequately express our grief and appreciation of a life that has so greatly impacted our parish community. She embodied the phrase, "see how they love one another." She reflected the wounded, loving Sacred Heart of Jesus.)

What does this liturgy have to say to our community and to me today? In what way is our community challenged? Do we still feel the same way about this liturgy as we did when we began? Has our original understanding been stretched, challenged, or affirmed?

The gospel demands a response.

How does our sharing and this biblical interpretation challenge our community and how does it challenge me? In what way does this gospel call our parish to action in the church, parish, neighborhood, or world? What is one concrete action we will take this week as a response to what was learned and shared today?

DOCTRINAL ISSUES

What church truth/teaching/doctrinal issue could be drawn from the liturgy for the feast of the Sacred Heart?

Participants suggest possible doctrinal themes that flow from the readings.

Possible Doctrinal Themes

Sacred Heart of Jesus; Trinity; Christology; charity-agape; paschal mystery; covenant

Present the doctrinal material at this time.

1. The facilitator gives input on a particular doctrinal issue of his/her prior choosing. OR
2. The group chooses a doctrinal issue from the list they created. They read together from the Doctrinal Appendix.

(The doctrinal issues are found in the Doctrinal Appendix in the back of this workbook. If you are choosing an issue from this resource, please refer to it now.)

Reflection questions centered around the chosen doctrinal theme can be found at the end of each topic in the Doctrinal Appendix. The questions are based on the five-step reflection process. If you choose a topic not included in the Doctrinal Appendix, craft your own questions according to the same five-step process.

Following the reflection questions you will be reminded to return to chapter 7, "Preparing the Catechetical Session," to assist you in crafting your own session.

Closing Prayer

Father,
we honor the heart of your Son
broken by man's cruelty,
yet symbol of love's triumph,
pledge of all that man is called to be.
Teach us to see Christ in the lives we touch,
to offer him living worship
by love-filled service to our brothers and sisters.
We ask this through Christ our Lord.[3]

---

[3]Sacred Heart: "Alternative Opening Prayer," *The Sacramentary.*

PRESENTATION OF THE LORD (FEBRUARY 2)

INTRODUCTORY RITES

Opening Song (or Entrance Antiphon)

Within your temple, we ponder your loving kindness, O God. As your name, so also your praise reaches to the ends of the earth; your right hand is filled with justice. (Ps 47:10–11)[1]

Blessing of Candles and Procession

The Lord will come with mighty power,
and give light to the eyes of all who serve him,
    alleluia.

Forty days ago we celebrated the joyful feast of the birth of our Lord Jesus Christ. Today we recall the holy day on which he was presented in the temple, fulfilling the law of Moses and at the same time going to meet his faithful people. Led by the Spirit, Simeon and Anna came to the temple, recognized Christ as their Lord, and proclaimed him with joy.

United by the Spirit, may we now go to the house of God to welcome Christ the Lord. There we shall recognize him in the breaking of the bread until he comes again in glory.

Then the priest joins his hands and blesses the candles.

Let us pray.
God, our Father, source of all light,
today you revealed to Simeon
your Light of revelation to the nations.
Bless + these candles and make them holy.
May we who carry them to praise your glory
walk in the path of goodness
and come to the light that shines for ever.
Grant this through Christ, our Lord.[2]

Opening Prayer

The facilitator of the session may lead the prayer. Others in the group may be asked to proclaim the readings.

All powerful Father,
Christ your Son became man for us
and was presented in the temple.
May he free our hearts from sin
and bring us into your presence.
We ask this through our Lord Jesus Christ, your
    Son,
who lives and reigns with you and the Holy Spirit,
one God, for ever and ever.[3]

LITURGY OF THE WORD

Let us listen to God's word.

The readings are proclaimed.

First Reading
Malachi 3:1–4

The reading from Malachi heralds the coming of the "messenger of the covenant." This messenger comes for judgment. The coming "Day of the Lord" will accomplish the purification of the people. We are to prepare by living the covenant.

The people had returned from exile and the temple had been rebuilt, but the people's response was lackluster. Those who turned away from God would be punished in the coming "Day of the Lord." Those who suffered while the wicked prospered would enjoy vindication on the "Day of the Lord." Placing this reading within this feast makes it clear how the church understands Malachi's prophecy. The presentation of Jesus in the temple is understood as the fulfillment of Malachi's prophecy.

Responsorial Psalm
Psalm 24:7–10

Second Reading
Hebrews 2:14–18

Jesus came to be the new high priest in the new covenant. He offered his life as a perfect sacri-

---

[1]Presentation of the Lord: "Entrance Antiphon," *The Sacramentary.*

[2]Presentation of the Lord: "Blessing of Candles and Procession," *The Sacramentary.*

[3]Presentation of the Lord: "Opening Prayer," *The Sacramentary.*

fice. By doing this, Jesus reconciled humanity with God. Jesus freely surrendered to death for the salvation of the world. He did this because of his faithfulness to Yahweh. Jesus' death was a passage to his glory, not to darkness. Because of Jesus' sacrifice, we are heirs to his resurrected life. We will die, but we will live with Jesus forever. Jesus' death was real. His suffering was real. He was a human being (with both a human and divine nature) and suffered as other human beings do. Like us in every way except sin, Jesus knows our suffering and is our advocate. He strengthens us and intercedes for us as we endure the trials of this life.

Gospel
Luke 2:22–40

Mary and Joseph take Jesus and present him in the temple.

STEP 1
NAMING ONE'S EXPERIENCE

What were your first impressions? What was your first response? What grabbed your attention? How did you feel?

Each person names his or her initial impression. Statements should be brief. No reasons should be given at this time. All simply listen without agreeing or disagreeing.

STEP 2
UNDERSTANDING

In a brief statement, what do you think this gospel is trying to convey?

STEP 3
INPUT FROM VISION/STORY/TRADITION

Liturgical Context

Jesus is the center of attention in today's gospel. The feast takes place forty days after Christmas and is centered around events that took place in the Jerusalem temple.

In antiquity, a woman was considered unclean for forty days after delivering a male child (eighty days after a female). She was to go to the temple and offer the priest a lamb and a young pigeon or turtledove or, if poor, two turtledoves. This was to be her sin offering, to make her ritually clean again.

Mary was dutifully following the law when she presented her son Jesus to the temple. Firstborn male children belonged to the Lord (Ex 13:2) and were to be taken to the temple so the parents could ransom them back with money. "In keeping with these regulations Mary and Joseph brought Jesus to the temple, and Mary offered the sacrifice that 'purified' her and at the same time ransomed her firstborn."[4]

It is possible that this feast was celebrated as early as the fifth century. The feast was a continuation of the Christmas event and its focus was clearly driven by today's gospel. While it is a feast strongly connected to the Nativity, it also has a paschal orientation.

The celebration included a procession. It began as a replacement for the pagan procession of expiation that took place every five years in February. To capture the original penitential flavor of the feast, purple vestments were worn (up to 1960).

The procession with candles reminds us that Simeon called Jesus "a revealing light to the gentiles" (Lk 2:32). This feast has also been referred to as Candlemas. In the middle of the eighth century the feast was designated the "Purification of Blessed Virgin Mary." The new calendar made clear that the feast was a feast of the Lord, not of Mary, and the change of name in 1969 captured the original intent of the feast. The blessing of candles dates back to around 1000 C.E. in Gaul.

There are two forms of procession and blessing that may be used. In the first form, people gather outside and process into church with blessed candles (perhaps singing the Canticle of Simeon, the *Nunc dimittis*: "Now Master, you may let your servant go in peace according to your word."). The simpler form has a representative group enter the church carrying candles in procession with the priest.

---

[4]*LY*, 150.

777

The temple events are the lens through which all the ritual prayers of the mass are viewed. The prayers of the mass reflect the biblical understanding of the feast. We are to be joyful and praise God forever, because we have seen the light of the Lord (Preface). His light has gone out to all the world. We share that light as we await the day he will return and bring us into everlasting life (Prayer After Communion).

Gospel Exegesis

The facilitator gives input regarding what critical biblical scholarship has to say about this text. The input includes insights as to how people would have heard the gospel in Jesus' time.

Today's episode with Simeon during the presentation of Jesus in the temple accomplishes far more than the actual event described. The Lord's mission and destiny are heralded and the law and the Old Testament's importance are underscored. This gospel pronounces of the mystery of Christ: "Jesus, by submitting to the prescriptions of the Law imposed on first-born sons, manifested as soon as he entered the world his obedience to God, his Father (Luke 2:49)."[5]

Simeon, representative of the just of Israel, understood salvation to be the dawning of light to all the nations. Simeon echoed the words of the prophets who attested to the universal mission of the messiah. Yet, even though this mission is inclusive of all people, it will not be easy. Those who accept Christ will be rejected, just as Christ will be rejected. Simeon prophesies about the division that will be brought about as a result of faith in Christ. Mary, as representative of all believers, is an example of a faithful servant who listens to God's word and acts upon it. We are to do the same.

The Eastern Church calls this the Feast of the Encounter. Through celebration of the liturgy and the biblical texts, we encounter the mystery of the *Living One Who Came to Bring Light to the Nations* and we are challenged to live in a radical new way because of it. God promised to send a messenger

to purify the temple, the priesthood, and the people. He sent his Son to be the light for the entire world.

Proclaim the gospel again.

Sometimes we gain new insights when we hear the text after the interpretation has been given. Someone from the group proclaims the gospel a second time.

STEP 4
TESTING

Conversation with the Liturgy and the Scriptures

Test your original understanding in dialogue with the text.

(You might consider breaking into smaller groups.)

How does your original understanding of this story compare with what was just shared? How does this story speak to your life?

Participants share an experience from their lives that connects with the biblical interpretation just shared.

What does this liturgy have to say to our community and to me today? Has our original understanding been stretched, challenged, or affirmed?

STEP 5
DECISION

The gospel demands a response.

In what way does this gospel call our parish to action in the church, parish, neighborhood, or world? Has this conversation with the exegesis of this liturgy changed or stretched my personal attitudes? What is one concrete action we will take this week as a response to what was learned and shared today?

DOCTRINAL ISSUES

What church truth/teaching/doctrinal issue

---

[5]*DL* (VII), 112.

778

could be drawn from the gospel for the Presentation of the Lord?

Participants suggest possible doctrinal themes that flow from the readings.

Possible Doctrinal Themes

Mystery of Christ, incarnation, evangelization, ecumenism

Present the doctrinal material at this time.

1. The facilitator gives input on a particular doctrinal issue of his/her prior choosing. OR
2. The group chooses a doctrinal issue from the list they created. They read together from the Doctrinal Appendix.

(The doctrinal issues are found in the Doctrinal Appendix in the back of this workbook. If you are choosing an issue from this resource, please refer to it now.)

Reflection questions centered around the chosen doctrinal theme can be found at the end of each topic in the Doctrinal Appendix. The questions are based on the five-step reflection process. If you choose a topic not included in the Doctrinal Appendix, craft your own questions according to the same five-step process.

Following the reflection questions you will be reminded to return to chapter 7, "Preparing the Catechetical Session," to assist you in crafting your own session.

Closing Prayer

Lord,
you fulfilled the hope of Simeon,
who did not die
until he had been privileged to welcome the Messiah.
May this communion perfect your grace in us
and prepare us to meet Christ
when he comes to bring us into everlasting life,
for he is Lord for ever and ever.[6]

---

[6]Presentation of the Lord: "Prayer After Communion," *The Sacramentary.*

SOLEMNITY OF JOSEPH, HUSBAND OF MARY (MARCH 19)

INTRODUCTORY RITES

Opening Song (or Entrance Antiphon)

The Lord has put his faithful servant in charge of his household. (Lk 12:42)[1]

Opening Prayer

The facilitator of the session may lead the prayer. Others in the group may be asked to proclaim the readings.

Let us pray
[that the Church will continue
the saving work of Christ]

Pause for silent prayer.

Father,
you entrusted our Savior to the care of St. Joseph.
By the help of his prayers
may your Church continue to serve its Lord, Jesus Christ,
who lives and reigns with you and the Holy Spirit,
one God, for ever and ever.[2]

LITURGY OF THE WORD

Let us listen to God's word.

The readings are proclaimed.

First Reading
2 Samuel 7:4–5, 12–14, 16

Today's reading from Samuel reminds us of Yahweh's promise that David's reign would endure forever. This promise is considered typological of the promise that would be fulfilled in the messianic reign of Jesus Christ. Jesus fulfilled the promise made to David, since Joseph was a descendant of David.

---

[1]Solemnity of Joseph, Husband of Mary: "Entrance Antiphon," *The Sacramentary.*

[2]Solemnity of Joseph, Husband of Mary: "Opening Prayer," *The Sacramentary.*

Responsorial Psalm
Psalm 89:2–3, 4–5, 27, 29

This psalm is a reflection on the promise made to David: David's house would endure forever and his reign would extend for all time.

Second Reading
Romans 4:13, 16–18, 22

Joseph is called "Just in the eyes of God" *(tzaddik).* It is the greatest accolade paid to anyone in biblical tradition. Anyone who played a role in the history of salvation was considered a model to follow and was thus entitled to be called "just." Paul's letter to the Romans seeks to teach the disciple how to become "just" like the *tzaddik.* Paul used Abraham as an example.

Abraham was righteous ("just") because of his faith in God. God did not grace Abraham because of his observance of the law. Abraham was elected completely through the grace of God and trusted that God would multiply his descendants even though the aged Sarah was childless. Abraham even stood firm in his trust of Yahweh when asked to sacrifice his son, Isaac.

Paul's letter to the Romans invites the reader to share Abraham's faith. We, too, are heirs of the promise made to Abraham. Our response is complete trust.

Gospel
Matthew 1:16, 18–21, 24

Joseph obeyed the angel and took Mary as his wife.

Or Luke 2:41–51

Jesus is left behind in the temple in Jerusalem as Mary and Joseph search for him.

STEP 1
NAMING ONE'S EXPERIENCE

What were your first impressions? What was your first response? What grabbed your attention? How did you feel?

Each person names his or her initial impression. State-ments should be brief. No reasons should be given at this time. All simply listen without agreeing or disagreeing.

STEP 2
UNDERSTANDING

In a brief statement, what do you think this gospel is trying to convey?

STEP 3
INPUT FROM VISION/STORY/TRADITION

Liturgical Context

The earliest evidence of observance of a devotion to Joseph, husband of Mary, can be traced back to the eighth century in Coptic calendars. A celebra-tion taking place on March 19 occurred in the twelfth century. Bernadine of Sienna, a Francis-can, fostered the celebration of the feast in honor of St. Joseph. A church was built in honor of Joseph in Nazareth during the crusades.

By the end of the sixteenth century Pope Sixtus IV established the feast for the church universal. Pope Gregory XV made it a holy day of obligation in 1621. Pius IX named Joseph the patron and protector of the universal church in 1870.

A preface in honor of St. Joseph was introduced in 1920 and was retained in the New Missal of 1970. Pope John XXIII added St. Joseph's name to the Roman canon in 1962. Since the feast falls in Lent, permission is granted to episcopal confer-ences to transfer it to another time.

In 1847 Pius IX established another feast in honor of St. Joseph and placed it on the third Sunday after Easter. This feast had been celebrated by the Carmelites of Italy and France since 1860. Pius X made it a first-class feast and moved it to the third Wednesday after Easter. Since this was a duplica-tion of the present solemnity, it was abolished by the Congregation of Rites in 1956.[3]

In the secular contemporary world, May 1 has been observed as a day in honor of the rights of the working person. Pius XII established a feast on May 1 in order to give the secular observance a Christian dimension. The pope also wished to highlight the rights of workers. The "Solemnity of St. Joseph the Worker, Husband of the Blessed Virgin Mary, Confessor and Patron of Working People" was retained in the new calendar as an optional memorial. The reason for reducing the rank of the feast is evidence of Rome's attempt to lessen the number of *idea feasts.*

The preface for this solemnity speaks of Joseph, the "just man" who served as protector in the in-fancy stages of the Incarnation event, protector of Mary, the Mother of God, and protector of Jesus, God's Son. Joseph served as earthly father in place of Jesus' natural father.

By being faithful to his mission of serving God, Joseph took his place in the annals of salvation his-tory. Joseph is named as a wise, loyal, selfless ser-vant. The liturgy opens by illuminating the charac-ter of Joseph: "The Lord has put his faithful servant in charge of his household" (Entrance Antiphon). We are exhorted to follow the example of Joseph in his ministry of service and care: "Father, with un-selfish love St. Joseph cared for your Son, born of the Virgin Mary. May we also serve you at your altar with pure hearts" (Prayer Over the Gifts).

Flowers are allowed in church on this lenten weekday and are therefore an appropriate adorn-ment for the St. Joseph shrine. An Italian tradi-tion, the St. Joseph's table originated as a meal for the poor. It was offered in thanksgiving and in honor of St. Joseph for answered prayer. The meal is comprised of meatless dishes. It is a wholesome combination of the lenten disciplines of prayer, fasting, and almsgiving. *Catholic House-hold Blessings and Prayers* provides a litany and do-mestic prayer for the day. The *Book of Blessings* provides an "Order of Blessing of St. Joseph's Table." "Joseph is the patron saint of Mexico, Canada, Bohemia (in the Czech Republic) and Belgium, too. He has become known as the pa-tron saint of the church, of fathers, of a happy death and of prayer."[4]

---

[3]*LY*, 230.

[4]*CC*, 60.

Gospel Exegesis

The facilitator gives input regarding what critical biblical scholarship has to say about this text. The input includes insights as to how people would have heard the gospel in Jesus' time.

Matthew 1:16, 18–21, 24

The genealogy of Matthew ends with Joseph, who was to play a role in God's messianic plan of salvation. Through the mediation of an angel, God revealed to Joseph the role he was to play in the lives of Mary and Jesus. It is through Joseph's genealogy that Jesus would be an heir to the promise made to David. When Jesus assumed Joseph's name, Jesus was legitimated as a descendant of David. When Joseph accepted Jesus as his son, he acknowledged Jesus' role as messiah. Joseph, as a righteous man, lived according to the law and was faithful to the will of God. All who follow Joseph's example are also righteous in the eyes of God.

Scripture does not credit Joseph with speaking a single word. Joseph's silence is the silence of one who lets God do the talking and simply and humbly follows God's commands. After the first two chapters in Matthew, Joseph is not heard from again. His role, according to Matthew, was assigned to the early life of Christ. He passed on his lineage to Jesus, he saved Jesus from Herod, and he brought his small family back to Galilee after the sojourn in Egypt. Joseph acted always at God's initiative, thus making him the personal representative of the Father at the side of the Son on earth. Joseph was a trustworthy guardian because he was faithful to God's word.

Joseph was not a wild-eyed dreamer. He was a man of action. But God revealed his intentions to Joseph through dreams, a common biblical medium of divine revelation. Joseph listened and followed God's leading. Joseph is a model for all who seek to do God's will.

Luke 2:41–51

Today's gospel from Luke serves as a transition from the infancy narratives to the adult manifestation of Christ. The event in today's story is more about Jesus than it is about his parents. It reflects and illuminates the mystery of the Incarnation and how the believer is to understand it. Jesus, Mary, and Joseph's pilgrimage to Jerusalem for the annual feast of Passover is of particular importance in the context of this passage. We are told that Jesus was twelve years old. This is Luke's way of telling the reader that Jesus was no longer a child and was now subject to the law.

The fact that Jesus remained in the temple after his parents left demonstrates Jesus' close connection to the sacred place. It was in this very same place that Jesus' future destiny would play itself out and lead to the cross on Calvary. However, in this scene, the learned teachers marvel at the wisdom of this budding would-be rabbi. We are not to sentimentalize this scene as that of a child prodigy amazing the scholars. We must look at this event through the lens of the crucifixion.

When Jesus responded to his anxious parents that he must be about his Father's business, we are told that they did not understand. They who lived with Jesus, his own parents, had to grow in understanding of his mission. As the words and experiences of Jesus' life unfolded, they would be able to reflect back on them and grow in understanding. Believers are thus encouraged in the face of their own doubts and lack of understanding.

Proclaim the gospel again.

Sometimes we gain new insights when we hear the text after the interpretation has been given. Someone from the group proclaims the gospel a second time.

STEP 4
TESTING

Conversation with the Liturgy and the Scriptures

Test your original understanding in dialogue with the text.

(You might consider breaking into smaller groups.)

How does your original understanding of this story compare with what was just shared? How does this story speak to your life?

Participants share an experience from their lives that connects with the biblical interpretation just shared.

What does this liturgy have to say to our community and to me today? Has our original understanding been stretched, challenged, or affirmed?

STEP 5
DECISION

The gospel demands a response.

In what way does this gospel call our parish to action in the church, parish, neighborhood, or world? Has this conversation with the exegesis of this liturgy changed or stretched our personal attitudes? What is one concrete action we will take this week as a response to what was learned and shared today?

DOCTRINAL ISSUES

What church truth/teaching/doctrinal issue could be drawn from the gospel for the Solemnity of Joseph, Husband of Mary?

Participants suggest possible doctrinal themes that flow from the readings.

Possible Doctrinal Themes

Incarnation, faith, mystery of Christ, St. Joseph, protector of the Universal Church

Present the doctrinal material at this time.

1. The facilitator gives input on a particular doctrinal issue of his/her prior choosing. OR
2. The group chooses a doctrinal issue from the list they created. They read together from the Doctrinal Appendix.

(The doctrinal issues are found in the Doctrinal Appendix in the back of this workbook. If you are choosing an issue from this resource, please refer to it now.)

Reflection questions centered around the chosen doctrinal theme can be found at the end of each topic in the Doctrinal Appendix. The questions are based on the five-step reflection process. If you choose a topic not included in the Doctrinal Appendix, craft your own questions according to the same five-step process.

Following the reflection questions you will be reminded to return to chapter 7, "Preparing the Catechetical Session," to assist you in crafting your own session.

Closing Prayer

Lord,
you nourish us at this altar
as we celebrate the feast of St. Joseph.
Protect your Church always,
and in your love watch over the gifts you have
    given us.
Grant this through Christ, our Lord.[5]

---

[5]Solemnity of Joseph, Husband of Mary: "Prayer After Communion," *The Sacramentary.*

SOLEMNITY OF THE ANNUNCIATION OF THE LORD (MARCH 25)

INTRODUCTORY RITES

Opening Song (or Entrance Antiphon)

As Christ came into the world, he said: Behold! I have come to do your will, O God. (Heb 10:5, 7)[1]

Opening Prayer

The facilitator of the session may lead the prayer. Others in the group may be asked to proclaim the readings.

Let us pray
[that Christ, the Word made flesh,
will make us more like him]

Pause for silent prayer.

God, our Father,
your Word became man and was born of the Virgin Mary.
May we become more like Jesus Christ,
whom we acknowledge as our redeemer, God and man.
We ask this through our Lord Jesus Christ, your Son,
who lives and reigns with you and the Holy Spirit,
one God, for ever and ever.[2]

LITURGY OF THE WORD

Let us listen to God's word.

The readings are proclaimed.

First Reading
Isaiah 7:10–14

King Ahaz was undecided on his course of action in the face of military conflict. Like other arrogant monarchs, Ahaz believed in his own self-sufficiency. He did not need the intervention of Yahweh in the affairs of state. The prophet was urging one course of action and Ahaz's advisers another. Isaiah offered a sign. Ahaz was encouraged to seek confirmation of Isaiah's promise, but his mind was already closed. It seemed to him that the obvious course of action was to make an alliance with a powerful nation and rise up against a weaker one. What could go wrong? He did not listen to the Lord's warning. Without a firm faith he would not stand.

God would keep his promise to David and the sign would remain—not to convince Ahaz, but rather to prove the truth of the prophet's word. The word referring to the *woman* with child was not the technical term for virgin. Scholars suggest that the woman, though a hazy character, is probably one of Ahaz's wives. The promised child was a sign himself. This woman would give birth to a child who would be a sign. The child would possess a unique destiny in salvation history. Isaiah's prophecy served as the foundation for Israel's messianic hope.

Christ is the obvious fulfillment of this messianic hope. Christ, Immanuel, is with us as his salvation plan unfolds before the world.

Responsorial Psalm
Psalm 40:7–8, 8–9, 10, 11

Second Reading
Hebrews 10:4–10

The letter to the Hebrews is primarily concerned with reflection upon the Jewish scriptures. The Lectionary omits a very important piece of Hebrews in which the humanity of Jesus is addressed at great length. It is perhaps the "New Testament's most profound and systematic discussion of what it means for Jesus to have been human."[3] This reading is particularly appropriate on this feast that celebrates the announcement of Jesus' birth. The reason for Christ's Incarnation is reparation

---

[1]Annunciation of the Lord: "Entrance Antiphon," *The Sacramentary.*

[2]Annunciation of the Lord: "Opening Prayer," *The Sacramentary.*

[3]*PTE,* 120–121.

for the sins of the world. With the coming of Jesus, the sacrifices of old are rendered meaningless. Jesus replaced the burnt offerings and sacrifices of the old covenant.

The Pauline community asserts that Jesus definitively assumed unto himself such oblations once and for all. One cannot meditate on the Incarnation without reflection upon the reason for it in the first place: the cross and resurrection.

Gospel
Luke 1:26–38

The angel Gabriel announces the birth of Jesus to Mary.

STEP 1
NAMING ONE'S EXPERIENCE

What were your first impressions? What was your first response? What grabbed your attention? How did you feel?

Each person names his or her initial impression. Statements should be brief. No reasons should be given at this time. All simply listen without agreeing or disagreeing.

STEP 2
UNDERSTANDING

In a brief statement, what do you think this gospel is trying to convey?

STEP 3
INPUT FROM VISION/STORY/TRADITION

Liturgical Context

The first hint of a celebration honoring the Annunciation of the Lord can be traced to the Council of Toledo in 656. Thirty years later the feast was celebrated in Rome. The March 25 date has had a dubious background. There is evidence that the feast was celebrated on December 18, a week prior to Christmas, in Spain around the year 1000. The feast is understood in the context of the Nativity event. The reform of the Vatican Council appropriately named it a feast of the Lord.

The feast strongly resonates with a sound Mariology. Mary is the Mother of God's Son who came to save the world through the paschal mystery—death, resurrection, and glorification. She is a venerated person in the history of salvation because God chose her and graced her to be the mother of Christ. The scriptural texts, the announcement of Jesus' birth, the promised Immanuel of Isaiah, and Paul's letter to the Hebrews regarding the self-gift of Christ to the world, give us the absolute lens through which we are to view and celebrate this event. It is a Christ event—it calls us to fix our gaze on Jesus Christ, Son of God, born of the Virgin Mary.

The introductory rites open the liturgy with a proclamation of Jesus' mission: He came to do his Father's will. This liturgy celebrates the God who sent his Son to become bone and flesh, to be born of a human, virgin mother, to experience life as all human beings experience it (except for the experience of sin) and to one day allow his human body to suffer, die, and rise again for the salvation of all. The Virgin Mary gave completely of herself. She gave her very womb to bear the will of the Father in the flesh.

The liturgy knows well the longing of the human heart and that only Jesus' presence will satisfy it. Mary intercedes for the waiting world (Alternative Opening Prayer) and asks that Jesus fill the void of incompleteness. The opening prayer asks that we become more like Jesus, our redeemer, who is both human and divine. The prayer over the gifts reminds us that the Incarnation of Christ was the beginning of the church. This feast is about Christ. It is a feast of the Lord. It is the cornerstone of our faith and celebrates the primary truths of the Christian faith: Jesus, the Father's only Son, our Lord, became a man and dwelt among us. "... By the power of the Holy Spirit he was born of the Virgin Mary, and became man. For our sake he was crucified under Pontius Pilate; he suffered, died and was buried. On the third day he rose again in fulfillment of the Scriptures; he ascended into heaven and is seated at the right hand of the Father. He will come again in glory to judge the living and the dead, and his kingdom will have no end. We believe in the Holy

Spirit, the Lord, the giver of life, who proceeds from the Father and the Son. With the Father and the Son he is worshiped and glorified...."[4]

Gospel Exegesis

The facilitator gives input regarding what critical biblical scholarship has to say about this text. The input includes insights as to how people would have heard the gospel in Jesus' time.

Luke's announcement story is patterned after other biblical birth announcements of extraordinary persons. The similarities are so strong that they place the contrasts in stark focus. Only twice in biblical tradition does an angel appear to a woman: Hagar (Gen 16:7–16) and Samson's mother (Judg 13: 1–25). The appearance of the angel is to announce to the reader that the events being foretold are part of God's plan of salvation for the world.

The angel's words are similar in the birth announcements of John and Jesus; there are differences, however, in the description of each child's role and identity. John is to be "great before the Lord," but Jesus will be "great and Son of the Most High." John will prepare the people, but Jesus will rule over them. John's role is temporary, Jesus' is endless. John is a prophet, Jesus is more than a prophet: he is the Son of God. Luke's readers are alerted to the graphic differences between John and Jesus and that Jesus is something far greater than a Davidic king.[5]

It is quite remarkable that Luke gave Mary such an important focus. The patriarchal biblical and secular world would have given little credence to the exalted role of a woman. Even more remarkable is the fact that it was Joseph who gave Jesus his legitimacy as heir to the Davidic dynasty. Luke Timothy Johnson maintains that Luke's intention remains unclear. It is possible that his treatment of Mary is a "historical reminiscence, special tradition, or Luke's predilection for presenting positive women figures (evident throughout his narrative)."[6]

In Matthew's account the emphasis is placed on the role of Joseph. Luke gives Mary center stage. Mary's name, a Semitic name (*Mariam* in Greek; *Miryam* in Hebrew), is derived from the Hebrew word for *height* or *summit*. In a feminine context it probably meant "excellence." It is not without significance that Mary's name is the same as that of the mother of Moses. Both are significant characters in God's salvation plan and both have similar stories. Luke tells us very little about Mary in the infancy narratives. The other characters are well introduced. Elizabeth, Joseph, Zechariah, Simeon, and Anna are all identified by their genealogy or their piety. Mary is not heralded as possessing any special characteristics. She is not called righteous, or an astute observer of the law. She is one of society's powerless: she is young in a culture that values age, a female in a man's world, and poor in an unequal economy. A woman's identity is validated through her husband and child—yet she has neither. The great paradox of this passage is that Luke understands God to be a God of surprise, "always reversing human expectations."[7]

We have to wait until the angel's proclamation before we are given a glimpse of how God considers Mary. "Hail, rejoice, Mary!" gives us a clue to her exalted status with God. We are told of her virginity and of her high standing with God. There is no question: Mary is a decent person, in spite of outward appearances. There is no hint of impropriety in Luke's gospel.

Mary is fearful at the angel's announcement. In biblical tradition, fear is a common reaction to angelic messengers. Mary is troubled that the angel said she "had found favor." She was a "favored one." That was an uncommon salutation in the New Testament. The Hebrew scriptures attest to people who were "favored": Noah, Moses, Gideon, Samuel. Perhaps Mary is troubled because a woman was being called "favored by God." A woman was named a key player in God's salvation plan. Perhaps Mary is troubled at the thought of the heavy burden usually placed on "those favored by God." The "favored of God" usually end up paying the ultimate price in their service of God.

---

[4] Nicene Creed, *The Sacramentary*.
[5] *GL*, 38–39.
[6] Ibid., 39.

---

[7] Ibid.

786

Gabriel's declaration to Mary that the Lord is with her is a reminder that she will participate in "God's action to save."[8] The angel announces to Mary that she is to bear a Son and tells her what she is to name him and what his role will be. Mary is incredulous. So was Zechariah. However, there is a difference. Mary's question asks how it could be possible in light of her virginity. Hers is a practical question. Zechariah's question is one of basic disbelief.

Mary's question keeps the story line in a suspenseful forward motion. Gabriel proceeds to tell her how all this will happen. The Holy Spirit will accomplish it. The Holy Spirit will overshadow and come upon her. These are not sexual metaphors for divine-human intercourse. Rather, they are simply statements that God will intervene and do what God intends.

Mary's assent, "be it done unto me according to your will," places her in the role of disciple. Disciples hear the word of God and act on it. All Mary needed to hear was the angel's assurance that it was by divine intervention, not by human design that she should be so blessed. "She prefigures her son's acceptance of God's will, despite the high price that it demands."[9]

The Incarnation is shrouded in obedience. The Son was obedient to the Father, Mary and Joseph were obedient to the word of God through the mediation of an angel. Faithful obedience to God's will is demanded of all faithful disciples. The ancient martyrologies referred to this feast as "The announcement of the divine incarnation to the Blessed Virgin Mary." Today it is less explicitly named "Annunciation of the Lord." "Today is the announcement of the first day of the new era of creation."[10]

Proclaim the gospel again.

Sometimes we gain new insights when we hear the text after the interpretation has been given. Someone from the group proclaims the gospel a second time.

---

[8]*CBP*, 67.
[9]Ibid., 69.
[10]*DL* (VII), 142.

STEP 4
TESTING

Conversation with the Liturgy and the Scriptures

Test your original understanding in dialogue with the text.

(You might consider breaking into smaller groups.)

How does your original understanding of this story compare with what was just shared? How does this story speak to your life?

Participants share an experience from their lives that connects with the biblical interpretation just shared.

What does this liturgy have to say to our community and to me today? Has our original understanding been stretched, challenged, or affirmed?

STEP 5
DECISION

The gospel demands a response.

In what concrete way does this gospel call our parish to action in the church, parish, neighborhood, or world? Has this conversation with the exegesis of this liturgy changed or stretched our personal attitudes? What is one specific action we will take this week as a response to what was learned and shared today?

DOCTRINAL ISSUES

What church truth/teaching/doctrinal issue could be drawn from the gospel for the Solemnity of the Annunciation of the Lord?

Participants suggest possible doctrinal themes that flow from the readings.

Possible Doctrinal Themes

Incarnation, Holy Spirit, role of Mary: mother of God, disciple, Christology

Present the doctrinal material at this time.

1. The facilitator gives input on a particular doc-
    trinal issue of his/her prior choosing. OR
2. The group chooses a doctrinal issue from the
    list they created. They read together from the
    Doctrinal Appendix.

(The doctrinal issues are found in the Doctrinal
Appendix in the back of this workbook. If you are
choosing an issue from this resource, please refer
to it now.)

Reflection questions centered around the chosen
doctrinal theme can be found at the end of each
topic in the Doctrinal Appendix. The questions
are based on the five-step reflection process. If you
choose a topic not included in the Doctrinal Appendix, craft your own questions according to the
same five-step process.

Following the reflection questions you will be reminded to return to chapter 7, "Preparing the
Catechetical Session," to assist you in crafting your
own session.

Closing Prayer

Father, all powerful and ever-living God,
we do well always and everywhere
to give you thanks through Jesus Christ our Lord.
He came to save mankind by becoming a man
     himself.
The Virgin Mary, receiving the angel's message in
     faith,
conceived by the power of the Holy Spirit
and bore your son in purest love.
In Christ, the eternal truth,
your promise to Israel was realized beyond all ex-
     pectations.
Through Christ the angels of heaven
offer their prayer of adoration
as they rejoice in your presence for ever.
May our voices be one with theirs
in their triumphant hymn of praise:
Holy, Holy, Holy Lord, God of power and might,
heaven and earth are full of your glory.
Hosanna in the highest.
Blessed is he who comes in the name of the Lord.
Hosanna in the highest.[11]

---

[11]Annunciation: "Preface," *The Sacramentary.*

SOLEMNITY OF THE BIRTH OF JOHN THE BAPTIST (JUNE 24)

INTRODUCTORY RITES

Opening Song (or Entrance Antiphon)

There was a man sent from God whose name was John. He came to bear witness to the light, to prepare an upright people for the Lord. (Lk 1:6–7; 17)[1]

Opening Prayer

The facilitator of the session may lead the prayer. Others in the group may be asked to proclaim the readings.

Let us pray
[that God will give us joy and peace]

Pause for silent prayer.

God, our Father,
you raised up John the Baptist,
to prepare a perfect people for Christ the Lord.
Give your Church joy in spirit
and guide those who believe in you
into the way of salvation and peace.
We ask this through our Lord Jesus Christ, your Son,
who lives and reigns with you and the Holy Spirit,
one God, for ever and ever.[2]

LITURGY OF THE WORD

Let us listen to God's word.

The readings are proclaimed.

First Reading
Isaiah 49:1–6

Isaiah foretold a *Suffering Servant,* especially chosen by God, who would suffer and in the end would lead people to salvation. In biblical history this figure eventually became associated with the messiah. Christianity easily saw the Suffering Servant to be a prefigure of Christ who suffered, died, was buried, and rose again for the salvation of the world.

The Suffering Servant figure was also reminiscent of other prophets who suffered so that others might come to recognize the Holy One upon his arrival. John the Baptist was understood as such a prophet.

His mission was difficult and discouraging. It was easy to lose heart. Prophets were acutely aware that they were driven and propelled by the power of Yahweh. The Servant in today's pericope was assured of God's confidence in the mission God had appointed him to accomplish. The prophetic message is to have everlasting consequences, reaching to the ends of the earth by the power of God. John's mission was to prepare the way for the *Anointed One of God.* His message was one of conversion and repentance. John would be misunderstood and in the end give his life for the *Word* he was sent to herald. But his message not only would reach to the ends of the earth, it would do so for all time. Today's prophetic message would extend to the end of the ages.

Responsorial Psalm
Psalm 139:1–3, 13–14, 14–15

Second Reading
Acts 13:22–26

On Paul's first missionary journey he preached in the synagogue at Pisidia. Paul addressed the people with a foundational truth that both the speaker and the audience shared: Israel was elected by God and David, also elected, was regarded as the king who found favor with God and to whom God made a promise. Unlike the political leaders of today, there were no "spin-doctors" to whitewash David's character. All of his faults were laid bare for biblical history to examine. However, David was memorialized as a larger-than-life character who repented, loved, and was loyal to his God. "Idealized by the biblical tradition in chronicles that are apologies David became the figure of the Messiah himself."[3] Thus, the messiah would come from David's dynasty and emerge

---

[1]Birth of John the Baptist: "Entrance Antiphon," *The Sacramentary.*

[2]Birth of John the Baptist: "Opening Prayer," *The Sacramentary.*

[3]*DL* (VII), 156.

from David's throne. All in Paul's audience could agree on that premise. There was nothing new until Paul spoke of the messiah in past tense terms. By implying that the messiah had already come, Paul threw them a curve. "Paul speaks in the past tense of the Messiah who has already come to Israel and identifies the Messiah with Jesus."[4]

Here is where Paul sparks controversy. This Jewish audience would not be coming with any such presupposition. Paul built on the foundation they knew and understood in order to help them see that within their cherished history lay the seeds of what God had already accomplished through Jesus. Paul's speech is an announcement that the promised messiah has indeed arrived and today sits on the Davidic throne by the power of his death and resurrection.

John heralded the advent of the Savior by preaching a baptism of repentance. He specifically gave testimony to Christ by attesting that a greater one than he was still to come. John was not the expected messiah: of this he was emphatic! He reminds us that we are to prepare our hearts for the reign of Christ in our lives. We are to turn from sin, change our lives and live the good news.

Gospel
Luke 1:57–66, 80

The birth of the Baptist is announced and he is named John.

STEP 1
NAMING ONE'S EXPERIENCE

What were your first impressions? What was your first response? What grabbed your attention? How did you feel?

Each person names his or her initial impression. Statements should be brief. No reasons should be given at this time. All simply listen without agreeing or disagreeing.

STEP 2
UNDERSTANDING

In a brief statement, what do you think this gospel is trying to convey?

STEP 3
INPUT FROM VISION/STORY/TRADITION

Liturgical Context

Jesus himself proclaimed to the world that John was more than a prophet: "the greatest of human beings." The fact that Jesus attested to his greatness and the fact that he was a martyr won him a venerated place among the saints of the early church. He was on a par with the apostles and Stephen.

Celebration of a feast in honor of John the Baptist dates back to the fourth century. The Greeks celebrated it on January 7, the day after Epiphany, the day that commemorated the baptism of the Lord. Since John baptized Jesus in the Jordan, the celebration of his feast was placed on the day following Epiphany. The West celebrated his feast on June 24, thus placing it six months prior to the Nativity of the Lord according to the scripture attesting to this time frame (Lk 1:36a).

Six churches were built in Rome in honor of John. By the sixth century a vigil was attached to the celebration and there were three assigned masses for the day. One of the masses was to be celebrated at the baptistry *(ad fontem)*.

The East established two other feasts in his honor, but the West maintained only one of them: the Beheading of John the Baptist on August 29. His birth is still commemorated in the Byzantine Church on September 24.

The solemnity has a vigil attached to it that includes most of the prayers from the old vigil mass in addition to the inclusion of a second reading, an alleluia verse, and the special preface.[5] This chapter will deal only with the mass of the day, however.

---

[4]*NULA* (II), 166.

[5]*LY,* 234.

The preface for this feast depicts God's favor bestowed on John. It describes his mission, his martyrdom, and his role in salvation through Christ. The opening prayer asks that we be guided to walk the path of salvation and peace. John, we are told, prepares us to become a perfect people (notice the present tense). The teaching of John will lead us to Christ. We ask for help to live, by the action of our lives, the mystery we celebrate (Vigil Prayer Over the Gifts). This is done in the shadow of John's message of repentance and gospel living.

"In the liturgy of the Church, a 'nativity' is not a birthday. Birthdays are anniversaries of a birth. Instead, a nativity is the birth itself. Today is not John the Baptist's birthday. Today John is born. That is what we sing in the liturgy today!"[6] We remember and make present the effects, implications, and mission of John the Baptist as we celebrate this feast. He is born anew to herald the same message of repentance and conversion.

Places around the world honor the feast day in various ways. People in Europe mark the feast by staying up all night and burning "St. John's fires." In Poland candles are placed on wreaths and floated downriver. In Morocco the Muslims also light fires in his honor. In Sweden people decorate cars, buses, doors, and a Maypole with green birch twigs. The pole is hoisted in the afternoon amid shouts of joy. In Lithuania people sweeten a cheese with honey, which is reminiscent of the food eaten by John. The cheese is prepared to look like the sun.

Gospel Exegesis

The facilitator gives input regarding what critical biblical scholarship has to say about this text. The input includes insights as to how people would have heard the gospel in Jesus' time.

Today's story is less about the announcement of John's birth and more about the naming of John. When John was named, his special identity and role in salvation history were announced. John was given his name on the day of his circumcision. It was a day of celebration and all expected John to be named after his father, Zechariah. Elizabeth, however, proclaimed that his name would be John (in obedience to the command given earlier by Gabriel). The gathered crowd was taken aback and approached Zechariah expecting him to rectify this breach of tradition. Zechariah, unable to speak, confirmed in writing that indeed the child's name was "John." The crowd was astonished!

In antiquity, people's names expressed their role, their character, and very often their mission in life. "Transcending all classifications, it is a person's proper word, speaking his unique identity and singular contribution to history."[7] However, it is not the meaning of John's name ("The Lord has been gracious") that sparks attention in this case; it is the fact that he was named by divine intervention. The fact that God intervened in John's conception and now intervened in his naming called attention to John's significant destiny. A child was born who enjoyed great favor with God. This was great news not only for his parents, but for all in their region.

Because Zechariah did not believe the angel's word that God would send them a child, he was subsequently struck dumb. His speech was restored when he responded to God's earlier directive and named his son *John*, blessing God as he did so. Everyone who heard or witnessed the event was afraid. Zechariah's ability to speak was understood by all as a sign from God that focused attention not on Zechariah's miracle, but on the person of John. All were alerted to the fact that this child was indeed favored by God and great things could be expected as a result. John's mission, however, remained cloaked in mystery.

The story ends with a fast-forward into John's adult life. We are taken to the edge of the desert to await his adult mission. The desert image alerts the reader that John is about to enter a time of preparation for his mission. In the scriptures, the desert signifies a barren area with low rainfall. Sometimes it is called the wilderness. In the bibli-

---

[6]*CC*, 94.

[7]*LK*, 26, 27.

cal perspective barren places are places where humans encounter God. In the Christian perspective, the desert is a symbol of inner pilgrimage leading to the experience of God.

Many of the salvific acts of the Old Testament occurred in the desert. *It was a place of death*. If people lost their way in the desert, they would surely die. *It was a place of protection and a place of testing*. In the story of Exodus, God led Israel through the desert for forty years. He fed them, provided water for their thirst, and showed them the way through the desert. God entered into a covenant with Israel and it became a people. God tested Israel through its forty-year sojourn. Many of God's dealings with Israel occurred in the desert. "Clearly the desert and God's plan for Israel were intimately bound together."[8] The desert is a place where God tests, forms, and prepares his chosen for their mission, just as God tested, formed, and prepared Israel for its mission in the promised land.

We are told that the child John grew up and matured in spirit. Such an announcement was a biblical formula used to depict the "harmonious development of a child marked before birth by divine grace and one whom 'the hand of the Lord' reposed."[9] John was destined to preach the good news of salvation from his very conception. God's favor rested on him; he could do no less.

John's mission is intimately bound to the mission of Christ. John preached conversion and repentance, thus preparing people to hear and accept Jesus' message. Today the church continues John's preaching mission. John preached a word that cost him his life. It was not a soft word, but a word that demanded *metanoia*, a complete turning of one's heart and life to God. Such preachers usually pay the ultimate price for their work. John paid with his head.

John reminds us that we must prepare the way for Christ to come into our hearts and to the hearts of all people everywhere. He invites us to become evangelists. John reminds us that we are to preach the good news and repent. He invites us to share the gospel and to change our lives.

---

[8]Craghan, "Desert," in *CPBDT*, 216.
[9]*DL* (VII), 159.

John reminds us that we are to give of our life-blood in pursuit of the gospel way of life. He invites us to become martyrs. John is our model who reaches out his hand and invites us to follow him, if we dare!

Proclaim the gospel again.

Sometimes we gain new insights when we hear the text after the interpretation has been given. Someone from the group proclaims the gospel a second time.

STEP 4
TESTING

Conversation with the Liturgy and the Scriptures

Test your original understanding in dialogue with the text.

(You might consider breaking into smaller groups.)

How does your original understanding of this story compare with what was just shared? How does this story speak to your life?

Participants share an experience from their lives that connects with the biblical interpretation just shared.

How does this liturgy challenge our community? How does it challenge me? Has our original understanding been stretched, challenged, or affirmed?

STEP 5
DECISION

The gospel demands a response.

In what way does this gospel call your parish to action in the church, parish, neighborhood, or world? Be concrete. Has this conversation with the exegesis of this liturgy changed or stretched your personal attitudes? Name one concrete action you will take this week as a response to what was learned and shared today.

DOCTRINAL ISSUES

What church truth/teaching/doctrinal issue could be drawn from the gospel for the Solemnity of the Birth of John the Baptist?

Participants suggest possible doctrinal themes that flow from the readings.

Possible Doctrinal Themes

Conversion, Christology, repentance

Present the doctrinal material at this time.

1. The facilitator gives input on a particular doctrinal issue of his/her prior choosing. OR
2. The group chooses a doctrinal issue from the list they created. They read together from the Doctrinal Appendix.

(The doctrinal issues are found in the Doctrinal Appendix in the back of this workbook. If you are choosing an issue from this resource, please refer to it now.)

Reflection questions centered around the chosen doctrinal theme can be found at the end of each topic in the Doctrinal Appendix. The questions are based on the five-step reflection process. If you choose a topic not included in the Doctrinal Appendix, craft your own questions according to the same five-step process.

Following the reflection questions you will be reminded to return to chapter 7, "Preparing the Catechetical Session," to assist you in crafting your own session.

Closing Prayer

God our Father,
the voice of John the Baptist challenges us to repentance
and points the way to Christ the Lord.
Open our ears to hear his message,
and free our hearts
to turn from our sins and receive the life of the gospel.
We ask this through Christ our Lord.[10]

---

[10]Birth of John the Baptist: "Alternative Opening Prayer," *The Sacramentary.*

Solemnity of Peter and Paul, Apostles (June 29)

INTRODUCTORY RITES

Opening Song (or Entrance Antiphon)

These men, conquering all human frailty, shed their blood and helped the Church to grow. By sharing the cup of the Lord's suffering, they became the friends of God.[1]

Opening Prayer

The facilitator of the session may lead the prayer. Others in the group may be asked to proclaim the readings.

Let us pray
[that we may remain true to the faith of the apostles]

Pause for silent prayer.

God our Father,
today you give us the joy
of celebrating the feast of the apostles Peter and
　　Paul.
Through them your Church first received the
　　faith.
Keep us true to their teaching.
Grant this through our Lord Jesus Christ, your
　　Son,
who lives and reigns with you and the Holy Spirit,
one God for ever and ever.[2]

LITURGY OF THE WORD

Let us listen to God's word.

The readings are proclaimed.

First Reading
Acts 12:1–11

Today's story of Peter's rescue from prison has a deeper significance than that which appears at first glance. It is a story that is reminiscent of other biblical stories of divine rescue. As such, it has a higher purpose than just relating the events of this particular story. "It [the story] recalls the power of God to rescue those chosen for God's mission, a power repeatedly demonstrated in the past."[3]

We are reminded of past events in which there is rescue from evil rulers. Peter's arrest is similar to Jesus' arrest in Luke 22:54. The reference to Passover is intentional. The reader is to make a parallel connection between Jesus' passion story and the story at hand. Jesus' disciples are experiencing the fate he assured them they would endure.

The Passover allusion also serves as a reminder of another past event, the exodus out of bondage in Egypt. The reader is asked to look below the surface for another type of exodus rescue, suggests Robert Tannehill. Peter's language in the later telling of his rescue is laced with exodus language: the Lord "rescued me from the hand of Herod." The command of the angel for Peter to rise and gird himself is reminiscent of the command to the Israelites to eat the Passover with their loins girded and sandals on their feet (Ex 12:11). The rescue of Peter serves as an exodus parable. "For the Church, it is still the time of the Exodus. During the night of this world, it prays with confidence, remembering the pasch of Christ and giving thanks for the marvels God has accomplished, including thanksgiving ahead of time for the crowning marvel: when Christ himself, and no longer an angel, will come back to 'snatch her finally and forever from the hands of all her enemies.'"[4]

Responsorial Psalm
Psalm 34:2–3, 4–5, 6–7, 8–9

Second Reading
2 Timothy 4:6–8, 17–18

---

[1]Peter and Paul, Apostles: "Entrance Antiphon," *The Sacramentary.*

[2]Peter and Paul, Apostles: "Opening Prayer," *The Sacramentary.*

[3]*NULA* (II), 151.

[4]*DL* (VII), 176.

Paul's second letter to Timothy is in the genre of a farewell discourse and exhortation. It is generally believed that Paul was not the author of this letter and that it was written somewhere near the second century. It is further believed that the letter contains fragments of Paul's original words. Those authentic fragments are believed to be the words of today's second reading. Paul is awaiting death from his prison cell as he writes to Timothy. (Please refer to Twenty-Seventh Sunday in Ordinary Time for further background information on 2 Timothy.) "Although he feels close to death (4:6–8), he writes to encourage and admonish his favorite delegate in *his* struggles."[5] *Life poured out like a libation* is language indicative of Greek thought. Libations of wine and oil were often associated with the Jewish liturgy of offering sacrifice. They were also used by the Greeks and the Romans. Wine was poured on the ground in homage to gods at banquets and festive occasions. Paul adapted the pagan notion as an image of his own life, being poured out in sacrifice for the sake of others.

When Paul mentioned that he had kept the faith (v. 7), he meant that through the witness of his life and adherence to the doctrine of Christ crucified, he endured in spite of persecution.

There is no new word for Timothy in this letter; it is simply a reiteration of what Timothy already knows and holds to be true. Paul challenges Timothy to remain steadfast to what he already knows.

In this fourth chapter of second Timothy, Paul presents himself as the model of suffering in hope. In spite of being opposed, Paul had remained strong in his ministry. Timothy is thus exhorted to remain steadfast through suffering and adherence to the gospel, just like Paul. Hope resonates through Paul's encouragement to Timothy. Paul is assured of God's love, God's reign, and God's protection until such time as he is taken safely to the heavenly reign. Paul would win the crown (an olive, laurel, or pine branch wreath was awarded to athletes at the end of a great feat of endurance) through his participation in Jesus' suffering, death, resurrection, and subsequent victory over evil.

---

[5] *WNT,* 391.

In the second part of today's pericope, Paul speaks of a *first hearing* that no doubt functioned like an arraignment to determine if charges would be leveled. It appears that no one came to Paul's defense at this first hearing. Some scholars suggest that the absence of support by Paul's Christian brothers and sisters might have been due in part to the Roman church's concerns about his orthodoxy. Paul assures Timothy that, with or without their support, Jesus was with him to strengthen and uphold, *to stand by his side and give him strength* (v. 17)

Gospel
Matthew 16:13–19

Peter confesses faith at Caesarea Philippi.

STEP 1
NAMING ONE'S EXPERIENCE

What were your first impressions? What was your first response? What grabbed your attention? How did you feel?

Each person names his or her initial impression. Statements should be brief. No reasons should be given at this time. All simply listen without agreeing or disagreeing.

STEP 2
UNDERSTANDING

In a brief statement, what do you think this gospel is trying to convey?

STEP 3
INPUT FROM VISION/STORY/TRADITION

Liturgical Context

The apostles, those first eyewitnesses to the Jesus event, were paid great homage by the early Christian church. Christ hand-picked them to carry out his mission of salvation to the world. He empowered the first apostles, particularly Peter, to form, strengthen, and build the church. They were the foundation upon which the future church would be built. The early community venerated these noble saints as evidenced by the devotion of Constantine who built a church in their honor.

Origins of a feast commemorating the apostles can be traced to the East where all twelve apostles were remembered in a single feast. Individual feasts were primarily celebrated in places where the tomb of each apostle was located or in places connected with memories of certain apostles.

The two great apostles, Peter and Paul, were martyred in Rome by Nero (54–68). Paul was beheaded and Peter was crucified. Even though there is nothing to suggest that these two martyrdoms occurred simultaneously, both apostles have been remembered on the same day since the mid-third century.

Three liturgies were celebrated in Rome on this feast. Peter was commemorated at a special liturgy celebrated on Vatican Hill in the church that was named after him. Paul was honored in a liturgy on the road to Ostia at St. Paul Outside the Walls. A liturgy commemorating both apostles was celebrated at the "catacombs" (near the present-day St. Sebastian's. It is believed that this is where their bodies or their heads were kept during the persecution of Valerian). Observance of three liturgies posed a hardship for the church of the eighth century, so St. Paul's feast was moved to the next day, even though he was still remembered on June 29. However, the revised Roman calendar removed Paul's feast from the calendar (June 30) except in the place that honors his name: The Roman Basilica of St. Paul.

By the third century, a feast commemorating both apostles extended to the church in Italy and North Africa. By the fifth century most Eastern and Western countries held similar observances. St. Ambrose attested to a vigil observance as early as 397.

The revised Roman calendar maintained the vigil as a mass for the evening preceding the solemnity. Some ritual texts such as the entrance antiphon, the second reading, the presidential prayers, and the preface are new. The opening prayer reminds us that it was through the apostles that the church received its initial faith. We ask for the strength to remain faithful to their teaching. The preface reminds us that each apostle was chosen to gather the church in unity, Peter as its fearless leader and Paul as its gifted preacher. We are reminded of the price each paid for his call to ministry. We too are called to lead and to preach the word of God by the action of our lives. Paul and Peter serve as models of faithful service.

> Father, all-powerful and ever-living God,
> we do well always and everywhere to give you
> thanks.
> You fill our hearts with joy
> as we honor your great apostles:
> Peter, our leader in faith,
> and Paul, its fearless preacher.
> Peter raised up the Church
> from the faithful flock of Israel.
> Paul brought your call to the nations,
> and became the teacher of the world.
> Each in his chosen way gathered into unity
> the one family of Christ.
> Both shared a martyr's death
> and are praised throughout the world.
> Now, with the apostles and all the angels and
> saints,
> we praise you for ever:
> Holy, holy, holy Lord, God of power might,
> heaven and earth are full of your glory.
> Hosanna in the highest.
> Blessed is he who comes in the name of the
> Lord.
> Hosanna in the highest.[6]

We continue to ask for their prayers in the ongoing ministry of word and sacrament in today's church reflected in the prayer over the gifts: "Lord, may your apostles join their prayers to our offering and help us to celebrate this sacrifice in love and unity."[7] We further ask that we be united in love through the breaking of bread in the sacrament of eucharist and through the teaching of the apostles. We are confident that the church will be renewed through our participation in the eucharist and through listening and responding to the teaching of the apostles:

---

[6]Peter and Paul, Apostles: "Preface," *The Sacramentary*.
[7]Peter and Paul, Apostles: "Prayer Over the Gifts," *The Sacramentary*.

Lord,
renew the life of your Church
with the power of this sacrament.
May the breaking of bread
and the teaching of the apostles
keep us united in your love.
We ask this through Christ our Lord.[8]

The celebration of this solemnity reminds us of the church's two-fold dimension: one and universal. Peter and Paul represent the diversity of ministries to further the mission of Christ on earth. "Peter and Paul are the two pillars of the Church, the one the shepherd of Christ's flock who governs from his 'chair' at Rome, the other the missionary, the 'Apostle of Nations' who went all over the world to found ecclesial communities everywhere and to strengthen, in the course of his apostolic journeys, those he had already established."[9]

Gospel Exegesis

The facilitator gives input regarding what critical biblical scholarship has to say about this text. The input includes insights as to how people would have heard the gospel in Jesus' time.

Peter's confession of faith, Jesus' pronouncement of the rigors of discipleship, and the envisioning of the transfiguration are turning points in Jesus' ministry in all three synoptic gospels. Matthew, however, adds the investiture of Peter by Jesus as leader and rock of the church.

Jesus asked the ultimate question of his disciples: "Who do you say that I am?" In answering they would profess faith in him. Peter's insight was astounding as he answered for the whole church. Jesus was overwhelmed at Peter's insight and praised his Father for revealing this truth to one with such childlike faith. Peter professed the faith of the church and was given the keys of the kingdom of God. Until the master's return, the keys will safeguard and protect the Master's property. When Jesus gave Peter the keys, it was a symbol of confidence. He was handing over his property for Peter. As new master of the house, Peter was to

lead as a servant and steward. The apostles were fully aware that they would be held accountable for their management of the property in the master's absence. "They were given their authority only for the service of their brethren (John 13:13-17)."[10]

Jesus, as head of the kingdom, or household, exercises authority in God's name. Jesus passes authority on to the church to "mediate salvation in the time between the earthly ministry of Jesus and the future coming of the kingdom."[11]

Enormous authority is given to Peter. Citing R. H. Hiers and J. Jeremias, Benedict Viviano maintains that according to rabbinic legislation, binding and loosing may refer to exorcism of the devil, "to the juridical acts of excommunication and of definitive decision-making (a form of teaching through legislation, policy setting)."[12] The disciples are given the authority to bind and loose in verse 18, but only Peter is the foundation and only Peter is given the keys.

In the gospel of Thomas, James, the leader of the Jewish Christians, was afforded a special role of leadership. The Gentile Christians would have preferred to have had Paul named as their foundational leader. Thus, the ecumenically sensitive Matthew named Peter as the rock, thus holding both communities together in peaceful, delicate balance. It was, after all, Peter who served as spokesman for Jesus in his earthly ministry. Peter may be the keeper of the keys, but in Matthew's ecclesiology, Christ is always present in the whole church and through the power of the Holy Spirit continues to guide the church as it waits for Jesus' return.

The apostles were stewards of Christ's salvation and servants of God's servants. Even though their ministries and their personalities were different, Peter and Paul had similarities. Peter denied Jesus; Paul persecuted him through his disciples. Peter was generous, presumptuous, often hesitant but steadfastly loyal. Paul was a proud Roman citizen who demanded his rightful title of apostle and

---

[8]Peter and Paul, Apostles: "Prayer After Communion," *The Sacramentary.*
[9]*DL* (VII), 162.

[10]Ibid., 181.
[11]Benedict T. Viviano, O.P., "The Gospel of Matthew," in *NJBC*, 659.
[12]Ibid.

owned his own fragility. Peter was loyal to the institution, but was not afraid to be challenged by the Spirit. Paul evangelized to the nations, but was resisted by his own people. Both were martyrs and gave their lives for the Christ they adored and served with ardent passion. We are to do no less.

Proclaim the gospel again.

Sometimes we gain new insights when we hear the text after the interpretation has been given. Someone from the group proclaims the gospel a second time.

STEP 4
TESTING

Conversation with the Liturgy and the Scriptures

Test your original understanding in dialogue with the text.

(You might consider breaking into smaller groups.)

How does your original understanding of this story compare with what was just shared? How does this story speak to your life?

Participants share an experience from their lives that connects with the biblical interpretation just shared.

How does this liturgy challenge your community? How does it challenge you? Has your original understanding been stretched, challenged, or affirmed?

STEP 5
DECISION

The gospel demands a response.

In what way does this gospel call your parish to action in the church, parish, neighborhood, or world? Be concrete. Has this conversation with the exegesis of this liturgy changed or stretched your personal attitudes? Name one concrete action you will take this week as a response to what was learned and shared today.

DOCTRINAL ISSUES

What church truth/teaching/doctrinal issue could be drawn from the gospel for the Solemnity of Peter and Paul, Apostles?

Participants suggest possible doctrinal themes that flow from the readings.

Possible Doctrinal Themes

Discipleship, apostleship, reign of God, martyrdom, the mystery of the church

Present the doctrinal material at this time.

1. The facilitator gives input on a particular doctrinal issue of his/her prior choosing. OR
2. The group chooses a doctrinal issue from the list they created. They read together from the Doctrinal Appendix.

(The doctrinal issues are found in the Doctrinal Appendix in the back of this workbook. If you are choosing an issue from this resource, please refer to it now.)

Reflection questions centered around the chosen doctrinal theme can be found at the end of each topic in the Doctrinal Appendix. The questions are based on the five-step reflection process. If you choose a topic not included in the Doctrinal Appendix, craft your own questions according to the same five-step process.

Following the reflection questions you will be reminded to return to chapter 7, "Preparing the Catechetical Session," to assist you in crafting your own session.

Closing Prayer

Let us pray
[one with Peter and Paul in our faith in
Christ the Son of the living God]

Pause for silent prayer.

Praise to you, the God and Father of our Lord
    Jesus Christ,
who in your great mercy
have given us new birth and hope

through the power of Christ's resurrection.
Through the prayers of the apostles Peter and Paul
may we who received this faith through their
      preaching
share their joy in following the Lord
to the unfading inheritance
reserved for us in heaven.
We ask this in the name of Jesus the Lord.[13]

OR

The Lord has set you firm within his Church,
which he built upon the rock of Peter's faith.
May he bless you with a faith that never falters.
      (Amen.)

The Lord has given you knowledge of the faith
through the labors and preaching of St. Paul.
May his example inspire you to lead others to
      Christ
by the manner of your life. (Amen.)

May the keys of Peter, and the words of Paul,
their undying witness and their prayers,
lead you to the joy of that eternal home
which Peter gained by his cross, and Paul by the
      sword. (Amen.)[14]

---

[13]Peter and Paul, Apostles: "Alternative Opening Prayer,"
The Sacramentary.

[14]Peter and Paul, Apostles: "Solemn Blessing," *The Sacramentary.*

Feast of the Transfiguration (August 6)

INTRODUCTORY RITES

Opening Song (or Entrance Antiphon)

In the shining cloud the Spirit is seen; from it the voice of the Father is heard: This is my Son, my beloved, in whom is all my delight. Listen to him. (See Mt 17:5)[1] (Or sung psalm or song)

Opening Prayer

The facilitator of the session may lead the prayer. Others in the group may be asked to proclaim the readings.

Let us pray
[that we may hear the Lord Jesus
and share his everlasting life]

    Pause for silent prayer.

God our Father,
in the transfigured glory of Christ your Son,
you strengthen our faith
by confirming the witness of your prophets,
and show us the splendor of your beloved sons
    and daughters.
As we listen to the voice of your Son,
help us to become heirs to eternal life with him
who lives and reigns with you and the Holy
    Spirit,
one God, for ever and ever.[2]

LITURGY OF THE WORD

Let us listen to God's word.

The readings are proclaimed.

First Reading
Daniel 7:9–10, 13–14

The prophet is not a fortune teller. He proclaims what he hears, but even he does not fully under-

stand all there is to know about the word he has been given. With time and the passage of events, the meaning becomes clearer. The prophet and his contemporaries do not necessarily see the prophetic word as foretelling specific future events.

Often it is only hindsight that gives meaning to the biblical prophecy. The New Testament uses much of Hebrew prophecy in that way. A past prophecy helps explain the meaning of present events. Daniel's vision helps explain the full implications of what the disciples witnessed on Mount Tabor.

The church often chooses scripture in its liturgy to shed light on specific mysteries. It does not give new meaning to the texts, but it uses them to further reveal the meaning of an event, feast, or specific celebration. Jesus, the Son of Man, is the *One* Daniel heralds in his vision.

In Daniel's vision the people of God are living in the midst of persecution and oppression. To all appearances, God appears to be powerless. An ageless, ancient personage takes his place on the throne. His white hair and garment give him a radiant brilliance. All attend to this magnificent person as he passes judgment on the good and the evil. Then another person appears, one like a son of man, who has been given authority over all the earth. The Ancient One gives this person everlasting authority. The term "son of man" originally referred to every member of the human race. It eventually came to refer to a perfect man, who was an image of God and was representative of the entire human race. This new man, unlike Adam, originates from heaven. Jesus is understood in the New Testament as this Son of Man. Jesus, the Son of Man, will establish the reign Daniel proclaims in this first reading. Jesus, Son of Man, does have dominion over all the earth. Jesus' reign is everlasting and the entire world bows before him.

Responsorial Psalm
Psalm 97:1–2, 5–6, 9

The Lord is king, the most high over all the earth.

---

[1]Feast of the Transfiguration: "Entrance Antiphon," *The Sacramentary.*

[2]Feast of the Transfiguration: "Opening Prayer," *The Sacramentary.*

Second Reading
2 Peter 1:16–19

Peter is exhorting his believers to embrace the message they have been given about Christ as an authentic and true word. It is a not a myth. Peter and the other disciples witnessed Jesus' glory themselves on top of Mount Tabor. The apostles experienced the presence of the risen Christ after his death. Their testimony is true and trustworthy. The church can count on their eyewitness account. The church's faith rests on the testimony of the apostles. The Christian professes belief in the resurrection and ascension into glory of Christ and understands it as an act of prophetic fulfillment. The gospel opens to us the meaning of past prophecy, but always points us to the future. Through his life, passion, death, and resurrection, Jesus fulfilled scripture and revealed to us its deepest meaning. Even though Christ was revealed in his glory on Tabor, we still await the final glory when all will stand with him in the light of heaven. We continue to wait for his final return but are sustained and nourished by the sacrament of Christ's word in the scripture and eucharist.

Gospel
Matthew 17:1–9

Jesus is transfigured before their eyes.

STEP 1
NAMING ONE'S EXPERIENCE

What were your first impressions? What was your first response? What grabbed your attention? How did you feel?

Each person names his or her initial impression. Statements should be brief. No reasons should be given at this time. All simply listen without agreeing or disagreeing.

STEP 2
UNDERSTANDING

In a brief statement, what do you think this gospel is trying to convey?

STEP 3
INPUT FROM VISION/STORY/TRADITION

Liturgical Context

The foundation for this feast rests with the fact that all three versions of the event in the synoptic gospels agree on what happened. Early in Lent our eyes are turned toward Mount Tabor in order to prepare us to encounter the glory of Christ crucified during the Triduum. Now, forty days before the feast of the Triumph of the Cross, we are once again asked to reflect in similar fashion. We are reminded that through Christ's passion and death he entered into glory. Once again, on August 6, we are invited into the glory and brilliance of Easter that reminds us of our ultimate destiny and eschatological hope—a share in the glory of Christ.

This feast dates back to the fourth century in the East. The monks of the desert were the first to pay particular attention to the transfiguration event. They reflected upon the transfigured glory of Christ as part of their mystic spirituality.

An official feast was observed in Spain around the tenth century and rapidly spread due (it is believed) to a heightened interest in the sacred sites of the Holy Land. Abbot Peter the Venerable established the feast and wrote an office for it at Cluny. Calistus III instituted it in Rome before he became pope (1455–1458). It was placed in the calendar in 1457 in thanksgiving for the victory over the Turks the previous year by John of Capistrano and John Hunyadi.

We are reminded in the opening prayer that the transfigured glory of Christ was foretold by the prophets of old. We ask that as we listen to and grow in Christ we may become heirs to his promise. The prayer over the gifts reminds us that through the power of the resurrected, glorified Christ, the gifts of bread and wine are made holy, transformed and become his body and blood.

> Lord, by the transfiguration of your Son,
> make our gifts holy,
> and by his radiant glory free us from our sins.[3]

---

[3]Feast of the Transfiguration: "Prayer Over the Gifts," *The Sacramentary.*

The celebration of this liturgy serves as a further reminder that every eucharistic liturgy is participation in the passion, death, resurrection, and ascension into the glory of Christ. Thus, through the power of Christ in the eucharist we are changed to become more like him.

Lord,
you revealed the true radiance of Christ
in the glory of his transfiguration.
May the food we receive from heaven
change us into his image.[4]

Gospel Exegesis

The facilitator gives input regarding what critical biblical scholarship has to say about this text. The input includes insights as to how people would have heard the gospel in Jesus' time.

All three synoptic gospels report the story of the transfiguration of Jesus on Mount Tabor. The accounts are very similar, yet distinct. As is customarily the case, each of the evangelists interpreted the events from his own unique perspective and for his own purposes.

Matthew and Mark both tell us that the event on Mount Tabor took place six days after Jesus announced that he would suffer and die. Luke insists that it was eight days later. This puts the event in close proximity to the death and resurrection and thus with the Passover of the Lord.

In order to interpret the mystery of the transfiguration, in itself inexpressible and indescribable, the evangelists employed a double literary structure.[5] They called upon two very well-known biblical characters of old who themselves had experienced God's manifestation. Both Elijah and Moses came face to face with God on a mountain in the Old Testament. The evangelists also draw on the apocalypses in the Book of Daniel.

All three gospels give approximately the same details. Jesus went up the mountain with Peter, James, and John. Suddenly Jesus changed in appearance; he was transfigured by a brilliant light

as Moses and Elijah appeared with him. Peter is dumbfounded, but speaks first. He does not understand what is happening. A voice from heaven thunders the same message that was announced at Jesus' baptism: "This is my beloved Son." The voice addresses the apostles and then the vision vanishes.

Jesus and the apostles are alone again and make their way down the mountain together. The apostles do not understand what they just experienced and therefore do not say anything to anyone. They do not, however, forget. They speak of it again after the resurrection when they interpret it in light of the resurrection, and they interpret the resurrection in light of their experience on Tabor.

The apostles, though the only privileged ones to witness the event, were given the experience for the sake of the entire church. The transfiguration was understood as a preview of Christ's resurrected glory. The transfiguration reminds the church and the people of God of the hope and the glory of the resurrection as we experience Jesus Christ crucified, and his persecution, trials, tribulations, suffering, doubts, and lack of hope. The transfiguration bolsters our spirit during those times that try our souls and our patience. When in the depths of hell, the transfiguration transports us to the heights of heaven.

Matthew's version of the transfiguration presents Christ as the one who will return to the world in glory at the end of time. Matthew's common theme of God's reign and the Old Testament tradition weaves its way into his account of the transfiguration. The kingdom was proclaimed by the prophets and established by Christ himself. Jesus will come again—when we do not know, but come he will. And the church will be waiting for his return. In the meantime, we are to put into action the words, life, and commands of our Master. We can be confident that Jesus will return because, even though none of us has seen him, the three apostles *did* see him in his resurrected glory. This is the hope to which we cling.

Jesus entered into God's glory. He sits at God's throne and from that throne he will judge both the living and the dead. We know him to be God's Son, the beloved one. We are to spend our lives preparing to meet him when he comes again.

---

[4]Feast of the Transfiguration: "Prayer After Communion," *The Sacramentary.*

[5]*DL* (VII), 193.

Great and significant events in Jesus' life take place on a mountain. It is a place of manifestation for Matthew. In Matthew's gospel the temptation of Jesus (4:8), his inaugural sermon (5:1), the sending of the apostles on the mission of the church, were all mountain-top events. The Lord will usher those who are his own into the light of glory on a high mountain at the end of time; Tabor evokes that image.

When the people of God are taken to the light of glory they will know the same transfiguration that Jesus experienced on Mount Tabor. They will shine with the light of God.

Moses and Elijah represent the law and the prophets—the entire scripture—the revealed word of God now fulfilled in the Christ event. We have seen his glory. Now we can go back down the mountain and share that glory with others until the day when it will be fully revealed to all the nations.

The language Matthew uses is reminiscent of the Easter language of the passion, death, and post-resurrection stories. The apostles are told "not to be afraid." Jesus "touched" them like he touched those he healed. They were told to "rise" just as Christ would rise. Jesus also tells the church not to be afraid, to rise, and to continue to march to the light of the glory that awaits us. We cannot just give lip service to our march, but we must back it up with our service in the kingdom of God. On that great and wonderful day we will joyfully go with Christ into the light of his glory.

(Please refer to the Second Sunday of Lent, Gospel Exegesis, for Mark's perspective.)

Proclaim the gospel again.

Sometimes we gain new insights when we hear the text after the interpretation has been given. Someone from the group proclaims the gospel a second time.

STEP 4
TESTING

Conversation with the Liturgy and the Scriptures

Test your original understanding in dialogue with the text.

(You might consider breaking into smaller groups.)

How does your original understanding of this story compare with what was just shared? How does this story speak to your life?

Participants share an experience from their lives that connects with the biblical interpretation just shared.

How does this liturgy challenge your community? How does it challenge you? Has your original understanding been stretched, challenged, or affirmed?

STEP 5
DECISION

The gospel demands a response.

In what way does this gospel call your parish to action in the church, parish, neighborhood, or world? Be concrete. Has this conversation with the exegesis of this liturgy changed or stretched your personal attitudes? Name one concrete action you will take this week as a response to what was learned and shared today.

DOCTRINAL ISSUES

What church truth/teaching/doctrinal issue could be drawn from the gospel for feast of the Transfiguration?

Participants suggest possible doctrinal themes that flow from the readings.

Possible Doctrinal Themes

Christology, Spirit of God, transfiguration, ascension, paschal mystery, resurrection, parousia, eschatology, mission of the church, evangelization, sacrament of baptism

Present the doctrinal material at this time.

1. The facilitator gives input on a particular doctrinal issue of his/her prior choosing. OR
2. The group chooses a doctrinal issue from the list they created. They read together from the Doctrinal Appendix.

(The doctrinal issues are found in the Doctrinal Appendix in the back of this workbook. If you are choosing an issue from this resource, please refer to it now.)

Reflection questions centered around the chosen doctrinal theme can be found at the end of each topic in the Doctrinal Appendix. The questions are based on the five-step reflection process. If you choose a topic not included in the Doctrinal Appendix, craft your own questions according to the same five-step process.

Following the reflection questions you will be reminded to return to chapter 7, "Preparing the Catechetical Session," to assist you in crafting your own session.

Closing Prayer

Lord,
you revealed the true radiance of Christ
in the glory of his transfiguration.
May the food we receive from heaven
change us into his image.
We ask this in the name of Jesus.[6]

---

[6]Feast of the Transfiguration: "Prayer After Communion," *The Sacramentary*.

Solemnity of the Assumption (August 15)

INTRODUCTORY RITES

Opening Song (or Entrance Antiphon)

All honor to you, Mary! Today you were raised above the choirs of angels to lasting glory with Christ.[1]

Opening Prayer

The facilitator of the session may lead the prayer. Others in the group may be asked to proclaim the readings.

Let us pray
[that the Virgin Mary will help us with her prayers]

Pause for silent prayer.

Almighty God,
you gave a humble virgin
the privilege of being the mother of your Son,
and crowned her with the glory of heaven.
May the prayers of the Virgin Mary
bring us to the salvation of Christ
and raise us up to eternal life.
We ask this through our Lord Jesus Christ, your
        Son,
who lives and reigns with you and the Holy
        Spirit,
one God for ever and ever. [2]

LITURGY OF THE WORD

Let us listen to God's word.

The readings are proclaimed.

First Reading
Revelation 11:19; 12:1–6, 10

This eschatological reading reminds us of previous prophets who spoke of Jerusalem's and the people's promised glory in the last days. The image of a woman in the pangs of childbirth emerges as a symbol of new life that can come to pass only in the fullness of time and only after enduring unavoidable pain.

It is tempting to think that Mary is the mother about to give birth to Christ, the child about to be born. However, the author was not thinking of Mary. Christ is about to come to birth in the lives of people. It is painful because it is accompanied by sorrow, persecution, and the daily struggle to persevere. The woman is a symbol of the church who exists in the midst of God's glory, yet nevertheless is bound to the struggles of this earthly sojourn. Christ protects and strengthens her as she passes from death to life.

Even though the author of Revelation was not referring to Mary in his vision, Christian tradition has always understood the woman as an image of Mary. The meaning is not changed, however. Mary is a symbol of the church who still gives birth to Christ in the lives of the faithful. "God willed this unique and marvelous divine motherhood to be the figure and exemplar of the fecundity of the virgin Church that also becomes a mother... the Church in the sacrament of baptism somehow continues Mary's virginal motherhood. We may offer one example of this teaching from our predecessor St. Leo the Great; in one of his Christmas sermons he says: '[Christ] placed in the baptismal font the source of his own origin in the womb of the Virgin: the power of the most high and the overshadowing of the water to give rebirth to the believer.'[3] And if we want to find the same idea in liturgical

---

[1]Vigil of the Assumption: "Entrance Antiphon," *The Sacramentary.*

[2]Vigil of the Assumption: "Opening Prayer," *The Sacramentary.*

[3]Leo the Great, *Tractatus* (In Nativitate Domini) 5: CCL 138, 123: SC 22 bis, 132; see also *Tractatus* (In Nativitate Domini) 1: CCL 138, 147; SC 22 bis, 178; *Tractatus* 63 (De Passione Domini) 6: CCL 138, 386; SC 74, 82. In *DOL, 1963–1979: Conciliar, Papal and Curial Texts,* Section 4: Sanctoral Cycle: A. Mary, 1213.

sources, we can cite the very beautiful *Illatio* [preface] of the Mozarabic liturgy: '[Mary] carried life in her womb; the Church, in the baptismal font. In the body of Mary Christ put on flesh; in the waters of the Church the baptized put on Christ.' "[4, 5]

Responsorial Psalm
Psalm 45:10, 11, 12, 16

The queen stands at your right hand, arrayed in gold.

Second Reading
1 Corinthians 15:20–26

There is no denying that Jesus rose from the dead. This is the core of our faith: Christ conquered death once and for all. Our salvation depends on it. All will live because of Christ, the "first fruit." When the first fruits of the harvest were offered, it was considered a sample of the entire harvest. Symbolically it was a rendering of the entire harvest to God. Thus, Christ offered himself completely for the human race. In that offering the entire human race was offered with him. Christ freed Adam's heirs from the stain of his sin. Christ's act of self surrender was definitive. His death and resurrection accomplished salvation for the entire world—once and for all. We still await the final day when he will return and establish his heavenly rule forever. We continue to remain vigilant until that last and final victory over death. When Jesus comes again, death will be no longer. In one last grand act, the human race will be resurrected into everlasting glory. Mary is a sign of the hope we all share as we await that great and glorious day.

Gospel
Luke 1:39–56

Mary sets out to see Elizabeth, the baby leaps in Mary's womb, and Mary proclaims the glory of God.

---

[4]M. Ferotin, *Le Liber Mozarabicus Sacramentorum* col. 56. In *DOL 1963–1979: Conciliar, Papal and Curial Texts*, Section 4: Sanctoral Cycle: A. Mary, 1213.

[5]*DOL 1963–1979: Conciliar, Papal and Curial Texts*, Section 4: Sanctoral Cycle: A. Mary, #19, #3917, p. 1213.

STEP 1
NAMING ONE'S EXPERIENCE

What were your first impressions? What was your first response? What grabbed your attention? How did you feel?

Each person names his or her initial impression. Statements should be brief. No reasons should be given at this time. All simply listen without agreeing or disagreeing.

STEP 2
UNDERSTANDING

In a brief statement, what do you think this gospel is trying to convey?

STEP 3
INPUT FROM VISION/STORY/TRADITION

Liturgical Context

Even after they had converted to Christianity, people who had formerly been pagans continued the practice of honoring their dead. They purged the paganism from their commemoration of dead ancestors by placing their memorial celebrations within the context of their faith in Christ and his resurrection. They sang hymns to Christ and eventually began the practice of gathering near the tombs of their ancestors on anniversaries of their death. If a person had been martyred, all gathered around his or her tomb to commemorate the anniversary of that person's death. These celebrations were eventually moved into the church. Commemoration of the most famous martyrs spread to the church at large.

Veneration of martyrs continued. Added to the list were those "confessors of faith," who had not spilt their blood, but had suffered prison, exile, or forced labor for the cause of Christianity. Virgins and mystics who had given their lives to the Lord's service of prayer and solitude were also included as persons to be venerated and remembered. A life of dedication and consecration was understood as a type of martyrdom. This is how the church's practice of venerating the saints evolved.

Mary's role in scripture seemed to end with the Pentecost event. We do not hear of her again. However, in 431 the third ecumenical council at Ephesus took action that resulted in the beginning of the cult of the Virgin Mary. The council declared that Christ was both God and man, refuting the teaching of Nestorius. Mary became the "Mother of God—Theotokos." Afterward, Pope Sixtus III (432–440) built a basilica in honor of the Mother of God—"St. Mary Major." The first liturgical observance centered around the feast of the Nativity both in the East and in the West.

There is evidence of apocryphal writings dating from the fourth century telling of Jesus' appearance to Mary two years after his ascension to tell her that she would soon be assumed into heaven. There were other apocryphal writings that spoke of Mary's death and of her being carried up to heaven.

The origin of this feast occurred in Jerusalem with a celebration that took place near the location where it is believed that Mary *rested* (*koimesis*, which in Greek means either rest of sleep or sleep of death) before entering Bethlehem. By the end of the fifth century the feast (Dormition of Mary) was celebrated at Gethsemane where Mary's tomb was venerated. The feast commemorated her death and entrance into heaven.

By the end of the sixth century this was made an obligatory feast in the East. The West celebrated a similar obligatory feast remembering her motherhood on January 1 in Rome. The August 15 date was established around the year 650 and the celebration centered around the glorification of the Virgin Mary. The term *dormition* was used until 770 when the word *assumption* appeared.

Since there were no authentic witnesses to the Marian events, the reticent church of the ninth century did not insist upon adherence to the doctrine of Mary's glorification. "For a long time the magisterium remains silent: It silently observes the dialogue between the intuitions of the 'lovers' of Mary and the reticence of the theologians, who respect above all the witness of the word of God, including its silences."[6] There were, however, nearly twenty feasts devoted to Mary in the Roman Calendar.

The church took a stronger position with regard to Mary in 1854 when Pius IX defined the Dogma of the Immaculate Conception and in 1950 when Pius XII defined the Assumption. The new calendar promulgated by Paul VI arranged the Marian feasts according to their importance; the feasts were "integrated in a clear way into the mystery of salvation through Christ, the true object of Christian faith and worship."[7]

> On August 15 we celebrate the glorious Assumption of Mary into heaven. It is the festival honoring the fullness of blessedness that was her destiny, the glorification of her immaculate soul and virginal body that completely conformed her to the risen Christ. This is a celebration that offers to the Church and to all humanity an exemplar and a consoling message, teaching us the fulfillment of our highest hopes: their own future glorification is happily in store for all those whom Christ has made his own brothers and sisters by taking on their "flesh and blood" (Heb. 2:14, see Gal. 4:4). The solemnity of the Assumption is continued on into the celebration of the Queenship of Mary on the octave day. She who is enthroned next to the King of Ages is contemplated as the radiant Queen and interceding Mother. These then are the four solemnities [Immaculate Conception, Mary Mother of God, the Annunciation, and the Assumption of Mary] that in their high rank as liturgical celebrations bring out the main truths related to the simple handmaid of the Lord.[8]

---

[6]M. Bobichon, *Marie dans la nouvelle Liturgie de la Parole*, tome 1, Pâque nouvelle (Lyon: Chalet, 1971), 110, in *DL* (VII), 202.

[7]Ibid.

[8]Paul VI, Apostolic Exhortation *Marialis cultus*, on rightly grounding and increasing Marian devotion, 2 February 1974: AAS 66 (1974) 113–168; Not 10 (1974) 153–197, in *DOL 1963–1979: Conciliar, Papal and Curial Texts*, Section 4: Sanctoral Cycle: A. Mary, #3904, p. 1208.

There are two masses for this solemnity: the vigil and the day of the feast. The vigil celebration focuses on "Mary's glory and her significance in the history of salvation. The Mother of our Savior, the Son of God, is already elevated to the glory of the elect, where she bears witness to the victory over death that will shine for all those who follow Christ, who hear the word of God and observe it."[9] The mass during the day reminds us of the self-offering of Mary and the foreshadowing of that same pasche in the church. Mary's joy at the birth of her Son is intimately connected to her sorrow at his death. The mass of the day celebrates Mary as the symbol of the church and a sign for all believers who journey toward their heavenly glory with Christ. Mary is a sign of hope for us all.

Gospel Exegesis

The facilitator gives input regarding what critical biblical scholarship has to say about this text. The input includes insights as to how people would have heard the gospel in Jesus' time.

Luke is not concerned with telling us a story about two pregnant relatives who meet one last time before their babies' birth. Nor is it a story that denotes Mary's concern and care for Elizabeth in her time of need. If that were the case, Luke would not have Mary departing when Elizabeth's need is obviously the greatest. Rather, through the literary devices inherent in story-telling, Luke provides a theology of God's plan of salvation through Jesus. The two mothers-to-be are gathered in praise of God for the work God is doing in and through them. In their gathering, the theological reality that John is the precursor of Jesus and that Jesus is the Savior who is superior to John is proclaimed. This is the point of the story.

There are four literary devices commonly used in Luke/Acts to illustrate God's plan. They are: previews and reviews, repeated or highlighted scriptural references, commission statements, and interpretive statements by reliable characters. Robert Tannehill suggests that there may be details in the story that review what God has already

done in the past and preview what God is about to do, "in a way that interprets these events."[10] Through the birth stories of both John and Jesus, Luke previews what God intends for humanity's redemption. Through various images and words, the reader knows that reference is being made to God's plan revealed throughout the scriptures.

Through allusions to scriptural passages and traditions, the reader is shown that "the law and the prophets are fulfilled in Jesus."[11] These same passages also express a particular understanding of God's purpose and are programs for action.[12] For example, when Elizabeth tells us that the baby leapt in her womb, the reader is reminded of the leaping of Rebekah's twin children, Jacob and Esau. According to biblical tradition, leaping in-utero foreshadowed a future relationship and "symbolized destinies that would be lived out by the children."[13] In John's leaping we are previewing a future relationship between Jesus and John.[14] Through the power of the Holy Spirit, Elizabeth is able to interpret John's leaping. John leapt in Elizabeth's womb because the destiny of the world was being fulfilled in the baby within Mary's womb.

The third literary device is the agent, the chosen instrument, "reliable persons commissioned by God to carry out God's purpose."[15] In this story both Elizabeth and Mary are those instruments. Both have been obedient to the will of God and, as a result, both bring God's intended plan of redemption to birth in the world. In biblical tradition, Mary leaving in haste refers to an "interior disposition that makes one act with fervor and zeal."[16] Mary is understood as great because of the child she will bear and is praised because of her relationship to Christ. Mary's role is christological. She has a role in God's liberating plan for the human race.

The fourth literary technique is the commission, the call and mission of the individual in question. When Elizabeth says, "...blessed is the fruit of

---

[9]*DL* (VII), 203–204.

[10]*NULA* (II), 20–38.

[11]Ibid., 21.

[12]Ibid., 22.

[13]*WWC*, 272.

[14]Karris, "The Gospel According to Luke," in *NJBC*, 681.

[15]*NULA* (II), 21.

[16]*DL* (I), 158.

your womb. Who am I that the mother of my Lord should come to me?" she prophesies about the mission of the child in Mary's womb. This child will bring salvation. He will be the fulfillment of God's plan. Luke wants to make it clear that both John and Jesus have a unique role to play. John will prepare the way and will be the bridge between the old covenant and the new covenant. John will help prepare hearts for giving birth to the advent of the Messiah. Jesus, however, is that messiah. Jesus is the One who will fulfill Israel's hopes. Luke insists that his community have no illusions about "who's who" in the eschatological events about to take place.

Mary and Elizabeth, two great women of scripture, listen to God and become the ultimate paradigm of disciple. In this scriptural text Mary becomes the great gift and model for the church. She listens, she responds, she obeys with fervor and zeal the voice of God and she acts on that Word. We, too, are exhorted to "go in haste," to go with zeal and fervor to live the call of the gospel and to share the mighty news it contains. Mary models for us the perfect liturgy. She listens, she gives thanks and praise, she responds in faith to the Word of God, and then she goes in haste.

Proclaim the gospel again.

Sometimes we gain new insights when we hear the text after the interpretation has been given. Someone from the group proclaims the gospel a second time.

STEP 4
TESTING

Conversation with the Liturgy and the Scriptures

Test your original understanding in dialogue with the text.

(You might consider breaking into smaller groups.)

How does your original understanding of this story compare with what was just shared? How does this story speak to your life?

Participants share an experience from their lives that connects with the biblical interpretation just shared.

How does this liturgy challenge our community? How does it challenge me? Has our original understanding been stretched, challenged, or affirmed?

STEP 5
DECISION

The gospel demands a response.

In what way does this gospel call your parish to action in the church, parish, neighborhood, or world? Be concrete. Has this conversation with the exegesis of this liturgy changed or stretched your personal attitudes? Name one concrete action you will take this week as a response to what was learned and shared today.

DOCTRINAL ISSUES

What church truth/teaching/doctrinal issue could be drawn from the gospel for the Solemnity of the Assumption of Mary?

Participants suggest possible doctrinal themes that flow from the readings.

Possible Doctrinal Themes

Mary, Mother of God, the Assumption of Mary, Mary, symbol of the church

Present the doctrinal material at this time.

1. The facilitator gives input on a particular doctrinal issue of his/her prior choosing. OR
2. The group chooses a doctrinal issue from the list they created. They read together from the Doctrinal Appendix.

(The doctrinal issues are found in the Doctrinal Appendix in the back of this workbook. If you are choosing an issue from this resource, please refer to it now.)

Reflection questions centered around the chosen doctrinal theme can be found at the end of each topic in the Doctrinal Appendix. The questions are based on the five-step reflection process. If you choose a topic not included in the Doctrinal Appendix, craft your own questions according to the same five-step process.

Following the reflection questions you will be reminded to return to chapter 7, "Preparing the Catechetical Session," to assist you in crafting your own session.

Closing Prayer

Lord,
may we who receive this sacrament of salvation
be led to the glory of heaven
by the prayers of the Virgin Mary.
We ask this in the name of Jesus the Lord.[17]

[17]Solemnity of the Assumption: "Prayer After Communion," *The Sacramentary.*

FEAST OF THE TRIUMPH OF THE CROSS (SEPTEMBER 14)

INTRODUCTORY RITES

Opening Song (or Entrance Antiphon)

We should glory in the cross of our Lord Jesus Christ, for he is our salvation, our life and our resurrection; through him we are saved and made free. (See Gal 6:14)[1]

Opening Prayer

The facilitator of the session may lead the prayer. Others in the group may be asked to proclaim the readings.

Let us pray
[that the death of Christ on the cross
will bring us to the glory of the
resurrection]

Pause for silent prayer.

God our Father,
in obedience to you
your only Son accepted death on the cross
for the salvation of mankind.
We acknowledge the mystery of the cross on earth.
May we receive the gift of redemption in heaven.
We ask this through our Lord Jesus Christ, your
    Son,
who lives and reigns with you and the Holy Spirit,
one God, for ever and ever.[2]

LITURGY OF THE WORD

Let us listen to God's word.

The readings are proclaimed.

First Reading
Numbers 21:4–9

The snake was a sign of danger, confusion, and even wisdom. In mythology the snake was a sign of fertility and rebirth. If a person was bitten by a snake and remained unharmed, it was a sign of some sort of divine protection. All these images creep into the telling of today's story.

The scene is the desert following Israel's escape from Egypt. The cast includes Moses and the people of Israel. The situation centers around the amnesia of Israel. The people had forgotten all that God had done for them. They obnoxiously believed that God took them to the desert to let them die. God was angered by their lack of faith and sent serpents among them. Many people died from the sting of these serpents. The people understood this tragedy to be a result of and punishment for their sin.[3] They prayed to be delivered. God told them to take a pole and fashion a serpent on the top of it. All who looked at the pole would be healed.

The serpent episode is typical of God's relationship with Israel. Israel sinned. God punished. The people repented and were converted wholeheartedly to the Lord who was ready to forgive their sins. The Christian tradition connected this reading and the image of the bronze serpent with the cross of Christ. Christ, elevated on the cross, was a sign of healing, salvation, and forgiveness.

Responsorial Psalm
Psalm 78:1–2, 34–35, 36–37, 38

Do not forget the works of the Lord!

Second Reading
Philippians 2:6–11

It is believed that Paul inserted this beautiful, previously crafted hymn into his letter to the Philippians. Some consider it a perfect expression of Pauline theology regarding the passion and death of Jesus. This hymn was probably used in ancient Christian liturgies and profoundly captures the essence and the paradox of Christian redemption. Jesus, through abject humiliation (see Fourth Sun-

---

[1] Feast of the Triumph of the Cross: "Entrance Antiphon," *The Sacramentary.*
[2] Feast of the Triumph of the Cross: "Opening Prayer," *The Sacramentary.*

---

[3] Israel understood all life to be ordered by God. They understood all blessings to be a result of God's benevolence and all tragedy to be a result of God's anger.

day of Lent, Cycle C, parable of prodigal son), offered the free gift of himself. Through such humiliation, salvation was won. Jesus left his rightful throne with Yahweh, descended into the midst of humanity and took the form of a slave, subject to the suffering and limitations of the human person. He allowed himself to be rejected, misunderstood, and treated like a slave and a criminal. Because of this free gift of self, this abasement, Jesus ascended back to the throne victorious. Because of the resurrection, humanity was and is offered freedom from the ravages of sin and death, and the promise of eternal life. Jesus, the perfect servant, model of all perfect servants, earned the rightful title, Lord, *Kyrios* (Greek), *Adonai* (Hebrew).

Paul was addressing the dissensions and factions in the Philippian community. He pleaded that all assume the posture of Jesus. If they would only assume the model of Christ's self-abasement, then harmony and peace would be restored to the community. Jesus could have claimed all the rights and privileges of royalty. But he did not. "He became sin"; he entered the human condition with all its defects and in the process emptied himself. The Philippian community was exhorted to embrace *kenosis,* a voluntary emptying of oneself in the manner of Jesus. Paul challenged his community to assume the humble stance of self-giver rather than give in to the lure of power and control. Jesus, emptied and poured-out, went willingly to his passion and death. We are to follow in his footsteps.

Gospel
John 3:13–17

Jesus tells Nicodemus that the Son of Man must be lifted up.

STEP 1
NAMING ONE'S EXPERIENCE

What were your first impressions? What was your first response? What grabbed your attention? How did you feel?

Each person names his or her initial impression. Statements should be brief. No reasons should be given at this time. All simply listen without agreeing or disagreeing.

STEP 2
UNDERSTANDING

In a brief statement, what do you think this gospel is trying to convey?

STEP 3
INPUT FROM VISION/STORY/TRADITION

Liturgical Context

In the early days of the church the cross was simply considered Jesus' instrument of execution. As Christianity evolved it became a multivalent symbol. It came to symbolize Christ's sacrificial death as well as Christ himself. It was also understood as a sign of Christianity.

Veneration of the cross is evidenced by the fourth century. The cross of Christ was found by Empress Helena on September 14, 320. Five years later, on September 13, two churches were consecrated in honor of the cross—Martyrium (the Church of the Cross), and the Resurrection (the Church of the Anastasis). Helena's discovered cross was displayed and venerated by the faithful on the next day, September 14, 325. The solemn observance became an annual event. Constantinople observed a similar feast by the fifth century and Rome by the seventh century. Those churches that had major relics of the cross showed the relics to the faithful in a solemn celebration called the *Exaltatio* (lifting-up).

During the eighth century, the people of Gaul celebrated a feast honoring the cross on May 3. A relic of the cross was captured by the Persians. It was subsequently recovered and carried in triumphant procession into Jerusalem. Rome placed this observance in the calendar and erroneously called it "Discovery of the Holy Cross." The September 14 feast was called "The Exaltation of the Holy Cross." The September feast was incorrectly designated as the feast to honor the restoration of the cross. Pope John XXIII rectified the situation and removed the May 3 observance from the calendar. The original meaning was restored to the September 14 feast.

The entrance antiphon gives us the theme for today's liturgy: we are to glory in the cross, for it is our salvation. The liturgy celebrates the salvation won for humanity by the sacrifice of Christ on the cross. The preface makes the comparison between the cross of Christ and the tree of paradise that was ultimately the sign of sin and death.

The cross is a sign of our identity as Christians. We sign ourselves with the cross. Catechumens are traced with the cross as a sign of God's strength and incorporation into the life of Christ. We sign ourselves with the cross when we enter and leave church; when we begin every liturgical celebration; when we eat a meal; and when we go to bed and wake up in the morning. The cross is the sign of Christ and the sign of the Christian life.

There are forty days from the feast of the Transfiguration on August 6 to the feast of the Holy Cross on September 14. This was once a period of pilgrimage to welcome the autumn season.

Gospel Exegesis

The facilitator gives input regarding what critical biblical scholarship has to say about this text. The input includes insights as to how people would have heard the gospel in Jesus' time.

Jesus was to be lifted up, like the serpent of Moses, as a sign of healing and salvation. Through the sign of the cross all who believe in Jesus will inherit eternal life. The cross, then, becomes the throne of glory, not the tool of an executioner. John insists that Jesus was "lifted up" on the cross. He uses coronation language rather than execution language. John's gospel reads like a royal liturgy. The language of crucifixion sounds like the installation of royalty upon a throne. The king is lifted up and crowned triumphant upon the throne of the cross.

Jesus willingly and knowingly went to his death. He was in control. It was a horrible death, but the torturous details are not the point of the story. Jesus, Son of Man, God-Man, saved the world from his throne of the cross. Those who looked upon Moses' serpent were saved. Those who look to the cross of Christ, believe in its power to save, and conform their lives to its power are also saved.

We are not to forget the gravity of sin, its lure and its death-dealing consequences. But today's liturgy is a joyful reminder that the cross is our hope in the midst of our sinfulness. This feast, situated halfway between the Triduum's celebration of the passion, death, and resurrection of Christ and the end of the liturgical year, serves as a midyear reality check. Every day is an opportunity to join in the sacrifice of Christ on the cross. Every liturgy remembers and makes present its saving power. Today's liturgy is an invitation to model Christ's saving action in our everyday lives. Do we love to the point of self-sacrifice, to the point of dying on the cross of our own selfishness?

Proclaim the gospel again.

Sometimes we gain new insights when we hear the text after the interpretation has been given. Someone from the group proclaims the gospel a second time.

STEP 4
TESTING

Conversation with the Liturgy and the Scriptures

Test your original understanding in dialogue with the text.

(You might consider breaking into smaller groups.)

How does your original understanding of this story compare with what was just shared? How does this story speak to your life?

Participants share an experience from their lives that connects with the biblical interpretation just shared.

How does this liturgy challenge our community? How does it challenge me? Has our original understanding been stretched, challenged, or affirmed?

STEP 5
DECISION

The gospel demands a response.

In what way does this gospel call your parish to action in the church, parish, neighborhood, or world? Be concrete. Has this conversation with the exegesis of this liturgy changed or stretched your personal attitudes? Name one concrete action you will take this week as a response to what was learned and shared today.

DOCTRINAL ISSUES

What church truth/teaching/doctrinal issue could be drawn from the gospel for Triumph of the Cross?

Participants suggest possible doctrinal themes that flow from the readings.

Possible Doctrinal Themes

Cross, redemptive suffering, paschal mystery

Present the doctrinal material at this time.

1. The facilitator gives input on a particular doctrinal issue of his/her prior choosing. OR
2. The group chooses a doctrinal issue from the list they created. They read together from the Doctrinal Appendix.

(The doctrinal issues are found in the Doctrinal Appendix in the back of this workbook. If you are choosing an issue from this resource, please refer to it now.)

Reflection questions centered around the chosen doctrinal theme can be found at the end of each topic in the Doctrinal Appendix. The questions are based on the five-step reflection process. If you choose a topic not included in the Doctrinal Appendix, craft your own questions according to the same five-step process.

Following the reflection questions you will be reminded to return to chapter 7, "Preparing the Catechetical Session," to assist you in crafting your own session.

Closing Prayer

Lord,
may this sacrifice once offered on the cross
to take away the sins of the world
now free us from our sins.
We ask this through Christ our Lord.[4]

[4]Feast of the Triumph of the Cross: "Prayer Over the Gifts," *The Sacramentary*.

Solemnity of All Saints (November 1)

INTRODUCTORY RITES

Opening Song (or Entrance Antiphon)

Let us all rejoice in the Lord and keep a festival in honor of all the saints. Let us join with the angels in joyful praise to the Son of God.[1]

Opening Prayer

The facilitator of the session may lead the prayer. Others in the group may be asked to proclaim the readings.

Let us pray
[that the prayers of all the saints
will bring us forgiveness for our sins]

> *Pause for silent prayer.*

Father, all powerful and ever-living God,
today we rejoice in the holy men and women
of every time and place.
May their prayers bring us your forgiveness and
    love.
We ask this through our Lord Jesus Christ, your Son,
who lives and reigns with you and the Holy Spirit,
one God for ever and ever. [2]

LITURGY OF THE WORD

Let us listen to God's word.

The readings are proclaimed.

First Reading
Revelation 7:2–4, 9–14

(Refer to the Thirty-Fourth Sunday in Ordinary Time for an overview of the Book of Revelation.)

Christ, who is risen, exalted, and appears in glory, is the primary theme of the book of Revelation.

After giving a word of encouragement to the seven churches, Christ reveals the turmoil that will take place in the great battle between good and evil at the end of time.

Today's liturgy celebrates the joy of martyrs who share Christ's glorification. They shared in Christ's passion through their martyrdom. This is John's second vision in which there is a large gathering of people. In this vision, the number of people is beyond counting. The first vision was in reference to Israel. This vision refers to everyone—all nations. The palm fronds that are held by the assembled are a sign of victory.

The great trial referred to in this pericope is the tribulation that will come at the end of the age. During these latter days of tribulation, God's faithful will experience persecution. The robes represent the interior, spiritual disposition of the individual. The soiled robes represent sin and the clean robes represent holiness. This cleanliness is associated with the sacrificial death of Jesus. Through Jesus' death and resurrection, the robes (interior lives) are washed clean.

Baptism is the means through which the person is transformed, washed clean by the blood of the Lamb, and made holy. "The fundamental allusion here seems to be repentance, conversion, and baptism taken together as a transformation of the person."[3]

The image of the last tribulation or the trial is an exhortation to persevere in conversion and *metanoia*. Perseverance will give people the necessary means to endure and share in the salvation offered through Jesus' paschal mystery. Some of those who persevere will be called to martyrdom.

Responsorial Psalm
Psalm 24:1–6

Lord, this is the people that longs to see your face.

---

[1] Solemnity of All Saints: "Entrance Antiphon," *The Sacramentary.*

[2] Solemnity of All Saints: "Opening Prayer," *The Sacramentary.*

[3] Adela Yarbro Collins, "The Apocalypse (Revelation)," in *NJBC*, 1006.

Second Reading
1 John 3:1–3

John's favorite message is the love of God for his people. If we would only keep God's love in our consciousness, then we would convert our entire lives to God. The world will not understand. We are not to provoke persecution, but persecution will be ours. Without the eyes of faith, Jesus' identity is incomprehensible to the world. Through God's love we are made his children. As God's children we share his divine nature. Because we are God's children we will share his glory at the end of time.

Gospel
Matthew 5:1–12

Jesus gives us the blueprint for living in his reign: the beatitudes.

STEP 1
NAMING ONE'S EXPERIENCE

What were your first impressions? What was your first response? What grabbed your attention? How did you feel?

Each person names his or her initial impression. Statements should be brief. No reasons should be given at this time. All simply listen without agreeing or disagreeing.

STEP 2
UNDERSTANDING

In a brief statement, what do you think this gospel is trying to convey?

STEP 3
INPUT FROM VISION/STORY/TRADITION

Liturgical Context

During the fourth century, martyrs were remembered at a celebration. The day of the celebration was different in each of the churches. In Syria it was celebrated on May 13. In Antioch it was celebrated on the day after Pentecost. The Greek Orthodox still observe this day and call it "All Saints Sunday." The Eastern Syrian liturgy observes the feast on the Friday after Easter.[4]

There is evidence that in Rome all three dates were observed. Pope Boniface IV accepted the Pantheon, a pagan temple, as a gift from Emperor Phocas. It was consecrated in honor of the Virgin Mary and martyrs on May 13, 609. Twenty-eight wagon loads of martyrs' bones were brought to the church from the catacombs. The pope named the feast assigned to May 13 the feast of All Saints.

In the eighth century in England and Ireland a feast in honor of All the Saints was celebrated on November 1. Pope Gregory IV gave permission to Louis the Pius, emperor of the West, to promulgate November 1 as the feast of "All Saints" for his entire kingdom. That date spread to the entire church and May 13 eventually disappeared. From the beginning the feast was assigned a vigil and by the fifteenth century an octave was also included. However, both vigil and octave were eliminated in the liturgical reform of 1955.

The feast remembers deceased friends, relatives, and ancestors who upon their death entered into heavenly glory. It also remembers the canonized saints. The liturgy seeks the intercessions of the saints who went before us. We ask that their prayers bring us forgiveness and love.

The feast also celebrates the Triune God who gathers the elect together in the courts of the heavenly Jerusalem to worship him. Every liturgy foreshadows our future participation in the heavenly banquet. This, however, is an extended meditation on the hope we celebrate. The praise and worship of God are at the center of this celebration.

Gospel Exegesis

The facilitator gives input regarding what critical biblical scholarship has to say about this text. The input includes insights as to how people would have heard the gospel in Jesus' time.

---

[4]*LY*, 228.

When Jesus returned from his ordeal in the desert, he went to Capernaum to announce the arrival of the messianic reign. He exhorted the people to repent. Jesus went up to a mountain and began to teach them. For Matthew, the mountain location was significant. It was a high place where human beings encounter divine authority. Moses went up the mountain to encounter God. Jesus, too, went up the mountain, the place of divine authority, and he sat down to teach the people. Matthew paints this picture with an exclamation point: he wants his audience to know that Jesus was speaking with the highest authority. He sat down to teach them as one who would rule from a royal throne.

Jesus began to exhort and encourage the people. In Jesus' reign, this is how it is to be. Jesus gives a blueprint for holiness. In a workshop given in 1995, Donald Senior noted that "The key to Matthew's gospel is that it is a call to doing things, not saying things." The sermon on the mount was a response to a crowd in need of healing. Matthew portrays Jesus as Teacher and Healer. Matthew's Jesus teaches for the transformation of people through the reign of God. Jesus' reign was not a future event, but a present reality.

There are four characteristics to the kingdom of God motif, says Senior.

1. soteriological: the kingdom is intended to rescue people from an intolerable situation.
2. theological: the kingdom reveals Israel's image of God. God cares enough to come and save Israel. God cares about the lives of the people.
3. eschatological: the final history is at hand.
4. community: the kingdom is a community effort. Individuals cannot experience the reign of God in isolation. Israel was a community. The transformation of our world was not an individual experience.[5]

---

[5]Donald Senior, "Gospel of Matthew," Workshop, Church of Our Savior, Oct. 1995.

Those who were listening to Jesus' message were experiencing the reign. The kingdom of God is now! Jesus gives the Christian the blueprint for sainthood. As we await the future heavenly glory of the heavenly Jerusalem, we live in this earthly reality. Thus, we are to be meek and clean of heart. We are to thirst after justice and hunger for righteousness. All these things lead the saints of God on their way to their final resting place where they will join all those saints who went before them. Joachim Jeremias asserts that good gospel living is sign and symptom of what happens when grace seizes a child of God. Donald Senior takes it another step. "The Beatitudes are what happens when grace seizes a child of God."

Proclaim the gospel again.

Sometimes we gain new insights when we hear the text after the interpretation has been given. Someone from the group proclaims the gospel a second time.

STEP 4
TESTING

Conversation with the Liturgy and the Scriptures

Test your original understanding in dialogue with the text.

(You might consider breaking into smaller groups.)

How does your original understanding of this story compare with what was just shared? How does this story speak to your life?

Participants share an experience from their lives that connects with the biblical interpretation just shared.

How does this liturgy challenge our community? How does it challenge me? Has our original understanding been stretched, challenged, or affirmed?

STEP 5
DECISION

The gospel demands a response.

In what way does this gospel call your parish to action in the church, parish, neighborhood, or world? Be concrete. Has this conversation with the exegesis of this liturgy changed or stretched your personal attitudes? Name one concrete action you will take this week as a response to what was learned and shared today.

DOCTRINAL ISSUES

What church truth/teaching/doctrinal issue could be drawn from the gospel for the feast of All Saints?

Participants suggest possible doctrinal themes that flow from the readings.

Possible Doctrinal Themes

Saints, eschatology, kingdom of God, soteriology

Present the doctrinal material at this time.

1. The facilitator gives input on a particular doctrinal issue of his/her prior choosing. OR
2. The group chooses a doctrinal issue from the list they created. They read together from the Doctrinal Appendix.

(The doctrinal issues are found in the Doctrinal Appendix in the back of this workbook. If you are choosing an issue from this resource, please refer to it now.)

Reflection questions centered around the chosen doctrinal theme can be found at the end of each topic in the Doctrinal Appendix. The questions are based on the five-step reflection process. If you choose a topic not included in the Doctrinal Appendix, craft your own questions according to the same five-step process.

Following the reflection questions you will be reminded to return to chapter 7, "Preparing the Catechetical Session," to assist you in crafting your own session.

Closing Prayer

Father, holy one,
we praise your glory reflected in the saints.

May we who share at this table
be filled with your love
and prepared for the joy of your kingdom,
where Jesus is Lord for ever and ever.[6]

---

[6]Solemnity of All Saints: "Prayer After Communion," *The Sacramentary.*

FEAST OF ALL SOULS (NOVEMBER 2)

INTRODUCTORY RITES

Opening Song (or Entrance Antiphon)

Just as Jesus died and rose again, so will the Father bring with him those who have died in Jesus. Just as in Adam all men die, so in Christ all will be made alive. (1 Thes 4:14; 1 Cor 15:22)[1]

Opening Prayer

The facilitator of the session may lead the prayer. Others in the group may be asked to proclaim the readings.

Let us pray
[for all our departed brothers and sisters]

Pause for silent prayer.

Merciful Father,
hear our prayers and console us.
As we renew our faith in your Son,
whom you raised from the dead,
strengthen our hope that all our departed brothers and sisters
will share in his resurrection,
who lives and reigns with you and the Holy
Spirit,
one God, for ever and ever.[2]

LITURGY OF THE WORD

The Readings

There are no set readings for today's liturgy. The Lectionary refers us to the readings for the masses for the dead. Any of the readings from the vast repertoire may be chosen. The large number of readings shed light on and reflect the inexhaustible meaning of death. The scriptures tell the story of past communities who struggled with the pain of death and thereby appropriated meaning for their lives. The word of God is a living word that has relevance today as similar communities struggle with similar issues. Scriptures "demonstrate how revelation can and must be constantly read in light of everyday life and the thought of people of all races and cultures. In this way, Scripture appears as a powerful and sure contribution to progress of thought, offering always new perspectives and lighting up its way."[3]

With nearly fifty different scripture passages included in masses for the dead, there is not sufficient space to provide an exegesis for all of them. It is important, however, to be aware of their purpose.

The Old Testament readings reveal the mystery of death as understood by believers five centuries before the birth of Jesus. These readings reflect the yearnings, questions, and queries of believers of those ancient times, the answers they received, and the meaning they were able to appropriate from their searching inquiries. The same questions are still asked today. Reflection on the Old Testament readings helps us understand how our ancestors grappled with the same questions about death that we ask today.

The psalms provide us with a timeless prayer book. Centuries of previous generations have been strengthened, consoled, encouraged, and exhorted by their use. Jewish and Christian faith have been nourished by the psalms. The psalms are always relevant. They reflect the longing, aching, and supplication of the human heart. They speak in honest, direct, and frank terms. They are so filled with faith and trust that they hold us up when we are tempted to despair in the midst of sorrow and pain. The healing words of the psalms console us and give us the courage to speak to God in words that we might be afraid to utter. The psalms connect us with others who have cried the same tears and suffered the same anguish. They also give us the means of direct dialogue with a God who is with us in the struggles of our everyday life.

---

[1]All Souls Day: "Entrance Antiphon," *The Sacramentary*.
[2]All Souls Day: "Opening Prayer," *The Sacramentary*.

[3]*DL* (VII), 260.

The New Testament writings include the Acts of the Apostles, the apostolic letters, and the book of Revelation. The Acts of the Apostles reflects the good news, the Christian kerygma, as proclaimed by the first Christian community. The apostolic letters are letters of encouragement written to early Christian communities who struggled with living the gospel in light of the Christ event. The letters were written to guide the faith of those first communities. The book of Revelation is a prophetic book that gives us a look at the last days and the fulfillment of the reign of Jesus Christ, the messiah. The New Testament readings in the masses for the dead are from these three literary genres. "Each one of these twenty-four texts takes up the central message of the preaching of the apostles while emphasizing one or more particular points, sometimes giving more concrete consequences of the basics of faith as proclaimed by the apostles."[4]

The gospels, beginning with Mark (ca. 64–69 C.E.) and ending with John (end of the first century), are witnesses to the life and mystery of Jesus Christ. They tell the story of his life, his teaching, and his saving actions. The evangelists were not seeking to produce historically accurate biographies, but rather to express the living faith of communities who experienced Christ and were brought to faith as a result of their experience. The gospel proclaims the good news of his life and mission. The one central message of the gospel is the paschal mystery: the life, passion, death, resurrection, ascension into glory and coming of the Spirit of Jesus Christ.

Jesus is the source of happiness. In the midst of despair, he is reason for hope. Jesus offers the human soul joy in the midst of suffering. Jesus came to save us all. He is the good shepherd who knows his sheep by name and gathers them all together to be with him. Jesus died and went to prepare a place for all of us who will one day join him and his Father in eternity.

Jesus broke the chains of death once and for all when he died on the cross. He understood death. Jesus knew that he had to die and that his death would bring about his glorification; yet he still suffered untold anguish. The human Christ gives the human race the hope to endure. Jesus suffered

and cried out. In our anguish we are consoled by the suffering Christ who conquered death in order for us to live eternally with him. The gospels for the masses for the dead express essential truths revealed either through Jesus' teaching or his actions. The mystery of death is laid before us and hope is placed in its path through reflection on the gospels for this day.

Liturgical Context

The pagans of antiquity kept memorials of dead relatives. Christians retained the practice of remembering their dead as long as it was consonant with their Christian faith. There is evidence of a celebration commemorating deceased relatives as early as the second century. The dead were prayed for and a mass was celebrated. The custom of the early church was to celebrate a remembrance of the deceased person three days after burial and on the one-year anniversary of the person's death. A later practice included an observance seven days following burial and then thirty and forty days after that.

In the seventh century, Bishop Isodore of Seville began a yearly commemoration of the souls of the dead. He ordered his monks to celebrate mass for this purpose on the day after Pentecost. By the ninth century the practice had spread and an office of the dead was added to the liturgy of the hours on the feast of All Saints.

In 998 "All Souls Day" was established when Abbot Odo of Cluny ordered that all monasteries celebrate a festal memorial of all the faithful departed. The practice spread but was not accepted in Rome until the thirteenth century.

Previously, if All Souls Day occurred on Sunday, the readings for the Sunday were given precedence. However, in the revised Roman Missal of 1970, the All Souls Day readings are given precedence. The missal provides three sets of prayers for this day. Each set contains an entrance antiphon, an opening prayer, a prayer over the gifts and a post-communion prayer. There are also five prefaces from which to choose.

This liturgy is intended to highlight the paschal nature of Christian death. The paschal mystery (the life, death, resurrection and ascension) of

---

[4]Ibid., 273.

Christ is the ultimate source of our hope. Previously used texts that hinted at the fear of God's judgment were replaced with texts that express Christian faith in the resurrection. The Easter pasch is at the heart of this celebration. All Souls Day celebrates the Christian's participation in the death and resurrection of Jesus. The entrance antiphon expresses this well: "Just as Jesus died and rose again, so will the Father bring with him all those who have died in Jesus. Just as in Adam all men die, so in Christ all will be made alive." We ask in the opening prayer that our hope be strengthened that our departed brothers and sisters will share in Christ's resurrection.

The ritual prayers reveal for us the church's perspective in relation to death, dying, and life after death. Any reflection on All Souls Day would necessarily require that the ritual texts from the liturgy of this day be prayed and reflected upon.

DOCTRINAL ISSUES

What church truth/teaching/doctrinal issue could be drawn from the celebration of All Souls Day?

Possible Doctrinal Themes

Death, eschatology, resurrection of the dead, heaven

Closing Prayer

Lord God,
may the death and resurrection of Christ
which we celebrate in this eucharist
bring the departed faithful to the peace of your
     eternal home.
We ask this in the name of Jesus.[5]

---

[5]All Souls Day: "Prayer After Communion," *The Sacramentary*.

Feast of the Dedication of the Basilica of St. John Lateran (November 9)

INTRODUCTORY RITES

Opening Song (or Entrance Antiphon)

Greatly to be feared is God in his sanctuary; he, the God of Israel, gives power and strength to his people. Blessed be God! (Ps 67:36)[1]

Opening Prayer

The facilitator of the session may lead the prayer. Others in the group may be asked to proclaim the readings.

God our Father,
from living stones, your chosen people,
you built an eternal temple to your glory.
Increase the spiritual gifts you have given to your
    Church,
so that your faithful people may continue to grow
into the new and eternal Jerusalem.
We ask this through our Lord Jesus Christ, your
    Son,
who lives and reigns with you and the Holy Spirit,
one God, for ever and ever.[2]

The Readings

The readings for today's liturgy are taken from the Commons of the Dedication of a Church.

Liturgical Context

The Basilica of St. John Lateran is the cathedral of the diocese of Rome. The pope is the bishop of this church. The name Lateran is derived from the reign of the Laterani family. The edict of Milan brought an end to persecution and Christianity became the official state religion. Older churches were refurbished and new ones were built. Emperor Constantine gave the Lateran

palace and the surrounding property to the Church of Rome. He had a church built on the grounds in 324. On November 9 Pope Sylvester I dedicated the new basilica built on the site that had once housed the imperial guard. He dedicated the basilica to the Holy Redeemer. It was damaged by earthquakes in the fourth and especially the tenth centuries and was rebuilt by Sergius III (904–911).

Since the twelfth century the second titular patron of the basilica has been St. John the Baptist. Later, St. John the Evangelist was also associated with the basilica. This is why it is referred to as St. John Lateran.

The palace was the home of the bishop up until 1304 when Pope Benedict XI was forced to leave Rome because of political uprisings. His successors made Avignon their residence until 1377. During this time the Lateran palace was unused. During Nicholas V's term as pope, the church offices were moved to the Vatican. However, the Basilica of the Lateran has always been the cathedral church of the bishop of Rome, the pope. The basilica of the Lateran was damaged by fire in 1308 and again in 1361. Pope Benedict XIII consecrated it in 1726. It has since been under constant reconstruction and renovation. Clement XII (1730–1740) had an inscription placed on the basilica: this church is "Mother and Head of all the churches of the City and the world." The annual commemoration of the dedication spread throughout the church as a result of the efforts of the Augustinian hermits.

This feast holds great importance because the Basilica of St. John Lateran is the cathedral of the universal church. The cathedral is a symbol of the unity of the church gathered around its bishop. The bishop of Rome is responsible for the unity of his own diocese and the entire church. Thus, the cathedral of Rome has great significance for the entire church. "Celebrating the anniversary of the cathedral that is the mother of all others founded

---

[1]Common of the Dedication of a Church (A. In the Dedicated Church): "Entrance Antiphon," *The Sacramentary.*

[2]Common of the Dedication of a Church (B. Outside the Dedicated Church): "Opening Prayer A," *The Sacramentary.*

down through the ages is to celebrate the Lord, who founded his Church in order to gather together in unity, under the crozier of Peter and his successors, all the children of God, wherever they may live."[3]

The celebration of the anniversary of the dedication of the Lateran Basilica expresses the unity of all local parish churches with the universal Church of Rome, founded by Peter and Paul. The pope, as head of the college of bishops "presides over the charity of all the Churches throughout the world."[4]

Churches elegant and churches humble are living testament to the presence of God and the faith of those who built them. We are to remember that the people are the living stones upon which the church is built. It is the only church that will live on at the end of time—the church as people of God.

DOCTRINAL ISSUES

What church truth/teaching/doctrinal issue could be drawn from the gospel for feast of the Dedication of St. John Lateran?

Possible Doctrinal Themes

Mystery of the church

Closing Prayer

Father,
you called your people to be your Church.
As we gather together in your name,
may we love, honor, and follow you
to eternal life in the kingdom you promise.
Grant this through our Lord Jesus Christ, your
    Son
who lives and reigns with you and the Holy Spirit,
one God, for ever and ever.[5]

---

[3]*DL* (VII), 280.

[4]Ibid., 290.

[5]Common of the Dedication of a Church (B. Outside the Dedicated Church): "Opening Prayer B," *The Sacramentary.*

SOLEMNITY OF THE IMMACULATE CONCEPTION (DECEMBER 8)

INTRODUCTORY RITES

Opening Song (or Entrance Antiphon)

I exult for joy in the Lord, my soul rejoices in my God; for he has clothed me in the garment of salvation and robed me in the cloak of justice, like a bride adorned with her jewels. (Is 61:10)[1]

Opening Prayer

The facilitator of the session may lead the prayer. Others in the group may be asked to proclaim the readings.

Let us pray
[that through the prayers of the sinless
Virgin Mary, God will free us from our sins]

 Pause for silent prayer.

Father,
you prepared the Virgin Mary
to be worthy mother of your Son.
You let her share beforehand
in the salvation Christ would bring
by his death,
and kept her sinless from the first
moment of her conception.
Help us by her prayers
to live in your presence without sin.
We ask this through our Lord Jesus Christ, your
  Son,
who lives and reigns with you and the Holy
  Spirit,
one God, for ever and ever.[2]

LITURGY OF THE WORD

Let us listen to God's word.

The readings are proclaimed.

---

[1]Solemnity of the Immaculate Conception: "Entrance Antiphon," *The Sacramentary.*

[2]Solemnity of the Immaculate Conception: "Opening Prayer," *The Sacramentary.*

First Reading
Genesis 3:9–15, 20

The sages of Israel meditated on the relationship between God and the sinner and the nature of sin. Their reflection was based on their historical experience of God and God's people. Israel understood misfortune to be punishment for sin. When they lived outside the law, tragedy befell them. However, even when God punished them, he loved them, offered forgiveness, and promised them future blessing. The very first telling of this story of grace and sin takes place in today's story of Adam and Eve in the garden. This is the first fall from grace into sin.

Sin is an act of rebellion on the part of the created person who believes he or she can survive without God. Sin cuts the person off from God. Today's story depicts two human beings who enjoyed trusted freedom with their Creator. They chose to rebel and thus became afraid of their Creator. Awareness of nudity was a sign of their poverty and lack of protection against destruction. Sin caused a lack of communion with God. This lack of communion caused dissension between Adam and Eve.

We are given no information about the serpent who tempted Eve. The serpent was sentenced to a life of crawling on his belly because of his evil action. The serpent will continue to do battle with the human race, but he will not be victorious. He will be destroyed by the offspring of the woman. "St. Jerome's (ca. 342–420) Latin translates the Hebrew neuter with a feminine pronoun. . . . It is a daughter of the woman, a new Eve, who will crush the head of the serpent."[3] This interpretation probably was not the original intent of the author of Genesis, but Christian tradition has interpreted the story in light of the Christ event.

Christian tradition understands Jesus as the new Adam who conquered sin and brought salvation.

---

[3]*DL* (VII), 300.

Mary is the new Eve, the mother of the Savior, whose victory was foretold after the fall. The Genesis reading sheds light on the mystery celebrated in this solemnity.

Responsorial Psalm
Psalm 98:1, 2–3, 3–4

Sing to the Lord a new song, for he has done marvelous deeds.

Second Reading
Ephesians 1:3–6, 11–12

The letter to the Ephesians begins with a liturgical prayer of thanksgiving. Its subject is God's plan of salvation, hidden throughout time, fulfilled in the person of Christ and revealed to all believers. Today's pericope refers especially to the Virgin Mary who was chosen beforetime to bear the Christ and to be holy in the sight of God. The apostle celebrates the work of salvation already accomplished by God through Jesus and in the Spirit. Ephesians asserts that we are chosen by God to be holy and without blemish. We are his adopted children and salvation is initiated solely through the love of God. Jesus was also part of the decision. With the Father, Jesus chose the human race for salvation just as he chose Israel as his own.

If we are so chosen, how much more, then, is Mary, the mother of Christ, chosen and blameless in the eyes of God. She is the perfect model of holiness for us.

Gospel
Luke 1:26–38

The angel appeared to Mary to tell her that she would conceive and bear a son.

STEP 1
NAMING ONE'S EXPERIENCE

What were your first impressions? What was your first response? What grabbed your attention? How did you feel?

Each person names his or her initial impression. Statements should be brief. No reasons should be given at this time. All simply listen without agreeing or disagreeing.

STEP 2
UNDERSTANDING

In a brief statement, what do you think this gospel is trying to convey?

STEP 3
INPUT FROM VISION/STORY/TRADITION

Liturgical Context

This feast celebrates the dogma that Mary was free from original sin from the first moment of her existence. Pope Pius XII promulgated the papal bull *Ineffabilis Deus* on December 8, 1854. The feast is still celebrated on this date. The doctrine of the Immaculate Conception holds that through the grace of God and the saving action of Christ, Mary was free from sin from the moment of her conception. Mary was born free of original sin.

While the Immaculate Conception is not found explicitly in scripture, there are texts that support it, such as today's Lectionary readings: victory over the serpent (Gn 3:15) and the angel's salutation to Mary as full of grace (Lk 1:28).

Special devotion to Mary that included a recognition of the uniqueness of her conception began around the seventh century in the East. In the twelfth century a feast in honor of the Immaculate Conception was celebrated in England.

However, controversy over the doctrine grew. Theologians such as Anselm, Bernard, Aquinas, and Bonaventure attested to Mary's sanctification in the womb, but they argued that she had to be affected by original sin even if for only a moment in order to be a recipient of Christ's redeeming grace. These objections were resolved by Duns Scotus (d. 1308) who asserted that Christ saves in two ways. "In one, he rescues from sin those already fallen. In the other, he preserves someone from being touched by sin even for an instant."[4] The Council of Trent (1545–1563) purposely

---

[4]Richard P. McBrien, "The Immaculate Conception," in *HCEC*, 655.

eliminated Mary from the doctrine on original sin. It asserted that she was sin-free her entire life. In 1846 the United States bishops named Mary in her Immaculate Conception as patroness of the country.

This feast is christological in that it centers on the salvation offered for sinful humanity. Jesus suffered, died, and was buried for the sins of the world. The doctrine of the Immaculate Conception celebrates Christ's victory over the evil powers of the world at Mary's conception. "In her very being, through the mercy of God, the grip of evil is broken. To the Catholic imagination it is fitting that grace be freely given to her from the first moment of her existence because of her role in being the faith-filled mother of Jesus. Her yes to God brought Christ into the world, through whom the ancient sin of Adam and Eve is overturned."[5] This feast reminds us that grace is freely given and is more powerful than sin.

We are not to lose sight of the season in which this celebration is situated. "During Advent the liturgy frequently brings Mary to mind. On 8 December the solemnity of the Immaculate Conception recalls the preparation for the Savior's coming at its origins (See Is 11:1 and 10) and also the happy beginning of the Church in its beauty without spot or wrinkle."[6]

Gospel Exegesis

The facilitator gives input regarding what critical biblical scholarship has to say about this text. The input includes insights as to how people would have heard the gospel in Jesus' time.

Luke's concern in this pericope is the unusual circumstance surrounding Jesus' conception. Verse 35 asserts that Jesus would be the promised Davidic Messiah, thus the meaning of Jesus' name: "Yahweh saves." Jesus was conceived through the power of the Holy Spirit in the womb of Mary and thus is the Son of God. Jesus' birth of the virgin Mary is evidence of his humanity.

St. Augustine developed this theology when he asserted that all people are sinful because of original sin. All people need Christ's salvation. We are all heirs of original sin because of sexual generation. Christ as Savior was sinless and did not inherit original sin. Thus, Jesus could not have become human through sexual procreation. When Christ was conceived by the Holy Spirit he avoided the stain of original sin and was sinless Savior of the world.

In Greco-Roman literature the hero's greatness was often explained by a story of the hero's miraculous conception. "Jesus was what he was because he was divinely begotten."[7]

One emphasis in Luke/Acts is that Jesus descended from the Davidic monarchy and is the fulfillment of messianic Jewish prophecy. Through the paschal mystery Jesus is the glorified, exalted Son of God who sits at the right hand of his Father. Christ rules from his Father's right hand and intercedes for the people. Through the power of divine intervention (miraculous conception) Jesus was Savior of the world: he lived, suffered, died, rose again, and ascended to sit at the right hand of his Father's throne.

Proclaim the gospel again.

Sometimes we gain new insights when we hear the text after the interpretation has been given. Someone from the group proclaims the gospel a second time.

STEP 4
TESTING

Conversation with the Liturgy and the Scriptures

Test your original understanding in dialogue with the text.

(You might consider breaking into smaller groups.)

Were there any new insights? Was there anything you had not considered before? How does your original understanding of this story compare with

---

[5]Ibid., 656.

[6]*DOL*, #467, Section 4, Sanctoral Cycle: A. Mary, #3901, #3, 1207.

[7]*RL*, 20.

what was just shared? How does this story speak to your life?

Participants share an experience from their lives that connects with the biblical interpretation just shared.

What was Luke trying to tell his community? What does he have to say to our community and to me today? Do we still feel the same way about this text as we did when we began? Has our original understanding been stretched, challenged, or affirmed?

STEP 5
DECISION

The gospel demands a response.

In what way does this gospel call your parish to action in the church, parish, neighborhood, or world? Be concrete. What are you called to do in response? Name one concrete action you will take this week as a response to what was learned and shared today.

DOCTRINAL ISSUES

What church truth/teaching/doctrinal issue could be drawn from the gospel for the feast of the Immaculate Conception?

Participants suggest possible doctrinal themes that flow from the readings.

Possible Doctrinal Themes

Immaculate Conception of Mary

Present the doctrinal material at this time.

1. The facilitator gives input on a particular doctrinal issue of his/her prior choosing. OR
2. The group chooses a doctrinal issue from the list they created. They read together from the Doctrinal Appendix.

(The doctrinal issues are found in the Doctrinal Appendix in the back of this workbook. If you are choosing an issue from this resource, please refer to it now.)

Reflection questions centered around the chosen doctrinal theme can be found at the end of each topic in the Doctrinal Appendix. The questions are based on the five-step reflection process. If you choose a topic not included in the Doctrinal Appendix, craft your own questions according to the same five-step process.

Following the reflection questions you will be reminded to return to chapter 7, "Preparing the Catechetical Session," to assist you in crafting your own session.

Closing Prayer

Born of the Blessed Virgin Mary,
the Son of God redeemed mankind.
May he enrich you with his blessings.
    Response: Amen.

You received the author of life through Mary.
May you always rejoice in her loving care.
    Response: Amen.

You have come to rejoice at Mary's feast.
May you be filled with the joys of the Spirit
and the gifts of your eternal home.
    Response: Amen.

May almighty God bless you,
the Father, and the Son + and the Holy Spirit.
    Response: Amen.[8]

---

[8]Solemnity of the Immaculate Conception: "Solemn Blessing Over the People," *The Sacramentary.*

DOCTRINAL APPENDIX

DOCTRINE AND THE LITURGICAL YEAR

This appendix contains doctrinal material that flows from and surfaces out of the experience of word and worship on Sunday. The church has always revered the scriptures in much the same way as it reveres the Body of Christ. The people of God are offered the bread of life at both the table of God's word and the table of the eucharist.[1]

The Second Vatican Council's document, *The Dogmatic Constitution on Divine Revelation*, asserts that sacred scripture and tradition are intimately connected. They flow from and through one another. They have the same purpose. Scripture is God communicating with human beings through human writers by the power of the Holy Spirit. Tradition provides us with the full message of God's word given to the apostles by Jesus and the Holy Spirit. Thus, all future generations are enlightened by what was handed on to us by the apostles. Through that inheritance the Spirit strengthens us to live a gospel life and spread the good news of salvation. "Therefore both sacred Tradition and sacred Scripture are to be accepted and venerated with the same sense of devotion and reverence"[2]

The church has always considered scripture and tradition to be the primary rule of faith. Theology's foundational roots hinge on the written word of God and sacred tradition. Through both, the mystery of Christ is encountered, bringing light and life to the believer. "Therefore, the 'study of the sacred page' should be very soul of sacred theology."[3]

As an introduction to this Doctrinal Appendix, basic principles regarding the core issues of tradition will be articulated once again for review. This appendix will address the central core of the church's teaching, the hierarchy of truths that comes to us from scripture and tradition that

began with the apostles and has continued through the ages. All other teachings of our faith are rooted and find meaning in those essential, primary truths. The church has many teachings that are not included in the "hierarchy of truths." This section will focus only on those that form the basis of our faith. This in no way diminishes the fact that we are to believe all that the church holds to be true. However, some truths hold more importance than others as they are foundational to all we believe.

The General Catechetical Directory asserts that "the message of salvation has a certain hierarchy of truths which the Church has always recognized when it composed creeds or summaries of the truths of the faith. Some truths of the faith are based on others as of a higher priority and are illumined by them."[4]

The hierarchy of truths is listed in both the General and National Catechetical Directory. These truths are grouped under four headings. Once again they are:

1. The mystery of God the Father, the Son, and the Holy Spirit, Creator of all things.

2. The mystery of Christ, the incarnate Word, who was born of the Virgin Mary and who suffered, died, and rose for our salvation.

3. The mystery of the Holy Spirit, who is present in the church, sanctifying it and guiding it until the glorious coming of Christ, our Savior and Judge.

4. The mystery of the church, which is Christ's Mystical Body, in which the Virgin Mary holds a preeminent place.

All other truths are informed by and in direct relation to the hierarchy of truths. These truths

---

[1] *The Dogmatic Constitution on Divine Revelation (Dei Verbum)*, in *The Documents of Vatican II,* ed. Walter M. Abbott, S.J. (New York: America Press, 1966), 125, #21.

[2] Ibid., #9.

[3] Ibid., #21, 24.

[4] General Catechetical Directory (GCD), in *The Catechetical Documents* (Chicago: Liturgy Training Publications, 1996), 33, #34.

are encountered and remembered ritually throughout the liturgical year through the Lectionary scriptures and in the feasts and seasons we celebrate.

The doctrinal issues in this appendix are thematic overviews. This chapter is not an attempt to provide a comprehensive rendering of all the articles of Catholic belief and practices. The primary sources used in this appendix are the documents of the church. All other resources provide supplemental background. We encourage you to study church documents, the rites of the church, the *Catechism of the Catholic Church,* historical context, and the related works of theologians in order to broaden your understanding.

This is not "everything you ever wanted to know about a topic." Rather, it provides a brief overview of post-biblical teaching or practice as it relates to the lived experience of past communities, flows from the gospel exegesis, and connects to the lived experience of people today. What is provided in this appendix is but a taste and is intended to provide a model that may be used to assist others in crafting doctrinal sessions not included in this workbook.

The facilitator may prepare material on a doctrinal issue or the group may choose and read together a doctrine from this appendix. The suggested themes may or may not be appropriate for each parish. It is not our intention to suggest that every parish should teach the same doctrine on a particular Sunday. Each community should decide for itself what issues of tradition are pertinent and best flow from the Sunday's readings and from the needs of the community.

This appendix will not include every doctrinal issue listed under the following list of core issues. Some of the topics are addressed within the body of the workbook, however. For example, the dominant symbols of the church are examined in the Easter Vigil section. One need only use that material in conjunction with the learning model used in these structured sessions.

The following list is a compilation of doctrinal themes that are inherent in and flow from the liturgical year.

CORE ISSUES OF FAITH IN THE LITURGICAL YEAR

Advent
Eschatology, Christ's Coming: Future, Present, Past, Son of Man, Parousia, Kingdom of God

Christmas
Incarnation, Epiphany/Manifestation, Holy Family, Christology

Lent
Renewal, Preparation, Penitence, Fasting, Conversion, Almsgiving, Practices of Prayer, Sin, Transfiguration, Grace, Providence, Soteriology

Easter Triduum
Paschal Mystery, Redemption, Vigil, Eucharist, Priesthood, Service, Justice; Dominant Symbols of the Church: Assembly, Light, Cross, Water, Oil, Laying on of Hands, Garment, Bread/Wine

Easter Season
Fifty Days, Ascension, Pentecost, Resurrection, Holy Spirit, Charisms, Ecclesiology, Discipleship, Hope

Ordinary Time
Trinity, Body and Blood of Jesus, Christian Witness, Sacraments, Death/Dying, Suffering, Beatitudes, Vocation, Moral Decision Making, Non-violence, Christian Stewardship, All Saints, All Souls, Sacred Heart, Solemnity Mary Mother of God, Assumption, Immaculate Conception, Saints, Kingdom of God

DOCTRINAL TOPICS

ADVENT

See Advent Overview.

ALL SAINTS

See Feast of All Saints.

ALL SOULS

See Feast of All Souls.

ALMSGIVING

See Lenten Overview.

ASCENSION

See Easter Overview and Feast of the Ascension.

ASSUMPTION

See Feast of the Assumption.

BAPTISM

See CHRISTIAN INITIATION: Part I—Baptism (Appendix). See Easter Vigil, Symbols of Water, Light, and Garment.

BODY AND BLOOD

See CHRISTIAN INITIATION: Eucharist (Appendix). See Easter Vigil, Symbol of Bread. See Feast of Corpus Christi.

BREAD

See Easter Vigil.

CHRISTIAN INITIATION

Through the sacrament of initiation people are freed from the power of sin and evil. They die and are buried with Christ and are raised again to new life. They receive the Spirit of adoption, making them children of God. With the entire church they celebrate the memorial of Christ's death and resurrection.

Through baptism people are incorporated in the life of Christ. They are formed as God's people and are forgiven their sins. They are elevated to the dignity of adopted children. They are a new creation in Christ through water and the Spirit, and thus are called children of God.

Christians more perfectly become the image of Christ when they are signed with the gift of the Holy Spirit in confirmation. They bear witness to Christ and strive to bring others to him.

They come to the Lord's table to eat and drink his Body and Blood so they may have eternal life and show the unity of God's people. They offer themselves with Christ, thereby sharing in his paschal mystery. They pray for an outpouring of the Holy Spirit so the human race may be brought together in unity as God's people. The three sacraments bring the faithful to full stature in Christ and empower them to carry out the mission of Christ in the church and the world.[1]

I. Baptism

Natural Sign
What is your experience of water in everyday life? How might water express something about the mystery of God? What is your present understanding of baptism? How would you articulate a definition? Complete this sentence: "Baptism is...."

Tradition: Biblical, Ecclesial, and Liturgical Signs
The sacraments of initiation (baptism, confirmation, and eucharist) free us from the power of darkness and evil. We are united to Christ and his paschal mystery, his death, burial and resurrection. We are adopted children of God by the power of the Holy Spirit and are incorporated

---

[1]Christian Initiation, *The Rites of the Catholic Church,* English translation prepared by the International Commission on English in the Liturgy (New York: Pueblo Publishing Co., 1976), p. 3, #s 1, 2.

into the Body of Christ in the celebration of the memorial of the paschal mystery—the eucharist.

"Baptism incorporates us into Christ and forms us into God's people. This first sacrament pardons all our sins, rescues us from the power of darkness, and brings us to the dignity of adopted children, a new creation through water and the Holy Spirit. Hence we are called and indeed are the children of God."[2] (See Colossians 1:13; Romans 8:15; Galatians 4:5.) The three sacraments of initiation allow us to carry out the mission of Christ in the world.

Baptism initiates us into God's reign and is the gateway to eternal life. It is the first sacrament offered by Christ who later entrusted it and his gospel to the church when he exhorted his disciples to "Go and make disciples of all the nations, and baptize them in the name of the Father, and of the Son, and of the Holy Spirit" (Mt 28:19). Through baptism, we are enlightened by the Spirit of God to live the gospel.

Baptism incorporates us into the church and into the house of God (Eph 2:22). We are made a royal priesthood. We are all united through the sacramental bond of baptism. We have been signed into this unchangeable effect through the anointing with chrism in the presence of God's people. Baptism, validly celebrated even by Christians with whom we are not in full communion, may never be repeated.[3]

Through the sign of water, baptism cleanses away every stain of sin, original and personal, and offers us a share in the life of Christ. We become his adopted children. Through the water of baptism we are reborn into Christ. The Blessed Trinity is invoked over the person who is baptized. The baptized enter into communion with the Father, the Son, and the Holy Spirit. The baptized are prepared for and led to this communion through biblical readings, the prayer of the community, and their own profession of faith in the Father, Son, and Spirit.[4]

This is all accomplished through the death and resurrection of Jesus Christ. We who are baptized are united to him in his death. We are buried with Christ and then are born again to new life in Christ. Baptism remembers and makes present the death and resurrection of Jesus, his paschal mystery. Through baptism we die to sin and are born to new life.[5] (See Ephesians 5:26, 2:5–6, 2:22; 1 Peter 2:9; 2 Peter 1:4; Romans 6:4–5, 8:15; Galatians 4–5; Titus 3:5; John 3:1, 5, 6:55; Matthew 28:19.)

Through the ritual of baptism we are anointed priest, prophet, and king. As priest we are called to serve, as prophet we are called to proclaim the good news, and as royalty we are called to lead.

Water used in baptism is to be true water, pure and clean. Immersion, a more suitable symbol denoting the death and resurrection of Christ (we go down into the waters and are buried in Christ and rise out of the waters to new life), or pouring can be used to lawfully administer the sacrament. The words for the conferral of baptism are: "I baptize you in the name of the Father, and of the Son and of the Holy Spirit."[6]

Refer to the symbol of water in the Easter Vigil chapter. A similar, separate reflection process centered around the symbol of water would be recommended and would include: natural sign of water in everyday life; biblical uses of water throughout the scriptures; ecclesial understanding of water throughout the history of the church; liturgical use of water.

Testing
Were there any new insights or clarifications? What might this doctrine have to do with my everyday life or the life of the community? What are the implications for living the Christian life?

Decision
What concrete action will I take as a result of this teaching?

Refer to chapter 7, "Preparing the Catechetical Session," if you intend to plan your catechetical session at this time.

---

[2] RCIA, #2.
[3] Ibid., #4.
[4] Ibid., #5.

---

[5] Ibid., #6.
[6] Ibid., #23.

II. Confirmation

Natural Sign

What is your experience of oil in everyday life? How does it speak to you about God? How would you explain the sacrament of confirmation?

Tradition: Biblical, Ecclesial, and Liturgical Signs

Confirmation is an initiation sacrament. The Rite of Confirmation #1 states that the baptized continue on the path of Christian initiation through the sacrament of confirmation. The joining of both baptism and confirmation signifies the unity of the paschal mystery, and the close connection between the work of the Son and the outpouring of the Holy Spirit. The Father, Son, and Spirit come to those who are baptized. Adults and children of catechetical age are to receive the sacraments of baptism, confirmation, and eucharist in a simple celebration.[7] The priest receives authority to confer confirmation at these celebrations from canon law itself.

The conferral of the Spirit at confirmation is the second stage of initiation, not a rite of passage into adulthood. Confirmation leads us more fully into our baptismal identity. Confirmation is not about ratifying an adult faith. It is the gift of the Spirit.

The initiatory character of confirmation and its connection with baptism and eucharist are based on the life, death, and resurrection of Christ. Confirmation is a sign of the paschal mystery. "This makes clear the specific importance of confirmation for sacramental initiation, by which the faithful members of the living Christ are incorporated into him and *configured* to him through baptism and through confirmation and the eucharist."[8]

One significant aspect of confirmation reform as set forth in the Apostolic Constitution or the Rite of Confirmation places the coming of the Spirit at Pentecost in center stage. The anointing with chrism is understood as having its basis in Jesus'

baptism and the outpouring of the Spirit on the disciples at Pentecost. "The descent of the Spirit at Jesus' baptism reflects a new and extraordinary vision of the pneumatic quality of baptism itself, and the intrinsic unity of the baptismal event: baptism and the outpouring of the Spirit are one mystery and sacrament."[9]

Those who are born anew in baptism receive the inexpressible Gift, the Holy Spirit himself who imparts a special strength. Confirmation, then, is closely related to eucharist. After being signed by baptism and confirmation, the faithful are then fully incorporated into the Body of Christ through participation in the eucharist. This is signified more fully in the new sacramental formula: "Be sealed with the Gift of the Holy Spirit." The Gift *is* the Spirit, not the gifts *of* the Spirit. Thus, confirmation makes us:

1. more completely the image of Christ and fills us with his Spirit so we may bear witness to him;
2. configured to Christ and strengthened by the Holy Spirit;
3. witnesses to Christ in order to build the Body of Christ in faith and love.

Confirmation so marks the recipient with the character of Christ that, like baptism, it also cannot be repeated. The seal of the Spirit marks our total being for Christ. We are forever in the service of Christ's mission and we are promised divine protection until the final day.

Confirmation completes baptism; eucharist completes initiation. It is eucharist that fully incorporates a person into the Body of Christ. Eucharist is the repeatable sacrament of initiation [Augustine]. We grow into our identity as fully initiated members of the Body of Christ through our sharing in the eucharist. Confirmation takes place within mass in order to stress the fundamental connection between confirmation and Christian initiation that culminates in the communion of Christ's Body and Blood. "Thus, even when confirmation is celebrated after first communion, the initiatory identity of Eucharist as the sacrament

---

[7]National Statutes of the RCIA, #14.

[8]"Rite of Confirmation—Apostolic Constitution," *The Rites of the Catholic Church*, English translation prepared by the International Commission on English in the Liturgy (New York: Pueblo Publishing Co., 1976), 290–297.

[9]Linda Gaupin, CDP, Ph.D., Specialized Certification for Sacramental Catechesis (Diocese of Orlando, Fla., 1996–1997), unpublished course text, 7.

which completes initiation should be maintained."[10]

Confirmation, therefore, is not an occasion of personal commitment to an adult faith. It is not a rite of adult passage, nor is it a sacrament of maturity. "Although Confirmation is sometimes called the 'sacrament of Christian maturity,' we must not confuse adult faith with the adult age of natural growth, nor forget that the baptismal grace is a grace of free, unmerited election and does not need 'ratification' to become effective."[11]

"Some are teaching that the main reason for the Rite of Baptism for Children is that infants be allowed at some point to accept for themselves the faith. That is where confirmation comes in. Response: This is pure fantasy. The rite says no such thing. Some are teaching that confirmation 'assists the transition into adult faith . . . it develops experiences of faith based upon both the individual and the community.' Response: This is the purpose of the eucharist."[12]

The sacrament of confirmation is conferred by anointing the candidates with chrism on the forehead and saying the words: "Receive the Gift of the Holy Spirit." *The anointing with chrism represents the apostolic laying on of hands and the anointing with the Holy Spirit.* The laying on of hands and accompanying prayer prior to the anointing with chrism does not belong to the substance of the rite yet it is to be held in high regard.

Refer to the Rite of Confirmation (chapter 5, III) for the scriptural passages that taken together shed light on the celebration of this sacrament.

Refer to the symbol of oil in the Easter Vigil chapter. A similar, separate reflection process centered around the symbol of oil would be recommended and would include: natural sign of oil in everyday life; biblical uses of oil throughout the scriptures; ecclesial understanding of oil throughout the history of the church; liturgical use of oil.

Testing
Were there any new insights? How would you articulate a definition of confirmation now? Have your

original assumptions been stretched in any way? How does this doctrine of confirmation have anything to do with living everyday life?

Decision
What action will I take as a result of today's sharing?

Refer to chapter 7, "Preparing the Catechetical Session," if you intend to plan your catechetical session at this time.

III. Eucharist

Natural Sign
What is your experience of bread and wine in everyday life? How do they speak to you about the nature of God? What is your present understanding of the sacrament of eucharist?

Tradition: Biblical, Ecclesial, and Liturgical Signs
Eucharist completes initiation. Those who have been elevated to the status of royal priesthood through baptism and configured to Christ through confirmation share with the entire community in the Lord's sacrifice of Calvary through the eucharist. The eucharist ["liturgy," *Constitution on the Sacred Liturgy,* #10] is the source and summit of all we do. All catechesis, all our efforts as Christian people lead us to full and active participation in the eucharistic banquet. Eucharist is a sacrament of unity and it strengthens the Body of Christ. The eucharistic celebration is carried out in response to the mandate of Christ to "Do this in memory of me."

In the liturgy the priest prays the words of eucharistic consecration and the bread and wine are changed into the Body and Blood of Christ. Under the appearance of bread and wine, Jesus, true God and true Man, "is substantially present, in a mysterious way, under the appearance of bread and wine."[13]

It is called *eucharist* (Greek: *eucharistein, eulogein*—recollection of the Jewish blessing in praise of God's work or redemption and sanctification) as it is a ritual action of praise and thanks to God.

The paschal mystery (passion, death, and resurrection of Christ) is celebrated anew in an un-

---

[10]Ibid., 9.
[11]*CCC,* 1308.
[12]Gaupin, 9.

---

[13]"Basic Teachings for Catholic Religious Education," in *CD,* #12.

bloody manner through the ministry of the priests. This holy meal recalls and makes present the Last Supper and it celebrates the unity we share in Christ. It also looks toward our participation in the heavenly banquet.

Bread and wine, the two symbols of eucharist, are changed into Christ's Body and Blood through the invocation of the Holy Spirit. We are nourished by the Body and Blood of Christ so that we may become a people more acceptable to God and that we may be capable of greater love for God and one another.

In the celebration of the eucharist the church gathers to celebrate the presence of Christ in the Body of Christ, the eucharistic assembly, in the proclamation of the word, in the presiding celebrant, and in the eucharistic elements. "To accomplish so great a work, Christ is always present in his Church.... He is present in the sacrifice of the Mass, not only in the person of his minister...but especially under the eucharistic elements.... He is present in his word since it is Christ himself who speaks when the holy scriptures are read in the Church. He is present lastly, when the Church prays and sings, for he promised: 'Where two or more are gathered together in my name, there am I in the midst of them' (Mt. 18:20)."[14]

The eucharist is foreshadowed in the Hebrew scriptures in the gesture of the king-priest Melchizedek who offered bread and wine (Gen 14:18). Bread and wine were offered under the old covenant as a sign of grateful thanks for the harvest and the Creator's benevolence. Bread and wine were significant symbols in the Passover meal that remembered the liberation out of Egypt's bondage into the promised land (Deut 8:3). The miracle of the loaves and fishes foreshadowed the eucharist in the multiplication, breaking, and distribution of the loaves to the crowd, prefiguring "the superabundance of this unique bread of his Eucharist."[15]

Jesus left a pledge of his love by leaving a memorial of his death and resurrection and commanding his followers to repeat the ritual action of this memorial until his return. "The three synoptic Gospels and St. Paul have handed on to us the account of the institution of the Eucharist; St. John, for his part, reports the words of Jesus in the synagogue of Capernaum that prepare for the institution of the Eucharist: Christ calls himself the bread of life, come down from heaven."[16] Jesus instituted this memorial on the night before he would die and in the process gave new and definitive meaning to the Passover event: Jesus passed from this life to his Father through his death and resurrection. This new Passover is anticipated in the eucharist that fulfilled the Passover of the old covenant and anticipates the last Passover of the entire church at the end of the age.[17]

The eucharist, center of the church's life, proclaims the paschal mystery of Christ and makes it present. The eucharist strengthens the community of believers as they embrace the cross and move forward to their final destination in heaven, where all the "elect will be seated at the table of the kingdom."[18]

Eucharist initiates conversion again and again. It invites and causes transformation. The bread is taken, blessed, broken, and shared; we too are taken, blessed, broken, and shared and in that way participate in the paschal mystery of Jesus. Eucharist strengthens our union in Christ, forgives our sins, makes us church, and empowers us to do good, promote the gospel, and serve the needs of the world. "Eucharist commits us to the poor."[19]

Refer to the symbols of bread and wine in the Easter Vigil chapter. A similar, separate reflection process centered around the symbols of bread and wine would be recommended and would include: natural signs of bread and wine in everyday life; biblical uses of bread and wine throughout the scriptures; ecclesial understanding of symbols of bread and wine throughout the history of the church; liturgical use of bread and wine.

Testing
Were there any new insights? How would you now finish this sentence: "Eucharist is..."?
What are the implications for living Christian life?
What is the challenge of eucharist?

---

[14]*CSL*, in *TLD*, #7.
[15]*CCC*, #1335.

[16]Ibid., #1338.
[17]Ibid., #1339–1340.
[18]Ibid., #1344.
[19]Ibid., #1397.

Decision
What am I/we going to do about it? What response am I going to make?

Refer to chapter 7, "Preparing the Catechetical Session," if you intend to plan your catechetical session at this time.

CHRISTMAS

See Overview of Christmas and the Sundays of the Christmas Season.

CHRISTOLOGY

See JESUS (Appendix).

CHURCH, MYSTERY OF

Natural Sign
Have you ever had an experience of being part of a community other than your church community? What were the things that attracted you to this community? Did you ever have the sense that a community you were part of possessed corporate power?

One of the first symbols of God's presence in the world is the church. There are many interchangeable terms for church—community, church, people of God, assembly—but they are all the same reality. God is present to the world through the visible, tangible sign of God's love, the church. "As a divine reality inserted into human history, the Church is a kind of sacrament. Its unique relationship with Christ makes it both sign and instrument of God's unfathomable union with humanity and of the unity of human beings among themselves. Part of the Church's mission is to lead people to a deeper understanding of human nature and destiny and to provide them with more profound experiences of God's presence in human affairs."[20]

Tradition: Biblical, Ecclesial, and Liturgical Signs
Please refer to Easter Vigil: Symbol of Church (p. 232), for information regarding the biblical understanding of church/community and for further historical elaboration.

---

[20]*NCD,* #63.

The Second Vatican Council redefined our understanding of church. The following principles are a summary of our theology as articulated in *Sharing the Light of Faith: The National Catechetical Directory.* "The Church is a mystery. It is a reality imbued with the hidden presence of God (From Pope Paul VI's opening allocution at the second session [September 19, 1963]." The Church is a gift coming from the love of God, Christ's redeeming action and the power of the Holy Spirit (National Catechetical Directory [NCD], #63). "As a divine reality inserted into human history, the Church is a kind of sacrament. Its unique relationship with Christ makes it both a sign and instrument of God's unfathomable union with humanity and of the unity of human beings among themselves" (NCD, #63). "...As a mystery, the Church cannot be totally understood or fully defined. Its nature and mission are best captured in scriptural parables and images, taken from ordinary life, which not only express truth about its nature but challenge the Church: for example, to become more a People of God, a better servant, more faithful and holy, more united around the teaching authority of the hierarchy" (NCD, #63).

The church is a community of believers, the people of God. We are called to become a new people, a royal priesthood, a people claimed by God to proclaim the greatness of God (1 Pet 2:9). Jesus freed us from sin and because of the saving waters of baptism we are called to believe, worship, and witness to his saving works.

We are one body in Christ (Rom 12:5). Through Jesus' death, resurrection, and glorification, he remains a living presence and head of his church, of which we are all members. *We celebrate this identity most especially in the eucharist.* Through the eucharist, we become the Body and Blood of Christ.

The church is servant and has a mission to heal and reconcile as Jesus did. The church is to live the gospel through the works of mercy, assisting the needy or anyone who is in need of our help. The church as servant acts out of love and concern, not for personal glory. One way the church is servant is through its teaching ministry in which it witnesses to the gospel and the power of God in the world.

The church is a sign of the reign of God. The church is evidence that God is alive in our midst.

In order to be that sign, the church "must be committed to justice, love and peace, to grace and holiness, truth and life, for these are the hallmarks of the kingdom of God" (NCD, #67).

The church is a pilgrim church. Aware of its sins, the church journeys to its final destination as it repents and overcomes patiently the trials and tribulations that come its way. In this way it demonstrates its steadfast faithfulness to the world.

"As mystery, people, one body in Christ, servant, sign of the kingdom, and pilgrim, the Church is conceived as God's family, whose members are united to Christ and led by the Spirit in their journey to the Father. The Church merits our prayerful reflection and wholehearted response" (NCD, # 68).

The church is one, holy catholic and apostolic. Unity is the substance of the church and is based on the unity of the Trinity. While unified, the church is diverse; this is expressed by the various liturgical rites within the church such as Catholic Coptic Rite, Ethiopian Rite, etc.

We express our unity through a profession of faith, apostolic succession, and the communal celebration of worship, especially the sacraments. Heresy, apostasy, and schism wound the unity of the church. The Catholic Church shares baptism, scripture, belief in the Trinity, and some sacraments with some ecclesial communities; it shares devotion to Mary, Mother of God, and some common liturgical texts with other ecclesial communities.

The symbol of church as people of God is a primary symbol in the liturgy. The gathered community is a sign of God's presence in our midst. Before the book is opened or the bread shared, God is experienced in the community. "For these people are the people of God, purchased by Christ's blood, gathered together by the Lord, nourished by the word. They are a people called to offer God the prayers of the entire human family, a people giving thanks in Christ for the mystery of salvation by offering his sacrifice. Finally, they are a people growing together into unity by sharing Christ's Body and Blood. These people are holy by their origin, but becoming ever more holy by conscious, active and fruitful participation in the mystery of the eucharist."[21] In every liturgical celebration the community is a primary experience of God's presence. We profess the mystery of the church in our ritual prayers and the creed, and through the eucharist we live its reality. Through all the ministries of the church, Christ is present. Thus, when the people participate and celebrate, the lector proclaims, the priest presides, the eucharistic minister serves, the cantor sings, the hospitality people welcome, etc., Christ is made manifest in our midst.

The church is a priestly, prophetic, and royal people. Through baptism and faith in God the church shares Christ's priestly role as leader. The church is consecrated a holy priesthood and a spiritual house. The church shares the prophetic ministry as it witnesses to God's reign in the world. The church is royal in its ministry of service to the poor and the needs of the world.

Testing
Are there any new insights? Have any of your original assumptions about church been stretched or affirmed? Does this teaching about church resonate with your experience of church in your own community? What are the areas of death/resurrection? What are some specific areas that are in need of growth?

Decision
What is the challenge and what action will I take as a result of this teaching on the mystery of the church?

Refer to chapter 7, "Preparing the Catechetical Session," if you intend to plan your catechetical session at this time.

CONFIRMATION

See CHRISTIAN INITIATION: Part II—Confirmation (Appendix). See Easter Vigil, Symbol of Oil.

CONVERSION

Natural Sign
Have you ever experienced making a change in direction in the course of your life? Have you ever changed your thinking or pattern of behavior?

---

[21] *GIRM*, in *TLD*, #5.

What prompted these changes? What did you learn from these experiences?

Tradition: Biblical, Ecclesial, and Liturgical Signs

The Sundays of Lent, in fact the entire liturgical year, invite us to embark on a journey of deep conversion. Since *conversion* is a word that is bounced around a great deal in evangelical parlance, it might be a beneficial exercise to explore the biblical understanding of conversion as we embark on the journey into its heart and spirit. In modern usage, conversion often refers to an event—a "born-again" experience of faith in Jesus Christ. "It boils down to a singular experience of being born again in Jesus Christ on a given occasion. It entails becoming a Christian and being saved on a given occasion."[22] This narrow vision helps the recipients of this one-time event to distance themselves from conversion's ongoing imperative. "It is usually 'other people' who need to heed the message. It is seldom directed inwardly to ourselves and even less to a call to societal or ecclesial change."[23] Ronald Wintherop cites a study by Beverly Roberts Gaventa (1986) in which she notes "three categories of personal change which are found in the NT: alternation, conversion, and transformation. She notes that the distinctions are not mutually exclusive, yet are distinctive enough for the following separate descriptions: 'Alternation is a relatively limited form of change that develops from one's previous behavior; conversion is a radical change in which past affiliations are rejected for some new commitment and identity; transformation is also a radical change, but one in which an altered perception reinterprets both past and present' (1986:12)."[24]

Conversion involves some form of change. Conversion is fluid, moving, and dynamic. When the Hebrew Scriptures refer to the human person they bespeak a united wholeness. The human being is not separated into body and spirit as in later Greek anthropology. The perspective of conversion in the scriptures involves the action of the whole person—body, mind, and spirit. Someone in need of conversion is a person who is in dire need of a change in direction for the course of his or her life. So great is their need that they are to stop dead in their tracks, make an about-face, and turn in the opposite direction from their original course. A big change—a monumental change!

Another interesting concept of conversion in the Hebrew Scriptures (OT) is the conversion of God. How presumptuous can we get? God in need of conversion? Not at all. Yet God repeatedly made changes in his course. God changed his plans and his direction as an act of love. God repented. "If you remain quietly in this land I will build you up, and not tear you down; I will plant you, not uproot you; for I regret the evil I have done you (Jer 42:10)." "From the OT perspective, then, God is a God of change and of integrity, one who can set limits on relating to the world and yet who can also have a change of heart when deemed appropriate."[25] God gives us the perfect model of conversion and repentance. If God can change his heart, then we in turn can do no less.

According to scriptural perspective, true repentance can only be accomplished through the grace of God. Human beings, in and of themselves, are incapable of true repentance. God will accomplish the repentance of his people by divine initiative; it will not be accomplished by human design.

Conversion in the Old Testament is often accompanied by "symbolic gestures and rituals."[26] The most observable ritual is the use of ritual cleansing, also prominent in the NT. Ezekiel's proclamation of God's sprinkling clean water upon Israel while offering a new heart, in place of Israel's stony heart, is indicative of Israel's ritual celebration of God's covenant and the ongoing journey of conversion with the People of God.

The New Testament understands conversion in terms of *metanoia* (change in one's mind and direction) and *epistrepho* (change in direction—a turning away from or toward). Conversion presupposes remorse for one's actions and is an act of repentance. As in the Old Testament, *conversion* involves a change in one's life and a turning toward God. "Whenever the nominal form of the word is used (twenty-two times in the NT), it is always in

---

[22] *CNT*, 4.
[23] Ibid., 5.
[24] Ibid., 6.

[25] Ibid., 14.
[26] Ibid., 15.

the singular rather than the plural form. This usage emphasizes conversion as a process rather than a once-for-all-time action."[27]

Both Testaments have spoken definitively on the issue of conversion. It is not a one-time event. It is always a movement either toward something or away from something. The primary perspective of the NT is turning away from sin and a turning toward God and Jesus.

Conversion in the Gospel of Matthew picks up the same theme that Mark develops: conversion goes hand-in-hand with faith and discipleship. However, Matthew nuances it even further. Matthew connects conversion with "bearing good fruit." True conversion will be evidenced in the fruit that it bears. From Matthew's perspective, "people reap exactly what they sow. . . . Matthew has a great concern that interior motivation be matched by exterior reality."[28]

Matthew insists that conversion involves an ethical response. It involves a personal choice with attached consequences. Conversion leads to salvation. Matthew ultimately embraces scripture's common understanding of conversion—a turning away from sin and foolishness and a turning toward God and new life.

Luke personalizes conversion. Rather than simply a call to the people or a nation, as in the OT, Luke insists on individual conversion. Luke's understanding of conversion has its basis in the mercy of God. Luke believed that conversion, repentance, forgiveness, and reconciliation pour forth from the free-flowing fountain of God's mercy. Luke's understanding of conversion, reconciliation, and the mercy of God is the cornerstone upon which our contemporary theology of the sacrament of reconciliation is built. Rather than an extended meditation on sin, the sacrament celebrates the fount of grace at the hands of our merciful God.

The *Constitution on the Sacred Liturgy* understands conversion as a call to faith in Jesus Christ. In the *Decree on the Church's Missionary Activity*, the Second Vatican Council asserted that conversion involves

awareness of being delivered from sin and led into the mystery of God's love (#13) and a personal relationship with him. The decree describes conversion as a spiritual journey, a process in which a person is gradually and progressively changed. Following the lead of scripture, the church understands conversion as a process, a journey, a change in outlook, behavior, and life. "When man accepts the Spirit of Christ, he establishes *a way of life* that is totally new and gratuitous."[29] Conversion is a turning toward or a return to God with our whole being. Conversion desires an end to sin and is a turning away from evil, "with repugnance toward the evil actions we have committed."[30] Conversion involves the commitment to change one's life, while trusting in the grace and mercy of God to accomplish the task.[31]

The liturgy invites conversion. Every liturgy—every sacrament—is a call to continued growth in Christ and participation in his life, death, and resurrection. Sacraments "not only presuppose faith, but by words and objects they also nourish, strengthen and express it. . . ."[32] "They do indeed impart grace but, in addition, the very act of celebrating them disposes the faithful most effectively to receive this grace in a *fruitful manner, to worship God duly and to practice charity* [italics mine]."[33] The liturgy assumes change and transformation. Every celebration is a call to action and ongoing growth in a person's relationship with God, one another, and the world.

Decision

How is our community in need of conversion at this time? How might I/we be challenged to be an agent of change within my/our community? In what way have I been cooperating with the grace of conversion in my life right now? What are the areas most in need of conversion and transformation at this time in my life? In what concrete way am I prompted to respond to the implications of this teaching in my family life, my work life, my parish life, or my civic and world communities?

---

[27]Ibid., 19.
[28]Ibid., 32.

---

[29]*GCD*, #60.
[30]*CCC*, 1431.
[31]Ibid.
[32]*CSL*, 59.
[33]Ibid.

Refer to chapter 7, "Preparing the Catechetical Session," if you intend to plan your catechetical session at this time.

CREATION

Natural Sign

Have you ever reflected upon the mystery of creation when gazing at a starlit sky, beholding the grandeur of a spring day, or gazing across the horizon at the beach's edge? How do such experiences speak to you about God?

Tradition: Biblical, Ecclesial, and Liturgical Signs

The creation of the world has been a fascination for peoples since the beginning of time. Ancient myths, as well as biblical themes and stories, have attempted to capture the mystery of the creation of the universe.

The Old Testament considers creation to be a primary motif or theme. God is the Creator and human beings and the world are the created. However, God is mostly described in the action of creating—not as Creator. "This creative activity is often referred to as stretching out the heavens (Is 40:22; 44:24; 45:12; 51:13), firmly establishing the earth (Ps 75:4; 93:1; 96:10; 104:5), or conquering the mythological beasts (Ps 74:13–15; 89:10f.; Is 51:9f.; Job 9:13)."[34]

Creation in the Old Testament was understood as an ordering of chaos rather than the creation of something out of nothing. This is best expressed in the creation account read at the Easter Vigil: "the world was a formless wasteland...." (Gen 1:2) God ordered creation by establishing all things in their rightful place—the water, the sky, the land, and the things contained within. The writers of Genesis probably drew upon the contemporary mythological account of creation known as *Enuma Elish*. In that account two gods were engaged in battle. One god represented chaos, the other order. Order won and chaos was defeated. The biblical authors drew upon this mythology as it shaped its own story of creation to fit Israel's monotheistic religion. God was thus understood as the warrior who restored order and took up residence in the new city, the Temple, and the

promised land where God reigns triumphant. The beginning of the world reflected the establishment of order and harmony. History and creation are intimately connected by the biblical authors. Thus, the goal of history is understood as the restoration of the perfect harmony and order that were established at the creation of the world.

Israel understood God to be the author of all creation. Israel believed that the world possessed an inherent order. To discover and live within this order resulted in peace and harmony. Those who were deemed capable of grasping this order were said to possess wisdom. If human beings were able to perceive this order through wisdom, then there must be a divine source of this order as well. Thus, wisdom and creation are intimately connected throughout scriptures. This is particularly evident in the Genesis story about the tree of knowledge of good and evil (Gen 2:9).

The creation of men and women is considered God's crowning creative achievement. "The creation of the human person is the climax of God's creative activity in this world. Made in God's likeness each person possesses a capacity for knowledge that is transcendent, love that is unselfish, and freedom for self-direction. Inherent in each unique human person called into existence by God, these qualities reflect the essential immortality of the human spirit."[35]

Biblical texts reveal nothing but praise in the face of God's grandeur in creation. All creation is called upon to worship God for the magnificence of his handiwork. The Old Testament embodies a portrait of the warrior God who, as benefactor and benevolent master of creation, chose man and woman to rule over the created order. They were chosen to live in harmony with all creation. They were in covenant relationship with God and with God's creation. They would subdue the earth and rule it. Thus, God would enter into reciprocal covenant relationship with the human race. God would provide and care for human beings. In return, human beings would love the Lord with their whole heart, body, soul, mind, and spirit. They would love one another, love themselves, and love and care for God's little ones—those who

---

[34] Dianne Bergant, C.S.A., "Creation," in *CPDBT*, 187.

[35] *NCD*, #85.

could not care for themselves. Humanity would respect and care for all of God's creation. This was understood as biblical justice.

The New Testament reflects the same images and themes inherent in the Old Testament. However, creation is understood in light of the Christ event. The New Testament perspective understands history as moving toward the culminating creation event: the paschal mystery of Jesus Christ. "Creation should be presented as directly related to the salvation accomplished by Jesus Christ. In reflecting on the doctrine of creation, one should be mindful not only of God's first action creating the heavens and the earth, but of His continuing activity in sustaining creation and working out human salvation."[36]

In the gospels, Jesus proclaims God's creative power and providence in the world. He insisted that all creation is good when he declared all foods clean (Mk 7:19). In the gospels creation is understood in terms of God's overall plan for the world. From the very beginning God's plan included the salvation of all the world.

Paul asserted Christ's role in creation, assigning to him the mediatory role of wisdom found in the Book of Proverbs. The pre-existence of Christ is hinted at throughout the scriptures. Creation comes to fullness and fulfillment through Jesus Christ. We were chosen in Christ from the very beginning of the world.

Jesus' sacrifice does not do away with the effects of sin, but humanity is heir to the final glory that awaits us. That is why all creation is said to groan in anticipation for the consummation of the created order.

St. Paul speaks of the new life of baptism in terms of "new creation." God's creative work continues in the life of Christians as they enter the waters of new birth to new life in Christ. It is the generative, creative work of God that continues in the life of baptized Christians. The old self dies and the new person puts on the new life in Christ—behavior is thus transformed. Human beings participate in the creative work of God when they enter into Jesus' ministry of reconciliation. This "new creation" through baptism assumes that the harmony established at the creation of the world is once again realized and human beings live in harmony with God, one another, and with the universe.

The fulfillment of creation will be complete at the consummation of the world when the old order will pass away and a new heaven and a new earth will be established. At that time all creation will live in glory with Christ at the right hand of God. Victory over evil will be final and complete and all creation will be eternally renewed.

Three principles have guided the church's theology of creation. First, creation is the handiwork of God. The world was created out of nothing. God alone is responsible. Evil will not win over God's creative power. Secondly, God's world is good. The litany professed in the Genesis account of creation is ultimate truth. "God saw that the world was good." The point is not to be missed. Even though sin and evil exist, the world is created good, and evil will not have the final say. In and of itself the world was not created evil. Evil entered the world after creation. Thus, creation is a gift from God and creation is good. Thirdly, God can be experienced through creation. Creation itself reveals God. Creation reveals God even before God is revealed to Israel and before God is revealed through Jesus. Creation mirrors God. Catholic Christianity affirms the sacramentality of creation.

Late in the nineteenth century, the literal account of creation was questioned due to the scientific data concerning evolution. Science and faith seemed to be at odds with each other. Science suggested that the world was epochs older than the Bible maintained. Science suggested that plants and animals inhabited the earth long before the appearance of humans. The literal account of creation was brought into serious question. Fundamentalists today still strictly adhere to the literalist view. Fundamentalism insists that the world was created four thousand years ago and took place over the span of six days. This theory is known as "creationism."[37] Creationism maintains that evolution is merely a scientific theory that cannot be proven.

---

[36]Ibid.

[37]Robert J. Schreiter, C.PP.S., "Grace: Pastoral Liturgical Tradition," in *CPDBT*, 191.

Most Christians, however, believe in the probability of evolution and hold that the creation story in Genesis is a theological rather than a historical account. The Genesis narrative is intended to show the ultimate power and authority of God, the Creator of all. The six days of creation are intended to manifest the God who brings order out of chaos and does it in orderly fashion. The theological reading serves the story without requiring one to explain all its contradictions, such as how light existed before the sun was created. Creation continues to be understood as the ongoing, dynamic action of God in creating and re-creating the world. We are in constant process. God continues to create anew. God continues to do a new thing in the lives of people.

"God manifests Himself through creation. 'Since the creation of the world, invisible realities, God's external power and divinity, have become visible, recognized through the things he has made' (Romans 1:20). The first chapter of Genesis tells us that God spoke and created all things."[38] The world was *spoken* into creation. Since the world came into being through the *Word,* "creation is a great symbol of Him."[39]

Every liturgy proclaims and heralds God's creative and generative work. Easter is understood in light of the re-creation of the world. "The joy of the resurrection renews the whole world, while the choirs of angels sing forever to your glory": (Easter Preface IV). "All things are of your making, all times and seasons obey your laws, but you chose to create man in your own image..." (Sundays in Ordinary Time V: Preface). The ongoing re-creative power of God elevates human nature to divine likeness. "Through your beloved Son you created our human family. Through him you restored us to your likeness" (Weekdays III: Preface). Every profession of faith is an odyssey of remembrance into the creative, generative power of God. It recalls the mystery of the Trinity and the genesis of salvation history. Every Rite of Sprinkling acknowledges the wonders of creation, particularly in the symbol of water. All the dominant symbols of the church have their genesis in the sacramentality of creation itself. Our sacramental symbols come to us from the "stuff" of everyday life. Things of the earth re-

mind us of God, reflect his image, and bring into the present his saving presence.

When the gifts of bread and wine are brought forward, those things, made of human hands that will become transformed by the power of the Spirit, we are transported into the mystery of Divine creation, and in the process we too are re-created. We become a new creation along with the transformed bread and wine. We, too, become the Body and Blood of Christ. Creation theology is the thread that underpins our understanding of sacraments.

> Blessed are you, Lord, God of all creation.
> Through your goodness we have this bread
>   to offer,
> which earth has given and human hands
>   have made.
> It will become for us the bread of life.
> By the mystery of this water and wine may
>   we come
> to share in the divinity of Christ, who humbled himself
> to share in our humanity.
> Blessed are you, Lord, God of all creation.
> Through your goodness we have this wine
>   to offer,
> fruit of the vine and work of human hands.
> It will become our spiritual drink.
> (Preparation of the Altar and Gifts, *The Sacramentary*)

In our liturgy we honor God's creation, the work of God's hands. All creation is understood as bowing in humble adoration of God, the Creator. "Therefore it is right to receive *the obedience of all creation,* the praise of the Church on earth, the thanksgiving of the saints in heaven..." (Preface: Weekdays III, P39, *The Sacramentary*).

Everything in creation is sanctified and made holy by the hand of our Creator God. We are made holy; the symbols of our faith are made holy and reveal the transcendence of God, and the earth is made holy. Our church cares for human activity, human life, what affects human life, and all human endeavor. Our church has a deep respect for things of the earth and for our world and its concerns. Evidence of such care is to be found in the Masses and the Prayers For Various Needs and Occasions, such as Masses For the Laity, For the Unity of Christians, For the Nations, For Those

---

[38] *NCD,* #51.

[39] Ibid.

Who Serve in Public Office, For Congress, For the President, For the Progress of Peoples, For Peace and Justice, In Time of War or Civil Disturbance, For the Blessings of Human Labor, For Productive Land, After the Harvest, In Time of Famine or For Those Who Suffer from Famine, For Refugees and Exiles, For Those Unjustly Deprived of Liberty, For Prisoners, For the Sick, For the Dying, In Time of Earthquake, For Rain, For Fine Weather, To Avert Storms, For Any Need, In Thanksgiving, For Charity, For Forgiveness of Sins, For Promoting Harmony, For the Family, For Relatives and Friends, For Our Oppressors, and For a Happy Death.

The *Book of Blessings* is given to the church to sanctify all of life's activities, from the work of our hands to the seeds that die in the earth to be born into new buds of life. Included in the *Book of Blessings* are blessings that reflect our great respect for the world, for life, for human labor, and for all human situations and activity such as: Order for the Blessing of Families and Members of Families, for Children, Blessing of Sons and Daughters, Blessing for Parents before Childbirth, for Mothers before Childbirth, for Mothers after Childbirth, Blessing of Parents after a Miscarriage, Blessing of Parents and an Adopted Child, on the Occasion of a Birthday, Orders for the Blessing of Elderly People Confined to Their Homes, Orders for the Blessing of the Sick, Order for the Blessing of Students and Teachers, Blessing of a Person Suffering from Addiction or from Substance Abuse, for the Victim of Crime or Oppression, Blessing of Seeds at Planting Time, Order for the Blessing of an Athletic Event, Order for the Blessing of a New Hospital, or other Facility for the Care of the Sick, Order for the Blessing of an Office, Shop, or Factory, Orders for the Blessing of Those Gathered at a Meeting, Order for the Blessing of Organizations Concerned with Public Need, Order for the Blessing of Travelers, Order for the Blessing of a New Building Site, a New Home, a New Religious House, a New School or University, a New Library, a Parish Hall or Catechetical Center, Centers of Social Communication, Gymnasium or a Field for Athletics, Blessing of Boats and Fishing Gear, Order for the Blessing of Various Means of Transportation, Order for the Blessing of Technical Installations or Equipment and the Blessing of Tools or Other Equipment for Work. The Masses for Various Needs and Occa-

sions and the myriad of Blessings provided in the *Book of Blessings* prove in triplicate that the church regards all life and human experience as sacred, holy, and worthy of honor.

Testing

How does the church's teaching on creation have any relevance for your life? In what way does the dynamic ongoing creative power of God impact your life? What are the implications of creation theology for the life of believers? What are the implications of creation in relation to baptism? How does the understanding of creation in terms of God's bringing order out of chaos speak to you? Is there any experience in your life that you might connect to this teaching? Have you ever experienced the creative power of God in your life? How does this teaching speak to your community?

Decision

What is the challenge inherent in this teaching? What is the invitation to change? In what way does this teaching invite a response? What one concrete action might you take as a result of this teaching?

Refer to chapter 7, "Preparing the Catechetical Session," if you intend to plan your catechetical session at this time.

CROSS

See Easter Vigil.

EASTER SEASON

See Overview of Easter Season, Easter Vigil, and the Sundays of Easter.

EASTER VIGIL

See Easter Vigil.

EPIPHANY

See Overview of Christmas and Feast of Epiphany.

ESCHATOLOGY

The Collegeville Pastoral Dictionary of Biblical Theology defines eschatology, from the Greek *eschatos,* last, as that which has to do with beliefs and ideas about the end time, and with the valuation of time and history in this perspective. "Most religious traditions have some set of beliefs about an ultimate future of the individual and of the earth, whether that future is envisioned as eternal, cyclic, or limited."[40]

Natural Sign

When we speak about the end of the world, what does it evoke in you? How do you feel when we speak about the end of your own world through death? If you were to articulate an understanding of what happens to us after we die, what would you say? How would you articulate an understanding of your faith tradition's belief in the afterlife and the end of time?

Tradition: Biblical, Ecclesial, and Biblical Signs

Eschatology is the area of theology that studies the last things. The last things refer to the final manifestation of God's loving relationship to humanity. Issues that fall under the umbrella of eschatology's concerns are "death, particular judgement, heaven, hell, purgatory, Second Coming of Christ, resurrection of the body, general judgment, consummation of all things in the perfection of the Kingdom of God."[41] Richard McBrien asserts that even though future oriented, these realities have already been accomplished in the present through people who live the life awarded to them by the death and resurrection of Jesus. "Our *judgment* will be the visible manifestation of the judgment of acquittal already rendered in Jesus Christ."[42]

All of time is sanctified by God. In the Christian perspective, eschatology refers to the sanctification of future time and hinges upon the life, death, and resurrection of Jesus. Eschatology's springboard is the reality of Jesus' first entrance into human history through his Incarnation, the resulting effects, and the future promise of eternal life at the end of time.

One type of eschatology found in the New Testament is apocalyptical. That is, it alludes to the end of the world with preceding signs and wonders. The end time is seen as a time in which evil is con-

quered and Jesus will come again on a cloud, summoning all the faithful to their final destination: life with all the saints in the heavenly kingdom. Apocalyptic literature is often rich in symbolic language and speaks powerfully of a present reality, not just some future expectation. Berard Marthaler states: "Apocalyptic literature is purported to be a revelation of the future, whereas in actuality it was most often a commentary on the times in which it was composed."[43] The book of Revelation is an example of apocalyptic literature. Often the purpose of such literature was to offer consolation to persecuted people in present crisis situations.

Another type of eschatology in the scriptures can be found in the synoptic gospels of Matthew, Mark, and Luke. This type of eschatology heralds the reign of God both now and in the future. God is celebrated as the ONE who reigns in our midst. God's presence demands nothing but the total giving of self in response: complete conversion and *metanoia*. The kingdom of God is present when people are gathered in the name of Jesus.

Another scriptural image for eschatology is that of banquet. In the Old Testament the image of feasting was used in reference to "heavenly happiness."[44] The Last Supper was also seen as eschatological. It signaled the beginning of the last days. That which Christ was sent to do was coming to completion, beginning with the Lord's Supper. Thus, every eucharistic celebration has remembrances and reminders of our eschatological center.

Another biblical principle of eschatology appears in the gospel of John and is referred to as *realized eschatology*. The term refers to the fulfillment of that which is awaited and hoped for. Thus, those who believe in Jesus are already living in the promise and imbued with the Spirit of his very presence.

The history of eschatology in the church developed over time. It moved through stages in which there were notions that after a thousand year reign the end would come. This understanding came from a literalist view of Revelation 20. It was

---

[40]Carolyn Osiek, R.S.C.J., "Eschatology," in *CPDBT*, 264.
[41]*CSM*, 1101-1105.
[42]Ibid., 1103.

---

[43]*CR*, 206.
[44]John J. Collins, "Eschatology," in *CPDBT*, 261–264.

an understanding easily reputed in the year 1001. The end, of course, did not arrive.

Later there was great debate concerning where people would go upon their death. Questions of location came to the fore. Where would the individual soul go? Were there interim places before the final beatific vision? It is out of such debate that our understandings of purgatory and the resurrected body come.

These understandings remained intact until the advent of biblical scholarship in recent times. There was a shift away from the concept of the individual and the locale of his or her final resting place toward a broader, more inclusive understanding of eschatology. Contemporary theology thinks more in terms of humanity's final collective relationship to the Creator as a people.

More recently, Marxism criticized the *future only oriented* Christian stance as an excuse to avoid engaging in the concerns of the world. From such critique emerged the perception that indeed God and humanity were to be coworkers in the work of transforming the world. Disciples are called to be actors in the ongoing theater of life. They are to be history makers.

Lest we negate the creed of the kingdom of God *yet to come* in favor of a narrower interpretation as only meaning the kingdom of God *here and now*, the Second Vatican Council redefined the church's theology in regard to eschatology. The church defined the reign of God as a transcendent future, yet acknowledged humanity's role to be active participants in changing the present world while awaiting the coming of the next *(Dogmatic Constitution on the Church)*.

Thus, we are to face death with courage and joy. We should be counseled about our belief in death, judgment, and eternity, but always with "consoling hope, as well as salutory fear."[45] The Lord's death has conquered death. In our funeral liturgy we proclaim that through the resurrection of Jesus we share in his life; we live, we die, and we shall live again. We are to look forward with hope as we real-

ize our responsibility toward our own eternal destiny and the destiny of the world. Evangelization, spreading the reconciling good news of Jesus, is no light matter when one considers the stakes.

The following citations are a few that reflect the eschatology of Israel, the gospels, and the early church:

Hebrew Scriptures
National Eschatology: Prophet Amos—professed the fall of the Northern Kingdom (9:8); Prophet Isaiah—insisted Southern Kingdom would stand (6:13); he also foretold the messianic reign (11:1–9).
Cosmic Eschatology: Prophet Isaiah—envisioned the new heaven and new earth (65:1); Prophet Jeremiah—spoke of the void earth (4:23); Prophet Ezra spoke about the end of the world (4 Ez 7:30).
Personal Eschatology: resurrection of the dead (Dn 12:2; 2 Mac 7).

New Testament
Christ's future return (Jn 21:22–23; Acts 1:11); parousia (Mt 24:29–31; Mk 13:24–27); eschatological reign of God (Mt 13:31–32, Mk 4:30–32); eschatological banquet (Mt 26:29; Mk 14:25; Lk 22:15–16); realized eschatology (Jn 14:6; 17:3); final judgment (Rev 13:1–8; Mt 19:28; Lk 22:30; 1 Cor 6:2–3).

Testing
In what way, if any, has your original understanding regarding the end times been stretched, challenged, or affirmed? Was there any new information for you? If so, what was it? In light of the material just presented, is there any implication for living the Christian life? Are there any implications for the wider church? In what way can we as church participate in helping people live in *realized eschatology*? How are the biblical themes of covenant, exodus, creation, and community evident in the post-biblical teachings about the end times, final judgment, eternal life, and resurrection of the body? In what way are these post-biblical teachings related to the scriptures of this Sunday's liturgy? In light of this sharing, how would you articulate a theology or an understanding of eschatology? Is it the same as your first understanding, or has it changed?

---

[45]"Basic Teaching for Catholic Religious Education," #25, p. 142.

Decision

How does this understanding of eschatology challenge me personally? How am I living the message? In what way do I need to grow? What is one concrete action I can take this week as a response to our sharing? Prepare to share the experience next week.

Refer to chapter 7, "Preparing the Catechetical Session," if you intend to plan your catechetical session at this time.

EUCHARIST

See Christian Initiation, Part III: Eucharist (Appendix).

FASTING

See Lenten Overview.

GARMENT

See Easter Vigil, Symbol of Garment.

GRACE

Natural Sign

What is the most precious gift you have ever been given? Why? What did the gift express to you? What was the meaning behind the gift? Did the gift bear any significance for your life? What does the word *grace* mean to you?

Tradition: Biblical, Ecclesial, and Liturgical Signs

The word *grace* conjures up a wide range of meaning both in theological as well as secular terms. Theologically the word can imply favor or kindnesses given by God to the human race, or gifts given by God to individuals, or the gift of thanks offered by human beings to God for God's many kindnesses. In everyday parlance the word implies a salutation of high honor, such as "Your Grace." The usage of the word *grace* in everyday speech, such as "There but for the grace of God go I," or "I hope that I have the grace to . . . ," is derived from theological origins. The genesis of both secular and theological forms is found in the concept of favor. Theologically the word suggests a relationship between God and God's children. It is a relationship in which God bestows on the human race God's complete, gratuitous, unmerited love. Grace is not an event, an object, a person, or an act of God, but rather the gratuitous self-gift of God to the human race. Grace is also the action of God in human history. Grace is union with God. Grace is not a holy bank account in the sky in which one deposits favor from God, only to have it withdrawn by some infraction of law. Throughout the ages the church has spent volumes exploring and meditating on the usage, implication, and meaning of the word *grace*.

The word grace in the Hebrew Scriptures means to "incline oneself favorably to another."[46] It is best understood in terms of the client-patron relationship of ancient Mediterranean cultures. When governments could not provide for the needs of their citizenry, the wealthy landowners entered into a relationship of favor with their less fortunate lower-class clients. The higher-class patron cared for the basic needs of the lower-class client. When a patron did not share his surplus, he was considered greedy. The patron enjoyed honorable acclaim and the client enjoyed benefits that could be obtained in no other way.

God was understood in similar terms. God was the patron of Israel. The election of Israel meant that God, the patron, took care of the needs of Israel, the client. Israel was totally dependent upon God. The client-patron relationship was not without strings attached. The patron would provide, but the client owed the patron allegiance. There was an intended response. The client would be grateful for the gifts rendered. When Israel was not grateful, when Israel sinned, they severed the client-patron relationship. God was an extraordinary patron, however, as he continually restored the client-patron relationship following a rupture on the part of Israel, the client. God bestows *grace* (favor) without end to God's client, Israel.

In the New Testament, Jesus Christ epitomizes the favor shown by God. No longer does Israel act like the client of the Patron, God, but now Christians enjoy a status not enjoyed before. Followers of Christ are true members of God's family. They are no longer clients, but enjoy status as children of the Patron's family.

---

[46]John J. Pilch, "Grace," in *CPDBT*, 397.

The word grace as used in the New Testament infers a refined theology of gratitude for the saving action of God accomplished through Jesus Christ. The biblical authors use the language of their Hebrew tradition to reflect their gratitude for God's election of Israel, and the subsequent inclusion of Gentiles in that election. The early Christians reflect their gratitude for the forgiveness of sins offered by Christ's sacrifice on Calvary. They are grateful for the new life of Christ in the Spirit, for the peace and shalom offered by this new life, for the love and transformation that are possible because of Christ's self-sacrifice. Christians are thankful for the anticipation they share in waiting for the final consummation of the world and Christ's return in glory. They did not, however, attempt to narrow this gratitude into one single concept called grace. The word *grace* is used, but in reference to a favor or blessing, to forgiveness, or to specific gifts called charisms. Grace is not used as the singular expression of the gift of God's self. Wherever the word is used, one can readily substitute the word gift or favor in its place. Only later in church history will the concept of *grace* take on a theology of its own.

The early Christians spoke of grace (*charis*) when describing the effects of the gift of Christ. The etymology (origin) of the word from both Latin and Greek can mean "(1) graciousness, attractiveness, charm, or (2) a favor granted to someone, or (3) the gratitude due to someone in response to a gift. Moreover, in both Greek and Latin the term can designate either the source of a gift in the giver or the effect of the gift in the recipient."[47]

The early church also connected the term grace (*charis*) to reflect a connection with the eucharist and Christ's presence in the assembly through the eucharist. Grace was that present and future gift of God's presence. The grace of Christ's presence is a foretaste of the eschatological pledge of eternal life.

Justin Martyr, an early Father of the Church (c. 100–165), understood God's grace as the universal gift of *God's Love* active in salvation history. According to Justin, all who lived according to

Christ, God's incarnate *Word* (who was active in human history since the beginning of time), would be beneficiaries of God's everlasting grace/ life/love. They need not necessarily accept the God of Israel or Christianity. Those who opposed God, or lived against the principles of Christ, would not be saved. Thus, pagans who lived an exemplary life would be heir to God's saving grace.

Later however, Cyprian of Carthage (c. 200–258) limited the beneficiaries. Only those who were in union with the Catholic Church could be saved. Cyprian's theology dominated much of Catholic theology until the Second Vatican Council. *The Pastoral Constitution on the Church in the Modern World* reaffirmed God's universal gift of love and salvation to all humanity.

A further defining event for Western theology in regard to grace was a result of the debate between St. Augustine of Hippo, and Pelagius, an English spiritual guide. Pelagius taught that people were created good by God, and because human beings were created good by God, they had the instinctive power, in and of themselves, to do good without God's help. Pelagius did acknowledge the need for grace, but understood grace as merely a necessary support, or aid, very much like a moral code, or the example of Christ or his teaching. Pelagius understood grace as an external support. Augustine, on the other hand, refuted the Pelagian heresy, and used St. Paul to prove his position. In Paul's letter to the Romans, Paul insists that human beings are saved through the power of Christ's death and resurrection, not by their own good works. For Augustine, grace was a gift from God that empowers the human will to do good—a completely gratuitous gift. He believed that human beings can do nothing to earn the necessary grace for salvation—that it is a free gift that empowers people to change their lives and live according to the law of love. "The mystery of grace is at the heart of Augustine's writings which include a sacramental view of reality that sees the 'vestiges of the Trinity' present throughout creation, an inner desire for God at the core of every human heart, and the Baptism as a share in the inner divine life of love."[48] Augustine asserted a "strong emphasis on grace as a divine force liberating the

---

[47]Leo D. Lefebure, "Grace: Pastoral Liturgical Tradition," in *CPDBT*, 400.

[48]Richard P. McBrien, "Grace," in *HCEC*, 578.

human will from the bondage of sin."[49] He believed that people are justified and made righteous through faith and God's grace. Pelagius insisted that if we were created good, that we must have the capacity to choose good, which is itself a gift from God, or God's grace, whereas Augustine taught that human beings are so tainted by the effects of original sin that only by grace are we able to live righteously. Grace is the "internal assistance of the Holy Spirit" needed to become a healed and transformed mind, body, soul, and spirit.

The Eastern Church developed an understanding of grace as empowerment to live righteously but also as participation in God's divine nature. Grace is a share of the divine life of God, our life as adopted children of God. Grace is the gift of God's self to humanity. Grace is participation in God's divine life. Grace is the new life of God's *created grace* within every human being. St. Athanasias draws upon this notion of grace in his teaching concerning the Incarnation of Christ. The Incarnation represents God's offer of divine self to humanity, whereby human beings are offered a share in God's divine life. "For Athanasias of Alexandria (c. 295–373), this is the central meaning of the incarnation: God became human so that humans could share in God's own life and become divine. Similarly, Cyril of Alexandria (d. 444) viewed grace as a state of communion with God, a state in which we become partakers of the divine nature."[50] (See the preface for Christmas.)

St. Thomas Aquinas of the Middle Ages posits an understanding of grace as everything that comes from God and similarly returns to God. Aquinas drew upon Augustine's healing notion of grace, but he also drew upon the Eastern tradition of grace as divinization—participation in the divine life of love. Aquinas made the distinction between created and uncreated grace. Uncreated grace is synonymous with the gift of love present in the Trinity—it is God's self. Created grace is the effect that God's love has on human beings who are captured by God's uncreated grace. Not only is human nature healed by this love, but human beings are elevated to divine status; they share and

participate in the divine life; they share God's life and love. It is beyond human capacity to attain this divine life. God elevates human nature through the gift of God's indwelling Spirit in the human soul. Grace allows human beings to enter into intimate relationship and friendship with the Trinity. Human beings become adopted heirs to what is natural and inherent to the Trinity—perfect love. This divinization was referred to as the "habit" of grace by Aquinas.

Later debates about faith and justification during the Reformation led to the Council of Trent's formulation of the theology of grace. Justification is the forgiveness of sins as well as the radical transformation of the baptized. The transformed person's new habit of grace allows that person to move from enmity with God to friendship with God. This habit of grace that leads to radical transformation empowers the person to act and live righteously by God's initiative, and by human participation in God's initiative. This did not stop the debate on the nature and effects of grace. It would continue over the centuries. Twentieth-century theologians attempted to recapture the notion of grace as the gratuitous gift of God's self and God's love to human beings. Theologians such as Karl Rahner (1984), Henri de Lubac (1991), Pierre Teilhard de Chardin (1955), and Edward Schillebeeckx reaffirmed the understanding of grace as God's self-offer of *Ultimate Love*. They also posited the belief in the human will as naturally directed and oriented to seek and encounter the living God. God desires relationship with human beings. Human beings are naturally predisposed and created to love and seek God, whether they are conscious of that fact or not. Rahner insisted that human beings are created with this natural predisposition to love God. It is God's gift of self-love to human beings. He called it the "supernatural existential," implying that such orientation for the love and seeking of God is the result of the unmerited, gratuitous action of God. This is eloquently expressed in the Weekdays IV Preface: "You have no need of our praise, yet our desire to thank you is itself gift. Our prayer of thanksgiving adds nothing to your greatness, but makes us grow in your grace, through Jesus Christ our Lord."

Rahner affirmed God's universal salvific will that all people be saved, while still maintaining salvation through the life, death, and resurrection of

---

    [49]Ibid.

    [50]Lefebure, "Grace: Pastoral Liturgical Tradition," in *CPDBT*, 401.

Jesus Christ. He insisted that people who live in fidelity to God's love found deep within their own hearts, whether consciously Christian or not, are living in the reality of God's love and God's salvation. He called such people "anonymous Christians."

Edward Schillebeeckx asserts that grace flourishes in the human heart when people stand in solidarity with those who suffer, and when human beings make the effort to resist the evil that permeates our world. Liberation theologians such as Leonardo Boff and Gustavo Gutierrez understand grace as the liberating power of God present in the midst of oppressed peoples and societies. Liberation theologians propose that grace is both gift and responsibility. We are gifted and empowered for action, and that action resides in solidarity with the whole human race—and especially the oppressed and exploited.

God's gift of self is manifest through divine revelation. The Spirit of God manifests God's self to human beings through natural, biblical, ecclesial, and liturgical signs. God's divine revelation calls for a response from human beings. This response is the grace of God's self within each human heart. This habit of grace within each person allows them to respond with mind, will, heart, and emotions—the total self. The inner dwelling of the Spirit disposes human beings to turn the heart and the will to God. This Spirit-presence is grace. "One believes in response to grace."[51] "Grace is God's generous and free gift to His people. It is union with God, a sharing in his life, the state of having been forgiven one's sins, of being adopted as God's own child and sustained by God's unfailing love. Grace is possible for us because of Christ's redemptive sacrifice."[52]

The sacraments are an effective means to experience God's grace. The sacraments are the gift of God's self to the church. "The sacraments are important means for bringing about the Christian's union with God in grace. They are sources of grace for individuals and communities, as well as remedies for sin and its effects."[53]

---

[51]*NCD*, #57.
[52]Ibid., #98.
[53]Ibid.

Grace is also understood to be present in creation itself. God's presence is mediated through the gift of this world, its resources, its art, its music, its treasures, its science and technology, its healing arts, and all things that enhance human life and dignity.

Testing
Were there any new insights for you, or anything you had not considered before? How would you articulate an understanding of grace? What is a habit of grace? How does one get it? What do you think it means that grace is participation in God's divine life? What does that mean for your everyday life? How does this teaching on grace invite transformation in your life? In what way can you relate to the liberation theologians' understanding of grace? How does it invite a response? How do you experience grace in creation? If grace is the gift of God's self to humanity, what is the human response in the face of such unmerited love? Do you know any anonymous Christians? What do they teach you about grace? How does the church celebrate grace in its liturgy? How might this teaching on grace speak to your community?

Decision
What is the challenge of the church's teaching on grace? How does this teaching concretely invite transformed behavior? What one specific thing might you do in response to this teaching?

Refer to chapter 7, "Preparing the Catechetical Session," if you intend to plan your catechetical session at this time.

HOLY FAMILY

See Feast of the Holy Family.

HOLY SPIRIT

See Trinity: God as Spirit (Appendix). See Feast of Pentecost. See Easter Season Overview. See Feast of the Baptism of the Lord.

INCARNATION

The Incarnation (from the Latin, *caro*, "flesh," "enfleshing") refers to God assuming human nature. It specifically refers to God becoming a human being when Jesus was conceived by the Holy Spirit in his mother, Mary. It also refers to the mystery of Christ, as one divine person, possessing a fully human and a fully divine nature.

Natural Sign

When we speak about the Incarnation, what does it evoke in you? How do you feel about the idea of God coming to earth in the person of Jesus? If you were to articulate an understanding of Incarnation, first, do you have such an understanding, and second, what is it? How would you [or could you] articulate an understanding of your faith tradition's belief in the Incarnation?

Tradition: Biblical, Ecclesial, and Liturgical Signs

Belief in the incarnation is a foundational truth. It is among the *hierarchy of truths*. The essence of being Christian is to accept the reality and the mystery of the Incarnation. Jesus, who was one with God, entered human history and took on a human nature. We are taught that Jesus became a human being to save us from our sins, to reconcile us with God (1 Jn 4:10; 4:14). We proclaim that truth every time we pray the Nicene Creed together in liturgy.

Another reason God took human form through Jesus is so that we all could experience God's unfathomable love. We humans are very stubborn sometimes. God understands us all too well. God knew that if he did not come to us in the flesh, we would never really believe the love God has for us. Unless someone could walk with us in our struggles, suffer with us in our pain, laugh with us in our joys, we would never really own the love that God has for us. Thus, Yahweh sent his Son to endure what all human beings have to endure, the struggles of life.

Jesus, the Son of God, also came to us to show us the way to God, to show us what it means to be a holy people. Jesus is the perfect model. As our brother, he showed us how to live by the example of his own life. Through his teaching we are shown what it means to be a holy people, a royal priesthood, a people set apart. Jesus came to offer us the law of love. He gave us the great commandment of love: we are to love God and one another. We are to lay down our lives for one another, just as Jesus laid down his life for us.

God became human in order for us to share in his divine nature. "For this is why the Word became man, and the Son of God became the Son of man: so that man, by entering into communion with the Word and thus receiving divine sonship, might become a son of God."[54] Sometimes this is the most difficult reality for people. We are so sure of our wretchedness that we find it difficult to accept that we share the divine nature of God through our incorporation into Jesus' Mystical Body. We *are* holy people. To echo the words of Genesis: God created male and female and God saw that it was good. By taking human form God elevated human nature and restored human dignity.

Jesus is not a divided self, part God and part human. The mystery we celebrate is that Jesus was fully human and fully divine at the same time. The first heresies denied that Jesus was fully human (Gnostic Docetism). According to the Arian heresy, Jesus was not from the same substance as the Father. In response, the Nicean Council stated that Jesus was begotten, not made. There never was a time when Jesus was not.

Jesus, as true God and true human being, possessed a human will and intellect. This will and intellect were subject to his divine will and intellect, the same will and intellect of Father and Son. The mystery of the Incarnation "sheds light both on the mystery of God and the mystery of human life."[55] Through the mystery of the Incarnation God is so dedicated to humanity and to creation (God's handiwork) that he exploded into human history to be one with us in all things. God desired to experience our humanity in its completeness: the joys and the struggles.

The Incarnation shows us what it means to be human and gives meaning and purpose to the human life. To live is to hunger for intimate relationship with God. For this we were created. Consequently, the Incarnation is good news for the human race. It expresses the potential goodness of every human life. How could human life be anything but potentially worthy if God was willing to take its form? While there is propensity for sin

---

[54]St. Irenaeus, Adv. Haeres. 3, 19, 1:PG7/1, 939, in *CCC*, p. 116, #460.

[55]*EC*, 659.

in human nature, the Incarnation gives us the hope and the means to enter deeply into relationship with God. It is the kind of relationship that God envisioned and desired at the creation of the world.

The messiah came to restore the perfect harmony created by God in the genesis event. Creation's perfect harmony consisted in right ordered relationships: God's perfect justice. Perfect justice is an ordering of relationships that places human beings in reciprocal covenant relationship with God, with one another, and with creation. God and humanity were to share an unbreakable bond and as a result were to enter into a similar union with one another. They were to offer God's justice and love to the powerless and to those difficult to love by the world's standards. This love was to be extended not necessarily because such persons deserved to be loved, but because God would do as much and wished that we do no less. Humanity's response was a sign of their love for God (or lack thereof).

However, people interrupted God's plan through sin. They turned from God and lost God's just and perfect kingdom. The *Word Made Flesh* was to restore creation's justly ordered design. The peace that accompanied Jesus' birth was nothing less than the restoration of God's first grand design. Through Jesus the relationships envisioned by God are possible.

The Advent/Christmas season highlights the Incarnation in the liturgical texts and scriptures celebrated throughout the season. Every eucharistic liturgy celebrates the Incarnation and professes it in ritual and prayer, Gloria, Creed, eucharistic prayers, etc.

Testing

In what way, if any, has your original understanding regarding the Incarnation been informed, stretched, challenged, or affirmed? Was there any new information for you? If so, what was it? In light of the material just presented, is there any implication for living the Christian life? What does this teaching have to say about the community's and your role in God's plan for the redemption of the human race? In what way is this post-biblical teaching related to the scriptures of this Sunday's liturgy? In light of this sharing, how would you articulate an understanding of the Incarnation? Is it the same as your first understanding, or has it changed?

Decision

How does this teaching about the Incarnation challenge our community? In what way is our community living the message we just shared? In what specific way is our community in need of transformation? Is there any concrete action I can take to be an agent of change in my community? How does this reflection concerning the Incarnation of Jesus challenge me personally? How am I living the message? In what way do I need to grow? What one concrete action can I take this week as a response to what we have shared?

Refer to chapter 7, "Preparing the Catechetical Session," if you intend to plan your catechetical session at this time.

JESUS

Natural Sign

Have you ever had a personal experience of Jesus in your life? Define what you believe about Jesus. What do you think the church teaches about Jesus Christ?

Tradition: Biblical, Ecclesial, and Liturgical Signs

Non-Christian sources do give testimony to the existence of Jesus. However, they give little or no historical information.

The New Testament answers the question of "Who is Jesus?" through the use of a multitude of titles that reflect his multi-faceted personhood and mission such as: Jesus the Prophet, Jesus the Suffering Servant of God, Jesus the High Priest, Jesus the Messiah, Jesus the Son of Man, Jesus the Lord, Jesus the Savior, Jesus the Word, Jesus the Son of God.

The gospels are the final, edited, redacted version of the oral and written remembrance of Christ proclaimed in the early church. The resurrection of Christ is the central pivot upon which the Christian kerygma hinges. It is the event that prompts the early church's faith in Christ as the promised messiah and Savior of the world. No one saw the resurrection, but many experienced Christ after the resurrection. Jesus' central message was the arrival of the reign of God that he proclaimed through parables, proverbial sayings, and the Lord's Prayer.

The church's understanding of Jesus grew gradually in the apostolic age especially between 100 and 700 with the primary focus centered on his nature. Doctrine in relation to Christ developed as a result of curiosity, controversies, and heresies.

The main question or problem centered around the divinity and the humanity of Christ. Belief in Jesus, the God-Man, was the cause of controversy. Jesus was both human and divine. To stress the divinity over the humanity undermines belief in Jesus' humanity. When Jesus' humanity is too greatly stressed his divinity is diminished. Balance is critical.

Heresies centered around belief in Christ's humanity and divinity prompted an articulation of the church's creed in relationship to Christ. The Council of Nicea definitively asserted the divinity of Christ and rejected the Arian heresy that stated that Jesus was made at a certain point in time. The Council attested to Jesus' oneness with the Father. The Council of Constantinople was concerned with upholding the humanity of Christ so that the effect of Christ's redemption not be minimized. The Council of Ephesus maintained that Jesus is both God and human at the same time and that Mary, his mother, is the mother of Jesus and the Mother of God (Theotokos). The Council attested to the two natures of Jesus: human and divine at the same time. The Council of Chaldeon affirmed Jesus' two distinct natures. He is fully human and fully divine and like us in all things except sin.

Doctrine in relation to Christ was firmly established in the historical period of 100–700 and forms the basis of our christology today. The church teaches that Jesus is the Word made flesh. God took on human form in order to accomplish his plan of salvation. He became human for us that we might be reconciled with God and saved for all eternity. He became human so that we would know God's love for us and so we would have an example of holiness. Jesus taught us what it means to be fully human and fully alive.

Jesus is truly God and truly human. He became man while remaining fully divine. Belief in the passion, death, and resurrection is at the heart of the Christian kerygma. Christ loved us to death. He died and rose again for the sins of the world. The blood ritual of the old covenant was replaced by the Christ's blood, the blood of the new covenant. Christ's sacrifice surpasses all other sacrifices. None is greater. Through Christ's death we are freed from sin; through his resurrection we are raised to new and eternal life. Jesus is the second person of the Blessed Trinity.

Jesus is the centerpiece of all liturgical celebrations, blessings, sacraments, private prayer, and devotions. He is the object and purpose of our gathering and the source of our prayer.

Testing
Were there any new insights? Have any of your original assumptions been stretched? How would you articulate an understanding about the church's belief in Christ in light of this presentation? What does belief in Christ have to do with everyday life?

Decision
How does this teaching about Christ challenge me personally? How am I living the message? In what way do I need to grow? What one concrete action can I take this week as a response to what was shared?

Refer to chapter 7, "Preparing the Catechetical Session," if you intend to plan your catechetical session at this time.

JUSTICE

Natural Sign
What does the word *justice* mean to you? What does justice mean in the secular world? How might you connect the secular understanding of justice with the spiritual understanding of justice?

Tradition: Biblical, Ecclesial, and Liturgical Signs
The command to care for the world's less fortunate, for the oppressed, and for the downtrodden is an ancient one. It begins with our understanding of creation and biblical justice. At the 1996 Orlando Catechetical Conference, the noted scripture scholar Walter Burghardt asserted that

biblical justice is fidelity to the demands of relationships, and to responsibilities that stem from our covenant with God.

> The Old Testament asked: what did it mean for an Israelite to live? They were united by bonds of family or covenant. In that framework or context, how is God just? God acts as God should: always faithful to his promise. God provides and God punishes violations. *God is always faithful.* When are we just? When we are in right relationship to our God, to our brothers and sisters, and to the earth. In the Genesis creation story everything was in right relationship to everything else. All were in covenant relationship with God. Because of this covenant the people of God were to welcome the stranger, feed the hungry, give a home to the alien—not because they deserved it, but because this is how God acted toward Israel. Deuteronomy said to love the stranger because God did. Justice of God, then, is fidelity to relationships, expressions of love. Not to execute justice was not to worship God.

God was Israel's caretaker (Ex 19:3–6; 20:2). Israel's response was to be faithful to the Law and the commandments (Ex 19:5; 20:1–17). This treaty between God and humanity demanded that Israel respond in obedience and trust. Deuteronomy insists that the love and mercy God shows to Israel is to be extended to everyone in their community and to foreigners. "... (J)ustice lives on in the world both by divine action and through those who fulfill the obligations of their covenant relationship with God."[56]

The prophets railed against Israel's inattention to the covenant. They professed God's mercy, compassion, and incredible patience in the face of Israel's injustice. The prophets clamored for a return to right relationship (*hesed*) with God. This meant a return to righteousness, justice, compassion, and steadfast kindness. Israel would be re-created and the harmony of paradise would be restored. This harmony meant that humanity was in right relationship with God. God would provide for human beings. God would love human beings and in return humanity would love as God loves. This love would be evident in behavior. Wherever and whenever God's children are not cared for, this is evidence of a ruptured covenant. The absence of justice is understood as complete darkness. Living in justice is living in the light. The practice of justice was synonymous with salvation.

Jesus demanded biblical justice for all people. He strongly challenged those who did not live according to the biblical command to live in right relationship. A primary motif in Luke/Acts is care and concern for the lowly, the marginalized, the sinner, and those on the fringe of society. Jesus insisted that the hallmark of his mission was that the poor have the good news preached to them. The main thread running through the garment of New Testament teaching is care and concern for all of God's people: the lowest of the low and the poorest of the poor. "The NT authors—especially Luke—are optimistic about the ability of the Church to ameliorate social injustice while awaiting the coming reign of God."[57]

The church's teaching on social justice is rooted in creation. God's creation is good. All humanity is created in the image and likeness of God, thereby possessing a divine status and dignity as God's children. As a result of this divine status, all people are entitled to live to their fullest human potential. In order to live according to their fullest potential, every human person is entitled to health, well-being, happiness, and the best possible opportunities to achieve the potential for which they were created. Biblical justice, therefore, is the right of every person on earth. The liturgy affirms the equal status of all people before God:

> Lord,
> you guide all creation with fatherly care,
> As you have given all men one common origin,
> bring them together peacefully into one family
> and keep them united in brotherly love.
> (Mass for Peace and Justice, "Alternative Opening Prayer," *The Sacramentary*)

---

[56] Gregory J. Polan, O.S.B., "Justice," in *CPDBT*, 511.

[57] J. Albert Harrill, "Justice," in *CPDBT*, 515.

The covenant forged with God at the creation of the world demands a moral response. The moral response of human beings involves living in right relationship with God and one another. Thus, every Christian has a moral responsibility to act justly toward all of God's people. Every person is called to an eternal destiny. Every person is redeemed by the blood of the cross. We are therefore to recognize Christ in all people and treat them accordingly. "We must be concerned for the spiritual condition of others and for their temporal condition. Our concern will therefore extend to their authentic freedom, their spiritual and moral well-being, their intellectual and cultural welfare, their material and physical needs (e.g. housing, food, health, employment, etc.). Such concern will be expressed in action, including efforts to build a cultural, social, and political order based on peace and justice—locally, nationally, and internationally."[58]

Any action that is contrary to the life, health, and well-being of others is an action contrary to the gospel. Any action or omission that fails to enhance human dignity violates biblical justice and the human responsibility to fulfill the covenant treaty and relationship with God.

Every liturgical celebration places us in harmony and solidarity with all of God's creation. The celebration of eucharist demands that we become the Body of Christ in the world, that we lay down our lives for all people. The *Catechism of the Catholic Church* asserts that eucharist commits us to the poor (1397). In the General Intercessions we exert our priestly role and intercede on behalf of the world's poor and suffering. The church heralds concern for peace and for lasting harmony in the world.

> God our Father,
> you reveal that those who work for peace
> will be called your sons.
> Help us to work without ceasing for that
> justice
> which brings true and lasting peace.
> (Mass for Peace and Justice: Opening
> Prayer, *The Sacramentary*)

---

[58] *NCD*, #105.

The liturgy reflects the church's concern for justice in the wide selection of masses set aside for various needs and occasions: For Persecuted Christians, For the Progress of Peoples, For Peace and Justice, In Time of War or Civil Disturbance, In Time of Famine or For Those Who Suffer from Famine, For Refugees and Exiles, For Those Unjustly Deprived of Liberty, For Prisoners, For the Sick, For the Dying, In Time of Earthquake, For Charity, For Forgiveness of Sins, For Promoting Harmony, For the Family, For Relatives and Friends, For Our Oppressors (*The Sacramentary*). The *Book of Blessings* also shows concern for issues of justice as evidenced by blessings for: Elderly People Confined to Their Homes, Blessing of the Sick, Blessing of a Person Suffering from Addiction or from Substance Abuse, Blessing of a Victim of Crime or Oppression, and the Blessing of Organizations Concerned with Public Need.

Testing
What are the implications of biblical justice for living the Christian life? What does this teaching have to do with your everyday life? Is there anyone that you know who does not enjoy the benefits demanded in this teaching? Where is there need for an attitude adjustment in relation to this teaching? How does this teaching invite transformation of your attitudes and behavior? Your community's attitudes and behavior? How do you feel about the concept that justice is a right and not simply charity? What are the implications?

Decision
What concrete action are you willing to take in response to this teaching? What does this teaching invite your community to do in response? What attitudes are in need of healing and transformation? What are the obstacles to changing your perspective and behavior in relation to this teaching?

Refer to chapter 7, "Preparing the Catechetical Session," if you intend to plan your catechetical session at this time.

KINGDOM OF GOD

Natural Sign
What does the term "kingdom of God" evoke in you? What does it call to mind? Have you ever had a personal experience of God's kingdom in your

life? If you were to give a definition of "the kingdom of God," what would it be? What do you think is meant by the term?

Tradition: Biblical, Ecclesial, and Liturgical Signs

The kingdom of God is now. There is evidence in scripture to make such an assertion. Jesus said that "the kingdom of God is at hand" (Mk 1:14-15). In obedience to his Father's will, Jesus initiates the kingdom of heaven in our midst, here and now, on earth.

As members of this kingdom we share in God's divine life. We call this gathering of God's people the church, the family of God. Jesus is the head of that family through his word, through signs that reveal God's reign, and through the sending of disciples to spread the good news. "The Word of the Lord is compared to a seed which is sown in a field; those who hear the Word with faith and become part of the little flock of Christ, have received the Kingdom itself" (*Lumen Gentium*, #5).

Jesus established his kingdom on earth. We are invited to be part of that kingdom by living Christ's paschal mystery. When we accept the daily dyings and risings of life, we share in Jesus' suffering, death, and resurrection.

Everyone is called to God's kingdom. It belongs to the poor and the lowly. Jesus identifies with the poor and those humble enough to hear his word. The condition for membership in God's kingdom is that we respond in love to the poor and less fortunate.

Sinners are welcome and are part of God's kingdom. They are invited to deep conversion and transformation.

We learn a great deal about God's kingdom through Jesus' parables. They challenge us to give all that we are to build God's kingdom—in word and action. "The parables highlight the social character of the kingdom. Jesus never presents the kingdom as a private affair between God and an individual. Rather, it is an active force in the world, a reconciling presence creating a sense of solidarity among people."[59]

We know the kingdom is at hand through the signs Jesus performed. Miracles strengthen faith. "The miracles of Jesus also confirm that the Kingdom has already arrived on earth" (*Lumen Gentium*, #5). We are not, however, to view them in a magical, manipulative way.

Jesus empowers the apostles to carry on his work in establishing the kingdom. That authority continues through the pope, bishops, priests, deacons, religious, and all God's people.

We live in God's kingdom now with hope in the kingdom yet to come. Through the story of the Transfiguration we are given a glimpse of God's heavenly kingdom. We will one day share in Jesus' transfigured glory when we join him in the eternal city.

We must not lose sight of that hope. Yet we live in the present. Our reality is that the kingdom of God is *now*. Jesus envisions a kingdom of peace where the lame walk, where the blind see, where people lay down their lives for one another and the poor and oppressed are cared for. When one looks at present day society it is often difficult to imagine such a kingdom. However, the kingdom of God *is at hand* when Christians gather in truth, hope, and love; when they live a gospel life, repent, change their lives, and spread the good news.[60]

The following gospel citations address the reign of God. The kingdom of God in Mark's gospel: "is at hand . . ." (1:15); purpose of the parables (4:11, 26, 30). The kingdom of God in Matthew's gospel: on earth, in heaven (6:10); parables—"kingdom is like . . ." (13:24, 31, 33–34, 44–45, 47; 18:23; 20:1; 22:2; 25:1). Kingdom of God in Luke's gospel: now and not yet (4:43; 8:1; 9:2, 11, 60, 62; 16:16). Kingdom of God in John's gospel: who is admitted? (3:1–5).

The kingdom of God is proclaimed at every liturgy when the gospel is proclaimed and the eucharist and the sacraments are celebrated. Every liturgy is a proclamation of the reign of God. The kingdom of God is definitely announced in the Lord's Prayer.

---

[59] *CR*, 223–227.

[60] Ibid.

Testing

In what way, if any, has your original understanding regarding the kingdom of God been stretched, challenged, or affirmed? Was there any new information for you? If so, what was it? In light of the material just presented, is there any implication for living the Christian life? What does this teaching have to say about the community's and your role in God's kingdom? Who is invited? What are the signs of God's kingdom? The biblical themes of the presence of God through his covenant, the exodus, creation, and community are evident in this teaching. How are those themes connected to this understanding of the kingdom of God?

In what way is this church teaching related to the scriptures of this Sunday's liturgy? In light of this sharing, how would you articulate an understanding of the kingdom of God now? Is it the same as your first understanding, or has it changed?

Decision

How does this teaching about the kingdom of God challenge our community? In what way is our community living the message we just shared? In what specific way is our community in need of transformation? Is there any concrete action you can take to be an agent of change in your community? How does this understanding of the kingdom of God challenge you personally? How are you living the message? In what way do you need to grow? What one concrete action can you take this week as a response to this sharing?

Refer to chapter 7, "Preparing the Catechetical Session," if you intend to plan your catechetical session at this time.

LAYING ON OF HANDS

See Trinity: God as Spirit (Appendix). See Easter Vigil: Symbol of Laying on of Hands.

LENT

See Lenten Overview and the Sundays of Lent.

LIGHT

See Easter Vigil: Symbol of Light.

MARY, MODEL FOR THE CHURCH

Natural Sign

What role, if any, does Mary play in your life? What does the image of mother evoke in you? What is your understanding of the church's teaching on Mary?

Tradition: Biblical, Ecclesial, and Liturgical Signs

The basis of the church's teaching regarding Mary is belief in Jesus Christ. As the first Christian, Mary is a model for how to reveal Christ to the world and how to live the Christian kerygma.

The *Catechism of the Catholic Church* calls Mary the "Eschatological Icon of the Church" (972). Through her we reflect upon what the church already is as it makes its journey of faith toward the final resting place in heaven.

Christ is the focus of Marian devotion. Church teaching about Mary is best summed up in the liturgical feasts of the year. Mary, Mother of God (Jan. 1) stresses the true nature of Christ—his humanity and divinity, and honors Mary as the Mother of God. The Annunciation honors the virginal conception of Christ by the power of the Spirit. The Immaculate Conception (Dec. 8) celebrates the utter graciousness of God toward humanity in that Mary was conceived without original sin due to grace, not merit. The Visitation (May 31) celebrates the working of the Spirit as Mary was inspired to visit her cousin Elizabeth. The Assumption of Mary (Aug. 15) into heaven was intended to strengthen our belief in the resurrection of the body. The feast also honors Mary who shares a unique union with God in Christ from the very beginning through the end of her life. The Queenship of Mary (Aug. 22) honors Mary as queen and mother of the human race. Our Lady of Sorrows (Sept. 15) remembers the suffering of Mary and reminds us that the church is united with Christ through suffering and death so that we may live eternally with him.[61]

Commentary in this workbook on the liturgical feasts honoring Mary offers a more elaborate and detailed analysis of various facets of Marian devo-

---

[61]Linda Gaupin, CDP, Ph.D., *Catholic Faith and Life: Catechist Training* (Diocese of Orlando, Fla., 1996). Unpublished course text, 81.

tion. Please refer to those feasts for further insights.

Testing
Were there any new insights? Is your understanding of the role of Mary expanded or affirmed? How might the role of Mary have anything to do with your everyday life? What are the implications for living the Christian kerygma?

Decision
In what way does this teaching call me to action in my life, in the church, or in the world? What action will I take as a result?

Refer to chapter 7, "Preparing the Catechetical Session," if you intend to plan your catechetical session at this time.

MORALITY: FOUNDATIONS

Natural Sign
If you were asked what it means to live a moral life, how would you respond? Complete this sentence: "Morality is. . . ."

Tradition: Biblical, Ecclesial, and Liturgical Signs
Morality refers to behaviors that flow from an individual's principled assumptions. Both the Hebrew scriptures (Old Testament) and the Christian scriptures (New Testament) view the totality of life, secular and the spiritual, as one. The Hellenistic world (Greek) and its philosophical constructions introduced to us a sense that we are divided between matters spiritual and temporal. This is called dualism. The scriptures paint an entirely different picture, however. All life is sacred and consecrated to God's saving presence. God wishes us to be happy and whole, not divided. The Hebrew understanding of wholeness is the right ordering of relationships (*hesed*), that is, right relationship to God, to one another, to the earth, and to oneself.

The Christian scriptures uphold a standard that speaks of moral behavior in terms of *just actions,* such as feeding the hungry and giving drink to the thirsty. In contrast with a fundamentalist approach to morality in which morality is founded on direct biblical revelation and directives,[62]

Catholic morality is based primarily on the biblical themes of creation, exodus, covenant, and cross. From a biblical and early church perspective, when one's morality was weighed, it was judged in light of discipleship. For example, before one was admitted for baptism, that person's readiness was discerned. The criteria for this discernment were based on the person's moral behavior. Was *metanoia* visible in the person's life? Was there a change, a turning from one thing toward another, a turn from one way of living to a new way of living in Christ? Early documents, such as the Didache, directed that catechumens be given clear instruction regarding the type of life they were to live after baptism. Baptism empowered them for incorporation into the life and mission of Christ.

Christian morality is based on the understanding posited by Thomas Aquinas that nature and supernature are graced by God. As human beings we possess dignity. God is infinitely present to all of life, thus all of life is graced by God. We have been told in the story of our human genesis that we are made in God's image. We are sacred because *we are*, not because of anything we have done. Jesus lives within us and teaches us what it means to be fully human. "All people seek happiness: life, peace, joy, wholeness and wholesomeness of being. The happiness human beings seek and for which they are fashioned is given in Jesus, God's supreme gift of love. He comes in the Father's name to bring the fulfillment promised to the Hebrew people and, through them, to all people everywhere. He is Himself our happiness and peace, our joy and beatitude."[63]

Through our union with God, who is communal by nature (Father, Son, and Spirit), we are *social beings*. We are intended to live in relationship. As human beings we live in the community of family, church, and world. We are destined for happiness insofar as we live in right ordered relationships

---

[62]It is interesting to note that fundamentalists often ignore the biblical directive to sell all you have and give to the

poor. "We don't take the bible that literally," is often the reply. In essence, they become their own redactors of biblical ethics. The result is a canon within the canon: a biblically interpreted moral code, delicatessen style. Biblical interpretation insists that the historical, cultural, and literary milieu of the text be considered when appropriating meaning for our contemporary culture.

[63]*Sharing the Light of Faith, NCD,* #100.

(*hesed*). When we respond in love to uphold the dignity of the human person we become fully human and fully alive. There is no room for an individualistic faith. We are ecclesial by nature and by design.

Our moral life is communal by nature and by design. Even our personal sins impact others in some way. Thus, our pursuit of happiness must be grounded in care and concern for others. Living a moral life demands that we uphold the ethical teaching of Christ in the gospel.

God created us with a free will. We have the power to choose the path for our lives. We are free to pattern our lives in conformity to God's will, to say yes or no to God. Human beings are free to choose between good and evil; thus we are called to responsibility. As a mature person of faith I am called to behave in a moral way because God desires it.

The church teaches that the moral law is expressed in different ways, all of which are connected. The moral law is expressed through eternal law, given by God who is the source of all law, through natural law, through revealed law (Old Covenant and New Covenant) and civil and ecclesiastical law. Moral law, then, hinges on more than the Ten Commandments. All forms of moral law find meaning in the life of Jesus.

For example, as a Christian, my choice to obey the civil law regarding the speed limit brings my Christian perspective into the choice. On a very practical level I do not disobey the civil law against speeding because I do not want to get a ticket. On a moral level, however, my choice to obey the law is illumined by my relationship with Christ. I am in covenant relationship with Jesus. Jesus loves me unconditionally. I, in turn, love Jesus and wish to act according to his design. We are all God's children and are graced by God. As a child of God, I have a responsibility to care for those around me. If I choose to place anyone in danger because of my actions, my relationships are not in right order. My relationship with Christ is strained because I have violated the law of love—care and concern for others. My relationship with my neighbor has been strained because I have placed others in harm's way. My relationship to myself is

strained because in order to live in *shalom*-peace[64] my life has to be ordered to the will of God. As I reflect upon the life of Jesus in the gospel, I am invited into relationship. That relationship demands a response. The response made in love helps give meaning to my life.

Testing
Were there any new insights? How would I answer the question, "Morality is . . ." in light of the tradition presented? What is the challenge of this doctrine?

Decision
What action will I take as a response to this presentation? How am I called to transformation? Be specific.

Refer to chapter 7, "Preparing the Catechetical Session," if you intend to plan your catechetical session at this time.

ORDINARY TIME

See Overview of Ordinary Time. See chapter 8, "Time and the Liturgical Cycle."

PAROUSIA

The term *parousia* (pronounced pahr-*oo*-see'-uh) is a Greek word meaning "presence" or "arrival." In the ancient Greek world, cities awaiting the arrival of dignitaries to their region would be awaiting their *parousia*. Paul uses the term in reference to himself when visiting the various communities. The term later was transferred to the belief in Jesus' second coming.

Natural Sign
What are your feelings in regard to the second coming of Jesus? Is it completely foreign to your experience or understanding or are you comfortable with the concept? Have you ever considered it before? What possible connection might there

---

[64]"When the heavenly hosts came announcing good news and peace to people of good will, *shalom*/peace was understood to mean wholeness. *Shalom* is a wholeness achieved only through the right ordering of relationships with God, one another, self, and the natural world.

be to your own personal life? What might you say if asked to explain what the parousia or second coming of Jesus is about? What do you think is meant by the term?

Tradition: Biblical, Ecclesial, and Liturgical Signs

Parousia is referred to as the glorious coming of Christ a second time, but is also related to the completion of God's plan of salvation for the human race, the final arrival of God's reign, the resurrection of the body on the last day, and final judgment. The coming of Jesus is the fulfillment of all God has been doing throughout salvation history. From the very beginning, at the creation of the world, God's master plan of salvation was intended to be accomplished through the life, death, and resurrection of Jesus Christ, the Son of God. Jesus is God's spoken Word that entered the lives of human beings. "The entire economy of salvation receives its meaning from the Incarnate Word. It prepared his coming; it manifests and extends his kingdom on earth from the time of his death and resurrection up to his second glorious coming, which *will complete the work of God.*"[65] Thus, when Jesus comes again, God's plan of salvation for the human race will be completed.

Our understanding of the parousia is expressed in our core truth, "the mystery of God the Father, the Son, and the Holy Spirit, Creator of all things; the mystery of Christ, the Incarnate Word, who was born of the Virgin Mary, and who suffered, died, and rose for our salvation, the mystery of the Holy Spirit, who is present in the Church, sanctifying it and guiding it until *the glorious coming of Christ,* our Savior and Judge; and the mystery of the Church, which is Christ's Mystical Body, in which the Virgin Mary holds a preeminent place."[66] We proclaim this truth every time we gather for liturgy when we pray the Nicene Creed, "...he will come again in glory to judge the living and the dead...." The parousia underscores the presence of Christ throughout all of salvation history, and the completion of the ultimate plan or process of salvation that began with the Incarnation, death, and resurrection of Jesus.[67]

The early church struggled with the reality that Jesus' second coming was not as imminent as they first had thought. In response, the evangelists formulated an understanding of God that put him beyond human time limitations. Believers were exhorted to view God's delay as a sign of "merciful opportunity for repentance."[68]

It is important not to consider the parousia as the return of Christ who has been absent all these long generations. "It is a breaking through of a presence that has been continuous throughout history."[69]

Jesus promised us that we would be judged at the end of time. Our hearts will be laid bare and all will be given a personal accounting of how they have or have not lived the law of love in their lives. Each person will be held accountable for the actions of his or her life and judged accordingly.

Jesus reigns today in the church through the Holy Spirit. However, the entire world has yet to recognize his reign. At the end of time Jesus will prevail victorious over the evil that permeates the world. Evil will be definitively squashed.

The church embraces the basic biblical understanding that human history has a purpose and that Jesus will win out over evil. Our doctrine is essentially a message of hope and consolation in the face of what often seems to be the ultimate victory of evil over good. We will one day experience a reversal and thus live in the eternal Presence where evil reigns no more.

The implication of the parousia is to be constantly on guard, to have our houses in order, to live in right relationship, and to assist in God's work of establishing justice in our temporal world.

Biblical passages that address the parousia (Jesus' second coming in glory and the final coming of God's reign, resurrection from the dead and final judgement) are the following:

Foreshadowed in the Old Testament:
   Genesis 49:8. Numbers 23:21. Isaiah 2:2–5; 9:2;

---

[65] *GCD*, #41.
[66] Ibid., #43.
[67] Zachary Hayes, O.F.M., "Parousia," in *NDT*, 743.

---

[68] Sean P. Kealy, "Parousia," in *CPDBT*, 692–694.
[69] Hayes, "Parousia," in *NDT*, 743–744.

11:6–16. Jeremiah 23:6. Daniel 7:13–14. Hosea 2:21–25. Zechariah 11:10.

New Testament:

Acts 1:11. 1 Corinthians 15:23. 1 Thessalonians 2:19; 3:13; 4:15; 5:23. 2 Thessalonians 1:7. 2 Timothy 4:1. Titus 2:13. Peter 1:7. 1 John 2:28; 3:2, 5, 8.

Gospels:

Matthew 10:23; 14:62; 16:27–28; 24:3, 27, 30, 36–37, 39. Mark 13:24. Luke 9:26; 12:40, 46; 17:20–37; 18:8; 21:27.

The parousia is addressed at every liturgical celebration that exhorts us to hope for the day when Christ will come again. ("Christ has died, Christ is risen; Christ will come again.") The season of Advent particularly looks toward that future day.

Testing

In what way, if any, has your original understanding regarding the second coming of Jesus been informed, stretched, challenged, or affirmed? Was there any new information for you? If so, what was it? In light of the material just presented, is there any implication for living the Christian life? What does this teaching have to say about the community's and your role in preparing for the parousia? In what way is this teaching related to the scriptures of this Sunday's liturgy? In light of this sharing, how would you articulate an understanding of the parousia? Is it the same as your first understanding, or has it changed?

Decision

How does this teaching about Jesus' second coming challenge our community? In what way is our community living the message we just shared? In what specific way is our community in need of transformation? Is there any concrete action I can take to be an agent of change in my community? How does this understanding of the parousia challenge me personally? How am I living the message? In what way do I need to grow? What one concrete action can I take this week as a response to what we have shared?

Refer to chapter 7, "Preparing the Catechetical Session," if you intend to plan your catechetical session at this time.

PASCHAL MYSTERY

Natural Sign

What images from everyday life might evoke the sense of dying and rising? If you were asked what it meant to die and rise again, how would you respond? Finish this sentence: "The paschal mystery is...."

Tradition: Biblical, Ecclesial, and Liturgical Signs

The paschal mystery refers to the essential elements of Christian redemption. It encompasses the passion, death, resurrection, and ascension of Jesus Christ that we celebrate every time we gather and especially at the church's premier celebration during Holy Week and Easter. God's plan for the salvation of the world was accomplished once and for all by the death and resurrection of Christ.

Jesus did not come to abolish the covenant, but rather to fulfill it (Mt 5:17–19). He revealed the deepest meaning of the law and reformed the sins against it (Heb 9:15). Jesus honored the temple and the Jewish feasts. Jesus used the temple to prefigure his own death as he announced the destruction of the temple and the entrance into the messianic age in which his body would become the new temple.

Jesus suffered at the hands of the chief priests and the scribes who handed him over to the authorities to be tortured and crucified (Mk 8:31; Mt 20:19). They sought his death because of his acts of forgiving sins, expelling demons, and healing people on the sabbath as well as his unusual stance regarding the ritual laws of purity. It did not sit well with the religious authorities that he ate with sinners and tax collectors. Some people even believed that Jesus was possessed and others accused him of blasphemy, false prophecy, and religious crimes punishable by the death penalty—stoning (Mk 2:7, 14–17; 3:1–6, 22; 7:14–23; 14:1. Mt 12:24. Jn 8:48; 10:20; 7:12, 52; 8:59; 10:31, 33).

God sent his only Son to demonstrate his love for us and Jesus freely died for our sins. He gave us a lasting memorial of his death and resurrection when he gave us his Body and Blood at the Last Supper. Jesus atoned for the sins of the world through his death and resurrection, thereby fulfilling the atoning mission of the Suffering Servant (CCC, #623). Jesus went down to the domain of the dead to release those who had died before him and were held captive by the power of death. He opened the doors to the heavenly kingdom.

The resurrection was attested to by the disciples who encountered Christ in his risen state. Through the resurrection Christ entered into his glory. The empty tomb and cloths are reminders that Christ escaped the power of death. Christ entered into heavenly glory in his full humanity at his ascension into heaven. Jesus went ahead of us to prepare a place for us to dwell with him for all eternity. The paschal mystery also includes the sending of the Spirit to be with the church until such time as Christ will return to judge the living and the dead according to their righteousness before God.

The paschal mystery includes salvation as foretold in the Hebrew scriptures, incorporation into Jesus' life, and the origins of the church and its sacramental life. We especially are united into the paschal mystery through the sacraments of initiation—baptism, confirmation, and eucharist.

Through the sacraments of initiation and especially through what Augustine referred to as the repeatable sacrament of initiation, eucharist, Christians are united with Christ's suffering, death, and resurrection; his passover from death to life. That is, Christians reenact and make present the paschal mystery when they take up their cross and unite their joys and sorrows with those of Jesus in the daily experience of their lives.

The paschal mystery is celebrated at every liturgy. This is why the Sunday celebration of eucharist is often referred to as an Easter event and why Easter is considered the Great Feast of Sunday. All the sacraments express incorporation into the paschal mystery of Christ.

In the sacrament of baptism an individual plunges into the life-giving waters and in so doing dies to sin and passes over into new life in Christ. Through the sacramental anointing of confirmation the Spirit is given and the person is configured to Christ, which seals him or her permanently with the life, death, and resurrection of Jesus. Through eucharist the faithful participate in the death and resurrection of Christ in the taking, blessing, breaking, and sharing of the eucharist at each eucharistic liturgy. The suffering, death, resurrection, and ascension of Christ and the sending of the Spirit are remembered and actualized at every celebration of eucharist.

Testing

Has your original understanding of the paschal mystery been affirmed, stretched, or challenged? Were there any new insights? Was there anything just shared that had not occurred to you before? What are the implications for everyday life? In what way have you experienced death and resurrection in your life? What are the implications for the church? In what way does the post-biblical teaching on paschal mystery have to do with this Sunday's readings? In light of this sharing, how would you articulate an understanding of the paschal mystery? Is it the same as your first understanding, or has it changed?

Decision

In what way do we as community live the message we just shared? Are there ways we need to grow in our understanding of what was shared? Where are the specific places where transformation is needed? How does the paschal mystery challenge me personally? How am I living it? In what way do I need to grow? What one concrete action can I take this week as a response to our sharing?

Refer to chapter 7, "Preparing the Catechetical Session," if you intend to plan your catechetical session at this time.

RECONCILIATION

Natural Sign

Have you ever experienced the forgiveness of someone close to you? Please explain. What did it teach you about reconciliation? How would you complete this sentence: "Reconciliation is . . ."?

Tradition: Biblical, Ecclesial, and Liturgical Signs

Please refer to the Rite of Penance (#386–394) for the scripture citations that are suggested in the Rite of Penance. These scriptural texts shed light on God's mercy experienced through his healing love and reconciliation.

The church exhorts men and women to repentance so that they may turn away from sin and be converted completely to the Lord (Rite of

Penance [RP], #1). We are called to reconciliation with God and the church. Every sin is an offense against God that disrupts our friendship with him. "The ultimate purpose of penance is that we should love God deeply and commit ourselves deeply to him"[70] Sinners who embrace the way of penance come back to the Father who loved us first, to Christ who gave himself up for us, and to the Spirit who has been abundantly poured upon us.

By the mystery of God's love we are joined in the bond of solidarity. The sin of one harms others and the holiness of one benefits others.[71] Penance always involves reconciliation with brothers and sisters who are harmed by our sins (RP, #5). Through the grace of Christ we are all to work for justice and peace in the world (RP, #6). Hence, we are to be cognizant of the social dimension of sin. "Men frequently join together to commit injustice (RP, #6)."

> Sin and its effects are visible everywhere: in exploitative relationships, loveless families, unjust social structures and policies, crimes by and against individuals and against creation, the oppression of the weak and the manipulation of the vulnerable, explosive tensions among nations and among ideological, racial and religious groups, and social classes, the scandalous gulf between those who waste goods and resources, and those who live and die amid deprivation and underdevelopment, wars and preparations for war. Sin is a reality in the world.[72]

Thus, we are to help each other do penance by working with others to realize justice and peace for all.

There are observable effects of reconciliation. We are converted to God with our whole heart. This conversion leads to sorrow for sin and the inten-

tion to live a new life. The intent to lead a new life is expressed through confession made to the church, through due satisfaction for sin and the promise to amend one's life. Pardon is granted through the church, which works by the ministry of priests (RP, #6).

Reconciliation occurs through the four components of the sacrament of penance. 1. Contrition: we are sorry for our sins and intend to sin no more. We are completely converted to Christ and turn our lives to the holiness and love of God in order to render ourselves more like Christ. 2. Confession: we examine our sin in light of God's mercy before God; we are sorry for our sins, and our heart is to be opened to God's minister, the priest. 3. Act of penance: True conversion is completed and evidenced by satisfaction for sins committed, amendment of conduct, and reparation of injury (suited to personal condition of each penitent). 4. Absolution is given through the sign of laying on of hands. God grants pardon to the sinner in sacramental confession and penance is completed.

> In the sacrament of penance the Father receives the repentant Son who comes back to him, Christ places the lost sheep on his shoulders and brings it back to the sheepfold, and the Holy Spirit sanctifies this temple of God again or lives more fully within it. This is finally expressed in a renewed and more fervent sharing of the Lord's table, and there is great joy at the banquet of God's church over the Son who has returned from afar.[73]

The church celebrates reconciliation through liturgical signs in the following manner: Rite of Reconciliation of individual penitents, Rite of Reconciliation of Several Penitents with Individual Confession and Absolution, Rite of Reconciliation of Several Penitents with General Confession and Absolution and Various Texts Used in the Celebration of Reconciliation, including sample nonsacramental penitential celebration. "Penitential celebrations, mentioned in the Rite of Penance (#36–37), are beneficial in fostering a spirit and

---

[70]Paul VI, Apostolic Constitution *Paenitenini,* February 17, 1966. AAS 57 (1965), 15–16. In Rite of Penance: *The Rites of the Catholic Church,* #5.

[71]Paul VI, Apostolic Constitution *Indulgentiarum doctrina,* Jan. 1, 1967, no. 4: AAS 59 (1967), 9; see Pius XII, encyclical *Mystici Corporis,* June 29, 1943. AAS 35 (1943), 213.

[72]*NCD,* #98.

[73]Rite of Penance, #6d.

virtue of penance among individuals and communities; they also help in preparing for a more fruitful celebration of the sacrament of penance. However, the faithful must be reminded of the difference between these celebrations and sacramental confession and absolution."[74]

Testing

Were there any new insights? How would you answer the following question now? "Reconciliation is. . . ."? What is the challenge? How are you called to live in a new way as a result of this doctrine?

Decision

What concrete action will I take as a result of this sharing?

Refer to chapter 7, "Preparing the Catechetical Session," if you intend to plan your catechetical session at this time.

SACRAMENTALITY

Sacramentality refers to the presence and encounter of God in all spheres of relationships and human endeavors.

Natural Sign

Do you remember a time when you experienced a sense of God's presence? How do you remember it? Describe it. What happened? How do you understand the meaning of the encounter you just described?

Tradition: Biblical, Ecclesial, and Liturgical Signs

In order to better understand sacraments it would be helpful to understand the concept of sacramentality on a purely human or anthropological level. Sacramentality is an activity that all human beings engage in by virtue of being in relationship. It is a process of discovery. People perform the rituals of life and in the process seek to appropriate meaning for their lives. Through sacramentality we give deeper meaning to the observable events around us. Moments of significant encounter, relational moments, form us and cause us to reflect on the meaning for our lives.

---

[74]Rite of Penance, Appendix II, #1.

In the scriptures the word sacrament is translated "mystery." It has a broad meaning and refers to God's plan and activity, revealed in Christ, for our salvation. The word sacramentality encompasses all the ways that God reaches out to us in the world. Any object, person, or thing that somehow brings God and people into contact, that reveals God's saving love, is understood as sacrament.

Sacramentality occurs whenever there is a precious encounter, a presence of God in any situation. Sacramentality embodies everyday moments of grace that have meaning for our lives. Wherever human beings are fully alive, God is present.

By our very nature, we Catholics are a sacramental people. We regard all creation as holy. We see God's life and energy in all created things, and we particularly set aside specific symbols from our natural world to speak and celebrate that reality.

The National Catechetical Directory states that there are four signs of God's presence: natural signs, biblical signs, ecclesial signs, and liturgical signs. Sacramentality is the essence of these signs. God is present throughout all human experience, through the natural signs in everyday life. God is sacramentally present in human experiences and relationships, in art, in music, in technology. God is sacramentally present in biblical signs, in the word of God spoken through the generations. God is revealed to us sacramentally (real presence) in the scriptures. God is truly (sacramentally) present to us in the church, through the living of our faith, through our beliefs and practices and through the service we perform in his name. God is sacramentally present to us in the rites of identity, passage, and celebration that we perform in the gathering and worship of God's people, the liturgy.

Even before Christ became human, there were rituals, blessings, signs, prayers, and gestures that spoke to the people about their identity and about a sacramental presence of God. The Spirit-guided church determined seven signs to be the most important and the most authentic because within them there appeared to be the very essence and life energy of Christ. Thus, there are seven unique signs that are especially determined to be sources of God's life and grace for the uplifting of the church. They are called the seven sacraments.

Testing
Had you ever considered the concept of sacramentality before? Were there any new insights? Was there anything just shared that had not occurred to you before? What are the implications for everyday life? In what way does sacramentality have anything to do with this Sunday's readings? How would you articulate an understanding of sacramentality?

Decision
How does sacramentality impact my life? How should I respond? How does this understanding of sacramentality challenge me personally? In what way do I need to grow? What one concrete action can I take this week as a response?

Refer to chapter 7, "Preparing the Catechetical Session," if you intend to plan your catechetical session at this time.

SACRAMENTS

Sacraments are the seven designated "liturgical rites of the church through which participants experience the love and power of God (grace) that flows from Christ's Passion, death and Resurrection."[75]

Natural Sign
Call to mind a particularly meaningful sacramental rite you have experienced. (Remember that people in the initiation process may or may not have had any church rituals. Thus, they instead might be asked: "Do you have a conscious memory of celebrating any church ritual or any other type of family or organization's ritual?") Please describe the experience. What happened? Based on your experience, how would you define *sacrament*? (Or, for a person in initiation, one might ask: "How would you explain the meaning of the word *ritual* in light of the experience you just shared?")

Tradition: Biblical, Ecclesial, and Liturgical Signs
The seven sacraments were not presented to us by Christ in specific formula and intent. One cannot

go to the scriptures and find the as-is liturgical rituals of sacraments. Their origins are reminiscent of the so-called Jewish sacraments. However, the spirit and meaning of the sacraments can be found in scripture through the life, ministry, and paschal mystery of Christ. We celebrate the mystery of salvation through the sacraments. They point us toward our eventual participation in the great banquet of heaven.

The term sacrament (from the Latin *sacramentum*, "oath," "pledge") refers to the seven liturgical rites of the church. Through the celebration of these rites people experience the love and grace of God and share in the paschal mystery of Christ, his life, passion, death, and resurrection. The seven sacraments are baptism, confirmation, eucharist, penance, anointing of the sick, holy orders, and matrimony.

The original word, *mysterion* (Greek "mystery"), was translated into the Latin word *sacramentum*. "A sacrament was an oath of allegiance made by a soldier in the military. Sometimes the soldier was branded on the arm with a sign of the general he was to serve."[76] An early church Father, Tertullian, used this image to refer to baptism. We are permanently consigned to the mission of God "through word 'oath' and visible 'sign' (brand) made possible through sharing in the Paschal Mystery of Christ."[77]

During the Middle Ages the church designated a list of seven sacraments. Prior to that time there had been a broader understanding of sacrament. It was understood to mean the power, love, and manifestation of God in any and all circumstances. Sacraments were also referred to as mysteries. The hidden nature of sacrament reflected God's hidden plan of salvation for all the world. God's plan was realized through the paschal mystery of Christ.

The theology of sacrament was developed during the scholastic period of the church (1100–1300). God offers salvation and strengthens the church through the sacraments that are instruments of God's grace. Sacraments unify the church and make holy its people. God's action is inherent in

---

[75]Richard McBrien, "Sacrament," in *HCEC*, 1146.

[76]Ibid.
[77]Ibid., 1147.

the sacramental signs. The familiar definition was "Sacraments are an outward sign, instituted by Christ, to give grace."

To expand the scholastic understanding of sacramental theology, modern sacramental catechesis "has emphasized that *Jesus Christ is the first sacrament.*"[78] Since the power of the sacraments flows from the life, passion, death, and resurrection of Jesus, he is our first sacrament. *The Church has also been referred to as sacrament since it is the living presence of Christ on earth until he comes again in glory.* The church as the Body of Christ is the instrument that "proclaims God's powerful love for humanity in and through the Paschal mystery."[79]

Christ himself, through the Holy Spirit, offers the grace and power that each sacrament expresses. Through the Holy Spirit the sacraments have the power of healing and transformation. Through the sacraments we are made more into the image of Christ. Thomas Aquinas stated: "Therefore a sacrament is a sign that commemorates what precedes it—Christ's Passion; demonstrates what is accomplished in us through Christ's Passion—grace; and prefigures what that Passion pledges to us—future glory."[80] In other words, through the sacraments, the passion of Jesus is remembered and made present. We are graced, given a share in his life, and are promised eternal life. Sacraments strengthen and empower us to cooperate with the life we have been given.

Sacraments have their genesis out of the signs and symbols of everyday life. Humanity experiences the spiritual world through symbols. Language, gestures, and actions express and communicate meaning on a very basic level. The elements of creation speak to us of the power and nature of God. Fire, water, light speak to us of God's presence and God's power. Actions of everyday life, washing, anointing, breaking bread, sharing a cup, can express for us the way God graces us and the way we offer praise and thanks for all of God's saving work. God takes the gifts made from human hands and through the power of the Holy Spirit makes them holy. The elements (bread, wine, water, oil, light, laying on of hands, cross, fire) are transformed into a new reality and in the process we are changed and transformed as well. It is not magic, but it is mystery. It is mystery when the church is able by the grace of the Holy Spirit to remember past events and actions, bring those events and actions into the present through story telling and symbolic ritual, and know that the same effect of the original event is a present, experienced reality.

Sacraments are celebrations of conversion and are related to life and human experience. They possess meaning on two levels, theoretical and practical. We understand conceptually what a sacrament means and we *experience* the meaning given to it through its celebration in the community.

The sacraments are not private. They are communal by nature and by intent. The Constitution on the Sacred Liturgy states: "Liturgical services are not private functions but are celebrations of the entire Church which is 'the sacrament of unity,' namely, the holy people united and organized under the authority of the bishops. Therefore, liturgical services pertain to the whole Body of the Church. They manifest it, and have effects upon it."[81] Thus, sacraments are celebrated through active participation of all the faithful. By virtue of our baptism we are consecrated a holy people. We are anointed priest, prophet, and king and therefore "may offer spiritual sacrifices."[82] "Rites that are meant to be celebrated in common, with the faithful present and actively participating, should as far as possible be celebrated in that way rather than by an individual and quasi-privately."[83] Sacramental celebration, therefore, is a communal response of word, song, prayer, and gesture to the God who calls us to life through Christ Jesus.

Sacraments assume celebration in faith. It is said that sacraments effect what they signify. When the celebration of a sacrament expresses a specific grace, for example, membership, cleansing, and empowerment for mission, it is not only bestowed on the person, but it is also operative in the life of the one who celebrates. However, since faith is assumed, the effects are dependent on the disposi-

---

[78]Ibid.

[79]Ibid.

[80]St. Thomas Aquinas, *Summa theologiae*, III, 60, 3.

[81]*CSL*, #26.

[82]*Lumen Gentium* 10; cf. 1 Pet 2:45.

[83]*CSL*, #27.

tion (faith, conversion) of the individual. One either cooperates with the grace or one does not. I used to be an excellent guitar player. Over the years I have had to use my keyboard talents more than my guitar playing skills. I no longer can play as I used to play. However, if I were to invest the time and energy into the practice of the guitar, my playing would rapidly improve. Sacraments operate in somewhat similar fashion. Grace (the presence of Christ) is there for the asking, but without faith it is not necessarily evident and operative in the life of the individual.

Sacraments call us to action. They are not simply gifts for our own spiritual benefit. They are intended to build up the entire church. That can happen only when its members live and act as children of God, when they live the paschal mystery and take what they have received into the world in order to transform it.

Testing
Was there anything just shared that had not occurred to you before? Were there any new insights? What are the implications of sacraments for living your everyday life? What difference do sacraments make to the wider church? In what way have sacraments made a difference in your life? What do sacraments have to do with this Sunday's readings? How would you explain sacraments to a stranger? Has your original understanding been changed, affirmed, or challenged in any way?

Decision
How do sacraments call for a response by the community? What are the implications of sacraments for the church? How do sacraments as described in this session challenge me personally? What one concrete action can I take this week as a response to our sharing?

Refer to chapter 7, "Preparing the Catechetical Session," if you intend to plan your catechetical session at this time.

SIN

Natural Sign
When we speak about sin, what does it mean to you? Have you ever given any thought to your own sinfulness? In what way? How would you articulate an understanding of your faith tradition's belief about sin?

Tradition: Biblical, Ecclesial, and Liturgical Signs
The etymology of the word sin means to "miss the mark" or, in a religious sense, "to fall short of God's will for us."[84] Human beings were created in the image and likeness of God. As such, we are holy in God's sight. However, since the beginning of time human beings have abused the freedom given to them by God. Men and women have turned away from God and attempted to be fulfilled apart from God.[85]

Sin wreaks havoc in the lives of people. It causes great sorrow and upheaval. People sin when their actions "knowingly and deliberately violate the moral law and in a serious matter also seriously offend God."[86] Most of us have experienced a time in our lives when our actions affected another person in a negative, hurtful, or destructive way. This is sin.

Throughout the history of salvation God has intervened in the lives of men and women in order to help them in their struggle against the forces of sin and evil. Sin was, is, and always will be a part of our lives. In the Old Testament sin was usually personified in terms of a character (e.g., the serpent in the garden). For the ancients, sin resulted in humanity's foolish belief that they could get along without God, or that they could be like God. The primary motif of the Old Testament scriptures is God in relationship to a people. God entered into covenant with Israel. Israel sinned; God invited it to repent; Israel repented, and God rescued and liberated it.

In both the Old and the New Testaments there is very little understanding of sin in personal terms. It is most commonly understood to be communal. Serious sins such as rebellion, infidelity, and sexual misconduct were seen as disturbances to community and family order and would be reprimanded accordingly. When people revolted by turning away from God completely, the punish-

---

[84]Robert J. Schreiter, C.PP.S., "Sin," in *CPDBT*, 921–922.
[85]*Dogmatic Constitution on the Church*, #13, in *DV* II.
[86]*GCD*, #62.

ment was either banishment from the community or death. It was believed that sinners brought such judgment down upon themselves.[87]

Jesus' primary role through his passion, death, and resurrection, was to free the human race of the effects of sin. God is alive for us in the person of his Son. The grace given to us by Jesus is far more abundant than the sins we commit. Through repentance for our sins we can share in the love and salvation offered by Jesus.[88]

Sin is the greatest obstacle men and women face in their efforts to love God and one another. There are different types of sin. Humanity is born into original sin, the first obstacle to a life of love. We are born into the human condition, a fallen state: "human nature . . . fallen, stripped of the grace that clothed it, injured in its own natural powers and subjected to the dominion of death, that is transmitted to all."[89]

Human beings as individuals commit personal sins. "It is willful rejection, either partial or total, of one's role as a child of God and a member of His people. By it sinners knowingly and deliberately disobey God's command to love Him, other people, and themselves in a morally right way."[90] By sins of omission (failing to do what one should do) or commission (willfully doing what one should not do) men and women turn from God's will. Personal sin begins within the heart of an individual and extends to behavior that defies God's greatest commandment to love God, neighbor, and self.

Grave sin, called mortal, seriously disrupts one's relationship with God. Mortal sin is committed with malice of intent, by deliberately choosing evil over good. Mortal sin assumes full consent and knowledge of the offense. Lesser sins, called venial, also impair that same relationship and can accumulate to the point of leading to more serious sin.[91]

Because God loves us, the entire human race is formed in an eternal bond of "supernatural solidarity, so much so that the sin of one harms the others just as the holiness of one benefits the others."[92] Penance calls us to reconcile with our brothers and sisters who are always harmed by our sins.[93] God calls us away from sin. This conversion constitutes a "profound change of the whole person by which one begins to consider, judge, and arrange his life according to the holiness and love of God."[94]

We are forgiven our sins and reconciled with God and one another through the sacraments of penance and eucharist. Through baptism our fallen nature is crucified with Christ so that the body of sin may be destroyed and we may no longer be slaves to sin, but rise with Christ and live for God (Rom 6:4–10). The sacrament of penance is like a second baptism. Rather than the water of baptism, there are tears of penance.[95]

The eucharist is also for the forgiveness of sins. In the liturgy we recall and make present Jesus' words, "Take and eat. This is my Body given up for you for the forgiveness of sins." We are forgiven by the death and resurrection of Jesus. We, in turn, take up our cross and offer our lives for the sins of others, just as Christ offered his life for us.

Sometimes we unconsciously trivialize the actual atrocity of sin. We reduce it to a laundry list of do's and don't's and fail to get inside the permeating and devastating aspects of another dimension of sin called *social sin*. It is very easy to relegate social sin to be out of our control, unrelated to us or our lives and, in essence, not our problem. We often fail to see that we are part of a global human village.

Sin occurs in both personal and social forms. Social sin is a concept that most of us have not had the occasion to consider. What is it? "Social sin represents, as it were, the accumulation of sinful acts that cre-

---

[87]James A. Fischer, "Sin—Old Testament," in *CPDBT*, 916–919.

[88]*GCD*, #62.

[89]Pope Paul VI, *Credo of the People of God* (June 30, 1968).

[90]*NCD*, #98.

[91]Ibid.

[92]Paul VI, Apostolic Constitution *Indulgentiarum doctrina*, January 1, 1967, no. 4: AAS 59 (1967), 9; see Pius XII, encyclical *Mystici Corporis*, June 29, 1943. AAS 35 (1943), 213.

[93]Rite of Penance, #5.

[94]Pope Paul VI, Apostolic Constitution *Paenitemini*, February 17, 1966.

[95]St. Ambrose, Letter 41:12: PL 16, 1116.

ate environments of oppression, racism, and sexism, environments of sinfulness so powerful and so pervasive that no one can escape them."[96]

How do we commit social sin? Social sin has seriously impacted the lives of innocent people around the world. This sinister reality was confronted in 1983 by a group of bishops gathered at the Synod of Reconciliation. As a result of this meeting, Pope John Paul II addressed the topic of social sin in an apostolic letter resulting from this Synod, "Reconciliation and Penance," Dec. 2, 1984.

The highlight of the letter's main points are as follows:

I: The presence of social sin exists in laws, policies, and social practices that result in the failure to respect or enhance the human dignity of certain groups within society.

II: Social sin is the accumulation of personal sins. Human beings contribute to social sin in a number of ways.

   a. Actions or omissions that cause or support the evil condition, that fail to enhance human dignity. (*"The School of the Americas is training guerrillas in the art of torture and warfare to use in Third World countries. That's the government's business, not mine."*)

   b. Actions or omissions that exploit the evil condition, that take advantage of people or situations for self-interest or gain. (*"I think I might hire an illegal immigrant. I can get a lady to clean my house for $2.00 an hour because she is desperate."*)

   c. Failure to avoid, eliminate, or at least limit the evil condition due to laziness, fear, indifference, the conspiracy of silence, or through secret complicity. (*"I know that my boss is knowingly discriminating against the minorities in my company and is falsifying records in order to get away with it. But I'll never tell anyone; it's none of my business."*)

   d. Another way personal sin contributes to social sin is when I take refuge in the impossibility of changing the evil condition with the attitude that there is nothing I can do. (*Henry Thoreau was imprisoned during the Mexican War. He thought the war was an attempt to gain control of other regions for the purpose of building their slave labor pool. He would not support the war and refused to pay taxes. When his friend, Ralph Waldo Emerson visited him in prison, he asked Thoreau why he was in jail. Thoreau very indignantly asked Emerson why he was not right there with him, as he too had been opposed to the war for the same reason. How many of us are that ready to put our money where our mouth is!*)

   e. When we sidestep the effort and sacrifice required to address the evil condition with the attitude, "I don't want to be bothered; it will put me out too much." (*"I would like to work at the soup kitchen on Tuesdays but it is the day I get my hair and nails done. Or... I am against abortion, but it is just too much fuss to do or say anything about it. Leave that to others!"*)

   f. When we rationalize with regard to why we cannot engage in actions to address the evil condition by thinking, "If I do that they will have my head on the platter." (*"I am very much against the practices of the World Bank because they deliberately charge interest that causes excessive suffering for the poor in Third World countries. If I take any action to speak up in any way, I will be fired from my position at the bank."*)

While social sin is communal, the responsibility belongs to individuals. Social sin is the amassment of our own personal sins. The effects of my sins are limited to those in somewhat close proximity. I sin due to an action or a failure to act and the consequences generally affect a small group of people. Personal sins are healed through the healing sacrament of reconciliation. Social sin, on the other hand, is intricate and ambiguous and affects a much larger group of people. It invades our laws, customs, and practices and thus the repercussions are immense. It is not easily healed as it usually involves a collective blindness. Sometimes social sin is even disguised as socially acceptable. We need to make it our business to see. (*A young man who grew up in New Orleans during the days of segregation was riding his daily bus. He witnessed a scene he had observed many other times: a black woman getting on the bus, only this time she attempted to enter it from the front rather than the rear.*

---

[96]Robert J. Schreiter, C.PP.S., "Sin," in *CPDBT,* 921–922.

The bus driver hit the woman. For the first time this young man's eyes were opened. He saw the evil of prejudice and its effects.)

The pope maintains that personal sin such as fear, greed, and selfishness is at the core of all social sin and that we must take responsibility for it. We respond to social sin with a communal mindset, an awareness that we are part of the human village. This begins with an inner disposition of solidarity with those who suffer any injustice, asserts the pope. One reason Jesus was killed was because of his unpopular, dangerous support for the poor and marginalized. He shook the status quo. He offered hope to the oppressed and unnerved those who were in positions of power.

The first place to begin to address our participation in social sin is to raise our consciousness to all evil, especially evil that robs human beings of their God-given right to dignity.[97]

Testing
In what way, if any, has your original understanding of sin been stretched, challenged, or affirmed? Was there any new information for you? If so, what was it? Was there anything you found to be uncomfortable about in this teaching? In light of the material just presented, is there any implication for living the Christian life? In what way is this post-biblical teaching related to the scriptures of this Sunday's liturgy? In light of this sharing, how would you articulate a theology or understanding of sin? Is it the same as your first understanding, or has it changed?

Decision
How does this teaching about sin challenge our community? In what way do we as community live the message we just shared? Are there ways we need to grow in our understanding of what was shared? Where are the specific places where transformation is needed? Is there any concrete action I can take to be an agent of change in my community? How does this understanding of sin challenge me personally? How am I living the message? In what way do I need to grow? What is one

specific action I can take this week as a response to our sharing?

Refer to chapter 7, "Preparing the Catechetical Session," if you intend to plan your catechetical session at this time.

TRINITY

Natural Sign
In what way have you experienced God in creation? How would you finish the following sentence: "The Trinity is..."?

Tradition: Biblical, Ecclesial, and Liturgical Signs
The mystery of the Trinity is essential to our faith. It is unique to the Christian faith: One God in three persons. The Hebrew scriptures do not provide a Trinitarian understanding of God. Israel contributed the concept of a mono-theistic God. In the Hebrew scriptures God is Creator, Author of all Life. Israel depicted God as Word (*dabar*), Spirit (*ruah*), Wisdom (*hokmah*), and Presence (*shekina*).

The New Testament does not clearly define the dogma of Trinity. Rarely is Jesus referred to as God, as it would identify him too closely with the Father. But his divinity is recognized. The word Trinity is not used, but there is a proclaimed experience of Triune God—Father, Son, and Spirit. This is referred to as the economic trinity—the experience of God's action in the world. Matthew's gospel has Jesus exhorting his disciples to go out and baptize all nations in the name of the Father, Son, and Spirit (28:19). The Trinity is experienced in Jesus' baptism in the Jordan when the Spirit descends upon him and the Father's voice is heard.

The apostolic age held fast to the doctrine of one God and defended this against pagan polytheism. There are references to the Trinity in early liturgies prior to a formalized doctrine on Trinity. There is a basic principle that states that from the church's prayer flows its creed (*lex orandi, lex credendi*). The church professed its belief through its prayer. The prayer of the church reflects the lived experience of the Triune God. From the experience of ritual prayer, the church formulated its official creed.

The Trinitarian creed was formulated as a result of heresies that crept into the church early in its history. Language is very limited when it comes

---

[97]Section on social sin adapted from "Grace and Sin," a presentation by Robert Duggan, North American Forum on the Catechumenate.

to explaining an inexplicable mystery. Notions from philosophical origins helped formulate the theology.

There were two schools of thought emanating from the Greek and Latin Fathers. The two schools were based on the distinctions between immanent trinity and economic trinity. The economic trinity (Greek Fathers) was based on the experience of God in the world, in the history of salvation. Humanity experienced God as creator, Son as redeemer, and Spirit as sanctifier. The term relates to the three "faces" or actions of God's manifestation. Economic trinity refers to the *mission* of God who sent the Son and the Spirit to accomplish the work of salvation.

Immanent trinity (Latin Fathers) refers to the relationship the Father, Son, and Spirit have with one another apart from the actions they have performed in the world. Immanent trinity centers on the "Oneness" of God, one divine nature. The inner life of God is Trinitarian. Outside the inner life, the actions of God are common to all three persons as there is only one nature. No person of the Trinity is less than the others.

The Arian heresy asserted that there was a time when Jesus *was not*. He was created by the Father. The divinity of the Holy Spirit was questioned by other heresies. The Council of Nicea (325 C.E.) resolved the heresies by establishing a creedal statement of faith, the Nicene Creed (proclaimed in every eucharistic liturgy).

The Council asserted that there is one God of three: co-equal and co-eternal. Jesus was begotten, not made. He always was with the Father. There was never a time he was not. He was with the Father, as was the Spirit, at the creation of the world. That is, all three always existed. The three persons are distinct, but not separate. The Son is of the same substance as the Father (*homoousios*). Father, Son, and Spirit work for our redemption. The Council of Constantinople in 553 attested to the one God in three persons (consubstantial Trinity). The Council of Toledo maintained that the "three persons do not share one divinity unto themselves, but each one is whole and entire."[98] They are distinct from one another, yet one. The term used to

designate this three persons and their distinctions is *hypostasis*. The Father is not the Son, the Son is not the Spirit, etc. God is one, but not solitary. The divine persons are distinct. They are distinct in the way they are related to each other. The Father generates, the Son is begotten, and the Holy Spirit proceeds.

The official church teaches that the Trinity is an absolute mystery. We do not understand it even after it has been revealed. Mystery transcends the capacity of our ordinary rational and conceptual powers. It goes beyond the scope of human imagination and everyday knowledge.

God as Father

The Father, unbegotten, acts only with the Son and the Spirit. The Father generates the Son and sends the Spirit. Jesus reveals the Father who is Father because of his relationship to Jesus, the Son. Jesus is Son only in relation to the Father.

God as Son

Jesus was eternally begotten of the Father. He was not made. Jesus is of the same essence as the Father—divine and coeternal (he always was). In John's gospel Jesus is referred to as the Word. One possible metaphor for trying to grasp the ineffable mystery is to see it in terms of the WORD image. If Jesus is the WORD of the Father, the WORD was always a part of the Father. God but spoke the Word and a part of Godself came forth from his very being.

It is through Jesus that the Father is expressed to us in our salvation history. The Son is the same unity, substance as the Father—thus it is not Sonship as we understand it in human terms.

God as Spirit

If Jesus is the Word, the truth of God's self that comes from his very being, then who is the Spirit? The Spirit is also God. The Word was spoken and Jesus was begotten. The life force, the breath that came forth from the mouth of God was the Spirit. From the truth of God's existence came the Son, begotten of the Father. From the truth of God as revealed to us by the Son comes love, the Spirit of God. If Jesus is the Word, or Truth of who God is, the Spirit is the action of the Truth: Love.

[98]Linda Gaupin, *Catholic Faith and Life*, 46.

God the Holy Spirit is another divine person who is with Jesus and the Father. The Spirit is given as gift from the Father, given to us through the Son. The Spirit communicates the Father to us and we are able to communicate in a personal relationship with the Father. The Holy Spirit is God communicating with us. Thus, the Holy Spirit is given in love and with that love comes reconciling and renewing power. The Spirit is of the same essence as the Father, but distinct. "The Spirit has the same essence of the Father, and yet is distinct from the Father and the Son. The Spirit proceeds from the Father through the Son. The procession is not a begetting, since this would lead to the supposition that there are two Sons, nor is the Spirit merely a mode [through] which the Son communicates himself to us. The Spirit originates from the Father and the Son, and has a distinct relationship to the Father and the Son."[99] Thus, they are three persons in one God, and the Spirit has a role in the saving mission throughout history.

The symbols of the Holy Spirit show us the nature and the activity of the Spirit in the church. Water signifies the Holy Spirit in baptism and is a sign of new birth. The gestation of first birth took place in water, so too, our birth in the divine life comes through water. Anointing is a sign of the presence of the Spirit. Christ in Hebrew means the *one anointed by God's Spirit*. The Holy Spirit anointed Jesus as "Christ."

By the power of the Spirit Mary conceived and Simeon could proclaim her son messiah. Through the Spirit power went out from Jesus through acts of healing and saving. The Spirit raised Jesus from the dead.

Fire as symbol signifies the transforming energy of the Spirit's actions. Jesus said of the Spirit, "I came to cast fire on the face of the earth, and would that it were already kindled." The tongues of *fire, cloud, and light* are manifestations of the Holy Spirit. They reveal God's transcendence, omnipotence and glory, (e.g., Moses on Sinai, at the tent of meeting, and the wandering in the desert).

---

[99]Ibid., 49.

The *seal* as symbol of the Spirit is similar to anointing. It indicates the effects of the anointing of the Spirit. The *hand* as sign of the Spirit demonstrates healing power. Jesus invokes the Spirit and heals the sick by the laying on of hands. The apostles would do the same. The *finger* is also a sign of the Holy Spirit. By the finger of God Jesus cast out demons (Lk 11:20). The dove (flood, baptism) is a traditional sign of the Spirit. Noah released a dove and the earth was again hospitable. The Spirit comes "like a dove" and remains in the purified hearts of the baptized (Mk 1:10).

What is the bottom line here? When all is said and done, it is God who created us, who sustains us, who will judge us, and who will give us eternal life. This is a God who is not removed from us. Our God is a God of absolute proximity, who is truly communicated to us in the flesh in history and within the human family. God is with us in the spiritual depths of our existence as well as in our unfolding history. God is in our everyday lives. God is the source of enlightenment and community.

We proclaim the Trinity in the liturgy in the greeting, the sign of the cross, the Gloria, the creed, the eucharistic prayers, the doxology, and the final blessings as well as in all the sacraments. Refer to the *Catechism of the Catholic Church*, #249–267.

Testing
Were there any new insights? How would you articulate an understanding of Trinity? How does this dogma have anything to do with everyday life? Have any of your original assumptions been stretched?

Decision
How does this teaching call us to action? What one action will you take as a response?

Refer to chapter 7, "Preparing the Catechetical Session," if you intend to plan your catechetical session at this time.

TRANSFIGURATION

See Feast of the Transfiguration and Second Sunday of Lent.

FOOTNOTE CODES

ACC	Brown, Raymond E., S.S. *An Adult Christ at Christmas.*	
AIRI	Yarnold, Edward, S.J. *The Awe-Inspiring Rites of Initiation.*	
BAL	Brown, Raymond E., S.S. *The Beatitudes According to Luke.*	
BOM	Brown, Raymond E., S.S. *The Birth of the Messiah.*	
BSM	Myers, Ched. *Binding the Strong Man.*	
CBC	Karris, Robert J., O.F.M., ed. *Collegeville Bible Commentary.*	
CBP	Reid, Barbara E. *Choosing the Better Part.*	
CC	Hynes, Mary Ellen. *Companion to the Calendar.*	
CCA	Brown, Raymond E., S.S. *A Coming Christ in Advent.*	
CCC	*Catechism of the Catholic Church.*	
CCHW	Brown, Raymond E., S.S. *A Crucified Christ in Holy Week.*	
CCT	Dues, Greg. *Catholic Customs and Traditions.*	
CD	*The Catechetical Documents: A Parish Resource.*	
CGOS	Brown, Raymond E. *Christ in the Gospels of the Ordinary Sundays.*	
CHBP	*Catholic Household Blessings and Prayers.*	
CL	Gaupin, Linda. *Catechesis for Liturgy.*	
CM	Kingsbury, Jack Dean. *Conflict in Mark.*	
CNT	Wintherop, Ronald D. *Conversion in the New Testament.*	
COMG	Kingsbury, Jack Dean. *The Christology of Mark's Gospel.*	
CONF	*Confessions of St. Augustine.*	
CPDBT	Stuhlmueller, Carroll, C.P., ed. *The Collegeville Pastoral Dictionary of Biblical Theology.*	
CR	Marthaler, Berard. *The Creed.*	
CSL	*Constitution on the Sacred Liturgy.*	
CSM	McBrien, Richard P. *Catholicism.*	
CWJ	Pilch, John J. *The Cultural World of Jesus.*	
CWJ-B	Pilch, John J. *The Cultural World of Jesus, Sunday by Sunday, Cycle B.*	
CY	Mazar, Peter. *To Crown the Year: Decorating the Year Through the Seasons.*	
DB	McKenzie, John L. *The Dictionary of the Bible.*	
DL	*Days of the Lord (Vols. I–VII).*	
DBT	Léon-Dufour, Xavier. *Dictionary of Biblical Theology.*	
DOB	McKenzie, John L. *The Dictionary of the Bible.*	
DOL	*Documents on the Liturgy.*	
DV(II)	Abbott, Walter M., S.J., ed. *The Documents of Vatican II.*	
EEC	Rordorf, Willy. *The Eucharist of the Early Christians.*	
EGW	Dunning, Jim. *Echoing God's Word.*	
GAP	Richards, Hubert. *The Gospel According to St. Paul.*	
GCD	*General Catechetical Directory.*	
GCY	Rahner, Karl. *The Great Church Year.*	
GEJ	Brown, Raymond E., S.S. *The Gospel and Epistles of John.*	
GIRM	*General Instruction of the Roman Missal.*	
GJ	Ellis, Peter F. *The Genius of John.*	
GL	Johnson, Luke Timothy. *The Gospel of Luke.*	
GNLY	*General Norms for the Liturgical Year and Calendar.*	
GWT	Dalton, William. *Galatians Without Tears.*	
HCEC	McBrien, Richard P., ed. *HarperCollins Encyclopedia of Catholicism.*	
HD	Crosby, Michael H. *The House of Disciples.*	
HTP	Scott, Bernard Brandon. *Hear Then the Parable.*	
IA	Karris, Robert J., O.F.M. *Invitation to Acts.*	
IM	Senior, Donald, C.P. *Invitation to Matthew.*	
IMC	Winjgaards, John, M.H.M. *Inheriting the Master's Cloak.*	
JGNP	Cassidy, Richard J. *John's Gospel in New Perspective.*	
JHT	Johnson, Sherman E. *Jesus and His Towns.*	
JHW	Collins, Raymond F. *John and His Witness.*	
JMJG	Karris, Robert J. *Jesus and the Marginalized in John's Gospel.*	
JP	Kealy, Sean P., C.S.Sp. *Jesus and Politics.*	
KG	Bright, John. *The Kingdom of God.*	
LAF, LF	Grassi, Joseph A. *Loaves and Fishes.*	
LK	LaVerdiere, Eugene, S.S.S. *Luke.*	
LM	*Lectionary for Mass: Introduction,* second editio typica, ICEL, 1985.	
LPT	Stockhausen, Carol L. *Letters in the Pauline Tradition.*	
LTS	Talbert, Charles H. *Learning Through Suffering.*	
LY	Adam, Adolf. *The Liturgical Year.*	
MAM	Anderson, Janice Cape, and Stephen D. Moore. *Mark and Method: New Approaches to Biblical Studies.*	

MARK	Harrington, Wilfrid, O.P. *Mark.*
MI	Hare, Douglas R.A. *Matthew, Interpretation: A Bible Commentary for Teaching and Preaching.*
MK	Harrington, Wilfrid, O.P. *Mark.*
MML	Flanagan, Neal M., O.S.M. *Mark, Matthew, Luke: A Guide to the Gospel Parallels.*
MRR	Jungman, Joseph A. *The Mass of the Roman Rite: Its Origins and Development.*
MSS	Richter, Klemens. *The Meaning of the Sacramental Symbols.* Linda Maloney, trans.
NAB	*New American Bible.*
NCD	*The National Catechetical Directory*
NDSW	Fink, Peter E., S.J., ed. *The New Dictionary of Sacramental Worship.*
NDT	Komonchak, Joseph A., Mary Collins, Dermot A. Lane, eds. *The New Dictionary of Theology.*
NJBC	Brown, Raymond E., S.S., et al., eds. *The New Jerome Biblical Commentary.*
NS	Beck, Robert R. *Nonviolent Story.*
NTI	Perrin, Norman, and Dennis C. Duling. *The New Testament: An Introduction.*
NULA	Tannehill, Robert C. *The Narrative Unity of Luke-Acts: A Literary Interpretation* (Vols. I and II).
OCSP	Brown, Raymond E., S.S. *Once and Coming Spirit at Pentecost.*
OLY	Talley, Thomas J. *Origins of the Liturgical Year.*
PAI	Kuntz, J. Kenneth. *The People of Ancient Israel: An Introduction to Old Testament Literature, History, and Thought.*
PCW	Byrne, Brendan, S.J. *Paul and the Christian Woman.*
PE	Karris, Robert J., O.F.M. *The Pastoral Epistles.*
PG	Collins, Raymond F. *Preaching the Gospels.*
PJGM	Senior, Donald, C.P. *The Passion of Jesus in the Gospel of Matthew.*
PL	Fuller, Reginald H. *Preaching the Lectionary.*
PNL	Fuller, Reginald H. *Preaching the New Lectionary.*
PTE	Collins, Raymond F. *Preaching the Epistles.*
PW	Jungman, Joseph A. *Public Worship: A Survey.* Clifford Howell, trans.
RCC	*Rites of the Catholic Church,* ICEL, 1988.
RCE	Brown, Raymond E., S.S. *A Risen Christ in Eastertime.*
RCIA	The Rite of Christian Initiation for Adults.
RF	Ramshaw, Gail. *Richer Fare for the Christian People.*
RJ	Talbert, Charles H. *Reading John.*
RJE	Brown, Raymond E., S.S. *A Retreat with John the Evangelist.*
RL	Talbert, Charles H. *Reading Luke.*
RM	Garland, David E. *Reading Matthew: A Literary and Theological Commentary on the First Gospel.*
RNT	Perkins, Pheme. *Reading the New Testament.*
ROT	Boadt, Lawrence, C.S.P. *Reading the Old Testament.*
RP	Rite of Penance. *Rites of the Catholic Church.* ICEL, 1976.
RT	Schneiders, Sandra. *The Revelatory Text.*
SB	Crosby, Michael H. *The Spirituality of the Beatitudes: Matthew's Challenge for First World Christians.*
SCOTL	Campbell, Anthony F., S.J. *The Study Companion to Old Testament Literature.*
SIR	Rybolt, John E. *Sirach. Collegeville Bible Commentary, Old Testament #21,* Robert J. Karris, O.F.M., ed.
SL	Jones, Cheslyn, Geoffrey Wainwright, Edward Yarnold, S.J., and Paul Bradshaw, eds. *The Study of Liturgy, Rev. ed.*
SWTLY	Gutierrez, Gustavo. *Sharing the Word Through the Liturgical Year.*
TCBD	Brown, Raymond E., S.S. *The Community of the Beloved Disciple.*
TCY	Mazar, Peter. *To Crown the Year: Decorating the Church Through the Seasons.*
TDJR	Stamps, Mary E., ed. *To Do Justice and Right Upon the Earth.*
TFC	Lee, Bernard J. *The Future Church of 140 B.C.E.*
TGJ	Marrow, Stanley B. *The Gospel of John.*
TI	Hughes, Philip Edgcumbe. *The True Image.*
TKG	Bright, John. *The Kingdom of God.*
TLD	Hoffman, Elizabeth, ed. *The Liturgy Documents.*
TWOW	Corbon, Jean. *The Wellspring of Worship.*
UOT	Anderson, Bernhard W. *Understanding the Old Testament,* Fourth Edition.
WBC	Camp, Claudia V. *The Women's Bible Commentary.*
WNT	Johnson, Luke Timothy. *The Writings of the New Testament: An Interpretation.*
WWC	Sanchez, Patricia Datchuck. *The Word We Celebrate.*

BIBLIOGRAPHY

Abbott, Walter M., S.J., ed. *The Documents of Vatican II.* New York: The Guild Press, 1966.

Adam, Adolf. *The Liturgical Year.* Collegeville: The Liturgical Press, 1979.

Anderson, Bernhard W. *Understanding the Old Testament.* Fourth Edition. Englewood Cliffs: Prentice-Hall, 1986.

Anderson, Janice Cape, and Stephen D. Moore. *Mark and Method: New Approaches to Biblical Studies.* Minneapolis: Fortress Press, 1992.

Beck, Robert R. *Nonviolent Story. Narrative Conflict Resolution in the Gospel of Mark.* Maryknoll: Orbis Books, 1996.

Bernard, St. (1090–1153). *Sermon 84 sur le Cantique des Cantiques*, 3. In *Invit'es aux noces*, trans. and ed. P.-Y. Emery. Paris: Descl'ee, 1979.

Boadt, Lawrence, C.S.P. *Reading the Old Testament.* New York/Mahwah: Paulist Press, 1984.

Bright, John. *The Kingdom of God.* New York: Abington, 1953.

Brown, Raymond E., S.S. *An Adult Christ at Christmas.* Collegeville: The Liturgical Press, 1978.

———. *The Beatitudes According to Luke. New Testament Essays.* Garden City: Doubleday Image Books, 1975.

———. *The Birth of the Messiah.* New York: Doubleday, 1977.

———. *Christ in the Gospels of Ordinary Sundays.* Collegeville: The Liturgical Press, 1998.

———. *A Coming Christ in Advent.* Collegeville: The Liturgical Press, 1988.

———. *The Community of the Beloved Disciple.* New York: Paulist Press, 1979.

———. *A Crucified Christ in Holy Week.* Collegeville: The Liturgical Press, 1986.

———. *The Gospel According to John.* Garden City: Doubleday, 1966.

———. *The Gospel and Epistles of John.* Collegeville: The Liturgical Press, 1988.

——— et al, eds. *The New Jerome Biblical Commentary.* Englewood Cliffs: Prentice Hall, 1990.

———. *Once and Coming Spirit at Pentecost.* Collegeville: The Liturgical Press, 1994.

———. *A Retreat with John the Evangelist.* Cincinnati: St. Anthony Messenger Press, 1998.

———. *A Risen Christ in Eastertime.* Collegeville: The Liturgical Press, 1991.

Byrne, Brendan, S.J. *Paul and the Christian Woman.* Collegeville: Liturgical Press, 1989.

Camp, Claudia. *The Women's Bible Commentary.* Louisville: Westminster/John Knox Press, 1992.

Campbell, Anthony F., S.J. *The Study Companion to Old Testament Literature. An Approach to the Writings of Pre-Exilic and Exilic Israel.* Collegeville: The Liturgical Press, 1992.

Cantalamessa, Raniero. *The Mystery of Easter.* Collegeville: The Liturgical Press, 1993.

Carson, D.A. *The Gospel According to John.* Grand Rapids: Eerdmans, 1991.

Cassidy, Richard J. *John's Gospel in New Perspective.* Maryknoll, NY: Orbis Books, 1992.

The Catechetical Documents: A Parish Resource. The Archdiocese of Chicago. Chicago: Liturgical Training Publications, 1996.

Catechism of the Catholic Church. Liguori: Liguori Publications, 1994.

Catholic Household Blessings and Prayers. Washington, D.C.: NCCB, 1988.

Collins, Raymond F. *John and His Witness.* Collegeville: The Liturgical Press, 1991.

———. *Preaching the Epistles.* Mahwah: Paulist Press, 1996.

———. *Preaching the Gospels.* Mahwah: Paulist Press, 1996.

Commetarius in Annum Liturgicum Instauratum. Published by the Consilium for the Implementation of the Constitution on the Sacred Liturgy.

Communities of Salt and Light: Reflection on the Social Mission of the Parish. Washington: NCCB, 1993.

Confessions of St. Augustine. Trans. F. J. Sheed. New York: Sheed and Ward, 1944.

Congregation for Divine Worship. *Actio Pastoralis.* "Instruction on Masses for Special Gatherings." May 15, 1969.

Corbon, Jean. *The Wellspring of Worship.* Matthew J. O'Connell, trans. New York: Paulist Press, 1988.

Crosby, Michael H. *The House of Disciples.* Maryknoll: Orbis Books, 1988.

———. *The Spirituality of the Beatitudes: Matthew's Challenge for First World Christians.* Maryknoll: Orbis Books, 1981.

Dalton, William. *Galatians Without Tears.* Collegeville: The Liturgical Press, 1992.

Days of the Lord, Vols. I–VII. Collegeville: The Liturgical Press, 1991–1994.

De Lubac, Henri. *Catholicism: A Study of Dogma in Relation to the Corporate Destiny of Mankind.* New York: New American Library, 1964.

Documents on the Liturgy. Collegeville: The Liturgical Press, 1982.

Dues, Greg. *Catholic Customs and Traditions.* Mystic: Twenty-Third Publications, 1992.

Dunning, Jim. *Echoing God's Word*. Arlington: North American Forum on the Catechumenate, 1993.

Ellis, Peter F. *The Genius of John*. Collegeville: The Liturgical Press, 1984.

Erdman, R. Charles. *The Second Epistle of Paul to the Corinthians*. Philadelphia: Westminster Press, 1966.

Fink, Peter E., S.J., ed. *The New Dictionary of Sacramental Worship*. Collegeville: The Liturgical Press, 1990.

Flanagan, Neal M., O.S.M. *Mark, Matthew, Luke: A Guide to the Gospel Parallels*. Collegeville: The Liturgical Press. 1978.

Fuller, Reginald H. *Preaching the Lectionary*. Collegeville: The Liturgical Press, 1974.

———. *Preaching the New Lectionary*. Collegeville: The Liturgical Press, 1984.

Garland, David E. *Reading Matthew: A Literary and Theological Commentary on the First Gospel*. New York: Crossroad, 1995.

Gaupin, Linda, C.D.P., Ph.D. Catechesis for Liturgy, Orlando, Florida, 1996.

———. "Special Certification in Sacramental Catechesis." Diocese of Orlando, Florida, October 23, 1996.

General Catechetical Directory. The Catechetical Documents: A Parish Resource. Chicago: Liturgy Training Publications, 1996.

General Instruction of the Roman Missal, ICEL, 1975. Chicago: Liturgy Training Publications, 1990.

Grassi, Joseph A. *Loaves and Fishes*. Collegeville: The Liturgical Press, 1991.

Gutierrez, Gustavo. *Sharing the Word Through the Liturgical Year*. Maryknoll: Orbis Books, 1997.

Hare, Douglas R.A. *Matthew, Interpretation: A Bible Commentary for Teaching and Preaching*. Louisville: John Knox Press, 1993.

Harrington, Wilfrid, O.P. *Mark*. Collegeville: The Liturgical Press, 1991.

Heschel, Abraham J. *The Prophets*. New York: Harper & Row, 1963.

Himes, Michael. "Jesus: Yesterday, Today and Forever." Workshop, National Conference of Catechetical Leadership, Orlando, Florida, April 13–17, 1997.

Hoffman, Elizabeth, ed. *The Liturgy Documents*. Chicago: Liturgy Training Publications, 1991.

Huck, Gabe. *The Three Days: Parish Prayer in the Paschal Triduum*. Chicago: Liturgy Training Publications, 1981.

Hughes, Philip Edgcumbe. *The True Image*. Grand Rapids: Eerdmans, 1989.

Hynes, Mary Ellen. *Companion to the Calendar*. Chicago: Liturgy Training Publications, 1993.

Jarrell, Stephen T. *Guide to the Sacramentary*. Chicago: Liturgy Training Publications, 1983.

Jeremias, Joachim. *The Eucharistic Words of Jesus*. London: SCM, 1966.

Johnson, Luke Timothy. *The Gospel of Luke*. Sacra Pagina Series, Vol. 3. Collegeville: The Liturgical Press, 1991.

———. *The Writings of the New Testament: An Interpretation*. Philadelphia: Fortress Press, 1966.

Johnson, Sherman E. *Jesus and His Towns*. Good News Studies 29. Wilmington: Michael Glazier, 1989.

Jones, Cheslyn, et al, eds. *The Study of Liturgy*. Revised Edition. New York: Oxford University Press, 1992.

Jungman, Joseph, A. *The Mass of the Roman Rite: Its Origins and Development*. Francis A. Brunner, C.SS.R., trans. Westminster: Christian Classics, Inc., Replica Edition, 1986.

———. *Public Worship: A Survey*. Clifford Howell, trans. Collegeville: The Liturgical Press, 1957.

Karris, Robert J., O.F.M., ed. *Collegeville Bible Commentary*. Collegeville: The Liturgical Press, 1986.

———. *Invitation to Acts*. Garden City: Doubleday and Company, Inc., 1978.

———. *Jesus and the Marginalized in John's Gospel*. Collegeville: The Liturgical Press, 1990.

———. *The Pastoral Epistles*. Wilmington: Michael Glazier, Inc., 1984.

Kavanaugh, Kieran, O.C.D. and Otilio Rodriguez, O.C.D., trans. *The Collected Works of St. John of the Cross*. Washington, D.C.: Institute of Carmelite Studies, 1979.

Kealy, Sean P., C.S.Sp. *Jesus and Politics*. Collegeville: The Liturgical Press. 1990.

Kingsbury, Jack Dean. *The Christology of Mark's Gospel*. Philadelphia: Fortress Press, 1983.

———. *Conflict in Mark: Jesus, Authorities, Disciples*. Minneapolis: Fortress Press, 1989.

Komonchak, Joseph A., et al, eds. *The New Dictionary of Theology*. Collegeville: The Liturgical Press, 1990.

Kuntz, J. Kenneth. *The People of Ancient Israel: An Introduction to Old Testament Literature, History, and Thought*. New York: Harper & Row, 1974.

LaVerdiere, Eugene, S.S.S. *Dining in the Kingdom of God*. Chicago: Liturgy Training Publications, 1994.

———. *Luke*. Wilmington: Michael Glazier Books, 1980.

Lee, Bernard J., ed. *Alternative Futures for Worship, Vol. 3; The Eucharist*. Collegeville: The Liturgical Press, 1987.

Léon-Dufour, Xavier. *Dictionary of Biblical Theology*. New York: The Seabury Press, 1967.

Liturgy of the Hours. New York: Catholic Book Publishing Co., 1975.

Marrow, Stanley B. *The Gospel of John.* New York/Mahwah: Paulist Press, 1995.

Marthaler, Berard. *The Creed.* Mystic: Twenty-Third Publications, 1987.

Mazar, Peter. *To Crown the Year: Decorating the Church Through the Seasons.* Chicago: Liturgy Training Publications, 1994.

McBrien, Richard P. *Catholicism.* Minneapolis: Winston Press, 1980.

———, ed. *HarperCollins Encyclopedia of Catholicism.* San Francisco: HarperCollins, 1995.

McDonnell, Rea, S.S.N.D. *The Catholic Epistles and Hebrews.* Wilmington: Michael Glazier, 1986.

McKenzie, John, L. *The Dictionary of the Bible.* New York: Collier Macmillan, 1965.

Mick, Laurence E., Timothy Fitzgerald DiCello, Kathleen Hughes, R.S.C.J. *Sourcebook for Sundays and Seasons.* Chicago: Liturgy Training Publications, 1995.

Migne, J. P., ed. *The Liturgy of the Hours, Vol. 2.* New York: Catholic Book Publishing Co., 1996.

Myers, Ched. *Binding the Strong Man. A Political Reading of Mark's Story of Jesus.* Maryknoll: Orbis Books, 1988.

The National Catechetical Directory. The Catechetical Documents. Chicago: Liturgy Training Publications, 1996.

Neyrey, J. "The Idea of Purity in Mark's Gospel." *Semeia, 35;* pp. 91–127 in *BSM,* 363.

Perkins, Pheme. *Reading the New Testament.* New York/Mahwah: Paulist Press, 1988.

Perrin, Norman, and Dennis C. Duling. *The New Testament: An Introduction. Second Edition.* New York: Harcourt Brace Jovanovich, Publishers, 1982.

Pilch, John J. *The Cultural World of Jesus.* Collegeville: The Liturgical Press, 1995.

———. *The Cultural World of Jesus. Sunday by Sunday, Cycle B.* Collegeville: The Liturgical Press, 1996.

Rahner, Karl. *The Great Church Year.* New York: Crossroad, 1993.

Ramshaw, Gail. *Richer Fare for the Christian People: Reflections on the Sunday Readings, Cycles A,B,C.* New York: Pueblo, 1990.

Reid, Barbara E. *Choosing the Better Part.* Collegeville: The Liturgical Press, 1996.

———. "The Gospel of Mark in the Liturgical Year." Workshop: Church of Our Saviour, Cocoa Beach, Florida, 1996.

Richards, Hubert. *The Gospel According to St. Paul.* Collegeville: The Liturgical Press, 1990.

Richter, Klemens. *The Meaning of the Sacramental Symbols.* Linda Maloney, trans. Collegeville: The Liturgical Press, 1990.

Rordorf, Willy. *The Eucharist of the Early Christians.* Matthew J. O'Connell, trans. New York: Pueblo, 1978.

Rybolt, John E., C.M. *Sirach,* Old Testament #21. *Collegeville Bible Commentary,* Robert J. Karris, O.S.M., ed. Collegeville: The Liturgical Press, 1986.

Sanchez, Patricia Datchuck. *The Word We Celebrate.* Kansas City: Sheed and Ward, 1986.

Schneiders, Sandra. *The Revelatory Text.* San Francisco: HarperCollins, 1991.

Scott, Bernard Brandon. *Hear Then the Parable.* Minneapolis: Fortress Press, 1989.

Senior, Donald, C.P. *Invitation to Matthew.* New York: Doubleday Image Books, 1977.

———. *The Passion of Jesus in the Gospel of Matthew.* Wilmington: Michael Glazier, 1985.

———. Workshop: "Gospel of Matthew." Church of Our Saviour, Cocoa Beach, Florida, October, 1995.

Stamps, Mary E., ed. *To Do Justice and Right Upon the Earth: Papers from the Virgil Michel Symposium on Liturgy and Social Justice.* Collegeville: The Liturgical Press, 1993.

Stockhausen, Carol L. *Letters in the Pauline Tradition, Ephesians, Colossians, I Timothy, II Timothy and Titus.* Wilmington: Michael Glazier, 1989.

Stuhlmueller, Carroll, C.P., ed. *The Collegeville Pastoral Dictionary of Biblical Theology.* Collegeville: The Liturgical Press, 1996.

Talbert, Charles H. *Learning Through Suffering.* Collegeville: The Liturgical Press, 1991.

———. *Reading John: A Literary and Theological Commentary on the Fourth Gospel and the Johannine Epistles.* New York: Crossroad, 1992.

———. *Reading Luke.* New York: Crossroad, 1992.

Talley, Thomas J. *Origins of the Liturgical Year.* Collegeville: The Liturgical Press, 1986.

Tannehill, Robert C. *The Narrative Unity of Luke-Acts: A Literary Interpretation.* Vols. I and II. Philadelphia: Fortress Press, 1986 and 1990.

Van Iersel, Bas. *Reading Mark.* Collegeville: The Liturgical Press, 1988.

Wijngaards, John, M.H.M. *Inheriting the Master's Cloak.* Notre Dame, Ind.: Ave Maria Press, 1985.

Wintherop, Ronald D., S.S. *Conversion in the New Testament.* Collegeville: The Liturgical Press, 1994.

Yarnold, Edward, S.J. *The Awe-Inspiring Rites of Initiation.* Second Edition. Collegeville: The Liturgical Press, 1994.

GLOSSARY

Abraham
See Second Sunday of Lent: first reading.

Anamnesis
See Twenty-Sixth Sunday: liturgical context; "Bread," Biblical sign: Easter Vigil; Third Sunday of Easter: liturgical context.

Anointing
The action of touching a person or thing with a substance such as oil, water, mud, blood, or fat in order to bring about a change, either in an external or internal manner. See also "Sign of Oil": Easter Vigil; "Service of Baptism": Easter Vigil (Confirmation); "Confirmation": Doctrinal Appendix; "Reconciliation": Doctrinal Appendix; See Fourth Sunday of Lent: first reading.

Anonymous Christian
See Feast of Christ the King.

Authority
Refer to Twenty-First Sunday in Ordinary Time.

Baptism
See "Symbol of Water": Easter Vigil; Service of Baptism: Easter Vigil; Sundays of Easter; Baptism of the Lord; Twenty-Fourth Sunday: second reading; "Baptism": Doctrinal Appendix; Overview of Easter.

Beatitude
"Technical term for a literary form found in both the OT and NT. A beatitude is a declaration of blessedness on the ground of some virtue or good fortune." (John L. McKenzie, *DOB*, 84) See Fourth Sunday in Ordinary Time.

Bible
From the Greek word *ta biblia* (the books), the Bible is a collection of literary works of various genres that unfold God's relationship with human beings over the course of human history. The Christian Bible is divided into two sections—Old Testament and New Testament. The Old Testament spans the historical experiences of the people of Israel from their beginning around 2,000 B.C.E. until the Maccabean Revolution, around a hundred and fifty years before the birth of Christ (before the Christian era, or before the Common era). The New Testament proclaims the story of Jesus Christ, Messiah, Son of God, Savior of the world, the long-expected One foretold by prophets of old—his kerygma (message) and the life and mission of his followers. See also: "Hebrew Scriptures" (below); "Symbol of Word": Easter Vigil; "Biblical Signs and Themes"—Chapter 2; "Scripture"—Chapter 3.

Bless
To bless in ancient Israel means to "invoke upon the faithful all that God is and all that he has done for his people." (Reginald H. Fuller, *PL*, 27) See *CCC*: 1078–1083, 1669, 2090, 2645. See Ninth Sunday: first reading; Mary, Mother of God: first reading.

Blood
See Palm Sunday: passion exegesis; Holy Thursday: first reading; "Symbol of wine/blood": Easter Vigil.

Bread
See "Symbol of Bread": Easter Vigil; "Eucharist": Doctrinal Appendix; Eighteenth Sunday: first reading, liturgical context.

Christology, John's
See Trinity Sunday.

Church/Community
See Corpus Christi: second reading; Fifth Sunday of Easter; Seventh Sunday of Easter: second reading; "Symbol of Church": Easter Vigil; see also "Church, Mystery of": Doctrinal Appendix; Seventh Sunday: gospel exegesis; Fifteenth, Seventeenth, Eighteenth, and Nineteenth Sundays: gospel exegesis; Twenty-First Sunday; Twenty-Third Sunday: gospel exegesis; Twenty-Fourth Sunday; Twenty-Fifth Sunday; Twenty-Seventh Sunday: first reading.

Cloud
A sign in scripture of divine presence and God's involvement in human affairs. See also *CCC*, 697.

Conversion
Refer to First Sunday of Lent: liturgical context; "Conversion": Doctrinal Appendix; See also Tenth Sunday: first reading; Twenty-Second Sunday: second reading; Christ the King: first reading.

Creation
See first reading from Genesis: Easter Vigil; First Sunday of Lent; Third Sunday in Advent; Fourth Sunday; "Creation": Doctrinal Appendix.

Cross
See Palm Sunday; Holy Thursday; Good Friday; "Symbol of Cross": Easter Vigil; Overview of Triduum; Feast of the Triumph of the Cross; Eighteenth Sunday: second reading; Sundays of the Easter Season; "Paschal Mystery": Doctrinal Appendix.

Day of the Lord
Thirty-First Sunday: first reading; Thirty-Third Sunday: second reading.

Death
See Third Sunday of Easter: first reading; Twelfth Sunday: second reading; Thirty-Second Sunday; Twenty-Eighth Sunday: first reading; "Death:" Doctrinal Appendix.

Desert
In biblical understanding, the desert was a place of encounter with God. See First Sunday of Lent.

Dust
In biblical understanding, dust referred to the dry surface of the ground out of which God fashioned human beings (Gn 2:7). It also meant *the ground of the grave*, which prompted another meaning of commonness and worthlessness, and sometimes death. Refer also to Ash Wednesday.

Ecumenism
Universal mission of the church. See Twentieth Sunday: liturgical context; Twenty-Fifth Sunday.

Election
Refers to the choice by God of a certain group of people. There is no intention to assume superiority or merit. The choice is due to the graciousness of God. Election demands a response in behavior and lifestyle in conformity with God's will. It is a privilege and responsibility. See also First Sunday of Lent; Symbol of Community: Easter Vigil.

Epiclesis
Refers to the action of calling down or invoking the power of the Holy Spirit to bless, consecrate, and transform that which is blessed. In the sacraments it is associated with the action of the laying on of hands. See also Symbol of "Laying on of Hands": Easter Vigil; Symbol of "Bread as Ecclesial Sign": Easter Vigil.

Epistle/Letter
An epistle is a literary composition intended for a wide audience, and not necessarily attached to a specific situation. A letter is a non-literary method of communication between individuals.

Eschatology
Thirty-Second Sunday; Thirty-Third Sunday: second reading; Transfiguration: gospel exegesis; "Eschatology": Doctrinal Appendix.

Eucharist
See Palm Sunday: passion exegesis; "Symbol of Bread/Wine": Easter Vigil; Holy Thursday; Third Sunday of Easter: liturgical context; Corpus Christi; See Eighteenth Sunday: first reading; Twenty-Eighth Sunday; "Eucharist": Doctrinal Appendix.

Eucharistic liturgy, Paul's original sketch of
See Corpus Christi.

Eucharistic prayer
See Seventh Sunday of Easter: gospel exegesis; Eighteenth Sunday.

Evangelization
See Eleventh Sunday: liturgical context; Twelfth Sunday: gospel exegesis.

Expulsion of the Christians from the synagogue
See Thirteenth Sunday.

Faith
See Nineteenth Sunday: gospel exegesis.

Faith/Works
See Ninth Sunday; Tenth Sunday; Eleventh Sunday; Thirtieth Sunday: second reading.

Fear of God
Fear was a common response to deities in antiquity. It involved two almost incongruous elements—terror in the face of transcendence and attraction and love that are expressed in feelings of contentment, guidance, and assurance. As the element of fear subsides, "fear of God" may move into the sphere of piety, religion, worship, and obedience. (*CCC*, 1831)

Finger of God
The finger of God throughout Hebrew Scriptures is a term reflecting God's power. It is similar in usage to the "hand" of God, also a symbol of divine power. The term is used in the New Testament in Luke 11:20 when Jesus drives out a demon "by the finger of God." It is used also as a means to show the ease with which Jesus performed his miracles. St. Ambrose, in the fourth century, made the comparison of the Son and Spirit with the hand and finger of God. There was no intention to minimize their role, or to imply that they were only a small portion of God. "It expresses the unity of power among the three in all their actions." (Dennis M. Sweetland, "Finger of God," in *CPDBT*, 334.) This understanding is articulated in later centuries in the hymn *Veni Creator Spiritus (766–856)*. The Spirit is cited as the "Finger of God's Right Hand." The term *finger of God* is used in the Vatican II document, *Dogmatic Constitution on the Church* #5, quoting a passage of Luke 11:20. It is a reference to the power of Christ's miracles as a sign that the reign of God was firmly established on this earth. See also "Symbol—Laying on of Hands": Easter Vigil. (*CCC*, 700.)

Fire
Fire is a symbol in scripture of the presence, action, and protection of God. It also refers to judgment, anger, testing, and purification. See also "Symbol of Fire/Light": Easter Vigil; Pentecost: first reading during the day; Service of Baptism. (*CCC*, 696)

Flesh
The biblical understanding of *flesh* refers to the way human beings act—positively or negatively.

Flesh could honor and obey God, but it could also rebel against God. It represents a person's totality. It also is the stage on which the struggles of the spirit are won or lost—the struggles of human passion. In the NT, *flesh* is also symbolic of the Incarnation, and the elevation of human dignity as a result. However, negative connotations of flesh have been passed on to us from previous generations. Even though church tradition teaches that flesh is not sinful, but created in goodness and sanctified by the Incarnation, vestiges of the heresy which denies that goodness remain with us today. However, one is not to deny the apparent ambiguous mystery—that flesh is mortal, beautiful, and weak. See Palm Sunday: passion exegesis; Corpus Christi: gospel exegesis; Fourteenth Sunday: second reading.

Forgiveness
See Pentecost; gospel exegesis; Twenty-Third Sunday: gospel exegesis; Twenty-Fourth Sunday; Sundays of Lent.

Garment
See "Symbol of Garment": Easter Vigil; Service of Baptism; Holy Thursday: gospel exegesis; Twenty-Eighth Sunday: gospel exegesis; Thirty-Second Sunday (wedding garment represents acts of righteousness and good deeds); Holy Family: second reading; Thirteenth Sunday, Cycle C.

Gehenna
The final place of eternal punishment in the Bible. The root of the word means "valley of Hinnom." This valley, located southwest of Jerusalem and running into the Kidron, was at one time the boundary between the tribe of Judah and the tribe of Benjamin. At one time this valley had the reputation of evil due to the idolatrous cult that offered religious sacrifices, including children, to the god Moloch. Jeremiah brought judgment and condemnation upon the Valley of Hinnom, which was later remembered by those who associated the valley with fiery damnation, hell, and the locus for final judgment. The NT made a clear distinction between Hades and Gehenna. Hades was a place where the ungodly were sent for temporary punishment. Gehenna was the place of final judgment and permanent punishment. Gehenna was the destination of those who refuse to accept the reign of God.

Grace

"Grace means favor, God's favor toward us. It can be creative, redemptive, or eschatological." (John J. Pilch, "Grace," in *CPDBT*, 397) According to NT understanding of *grace*, the favor (*grace*) God gives is God's Son, Jesus Christ. Grace is God revealing godself to human beings. See Tenth Sunday: gospel exegesis; Twentieth Sunday: second reading; Twenty-Fifth Sunday; "Grace": Doctrinal Appendix; Third Sunday of Lent: second reading.

Hand

See "Symbol: Laying on of Hands": Easter Vigil; "Service of Baptism": confirmation; "Confirmation," "Reconciliation": Doctrinal Appendix. (*CCC*, 699)

Heart

The heart is at the center of a person's entire life—the place where he or she meets God. In biblical anthropology the heart is the source of feelings, desires, longings, understanding, and decision, and conversion (*metanoia*) results in positively changing all of these. The antithesis consists in closing one's mind and heart, resulting in "hardness of heart." (Thomas P. McCreesh, O.P., "Heart"; Diane Bergant, C.S.A., "Hardness of Heart," in *CPDBT*, 424, 408)

Hebrew Scriptures

For Jewish people, there is only one canon—the Hebrew Bible. "Old Testament" is a Christian designation to distinguish between the first and second testaments. The Hebrew Bible is one book composed of three parts—the Law (Torah), the Prophets, and the Writings. Since the Jewish Hebrew Bible and the Christian Old Testament are fundamentally the same, except for the arrangement, many scholars today prefer the more inclusive term—Hebrew Scriptures—as a reference for the Old Testament. Some books not included in the Hebrew Bible were, at one time, read enthusiastically and regularly by the Jewish people but, for some reason, were not included in their canon. These were included in the Christian Bible, however. The early Christians were Greek-speaking people. They read the scriptures of the Old Testament, known as the *Septuagint*, from a Greek source originating in Alexandria, Egypt around the third century B.C.E. The arrangement of books in this translation was different from the arrangement in the Hebrew Bible. "The Prophets" were placed last, and some of the books that did not make their way into the Hebrew canon were included.

After the Reformation, Protestants restricted the number of books in the canon of the Old Testament to only those included in the Hebrew Bible. The books not included were put in a special section called the "Apocrypha" (hidden or secret works), with the explanation that they are worthy of reading, but are not on the same par as the rest of the scriptures. The Catholic Church, on the other hand, officially determined that the above mentioned books are deserving of canonical recognition. Thus, the Catholic canon is seven books longer than the Protestant and Jewish canons. Eastern Orthodox churches recognize the seven extra books as well. See also: "Symbol of Word": Easter Vigil; Biblical Signs and Themes: Chapter 2; "Scripture": Chapter 3. See also Holy Family: first reading.

Hermeneutics

The science of interpretation—the principles by which a statement or text is interpreted.

Holy Spirit

See Baptism of the Lord; Triduum; Sundays of Easter; Pentecost; Trinity Sunday; Good Friday: gospel exegesis.

Hospitality

Ancient cultures believed that the extension of hospitality, especially to strangers, was a religious act. Hospitality was a very important responsibility for Israel. The people knew well what it meant to be a stranger in a foreign land. Divine hospitality was a common metaphor for God's protection and care for Israel. The NT extends this hospitality a step further by insisting that the poor, oppressed, outcasts, and marginalized are to be recipients of hospitality. Offering such hospitality is the same as offering it to Christ himself. Lack of hospitality has serious implications, as indicated by the story of Sodom and Gomorrah (see below). See "Bread—Biblical Sign": Easter Vigil; Third Sunday of Easter: gospel exegesis; Eleventh and Thirteenth Sundays: gospel exegesis; Twenty-Eighth Sunday: first reading.

Human Dignity
See Easter Vigil: first reading; Easter Sunday: second reading; Christmas, Mass at Midnight: liturgical context; Fourth Sunday of Lent: second reading; Twelfth Sunday: gospel exegesis; Easter Vigil: first reading; Seventeenth Sunday: second reading; Trinity: gospel exegesis.

Incarnation
See Second Sunday of Advent; Overview of Advent and the Sundays of Advent; See Overview of the Christmas Season and the Sundays of the Christmas season; Trinity Sunday; Twenty-Sixth Sunday: second reading; "Incarnation": Doctrinal Appendix.

Jubilee Year
Israel established a jubilee year in order to bring about economic and social justice in Israel. "The law freed Israelite slaves and returned ancestral land to its original owners. Although the law may never have been practiced, the Jubilee became a symbol of hope in OT literature and in the Gospel of Luke." (Kathleen M. O'Connor, "Jubilee Year," in *CPDBT*, 501)

Judgment
See also Seventeenth Sunday; Thirty-First Sunday: first reading; Christ the King: first reading

Justice, biblical
See Fourth Sunday; Twenty-Fifth Sunday: gospel exegesis; Thirtieth Sunday; Second and Third Sundays of Advent; "Justice": Doctrinal Appendix; *hesed*: Holy Family, first reading; Symbol of Community: Easter Vigil.

Kerygma
The message of the gospel—the word that was originally proclaimed. See First Sunday of Advent: second reading; Twelfth, Seventeenth, Twenty-First, and Thirty-First Sundays: gospel exegesis.

Kingdom of God/Reign of God
Jesus' death and resurrection signaled the end of an age and the beginning of the messianic age. The purpose of Jesus' mission was to establish God's reign on earth until he returns in glory. The reign of God is both a present and future reality. The intention of the parables is to proclaim the reign of God. Scholars suggest that rather than refer to the *kingdom of God*, we call it instead the *reign of God*. Kingdom refers to a place where someone lives. Reign, as it is described in the parables, suggests a *way to live*. See Fifteenth Sunday, Seventeenth Sunday: gospel exegesis; Twenty-Seventh Sunday: first reading; Twenty-Eighth Sunday: gospel exegesis; Second Sunday of Advent; "Kingdom of God": Doctrinal Appendix.

Law
Fourth Sunday of Lent: first reading; Seventh Sunday: gospel exegesis; Twenty-Ninth Sunday: gospel exegesis.

Light
See "Symbol of Light/Fire": Easter Vigil; Epiphany; Christmas Overview; Sundays of Christmas Season; Fourth Sunday in Lent; Thirty-First Sunday: first reading; Second Sunday of Advent: second reading.

Love of God/neighbor
Seventh Sunday: first reading; Thirtieth Sunday; Twenty-Third Sunday: second reading.

Manifestation
See Epiphany, Sundays of Christmas Season; Pentecost, Mass During the Day: first reading; Sundays of the Easter Season; Nineteenth Sunday: gospel exegesis.

Mary, Mother of God
See Solemnity of Mary, Mother of God, Immaculate Conception; "Mary, Model for the Church": Doctrinal Appendix.

Meal/Banquet/Feast
See Twenty-Eighth Sunday: first reading: Eighteenth Sunday.

Meekness
See Fourth Sunday; Fourteenth Sunday: first reading.

Miracles
See Signs/Miracles below.

Morality
See Sixth Sunday of Easter: gospel exegesis; Fourth Sunday: gospel exegesis; Twenty-Second Sunday: second reading.

Mountains
Sixth Sunday of Easter: gospel exegesis.

Name, biblical understanding
See Mary, Mother of God.

Non-Violence
See Seventh Sunday; Twenty-Third Sunday: gospel exegesis.

Oil
"Symbol of Oil": Easter Vigil; Sacraments of baptism, confirmation, penance; Thirty-Second Sunday.

Paranesis
A moral exhortation or instruction and common literary form of the ancient Hellenistic, Christian, and Jewish world. Christian tradition freely employed this common form of moral imperative. See Third Sunday of Advent: second reading.

Parousia
See First Sunday of Advent.

Paschal Mystery
See Triduum; Symbol of Cross: Easter Vigil; Third Sunday of Easter: liturgical context; Sundays of Easter; Twelfth Sunday: second reading; Thirteenth Sunday; Fifteenth and Eighteenth Sundays: second reading; Twenty-First Sunday: gospel exegesis; Twenty-Second Sunday: second reading; Overviews of Triduum, Easter Season; "Paschal Mystery": Doctrinal Appendix.

Pentateuch
The first five books of the Old Testament: Genesis, Exodus, Leviticus, Numbers, Deuteronomy.

Pericope
The particular portion or segment of scripture that is chosen for a specific proclamation.

Poverty
See Fourth Sunday.

Prayer
See Nineteenth Sunday: gospel exegesis; Trinity Sunday.

Prophets and Prophecy
Prophets—ministers of God's word—were trained for their service. They did not just sit and wait for the Lord to speak to them. Some prophets were trained to serve in the temple and were known as temple prophets. Even though some prophets were trained professionally for their service, others did emerge outside the system (see Amos 7:14–15). Prophecy was in the form of warning, encouragement, judgment, praise, thanks, exhortation and reassurance, prediction of future events, and interpretation of past events. Prophets were messengers of the Lord and delivered God's word to the people. See also Third Sunday of Easter: gospel exegesis; Epiphany: first reading; Thirty-First Sunday: gospel exegesis.

Religious Intolerance
See Sixteenth Sunday.

Resurrection
Triduum; Sundays of Easter: Pentecost; Ascension; Trinity Sunday.

Revelation
See Trinity Sunday.

Sacrifice
See Fifth Sunday of Easter: second reading; Tenth Sunday: gospel exegesis; Eighteenth Sunday.

Shepherd
See Fourth Sunday of Easter; Feast of Christ the King: first reading and gospel exegesis.

Signs/Miracles
Hebrew Scriptures: Signs are evidence of God's presence and power. They are the way in which God communicates to people. They need to be interpreted. "A sign is a vehicle of communication—an action, condition, quality, occurrence, visible object, or linguistic unity—that conveys meaning. Most often it is a significant event, action, or other vehicle of communication that reveals God's intention or presence." (John J. Pilch, "Sign/Symbol," in *CPDBT*, 911) "The purpose of a sign is to make visible, to confirm dramatically, the truth and power of Yahweh's word spoken by the prophet. A sign does not necessarily have to be a miracle, in our sense of the word, for its significance is not so much in the unusual character as in its power to confirm a prophetic word spoken in threat or promise." (Bernard W. Anderson, *UOT*, 331–334)

New Testament: Much of John's gospel is intent on authenticating Jesus' identity. His miracles play a key role in that discussion. The scriptures provide us with various perspectives regarding Jesus' miracles. Luke/Acts proposes a positive view of Jesus' miracles. In Luke's gospel and in the Acts of the Apostles, Jesus' miracles are the impetus for faith (Lk 4:31–5:11). The disciples' miracles proclaim and promote the growth of the faith (Acts 3:1–4: 4; 5:12–14; 8:6–8; 13:4–12). Mark's view is not as positive as Luke/Acts. He reflects a negative perspective. Mark reminds us that Jesus' miracles are not accepted by everyone. He reminds us that our faith is not to be completely based on Christ's miracles, but also on the power of the cross (Mk 8:14–21, 22–26, 27–31). John's gospel posits a complex, multivalent understanding of Jesus' miracles, called signs. They sometimes elicit faith (4:53; 10:41–42; 11:45, 47–48; 14:11). Not everyone believes in Jesus because of his miracles. Signs are often ambiguous (10:25–26; 11:45–48). Some people are interested in Jesus' miracles or signs simply for their own self-interest (physical benefits, 6:26). Some see them as a threat to Israel's security (11:46–48). Some believe that Jesus' signs are not from God because his regular behavior does not conform to certain standards (9:16, 30, 34). Scripture anticipated the rejection of Jesus' signs (12:37–40). People who accept Jesus' signs often possess some initial faith (2:11; 4:46–54; 20:30–31; 21:6–7). Sometimes the contrary is true, however (2:23; 3:2; chap. 9; 11:45). If faith already exists, Jesus' miracles strengthen and deepen it (2:11; 4:46–54; 20:30–31). The early Christian community believed that they shared Jesus' power and thus were agents of his miracle-working activity. John's community believed that they were agents of Jesus' signs continued in the life of the community. However, the miracles, in and of themselves, do not authenticate Jesus' mission. (Charles H. Talbert, *RJ*, 103–104) See also Fourth Week of Advent: first reading.

Sin

See Sundays of Lent; Seventeenth Sunday; Thirty-First Sunday: first reading; Overview of Lent; "Sin": Doctrinal Appendix.

Sodom and Gomorrah

See Genesis, chapters 18, 19. Don C. Benjamin asserts that the story of Sodom and Gomorrah is about hospitality: "...strangers appear, Lot's household protects them, and they bless it with life." There was a definitive protocol regarding hospitality in antiquity. It helped to test whether a person was a friend or an enemy. In the story of Sodom and Gomorrah, the strangers pass the first test with flying colors when they decline the first invitation. They become official guests with the gesture of foot washing. Another test was to observe the stranger's table manners. If they responded appropriately it was apparent that they understood the mores of their host. However, in this instance, before the test is completed, the young warriors and men in leadership gather and decide on their own that the visitors are enemies. Their punishment would be rape (similar to what was experienced by David's messenger before he was released by the Ammorites). The sexual implications in that culture were not understood as they are today. Sexual activity was considered to be part of the realm of contractual agreement. Monarchs had hundred of wives because they were in contractual agreement with other nations. Homosexual or heterosexual rape was a sign of a broken treaty. We are understandably shocked when Abraham offered his daughters in return for the strangers' lives. While not certain, scholars believe that this was an act of offering Abraham's own self to save the guests. It was believed that dead parents live on in their children. Since it is the children who must care for aged parents, by offering his daughters he was in essence saying, "Here, take my only hope of survival. I will be destined to live a life of poverty and destitution because of the death of my daughters." The sin of Sodom and Gomorrah was its refusal to extend hospitality to the strangers.

Son of Man

"In the OT Son of Man is a synonym for a human being. In Daniel 7:13 Son of Man is used to indicate that of a symbolic figure of the last days in human experience. In the NT Jesus seems to have used Son of Man in two different ways: as a way of referring to himself, and in reference to Daniel 7:13. After Jesus' death and resurrection, his followers expressed their expectation that he would come again by identifying him with the Son of Man of Daniel 7:13. Outside of the gospel tradition Son of Man was little used by the first-century Church. It was revived in the Patristic era as an expression of Jesus' humanity." (Terrance Callan, "Son of Man," in *CPDBT*, 937)

Soteriology

The study of salvation—the discipline that examines the mystery of salvation embodied in the passion, death, resurrection, ascension of Jesus. See Twenty-Second Sunday: second reading; Twenty-Eighth and Twenty-Ninth Sundays: gospel exegesis; Christ the King.

Stewardship

See Thirty-Third Sunday: gospel exegesis; Eighth Sunday.

Submission of wives

Holy Family: second reading.

Suffering

See Second Sunday of Lent: second reading; Second Sunday of Easter: second reading; Fourth Sunday of Easter: second reading; Sixth Sunday of Easter: liturgical context; Seventh Sunday of Easter: second reading; Fifteenth and Sixteenth Sundays: second reading.

Symbol

A sign that embodies what it is intended to signify. It is almost synonymous with sacrament. It is a sign which is intimately connected to that which it signifies. For further explanation refer to the section of the Easter Vigil that explains symbols. See also *CCC*, 1146–1149.

Temptation

See First Sunday of Lent: gospel exegesis.

Time

See Seventh Sunday of Easter: gospel exegesis; Chapter 8: sacred time, liturgical calendar; see Overview of Ordinary Time.

Trinity

See Sixth Sunday of Easter: gospel exegesis; Easter; Trinity Sunday; Mary, Mother of God: first reading; "Trinity": Doctrinal Appendix.

Typology

Typology is a way of interpreting the scriptures in light of God's plan of salvation, understood as having begun with people and events of past genera-

tions. Typology asserts that some of those people and events looked forward to (foreshadowed) future events, truths, and realities. For example, OT persons or events foreshadowed a New Testament truth, event, or reality. In the Book of Hebrews the Old Testament liturgy foreshadows the heavenly liturgy inaugurated by Jesus. "In the Church's pastoral and liturgical tradition typology emphasizes the continuity between the Testaments. It also underscores the abiding presence of God among those who believe." (Demetrius R. Dumm, O.S.B., "Type," in *CPDBT*, 1026) See also Epiphany: first reading; Holy Family: gospel exegesis; Eighteenth Sunday: gospel exegesis.

Water

See "Symbol of Water": Easter Vigil; Easter Vigil Readings; Pentecost Vigil: gospel exegesis; "Baptism": Doctrinal Appendix; See Third Sunday of Lent.

Word

See also Easter Vigil: fifth and sixth readings; Third Sunday of Easter: liturgical context; "Hebrew Scriptures" (above); Symbol of Word: Easter Vigil; Fourteenth Sunday: gospel exegesis; Fifteenth Sunday: first reading, liturgical context; Seventeenth Sunday: gospel exegesis; Thirty-First Sunday: gospel exegesis; Biblical Signs and Themes: Chapter 2; "Scripture": Chapter 3; Overview of Cycle A.

Doctrinal Index

This index of doctrinal topics lists relevant church documents and official sources. Document titles are abbreviated; for more information on these sources, see the listing of documents that follows the index.

DOCTRINAL TOPICS

ADVENT DOL 442 nos 39–42, 467 nos 3–4; CB 235; GNLY 39–42; LM 11; CCC 522–524

ALL SOULS CB 395; DOL 478

ALMSGIVING CCC 575, 1032, 1434, 1438, 2101, 2447, 2462

ANOINTING AND PASTORAL CARE OF THE SICK RA Apostolic Constitution, RA 1–40; DOL 408–409, 412; NCD 127–128; SC 73–75; CCC 1520–1525

ASCENSION CCC 659–664, 668–673

ASSUMPTION DOL 467 no 6; CCC 966, 974

BAPTISM (see Christian Initiation)

BEATITUDES CCC 1716–1724; BT 19; NCD 105

BREAD GIRM 281–285; CCC 1329, 1333–1340, 1355

BODY OF CHRIST DOL 176 no 35–39, 44, 64–72; 179 no 6–8; CCC 775–776, 779, 789, 791, 792, 805, 807

CHRISTMAS GNLY 32–38; LM 95; AD 3; LM 12; CCC 525–534

CHRISTIAN INITIATION

BAPTISM RCIA INTRO 1–35; GS 11; LG 10–17; GCD 11, 57; NCD 116–117; SC 7; UR 22; DOL 301 no 33; CCC 1213–1274 (Role of baptized: priest, prophet, and king CCC 901–913)

CONFIRMATION RC Apostolic Constitution, RA 1, 9, 13; RCIA INTRO 2; LG 11, GCD 11; CCC 698, 1183, 1272–1274, 1285–1314; NCD 118–119; DOL 304, 305 nos 1–19

EUCHARIST RCIA INTRO 2; LG 7, 11; DOL 169 no 58, 176 no 70, 177; GIRM INTRO 2–5; GIRM 1–2, 7–8, 62; AA 8; GCD 12, 58; NCD 120–122; CCC 1322–1405; SC 47; Influence of eucharistic celebration on daily life: DOL 179 no 13; Adoration of eucharist: DOL 179 no 49, 50; Mystery of the eucharist: DOL 184, 185, 189, 191

CHURCH, MYSTERY LG 1–16; GCD 20–23, 65–67; DOL 4 no 3, 176 no 37–38; NCD 30, 56–59; 63–73; 93–96; TJD 12; CCC 774–776, 811–829, 1396

COMMUNION DOL 177, 179 nos 3b, 31–32, 34; 183; 188

CONFIRMATION (see Christian Initiation)

CONVERSION SC 9; DH 10; DV 5; RP 6; DOL 191, 193, 378 NCD 99, RCIA 36, 37; CCC 1989

CREATION LG 1; GCD 51; NCD 51, 85; CCC 280–314

CROSS LG 3, 38; CB 1011; DOL 176 no 34; CCC 517, 618, 662, 1235

DEATH/DYING GS 18, 22; AG 18; OCF 1–7, 18–19, 22; NCD 108; RA 26–34; SC 81; BT 25

DIGNITY OF HUMAN PERSON GS 3,12, 27; AG 18; AA 6; DH 1, 9; GCD 60

DISCIPLESHIP AA 6, 8; NCD 72, 152–154; CCC 425, 654, 618, 1816

EASTER SEASON GNLY 22–26; LM 11–102; CB 371; CCC 1169; NCD 144

EASTER TRIDUUM GNLY 18–21; LM 99; CB 295–332; 68–639; SC 102

ECUMENISM UR 1–24; DOL 6 nos 2–8, 178 no 10

ESCHATOLOGY LG 39; GCD 25; NCD 109–110; BT 25; OCF 1–8; CCC 958, 1020–1050, 1088–1090, 1402, 1662, 1681; SC 8

EUCHARIST (see Christian Initiation)

EVANGELIZATION AA 6, 8; EN 6–82; AD 1–22; 35–36; RCIA 36–40; DOL 66 no 2, 189; CCC 858–859

FAITH GCD 15, 22–24 57–59; DV 5; NCD 15, 22; RCIA 211; DH 10; CCC 142–175

FASTING CCC 1434, 2043

FIRE CCC 696

GARMENT RCIA 214, 320; CCC 1243–1244

GRACE GS 57; NCD 98; CCC 1996–2005

HIERARCHY OF TRUTHS GCD 43; BR INTRO; NCD 43,47; CCC 90, 234

HOLY ORDERS PO 1–9; GCD 57; NCD 132–133

HOLY SPIRIT (see Trinity)

INCARNATION AD 3; BT 4; GCD 52–54; NCD 87; CCC 456–478, 653

JESUS (see Trinity)

JUSTICE LG 27–32, 69–72; EJFA 48–78; NCD 162, 165; CCC 1397; TJD 10–11

KINGDOM OF GOD LG 36; GS 45; CCC 541–560,675, 677

LAYING ON OF HANDS DOL 306; RC 9; RA 5–6; CCC 1288, 1668; 1556

LENT SC 109–110; GNLY 27–31; LM 13; RCIA 138

LIGHT RCIA 230, LG 1; NCD 117, CCC 699, 700, 697, 1243

LITURGICAL YEAR SC 102; GNLY 1,17; CB 228; LM 7

LITURGY SC 10; DOL 21, 22 no 19, 176 no 35; CCC 1069–1075, 1077–1124

LORD'S PRAYER GIRM 56; CCC 2601, 2777–2856

MARY, MODEL FOR THE CHURCH LG 60–69; SC 103; GCD 24; BT 24; NCD 106

MASS GIRM 1–58; DOL 176 nos 1–55; 179 3b–g, 12, 193; CCC 1332, 1382

MATRIMONY RMa 1–7; GCD 59; AA 11; NCD 131; AA 11; GS 47–52; LG 11; SC 77–78; DOL 169 no 59

MERCY OF GOD RP 1–11; CCC 1991–1992, 1994

MORAL CONSCIENCE GS 15–16; NCD 103, 190; DH 3, 14

MORALITY: FOUNDATIONS GCD 19, 63–64; NCD 101–105; BT 15,17–19

NEW TESTAMENT DV 17–20; CCC 124–128

OIL RC 9; RBO 1–5; RA 5–15, 20–29; RCIA INTRO 2, 214; NCD 117; CCC 695, 1241, 1291, 1289, 1294–1296

OLD TESTAMENT DV 14–16; CCC 121–123

ORDINARY TIME GNLY 43–44; LM 15, 103–110; CB 377–380

PASCHAL MYSTERY GS 38; RCIA INTRO 1, 5, 6; AG 38; SC 106; GIRM 2; OCF 2, 3; CCC 444–445; 654, 1067–1068, 1164, 1363–1364, 2175

PENANCE (see Reconciliation)

PENTECOST LG 4, 19–20, 24; AG 4; CCC 731–741

PRAYER SC 9–13; BT-INTRO; DOL 53, 55; NCD 140–145; CCC 2558–2565, 2566–2745; 2598–2622

PRAYER FORMS CCC 2626–2643

RECONCILIATION/PENANCE RP-INTRO, 1–11; LG 11; DOL 191; GCD 11; NCD 124–126

RESURRECTION LG 36; BT 4, 8; NCD 87 CCC 638–655

REVELATION DV 2–6, 21–24; GCD 10–14; NCD 48–55; CCC 51–67

SACRAMENTS SC 59; DOL 169 nos 55–57; LG 11; GIRM 346; GCD 10–11, 55; NCD 97, 114; BT 10–13; CCC 1113–1130, 1145–1158

SAINTS LG 49–51; SC 104, 111; LM 5; NCD 107; CCC 957, 2030

SALVATION DV 2; GCD 37–44, 62; BT 1, 5–6, 8, 22–23; NCD 85, 96; AA 5–6; GIRM 2

SCRIPTURE DV 11–26; CCC 101–133; LM 1

SERVICE/MISSION LG 27; AA 2–3, 8, 10; RCIA 75–76; TJD 27–32; DOL 179 no 13

SIN GS 13; NCD 98–99; GCD 62; BT 15–16, 19; RCIA 211; RP 5; AA 7; CCC 385–412

SOCIAL JUSTICE NCD 149–171; CCC 1928–1942

SUFFERING GS 22; RA INTRO 1–3; CCC 164, 1508, 1521

TRANSFIGURATION CCC 554–56, 568

TRANSUBSTANTIATION DOL 176 no 46–55

TRINITY GCD 1, 41, 47; DV 2; NCD 83, RCIA 200; CCC 233–260, 290–292

FATHER LG 2–4; GCD 41; NCD 51; CCC 238–242, 248, 254, 268–274, 279, 286–288

JESUS LG 3–4; GS 22; AD 3; DV 17; GCD, 4, 6, 8, 50, 53–55; NCD 53, 87–91; CCC 249–267; BT 4–9; GS 45

HOLY SPIRIT LG 4, 12; AD 3; RC Apostolic Constitution, RC 2; GCD 9, 41; NCD 54, 92; BT 9; CCC 687–741, 1091–1109; 1286; 1289

WATER RCIA INTRO 5, 18–22, 213; CCC 694, 1217–1222; OCF 8

WORD OF GOD LM 1, 3, 10; DV 10–21; CCC 109–120

Note: This is by no means an exhaustive listing of topics or documentation for the topics listed. This index merely scratches the surface and serves as a point of departure for those interested in further exploration of such topics.

DOCUMENTS

AA   *Apostolicam actuositatem:* The Decree on the Apostolate of the Laity, Vatican Council II, November 18, 1965. (Can be found in *The Documents of Vatican II,* edited by Walter M. Abbott, S.J., New York: Guild Press, America Press, Association Press, 1966.)

AG   *Ad gentes:* Decree on the Church's Missionary Activity, Vatican Council II, December 7, 1965. (Can be found in *The Documents of Vatican II,* edited by Walter M. Abbott, S.J., New York: Guild Press, America Press, Association Press, 1966.)

BT   *Basic Teachings for Catholic Religious Education,* NCCB, 1973. (Can be found in *The Catechetical Documents: A Parish Resource,* Chicago: Liturgy Training Publications, 1996.)

CB   *Ceremonial of Bishops,* ICEL, 1989. (Can be found in *The Liturgy Documents: A Pastoral Resource,* Chicago: Liturgy Training Publications, 1990.)

CCC   *Catechism of the Catholic Church,* USCC-Libreria Editrice Vaticana, 1994.

DH   *Dignitatis humanae:* Declaration on Human Freedom, Vatican Council II, December 7, 1965. (Can be found in *The Documents of Vatican II,* edited by Walter M. Abbott, S.J., New York: Guild Press, America Press, Association Press, 1966.)

DOL   *Documents on the Liturgy 1963–1979, Conciliar, Papal and Curial and Liturgical Texts,* Collegeville: The Liturgical Press, 1982.

DV   *Dei verbum:* Dogmatic Constitution on Divine Revelation, Vatican Council II, Nov. 18, 1965. (Can be found in *The Documents of Vatican II,* edited by Walter M. Abbott, S.J., New York: Guild Press, America Press, Association Press, 1966.)

EJFA   *Economic Justice for All,* NCCB, 1986.

EN   *Evangelii Nuntiandi:* On Evangelization in the Modern World, Paul VI, December 8, 1975. (Can be found in *The Catechetical Documents: A Parish Resource,* Chicago: Liturgy Training Publications, 1996.)

GIRM   *General Instruction of the Roman Missal,* ICEL, 1975. (Can be found in *The Liturgy Documents: A Parish Resource,* Chicago: Liturgy Training Publications, 1990.)

GCD   *General Catechetical Directory,* Sacred Congregation for the Clergy, 1971. (Can be found in *The Catechetical Documents: A Parish Resource,* Chicago: Liturgy Training Publications, 1996.)

GS   *Gaudium et spes:* The Pastoral Constitution on the Church in the Modern World, Vatican Council II, December 7, 1965. (Can be found in *The Documents of Vatican II,* edited by Walter M. Abbott, S.J., New York: Guild Press, America Press, Association Press, 1966.)

HLS   *This Holy and Living Sacrifice for the Celebration and Reception of Communion under Both Kinds,* USCC, 1985. (Can be found in *The Liturgy Documents: A Parish Resource.* Chicago: Liturgy Training Publications, 1990.)

LG   *Lumen gentium:* Dogmatic Constitution on the Church, Vatican Council II, 1965. (Can be found in *The Documents of Vatican II,* edited by Walter M. Abbott, S.J., New York: Guild Press, America Press, Association Press, 1966.)

LM   *Lectionary for Mass: Introduction,* second editio typica, ICEL, 1985. (Can be found in *The Liturgy Documents: A Parish Resource,* Chicago: Liturgy Training Publications, 1990.)

NCD   *Sharing the Light of Faith: National Catechetical Directory,* NCCB, 1978 (Can be found in *The Catechetical Documents: A Parish Resource,* Chicago: Liturgy Training Publications, 1996.)

OCF   *Order of Christian Funerals,* ICEL, 1990.

PO   *Presbyterorum ordinis:* Decree on the Ministry and Life of Priests, Vatican Council II, 1966. (Can be found in *The Documents of Vatican II,* edited by Walter M. Abbot, S.J., New York: Guild Press, America Press, Association Press, 1966.)

RA   Rite of Anointing and Pastoral Care of the Sick, *Rites of the Catholic Church,* ICEL, 1976.

RBO   Rite of Blessing of Oils and Rite of Consecration of Chrism: Introduction, *Rites of the Catholic Church,* ICEL, 1976.

RCIA   *Rite of Christian Initiation of Adults,* ICEL, 1988.

RC   Rite of Confirmation, *Rites of the Catholic Church,* ICEL, 1976.

RMa   Rite of Marriage, *Rites of the Catholic Church,* ICEL, 1976.

RP   Rite of Penance, *Rites of the Catholic Church,* ICEL, 1976.

RO   Rite of Ordination of Deacons, Presbyters, and Bishops, *Rites of the Catholic Church,* ICEL, 1976.

SC   *Sacrosanctum concilium:* Constitution on the Sacred Liturgy, Vatican Council II, December 4, 1964. (Can be found in *The Documents of Vatican II,* edited by Walter M. Abbott, S.J., New York: Guild Press, America Press, Association Press, 1966, OR *The Liturgy Documents: A Parish Resource,* Chicago: Liturgy Training Publications, 1990.)

UR   *Unitatis redintegratio:* The Decree on Ecumenism, Vatican Council II, November 21, 1964. (Can be found in *The Documents of Vatican II,* edited by Walter M. Abbott, S.J., New York: Guild Press, America Press, Association Press, 1966.)

TJD   *To Teach as Jesus Did,* NCCB, 1972. (Can be found in *The Catechetical Documents: A Parish Resource,* Chicago: Liturgy Training Publications, 1996.)